The Victoria and Albert Museum

A Bibliography and Exhibition Chronology, 1852–1996

"This museum will be like a book
with its pages always open"

Henry Cole, 16 November 1857[1]

[1]*The functions of the Science and Art Department*, Introductory addresses on the functions of the Science and Art Department and the South Kensington Museum (v.1857.005)

The Victoria and Albert Museum

A Bibliography and Exhibition Chronology, 1852–1996

Compiled by

Elizabeth James

National Art Library

Fitzroy Dearborn Publishers

LONDON · CHICAGO

in association with

The Victoria and Albert Museum

© The Board of Trustees of the Victoria and Albert Museum 1998

Published by
FITZROY DEARBORN PUBLISHERS
310 Regent Street
London WIR 5AJ
England

and

70 East Walton Street
Chicago, Illinois 60611
USA

British Library Cataloguing in Publication Data
The Victoria and Albert Museum : a bibliography and
   exhibition chronology
   1. Victoria and Albert Museum – History.   2. Exhibitions –
   England – London – History   3. Exhibitions – England – London
   – Bibliography
   I. James, Elizabeth
   069'.0942134

ISBN 1–884964–95–8

Library of Congress Cataloging in Publication Data is available

First published in the UK and USA 1998

Book design by Humphrey Stone
Cover design by Philip Lewis

Typeset by The Florence Group, Stoodleigh, Devon
Printed by the Bath Press, UK

Cover illustration
The arch above the main entrance to the Victoria and Albert Museum (building designed by Sir Aston Webb). The statue of Prince Albert was made by Alfred Drury.

CONTENTS

LIST OF ILLUSTRATIONS

between pages 388 and 389

All photographs by V&A Photographic Studio. Cover illustration by James Stevenson; all others except no. 7 by Dominic Naish.

ACKNOWLEDGMENTS

The original project to catalogue all the publications of the Victoria and Albert Museum, establish a complete collection of them, and publish a bibliography, was conceived and proposed by Jane Savidge and Douglas Dodds, respectively Chief Cataloguer and Head of Collection Management at the National Art Library. In directing the Project, and the compilation of this book, they have both contributed a very great deal of editorial and technical work.

Without funds from the Museum's Research Department and the Friends of the V&A the Project could not have got under way.

In the National Art Library, many people have contributed in different ways. Acknowledgments are particularly due to Deborah Harris, Sehnaz Hassan, Chris McKay, the indefatigable Maureen Mulvanney and all staff at the Museum Registry, Helen Pye-Smith, Elizabeth Salmon, Mandy Sullivan, Jan van der Wateren and Gerry White. Katie Hill and Sarah Macdonald worked as project assistants during the first year. Gillian Varley generously assisted with proofreading as well as contributing editorial expertise. Justine Hunt and Margarida Bicas Pereira did useful research during placements at the NAL. Previous work done by Marjorie Finnis laid the foundations for this enterprise.

Throughout the V&A there are few who have not at some time helped by providing access to Departmental libraries, answering queries, sharing their knowledge to correct and augment references, or encouraging the project by their support. To every one, we are grateful. Anthony Burton took a particular interest, and contributed information and documents, as did Clive Wainwright. Halina Pasierbska facilitated access to the library at the Bethnal Green Museum of Childhood, Claire Hudson and Helen Smith to that at the Theatre Museum. Former V&A curators also responded kindly to requests for information: Elizabeth Bonython, David Coachworth, Geoff Opie. Ken Jackson and Dominic Naish, in the V&A Photographic Studio, were accommodating beyond the call of duty. David Anderson contributed the quotation that forms our epigraph.

Thanks to Pauline Dingley, Librarian of the Science Museum, for giving access to its South Kensington collection (and encouragement to a fellow-bibliographer); to Hamish Todd at the British Library, for kindly checking Japanese transliterations; to Gerard Forde at the Design Museum, and Stephen Bayley, for information on Boilerhouse exhibitions; to Harry Gilonis, for enormous amounts of checking and proofreading.

We are extremely grateful to Michael Conforti for contributing a Foreword from the international perspective.

Responsibility for errors and omissions lies with the compiler. A work such as this is almost infinitely improveable, and corrections will be gladly received and recorded by the National Art Library.

The compiler wishes to acknowledge all the staff at Fitzroy Dearborn, who made the final stages of this long project happier; and especially the work of Gordon Lee and Delia Gaze. Publisher Daniel Kirkpatrick's inspirational pragmatism has seen me through. I appreciated feedback and advice from Mary Butler at V&A Publications, and I am glad to acknowledge personal debts of gratitude for practical and moral support to my colleagues John Meriton, Bernadette Archer and Mandy Sullivan, to Valerie Holman, to Michael Wilson who also assisted with indexing, to G. Ingli James; above all to Harry Gilonis. And without the intervention of Carlo Dumontet this book might not have been.

ELIZABETH JAMES

DIRECTOR'S FOREWORD

One of the duties a museum should take seriously is to make available information about its own history, the growth of the collections, changing policies and interpretations. The catalogue of the Victoria and Albert Museum's publications and list of its exhibitions is evidence of our commitment to that ideal. Publication is timely as it reflects the progress of the Museum at the approach of its 150th anniversary and of the London opening in 1999 of *A Grand Design*, the exhibition constructed to celebrate the Victoria and Albert Museum's achievements.

The V&A has always been a conduit for art and design ideas in Britain, and the development of the collections and definitive gallery displays has been supplemented by a commitment to outreach, circulation and exchange. The Museum's publications, exhibitions and displays have had scholarly significance and been of considerable popularity, exerting a strong influence, particularly in the re-evaluation of artists' and designers' reputations, and influencing contemporary fashions and trends. Some publications have long remained key references for subsequent art and design histories.

From its inception, the Museum has vigorously published catalogues and learned works on exhibitions, collections and topical research concerns. Many exhibitions, both internal and extramural, have left a printed record, however ephemeral. The project to catalogue all V&A publications has for the first time consolidated the canon and provides as near a complete listing as is possible. This was achieved by cataloguing all relevant material in the National Art Library and departmental Museum libraries, researching and including items missing from these collections, and creating a separate archival collection within the Library. Integral with the compilation of the catalogue has been the parallel listing in detail of the exhibitions and displays mounted by the Museum.

The project is part of the National Art Library's programme of providing access to all documents relating to the V&A's history. The effort includes the establishment of the Archive of Art and Design and accepting custody of the Museum Archive (which material complements the information in this book), the recently completed project to catalogue all 1851 Great Exhibition material in the Library, and proposals to catalogue the papers of the Museum's first Director, Sir Henry Cole.

The material here published was first assembled and organized in the Library's computer system, and is therefore available among the Library's catalogue and supplementary databases. Its transformation into book form, an exacting process both technically and editorially, has added value to the information. The book has been for centuries the West's dominant communication technology, one which is by no means superseded. By contrast with the ways in which electronic information is delivered, a book's scope is immediately comprehended; it is clear and readable; above all the book is a portable object and its format is permanent. In itself it becomes an historic document of the state of knowledge and angle of interest at the time of publication.

This is the most comprehensive bibliographic reference source of its kind published by a major art museum and the work should serve as useful scholarly reference book and a great contribution towards the history of a world-ranking cultural institution.

ALAN BORG
Director

FOREWORD

It is well known that the Victoria and Albert Museum houses one of the premier collections of applied arts. We may be less conscious of the fact that throughout its history the V&A has not only been an active force in design education but a model for public educational initiatives by museums throughout the world. The V&A established this reputation through extensive lecture programmes, circulating exhibitions and the enormous number of publications it has supported from the moment the Museum was founded in the 1850s.

The V&A, or South Kensington Museum as it was then called, was the museum to imitate in the 19th century. It inspired a number of similar institutions focused on design education, particularly in continental Europe where thirty such museums were established in Germany alone from 1860 to the 1890s. In addition, virtually every North American museum founded in the 1870s and 1880s, from New York's Metropolitan to Boston, from Cincinnati to St. Louis, owes much of its earliest stated mission to the example of South Kensington. What attracted these institutions to the South Kensington example was the public education initiatives of the museum, made famous by its enormous programme of lectures and publications. As soon as the Museum was established it began to publish catalogues of its holdings, and they appeared at a rapid rate throughout its first decades of operation. With the development of materials-based curatorial departments in the 1890s the Museum began to support a level of specialised scholarship and connoisseurship in the applied arts that set an international standard in the field. Books on subjects ranging from German metalwork to Italian sculpture to Japanese ceramics, and exhibitions focused on a variety of subjects and periods of artistic production, have contributed to our understanding of the history of material culture.

Now as the Museum approaches its 150th anniversary, it is advancing the educational goals represented in its publication programme by commissioning volumes that address more varied public interests and a broader range of intellectual perspectives, interpreting objects within a wider frame of reference. In this redirection the publications programme continues to be a primary expression of the Museum's commitment to scholarship and public access. It is this tradition of publication, a tradition probably second to none among museums in the West, that we honour with this Bibliography, a volume that allows the books published by the Victoria and Albert Museum over the years to be accessible to an even greater number of potential users.

MICHAEL CONFORTI
Director, Sterling and Francine Clark Art Institute,
Williamstown, Massachusetts

INTRODUCTION

This book makes available for the first time chronological, indexed lists of all the publications and exhibitions of the Victoria and Albert Museum during the first 144 years of its existence. While it aims to be comprehensive, any additions and amendments resulting from its appearance are valuable in increasing the sum of accurate knowledge about the institution.[1] In order to clarify exactly what the work covers, this introduction begins with an outline of the V&A itself, including a brief account of its subdivisions and satellites. An explanation of the book's contents and arrangement follows on p. xxiii. Detailed keys to usage are located at the beginning of the Bibliography sections (p. 3, p. 387), the Exhibitions list (p. 517) and each Index.

From the Museum of Ornamental Art, to South Kensington Museum, to the V&A[2]

In the 1830s, British anxieties about competition for trade in manufactured goods led to a desire in Government to improve national product design and ornamentation. A network of art and design teaching institutions was established by the Board of Trade, centred on the Government School of Design in London, where new teaching systems and techniques were developed to meet the needs of industrial, rather than fine, artists.[3] These schools were not without problems, but the design reform movement achieved a triumphant entry into the general public's consciousness, both in Britain and inter-

---

[1] The information published here is derived from the online catalogue and exhibition list of the National Art Library. These are accessible via the Internet, at http://www.nal.vam.ac.uk/. They will be updated as and when additional details come to light, and any future edition of the book revised accordingly.

[2] The history of the Museum is not rehearsed in detail here. *History of the Victoria and Albert Museum* ... (V.1906.009) is a useful outline of the early period. The standard work on the building and development of the institution is John Physick, *The Victoria and Albert Museum: the history of its building* (V.1982.032). On the history of the collections, see Anna Somers Cocks, *The Victoria and Albert Museum: the making of the collection* (VR.1980.012), and Clive Wainwright, *The making of the applied arts collections at the South Kensington Museum* (London: V&A, forthcoming, due 2002). An 'intellectual history' of the V&A is also forthcoming: Anthony Burton, *Vision and accident: the story of the V&A* [provisional title] (London: V&A, due 1999). A great deal of recent research, and an illustrated chronology, are contained in the catalogue of an exhibition touring in North America, 1997–1999: Malcolm Baker and Brenda Richardson, general editors, *A grand design: the art of the Victoria and Albert Museum* (London: V&A; New York: Abrams, with the Baltimore Museum of Art, 1997). See also Barbara Morris, *Inspiration for design: the influence of the Victoria and Albert Museum* (V.1986.023), and, for a booklet summary, *The history of the Victoria & Albert Museum*, 2nd ed. (V.1976.031).

[3] See Quentin Bell, *The Schools of Design: the first state-supported art schools in England* (London: Routledge & Kegan Paul, 1963), and Christopher Frayling, *The Royal College of Art: one hundred years of art and design* (London: Barrie & Jenkins, 1987).

nationally, with the Great Exhibition of 1851. This massive international trade fair was held at Hyde Park in the innovative 'Crystal Palace', a pavilion of iron and glass, with British manufactured products displayed alongside those of their international competitors in a carnival atmosphere blending hospitality and rivalry. There were more than 6 million visitors to the Exhibition, and the resulting substantial profit contributed to the establishment of the Museum and its collections.[4]

The Museum's pre-history ends, and its history begins, in 1852. A new government body, the Department of Practical Art, was created under the Board of Trade, to take charge of art and design education in Britain and to establish "Museums, by which all classes might be induced to investigate those common principles of taste, which may be traced in the works of excellence of all ages".[5] As a result the Museum of Ornamental Art opened to the public in May of that year. The Museum was founded on collections which had originally been assembled solely for the use of students at the School of Design, now renamed the Central Training School. Those collections already included important purchases from the international trade fair in Paris in 1844, and were significantly strengthened by acquisitions from the Great Exhibition. One room, notoriously, was devoted to a 'Chamber of Horrors' – examples of *bad* design.[6]

School and Museum were both temporarily accommodated in Marlborough House, a royal residence, thanks to the support of Prince Albert, Queen Victoria's Consort, who had a committed interest in design reform. Albert was President of the Society for the Encouragement of Arts, Manufacturers and Commerce, and also of the Royal Commission for the Great Exhibition. He was closely associated with Henry Cole,[7] whose role in organising the Great Exhibition, running the Science and Art Department, and creating and shaping the Museum makes him the single most important figure in the history of the V&A.

The next few years saw some changes. The Department of Practical Art was almost immediately redesignated the Department of Science and Art, and in 1856 its management was transferred from the Board of Trade to the Privy Council's Committee on Education, alongside the Education Department. It thus came under the control of Henry Cole, who had been appointed Secretary of that Department.[8] Profits from the Great Exhibition were used to purchase the main part of the V&A's present site in

---

[4]The Royal Commission for the Great Exhibition of 1851 still disburses its funds to "increase the means of industrial education and extend the influence of science and art upon productive industry" according to its Charter, mainly by funding post-doctoral research for scientists intending to work in British industry. In 1994–6 it funded the cataloguing of the National Art Library's large holdings of Great Exhibition and related publications and archives. These are now listed on the NAL's Computer Catalogue. See footnote 1 for Internet address.

[5]*First report of the Department of Practical Art* (VRP.1853.001), p. 2.

[6]See V.1852.001, Appendix C. "I was ashamed of the pattern of my own trowsers for I saw a piece of them hung up there as a horror", wailed Henry Morley's 'Mr Crumpet' in *Household words* (editor, Charles Dickens) no. 141 (4 Dec. 1852).

[7]1808–1872. Cole's name recurs throughout in all accounts of the South Kensington Museum, the Great Exhibition and the Departments of Education and of Science and Art. See Elizabeth Bonython, 'Henry Cole: first Director of the V&A', in *The V&A album* 1 (VP.1982.001), and the same author's *King Cole: a picture portrait of Sir Henry Cole . . .* (V.1982.022). A full biography by Elizabeth Bonython and Anthony Burton is to be published by the V&A in 2001.

[8]See: 'History of the Science and Art Department of the Committee of Council on Education since its creation' in *Thirtieth report of the Science and Art Department* (1883), pp. ix–cxii; Harry Butterworth, *The Science and Art Department 1853–1900* (Ph.D. thesis, University of Sheffield, 1968); Arnold S. Levine, *The politics of taste: the Science and Art Department of Great Britain 1852–1873* (Ph.D. thesis, University of Wisconsin, 1972).

South Kensington, and by 1857 it was ready to accommodate the whole Science and Art establishment, including the administration, the School and the Museum. Gradually the latter became known as the South Kensington Museum.[9] The complex history of an almost continuous programme of building and reorganisation on this site has been extensively researched by John Physick.[10] At one of her last public engagements, on 7 May 1899, Queen Victoria laid the foundation stone of the new Aston Webb building, whose 720-foot façade now fronts onto the Cromwell Road. At the same time she bestowed upon it the name 'Victoria and Albert Museum'.

Although the V&A is known today as the UK's national museum of art and design, the South Kensington Museum reflected the wider remit of the Science and Art Department. From the outset there were collections of **Food**, **Animal Products** (both later moved to Bethnal Green), models of **Machinery**, and **Construction/Building Materials**. The **Patent Commissioners' museum** of inventions was transferred to South Kensington in 1852, and its contents and library were later fully amalgamated with the other science collections. The Royal Society of Arts deposited its **Education** collection of teaching apparatus and books; these evolved into the **Science Collections for Teaching and Research**, and the **Science Library**. By the 1870s there were collections of **Naval Models/Marine Engineering** contributed by the Admiralty; **Economic Entomology and Forestry**; and **Fish Culture**.[11] These became consolidated in the galleries on the western side of Exhibition Road, and from the 1880s onwards were subject to a number of reports and reorganisations. By the time the Aston Webb building opened in 1909 the Science Museum existed as a separate entity.[12]

The art collections at South Kensington

The curatorial subdivision of the V&A's art collections according to their material type was first instituted in 1896 and extended by the Committee of Re-Arrangement in 1908.[13] Today the departments are as follows:

---

[9]Compare v.1863.005 and v.1863.005a.

[10]Op. cit. Today the V&A occupies the whole site. The remaining departments of the Royal College of Art moved to its Kensington Gore premises in 1990, and its former building was subsequently refitted for the Museum's use. At the time of writing, the V&A is planning to develop the last available space, with a major new building designed by Daniel Libeskind.

[11]In fact a working fish hatchery, privately owned and run by Francis Buckland.

[12]The following references on the history of the Science Museum were supplied by the Science Museum Library: Frank Greenaway, *A short history of the Science Museum* (London: H.M.S.O., 1951); *The Science Museum: the first 100 years* (London: H.M.S.O., 1957); L.R. Day, 'A short history of the Science Museum' in *Science Museum review* (1978); David Follett, *The rise of the Science Museum under Henry Lyons* (London: Science Museum, 1978); Mari Williams 'Science, education and museums in Britain, 1870–1914' in *History and technology* 10, no. 1 (1993).

[13]The principle of displaying the collections in material-based areas is generally attributed to the the 1908 Committee (Report, VR.1908.002) but administratively it already existed, in that specialist keepers were allocated to Ceramics, Metalwork, Sculpture, Textiles and Woodwork in 1896. The materials-based classification was reaffirmed in 1899 by the Walpole Committee, appointed to advise on the reorganisation of the Departments of Education and of Science and Art (resulting in the latter's dissolution). The Walpole report is quoted by the 1908 Committee, op. cit. Thanks to Anthony Burton for clarification of this point, documented by his research in papers relating to the Select Committee on the Science and Art Department, 1897–1898. A full account will appear in his history of the V&A (*see footnote* 2).

— Ceramics and Glass

— **Furniture and Woodwork**[14]
Formerly Department of Woodwork; and from 1984 to 1990 designated Furniture and Interior Design.

— **Metalwork, Silver and Jewellery**[15]
Formerly Department of Metalwork. The collections also include clocks and watches, armour and a large number of electrotypes (reproductions cast in metal).

— **Sculpture**[16]
Formerly called Architecture and Sculpture. The national collection of post-classical sculpture also includes numerous plaster casts. Reproductions were as important as original objects for the Museum's educational purposes, and it commissioned casts and electrotypes on a very large scale, as well as photographic and print illustrations of architecture and art objects.[17]

— **Textiles and Dress**[18]
Formerly Department of Textiles.

— **Prints, Drawings and Paintings**[19]
The paintings collection at South Kensington was founded in 1857 with a large gift of British oil paintings from John Sheepshanks, whose aim was to establish a National Gallery of British Art. The Museum performed this function until towards the end of the 19th century, when another 'National Gallery of British Art' was opened at Millbank in 1897, as a division of the National Gallery. In 1908 this became the Tate Gallery, and took over the national remit to collect British painting. The V&A, however, retained the Sheepshanks gift and many other important acquisitions including collections of John Constable's work and of portrait miniatures, as well as foreign paintings.

The Department of Engraving, Illustration and Design (E.I.&D.) was created in 1909. Until that time, prints and drawings had been the province of the National Art Library. Much later, in 1977, the Department likewise took over from the Library the museum's photography collection. In 1960 E.I.&D. was renamed Prints and Drawings and placed under the responsibility of the Keeper of Paintings. The sections were formally merged in 1986. For a short period around 1990 it was also known as Designs, Prints and Drawings.

---

[14]See 'Furniture collecting at the Victoria and Albert Museum: a summary history', in Christopher Wilk, ed., *Western furniture, 1350 to the present day, in the Victoria and Albert Museum, London* (v.1996.039).

[15]See *Metalwork*, Victoria & Albert Museum departmental guides (v.1980.031).

[16]See 'The formation of the Collection' in Paul Williamson, ed., *European sculpture at the Victoria and Albert Museum* (v.1996.014).

[17]In order to gain access to monuments and sculptures all over Europe, Henry Cole negotiated the Convention for promoting universal reproduction of works of art for the benefit of museums of all countries. See *Catalogues of reproductions of objects of art: in metal, plaster and fictile ivory, chromolithography, etching and photography . . .* (v.1869.004).

[18]See *Textiles and dress*, Victoria & Albert Museum departmental guides (v.1978.091).

[19]See C.M. Kauffmann, *Paintings, water-colours and miniatures*, Victoria & Albert Museum departmental guides (v.1978.070); H. Barkley, ed., *Handbook to the Departments of Prints, Drawings & Photographs and Paintings* (v.1982.008); Mark Haworth-Booth, 'The national collection of the art of photography' in *Photography, an independent art: photographs from the Victoria and Albert Museum 1839–1996* (London: V&A Publications, 1997).

Two departments are geographically-based:

— The **Indian and South-East Asian Department**[20] originated in the East India Company's 'India Museum', founded in 1801. In 1879 most of its holdings were transferred to galleries on the west side of Exhibition Road, where they were joined by the extensive Indian collections that had already been acquired by the South Kensington Museum from 1851 onwards. The department was referred to as the 'Indian Section', or (after 1909) the 'Indian Museum'. In 1955 the building was demolished and the collection moved to the main Museum premises.

— The **Far Eastern Department** was founded in 1970, taking over most of the Chinese, Japanese and Korean holdings from the other collections.

Two other art institutions were temporarily part of the South Kensington complex. An **Architectural Museum** was housed there from 1857 to 1867.[21] The **National Portrait Gallery** was brought to the galleries on the western side of Exhibition Road in 1869. Following a fire in 1885 the pictures were transferred to Bethnal Green where they remained for ten years until moving to the present National Portrait Gallery.[22]

National Art Library[23]

The National Art Library has its origins in the reference collection of "casts, examples, books, &c"[24] assembled for the use of the students and Council members of the Government School of Design which opened in 1837. In 1842 a lending library was added.[25] Like the Museum, the Library was first opened to the general public in 1852. In the tradition of the original collection, the new Librarian was also Keeper of Casts, demonstrating the assumption that books and objects were equivalent insofar as their illustrative and educational functions were concerned. The Library's 'National' appellation dates from the late 1860s.[26] Today the Library still performs curatorial as

---

[20]See *Indian art*, Victoria & Albert Museum departmental guides (v.1978.043).

[21]The museum was founded in 1851 in Westminster, and returned there in 1867. It became known as the Royal Architectural Museum in 1870, and was maintained by the Architectural Association until 1916, when the Association had to move premises. Most of the collections were then transferred back to the V&A permanently.

[22]St Martin's Place, near Trafalgar Square.

[23]Historical accounts of the Library include: W.H.J. Weale, 'The history and cataloguing of the National Art Library', in *Transactions and proceedings of the Second International Library Conference* (London, 1897); Anthony Burton, 'The history of the Victoria and Albert Museum Library' (unpublished lecture, 1974); Edmund M.B. King, *The South Kensington Art Library: a study of its origins and development until 1900* (M.A. thesis, University of London, 1975); Chiara Barontini, *From the Library of the School of Design to the National Art Library: 150 years of art librarianship* (M.A. thesis, University College, London, 1993); Jan van der Wateren & Rowan Watson, eds., *The National Art Library: a policy for the development of the collections* (v.1993.011); Eva White, *The first years of the National Art Library 1837–1853: from the School of Design to the Department of Practical Art* (v.1994.005); Chiara Barontini, *The National Art Library and its buildings: from Somerset House to South Kensington* (v.1995.018).

[24]Minutes of the Council of the School of Design. Meeting of 19 Dec. 1836. Quoted by Eva White, op. cit.

[25]One catalogue is known in the National Art Library: *Catalogue of the lending library comprising works on art, useful knowledge & miscellaneous literature* (London: printed by W. Clowes and Sons, 1848).

[26]See v.1869.011.

well as documentary functions, in relation to its collections of illuminated manuscripts, calligraphy, fine bindings, book illustration, artists' books, comics and other genres of the book arts; however its prints and drawings, and photographs, were transferred to the Prints and Drawings Department in 1909 and 1977 respectively, as noted above.

Other Departments

Chief among the other departments responsible for publications or exhibitions are:

Circulation[27]

The Circulation Department administered the V&A's programme of travelling exhibitions to educational establishments and provincial museums. After 1909 it was empowered to acquire objects directly, rather than merely assemble collections from the existing holdings of other departments. Circulation was the first department to start acquiring 20th-century objects. In 1975 it was subsumed into a department of Education and Regional Services, but was subsequently disbanded in 1978 when the Museum, under financial pressure, decided to abandon travelling exhibitions.

Conservation

The Conservation Department was created in 1960, replacing the old 'art workshops', where craftsmen carried out repairs and restoration, with a modern, scientifically-based unit. It has expanded from a staff of about half a dozen to more than fifty, organised in specialist groups. Since 1989 the Department has co-operated with the Royal College of Art in running a Joint Conservation Course awarding M.A. and M.Phil. degrees; and it also publishes a quarterly journal.[28]

Education

The V&A was established for explicitly educational purposes, and its educational role is inherent in all its activities. For most of its history the Museum was part of the government department responsible for education, and it has always had a commitment to broadening public access to cultural resources and cultural activities. Public lectures, guided tours and courses by curators and other specialists have been a distinctive feature of the V&A's service from the beginning, but it was not until 1966 that a separate Education Department was created. Its prominence and mission have varied over time; during the 1990s the Museum re-established a commitment to the schools sector, and developed in addition a wide range of services for community groups and adult learners.

Research

A separate Research Department was set up in 1989, to allow V&A curators periods of time away from their normal duties, in order to concentrate on particular projects, such as writing a book or researching an exhibition. Additionally, appointments are

---

[27] *V & A Museum Circulation Department: its history and scope* (V.1950.024).

[28] *V&A conservation journal* (VP.1991.001).

made directly to the Department, usually for a fixed term, and scholars are brought into the Museum for periods of time on a Fellowship basis. The Department also runs M.A. courses on the History of Design, jointly with the Royal College of Art.[29]

The Boilerhouse Project (1981–1986)

This project was run by the Conran Foundation, which had been set up by designer and businessman Terence Conran, founder of the interior design chain store Habitat. Between 1981 and 1986 the Project mounted a series of popular exhibitions in a renovated building in the V&A's old boilerhouse yard. Though independent of the V&A, the Boilerhouse was closely associated with the Museum, and its active programme of exhibitions and associated publications on design is therefore documented here.[30]

Branch museums and outstations

Bethnal Green Museum of Childhood[31]

By the mid-1860s the South Kensington Museum was ready to replace the prefabricated iron structure in which it had first opened. The iron buildings were to be made available for new museums in other parts of London.[32] In the event only one such museum came about, and it remained connected to its South Kensington parent rather than being a wholly independent institution. The 'Bethnal Green Branch Museum' opened in East London in 1872, with a mixture of exhibits, as at South Kensington. The scientific collections, of Animal Products and of Food, were transferred there, where they remained until the late 1920s. Among the numerous private long- or short-term loans were important art collections, such as that of Richard Wallace, and the Chantrey Bequest to the Royal Academy.[33] As mentioned above, the National Portrait Gallery's pictures were displayed there from 1885 to 1895. After the first World War the Bethnal Green Museum was reorganised chiefly to present 19th-century arts, and particularly those relevant to its local industries: furniture, shoemaking and silk weaving. Later a special emphasis was given to costume, and for a few years BGM became the London showplace for the V&A's Circulation Department travelling exhibitions. However, from early in the 20th century there had been a commitment in the V&A to collections and activities relevant to children, and Roy Strong, while Director, recognised that there was sufficient material within the two museums to devote Bethnal Green to the history of childhood. This was implemented in 1974, and today it is officially recognised as the National Museum of Childhood.

---

[29]The course was first set up under the Education Department in 1982/3, but following reorganisation in that Department it was transferred to the administrative aegis of the National Art Library until the Research Department was created.

[30]Conran subsequently opened the Design Museum in London's Docklands.

[31]*Bethnal Green Museum of Childhood* (v.1993.004).

[32]See *Local metropolitan museums: reports of the proceedings* ... (VR.1865.002).

[33]See C.C. Black, *Catalogue of the collection ... lent for exhibition ... by Sir Richard Wallace* (v.1872.009 and numerous reprints). This collection was later established as a museum in its own right. The Chantrey Bequest became a founding collection of the Tate Gallery.

Theatre Museum[34]

The major founding collection of theatrical material was that of Gabrielle Enthoven, comprising playbills, prints and designs, acquired by the V&A in 1924. The Theatre Museum itself, however, came into existence largely through external public campaigns. The British Theatre Museum Association (BTMA) was created in 1957, operating at Leighton House, in Kensington, where it was able to display some of its holdings to the public. A new initiative, instigated in 1968, gained the support of both the V&A and the BTMA, and thus the two collections were brought together. Exhibitions were organised, within the V&A and elsewhere, from 1975. Following a lengthy search for suitable premises, the Museum opened in Covent Garden, appropriately close to London's theatre quarter, in 1987. Its pre-eminence was officially affirmed in 1991 when it was granted the title 'National Museum of the Performing Arts'.

Wellington Museum[35]

Apsley House, at Hyde Park Corner ('Number One, London'), has been the home of the Dukes of Wellington since 1817, when it was bought by the first Duke, victor of Waterloo. In 1947 it was presented to the nation by the seventh Duke, since when it has been administered by the V&A as a museum, with the family remaining in residence. The first Duke's own collections of paintings, sculpture, furniture, porcelain, silver, medals and memorabilia are on display.

Museum Archives

The Museum Archives are managed by the National Art Library.

The **Archive of Art and Design** was set up in 1977 to collect archive material from individuals, firms and associations active in design and the decorative arts. It has been open to the public since 1978, first at South Kensington, then at Neil House, Aldgate, and from 1985 at Blythe House, Olympia.[36]

The **V&A Archive** is the Museum's repository of its official papers, also at Blythe House and under the management of the National Art Library since 1993.

Ham House and Osterley Park House

Ham and Osterley are stately homes in Middlesex, both given to the National Trust in the late 1940s and administered by the V&A until 1991. Publications relating to the houses during this period are therefore included in the bibliography.

The Museum's Publications

Strictly speaking, the Museum has not itself been the publisher of most of its own books. The catalogues and other works that began to be produced by the Department

---

[34]See Jean Scott Rogers, *Stage by stage: the making of the Theatre Museum* (V.1985.042).

[35]Simon Jervis & Maurice Tomlin, *Apsley House, Wellington Museum* (V.1996.004).

[36]It is intended that the Archive will be reunited with the Library with the removal of both to a new location early in the 21st century.

of Science and Art and its new Museum were mainly official Government publications, whose actual production was arranged and financed by Her Majesty's Stationery Office (H.M.S.O.).[37] Further research would be needed to give a detailed account of the transactions between the different parties involved. Correspondence in the V&A Archive, dating back to the 19th century, certainly records clashes arising from the division of editorial and financial responsibilities. The Department's educational mission, and its desire to promulgate good design by example as well as by precept, ensured that affordability and quality were priorities, whereas 'economic' considerations were paramount to H.M.S.O.'s Controller and to the Treasury, in all matters from choice of printers to the selling price of catalogues.[38]

The Museum's own Catalogue Stall[39] was the main retail outlet for its publications, with H.M.S.O. responsible for their commercial distribution. They were also sent free to art schools and to other museums and scholarly institutions nationally and internationally.[40]

In 1976 the V&A appointed a Publications Officer for the first time.[41] H.M.S.O. continued to publish all the Museum's books and catalogues of any substance until the early 1980s, when some major publications began to appear with the Museum's own name given as publisher. For several years in-house publishing expanded rapidly, as can be observed in the Bibliography. However, the National Heritage Act of 1983 resulted in significant changes to the V&A's status.[42] The Act stated that the management of some national museums should be delegated to Boards of Trustees, who would be answerable to the Treasury via the Office of Arts and Libraries.[43] The V&A's Trustees soon found that publications would have to come under much tighter financial control, and within a couple of years the publishing programme was sharply reined in.[44] With a small in-house team and a greater dependence on co-publication the V&A did manage to continue producing books through the 1980s and early 1990s, as the link with H.M.S.O. was gradually dissolved.[45]

---

[37]Or His Majesty's . . . (1901–1952).

[38]Official records held at the Museum Archive concerning publications include: Ed.84.153, 157–163 ('Publication and sales of books on art to the general public', 1862–1935); VA.400 series (Registered papers relating to publications), 1959–. Records have been heavily weeded.

[39]The Catalogue Stall became the Museum Shop, and began stocking commercial publications as well as those relating to the V&A, in 1976.

[40]The exchange of publications continues today, administered by the National Art Library which has about 750 exchange partners worldwide. The value of the publications coming in to the Museum offsets the cost of sending V&A publications out.

[41]Recorded in *Review of the years 1974–1978* (VP.1981.001), p. 105. The exact date of the first appointment is not clear.

[42]In 1900 the Department of Science and Art had been replaced by a Board of Education, itself superseded by the Ministry of Education in 1944 and by the Department of Education and Science in 1964. These changes did not fundamentally affect the way the Museum was governed.

[43]Later the Department of National Heritage and currently Department for Culture, Media and Sport.

[44]"Since 1985, financial pressures have forced the Museum to scale down its publishing activities . . . in line with the Trustees' brief to become profitable", *Victoria and Albert Museum: report of the Board of Trustees, 1st April 1986–31st March 1989* (VP.1986.001), p. 13. A catalogue of V&A publications for sale in 1984 announces many forthcoming titles that were never published.

[45]H.M.S.O. was itself reconstituted on more commercial lines, and is still occasionally used by the Museum, e.g. Michael Archer, *Delftware, the tin-glazed earthenware of the British Isles: a catalogue of the collection in the Victoria and Albert Museum* (London: The Stationery Office in association with the Victoria and Albert Museum, 1997).

At the time of writing, however, V&A publishing is in revival. In 1995 the management of V&A Publications was transferred to **V&A Enterprises,** the trading company established as a result of the 1983 change in status. New staff were appointed, and the Museum's own imprint was formally relaunched in 1996, with an affirmed policy of publishing key titles itself. Museum curators are still strongly represented on the Publications Committee which considers all proposals. Profitability is the aim,[46] through popular publications that disseminate awareness of the V&A's collections and also help to underwrite the production of collection catalogues and other academically important works.

Co-operation and collaboration in publishing

In addition to the collaborations and negotiations already implied in this sketch of its publishing over the years, the V&A has engaged in relationships with a variety of external publishing bodies. Sometimes the Museum actively seeks publishing partners; on other occasions the proposal comes from the potential partner. Variable elements in these arrangements include: the distribution of editorial initiative and control; copyright and financial liability; and the degree and kind of Museum participation in writing and/or illustrating the text.

From 1872 onwards, the established firm of Chapman and Hall published for the Department of Science and Art a series of popular introductions to various aspects of the arts: the *South Kensington Museum art handbooks.* The first few titles were reprints of the introductions to the Museum's official catalogues. These were sufficiently successful to encourage the commissioning of further titles, and a sister series of *Science handbooks.* The series continued for 40 years.[47]

Since Owen Jones's celebrated *Grammar of ornament,*[48] there has been a market niche for high-quality colour illustrations of ornamental designs. In the 1880s the pioneering lithographic and facsimile printer William Griggs was engaged to issue plates of objects in the Museum, in parts.[49] A century later, Webb & Bower published the *V&A colour books,* popular, stylishly designed compilations of ornamental motifs from V&A objects, with introductory texts by curators. These however are as much in the style of keepsakes as of working patterns for designers.[50]

Some books are published externally because the Museum is unable to undertake them in-house. A note in a book published in 1947 states, "The book is one which in normal times the Museum would have probably published itself",[51] presumably referring to post-war exigencies. In the late 1980s and early 1990s some important co-publications reflect the Museum's need for support in a difficult financial climate. Today co-publication is more likely to be undertaken for positive, strategic reasons: the book you are now reading was entrusted to an external firm with specific expertise in publishing and marketing art reference books.

---

[46]It has been achieved in 1998.

[47]See Series index.

[48]Owen Jones, *The grammar of ornament: illustrated by examples from various styles of ornament: one hundred folio plates, drawn on stone by F. Bedford, and printed in colours* ... (London: Day and Son, 1856).

[49]*Portfolios of industrial art* (VRP.1881.002).

[50]See Series index. The series also won critical approbation, in the form of a Design and Art Direction award in 1986.

[51]Leigh Ashton, ed., *Style in sculpture* (VR.1947.005).

In some cases, permission or co-operation is sought for works wholly about the Museum, but the V&A nevertheless plays no part in their publication. The borderline between this and a real 'association' can be hard to define. Until the early years of the 20th century, publishers and individuals solicited the right merely to have their books sold at the Museum "under the sanction of the Department of Science and Art", as proudly printed on their title pages. Some of these 'sanctioned' works, however, seem as close to 'official' as makes no difference.[52]

In addition to collaborating with various book publishers, the Museum has twice acquired commercial partners in attempts to establish a substantial art periodical. The *Yearbook* and the *Album*[53] each contained useful and well-written articles, but both were relatively short-lived.[54]

The V&A is associated with several specialist decorative arts societies such as the Costume Society, the Furniture History Society and the Oriental Ceramics Society, and has from time to time produced (usually relatively modest) publications for them.

Scope and Arrangement of this Book

There are four bibliographical sequences, plus a list of exhibitions and displays. All sequences are arranged in chronological order. References in each sequence are given a mnemonic prefix:

V.	=	Publications of the Victoria and Albert Museum
		i.e. printed works published by, for, or in association with the Victoria and Albert Museum, its ancestor institutions and its outstations, as detailed above, since 1852. All known editions and reprints are listed, in their own year of issue. The reader interested in collating all printings of a title can use the Title index to do so.
VP.	=	Periodical publications
VR.	=	Publications related to, but not published by, the V&A
		i.e. works closely relating to the Museum but apparently not published by, for, or in explicit association with it.
VRP.	=	Related periodicals and part works.
VX.	=	Exhibitions and displays
		i.e. those held at the Museum, on any of its sites, plus those which it has organised elsewhere.

Publications

The distinction between 'V&A publications proper' and 'Related publications' has been made in order to present more clearly the Museum's role *as* publisher, without losing

---

[52]E.g. Arundel Society for Promoting the Knowledge of Art, *Chromolithographs of the principal objects of art in the South Kensington Museum* (VRP.1868.001), "With the sanction of the Science and Art Department ... for the use of Schools of Art and amateurs"; or William Clowes and Sons [later Spottiswoode & Co.], *A guide to the South Kensington Museum* (VR.1865.001 and passim to VR.1908.001).

[53]VP.1969.001 (1969–1974) and VP.1982.001 (1982–1989) respectively.

[54]In 1998, *V&A magazine* was launched by the Friends of the V&A. It doubles as their own journal (formerly VP.1994.001) and provides current information about displays, courses, activities, events etc. at the V&A (previously supplied by the free publication *In-view*, VP.1988.001) plus topical articles and stylish illustrations.

sight of a large amount of other relevant and useful material. In order to be included in the main bibliography, a publication must contain an explicit statement that it was published or co-published by the Museum;[55] or, in the case of H.M.S.O. imprints other than government reports, the V&A must be prominently named.

Both sequences consist mostly of publications conforming to normal commercial standards of production, intended for general distribution though not necessarily for sale. Genres include:

— bibliographies;
— catalogues of the collections;
— exhibition catalogues;
— facsimiles;
— guides to the whole Museum or parts of it;
— handbooks to subjects;
— illustrations of Museum collections, in sets of printed plates or microforms;
— monographs, both introductory and research level;
— picture books of objects by material type, function or motif;
— reports;
— technical guides to crafts;
— sound recordings of music played on instruments in the collection.

Exclusions

The following categories are mainly excluded, though a few exceptions have been made for items that seem especially interesting:

— documents intended for internal staff circulation only;
— printed matter such as posters, postcards, diaries and other stationery items;
— catalogues listing merchandise or publications for sale;
— publicity leaflets and handout plans of galleries;
— ephemera associated with exhibitions and displays.

It should be borne in mind that there are many publications by V&A staff that fall outside the limits of this book. Since 1990 the Museum has published a research report in which these are recorded.[56]

Exhibitions and displays

Naturally there are close links between the Museum's publishing and exhibiting programmes. Not only are exhibitions often accompanied by catalogues or other related publications, but they are sometimes also based on, or used to launch, books.[57] The

---

[55]The lack of such explicit statements is in retrospect often surprising, e.g. Anna Somers Cocks, *The Victoria and Albert Museum: the making of the collection* (VR.1980.012), which has every other sign of being an 'official' Museum publication. (The V&A seems also to have taken a relaxed view of copyrights at the end of the H.M.S.O. period, up to and after the change to Trustee status. Crown copyright had invariably applied in H.M.S.O. publications; today V&A staff publications are copyright to the V&A.)

[56]VP.1990.001. From 1997 the report is published biennially. Details of all staff publications are entered also on the NAL's Computer Catalogue. See footnote 1 for Internet address.

[57]"Exhibition books are a key category in the relaunched V&A Publications policy ... [with] close collaboration in the planning stages of the exhibitions programme", Mary Butler, Head of V&A Publications, memo to the compiler, 28 May 1998.

exhibitions are here cross-referenced to the publications lists, in order to bring out these links.

An exhibition is considered to be essentially a temporary arrangement, and a display is a small-scale exhibition. There are several categories of exhibition represented in this book:

— those organised by, and shown at, the Museum, its branches and outstations;
— those organised by the Museum for circulation elsewhere;
— those shown at, but not organised by, the Museum (including Boilerhouse Project exhibitions);
— those organised externally, for exhibition elsewhere, but wholly representing Museum collections.

All exhibitions and displays for which published evidence has been found are listed, including a few which were publicised but did not in fact take place.[58] Displays of single objects from the Museum's own collections are excluded.[59]

Loan collections in

From the Museum's inception, the permanent collections were supplemented by many objects and collections on short-term loan from private collectors, and often from royal collections. Some were later acquired, by purchase or bequest. After the move to South Kensington, a permanent 'loan court' was established. All loans were recorded in the annual reports of the Science and Art Department, and later also listed separately.[60] The Museum published catalogues of some, and these appear in the bibliography. Loans are included here selectively: if explicitly referred to as 'exhibitions', if of definite fixed duration, or if felt to be especially important.[61]

Loan collections out, and the Circulation Department

In 1850, "a travelling collection of works of art was established at the Central School of Design at Somerset House, and lent in rotation to the provincial schools".[62] In 1852 this function was taken over by the Museum. Collections of objects were also contributed to regional exhibitions, often supplemented by loans from collectors in the area and works by students of the local art schools. "Far more important, it [the Museum] also took over the principle of lending a part of its treasures to the provinces",[63] a principle which was energetically put into practice from 1852 until the dissolution of the Circulation Department in 1978. Some information about travelling exhibitions can be derived from published sources, but in general itineraries cannot easily be reconstructed.[64] Those Circulation exhibitions known to have been shown at South Kensington or Bethnal Green appear in the Exhibitions list.

---

[58]E.g. 'The gold reliquary of Charles the Bold' (VX.1980.005), cancelled due to a strike.

[59]E.g. 'Masterpiece of the week' (a series in the 1930s).

[60]*List of art objects in the South Kensington Museum ... lent during the year ...* (VP.1871.001).

[61]E.g. Heinrich Schliemann's Trojan artefacts (VX.1877.001).

[62]*V&A Museum Circulation Department: its history and scope* (V.1950.024).

[63]ibid. See also *Report on the system of circulation of art objects on loan from the South Kensington Museum for exhibition* (VR.1881.001).

[64]*Report[s] of the Department of Science and Art* (VRP.1853.001); *The National Museum Loan Service: the year's work* (VP.1966.001). Annual catalogues record all exhibitions offered for loan from c.1950: see VP.1950.001, VP.1950.002. The Museum Archive holds the records that survive of the Circulation Department, but these are incomplete.

Crafts Council

The work of British craftspeople has been exhibited and sold in the V&A Shop since 1974. These displays are not included here, but they are recorded in the Crafts Council's own published annual reports.

International exhibitions

As described earlier, the foundation of the V&A is closely connected with the Great Exhibition of 1851. The Exhibition's success funded the Museum's establishment at South Kensington, and a selection of works from the Exhibition was acquired by the Museum. The Exhibition also inaugurated an era of large international trade fairs in Europe and North America.[65] In 1862 another such event was staged in South Kensington, in new buildings on the west side of Exhibition Road, opposite the Museum.[66] A four-year annual series followed in 1871–74, and a further series in 1883–86 was based around themes: Fisheries, Health, 'Inventions', and the Colonies and India, respectively.These exhibitions were organised by the Royal Commission for the Exhibition of 1851 and not by the Department of Science and Art, but they have been given nominal entries in the chronology to mark their relation to the Museum's history. The physical proximity of the exhibition buildings meant that the Museum, as well as the School of Design, was able to make use of them at other times.

Students' competition entries

An annual competition was held for students at the Government art schools all over the British Isles. The entries were sent in and judged, then displayed at the South Kensington School of Design. Not Museum exhibitions as such, they are not listed here,[67] but further information can be found in the annual reports of the Science and Art Department.

Indexes

Four indexes provide access to the Publications and Exhibitions lists, by name, title, series and subject.

Name index

All names occurring in the bibliography and exhibition chronology are indexed. Personal names include authors, contributors, editors, artists and collectors. Institutional names include houses, parks and gardens, churches, events (e.g. American Festival) and government departments, as well as museums and galleries, and firms, including publishers and printers. Names of publications (e.g. newspapers) are in the Title index.

---

[65]See Paul Greenhalgh, *Ephemeral vistas: the Expositions universelles, Great Exhibitions and World's Fairs* (Manchester University Press, 1988).

[66]See *Some account of the buildings designed by Francis Fowke, Capt. R.E., for the International Exhibition of 1862, and future decennial exhibitions of the works of art and industry* (VR.1861.001).

[67]With the exception of vx.1858.002 and vx.1896.003, retrospectives of winning works from previous years, and vx.1914.006, which was, exceptionally, held on Museum premises.

Title index

Indexed here are short titles of the books, exhibitions and periodical articles listed in the bibliographies and exhibition chronology. There are additional index entries for distinctive subtitles or alternative titles, and essays within books. Titles consisting of generic terms such as Report are not indexed. Titles consisting solely or substantially of names (e.g. *Apsley House, Wellington Museum; Reynolds Stone, 1909–1979*) are also excluded. Publications and exhibitions of this kind may be located using the Name index.

Series index

An index to series published by the V&A (not covering related works), with lists of all known titles in each series.

Subject index

Subject access is provided to all sections of the bibliography and the exhibition chronology. The aims of the subject index are objectivity, comprehensiveness and simplicity. The subject of each item – book, article or exhibition – is broadly summarised in one or more key words. Subject terms and geographic names are derived mainly from the entries themselves. Extensive cross-references have been added, from general headings to specific topics and/or to the other indexes, to give a broader view and suggest relative quantities of material.

Sources of Information

The bibliography has been created by converting and editing records from the National Art Library's Computer Catalogue.[68] The Library has established a special collection of V&A publications and exhibition catalogues, and items found in the Museum's other Departments, the Branch Museums' libraries and the Science Museum, are also recorded. Additional entries are derived from bibliographic sources including the British Library catalogue and the international OCLC database. It is unlikely, however, that the lists are absolutely complete, and the Library would welcome notification of omissions.

All items have been examined, unless otherwise stated. Inconsistencies and omissions in the physical descriptions of the publications arise from the fact that some have been seen only in rebound or damaged copies.

For the Exhibitions list, information has been collated from sources which include catalogues held in the National Art Library, published reports, magazine listings, press releases and internal lists. The amount of activity, and the extent of surviving evidence for it, are variable, and here lacunae are more than likely. Uncertainties tend to attach to exhibitions and displays – they may change their dates, and be known by variant titles. Again, further information would be welcomed.

---

[68]See footnote 1 for the Internet address.

PUBLICATIONS OF THE
VICTORIA AND ALBERT MUSEUM
1852–1996

The construction of entries is based on the standard cataloguing format used in the National Art Library[1]. Titles and statements of responsibility – author, editor etc. – are transcribed verbatim from title pages, but other elements of the description, and all punctuation, are formalised according to the rules.

Explanation of entries:

Citation number[a]	V.1913.005
Title[b]	*Japanese colour prints* / by Edward F. Strange. 4th ed.
Publication[c]	London : H.M.S.O., 1913 ("E & S", printer).
Physical description[d]	x, 169 p., lxxxiv leaves of plates : ill. ; 19 cm.
Series title	(Victoria and Albert Museum handbooks)
Notes[e]	At head of title: Victoria and Albert Museum, Department of Engraving, Illustration and Design. — V & A Publication no. 89 E.I.D.[f] — Index of artists' names. — Printing: 11/13. — Wrappers.
	Copy note[g]: Some copies 22 cm.

V.1971.034	*Sports photographs by Gerry Cranham : a Victoria and Albert Museum loan exhibition.*
	[London : The Museum, 1971.][h]
	1 sheet, folded [6] p.) 1 ill. ; 11 cm.
	Texts by Geoffrey Nicholson, George Hughes. Acknowledgements / Hugh Wakefield. — "The 56 pictures shown in the present travelling version are still correctly described by their original catalogue numbers, but their sequence is no longer a complete one."–p. [7][i].
Cross reference	EXHIBITION: vx[j].1971.006

[a] Standard prefix, year of publication, running number.
[b] Title : subtitle if present / statement of responsibility; further statement/s of responsibility. Edition
[c] Place : Publisher, date (Printer or other manufacturer).
[d] Number of pages [in square brackets if unnumbered]: illustrations; height (x width if wider than high, or if width less than half of height), rounded up.
[e] Long dash (—) separates notes by category; slash (/) is used, as in title, for statements of authorship.
[f] H.M.S.O. order number.
[g] Variant aspects of particular copy seen.
[h] Square brackets used for information derived from other than usual source.

[1]The primary tool is Gorman, Michael and Paul W. Winkler, eds., *Anglo-American cataloguing rules* 2nd ed., 1988 revision. Canadian Library Association, Library Association Publishing, American Library Association, 1988.

ⁱ Quoted information in notes is from title page or verso, unless otherwise indicated.
^j Citation number in exhibition chronology, starts p. 517.

Multiple editions and issues in the same year of publication

Second and subsequent issues or editions of a title in the same year are given the same citation number with an alphabetical suffix. Only the variant details are given:

V.1875.001	*Ancient and modern furniture and woodwork* / by John Hungerford Pollen.
	[London] : Published for the Committee of Council on Education, by Chapman and Hall, [1875] (Dalziel Brothers, printers, Camden Press).
	vii, 143 p. : ill. ; 20 cm.
	(South Kensington Museum art handbooks ; no. 3)
	Index.
V.1875.001A	[Large paper ed. with additional illustrations]
	(Printed by Virtue and Co.)
	vii, 143 p., [11] leaves of plates : ill. ; 27 cm.
	Additional illustrations are etchings. — Edition of fifty.

Abbreviations and usages:

At head (or foot) of title	At the top (or bottom) of the title page
boards	upper and lower covers of a book
cm.	centimetres
col.	colour/ed
concordance	indexes Museum numbers to catalogue numbers in a publication
ed.	edition
et seq.	and following
facsims.	facsimiles
H.M.S.O.	Her (or His) Majesty's Stationery Office
ISBN	International Standard Book Number
ISSN	International Standard Serial Number
ill.	illustration/s
imp.	imprint, printing
Lugt	*Repertoire des catalogues de ventes publiques* . . . . La Haye : M. Nijhoff, 1938–
'marks'	book includes tables of makers' marks: ceramics, silver, etc.
Museum numbers	inventory numbers assigned to acquisitions
numerical index	as concordance, above
OCLC	Online Catalog Library Center bibliographic database
p.	page/s
pbk.	paperback
port/s.	portrait/s
printing: [e.g.] 9/17	printing date, month/year
repr.	reprint/ed
rev.	revised
sized	(of paper) coated, often with china clay, to give a shiny printing surface

s.l.   place (of publication) unknown: 'sine loco'
s.n.   name (of publisher) unknown: 'sine nomine'
v., vol.   volume
wrappers   any limp or paperback binding

1852

V.1852.001   *Appendix to a catalogue of the articles of ornamental art in the*
              Museum of the Department : for the use of students and
              manufacturers, and the consultation of the public.
              London : Printed by George E. Eyre and William Spottiswoode for
              H.M.S.O., 1852.
              32 p. : ill. ; 22 cm.
              At head of title: Department of Practical Art. — Appendix A: Principles of practical art.
              Appendix B: Instruction in practical art in foreign schools / W. Dyce. Appendix C:
              Examples of false principles in decoration.
              EXHIBITION: VX.1852.001

V.1852.002   *A catalogue of the articles of ornamental art in the Museum of the*
              Department : for the use of students and manufacturers, and the
              consultation of the public. 3rd ed.
              London : Printed by George E. Eyre and William Spottiswoode for
              H.M.S.O., 1852.
              55 p. ; 21 cm.
              At head of title: Department of Practical Art. — "With appendices, published
              separately." — CONTENTS: Introduction / Henry Cole, Owen Jones, Richard
              Redgrave. Postscript / Henry Cole. Observations / by Owen Jones. — [Catalogue of the
              6 divisions of the Museum, i.e. Woven fabrics; Metal work; Pottery; Glass; Furniture
              and upholstery, wood carvings, papier mâché and japanned wares; Various].

V.1852.003   *A catalogue of the articles of ornamental art in the Museum of the*
              Department : for the use of students and manufacturers, and the
              consultation of the public. 3rd ed.
              London : Printed by George E. Eyre and William Spottiswoode for
              H.M.S.O., 1852.
              110 p. : ill. ; 21 cm.
              At head of title: Department of Practical Art. — "With appendices". — CONTENTS:
              v.1852.002, v.1852.001. v.1852.006 continuously paged.

V.1852.004   *A catalogue of the articles of ornamental art, selected from the*
              Exhibition of the Works of Industry of all Nations in 1851, and
              purchased by the government : prepared at the desire of the Lords of
              the Committee of Privy Council for Trade.
              London : Published for the Department of Practical Art by Chapman
              and Hall, [1852] (Printed by W. Clowes and Sons).
              v, 7–96 p. ; 22 cm.

At head of title: Department of Practical Art. — "With an appendix." — CONTENTS: Introduction [dated: 17th May, 1852] / Henry Cole, Owen Jones, Richard Redgrave. Observations / Owen Jones. A catalogue. Appendix A: Principles of practical art [extracts from Richard Redgrave, J.R. Herbert, Digby Wyatt]. Appendix B: Instruction in practical art in foreign schools / William Dyce. Prospectus [of the] Department of Practical Art.

V.1852.004A   [Another issue]

v, 7–101 p.

Introduction dated: "May 17, 1852."

V.1852.005   *A catalogue of the articles of ornamental art, selected from the Exhibition of the Works of Industry of all Nations in 1851, and purchased by the government : prepared at the desire of the Lords of the Committee of Privy Council for Trade.* [2nd ed.?]

London : Printed by George E. Eyre and William Spottiswoode for H.M.S.O., 1852. (W. Clowes and Sons, printer).

[?], 98, [2] p. : ill. ; 22 cm.

Catalogued from an incomplete copy . . . [Sept. 1852?].

Appendix A: Principles of practical art . . . / Richard Redgrave. Appendix B: Instruction in practical art in foreign schools / William Dyce. Appendix C: Examples of false principles in decoration. Prospectus [of the] Department of Practical Art.

EXHIBITION: VX.1852.001

V.1852.006   *Department of Practical Art. 1. A brief statement of the contents of the Museum. 2. Prospectus of the Department, setting forth the rules and fees appointed to be taken in the management of the Museum, Library, special classes, schools of ornamental art, and teaching of elementary drawing.*

London : Printed by George E. Eyre and William Spottiswoode for H.M.S.O., 1852.

22, [2] p. ; 22 cm.

Caption title. — Museum : Contents of the rooms, passages &c open to the public. Prospectus : Department of Practical Art, Marlborough House, Pall Mall, London, under the authority of the Board of Trade.

1853

V.1853.001   *Catalogue of specimens of cabinet work exhibited at Gore House, Kensington.*

London : Printed by George E. Eyre and William Spottiswoode for H.M.S.O., 1853.

39 p. ; 22 cm.

At head of title: Board of Trade, Department of Science and Art. — "As the space at Marlborough House is now fully occupied by the Museum and special classes, permission has been obtained . . . to use such accommodations as may be afforded by Gore House . . ."–t.p. verso.

EXHIBITION: VX.1853.XXX.001

V.1853.002   *A catalogue of the articles of ornamental art in the Museum of the Department : for the use of students and manufacturers, and the consultation of the public.* 4th ed.

London : Printed by George E. Eyre and William Spottiswoode for
H.M.S.O., 1853.

64 p. ; 21 cm.

At head of title: Department of Practical Art. — "With appendices, published
separately." — "February 1853."— CONTENTS: Introduction / Henry Cole, Owen
Jones, Richard Redgrave. Postscript / Henry Cole. Observations / by Owen Jones. —
[Catalogue of the divisions of the Museum, i.e. Woven fabrics; Metal work; Pottery;
Glass; Furniture and upholstery, wood carvings, papier mâché and japanned wares;
Various].

v.1853.003   *A catalogue of the Museum of Ornamental Art at Marlborough
House, Pall Mall : for the use of students and manufacturers, and the
public.* 5th ed.
London : Printed by George E. Eyre and William Spottiswoode for
H.M.S.O., 1853.

156 p. : ill. ; 21 cm.

At head of title: Department of Science and Art. — "With explanatory and critical
remarks and appendices." — "May 1853."

CONTENTS: Introduction. General arrangement of the Museum. Examples of false
principles in decoration. A catalogue of the objects in the Museum (Division I, Furniture
and upholstery, wood carvings, papier mâché and japanned wares; Division II, Glass;
Division III, Metal work; Division IV, Pottery; Division V, Various; Division VI, Woven
fabrics). Observations on some of the specimens of metal work / by Professor Semper.
Observations on lace / by Octavius Hudson. Appendix A. Formation of the Museum
(Report of the Committee appointed by the Board of Trade for the disposal of the
Parliamentary grant of £5,000 for the purchase of articles from the Exhibition of 1851)
/ Henry Cole, Owen Jones, Richard Redgrave. Appendix B. Extracts [from Richard
Redgrave and William Dyce] illustrating the principles of practical art. Appendix C.
Observations on the collection of Indian examples / by Owen Jones. Appendix D.
Principles of decorative art . . . / by Owen Jones. Appendix E. Principles of science and
art, being the conclusion of Professor Forbes's lecture on animal forms. Prospectus of
the Board of Trade Department of Science and Art.

v.1853.004   *A descriptive catalogue of a collection of oriental and old Sèvres
porcelain, the property of Her Majesty The Queen : deposited for
exhibition in the Museum of the Department* / by J.C. Robinson.
London : Printed by George E. Eyre and William Spottiswoode for
H.M.S.O., 1853.

16 p. ; 22 cm.

At head of title: Department of Science and Art.

v.1853.004A   [Another issue]
18 p ; 22 cm.

At head of title: Department of Science and Art, Division for Art.

v.1853.005   *Prospectus of the Library of the Section of Art at Marlborough House*
/ by R.N. Wornum.
London : Printed by George E. Eyre and William Spottiswoode for
H.M.S.O., 1853.

14 p. ; 22 cm.

At head of title: Department of Science and Art. — Bibliography: p. 11–14.

1854

V.1854.001   *Catalogue of ornamental casts in the possession of the Department.*
Third division, the Renaissance styles / by R.N. Wornum.
London : Printed by George E. Eyre and William Spottiswoode for
H.M.S.O. and published by Longman, Brown, Green and Longmans,
1854.
54 p., [26] leaves of plates (some folded) : ill. ; 25 cm.
At head of title: Board of Trade Department of Science and Art. Cover title: Ornamental
casts. Renaissance. — "With illustrations on wood, engraved by the female students of
the wood engraving class." — Plates printed in brown. Maroon cloth covered boards
blind stamped with border design. Title stamped in gold.

V.1854.002   *A catalogue of the Museum of Ornamental Art át Marlborough*
House, Pall Mall . . . : with explanatory and critical remarks and
appendices. 6th ed.
London : Printed by George E. Eyre and William Spottiswoode for
H.M.S.O., 1854.
111 p. : ill. ; 21 cm.
At head of title: Board of Trade, Department of Science and Art. — "March 1854." —
CONTENTS: Introduction. A catalogue of the objects in the Museum (Division I,
Furniture and upholstery, wood carvings, papier mâché and japanned wares; Division II,
Glass; Division III, Metal work; Division IV, Pottery; Division V, Various; Division VI,
Woven fabrics). Observations on some of the specimens of metal work, enamels, &c. /
by Professor Semper. Observations on lace / by Octavius Hudson. Appendices A-E as
V.1853.003. Appendix F: Extracts from Sir Gardiner [i.e. Gardner] Wilkinson.

1855

V.1855.001   *An account of the Library of the Division of Art at Marlborough*
House : with a catalogue of the principal works, classified for the use
of visitors to the library / by Ralph N. Wornum.
London : Printed by George E. Eyre and William Spottiswoode for
H.M.S.O., 1855.
240 p. ; 21 cm.
At head of title: Department of Science and Art. — Includes index to classes.

V.1855.001A   [Another ed.]
263 p. ; 21 cm.
Includes indexes to classes and to authors' names.

V.1855.002   *Catalogue of a collection of works of decorative art : being a selection*
from the Museum at Marlborough House, circulated for exhibition in
provincial schools of art / by J.C. Robinson.
London : Printed by George E. Eyre and William Spottiswoode for
H.M.S.O., 1855.
87 p. ; 24 cm.
At head of title: Board of Trade, Department of Science and Art. — "June 1855." —
"Under revision." — Includes copy of Board of Trade circular on the circulation of art
objects from the Museum to local schools of art, signed Henry Cole, Lyon Playfair. —
Index to classes.
EXHIBITION: VX.1855.XXX.001

V.1855.003   *A catalogue of the Museum of Ornamental Art, at Marlborough*
              House, Pall Mall / by J.C. Robinson. Part 1.
              London : Printed by George E. Eyre and William Spottiswoode for
              H.M.S.O. and published by Chapman and Hall, 1855.
              90 p., [7] leaves of plates, folded : ill. ; 24 cm.
              At head of title: Board of Trade, Department of Science and Art. — "May 1855." —
              "Under revision." — Division 1, Sculpture: Carvings &c in marble, alabaster, stone,
              wood, ivory, and other materials; Art bronzes; Terra cottas and models in wax, plaster
              &c. Division 2, Painting: Wall decoration; Paper hangings; Illuminations; Printing;
              Designs &c. Division 3, Glyptic and numismatic art: Cameos and intaglios in hard
              stones and in shell; Medals, seals &c. Divison 4, Mosaics: Mosaics of calcareous stones;
              Pietra dura work; Glass mosaics; *Marqueterie; Intarsiatura; Parquetage; "Buhl"* and
              Picqué work; Straw mosaic &c. Division 5, Furniture and general upholstery. Division
              6, Basket work. Division 7, Leather work: Stamped work; Bookbinding &c. Division 8,
              Japanned or lacquered work. Division 9, Glass painting. Division 10, Glass
              manufactures. Division 11, Enamels. Division 12, Pottery. Division 13, Works in metal:
              Wrought, cast and stamped works in general; Chasing, engraving, etching &c.;
              Instruments and utensils; Locksmiths' works; Goldsmiths' works; *Damasquinerie* or
              inlaying; *Niello* work. Division 14, Arms, armour and accoutrements; Division 15,
              Watch and clock work; Division 16, Jewellery: Personal ornaments; Objects in precious
              metals. Division 17, Textile fabrics: Costumes and garment tissues; Lace; Embroidery;
              Carpets; Hangings &c.; Woven fabrics in grass, straw &c. — Appendix A. Formation of
              the Museum (Report of the Committee appointed by the Board of Trade for the disposal
              of the Parliamentary grant of £5,000 for the purchase of articles from the Exhibition of
              1851) / Henry Cole, Owen Jones, Richard Redgrave. Appendix B. Extracts [from
              Richard Redgrave and William Dyce] illustrating the principles of practical art. — Grey
              wrappers.

V.1855.003A   [2nd ed.]
              108 p., [19] leaves of plates.
              "October 1855."

1856

V.1856.001   *Catalogue of a collection of objects of ornamental art formed by M.*
              Soulages of Toulouse / by J. Webb.
              London : Printed by George E. Eyre and William Spottiswoode for
              H.M.S.O., 1856.
              13 p. ; 21 cm.
              EXHIBITION: VX.1857

V.1856.002   *Catalogue of a collection of works of decorative art : being a selection*
              from the Museum at Marlborough House, circulated for exhibition in
              provincial schools of art / by J.C. Robinson. 4th ed.
              London : Printed by George E. Eyre and William Spottiswoode for
              H.M.S.O., 1856.
              87 p. ; 24 cm.
              At head of title: Board of Trade, Department of Science and Art. — "January 1856." —
              Includes copy of Board of Trade circular on the circulation of art objects from the
              Museum to local schools of art, signed Henry Cole, Lyon Playfair. — Index to classes.
              — Blue wrappers. — 2nd and 3rd eds. not traced.
              EXHIBITION: VX.1855.XXX.001

V.1856.002A   [Another ed.]
              "November 1856." — Unseen. Record from National Art Library catalogue of
              acquisitions before 1890.

v.1856.003   *A catalogue of the Museum of Ornamental Art at Marlborough House, Pall Mall* / by J.C. Robinson. Part I. Abridged 2nd ed.
London : Printed by George E. Eyre and William Spottiswoode for H.M.S.O., 1856.
47 p. ; 22 cm.
At head of title: Board of Trade, Department of Science and Art. — "Under revision."

v.1856.004   *A catalogue of the Museum of Ornamental Art, at Marlborough House, Pall Mall* / by J.C. Robinson. Part I. 3rd ed.
London : Printed by George E. Eyre and William Spottiswoode for H.M.S.O. and published by Chapman and Hall, 1856.
128 p., [26] leaves of plates : ill. ; 24 cm.
At head of title: Board of Trade Department of Science and Art. — "January 1856." — "Under revision". — Appendices A-B as v.1853.003. — Grey wrappers.

v.1856.005   *Inventory of the objects forming the collections of the Museum of Ornamental Art* / by J.C. Robinson.
London : Printed by George E. Eyre and William Spottiswoode for H.M.S.O., 1856.
73 p. ; 22 cm.
General classification: I, Sculpture. II, Glyptic and numismatic art. III, Mosaics. IV, Painting. V, Japanned or lacquer ware. VI, Glass painting. VII, Enamels. VIII, Pottery. IX, Glass manufactures. X, Works in metal. XI, Watches and clocks. XII, Jewelry [sic] and decorative objects in precious materials. XIII, Arms, armour and accoutrements. XIV, Furniture and general upholstery. XV, Leather work. XVI, Basket work. XVII, Textile fabrics. XVIII, Bookbinding and book decoration generally. XIX, Ornamental designs, drawings, engravings &c.

1857

v.1857.001   *A brief guide to the collection of animal products.*
[London : H.M.S.O.?, 1857] (Printed by W. Clowes and Sons).
16 p. ; 22 cm.
Caption title. At head of title: South Kensington Museum.

v.1857.002   *Catalogue of the Educational Division of the South Kensington Museum.*
London : Printed by George E. Eyre and William Spottiswoode for H.M.S.O., 1857.
xvi, 159 p. ; 23 cm.
Copy note: Bound with catalogues of commercial publishers and suppliers of educational materials.

v.1857.003   2nd ed.
xxiv, 181 p.
"Corrected to November 1857."

v.1857.004   *Catalogue of the Soulages collection : being a descriptive inventory of a collection of works of decorative art, formerly in the possession of M. Jules Soulages of Toulouse, now by permission of the Committee of Privy Council for Trade exhibited to the public at the Museum of Ornamental Art, Marlborough House* / by J.C. Robinson.

London : Printed by George E. Eyre and William Spottiswoode for
H.M.S.O., 1857.
18 p. ; 22 cm.
"January 1857."

v.1857.005   *The functions of the Science and Art Department* / by Henry Cole.
London : Chapman and Hall, Agents to the Science and Art
Department of the Committee of Council on Education, 1857 (Printed
by Eyre and Spottiswoode).
32 p., ; 18 cm.
(Introductory addresses on the Science and Art Department and the
South Kensington Museum ; no. 1)
"Delivered on 16th Nov. 1857."

v.1857.006   *Inventory of the pictures, drawings, etchings &c. in the British Fine
Art Collections deposited in the new gallery at Cromwell Gardens,
South Kensington : being for the most part the gift of John
Sheepshanks, Esq.*
London : Printed by George E. Eyre & William Spottiswoode for
H.M.S.O., 1857.
24 p. ; 22 cm.
Introduction / by Richard Redgrave.

v.1857.007   *On a national collection of architectural art* / by James Fergusson.
London : Chapman and Hall, Agents to the Science and Art
Department of the Committee of Council on Education, 1857 (Printed
by Eyre and Spottiswoode).
22 p. ; 18 cm.
(Introductory addresses on the Science and Art Department and the
South Kensington Museum ; no. 6)
"Delivered on 21st Dec. 1857."

v.1857.008   *On scientific institutions in connexion with the Department of Science
and Art* / by Lyon Playfair.
London : Chapman and Hall, Agents to the Science and Art
Department of the Committee of Council on Education, 1857 (Printed
by Eyre and Spottiswoode).
32 p. ; 18 cm.
(Introductory addresses on the Science and Art Department and the
South Kensington Museum ; no. 3)
Date of lecture not recorded.

v.1857.009   *On the gift of the Sheepshanks collection : with a view to the
formation of a national gallery of British art* / by Richard Redgrave.
London : Chapman and Hall, Agents to the Science and Art
Department of the Committee of Council on Education, 1857 (Printed
by Eyre and Spottiswoode).
31 p. : ill. ; 18 cm.
(Introductory addresses on the Science and Art Department and the
South Kensington Museum ; no. 2)
Date of lecture not recorded.

V.1857.010   *Supplement (A. to December 1856) to the catalogue of the Library of the Division of Art, in alphabetical order.*
London : Printed by George E. Eyre and William Spottiswoode for H.M.S.O., 1857.
61 p. ; 21 cm.
At head of title: Department of Science and Art.

1858

V.1858.001   *Appendix to the inventory of the objects forming the collections of the Museum of Ornamental Art.*
London : Printed by George E. Eyre and William Spottiswoode for H.M.S.O., [1858].
15 p. ; 22 cm.
Caption title. — Divisions as v.1856.005, except: III, Mosaics, marquetry and various objects. XII, Jewellery, personal ornaments and objects in precious materials. XVII, Textile fabrics, costumes etc. [XIX not present].

V.1858.002   *British sculpture in connection with the Department of Science and Art* / by John Bell.
London : Chapman and Hall, 1858 (W. Clowes and Sons).
32 p. ; 18 cm.
(Introductory addresses on the Science and Art Department and the South Kensington Museum)
"Delivered 19th April 1858."

V.1858.003   *Catalogue of a collection of works of decorative art : being a selection from the Museum at South Kensington, circulated for exhibition in provincial schools of art* / by J.C. Robinson.
6th ed.
London : [H.M.S.O.], 1858.
"March 1858." — Unseen. Record from National Art Library catalogue of acquisitions before 1890. — 5th ed. not traced.
EXHIBITION: VX.1855.XXX.001

V.1858.004   *Catalogue of the collection of animal products* . . . .
London, 1858.
Unseen. Record from National Art Library catalogue of acquisitions before 1890.

V.1858.005   *Catalogue of the Educational Division of the South Kensington Museum.* 3rd ed.
London : Printed by George E. Eyre and William Spottiswoode for H.M.S.O., [1858].
xxiv, 191 p. ; 23 cm.
"Corrected to April 1858."
Copy note: Bound with catalogues of commercial publishers and suppliers of educational materials.

V.1858.006   *A catalogue of the pictures, drawings, etchings, &c. in the British Fine Art Collections deposited in the new gallery at South Kensington : being for the most part the gift of John Sheepshanks, Esq.*
London : Printed by George E. Eyre and William Spottiswoode for H.M.S.O., 1858.

102 p. : plan ; 24 cm.
Includes: Minute / Lyon Playfair; Introduction / by Richard Redgrave. — Index. —
Wrappers, with plan.

V.1858.007   *A description of the building at South Kensington, erected to receive
the Sheepshanks collection of pictures : with plans and illustrations /*
by Francis Fowke.
London : Chapman and Hall, Agents to the Science and Art
Department of the Committee of Council on Education, 1858 (Printed
by George E. Eyre and William Spottiswoode).
34 p. (1 folded) : ill., plans ; 24 cm.
p. 32–34: South Kensington Museum of Pictures, Sculpture, Education, Architecture,
Building Materials, Patented Inventions and Products of the Animal Kingdom:
arrangements for the winter session. The Metropolitan Schools of Art . . . . Library. —
Green-grey wrappers with diagram.

V.1858.008   *On the Central Training School for Art /* by Richard Burchett.
London : Chapman and Hall, Agents to the Science and Art
Department of the Committee of Council on Education, 1858 (Printed
by Eyre and Spottiswoode).
32 p. ; 18 cm.
(Introductory addresses on the Science and Art Department and the
South Kensington Museum ; no. 4)
"Delivered 7th Dec. 1857."

V.1858.009   *On the Museum of Art /* by J.C. Robinson.
London : Chapman and Hall, Agents to the Science and Art
Department of the Committee of Council on Education, 1858 (Printed
by Eyre and Spottiswoode).
29 p. ; 18 cm.
(Introductory addresses on the Science and Art Department and the
South Kensington Museum; no. 5)
"Delivered 14th Dec. 1857."

1859

V.1859.001   *Catalogue of the collection illustrating construction and building
material in the South Kensington Museum.*
London : Printed by George E. Eyre and William Spottiswoode for
H.M.S.O., 1859.
111 p. ; 22 cm.
Wrapper title: Classed catalogue of the Museum of Construction in the South
Kensington Museum.

V.1859.002   *Catalogue of the Educational Division of the South Kensington
Museum.* 4th ed.
London : Printed by George E. Eyre and William Spottiswoode for
H.M.S.O., [1859].
xxviii, 253 p. ; 23 cm.
"Corrected to December 1859."
Copy notes: Bound with catalogues of commercial publishers and suppliers of
educational materials.

V.1859.002A   [Another issue]
"Corrected to March 1859."
Unseen; record in National Art Library catalogue of acquisitions before 1890.

V.1859.003   *A catalogue of the pictures, drawings, etchings, &c. in the British Fine Art Collections deposited in the new gallery at South Kensington : being for the most part the gift of John Sheepshanks, Esq.* [Rev. ed.]
London : Printed by George E. Eyre and William Spottiswoode, 1859.
104 p. ; 24 cm.
Includes: Minute / Lyon Playfair; Introduction / by Richard Redgrave. — Index. — Wrappers, with plan.

V.1859.003A   [Another issue]
110 p. ; 22 cm.
Copy note: "7th thousand".

V.1859.004   *A guide to the food collection in the South Kensington Museum* / by Edwin Lankester.
London : Printed by George E. Eyre and William Spottiswoode for H.M.S.O., 1859.
96 p. ; 21 cm.

V.1859.005   *Inventory of the pictures, drawings, etchings, &c. in the British Fine Art Collections deposited in the new gallery, South Kensington : being for the most part the gift of John Sheepshanks, Esq.*
London : Printed by George E. Eyre and William Spottiswoode for H.M.S.O., 1859.
29 p. ; 21 cm.
Introduction / by Richard Redgrave.

V.1859.006   *Photographic illustrations of works in various sections of the collection : the objects selected by J.C. Robinson and photographed by C. Thurston Thompson.*
London : Published by authority of the Science and Art Department of the Committee of Council on Education, 1859.
48 leaves of plates : all ill. ; 51 cm.
At head of title: Museum of Art, South Kensington. — Published in twelve parts. — Photographs pasted onto leaves.

V.1859.007   *Price list of reproductions of objects of art selected from the South Kensington Museum, and from various other public and private collections : produced for the use of schools of art and for general purposes of public instruction : electrotypes, casts, photographs, &c.*
London : Printed by George E. Eyre and William Spottiswoode for H.M.S.O., 1859.
16 p. ; 22 cm.
At head of title: Department of Science and Art. — Elkington's electrotypes. Franchi's electrotypes. Franchi's casts in fictile ivory and plaster. Brucciani's casts in plaster. Photographs by C. Thurston Thompson.

V.1859.008   *Price list of reproductions of works of art by means of photography, electrotyping, casting &c. selected from the South Kensington Museum, and from various other public and private collections : produced for the use of schools of art and public instruction generally*
. . . .

London : Printed by George E. Eyre and William Spottiswoode for
H.M.S.O., 1859.

39 p. ; 22 cm.

At head of title: Committee of Council on Education, Department of Science and Art. —
"With a historical sketch of the cartoons by Raffaelle at Hampton Court, and
descriptive notices of other works in the series of photographs." — Text on the Raphael
cartoons signed "G.W." [i.e. George Wallis?]. — Lists: Photographs, comprising official
photographs of the Science and Art Department; official photographs of the British
Museum; various series by C. Thurston Thompson. Elkington's electrotypes. Franchi's
electrotypes. Franchi's casts in fictile ivory and plaster. Brucciani's casts in plaster.
Arundel Society's publications.

1860

V.1860.001   *Catalogue of the circulating collection of works of art selected from
the Museum at South Kensington : intended for temporary exhibitions
in provincial schools of art* / by J.C. Robinson.
London : Printed by George E. Eyre and William Spottiswoode, for
H.M.S.O., 1860.

97 p. ; 22 cm.

At head of title: Science and Art Department of the Committee of Council on Education.
— "July 1860." — Index to classes.

EXHIBITION: VX.1860.XXX.001

V.1860.002   *Catalogue of the collection of animal products, South Kensington
Museum.* 2nd ed.
London : Printed by George E. Eyre and William Spottiswoode for
H.M.S.O., 1860.

viii, 120 p., 2, [2], [4], 4, 4 p., [5] leaves of advertisements ; 21 cm.

Preface / Edgar A. Bowring. Compiled by P.L. Simmonds. — "Since the publication of
the first edition of this catalogue, the whole of the "Collection of Animal Products" has
been presented by Her Majesty's Commissioners for the Exhibition of 1851 to the
Science and Art Department . . . It . . . forms one of the three public museums devoted to
the industrial products of the Mineral, Vegetable and Animal Kingdoms. The Mineral
Products are deposited at Jermyn Street, the Vegetable Products at Kew, and the Animal
Products . . . form part of the Museum at South Kensington."–p. v.

V.1860.003   *Catalogue of the Educational Division of the South Kensington
Museum.* 5th ed.
London : Printed by George E. Eyre and William Spottiswoode for
H.M.S.O., [1860].

xxviii, 286, [2] p. ; 23 cm.

"Corrected to February 1860."

V.1860.004   6th ed.

xxvii, 332, [2] p.

Wrappers title: Classed catalogue of the Educational Division of the South Kensington
Museum. — "Corrected to December 1860."

V.1860.005   *A catalogue of the pictures, drawings, etchings, &c. in the British Fine
Art Collections deposited in the new gallery at South Kensington :
being for the most part the gift of John Sheepshanks.*
London : Printed by George E. Eyre and W. Spottiswoode for
H.M.S.O., 1860.

103 p. ; 21 cm.

Includes: Minute / Lyon Playfair; Introduction / by Richard Redgrave.
Copy notes: "10th thousand", "13th thousand" seen.

V.1860.006   *A guide to the food collection in the South Kensington Museum* / by
Edwin Lankester. 2nd ed.
London : Printed by George E. Eyre and William Spottiswoode for
H.M.S.O., 1860.
103 p. ; 21 cm.
"February 1860."

V.1860.007   3rd ed.
viii, 149 p.
"November 1860."

V.1860.008   *Inventory of the British water colour paintings in the Fine Arts
Collections at South Kensington* / with an introduction by R.
Redgrave.
London : Printed by George E. Eyre and William Spottiswoode for
H.M.S.O., 1860.
16 p. ; 21 cm.
Copy note: Annotated in pen at colophon: "April".

V.1860.008A   [Another issue]
22 p. ; 21 cm.
Copy note: Annotated in pencil at colophon: "July".

V.1860.009   *Inventory of the objects forming the collections of the Museum of
Ornamental Art at South Kensington* / edited by J.C. Robinson.
London : Printed by George E. Eyre and William Spottiswoode for
H.M.S.O., 1860.
127 p. ; 22 cm.
At head of title: Science and Art Department of the Committee of Council on Education.
— "Under revision." – General classification: I, Sculpture. II, Glyptic and numismatic
art. III, Mosaics, marquetry &c. IV, Painting. V, Japanned or lacquer ware. VI, Glass
painting. VII, Enamels on metal. VIII, Pottery. IX, Glass manufactures. X, Works in
metal. XI, Watch and clock work. XII, Jewelry [sic], personal ornaments, and objects in
precious materials. XIII, Arms, armour and accoutrements. XIV, Furniture, upholstery
&c. XV, Leather work. XVI, Basket and other work in vegetable fibre. XVII, Textile
fabrics. XVIII, Bookbinding and book decoration generally. — Includes list of donors.
— Copies known with Notices dated January, and October. There may also have been
issues in February, July, November. — Blue wrappers.

V.1860.010   *Notice of works of mediaeval and Renaissance sculpture, decorative
furniture, &c. acquired in Italy, in the early part of the year 1859, for
the South Kensington Museum, by J.C. Robinson, F.S.A., ...*
London : Printed by George E. Eyre and William Spottiswoode for
H.M.S.O., 1860.
14 p. ; 21 cm.
At head of title: Science and Art Department of the Committee of Council on Education.

V.1860.011   *Price list of reproductions of works of art by means of photography,
electrotyping, casting &c. selected from the South Kensington
Museum, and from various other public and private collections :
produced for the use of schools of art and public instruction generally
. . . .*

London : Printed by George E. Eyre and William Spottiswoode for H.M.S.O., 1860.

39 p. ; 22 cm.

At head of title: Committee of Council on Education, Department of Science and Art. — "With a historical sketch of the cartoons by Raffaelle at Hampton Court, and descriptive notices of other works in the series of photographs." — Contents as v.1859.008. — "Notice", p. [2], dated 23rd January 1860.

V.1860.011A   [Another isssue]

42 p. ; 22 cm.

"September 1860."

1861

V.1861.001   *Catalogue of the Art Library* / J.C. Robinson.
London : Printed by George E. Eyre and William Spottiswoode for H.M.S.O., 1861.

272 leaves ; 34 cm.

At head of title: Science and Art Department of the Committee of Council on Education. — "Under revision."

Copy note: Printed as proofs, on one side of the sheets only.

V.1861.002   *Catalogue of the circulating collection of works of art selected from the Museum at South Kensington : intended for temporary exhibitions in provincial schools of art* / by J.C. Robinson.
London : [H.M.S.O.], 1861.

May 1861. — Unseen. Record from National Art Library catalogue of acquisitions before 1890.

V.1861.003   *Catalogue of the collection illustrating construction and building materials in the South Kensington Museum* / edited by Henry Sandham. 2nd ed.
London : Printed by George E. Eyre and William Spottiswoode for H.M.S.O., 1861.

213 p. : plan ; 22 cm.

At head of title: Science and Art Department of the Committee of Council on Education. — "Under revision."

V.1861.003A   [Another issue]

230 p. ; 22 cm.

V.1861.004   *Catalogue of the collection of animal products . . . .*
London, 1861.

Unseen. Record from National Art Library catalogue of acquisitions before 1890.

V.1861.005

Inventory of the objects forming the collections of the Museum of Ornamental Art at South Kensington / edited by J.C. Robinson.
London : Printed by George E. Eyre and William Spottiswoode for H.M.S.O., 1860 [sic].

176 p. ; 22 cm.

At head of title: Science and Art Department of the Committee of Council on Education. — "Under revision." – General classification: as v.1860.009. — Notice dated March 1861. — Includes list of donors. — Blue wrappers.

V.1861.005A   [Another issue]
                1861.
                178 p.
                Notice dated May 1861.

1862

V.1862.001   *Catalogue of the Art Library, South Kensington Museum / J.C.*
                Robinson.
                London : Printed by George E. Eyre and William Spottiswoode for
                H.M.S.O., 1862.
                334 p. ; 22 cm.
                At head of title: Science and Art Department of the Committee of Council on Education.
                — "This catalogue has been prepared for the use of the students frequenting the Art
                Library, and for the provincial schools which have the privilege of obtaining books on
                loan; it is not published for sale"–t.p. verso. — Printing: 11/62.

V.1862.002   *A catalogue of the British Fine Art Collections at South Kensington :*
                being for the most part the gifts of John Sheepshanks and Mrs.
                Ellison.
                London : [Printed by George E. Eyre and William Spottiswoode for
                H.M.S.O.], 1862.
                104 p. ; 22 cm.
                Includes: Foundation of the collections, Mr Sheepshanks' Deed of Gift; Minute of the
                Lords of the Privy Council . . . / Lyon Playfair. Introduction / by Richard Redgrave. —
                Numerical index. — Grey wrappers.
                Copy note: "18th thousand."

V.1862.003   *Catalogue of the collection illustrating construction and building*
                materials in the South Kensington Museum / edited by Henry
                Sandham. 3rd ed.
                London : Printed by George E. Eyre and W. Spottiswoode for
                H.M.S.O., 1862.
                241 p. : ill., plan ; 22 cm.
                At head of title: Science and Art Department of the Committee of Council on Education.
                — Regulations for the guidance of contributors to the Museum of Construction / Henry
                Cole. — Index to exhibitors. — Printing: 11/62.

V.1862.004   *Catalogue of the collection of animal products . . . .*
                London, 1862.
                Unseen. Record from National Art Library catalogue of acquisitions before 1890.

V.1862.005   *Catalogue of the Educational Division of the South Kensington*
                Museum. 7th ed.
                London : Printed by George E. Eyre and William Spottiswoode for
                H.M.S.O., [1862].
                xxiv, 368 p. ; 23 cm.
                "Corrected to July 1862."

V.1862.006   *Catalogue of the special exhibition of works of art of the mediaeval,*
                Renaissance, and more recent periods, on loan at the South
                Kensington Museum, June 1862 / edited by J.C. Robinson.

London : Printed by George E. Eyre and William Spottiswoode for
H.M.S.O., 1862.

721 p. ; 22 cm.

Title page is that of Part I. At head of title: Science and Art Department of the
Committee of Council on Education. — "Under revision" (all parts). — Copy of minute
directing the formation of the collection, by Henry Cole. — Includes list of contributors.

CONTENTS: Part I. Section 1, Sculptures in marble, terra cotta &c. 2, Carvings in
ivory. 3, Art bronzes. 4, Furniture. 5, Objects of ancient Irish and Anglo-Saxon art. 6,
Various works of mediaeval art, ecclesiastical utensils &c. 7, "Henri Deux" ware. Part
II. Section 8, Bernard Palissy ware. 9, Sèvres porcelain. 10, Limoges painted enamels.
11, Portrait miniatures. 12, Ecclesiastical vestments, tissues and embroideries. 13,
Decorative plate belonging to the Universities of Oxford and Cambridge. Part III.
Section 14, Persian ware. 15, Porcelain and other pottery of various manufactories. 16,
English porcelain, stonewares &c. . . . . 17, Snuff-boxes, bijouterie &c. 18,
Decorative arms and armour. 19, Miscellaneous enamels. 20, Glass. Part IV. Section 21,
Majolica wares. 22, Decorative plate &c contributed by the various Companies of the
City of London. 23, Plate and other objects contributed by various corporate bodies. 24,
Plate of English manufacture. 25, Decorative plate . . . of various foreign origin. 26,
Damascened work. 27, Locks, keys, and other objects in wrought iron. 28, Antique and
other engraved gems. 29, Addenda and miscellaneous objects. Part V. Section 30,
Illuminations and illuminated manuscripts. 31, Bookbindings. 32, Rings. 33, Jewellery,
personal ornament, gems. 34, Clocks and watches. 35, Vases and other objects in rock
crystal, sardonyx &c. 36, Historical relics. 37, Miscellaneous objects. 38, Addenda
Part II.

Authors: Ch. Baily and G. Russell French: 22; James Beck: 11, 31, 36; W. Chaffers: 9,
27, 33, 34, 35; W. Chaffers, revised by J. Beck: 24; W. Chaffers, revised by J.C.
Robinson: 15, 16, 17, 18, 25; Daniel Rock: 12; A.W. Franks: 2, 10, 19, 20; Richard R.
Holmes: 30; E. Stanley Poole: 26; J.C. Robinson: 1, 3, 4, 6, 7, 8, 9 (introductory notice),
14, 21, 28, 29 (Part I); R.H.S. Smith: 5, 13, 29 (part), 37, 38; Edmund Waterton: 32.

EXHIBITION: VX.1862.001

V.1862.007 *Italian sculpture of the Middle Ages and period of the revival of art : a
descriptive catalogue of the works forming the above section of the
Museum, with additional illustrative notices* / by J.C. Robinson.
London : Chapman and Hall, for the Science and Art Department of
the Committee on Council on Education, 1862 (Chiswick Press,
printed by Whittingham and Wilkins).

xxxi, 192 p., [20] leaves of plates : ill. ; 26 cm.

Includes indexes of artists and schools, and of Museum numbers. — White cloth
covered boards with heraldic devices in gold on upper, blind on lower.

V.1862.008 *Special exhibition of objects of art on loan in the new South Court of
the Art Museum, South Kensington, June 1862 : list of contributors,
and abstract of their respective loans.*
London : Printed by George E. Eyre and William Spottiswoode for
H.M.S.O., 1862.

9 p. ; 22 cm. + 1 leaf.

At head of title: Science and Art Department of the Committee of Council on Education.
— Leaf loosely inserted: Objects contributed to the special exhibition by Her most
gracious Majesty the Queen, from royal collections at Windsor Castle and Buckingham
Palace.

EXHIBITION: VX.1862.001

1863

V.1863.001　　　*A catalogue of the British Fine Art Collections at South Kensington :*
being for the most part the gifts of John Sheepshanks and Mrs.
Ellison.
London : [Printed by George E. Eyre and William Spottiswoode for
H.M.S.O.], 1863.
107 p. ; 22 cm.
Contents as V.1862.002. — Grey wrappers.
Copy note: "21st thousand".

V.1863.002　　　*Catalogue of the circulating collection of works of art selected from*
the Museum at South Kensington : intended for temporary exhibitions
in provincial schools of art / by J.C. Robinson.
London : [H.M.S.O.], 1863.
January 1863. — Unseen. Record from National Art Library catalogue of acquisitions
before 1890.
EXHIBITION: VX.1860.XXX.001

V.1863.003　　　*Catalogue of the special exhibition of works of art of the mediaeval,*
Renaissance, and more recent periods : on loan at the South
Kensington Museum, June 1862 / edited by J. C. Robinson. Rev. ed.
London : Printed by George E. Eyre and William Spottiswoode for
H.M.S.O., [1863].
xvi, 766 p. ; 23 cm.
At head of title: Science and Art Department of the Committee of Council on Education.
— "January 1863." — "General index."
Copy notes: Printing: 3/63.
EXHIBITION: VX.1862.001

V.1863.003A　　[Large paper ed.]
26 cm.
Copy notes: Printing: 6/63.

V.1863.003B　　[Larger paper ed.]
29 cm.

V.1863.004　　　*A guide to the food collection in the South Kensington Museum* / by
Edwin Lankester. "3rd ed."
London : Printed by George E. Eyre and William Spottiswoode for
H.M.S.O., 1863.
vi, 129 p. ; 21 cm.
"February 1863." — Varies from V.1860.007.

V.1863.005　　　*Inventory of the objects forming the art collections of the Museum at*
South Kensington.
London : Printed by George E. Eyre and William Spottiswoode for
H.M.S.O. and sold by Chapman and Hall, 1863.
xxv, 178 p. ; 22 cm.
At head of title: Science and Art Department of the Committee of Council on Education.
— "Under revision." — "The Collections are now regulated by the following Minute
..." / Henry Cole. A brief account of the formation of the ornamental art collections. –
Includes list of donors, index to artists and producers, objects types. — 'Provisional
classification': as V.1860.009, except: II, Medals and engraved gems. — Blue wrappers.
— Printing: 12/63.

V.1863.005A   *Inventory of the objects forming the collections of the Museum of Ornamental Art at South Kensington.*
London : Printed by George E. Eyre and William Spottiswoode for H.M.S.O., 1863.
iii, 189 p. ; 22 cm.
At head of title: Science and Art Department of the Committee of Council on Education. — "Under revision." – General classification: as v.1860.009. — Notice dated April 1863. — A brief account of the formation of the ornamental art collections. – Includes list of donors. — Blue wrappers.

V.1863.006   *Inventory of the pictures, drawings, etchings &c. in the British Fine Art Collections deposited in the new gallery, South Kensington : being for the most part the gift of John Sheepshanks, Esq. and Mrs. Ellison.*
[New ed.]
London : H.M.S.O., 1863 (Printed by George E. Eyre and William Spottiswoode).
28 p. ; 22 cm.
Introduction / by Richard Redgrave.

V.1863.007   *A list of the wedding presents accepted by Their Royal Highnesses the Prince and Princess of Wales and exhibited by Their Royal Highnesses' permission at the South Kensington Museum, April 1863.*
London : Printed by George E. Eyre and William Spottiswoode for H.M.S.O. and sold by Chapman and Hall, 1863.
10 p. ; 21 cm.
"Under revision." — Notice / Henry Cole.
EXHIBITION: vx.1863.001

1864

V.1864.001   *A catalogue of the exhibition of stained glass, mosaics, etc. : designed and executed by British artists, arranged in the north and west cloisters of the South Kensington Museum, under the National Art Training Schools.*
London : Printed by George E. Eyre and William Spottiswoode for H.M.S.O., 1864.
11 p. ; 22 cm.
At head of title: Science and Art Department, South Kensington Museum. — Preface by T. Gambier Parry, R. Burchett. — List of exhibitors. — Printing: 6/64.
EXHIBITION: vx.1864.001

V.1864.002   *A catalogue of the pictures, drawings, sketches etc., of the late William Mulready, Esq., R.A. (1786–1863). Part I, The oil paintings.*
London : Printed by George Edward Eyre and William Spottiswoode for H.M.S.O., 1864.
23 p. ; 21 cm.
At head of title: Science and Art Department, South Kensington Museum. — Printing: 3/64. — Generally found bound with v.1864.003.

V.1864.003   *A catalogue of the pictures, drawings, sketches etc. of the late William Mulready, Esq., R.A. (1786–1863). Part II, The drawings, sketches, etc.*

London : Printed by George Edward Eyre and William Spottiswoode for H.M.S.O., 1864.

26 p. ; 21 cm.

At head of title: Science and Art Department, South Kensington Museum. — Printing: 3/64. — Generally found bound with v.1864.002.

v.1864.004   *Inventory of the objects forming the art collections of the Museum at South Kensington.*
London : Printed by George E. Eyre and William Spottiswoode for H.M.S.O. and sold by Chapman and Hall, 1864.

xxv, 178 p. ; 22 cm.

At head of title: Science and Art Department of the Committee of Council on Education. — "Under revision." — "The Collections are now regulated by the following Minute …" / Henry Cole. A brief account of the formation of the ornamental art collections. — Includes list of donors, index to artists and producers, objects types. — 'Provisional classification' as v.1863.005. — Printing: 2/64.

v.1864.005   *Price list of mounted photographs printed from negatives taken for the Science and Art Department by the official photographer, C. Thurston Thompson . . . .*
London : Chapman and Hall, Agents to the Science and Art Department for the sale of photographs, [1864] (Printed by George E. Eyre and William Spottiswoode for H.M.S.O.).

32 p. ; 22 cm.

Caption title. At head of title: Science and Art Department of the Committee of Council on Education. — Printing: 6/64.

v.1864.006   *Supplemental list of loans to the art-collections.*
[s.l. : s.n.], 1864 (Strangeways & Walden, printers).

197 p. ; 22 cm.

At head of title: Science and Art Department, South Kensington Museum. — Ivory wrappers. — Possibly an internal document only.

1865

v.1865.001   *Catalogue of the circulating collection of works of art selected from the Museum at South Kensington : intended for temporary exhibitions in provincial schools of art* / by J.C. Robinson.
London : [H.M.S.O.], 1865.

May 1865. — Unseen. Record from National Art Library catalogue of acquisitions before 1890.

v.1865.002   *Catalogue of the Educational Division of the South Kensington Museum.* 8th ed.
London : Printed by George E. Eyre and William Spottiswoode for H.M.S.O., [1865].

xxvii, 419 p. ; 23 cm.

"Corrected to January 1865." — Printing: 2/65.

v.1865.003   *Catalogue of the naval models in the South Kensington Museum.*
London : Printed by George E. Eyre and William Spottiswoode, 1865.

279 p. : ill. ; 22 cm.

Part I. Admiralty collection of models, &c. Part II. Collection of models from private sources. Photographic illustrations. — Unseen. Record from British Library catalogue and OCLC.

V.1865.004   *Catalogue of the naval models in the South Kensington Museum.*
               [Appendix]
               London : Printed by George E. Eyre and William Spottiswoode, for
               H.M.S.O., 1865.
               160 p. ; 21 cm.
               Part I. Admiralty collection of models, &c. Part II. Collection of models from private
               sources. — Index, to the catalogue and appendix. — Blue wrappers.

V.1865.005   *Catalogue of the special exhibition of portrait miniatures on loan at
               the South Kensington Museum, June 1865.*
               London : Printed by Whittingham and Wilkins, 1865.
               xxii, 340 p. ; 25 cm.
               At head of title: Science and Art Department of the Committee of Council on Education.
               — Minute / Henry Cole. Introductory notice / Samuel Redgrave. — General index, list
               of lenders, biographical notices of artists. — Printed with borders and decorated initials.
               EXHIBITION: VX.1865.001

V.1865.005A   [Large paper ed.]
               28 cm.
               Wrappers. — Page of corrections bound in at end.

V.1865.006   *Notes on the Cartoons of Raphael now in the South Kensington
               Museum : also on Raphael's other works* / prepared for the Science
               and Art Department, by Charles Ruland.
               London : Printed by George E. Eyre and William Spottiswoode for
               H.M.S.O., 1865.
               55p. ; 22 cm.
               "Under revision."

V.1865.007   *A short introduction to the gallery of naval models.*
               London : Printed by George E. Eyre and William Spottiswoode for
               H.M.S.O., 1865.
               20 p. ; 22 cm.
               Printing: 4/65.

1866

V.1866.001   *A catalogue of the British Fine Art Collections at South Kensington :
               being for the most part the gifts of John Sheepshanks and Mrs.
               Ellison.*
               London : [Printed by George E. Eyre and William Spottiswoode for
               H.M.S.O.], 1866.
               112 p. ; 22 cm.
               Contents as V.1862.002.
               Copy note: "24th thousand."

V.1866.002   *Catalogue of the first special exhibition of national portraits ending
               with the reign of King James the Second : on loan to the South
               Kensington Museum, April 1866.*
               London : [s.n.], 1866 (printed by Strangeways and Walden).
               xi, [i blank], 191 p ; 21 cm.
               At head of title: Science and Art Department of the Committee of Council on Education.
               — Introductory notice by Samuel Redgrave. — Indexes of lenders, painters and
               portraits.

Copy notes: "First thousand".
EXHIBITION: vx.1866.001

V.1866.002A   [Another issue]
172 p.
Lacking indexes.
Copy notes: "Third thousand", "Fourth thousand".

V.1866.002B   [Rev. ed.]
xi, [i], 202 p. ; 26 cm.
Appendix: p. [193]–202 consists of notes on the pictures mainly relating to attributions.

V.1866.003   *Catalogue of the special exhibition of oil paintings, water-colour drawings, architectural and other studies by the late Godfrey Sykes : at the South Kensington Museum, June 1866.*
London : Printed by George E. Eyre and William Spottiswoode for H.M.S.O., 1866.
15 p. ; 22 cm.
Cover title. At head of title: Science and Art Department of the Committee of Council on Education. — Introduction / J.H. Pollen. — Printing: 6/66. — Grey wrappers.
EXHIBITION: vx.1866.002

V.1866.004   *A description of the building at South Kensington, erected to receive the Sheepshanks collection of pictures* / by Francis Fowke.
London : Chapman and Hall, Agents to the Science and Art Department of the Committee of Council on Education, 1866 (Printed by George E. Eyre and William Spottiswoode).
35 p. (2 folded) : ill., plans ; 24 cm.
"With plans and illustrations." — Text dated 1858. — Appendix A: Report of the Commission appointed to consider the subject of lighting picture galleries by gas. — Printing: 5/66. — Grey wrappers with diagram.

V.1866.005   *A list of the museums in France : prepared for the use of the South Kensington Museum.*
London: [s.n.], 1866.
[6] p. ; 23 cm.
With introduction by the Secretary, South Kensington Museum.

V.1866.006   *A list of the principal libraries in Europe and the United States of America : compiled from various sources for the use of the Science and Art Department of the Committee of Council on Education.*
London : South Kensington Museum, 1866.
[4], 29 p. ; 25 cm.
"Proof. Under revision." — Prefatory remarks / J.H. Pollen, Art Library, South Kensington Museum.

V.1866.007   *Notes on the Cartoons of Raphael now in the South Kensington Museum : and on Raphael's other works* / prepared for the Science and Art Department, by Charles Ruland.
London : Printed by George E. Eyre and William Spottiswoode for H.M.S.O., 1866.
55p. ; 22 cm.
"Under revision." — Printing: 6/66. — Grey wrappers.

1867

v.1867.001   *A catalogue of the British Fine Art Collections at South Kensington :
              being for the most part the gifts of John Sheepshanks and Mrs.
              Ellison.*
              London : [Printed by George E. Eyre and William Spottiswoode for
              H.M.S.O.], 1867.
              120 p. ; 22 cm.
              Contents as v.1862.002. — Grey wrappers.
              Copy note: "25th thousand."

v.1867.002   *Catalogue of the Educational Division of the South Kensington
              Museum.* 8th ed.
              London : Printed by George E. Eyre and William Spottiswoode for
              H.M.S.O., [1867].
              xxvii, 419, 54 p. ; 23 cm.
              New issue, with a supplement brought down to January 1867. — Printing (suppl.):
              5/67.

v.1867.003   *Catalogue of the second special exhibition of national portraits
              commencing with the reign of William and Mary and ending with the
              year MDCCC, on loan to the South Kensington Museum, May 1,
              1867.*
              London : [s.n.], 1867 (Printed by Strangeways and Walden).
              x, 11–87 p. ; 22 cm.
              At head of title: Science and Art Department of the Committee of Council on Education.
              — Introductory notice / Sam. Redgrave. — Half bound in leather; boards covered in
              blue cloth with diagonal dot-and-ribbon grain. Or wrappers.
              Copy note: "Tenth thousand".
              EXHIBITION: vx.1867.001

v.1867.004   [Rev. ed., with indexes]
              208 p. ; 26 cm.

v.1867.005   *List of the electrotype reproductions in the Art Division of the
              Museum at South Kensington.*
              London : Printed by George E. Eyre and William Spottiswoode for
              H.M.S.O., 1867.
              45 p. ; 21 cm.
              (Reproductions ; Part 1)
              At head of title: Science and Art Department of the Committee of Council on Education.
              — "Proof under correction."

v.1867.006   *Notes for a universal art inventory of works of fine art which may be
              found throughout the continent of Europe, for the most part in
              ecclesiastical buildings and in connexion with architecture : compiled
              for the use of the South Kensington Museum and the Schools of Art in
              the United Kingdom* / edited by Henry Cole.
              London : Printed by George E. Eyre and William Spottiswoode for
              H.M.S.O., 1867.
              x, 148 p. ; 33 cm.
              At head of title: Science and Art Department. — "Proof under revision." — Blue
              wrappers.

1868

V.1868.001   *Catalogue of pictures of the Dutch and Flemish schools : the property*
of Mrs Henry Thomas Hope : on loan to the South Kensington
Museum.
London : Printed by George E. Eyre and William Spottiswoode for
H.M.S.O., 1868.
12 p. ; 21 cm.
At head of title: Science and Art Department of the Committee of Council on Education.
— Printing: 9/68.

V.1868.002   *Catalogue of the third and concluding exhibition of national portraits,*
commencing with the fortieth year of the reign of George the Third
and ending with the year MDCCCLXVII : on loan to the South
Kensington Museum, April 13, 1868.
London : [s.n.], 1868 (printed by Strangeways and Walden).
x, 182 p. ; 22 cm.
At head of title: Science and Art Department of the Committee of Council on Education.
Introductory notice / Sam. Redgrave. — Indexes of lenders, painters and portraits.
EXHIBITION: VX.1868.001

V.1868.002A   [Large paper ed.]
26 cm.
Half bound in leather with gold rules; boards covered in green cloth with diagonal dot-
and-ribbon grain.

V.1868.003   *Catalogue of the third and concluding exhibition of national portraits,*
commencing with the fortieth year of the reign of George the Third
and ending with the year MDCCCLXVII : on loan to the South
Kensington Museum, April 13, 1868. Rev. ed. with indexes.
London : [s.n.], 1868 (printed by Strangeways and Walden).
x, 210 p. ; 22 cm.
At head of title: Science and Art Department of the Committee of Council on Education.
— "Under revision." — Introductory note / Sam. Redgrave. — Indexes of lenders,
painters and portraits. — Buff wrappers.
Copy note: "Eleventh thousand."
EXHIBITION: VX.1868.001

V.1868.004   *List of the objects obtained during the Paris Exhibition of 1867, by*
gift, loan or purchase and now exhibited in the South Kensington
Museum.
London : Printed by George E. Eyre and William Spottiswoode for
H.M.S.O., 1868.
vii, 64 p. ; 21 cm.
At head of title: Science and Art Department. — "Under revision." — List of official
catalogues and books &c. collected at the Paris Exposition Universelle: p. 55–62. —
Printing: 4/68.

1869

V.1869.001   *Catalogue of the armour and miscellaneous objects of art known as*
the Meyrick collection : lent by Colonel Meyrick, of Goodrich Court,
Herefordshire, and exhibited at the South Kensington Museum / with
an introduction by J.R. Planché.

London : Printed by George E. Eyre and William Spottiswoode for
H.M.S.O., 1869.

xviii, 120 p. ; 21 cm.

Printing: 3/69. — Grey wrappers.

EXHIBITION: vx.1868.003

v.1869.002   *A catalogue of works illustrative of decorative art :
chromolithographs, etchings and photographs of objects of art :
chiefly selected from the South Kensington Museum : produced for
the use of schools of art, for prizes, and generally for public
instruction : published by the Arundel Society for Promoting the
Knowledge of Art.*
London : Printed by George E. Eyre and William Spottiswoode for
H.M.S.O., 1869.

32 p. ; 21 cm.

At head of title: Science and Art Department of the Committee of Council on Education,
South Kensington Museum. — Printing: 6/69.

v.1869.003   *Catalogue (with an appendix) of the naval models in the South
Kensington Museum.*
London : Printed by George E. Eyre and William Spottiswoode, for
H.M.S.O., 1869.

279, 160 p. ; 21 cm.

Added t.p.: Appendix to the catalogue of naval models in the South Kensington
Museum : with table of contents and index to the whole catalogue — Part I. Admiralty
collection of models, etc. Part II. Collection of models from private sources. Appendix
and index. — Printing: 7/65 (main work); 6/69 (Appendix). — Blue wrappers.

v.1869.004   *Catalogues of reproductions of objects of art : in metal, plaster and
fictile ivory, chromolithography, etching and photography : selected
from the South Kensington Museum, continental museums, and
various other public and private collections : produced for the use of
schools of art, for prizes, and for general purposes of public
instruction.*
London : Printed by George E. Eyre and William Spottiswoode for
H.M.S.O., 1869.

1 v. ; 22 cm.

At head of title: Science and Art Department of the Committee of Council on Education,
South Kensington Museum. — 7 works bound together (one in two parts) as issued,
with collective title page: v.1869.006, v.1869.008, v.1869.009, v.1869.002,
VR.1867.001, VR.1867.003, VR.1867.004. — Includes: Convention for promoting
universal reproduction of works of art for the benefit of museums of all countries. — In
red cloth covered boards, half bound in red morocco. Marbled end papers.

v.1869.005   *Catalogues of reproductions of objects of art : in metal, plaster and
fictile ivory, chromolithography, etching and photography : selected
from the South Kensington Museum, continental museums, and
various other public and private collections : produced for the use of
schools of art, for prizes, and for general purposes of public
instruction.*
London : Printed by George E. Eyre and William Spottiswoode for
H.M.S.O., 1869.

1 v. ; 22 cm.

At head of title: Science and Art Department of the Committee of Council on Education, South Kensington Museum. — 8 works bound together (one in two parts) as issued, with collective title page. — Contents as V.1869.004, plus VR.1868.005. — In red cloth covered boards, half bound in red morocco. Marbled end papers.

V.1869.006   *Inventory of the electrotype reproductions of objects of art : selected from the South Kensington Museum, continental museums, and various other public and private collections : produced for the use of schools of art, for prizes, and generally for public instruction.*
London : Printed by George E. Eyre and William Spottiswoode for H.M.S.O., 1869.
viii, 58p.; 21 cm.
(Reproductions ; Part I)
At head of title: Science and Art Department of the Committee of Council on Education, South Kensington Museum. — Indexes to countries, objects and dates. — Printing: 6/69. — Ivory wrappers.

V.1869.007   *Inventory of the food collection : arranged in alphabetical order.*
London : Printed by George E. Eyre and William Spottiswoode for H.M.S.O., 1869.
107 p. ; 21 cm.
At head of title: Science and Art Department of the Committee of Council on Education, South Kensington. — Printing: 3/69. — Grey wrappers.

V.1869.008   *Inventory of the plaster casts of objects of art : collected from various sources on the continent and in Great Britain and Ireland : with wax impressions of seals in the British Museum : produced for the use of schools of art, and for general purposes of public instruction.*
London : Printed by George E. Eyre and William Spottiswoode for H.M.S.O., 1869.
viii, 47 p. ; 21 cm.
(Reproductions ; Part II)
At head of title: Science and Art Department of the Committee of Council on Education, South Kensington Museum. — Printing: 6/69. — Ivory wrappers.

V.1869.009   *Inventory of the reproductions in fictile ivory from ivory carvings : selected from the South Kensington Museum, continental museums, and various other public and private collections : produced for the use of schools of art, for prizes, and for general purposes of public instruction.*
London : Printed by George E. Eyre and William Spottiswoode for H.M.S.O, 1869.
vii, 38 p. ; 21 cm.
(Reproductions ; Part III)
At head of title: Science and Art Department of the Committee of Council on Education, South Kensington Museum. — Printing: 7/69. — Ivory wrappers.

V.1869.010   *List of electrotype reproductions in the South Kensington Museum.*
London : Printed by George E. Eyre and William Spottiswoode for H.M.S.O., 1869.
71 p. ; 21 cm.
Caption title. — Printing: 2/69.

v.1869.011   *Notes on the National Art Library, South Kensington Museum. No. 1,
               1869.*
               London : Printed by George E. Eyre and William Spottiswoode for
               H.M.S.O., 1869.
               8 p. ; 21 cm.
               Caption title. At head of title: Science and Art Department of the Committee of Council
               on Education. — Printing: 7/69.

1870

v.1870.001   *A catalogue of the British Fine Art Collections in the South
               Kensington Museum : including the gifts of John Sheepshanks Esq.,
               Mrs. Ellison, and part of the bequest of the Rev. Chauncy Hare
               Townshend.*
               London : [Printed by George E. Eyre and William Spottiswoode for
               H.M.S.O.], 1870.
               147 p. ; 22 cm.
               Contents as v.1862.002.
               Copy note: "26th thousand."

v.1870.002   *Catalogue of the coloured drawings and engravings of ancient mosaics
               made for, and collected by, the late Dr. Robert Wollaston, and
               presented to the South Kensington Museum by Mrs. Wollaston, 1867.*
               London : Printed by George E. Eyre and William Spottiswoode and
               sold by Chapman and Hall, 1870.
               15 p. ; 22 cm.
               At head of title: Science and Art Department of the Committee of Council on Education,
               South Kensington Museum. — "Presented . . . to the National Art Library of the South
               Kensington Museum"–p. 3.

v.1870.003   *Catalogue of the loan exhibition of fans, MDCCCLXX.*
               London : Chapman and Hall, Agents to the Department, 1870
               (Printed by Strangeways and Walden).
               viii, 66 p. ; 23 cm.
               At head of title: Science and Art Department, South Kensington Museum. —
               Introduction / Sam. Redgrave. — Buff wrappers.
               EXHIBITION: vx.1870.001

v.1870.003A   [Large paper ed.]
               "large paper copy with illustrations, distributed to contributors"–*Eighteenth report of
               the Department of Science and Art* (1871), p. xxv. Unseen.

v.1870.004   *Catalogues of reproductions of objects of art : in metal, plaster, and
               fictile ivory, chromolithography, etching and photography : selected
               from the South Kensington Museum, continental museums and
               various other public and private collections : produced for the use of
               schools of art, for prizes, and for general purposes of public
               instruction.*
               London : Printed by George E. Eyre and William Spottiswoode for
               H.M.S.O., 1870.
               1 v. ; 22 cm.

At head of title: Science and Art Department of the Committee of Council on Education, South Kensington Museum.

7 works bound together (one in two parts) as issued, with collective title page. — In red cloth covered boards, half bound in red morocco. Marbled end papers. — Contents are identical to v.1869.004.

v.1870.005   *Collection of pictures and other objects belonging to the Marquis of Westminster : lent for exhibition to the South Kensington Museum.*
London : Printed by George E. Eyre and William Spottiswoode, 1870.
7 p. ; 21 cm.
Caption title. — Printing: 11/70.

v.1870.006   *A descriptive catalogue of gems, precious stones and pearls : bequeathed to the South Kensington Museum by the Rev. Chauncy Hare Townshend M.A.* / by James Tennant.
London : Printed by George E. Eyre and William Spottiswoode [for H.M.S.O.] and sold by Chapman and Hall, 1870.
23 p. ; 22 cm.
Cover title: Catalogue of gems and precious stones . . . . At head of title: Science and Art Department of the Committee of Council on Education, South Kensington Museum. — Index. — Printing: 2/70. — Ivory wrappers.

v.1870.007   *A descriptive catalogue of the musical instruments in the South Kensington Museum* / by Carl Engel.
London : Printed by George E. Eyre and William Spottiswoode and sold by Chapman & Hall, 1870.
82 p. : ill., music ; 21 cm.
At head of title: Science and Art Department of the Committee of Council on Education, South Kensington Museum. — Index. — Wrappers.

v.1870.008   *The first proofs of the universal catalogue of books on art : compiled for the use of the National Art Library and the schools of art in the United Kingdom.*
London : Chapman and Hall, and at the office of *Notes and queries*, 1870 (Printed by Spottiswoode and Co.).
2v. (xvi, 1030 p.; p. 1060–[2188]) ; 22 cm.
At head of title: Science and Art Department of the Committee of Council on Education, South Kensington. "By order of the Lords of the Committee of Council on Education"–t.p. — Edited by John Hungerford Pollen. Preface signed: Henry Cole. — " . . . circulated for the purpose of obtaining additional information and corrections"–t.p. verso. — "Not only the books in the library, but all books printed and published, at the date of the issue of the Catalogue, that could be required to make the library perfect"–p. iv. — Vol. I, A to K. Vol. II, L to Z.

Proof-sheets first published in *Notes and queries*, 1868–1870, as 4 and 12 page supplements; widely circulated for additions and corrections, which were incorporated in these "first proofs". The work was discontinued on account of a lack of funds, and, except for a supplementary volume published in 1877, no further revisions were ever issued; the sections "Illustrated Bibles and liturgies", "Catalogues", "Periodicals" and "Societies" which it was proposed to issue separately at the end of the alphabet, remain unpublished.

Boards in brown sand grain cloth; half bound in honey-coloured leather with title stamped in gold on spine.

Copy note: One copy has additional p. i-x: Extracts of correspondence and papers on the subject of the Universal art catalogue, bound in after p. ix.

V.1870.008A *Universal catalogue of books on art : comprehending painting,*
sculpture, architecture, decoration, coins, antiquities, &c.
London : Published by Chapman & Hall and at the office of *Notes*
and queries, 1870.
2187 p. ; 22 cm.

Title from wrappers. At head of title: Science and Art Department of the Committee of
Council on Education, South Kensington. Proof sheets circulated for the purpose of
obtaining additions and corrections. — Part I: Letter A (Issued in *Notes and queries*). –
Part II: Letters B-C (Issued in *Notes and queries*). – Part III: Letters D-E. – Part IV:
Letters F-G. – Part V: Letters H-K (Issued in *Notes and queries*). – Part VI: Letter L. Part
VII: Letters M-N. – Part VIII: Letters O-P. – Part IX: Letters Q-R. – Part X: Letters S-U.
– Part XI: Letters V-Z (Issued in *Notes and queries*). With collective title page for Vol.
II, L-Z.

V.1870.009 *Textile fabrics : a descriptive catalogue of the collection of church-*
vestments, dresses, silk stuffs, needlework and tapestries, forming that
section of the Museum / by Daniel Rock.
London : Published for the Science and Art Department of the
Committee of Council on Education [by] Chapman and Hall, 1870
(Chiswick Press, printed by Whittingham and Wilkins).
clxviii, 356 p., [20] leaves of plates : ill. (some col.) ; 26 cm.

At head of title: South Kensington Museum. — General and geographical indexes. —
Chromolithographs printed by Vincent Brooks Day & Son.

Copy note: Half bound in leather; boards covered in green morocco grain cloth.

V.1870.010 *Universal art inventory : consisting of brief notes of works of fine and*
ornamental art executed before A.D. 1800, chiefly to be found in
Europe, especially in connexion with architecture and for the most
part existing in ecclesiastical buildings : compiled for the use of the
South Kensington Museum and the Schools of Art in the United
Kingdom. Part I, containing mosaics and stained glass / edited by
Henry Cole.
London : Printed by George E. Eyre and William Spottiswoode for
H.M.S.O., 1870.
xxiv, 151 p. ; 21 cm.

At head of title: Science and Art Department. — "Edition for 1870–71 under revision."
— "Titles of books on mosaics": p. xxi-xxiv. — Printing: 2/70. — Wrappers.

1871

V.1871.001 *A catalogue of Anglo-Saxon and other antiquities discovered at*
Faversham in Kent : and bequeathed by William Gibbs . . . to the
South Kensington Museum / compiled by C. Roach Smith.
London : Printed by George E. Eyre and William Spottiswoode [for
H.M.S.O.] and sold by Chapman & Hall, 1871.
25 p. : ill. ; 24 cm.

At head of title: Science and Art Department of the Committee of Council on Education,
South Kensington Museum. Printing: 3/71. — Wrappers.

V.1871.002 *A descriptive catalogue of the lace and embroidery in the South*
Kensington Museum / by Mrs Bury Palliser.
London : Printed by George E. Eyre and William Spottiswoode for
H.M.S.O., 1871.

60p., [14] leaves of plates : ill. ; 22 cm.
At head of title: Science and Art Department of the Committee of Council on Education.
Half title: Catalogue of the lace in the South Kensington Museum. — "With fourteen
illustrations." — "List of books on lace in the Art Library, South Kensington Museum":
p. 57–58. Index of Museum numbers.

V.1871.003   *Extracts from foreign reports and art publications relative to the*
establishment of the South Kensington Museum and the National Art
Training Schools.
[London : Science and Art Dept.?, 1871] (George E. Eyre and William
Spottiswoode, printers).
21 p. ; 34 cm.
Compilation of complimentary references, taken from foreign reports, documents and
periodicals (translated into English), dated 1864–1869. — Includes extracts from the
reports of the French jurors at the International Exhibition of 1862. — Index.

V.1871.004   *A first list of buildings in England having mural or other painted*
decorations of dates previous to the middle of the 16th century
(compiled for the use of schools of art in the United Kingdom).
London : Printed by George E. Eyre and William Spottiswoode and
sold by Chapman and Hall, 1871.
24 p. ; 22 cm.
At head of title: Science and Art Department of the Committee of Council on Education,
South Kensington Museum. — Prefatory notice by R.H. Soden Smith.

V.1871.005   *List of the bequests and donations to the Department of Science and*
Art, South Kensington Museum : completed to 31st December 1870.
London : Printed by George Edward Eyre and William Spottiswoode,
for H.M.S.O., 1871.
92 p. ; 33 cm.
At head of title: Department of Science and Art of the Committee of Council on
Education, South Kensington. — Alphabetical and classified indexes of donors.

V.1871.006   *Notes on monuments of early Christian art : sculptures and catacomb*
paintings.
London : Printed by George E. Eyre and William Spottiswoode and
sold by Chapman and Hall, September 1871.
1 v. ; 22 cm.
At head of title: Science and Art Department of the Committee of Council on Education,
South Kensington Museum. — Written by J.W. Appell. — Catalogued from an
incomplete copy.

1872

V.1872.001   *Babbage's calculating machine or difference engine : a description of a*
portion of this machine put together in 1833 and now exhibited by
permission of the Board of Works, in the Education Division of the
South Kensington Museum.
London : [H.M.S.O.?], 1872.
8 p. : 1 ill. ; 24 cm.
At head of title: Science and Art Department. — By B. Herschel Babbage. — Grey
wrappers.

v.1872.002

A brief guide to the animal products collection.
London : Printed by George E. Eyre and William Spottiswoode for
H.M.S.O., 1872.

28 p. ; 22 cm.

Caption title: A brief guide to the collection of animal products. At head of title: Science
and Art Department of the Committee of Council on Education; Bethnal Green Branch
of the South Kensington Museum. — Introduction by Henry Cole. — "First issue." —
Printing: 7/72.

v.1872.003

A brief guide to the food collection.
London : Printed by George E. Eyre and William Spottiswoode for
H.M.S.O., 1872.

20 p. ; 21 cm.

At head of title: Science and Art Department of the Committee of Council on Education.
— Introduction by Henry Cole. — "First issue." — Printing: 7/72. — Grey wrappers.

v.1872.004

*A catalogue of a collection of models of ruled surfaces, constructed by
M. Fabre de Lagrange : with an appendix containing an account of the
application of analysis to their investigation and classification /* by
C.W. Merrifield.
London : Printed by George E. Eyre and William Spottiswoode for
H.M.S.O., 1872.

41 p., xii leaves of plates : ill. ; 21 cm.

At head of title: Science and Art Department of the Committee of Council on Education,
South Kensington Museum. — Photographs pasted in. — Printing: 11/72.

v.1872.005

*Catalogue of Chinese objects in the South Kensington Museum, with
an introduction and notes /* by C. Alabaster.
London : Printed by George E. Eyre and William Spottiswoode for
H.M.S.O., 1872.

80 p.; 21 cm.

At head of title: Science and Art Department of the Committee of Council on Education,
South Kensington Museum. — Index. — Printing: 7/72. — Grey wrappers.

v.1872.006

*Catalogue of selections from the objects of science and art collected by
His Royal Highness together with water-colour sketches and drawings
in illustration of the cruise, expressly executed by Messrs. O.W.
Brierly and N. Chevalier : lent for exhibition in the South Kensington
Museum.* 2nd ed.
London : H.M.S.O., 1872 (George E. Eyre and William Spottiswoode,
printers).

78 p. : map ; 22 cm.

At head of cover: Science and Art Department of the Committee of Council on
Education. — First ed. (?) entitled Catalogue of water-colour sketches and drawings in
illustration of the cruise . . . together with selections from the objects . . . . "Under
revision." — "The cruise of His Royal Highness the Duke of Edinburgh, K.G., round
the world in H.M.S. 'Galatea', in the years 1867, 1868, 1869, 1870, 1871." —
Coloured chart on fold-out leaf.
EXHIBITION: vx.1872.001

v.1872.007

"3rd ed."

v.1872.008

*Catalogue of the collection of objects selected from the Museum at
South Kensington to be contributed on loan for twelve months (until
June 1873) to the Midland Counties Museum of Science and Art,
Nottingham.*

London : Printed by George E. Eyre and William Spottiswoode for
H.M.S.O., 1872.
xi, 79 p. ; 21 cm.
Introduction by George Wallis. — Printing: 6/72. — Wrappers.

v.1872.009   *Catalogue of the collection of paintings, porcelain, bronzes, decorative
furniture, and other works of art : lent for exhibition in the Bethnal
Green Branch of the South Kensington Museum by Sir Richard
Wallace, Bart., June 1872* / by C.C. Black.
London : Printed by George E. Eyre and William Spottiswoode for
H.M.S.O., 1872.
ix, 104 p. ; 22 cm.
At head of title: Science and Art Department of the Committee of Council on Education,
South Kensington; Bethnal Green Branch Museum. — "Under revision." —
Introduction by Henry Cole. — Stone-coloured wrappers.

v.1872.010   2nd ed.
ix, 107 p.

v.1872.011   3rd ed.
xi, 109 p.

v.1872.012   4th ed.
xi, 114 p.

v.1872.013   5th ed.
xi, 125 p.

v.1872.014   "6th ed."

v.1872.015   *Catalogue of the loan exhibition of ancient and modern jewellery and
personal ornaments, MDCCCLXXII.*
London : [s.n.], [1872] (Printed by John Strangeways).
96 p. ; 22 cm.
At head of title: Science and Art Department, South Kensington Museum. — "First
issue"–t.p. — Introductory remarks / R.H. Soden Smith. — List of precious gems and
other materials used in jewellery, with explanatory notes, p. 18–23.
EXHIBITION: vx.1872.003

v.1872.015A   Second issue
110 p. ; 21 cm.
Includes Addenda, and list of contributors. — Grey wrappers.

v.1872.016   *Catalogue of the special exhibition of ancient musical instruments :
MDCCCLXXII.*
London, [1872] (John Strangeways, printer).
ix, 48 p. ; 21 cm.
At head of title: Science and Art Department, South Kensington Museum. — "Under
revision." — Introduction signed "C.E." [i.e. Carl Engel]. — Grey wrappers.
EXHIBITION: vx.1872.002

v.1872.017   *Catalogue of water-colour sketches and drawings in illustration of the
cruise, expressly executed by Messrs. O.W. Brierly and N. Chevalier :
together with selections from the objects of science and art collected
by His Royal Highness, and lent for exhibition in the South
Kensington Museum.*

London : H.M.S.O., 1872 (George E. Eyre and William Spottiswoode, printers . . .).

72 p. : map ; 22 cm.

At head of cover: Science and Art Department of the Committee of Council on Education. — "The cruise of His Royal Highness the Duke of Edinburgh, K.G., round the world in H.M.S. 'Galatea', in the years 1867, 1868, 1869, 1870, 1871." — "Under revision." — Coloured chart on fold-out leaf.

EXHIBITION: vx.1872.001

v.1872.018   *Ceremonial of the opening of the Bethnal Green Museum by His Royal Highness the Prince of Wales, on behalf of Her Majesty the Queen, on Monday the 24th of June 1872 at a quarter-past twelve o'clock.*

[London : s.n., 1872.]

[4] p. ; 24 cm.

Grey wrappers.

v.1872.019   *Classified and descriptive catalogue of the art objects of Spanish production in the South Kensington Museum* / with an introduction and notes by Juan F. Riaño.

London : Printed by George E. Eyre and William Spottiswoode for H.M.S.O., 1872.

xliv, 75 p. ; 21 cm.

At head of title: Science and Art Department of the Committee of Council on Education, South Kensington Museum. — Index. — Printing: 6/72. — Grey wrappers.

v.1872.020   *A classified and priced list of objects of art, reproduced in metal by various processes : as they appear in the South Kensington Museum.*

London : Printed by George E. Eyre and William Spottiswoode [for H.M.S.O.] and sold by Chapman & Hall, 1872.

viii, 76 p. ; 21 cm.

At head of title: Science and Art Department of the Committee of Council on Education, South Kensington Museum. — "Reproductions in metal"–t.p. — Geographical and chronological indexes. — Printing: 1/72.

v.1872.021   *A description of the ivories, ancient and mediaeval, in the South Kensington Museum* / with a preface by William Maskell.

London : Published for the Science and Art Department of the Committee of Council on Education by Chapman & Hall, 1872 (Printed by George Edward Eyre and William Spottiswoode, for H.M.S.O.).

cvii, 211 p., [24] leaves of plates : ill. ; 26 cm.

Half title: Ancient & mediaeval ivories in the South Kensington Museum. — Chronological, geographical, general and object indexes. — Photographic illustrations printed by the Permanent Printing Company using the Woodbury process. — Dark green bubble grain cloth covered boards, quarter bound in leather; title stamped in gold on spine.

v.1872.021A   [Large paper ed.; additional photographs.]

cvii, 211 p., [39] leaves of plates : ill. ; 29 cm.

Green sand grain cloth covered boards, half bound in green leather; on spine title stamped in gold.

v.1872.022   *Drawings of the glass cases in use for the exhibition of objects in the South Kensington Museum.*

[London : For the Museum?], 1872.
[1], 4 p., 21 leaves of plates, some folded : chiefly ill. ; 29 cm.
Preface by Henry Cole.

v.1872.023   *A five-years' cruise round the world (1867 to 1871) by H.R.H. the
Duke of Edinburgh, K.G., Captain of H.M.S. 'Galatea' : a guide to
the works of art and science collected by His Royal Highness, and lent
for exhibition in the South Kensington Museum, February, 1872.*
London : [s.n., 1872?] (Printed by John Strangeways).
66, [4] p., 1 folded leaf of plates : tinted map, plan ; 21 cm.
Preface signed "A.S.C." [i.e. Alan Summerly Cole]. — Map and plan printed by Vincent
Brooks Day & Son. — Grey wrappers with red rule.
EXHIBITION: vx.1872.001

v.1872.024   *A guide to the works of art and science collected by Captain His
Royal Highness the Duke of Edinburgh, K.G., during his five-years'
cruise round the world in H.M.S. 'Galatea' (1867–1871) : and lent for
exhibition in the South Kensington Museum, February 1872* 2nd ed.
London : [s.n., 1872?] (printed by John Strangeways).
74, [4] p., 1 folded leaf of plates : tinted map, music, plan ; 21 cm.
Preface signed "A.S.C." [i.e. Alan Summerly Cole]. — Map and plan printed by Vincent
Brooks Day & Son.
EXHIBITION: vx.1872.001

v.1872.025   "3rd ed."

v.1872.025A   [with extra illustrations]
74, [4] p., [9] leaves, 1 folded, of plates : ill., tinted map, music, plan ;
21 cm.
Photographic illustrations pasted in.

v.1872.026   4th ed.
Some copies lack map.

v.1872.027   *Inventory of the food collection : arranged in alphabetical order.*
London, 1872.
Unseen. Record from National Art Library catalogue of acquisitions before 1890.

v.1872.028   *A list of buildings in England having mural or other painted
decorations : of dates previous to the middle of the 16th century :
(compiled for the use of schools of art in the United Kingdom).*
London : Printed by George E. Eyre and William Spottiswoode, and
sold by Chapman and Hall [for H.M.S.O.], 1872.
57 p. ; 21 cm.
At head of title: Science and Art Department of the Committee of Council on Education,
South Kensington Museum. Previously entitled A first list of buildings in England . . . .
— Introductory notice by R.H. Soden Smith. — Printing : 10/72.

v.1872.029   *Monuments of early Christian art : sculptures and catacomb paintings
: illustrative notes, collected in order to promote the reproduction of
remains of art belonging to the early centuries of the Christian era* / by
J.W. Appell.
London : Printed by George E. Eyre and William Spottiswoode and
sold by Chapman and Hall, 1872.
68 p. : ill. ; 23 cm.

"Under revision." — Previous title: Notes on monuments of early Christian art. — Apparently published under the aegis of the South Kensington Museum, where the author was Assistant Keeper. — Includes bibliographic references. — Printing: 8/72. — Brown sand grain cloth covered boards; front and spine stamped in gold with title.

v.1872.030   *Notes on the history of lace* / by Mrs Bury Palliser.
London : Printed by George E. Eyre and William Spottiswoode for H.M.S.O., 1872.
39 p., [14] leaves of plates : ill. ; 21 cm.
"To which is added, *A catalogue of specimens of lace selected from the Museum at South Kensington contributed as a loan to the Midland Counties Museum of Science and Art, Nottingham : with fourteen illustrations* — t.p.".— Printing: 5/72. — Wrappers.

1873

v.1873.001   *A catalogue of Anglo-Saxon and other antiquities discovered at Faversham in Kent and bequeathed by William Gibbs . . . to the South Kensington Museum* / compiled by C. Roach Smith. 2nd ed.
London : Printed by George E. Eyre and William Spottiswoode; sold by Chapman & Hall, 1873.
xxiii, 25 p. ; 24 cm.
At head of title: Science and Art Department of the Committee of Council on Education, South Kensington Museum. — Bibliography: p. xxii-xxiii. . — Printing: 11/73. — Wrappers.

v.1873.002   *Catalogue of the collection of objects selected from the Museum at South Kensington to be contributed on loan for twelve months (until June 1874) to the Midland Counties Museum of Science and Art, Nottingham : second year, 1873–74.*
London : Printed by George E. Eyre and William Spottiswoode, for H.M.S.O., 1873.
67 p. ; 21 cm.
At head of title: Science and Art Department of the Committee of Council on Education. — Introduction by George Wallis. — Printing: 6/73. — Grey wrappers.

v.1873.003   *Catalogue of the collection of paintings, porcelain, bronzes, decorative furniture, and other works of art : lent for exhibition in the Bethnal Green Branch of the South Kensington Museum by Sir Richard Wallace, Bart., June 1872* / by C.C. Black. 7th ed.
London : Printed by George E. Eyre and William Spottiswoode for H.M.S.O., 1872.
xi, 151 p. ; 22 cm.
At head of title: Science and Art Department of the Committee of Council on Education, South Kensington; Bethnal Green Branch Museum. — "Under revision." — Introduction by Henry Cole. — Printing: 3/73.

v.1873.004   "8th ed."
Printing: 12/73.

v.1873.005   *Catalogue of the loan exhibition of ancient and modern jewellery and personal ornaments, MDCCCLXXII.*
London : [s.n.], 1873 (Printed by John Strangeways).
111 p., xiv leaves of plates : ill. ; 28 cm.

At head of title: Science and Art Department, South Kensington Museum. — Introductory remarks signed "R.H.S.S." [i.e. R.H. Soden Smith]. — "List of precious gems and other materials used in jewellery..."–p. 18–23. — Index of contributors. — Photographic illustrations pasted in. — Buff wrappers.
EXHIBITION: vx.1872.003

v.1873.006   *Catalogue of the special exhibition of ancient musical instruments, MDCCCLXXII.*
London : [s.n.], [1873] (Printed by John Strangeways).
xi, 48 p., xvi leaves of plates. ill. ; 28 cm.
At head of title: Science and Art Department, South Kensington Museum. — Introduction signed "C.E." [i.e. Carl Engel]. — Date from wrappers. — Index of lenders. — Photographic illustrations pasted in.
EXHIBITION: vx.1872.002

v.1873.007   *Catalogue of the special loan exhibition of decorative art needlework made before 1800 : MDCCCLXXIII.*
London : Printed by George E. Eyre and William Spottiswoode for H.M.S.O., 1873.
vii, 54 p. ; 21 cm.
At head of title: Science and Art Department of the Committee of Council on Education, South Kensington Museum. Notice / Alan S. Cole. — Printing: 6/73. — Stone-coloured wrappers.
EXHIBITION: vx.1873.001

v.1873.008   *A descriptive catalogue of the lace in the South Kensington Museum /* by Mrs. Bury Palliser. 2nd ed.
London : Printed by George E. Eyre and William Spottiswoode for H.M.S.O., 1873.
73 p., [14] leaves of plates : ill. ; 22 cm.
At head of title: Science and Art Department of the Committee of Council on Education. Half title: Catalogue of the lace in the South Kensington Museum. Previous ed.: entitled A descriptive catalogue of the lace and embroidery . . . . — "With fourteen illustrations." — "List of books on lace in the Art Library, South Kensington Museum": p. 69–71.

v.1873.009   *A descriptive catalogue of the maiolica, Hispano-Moresco, Persian, Damascus, and Rhodian wares in the South Kensington Museum : with historical notes, marks, & monograms /* by C. Drury E. Fortnum.
London : Published for the Science and Art Department of the Committee of Council on Education . . . sold by Chapman and Hall, 1873 (Printed by George E. Eyre and William Spottiswoode).
cix, 699 p., [12] leaves of plates : ill. (some col.) ; 26 cm.
Bibliography: p. 657–665. General and numerical indexes.— Colour plates, pasted in. — Green bubble grain cloth covered boards, quarter bound in leather; title stamped in gold on spine.

v.1873.010   *Illustrated catalogue of electrotype reproductions of works of art from originals in the South Kensington Museum.*
London : Printed by George Edward Eyre and William Spottiswoode for H.M.S.O., 1873.
vi, 41 p. : ill. ; 28 cm.
At head of title: Science and Art Department of the Committee of Council on Education, South Kensington Museum. — Photographic illustrations pasted in. — Grey paper boards, quarter bound in brown leather. — Printing: 7/73.

V.1873.011   *Report on the collection of Persian articles in the South Kensington Museum by* / R. Murdoch Smith.
London : Printed by George E. Eyre and William Spottiswoode for H.M.S.O., 1873.
15 leaves ; 33 cm.
At head of title: Science and Art Department of the Committee of Council on Education, South Kensington Museum. — Includes: Catalogue of objects of Persian art in the South Kensington Museum with remarks. — Wrappers.

1874

V.1874.001   *Ancient & modern furniture and woodwork in the South Kensington Museum* / described with an introduction by John Hungerford Pollen.
London : Published for the Science and Art Department of the Committee of Council on Education by Chapman and Hall, 1874 (Printed by George E. Eyre and William Spottiswoode for H.M.S.O.).
ccli, 415 p., [16] leaves of plates : ill. (1 col.) ; 26 cm.
Includes bibliographic references. General and numerical indexes, index to artists. — Photographs printed by the Permanent Printing Company, using the Woodbury process. 1 chromolithograph. — Printing: 11/73. — Dark green cloth covered boards, quarter bound in brown leather, stamped in gold on spine.

V.1874.001A   [Large paper ed.].
28 cm.
Green cloth covered boards, half bound in green leather.

V.1874.002   *Catalogue of mercantile, marine and naval models in the South Kensington Museum : with classified table of contents and an alphabetical index of subjects.*
London : Printed by George E. Eyre and William Spottiswoode, for H.M.S.O., 1874.
108 p. ; 21 cm.
At head of title: Science and Art Department of the Committee of Council on Education. — Preface / H. Sandham. — Printing: 11/74. — Blue wrappers.

V.1874.003   *Catalogue of the anthropological collection lent by Colonel Lane Fox for exhibition in the Bethnal Green Branch of the South Kensington Museum, June 1874* / by Colonel Lane Fox.
London : Printed by George E. Eyre and William Spottiswoode for H.M.S.O., 1874.
xv, 184 p., xiv leaves of plates : ill. ; 22 cm.
At head of title: Science and Art Department of the Committee of Council on Education, South Kensington. — Part I: Typical human skulls and hair of different races. Part II: Weapons. — Printing: 6/74. — Stone-coloured wrappers.

V.1874.004   *Catalogue of the collection of paintings, porcelain, bronzes, decorative furniture and other works of art : lent for exhibition in the Bethnal Green Branch of the South Kensington Museum by Sir Richard Wallace, June 1872* / by C.C. Black. 8th ed.
London : Printed by George E. Eyre and William Spottiswoode for H.M.S.O., 1874.
xi, 151 p. ; 22 cm.

At head of title: Science and Art Department of the Committee of Council on Education, South Kensington; Bethnal Green Branch Museum. — Introduction / Henry Cole. — Biographical index of painters: p. 49–94. — Printing: 12/73. — Stone-coloured wrappers.

v.1874.005   *A catalogue of the National Gallery of British Art at South Kensington : with a supplement containing works by modern foreign artists and old masters.* New ed.
London : Printed by George E. Eyre and William Spottiswoode for H.M.S.O., 1874.
iv, 185 p. ; 22 cm.
At head of title: Department of Science and Art of the Committee of Council on Education, South Kensington Museum. Half-title: National Gallery of British Art. — Introductions by Richard Redgrave. — Includes: Report of the Commission appointed to consider the subject of lighting picture galleries by gas (1859): p. 34–35. — Indexes to painters, and gifts and bequests. — Printing: 5/74. — Stone-coloured wrappers.

v.1874.006   *Catalogue of the objects of Indian art exhibited in the South Kensington Museum : illustrated by woodcuts and by a map of India showing the localities of various art industries* / by H.H. Cole.
London : Printed by George E. Eyre and William Spottiswoode and sold by Chapman & Hall, 1874.
x, 352 p. : ill., fold. map, 16 leaves of plates ; 22 cm.
At head of title: Science and Art Department of the Committee of Council on Education, South Kensington Museum. Half-title: Indian art in the South Kensington Museum. — "Catalogue of the collection of Indian objects lent by Mr. William Tayler": p. [272]–319. — General and numerical indexes. — Printing: 10/74. — Bound in brown patterned sand grain cloth.

v.1874.006A   [Large paper ed.]

v.1874.007   *Catalogue of the special loan exhibition of decorative art needlework made before 1800 : held in 1873.*
London : [s.n.], 1874 (Printed at the Chiswick Press).
xiii, [3], 122 p., [18] leaves of plates : ill. ; 28 cm.
At head of title: Science and Art Department of the Committee of Council on Education, South Kensington Museum. — Notice / Alan S. Cole. — Bibliography of works to be found in the National Art Library: p. 119–122. Index of lenders' names. — Photographic illustrations pasted in. — Grey paper covered boards; quarter bound in brown leather with title stamped in gold on spine, printed on upper board.
EXHIBITION: vx.1873.001

v.1874.008   *Catalogue of the special loan exhibition of enamels on metal : MDCCCLXXIV*
London : Printed by George E. Eyre and William Spottiswoode for H.M.S.O., 1874.
xiii, 185 p. ; 21 cm.
At head of title: Science and Art Department of the Committee of Council on Education, South Kensington Museum. — Preface / John Hungerford Pollen. — Printing: 7/74.
EXHIBITION: vx.1874.001

v.1874.009   *Classed catalogue of the objects in the Art Division of the Museum at South Kensington, for the years 1852 to the end of 1870.*
London : Printed by George E. Eyre and William Spottiswoode for H.M.S.O., 1874.
32 cm.

At head of title: Science and Art Department of the Committee of Council on Education. — Buff wrappers.

V.1874.009A   Division I
               Not traced.

V.1874.009B   Division II
               Not traced.

V.1874.009C   Division III. Carvings in ivory, bone and horn. — 15 leaves.

V.1874.009D   Division IV. Woodwork. — 34 leaves.

V.1874.009E   Division V. Metal work. — 58 leaves.

V.1874.009F   Division VI. Coins, medals, medallions and embossed plaques.
               — 33 leaves.

V.1874.009G   Division VII. Arms and armour. — 9 leaves.

V.1874.009H   Division VIII. Silversmiths' work including plate. — 23 leaves.

V.1874.009I   Division IX. Jewellery and goldsmiths' work. — 85 leaves.

V.1874.009J Division X. Enamels on metal. — 17 leaves.

V.1874.010   *A description of the architecture and monumental sculpture in the
             south-east court of the South Kensington Museum* / by John
             Hungerford Pollen.
             London : Printed by George E. Eyre and William Spottiswoode for
             H.M.S.O., 1874.
             98 p. : ill. ; 21 cm.
             Cover title. At head of title: Science and Art Department of the Committee of Council
             on Education, South Kensington Museum. — General and numerical indexes. —
             Printing: 3/74. — Ivory wrappers.

V.1874.010A [Another issue]
             25 cm.
             Printing: 5/74. — Brown patterned-sand grain cloth covered boards.

V.1874.011   *A description of the Trajan column* / by John Hungerford Pollen.
             London : Printed by George E. Eyre and William Spottiswoode, and
             sold by Chapman & Hall, 1874.
             [4], 181 p., [1] leaf of plates : ill., plan ; 22 cm.
             At head of title: Science and Art Department of the Committee of Council on Education,
             South Kensington Museum. — Description based on casts at the South Kensington
             Museum. — Includes bibliographic references. Index. — Printing: 3/74. — Brown
             patterned-sand grain cloth covered boards; title stamped in gold.

V.1874.012   *A descriptive catalogue of the musical instruments in the South
             Kensington Museum : preceded by an essay on the history of musical
             instruments* / by Carl Engel. 2nd ed.
             London : Printed by George E. Eyre and William Spottiswoode for
             H.M.S.O., 1874.
             vii, 402 p., [6] leaves of plates : ill., music ; 26 cm.

At head of title: Science and Art Department of the Committee of Council on Education, South Kensington Museum. Half-title: Musical instruments in the South Kensington Museum. — Appendix 2: Some account of the special exhibition of ancient musical instruments in the South Kensington Museum, anno 1872. — General and numerical indexes. — Photographic plates pasted in. — Boards in green morocco grain cloth; quarter bound in leather.

V.1874.012A   [Large paper ed.]
                29 cm.
                Green pebble grain cloth, half bound in green leather.

V.1874.013   *Dyce collection : a catalogue of the paintings, miniatures, drawings, engravings, rings, and miscellaneous objects bequeathed by the Reverend Alexander Dyce.*
                London : Printed by George E. Eyre and William Spottiswoode for H.M.S.O., 1874.
                vi, 326 p. ; 26 cm.
                At head of title: Science and Art Department of the Committee of Council on Education, South Kensington Museum. — Paintings and miniatures / by Samuel Redgrave. Drawings, and Prints and etchings / by George William Reid. Rings and miscellaneous objects / by Charles C. Black. — Index. — Printing: 4/74. — Boards in green morocco grain cloth; quarter bound in leather.

V.1874.014   *Illustrated catalogue of a collection of ancient cutlery lent by M. Achille Jubinal to the South Kensington Museum.*
                London : Printed by George E. Eyre and William Spottiswoode for H.M.S.O., 1874.
                25 p., xviii leaves of plates : ill. ; 28 cm.
                At head of title: Science and Art Department of the Committee of Council on Education.

V.1874.015   *An inventory of plaster casts in various styles including the antique and the Renaissance : acquired by the South Kensington Museum.*
                London : Printed by George E. Eyre and William Spottiswoode for H.M.S.O., 1874.
                viii, 85 p. ; 21 cm.
                At head of title: Science and Art Department of the Committee of Council on Education, South Kensington Museum. — Geographical and chronological indexes. — Printing: 11/74.

1875

V.1875.001   *Ancient and modern furniture and woodwork* / by John Hungerford Pollen.
                [London] : Published for the Committee of Council on Education, by Chapman and Hall, [1875] (Dalziel Brothers, printers, Camden Press).
                vii, 143 p. : ill. ; 20 cm.
                (South Kensington Museum art handbooks ; no. 3)
                Index.

V.1875.001A   [Large paper ed. with additional illustrations.]
                (Printed by Virtue and Co.).
                vii, 143 p., [11] leaves of plates : ill. ; 27 cm.
                Additional illustrations are etchings. — Edition of fifty.

v.1875.002   *Catalogue of models of machinery, drawings, tools, &c. in the South*
              Kensington Museum : with classified table of contents, and an
              alphabetical index of subjects.
              London : Printed by George E. Eyre and William Spottiswoode for
              H.M.S.O., 1875.
              49 p. ; 22 cm.
              At head of title: Science and Art Department of the Committee of Council on Education.
              — Preface / H. Sandham. — Subject index. — Printing: 6/75.

v.1875.003   *Catalogue of the collection of munitions of war, &c., in the South*
              Kensington Museum : with classified table of contents and an
              alphabetical list of subjects.
              London : Printed by George E. Eyre and William Spottiswoode for
              H.M.S.O., 1875.
              68 p. ; 22 cm.
              At head of title: Science and Art Department of the Committee of Council on Education.
              — Preface by Henry Sandham. — Printing: 12/75.

v.1875.004   *Catalogue of the collection of objects selected from the Museum at*
              South Kensington and contributed on loan to the Wedgwood
              Memorial Institute, Burslem, 1875.
              London : Printed by George E. Eyre and William Spottiswoode for
              H.M.S.O., 1875.
              22 p. ; 21 cm.
              At head of title: Science and Art Department of the Committee of Council on Education.
              — Printing: 1/75. — Wrappers.

v.1875.005   *Catalogue of the collection of paintings, porcelain, bronzes, decorative*
              furniture, and other works of art : lent for exhibition in the Bethnal
              Green Branch of the South Kensington Museum by Sir Richard
              Wallace, Bart., M.P., June 1872 to April 1875 / by C.C. Black. 9th ed.
              London : Printed by George E. Eyre and William Spottiswoode for
              H.M.S.O., 1875.
              xi, 151 p. ; 29 cm.
              At head of title: Science and Art Department of the Committee of Council on Education,
              South Kensington. — Introduction / Henry Cole. — Printing: 5/75. — Dark green
              bubble grain cloth, half bound in green leather. — Edition of 50.

v.1875.006   *Catalogue of the special loan exhibition of enamels on metal held at*
              the South Kensington Museum in 1874.
              London : [s.n.], 1875 (Printed at the Chiswick Press by Whittingham
              and Wilkins).
              xx, 149 p., [xv] leaves of plates : ill. ; 29 cm.
              At head of title: Science and Art Department of the Committee of Council on Education.
              — Preface / John Hungerford Pollen. — General index, index of lenders. — Grey paper
              covered boards, quarter bound in leather.
              EXHIBITION: vx.1874.001

v.1875.007   *Descriptive catalogue of the collection illustrating the utilization of*
              waste products.
              London : Printed by George E. Eyre and William Spottiswoode, for
              H.M.S.O., 1875.
              79 p. ; 22 cm.

At head of title: Science and Art Department of the Committee of Council on Education, South Kensington; Bethnal Green Branch of the South Kensington Museum. — Index. — Printing: 8/75. — Wrappers.

v.1875.008   *Dyce collection : a catalogue of the printed books and manuscripts bequeathed by the Reverend Alexander Dyce.*
London : Printed by George E. Eyre and William Spottiswoode for H.M.S.O., 1875.
2v. (xxiv, 462 p. ; 448p.) : port. ; 26 cm.
At head of title: Science and Art Department of the Committee of Council on Education, South Kensington Museum. — I: Manuscripts. Printed books A–K. II: Printed books L–Z. — Alexander Dyce : a biographical sketch / John Forster. — Dark blue green pebble grain cloth covered boards, quarter bound in leather, green end-papers; or wrappers. — Printing: 2/75 (I); 12/75 (II).

v.1875.009   *A first list of examples of stained and painted glass in the United Kingdom, of dates previous to 1820.*
[London : s.n., 1875] ("E. & S.", printer).
[1], 28 leaves, 4 p. ; 35 cm.
Paged proofs. — "List of books from which notices of painted glass have been taken": p. [i]. Topographical index.
Copy notes: Printing: (i) "List of books . . ." 5/75; List 2/75; Topographical index 3/75; (ii) Topographical index 5/75; (iii) 9/75.

v.1875.010   *Inventory of the food collection : arranged in alphabetical order.*
London : Printed by George E. Eyre and William Spottiswoode for H.M.S.O., 1875.
At head of title: Science and Art Department of the Committee of Council on Education, South Kensington. Bethnal Green Branch of the South Kensington Museum. — "(Corrected to June 1874.)" — Printing: 4/75.

v.1875.011   *Ivories ancient and mediaeval* / by William Maskell.
London : Published for the Committee of Council on Education by Chapman and Hall, [1875] (Printed by Charles Dickens and Evans, Crystal Palace Press).
viii, 124 p. : ill. ; 20cm.
(South Kensington Museum art handbooks ; no. 2)
"With numerous woodcuts." — Prefatory note dated August 1875. — Index.

v.1875.011A   [Large paper ed. with additional illustrations]
viii, 124 p., [9] leaves of plates : ill. ; 27 cm.
Additional illustrations are etchings. — Edition of fifty.

v.1875.012   *A list of works on pottery and porcelain in the National Art Library : including those containing references to the subject or illustrations : (compiled for the use of students and visitors).*
London : Printed by George E. Eyre and William Spottiswoode for H.M.S.O., 1875.
22 p. ; 21 cm.
At head of title: Science and Art Department of the Committee of Council on Education, South Kensington Museum. — Notice / R.H. Soden-Smith. — Index. — White wrappers.

v.1875.013   *Maiolica* / by C. Drury E. Fortnum.
[London] : Published for the Committee of Council on Education by Chapman and Hall, [1875?] (Bradbury, Agnew & Co., Printers).

vii, 192 p. : ill. ; 20 cm.
(South Kensington Museum art handbooks ; no. 4)
Index.
Copy note: "Fourth thousand."

V.1875.013A   [Large paper ed. with additional illustrations]
vii, 192 p., [4] leaves of plates : ill. (some col.) ; 27 cm.

V.1875.014   *Musical instruments* / by Carl Engel.
London : Published for the Committee of Council on Education by
Chapman and Hall, 1875 (Printed by Virtue and Co.).
vii, 128 p. : ill. ; 20 cm.
(South Kensington Museum art handbooks ; no. 5)
Includes index. — Errata slip inserted.
Copy note: One copy bears erroneous? colophon: Printed by Taylor and Co.

V.1875.014A   [Another issue]
With corrections (p. 107–8).

V.1875.014B   [Large paper ed. with additional illustrations]
vii, 128 p., [1] leaf of plates : ill. ; 27 cm.
Additional illustrations are etchings. — Errata slip inserted — Edition of fifty.

1876

V.1876.001   *Catalogue of a collection of articles of Japanese art lent for exhibition
by W.J. Alt.*
London : Printed by George E. Eyre and William Spottiswoode for
H.M.S.O., 1876.
ix, 109 p. ; 22 cm.
At head of title: Science and Art Department of the Committee of Council on Education,
South Kensington; Bethnal Green Branch Museum. — Printing: 6/76.

V.1876.002   *Catalogue of a collection of oriental porcelain and pottery lent for
exhibition by A.W. Franks.*
London : Printed by George E. Eyre and William Spottiswoode for
H.M.S.O., 1876.
xvi, 124 p., 14 leaves of plates ; 22 cm.   ☾
At head of title: Science and Art Department of the Committee of Council on Education,
South Kensington; Bethnal Green Branch Museum. — Marks. — Printing: 6/76. —
Wrappers.

V.1876.003   *Catalogue of Persian objects in the South Kensington Museum.*
London : Printed by George E. Eyre and William Spottiswoode for
H.M.S.O., 1876.
129 p. ; 20 cm.
At head of title: Science and Art Department of the Committee of Council on Education.
— Printing: 3/76. — Grey wrappers.

V.1876.004   *Catalogue of the collection illustrating construction and building
materials in the South Kensington Museum.* New ed.
London : Printed by George E. Eyre and William Spottiswoode for
H.M.S.O., 1876.
xvi, 255 p. ; 22 cm.

At head of title: Science and Art Department of the Committee of Council on Education. — Preface / H. Sandham. — "With classified table of contents, and an alphabetical index of subjects [actually 'objects'] and exhibitors." — Printing: 9/76.

Copy note: Additional entries printed on grey paper, tipped in.

v.1876.005   *Catalogue of the Educational Division of the South Kensington Museum.* 9th ed.
London : Printed by George E. Eyre and William Spottiswoode for H.M.S.O., 1876.
xx, 618, 55, [1] p. 21 cm.
With a supplement brought down to November 1875. — Printing: 12/75.

v.1876.006   *A catalogue of the National Gallery of British Art at South Kensington : with a supplement containing works by modern foreign artists and old masters.* New ed.
London : Printed by George E. Eyre and William Spottiswoode for H.M.S.O., 1876.
v, 191 p. ; 22 cm.
At head of title: Department of Science and Art of the Committee of Council on Education, South Kensington Museum. Spine title: National Gallery of British Art, South Kensington. — Contents as v.1874.005. — Grey wrappers.

v.1876.007   *Catalogue of the special loan collection of scientific apparatus at the South Kensington Museum, 1876.*
London, 1876.
xliii, 617 p.
Unseen. Record from OCLC.
EXHIBITION: vx.1876.001

v.1876.008   *Catalogue of the special loan collection of scientific apparatus at the South Kensington Museum, MDCCCLXXXVI.* 2nd ed.
London : Printed by George E. Eyre and William Spottiswoode for H.M.S.O., 1876.
xlvii, 957 p. : ill., plan ; 21 cm.
Printing: 6/76.
EXHIBITION: vx.1876.001

v.1876.009   *A classified and priced list of objects of art, reproduced in metal by various processes, as they appear in the South Kensington Museum.*
London : Printed by George E. Eyre and William Spottiswoode for H.M.S.O., 1876.
viii, 96 p.; 21 cm.
At head of title: Science and Art Department of the Committee of Council on Education, South Kensington Museum. — "Reproductions in metal"–t.p. — Geographical and chronological indexes. — Printing: 5/76. — Grey wrappers.

v.1876.010   *A companion to the pictures and sculptures, and works of decorative art in the Bethnal Green Museum* / by F.G. Stephens.
London : Printed by George E. Eyre and William Spottiswoode for H.M.S.O., 1876.
39 p.; 21 cm.
At head of title: Science and Art Department of the Committee of Council on Education, South Kensington; Bethnal Green Branch of the South Kensington Museum. — Printing: 6/76. — Wrappers.

V.1876.011   *Conferences held in connection with the special loan collection of*
              scientific apparatus, 1876. Chemistry, biology, physical geography,
              geology, mineralogy and meteorology.
              London : Published for the Lords of the Committee of Council on
              Education by Chapman and Hall, [1876?] (Printed by Vincent Brooks,
              Day and Son).
              xi, 420 p. : ill. ; 21 cm.
              At head of title: South Kensington Museum. — Bound in dark green rib grain cloth.
              EXHIBITION: vx.1876.001

V.1876.012   *Conferences held in connection with the special loan collection of*
              scientific apparatus, 1876. Physics and mechanics.
              London : Published for the Lords of the Committee of Council on
              Education by Chapman and Hall, [1876?] (Printed by Vincent Brooks,
              Day and Son).
              viii, 441 p. : ill. ; 21 cm.
              At head of title: South Kensington Museum. — Bound in dark green rib grain cloth.
              EXHIBITION: vx.1876.001

V.1876.013   *A descriptive catalogue of the bronzes of European origin in the*
              South Kensington Museum / with an introductory notice by C. Drury
              E. Fortnum.
              London : Printed by George E. Eyre and William Spottiswoode and
              sold by Chapman & Hall, 1876.
              ccx, 248 p., [34] leaves of plates : ill. ; 26 cm.
              At head of title: Science and Art Department of the Committee of Council on Education;
              South Kensington Museum. — Bibliography: p. ccix-ccx. — Index. — Etchings, and
              photographs printed by the Permanent Printing Co., using the Woodbury process. —
              Dark green bubble grain cloth covered boards; quarter bound in leather; title stamped in
              gold on spine.

V.1876.014   *A descriptive catalogue of the fictile ivories in the South Kensington*
              Museum : with an account of the continental collections of classical
              and mediaeval ivories / by J.O. Westwood.
              London : Printed by George E. Eyre and William Spottiswoode; sold
              by Chapman and Hall, 1876.
              xv, 547 p., [9] leaves of plates : ill. ; 26 cm.
              At head of title: Science and Art Department of the Committee of Council on Education,
              South Kensington Museum. Half-title: Fictile ivory casts in the South Kensington
              Museum. — Numerical and subject indexes, index of collections. — Photographs
              printed by the Permanent Printing Co. using the Woodbury process; wood engravings.
              — Printing: 1/76. — Dark green pebble grain cloth covered board, quarter bound in
              leather.
              Copy notes: One copy is 29 cm.

V.1876.015   *A descriptive catalogue of the historical collection of water-colour*
              paintings in the South Kensington Museum / with an introductory
              notice by Samuel Redgrave.
              London : Chapman and Hall for the Science and Art Department of
              the Committee of Council on Education, 1876.
              viii, 242 p., [21] leaves of plates : ill. (some col.) ; 26 cm.
              Half-title: Water-colour paintings in the South Kensington Museum. — Name and
              subject indexes. — Illustrations consist of etchings ("the work of students in training as

art teachers in the etching class at the South Kensington Art Schools"–p. viii),
chromolithographs printed by Vincent Brooks, Day & Son, and tinted photographs. —
Dark green sand grain cloth covered boards, quarter bound in leather.

v.1876.016   *Drawings of glass cases in the South Kensington Museum, with*
               suggestions for the arrangement of specimens.
               [London] : Printed for the Committee of Council on Education by
               Vincent Brooks, Day & Son, 1876.
               [99] leaves : ill. (some col.) ; 29 cm.
               At head of title: Science and Art Department of the Committee of Council on Education,
               South Kensington Museum. — "Note" dated January 1877. — Grey paper covered
               boards, quarter bound in blue leather.

v.1876.017   *Food : some account of its sources, constituents and uses* / by A.H.
               Church.
               [London] : Published for the Committee of Council on Education by
               Chapman and Hall, 1876 (Charles Dickens and Evans, Crystal Palace
               Press, printer).
               viii, 224 p. ; 20 cm.
               (South Kensington Museum science handbook; Branch Museum,
               Bethnal Green)
               Includes index.

v.1876.018   *Free evening lectures delivered in connection with the special loan*
               collection of scientific apparatus, 1876.
               London : Published for the Lords of the Committee of Council on
               Education by Chapman and Hall, [1876?] (Printed by Taylor and
               Co.).
               vii, 524 p. : ill. ; 21 cm.
               At head of title: South Kensington Museum. — Dark green rib grain cloth covered
               boards.
               EXHIBITION: vx.1876.001

v.1876.019   *Guide théorique pour l'exposition d'appareils scientifiques du Musée*
               de South Kensington, 1876.
               Paris ; London ; Librairie Hachette et Cie, [1876?] (Virtue et cie,
               printer).
               xviii, 345 p. : ill. ; 21 cm.
               Translation of: v.1876.020. — "Préparé à la requête des Lords du Conseil
               d'Education." — Bound in style of South Kensington Museum science handbooks (see
               Series Index).
               EXHIBITION: vx.1876.001

v.1876.020   *Handbook to the special loan collection of scientific apparatus,*
               1876.
               London : Prepared at the request of the Committee of Council on
               Education and published for them by Chapman and Hall, [1876]
               (Printed by Virtue and Co.).
               xxvii, 339 p. : ill., plan ; 20 cm.
               (South Kensington Museum science handbooks)
               At head of title: South Kensington Museum. — Plan pasted on to front endpapers. —
               Also issued: New York : Scribner, Welford and Armstrong, 1877.
               Copy note: One copy: "Sixth thousand", 8 p. of advertisements bound in to wrappers.
               EXHIBITION: vx.1876.001

V.1876.021   *Handbuch, enthaltend Aufsätze über die exacten Wissenschaften und ihre Anwendungen. Deutsche Ausgabe, herausgegeben durch Rudolf Biedermann.*
London : Chapman and Hall, 1876 (Gedruckt bei Wertheimer, Lea and Co.).
xx, 402 p.
At head of title: Internationale Ausstellung wissenschaftlicher Apparate im South Kensington Museum, London, 1876. — Translation of v.1876.020. — Bound in style of South Kensington Museum science handbooks (see Series index). — On wrapper: A. Ascher & Co., Berlin [as publisher].
Copy note: 8 p. of advertisements (English) bound in to wrappers.
EXHIBITION: VX.1876.001

V.1876.022   *The industrial arts : historical sketches, with numerous illustrations.*
London : Published for the Committee of Council on Education by Chapman and Hall, [1876].
xiv, 276 p. : ill. ; 20 cm.
(South Kensington Museum art handbooks)
Preface signed: "W.M." [i.e. William Maskell].
Unseen. Record from OCLC.

V.1876.023   *The industrial arts : historical sketches*
London : Published for the Committee of Council on Education by Chapman and Hall, [187–?] (Printed by Taylor and Co.).
ill. ; 20 cm
At head of title: South Kensington Museum. — "Sold in all Museums in connection with the Science and Art Department." — Issued in parts. Title and publication details taken from I. Gold and silver work.
Copy notes: National Art Library's copies are bound together with t.p. of I. Gold and silver work.

V.1876.023A   I. *Gold and silver work.*
32 p.

V.1876.023B   II. *Bronze, copper and iron.*
16 p.

V.1876.023C   III. *Enamels.*
16 p.

V.1876.023D   IV. *Furniture.*
22 p.

V.1876.023E   V. *Ivories.*
22 p.

V.1876.023F   VI. *Pottery and porcelain.*
24, 19 p.
Part I. Part II.

V.1876.023G   VII. *Maiolica.*
24 p.

V.1876.023H   VIII. *Glass.*
22 p.

V.1876.023I   IX. *Mosaics.*
14 p.

v.1876.023J   X. *Arms and armour.*
                 10 p.

v.1876.023K   XI. *Textiles.*
                 16 p.

v.1876.023L   XII. *Lace.*
                 18 p.

v.1876.024   *Manual of design* / compiled from the writings and addresses of
Richard Redgrave by Gilbert R. Redgrave.
[London] : Published for the Committee of Council on Education by
Chapman and Hall, [1876] (Charles Dickens and Evans, Crystal
Palace Press, printer).
viii, 173 p. : ill. ; 20 cm.
(South Kensington Museum art handbooks ; no. 6)
Preface dated May 1876.

v.1876.024A   [Large paper ed.]
27 cm.

v.1876.025   *Persian art* / by R. Murdoch Smith.
[London] : Published for the Committee of Council on Education by
Chapman and Hall [1876] (Printed by Taylor and Co.).
[4], 60 p., [5] p. of plates (1 folded), 8 p. of advertisements : ill., map ;
20 cm.
(South Kensington Museum art handbooks)
Includes in Appendix: Classified abstract of the objects forming the Persian collection in
the South Kensington Museum.

v.1876.026   *A priced inventory of the casts in 'fictile ivory' in the South
Kensington Museum : arranged in order of acquisition, with classified
indexes.*
London : Printed by George E. Eyre and William Spottiswoode [for
H.M.S.O.] and sold by Chapman and Hall, 1876.
viii, 88 p. ; 21 cm.
At head of title: Science and Art Department of the Committee of Council on Education,
South Kensington Museum. — "Reproductions of carved ivories." — Indexes of objects,
museums and other collections, South Kensington Museum numbers, and a
chronological index. — Printing: 1/76. — Ivory wrappers.

v.1876.027   *Textile fabrics* / by Daniel Rock.
[London] : Published for the Committee of Council on Education by
Chapman and Hall, 1876 (Printed by Taylor and Co.).
116 p., 10 p. of advertisements : ill. ; 20 cm.
(South Kensington Museum art handbooks ; no. 1)
"With numerous woodcuts." — Includes index.

v.1876.027A   [Large paper ed. with additional illustrations.]
116 p., [7] leaves of plates : ill. (1 col.) ; 27 cm.
Additional illustrations are etchings, and one chromolithograph. — Edition of fifty.

v.1876.028   *Universal art inventory : consisting of brief notes of works of fine and
ornamental art executed before A.D. 1800, chiefly to be found in
Europe, especially in connexion with architecture and for the most*

part existing in ecclesiastical buildings : compiled for the use of the South Kensington Museum and the Schools of Art in the United Kingdom. Part II, containing (a) goldsmiths' work and enamels, and (b) ivories / edited by Henry Cole.
London : Printed by George E. Eyre and William Spottiswoode for H.M.S.O., 1876.
xv, 197 p. ; 21 cm.
At head of title: Science and Art Department. — "Edition for 1876 under revision"–t.p. — "List of books on goldsmith's [sic] work and ivories": p. xiii-xv. — Printing: 1/76. — Wrappers.

v.1876.029   *Universal art inventory : consisting of brief notes of works of fine and ornamental art executed before A.D. 1800, chiefly to be found in Europe, especially in connexion with architecture and for the most part existing in ecclesiastical buildings : compiled for the use of the South Kensington Museum and the Schools of Art in the United Kingdom. Part III, containing metal work: (a) bronze, brass, copper and lead, (b) foreign monumental brasses, (c) iron work* / compiled by H. Lindsay Cole and edited by Henry Cole.
London : Printed by George E. Eyre and William Spottiswoode for H.M.S.O., 1876.
vii, 135 p. ; 21 cm.
At head of title: Science and Art Department. — "Edition for 1876 under revision"–t.p. — "Titles of books on metal work": p. v-vii. — Printing: 11/76. — Wrappers.

1877

v.1877.001   *Animal products : their preparation, commercial uses, and value* / By P.L. Simmonds.
[London] : Published for the Committee of Council on Education by Chapman and Hall, 1877 (Bradbury, Agnew & Co., Printers).
xx, 416 p. : ill. ; 21 cm.
(South Kensington Museum science handbooks; Branch Museum, Bethnal Green)
Includes index.

v.1877.002   *Bericht über die Ausstellung wissenschaftlicher Apparate im South Kensington Museum, zu London, 1876 : zugleich vollständiger und beschreibender Katalog des Ausstellung . . .* / zusammengestellt von Rudolf Biedermann.
London : [s.n.], 1877 (John Strangeways, printer).
li, 1063 p., [6] leaves of plates (some folded) : ill., plan ; 22 cm.
Einleitung / F.R. Sandford. — Dark green cloth covered boards.
EXHIBITION: vx.1876.001

v.1877.003   *Bronzes* / by C. Drury E. Fortnum.
[London] : Published for the Committee of Council on Education by Chapman and Hall, [1877] (Charles Dickens and Evans, Crystal Palace Press, printer).
viii, 162 p. : ill. ; 20 cm.
(South Kensington Museum art handbooks)
Includes index. — "With numerous woodcuts."

V.1877.003A   [Large paper ed. with additional illustrations]
viii, 162 p., [13] leaves of plates : ill. ; 27 cm.
Additional illustrations are etchings.

V.1877.004   *Catalogue of the Doubleday collection of lepidoptera. Part I, British lepidoptera.*
[London] : Published for the Committee of Council on Education by Chapman and Hall, [1877] (Bradbury, Agnew & Co., printers).
[4], 32 p. ; 20 cm.
(South Kensington Museum science handbooks; Branch Museum, Bethnal Green)
Half-title: Doubleday collection of lepidoptera. Caption title: Catalogue of
Mr. Doubleday's collections of lepidoptera, deposited in the Bethnal Green Branch of
the South Kensington Museum. — Prepared by Andrew Murray and collated with the
collection by A.B. Farn.

V.1877.005   *Catalogue of the Doubleday collection of lepidoptera. Part II, European lepidoptera.*
[London] : Published for the Committee of Council on Education by Chapman and Hall, [1877] (Bradbury, Agnew & Co., printers).
36 p. ; 20 cm.
(South Kensington Museum science handbooks; Branch Museum, Bethnal Green)
Cover title. Caption title: Catalogue of Mr. Doubleday's collections of lepidoptera,
deposited in the Bethnal Green Branch of the South Kensington Museum. — Index.

V.1877.006   *Catalogue of the special loan collection of scientific apparatus at the South Kensington Museum : MDCCCLXXVI.* 3rd ed.
London : Printed by George E. Eyre and William Spottiswoode, for H.M.S.O., 1877.
lviii, 1084 p., [6] leaves of plates (1 folded) : ill., plan ; 22 cm.
At head of title: Science and Art Department of the Committee of Council on
Education.
EXHIBITION: VX.1876.001

V.1877.007   *Christian mosaic pictures : a catalogue of reproductions of Christian mosaics exhibited in the South Kensington Museum* / by J.W. Appell.
London : Printed by George E. Eyre and William Spottiswoode for H.M.S.O., 1877.
25 p. ; 22 cm.
Includes bibliographic references. — Printing: 12/76. — Ivory wrappers.

V.1877.008   *A descriptive catalogue of gems, precious stones and pearls : bequeathed to the South Kensington Museum by the Rev. Chauncy Hare Townshend M.A.* / by James Tennant.
London : Printed by George E. Eyre and William Spottiswoode [for H.M.S.O.] and sold by Chapman and Hall, 1877.
23 p. ; 22 cm.
At head of title: Science and Art Department of the Committee of Council on Education,
South Kensington Museum. Cover title: Catalogue of gems and precious stones . . . . —
Index. — Printing: 1/77. — Ivory wrappers.

v.1877.009   *Economic entomology* / by Andrew Murray. *Aptera.*
[London] : Prepared at the request of the Lords for the Committee of
Council on Education, and published for them by Chapman and Hall,
[1877] (Bradbury, Agnew & Co., printers).
xxiii, 433 p. : ill. ; 21 cm.
(South Kensington Museum science handbooks)
Includes index.

v.1877.010   *List of a collection of studies in oil colour representing the botany and
landscapes of various countries, painted on the spot by Miss Marianne
North.*
London : Printed by George E. Eyre and William Spottiswoode for
H.M.S.O., 1877.
19 p. ; 22 cm.
Cover title. At head of title: Science and Art Department of the Committee of Council
on Education, South Kensington Museum. — Printing: 12/77. — Wrappers.

v.1877.011   *List of the collection of water-colour paintings, the gift and bequest of
William Smith, Esq., F.S.A., 1871 and 1876.*
London : Printed by George E. Eyre and William Spottiswoode for
H.M.S.O., 1877.
16 p. ; 21 cm.
At head of title: Science and Art Department of the Committee of Council on Education,
South Kensington Museum. — Printing: 2/77.

v.1877.012   *Plain words about water* / by A.H. Church.
London : Published for the Committee of Council on Education by
Chapman and Hall, 1877 (Charles Dickens and Evans, Crystal Palace
Press, printer).
36 p. : ill. ; 21 cm.
(South Kensington Museum science handbooks)

v.1877.013   *Supplement to the universal catalogue of books on art : compiled for
the use of the National Art Library and the schools of art in the
United Kingdom.*
London : Printed for H.M.S.O. by George E. Eyre and William
Spottiswoode, 1877.
654 p. ; 22 cm.
At head of title: Science and Art Department of the Committee of Council on Education,
South Kensington. Half title: Universal catalogue of books on art. Supplementary
volume. (Proofs under revision.) — "By order of the Lords of the Committee of Council
on Education." — Printing: 12/74.

1878

v.1878.001   *Ancient and modern gold and silver smiths' work : in the South
Kensington Museum* / described with an introduction by John
Hungerford Pollen.
London : Printed by George E. Eyre and William Spottiswoode and
sold by Chapman & Hall, 1878.
cxcix, 415 p., [15] leaves of plates : ill. (1 col.) ; 26 cm.

At head of title: Science and Art Department of the Committee of Council on Education, South Kensington Museum. Half-title: Gold and silver smiths' work in the South Kensington Museum. — Title printed in red. — Indexes of objects and Museum numbers, and general index. — 1 chromolithograph; etchings, "the work of students . . . in the etching class at the South Kensington Art Schools"–p. viii. — Printing: 8/78. — Dark green pebble grain cloth covered boards; half bound in brown leather; title stamped in gold on spine. Dark brown end-papers.

V.1878.001A   [Large paper ed.]
29 cm.
Green patterned sand grain cloth covered boards, half bound in green leather.

V.1878.002   *Catalogue of a collection of oriental porcelain and pottery lent for exhibition by A.W. Franks . . . . 2nd ed.*
London : Printed by George E. Eyre and William Spottiswoode for H.M.S.O., 1878.
xviii, 246 p., xviii, A-G leaves of plates : ill. ; 22 cm.
At head of title: Science and Art Department of the Committee of Council on Education, South Kensington, Bethnal Green Branch Museum. — Marks. — Printing: 3/78. — Bound in dark tan cloth lettered in gold.

V.1878.003   *Catalogue of a special loan collection of furniture* / with an introduction by George Wallis. 2nd ed.
London : Printed by George E. Eyre and William Spottiswoode for H.M.S.O., 1878.
72 p. : ill. ; 22 cm.
At head of title: Science and Art Department of the Committee of Council on Education, South Kensington; Bethnal Green Branch Museum. — "With forty-four illustrations." — Printing: 8/78. — Ivory wrappers, or brown sand grain cloth covered boards with rules and gold lettering. Dark green end-papers. — First ed. (same year) not traced.
EXHIBITION: VX.1878.BGM.001

V.1878.004   *Catalogue of ship models and marine engineering in the South Kensington Museum : with classified table of contents and an alphabetical index of exhibitors and subjects.*
London : Printed by George E. Eyre and William Spottiswoode for H.M.S.O., 1878.
iv, 167 p. ; 21 cm.
At head of title: Science and Art Department of the Committee of Council on Education. — Preface / H. Sandham. — Printing: 1/78. — Blue wrappers.

V.1878.005   *A catalogue of the National Gallery of British Art at South Kensington : with a supplement containing works by modern foreign artists and old masters.* New ed.
London : Printed by George E. Eyre and William Spottiswoode for H.M.S.O., 1878.
vi, 203 p. ; 22 cm.
At head of title: Department of Science and Art of the Committee of Council on Education, South Kensington Museum. Half-title: National Gallery of British Art. — Introductions by Richard Redgrave. — Indexes to collections and painters. — Printing: 12/78.

V.1878.006   *Classified list of photographs of paintings and drawings, published by authority of the Department.*
London : Printed by George E. Eyre and William Spottiswoode for H.M.S.O., 1878.

167, [1] p. ; 22 cm.

At head of title: Science and Art Department of the Committee of Council on Education, South Kensington Museum. — "Complete sets of the photographs ... may be consulted in the National Art Library"–p. 3. — Printing: 4/78.

v.1878.007   *A descriptive catalogue of Swiss coins in the South Kensington Museum : bequeathed by the Reverend Chauncy Hare Townshend /* with introductory and historical notes by Reginald Stuart Poole.
London : Printed by George E. Eyre and William Spottiswoode, and sold by Chapman and Hall, 1878.
xix, 673, [1] p. ; 26 cm.

At head of title: Science and Art Department of the Committee of Council on Education, South Kensington Museum. Half-title: Swiss coins in the South Kensington Museum. — General index; indexes of denominations, subjects, inscriptions and engravers. — Printing: 5/78. — Part of title printed in red. Green pebble grain cloth covered boards. Quarter bound in leather. Title in gold on spine.

v.1878.008   *A descriptive catalogue of the glass vessels in the South Kensington Museum /* with an introductory notice by Alexander Nesbitt.
London : Printed by George E. Eyre and William Spottiswoode and sold by Chapman and Hall, 1878.
clx, 218 p., xxi leaves of plates : ill. (some col.) ; 26 cm.

At head of title: Science and Art Department of the Committee of Council on Education, South Kensington Museum. — Numerical and general indexes. — Title partly printed in red. — Illustrations include nine chromolithographs printed by Vincent Brooks, Day & Son, pasted in. — Printing: 5/78. — Green pebble grain cloth covered boards. Quarter bound in leather. Title in gold on spine.

v.1878.009   *Glass /* by Alexander Nesbitt.
[London] : Printed for the Committee of Council on Education by Chapman and Hall, [1878?].
viii, 143 p. : ill. ; 20 cm.
(South Kensington Museum art handbooks)

"With numerous woodcuts." — T.p. verso: Dalziel Bros., Camden Press. — Index.

v.1878.009A   [Large paper ed. with additional illustrations]
viii, 143 p., [8] leaves of plates : ill. (some col.) ; 27 cm.

"... chromolithographs inserted in fifty copies on large paper." Plates pasted in.

v.1878.010   *A list of works on furniture in the National Art Library.*
London : Printed by George E. Eyre and William Spottiswoode for H.M.S.O., 1878.
10p. ; 22 cm.

At head of title: Science and Art Department of the Committee of Council on Education, South Kensington. — Note signed "R.H.S.S." [i.e. R.H. Soden Smith]. — Printing: 6/78.

v.1878.011   *Tapestry /* by Alfred de Champeaux.
[London] : Published for the Committee of Council on Education by Chapman and Hall, [1878] (Charles Dickens and Evans, Crystal Palace Press).
vi, 78 p., [2] leaves of plates, 1 folded, 10 p. of advertisements : ill. ; 20 cm.
(South Kensington Museum art handbooks)

"Translated from the French by Mrs. R.F. Sketchley." — "List of the principal works relating to the history of tapestry": p. [66]–68.

1879

V.1879.001   *Catalogue of the maps, plans, and views of London and Westminster*
              collected by the late Mr. Frederick Crace : lent for exhibition in the
              South Kensington Museum by Mr. John Gregory Crace.
              London : Printed by George E. Eyre and William Spottiswoode for
              H.M.S.O., 1879.
              viii, 152 p. ; 20 cm.
              At head of title: Science and Art Department of the Committee of Council on Education,
              South Kensington. Half-title: Catalogue of the Crace collection of maps, plans and views
              of London. — Printing: 1/79.

V.1879.002   *Gold and silver smiths' work* / by John Hungerford Pollen.
              London : Published for the Committee of Council on Education
              by Chapman and Hall, [1879?] (R. Clay, Sons, and Taylor,
              printers).
              viii, 160 p. : ill. ; 20 cm.
              (South Kensington Museum art handbooks)
              Cover title: Gold and silver. — "With numerous woodcuts." — Index.

V.1879.002A   [Large paper ed. with additional illustrations.]
              viii, 160 p., [15] leaves of plates : ill. (1 col.) ; 27 cm.
              Additional illustrations are 1 chromolithograph, and etchings "the work of the students
              . . . in the etching class at the South Kensington Art Schools".

V.1879.003   *The industrial arts in Spain* / by Juan F. Riaño.
              London : Chapman and Hall for the Committee of Council on
              Education, 1879 (Bradbury, Agnew & Co., printer).
              viii, 276 p., 1 folded leaf of plates : ill. ; 20 cm.
              (South Kensington Museum art handbooks)
              Cover title: Spanish arts. — "With numerous woodcuts."

V.1879.004   *A list of books on lace and needlework in the National Art Library :*
              (compiled for the use of students and visitors).
              London : Printed by George E. Eyre and William Spottiswoode for
              H.M.S.O., 1879.
              16 p. ; 21 cm.
              At head of title: Science and Art Department of the Committee of Council on Education,
              South Kensington Museum. — Notice / R.H. Soden-Smith. — Printing: 2/79.

V.1879.005   *Memorandum upon the formation, arrangement and administration of*
              the South Kensington Museum.
              London : [s.n.], 1879.
              18 p.; 23 cm.
              At head of title: Science and Art Department of the Committee of Council on Education,
              South Kensington.

V.1879.006   *Some account of the armorial bearings upon the chimney breast,*
              centre, and sides, in the Palais de Justice, Bruges, repeated in the cast
              in the South Kensington Museum / by Daniel Parsons.
              London : [s.n.], 1879.
              16 p. ; 22 cm.
              At head of title: Science and Art Department of the Committee of Council on Education,
              South Kensington.

v.1879.007   *Universal art inventory : consisting of brief notes of works of fine
              and ornamental art executed before A.D. 1800, chiefly to be found in
              Europe, especially in connexion with architecture and for the most
              part existing in ecclesiastical buildings : compiled for the use of the
              South Kensington Museum and the Schools of Art in the United
              Kingdom. Part IV, containing woodwork, sculpture in marble,
              alabaster, stone &c* / compiled by H. Lindsay Cole and edited by
              Henry Cole.
              London : Printed by George E. Eyre and William Spottiswoode for
              H.M.S.O., 1879.
              viii, 382 p. ; 21 cm.
              At head of title: Science and Art Department. — "Titles of books on woodwork":
              p. vi–vii. "Titles of books on sculpture": p. viii. — Printing: 8/79. — Wrappers.

1880

v.1880.001   *Catalogue of models of machinery, drawings, tools, &c. in the South
              Kensington Museum : with classified table of contents, and an
              alphabetical index of exhibitors and subjects.*
              London : Printed by George E. Eyre and William Spottiswoode for
              H.M.S.O., 1880.
              194 p. ; 22 cm.
              At head of title: Science and Art Department of the Committee of Council on Education.
              — Printing: 2/80.

v.1880.002   *Catalogue of the collection of munitions of war . . . .*
              1880.
              Unseen. Record from National Art Library catalogue of acquisitions before 1890.

v.1880.003   *The commercial products of the animal kingdom employed in the arts
              and manufactures : shown in the collection of the Bethnal Green
              Branch of the South Kensington Museum* / briefly described by P.L.
              Simmonds.
              London : Printed by George Edward Eyre and William Spottiswoode
              for H.M.S.O., 1880.
              96 p. : ill. ; 31 cm.
              At head of title: Science and Art Department of the Committee of Council on
              Education, South Kensington. — "With more than 150 illustrations." — Printing:
              1/80.

v.1880.004   *Food : some account of its sources, constituents and uses* / by A.H.
              Church. Repr.
              [London] : Published for the Committee of Council on Education by
              Chapman and Hall, 1880 (Charles Dickens and Evans, Crystal Palace
              Press, printer).
              viii, 224 p. ; 20 cm.
              (South Kensington Museum science handbooks; Branch Museum,
              Bethnal Green)
              Copy note: "Fourth thousand".

v.1880.005   *Handbook of the Dyce and Forster collections in the South
                Kensington Museum : with engravings and facsimiles.*
                London : Published for the Committee of Council on Education by
                Chapman and Hall, Ltd., [1880?] (Charles Dickens and Evans, Crystal
                Palace Press).
                viii, 105 p., [19] leaves of plates : ill., facsims., ports. ; 20 cm.
                (South Kensington Museum art handbooks)

v.1880.005A   [Large paper ed.]
                27 cm.

v.1880.006   *India Museum : inventory of the collection of examples of Indian art
                and manufactures transferred to the South Kensington Museum.*
                London : Printed by George E. Eyre and William Spottiswoode for
                H.M.S.O., 1880.
                [4], 190 p., 1a–287a ; 34 cm.
                At head of title: Science and Art Department of the Committee of Council on Education,
                South Kensington. — Printing: 2/80. — Maroon rib grain cloth covered boards; ruled
                border with sprig design in corners, stamped blind; title in gold on spine. Primrose end-
                papers.

v.1880.007   *The industrial arts of India* / by George C.M. Birdwood.
                [London] : Published for the Committee of Council on Education by
                Chapman and Hall, [1880] (Printed by R. Clay, Sons, and Taylor).
                2 v. (xv, 168 p., [1] folded leaf, 42 leaves of plates ; viii, 176 p., p.
                43–76 of plates) : ill., maps; 20 cm.
                (South Kensington Museum art handbooks)
                Title on cover and spine: Indian arts. — "With maps and woodcuts." — In two
                volumes. Vol. I: Part I, The Hindu pantheon. Part II. The master handicrafts of India [4
                chapters]. Vol. II: Part II. The master handicrafts of India (continued).
                Copy note: 4 p. of advertisements at end.

v.1880.007A   [Another issue]
                2 v. (xvi, 130 p., [1] folded leaf, leaves A-O of plates; p. [131]–344, 76
                leaves of plates)
                "In two parts." — [Vol. 1] Part I. The Hindu pantheon. [Vol. 2] Part II. The master
                handicrafts of India.
                Copy note: [2], 8, [4], [12] p. of advertisements bound in.

v.1880.008   *Japanese pottery : being a native report* / with an introduction and
                catalogue by Augustus W. Franks.
                London : Published for the Committee of Council on Education by
                Chapman and Hall, 1880.
                xvi, 112 p. : ill. ; 20 cm.
                (South Kensington Museum art handbooks)
                Prepared by M. Shioda, translated by T. Asami. — Includes list of potters and
                decorators who exhibited at the Paris Exhibition, 1878.

v.1880.008A   [Large paper ed.]
                27 cm.

v.1880.009   *A list of works on heraldry, or containing heraldic illustrations, in the
                National Art Library : (compiled for the use of students and visitors).*
                London : Printed by George E. Eyre and William Spottiswoode for
                H.M.S.O., 1880.

31 p. ; 22 cm.
At head of title: Science and Art Department of the Committee of Council on Education,
South Kensington Museum. — Introductory notice by R.H. Soden-Smith.

V.1880.010   *Persian art* / by Major R. Murdoch Smith. 2nd ed. enl.
[London] : Published for the Committee of Council on Education by
Chapman and Hall, [1880?] (Printed by Virtue and Co. Ltd.).
viii, 103 p., 1 folded leaf of plates : ill., map ; 20 cm.
(South Kensington Museum art handbooks)

1881

V.1881.001   *The analysis and adulteration of foods* / by James Bell. *Part I, Tea,
coffee, cocoa, sugar, &c.*
[London] : Published for the Committee of Council on Education by
Chapman and Hall, 1881 (Charles Dickens and Evans, Crystal Palace
Press).
[6], 120 p. : ill. ; 20 cm.
(South Kensington Museum science handbooks; Branch Museum,
Bethnal Green)
Copy notes: [18] p. of advertisements bound into wrappers. — Found in covers lettered
"South Kensington Museum art handbooks".

V.1881.002   *A catalogue of the first circulating historical series of water-colour
paintings illustrative of the rise and progress of the art in England :
selected from the National Gallery of British Art at South Kensington.*
London : Printed by George E. Eyre and William Spottiswoode for
H.M.S.O., 1881.
Unseen. Record from National Art Library Catalogue of acquisitions before 1890.

V.1881.003   *A catalogue of the second circulating historical series of water-colour
paintings illustrative of the rise and progress of the art in England :
selected from the National Gallery of British Art at South Kensington.*
London : Printed by George E. Eyre and William Spottiswoode for
H.M.S.O., 1881.
14 p. ; 21 cm.
At head of title: Science and Art Department of the Committee of Council on Education,
South Kensington Museum. — Introduction by Richard Redgrave, abridged from
V.1878.005. — Printing: 12/81. — Stone-coloured wrappers.

V.1881.004   *Catalogue of the special loan exhibition of Spanish and Portuguese
ornamental art : South Kensington Museum, 1881* / edited by J.C.
Robinson.
London : Chapman & Hall, 1881 (Printed for the Committee of
Council on Education by R. Clay, Sons, and Taylor).
211 p. ; 21 cm.
At head of title: Science and Art Department of the Committee of Council on Education.
— Items 704–1576 are from the Museum's own collections. — Index of lenders..
EXHIBITION: vx.1881.001

V.1881.004A   [Large paper ed.]
Grey paper covered boards, quarter bound in brown leather.

V.1881.005   *Catalogue of the water-colour drawings of Indian views, groups, &c.*
              executed and lent for exhibition in the South Kensington Museum by
              William Carpenter.
              London : Printed by George E. Eyre and William Spottiswoode for
              H.M.S.O., 1881.
              15 p. ; 25 cm.
              At head of title: Science and Art Department of the Committee of Council on Education,
              South Kensington. — Printing: 1/81.

V.1881.006   *The chemistry of foods : with microscopic illustrations* / by James Bell.
              Part I, Tea, coffee, cocoa, sugar, etc.
              [London] : Published for the Committee of Council on Education by
              Chapman and Hall, [1881?] (Charles Dickens and Evans, Crystal
              Palace Press).
              [6], 120 p. : ill. ; 20 cm.
              (South Kensington Museum science handbooks; Branch Museum,
              Bethnal Green)
              Contents identical to v.1881.001. Possibly a later reprint.
              Copy note: Found in covers lettered "South Kensington Museum art handbooks".

V.1881.007   *College and corporation plate : a handbook to the reproductions of*
              silver plate in the South Kensington Museum, from celebrated English
              collections / by Wilfred Joseph Cripps.
              [London] : Published for the Committee of Council on Education by
              Chapman and Hall, 1881 (R. Clay, Sons, and Taylor, printer).
              xii, 155 p., [16] p. of advertisements : ill. ; 20 cm.
              (South Kensington Museum art handbooks)
              Includes index.

V.1881.007A   [Large paper ed.]
              xii, 155 p. : ill. ; 27 cm.

V.1881.008   *A descriptive catalogue of the collection of lace in the South*
              Kensington Museum / by Mrs. Bury Palliser. 3rd ed., rev. and enl. by
              Alan S. Cole.
              London : Printed by George E. Eyre and William Spottiswoode for
              H.M.S.O., 1881.
              xliii, 144 p., xxi leaves of plates : ill. ; 22 cm.
              At head of title: Science and Art Department of the Committee of Council on Education,
              South Kensington. Previous ed. entitled A descriptive catalogue of the lace . . . .
              — "with numerous illustrations." — "List of books on lace in the National Art
              Library": p. 123–129. Numerical and general indexes. — Printing: 12/81.

V.1881.008A   [Large paper ed.]
              29 cm.
              Edition of fifty.

V.1881.009   *Handbook of the collection illustrative of the wild silks of India in the*
              Indian Section of the South Kensington Museum : with a catalogue of
              the collection and numerous illustrations / by Thomas Wardle.
              London : Printed by George E. Eyre and William Spottiswoode, for
              H.M.S.O., 1881.

xii, 97 p., 98–163 leaves (1 folded) : ill., maps ; 22 cm.

At head of title: Science and Art Department of the Committee of Council on Education, South Kensington. — Index. — Wrappers.

V.1881.010   *List of objects of art reproduced in metal by various processes, as they appear in the South Kensington Museum. Part I, Examples of which copies may be supplied by the electrotypists.*
London : Printed by George E. Eyre and William Spottiswoode for H.M.S.O., 1881.

iii, 93 p. ; 22 cm.

At head of title: Science and Art Department of the Committee of Council on Education, South Kensington Museum. — Geographical and chronological indexes. — Printing : 5/81.

V.1881.011   *List of papers and periodicals received in the National Art Library, 1881.*
London : [s.n.], 1881.

8 p. ; 21 cm.

At head of title: Science and Art Department of the Committee of Council on Education, South Kensington. — Includes subscription prices.

V.1881.012   *List of the bequests and donations to the Department of Science and Art, South Kensington Museum : completed to 31st December 1880.*
London : Printed by George Edward Eyre and William Spottiswoode, 1881.

153 p. ; 33 cm.

At head of title: Department of Science and Art of the Committee of Council on Education, South Kensington. — Subject and donor indexes. — Printing: 11/81. — Wrappers.

V.1881.013   *A list of works on costume in the National Art Library : (compiled for the use of students and visitors).*
London : Printed by Eyre and Spottiswoode for H.M.S.O., 1881.

70 p. ; 21 cm.

At head of title: Science and Art Department of the Committee of Council on Education, South Kensington Museum. — Preface / R.H. Soden Smith. — Stone-coloured wrappers.

V.1881.014   *A list of works on painting in the National Art Library : (compiled for the use of students and visitors).*
London : Printed by George E. Eyre and William Spottiswoode for H.M.S.O., 1881.

47 p. ; 21 cm.

At head of title: Science and Art Department of the Committee of Council on Education, South Kensington Museum. — Notice / R.H. Soden-Smith — Printing: 6/81. — Buff wrappers.

1882

V.1882.001   *Catalogue of ship models and marine engineering in the South Kensington Museum : supplement.*
London : [H.M.S.O.], 1882.

24 p. ; 21 cm.

At head of title: Science and Art Department of the Committee of Council on Education. — Index.

v.1882.002   *Catalogue of the collection of munitions of war . . . .*
              1882.
              Unseen. Record from National Art Library catalogue of acquisitions before 1890.

v.1882.003   *Catalogue of the Jones Bequest in the South Kensington*
              Museum.
              London : Printed by Eyre and Spottiswoode for H.M.S.O., 1882.
              82 p. ; 20 cm.
              At head of title: Science and Art Department of the Committee of Council on Education.
              — Printing: 1/83. — Grey wrappers.

v.1882.004   *The industrial arts of Denmark : from the earliest times to the Danish*
              conquest of England / by J.J.A. Worsaae.
              [London] : Published for the Committee of Council on Education by
              Chapman and Hall, 1882 (R. Clay, Sons, and Taylor, printers).
              xii, 206 p., 1 folded leaf of plates : ill., map ; 20 cm.
              (South Kensington Museum art handbooks)
              Title on cover and spine: Danish arts. — "With map and woodcuts." — "In the summer
              of 1882, a special loan exhibition of the industrial arts of Denmark, Norway and
              Sweden was held in the South Kensington Museum . . ."
              EXHIBITION: vx.1882.001

v.1882.004A   [Another issue]
              xii, 119 p., viii, 86 p.
              Contents as v.1882.004 but in two parts, bound together, with separate t.p.
              and contents pages. — Part I: The Stone Age. The Bronze Age. Part II: The
              Iron Age.
              Copy note: Series title on cover Victoria and Albert Museum art handbook.

v.1882.005   *A list of works on gold and silversmiths' work and jewellery in the*
              National Art Library : (compiled for the use of students and
              visitors).
              London : Printed by G.E.B. Eyre and William Spottiswoode for
              H.M.S.O., 1882.
              62 p. ; 20 cm.
              At head of title: Science and Art Department of the Committee of Council on Education,
              South Kensington Museum. — Notice / R.H. Soden-Smith. — Blue wrappers.
              Copy notes: Printings: 10/82, 11/82.

v.1882.006   *A list of works on ornament in the National Art Library : (compiled*
              for the use of students and visitors).
              London : Printed by Eyre and Spottiswoode for H.M.S.O., 1882.
              101 p. ; 21 cm.
              At head of title: Science and Art Department of the Committee of Council on Education,
              South Kensington Museum. — Notice / R.H. Soden-Smith. — Printing: 9/82. — Buff
              wrappers.

v.1882.007   *A list of works on sculpture in the National Art Library : (compiled*
              for the use of students and visitors).
              London : Printed by George E. Eyre and William Spottiswoode for
              H.M.S.O., 1882.
              31 p. ; 21 cm.
              At head of title: Science and Art Department of the Committee of Council on Education,
              South Kensington Museum. — Printing: 5/82. — Buff wrappers.

v.1882.008   *Maiolica* / by C. Drury E. Fortnum. Repr.
              [London] : Published for the Committee of Council on Education by
              Chapman and Hall, 1882 (R. Clay, Sons, and Taylor, printer).
              vii, 192 p. : ill. ; 20 cm.
              (South Kensington Museum art handbooks ; no. 4)
              "With numerous woodcuts." — Index.

1883

v.1883.001   *Catalogue of the collection of paintings lent for exhibition by the
              Marquis of Bute, K.T.* / by Jean Paul Richter.
              London : Printed by George E.B. Eyre and William Spottiswoode for
              H.M.S.O., 1883.
              82 p. ; 21 cm.
              At head of title: Science and Art Department of the Committee of Council on Education,
              South Kensington; Bethnal Green Branch Museum. — Index. — Printing: 6/83. — Buff
              wrappers.

v.1883.002   *The chemistry of foods : with microscopic illustrations* / by James Bell.
              Part II, Milk, butter, cheese, cereal foods, prepared starches, &c.
              [London] : Published for the Committee of Council on Education by
              Chapman and Hall, 1883 (Charles Dickens and Evans, Crystal Palace
              Press).
              vi, [2], 177 p. : ill. ; 20 cm.
              (South Kensington Museum science handbooks; Branch Museum,
              Bethnal Green)
              Cover series title: South Kensington Museum art handbook

v.1883.003   *Gold and silver smiths' work* / by John Hungerford Pollen.
              London : Published for the Committee of Council on Education by
              Chapman and Hall, 1883.
              viii, 160 p. : ill. ; 20 cm.
              (South Kensington Museum art handbooks)
              Cover title: Gold and silver. — Includes index.

v.1883.004   *Handbook of the Jones collection in the South Kensington Museum.*
              [London] : Published for the Committee of Council on Education by
              Chapman and Hall, 1883 (R. Clay, Sons, and Taylor, printer).
              viii, 160 p., [1] leaf of plates : ill., 1 port. ; 20 cm.
              (South Kensington Museum art handbooks)
              "With portrait and woodcuts."

v.1883.004A   [Large paper ed.]
              viii, 160 p., [1] leaf of plates : ill., 1 port. ; 26 cm.
              Lacks series statement.

v.1883.005   *The industrial arts of Scandinavia in the pagan time* / by Hans
              Hildebrand.
              London : Published for the Committee of Council on Education by
              Chapman and Hall, 1883 (R. Clay, Sons, and Taylor, printer).
              viii, 150 p. : ill. ; 20 cm.
              (South Kensington Museum art handbooks)

Cover title: Scandinavian arts. — Companion volume to v.1882.004.
EXHIBITION: vx.1882.001

v.1883.006   *Inventory of reproductions in metal : comprising, in addition to those*
available for sale to the public, electrotypes bought or made specially
for the use of the South Kensington Museum, and schools of art, by
permission of the respective owners. Part I, Examples of which copies
may be supplied by the electrotypists.
London : Printed by George E.B. Eyre and William Spottiswoode for
H.M.S.O., 1883.
[2], 72 p. ; 33 cm.
At head of title: Science and Art Department of the Committee of Council on
Education, South Kensington Museum. "For official use." — Indexes to objects and
artists (electrotypes); names and subects, artists (medals). — Printing: 4/83. —
Wrappers.

v.1883.006A   *Inventory of reproductions in metal : comprising, in addition to those*
available for sale to the public, electrotypes bought or made specially
for the use of the South Kensington Museum, and schools of art, by
permission of the respective owners.
London : Printed by Eyre and Spottiswoode for H.M.S.O., 1883.
iv, 72 p. ; 33 cm.
At head of title: Science and Art Department of the Committee of Council on
Education, South Kensington Museum. "For official use." —"The examples marked
with an asterisk before the number cannot be supplied by the electrotypists without
the special permission of the owners." — Printing: 8/83. — Seen only as part of
v.1886.003.

v.1883.007   *Inventory of reproductions in metal. Part II, Works of art in private*
collections, reproduced for the South Kensington Museum by special
permission of the owners.
London : Printed by George E.B. Eyre and William Spottiswoode for
H.M.S.O., 1883.
iv, 26 p. ; 33 cm.
At head of title: Science and Art Department of the Committee of Council on Education,
South Kensington Museum. "For official use." — "Not for sale"–t.p. — Indexes to
objects and owners. — Printing: 4/83. — Wrappers.

v.1883.008   *A list of books and photographs in the National Art Library*
illustrating armour and weapons : (compiled for the use of students
and visitors).
London : Printed by G.E.B. Eyre and William Spottiswoode for
H.M.S.O., 1883.
68 p. ; 20 cm.
At head of title: Science and Art Department of the Committee of Council on Education,
South Kensington Museum.

v.1883.009   *A list of buildings in Great Britain and Ireland having mural and other*
painted decorations : of dates prior to the latter part of the sixteenth
century, with historical introduction and alphabetical index of subjects
/ by C.E. Keyser. 3rd ed., enl.
London : Printed by Eyre and Spottiswoode for H.M.S.O. and sold at
the South Kensington Museum, 1883.
xciii, 402 p. 22 cm.

At head of title: Science and Art Department of the Committee of Council on Education, South Kensington Museum. Previous ed. entitled A list of buildings in England .... — "Compiled for the use of schools of art in the United Kingdom." — Indexes of objects, subjects, saints. — Printing: 10/83.

V.1883.010   *A list of works on ornament in the National Art Library : (compiled for the use of students and visitors).* 2nd ed.
London : Printed by Eyre and Spottiswoode for H.M.S.O., 1883.
102 p. ; 22 cm.
At head of title: Science and Art Department of the Committee of Council on Education, South Kensington Museum.

V.1883.011   *A list of works on painting in the National Art Library : (compiled for the use of students and visitors).* 2nd ed.
London : Printed by Eyre and Spottiswoode for H.M.S.O., 1883.
vii, 157 p. ; 22 cm.
At head of title: Science and Art Department of the Committee of Council on Education, South Kensington Museum. — Printing: 1/84. — Wrappers.

V.1883.012   *Plain words about water* / A.H. Church. New ed.
London : Chapman and Hall, 1883.
36 p. ; 20 cm.
(South Kensington Museum science handbooks)
Unseen. Record from OCLC.

V.1883.013   *Precious stones considered in their scientific and artistic relations : with a catalogue of the Townshend collection of gems in the South Kensington Museum* / by A.H. Church.
London : Printed for the Committee of Council on Education by Chapman and Hall, 1883.
viii, 111 p., [5] leaves of plates : ill. (1 col.) ; 20 cm.
(South Kensington Museum art handbooks)
Charles Dickens and Evans, Crystal Palace Press–t.p. verso. — "Bibliographical notes": p. 95. Index.

1884

V.1884.001   *A catalogue of the National Gallery of British Art at South Kensington : with a supplement containing works by modern foreign artists and old masters. Part I, Oil paintings.* New ed.
London : Printed by Eyre and Spottiswoode for H.M.S.O., 1884.
v, 133 ; 22 cm.
At head of title: Department of Science and Art of the Committee of Council on Education, South Kensington Museum. Spine title: National Gallery of British Art, South Kensington. — Introduction / by Richard Redgrave. — Index of gifts and bequests, and index of painters. — Printing: 6/84. — Wrappers.

V.1884.002   *A catalogue of the National Gallery of British Art at South Kensington : with a supplement containing works by modern foreign artists. Part II, Water colour paintings.* New ed.
London : Printed by Eyre and Spottiswoode for H.M.S.O., 1884.
v, 145 p. ; 22 cm.

At head of title: Department of Science and Art of the Committee of Council on
Education, South Kensington Museum. Spine title: National Gallery of British Art,
South Kensington. — Introduction / by Richard Redgrave. — Index of gifts and
bequests, and index of painters.— Printing: 6/84. — Wrappers.

v.1884.003   *A descriptive catalogue of the collection of casts from the antique in
the South Kensington Museum* / by Walter Copland Perry.
London : Printed by Eyre and Spottiswoode for H.M.S.O.,
1884.
xviii, 122 p. ; 22 cm.
At head of title: Science and Art Department of the Committee of Council on Education.
South Kensington. — Printing: 8/84.

v.1884.004   *English earthenware : a handbook to the wares made in England
during the seventeenth and eighteenth centuries as illustrated by
specimens in the national collections* / by A.H. Church.
[London] : Published for the Committee of Council on Education, by
Chapman and Hall, 1884 (R. Clay, Sons, and Taylor [printer]).
xiv, 123 p., [65] leaves of plates : ill. ; 20 cm.
(South Kensington Museum art handbooks)
"With numerous woodcuts." — "Bibliographical notes ": p. [xv]–xvi. Index. — Grey
wrappers with advertisements; dark green cloth covered boards stamped in gold and
black and blind with title, device and rules.

v.1884.004A   [Large paper ed.]
27 cm.
Bound with this are title page and prelims. including "Additions and corrections", taken
from *English pottery*, comprising *English earthenware* and the same author's *English
porcelain*.

v.1884.005   *French pottery* / by Paul Gasnault and Edouard Garnier.
[London] : Published for the Committee of Council on Education by
Chapman and Hall, 1884 (Charles Dickens and Evans, Crystal Palace
Press, printer).
viii, 183 p. : ill. ; 20 cm.
(South Kensington Museum art handbooks)
"With illustrations and marks." — Index. — "Translated from the French by M.P.
Villars."

v.1884.006   *The industrial arts of India* / by George C.M. Birdwood. New ed.
London : Chapman and Hall for the Committee of Council on
Education, 1884.
2 v. in 1 (438 p., 1 folded) : ill., map ; 20 cm.
(South Kensington Museum art handbooks)
Unseen. Record from OCLC.

v.1884.007   *A list of works on heraldry, or containing heraldic illustrations, in the
National Art Library : (compiled for the use of students and visitors).*
2nd ed.
London : Printed by Eyre and Spottiswoode for H.M.S.O.,
1884.
75 p. ; 22 cm.
At head of title: Science and Art Department of the Committee of Council on Education,
South Kensington Museum. — Introductory notice by R.H. Soden-Smith. — Printing:
2/84. — Buff wrappers.

v.1884.008   *Russian art and art objects in Russia : a handbook to the reproductions of goldsmiths' work and other art treasures from that country in the South Kensington Museum* / by Alfred Maskell.
[London] : Published for the Committee of Council on Education by Chapman & Hall, 1884 (R. Clay, Sons, and Taylor, printer).
xii, 278 p., xxiv leaves of plates : ill., plan ; 20 cm.
(South Kensington Museum art handbooks)

1885

v.1885.001   *English porcelain : a handbook to the china made in England during the eighteenth century as illustrated by specimens chiefly in the national collections* / by A.H. Church.
[London] : Published for the Committee of Council on Education, by Chapman and Hall, 1885 (Richard Clay & Sons, printer).
xiii, 99 p., [40] leaves of plates, 16 p. of advertisements : ill. ; 20 cm.
(South Kensington Museum art handbooks)
"With numerous woodcuts." — "Bibliographical notes": leaf preceding p. [1]. Index.
Copy note: Date on wrappers of one copy: 1886.

v.1885.001A   [Large paper ed.]
27 cm.

v.1885.002   *Japanese pottery : being a native report* / with an introduction and catalogue by Augustus W. Franks. Repr.
London : Published for the Committee of Council on Education by Chapman and Hall, [1885] (Charles Dickens and Evans, Crystal Palace Press).
xvi, 112 p., 16 p. of advertisements : ill. ; 20 cm.
(South Kensington Museum art handbooks)
"With illustrations and marks." — Date from wrappers. — Prepared by M. Shioda, translated by T. Asami. — Includes list of potters and decorators who exhibited at the Paris Exhibition, 1878. Index.

v.1885.003   *Labels for the collection of casts from the antique in the South Kensington Museum.*
London : Printed by Eyre and Spottiswoode for H.M.S.O., 1885.
32 p. ; 22 cm.
At head of title: Science and Art Department of the Committee of Council on Education. South Kensington.

v.1885.004   *A list of books and pamphlets in the National Art Library on pottery and porcelain : (compiled for the use of students and visitors).* 2nd ed.
London : Printed by Eyre and Spottiswoode for H.M.S.O., 1885.
ix, 147 p. ; 22 cm.
At head of title: Science and Art Department of the Committee of Council on Education, South Kensington Museum. — Notice / R.H. Soden Smith. — Printing: 5/85. — Buff wrappers.

v.1885.005   *Schreiber collection : catalogue of English porcelain, earthenware, enamels &c. : collected by Charles Schreiber Esq., M.P. and the Lady Charlotte Elizabeth Schreiber, and presented to the South Kensington Museum in 1884.*

London : Printed by Eyre and Spottiswoode for H.M.S.O., 1885.
xi, 241 p., viii leaves of plates : ports. ; 22 cm.
"List of books referred to": p. 213–215. Index. Marks.
Copy note: Pasted in: Schreiber collection : additional examples received in 1889 (3 p.).

v.1885.005A   [Large paper ed.]

1886

v.1886.001   *Food-grains of India* / by A.H. Church.
London : Published for the Committee of Council on Education by
Chapman and Hall, 1886 (Charles Dickens and Evans, Crystal Palace
Press).
viii, [4], 180 p. : ill. ; 27 cm.
(South Kensington Museum science handbooks)
"Bibliographical notes"–p. [xii].

v.1886.002   *Index to electrotypes acquired in the years 1852 to 1883.*
[London : Printed by Eyre and Spottiswoode for H.M.S.O, 1886.]
19 p. ; 33 cm.
Caption title.

v.1886.003   *Inventory of reproductions in metal . . . .*
v.1883.006a and v.1886.002 issued together; cover date 1886.

v.1886.004   *A list of books and pamphlets in the National Art Library of the
South Kensington Museum, illustrating gems : (compiled for the use of
students and visitors).*
London : Printed by Eyre and Spottiswoode for H.M.S.O., 1886.
27 p. ; 20 cm.
At head of title: Science and Art Department of the Committee of Council on Education.

v.1886.005   *A list of books and pamphlets in the National Art Library, South
Kensington Museum, illustrating seals : (compiled for the use of
students and visitors).*
London : Printed by Eyre and Spottiswoode for H.M.S.O., 1886.
iv, 46 p. ; 22 cm.
At head of title: Science and Art Department of the Committee of Council on Education,
South Kensington Museum.

v.1886.006   *List of books in the National Art Library, South Kensington Museum,
on anatomy, human and comparative : (compiled for the use of
students and visitors).*
London : Printed by Eyre and Spottiswoode for H.M.S.O., 1886.
24 p. ; 21 cm.

v.1886.007   *A list of works illustrating sculpture in the National Art Library of the
South Kensington Museum : (compiled for the use of students and
visitors).* 2nd ed.
London : Printed by Eyre and Spottiswoode for H.M.S.O., 1886.
viii, 154 p. ; 22 cm.
At head of title: Science and Art Department of the Committee of Council on Education,
South Kensington Museum. — Printing: 4/86. — Wrappers.

1887

V.1887.001   *Catalogue of a collection of oil paintings, water-colour drawings and engravings, enamel paintings, sculpture, bronzes, &c. : bequeathed by the late Joshua Dixon, Esq.* 2nd ed.
London : Printed by Eyre and Spottiswoode for H.M.S.O., 1887.
18 p. ; 22 cm.
At head of title: Department of Science and Art of the Committee of Council on Education; Bethnal Green Branch Museum. — First ed. not traced.

V.1887.002   *Classified list of photographs of works of decorative art in the South Kensington Museum, and other collections.*
London : Printed for H.M.S.O., by Eyre and Spottiswoode, 1887.
308 p. ; 22 cm.
At head of title: Department of Science and Art of the Committee of Council on Education. — Printing: 8/87.

V.1887.003   *A descriptive catalogue of a collection of tapestry-woven and embroidered Egyptian textiles in the South Kensington Museum* / by Alan S. Cole.
London: Printed by Eyre and Spottiswoode for H.M.S.O., 1887.
xvii, 70 p. ; 22 cm.
At head of title: Department of Science and Art of the Committee of Council on Education. — Printing: 7/87. — Wrappers.

V.1887.004   *A descriptive catalogue of the collection of casts from the antique in the South Kensington Museum* / by Walter Copland Perry. 2nd ed.
London : Printed by Eyre and Spottiswoode for H.M.S.O., 1887.
xviii, 128 p. ; 22 cm.
At head of title: Science and Art Department of the Committee of Council on Education, South Kensington.

V.1887.005   *Early Christian art in Ireland* / by Margaret Stokes.
[London] : Published for the Committee of Council on Education by Chapman and Hall, 1887 (Charles Dickens and Evans, Crystal Palace Press).
xvi, 210 p., [1] folded leaf : ill. ; 20 cm.
(South Kensington Museum art handbooks)
"With one hundred and six woodcuts." — Bibliography: p. 198. Chronology on folded leaf.

V.1887.006   *A list of books and pamphlets in the National Art Library of the South Kensington Museum, illustrating glass : (compiled for the use of students and visitors).*
London : Printed by Eyre and Spottiswoode for H.M.S.O., 1887.
47 p. ; 20 cm.
At head of title: Science and Art Department of the Committee of Council on Education, South Kensington Museum.

V.1887.007   *A list of books and pamphlets in the National Art Library, South Kensington Museum, containing biographies of artists : and of others connected with the history of art : (compiled for the use of students and visitors).*
London : Printed by Eyre and Spottiswoode for H.M.S.O., 1887.
261 p. ; 21 cm.

v.1887.008   *A list of books and pamphlets in the National Art Library, South
              Kensington Museum, illustrating gold and silversmiths' work and
              jewellery : (compiled for the use of students and visitors).* 2nd ed.
              London : Printed by Eyre and Spottiswoode for H.M.S.O.,
              1887.
              91 p. ; 20 cm.
              At head of title: Science and Art Department of the Committee of Council on Education.
              — First published 1882.

v.1887.009   *Supplement to Art Library catalogue.*
              [London : Printed by Eyre and Spottiswoode for H.M.S.O., 1887.]
              80 leaves ; 21 cm.
              Printing: 1/87. — 50 copies printed.

v.1887.010   *Tapestry /* by Alfred de Champeaux. Repr.
              [London] : Published for the Committee of Council on Education by
              Chapman and Hall, [1887] (Charles Dickens and Evans, Crystal
              Palace Press).
              vi, 78 p., [2] leaves of plates, 1 folded : ill. ; 20 cm.
              (South Kensington Museum art handbooks)
              "Reprinted from stereotype plates, May 1887." — "Translated from the French by Mrs.
              R.F. Sketchley." — "List of the principal works relating to the history of tapestry":
              p. [66]–68. Index.
              Copy notes: "1889" – Wrappers.

1888

v.1888.001   *The art of the Saracens in Egypt /* by Stanley Lane-Poole.
              [London] : Published for the Committee of Council on Education by
              Chapman and Hall, 1888 (Printed by J.S. Virtue & Co.).
              xviii, 312 p., 16 p. of advertisements : ill. ; 20 cm.
              (South Kensington Museum art handboooks)
              Cover title: Saracenic art. Series title on cover only. — "With 108 woodcuts." — Index.
              — First published 1886, not in connection with the Museum.

v.1888.002   *Catalogue of a collection of silversmiths' work, porcelain, furniture
              and other examples of art manufacture : lent for exhibition by the
              Hon. W.F.B. Massey Mainwaring and Mrs Massey Mainwaring.* 2nd
              ed.
              London : William Clowes and Sons Ltd., 1888.
              151 p. ; 18 cm.
              At head of title: Department of Science and Art of the Committee of Council on
              Education, Bethnal Green Branch of the South Kensington Museum. — The collection
              was shown at South Kensington from 1874 and removed to Bethnal Green in 1888. —
              Original ed. not traced.

v.1888.003   *Catalogue of sky sketches from September 1883 to September 1886,
              by William Ascroft : illustrating optical phenomena attributed to the
              eruption at Krakatoa, in the Java Straits, August 27th, 1883 : lent for
              exhibition in the South Kensington Museum.*
              London : Printed by Eyre and Spottiswoode and sold at the South
              Kensington Museum, 1888.
              18 p. ; 22 cm.

At head of title: Department of Science and Art of the Committee of Council on Education.

v.1888.004   *A catalogue of the National Gallery of British Art at South Kensington : with a supplement containing works by modern foreign artists and old masters. Part I, Oil paintings.* New ed.
London : Printed by Eyre and Spottiswoode for H.M.S.O., 1888.
v, 162 ; 22 cm.
At head of title: Department of Science and Art of the Committee of Council on Education, South Kensington Museum. Spine title: National Gallery of British Art, South Kensington. — Introduction / by Richard Redgrave. — Index of gifts and bequests, and index of painters. — Printing: 11/88. — Wrappers.

v.1888.005   *A catalogue of the National Gallery of British Art at South Kensington : with a supplement containing works by modern foreign artists. Part II, Water colour paintings.* New ed.
London : Printed by Eyre and Spottiswoode for H.M.S.O., 1888.
v, 187 p.) ; 22 cm.
At head of title: Department of Science and Art of the Committee of Council on Education, South Kensington Museum. — Spine title: National Gallery of British Art, South Kensington. — Introduction / by Richard Redgrave. — Index of gifts and bequests, and index of painters. — Printing: 11/88. — Wrappers.

v.1888.005A   *A catalogue of the National Gallery of British Art at South Kensington : with a supplement containing works by modern foreign artists.*
v.1888.004 and v.1888.005 cased together in brown patterned sand grain. — No collective title page.

v.1888.006   *A descriptive catalogue of the collections of tapestry and embroidery in the South Kensington Museum* / by Alan S. Cole.
London : Printed by Eyre and Spottiswoode for H.M.S.O., 1888.
[8], 432 p. ; 23 cm.
At head of title: Department of Science and Art of the Committee of Council on Education. — "List of some of the books on making embroidery and tapestry in the National Art Library": p. 426–432. General and numerical indexes. — Printing: 12/87. — Brown sand grain cloth covered boards; title stamped in gold. Dark green end-papers.

v.1888.006A   [Large paper ed.]
29 cm.
Printing: 1/88. — Dark green pebble grain cloth covered boards, half bound in green leather. — Edition of 12 copies.

v.1888.006B   [Very large paper, with illustrations]
[8], 432 p., [15] leaves of plates, some folded : ill. (some col.) ;
40 cm.
Green cloth boards, half bound in green leather. — Edition of 6 copies.

v.1888.007   *Exhibition of the jubilee presents lent by Her Majesty the Queen : catalogue.*
London : [s.n.], 1888 (Harrison & Sons, printers).
79 p. ; 18 cm.
At head of title: Department of Science and Art of the Committee of Council on Education, Bethnal Green Branch Museum. — Grey wrappers, with royal arms, border and decorations.
EXHIBITION: VX.1888.BGM.001

v.1888.008 *Forster collection : a catalogue of the printed books bequeathed by John Forster, Esq., Ll.D., with index.*
London : Printed by Eyre and Spottiswoode for H.M.S.O., 1888.
xxviii, 710 p., [1] leaf of plates : 1 port. ; 26 cm.

At head of title: Science and Art Department of the Committee of Council on Education, South Kensington Museum. Half title: Forster collection : printed books. — John Forster / W. Elwin. — Index. — Printing: 2/88. — Dark blue-green pebble grain cloth covered boards, quarter bound in leather with title stamped in gold on spine.

v.1888.009 *The industrial arts : historical sketches, with numerous illustrations.*
New ed.
[London] : Published for the Committee of Council on Education by Chapman and Hall, 1888 (Richard Clay & Sons, printer).
xiv, 276 p., 8 p. of advertisements : ill. ; 20 cm.
(South Kensington Museum art handbooks)

Preface signed: "W.M." [i.e. William Maskell]. — "In two parts": I. Gold and silver work, Bronze, Copper and iron, Enamels, Furniture, Ivories. II. Pottery and porcelain, Maiolica, Glass, Mosaics, Arms and armour, Textile fabrics, Lace [reprinted from 1881.008]. — "Reprinted from electrotype plates, December 1888."
Copy notes: undated copies issued in 'Victoria and Albert Museum art handbook' covers, i.e. after 1899.

v.1888.010 *A list of books and pamphlets in the National Art Library, South Kensington Museum, illustrating architecture of the Renaissance and later periods, to the close of the 18th century.*
London : Printed by Eyre and Spottiswoode for H.M.S.O., 1888.
65 p. ; 20 cm.

At head of title: Department of Science and Art of the Committee of Council on Education. — Notice / R.H. Soden-Smith. — Printing: 7/88. — Buff wrappers.

v.1888.011 *A list of books and pamphlets in the National Art Library, South Kensington Museum, on drawing, geometry and perspective : (compiled for the use of students and visitors).*
London : Printed by Eyre and Spottiswoode for H.M.S.O., 1888.
viii, 9–92 p. ; 20 cm.

At head of title: Science and Art Department of the Committee of Council on Education. — Notice / R.H. Soden-Smith. — Printing: 12/88.

v.1888.012 *A list of books and pamphlets in the National Art Library, South Kensington Museum. Textile fabrics. Lace and needlework.*
London : Printed by Eyre and Spottiswoode for H.M.S.O., 1888.
85 p. ; 22 cm.

At head of title: Department of Science and Art of the Committee of Council on Education. — Part 1. Illustrating textile fabrics. Part 2. Lace and needlework.

v.1888.013 *List of catalogues of collections &c, also sale catalogues, in the National Art Library : 1888.*
[London : H.M.S.O.?, 1888.]
83 p. ; 21 cm.

Cover title. — Printing :1/90. — Ivory wrappers.

v.1888.014 *List of objects of art reproduced in metal in the South Kensington Museum. Part I, Examples of which copies may be supplied by the electrotypists.*

London : Printed by Eyre and Spottiswoode for H.M.S.O., 1888.
x, 163 p. 21 cm.

At head of title: Department of Science and Art of the Committee of Council on
Education. Cover title: Reproductions in metal : list of objects of art reproduced in
metal by various processes : as they appear in the South Kensington Museum. —
Convention for promoting reproduction of works of art: p. iii-vii. — List of private
collections. Index of objects and artists' names, numerical and chronological indexes.

v.1888.015   *Supplement to Art Library catalogue.*
[London : Printed by Eyre and Spottiswoode for H.M.S.O., 1888.]
127 p. ; 21 cm.

Printing: 2/88. — 50 copies printed.

1889

v.1889.001   *Catalogue of ship models and marine engineering in the South
Kensington Museum : with classified table of contents, and an
alphabetical index of exhibitors and subjects.*
London : Printed by Eyre and Spottiswoode for H.M.S.O., 1889.
352 p. : 22 cm.

At head of title: Department of Science and Art of the Committee of Council on
Education. — Preface signed "H.S." [i.e. Henry Sandham]. — Printing: 6/89.

v.1889.002   *Food : some account of its sources, constituents and uses* / by A.H.
Church. New ed., rev. and enl.
[London] : Published for the Committee of Council on Education by
Chapman and Hall, 1889.
viii, 252 p. ; 20 cm.
(South Kensington Museum science handbooks; Branch Museum,
Bethnal Green)

Unseen. Record from OCLC.

v.1889.003   *A list of books and pamphlets in the National Art Library, South
Kensington Museum, on coins and medals : (compiled for the use of
students and visitors).*
London : Printed by Eyre and Spottiswoode for H.M.S.O., 1889.
88 p. ; 20 cm.

At head of title: Department of Science and Art of the Committee of Council on
Education.

v.1889.004   *A list of books and pamphlets in the National Art Library, South
Kensington Museum, on construction, engineering and machinery :
(compiled for the use of students and visitors).*
London : Printed by Eyre and Spottiswoode for H.M.S.O., 1889.
68 p. ; 20 cm.

At head of title: Department of Science and Art of the Committee of Council on
Education.

v.1889.005   *List of medals, medallions, and plaques, reproduced in metal in the
South Kensington Museum.*
London : Printed by Eyre and Spottiswoode for H.M.S.O., 1889.
vii, 79 p. ; 22 cm.

At head of title: Department of Science and Art of the Committee of Council on
Education. — Printing: 3/89. — Buff wrappers.

v.1889.006   *List of the bequests and donations to the Department of Science and
               Art, South Kensington Museum : completed to 31st December 1888.*
               1889.
               Unseen. Record from National Art Library Author catalogue.

v.1889.007   *Marine engines and boilers* / by George C.V. Holmes.
               [London] : Published for the Committee of Council on Education, by
               Chapman and Hall, 1889 (Charles Dickens and Evans, Crystal Palace
               Press, printer).
               xii, 135 p., [1] leaf of plates : ill. ; 20 cm.
               (South Kensington Museum science handbooks)
               "With sixty-nine woodcuts." — Index.
               Copy note: Bound in: A catalogue of books published by Chapman & Hall (40 p.).
               "November 1889.".

v.1889.008   *Supplement to Art Library catalogue.*
               [London : Printed by Eyre and Spottiswoode for H.M.S.O., 1889.]
               669 p. ; 21 cm.
               Printing: 10/89. — 50 copies printed.

1890

v.1890.001   *A brief guide to the various collections in the Bethnal Green Branch of
               the South Kensington Museum* / by Charles H. Derby.
               London : Printed by George E. Eyre and William Spottiswoode for
               H.M.S.O., 1890.
               48 p. : ill. ; 22 cm.
               At head of title: Department of Science and Art of the Committee of Council on
               Education. — Printing: 12/90. — Purple wrappers.

v.1890.002   *Catalogue of a collection of oil paintings, water-colour drawings and
               engravings, enamel paintings, sculpture, bronzes, &c. : bequeathed by
               the late Joshua Dixon, Esq.* 3rd. ed.
               London : Printed by Eyre and Spottiswoode for H.M.S.O., 1890.
               18[?] p. ; 22 cm.
               At head of title: Department of Science and Art of the Committee of Council on
               Education, Bethnal Green Branch Museum. — Printing: 10/90. — Wrappers.
               Catalogued from a possibly incomplete copy.

v.1890.003   *Catalogue of machinery, models, &c., in the Machinery and
               Inventions Division of the South Kensington Museum* / with
               descriptive and historical notes by E.A. Cowper.
               London : Printed by Eyre and Spottiswoode for H.M.S.O., 1890.
               214 p. ; 25 cm.
               At head of title: Department of Science and Art of the Committee of Council on
               Education. Includes: "Mining and metallurgical appliances. Textile machinery. Paper-
               making and printing machinery. Agricultural implements. Machine tools. Lighting
               appliances. Telegraphic apparatus. etc., etc." — Index. — Printing: 2/90.

v.1890.004   *The industrial arts in Spain* / by Juan F. Riaño.
               London : Published for the Committee of Council on Education by
               Chapman and Hall, 1890 (Richard Clay and Sons Ltd., printer).
               viii, 276 p., 1 folded leaf of plates : ill. ; 20 cm.

(South Kensington Museum art handbooks)

Half-title: Spanish industrial arts. Cover title: Spanish arts. — "With numerous woodcuts."

Copy note: Found in covers lettered Victoria and Albert Museum art handbook, i.e. after 1899.

v.1890.005   *A priced inventory of the casts in fictile ivory in the South Kensington Museum : arranged in order of acquisition, with classified indexes.*
London : Printed by Eyre and Spottiswoode and sold in the South Kensington Museum, 1890.

112 p. ; 21 cm.

At head of title: Department of Science and Art of the Committee of Council on Education. — "Reproductions of carved ivories." — Caption: Reproductions of ivories. Inventory of fictile casts in the South Kensington Museum. — Chronological index. Indexes of collections. Museum numbers of originals and fictiles, numbers in v.1876.014.

v.1890.006   *Supplement to Art Library catalogue : publications of the Science and Art Department.*
[London : H.M.S.O., 1890 ("E & S", printer).

15 p. ; 21 cm.

Printing: 3/90. — 50 copies printed.

1891

v.1891.001   *Appendix to the classified list of photographs of works of decorative art in the South Kensington Museum, and other collections.*
London : Printed for H.M.S.O., by Eyre and Spottiswoode, 1891.

49 p. ; 22 cm.

At head of title: Department of Science and Art of the Committee of Council on Education. — Printing: 6/91. — Stone-coloured wrappers.

v.1891.002   *A brief guide to the various collections in the Bethnal Green Branch of the South Kensington Museum* / by Charles H. Derby. 2nd ed.
London : Printed for H.M.S.O. by Eyre and Spottiswoode, 1891.

47 p. : ill. ; 22 cm.

At head of title: Department of Science and Art of the Committee of Council on Education. — Printing: 6/91.

v.1891.003   *A catalogue of pictures of the Dutch and Flemish schools lent to the South Kensington Museum by Lord Francis Pelham Clinton-Hope.*
London : Printed by Eyre and Spottiswoode for H.M.S.O., 1891.

16 p. ; 25 cm.

At head of title: Department of Science and Art of the Committee of Council on Education. — Index of artists.

v.1891.004   *A catalogue of the Prescott-Hewett gift of water-colour paintings forming part of the National Gallery of British Art at South Kensington.*
London : Printed for H.M.S.O. by Eyre and Spottiswoode, 1891.

8 p. ; 25 cm.

At head of title: Department of Science and Art of the Committee of Council on Education. — Printing: 10/91. — Buff wrappers.

V.1891.005   *Catalogue of the science collections for teaching and research in the South Kensington Museum. Part III, Chemistry.*
London : Printed by Eyre and Spottiswoode for H.M.S.O., 1891.
[4], 69 p. ; 23 cm.
At head of title: Department of Science and Art of the Committee of Council on Education. — Includes list of contributors. — Printing: 2/91.

V.1891.006   *Catalogue of the science collections for teaching and research in the South Kensington Museum. Part VII, Biology.*
London : Printed for H.M.S.O. by Eyre and Spottiswoode, 1891.
ii, 114 p. ; 25 cm.
At head of title: Department of Science and Art of the Committee of Council on Education. — Includes list of contributors. — Printing: 8/91.
Copy note: Reissued in or after 1899 with new t.p. : Catalogue of the science collections for teaching and research in the Victoria and Albert Museum.

V.1891.007   *Catalogue of the Science Library in the South Kensington Museum.*
London : Printed by Eyre and Spottiswoode for H.M.S.O., 1891.
viii, 501 p. ; 26 cm.
At head of title: Department of Science and Art of the Committee of Council on Education. — "The following catalogue . . . is really a tenth edition . . . of the science portion of the *Catalogue of the Educational Division of the South Kensington Museum* [v.1876.005]."–p. v-vi. — Printing: 3/91. —
Boards covered in green wave-grain cloth, printed in gold. Primrose end-papers.

V.1891.008   *A supplemental descriptive catalogue of embroideries and tapestry-woven specimens acquired for the South Kensington Museum, between 1886 and June 1890* / by Alan S. Cole.
London : Printed by Eyre and Spottiswoode for H.M.S.O. : Sold at the South Kensington and Bethnal Green Museums, 1891.
[49] p. ; 25 cm.
At head of title: Department of Science and Art of the Committee of Council on Education, London, S.W. — Includes bibliographic references.— Printing: 5/91. — Buff wrappers.

V.1891.009   *A supplemental descriptive catalogue of specimens of lace acquired for the South Kensington Museum, between June 1880 and June 1890* / by Alan Cole.
London : Printed by Eyre and Spottiswood for H.M.S.O., 1891.
46 p., [15 leaves of plates] : ill., ports. ; 25 cm.
At head of title: Department of Science and Art of the Committee of Council on Education. — Printing: 5/91.

V.1891.010   *A supplemental descriptive catalogue of tapestry-woven and embroidered Egyptian textiles, acquired for the South Kensington Museum between 1886 and June 1890* / by Alan S. Cole.
London : Printed for H.M.S.O. by Eyre and Spottiswoode : Sold at South Kensington and Bethnal Green Museums, 1891.
57 p. ; 25 cm.
At head of title: Department of Science and Art of the Committee of Council on Education, London, S.W. — Includes bibliographic references. — Buff wrappers.

V.1891.011   *Supplementary list of medals, medallions and plaques reproduced in metal in the South Kensington Museum.*
London : [H.M.S.O.?], 1891 (Printed by Eyre and Spottiswoode).

p. 81–98 ; 22 cm.

At head of title: Department of Science and Art of the Committee of Council on Education. — Indexes to names and subjects, artists, and Museum numbers. — Printing: 4/91. — Buff wrappers.

1892

V.1892.001   *A brief guide to the various collections in the Bethnal Green Branch of the South Kensington Museum* / by Charles H. Derby. 4th ed.
London : Printed for H.M.S.O. by Eyre and Spottiswoode, 1892.
47 p. : ill. ; 22 cm.

At head of title: Department of Science and Art of the Committee of Council on Education. — Printing: 8/92. — Pink wrappers.

V.1892.002   *Catalogue of the collection of metallurgical specimens formed by the late John Percy Esq., M.D., F.R.S., now in the South Kensington Museum* / by J.F. Blake ; with an introduction by Professor Roberts-Austen.
London : Printed for H.M.S.O. by Eyre and Spottiswoode, 1892.
xi, 435 p. ; 25 cm.

At head of title: Department of Science and Art of the Committee of Council on Education. Cover title: Catalogue of the Percy collection of metallurgy in the South Kensington Museum. — Dark blue sand grain cloth covered boards, rules, title stamped in gold.

V.1892.003   *Catalogue of the science collections for teaching and research in the South Kensington Museum. Part I, Mathematics and mechanics.*
London : Printed for H.M.S.O. by Eyre and Spottiswoode, 1892.
iv, 152 p. ; 23 cm.

At head of title: Department of Science and Art of the Committee of Council on Education. — Includes list of contributors. — Printing: 12/91.

V.1892.004   *Catalogue of the science collections for teaching and research in the South Kensington Museum. Part IV, Metallurgy.*
London : Printed for H.M.S.O. by Eyre and Spottiswoode, 1892.
24 p. ; 23 cm.

At head of title: Department of Science and Art of the Committee of Council on Education. — Includes list of contributors. — Printing: 11/92.

V.1892.005   *Catalogue of the science collections for teaching and research in the South Kensington Museum. Part VI, Mineralogy and geology.*
London : Printed for H.M.S.O. by Eyre and Spottiswoode, 1892.
iv, 73 p. ; 23 cm.

At head of title: Department of Science and Art of the Committee of Council on Education. — Includes list of contributors. — Printing: 1/92.

V.1892.006   *The industrial arts of Scandinavia : in the pagan time* / by Hans Hildebrand. New ed.
[London] : Published for the Committee of Council on Education by Chapman and Hall, 1892 (Richard Clay & Sons Ltd., printer).
viii, 150 p. : ill. ; 20 cm.
(South Kensington Museum art handbooks)

Cover title: Scandinavian arts. — "With numerous woodcuts."
Copy note: Found in covers lettered Victoria and Albert Museum art handbook, i.e.
after 1899.

v.1892.007   *Maiolica* / by C. Drury E. Fortnum. ["New ed."?]
[London] : Published for the Committee of Council on Education by
Chapman and Hall, 1892 (Richard Clay and Sons Ltd., printer).
vii, 192 p. : ill. ; 20 cm.
(South Kensington Museum art handbooks ; no. 4)
"With numerous woodcuts." — Index.
Copy note: "Sixth thousand". One copy in grey wrappers, bearing date 1891, and
"New edition". Found in covers lettered Victoria and Albert Museum art handboooks.

v.1892.008   *Report on the analysis of various examples of oriental metal-work,
&c. : in the South Kensington Museum and other collections* / made
under the direction of W.C. Roberts-Austen, by Arthur Wingham.
London : Printed for H.M.S.O. by Eyre and Spottiswoode, 1892.
54 p. : ill. ; 25 cm.
At head of title: Department of Science and Art of the Committee of Council on
Education. — Introduction by W.C. Roberts-Austen. — Printing: 12/91.

1893

v.1893.001   *A brief guide to the various collections in the Bethnal Green Branch of
the South Kensington Museum* / by Charles H. Derby. 6th ed.
London : Printed by Eyre and Spottiswoode for H.M.S.O., 1893.
47 p. : ill. ; 22 cm.
At head of title: Department of Science and Art of the Committee of Council on
Education. — Printing: 10/93. — Pink wrappers.

v.1893.002   *Catalogue of the Education Library in the South Kensington Museum.*
London : Printed for H.M.S.O. by Eyre and Spottiswoode, 1893.
viii, 234 p. ; 26 cm.
At head of title: Department of Science and Art of the Committee of Council on
Education. — "The following catalogue is really a 10th ed. . . . of portions of the
Catalogue of the Educational Division of the South Kensington Museum [v.1876.005]."
— Printing: 11/93. — Boards covered in green wave-grain cloth, printed in gold.
Primrose end-papers.

v.1893.003   *A catalogue of the National Gallery of British Art at South
Kensington : with a supplement containing works by modern foreign
artists and old masters. Part I, Oil paintings.* New ed.
London : Printed by Eyre and Spottiswoode for H.M.S.O.,
1893.
191 p. ; 23 cm.
At head of title: Department of Science and Art of the Committee of Council on
Education, South Kensington Museum. — Printing: 4/93. — Wrappers.

v.1893.004   *A catalogue of the National Gallery of British Art at South
Kensington : with a supplement containing works by modern foreign
artists. Part II, Water colour paintings, &c.* New ed.
London : Printed for H.M.S.O. by Eyre and Spottiswoode, 1893.
237 p. ; 23 cm.
Printing: 8/93. — Wrappers.

V.1893.004A   *A catalogue of the National Gallery of British Art at South
                Kensington : with a supplement containing works by modern foreign
                artists.*
                v.1893.003 and v.1893.004 cased together in brown sand grain cloth; title stamped in
                gold on cover and spine.

V.1893.005   *Food : some account of its sources, constituents and uses /* by A.H.
                Church. Repr.
                [London] : Published for the Committee of Council on Education by
                Chapman and Hall, 1893 (Charles Dickens and Evans, Crystal Palace
                Press).
                viii, 252 p. ; 20 cm.
                (South Kensington Museum science handbooks ; Branch Museum,
                Bethnal Green)
                "some more recent statistics have been introduced, while a few mistakes and misprints
                have been corrected"–p. [iv]. — Index.
                Copy note: "14th thousand."

V.1893.006   *Forster collection : a catalogue of the paintings, manuscripts,
                autograph letters, pamphlets, etc., bequeathed by John Forster, Esq.,
                Ll.D : with indexes.*
                London : Printed for H.M.S.O. by Eyre and Spottiswoode, 1893.
                261 p. ; 26 cm.
                At head of title: Science and Art Department of the Committee of Council on
                Education, South Kensington Museum. — Note signed "R.F.S." [i.e. R.F. Sketchley]. —
                Includes index to the manuscripts and autograph letters. — Printing: 6/93. — Library's
                copies in dark blue-green bubble grain cloth, quarter bound in leather with title stamped
                in gold on spine. Black end-papers.

V.1893.007   *Ironwork : from the earliest times to the end of the mediaeval period /*
                by J. Starkie Gardner.
                [London] : Published for the Committee of Council on Education by
                Chapman and Hall, 1893 (Printed by William Clowes and Sons).
                x, 152 p. : ill. ; 20 cm.
                (South Kensington Museum art handbooks)
                "With fifty-seven illustrations." — Includes index.

V.1893.008   *Japanese art. Japanese books and albums of prints in colour in the
                National Art Library, South Kensington.*
                London : Printed for H.M.S.O., by Eyre and Spottiswoode, 1893.
                94 p. ; 22 cm.
                At head of title: Department of Science & Art of the Committee of Council on
                Education. — Compiled by Edward F. Strange. — Wrappers.

1894

V.1894.001   *Bookbindings and rubbings of bindings in the National Art Library,
                South Kensington. II, Catalogue.*
                London : Printed for H.M.S.O. by Eyre and Spottiswoode,
                1894.
                329 p. ; 23cm.
                At head of title: Department of Science & Art of the Committee of Council on
                Education. — By James Weale. — For introduction, see v.1898.001.

v.1894.002   *A brief guide to the various collections in the Bethnal Green Branch of
              the South Kensington Museum* / by Charles H. Derby.
              London : Printed for H.M.S.O. by Eyre and Spottiswoode, 1894.
              47 p. : ill. ; 22 cm.

v.1894.003   *Catalogue of machinery, models, &c., in the Machinery and
              Inventions Division of the South Kensington Museum : with
              descriptive and historical notes. Part I, Steam engines and other
              motors, locomotives and railways, dynamos and electrical fittings,
              mechanical measuring appliances, pumps and lifting machinery, power
              transmission.*
              London : Printed for H.M.S.O. by Eyre and Spottiswoode, 1894.
              180 p. 25 cm.
              At head of title: Department of Science and Art of the Committee of Council on
              Education. — Indexes of objects and contributors. — Printing : 7/94.

v.1894.004   *Catalogue of the science collections for teaching and research in the
              South Kensington Museum. Part II, Physics.*
              London : Printed for H.M.S.O. by Eyre and Spottiswoode, 1894.
              v, 195 p. ; 23 cm.
              At head of title: Department of Science and Art of the Committee of Council on
              Education. — Includes list of contributors. — Printing: 8/94.

v.1894.005   *English porcelain : a handbook to the china made in England during
              the eighteenth century as illustrated by specimens chiefly in the
              national collections* / by A. H. Church. Repr.
              London : Published for the Committee of Council on Education, by
              Chapman and Hall, 1894 (Richard Clay & Sons, printer).
              xiii, 99 p., [40] leaves of plates, 16 p. of advertisements : ill. ; 20 cm.
              (South Kensington Museum art handbooks)
              "With numerous woodcuts." — "Bibliographical notes": leaf preceding p. [1]. — Index.

1895

v.1895.001   *A catalogue of books which can be lent to schools of art.*
              London : Printed by Eyre and Spottiswoode, 1895.
              77 p. ; 22 cm.
              At head of title: Department of Science and Art. — "Under revision." — Printing:
              10/95.
              Copy note: Printed on one side of the page.

v.1895.002   *A catalogue of engraved national portraits in the National Art Library*
              / with a prefatory note by Julian Marshall.
              London : Printed for H.M.S.O. by Eyre and Spottiswoode, 1895.
              v, 523 p. ; 22 cm.
              At head of title: Department of Science and Art of the Committee of Council on
              Education, South Kensington Museum. — Printing: 3/96. — Brown patterned sand
              grain cloth covered boards; title stamped in gold.

v.1895.003   *Catalogue of prints in the National Art Library.*
              [London : H.M.S.O., 1895] ("E. & S.", printer).
              45 leaves ; 34 cm.
              Caption title. — Proofs? — Printing: 4/95. — 50 copies.

v.1895.004   *Catalogue of the science collections for teaching and research in the South Kensington Museum. Part V, Physiography.*
London : Printed for H.M.S.O. by Eyre and Spottiswoode, 1895.
[iv], 125 p. ; 24 cm.
At head of title: Department of Science and Art of the Committee of Council on Education. — Includes list of contributors. — Printing: 6/95.

v.1895.005   *Classed catalogue of printed books. Ceramics* / National Art Library, South Kensington.
London : Printed for H.M.S.O. by Eyre and Spottiswoode, 1895.
xi, 352 p. ; 25 cm.
At head of t.p.: Department of Science & Art of the Committee of Council on Education.

v.1895.006   *List of the bequests and donations to the Department of Science and Art for the South Kensington Museum : completed to 31st December 1894.*
London : Printed for H.M.S.O. by Eyre and Spottiswoode, 1895.
201 p. ; 33 cm.
At head of title: Department of Science and Art of the Committee of Council on Education, London. — Index of donors — Printing: 9/95. — Wrappers.

v.1895.007   *Supplement to the catalogue of the Science Library in the South Kensington Museum : (additions from April 1891 to April 1895).*
London : Printed for H.M.S.O., by Eyre and Spottiswoode, 1895.
iv, 118 p. ; 26 cm.
Index. — Printing: 6/95.

v.1895.008   *A supplemental descriptive catalogue of specimens of lace acquired for the South Kensington Museum, between June 1890 and June 1895* / by Alan S. Cole.
London : Printed for H.M.S.O., by Eyre and Spottiswoode, 1895.
48 p. ; 23 cm.
At head of title: Science and Art Department of the Committee of Council on Education, South Kensington Museum. Index of Museum numbers. — Printing: 3/96. — Wrappers.

1896

v.1896.001   *A brief guide to the collections in the Museum of Science and Art, Bethnal Green (Branch of the South Kensington Museum).*
London : Printed by Eyre and Spottiswoode for H.M.S.O., 1896.
49 p. : ill. ; 22 cm.
At head of title: Department of Science and Art of the Committee of Council on Education. — Printing: 5/96. — Grey wrappers.

v.1896.002   *Catalogue of a collection of continental porcelain* / lent and described by Sir A. Wollaston Franks.
London : Printed for H.M.S.O. by Eyre and Spottiswoode, 1896.
viii, 109 p., xv leaves of plates : ill. ; 25 cm.
At head of title: Science and Art Department of the Committee of Council on Education, South Kensington, Bethnal Green Branch Museum. — Index. Marks.— Printing: 10/96.

V.1896.002A   [Large paper ed.]
               29 cm.

V.1896.003   *Catalogue of a special loan collection of English furniture and figured*
               silks : manufactured in the 17th and 18th centuries / with an
               introduction by John H. Pollen.
               London : Printed for H.M.S.O. by Eyre and Spottiswoode, 1896.
               145 p. ; 25 cm.

               At head of title: Department of Science and Art of the Committee of Council on
               Education, South Kensington. — Printing: 10/96.
               EXHIBITION: VX.1896.BGM.001

V.1896.003A   [Large paper ed.]
               29 cm.

               Dark green pebble grain cloth covered boards, quarter bound in leather.

V.1896.004   *Catalogue of machinery, models etc., in the Machinery and*
               Inventions Division of the South Kensington Museum : with
               descriptive and historical notes. Part I, Steam engines and other
               motors, locomotives and railways, dynamos and electrical fittings,
               mechanical measuring appliances, pumps and lifting machinery,
               power transmission. 2nd ed.
               London : Printed for H.M.S.O. by Eyre and Spottiswoode, 1896.
               203 p. ; 25 cm.

               At head of title: Department of Science and Art of the Committee of Council on
               Education. — Indexes of objects and contributors. — Printing: 5/96.

V.1896.005   *Catalogue of prints in the National Art Library. II.*
               [London : H.M.S.O., 1896] ("E. & S.", printer).
               47 leaves ; 34 cm.

               Caption title. — Proofs? — Printing: 4/96.

V.1896.006   *Ironwork. Part II, being a continuation of the first handbook and*
               comprising from the close of the mediaeval period to the end of the
               eighteenth century / by J. Starkie Gardner.
               [London] : Published for the Committee of Council on Education by
               Chapman and Hall, 1896 (William Clowes and Sons [printer]).
               xvi, 202 p. : ill. ; 20 cm.
               (South Kensington Museum art handbooks)

               Appendix: Alphabetical list of illustrations of ironwork published in France between the
               sixteenth and eighteenth centuries [with museum locations]. — Index.
               Copy note: Found in covers lettered Victoria and Albert Museum art handbook, i.e.
               after 1899.

V.1896.007   *A supplemental descriptive catalogue of embroideries and tapestry-*
               woven specimens acquired for the South Kensington Museum between
               July 1890 and 1894 / by Alan S. Cole.
               London : Printed for H.M.S.O. by Eyre and Spottiswoode : Sold at the
               South Kensington and Bethnal Green Museums, 1896.
               66 p. ; 25 cm.

               At head of title: Science and Art Department of the Committee of Council on
               Education, South Kensington Museum. — Includes bibliographic references. — Printing:
               1/97.

V.1896.008   *A supplemental descriptive catalogue of tapestry-woven and*
embroidered Egyptian textiles acquired for the South Kensington
Museum between June 1890 and December 1893 / by Alan S. Cole.
London : Printed for H.M.S.O. by Eyre and Spottiswoode : Sold at
South Kensington and Bethnal Green Museums, 1896.
23 p. ; 25 cm.
At head of title: Department of Science and Art of the Committee of Council on
Education, London, S.W. — Includes bibliographic references. — Printing: 12/96. —
Ivory wrappers.

1897

V.1897.001   *A brief guide to the collections in the Bethnal Green Branch of the*
South Kensington Museum.
London : Printed for H.M.S.O. by Eyre and Spottiswoode, 1897.
30 p., [9] leaves of plates : ill., plans ; 22 cm.
Printing: 7/97. — Notice pasted in, concerning removal of Chantrey Bequest
paintings.

V.1897.002   *Catalogue of machinery, models, &c., in the Machinery and*
Inventions Division of the South Kensington Museum : with
descriptive and historical notes. Part II, Mining and metallurgical
appliances; textile machinery; paper-making and printing machinery;
agricultural implements; machine tools; lighting appliances;
telegraphic apparatus, etc., etc.
London : Printed for H.M.S.O. by Eyre and Spottiswoode, 1897.
314 p. ; 25 cm.
At head of title: Science and Art Department of the Committee of Council on Education.
— Printing: 7/97. — Blue wrappers.

V.1897.003   *A catalogue of the second circulating collection of water-colour*
paintings of the British school : illustrating the rise and progress of the
art : selected from the National Gallery of British Art at the South
Kensington Museum.
London : Printed for H.M.S.O., by Eyre and Spottiswoode, 1897.
32 p. ; 22 cm.
At head of title: Department of Science & Art of the Committee of Council on
Education. — Introduction taken from v.1884.002. — Index. — Printing: 8/97.— Pink
wrappers.

1898

V.1898.001   *Bookbindings and rubbings of bindings in the National Art Library,*
South Kensington Museum / by W.H. James Weale. *I, Introduction.*
London : Printed for H.M.S.O. by Eyre and Spottiswoode, 1898.
cl p. ; 23 cm.
At head of title: Department of Science & Art of the Committee of Council on
Education. — For Catalogue, see v.1894.001.

V.1898.002   *A brief guide to the collections in the Bethnal Green Branch of the*
South Kensington Museum.
London : Printed for H.M.S.O. by Wyman & Sons, 1898.

30, [2] p., [8] leaves of plates : ill., plans ; 22 cm.
At head of title: Department of Science and Art of the Committee of Council on Education. — Includes photographic illustrations. — Printing: 7/98. — Pink wrappers.

v.1898.003   *A catalogue of the first circulating collection of water-colour paintings of the British school : illustrating the rise and progress of the art : selected from the National Gallery of British Art at the South Kensington Museum.*
London : Printed for H.M.S.O., by Wyman and Sons, 1898.
57 p. ; 21 cm.
At head of title: Department of Science and Art of the Committee of Council on Education. — Introduction adapted from v.1884.002. — Index.— Printing: 8/98. — Grey wrappers.

v.1898.004   *Catalogue of the loan collection of lithographs, South Kensington Museum, 1898–99.*
[London : Printed for H.M.S.O.], 1898.
viii, 262 p.
Unseen. Record from British Library catalogue.
EXHIBITION: vx.1898.001

v.1898.005   *Classified list of photographs of works of decorative art in the South Kensington Museum, and other collections. Part I, Woodwork.*
London : Printed for H.M.S.O. by Wyman & Sons, [1898].
67 p. ; 25 cm.
At head of title: Department of Science and Art of the Committee of Council on Education. — Indexes, to lenders and localities, and Museum numbers. — Printing: 1/98.

v.1898.006   *English porcelain : a handbook to the china made in England during the eighteenth century as illustrated by specimens chiefly in the national collections* / by A.H. Church. Repr.
London : Published for the Committee of Council on Education by Chapman and Hall, [1898?], Richard Clay & Sons, printer).
xiii, 99 p., [40] leaves of plates : ill. ; 20 cm.
(South Kensington Museum art handbooks)
"With numerous woodcuts." Additional note at end of Preface, dated 1898. — "Bibliographical notes": leaf preceding p. [1]. Index.

v.1898.007   *Japanese art. II, Books relating to Japanese art in the National Art Library, South Kensington Museum.*
London : H.M.S.O., 1898.
37, [2] p. ; 21 cm.
At head of t.p.: Department of Science & Art of the Committee of Council on Education — Printing: 1/98.

v.1898.008   *Persian decoration : architectural drawings, designs and sketches from the collection dispersed at the death of Mirza Akber, architect to the court of Persia; acquired for the National Art Library, South Kensington Museum, from the Oostads Khodadad and Akber, master builders of Teheran, by C. Purdon Clarke . . ., 1876.*
London : Printed for H.M.S.O. by Wyman & Sons, 1898.
8 p. ; 24 cm.
At head of title: Department of Science & Art of the Committee of Council on Education. — Edition of 25 copies.

v.1898.009   *South Kensington Museum : Oriental collections.*
                 [London : H.M.S.O.], 1898 (Wy. & S.)
                 4 p. : 1 plan ; 25 cm.

                 Caption title. At head of title: Department of Science and Art of the Committee of
                 Council on Education. — "January 1898"–p. [1]. — Printing: 2/98.

1899

v.1899.001   *A brief guide to the collections in the Bethnal Green Branch of the*
                 Victoria and Albert Museum, South Kensington.
                 London : Printed for H.M.S.O. by Wyman & Sons, 1899.
                 32 p., [8] leaves of plates : ill., plans ; 22 cm.

                 At head of title: Department of Science and Art of the Committee of Council on
                 Education. — Includes photographic illustrations. — Printing: 10/99. — Pink wrappers.

v.1899.002   *Catalogue of a collection of pottery and porcelain illustrating popular*
                 British history : lent by Henry Willett . . . .
                 London : Printed for H.M.S.O. by Wyman and Sons, 1899.
                 [7], 123 p., [12] leaves of plates : ill. ; 22 cm.

                 At head of title: Department of Science and Art of the Committee of Council on
                 Education; The Bethnal Green Branch of the South Kensington Museum. — Printing:
                 10/99.

v.1899.003   *A catalogue of books available for loan to schools of art.*
                 London : Printed by Wyman and Sons, 1899.
                 156 p. ; 22 cm.

                 At head of title: Department of Science and Art. — "Under revision." — Author index.
                 — Printing: 9/99. — Tan wrappers.

v.1899.004   *Catalogue of the botanical models, diagrams and specimens in the*
                 South Kensington Museum (Western galleries).
                 London : Printed for H.M.S.O. by Wyman & Sons, 1899.
                 25 p. ; 25 cm.

                 At head of title: Department of Science and Art of the Committee of Council on
                 Education. — Printing: 3/99.

v.1899.005   *A catalogue of the first circulating collection of water-colour paintings*
                 of the British school : illustrating the rise and progress of the art :
                 selected from the National Gallery of British Art at the Victoria and
                 Albert Museum, South Kensington.
                 London : Printed for H.M.S.O., by Wyman and Sons, 1899.
                 57 p. ; 21 cm.

                 At head of title: Department of Science and Art of the Committee of Council on
                 Education. — Introduction adapted from v.1884.002. — Index. — Printing: 8/99. —
                 Grey wrappers.

v.1899.006   *Catalogue of the loan collection of lithographs, South Kensington*
                 Museum, 1898–99. 2nd ed.
                 London : Printed by Wyman & Sons for H.M.S.O., 1898 [i.e. 1899].
                 xvi, 264 p. ; 22 cm.

                 At head of title: Department of Science & Art of the Committee of Council on
                 Education. — Introduction by Edward F. Strange. — Index. List of contributors. —
                 Printing: 1/99.
                 EXHIBITION: vx.1898.001

v.1899.007   *Catalogue of the naval and marine engineering collection in the*
              Science Division of the Victoria and Albert Museum, South
              Kensington : with descriptive and historical notes.
              London : Printed for H.M.S.O. by Wyman and Sons, 1899.
              311 p. ; 25 cm.
              At head of title: Department of Science and Art of the Committee of Council on
              Education. — "War and mercantile vessels; yachts, boats, tugs, barges etc.; ship design
              and construction; life-saving appliances. Marine engines and boilers; paddle-wheels and
              screw propellers; steering appliances; auxiliary machinery"–t.p. — Index. List of donors
              and contributors. — Printing: 7/99.

v.1899.008   *Ceremonial for laying the first stone of the Victoria and Albert*
              Museum, by Her Majesty the Queen, at South Kensington, on
              Wednesday the 17th May 1899 at 4.30 o'clock.
              [London : s.n. ; 1899] (Harrison and Sons, printers).
              1 sheet (4 p.) ; 33 cm.
              Royal coat of arms at head of title.

v.1899.009   *Classified list of photographs of works of decorative art in the South*
              Kensington Museum, and other collections. Part II, Pottery and glass.
              London : Printed for H.M.S.O. by Wyman & Sons, 1899.
              74 p. ; 25 cm.
              At head of title: Department of Science and Art of the Committee of Council on
              Education. — Indexes, to lenders and localities, and Museum numbers. — Printing:
              5/99. — Buff wrappers.

1900

v.1900.001   *Ancient and modern ships. Part I, Wooden sailing-ships* / by George
              C.V. Holmes.
              London : Published for the Board of Education by Chapman & Hall,
              1900 (Printed by William Clowes and Sons Ltd.).
              xv, 164 p. : ill. ; 20 cm.
              (Victoria and Albert Museum science handbook)
              "With seventy-four woodcuts." — Includes index.

v.1900.002   *An annotated catalogue of drawings of old London* / by Philip
              Norman.
              London : Printed for H.M.S.O. by Wyman and Sons, 1900.
              46 p., [7] leaves of plates : ill. ; 22 cm.
              At head of title: Board of Education, South Kensington. — Index. — Printing: 10/00.

v.1900.003   *A brief guide to the collections in the Bethnal Green Branch of the*
              Victoria and Albert Museum, South Kensington.
              London : Printed for H.M.S.O. by Wyman & Sons, 1900.
              33 p., [8] leaves of plates : ill., plans ; 22 cm.
              At head of title: Board of Education, South Kensington. — Printing: 7/00. — Pink
              wrappers.

v.1900.004   *Catalogue of the science collections for teaching and research in the*
              Victoria and Albert Museum, South Kensington. Physiography, Part
              II, Meteorology, including terrestrial magnetism.
              London : Printed for H.M.S.O. by Wyman and Sons, 1900.

[4], 60 p. ; 24 cm.
At head of title: Board of Education, South Kensington. — Includes list of contributors.
— Printing: 10/00.

V.1900.005   *Catalogue of the third circulating collection of water-colour paintings*
of the British school : illustrating the rise and progress of the art :
selected from the National Gallery of British Art at the Victoria and
Albert Museum, South Kensington.
London : Printed for H.M.S.O. by Wyman and Sons, 1900.
29 p. ; 21 cm.
At head of title: Board of Education, South Kensington. — Printing: 6/1900.

1901

V.1901.001   *Catalogue of photographs consisting of historical and architectural*
subjects and studies from nature : chiefly contributed by Sir J.
Benjamin Stone, M.P.
London : Printed for H.M.S.O. by Wyman and Sons, 1901.
24 p. : 1 ill. ; 21 cm.
At head of title: Board of Education, South Kensington. Victoria and Albert Museum.
— Includes: "Photographs selected from the National Art Library." — Printing: 11/01.
— Grey wrappers.
EXHIBITION: VX.1901.002

V.1901.002   *Catalogue of the loan exhibition of modern illustration held at the*
Victoria and Albert Museum, South Kensington, 1901.
London : William Clowes and Sons, [1901?].
152 p. : plan ; 22 cm.
At head of t.p.: Board of Education, Secondary Branch. — "Under revision." —
Introduction by Henry B. Wheatley. — Index of artists; list of contributors.
Copy note: p. 153–176 of advertisements, with index.
EXHIBITION: VX.1901.001

V.1901.002A   [Another issue]
— Lacks 'Under revision' note. "Addenda" (p. [148]).
EXHIBITION: VX.1901.001

V.1901.003   *Catalogue of the mechanical engineering collection in the Science*
Division of the Victoria and Albert Museum, South Kensington : with
descriptive and historical notes. Part 1, Steam engines and other
motors; locomotives and railways; dynamos and electrical fittings;
mechanical measuring appliances; pumps and lifting machinery; power
transmission. 3rd ed., rev.
London : Printed for H.M.S.O. by Wyman and Sons, 1901.
298 p. ; 25 cm.
At head of title: Board of Education, South Kensington. Previous ed. entitled
Catalogue of machinery, models etc. . . . . — Index. — Printing: 6/01. — Blue
wrappers.

V.1901.004   *Classified list of photographs of works of decorative art in the Victoria*
and Albert Museum, and other collections. Part III, Textile fabrics
and lace.

London : Printed for H.M.S.O. by Wyman and Sons, 1901.

47 p. ; 25 cm.

At head of title: Board of Education, South Kensington. — Indexes of lenders and localities, and of Museum numbers. — Printing: 9/01.

V.1901.005   *Classified list of photographs of works of decorative art in the Victoria and Albert Museum, and other collections. Part IV, Silversmiths' work, jewellery, enamels, crystals, jade etc.*
London : Printed for H.M.S.O. by Wyman & Sons, 1901.

47 p. ; 25 cm.

At head of title: Board of Education, South Kensington. — Indexes, of lenders and localities, and of Museum numbers. — Printing: 11/01.

V.1901.006   *Historical introduction to the collection of illuminated letters and borders in the National Art Library, Victoria and Albert Museum* / by John W. Bradley.
London : Printed for H.M.S.O. by Eyre and Spottiswoode, 1901.

182 p., 19 leaves of plates : ill. ; 21 cm.

At head of title: Board of Education, South Kensington. — Preface signed "G.H.P." [i.e. G.H. Palmer]. — Bibliography: p. 179–182. — Printing: 10/01. — Ivory-coloured wrappers.

V.1901.007   *Italian wall decorations of the 15th and 16th centuries : a handbook to the models, illustrating interiors of Italian buildings, in the Victoria and Albert Museum, South Kensington.*
London : Chapman & Hall, 1901 (Gilbert and Rivington [printer]).

xiv, 112 p., [30] leaves of plates : ill., plans ; 20 cm.

(Victoria and Albert Museum art handbook)

The "Paradiso" of Isabella d'Este in the ducal palace, Mantua, by C. Yriarte. Chapel of St. Peter Martyr in the church of Sant' Eustorgio, Milan, by L. Beltrami. Chapel of St. Catherine in the church of San Maurizio, Milan, by L. Beltrami. The "Appartamento Borgia" in the Vatican, Rome, by F.W. Woodhouse. The "Villa Madama", near Rome, by F.W. Woodhouse. The "Sala del cambio", or the Hall of Exchange, Perugia, by L. Manzoni. The chapel in the Medici, now called Riccardi, palace, Florence, by G. Carocci. The Macchiavelli palace, Florence, by W.H. Allen. — Index.

V.1901.008   *List of the bequests and donations to the South Kensington Museum, now called the Victoria and Albert Museum : completed, to 31st December 1900.*
London : Printed for H.M.S.O. by Wyman & Sons, 1901.

293 p. ; 33 cm.

At head of title Board of Education, South Kensington, London. — "Under revision." — Donor index.

V.1901.009   *National Art Library, Victoria and Albert Museum : classed catalogue of printed books : heraldry.*
London : Printed for H.M.S.O. by Wyman and Sons Ltd., 1901.

186 p., 16 leaves of plates : ill. ; 25 cm.

At head of title: Board of Education. South Kensington. — Preface by G.H. Palmer. — Bibliography: p. 150–158. Indexes of names and subjects. — Printing: 6/01.

1902

V.1902.001   *A brief guide to the collections in the Bethnal Green Branch of the Victoria and Albert Museum, South Kensington.*
London : Printed for H.M.S.O. by Wyman & Sons, 1902.
32 p., [8] leaves of plates : ill., plans ; 22 cm.
At head of title: Board of Education, South Kensington. — Includes photographic illustrations. — Printing: 9/02. — Pink wrappers.

V.1902.002   *Drawings by British artists in the National Art Library, Victoria and Albert Museum. I, Pictorial subjects; drawings from life; anatomical studies.*
London : Printed for H.M.S.O. by Wyman and Sons, 1901 [i.e. 1902?].
38 p. ; 25 cm.
At head of title: Board of Education, South Kensington. — "Under revision." — Printing: 4/02.

V.1902.003   *Regulations relating to museums and institutions (from 1st August 1902 to July 1903).*
London : Printed for H.M.S.O. by Wyman and Sons, 1902.
vi, 148 p. ; 25 cm.
(Cd. 1218)
At head of title: Board of Education. — "Presented to Parliament by command of His Majesty." — Printing: 8/02.

1903

V.1903.001   *A brief guide to the collections in the Bethnal Green Branch of the Victoria and Albert Museum, South Kensington.*
London : Printed for H.M.S.O. by Wyman & Sons, 1903.
32 p., [10] leaves of plates : ill., plans ; 22 cm.
At head of title: Board of Education, South Kensington. — Includes chronological list of the principal loan collections from 1872. — Printing: 8/03. —Pink wrappers.

V.1903.002   *Catalogue of prints. I, Modern etchings of the foreign schools in the National Art Library, Victoria and Albert Museum.*
London : Printed for H.M.S.O. by Wyman and Sons, 1903.
275 p. ; 22 cm.
At head of title: Board of Education. South Kensington. Caption title: Catalogue of prints in the National Art Library. — Compiled by Martin Hardie. — Index. — Printing: 10/03.

V.1903.003   *Catalogue of the loan exhibition of British engraving and etching held at the Victoria and Albert Museum, South Kensington, 1903.*
London : Printed for H.M.S.O. by Wyman and Sons, 1903.
150 p. ; 24 cm.
At head of title: Board of Education, South Kensington. — Index of etchers and engravers. — Printing: 7/03.
EXHIBITION: VX.1903.001

V.1903.004   *Stained glass* / by Lewis F. Day.
London : Published for the Board of Education by Chapman & Hall, 1903.

xii, 155 p., [25] leaves of plates : ill. ; 20 cm.
(Victoria and Albert Museum art handbook)
"With numerous illustrations." — "Inventory of stained glass exhibited in the
Museum"–p. [102]–112 — Index.

1904

V.1904.001　　*A brief guide to the collections in the Bethnal Green Branch of the
Victoria and Albert Museum, South Kensington.*
London : Printed for H.M.S.O. by Wyman & Sons, 1904.
31 p., [7] leaves of plates : ill., plans ; 22 cm.
At head of title: Board of Education, South Kensington. — Includes chronological list of
the principal loan collections from 1872. — Printing: 9/04. — Pink wrappers.

V.1904.002　　*Catalogue of an exhibition of paintings by George Morland : held at
the Victoria and Albert Museum, South Kensington, 1904.*
London : Printed for H.M.S.O., by Wyman and Sons, 1904.
14 p. : port. ; 21 cm.
At head of title: Board of Education, South Kensington. — Bibliography: p. 4. —
Printing: 5/04.
EXHIBITION: VX.1904.001

V.1904.003　　"2nd ed."
Printing: 6/04.

V.1904.004　　*The catalogue of the Constantine Alexander Ionides collection.*
London : Printed for H.M.S.O. by Wyman and Sons, 1904.
iii, 83 p. ; 22 cm.
At head of title: Board of Education, South Kensington; Victoria and Albert Museum.
— Index. — Printing: 7/04. — Grey wrappers.

V.1904.005　　*Catalogue of the first circulating collection of water-colour paintings
of the British school : illustrating the rise and progress of the art :
selected from the National Gallery of British Art at the Victoria and
Albert Museum, South Kensington.*
London : Printed for H.M.S.O., by Wyman and Sons, 1904.
57 p. ; 21 cm.
Printing: 7/04. — Grey wrappers.
EXHIBITION: VX.1904.BGM.001

V.1904.006　　*Chinese art* / by Stephen W. Bushell. *Vol. I.*
London : Printed for H.M.S.O. by Wyman and Sons, 1904.
156 p. [86] leaves of plates : ill. ; 20 cm.
(Victoria and Albert Museum art handbooks)
At head of title: Board of Education, South Kensington, Victoria and Albert Museum.
Series title on cover only. — "With 104 illustrations." — Index. — Printing: 11/04.

V.1904.007　　*English earthenware made during the 17th and 18th centuries :
illustrated by specimens in the national collections* / by A.H. Church.
Rev. ed.
London : Printed for H.M.S.O., by Wyman and Sons, Ltd., 1904.
xiii, [67] leaves of plates : ill. ; 20 cm.
(Victoria and Albert Museum art handbooks)

At head of title: Board of Education, South Kensington, Victoria and Albert Museum.
First ed. entitled English earthenware : a handbook to the wares . . . . —
"Bibliographical notes"–p. [xv]. — Printing: 7/04.

V.1904.008   *English porcelain made during the eighteenth century : illustrated by*
              specimens in the national collections / by A.H. Church. Rev. ed.
              London : Printed for H.M.S.O., by Wyman and Sons, 1904.
              xii, 113 p., [43] leaves of plates : ill. ; 20 cm.
              (Victoria and Albert Museum art handbooks)
              At head of title: Board of Education, South Kensington, Victoria and Albert Museum.
              — "With numerous illustrations." — "Bibliographical notes": p. [xi]–xii. Index.

V.1904.009   *Japanese colour prints* / by Edward F. Strange.
              London : Printed for H.M.S.O., by Wyman and Sons, 1904.
              viii, 148 p., lxxxiv leaves of plates : ill. ; 23 cm.
              (Victoria and Albert Museum art handbooks)
              At head of title: Board of Education, South Kensington, Victoria and Albert Museum.

V.1904.010   *Tools and materials used in etching and engraving.*
              London : Printed for H.M.S.O. by Wyman and Sons, 1904.
              15 p. ; 22 cm.
              Cover title. At head of title: Board of Education, South Kensington. — "This collection
              has been prepared in the Engraving School of the Royal College of Art, by the assistant
              teacher, Miss C.M. Pott, R.E., under the direction of Mr. Frank Short, R.E., who has
              also supplied the following technical notes"–p. 3. — Printing: 1/04.

1905

V.1905.001   *Catalogue of the loan exhibition of process engraving : held at the*
              Victoria and Albert Museum, South Kensington, 1905.
              London : Printed for H.M.S.O. by Wyman and Sons, 1905.
              xx, 64 p. ; 24 cm.
              Exhibition catalogue. — At head of title: Board of Education, South Kensington.
              EXHIBITION: vx.1905.001

V.1905.002   *Catalogue of the science collections for teaching and research in the*
              Victoria and Albert Museum. Part II, Physics. 2nd ed.
              London : Printed for H.M.S.O. by Wyman and Sons, 1905.
              iv, 295 p. ; 25 cm.
              At head of title: Board of Education, South Kensington. — Includes bibliographic
              references, list of contributors, and index. — Printing: 1/05.

V.1905.003   *Chinese art* / by Stephen W. Bushell. *Vol. I.*
              London : Printed for H.M.S.O. by Wyman and Sons, 1904, 'reprinted
              1905'.
              156 p. [86] leaves of plates : ill. ; 20 cm.
              (Victoria and Albert Museum art handbooks)
              At head of title: Board of Education, South Kensington, Victoria and Albert Museum.
              Printing: 6/05.

V.1905.003A   Large paper ed.
              London : Printed for H.M.S.O. by Wyman and Sons, 1905.
              30 cm.
              Printing: 8/05.

V.1905.004   *English porcelain made during the eighteenth century : illustrated by specimens in the national collections* / by A.H. Church. Rev. ed.
London : Printed for H.M.S.O., by Wyman and Sons, 1904 (reprinted 1905).
xii, 113 p., [43] leaves of plates : ill. ; 20 cm.
(Victoria and Albert Museum art handbooks)
At head of title: Board of Education, South Kensington, Victoria and Albert Museum. — "With numerous illustrations." — "Bibliographical notes": p [xi]–xii. Index.

V.1905.005   *J.A. McNeill Whistler : etchings, etc., in the National Art Library, Victoria and Albert Museum, with a bibliography.*
London : Printed for H.M.S.O. by Wyman and Sons, 1905.
18 p. ; 21 cm.
At head of title: Board of Education, South Kensington. — Compiled by Martin Hardie. — Prints later transferred to the Department of Prints and Drawings, Victoria and Albert Museum. — Bibliography: p. 10–18.

V.1905.006   *Precious stones considered in their scientific and artistic relations: with a catalogue of the Townshend collection* / by A.H. Church. New ed.
London : Printed for H.M.S.O. by Wyman & Sons, 1905.
x, 135 p., [5] leaves of plates : ill. (1 col.) ; 22 cm.
(Victoria and Albert Museum art handbooks)
At head of title: Board of Education, South Kensington, Victoria and Albert Museum. — "Bibliographical notes": p. [ix]–x. — "the coloured illustration of the dichroism and spectra of precious stones was prepared and printed under Professor Church's supervision, and at his expense"–*Report for the year 1905 on the Victoria and Albert Museum* ... (1907), p. 8.

V.1905.007   *Regulations relating to the Victoria and Albert Museum, the Bethnal Green Branch Museum, and the Museum of Practical Geology, Jermyn Street.*
London : Printed for H.M.S.O. by Wyman and Sons, 1905.
34 p. ; 24 cm.
At head of title: Board of Education. — List of official publications (Board of Education): p. 23–34. — Printing: 12/05. — Wrappers.

V.1905.008   *Victoria and Albert Museum : art collections in the main building.*
[London : H.M.S.O., 1905] ("Wy. & S.", printer).
8 p. : plans ; 25 cm.
At head of title: Board of Education, South Kensington. — Printing: 8/05.

1906

V.1906.001   *Ancient and modern ships. Part I, Wooden sailing-ships* / by Sir George C.V. Holmes. (Rev.)
London : Printed for H.M.S.O. by Wyman and Sons, 1906.
xv, 168 p. xii, 219 p., [1] leaf of plates : ill. ; 22 cm.
(Victoria and Albert Museum science handbooks)
At head of title: Board of Education, South Kensington; Victoria and Albert Museum. — "with seventy-four illustrations." — Index. — Printing: 10/06.

V.1906.002   *Ancient and modern ships. Part II, The era of steam, iron & steel* / by Sir George C.V. Holmes.
London : Printed for H.M.S.O. by Wyman and Sons, 1906.

xii, 219, p., [2] folded leaves, [41] leaves of plates, 2 folded : ill. ; 22 cm.
(Victoria and Albert Museum science handbook)
At head of title: Board of Education, South Kensington; Victoria and Albert Museum. — "With 102 illustrations." — Index. — Printing: 10/06. — Errata slip inserted.

V.1906.003   *A brief guide to the collections in the Bethnal Green Branch of the Victoria and Albert Museum, South Kensington.*
London : Printed for H.M.S.O. by Wyman & Sons, 1906.
32 p., [10] leaves of plates : ill., plans ; 22 cm.
At head of title: Board of Education, South Kensington. — Includes chronological list of the principal loan collections from 1872. — Printing: 10/06. — Pink wrappers.

V.1906.004   *Catalogue of prints. II, Modern etchings and aquatints of the British and American schools in the National Art Library, Victoria and Albert Museum.*
London : Printed for H.M.S.O. by Wyman and Sons, 1906.
364 p. ; 22 cm.
At head of title: Board of Education, South Kensington. Caption title: Catalogue of prints in the National Art Library. — Compiled by Martin Hardie. — Printing: 2/06.

V.1906.005   *Catalogue of the science collections for teaching and research in the Victoria and Albert Museum. Part III, Chemistry.* New ed.
London : Printed for H.M.S.O. by Wyman and Sons, 1906.
[2] 88 p. ; 24 cm.
At head of title: Board of Education, South Kensington. — Index. List of contributors. — Printing: 1/06.

V.1906.006   *Catalogue of the science collections for teaching and research in the Victoria and Albert Museum. Part IV, Metallurgy.* New imp.
London : H.M.S.O., 1906.
24 p. ; 24 cm.
At head of title: Board of Education, South Kensington. — Includes list of contributors. — Reissue of v.1892.004 with new t.p. — Printing: 11/92 (text), 8/06 (t.p.).

V.1906.007   *Catalogue of the third circulating collection of water-colour paintings of the British school : illustrating the rise and progress of the art : selected from the National Gallery of British Art at the Victoria and Albert Museum, South Kensington.*
London : Printed for H.M.S.O., by Wyman and Sons, 1906.
29 p. ; 21 cm.
Printing: 11/06.

V.1906.008   *Chinese art* / by Stephen W. Bushell. Vol. II.
London : Printed for H.M.S.O. by Wyman and Sons, 1906.
145 p., [127] leaves of plates: ill. ; 22 cm.
(Victoria & Albert Museum art handbooks)
At head of title: Board of Education, South Kensington, Victoria and Albert Museum — Printing: 1/06.

V.1906.008A   [Large paper ed.]
30 cm.
Printing: 7/06.

v.1906.009   *History of the Victoria and Albert Museum (formerly the South
              Kensington Museum), the Bethnal Green Museum, and the Museum
              of Practical Geology, Jermyn Street.*
              [London : H.M.S.O., 1906] ("Wy. & S.", printer).
              37 p. ; 25 cm.
              Caption title. — "...reprinted with some minor alterations and corrections from the
              Calendar of the Department of Science and Art, 1900." — Printing: 8/06.

v.1906.010   *Japanese pottery : being a native report* / with an introduction and
              catalogue by Sir Augustus W. Franks. 2nd ed.
              London : Printed for H.M.S.O. by Wyman and Sons, 1906.
              xxi, 119 p., [30] leaves of plates : ill. ; 22 cm.
              (Victoria and Albert Museum art handbooks)
              At head of title: Board of Education, South Kensington, Victoria and Albert Museum.
              — "With illustrations and marks." — Prepared by M. Shioda, translated by T. Asami.
              — "A list of books, etc., relating to Japanese ceramics": p. [106]–113. Index. —
              Printing: 2/06.

v.1906.011   *List of samplers in the Victoria and Albert Museum, South
              Kensington.*
              London : Printed for H.M.S.O. by Wyman & Sons, 1906.
              21 p., [1] leaf of plates : ill. ; 22 cm.
              At head of title: Board of Education, South Kensington. — Bibliography: p. 4.
              Numerical index. — Printing: 9/06. — Grey wrappers. — "It was decided to issue cheap
              lists of the various classes of objects in the Museum, of which [this is] the first"–*Report
              for the year 1906 on the Victoria and Albert Museum . . .* (1908), p. 10.

v.1906.012   *Regulations relating to the Victoria and Albert Museum, the Bethnal
              Green Branch Museum, and the Museum of Practical Geology,
              Jermyn Street.*
              London : Printed for H.M.S.O. by Wyman and Sons, 1906.
              37 p. : plan ; 26 cm.
              At head of title: Board of Education. — List of official publications (Board of
              Education): p. 25–37. — Printing: 1/07.

1907

v.1907.001   *Catalogue of prints. Supplement VII (31 March 1907), The work of
              Virgil Solis (1514–1562).*
              [London] : National Art Library, 1907.
              31 p. ; 21 cm.
              Caption title. — Bibliography: p. 30–31.

v.1907.002   *Catalogue of the first circulating collection of water-colour
              paintings of the British school : illustrating the rise and progress
              of the art : selected from the Victoria and Albert Museum, South
              Kensington.*
              London : Printed for H.M.S.O., by Wyman and Sons, 1907.
              57 p. ; 21 cm.
              At head of title: Board of Education, South Kensington, S.W. — Introduction by
              S. Redgrave, from v.1893.004. — Index. — Printing: 5/07.

V.1907.003   *Catalogue of the mechanical engineering collection in the Science Division of the Victoria and Albert Museum, South Kensington : with descriptive and historical notes. Part I.* 4th ed., with a supplement containing illustrations.
London : Printed for H.M.S.O. by Wyman and Sons, 1907.
419 p., xii leaves of plates : ill. ; 24 cm.
At head of title: Board of Education, South Kensington. — "Steam engines and other motors; locomotives and railways; dynamos and electrical fittings; mechanical measuring appliances; pumps and lifting machinery; power transmission." — Index. List of donors and contributors. — Printing: 10/07. — Blue wrappers.

V.1907.004   *A catalogue of the second circulating collection of water-colour paintings of the British school : illustrating the rise and progress of the art : selected from the National Gallery of British Art at the Victoria and Albert Museum, South Kensington.*
London : Printed for H.M.S.O., by Wyman and Sons, 1907.
35 p. ; 21 cm.
At head of title: Board of Education, South Kensington. — Original title: A catalogue of the second circulating historical series of water-colour paintings. — p. 1–8 have been extracted, and t.p. pasted to p. 9. Slip tipped in: "The introduction formerly issued with this catalogue is under revision". — Index. — Pink wrappers.

V.1907.005   *Chinese art* / by Stephen W. Bushell.
Unseen. A reprint of this date is recorded in V.1924.011–012.

V.1907.006   *Eastern art objects : catalogue of a collection lent by Lord Curzon of Kedleston, G.C.S.I., G.C.I.E., P.C.*
London : Printed for H.M.S.O. by Wyman & Sons, 1907.
57 p. ; 22 cm.
At head of title: Board of Education, Bethnal Green Branch of the Victoria and Albert Museum.— Printing: 10/07. — Grey wrappers.

V.1907.007   *English ecclesiastical embroideries (XIIIth to XVIth century) in the Victoria and Albert Museum, South Kensington.*
London : Printed for H.M.S.O., by Wyman & Sons, Ltd., 1907.
29 p., [3] leaves of plates : ill. ; 22 cm.
At head of title: Board of Education, South Kensington. — "With three illustrations." — Compiled by Eric Maclagan. Heraldic notes by A. Van de Put. — Indexes of objects and Museum numbers. — Printing: 5/07.

V.1907.008   *Ironwork* / by J. Starkie Gardner. *Part I, From the earliest times to the end of the mediaeval period.* 2nd ed.
London : Printed for H.M.S.O. by Wyman and Sons, 1907.
ix, 144 p., [52] leaves of plates : ill. ; 20 cm.
(Victoria and Albert Museum art handbooks)
At head of title: Board of Education, South Kensington, Victoria and Albert Museum. — "with ninety-two ilustrations." — Index. — Printing: 4/07.

V.1907.009   *The National Gallery of British Art, Victoria and Albert Museum. Part I, Catalogue of oil paintings by British artists and foreigners working in Great Britain.*
[London] : Printed for H.M.S.O. by Darling & Son, 1907.
xiv, 167 p. ; 21 cm.
At head of title: Board of Education, South Kensington. — Foundation of the collection / Lyon Playfair. — Indexes of portraits and authors illustrated. — Printing: 9/1907.

V.1907.010   *A series of twelve Delft plates illustrating the tobacco industry :*
              presented by J.H. Fitzhenry, Esq. to the Victoria and Albert Museum.
              London : Printed for H.M.S.O., by Wyman & Sons, 1907.
              [28] p., 13 leaves of plates : ill. (1 col.) ; 29 cm.
              At head of title: Board of Education, South Kensington. — Short bibliography. —
              Printing: 4/07.

V.1907.011   *Supplement containing illustrations of catalogue of the mechanical*
              engineering collection in the Science Division of the Victoria and
              Albert Museum, South Kensington, Part I.
              London : Printed for H.M.S.O. by Wyman and Sons Ltd., 1907.
              1 leaf, xii leaves of plates : ill. ; 24 cm.
              At head of title: Board of Education, South Kensington. — Printing: 12/07. — Blue
              wrappers.

1908

V.1908.001   *Ancient & modern furniture and woodwork. Vol. I.* / by John
              Hungerford Pollen ; revised by T.A. Lehfeldt. 2nd ed., rev.
              London : Printed for H.M.S.O. by Wyman and Sons, 1908.
              ix, 141 p., [52] leaves of plates : ill. ; 21 cm.
              (Victoria and Albert Museum art handbook)
              At head of title: Board of Education, South Kensington, Victoria and Albert Museum.
              — "It was intended that Mr. Pollen's small handbook published in 1875 should be
              revised and extended to two parts so as to include a history of English and foreign
              furniture and woodwork, but Mr. Pollen's death occurred at a time when he had
              prepared only part of the book comprising the general introduction to woodwork and
              the description of English furniture in the Museum"–Preface. — "with illustrations". —
              Indexes of lenders and Museum numbers. — Printing: 10/08.

V.1908.002   *A brief guide to the collections in the Bethnal Green Branch of the*
              Victoria and Albert Museum, South Kensington.
              London : Printed for H.M.S.O. by Wyman & Sons, 1908.
              32 p., [10] leaves of plates : ill., plans ; 22 cm.
              At head of title: Board of Education, South Kensington. — Printing: 1/08. — Pink
              wrappers.

V.1908.003   *Catalogue of illuminated manuscripts. Part II, Miniatures, leaves and*
              cuttings.
              London : Printed for H.M.S.O. by Wyman and Sons, 1908.
              107 p., [24] leaves of plates : ill., facsims. ; 22 cm.
              At head of title: Board of Education, South Kensington. — "The attributions...have been
              supplied or revised by S.C. Cockerell. The descriptions also were made by him, in
              conjunction with Edward F. Strange...who has completed the catalogue"–t.p. verso. —
              Subject index. — Printing: 8/08.
              Part I has not yet been published. Copies of a draft are held at the National Art Library:
              Catalogue of illuminated manuscripts. Part I, Illuminated & calligraphic manuscripts in
              the Library (volumes). London, 1957. 2 v. ; 34 cm.

V.1908.004   *Catalogue of prints : the "Liber studiorum" of J.M.W. Turner, R.A.,*
              in the Victoria and Albert Museum.
              London : Printed for H.M.S.O. by Wyman and Sons, 1908.
              v, 36 p., [2] leaves of plates : ill. ; 22 cm.
              At head of title: Board of Education. — Compiled by E.F. Strange. — Bibliography:
              p. 22–28.

V.1908.005   *Catalogue of prints : wood engravings after Sir John Everett Millais,*
              bart., P.R.A., in the Victoria and Albert Museum.
              London : Printed for H.M.S.O., by Wyman and Sons, 1908.
              33 p., [4] leaves of plates : ill. ; 22 cm.
              At head of title: Board of Education. South Kensington. — Introduction signed "M.H."
              [i.e. Martin Hardie]. — Bibliography: p. 31–33. — Grey wrappers.

V.1908.006   *Catalogue of the circulating collection of illuminated manuscripts*
              (leaves and cuttings) : selected from the Victoria and Albert Museum,
              South Kensington.
              London : Printed for H.M.S.O. by Wyman and Sons, 1908.
              16 p., [2] leaves of plates : ill. ; 22 cm.
              At head of title: Board of Education, South Kensington, S.W. — Compiled by E.F.
              Strange.— Printing: 6/08. — Grey wrappers. — "Note" tipped in at front.

V.1908.007   *Catalogue of the first circulating collection of water-colour paintings*
              of the British school : illustrating the rise and progress of the art :
              selected from the Victoria and Albert Museum, South Kensington.
              London : Printed for H.M.S.O., by Eyre & Spottiswoode, 1908.
              [1] p., p. [9]–56 ; 22 cm.
              At head of title: Board of Education, South Kensington, S.W. — "The introduction
              formerly issued with this catalogue is under revision"–t.p. verso. — Index. — Grey
              wrappers.

V.1908.008   *Catalogue of the mechanical engineering collection in the Science*
              Division of the Victoria and Albert Museum, South Kensington : with
              descriptive and historical notes. Part II, Mining and metallurgical
              appliances; textile machinery; paper-making and printing machinery;
              agricultural implements; machine tools; lighting appliances;
              telegraphic apparatus. 2nd ed.
              London : Printed for H.M.S.O. by Eyre and Spottiswoode, 1908.
              369 p. ; 25 cm.
              At head of title: Board of Education, South Kensington. Previous ed. entitled: Catalogue
              of machinery, models etc. . . . . — Index. List of donors and contributors. — Printing:
              11/08. — Blue wrappers.

V.1908.009   *A catalogue of the miniatures.*
              London : Printed for H.M.S.O. by Wyman and Sons, 1908.
              vii, 66 p., [1], [26] leaves of plates : ports. ; 22 cm.
              At head of title: Board of Education, South Kensington. Victoria and Albert Museum.
              — Bibliography: p. vii.

V.1908.010   *Classification for works on pure and applied science in the Science*
              Library, Victoria & Albert Museum.
              London : Printed for H.M.S.O. by Wyman and Sons, 1908.
              120 p. ; 25 cm.
              At head of title: Board of Education, South Kensington.

V.1908.011   *Eastern art objects : catalogue of a collection lent by Lord Curzon of*
              Kedleston, G.C.S.I., G.C.I.E., P.C.
              London : Printed for H.M.S.O. by Eyre and Spottiswoode, 1908.
              60 p. ; 22 cm.
              At head of title: Board of Education, Bethnal Green Branch of the Victoria and Albert
              Museum. — Printing: 1/09. — Grey wrappers.

V.1908.012   *J.A. McNeill Whistler : etchings, etc., in the Art Library, Victoria and
               Albert Museum, with a bibliography.* 2nd ed., enl.
               London : Printed for H.M.S.O. by Wyman and Sons, 1908.
               31 p. : 1 port. ; 21 cm.
               At head of title: Board of Education, South Kensington. — Compiled by Martin Hardie.
               — Bibliography: p. 20–31. — Printing: 4/08.— Grey wrappers.

V.1908.013   *Japanese colour prints* / by Edward F. Strange. 2nd ed.
               London : Printed for H.M.S.O., by Wyman and Sons, 1908.
               viii, 150 p., lxxxiv leaves of plates : ill. ; 22 cm.
               (Victoria and Albert Museum handbooks)
               At head of title: Board of Education, South Kensington, Victoria and Albert Museum.
               — Printing: 4/08.

V.1908.014   *Japanese colour prints : catalogue of prints by Utagawa Toyokuni I in
               the National Art Library, Victoria and Albert Museum.*
               London : Printed for H.M.S.O., by Wyman and Sons, 1908.
               iv, 18 p., [3] leaves of plates : ill. ; 22 cm.
               At head of title: Board of Education, South Kensington. — Compiled by Edward F.
               Strange. — "Books of reference": p. 17–18. — Printing: 10/07. — Grey wrappers.

V.1908.015   *Musical instruments* / by Carl Engel. Rev. ed.
               London : Printed for H.M.S.O. by Wyman and Sons, 1908.
               x, 146 p., [52] leaves of plates : ill. ; 22 cm.
               (Victoria and Albert Museum art handbooks)
               At head of title: Board of Education, South Kensington, Victoria and Albert Museum.
               — "With seventy-eight illustrations." — Dark green cloth covered boards, stamped in
               gold and black with titles and device. — Printing: 10/08.
               Copy note: One copy, possibly proofs, in grey wrappers; printing 3/08.

V.1908.016   *The National Gallery of British Art, Victoria and Albert Museum :
               abridged catalogue of oil paintings by British artists and foreigners
               working in Great Britain.*
               London : Printed for H.M.S.O., by Wyman and Sons, 1908.
               xiii, 132 p., xxv leaves of plates : ill., ports. ; 22 cm.
               At head of title: Board of Education, South Kensington. — "Twenty-five illustrations."
               "Principal works consulted in the compilation of the catalogue": p. vi. — List of donors,
               topographical index, indexes of portraits and of authors whose work is illustrated in the
               paintings. — Printing: 10/08. — Grey cloth covered boards; title stamped in gold. —
               "Containing only works exhibited in the galleries."

V.1908.017   *The National Gallery of British Art, Victoria and Albert Museum.
               Part II, Catalogue of water colour paintings by British artists and
               foreigners working in Great Britain.*
               London : Printed for H.M.S.O. by Wyman and Sons, 1908.
               vii, 429 p. ; 22 cm.
               At head of title: Board of Education, South Kensington. — List of donors; topographical
               index; indexes of portraits and of authors illustrated. — Printing: 4/08.

V.1908.018   *Precious stones considered in their scientific and artistic relations:
               with a catalogue of the Townshend collection* / by A.H. Church.
               3rd ed.
               London : Printed for H.M.S.O. by Wyman & Sons, 1908.
               x, 139 p., [5] leaves of plates : ill. (1 col.) ; 22 cm.
               (Victoria and Albert Museum art handbooks)

At head of title: Board of Education, South Kensington, Victoria and Albert Museum. — "Bibliographical notes": p. [ix]–x.

v.1908.019   *Regulations relating to the Victoria and Albert Museum, the Bethnal Green Branch Museum, and the Museum of Practical Geology, Jermyn Street.*
London : Printed for H.M.S.O. by Wyman and Sons, 1908.
21, 11, 8 p. : plan ; 25 cm.
(Cd. 4225)
At head of title: Board of Education. — Incorporates two lists (11 p., 8 p.) of official publications of the Board of Education. — Buff wrappers.

v.1908.020   *Supplement containing illustrations of the mechanical engineering collection in the Science Division of the Victoria and Albert Museum, South Kensington.*
London : Printed for H.M.S.O. by Eyre and Spottiswoode, 1908.
[4] p., xii leaves of plates : all ill., maps ; 25 cm.
At head of title: Board of Education, South Kensington. — Printing: 11/08.

v.1908.021   *Topographical index to measured drawings of architecture which have appeared in the principal British architectural publications.*
London : Printed for H.M.S.O. by Wyman and Sons, 1908.
68 p. ; 22 cm.
At head of t.p.: Board of Education, South Kensington, Victoria and Albert Museum. — Catalogue compiled by E.F. Strange. — "With one or two exceptions, [the publications] can be referred to in the National Art Library"–p. [3]. — Printing 12/07. — Grey wrappers.

v.1908.022   *Victoria and Albert Museum : art collections in the main building.*
[London H.M.S.O., 1908] ("Wy. & S.", printer).
8 p. : plans ; 25 cm.
At head of title: Board of Education, South Kensington. — Printing: 2/08.

1909

v.1909.001   *Catalogue of the Phené Spiers collection of architectural drawings to 31st December, 1908.*
[s.l. : s.n., 1909]
78 p. ; 19 cm.
At head of title: Victoria and Albert Museum (Art). Engraving, Illustration and Design. — "List of donors to the Phené Spiers collection of architectural drawings": p. 78.

v.1909.002   *Chinese art* / by Stephen W. Bushell. *Vol. I.* 2nd ed., rev.
London : Printed for H.M.S.O. by Eyre and Spottiswoode, 1909.
160 p. [86] leaves of plates : ill. ; 20 cm.
(Victoria and Albert Museum art handbooks)
At head of title: Board of Education, South Kensington, Victoria and Albert Museum. — Printing: 1/09.

v.1909.002A   [Large paper ed.]
Unseen. Advertised in v.1909.002.

v.1909.003   *Chinese art* / by Stephen W. Bushell. *Vol. II.* "2nd ed., rev."
London : Printed for H.M.S.O. by Eyre and Spottiswoode, 1909.
153 p., [127] leaves of plates : ill. ; 20 cm.

(Victoria and Albert Museum art handbooks)
At head of title: Board of Education, South Kensington, Victoria and Albert Museum. — "with 135 illustrations and 113 marks and seals." — Vol. 2 may not be revised for this new edition. It retains previous chapter numbers and index entries. — Printing: 1/09. — Slip inserted, concerning the death of the author.

V.1909.003A   [Large paper ed.]
                Unseen. Advertised in v.1909.003.

V.1909.004   *Guide to the Victoria and Albert Museum, South Kensington.*
                London : Printed for H.M.S.O. by Eyre and Spottiswoode, 1909.
                54 p. ; 24 cm.
                Preface by Cecil Smith. — "This guide is intended to indicate briefly the nature of the re-arrangement of the collections in the combined old and new buildings."–Preface. — Includes: The Victoria and Albert Museum: short description of the buildings / Aston Webb. — Printing: 6/09. — Wrappers.

1910

V.1910.001   *A brief guide, with plans and illustrations, to the Bethnal Green Museum.*
                London : H.M.S.O., 1910 (Printed by Eyre and Spottiswoode).
                30 p., [8] leaves of plates : ill., plans; 22 cm.
                At head of title: Board of Education. — Printing: 10/10. — Green wrappers.

V.1910.002   *Chinese art* / Stephen W. Bushell. *Vol. I.* [2nd ed., reissue]
                London : Printed for H.M.S.O., 1910 ("E & S", printer, 1911 printing).
                xi, 148 p., [88] leaves of plates : ill. ; 20 cm.
                (Victoria and Albert Museum handbooks)
                At head of title: Victoria and Albert Museum. — Index. — Printing: 2/11.

V.1910.003   *Chinese art* / Stephen W. Bushell. *Vol. II.* [2nd ed., reissue]
                London : Printed for H.M.S.O., 1910 ("E & S", printer, 1911 printing).
                xiii, 158 p., 142 leaves of plates : ill. ; 20 cm.
                (Victoria and Albert Museum handbooks)
                At head of title: Victoria and Albert Museum. This may be the first true 2nd ed. of Vol. II, with renumbered chapters and expanded index. Bears no note re edition. Style of title page differs from earlier and later issues. — Index. — Printing: 2/11.

V.1910.004   *Eastern art objects : catalogue of a collection lent by Lord Curzon of Kedleston, G.C.S.I., G.C.I.E., P.C.*
                London : H.M.S.O., 1910 ("E & S", printer).
                60 p. ; 22 cm.
                At head of title: Bethnal Green Museum. — V & A Publication no. 65 B.G.M.— Printing: 11/10. — Grey wrappers.

V.1910.005   *Guide to the Victoria and Albert Museum, South Kensington.*
                London : Printed for H.M.S.O. by Eyre and Spottiswoode, 1910.
                63 p. , [4] folded leaves : col. plans ; 25 cm.
                At head of title: Board of Education. — Introduction by Cecil Smith, dated June 1910. — Printing: 6/10. — Grey wrappers.

V.1910.005A   [Illustrated ed.]
63 p., [35] leaves of plates (4 folded) : ill., col. plans ; 24 cm.
Cover title: A brief guide, with plans and illustrations, to the Victoria & Albert
Museum. — Note concerning the rearrangement of galleries, printed on green paper,
tipped in.
Copy note: Printing: 9/10 seen.

V.1910.006   *A guide to the Victoria & Albert Museum : with plans.*
London : H.M.S.O., 1910.
60 p., [4] leaves of plates, folded : col. plans ; 24 cm.
At head of title: Board of Education. — Introduction by Cecil Smith, dated December
1910.— Printing: 12/10. — Green slip bound in at front, relating to the Salting bequest.

V.1910.007   *Japanese colour prints* / by Edward F. Strange. [3rd ed.]
London : Printed for H.M.S.O. by Eyre and Spottiswoode, 1910.
viii, 169 p., lxxxiii leaves of plates : ill. ; 22 cm.
(Victoria and Albert Museum art handbooks)
At head of title: Victoria & Albert Museum.

V.1910.008   *The "Liber studiorum" of J.M.W. Turner, R.A., in the Victoria and
Albert Museum.* 2nd ed.
London : Printed for H.M.S.O., 1910 ("E.& S.", printer).
viii, 34 p., [2] leaves of plates : ill. ; 22 cm.
At head of title: Board of Education. — Compiled by E.F. Strange. — Bibliography: p.
24–26. Indexes of engravers and subjects. — Printing: 11/10. — Grey wrappers.

V.1910.009   *Tools and materials used in etching and engraving : a descriptive
catalogue of a collection exhibited in the Museum.*
London : H.M.S.O., 1910 ("E. & S.", printer).
16 p. ; 25 cm.
At head of title: Victoria and Albert Museum. — Note / E.F. Strange. — Printing: 10/10.

V.1910.010   *Victoria & Albert Museum : general regulations for the use of the
Museum by the public.*
[London : H.M.S.O.?], 1910 ("E.& S.", printer).
4 p. ; 24 cm.
(Rules ; 1)
At head of title: Board of Education. — Signed "Cecil Smith." — Printing: 9/10.
Copy note: One copy printed 7/13.

V.1910.011   *Victoria & Albert Museum : regulations.*
[London : H.M.S.O.], 1910.
Cover title. At head of title: Board of Education. — Consists of v.1910.010,
v.1910.012–v.1910.016 bound together, with contents page (Regulations of the
Victoria and Albert Museum, 1910) in dark green wrappers.

V.1910.012   *Victoria & Albert Museum : regulations for photographing museum
objects.*
[London : H.M.S.O.?], 1910.
3 p. ; 24 cm.
(Rules ; 3)
At head of title: Board of Education. — Signed "Cecil Smith."

V.1910.013   *Victoria & Albert Museum : regulations for sketching or drawing
museum objects.*

[London : H.M.S.O.?], 1910.
4 p. ; 24 cm.
(Rules ; 2)
At head of title: Board of Education. — Signed "Cecil Smith."

V.1910.014   *Victoria and Albert Museum : regulations for the use by the public of*
the Library reading rooms.
[London : H.M.S.O.?, 1910?]
1 sheet (2 p.) ; 24 cm.
(Rules ; 4)
Signed "Cecil Smith."

V.1910.015   *Victoria and Albert Museum : regulations for the use by the public of*
the students' room of the Department of Engraving, Illustration and
Design.
[London : H.M.S.O.?, 1910?]
1 sheet (2 p.) ; 24 cm.
(Rules ; 5)
Signed "Cecil Smith."

V.1910.016   *Victoria and Albert Museum : regulations relating to the reception of*
works of art . . . .
[London : H.M.S.O.?, 1910?]
1 sheet ; 24 cm.
(Rules ; 6)
(Rules ; 7)
Both sides signed "Cecil Smith." — Regulations relating to the reception of works of art
on loan (Rules ; 6). – Regulations relating to the reception of works of art on approval
for purchase (Rules ; 7).

1911

V.1911.001   *A brief guide to the Victoria & Albert Museum : with plans.*
London : H.M.S.O., 1911 ("E & S", printer).
64 p., [4] leaves of plates, folded : col. plans ; 24 cm.
At head of title: Board of Education. — Introduction by Cecil Smith, dated December
1910. — Subject index. — Printing: 10/11. — Slip bound in between pages 4 and 5,
relating to the Salting bequest. Note slips inserted at p. 19, 25, 41.

V.1911.002   *A brief guide, with plans & illustrations, to the Victoria & Albert*
Museum. London : H.M.S.O., 1910 ("E & S", printer).
64 p., [35] leaves of plates, 4 folded : col. plans. ; 24 cm.
At head of title: Board of Education. — Introduction by Cecil Smith, dated December
1910. — Subject index. — Printing: 9/11. — . Slip bound in between pages 4 and 5,
relating to the Salting bequest. Note slips inserted at pp. 19, 25, 41.

V.1911.003   *English earthenware made during the 17th and 18th centuries /*
Sir Arthur H. Church. Rev.
London : Printed for H.M.S.O., 1911.
xviii, 154 p., [67] leaves of plates : ill. ; 22 cm.
(Victoria and Albert Museum art handbooks)
At head of title: Victoria and Albert Museum. — "Bibliographical notes": p. [xvii]–xviii.
Index. — Printing: 2/11.

V.1911.004   *English ecclesiastical embroideries of the XIII to XVI centuries.* Rev. repr.
London : H.M.S.O., 1911.
[4], 45 p., 1 leaf of plates : 1 ill. ; 22 cm
At head of title: Victoria & Albert Museum catalogues. — By Eric Maclagan. Note signed "A.F.K" [i.e. A.F. Kendrick]. Heraldic notes by A. Van de Put. — General and numerical indexes. — Printing: 2/12. — Wrappers.

V.1911.004A   [Illustrated ed.]
[4] 45, iii p., xxxiii leaves of plates (1 folded) : ill. ; 22 cm.
Paper covered boards.

V.1911.005   *English porcelain of the eighteenth century* / by Sir A.H. Church. [3rd] rev. ed.
London : H.M.S.O., 1911 ("E & S", printer).
xii, 120 p., [43] leaves of plates : ill. ; 20 cm.
(Victoria and Albert Museum handbooks)
At head of title: Victoria and Albert Museum. Previous title: English porcelain made during the eighteenth century. — "Bibliographical notes": p. [xi]–xii. — Printing: 9/11.

V.1911.006   *General guide to the collections : (with plans).* Rev. and repr.
London : H.M.S.O., 1911 ("E & S", printer).
81 p., [4] folded leaves of plates: col. plans ; 25 cm.
At head of title: Victoria & Albert Museum guides. — "Alphabetical index of objects": p. 72–76. — Printing: 12/11. — Grey wrappers.

V.1911.007   *General guide to the collections : with plans & 36 illustrations.* Rev. and repr.
London : H.M.S.O., 1911.
81 p., [40] leaves of plates (4 folded) : ill., facsims., col. plans ; 24 cm.
At head of title: Victoria & Albert Museum guides. — Introduction / Cecil Smith. — "Alphabetical index of objects": p. 72–76. — Printing: 12/11. — Blue wrappers.

V.1911.008   *The Salting collection.*
London : H.M.S.O., 1911 ("E & S", printer).
53 p., [14] leaves of plates : ill., port. ; 25 cm.
At head of title: Victoria & Albert Museum guides. — "With 14 illustrations." — Captions to plates printed on inserted tissues. — Printing: 3/11. — Blue wrappers. — Erratum slip tipped in before p. [3].

V.1911.008A   [Another issue.]
[16] leaves of plates
"With 16 illustrations." — Printing: 6/11.

1912

V.1912.001   *A brief guide, with plans and illustrations, to the Bethnal Green Museum.*
London : H.M.S.O., 1912 (printed by Eyre and Spottiswoode).
30 p., [8] leaves of plates : ill., plans; 22 cm.
At head of title: Board of Education. — Includes chronological list of the principal loan collections from 1872. — Printing: 5/12. — Grey wrappers.

V.1912.002   *Capetown [sic] Cathedral memorial of the South African war,*
                1899-1902 : the illuminated record of the names of those who died in
                the war.
                [London : Victoria and Albert Museum?, 1912.]
                [4] p. ; 25 cm.
                At head of title: Victoria and Albert Museum, Room 72.
                EXHIBITION: VX.1912.003

V.1912.003   *Catalogue of an exhibition of Indian drawings : (chiefly Rajput*
                illuminated tempera paintings) : lent by H.H. the Maharaja Gaekwar
                of Baroda, G.C.S.I. : from the Baroda State Museum collection.
                [London : Victoria and Albert Museum, 1912.]
                26 leaves : ill. ; 33 cm.
                Cover title. At head of title: Victoria and Albert Museum Indian Section, 1912. —
                Printed catalogue text interleaved with photographic illustrations pasted on to green
                paper.

V.1912.004   *Dickens exhibition : March to October, 1912.*
                London : H.M.S.O., 1912 ("E & S", printer).
                63 p., 1, 7 leaves. of plates : ill., 1 port. ; 25 cm.
                At head of title: Victoria & Albert Museum guides. — "With 8 illustrations". — Preface
                Cecil Smith. — Pt. I: Books, manuscripts, and autographs. Pt. II: Illustrations, portraits,
                &c. Pt. III: Photographs. — Printing: 3/12. — Blue wrappers.
                EXHIBITION: VX.1912.001

V.1912.004A   [Another issue]
                63 p. ; 25 cm.
                Revised and reprinted without illustrations. — Printing: 4/12. — Grey wrappers.

V.1912.005   *Etchings by J.A. McN. Whistler : with a bibliography.* 3rd ed., enl.
                London : H.M.S.O., 1912.
                30 p. : 1 port. ; 25 cm.
                At head of title: Victoria & Albert Museum catalogues. Previous title: J.A.McN.
                Whistler : etchings etc. — Bibliography: p. 19-30. — Printing: 1/13. — Grey wrappers.

V.1912.006   *Japanese pottery : being a native report* / with an introduction and
                catalogue by Augustus W. Franks.
                London : H.M.S.O., 1912.
                xx, 129 p., [30] leaves of plates : ill. ; 22 cm.
                (Victoria and Albert Museum art handbooks)
                Prepared by M. Shioda, translated by T. Asami. — Bibliography: p. [114]-123.

V.1912.007   *Loan exhibition of tapestries, carpets and silk fabrics from the*
                Mobilier national, Paris : July to October 1912.
                London, H.M.S.O., 1912 ("E & S", printer).
                9 p. ; 25 cm.
                At head of title: Victoria & Albert Museum guides. — Introductory note / Cecil Smith.
                — Printing: 7/12. — Grey wrappers.
                EXHIBITION: VX.1912.005

V.1912.007A   Illustrated ed.
                9 p., 4 leaves of plates : ill. ; 25 cm.
                Blue wrappers. — "First printed July 1912. Reprinted September and October 1912."
                Copy notes: Printings: 10/12, 12/12.

1913

V.1913.001 *Drawings of old London* / by Philip Norman. [2nd ed., rev.]
London : H.M.S.O., 1913.
iv, 46 p., [8] leaves of plates : ill. ; 25 cm.
At head of title: Victoria & Albert Museum catalogues. Original title: An annotated catalogue of drawings of old London. — V & A Publication no. 85 E.I.D.

V.1913.002 *General guide to the collections : (with plans & 38 illustrations).* 4th. ill. ed.
London : H.M.S.O., 1913 ("E & S", printer).
108 p., [42] leaves of plates (4 folded) : ill., col. plans ; 24 cm.
At head of title: Victoria & Albert Museum guides. Introduction and Note / Cecil Smith. Text by Aston Webb on the new buildings, extracted from v.1909.004. — "Alphabetical index of objects": p. 96–101. — Printing: 5/13. — Blue wrappers.

V.1913.003 *Guide to the English costumes presented by Messrs. Harrods Ltd.*
London : Printed under the authority of H.M.S.O., 1913.
iv, 20 p., 16 leaves of plates : ill. ; 25 cm.
At head of title: Victoria and Albert Museum, Department of Textiles. — The collection was formed by Talbot Hughes. — V & A Publication no. 90 T.

V.1913.004 *Guide, with plans and illustrations, to the Bethnal Green Museum.*
London : H.M.S.O., 1913 (Printed by Eyre and Spottiswoode).
[4] p., 28 p., [i], vii leaves of plates : ill., plans; 22 cm.
At head of title: Board of Education. — V & A Publication no. 92 B.G.M. — Printing: 2/14. — Grey wrappers. — Note pasted in, concerning opening hours.

V.1913.005 *Japanese colour prints* / by Edward F. Strange. 4th ed.
London : Printed for H.M.S.O., 1913 ("E & S", printer).
x, 169 p., lxxxiv leaves of plates : ill. ; 19 cm.
(Victoria and Albert Museum handbooks)
At head of title: Victoria and Albert Museum, Department of Engraving, Illustration and Design. — V & A Publication no. 89 E.I.D. — Index of artists' names. — Printing: 11/13.
Copy note: Some copies 22 cm.

V.1913.006 *Japanese colour prints by Utagawa Toyokuni I.* [New ed.]
London : H.M.S.O., 1913 ("E & S", printer).
19 p., [6] leaves of plates : ill. ; 25 cm.
At head of title: Victoria and Albert Museum catalogues. — V & A Publication no. 80 E.I.D. — Compiled by Edward F. Strange. — "Books of reference": p. 18–19. — Printing: 9/13. — Grey wrappers.

V.1913.007 *Japanese colour-prints lent by R. Leicester Harmsworth, Esq., M.P. : November 1913 to March 1914.*
London : Printed under the authority of H.M.S.O., 1913
("E & S", printer).
44 p. front., 23 pl. 25 cm.
V & A Publication no. 88 E.I.D. — Compiled and written by Edward F. Strange. Note / Cecil Smith. — Printing: 11/13. — Blue wrappers.
EXHIBITION: vx.1913.002

V.1913.008 *List of books available for loan to schools of art and art classes.*
London : Printed by H.M.S.O., 1913.
156 p. ; 22 cm.

At head of title: Victoria and Albert Museum. — "Under revision." — Note / Cecil Smith.— Author index. — Printing: 10/13. — Blue wrappers.

V.1913.009   *Loan exhibition of tapestries, carpets and silk fabrics from the Mobilier national, Paris : Victoria & Albert Museum, July-November MCMXII.*
[London : The Museum, 1913.]
[12] p., xxv leaves of plates : ill. ; 57 cm.
A complete set of photographs of objects in the exhibition, pasted onto grey board, with decorative borders. — Notes written by officers of the Textiles Department, Victoria & Albert Museum.
EXHIBITION: VX.1912.005

V.1913.010   *Old English pattern books of the metal trades : a descriptive catalogue of the collection in the Museum : illustrated.*
London : Printed under the authority of H.M.S.O., 1913 ("E & S", printer).
38 p., xxiv leaves of plates : ill., 1 facsim. ; 25 cm.
At head of title: "Victoria and Albert Museum catalogues"; Department of Engraving, Illustration, & Design. — V & A Publication no. 87 E.I.D. — Compiled by W.A. Young. Note / Cecil Smith. — Printing: 11/13. — Grey wrappers.

V.1913.011   *Precious stones considered in their scientific and artistic relations : a guide to the Townshend collection* / by Sir A.H. Church.
London : H.M.S.O., 1913.
xiv, 164 p., [5] leaves of plates : ill. (1 col.) ; 22 cm.
(Victoria and Albert Museum handbooks)
At head of title: Victoria and Albert Museum. — V & A Publication no. 84 M. — "Bibliographical notes": p. [ix]–x. — Printing: 7/13. — Grey wrappers.

V.1913.012   *Stained glass* / Lewis F. Day. Repr.
London : H.M.S.O., 1913 ("E & S", printer).
iv, 115 p., [32] leaves of plates : ill. ; 22 cm.
(Victoria and Albert Museum handbooks)
At head of title: Victoria and Albert Museum. — "Inventory of stained glass exhibited in the Museum": p. [102]–112. — Index. — Printing: 1/13. — Wrappers or green cloth boards.

V.1913.013   *Tapestries. Part I.*
London : Printed under the authority of H.M.S.O., 1913.
[6 leaves] : ill. ; 38 cm.
(Victoria and Albert Museum portfolios)
Cover title. — "Chinoiseries", English, 17–18th cent.; Susanna & the elders, Flemish, circa 1500; The three fates, Brussels, 16th cent.

V.1913.014   *Tools and materials illustrating the Japanese method of colour-printing : a descriptive catalogue of a collection exhibited in the Museum.*
London, H.M.S.O., 1913 ("E & S", printer).
22 p., 3 leaves of plates : ill. ; 25 cm.
At head of title: Victoria & Albert Museum catalogues. Prepared by Edward F. Strange. Prefatory note / Cecil Smith. — "Books of reference": p. 22. — Printing: 3/13. — Grey wrappers.

1914

V.1914.001   *Catalogue of paintings of the new Calcutta School : lent by the Indian Society of Oriental Art, Calcutta, April & May 1914.*
London : H.M.S.O., 1914 ("E & S", printer).
32 p. ; 25 cm.
At head of title: Victoria & Albert Museum, Indian Section. — V & A Publication no. 97 T [sic]. — Compiled and written by A.J.D. Campbell. Introduction by C. Stanley Clarke. Prefatory note / Cecil Smith. — Printing: 4/14. — Wrappers.
EXHIBITION: VX.1914.002

V.1914.002   *Catalogue of sculpture by Auguste Rodin.*
London : Printed under the authority of H.M.S.O., 1914 ("E & S", printer).
22 p., [1], xv leaves of plates : ill., port. ; 25 cm.
At head of title: Victoria and Albert Museum Department of Architecture and Sculpture — V & A Publication no. 103 A & S. — Prefatory note / Cecil Smith. Written by E.R.D. Maclagan. — Bibliographical note: p. 21–22.— Printing: 12/14. — Blue wrappers.

V.1914.003   *Catalogue of tapestries* / by A.F. Kendrick.
London : H.M.S.O., 1914 ("E & S", printer).
104 p., 1, xviii leaves of plates : ill. ; 25 cm.
At head of title: Victoria and Albert Museum, Department of Textiles. — V & A Publication no. 91 T. — Appendices: Supplementary notes, by Mr. A. Van de Put, upon the heraldry of certain tapestries described in this Catalogue. List of useful works on tapestry in the Library of the Museum (p. 90–95). — Printing: 4/14 — Boards covered in blue paper.

V.1914.004   *Chinese art* / Stephen W. Bushell. *Vol. I.* 2nd ed., repr.
London : H.M.S.O., 1914 ("E & S", printer).
xi, 148 p., [86] leaves of plates : ill. ; 20 cm.
(Victoria and Albert Museum handbooks)
V & A Publication no. 102. — Index. — Printing: 11/14.

V.1914.005   *General guide to the collections : (with plans).* 7th ed.
London : H.M.S.O., 1914 ("E & S", printer).
108 p., [4] folded leaves : col. plans ; 25 cm.
At head of title: Victoria & Albert Museum guides. — "Alphabetical index of objects." — Printing: 3/14. — Grey wrappers.

V.1914.006   *General guide to the collections : (with plans & 38 illustrations).*
5th. ill. ed.
London : H.M.S.O., 1914 ("E & S", printer).
ii, 108 p., [42] leaves of plates, some folded : ill., col. plans, ports. ;
25 cm.
At head of title: Victoria & Albert Museum guides. — V & A Publication no. 93. — Includes index of objects. — Printing: 3/14. — Blue wrappers.

V.1914.007   *General guide to the collections : (with plans & 45 illustrations).*
6th. ill. ed.
[49] leaves of plates.
Printing: 9/14.

V.1914.008　　*Guide to an exhibition of tapestries, carpets and furniture lent by the Earl of Dalkeith : March to May 1914.*
London : H.M.S.O., 1914 ("E & S", printer).
27 p., 15 leaves of plates : ill, ; 25 cm.
At head of title: Victoria & Albert Museum, Department of Textiles. — V & A Publication no. 95 T. — Prepared by A.F. Kendrick with the assistance of A.D.H. Smith, F.F.L. Birrell. "Mr A. Van de Put is responsible for the heraldry"–Prefatory note / Cecil Smith. — Typed amendment pasted in at p. 21. — Blue wrappers.
EXHIBITION: VX.1914.005

V.1914.009　　2nd. illustrated ed. with four extra plates, April 1914.
27 p., [20] leaves of plates : ill, ; 25 cm.

V.1914.010　　3rd ed., April 1914.
27 p. ; 25 cm.

V.1914.011　　*Guide to the Bayeux tapestry.*
London : Printed under the authority of H.M.S.O., 1914 ("E & S", printer).
42 p., xi, [11] leaves of plates : ill. ; 25 cm.
At head of title: Victoria & Albert Museum, Department of Textiles. — V & A Publication no. 100 T. — Guide prepared by F.F.L. Birrell, cf. Note, p. 101. Prefatory note / Cecil Smith. Note, signed "A.F.K." [i.e. A.F. Kendrick]. — Bibliography: p. 36. Index. — Printing: 11/14.— Blue wrappers.

V.1914.012　　*Ironwork. Part 1, From the earliest times to the end of the mediaeval period /* J. Starkie Gardner. 3rd ed., rev.
London : H.M.S.O., 1914.
ix, 161 p., [104] leaves of plates : ill. ; 22 cm.
(Victoria and Albert Museum art handbooks)
V & A Publication no. 98 M.

V.1914.013　　*The panelled rooms. I, The Bromley room.*
London : Printed under the authority of H.M.S.O., 1914 ("E & S", printer).
23 p., [1], xvi leaves of plates : ill. ; 25 cm.
At head of title: Victoria and Albert Museum, Department of Woodwork. — V & A Publication no. 104 W. — Written by H. Clifford Smith. — Bibliography: p. 22–23. — Printing: 12/14. — Blue paper covered boards.

V.1914.014　　*The panelled rooms. II, The Clifford's Inn room.*
London : Printed under the authority of H.M.S.O., 1914.
16 p., xii leaves of plates : ill., geneal. table, plan ; 25 cm.
At head of title: Victoria and Albert Museum, Department of Woodwork. — V & A Publication no. 105 W. — Written by Oliver Brackett. — Bibliography: p. 16.

V.1914.015　　*Tapestries. Part II.*
London : Printed under the authority of H.M.S.O., 1914.
[6] leaves : ill. ; 38 cm.
(Victoria and Albert Museum portfolios)
Cover title. — Children playing. English, 17th cent. — V & A publication no. 99T.

V.1914.016　　*Tools and materials used in etching and engraving : a descriptive catalogue of a collection exhibited in the Museum.* 3rd ed.
London : Printed under the authority of H.M.S.O., 1914 ("E & S", printer).

18 p. ; 25 cm.
At head of title: Victoria and Albert Museum. Department of Engraving, Illustration
and Design. — V & A Publication no. 101 E.I.D. — Note / Martin Hardie. — Printing:
11/14. — Grey wrappers.

V.1914.017   *Victoria & Albert Museum : regulations for the use by the public of
the Library reading rooms.*
[London : H.M.S.O.], 1914 ("E & S", printer).
1 sheet, folded ([4] p.) ; 24 cm.
At head of title: Board of Education. — "Rules 4" (p. [2]). — Signed: Cecil Smith. —
Printing: 7/14.

1915

V.1915.001   *Catalogue of a collection of miniatures in plumbago etc. lent by
Francis Wellesley, Esq., 1914–1915.*
London : Printed under the authority of H.M.S.O., 1915
("E & S", printer).
iv, 22 p., 11 leaves of plates : ports. ; 25 cm.
At head of title: Victoria and Albert Museum, Department of Paintings. — "With 13
illustrations." — V & A Publication no. 108 P. — Prefatory note / Cecil Smith.
Introductory note signed "B.S.L." [i.e. Basil Long]. — Indexes of artists and of portraits.
— Printing: 6/15. — Blue wrappers.
EXHIBITION: VX.1914.003

V.1915.002   *Catalogue of a collection of miniatures lent in 1914–15 by Henry J.
Pfungst, Esq., F.S.A.*
London : Printed under the authority of H.M.S.O., 1915
("E & S", printer).
[6], 25 p., 1, xi leaves of plates : ill., ports. ; 25 cm.
At head of title: Victoria and Albert Museum. Department of Paintings. — "With 12
illustrations." — V & A Publication no. 110 P. — "The catalogue, which is based on
material supplied by the lender, with annotations by Mr. R.W. Goulding, has been
compiled by Mr. Basil S. Long"–Prefatory note / Cecil Smith. — Indexes of artists and
of portraits. — Printing: 7/15. — Blue wrappers.
EXHIBITION: VX.1914.004

V.1915.003   *Catalogue of Algerian embroideries.*
London : Printed under the authority of H.M.S.O., 1915.
14 p., iii leaves of plates : ill. ; 24 cm.
At head of title: Victoria and Albert Museum, Department of Textiles. — V & A
Publication no. 118 T.

V.1915.004   *Catalogue of English porcelain, earthenware, enamels and glass etc. :
collected by Charles Schreiber, Esq., M.P., and the Lady Charlotte
Elizabeth Schreiber, and presented to the Museum in 1884. Vol. I,
Porcelain* / by Bernard Rackham.
London : Published under the authority of H.M.S.O., 1915
("E & S", printer).
xviii, 186 p., 96 leaves of plates : ill. ; 25 cm.
At head of title: Victoria and Albert Museum, Department of Ceramics. — V & A
Publication no. 101 C. — Bibliography: p. xv-xviii. — Grey wrappers or blue cloth
covered boards, title in gold on spine; white dust-jacket.

V.1915.005   *Catalogue of samplers.* 2nd. ed.
London : Printed under the authority of H.M.S.O., 1915
("E & S", printer).
vii, 47 p., x leaves of plates : ill. ; 25 cm.
At head of title: Victoria and Albert Museum, Department of Textiles. Previous ed.:
List of samplers. — V & A Publication no. 115 T. — "This work has been entrusted to
Mr. P.G. Trendell"–Note / A.F. Kendrick. — "List of useful works on samplers in the
Library of the Museum": p. 41–42. General and numerical indexes. — Printing: 12/15.
— Blue wrappers.

V.1915.006   *Collection of tapestries, carpets, embroideries and furniture lent by the*
Duke of Buccleuch : Victoria and Albert Museum, March to July
1914.
[London? :H.M.S.O.?, 1915.]
23 p. ; 34 cm.
Introduction / Cecil Smith. — Grey wrappers, title and captions printed in red. —
Explanatory booklet, accompanying v.1915.007. In envelope inside front cover of first
vol.
EXHIBITION: vx.1914.005

V.1915.007   *Collection of tapestries, carpets, embroideries and furniture lent by the*
Duke of Buccleuch : Victoria and Albert Museum, March to July
1914. Plates I-XXXVIII.
[London?: H.M.S.O.?, 1915.]
2 v. (lxxvi leaves of plates) : all ill. ; 58 cm.
Complete set of photographs of objects in the exhibition, pasted onto grey card, with
decorative borders. Wrappers, white cloth covered boards stamped in gold. In slip case
with v.1915.006.
EXHIBITION: vx.1914.005

V.1915.008   *Eastern works of art : catalogue of a collection lent by Earl Curzon of*
Kedleston, G.C.S.I., G.C.I.E., P.C. 3rd ed.
London : Printed under the authority of H.M.S.O., 1915
("E & S", printer).
66 p. ; 22 cm.
At head of title: Bethnal Green Museum. Previous title : Eastern art objects. — V & A
Publication no. 114 B.G.M. — Printing: 9/15. — Grey wrappers.

V.1915.009   *Guide sommaire.*
[London : Victoria and Albert Museum, 1915?]
16 p. : plans ; 25 cm.
Cover title. At head of title: Musée Victoria et Albert. — Unseen. Record from OCLC
and *Report for the year 1915 on the Victoria and Albert Museum and the Bethnal
Green Museum*, p. 9.

V.1915.010   *Guide to the collection of carpets.*
London : Printed under the authority of H.M.S.O., 1915.
96 p., xlvii leaves of plates : ill. ; 26 cm.
At head of title: Victoria and Albert Museum, Department of Textiles. — V & A
Publication no. 111 T. — Introductory note / A.F. Kendrick. — "List of useful works on
carpets in the Library of the Museum": p. 83–87.

V.1915.011   *List of photographs of objects in the Victoria and Albert Museum.*
Part VIII, Department of Woodwork.
London : H.M.S.O., 1915 ("E & S", printer).

7 parts : ill. ; 24 cm.
(List ; no. 38)

Caption title. Cover title: List of photographs of objects in the Museum. "Under
revision"–caption. — Numerical index. — Wrappers.

V.1915.011A   *Section A, English woodwork and furniture.*
28 p., iv p. of plates.
(V. & A.M. list ; no. 28a [i.e.38a])
Printing: 1/15.

V.1915.011B   *Section B, French furniture and woodwork.*
35 p., iv p. of plates.
(List ; no. 38b)
Printing: 6/15.

V.1915.011C   *Section C, Dutch, Flemish, German, Swiss, Icelandic and
Norwegian furniture and woodwork.*
11 p., ii leaves of plates : ill. ; 24 cm.
(List ; no. 38c)
Printing: 9/15.

V.1915.011D   *Section D, Italian, Portuguese and Spanish furniture and
woodwork.*
21 p., iv p. of plates : ill. ; 24 cm.
(List ; no. 38d)

V.1915.011E   *Section E, Muhammadan, Far Eastern and miscellaneous
furniture and woodwork.*
12 p., ii leaves. of plates : ill. ; 24 cm.
(List ; no. 38e)

V.1915.011F   *Section F, Leatherwork.*
9 p., ii p. of plates.
(List ; no. 38f)
Printing: 11/15.

V.1915.011G   *Section G, Musical instruments.*
10 p., ii leaves of plates.
(List ; no. 38g)
Printing: 11/15.

V.1915.012   *List of rubbings of brasses : classified and arranged in chronological
order.*
London : Printed under the authority of H.M.S.O., 1915
("E & S", printer).
xx, 115 p. 56 pl. 25 cm.

At head of title: Victoria & Albert Museum, Department of Engraving, Illustration and
Design. — Compiled by H.W. Prior. Prefatory note / Cecil Smith. — Includes indexes of
names and places. — Printing: 7/15. — Errata slip pasted in.

V.1915.013   *List of samplers in the Victoria and Albert Museum, South
Kensington.*
London : Printed for H.M.S.O. by Wyman & Sons, 1915.
21 p. : 1 ill. ; 22 cm.

At head of title: Board of Education, South Kensington. — Bibliography: p. 4.

V.1915.014   *The panelled rooms. III, The boudoir of Madame de Serilly.*
London : Printed under the authority of H.M.S.O., 1915
("E & S", printer).
26 p., [1], xi leaves of plates : ill. ; 25 cm.
At head of title: Victoria and Albert Museum, Department of Woodwork. — V & A
Publication no. 109 W. — Written by Oliver Brackett. — Bibliography: p. 25–26.—
Printing: 8/15. — Blue paper covered boards.

V.1915.015   *The panelled rooms. IV, The inlaid room from Sizergh Castle.*
London : Printed under the authority of H.M.S.O., 1915
("E & S", printer).
34 p., [1], xv leaves of plates : ill. ; 25 cm.
At head of title: Victoria and Albert Museum, Department of Woodwork. — V & A
Publication no. 116 W. — Written by H. Clifford Smith. — Bibliography: p. 33–34. —
Printing: 12/15. — Blue paper covered boards.

V.1915.016   *Tapestries. Part III.*
London : Printed under the authority of H.M.S.O., 1915.
[19] leaves : ill. ; 38 cm.
(Victoria and Albert Museum portfolios)
Cover title. — V & A publication no. 112T. — Tapestry maps. English, 16th and 17th
cent.

1916

V.1916.001   *Catalogue of English ecclesiastical embroideries of the XIII. to XVI.
centuries.* 3rd ill. ed.
London : Published under the authority of H.M.S.O., 1916
("E & S", printer).
viii, 47 p., xxviii leaves of plates : ill. ; 25 cm.
At head of title: Victoria & Albert Museum, Department of Textiles. — V & A
Publication no. 117 T. — First ed. by Eric D. Maclagan (entitled English ecclesiastical
embroideries). Note on heraldry by A. Van de Put. Prefatory note / A.F. Kendrick. —
"Books of reference": p. 43–44. General and numerical indexes. — Printing: 3/16 —
Blue wrappers.

V.1916.002   *Eighty-two miniatures from the collection lent by the Duke of
Buccleuch, 1916–1917.*
London : Published under the authority of H.M.S.O., 1916
("C.P.", printer).
7 p., 48 p. of plates : ports. ; 19 cm.
At head of title: Victoria and Albert Museum. V & A Publication no. 121 P. —
Prefatory note / Cecil Smith. — Index of artists. — Printing: 8/16, 9/16. —
Grey wrappers, with port. — "Owing to the absence on active service of the senior
officers of the Department of Paintings it has not been possible to devote to this very
interesting collection the research necessary for issuing a catalogue raisonné"–Prefatory
note.
EXHIBITION: vx.1916.005

V.1916.003   *List of photographs of objects in the Museum. Part I, Department of
Architecture and Sculpture.*
London : H.M.S.O., 1916.
3 parts : ill. ; 24 cm.

(V. & A. M. list ; no. 31)
Caption title. Cover title: List of photographs of objects in the Museum. "Under revision"–caption. — Numerical index. — Wrappers.

V.1916.003A   *Section A, Italian sculpture.*
              30 p., iv p. of plates.
              (List ; no. 31a)
              Printing: 7/16.

V.1916.003B   *Section B, Sculpture other than Italian.*
              20 p., iv p. of plates.
              (List ; no. 31b)
              Printing: 8/16.

V.1916.003C   *Section C, Architectural details and mosaics.*
              12 p., ii leaves of plates.
              (List ; no. 31c)
              Printing: 12/16.

V.1916.004   *Ninety-six miniatures from the collection lent by the Duke of Buccleuch, 1916–1917.* 2nd ed., enl.
             London : Published under the authority of H.M.S.O., 1916.
             7 p., 56 p. of plates : ports. ; 19 cm.
             At head of title: Victoria and Albert Museum. Previous title: Eighty-two miniatures . . . .
             — V & A Publication no. 121 P. — Compiled by H.A. Kennedy. — Printing: 10/16. —
             Green wrappers with port.
             EXHIBITION: vx.1916.005

V.1916.005   *Note on domestic interior paintings and wall-papers.*
             [London : Victoria and Albert Museum, 1916.]
             5 leaves ; 22 cm.
             EXHIBITION: vx.1916.003

V.1916.006   *Shakespeare exhibition : 1916.*
             [London : H.M.S.O., 1916.]
             [2], ii, 20 p., 1 leaf of plates : ill. ; 20 cm.
             At head of title: Victoria and Albert Museum. — Prefatory note / Cecil Smith. —
             Stapled; blue wrappers. — Addendum slip pasted in at end, concerning access to the
             books in the exhibition.
             EXHIBITION: vx.1916.002

V.1916.007   2nd ed., rev.

1917

V.1917.001   *Catalogue of an exhibition of drawings chiefly by Dr. Thomas Monro, 1917.*
             [London : H.M.S.O.], 1917.
             12 p., viii leaves of plates : ill. ; 19 cm.
             At head of title: Victoria and Albert Museum. — V & A Publication no. 124 E.I.D. —
             Catalogue and introduction prepared by A.K. Sabin. — Blue wrappers.
             EXHIBITION: vx.1917.006

V.1917.002   *Catalogue of furniture from Montagu House, Devonshire House and Grosvenor House : lent by the Duke of Buccleuch, the Duke of*

Devonshire and the Duke of Westminster.
London : Printed under the authority of H.M.S.O., 1917 (Printed by Chiswick Press).
iv, 14, [1], xii p. of plates : ill. ; 19 cm.
At head of title: Victoria and Albert Museum, Department of Woodwork. — V & A Publication no. 122 W. — "prepared by Oliver Brackett."–Introductory note / Cecil Smith. — Printing: 2/17. — Grey wrappers. — Published on the occasion of the removal of furniture from the three houses to the Museum, due to their being requisitioned for war purposes.

V.1917.003   *Catalogue of the Herbert Allen collection of English porcelain /* by Bernard Rackham.
London : H.M.S.O., 1917 ("E & S", printer)
xvi, 168 p., 99 leaves of plates : ill. ; 26 cm.
At head of title: Victoria and Albert Museum, Department of Ceramics. — V & A Publication no. 123C. — Prefatory note / Cecil Smith. — Bibliography: p. xiii–xvi. Index. — Blue wrappers, or blue cloth covered boards, lettered in gold.

V.1917.004   *David Garrick's bedroom furniture.*
[London : Victoria and Albert Museum], 1917.
[4] p., 1 leaf of plates : ill. ; 25 cm.
Cover title. At head of title: Victoria and Albert Museum. Caption title: The furniture of David Garrick's bedroom, formerly in his villa at Hampton.

V.1917.005   *State bedstead from Boughton House : given by the Duke of Buccleuch, K.T.*
[London : Victoria and Albert Museum], 1917.
[4] p., 1 leaf of plates : ill. ; 25 cm.
At head of title: Victoria and Albert Museum.

1918

V.1918.001   *Catalogue of the Le Blond collection of Corean pottery /* by Bernard Rackham.
London : H.M.S.O., 1918 (Printed by R. Clay and Sons).
viii, 48 p., 48 p. of plates : ill. (1 col.) ; 26 cm.
At head of title: Victoria and Albert Museum, Ceramics Department. — V & A Publication no. 126C. — Bibliography: p. vii-viii. — Blue cloth covered boards; title stamped in gold on front and spine.

V.1918.002   *Mogul paintings, period of the Emperors Jahangır & Shah Jahan 1605–1658, and Persian calligraphy formerly in the imperial collection at Delhi : lent by Lady Wantage to the Victoria and Albert Museum, 1917.*
[London : H.M.S.O.?, 1918.]
[3] leaves, [2] p., 33 leaves, 33 [i.e. 64] leaves of plates : ill. ; 56 cm.
At head of cover: Victoria and Albert Museum. — Prefatory note / Cecil H. Smith. Introduction / C. Stanley Clarke. — Photographs pasted on both sides of grey cardboard leaves with printed borders, interleaved with caption pages. Title partly printed in green, with decoration. Case half bound; green cloth and vellum.
EXHIBITION: VX.1917.IND.001

v.1918.003   *Notes on an exhibition of rubbings of monumental brasses, 1918.*
[London : H.M.S.O., 1918.]
12 p., iv p. of plates : ill. ; 19 cm.

At head of title: Victoria and Albert Museum. — V & A Publication no. 127 E.I.D. —
Written by A.K. Sabin. Prefatory note / Cecil H. Smith. — Stapled, blue wrappers.
EXHIBITION: vx.1918.002

v.1918.004   *One hundred miniatures from the collection lent by the Duke of*
Buccleuch : with a brief guide to the collection. [3rd ed. enl.]
London : H.M.S.O., 1918.
27 p., 58 p. of plates, ports., 19 cm.

Previous title: Ninety-six miniatures . . . . — Includes indexes. — Printing: 2/18. — Grey
wrappers.
EXHIBITION: vx.1916.005

1919

v.1919.001   *Catalogue of furniture from Montagu House, Devonshire House and*
Grosvenor House : lent by the Duke of Buccleuch, the Duke of
Devonshire and the Duke of Westminster. 2nd ed., rev.
London : H.M.S.O., 1919 ("E & S", printer).
iv, 15 p., [1], xiv p. of plates : ill. ; 18 cm.

At head of title: Victoria and Albert Museum, Department of Woodwork. — By Oliver
Brackett — Printing: 5/19. — Grey paper covered boards.

v.1919.002   *Catalogue of modern wood-engravings* / by Martin Hardie.
London : Printed under the authority of H.M.S.O., 1919
("E & S", printer).
419 p., [1], l p. of plates ; ill. : 25 cm.

At head of title: Victoria and Albert Museum, Department of Engraving, Illustration
and Design. — V & A Publication no. 113 E.I.D. — "Books of reference": p. 401–414.
— Printing: 7/19. — Grey wrappers.

v.1919.003   *Catalogue of the war memorials exhibition, 1919.*
London : Printed under the authority of H.M.S.O., 1919.
89, iii p. ; 18 cm.

At head of title: Victoria and Albert Museum, organised in co-operation with the Royal
Academy War Memorials Committee. — [V & A] Publication no. 130. — Prefatory
note / Cecil H. Smith. — Index of artists. — Stapled, blue wrappers.
EXHIBITION: vx.1919.001

v.1919.004   *Chinese art* / Stephen W. Bushell. 2nd ed., rev. [repr.]
London : H.M.S.O., 1919.
2 v. : ill. ; 33 cm.

At head of title: Victoria and Albert Museum. — V & A publication no. 102.
Unseen. Record from OCLC.

v.1919.005   *Guide to the Japanese textiles. Part I, Textile fabrics* / by A.D. Howell
Smith.
London : Printed under the authority of H.M.S.O., 1919.
xi, 68 p., xxiv p. of plates : ill. ; 24 cm.

At head of title: Victoria and Albert Museum, Department of Textiles. — V & A
Publication no. 119 T. — Bibliography: p. 51–53. — Printing: 12/19. — Blue wrappers.

1920

V.1920.001   *Accounts of Chippendale, Haig & Co. for the furnishing of David*
              Garrick's house in the Adelphi.
              London : H.M.S.O., 1920.
              20 p. : ill. ; 25 cm.
              At head of title: Victoria & Albert Museum, Department of Woodwork. — V & A
              Publication no. 125 W. — Prefatory note / Cecil Harcourt Smith. Introduction signed
              "O.B." [i.e. Oliver Brackett]. — Stapled, grey wrappers. — Note pasted in, concerning
              Chippendale's birthplace.

V.1920.002   *Brief guide.*
              [London : Victoria and Albert Museum, 1920.]
              [2], 13, [1] p., [1] leaf, 2 p. of plates : ill., plans ; 19 cm.
              At head of title: Victoria and Albert Museum. — "July 1920." — Index. — Stapled,
              grey wrappers.

V.1920.003   *Catalogue of English silversmiths' work (with Scottish and Irish) : civil*
              and domestic / introduction by W.W. Watts.
              London : Printed under the authority of H.M.S.O., 1920
              ("E & S", printer).
              75 p., 64 p. of plates : ill. ; 25 cm.
              At head of title: Victoria and Albert Museum, Department of Metalwork. — V & A
              Publication no. 132 M. — Prefatory note / Cecil H. Smith. — Bibliography: p. 71–72.
              Index. — Printing: 8/20. — Blue wrappers, or blue cloth covered boards; title stamped
              in gold.

V.1920.004   *Catalogue of textiles from burying-grounds in Egypt. Vol. I, Graeco-*
              Roman period / by A. F. Kendrick.
              London : Published under the authority of H.M.S.O., 1920.
              x, 142 p., xxxii p. of plates : ill. ; 25 cm.
              At head of title: Victoria and Albert Museum, Department of Textiles. — V & A
              Publication no. 129 T. — Includes bibliographies. — Printing: 11/20. — Blue cloth
              covered boards, title stamped in gold.

V.1920.005   *Eastern works of art : catalogue of a collection lent by Earl Curzon of*
              Kedleston, G.C.S.I., G.C.I.E., P.C. 4th ed.
              London : Printed under the authority of H.M.S.O., 1920 ("E & S",
              printer).
              66 p. ; 22 cm.
              At head of title: Bethnal Green Museum. — Printing: 11/19. — Grey wrappers.

V.1920.006   *Guide to the collection of carpets.* 2nd ed., rev.
              London : Printed under the authority of H.M.S.O., 1920 ("O.U.P.",
              printer.)
              viii, 88 p., [24] leaves of plates : ill. ; 24 cm.
              At head of title: Victoria and Albert Museum, Department of Textiles. — V & A
              Publication no. 111 T. — Written by A.F. Kendrick. — "A list of useful works on
              carpets in the library of the Museum": p. 73–77. General and numerical indexes. —
              Blue wrappers.

V.1920.007   *Guide to the Japanese textiles. Part II, Costume* / by Albert J. Koop.
              London : Printed under the authority of H.M.S.O., 1920.
              [vii], 64 p., [6] leaves of plates : ill. ; 24 cm.

At head of title: Victoria and Albert Museum, Department of Textiles. Prefatory note /
Cecil Harcourt Smith. — V & A Publication no. 120 T. — Bibliography: p. 55–56.
Index of Japanese technical terms; general and numerical indexes. — Printing: 5/19. —
Blue wrappers.

V.1920.008   *Japanese colour prints by Utagawa Toyokuni I.*
                 London : Published under the authority of H.M.S.O., 1920.
                 19 p., [1] vii leaves of plates : ill. ; 25 cm.
                 At head of title: Victoria and Albert Museum, Department of Engraving, Illustration
                 and Design. — V & A Publication no. 80 E.I.D. — Compiled by Mr. Edward F.
                 Strange. Note / Cecil H. Smith. — "Books of reference": p. 18–19. — Printing: 3/20. —
                 Grey wrappers.

V.1920.009   *List of photographs of objects in the Victoria and Albert Museum.*
                 Part V, Department of Metalwork.
                 London : H.M.S.O., 1920.
                 <2> parts : ill. ; 24 cm.
                 Caption title. Cover title: List of photographs of objects in the Museum. — V. & A.M.
                 list no. 35. "Under revision"–caption. — Numerical index. — Wrappers.
                 Sections a–d not identified.

   V.1920.009E   *Section E, Architectural and decorative wrought ironwork;*
                 locksmiths' work and door furniture; fire-backs, fire place
                 implements and lighting apparatus; chests.
                 33 p., iv p. of plates.
                 (List ; no. 35e)
                 Printing: 7/20.

   V.1920.009F   *Section F, Chinese bronzes; Chinese enamels; Japanese*
                 bronzes, enamels, armour, swords and sword furniture;
                 Saracenic metalwork; other near-Eastern metalwork.
                 15 p., ii p. of plates.
                 (List ; no. 35f)
                 Printing: 12/20.

V.1920.010   *List of photographs of objects in the Victoria and Albert Museum.*
                 Part VIII, Department of Woodwork. Section C, Dutch, Flemish,
                 German, Swiss, Icelandic and Norwegian furniture and woodwork.
                 London : H.M.S.O., 1920.
                 13 p., ii leaves of plates : ill. ; 24 cm.
                 (List ; no. 38c)
                 Caption title. Cover title: List of photographs of objects in Museum. — "Under
                 revision"–caption. — Printing: 5/20. — Numerical index. — Wrappers.

V.1920.011   *Notes on carpet-knotting and weaving.*
                 London, H.M.S.O., 1920.
                 vii, 26, [2] p. : ill. ; 19 cm.
                 At head of title: Victoria and Albert Museum, Department of Textiles. — V & A
                 Publication no. 136 T. — "The pamphlet is the work of Mr. C.E.C. Tattersall, of this
                 department"–Prefatory note / A. F. Kendrick. — Blue wrappers.

V.1920.012   *The panelled rooms. V, The Hatton Garden room.*
                 London : Published under the authority of H.M.S.O., 1920 ("E & S",
                 printer).
                 19 p., [1], ix leaves of plates : ill. ; 25 cm.

At head of title: Victoria and Albert Museum, Department of Woodwork. — V & A
Publication no. 134 W. — Text by Oliver Brackett. Prefatory note / Cecil H. Smith. —
Bibliography: p. 15–16. — Printing: 4/20. — Blue paper covered boards. — The
panelled room was formerly in no. 26 Hatton Garden, London.

1921

V.1921.001   *Armenian architecture from the 6th to the 13th century : catalogue of
an exhibition of drawings of architectural details and ornament by A.
Fetvadjian : 1921.*
[London : H.M.S.O., 1921.]
12 p., iv p. of plates : ill. ; 19 cm.
At head of title: Victoria and Albert Museum. Department of Engraving, Illustration &
Design. — V & A Publication no. 145 E.I.D. — Introduction by W.R. Lethaby.
Prefatory note / Cecil H. Smith. — Bibliography: p. 12. — Stapled, blue wrappers.
EXHIBITION: VX.1921.005

V.1921.002   *Brief guide to the Chinese embroideries.*
London : Published under the authority of H.M.S.O., 1921.
12 p., viii p. of plates : ill. ; 19 cm.
At head of title: Victoria and Albert Museum. Department of Textiles. — V & A
Publication no. 144 T. — Bibliography: p. 8–9. — Printing: 8/21. — Pale blue
wrappers.

V.1921.003   *Catalogue of drawings of old London : illustrated /* by Philip Norman.
3rd ed., rev. and repr.
London : Published under the authority of H.M.S.O., 1921.
[4], 50 p., [8] leaves of plates : ill. ; 25 cm.
At head of title: Victoria and Albert Museum. Previous title: Drawings of old London.
— V & A Publication no. 85 E.I.D. — Note to 3rd ed. / Cecil H. Smith. — Index. —
Printing: 4/21. — Grey wrappers.

V.1921.004   *Catalogue of textiles from burying-grounds in Egypt. Vol II, Period of
transition and of Christian emblems /* by A.F. Kendrick.
London : Published under the authority of H.M.S.O., 1921.
vii, 108 p., [1] leaf, xxii p. of plates : ill. ; 25 cm.
At head of title: Victoria and Albert Museum Department of Textiles. — Bibliography:
p. 92–95. General and numerical indexes. — Printing: 11/21. — Blue cloth covered
boards, title stamped in gold.

V.1921.005   *Catalogue of works by James A.McN. Whistler : with a bibliography.*
4th ed.
London : Published under the authority of H.M.S.O., 1921.
32 p., 1 leaf of plates : port. ; 24 cm.
At head of title: Victoria and Albert Museum, Department of Engraving, Illustration
and Design. Previous title: Etchings by J.A.McN. Whistler. — V & A Publication no. 74
E.I.D. — Compiled by Martin Hardie. — Bibliography: p. 19–31 (includes newspaper
cuttings). — Printing: 5/21. — Grey wrappers.

V.1921.006   *Catalogue of works by William De Morgan.*
London : Published under the authority of H.M.S.O., 1921.
18 p., xvi p. of plates : ill. ; 19 cm.
At head of title: Victoria and Albert Museum, Department of Ceramics. — V & A
Publication no. 143C. — Prepared by William King "under the supervision of Mr
Bernard Rackham"–Prefatory note / Cecil H. Smith. — Printing: 4/21.

V.1921.007   *Chinese art* / Stephen W. Bushell. 2nd ed., rev. [repr.]
London : H.M.S.O., 1921.
2 v. : ill. ; 22 cm.

At head of title: Victoria and Albert Museum. — V & A publication no. 102.
Unseen. Record from OCLC, British Library Catalogue.

V.1921.008   *The Franco-British exhibition of textiles : 1921.*
London : Published under the authority of H.M.S.O., 1921.
28, [3] p., xvi p. of plates : ill. ; 18 cm.

Cover title: The Franco-British exhibition of textiles in the Victoria and Albert Museum
1921. — V & A Publication no. 141 T.
Copy note: Supplement (3 p.) pasted in at end.
EXHIBITION: vx.1921.001

V.1921.008A   [Another issue]
[4], 28 p., [1] leaf, xvii p. of plates : ill. ; 19 cm.

Two printing dates given: 3/21, 4/21. — Blue wrappers.

V.1921.009   Rev. ed.
[4], 28 p., xvii p. of plates : ill. ; 21 cm.

Printing: 5/21.

V.1921.010   *Guide to the Bayeux tapestry* / by F.F.L. Birrell. [2nd ed.]
London : Printed under the authority of H.M.S.O., 1921.
[6], 34 p., [1], xii p. of plates : ill. ; 25 cm.

At head of title: Victoria & Albert Museum, Department of Textiles. — V & A
Publication no. 100 T. — Prefatory note / Cecil H. Smith. — Bibliography: p. 28. Index.
— Printing: 6/21. — Blue wrappers.

V.1921.011   *List of lantern slides available for loan.*
London : Published under the authority of H.M.S.O., 1921 (I L N &
S, printer).
vi, 118 p. ; 25 cm.

At head of title: Victoria and Albert Museum. — V & A Publication no. 138 Circ. —
Introduction / Cecil Harcourt Smith. — Printing: 1/21.

V.1921.012   *List of photographs of objects in the Victoria and Albert Museum.
Part VIII, Department of Woodwork.*
London : H.M.S.O., 1921.
(V.&A.M. list ; no. 38)

Caption title. Cover title: List of photographs of objects in Museum. "Under
revision"–caption. — Numerical index. — Wrappers.

    V.1921.012A   *Section A, English woodwork and furniture.*
36 p., iv p. of plates : ill. ; 24 cm.
(List ; no. 38a)
Printing: 3/21.

    V.1921.012B   *Section B, French furniture and woodwork.*
London : H.M.S.O., 1921.
42 p., iv p. of plates : ill. ; 24 cm.
(List ; no. 38b)
Printing: 1/21.

V.1921.013   *List of water-colour paintings of the British school in the third*
              circulating collection.
              London : Printed under the authority of H.M.S.O., 1921 (M.P. Co.,
              printer).
              8 p. ; 18 cm.
              At head of title: Victoria and Albert Museum. — V & A Publication no. 52b Circ. —
              Printing: 2/21. — Grey wrappers.

V.1921.014   *Notes on printing and bookbinding : a guide to the exhibition of tools*
              and materials used in the processes / by S.T. Prideaux.
              London : Printed under the authority of H.M.S.O., 1921.
              40 p., 16 p. of plates : ill. ; 19 cm.
              At head of title: Victoria and Albert Museum. — V & A Publication no. 137 Lib. —
              Bibliographical note p. 31. — In blue wrappers. — Errata slip pasted in to Plate 7.

V.1921.015   *A selection of drawings by old masters in the Museum collections* /
              with a catalogue and notes by Henry Reitlinger.
              London : Printed under the authority of H.M.S.O., 1921 ("E & S",
              printer).
              [8], 68 p., [1], xxxix p. of plates : ill. ; 25 cm.
              At head of title: Victoria and Albert Museum. — V & A Publication no. 142 E.I.D. —
              Preface / Cecil H. Smith. Drawings by old masters, Introduction / Martin Hardie. —
              Printing: 8/21. — Blue wrappers, or red cloth covered boards.
              EXHIBITION: VX.1920.002

1922

V.1922.001   *Analysed specimens of English porcelain* / by Herbert Eccles &
              Bernard Rackham.
              London : Published under the authority of H.M.S.O., 1922.
              53 p., xvi p. of plates : ill. ; 19 cm.
              At head of title: Victoria and Albert Museum, Department of Ceramics. — V & A
              Publication no. 151C. — Bibliography: p. 6. — "First printed December, 1922." —
              Printing: 1/23. — Blue wrappers.

V.1922.002   *Brief guide to the Jones collection.*
              London : Published under the authority of H.M.S.O., 1922.
              14 p., 16 p. of plates : ill., ports. ; 19 cm.
              At head of title: Victoria and Albert Museum. — Printing: 11/21. — Blue wrappers. —
              "Note" and erratum slip tipped in.

V.1922.003   *Brief guide to the Persian woven fabrics.*
              London : Published under the authority of H.M.S.O., 1922.
              14 p., xvi p. of plates : ill. ; 19 cm.
              At head of title: Victoria and Albert Museum, Department of Textiles. — V & A
              Publication no. 148 T. — Works for fuller information on subject: p. 8–9. — Printing:
              4/22. — Blue wrappers.

V.1922.004   *Catalogue of casts for schools : including casts of most of the statues*
              which the Board of Education have approved, in their regulations for
              the art examinations, as suitable for study in Schools of Art.

Addendum [v.1921.016] *Indian drawings: twelve Mogul paintings of the school of Humāyūn (16th century)*
illustrating the Romance of Amīr Hamzah / text by C. Stanley Clarke. — London: Printed under the authority
of H.M.S.O., 1921. — 1, 4 p., [12] leaves, 12 leaves of plates: ill.; 40 cm. — (Victoria and Albert Museum
portfolios) — Cover title. Prefatory note / Cecil Harcourt Smith. Wrappers.

London : Victoria and Albert Museum, Department of the Sale of
Casts (including casts of sculptures etc. at the British Museum, in
succession to D. Brucciani & Co.), [192–?].
29 p., [28] p. of plates : ill. ; 28 cm.
"Notice" dated October 1922. — Brown wrappers.

V.1922.005   *Catalogue of chalices & other communion vessels* / by W.W. Watts.
London : Printed under the authority of H.M.S.O., 1922.
vi, 78 p., 28 p. of plates : ill. ; 25 cm.
At head of title: Victoria and Albert Museum, Department of Metalwork. — V & A
Publication no. 147 M. — One prefatory note by Cecil H. Smith. — Bibliography: p.
71–72. — Printing: 9/22 . — Blue wrappers.

V.1922.006   *Catalogue of samplers.* 3rd ed.
London : Printed under the authority of H.M.S.O., 1922.
vi, 65 p., [13] p. of plates : ill. ; 24 cm.
At head of title: Victoria and Albert Museum, Department of Textiles. — V & A
Publication no. 115 T. — Bibliography: p. 54–55. — Printing: 12/21; 6/22. — Blue
wrappers.

V.1922.007   *Catalogue of textiles from burying-grounds in Egypt. Vol. III, Coptic
period* / by A.F. Kendrick.
London : Published under the authority of H.M.S.O., 1922.
vii, 107 p., [1] leaf, xxxii p. of plates : ill. ; 25 cm.
At head of title: Victoria and Albert Museum, Department of Textiles — V & A
publication no. 153T. — Bibliography: p. 93–96. General and numerical indexes —
Printing: 12/22. — Blue wrappers or blue cloth covered boards.

V.1922.008   *Catalogue of the Jones collection. Part I, Furniture* / by Oliver Brackett.
London : Printed under the authority of H.M.S.O., 1922.
viii, 36 p., 48 p. of plates : ill. ; 25 cm.
At head of title: Victoria and Albert Museum. — V & A Publication no. 149. — Preface
/ Cecil H. Smith. — Bibliography: p. 32–33. — Errata slip inserted.

V.1922.009   *The Franco-British exhibition of textiles 1921.*
London : Published under the authority of H.M.S.O., 1922 (Printed at
the Oxford University Press by Frederick Hall).
vii, 26 p., l plate : ill. ; 31 cm.
At head of title: Victoria and Albert Museum. — Dark blue cloth covered boards, half
bound in dark blue leather. Marbled end papers, blue and gold. — Limited edition of
300 copies.
EXHIBITION: VX.1921.001

V.1922.010   *Indian drawings : thirty Mogul paintings of the school of Jahāngīr
(17th century) and four panels of calligraphy in the Wantage bequest* /
text by C. Stanley Clarke.
London : Printed under the authority of H.M.S.O., 1922.
4 p., 24 leaves, 24 leaves of plates : ill. ; 40 cm.
(Victoria and Albert Museum portfolios)
Cover title. — V & A Publication no. 152 I.S. — Prefatory note / Cecil Harcourt Smith.
— Grey wrappers.

V.1922.011   *Ironwork. Part III, A complete survey of the artistic working of iron
in Great Britain from the earliest times* / J. Starkie Gardner.
London : Published under the authority of H.M.S.O., 1922.
197 p., [46] leaves of plates : ill. ; 23 cm.

At head of title: Victoria and Albert Museum. — V & A Publication no. 131 M —
Prefatory note / Cecil H. Smith. — General and topographical indexes.

V.1922.012   *The Japanese theatre : catalogue of an exhibition of Japanese
              theatrical art.*
              London : Published under the authority of H.M.S.O., 1922.
              21 p., 2 p. of plates : ill. ; 18 cm.
              V & A Publication no. 150 E.I.D. — Written by E.F. Strange. Prefatory note / Cecil
              Harcourt Smith. — Printing: 5/22. — Blue wrappers.
              EXHIBITION: VX.1922.004

V.1922.013   *The panelled rooms. I, The Bromley room.* Rev. and repr.
              London : Printed under the authority of H.M.S.O., 1922 ("E & S",
              printer).
              21 p., xvii p. of plates : ill. ; 25 cm.
              At head of title: Victoria and Albert Museum, Department of Woodwork. — V & A
              Publication no. 104 W. — Written by H. Clifford Smith. — Introductory note by
              Edward F. Strange. — Bibliography: p. 20–21. — Printing: 4/22. — Blue paper covered
              boards.

V.1922.014   *The panelled rooms. II, The Clifford's Inn room.* Rev. ed.
              London : Printed under the authority of H.M.S.O., 1922.
              vi, 10 p., xii leaves of plates : ill., geneal. table, plan ; 25 cm.
              At head of title: Victoria and Albert Museum, Department of Woodwork. — V & A
              Publication no. 105 W. — Written by Oliver Brackett. — Bibliography: p. 9–10.

1923

V.1923.001   *Brief guide to the Turkish woven fabrics.*
              London : Published under the authority of H.M.S.O., 1923.
              22 p., xvi p. of plates : ill. ; 19 cm.
              At head of title: Victoria and Albert Museum, Department of Textiles. — V & A
              Publication no. 148 T. — [Written by Howell Smith]. — Bibliography: p. 15–16. —
              Printing: 9/23. — Blue wrappers.

V.1923.002   *Catalogue of English furniture & woodwork. Vol. I, Gothic and early
              Tudor* / by H. Clifford Smith.
              London : Printed under the authority of H.M.S.O., 1923.
              viii, 68 p., 56 p. of plates : ill. ; 25 cm.
              At head of title: Victoria and Albert Museum, Department of Woodwork. — V & A
              Publication no. 154 W. — Bibliography: p. 60–61.

V.1923.003   *Catalogue of miniatures, leaves, and cuttings from illuminated
              manuscripts.* Rev. ed.
              London : Printed under the authority of H.M.S.O., 1923.
              101 p., [26] leaves of plates ; 23 cm.
              At head of title: Victoria and Albert Museum, Department of Engraving, Illustration
              and Design. First ed. entitled Catalogue of illuminated manuscripts. Part I. — V & A
              Publication no. 60 E.I.D. — Prefatory note by Cecil Harcourt Smith. Introduction
              signed "E.F.S." [i.e. E.F. Strange]. — Subject index. — Printing: 10/23. — Grey
              wrappers.

V.1923.004   *Catalogue of the Herbert Allen collection of English porcelain* / by
              Bernard Rackham. 2nd ed.
              London : H.M.S.O., 1923.
              xvi, 172 p., 99 p. of plates : ill., port. ; 25 cm.

At head of title: Victoria and Albert Museum Department of Ceramics. — V & A
Publication no. 123C. — "December 1922"–colophon. — Bibliography: p. xi-xiii. —
Grey wrappers.

V.1923.005   *Catalogue of the Jones collection. Part III, Paintings and miniatures* /
by Basil S. Long.
London : Printed under the authority of H.M.S.O., 1923.
xii, 148 p., 59, [1] p. of plates : ill. ; 25 cm.
At head of title: Victoria and Albert Museum. — V & A Publication no. 158. — Preface
/ Cecil H. Smith. — Includes bibliographic references. Indexes of artists, portraits,
subjects and Museum numbers. — Printing: 11/23. — Blue wrappers or blue cloth
covered boards, title stamped in gold.

V.1923.006   *A catalogue of the principal works of art at Chequers* / with an
introduction by Viscount Lee of Fareham.
London : Published under the authority of H.M.S.O., 1923.
vii, 130 p., [1], liv leaves of plates : ill., ports. ; 25 cm.
"The greater part of the collections have been catalogued by officers of the Victoria &
Albert Museum"–Preface Cecil Harcourt Smith. — Index. — Blue wrappers.

V.1923.006A   Special ed.
Special ed. limited to 100 copies. — Boards in blue cloth, half bound in vellum. Leather
label on spine.

V.1923.007   *Dutch tiles, the Van den Bergh gift : a guide to the collection given to
the Museum by Henry Van den Bergh, Esquire, through the National
Art-Collections Fund* / by Bernard Rackham.
London : Published under the authority of the Board of Education,
1923.
32 p., xvi p. of plates : ill. ; 19 cm.
At head of title: Victoria and Albert Museum Department of Ceramics. — V & A
Publication no. 163 C. — Bibliography: p. 4. — Printing: 11/23.— Blue wrappers. —
"Erratum" slip inserted p. 22.

V.1923.008   *Facsimiles of Theban wall-paintings by Nina de Garis Davies, lent by
Alan H. Gardiner : 1923.*
[London : H.M.S.O., 1923.]
16 p., [4] leaves of plates : ill. ; 19 cm.
At head of title: Victoria and Albert Museum. — Prepared by Martin Hardie and J.
Laver. Prefatory note by Cecil Harcourt Smith. The nature of Theban tomb paintings /
"A.H.G." . Egyptian wall painting / "Nina de G.D.". — Stapled, beige wrappers.
EXHIBITION: vx.1923.003

V.1923.009   *Japanese colour prints* / by Edward F. Strange. 5th ed.
London, H.M.S.O., 1923.
x, 165 p., lxxxiv p. of plates : ill. ; 20 cm.
(Victoria and Albert Museum art handbooks)
At head of title: Victoria and Albert Museum. Department of Engraving, Illustration
and Design. — V & A Publication no. 89 E.I.D. — Printing: 8/23.

V.1923.010   *Loan exhibition of drawings by Auguste Ravier (1814–1895) : 1923.*
[London : H.M.S.O., 1923.]
9 p., [2] leaves of plates : ill. ; 20 cm.
At head of title: Victoria and Albert Museum. — Prefatory note / Cecil Harcourt Smith.
Auguste Ravier / Paul Jamot. — Stapled, blue wrappers.
EXHIBITION: vx.1923.005

V.1923.011   *Water-colours in the Dixon bequest : twenty-four reproductions with biographical notes on the artists.*
[London : H.M.S.O., 1923.]
27 p., xxiv p. of plates : ill. ; 19 cm.
At head of title: Bethnal Green Museum. — V & A Publication no. 155 B.G.M. — Prepared by Arthur K. Sabin. Prefatory note / Cecil Harcourt Smith. — Printing: 5/23. — Grey wrappers.

1924

V.1924.001   *Brief guide.*
[London : Victoria and Albert Museum, 1924.]
14 p., [1], 2 p. of plates : ill., plans ; 19 cm.
At head of title: Victoria and Albert Museum. — "May 1924." — Index of collections. — Stapled, grey wrappers.

V.1924.002   *Brief guide to the Oriental painted, dyed and printed textiles.*
London : Published under the authority of the Board of Education, 1924 (Printed by H.M.S.O. Press, Harrow).
32 p., xvi, [1] p. of plates : ill. ; 19 cm.
At head of title: Victoria and Albert Museum, Department of Textiles. — V & A Publication no. 170 T. — Prepared by A.D. Howell Smith. Prefatory note signed "A.F.K." [i.e. A.F. Kendrick]. — Bibliography: p. 23–25. — Printing: 11/24. — Blue wrappers.

V.1924.003   *Brief guide to the Western painted, dyed and printed textiles.*
London : Published under the authority of the Board of Education, 1924.
30 p., [1], xvi p. of plates : ill. ; 19 cm.
At head of title: Victoria and Albert Museum, Department of Textiles. — V & A Publication no. 165 T. — Prepared by A.D. Howell Smith." — Bibliography: p. 21–22. — Printing: 4/24.

V.1924.004   *Catalogue of English porcelain, earthenware, enamels and glass : collected by Charles Schreiber, Esq., M.P., and the Lady Charlotte Elizabeth Schreiber, and presented to the Museum in 1884. Vol. III, Enamels and glass / by Bernard Rackham.*
London : Published under the authority of the Board of Education, 1924.
[8], 102 p., 48 p. of plates : ill. ; 25 cm.
At head of title: Victoria and Albert Museum, Department of Ceramics. — V & A Publication no. 172C. — Prefatory note / Eric Maclagan. — Bibliography: p. 93. General and numerical index. — Grey wrappers or blue cloth covered boards, title in gold on spine; white dust-jacket.

V.1924.005   *Catalogue of Italian plaquettes / by Eric Maclagan.*
London : Published under the authority of the Board of Education, 1924.
vii, 87 p., 1, xvi p. of plates : ill. ; 25 cm.
At head of title: Victoria and Albert Museum, Department of Architecture and Sculpture. — V & A Publication no. 167A. — Prefatory note / Cecil H. Smith. — Bibliography: p. 78–79. Indexes of artists, Museum numbers and subjects. — Blue cloth covered boards, lettered in gold. — Includes "Other plaquettes in the Department of Metalwork".

V.1924.006 *Catalogue of Japanese lacquer. Part I, General* / by Edward F. Strange.
London : Printed under the authority of H.M.S.O., 1924.
viii, 193 p., 1 leaf, xlviii p. of plates : ill. ; 25 cm.
At head of title: Victoria and Albert Museum, Department of Woodwork. — V & A
Publication no. 159 W — Introductory note / Cecil H. Smith. — "Books of reference":
v. 1, p. 193. Indexes of artists and donors, and glossaries of technical terms. — Printing:
12/24. — Blue wrappers, or blue cloth covered boards.

V.1924.007 *Catalogue of Muhammadan textiles of the medieval period* / by A.F.
Kendrick.
London : Published under the authority of the Board of Education,
1924 ("W.H.S.", printer).
vii, 74 p., xxiv p. of plates : ill. ; 25 cm.
At head of title: Victoria and Albert Museum, Department of Textiles. — V & A
Publication no. 164 T. — Prefatory note / Cecil Smith. — Includes bibliographic
references. General and numerical indexes. — Printing: 11/23. — Blue cloth covered
boards; title stamped in gold on front. Or blue wrappers.

V.1924.008 *Catalogue of pastoral staves* / by W.W. Watts.
London : Published under the authority of the Board of Education,
1924 ("W.H.S.", printer).
v, 40 p., [1], 20 p. of plates : ill. ; 25 cm.
At head of title: Victoria and Albert Museum, Department of Metalwork. — V & A
Publication no. 162 M. — Prefatory note / Cecil H. Smith. — Bibliography: p. 37.
Numerical and subject indexes. — Printing: 10/23. — Blue cloth covered boards; or
blue wrappers.

V.1924.009 *Catalogue of tapestries* / by A.F. Kendrick. 2nd ed.
London : Printed under the authority of the Board of Education, 1924.
viii, 102 p., [36] p. of plates : ill. ; 26 cm.
At head of title: Victoria and Albert Museum, Department of Textiles. — V & A
Publication no. 91 T. — Prefatory note / Cecil H. Smith. — Bibliography: p. 86–92.
General and numerical indexes. — Printing: 3/24. — Blue wrappers; blue cloth covered
boards.

V.1924.010 *Catalogue of the Jones collection. Part II, Ceramics, ormolu,
goldsmiths' work, enamels, sculpture, tapestry, books and prints.*
London : Printed under the authority of the Board of Education, 1924.
viii, 124 p., 79, [1] p. of plates : ill. ; 25 cm.
At head of title: Victoria and Albert Museum. — V & A publication no. 157. —
Prefatory note / Cecil H. Smith. Notes preceding sections on Ceramics, Metalwork and
enamels, Sculpture, Books and prints, by Bernard Rackham, W.W. Watts, Eric
Maclagan and G.H. Palmer respectively. — Includes bibliographies. General and
numerical indexes. — Printing: 6/24. — In blue wrappers or blue cloth covered boards
with title stamped in gold.

V.1924.011 *Chinese art* / Stephen W. Bushell. *Vol. I.* 2nd ed., repr.
London : Published under the authority of the Board of Education,
1924 (Printed by H.M.S.O.).
xii, 142 p., [88] leaves of plates : ill. ; 22 cm.
At head of title: Victoria and Albert Museum. — V & A Publication no. 69. — Index.
— Printing: 2/24. — Grey wrappers.

V.1924.012 *Chinese art* / Stephen W. Bushell. *Vol. II.* 2nd ed., repr.
London : Published under the authority of the Board of Education,
1924 (Printed by H.M.S.O.).
xii, 158 p., [127] leaves of plates : ill. ; 22 cm.

At head of title: Victoria and Albert Museum. — V & A Publication no. 69. — Index. — Printing: 5/24. — Grey wrappers.

V.1924.013   *Guide to the collection of costumes.* [Rev. ed.]
London : Published under the authority of the Board of Education, 1924.
viii, 42 p., xxxvi leaves of plates : ill. ; 25 cm.
At head of title: Victoria and Albert Museum, Department of Textiles. Original title: Guide to the English costumes presented by Messrs. Harrods Ltd. — V & A Publication no. 90 T. — Printing: 7/24. — Grey wrappers; or blue cloth covered boards. — Revised and enlarged to include the other costumes in the Museum collection.

V.1924.014   *List of illuminated leaves & cuttings in the travelling series.* 2nd ed., rev, and enl.
London : Published under the authority of the Board of Education, 1924.
viii, 24 p., 16 p. of plates : ill. ; 19 cm.
Previous title: Catalogue of the circulating collection of illuminated manuscript (leaves and cuttings) . . . . V & A Publication no. 62 Circ. — Compiled by H.A. Kennedy. — Bibliography: p. vii-viii. — Printing: 3/24. — Errata slip pasted in.
EXHIBITION: VX.1924.BGM.002

V.1924.015   *The memorial roll of the Royal Army Medical Corps : designed by Graily Hewitt and exhibited in Room 72 : February 1st–29th 1924.*
London : Victoria & Albert Museum, 1924.
7 p., [6] leaves of plates : ill. ; 19 cm.
EXHIBITION: VX.1924.001

V.1924.016   *The panelled rooms. VI, The Waltham Abbey room.*
London : Published under the authority of the Board of Education, 1924.
24 p., [1], xvi p. of plates : ill. ; 25 cm.
At head of title: Victoria and Albert Museum, Department of Woodwork. — V & A Publication no. 166 W. — Written by H. Clifford Smith. Prefatory note / Cecil H. Smith. — Bibliography: p. 23–24. — Printing 8/24. — Blue paper covered boards.

V.1924.017   *Precious stones considered in their scientific and artistic relations : a guide to the Townshend collection* / by Sir A.H. Church. Repr.
London : Published under the authority of the Board of Education, 1924.
xvi, 164 p., [5] leaves of plates : ill. (1 col.) ; 22 cm.
(Victoria and Albert Museum handbooks)
At head of title: Victoria and Albert Museum. — V & A Publication no. 84 M. — "Bibliographical notes": p. xi-xii. — Printing: 7/24. — Grey wrappers, or dark green cloth covered boards.

V.1924.018   *Tools and materials illustrating the Japanese method of colour-printing : a descriptive catalogue of a collection exhibited in the Museum* / by Edward F. Strange.
London : Published under the authority of the Board of Education, 1924.
24 p., [ii] leaves of plates : ill. ; 25 cm.
At head of title: Victoria & Albert Museum, Department of Engraving, Illustration and Design. — Prefatory note / Cecil H. Smith. — "Books of reference": p. 24. — Printing: 11/24. — Stapled, grey wrappers.

1925

V.1925.001   *Brief guide to the Chinese woven fabrics.*
London : Published under the authority of the Board of Education,
1925.
34 p., 1, xvi p. of plates : ill. ; 19 cm.
At head of title: Victoria and Albert Museum, Department of Textiles. — V & A
Publication no. 175 T. — By A. D. Howell Smith. — Bibliography: p. 24–26. —
Printing: 9/25. — Blue wrappers.

V.1925.002   *The Bryan bequest.*
London : Published under the authority of the Board of Education,
1925 (Charles Whittingham and Griggs, printers, Chiswick Press).
[108] p. : ill. ; 25 cm.
At head of title: Victoria and Albert Museum. — V & A Publication no. 168. —
Prefatory note / Eric Maclagan. — Includes bibliographic references. — Title and
captions printed in green. Grey wrappers.

V.1925.003   *Catalogue of Chinese lacquer* / by Edward F. Strange.
London : Printed under the authority of H.M.S.O., 1925.
vii, 36 p., xliv, [1] p. of plates : ill. ; 25 cm.
At head of title: Victoria and Albert Museum, Department of Woodwork. — V & A
Publication no. 161 W. — Includes list of donors. — Printing: 5/25. — Blue wrappers or
cloth covered boards, lettered in gold.

V.1925.004   *Catalogue of drawings & prints relating to Hackney and Bethnal
Green.*
London : Published under the authority of the Board of Education,
1925 (Printed at the Oxford University Press by Frederick Hall).
48 p., xii p. of plates ; 19 cm.
At head of title: Bethnal Green Museum. — V & A Publication no. 169 B.G.M. —
Prepared by A.K. Sabin. Prefatory note / Eric Maclagan. — "Books of reference":
p. 25. — Grey wrappers.
EXHIBITION: VX.1925.BGM.002

V.1925.005   *Catalogue of early medieval woven fabrics* / by A.F. Kendrick.
London : Printed under the authority of the Board of Education, 1925
(Printed at the Oxford University Press by Frederick Hall).
vii, 73 p., 1, xxiv p. of plates : ill. ; 25 cm.
At head of title: Victoria and Albert Museum, Department of Textiles. — V & A
Publication no. 174 T. — Prefatory note / Eric Maclagan. — Includes bibliographic
references. General and numeric indexes. — Blue cloth covered boards; title stamped in
gold on cover and spine. Or blue wrappers.

V.1925.006   *Catalogue of Japanese lacquer. Part II, Medicine cases (Inrō)* / by
Edward F. Strange.
London : Printed under the authority of H.M.S.O., 1925.
xix, 162 p., 1 leaf, xxxvii p. of plates : ill. ; 25 cm.
At head of title: Victoria and Albert Museum, Department of Woodwork. — V & A
publication no. 160 W. — Introductory note / Eric Maclagan. — Includes bibliographic
references. Indexes of grounds, artists, donors. Includes glossary of technical terms. —
Printing : 5/25. — Blue wrappers or blue cloth covered boards.

V.1925.007   *Catalogue of sculpture by Auguste Rodin.* 2nd ed.
London : Published under the authority of the Board of Education,
1925.
24 p., xx p. of plates : ill., port. ; 25 cm.
At head of title: Victoria and Albert Museum, Department of Architecture and
Sculpture. — V & A publication no. 103A. — Text by E.R.D. Maclagan. — Includes
bibliographic references. — Blue wrappers.

V.1925.008   *Catalogue of the Constantine Alexander Ionides collection. Vol. I,
Paintings in oil, tempera and water-colour, together with certain of
the drawings* / by Basil S. Long.
London : Printed under the authority of the Board of Education, 1925.
viii, 69 p., 35 p. of plates : ill., ports. ; 25 cm.
At head of title: Victoria and Albert Museum. — "With 36 illustrations." — V & A
Publication no. 171. — Introduction / Eric Maclagan. — Includes bibliographic
references. Index of artists. — Printing: 2/25. — Blue wrappers or blue cloth covered
boards; title stamped in gold. — No further vols. published.

V.1925.009   *Catalogue of works by William De Morgan.* 2nd ed.
London : Published under the authority of the Board of Education,
1925.
[6], 19 p., xvi p. of plates : ill. ; 19 cm.
At head of title: Victoria and Albert Museum, Department of Ceramics. — V & A
Publication no. 143C. — By William King. Prefatory note to 2nd ed. / Eric Maclagan.
— Printing: 12/25. — Blue wrappers.

V.1925.010   *List of lantern slides available for loan. I, Painted decoration & oil
paintings. II, Paintings in water-colour.*
London : Published under the authority of the Board of Education,
1925 (Printed at the Oxford University Press).
63 p. ; 25 cm.
At head of title: Victoria and Albert Museum, Department of Circulation. —
Introduction / Eric Maclagan. — V & A Publication no. 173 Circ. — Blue wrappers.

V.1925.011   *The panelled rooms. III, The boudoir of Madame de Serilly.*
[2nd. ed.]
London : Printed under the authority of H.M.S.O., 1925.
25, [1] p., xi leaves of plates : ill. ; 25 cm.
At head of title: Victoria and Albert Museum, Department of Woodwork. — V & A
Publication no. 109 W. — Note to second edition / Eric Maclagan, p. [3]. — Written by
Oliver Brackett. — Bibliography: p. 23–25. — Printing : 2/25. — Blue paper covered
boards.

V.1925.012   *A picture book of English alabaster carvings.*
London : Published under the authority of the Board of Education,
1925 (Printed by Waterlow & Sons).
[4], 20 p. of plates : chiefly ill. ; 19 cm.
([Picture book] ; no. PB1)
At head of title: Victoria & Albert Museum. — Includes bibliographic references. —
Red wrappers.

V.1925.013   *A picture book of English chairs.*
London : Published under the authority of the Board of Education,
1925 (Printed by Waterlow & Sons).
[4] p., 20 p. of plates : ill. ; 19 cm.

([Picture book] ; no. PB4)
At head of title: Victoria & Albert Museum. — Red wrappers.

V.1925.014   *A picture book of English miniatures.*
London : Published under the authority of the Board of Education,
1925 (Printed by Waterlow & Sons).
[4] p., [20] p. of plates : ill. ; 19 cm.
([Picture book] ; no. PB3)
At head of title: Victoria & Albert Museum. — Red wrappers.

V.1925.015   *A picture book of English porcelain figures.*
London : Published under the authority of the Board of Education,
[1925] (Printed by Waterlow & Sons).
[4] p., 20 p. of plates : ill. ; 19 cm.
([Picture book] ; no. PB2)
At head of title: Victoria & Albert Museum. — Red wrappers.

V.1925.016   *Tools and materials used in etching and engraving : descriptive
catalogue of a collection exhibited in the Museum.* 4th ed.
London : Published under the authority of the Board of Education,
1925 (Charles Whittingham and Griggs, Chiswick Press, printer).
38 p. ; 19 cm.
At head of title: Victoria and Albert Museum, Department of Engraving, Illustration &
Design. — V & A Publication no. 101 E.I.D. — Note / Martin Hardie. — Stapled, blue
wrappers.

1926

V.1926.001   *Brief guide to the Peruvian textiles.*
London : Published under the authority of the Board of Education,
1926 (Charles Whittingham and Griggs, Chiswick Press, printer).
39 p., xvi, [1] p. of plates : ill. ; 18 cm.
At head of title: Victoria and Albert Museum, Department of Textiles. — V & A
Publication no. 176 T. — Written by Howell Smith. Prefatory note / Eric Maclagan. —
Bibliography: p. 22–26. — Pale blue wrappers.

V.1926.002   *Catalogue of an exhibition of drawings, etchings & woodcuts by
Samuel Palmer and other disciples of William Blake : October
20–December 31, 1926* / with an introduction and notes by A.H.
Palmer.
London : Published under the authority of the Board of Education,
1926 ("W.H.S.", printer).
vii, 87 p., xxxii p. of plates : ill., facsim., port. ; 25 cm.
At head of title: Victoria and Albert Museum, Department of Engraving, Illustration
and Design. — V & A Publication no. 178 E.I.D. — Prefatory note / Eric Maclagan. —
Printing: 9/26. — Blue wrappers.
EXHIBITION: VX.1926.003

V.1926.003   *An exhibition of works of art belonging to the Livery Companies of
the City of London.*
London : Published under the authority of the Board of Education
1926 (Chiswick Press, Charles Whittingham and Griggs, printers).
79 p. ; 19 cm.

At head of title: Victoria and Albert Museum. — Prepared by W.W. Watts. — Includes index. — Blue wrappers.
EXHIBITION: vx.1926.002

v.1926.004   *A guide to the Salting collection* / Victoria and Albert Museum. 3rd ed.
London : Published under the authority of the Board of Education, 1926 (Charles Whittingham and Griggs, Chiswick Press, printer).
63 p., 16 p. of plates : ill. ; 25 cm.
At head of title: Victoria and Albert Museum. — V & A Publication no. 67. — First published under title: The Salting collection. — Numerical index. — Blue wrappers.

v.1926.005   *A picture book of Byzantine art.*
London : Published under the authority of the Board of Education, 1926 (Printed by Waterlow & Sons).
[4] p., 20 p. of plates : ill. ; 19 cm.
([Picture book] ; no. PB14)
Bibliography. — Orange wrappers.

v.1926.006   *A picture book of dolls and dolls' houses.*
London : Published under the authority of the Board of Education, 1926 (Printed by Waterlow & Sons).
[4] p., 20 p. of plates : ill. ; 19 cm.
([Picture book] ; no. PB13)
At head of title: Victoria & Albert Museum. — Orange wrappers.

v.1926.007   *A picture book of English chests and cabinets.*
London : Published under the authority of the Board of Education, 1926 (Printed by Waterlow & Sons).
[4] p., 20 p. of plates ; chiefly ill. ; 19 cm.
([Picture book] ; no. PB10)
At head of title: Victoria & Albert Museum. — Red wrappers.

v.1926.008   *A picture book of English embroideries : Elizabethan & Stuart.*
London : Published under the authority of the Board of Education, 1926 (Printed by Waterlow & Sons).
[4] p., 20 p. of plates : chiefly ill. ; 19 cm.
([Picture book] ; no. PB5)
At head of title: Victoria & Albert Museum. — Red wrappers.

v.1926.009   *A picture book of English glass.*
London : Published under the authority of the Board of Education, 1926 (Printed by Waterlow & Sons).
[4] p., 20 p. of plates : ill. ; 19 cm.
([Picture book] ; no. PB7)
At head of title: Victoria & Albert Museum. — Red wrappers.

v.1926.010   *A picture book of English lace.*
London : Published under the authority of the Board of Education, 1926 (Printed by Waterlow & Sons).
[4] p., 20 p. of plates : ill. ; 19 cm.
([Picture book] ; no. PB11)
At head of title: Victoria & Albert Museum. — Bibliography. — Red wrappers.

V.1926.011   *A picture book of English wrought-iron work.*
London : Published under the authority of the Board of Education,
1926 (Printed by Waterlow & Sons).
[4] p., 20 p. of plates : ill. ; 19 cm.
([Picture book] ; no. PB6)
At head of title: Victoria & Albert Museum. — Bibliography. — Red wrappers.

V.1926.012   *A picture book of Persian pottery.*
London : Published under the authority of the Board of Education,
1926 (Printed by Waterlow & Sons).
[4] p., 20 p. of plates : ill. ; 19 cm.
([Picture book] ; no. PB15)
At head of title: Victoria & Albert Museum. — Orange wrappers.

V.1926.013   *A picture book of Sheffield plate.*
London : Published under the authority of the Board of Education,
1926 (Printed by Waterlow & Sons).
[4] p., 20 p. of plates : ill. ; 19 cm.
([Picture book] ; no. PB12)
At head of title: Victoria & Albert Museum. — Includes bibliographic references. —
Red wrappers.

V.1926.014   *A picture book of the pre-Raphaelites and their school.*
London : Published under the authority of the Board of Education,
1926 (Printed by Waterlow & Sons).
[4] p., 20 p. of plates : ill. ; 19 cm.
([Picture book] ; no. PB16)
At head of title: Victoria & Albert Museum. — Orange wrappers.

V.1926.015   *A picture book of the work of Alfred Stevens.*
London : Published under the authority of the Board of Education,
1926 (Printed by Waterlow & Sons).
[4] p., 20 p. of plates ; 19 cm.
([Picture book] ; no. PB8)
At head of title: Victoria & Albert Museum. — Bibliography. — Red wrappers.

V.1926.016   *A picture book of the work of John Constable.*
London : Published under the authority of the Board of Education,
1926 (Printed by Waterlow & Sons).
[4] p., [20] p. of plates : ill. ; 19 cm.
([Picture book] ; no. PB9)
At head of title: Victoria & Albert Museum. — Bibliography. — Red wrappers.

1927

V.1927.001   *Catalogue of carvings in ivory* / by Margaret H. Longhurst. *Part I, Up
to the thirteenth century.*
London : Published under the authority of the Board of Education,
1927 (Printed at the Curwen Press).
xiv, 102 p., lxxvi p. of plates : ill. ; 26 cm.
At head of title: Victoria and Albert Museum, Department of Architecture and
Sculpture. — V & A Publication no. 179 A. — Prefatory note / Eric Maclagan. —
Bibliography: p. 95–96. General and numerical indexes. — Blue wrappers.

V.1927.002   *Catalogue of English furniture & woodwork. Vol. III, Late Stuart to Queen Anne* / by Oliver Brackett.
London : Printed under the authority of the Board of Education, 1927 (Curwen Press, printer).
viii, 52 p., 56 p. of plates : ill. ; 25 cm.
At head of title: Victoria and Albert Museum, Department of Woodwork. — V & A Publication no. 181 W. — Preface / Eric Maclagan. — Bibliography: p. 44–45. Includes general and numerical indexes; list of donors.

V.1927.003   *Catalogue of water colour paintings by British artists and foreigners working in Great Britain*. Rev. ed.
London : Printed under the authority of the Board of Education, 1927 (Printed by T. and A. Constable at the University Press, Edinburgh).
xiv, 635 p., [20] p. of plates : ill. ; 22 cm.
At head of title: Victoria and Albert Museum. — V & A Publication no. 57 P. — ". . .revised by B.S. Long, Assistant Keeper in the Department of Paintings, with the assistance of F.W. Stokes"–p. iv. Note / Eric Maclagan. — Includes brief biographical notices of the painters. Indexes of artists, place names, portraits, subjects, authors illustrated. — Salmon wrappers.

V.1927.004   *Exhibition of I. Modern French and Russian designs for costume and scenery : II. Playbills and prints : selected examples from the Gabrielle Enthoven collection*.
[London? : Board of Education?, 1927?]
22 p., [6] p. of plates : ill. ; 22 cm.
At head of title: Victoria and Albert Museum. — Prefatory note by Eric Maclagan. — Blue wrappers.
EXHIBITIONS: VX.1927.003; VX.1927.004

V.1927.005   *An exhibition of works of art belonging to the Livery Companies of the City of London*. Rev. and ill. ed.
London : Published under the authority of the Board of Education, 1927 (Charles Whittingham and Griggs, printers, Chiswick Press).
81 p., lxxx p. of plates : ill. ; 25 cm.
At head of title: Victoria and Albert Museum. — V & A Publication no. 177. — Prepared by Mr. W.W. Watts. Preface / Eric Maclagan. — Index of companies. — Orange cloth covered boards, title stamped in gold.
EXHIBITION: VX.1926.002

V.1927.006   *Guide to the later Chinese porcelain : periods of K'ang Hsi, Yung Chêng and Ch'ien Lung* / by W.B. Honey.
London : Published under the authority of the Board of Education, 1927 (Printed at the University Press, Oxford, by John Johnson).
xxi, 123 p., 120 p. of plates : ill. ; 25 cm.
At head of title: The Victoria and Albert Museum Department of Ceramics. Half-title: Chinese porcelain: periods of K'ang Hsi, Yung Chêng and Ch'ien Lung. — V & A Publication no. 183C. — Preface / Eric Maclagan. — "Selected bibliography": p. xi-xii. Index. Marks. — Grey wrappers or red cloth covered boards.

V.1927.007   *Ironwork. Part 1, From the earliest times to the end of the mediaeval period* / by J. Starkie Gardner. 4th ed. rev by W.W. Watts.
London : Printed under the authority of the Board of Education, 1927.
xi, 146 p., 63 p. of plates : ill. ; 22 cm.
At head of title: Victoria and Albert Museum. — Prefaces by Cecil Smith, Eric Maclagan. — General and topographical indexes. — Brown wrappers.

V.1927.008   *Notes on carpet-knotting and weaving* / by C.E.C. Tattersall. 2nd ed.
               London : Published under the authority of the Board of Education,
               1927 (H.M.S.O. Press, Harrow).
               50 p., [1], xii p. of plates : ill. ; 19 cm.
               At head of title: Victoria and Albert Museum. Department of Textiles. — V & A
               Publication no. 136 T. — Blue wrappers.

V.1927.009   *A picture book of 15th century Italian book illustrations.*
               London : Published under the authority of the Board of Education,
               1927 (Printed by Waterlow & Sons).
               [4] p., 20 p. of plates : ill. ; 19 cm.
               ([Picture book] ; no. PB25)
               At head of title: Victoria & Albert Museum. — Includes bibliography. — Green
               wrappers.

V.1927.010   *A picture book of bookbindings. Part I, Before 1550.*
               London : Published under the authority of the Board of Education,
               1927 (Printed by Waterlow & Sons).
               [4] p., 20 p. of plates : ill. ; 19 cm.
               ([Picture book] ; no. PB17)
               At head of title: Victoria & Albert Museum. — Tan wrappers.

V.1927.011   *A picture book of bookbindings. Part II, 1550–1800.*
               London : Published under the authority of the Board of Education,
               1927 (Printed by Waterlow & Sons).
               [4] p., 20 p. of plates : ill. ; 19 cm.
               ([Picture book] ; no. PB18)
               At head of title: Victoria & Albert Museum. — Tan wrappers.

V.1927.012   *A picture book of children in sculpture.*
               London : Published under the authority of the Board of Education,
               1927 (Printed by Waterlow & Sons).
               [4] p., 20 p. of plates : ill. ; 19 cm.
               ([Picture book] ; no. PB22)
               At head of title: Victoria & Albert Museum. — Orange wrappers.

V.1927.013   *A picture book of English silver spoons.*
               London : Published under the authority of the Board of Education,
               1927 (Printed by Waterlow & Sons).
               [4] p., 20 p. of plates : ill. ; 19 cm.
               ([Picture book] ; no. PB24)
               At head of title: Victoria & Albert Museum. — Includes bibliography. — Green
               wrappers.

V.1927.014   *A picture book of English tables.*
               London : Published under the authority of the Board of Education,
               1927 (Printed by Waterlow & Sons).
               [4] p., 20 p. of plates : ill. ; 19 cm.
               ([Picture book] ; no. PB27)
               At head of title: Victoria & Albert Museum — Green wrappers.

V.1927.015   *A picture book of Japanese sword guards.*
               London : Published under the authority of the Board of Education,
               1927 (Printed by Waterlow & Sons).

[4] p., 20 p. of plates : ill. ; 19 cm.
([Picture book] ; no. PB19)
At head of title: Victoria & Albert Museum. — Orange wrappers.

V.1927.016   *A picture book of medieval enamels.*
London : Published under the authority of the Board of Education,
1927 (Printed by Waterlow & Sons).
[4] p., 20 p. of plates : ill. ; 19 cm.
([Picture book] ; no. PB20)
At head of title: Victoria & Albert Museum. — Orange wrappers.

V.1927.017   *A picture book of portrait busts.*
London : Published under the authority of the Board of Education,
1927 (Printed by Waterlow & Sons).
[4] p., 20 p. of plates ; 19 cm.
([Picture book] ; no. PB23)
At head of title: Victoria & Albert Museum. — Orange wrappers.

V.1927.018   *A picture book of the Raphael cartoons.*
London : Published under the authority of the Board of Education,
1927 (Printed by Waterlow & Sons).
[4] p., 20 p. of plates ; 19 cm.
([Picture book] ; no. PB21)
At head of title: Victoria & Albert Museum. — Bibliography. — Orange wrappers.

V.1927.019   *A picture book of Wedgwood ware.*
London : Published under the authority of the Board of Education,
1927 (Printed by Waterlow & Sons).
[4] p., 20 p. of plates : 19 cm.
([Picture book] ; no. PB26)
At head of title: Victoria & Albert Museum. — Green wrappers. — "Corrigenda" slip
tipped in.

1928

V.1928.001   *Brief guide to the Persian woven fabrics.*
London : Published under the authority of the Board of Education,
1928.
20 p., [1], xvi p. of plates : ill. ; 19 cm.
At head of title: Victoria and Albert Museum, Department of Textiles. — V & A
Publication no. 148 T. — Bibliography: p. 13. — Printing: 3/28. — Blue
wrappers.

V.1928.002   *Catalogue of English porcelain, earthenware, enamels and glass :
collected by Charles Schreiber, Esq., M.P., and the Lady Charlotte
Elizabeth Schreiber, and presented to the Museum in 1884. Vol. I,
Porcelain* / by Bernard Rackham. [2nd ed.]
London : Published under the authority of the Board of Education,
1928 (Printed . . . at the Mayflower Press, Plymouth, William Brendon
& Son).
xviii, 226 p., 96 p. of plates : ill. ; 25 cm.

At head of title: Victoria and Albert Museum, Department of Ceramics. — V & A Publication no. 101C. — Prefatory note / Eric Maclagan. — Bibliography: p. xv-xviii. General and numerical indexes. — Grey wrappers or blue cloth covered boards, title in gold on spine; white dust-jacket.

v.1928.003   *List of photographs of objects in the Victoria & Albert Museum. Part VIII, Department of Woodwork. Section G, Musical instruments.*
London : Printed under the authority of the Board of Education, 1928.
11 p., ii p. of plates : ill. ; 24 cm.
(List ; no. 38g)
Caption title. Cover title: List of photographs of objects in Museum. "Under revision"–caption. — Printing: 10/28. Numerical index. — Wrappers.

v.1928.004   *Mosaics and frescoes in Kahrié-Djami Constantinople, copied by Dmitri Ismailovitch.*
[London : Victoria and Albert Museum?, 1928.]
8 p., [4] p. of plates : ill. ; 20 cm.
Written by M. Clayton. Prefatory note, Eric Maclagan. — Grey wrappers.
EXHIBITION: vx.1928.004

v.1928.005   *The panelled rooms. IV, The inlaid room from Sizergh Castle.* Rev. and repr.
London : Printed under the authority of H.M.S.O., 1928 (H.M.S.O. Press, printer, Harrow).
32 p., xv p. of plates : ill. ; 25 cm.
At head of title: Victoria and Albert Museum, Department of Woodwork. — V & A Publication no. 116 W. — Written by H. Clifford Smith. "Note to revised edition" by Eric Maclagan — Bibliography: p. 31–32. — Printing : 2/28. — Blue paper covered boards. — Errata slip tipped in.

v.1928.006   *A picture book of Chinese pottery figures.*
London : Published under the authority of the Board of Education, 1928 (Printed by Waterlow & Sons).
[2] p., 20 p. of plates : chiefly ill. ; 19 cm.
([Picture book] ; no. PB33)
At head of title: Victoria & Albert Museum. — Bibliography. — Green wrappers.

v.1928.007   *A picture book of English chimneypieces.*
London : Published under the authority of the Board of Education, 1928 (Printed by Waterlow & Sons).
[4] p., 20 p. of plates : ill. ; 19 cm.
([Picture book] ; no. PB34)
At head of title: Victoria & Albert Museum. — Green wrappers.

v.1928:008   *A picture book of English embroideries. Part I, Elizabethan.* Rev. ed.
London : Published under the authority of the Board of Education, 1928 (Printed by Waterlow & Sons).
[4] p., 20 p. of plates : ill. ; 19 cm.
([Picture book] ; no. PB5)
At head of title: Victoria & Albert Museum. — Bibliography. — Green wrappers. — First published combined with v.1928.009.

v.1928.009   *A picture book of English embroideries. Part II, Stuart.* Rev. ed.
London : Published under the authority of the Board of Education, 1928 (Printed by Waterlow & Sons).

[4] p., 20 p. of plates : ill. ; 19 cm.
([Picture book] ; no. PB28)
At head of title: Victoria & Albert Museum. — Bibliography. — Green wrappers. —
First published combined with v.1928.008.

v.1928.010   *A picture book of English embroideries. Part III, Georgian.*
London : Published under the authority of the Board of Education,
1928 (Printed by Waterlow & Sons).
[4] p., 20 p. of plates : ill. ; 19 cm.
([Picture book] ; no. PB31)
At head of title: Victoria & Albert Museum. — Bibliography. — Green wrappers.

v.1928.011   *A picture book of English mirrors.*
London : Published under the authority of the Board of Education,
1928 (Printed by Waterlow & Sons).
[4] p., 20 p. of plates : 19 cm.
([Picture book] ; no. PB29)
At head of title: Victoria & Albert Museum. — Green wrappers.

v.1928.012   *A picture book of Roman alphabets.*
London : Published under the authority of the Board of Education,
1928 (Printed by Waterlow & Sons).
24 p. : ill. ; 19 cm.
([Picture book] ; no. PB32)
At head of title: Victoria & Albert Museum. — Green wrappers.

v.1928.013   *A picture book of Victorian paintings.*
London : Published under the authority of the Board of Education,
1928 (Printed by Waterlow & Sons).
[4] p., 20 p. of plates : ill. ; 19 cm.
([Picture book] ; no. PB30)
At head of title: Victoria & Albert Museum. Cover title: A picture book of early
Victorian paintings. — Green wrappers.

v.1928.014   *Victoria & Albert Museum : brief guide.*
[London : H.M.S.O.], 1928 (Printed by William Clowes & Sons).
19 p., [1] leaf, 2 p. of plates : ill., plans ; 22 p.
"June 1928." — Index. — Stapled. Yellow wrappers.

1929

v.1929.001   *Brief guide to the Persian embroideries.*
London : Published under the authority of the Board of Education,
1929 (Printed by William Brendon & Sons, Mayflower Press,
Plymouth).
19 p., xvi, [1] p. of plates: ill. ; 18 cm.
At head of title: Victoria and Albert Museum, Department of Textiles. — V & A
Publication no. 184 T. — "The Guide has been prepared by Mr. Leigh Ashton . . . under
the direction of Mr. A.J.B. Wace"–Prefatory note / Eric Maclagan. — Bibliography:
p. 15. — Blue wrappers.

V.1929.002   *Catalogue of carvings in ivory* / by Margaret H. Longhurst.
             Part II.
             London : Published under the authority of the Board of Education,
             1929 (William Brendon and Son, Plymouth, printer).
             xvi, 150 p., [1] leaf, xcvi p. of plates) : ill. ; 26 cm.
             At head of title: Victoria and Albert Museum, Department of Architecture and
             Sculpture. — V & A Publication no. 186 A. — Prefatory note / Eric Maclagan. —
             Bibliography: p. 133–134. General and numerical indexes. — Blue wrappers.

V.1929.003   *Catalogue of English furniture & woodwork. Vol. I, Gothic and early*
             Tudor / by H. Clifford Smith. Rev.
             London : Printed under the authority of the Board of Education, 1929
             (Percy Lund, Humphries & Co., printer).
             viii, 92 p., 60 p. of plates : ill. ; 25 cm.
             At head of title: Victoria and Albert Museum, Department of Woodwork. — V & A
             Publication no. 154 W. — Preface to the second edition / Eric Maclagan. —
             Bibliography: p. 80–81. Includes general and numerical indexes. — Blue wrappers, or
             blue cloth covered boards.

V.1929.004   *Catalogue of rubbings of brasses and incised slabs : classified and*
             arranged in chronological order / by Muriel Clayton. Rev. ed.
             London : Published under the àuthority of the Board of Education,
             1929 (Printed by T. and A. Constable at the University Press,
             Edinburgh).
             xiv, 250 p., 72 p. of plates : ill. ; 25 cm.
             At head of title: Victoria and Albert Museum, Department of Engraving, Illustration
             and Design. — Previously List of rubbings of brasses. — V & A Publication no. 107
             E.I.D. — "Books of reference": p. 32–33. Indexes of names and places. — Dark green
             wrappers.

V.1929.005   *Catalogue of wall-papers* / by C.C. Oman.
             London : Published under the authority of the Board of Education,
             1929 (Printed by T. and A. Constable Ltd. at the University Press,
             Edinburgh).
             viii, 114 p., xxiv p. of plates : ill. ; 25 cm.
             At head of title: Victoria and Albert Museum, Department of Engraving, Illustration
             and Design. — V & A Publication no. 185 E.I.D. — Includes bibliographic references.
             Indexes of places and of designers and manufacturers. — Green wrappers.

V.1929.006   *Exhibition of miniatures by George Engleheart, J.C.D. Engleheart and*
             Thomas Richmond : May-June 1929.
             London : Published under the authority of the Board of Education,
             1929 (Printed by William Clowes and Sons).
             31 p., 8 p. of plates : ports. ; 19 cm.
             At head of title: Victoria and Albert Museum. — V & A Publication no. 188 P. —
             Prefatory note / Eric Maclagan. Introduction / Basil S. Long. — Indexes of owners and
             portraits. — Buff wrappers.
             EXHIBITION: VX.1929.004

V.1929.007   *List of photographs of objects in the Victoria and Albert Museum.*
             Part VIII, Department of Woodwork. Section F, Leatherwork.
             London : Printed under the authority of the Board of Education, 1929.
             10 p., ii p. of plates : ill. ; 24 cm.
             (List ; no. 38f)

Caption title. Cover title: List of photographs of objects in Museum. "Under revision"–caption. — Printing: 2/29. — Numerical index. — Wrappers.

V.1929.008   *The panelled rooms. V, The Hatton Garden room.* 2nd ed.
London : Published under the authority of the Board of Education, 1929.
18 p., 10 p. of plates : ill. ; 25 cm.
At head of title: Victoria and Albert Museum, Department of Woodwork. — V & A Publication no. 134 W. — Text by Oliver Brackett. Note to second edition / Eric Maclagan. — Bibliography: p. 15–16. — Blue paper covered boards. — Originally printed 1920; this reprint is the same except for a few additions to the bibliography.

V.1929.009   *A picture book of English domestic silver. Part I, 14th–16th century.*
London : Published under the authority of the Board of Trade, 1929 (Printed by Waterlow & Sons).
[4] p., 20 p. of plates : ill. ; 19 cm.
([Picture book] ; no. PB36)
At head of title: Victoria & Albert Museum. — Bibliography. — Maroon wrappers.

V.1929.010   *A picture book of English domestic silver. Part II, 17th century.*
London : Published under the authority of the Board of Education, 1929 (Printed by Waterlow & Sons).
[4] p., 20 p. of plates : ill. ; 19 cm.
([Picture book] ; no. PB42)
At head of title: Victoria & Albert Museum. — Bibliography. — Maroon wrappers.

V.1929.011   *A picture book of English embroideries. Part IV, Chair seats.*
London : Published under the authority of the Board of Education, 1929 (Printed by Waterlow & Sons).
[4] p., 20 p. of plates : ill. ; 19 cm.
([Picture book] ; no. PB35)
At head of title: Victoria & Albert Museum. — Maroon wrappers.

V.1929.012   *A picture book of English glass.* Rev.
London : Published under the authority of the Board of Education, 1929 (Printed by Waterlow & Sons).
[4] p., 20 p. of plates : ill. ; 19 cm.
([Picture book] ; no. PB7)
At head of title: Victoria & Albert Museum. — Bibliography. — Red wrappers.

V.1929.013   *A picture book of English miniatures.* Rev.
London : Published under the authority of the Board of Education, 1929 (Printed by Waterlow & Sons).
[4] p., [20] p. of plates : ill. ; 19 cm.
([Picture book] ; no. PB3)
At head of title: Victoria & Albert Museum. — Red wrappers.

V.1929.014   *A picture book of English porcelain figures.* Rev.
London : Published under the authority of the Board of Education, 1929 (Printed by Waterlow & Sons).
[4] p., 20 p. of plates : ill. ; 19 cm.
([Picture book] ; no. PB2)
At head of title: Victoria & Albert Museum. — Red wrappers.

V.1929.015   *A picture book of English wrought-iron work.*
London : Published under the authority of the Board of Education,
1926 (Printed by Waterlow & Sons, 1929).
[4] p., 20 p. of plates : ill. ; 19 cm.
([Picture book] ; no. PB6)
At head of title: Victoria & Albert Museum. — Includes bibliography. — Red
wrappers.

V.1929.016   *A picture book of German porcelain figures.*
London : Published under the authority of the Board of Education,
1929 (Printed by Waterlow & Sons).
[4] p., 20 p. of plates : ill. ; 19 cm.
([Picture book] ; no. PB40)
At head of title: Victoria & Albert Museum. — Maroon wrappers.

V.1929.017   *A picture book of keyboard musical instruments.*
London : Published under the authority of the Board of Education,
1929 (Printed by Waterlow & Sons).
[4] p., 20 p. of plates : ill. ; 19 cm.
([Picture book] ; no. PB37)
At head of title: Victoria & Albert Museum. — Maroon wrappers.

V.1929.018   *A picture book of peasant pottery.*
London : Published under the authority of the Board of Education,
1929 (Printed by Waterlow & Sons).
[4] p., 20 p. of plates : ill. ; 19 cm.
([Picture book] ; no. PB39)
At head of title: Victoria & Albert Museum. — Maroon wrappers.

V.1929.019   *A picture book of the work of Peter De Wint.*
London : Published under the authority of the Board of Education,
1929 (Printed by Waterlow & Sons).
[4] p., 20 p. of plates : ill. ; 19 cm.
([Picture book] ; no. PB41)
At head of title: Victoria & Albert Museum. — Maroon wrappers.

V.1929.020   *A picture book of Turkish pottery.*
London : Published under the authority of the Board of Education,
1929 (Printed by Waterlow & Sons).
[4] p., 20 p. of plates : ill. ; 19 cm.
([Picture book] ; no. PB38)
At head of title: Victoria & Albert Museum. — Maroon wrappers.

1930

V.1930.001   *100 masterpieces. [i], Early Christian and mediaeval.*
London : Published under the authority of the Board of Education,
1930 (Printed by Waterlow & Sons).
[4] p., 100 p. of plates : chiefly ill. ; 19 cm.
At head of title: Victoria & Albert Museum. — V & A Publication no. 191. —
Introduction / Eric Maclagan. — Buff wrappers with all-over pattern in three colours.

V.1930.002   *Catalogue of an exhibition of hand-woven Finnish rugs : Victoria and Albert Museum, February–March 1930.*
[London : Victoria and Albert Museum?, 1930.]
1 sheet, folded ([3] p.) ; 28 cm.
EXHIBITION: vx.1930.002

V.1930.003   *Catalogue of English ecclesiastical embroideries of the XIII. to XVI. centuries.* 4th ill. ed.
London : Published under the authority of the Board of Education, 1930 (Printed by William Clowes and Sons).
68 p., xl p. of plates : ill. ; 25 cm.
<small>At head of title: Victoria & Albert Museum, Department of Textiles. — V & A Publication no. 117 T. — "The whole catalogue has . . . been thoroughly revised, and the introduction largely rewritten by Mr. P.G. Trendell . . . The heraldic notes for the greater part, and the appendix on the heraldry of the Syon cope are due . . . to Mr. A. Van de Put"–Preface / Eric Maclagan. — Bibliography: p. 57–60. Index. — Brown wrappers.</small>

V.1930.004   *Catalogue of English furniture & woodwork. Vol. II, Late Tudor and early Stuart /* by H. Clifford Smith.
London : Printed under the authority of the Board of Education, 1930 (Chiswick Press, Charles Whittingham and Griggs, printers).
xii, 55 p., 52 p. of plates : ill. ; 25 cm.
<small>At head of title: Victoria and Albert Museum, Department of Woodwork. — V & A Publication no. 180 W. — Preface / Eric Maclagan. — Bibliography: p. 80–81. General and numerical indexes, list of donors. — Wrappers or blue cloth covered boards.</small>

V.1930.005   *Catalogue of English porcelain, earthenware, enamels and glass : collected by Charles Schreiber Esq., M.P., and the Lady Charlotte Elizabeth Schreiber, and presented to the Museum in 1884. Vol. II, Earthenware /* by Bernard Rackham.
London : Published under the authority of the Board of Education, 1930.
xii, 139 p., 86 p. of plates : ill. ; 25 cm.
<small>At head of title: Victoria and Albert Museum, Department of Ceramics. — V & A Publication no. 187C. — Grey wrappers or blue cloth covered boards, title in gold on spine; white dust-jacket. — Bibliography: p. xi-xii.</small>

V.1930.006   *Catalogue of rings /* by C.C. Oman.
London : Published under the authority of the Board of Education, 1930 (Printed by T. and A. Constable at the University Press, Edinburgh).
xvi, 154 p., [1], xxxix p. of plates : ill. ; 25 cm.
<small>At head of title: Victoria and Albert Museum Department of Metalwork. — V & A Publication no. 190 M. — Prefatory note / Eric Maclagan. — "List of the principal works referred to": p. xv-xvi. General and numerical indexes. — Dun wrappers. Or red cloth covered boards.</small>

V.1930.007   *Catalogue of the Jones collection. Part I, Furniture /* by Oliver Brackett. 2nd ed., rev.
London : Printed under the authority of the Board of Education, 1930 (Percy Lund, Humphries & Co., printer).
viii, 36 p., 48 p. of plates : ill. ; 25 cm.

At head of title: Victoria and Albert Museum. — V & A Publication no. 149. — Preface
to the second ed. / Eric Maclagan. — Bibliography: p. 32–33. General and numerical
indexes — Blue wrappers or cloth covered boards.

V.1930.008　　　*A Christmas picture book.*
London : Published under the authority of the Board of Education,
1930 (Printed by Waterlow & Sons).
[4] p., 20 p. of plates : ill. ; 19 cm.
([Picture book] ; no. PB43)
At head of title: Victoria and Albert Museum. — Decorated wrappers.

V.1930.009　　　*Exhibition of English mediaeval art, 1930.*
London : Published by authority of the Board of Education, 1930
(Printed at the Kynoch Press, Birmingham).
[6], 194 p. ; 22 cm.
At head of title: Victoria & Albert Museum. — "Under revision." — V & A Publication
no. 193. — Introduction / Eric Maclagan. — Bibliographic note: p. [6]. Index of lenders.
— Wrappers (unseen) presumably as v.1930.009a.
EXHIBITION: vx.1930.003

V.1930.009A　　[Rev. ed.]
[6], 199 p. ; 22 cm.
Cover title: English mediaeval art. — "First printed May, 1930; revised August, 1930."
— Includes index of objects. — Buff wrappers with geometric illustration and label-style
title printed in black.

V.1930.010　　　*Exhibition of English mediaeval art, 1930 : illustrations.*
London : Published by authority of the Board of Education, 1930
(Printed by Percy Lund, Humphries & Co.).
x p., 100 p. of plates : ill. ; 21 cm.
V & A Publication no. 194. — Tan wrappers with ill.
EXHIBITION: vx.1930.003

V.1930.011　　　*An exhibition of Wedgwood ware : held in commemoration of the
bi-centenary of the birth of Josiah Wedgwood, 1730–1795.*
[London : Victoria and Albert Museum, 1930.]
[4] p. ; 24 cm.
At head of title: Victoria and Albert Museum, Department of Ceramics.
EXHIBITION: vx.1930.004

V.1930.012　　　*Guide to the collection of lace* / by P.G. Trendell.
London : Published under the authority of the Board of Education,
1930 (Printed at the Kynoch Press).
viii, 18 p., 1 leaf, xxxii p. of plates : ill. ; 24 cm.
At head of title: Victoria and Albert Museum, Department of Textiles. — V & A
Publication no. 189 T. — Preface / Eric Maclagan. — "List of useful books on lace in
the Library of the Museum": p. 15–16. Index. — Maroon wrappers. Or maroon cloth
covered boards; title stamped in gold.

V.1930.013　　　*Hand-list of miniature portraits and silhouettes* / by Basil S.
Long.
London : Published under the authority of the Board of Education,
1930.
xv, 114 p., 40 p. of plates : ill., ports. ; 26 cm.

At head of title: Victoria and Albert Museum. Department of Paintings. Cover title: Illustrated hand-list of miniature portraits and silhouettes. — "With 177 reproductions." — V & A Publication no. 192. — Preface / Eric Maclagan. — Indexes of portraits, subjects; list of donors. — Red wrappers.

V.1930.014   *Ironwork. Part 2, Continental ironwork of the Renaissance and later periods* / by J. Starkie Gardner. [2nd ed.], rev. and enl. by W.W. Watts
London : Published under the authority of the Board of Education, 1930.
xii, 124 p., 44 p. of plates : ill. ; 23 cm.
At head of title: Victoria and Albert Museum. — Preface to 2nd ed. / Eric Maclagan. — V & A publication no. 195 M. — Includes list of designs in the Department of Engraving, Illustration and Design. General and topographical indexes, and index of designers and craftsmen. Bibliography: p. [187]–192. — First ed. v.1896.006.

V.1930.015   *A picture book of English chairs*. Repr.
London : Published under the authority of the Board of Education, 1930 (Printed by Waterlow & Sons).
[4] p., 20 p. of plates : ill. ; 19 cm.
([Picture book] ; no. PB4)
At head of title: Victoria & Albert Museum. — Red wrappers.

V.1930.016   *A picture book of English chests, cupboards and cabinets*. Rev.
London : Published under the authority of the Board of Education, 1930 (Printed by Waterlow & Sons).
[4] p., 20 p. of plates : ill. ; 19 cm.
([Picture book] ; no. PB10)
At head of title: Victoria & Albert Museum. Original title: A picture book of English chests and cabinets. — Red wrappers.

V.1930.017   *A picture book of leatherwork*.
London : Published under the authority of the Board of Education, 1930 (Printed by Waterlow & Sons).
[4] p., 20 p. of plates : ill. ; 19 cm.
([Picture book] ; no. PB44)
At head of title: Victoria & Albert Museum. — Red wrappers.

V.1930.018   *Li tre libri dell'arte del vasaio : nei quai si tratta non solo la pratica ma brevemente tutti gli secreti di essa : cosa, che per sino al di, d'oggi èe stata sempre tenuta ascosta* / del Cipriano Piccolpasso.
[London? : H.M.S.O.? 1930].
3 v. : ill. ; 30 cm.
Spine title : Arte del vasaio. — Photographic reproduction of the 1557(?) manuscript in the National Art Library.

V.1930.019   *Victoria & Albert Museum : brief guide*.
[London : H.M.S.O.], 1930 (Printed by William Clowes & Sons).
18 p., [3] p. of plates : ill., plans ; 22 cm.
Index. — Printing: 6/30. — Stapled. Yellow wrappers.

1931

V.1931.001 *100 masterpieces. [ii], Renaissance and modern.*
London : Published under the authority of the Board of Education,
1931 (Printed by Waterlow & Sons).
[2] p., 100 p. of plates : ill. ; 20 cm.
V & A Publication no. 196. — Introduction / Eric Maclagan. — Buff wrappers with
overall pattern in three colours.

V.1931.002 *100 masterpieces. [iii], Mohammedan and Oriental.*
London : Published under the authority of the Board of Education,
1931 (Printed by Waterlow & Sons).
[4] p., 100 p. of plates : chiefly ill. ; 20 cm.
At head of title: Victoria & Albert Museum. — V & A Publication no. 202. —
Introduction / Eric Maclagan. — Buff wrappers with all-over pattern in 3 colours.

V.1931.003 *Brief guide to the Chinese embroideries.* Rev.
London : Published under the authority of the Board of Education,
1931 (Printed by William Clowes and Sons).
12 p., 1, viii p. of plates : ill. ; 19 cm.
At head of title: Victoria and Albert Museum. Department of Textiles. — V & A
Publication no. 144 T. — Select bibliography: p. 8–9. — Printing: 8/31. — Pale blue
wrappers.

V.1931.004 *Brief guide to the Turkish woven fabrics.* 2nd ed.
London : Published under the authority of the Board of Education,
1931 (Printed by Charles Whittingham and Griggs, Chiswick Press).
29 p., xvi p. of plates : ill. ; 19 cm.
At head of title: Victoria and Albert Museum, Department of Textiles. — V & A
Publication no. 148 T. — Re-written by A.J.B. Wace, with the assistance of C.E.C.
Tattersall. Preface / Eric Maclagan. — Bibliography: p. 29. — Dark green wrappers with
illustration.

V.1931.005 *Catalogue of English furniture & woodwork. Vol. IV, Georgian* / by
Ralph Edwards.
London : Printed under the authority of the Board of Education, 1931
(Printed by the Shenval Press).
viii, 95 p., 58 p. of plates : ill. ; 25 cm.
At head of title: Victoria and Albert Museum, Department of Woodwork. — V & A
Publication no. 201 W. — Preface / Eric Maclagan. — Bibliography: p. 80–82. General
and numerical indexes. — Grey wrappers, or blue cloth covered boards.

V.1931.006 *Dutch tiles, the Van den Bergh gift : a guide to the collection given to
the Museum by Henry Van den Bergh, Esquire, through the National
Art-Collections Fund* / by Bernard Rackham. 2nd ed.
London : Published under the authority of the Board of Education,
1931 (Printed by William Clowes & Sons).
35, [1] p., xx p. of plates : ill. ; 19 cm.
V & A publication no. 163C. — "Written . . . with the help of Mr. Herbert
Read"–Preface. Preface to 2nd ed. / Eric Maclagan. — Bibliography: p. 5. — Printing:
5/31. — Blue wrappers.

V.1931.007 *Exhibition of British and foreign posters.*
[London] : Published under the authority of the Board of Education,
1931 (Printed at the Kynoch Press, Birmingham).
72 p., viii leaves of plates : ill. ; 19 cm.

V & A Publication no. 200. — Written by Martin Hardie. Prefatory note / Eric Maclagan. — Includes indexes of donors and artists. — Pink wrappers, with illustration.
EXHIBITION: VX.1931.006

V.1931.008   *Guide to the Bayeux tapestry* / by F.F.L. Birrell. 3rd ed.
London : Printed under the authority of the Board of Education, 1931.
[6], 35 p., [1], xii p. of plates : ill. ; 25 cm.
At head of title: Victoria & Albert Museum. Department of Textiles. — V & A Publication no. 100 T. — Preface to the third edition / Eric Maclagan. — Bibliography: p. 28–29. Index. — "Printed under the authority of H.M.S.O. by William Clowes & Sons"–colophon, p. [35]. — Printing: 11/31. — Blue wrappers. — The Victoria and Albert Museum possesses two copies of the Bayeux Tapestry.

V.1931.009   *Guide to the collection of carpets.* 3rd ed. rev.
London : Published under the authority of the Board of Education, 1931.
68 p., [53] p. of plates : ill. ; 25 cm.
At head of title: Victoria & Albert Museum, Department of Textiles. — V & A Publication no. 111 T. — Revised by C.E.C. Tattersall. — Bibliography: p. 56–60.

V.1931.010   *Japanese colour prints* / by Edward F. Strange. 6th ed.
London, H.M.S.O., 1931 (Printed by William Clowes and Sons).
xii, 164 p., lxxxiv p. of plates : ill. ; 22 cm.
At head of title: Victoria and Albert Museum, Department of Engraving, Illustration and Design. — V & A Publication no. 89 E.I.D. — Note to 5th ed. / Eric Maclagan. — Includes bibliographic references. Chronology; signatures; index of artists. — Printing: 3/31. — Brown cloth covered boards; title stamped in gold. Or grey wrappers.

V.1931.011   *Paper casts and photographs of the mosaics in the Mosque of the Omeyyads at Damascus.*
London, 1931.
4 p.
Unseen. Record from OCLC.
EXHIBITION: VX.1931.001

V.1931.012   *A picture book in colour. I.*
[London] : Published under the authority of the Board of Education, 1931 (Printed at the Kynoch Press, Birmingham).
[2] leaves, 20 leaves of plates : col. ill. ; 17 cm.
At foot of title: Victoria and Albert Museum. — V&A Publication no. 197. — Wrappers with geometric design in red, black and white; title label pasted on.

V.1931.013   *A picture book in colour. II.*
London : Published under the authority of the Board of Education, 1931 (Printed at the Kynoch Press, Birmingham).
[2] leaves, 20 leaves of plates : col. ill. ; 11 x 17 cm.
At foot of title: Victoria and Albert Museum. — V & A Publication no. 198. — Wrappers with geometric design in red, black and white; title label pasted on.

V.1931.014   *A picture book of French art. I, Mediaeval.*
London : Published under the authority of the Board of Education, 1931 (Printed by Waterlow & Sons).
[4] p., 20 p. of plates : ill. ; 19 cm.
([Picture book] ; no. PB45)
At head of title: Victoria & Albert Museum. — Red wrappers.

V.1931.015   *A picture book of French art. II, Renaissance.*
               London : Published under the authority of the Board of Education
               1931 (Printed by Waterlow & Sons).
               [4] p., 20 p. of plates : ill. ; 19 cm.
               ([Picture book] ; no. PB46)
               At head of title: Victoria & Albert Museum. — Red wrappers.

V.1931.016   *A picture book of French art. III, Eighteenth century.*
               London : Published under the authority of the Board of Education
               1931 (Printed by Waterlow & Sons).
               [4] p., 20 p. of plates : ill. ; 19 cm.
               ([Picture book] ; no. PB47)
               At head of title: Victoria & Albert Museum. — Red wrappers.

V.1931.017   *A picture book of French art. IV, Nineteenth century.*
               London : Published under the authority of the Board of Education,
               1931 (Printed by Waterlow & Sons).
               [4] p., 20 p. of plates : ill. ; 19 cm.
               ([Picture book] ; no. PB48)
               At head of title: Victoria & Albert Museum. — Red wrappers.

V.1931.018   *The silk weavers of Spitalfields and Bethnal Green : with a catalogue
               and illustrations of Spitalfields silks* / by A.K. Sabin.
               London : Published under the authority of the Board of Education,
               1931.
               39 p., 6 leaves of plates : ill. ; 19 cm.
               At head of title: Bethnal Green Museum. Cover title: The silkweavers of Spitalfields and
               Bethnal Green. — V & A Publication no. 199 BGM. — Prefatory note / Eric Maclagan.
               — Grey wrappers with title and decoration printed in green and red.

V.1931.019   *[Victoria & Albert Museum : brief guide.*
               London : H.M.S.O., 1931.]
               19 p., 3 plates.
               Unseen. Listed in *List of publications : Victoria and Albert Museum* (London : Board of
               Education, July 1933).

1932

V.1932.001   *Catalogue of Italian sculpture* / by Eric Maclagan and Margaret H.
               Longhurst.
               London : Published under the authority of the Board of Education,
               1932 (Printed at the University Press, Oxford, by John Johnson).
               2 v. (xvi, 182 p., [1] leaf of plates ; xix p., 120 p. of plates) : ill. ; 26
               cm.
               At head of title: Victoria and Albert Museum, Department of Architecture and
               Sculpture. — (I): Text. (II): Plates. — "List of authorities quoted": p. xv-xvi. Index of
               artists and Museum numbers. — Dark green cloth covered boards or grey wrappers.

V.1932.002   *Notes on quilting.*
               London : Published under the authority of the Board of Education,
               1932 (Birmingham : Kynoch Press).
               14 p., [1], 16 p. of plates : ill. ; 19 cm.

At head of title: Victoria and Albert Museum, Department of Textiles. — "Select bibliography": p. 9. — Yellow textured wrappers.

V.1932.003   *A picture book of arms and armour.*
London : Published under the authority of the Board of Education, 1932 (Printed by Waterlow & Sons).
[4] p., 20 p. of plates : ill. ; 19 cm.
([Picture book] ; no. PB50)
At head of title: Victoria & Albert Museum. — Red wrappers.

V.1932.004   *A picture book of Corean pottery.*
London : Published under the authority of the Board of Education, 1932 (Printed by Waterlow & Sons).
[4] p., 20 p. of plates : ill. ; 19 cm.
([Picture book] ; no. PB51)
At head of title: Victoria & Albert Museum. — Red wrappers.

V.1932.005   *A picture book of English mediaeval wall-paintings.*
London : Published under the authority of the Board of Education, 1932 (Printed by Waterlow & Sons).
[4] p., [20] p. of plates : ill. ; 19 cm.
([Picture book] ; no. PB49)
At head of title: Victoria & Albert Museum. — Red wrappers.

V.1932.006   *A picture book of flowers in English embroidery.*
London : Published under the authority of the Board of Education, 1932 (Printed by Waterlow & Sons).
[4] p., [20] p. of plates : ill. ; 19 cm.
([Picture book] ; no. PB52)
At head of title: Victoria & Albert Museum. — Red wrappers.

V.1932.007   *Victoria & Albert Museum : brief guide.*
[London : H.M.S.O., 1932.]
18, [1] p., 2 p., 1 leaf of plates : ill. ; 21 cm
"July 1932." — Index. — Stapled. Yellow wrappers.

1933

V.1933.001   *Costume illustration : an index to the more important material in the library, with annotations and shelfmarks* / compiled by C.H. Gibbs-Smith.
London : [s.n.], 1933.
1 v., unpaged ; 34 cm.
At head of title: Victoria and Albert Museum. At head of second (typed) t.p.: Victoria and Albert Museum Library.

V.1933.002   *Exhibition of English mediaeval art, 1930 : illustrations.* 2nd ed.
London : Published by authority of the Board of Education, 1933 (Charles Whittingham and Griggs, printers, Chiswick Press).
x p., 100 p. of plates : ill. ; 21 cm.
At head of title: Victoria & Albert Museum. Cover title: English mediaeval art : illustrations. — V & A Publication no. 194. — Tan card wrappers with title and illustration printed in dark blue.
EXHIBITION: vx.1930.003

V.1933.003 *Guide to Italian maiolica* / by Bernard Rackham.
London : Published under the authority of the Board of Education,
1933 (Printed at the Kynoch Press, Birmingham).
xvi, [2], 97 p., 48 p. of plates : ill. ; 26 cm.
At head of title: Victoria and Albert Museum. — Preface / Eric Maclagan. —
Bibliography: p. [xi]–[xvii]. Numerical and subject indexes, and index of authors in the
bibliography. — Tan wrappers or cloth covered boards.

V.1933.004 *Notes on carpet-knotting and weaving* / by C.E.C. Tattersall. 3rd ed.
London : Published under the authority of the Board of Education,
1933 ("W.C. & S.", printer).
49 p., xii, [1] p. of plates : ill. ; 18 cm.
At head of title: Victoria and Albert Museum, Department of Textiles. — Preface / Eric
MacLagan. — Printing: 2/33. — Blue wrappers.

V.1933.005 *A picture book of bookbindings. Part I, Before 1550.* Rev.
London : Published under the authority of the Board of Education,
1933 (Printed by Waterlow & Sons).
[4] p., 20 p. of plates : ill. ; 19 cm.
([Picture book] ; no. PB17)
At head of title: Victoria & Albert Museum. — Orange wrappers.

V.1933.006 *A picture book of bookbindings. Part II, 1550–1800.* Rev.
London : Published under the authority of the Board of Education,
1933 (Printed by Waterlow & Sons).
[4] p., 20 p. of plates : ill. ; 19 cm.
([Picture book] ; no. PB18)
At head of title: Victoria & Albert Museum. — Orange wrappers.

V.1933.007 *A picture book of English embroideries. Part I, Elizabethan.* Rev. repr.
London : Published under the authority of the Board of Education,
1933 (Printed by Waterlow & Sons).
[4] p., 20 p. of plates : ill. ; 19 cm.
([Picture book] ; no. PB28)
At head of title: Victoria & Albert Museum. — Bibliography. — Orange wrappers. —
Previously Picture book no. 5.

V.1933.008 *A picture book of English embroideries. Part II, Stuart.* Rev. repr.
London : Published under the authority of the Board of Education,
1933 (Printed by Waterlow & Sons).
[4] p., 20 p. of plates : ill. ; 19 cm.
([Picture book] ; no. PB28)
At head of title: Victoria & Albert Museum. — Bibliography. — Orange wrappers.

V.1933.009 *A picture book of English tables.* Rev. repr.
London : Published under the authority of the Board of Education,
1933 (Printed by Waterlow & Sons, 1933 printing).
[4] p., 20 p. of plates : ill. ; 19 cm.
([Picture book] ; no. PB27)
At head of title: Victoria & Albert Museum. — Tan wrappers.

V.1933.010 *A picture book of Gothic sculpture.*
London : Published under the authority of the Board of Education,
1933 (Printed by Waterlow & Sons).

[4] p., 20 p. of plates : ill. ; 19 cm.
([Picture book] ; no. PB53)
Bibliography: p. [2]. — Orange wrappers.

V.1933.011　　A *picture book of Persian pottery.* Rev.
London : Published under the authority of the Board of Education,
1933 (Printed by Waterlow & Sons).
[4] p., 20 p. of plates : ill. ; 19 cm.
([Picture book] ; no. PB15)
At head of title: Victoria & Albert Museum. — Orange wrappers printed in black.

V.1933.012　　*Victoria & Albert Museum : brief guide.*
London : Printed under the authority of H.M.S.O. by William Clowes
& Sons, 1933.
18, [2] p., [1] leaf, 2 p. of plates : ill., plans ; 22 cm.
"November 1933." — Index of collections. — Stapled. Orange wrappers.

1934

V.1934.001　　*Catalogue of an exhibition in celebration of the centenary of William
Morris : held at the Victoria and Albert Museum, February 9–April 8.*
London : Published under the authority of the Board of Education,
1934 (Curwen Press, printer).
42, [2] p., [1], xi p. of plates : ill. ; 19 cm.
Cover title: Centenary of William Morris: catalogue of exhibition, 1934. — Foreword /
Eric Maclagan. Introduction / J.W. Mackail. — Includes list of lenders. — Wrappers
with William Morris design, and label-style title, printed in green.
EXHIBITION: VX.1934.001

V.1934.002　　*Exhibition of English silversmiths' work.*
[London : Victoria and Albert Museum? 1934.]
1 sheet, folded, [4] p. ; 19 cm.
Caption title.
EXHIBITION: VX.1934.005

V.1934.003　　*A picture book of dolls and dolls' houses.* Repr.
London : Published under the authority of the Board of Education,
1934 (Printed by Waterlow & Sons).
[4] p., 20 p. of plates : ill. ; 19 cm.
([Picture book] ; no. PB13)
At head of title: Victoria & Albert Museum. — Bibliography (3 items). — Red
wrappers.

V.1934.004　　*A picture book of English embroideries. Part III, Georgian.*
London : Published under the authority of the Board of Education,
1928 (Printed by Waterlow & Sons, 1934).
[4] p., 20 p. of plates : ill. ; 19 cm.
([Picture book] ; no. PB31)
At head of title: Victoria & Albert Museum. — Bibliography. — Red wrappers.

V.1934.005　　*A picture book of the work of John Constable.*
London : Published under the authority of the Board of Education,
1926 (Printed by Waterlow & Sons, 1934).

[4] p., [20] p. of plates : ill. ; 19 cm.
([Picture book] ; no. PB9)
At head of title: Victoria & Albert Museum. — Bibliography. — Red wrappers.

V.1934.006 *The three books of the potter's art : which treat not only of the*
practice but also briefly of all the secrets of this art, a matter which
until today has always been kept concealed / by Cavaliere Cipriano
Piccolpasso . . . .
London : Victoria and Albert Museum, under the authority of the
Board of Education, 1934 (Printed and bound at the Curwen Press;
collotype plates printed by Waterlow and Sons).
xxii, 85 p., 80 p. of plates : ill. ; 38 cm.
Added t.p.: Li tre libri dell' arte del vasaio nei quai si tratta non solo la practica ma
brevemente tutti gli secreti di essa, cosa che per sino al di d'oggi è stata sempre tenuta
ascosta del cavaliere Cipriano Piccolpasso Durantino. — "In the original Italian, with
translation and an introduction by Bernard Rackham . . . and Albert Van de Put"–
t.p. — Bibliography: p. xxi-xxii. — Tabby cloth covered boards; cream dust jacket. —
"750 copies of this book have been printed, of which 500 copies are for sale in England
and 250 copies for sale in the United States of America." — National Art Library
manuscript L.7446–1861.

V.1934.007 *Victoria & Albert Museum : brief guide.*
London : Printed under the authority of H.M.S.O. by William Clowes
& Sons, 1933.
18, [2] p., [1] leaf, 2 p. of plates : ill., plans ; 22 cm.
"March 1934." — Index of collections. — Stapled. Orange wrappers.

V.1934.008 *Water-colours in the Dixon bequest : twenty-four reproductions with*
biographical notes on the artists. Repr.
[London] : Published under the authority of the Board of Education,
1934 (Printed by William Clowes & Sons).
24 p., 24 p. of plates : ill. ; 18 cm.
At head of title: Bethnal Green Museum. — Written by Arthur K. Sabin. Note to reprint
/ Eric Maclagan. — Printing: 3/34. — Brown wrappers.

1935

V.1935.001 *Catalogue of Algerian embroideries* / by A.J.B. Wace. Rev. ed.
London : Published under the authority of the Board of Education,
1935 (Printed by William Clowes and Sons).
38 p., 7 p. of plates : ill. ; 19 cm.
At head of title: Victoria and Albert Museum, Department of Textiles. — Rewritten by
A.J.B. Wace. Preface by Eric Maclagan. — Bibliography: p. [23]. — Grey wrappers
printed in red.

V.1935.002 *Exhibition of English pottery and porcelain.*
[London : Victoria and Albert Museum ?, 1935.]
1 sheet, folded [4] p. ; 24 cm.
Caption title.
EXHIBITION: VX.1935.002

V.1935.003 *The Haynes Grange room* / by H. Clifford Smith.
London : Printed under the authority of the Board of Education, 1935
(Printed at the University Press, Oxford, by John Johnson).

27 p., [1], xiii p. of plates : ill., plan ; 26 cm.
At head of title: Victoria and Albert Museum, Department of Woodwork. — Prefatory
note / Eric Maclagan. — Bibliography: p. 27. — Grey paper covered boards. — The
room was previously at Houghton House.

V.1935.004   *The Victoria and Albert Museum : a short illustrated guide.*
[London] : Published under the authority of the Board of Education,
1935 (Printed by William Clowes & Sons).
31, [1] p. : ill., plans ; 21 cm.
Index to objects. — Printing: 2/35. — Cream wrappers printed in red, with a drawing of
the Museum.

1936

V.1936.001   *Catalogue of casts of elementary ornaments : fruits, leaves, vegetables,
etc. from nature, fishes, various (consisting of vases, shells etc.), and
certain heads and other parts of animals and birds treated as reliefs.*
[London : Victoria and Albert Museum, 1936?]
9 p. ; 29 cm.
Caption title. At head of title: Victoria and Albert Museum. — Apparently supplements
v.1936.002. (Printing order no. D 47543–1.) — Reproduced from typescript, stapled.

V.1936.002   *Catalogue of plaster casts.*
London : Victoria and Albert Museum, 1936.
69 p. ; 28 cm.
Cover title. At head of title: "1 April 1936." — "The long established business of D.
Brucciani & Co. Limited, makers of plaster casts, was taken over by the Board of
Education in 1922 . . . and is now included in the normal activities of the Victoria and
Albert Museum." — Reproduced from typescript. Ivory wrappers.

V.1936.003   *Chinese art : the Eumorfopoulos collection.*
London : Published under the authority of the Board of Education,
1936 (Printed by the Shenval Press).
23 p., 6, [1] p. of plates : ill. ; 19 cm.
Preface / George Hill, Eric Maclagan. — Grey wrappers printed in green.
EXHIBITION: vx.1935.003

V.1936.004   *Commemorative catalogue of an exhibition of models and designs by
Sir Alfred Gilbert : held at the Victoria and Albert Museum, Autumn
1936 /* E. Machell Cox.
[s.l. : s.n., 1936] (Printed at the University Press, Oxford, by John
Johnson).
35 p., [1], xxiii leaves of plates : ill. ; 26 cm.
Grey wrappers.
EXHIBITION: vx.1936.005

V.1936.004A   [Limited ed.]
"This edition, a tribute of admiration from Sigismund Goetze, is limited to one hundred
copies"–t.p. — Grey cloth covered boards, title stamped in gold.

V.1936.005   *Costume : an index to the more important material in the Library,
with annotations & shelfmarks, together with a guide to other
documentary material in the Museum /* by C.H. Gibbs-Smith. 2nd ed.
[rev.]
London : [s.n.], 1936.

211 leaves ; 36 cm.

At head of title: Victoria and Albert Museum, London. — "Vol. I, Sections I to III"–t.p.
In fact, work consists of 10 sections and 3 appendices and appears to be complete.
Variant t.p.: Costume bibliography : an index . . . . — Reproduced from typescript.

V.1936.006   *English pottery old and new.*
[London] : Published under the authority of the Board of Education,
1936 (Printed by Walter Lewis at the University Press, Cambridge).
56 p. : ill. ; 17 cm.

At head of title: Victoria and Albert Museum. — Prefatory note / Eric Maclagan, Frank
Pick. — Cover designed by E. McKnight Kauffer. — Boards covered in sized paper with
photographic illustration. Spine in blue cloth.
EXHIBITION: vx.1935.002

V.1936.007   *Exhibition of English domestic metalwork.*
[London : Victoria and Albert Museum? , 1936.]
1 sheet, folded [4] p. ; 20 cm.
EXHIBITION: vx.1936.003

V.1936.008   *A guide to the collections of stained glass* / by Bernard Rackham.
London : Printed under the authority of the Board of Education, 1936
(Printed by W. Lewis at the University Press, Cambridge).
xi, 140 p., 64 p. of plates : ill. ; 25 cm.

At head of title: Victoria and Albert Museum, Department of Ceramics. — Preface /
Eric Maclagan. — Bibliography: p. xi. Index of names and subjects, numerical index. —
Grey wrappers printed in dark blue, or blue cloth covered boards with title stamped in
gold on front and spine.

V.1936.009   *Illustrated supplement to the catalogue of plaster casts.*
London : Victoria and Albert Museum, [1936?] (Printed by William
Clowes and Sons).
23 p. : chiefly ill. ; 29 cm. + 3 p.

Accompanied by reproduced typescript index from the illustrations to the entries in the
Catalogue of plaster casts. (Printing order no. D 47994–1.)
Copy note: Another, printing 11/38, cross refers to v.1939.001.

1937

V.1937.001   *Brief guide to Persian embroideries.* [Repr.]
London : Published under the authority of the Board of Education,
1937 (Printed at the Chiswick Press).
19 p., xvi, [1] p. of plates: ill. ; 18 cm.

At head of title: Victoria and Albert Museum, Department of Textiles. Cover title:
Brief guide to the Persian embroideries. — V & A Publication no. 184 T. —
"The Guide has been prepared by Mr. Leigh Ashton . . . under the direction of
Mr. A.J.B. Wace"–Prefatory note / Eric Maclagan. — Bibliography: p. 15. — Green
wrappers.

V.1937.002   *Brief guide to the Persian woven fabrics.*
London : Published under the authority of the Board of Education,
1937 (William Brendon and Son, Plymouth, printer).
20 p., [1], xvi p. of plates : ill. ; 19 cm.

At head of title: Victoria and Albert Museum, Department of Textiles. — V & A
Publication no. 148 T. — Bibliography: p. 13. — Green wrappers.

V.1937.003   *Kings and queens of England, 1500–1900.*
London : Published under the authority of the Board of Education,
1937 (Lund Humphries, printer).
[4], 50 p., [1] leaf of plates : ill., geneal. table, ports. ; 18 cm.
At head of title: Victoria and Albert Museum. — Prefatory note / Eric Maclagan. —
Yellow wrappers printed on front with overall design and title, in tan.
EXHIBITION: VX.1937.003

V.1937.004   *A picture book of English chairs.*
London : Published under the authority of the Board of Education,
1937 (Printed by Waterlow & Sons).
[4] p., 20 p. of plates : ill. ; 19 cm.
([Picture book] ; no. PB4)
At head of title: Victoria & Albert Museum. — Red wrappers.

V.1937.005   *A picture book of English costume. Part 1, 17th century.*
London : Published under the authority of the Board of Education,
1937 (Printed by Waterlow & Sons).
[4] p., 20 p. of plates : ill. ; 19 cm.
([Picture book] ; no. PB54)
At head of title: Victoria & Albert Museum. — Bibliography. — Red wrappers.

V.1937.006   *A picture book of English costume. Part 2, 18th century.*
London : Published under the authority of the Board of Education,
1937 (Printed by Waterlow & Sons).
[4] p., 20 p. of plates : ill. ; 19 cm.
([Picture book] ; no. PB55)
At head of title: Victoria & Albert Museum. — Includes bibliographic references. —
Red wrappers.

V.1937.007   *A picture book of the Raphael cartoons.* Repr.
London : Published under the authority of the Board of Education,
1937 (Printed by Waterlow & Sons).
[4] p., 20 p. of plates : ill. ; 19 cm.
([Picture book] ; no. PB21)
At head of title: Victoria & Albert Museum. — Bibliography. — Red wrappers.

V.1937.008   *The Victoria and Albert Museum : a short illustrated guide.* Rev.
[London] : Published under the authority of the Board of Education,
1937 (Printed by William Clowes & Sons).
31 p. : ill., plans ; 21 cm.
Index to objects. — Cinnamon wrappers, with drawing of the Museum.

V.1937.009   *Victoria and Albert Museum : regulations for sketching, drawing and
the examination of museum objects.*
[London : H.M.S.O. under the authority of the Board of Education?,
1937.]
1 sheet, folded (4 p.) ; 25 cm.
At head of title: Board of Education. — "Rules 2." — Signed: Eric Maclagan. —
Printing: 3/37.

1938

V.1938.001 *Bethnal Green Museum : a short illustrated guide.*
[London] : Published under the authority of the Board of Education,
1938 (Printed by William Clowes and Sons).
27 p. : ill. ; 22 cm.
Green wrappers.

V.1938.002 *Brief guide to the Chinese woven fabrics.* Rev.
London : Published under the authority of the Board of Education,
1938 (Printed by the Shenval Press).
34 p., xvi p. of plates : ill. ; 19 cm.
At head of title: Victoria and Albert Museum Department of Textiles. — Written by
A.D. Howell Smith. Prefatory note / C.E.C.T[attersall]. — Bibliography: p. 24–26. —
Green wrappers.

V.1938.003 *Brief guide to the Western painted, dyed and printed textiles.* Rev.
London : Published under the authority of the Board of Education,
1938 (Printed by the Shenval Press).
32 p., xvi p. of plates : ill. ; 19 cm.
At head of title: Victoria and Albert Museum, Department of Textiles. — Revised by
Muriel Clayton. Prefatory note / C.E.C.T[attersall]. — Bibliography: p. 23. — Lavender
wrappers.

V.1938.004 *Catalogue of English domestic embroidery of the sixteenth &*
seventeenth centuries / by John L. Nevinson.
London : Published under the authority of the Board of Education,
1938 (Printed by Walter Lewis at the University Press, Cambridge).
xxviii, 107, 1 p., 1, lxxii p. of plates : ill. (1 col.) ; 25 cm.
At head of title: Victoria and Albert Museum, Department of Textiles. — Preface /
Eric Maclagan. — Bibliographies. General and numerical indexes. — Grey card wrapper
printed in orange or tan cloth covered boards, title stamped in black.

V.1938.005 *Notes on applied work and patchwork.*
London : Published under the authority of the Board of Education,
1938 (Shenval Press, printer).
18 p., 1 l. front., 16 pl. on 8 l. 18 1/2 cm.
At head of title: Victoria and Albert Museum, Department of Textiles. — "Select
bibliography": p. 13. — Yellow textured wrappers.

V.1938.006 *A picture book of English cupboards, cabinets and bookcases.* Rev.
London : Published under the authority of the Board of Education,
1938 (Printed by the Vandyck Printers).
[4] p., 20 p. of plates : ill. ; 19 cm.
([Picture book] ; no. PB10)
At head of title: Victoria & Albert Museum. — Previous title: A picture book of English
chests, cupboards and cabinets. — Dark green wrappers.

V.1938.007 *A picture book of English embroideries. Part IV, Chair seats and chair*
backs.
London : Published under the authority of the Board of Education,
1938 (Printed by the Vandyck Printers).
[4] p., 20 p. of plates : ill. ; 19 cm.
([Picture book] ; no. PB35)

At head of title: Victoria & Albert Museum. — Includes bibliographic references. — Dark green wrappers.

v.1938.008   *A picture book of flowers in English embroidery.* Rev.
London : Published under the authority of the Board of Education, 1938 (Printed by the Vandyck Printers).
[4] p., 20 p. of plates : ill. 19 cm.
([Picture book] ; no. PB52)
At head of title: Victoria & Albert Museum. — Dark green wrappers.

v.1938.009   *A picture book of Roman alphabets.* Rev. ed.
London : Published under the authority of the Board of Education, 1938 (Printed by the Vandyck Printers).
24 p. : ill. ; 19 cm.
([Picture book] ; no. PB32)
At head of title: Victoria & Albert Museum. — Dark green wrappers.

v.1938.010   *Technical exhibit of woven and printed furnishing textiles.*
[London : Victoria and Albert Museum, 1938?]
[4] p. ; 22 cm.
At head of title: Department of Engraving, Illustration and Design.
EXHIBITION: vx.1938.002

1939

v.1939.001   *Catalogue of an exhibition of early photographs : to commemorate the centenary of photography, 1839–1939.*
[London : Victoria and Albert Museum, 1939.]
5 p. ; 24 cm.
At head of title: Victoria and Albert Museum. — Printing: 12/38. — Reproduced typescript, stapled.
EXHIBITION: vx.1939.001

v.1939.002   *Catalogue of plaster casts.* [New ed.]
London : Victoria and Albert Museum, 1939.
73 p. ; 27 cm.
Cover title. At head of title: January 1939; All previous catalogues cancelled. — Printing: 10/38. — Stapled in white wrappers, spine taped in black.

v.1939.003   *Exhibition of tiles and tilework, old and new.*
[London : Victoria and Albert Museum, 1939.]
1 sheet, folded ([4] p.) ; 24 cm.
Caption title. At head of title: Victoria and Albert Museum.
EXHIBITION: vx.1939.002

v.1939.004   *A guide to the collection of tiles* / by Arthur Lane.
London : Published under the authority of the Board of Education, 1939 (Printed by the Shenval Press).
xi, 75 p., 48, [1], p. of plates : ill. ; 26 cm.
At head of title: Victoria and Albert Museum, Department of Ceramics. — Preface / Eric Maclagan. — Bibliographies at end of each chapter. Subject and numerical indexes. — Green wrappers, or cloth boards.

V.1939.005   *Historical notes on an exhibition of early photography.*
[London : National Art Library, 1939.]
1 sheet, folded, (4 p.) ; 22 cm.
At head of title: Victoria and Albert Museum.
EXHIBITION: vx.1939.001

V.1939.006   *Notes on carpet-knotting and weaving* / by C.E.C. Tattersall. 4th ed.
London : Published under the authority of the Board of Education,
1939 (William Clowes and Sons, printer).
42 p., 1 leaf, 12 p. of plates : ill. ; 19 cm.
At head of title: Victoria and Albert Museum, Department of Textiles. — Yellow
textured wrappers.

V.1939.007   *The Victoria and Albert Museum : a short illustrated guide.* Rev. ed.,
repr.
[London] : Published under the authority of the Board of Education,
1939 (Printed by William Clowes & Sons).
31 p. : ill., plans ; 20 cm.
Index to objects. — Printing: 8/39. — Cinnamon wrappers with drawing of the
Museum.

1940

V.1940.001   *Catalogue of Italian maiolica* / by Bernard Rackham.
London : Published under the authority of the Board of Education,
1940 (Printed by the Shenval Press).
2 v. (xxiii, 485 p., [1] leaf of plates) : ill. ; 26 cm.
At head of title: Victoria and Albert Museum Department of Ceramics. — Preface / Eric
Maclagan. — Vol. I. Text. Vol. II. Plates. — Bibliography: Vol. I, p. xix-xxiii. "Key to
shapes." General and numerical indexes. — Cloth boards or brown wrappers.

1941

V.1941.001   *Handbook to the W.G. Gulland bequest of Chinese porcelain :
including some notes on the subjects of the decoration.*
London : Board of Education, 1941.
57 p., xlviii p. of plates : ill. ; 21 cm.
At head of title: Victoria and Albert Museum. — Includes: The subjects of decoration on
Chinese porcelain / W.A. Thorpe. European influences on Chinese porcelain / Leigh
Ashton. — Buff card wrappers. — 12 copies only produced. — "The greater part of the
bequest has been assigned to the Department of Circulation"–p. 8.

1942

V.1942.001   *Catalogue of an exhibition of water colour drawings and sculpture,
1919–1939 : exhibited in Room 74, March to August 1942.*
[London : Victoria and Albert Museum, 1942.]
8 leaves ; 25 cm.
At head of title: Victoria and Albert Museum, Department of Paintings. — Cyclostyled
typescript.
EXHIBITION: vx.1942.001

1943

V.1943.001   *Catalogue of the drawings of the old masters from the Witt*
              collection : exhibited in Room 74, January to May, 1943.
              [London : Victoria and Albert Museum, 1943.]
              34 leaves ; 25 cm.
              At head of title: Victoria and Albert Museum, Department of Paintings. — Cyclostyled
              typescript.
              EXHIBITION: VX.1943.001

1945

V.1945.001   *Memorial exhibition to Edward Johnston : born 1872–died 1944 :*
              calligrapher : October-December 1945.
              [London : Victoria and Albert Museum, 1945] (Curwen Press,
              printer).
              16 p. : facsim. ; 18 cm.
              Cover title. — Foreword / Leigh Ashton. — Stapled; yellow wrappers.
              EXHIBITION: VX.1945.002

1946

V.1946.001   *Glass : a handbook for the study of glass vessels of all periods and*
              countries & a guide to the Museum collection / by W.B. Honey.
              London : Published under the authority of the Ministry of Education,
              1946 (Printed by the Shenval Press).
              xii, 169 p., 72 p. of plates : ill. ; 26 cm.
              Includes bibliographies. — Green wrappers.

1947

V.1947.001   *Costume illustration : the nineteenth century* / introduction by James
              Laver.
              London : Printed under the authority of the Ministry of Education,
              1947.
              8 p., [60] p. of plates : ill. ; 25 cm.
              (Large picture books ; no. 2)
              At head of title: Victoria and Albert Museum. — Cover title: Nineteenth century
              costume. — Foreword / Leigh Ashton. — Decorated wrappers printed in puce and
              black.

V.1947.002   *Drinking glasses.*
              London : Published under the authority of the Ministry of Education,
              1947 (Designed and printed by Lund Humphries).
              [4] p., 28 p. of plates : ill. ; 19 cm.
              (Small picture books ; no. 1)
              At head of title: Victoria and Albert Museum. — Introduction signed "W.B.H." [i.e.
              W.B. Honey]. — Grey wrappers, title printed in green; scribble decoration in blue.

V.1947.003   *English samplers.*
              London : Published under the authority of the Ministry of Education,
              1947 (Designed and printed by Lund Humphries).

[6] p., 26 p. of plates : ill. ; 18 cm.
(Small picture books ; no. 4)

At head of title: Victoria and Albert Museum. — Cover title: Samplers. — Introduction signed "G.B." [i.e. Gerard Brett]. — Includes technical notes. — Stapled; pink wrappers, with decoration, printed in blue and brown.

V.1947.004   *Exhibition of Wellington relics, June-August 1947 : catalogue.*
[London : Victoria and Albert Museum?, 1947.]
ii, 17 p. ; 20 cm.

Cover title. Caption title: Works of art and personal relics of the 1st Duke of Wellington: a selection kindly lent from his collections by His Grace the Duke of Wellington, for exhibition at the Victoria and Albert Museum. — Foreword / Leigh Ashton. — Printing: 5/47. — Printed typescript, stapled; buff wrappers printed in red.
EXHIBITION: VX.1947.006

V.1947.005   *Flowers in English embroidery.*
London : Published under the authority of the Minister of Education, 1947 (Designed and printed by Lund Humphries).
[6] p., 26 p. of plates : ill. ; 18 cm.
(Small picture book ; no. 2)

At head of title: Victoria and Albert Museum. — Introduction signed "G.B." [i.e. Gerard Brett]. — Includes technical notes. — Stapled; grey wrappers, with decorative title border, printed in rust and salmon.

V.1947.006   *Georgian furniture* / introduction by Ralph Edwards.
London : Published under the authority of the Ministry of Education, 1947 (Printed by Lund Humphries).
20 p., [100] p. of plates : ill. ; 25 cm.
(Large picture book ; no. 1)

Foreword / Leigh Ashton. — Includes bibliographic references. — Grey wrappers, with title and decoration on front cover printed in pink and ochre.

V.1947.007   *Nicholas Hilliard and Isaac Oliver : an exhibition to commemorate the 400th anniversary of the birth of Nicholas Hilliard* / monograph and catalogue by Graham Reynolds.
London : Published under the authority of the Ministry of Education, 1947 (Printed by the Shenval Press).
46 p., xlviii p. of plates : ill., ports. ; 25 cm.
(Victoria and Albert Museum handbooks ; no. 2)

Cover title: Nicholas Hilliard, 1547–1947. — Foreword / Leigh Ashton. — Bibliography: p. 21–22. Indexes of portraits and lenders. — Dust-jacket around wrappers, printed black and white on red.
EXHIBITION: VX.1947.005

V.1947.008   *Porcelain figures.*
London : Published under the authority of the Ministry of Education, 1947 (Printed by Lund Humphries).
[4] p., 28 p. of plates : ill. ; 19cm.
(Small picture book ; no. 3)

At head of title: Victoria and Albert Museum. — Introduction signed "W.B.H." [i.e. W.B. Honey]. — Stapled; buff wrappers, with decorative title border, printed in brown and blue.

Addendum [v.1947.009] *The Victoria and Albert Museum and its history.* — London : Victoria and Albert Museum, 1947. — 1 sheet ([2] p.); 25 cm. — Text dated January 1947. Printed in blue.

1948

V.1948.001 *Casts on sale to the public : a selected list.*
[London : Victoria and Albert Museum], 1948.
11 p. ; 33 cm.
Cover title. At head of title: Victoria and Albert Museum. — "January 1948." —
Printed typescript, stapled.

V.1948.002 *Christmas picture book.*
London : H.M.S.O., 1948 (Printed by Benham & Co., Colchester).
[4] p., [14] leaves of plates : ill. ; 18 cm.
(Small picture book ; no. 18)
At head of title: Victoria and Albert Museum. — Stapled; dark red wrappers with ill.
and border of stylised ferns around rules.

V.1948.003 *Elizabethan art.*
London : Published under the authority of the Ministry of Education,
1948 (Designed and printed by Lund Humphries).
[4] p., 28 p. of plates : ill. ; 18 cm.
(Small picture book ; no. 8)
At head of title: Victoria and Albert Museum. — Introduction signed by "G.R."
[i.e. Graham Reynolds]. — Stapled; grey wrappers; title with decorative border printed
in brown and green.

V.1948.004 *Elizabethan embroidery.*
London : Published under the authority of the Ministry of Education,
1948 (Designed and printed by Lund Humphries).
[3] p., 26 p. of plates : ill. ; 19 cm.
(Small picture book ; no. 5)
At head of title: Victoria and Albert Museum. Cover title: Elizabethan embroideries. —
Introduction signed: G.B. [i.e. Gerard Brett]. — Grey wrappers with green floral design
on front; title printed in black.

V.1948.005 *Indian art.*
London : Published under the authority of the Ministry of Education,
1948 (Designed and printed by Lund Humphries).
[4] p., 28 p. of plates : ill. ; 19 cm.
(Small picture book ; no. 7)
At head of title: Victoria and Albert Museum. — Introduction signed "J.C.I."
[i.e. J.C. Irwin]. — Stapled; salmon wrappers with title and motif printed in purple and
sky blue.

V.1948.006 *Portrait drawings.*
London : Published under the authority of the Ministry of Education,
1948 (Printed by Jarrold & Sons, Empire Press, Norwich).
[4] p., 28 p. of plates : ill. ; 19 cm.
(Small picture books ; no. 12)
At head of title: Victoria and Albert Museum. — Introduction signed "J.M." [i.e.
Jonathan Mayne?]. — Stapled; buff wrappers with decorated title printed in blue and
pink.

V.1948.007 *Portrait miniatures.*
London : Published under the authority of the Ministry of Education,
1948 (Printed by Jarrold & Sons Ltd, Empire Press, Norwich).
[4] p., xxviii p. of plates : ports. ; 19 cm.

(Small picture books ; no. 11)

At head of title: Victoria and Albert Museum. — Introduction signed "G.R." [i.e. Graham Reynolds]. — Stapled; grey wrappers printed in blue; grey border.

V.1948.008   *Tea-pots in pottery and porcelain.*
London : Published under the authority of the Ministry of Education, 1948 (Printed by Jarrold & Sons, Empire Press, Norwich).
[4] p., 28p. of plates : ill. ; 13 x 19 cm.
(Small picture books ; no. 9)

At head of title: Victoria and Albert Museum. Cover title: Teapots. — Introduction signed: A.L. [i.e. Arthur Lane]. — Stapled; cream wrappers, decorated, printed in black and grey.

V.1948.009   *Tudor domestic silver.*
London : Published under the authority of the Ministry of Education, 1948 (Designed and printed by Lund Humphries).
[5] p., 27 p. of plates : ill. ; 18 cm.
(Small picture book ; no. 6)

At head of title: Victoria and Albert Museum. — Introduction signed: "C.C.O." [i.e., Charles Chichele Oman]. — Stapled; grey wrappers with decoration; printed in grey and indigo.

V.1948.010   *Victorian paintings.*
London : Published under the authority of the Ministry of Education, 1948 (Printed by Jarrold & Sons, Empire Press, Norwich).
[4] p., 28 p. of plates : ill. ; 18 cm.
(Small picture books ; no. 10)

At head of title: Victoria and Albert Museum. — Introduction signed "G.R." [i.e. Graham Reynolds]. — Stapled; buff wrappers with illustration; title printed in ochre.

1949

V.1949.001   *The art of the book-jacket* / by Charles Rosner.
London : Published for the Victoria and Albert Museum by H.M.S.O., 1949 (Printed by Benham & Co., Colchester).
12 p. ; 22 cm.

Wrappers with turn-ins; calligraphic title printed in grey, white and red, one version on pale orange, another on pale mauve; designed by Hans Tisdall.
EXHIBITION: VX.1949.006

V.1949.002   *The art of the book jacket : an international exhibition of book-jackets from 19 countries : catalogue.*
[London : Victoria and Albert Museum, 1949.]
33 p. ; 33 cm.
Cover title. At head of title: Victoria and Albert Museum. — Printed typescript, stapled; buff wrappers.
EXHIBITION: VX.1949.006

V.1949.003   *Charles II domestic silver.*
London : H.M.S.O., 1949 (Printed by Benham & Co., Colchester).
[6] p., [26] p. of plates : ill. ; 18 cm.

Addendum [v.1948.011] *The Victoria and Albert Museum and its history.* — London : Victoria and Albert Museum, 1947. — 1 sheet ([2] p.); 33 cm. — Text signed "C.H. G-S" [i.e. Charles Gibbs-Smith], dated April 1948. Revision of v.1947.009

(Small picture book ; no. 17)

At head of title: Victoria and Albert Museum. — Introduction signed C.C.O.
[i.e. Charles Chichele Oman]. — Wrappers, decorated title printed black and white on
grey.

V.1949.004   *Christmas picture book.*
London : H.M.S.O., 1949 (Printed by Benham & Co., Colchester).
[4] p., [28] p. of plates : ill. ; 18 cm.
(Small picture book ; no. 18)

At head of title: Victoria and Albert Museum. — Buff wrappers with illustration and
decorative borders; printed black, blue, red and gold.

V.1949.005   *The development of European book-binding.*
[London : H.M.S.O., 1949] ("C.P.", printer).
1 sheet, folded ([4] p.) ; 25 cm.
(Victoria & Albert Museum introductory leaflet ; no. 1)

Caption title. — "prepared by the Circulation Department of the Victoria and Albert
Museum, in conjunction with the Department's travelling exhibition of European bookbinding"–p. [4]. — Printing: 6/49.

V.1949.006   *Donatello's relief of the Ascension with Christ giving the keys to St.
Peter* / by John Pope-Hennessy.
London : H.M.S.O., 1949 (Printed at the Kynoch Press, Birmingham).
12 p., [1], 12 p. of plates (1 folded) : ill. ; 25 cm.
(Museum monograph ; no. 1)

Green wrappers. Title printed to resemble label.

V.1949.007   *Early Christian and Byzantine art.*
London : H.M.S.O., 1949 (Printed by Benham & Co., Colchester).
[4] p., 28 p. of plates : ill. ; 18 cm.
(Small picture book ; no. 14)

At head of title: Victoria and Albert Museum. — Introduction signed "G.B." [i.e.
Gerard Brett?]. — Buff wrappers with decorated title and borders: red, green and black.

V.1949.008   *Early mediaeval art in the north.*
London : H.M.S.O., 1949 (Printed by Benham & Co., Colchester).
[6] p., [26] p. of plates : ill. ; 19cm.
(Small picture book ; no. 19)

At head of title: Victoria and Albert Museum. — Introduction signed "J.B."
[i.e. John Beckwith]. — Wrappers; calligraphic title printed in reverse on light brown.

V.1949.009   *European printed textiles.*
London : H.M.S.O., 1949 (Printed at the Kynoch Press, Birmingham).
14 p., [54] p. Of plates : ill. ; 25 cm.
(Large picture book ; no. 4)

At head of title: Victoria and Albert Museum. — Prepared by Gerard Brett. Foreword /
Leigh Ashton. — Bibliography: p. 11. — Cream card wrappers; title and all-over
decoration printed in maroon.

V.1949.010   *Figure drawings.*
London : H.M.S.O., 1949 (Printed by Benham & Co., Colchester).
[4] p., 28 p. of plates : ill. ; 18 cm.
(Small picture book ; no. 13)

At head of title: Victoria and Albert Museum. — Introduction signed "B.E.R."
[i.e. Brian Reade]. — Tan card wrapper, with illustration.

V.1949.011   *French paintings.*
                 London : H.M.S.O., 1949 (Printed at the Kynoch Press, Birmingham).
                 [4] p., 32 p. of plates : ill. ; 25 cm.
                 (Large picture book ; no. 3)
                 At head of title: Victoria and Albert Museum. — Text signed "G.R."
                 [i.e. Graham Reynolds]. — Wrappers coloured brown, with illustrative title.

V.1949.012   *A guide : June 1949.*
                 London : H.M.S.O., 1949 ("C.P.", printer).
                 35 p. ; 1 ill., 1 plan ; 25 cm.
                 At head of title: Victoria and Albert Museum — Stapled.

V.1949.012A   [Another issue]
                 September 1949.

V.1949.013   *Notes on applied work and patchwork.*
                 London : H.M.S.O., 1949 (McCorquodale & Co., printer).
                 18 p., 16 leaves of plates : ill. ; 18 cm.
                 At head of title: Victoria and Albert Museum. — Bibliography: p. 13. — Buff wrappers
                 with illustration.

V.1949.014   *Notes on carpet-knotting and weaving* / by C.E.C. Tattersall. 4th ed.,
                 reprint.
                 London : Published under the authority of the Board of Education,
                 1949 (McCorquodale & Co., printer).
                 42 p., xii, [1] p. of plates : ill. ; 19 cm.
                 At head of title: Victoria and Albert Museum. — Green wrappers with device.

V.1949.015   *Notes on quilting.* Repr.
                 London : H.M.S.O., 1949 (Printed by McCorquodale & Co.).
                 14 p., [1], 16 p. of plates : ill. ; 19 cm.
                 At head of title: Victoria and Albert Museum. — Prefatory note / Leigh Ashton.—
                 "Select bibliography": p. 9. — Grey wrappers with illustration.

V.1949.016   *The Virgin with the laughing Child* / by John Pope-Hennessy.
                 London : H.M.S.O., 1949 (Printed at the Kynoch Press, Birmingham).
                 10 p., [1], 12 p. of plates : ill. ; 25 cm.
                 (Museum monograph ; no. 2)
                 At head of title: Victoria and Albert Museum. — Foreword / Leigh Ashton. —
                 Bibliography: p. 10. — Wrappers, coloured tan, with photograph.

1950

V.1950.001   *Bookbindings* / by John P. Harthan.
                 London : H.M.S.O., 1950 (Printed by John Wright & Sons at the
                 Stonebridge Press, Bristol).
                 26 p., [64] p. of plates : ill. ; 22 cm.
                 (Illustrated booklet ; no. 2)
                 At head of title: Victoria & Albert Museum. — Bibliography: p. 17–18. Glossary. —
                 Cream wrappers, printed in gold.

V.1950.002   *Brief guide to Oriental painted, dyed and printed textiles.* Rev. ed.
                 London : H.M.S.O., 1950 (Printed by Benham & Co., Colchester).
                 20 p., [17] p. of plates : ill. ; 18 cm.

(Brief guide ; no. 3 [sic])

At head of title: Victoria and Albert Museum. — First ed. entitled Brief guide to the
Oriental painted, dyed and printed textiles. — Bibliography: p. 15. — Red wrappers
with decoration.

V.1950.003   *Brief guide to Persian embroideries.* Rev. ed.
London : H.M.S.O., 1950 (Printed by Benham and Co., Colchester).
11 p., 16 p. of plates : ill. ; 18 cm.
(Brief guide ; no. 2)

At head of title: Victoria and Albert Museum. Caption title: Brief guide to the Persian
embroideries .— Bibliography: p. 9. — Orange wrappers with decoration.

V.1950.004   *Brief guide to Persian woven fabrics.* [Rev. ed.]
London : H.M.S.O., 1950 (John Wright & Sons, printer, Bristol).
31 p. : ill. ; 18 cm.
(Brief guide ; no. 1)

At head of title: Victoria and Albert Museum. — First ed. entitled Brief guide to the
Persian woven fabrics. — Bibliography: p. 10. — Orange wrappers with ill.

V.1950.005   *Brief guide to Turkish woven fabrics.* Rev. ed.
London : H.M.S.O., 1950 (Printed by Benham & Co., Colchester).
23 p., 20 p. of plates : ill. ; 18 cm.
(Brief guide ; no. 3 [sic])

At head of title: Victoria and Albert Museum. — First ed. entitled Brief guide to the
Turkish woven fabrics. — Bibliography: p. 17. — Green wrappers with decoration.

V.1950.006   *Catalogue of English domestic embroidery of the sixteenth &*
seventeenth centuries / by John L. Nevinson. Repr.
London : H.M.S.O.,1950 (Printed by McCorquodale & Co.).
xxviii, 109, [1] p., [1], lxxii p. of plates : ill. (1 col.) ; 25 cm.

At head of title: Victoria and Albert Museum, Department of Textiles. — Preface to
second edition / Leigh Ashton: "Slight corrections have been made . . ., the bibliography
has been brought up to date." — Appendix: Accessions 1938–1948. — Bibliographies.
General and numerical indexes. — Grey wrappers, printed in orange.

V.1950.007   *Constable.*
London : H.M.S.O., 1950 (Printed by Benham & Co., Colchester).
[15] p., 33 p. of plates : ill. ; 19 cm.
(Small picture book ; no. 23)

Introduction signed "G.R." [i.e. Graham Reynolds]. — Olive green wrappers, with
illustration.

V.1950.008   *Dolls and dolls' houses.*
London : H.M.S.O., 1950 (Printed by McCorquodale & Co.).
[4] p., 28 p. of plates : ill. ; 18 cm.
(Small picture book ; no. 16)

At head of title: Victoria and Albert Museum. — Introduction signed "M.W."
[i.e. C.M. Weekley]. — Includes bibliographic references. — White wrappers with
coloured illustrated title.

V.1950.009   *Early Stuart silver.*
London : H.M.S.O., 1950 (Bristol : Printed by John Wright & Sons).
[4] p., [14] leaves of plates : ill. ; 18 cm.
(Small picture book ; no. 24)

At head of title: Victoria & Albert Museum. — Introduction signed "C.C.O." [i.e.
Charles Oman]. — Wrappers coloured grey.

V.1950.010
English samplers. Repr.
London : H.M.S.O., 1950 (Printed at the Curwen Press).
vi p., 26 p. of plates : ill. ; 18 cm.
(Small picture book ; no. 4)
At head of title: Victoria and Albert Museum. — Introduction signed "G.B."
[i.e. Gerard Brett]. — Grey wrappers with design in grey; title printed in red.

V.1950.011
English wrought-iron work.
London : H.M.S.O., 1950 (Printed by Benham and Co., Colchester).
[4] p. [14] leaves of plates : ill. ; 18 cm.
(Small picture book ; no. 20)
At head of title: Victoria and Albert Museum. — Introduction signed "J.F.H."
[i.e. John Hayward]. — Bibliography. — White wrappers, with decoration, and label-
style title, printed in orange and black.

V.1950.012
Exhibition of British stage design : from 19 April to 23 July 1950.
London : Victoria and Albert Museum, [1950].
1 sheet, folded ([2] p.) ; 22 cm.
Cover title, partly printed in red.
EXHIBITION: VX.1950.004

V.1950.013
Exhibition of Polish book illustration and book covers : catalogue.
[London : Victoria and Albert Museum, 1950.]
13 p. : ill. ; 21 cm.
Cover title.

V.1950.014
*Fifty masterpieces of pottery, porcelain, glass vessels, stained glass,
painted enamels.*
London : H.M.S.O., 1950 (Printed by F. Mildner & Sons).
103 p. : ill. ; 15 x 15 cm.
At head of title: Victoria & Albert Museum. Cover title: 50 masterpieces of pottery &
glass. — Card wrappers with device and geometrical border, printed on blue.

V.1950.015
Figure drawings.
London : H.M.S.O., 1949 (Colchester : Benham & Co., printer).
[4] p., 28 p. of plates : ill. ; 18 cm.
(Small picture book ; no. 13)
At head of title: Victoria and Albert Museum. — "June 1950." — Introduction signed
"B.E.R." [i.e. Brian Reade]. — Tan card wrappers, with illustration.

V.1950.016
Flowers in English embroidery.
London : H.M.S.O., 1950 (Printed by Benham & Co.).
[6] p., 26 p. of plates : ill. ; 18 cm.
(Small picture book ; no. 2)
At head of title: Victoria and Albert Museum. — Introduction signed "G.B."
[i.e. Gerard Brett]. — Card wrappers with coloured illustration on front; printed on
black.

V.1950.017
The Great Exhibition of 1851 : a commemorative album / compiled
by C.H. Gibbs-Smith.
London : H.M.S.O., 1950 (Printed by W.S. Cowell, Ipswich).
142 p. : ill. ; 22 cm.
At head of title: Victoria & Albert Museum. — Foreword / Leigh Ashton. —
Bibliography: p. 40. — Wrappers, with illustration, printed in yellow and maroon.
EXHIBITION: VX.1951.003

V.1950.018   *Guide to the Victoria & Albert Museum.* Rev. ed.
London : H.M.S.O., 1950 (Printed by Cheltenham Press).
74 p. : 1 ill., plans ; 25 cm.
Previously entitled: A guide. — "Winter 1949–50." — Printing: 1–50 (wrapper). — Stapled; orange wrappers printed in red-brown. — Loosely inserted: Supplement to the Victoria & Albert Museum guide : February 1950. 2, [2] p. ; 21 cm.

V.1950.018A   [Another issue]
"Autumn 1950." — Printing: 9–50 (wrappers). — Loosely inserted: Supplement to the Victoria & Albert Museum guide: May 1950; Victoria and Albert Museum guide : Supplement (Nov. 1950). Both 5 [1] p. ; 21 cm;. 5 [1] p. ; 21 cm.

V.1950.019   *Ham House : a guide* / by Ralph Edwards and Peter Ward-Jackson.
London : H.M.S.O., 1950 ("C.P. Ltd.", printer).
41 p. : ill. plans, ports. ; 21 cm.
At head of title: Victoria and Albert Museum. — Introductory note / Leigh Ashton. — Bibliography: p. 41. — Printing: 4/50. — Buff wrappers with decoration printed in brown, and engraved illustration.

V.1950.019A   [Another issue]
Reprinted June 1950.

V.1950.020   *Handbook to the W.G. Gulland bequest of Chinese porcelain : including some notes on the subjects of the decoration.* Repr.
London : H.M.S.O., 1950 (Printed at the Curwen Press).
57 p., xlviii p. of plates : ill. ; 21 cm.
At head of title: Victoria and Albert Museum. — Preface to the second edition / Leigh Ashton. The subjects of decoration on Chinese porcelain / W.A. Thorpe. European influences on Chinese porcelain / Leigh Ashton. — "The greater part of the bequest has been assigned to the Department of Circulation"–p. 5. — Grey wrappers, printed in red.

V.1950.021   *The history of Ham House* / by Ralph Edwards and Peter Ward-Jackson.
London : H.M.S.O., [1950].
10 p. ; 20 cm.
At head of title: Victoria and Albert Museum. — Date at end of text: "June 1950." — Stapled; no cover.

V.1950.022   *The Raphael cartoons* / introduction by John Pope-Hennessy.
London : H.M.S.O., 1950 (Printed by Waterlow & Sons).
10 p., 30 p. of plates : ill. ; 19 x 25 cm.
(Large picture book ; no. 5)
At head of title: Victoria & Albert Museum. — Foreword by Leigh Ashton. — Buff wrappers with decorated title, partly printed in purple.

V.1950.023   *Romanesque art.*
London : H.M.S.O., 1950 (Benham & Co., Colchester).
[4] p., 28 p. of plates : ill. ; 18 cm.
(Small picture book ; no. 15)
At head of title: Victoria and Albert Museum.

V.1950.024   *V & A Museum Circulation Department : its history and scope.*
London : Victoria and Albert Museum, [1950?] (Curwen Press,
printer).
7 p., [4] p. of plates : ill. ; 25 cm.
Pale green wrappers printed in brown.

1951

V.1951.001   *Arms and armour of old Japan* / by B.W. Robinson.
London : H.M.S.O., 1951 (Printed by F. Mildner & Sons).
18 p., 26 p. of plates : ill. ; 22 cm.
(Illustrated booklet ; no. 6)
At head of title: Victoria & Albert Museum. Cover title: Arms & armour of old Japan.
— Buff wrappers with illustration printed in tan.

V.1951.002   *British water-colours* / by Graham Reynolds.
London : H.M.S.O., 1951 (Printed at the Curwen Press).
56 p. : ill. ; 14 x 22 cm.
(Illustrated booklet ; no. 4)
At head of title: Victoria & Albert Museum. — Cover design by R.H. Mabey. — Card
wrapper, decorated title printed on grey.

V.1951.003   *Catalogue of a loan exhibition of Persian miniature paintings from
British collections.*
London : Printed for the Victoria and Albert Museum by H.M.S.O.,
[1951].
iv, 36 p. ; 20 cm.
Cover title. — Foreword / B.W. Robinson. — Includes bibliographic references. Index of
lenders. — Printing: 11/51. — Stapled; blue wrappers printed in black.
EXHIBITION: VX.1951.IND.002

V.1951.004   *Catalogue of drawings in the 'Recording Britain' collection given by
the Pilgrim Trust to the Victoria and Albert Museum.*
[London : The Museum, 1951.]
229 p. ; 22 cm.
Duplicated typescript.

V.1951.005   *Christmas picture book.* [Repr.]
London : H.M.S.O., 1951 (Colchester : Printed by Benham & Co.).
[4] p., [14] leaves of plates : ill. ; 18 cm.
(Small picture book ; no. 18)
At head of title: Victoria and Albert Museum. — Buff wrappers with illustration printed
blue and gold; decorative border in red.

V.1951.006   *Constable.* [Repr.].
London : H.M.S.O., 1951 (Colchester : Benham & Co., printer).
[48] p. : ill. ; 19 cm.
(Small picture book ; no. 23)
At head of title: Victoria & Albert Museum. — Introduction signed "G.R."
[i.e. Graham Reynolds]. — Olive green wrappers, with illustration.

V.1951.007   *Costume illustration : the seventeenth and eighteenth centuries* /
introduction by James Laver.
London : H.M.S.O., 1951 (Cover [printed] by Waterlow & Sons; text
and plates by W.S. Cowell, Ipswich).
10 p., [86] p. of plates : ill. ; 25 cm.
(Large picture book ; no. 9)
At head of title: Victoria and Albert Museum. Cover title: 17th and 18th century
costume. — Foreword / Leigh Ashton. — Wrappers, with colour illustration, printed on
tan.

V.1951.008   *Costume illustration : the nineteenth century* / introduction by James
Laver. Repr.
London : H.M.S.O., 1947 (Cover [printed] by Fosh & Cross ; text and
plates by the Curwen Press, 1951).
8 p., [60] p. of plates : ill. ; 25 cm.
(Large picture book ; no. 2)
At head of title: Victoria and Albert Museum. Cover title: 19th century costume. —
Foreword / Leigh Ashton. — Wrappers with colour illustration, printed on red.

V.1951.009   *Dolls and dolls' houses.* Repr.
London : H.M.S.O., 1950 (Printed by W.S. Cowell Ltd., Ipswich,
1951 printing).
[4] p., 28 p. of plates : ill. ; 18 cm.
(Small picture book ; no. 16)
At head of title: Victoria and Albert Museum. — Introduction signed "M.W."
[i.e. C.M. Weekley]. — Short bibliography.
— White wrappers with coloured illustrated title.

V.1951.010   *Early Christian and Byzantine art.* Repr.
London : H.M.S.O., 1951.
[4] p., 28 p. of plates : ill. ; 18 cm.
(Small picture book ; no. 14)
(V.1951.010)
At head of title: Victoria and Albert Museum. — Introduction signed "G.B."
[i.e. Gerard Brett]. — Buff wrappers with decorated title and borders: red, green and
black.

V.1951.011   *Elizabethan embroidery.* Repr.
London : H.M.S.O., 1951 (Printed by W.S. Cowell Ltd., Ipswich).
[6] p., 26 p. of plates : ill. ; 19 cm.
(Small picture book ; no. 5)
At head of title: Victoria and Albert Museum. — Introduction signed: "G.B."
[i.e. Gerard Brett]. — Includes technical notes. — Coloured all-over decoration on
wrappers; title printed label-style in red and yellow.

V.1951.012   *English embroidery* / by Barbara J. Morris.
London : H.M.S.O., 1951 (Printed by Waterlow & Sons).
48 p. : ill. ; 22 cm.
(Illustrated booklet ; no. 1)
At head of title: Victoria & Albert Museum. Cover title: The history of English
embroidery. — Bibliography: p. 15. Includes technical notes. — Cover design by
D.H. McKay. — Grey card wrappers printed in green and pink.

V.1951.013   *English samplers.* [Repr.]
London : H.M.S.O., 1951 (Printed at the Curwen Press).
vi p., 26 p. of plates : ill. ; 18 cm.
(Small picture book ; no. 4)

At head of title: Victoria and Albert Museum. — Introduction signed "G.B.".
[i.e. Gerard Brett]. — Buff wrappers with design in red; title printed in green.

V.1951.014   *European armour* / by J.F. Hayward.
London : H.M.S.O., 1951 (Printed by F. Mildner & Sons).
58 p. : ill. ; 21 cm.
(Illustrated booklet ; no. 5)

At head of title: Victoria & Albert Museum. Cover title: Armour. — Includes
bibliographic references. — Grey card wrappers printed with ill. in black and title in
blue.

V.1951.015   *Fifty masterpieces of metalwork.*
London : H.M.S.O., 1951 (Printed by F. Mildner & Sons).
103 p. : ill. ; 16 cm.

At head of title: Victoria & Albert Museum. — Card wrappers; title and device printed
on tan.

V.1951.016   *Fifty masterpieces of sculpture.*
London : H.M.S.O., 1951 (Printed by F. Mildner & Sons).
103 p. : ill. ; 15 cm.

At head of title: Victoria & Albert Museum. — Orange wrappers printed in black and
white.

V.1951.017   *Fifty masterpieces of textiles.*
London : H.M.S.O., 1951 (Printed by F. Mildner & Sons).
103 p. : ill. ; 15 cm.

At head of title: Victoria & Albert Museum. — Card wrappers; title and device printed
on pink.

V.1951.018   *Flowers in English embroidery.* Repr.
London : H.M.S.O., 1950 (Printed by W.S. Cowell Ltd., Ipswich,
1951).
[6] p., 26 p. of plates : ill. ; 18 cm.
(Small picture book ; no. 2)

At head of title: Victoria and Albert Museum. — Introduction signed "G.B."
[i.e. Gerard Brett] — Includes technical notes. — Card wrappers with coloured
illustration on front; printed on black.

V.1951.019   *Georgian furniture* / introduction by Ralph Edwards. Repr.
London : H.M.S.O., 1951 (Printed by John Wright and Sons at the
Stonebridge Press, Bristol).
20 p., [106] p. of plates : ill. ; 25 cm.
(Large picture book ; no. 1)

At head of title: Victoria & Albert Museum.— Foreword / Leigh Ashton. — Includes
bibliographic references. — Tan wrappers with cover decoration.

V.1951.020   *Guide to the Victoria & Albert Museum.* Rev. ed.
London : H.M.S.O., 1951 (Printed by Cheltenham Press).
86 p. : plans. ; 25 cm.

"Spring 1951." — Stapled; pink wrappers. — "For recent changes, see the loose
supplement inserted."

Supplement and corrections issued on single small sheets, dated January, March, April.

V.1951.021   *Ham House : a guide* / by Ralph Edwards and Peter Ward-Jackson.
2nd ed., rev. and enl.
London : H.M.S.O., 1951 (Printed at the Curwen Press).
60, [1] p. : ill., plans ; 21 cm.
Printing: 6/51. — Cream wrapper with illustration, and decoration printed in green.

V.1951.022   *A history of the English chair* / by Ralph Edwards.
London : H.M.S.O., 1951 (Printed at the Curwen Press).
30 p., [60] leaves of plates : ill. ; 25 cm.
At head of title: Victoria and Albert Museum. Cover title: English chairs. — Foreword /
Leigh Ashton. — Includes bibliographic references. — Green wrappers with border rule
in grey.

V.1951.023   *Indian embroidery.*
London : H.M.S.O., 1951 (Printed by W.S. Cowell Ltd., Ipswich).
9 p., [13] p. of plates : ill. ; 25 cm.
(Large picture book ; no. 7)
At head of title: Victoria and Albert Museum. — Written by John Irwin. Foreword /
Leigh Ashton. — Bibliography: p. 6. — Card wrappers with coloured illustration,
printed on green.

V.1951.024   *Queen Anne domestic silver.*
London : H.M.S.O., 1951 (Printed by F. Mildner & Sons).
[4] p., [28] p. of plates : ill. ; 18 cm.
(Small picture book ; no. 25)
At head of title: Victoria and Albert Museum. — Wrappers; title printed in decorative
border; grey background.

V.1951.025   *Supplement to the catalogue of water colour paintings by British
artists and foreigners working in Great Britain.*
ii, 98 p. ; 22 cm.
At head of title: Victoria and Albert Museum. — Compiled by J.H. Mayne. — List of
donors; index of place names. — Printing: 6/51. — Stapled; tan wrappers.

V.1951.026   *Swords & daggers* / by J.F. Hayward.
London : H.M.S.O., 1951 (Printed by Benham & Co., Colchester).
10 p., 32 p. of plates : ill. ; 22 cm.
(Illustrated booklet ; no. 3)
At head of title: Victoria and Albert Museum. — Wrappers; illustrated title printed in
black and red.

V.1951.027   *Tea-pots in pottery and porcelain.* Repr.
London : H.M.S.O., 1951 (Printed by W.S. Cowell Ltd., Ipswich).
[4] p.], 28 p. Of plates : ill. ; 12 x 18 cm.
(Small picture book ; no. 9)
At head of title: Victoria & Albert Museum. — Signed "A.L." [i.e. Arthur Lane]. —
Cream wrappers with photographic illustration and decoration printed in pink and
green.

1952

V.1952.001   *The centenary of the Victoria & Albert Museum* / by Sir Leigh Ashton.
[London : The Museum, 1952.]
8 p. ; 25 cm.
Caption title. — Stapled. No cover.

v.1952.002
Easter picture book.
London : H.M.S.O., 1952 (Printed by W.S. Cowell Ltd., Ipswich).
29 p. of plates, [1] p. : chiefly ill. ; 19 cm.
(Small picture book ; no. 30)
At head of title: Victoria and Albert Museum. — Tan wrappers with illustration and border; printed in green and black.

v.1952.003
English medieval silver.
London : H.M.S.O., 1952 (Printed by W.S. Cowell Ltd., Ipswich).
6 p., 25 p. of plates : ill. ; 18 cm.
(Small picture book ; no. 27)
Card wrappers, printed in grey with design.

v.1952.004
English prehistoric pottery.
London : H.M.S.O., 1952 (Ipswich : Printed by W.S. Cowell Ltd.; cover by Fosh & Cross).
[4] p., [28] p. of plates : ill. ; 19 cm.
(Small picture book ; no. 26)
At head of title: Victoria and Albert Museum. — By Hugh Wakefield. — Card wrappers with illustration, border and title in reverse on earth colour. — "The pottery illustrated . . . is all from a collection which has been gathered together by the Circulation Department of the Museum . . . the bulk of the material has been lent . . . by . . . the British Museum"–foreword.

v.1952.005
Exhibition of the Brunswick art treasures, 1952.
[London : H.M.S.O.?, 1952.]
7 [i.e. 8] p. ; 22 cm.
Caption title. At head of title: Victoria and Albert Museum. — Printing: 5/52. — No cover.
EXHIBITION: vx.1952.002

v.1952.006
Exhibition of Victorian and Edwardian decorative arts : catalogue.
London : H.M.S.O., 1952 (Text [printed] by Cheltenham Press; cover by Sanders Phillips & Co.).
149 p. ; 25 cm.
At head of title: Victoria & Albert Museum. Cover title: Catalogue of an exhibition of Victorian & Edwardian decorative arts. — Foreword / Leigh Ashton. Introduction / Peter Floud. — Includes bibliographic references. Indexes of artists, designers and manufacturers, and of lenders. — Printing: 10/52. — Card wrappers; printed with red allover design; label style title.
EXHIBITION: vx.1952.005

v.1952.007
Figure drawings. Repr.
London : H.M.S.O., 1952 (Printed by W.S. Cowell Ltd., Ipswich).
[4] p., 28 p. of plates : ill. ; 18 cm.
(Small picture book ; no. 13)
At head of title: Victoria and Albert Museum. — Introduction signed "B.E.R." [i.e. Brian Reade]. — Card wrappers coloured tan, with illustration on front.

v.1952.008
Glass table-ware. Repr.
London : H.M.S.O., 1952 (Printed by W.S. Cowell Ltd., Ipswich).
[4] p., 28 p. of plates : ill. ; 18 cm.
(Small picture book ; no. 1)
At head of title: Victoria and Albert Museum. Cover title: Glass. Original title: Drinking glasses. — Introduction signed "W.B.H." [i.e. W.B. Honey]. — Wrappers with illustration printed on grey.

V.1952.009   *The history of the Victoria & Albert Museum.*
               London : H.M.S.O., 1952 (Printed by W.S. Cowell Ltd., Ipswich).
               32 p. : ill. ; 16 cm.
               (Small picture book ; no. 31)
               Foreword by Sir Leigh Ashton. Prepared by C.H. Gibbs-Smith and Katharine
               Dougharty. — Stapled; cream wrappers, printed in blue and buff.

V.1952.010   *Indian art.* [Repr.]
               London : H.M.S.O., 1952 (Ipswich : Printed by W.S. Cowell Ltd.).
               [4] p., 28 p. of plates : ill. ; 19 cm.
               (Small picture book ; no. 7)
               At head of title: Victoria & Albert Museum. — Introduction signed "J.C.I."
               [i.e. John Irwin]. — Salmon card wrappers with illustrations.

V.1952.011   *Indian painting in the Punjab hills* / essays by W.G. Archer.
               London : H.M.S.O., 1952 (Ipswich : Printed by W.S. Cowell Ltd.).
               98 p. : ill. (1 col.), map ; 25 cm.
               (Monograph ; no. 3)
               At head of title: Victoria and Albert Museum. — Bibliographic references included in
               "Notes" (p. 85–92). — Buff wrappers; title printed in red; decorative borders.

V.1952.012   *Italian Gothic sculpture in the Victoria & Albert Museum* / by John
               Pope-Hennessy.
               London : H.M.S.O., 1952 (Printed by W.S. Cowell Ltd., Ipswich).
               30 p., 32 p. of plates : ill. ; 25 cm.
               (Museum monograph ; no. 5)
               At head of title: Victoria & Albert Museum. — Foreword / Leigh Ashton. — Cream
               wrappers with photograph; title printed reversed-out on dark red.

V.1952.013   *Japanese colour-prints* / introduction by Arthur W. Ruffy.
               London : H.M.S.O., 1952 (Printed by W.S. Cowell Ltd., Ipswich).
               24 p., 111 p. of plates : ill. ; 25 cm.
               (Large picture book ; no. 8)
               At head of title: Victoria & Albert Museum. Cover title: Japanese colour prints. —
               Foreword / Leigh Ashton. — Prints reproduced in b&w. Wrappers with colour
               illustration, printed on buff.

V.1952.014   *Masterpieces in the Victoria & Albert Museum.*
               London : H.M.S.O., 1952 (Printed by W.S. Cowell Ltd., Ipswich).
               [144] p. : chiefly ill. ; 25 cm.
               Foreword / by Sir Leigh Ashton. — Boards in blue cloth with title blind-stamped and
               image in gold, on front, pictorial dust-jacket, title printed in blue. Or pictorial wrappers.

V.1952.015   *Mid-Georgian domestic silver.*
               London : H.M.S.O., 1952 (Ipswich : Printed by W.S. Cowell Ltd.).
               [32] p. : ill. ; 18 cm.
               (Small picture book ; no. 28)
               At head of title: Victoria and Albert Museum. — Wrappers, decorated title, printed on
               grey.

V.1952.016   *A nonsense alphabet* / by Edward Lear.
               London : H.M.S.O., 1952 (Sanders Phillips & Co., printer).
               [36] p. : ill. ; 12 x 18 cm.
               (Small picture book ; no. 32)

At head of title: Victoria & Albert Museum. — Introduction by Brian Reade. — Salmon
card wrapper with illustration.

V.1952.017   *Persian paintings* / by B.W. Robinson.
               London : H.M.S.O., 1952 (Printed by W.S. Cowell Ltd., Ipswich).
               8 p., [28] p. of plates : ill. ; 24 cm.
               (Large picture book ; no. 6)
               At head of title: Victoria and Albert Museum. — Bibliography: p. 6. — Buff wrappers
               with decorative title in red and blue.

V.1952.018   *Porcelain figures.* [2nd imp.]
               London : H.M.S.O., 1952 (Printed by W.S. Cowell Ltd., Ipswich).
               [4] p., 28p. of plates : ill. ; 19 cm.
               (Small picture book ; no. 3)
               At head of title: Victoria and Albert Museum. — Introduction "W.B.H."
               [i.e. W.B. Honey]. — Card wrappers, with colour photograph, printed on pink.

V.1952.019   *Regency domestic silver.*
               London : H.M.S.O., 1952 (Printed by W.S. Cowell Ltd., Ipswich).
               [4] p., [16] leaves of plates : ill. ; 19 cm.
               (Small picture book ; no. 33)
               At head of title: Victoria and Albert Museum. — Card wrapper; title and outline
               illustration printed on grey.

V.1952.020   *Romanesque art.*
               London : H.M.S.O., 1950 (Printed by W.S. Cowell Ltd., Ipswich,
               1952).
               [4] p., 28 p. of plates : ill. ; 18 cm.
               (Small picture book ; no. 15)
               At head of title: Victoria and Albert Museum. — Introduction signed "J.B."
               [i.e. John Beckwith]. — Card wrappers; illustration, border and title in reverse on
               black.

V.1952.021   *Supplement to the Wellington Museum guide : the paintings (arranged
               by rooms, and from the left inside each doorway).*
               [s.l.] : Printed in Great Britain for H.M.S.O., 1952.
               xvi p. ; 21 cm.
               Caption title. — Index of painters. — Stapled. No cover.

V.1952.022   *Victoria & Albert Museum guide.* Rev. ed.
               London : H.M.S.O., 1952 (Printed by Cheltenham Press).
               120 p. : plans ; 25 cm.
               Previously entitled Guide to the Victoria & Albert Museum. — Edited by the
               Department of Museum Extension Services. — Index. — Printing: 5–52. — Blue
               wrappers, printed in brown.

V.1952.023   *Victorian and Edwardian decorative arts.*
               London : H.M.S.O., 1952 (Printed by W.S. Cowell Ltd., Ipswich).
               39 p. : ill. ; 18 cm.
               (Small picture book ; no. 34)
               At head of title: Victoria & Albert Museum. — "Issued in conjunction with the
               exhibition . . . held . . . to commemorate the centenary of the foundation of the Museum
               of Ornamental Art"–p. [2]. — Introduction signed "P.F." [i.e. Peter Floud]. — Buff
               wrappers with title panel and border in brown.
               EXHIBITION: VX.1952.005

V.1952.024   *The Virgin and Child by Agostino di Duccio* / by John Pope-Hennessy.
                London : H.M.S.O., 1952 (Printed by W.S. Cowell Ltd., Ipswich).
                16 p., [1], 10 p. of plates : ill. ; 25 cm.
                (Museum monograph ; no. 6)
                At head of title: Victoria and Albert Museum. — Cream card wrapper. Front cover
                printed with photograph, on grey.

V.1952.025   *The Wellington Museum, Apsley House : a guide* / by C.H. Gibbs-
                Smith and H.V.T. Percival.
                London : H.M.S.O., 1952 (Printed by W.S. Cowell Ltd., Ipswich).
                31 p., [8] p. of plates : ill., facsim., plan, ports. ; 22 cm. + xvi p.
                Cover title: Apsley House : a guide to the Wellington Museum. — "July 1952." —
                Foreword by Sir Leigh Ashton. — "Note. This provisional edition of the guide
                does not include a description of the pictures, which are dealt with in the loose
                supplement issued with this guide [i.e. v.1952.021]"–t.p. verso. — Bibliography:
                p. 31. — Stapled; cream wrappers with graphic illustration, printed black and in
                reverse, on red.

V.1952.025A   [Reissue]
                (Printed at the Curwen Press).
                Errata slip: Corrections to the picture supplement.

V.1952.025B.   2nd imp., corr.
                London : H.M.S.O., 1952 (Printed at the Curwen Press).
                "August 1952."

V.1952.026   *The Wellington Museum, Apsley House : a guide* / by C.H. Gibbs-
                Smith and H.V.T.Percival. 2nd (rev.) ed.
                London : H.M.S.O., 1952 (Printed by W.S. Cowell Ltd., Ipswich).
                51 p., [8] p. of plates : ill., facsim., plan, ports. ; 22 cm.
                Cover title: Apsley House : a guide to the Wellington Museum. — "October 1952." —
                Foreword / Sir Leigh Ashton. — Bibliography: p. 51. — Stapled; cream wrappers with
                graphic illustration, printed black and in reverse, on red. — Includes the paintings.

1953

V.1953.001   *Adam silver.*
                London : H.M.S.O., 1953 (Printed by W.S. Cowell Ltd., Ipswich).
                [4] p., [28] p. of plates : ill. ; 19 cm.
                (Small picture book ; no. 35)
                At head of title: Victoria & Albert Museum. — Wrappers with ill. printed white on
                grey.

V.1953.002   *Bazaar paintings of Calcutta : the style of Kalighat* / by W.G. Archer.
                London : H.M.S.O., 1953 (Printed by W.S. Cowell Ltd., Ipswich).
                76 p. : ill. ; 25 cm.
                (Museum monograph ; no. 7)
                At head of title: Victoria & Albert Museum. — Foreword / Leigh Ashton. —
                Bibliography: p. 16–17. Index.— Wrappers with colour illustration, printed on yellow.
                EXHIBITION: VX.1953.IND.002

V.1953.003   *Constable.* Repr.
                London : H.M.S.O., 1950 (Printed by W.S. Cowell Ltd., Ipswich,
                1953).

[14 p.], 33 p. of plates : ill. ; 19 cm.
(Small picture book ; no. 23)
At head of title: Victoria & Albert Museum. — Introduction signed "G.R."
[i.e. Graham Reynolds]. — Olive green wrappers, with illustration.

V.1953.004   *Early mediaeval art in the north.* Repr.
London : H.M.S.O., 1949 (Printed by W.S. Cowell Ltd., Ipswich, 1953).
[5] p., [27] p. of plates : ill. ; 19 cm.
(Small picture book ; no. 19)
At head of title: Victoria and Albert Museum. — Introduction signed "J.B."
[i.e. John Beckwith]. — Wrappers; calligraphic title printed in reverse on light brown.

V.1953.005   *Elizabethan art.* Repr.
London : H.M.S.O., 1953 (Printed by W.S. Cowell Ltd., Ipswich).
4 p., 28 p. of plates : ill. ; 18 cm.
(Small picture book ; no. 8)
At head of title: Victoria and Albert Museum. — Introduction signed "G.R."
[i.e. Graham Reynolds]. — Green decorated wrappers, printed in black and red.

V.1953.006   *Elizabethan embroidery.* 3rd imp.
London : H.M.S.O., 1953 (Printed by W.S. Cowell Ltd., Ipswich).
[6] p., 26 p. of plates : ill. ; 18cm.
(Small picture book ; no. 5)
At head of title: Victoria and Albert Museum. — Introduction signed "G.B."
[i.e. Gerard Brett]. — Includes technical notes. — Cream decorated wrappers, printed in black and red.

V.1953.007   *Exhibition at the Bethnal Green Museum to commemorate the bicentenary of the birth of Thomas Bewick, 1753-1828 : catalogue.*
London : H.M.S.O., 1953.
31 p. : ill. ; 19 cm.
At head of title: Victoria & Albert Museum. Cover title: Bicentenary of Thomas Bewick : Bethnal Green Museum exhibition catalogue. — Foreword / Leigh Ashton. — Printing: 8/53. — Stapled; illustration and title stretch across whole wrappers.
EXHIBITION: VX.1953.BGM.001

V.1953.008   *Exhibition of works by John Constable, R.A. : 1953.*
[London : Victoria and Albert Museum, 1953] ("S.P. & S.", printer).
7 p. ; 22 cm.
Caption title. At head of title: Victoria and Albert Museum. — Text by Graham Reynolds. — Stapled, no cover.

V.1953.009   *The golden age of Dutch silver.*
London : H.M.S.O., 1953 (Printed by W.S. Cowell Ltd., Ipswich).
[6] p., [14] leaves of plates : ill. ; 19 cm.
(Small picture book ; no. 29)
At head of title: Victoria & Albert Museum. — Text signed "C.C.O."
[i.e. Charles Oman]. — Card wrappers, decorated title printed in reverse on grey.

V.1953.010   *An introduction to practical embroidery : a new approach to embroidery design* / commissioned by the Circulation Department of the Victoria & Albert Museum and designed and carried out by Iris M. Hills.
London, H.M.S.O., 1953 (Printed by C.B.H.).

25 p. : col. ill. ; 33 cm.
At head of title: Victoria & Albert Museum. — Foreword / Leigh Ashton.
Introduction / Barbara Morris. — Orange cloth covered boards, title and design
embossed in white.

V.1953.011   *A nonsense alphabet* / by Edward Lear. 2nd imp.
London : H.M.S.O., 1952 (Printed by Sanders Phillips & Co.,
1953).
[36] p. : ill. ; 12 x 18 cm.
(Small picture book ; no. 32)
At head of title: Victoria & Albert Museum. — Introduction by Brian Reade. — Salmon
card wrapper with illustration.

V.1953.012   *Osterley Park : a guide* / by Peter Ward-Jackson.
London : H.M.S.O., 1953 (Text [printed] by Cheltenham Press, cover
by Sanders Phillips & Co.).
17 p. ; 22 cm.
At head of title: Victoria & Albert Museum. — Cover title: Guide to Osterley Park.
Introductory note / Leigh Ashton. — Bibliographic references. — Stapled; card
wrappers, printed black and white on grey.

V.1953.013   *Portrait drawings.*
London : H.M.S.O., 1953 (Text [printed] by W.S. Cowell Ltd., cover
by Sanders Phillips & Co.).
[4] p., 28 p. of plates : ports. ; 19 cm.
(Small picture book ; no. 12)
At head of title: Victoria and Albert Museum. — Card wrappers with illustration,
printed on grey.

V.1953.014   *Victorian paintings.*
London : H.M.S.O., 1948 (Printed by W.S. Cowell Ltd., Ipswich,
1953 printing).
[4] p., 28 p. of plates : ill. ; 18 cm.
(Small picture book ; no. 10)
At head of title: Victoria and Albert Museum. — Introduction signed "G.R."
[i.e. Graham Reynolds]. — Buff wrappers with illustration; title printed in red.

1954

V.1954.001   *Baroque, rococo & neo-classical sculpture* / by H.D. Molesworth.
[London] : H.M.S.O., 1954 (Printed by Clarke & Sherwell,
Northampton).
viii p., 48 p. of plates : ill. ; 29 cm.
(Large picture book ; no. 11)
At head of title: Victoria and Albert Museum. Cover title: Baroque sculpture. —
"This series of plates . . . the best examples of baroque, rococo and neo-classical
sculpture in the Victoria and Albert Museum". — Wrappers with photographs.

V.1954.002   *Catalogue of an exhibition of royal plate from Buckingham Palace
and Windsor Castle, by gracious permission of Her Majesty the
Queen.*
[London] : Published for the Victoria and Albert Museum by
H.M.S.O., 1954 (Printed by Fosh & Cross).
50 p. ; 22 cm.

Cover title: An exhibition of royal plate from Buckingham Palace & Windsor Castle. — Foreword / Leigh Ashton. Introduction / Charles Oman. Catalogue entries by John Hayward. — Printing: 2/54. — Stapled; grey wrappers.
EXHIBITION: vx.1954.001

V.1954.003   *English embroidery* / by Barbara J. Morris. Repr.
London : H.M.S.O., 1954 (Text [printed] by W.S. Cowell Ltd., cover by Sanders Phillips & Co).
15 p., 33 p. of plates : ill. ; 22 cm.
(Illustrated booklet ; no. 1)
At head of title: Victoria & Albert Museum. Cover title: The history of English embroidery. — Bibliography: p. 15. Includes technical notes. — Cover design by D.H. McKay. — Wrappers printed in green and pink on grey.

V.1954.004   *Exhibition of Rococo art from Bavaria : catalogue.*
[London] : H.M.S.O., 1954.
32 p. ; 25 cm. + 1 sheet.
Cover title. — Foreword / Leigh Ashton. Introduction / Theodor Müller. — Bibliography: p. 32. — List of lenders. — Printing: 10/54. — Stapled; buff wrappers; title printed in red.— Additions and corrections on separate sheet.
EXHIBITION: vx.1954.004

V.1954.004A   [Corrected]
32 p. ; 25 cm.
Printing: 11/54. — White wrappers.

V.1954.005   *Flowers in English embroidery.* 4th imp.
London : H.M.S.O., 1954 (Printed by W.S. Cowell Ltd., Ipswich).
[6] p., 26 p. of plates : ill. ; 18 cm.
(Small picture book ; no. 2.)
At head of title: Victoria & Albert Museum. — Introduction signed "G.B." [i.e. Gerard Brett]. — Card wrappers; with coloured illustration; printed on black.

V.1954.006   *Guide to the exhibition of Queen Mary's art treasures : May 26 to December 31, 1954.*
[London] : H.M.S.O., 1954.
23 p. ; 25 cm. + 1 sheet.
Cover title. At head of title: Victoria & Albert Museum, London. — Compiled by C.H. Gibbs-Smith and H.V. Percival. Foreword by Leigh Ashton. — Printing: 5/54. — Printed in blue. — Additions and corrections on separate sheet.
EXHIBITION: vx.1954.002

V.1954.006A   Repr. with minor corrections
23 p. ; 25 cm.
Printing: 6/54.

V.1954.006B   3rd imp.
Printing: 9/54.

V.1954.007   *International colour woodcuts : an exhibition arranged by the Victoria & Albert Museum, 1954–55.*
[London] : Published for the Victoria & Albert Museum by H.M.S.O., 1954 (Printed by W.S. Cowell Ltd., Ipswich).
[16] p., [4] p. of plates : ill. 22 cm.
Foreword / Leigh Ashton. — Cover designed by Frank Martin. — Wrappers with design in blue and brown.
EXHIBITION: vx.1954.005

v.1954.008   *Osterley Park : a guide* / by Peter Ward-Jackson. 2nd ed.
              London : H.M.S.O., 1954 (Text [printed] by Cheltenham Press; cover
              by Sanders Phillips & Co.).
              19 p., [8] p. of plates : ill., map, plan ; 22 cm.
              At head of title: Victoria & Albert Museum. — Introductory note / Leigh Ashton. —
              Includes bibliographic references. — Printing: 3/54.

v.1954.009   *A provisional check list of writing books & books on calligraphy :
              received in the library before 1890 and not in the current subject index
              : revised up to June, 1954* / J.I. Whalley.
              [London : National Art Library, 1954.]
              [13] leaves ; 33 cm.
              Includes bibliography. — Photographed pages of a typescript, bound together.

v.1954.010   *Queen Mary's art treasures.*
              London : H.M.S.O., 1954 (Text [printed] by W.S. Cowell Ltd.; cover
              by Sanders Phillips & Co.).
              5 [i.e. 6] p., [1], 18 p. of plates : ill., port. ; 25 cm.
              At head of title: Victoria and Albert Museum. — Introduction by Sir Leigh Ashton. —
              Wrappers, title and device printed in blue and white on blue.
              EXHIBITION: vx.1954.002

v.1954.011   *Rococo art from Bavaria : illustrations from the exhibition held at the
              Victoria & Albert Museum.*
              London : H.M.S.O., 1954 (Printed by W.S. Cowell Ltd., Ipswich).
              [4] p., 12 p. of plates : ill. ; 18 cm.
              Pink wrappers printed in purple.
              EXHIBITION: vx.1954.004

v.1954.012   *Royal plate from Buckingham Palace and Windsor Castle.*
              London : H.M.S.O. ; 1954 (Printed by W.S. Cowell Ltd., Ipswich).
              [4] p., 28 p. of plates : ill. ; 18 cm.
              (Small picture book ; no. 37)
              At head of title: Victoria and Albert Museum. — Introduction signed "C.C.O."
              [i.e. Charles Oman]. — Card wrappers, front printed on red.
              EXHIBITION: vx.1954.001

v.1954.013   Samson and a Philistine *by Giovanni Bologna* / by John Pope-
              Hennessy.
              London : H.M.S.O., 1954 (Printed by W.S. Cowell Ltd., Ipswich).
              20 p., 14 p. of plates : ill. ; 25 cm.
              (Museum monograph ; no. 8)
              Sized card wrapper. Photograph on front. Green at rear.

v.1954.014   *A second Christmas picture book.*
              London : H.M.S.O., 1954 (Printed by W.S. Cowell Ltd., Ipswich).
              [4] p., 28 p. of plates : ill. ; 18 cm.
              (Small picture book ; no. 38)
              At head of title: Victoria and Albert Museum. — Cream wrappers, with illustration and
              border, printed in orange, blue, gold and black.

v.1954.015   *Victoria & Albert Museum guide.* Rev. ed.
              London : H.M.S.O., 1954 (Printed by Cheltenham Press).
              116 p. : plans ; 25 cm.

Edited by the Department of Museum Extension Services. — "Spring 1954." — Index.
— Printing: 6–54. — Wrappers, printed in black and white on red.

V.1954.016   *The Wellington plate : Portuguese service (a baixela Wellington)* / by
Charles Oman.
London : H.M.S.O., 1954 (Printed by W.S. Cowell Ltd., Ipswich).
11 p., [28] p. of plates : ill. ; 25 cm.
([Museum monograph ; no. 4])
Foreword / Leigh Ashton. — Bibliography: p. 11. — Card wrapper with photographic
illustration.

1955

V.1955.001   *Bazaar paintings from Calcutta : catalogue of an exhibition lent by the
Victoria and Albert Museum, London.*
[London : H.M.S.O., 1955] (Printed by W.S. Cowell Ltd., Ipswich).
[8] p. ; 20 cm.
Cover title. — "Circulation exhibition catalogue no. 1." — Introduction signed "C.H."
[i.e. Carol Hogben?]. — Wrappers coloured yellow with coloured illustration.

V.1955.002   *Early Christian and Byzantine art.* 3rd imp.
London : H.M.S.O., 1955 (Printed by W.S. Cowell Ltd., Ipswich).
[4] p., 28 p. of plates : ill. ; 18 cm.
(Small picture book ; no. 14)
At head of title: Victoria and Albert Museum. — Introduction signed "G.B."
[i.e. Gerard Brett]. — Buff wrappers with decorated title and borders: red, green and
black.

V.1955.003   *English chintz.*
London : H.M.S.O., 1955 (Printed by W.S. Cowell Ltd., Ipswich).
[8] p., 32 p. of plates : ill. ; 18 cm.
(Small picture book ; no. 22)
At head of title: Victoria & Albert Museum. — Cover design by Roger Nicholson. —
Pink wrappers with decorated title printed in pink and green.
EXHIBITION: VX.1955.XXX.002

V.1955.004   *English chintz : two centuries of changing taste : an exhibition
assembled by the Victoria and Albert Museum at the Cotton Board,
Colour, Design and Style Centre, Manchester.*
London : H.M.S.O., 1955 (Cover printed by W.S. Cowell Ltd.,
Ipswich).
v, 58 p. ; 22 cm.
Cover title: Catalogue of an exhibition of English chintz: two centuries of changing taste
. . . . — Foreword / Donald Tomlinson. Introduction / Peter Floud. — Includes
bibliographic references. Index of designers, printers and merchants. Includes index. —
Cover design by Roger Nicholson. — Printing: 12/55. — Stapled; blue wrappers with
pictorial design printed in pink and black.
EXHIBITION: VX.1955.XXX.002

V.1955.005   *English embroidered pictures : lent by the Circulation Department,
Victoria and Albert Museum.*
London : H.M.S.O., 1955 (Printed by W.S. Cowell Ltd., Ipswich).
1 sheet, folded ([5] p.) ; 18 cm.
Printed in red on grey.

v.1955.006 *English wrought-iron work.* 3rd imp.
London : H.M.S.O., 1950 (Printed by W.S. Cowell Ltd., Ipswich, 1955).
[5] p. 27 p. of plates : ill. ; 18 cm.
(Small picture book ; no. 20)
At head of title: Victoria and Albert Museum. — Text signed "J.F.H." [i.e. John Hayward]. — Includes bibliography. — Cream card wrappers with black decoration and title printed label-style on orange. — 2nd imp. not traced.

v.1955.007 *European firearms* / by J.F. Hayward.
London : H.M.S.O., 1955 (Printed by W.S. Cowell Ltd., Ipswich).
[4], 53 p., xxxiv p. of plates : ill. ; 25 cm.
At head of title: Victoria and Albert Museum. — Foreword / Leigh Ashton. — Bibliography: p. 22. — Grey wrappers with illustration, printed in black and red. — "this work is . . . a guide to the Museum collection of firearms."

v.1955.008 *Exhibition of designs for theatrical decor and costume in England : held at the Victoria and Albert Museum, July 1st to July 31st, 1955.*
[London : The Museum?, 1955.]
8 p. ; 33 cm.
Duplicated typescript.
EXHIBITION: vx.1955.005

v.1955.009 *Fifty masterpieces of woodwork.*
London : H.M.S.O., 1955 (Printed by W.S. Cowell Ltd., Ipswich).
[103] p. : ill. ; 16 cm.
At head of title: Victoria & Albert Museum. Cover title: 50 masterpieces of woodwork. — Wrappers, coloured brown.

v.1955.010 *A history of English furniture.*
London : H.M.S.O., 1955 (Printed by W.S. Cowell Ltd., Ipswich).
26 p., 52 p. of plates : ill. ; 22 cm.
(Illustrated booklet ; no. 7)
At head of title: Victoria & Albert Museum. — Bibliography: p. 20. — Cover design by Edward Hughes. — Sized card wrapper with illustration printed on green.

v.1955.011 *Notes on carpet-knotting and weaving* / by C.E.C. Tattersall. 4th ed.; 3rd imp. with amendments.
London : H.M.S.O., 1955 (Printed by W.S. Cowell Ltd., Ipswich).
42 p., [1], xii p. of plates : ill. ; 19 cm.
At head of title: Victoria and Albert Museum. — Prefatory note / Leigh Ashton. — Bibliography: p. 38. — Buff wrappers with illustrations and title panel printed in red and black.

v.1955.012 *Shawls : a study in Indo-European influences* / by John Irwin.
London : H.M.S.O., 1955 (Printed by W.S. Cowell Ltd., Ipswich).
v, 66 p., 7, [48] p. of plates : ill. (some col.) ; 25 cm.
(Museum monograph ; no. 9)
At head of title: Victoria & Albert Museum. — Foreword / Leigh Ashton. — Bibliography: p. 52–55. Index. — Wrappers with title and illustration printed in red on yellow.

v.1955.013 *Sheffield plate.*
London : H.M.S.O., 1955 (Printed by W.S. Cowell Ltd., Ipswich).
[5] p., 30 p. of plates : ill. ; 18 cm.
(Small picture book ; no. 39)

At head of title: Victoria & Albert Museum. — Text signed "J.H." [i.e. John Hayward]. — Wrappers; printed in reverse on grey, with illustration.

V.1955.014   *Sophie Fedorovitch, 1893–1953 : a memorial exhibition of designs for ballet, opera and stage, arranged by the Victoria and Albert Museum.*
[London] : H.M.S.O., 1955 (Text [printed] by W.S. Cowell Ltd., Ipswich; cover by the Baynard Press).
16 p., [8] p. of plates : ill. ; 25 cm.
Cover title: Sophie Fedorovitch : an exhibition presented by the Victoria & Albert Museum. — Prepared by Carol Hogben. Tributes by Frederick Ashton, Marie Rambert, Richard Buckle. — Index of lenders. — Card wrappers with coloured illustration.
EXHIBITION: VX.1955.007

V.1955.015   *[Tea-pots in pottery and porcelain. 3rd imp?*
London : H.M.S.O., 1955.
[4] p., 28 p. of plates : ill. ; 13 x 19 cm.
(Small picture book ; no. 9)]
Not certain to exist. Cf. v.1957.013.

V.1955.016   *Turkish pottery.*
London : H.M.S.O., 1955 (Printed by W.S. Cowell Ltd., Ipswich).
[4] p., 28 p. of plates : ill. ; 18 cm.
(Small picture book ; no. 21)
At head of title: Victoria & Albert Museum. — Introduction signed "A.L." [i.e. Arthur Lane] — Card wrappers with decoration, in blue and green.

V.1955.017   *The Wellington Museum, Apsley House : a guide* / by C.H. Gibbs-Smith and H.V.T. Percival. 2nd ed., with amendments.
London : H.M.S.O., 1952 (Printed by W.S. Cowell Ltd., Ipswich, 1955).
51 p., [4] leaves of plates : ill., ports. ; 22 cm.
Cover title: Apsley House : a guide to the Wellington Museum. — Foreword / by Sir Leigh Ashton. — Bibliography: p. 51. — Stapled; cream wrappers with graphic illustration, printed black and in reverse, on red.

1956

V.1956.001   *English alabasters from the Hildburgh collection.*
London : H.M.S.O., 1956 (Printed by W.S. Cowell Ltd., Ipswich).
[4] p., 28 p. of plates : ill. ; 18 cm.
(Small picture book ; no. 36)
At head of title: Victoria & Albert Museum. — Introduction signed "T.H." [i.e. Terence Hodgkinson] — Bibliography: p. [4]. — Card wrappers; photograph on front, printed on dark green with floral motif.

V.1956.002   *English cutlery : sixteenth to eighteenth century* / J.F. Hayward.
London : H.M.S.O., 1956 (Printed by W.S. Cowell Ltd., Ipswich).
44 p. : ill. ; 21 cm.
At head of title: Victoria and Albert Museum. — Foreword / Trenchard Cox. — Pale blue wrappers with illustrated title. — "First published 1957 [sic]"- colophon.

V.1956.003   *English watches* / J. F. Hayward.
London : H.M.S.O., 1956 (Printed by W.S. Cowell Ltd., Ipswich).
[4], 10, [2] p., 47 p. of plates : ill. ; 21 cm.
At head of title: Victoria and Albert Museum. — Foreword / Trenchard Cox. —
Bibliography: p. [11]. — Cream card wrappers with illustrated title.

V.1956.004   *Exhibition of medieval paintings from Norwich (St. Michael at Plea)* :
18th July to 28th October 1956.
[London : H.M.S.O., 1956] (Printed by W.S. Cowell Ltd., Ipswich).
[7] p. ; 24 cm.
At head of title: Victoria and Albert Museum, London. — Preface / Trenchard Cox,
Anthony Blunt. Catalogue and introduction / by Pamela Tudor-Craig. — Short
bibliography. — Stapled. No cover.
EXHIBITION: VX.1956.008

V.1956.005   *A nonsense alphabet* / by Edward Lear. 3rd imp.
[London : H.M.S.O., 1956.
[36] p. : ill. ; 12 x 18 cm.
(Small picture books ; no. 32)]
Unseen. Listed in 4th imp. (V.1960.018).

V.1956.006   *Osterley Park : a guide* / by Peter Ward-Jackson. 2nd ed., 2nd imp.
with amendments.
London : H.M.S.O., 1954 (Text [printed] by Cheltenham Press; cover
by Sanders Phillips & Co., 1956).
19 p., [8] p. of plates : ill., plans ; 21 cm.
At head of title: Victoria & Albert Museum. Cover title: Guide to Osterley Park :
illustrated. — Introductory note / Trenchard Cox. — Includes bibliographic references.
— Printing: 3/56. — Grey card wrappers, printed in white and black.

V.1956.007   *Victoria & Albert Museum guide.* Rev. ed.
London : H.M.S.O., 1956 (Printed by Cheltenham Press).
110 p. : plans ; 25 cm.
Edited by the Department of Museum Extension Services. — "Spring 1956." — Index.
— Printing: 2–56. — Wrappers, printed in black and white on red.

1957

V.1957.001   *Chinese porcelain of the Ch'ing dynasty.*
London : H.M.S.O., 1957 (Printed by W.S. Cowell Ltd., Ipswich).
[4] p., 28 p. of plates : ill. ; 19 cm.
([Small picture book ; no. 41])
At head of title: Victoria & Albert Museum. — Introduction signed "A.L."
[i.e. Arthur Lane]. — Grey wrappers printed in blue and red.

V.1957.002   *English chairs* / with an introduction by Ralph Edwards. [Amended
repr.]
London : H.M.S.O., 1951 (Text [printed] by W.S. Cowell; cover by
Fosh & Cross, 1957).
26 p., [120] p. of plates : ill. ; 25 cm.
(Large picture book ; no. 10)
At head of title: Victoria & Albert Museum. Original title: A history of the English
chair. — Foreword / Trenchard Cox. — Includes bibliographic references. — Cream
wrappers with illustration.

V.1957.003   *Figure drawings.* 5th imp.
               London : H.M.S.O., 1949 (Printed by W.S. Cowell Ltd., Ipswich,
               1957).
               [4] p., 28 p. of plates : ill. ; 18 cm.
               (Small picture book ; no. 13)
               At head of title: Victoria and Albert Museum. — Introduction signed "B.E.R."
               [i.e. Brian Reade]. — Tan card wrappers, with illustration. — 4th imp. not traced.

V.1957.004   *Flowers in English embroidery.* 5th imp.
               London : H.M.S.O., 1947 (Printed by W.S. Cowell Ltd., Ipswich,
               1957).
               [6] p., 26 p. of plates : ill. ; 18 cm.
               (Small picture book ; no. 2)
               At head of title: Victoria & Albert Museum. — Introduction signed "G.B."
               [i.e. Gerard Brett]. — Includes technical notes. — Card wrappers; with coloured
               illustration; printed on green-grey.

V.1957.005   *French paintings.* 2nd imp., rev.
               London : H.M.S.O., 1949 (Printed by W.S. Cowell Ltd., Ipswich,
               1957).
               [4] p., 32 p. of plates : ill. ; 25 cm.
               (Large picture book ; no. 3)
               At head of title: Victoria and Albert Museum. — Introduction signed "G.R."
               [i.e. Graham Reynolds]. — Wrappers coloured brown, with illustrative title.

V.1957.006   *Ham House : a guide* / by Ralph Edwards and Peter Ward-Jackson.
               3rd ed., rev. and enl.
               London, H.M.S.O., 1957 (Printed at the Curwen Press).
               60, [1] p., 1 leaf of plates : ill., plans ; 22 cm.
               At head of title: Victoria and Albert Museum. — Introductory note / Trenchard Cox. —
               Bibliography: p. 60.

V.1957.007   *Henry Herbert Harrod bequest.*
               London : H.M.S.O., 1957.
               iii, 208 p. ; 22 cm.
               (Department of Engraving, Illustration and Design and Department of
               Paintings accessions, 1948, Vol. II)
               At head of title: Victoria and Albert Museum.

V.1957.008   *Hispano Moresque pottery.*
               London : H.M.S.O., 1957 (Printed by W.S. Cowell Ltd., Ipswich).
               [4] p., 28 p. of plates : ill. ; 18 cm.
               (Small picture book ; no. 40)
               At head of title: Victoria & Albert Museum. — Introduction signed "A.L."
               [i.e. Arthur Lane]. — Buff wrappers with decorative design in ochre; title printed in
               blue.

V.1957.009   *Medieval Near Eastern pottery.*
               London : H.M.S.O., 1957 (Printed by W.S. Cowell Ltd., Ipswich;
               cover by Fosh & Cross).
               [4] p., 28 p. of plates : ill. ; 18 cm.
               (Small picture book ; no. 42)
               At head of title: Victoria and Albert Museum. — Introduction signed "A.L." [i.e. Arthur
               Lane]. — Cream wrappers printed with design in russet and green.

V.1957.010   *Porcelain figures.* 3rd imp.
London : H.M.S.O., 1957 (Printed by W.S. Cowell Ltd., Ipswich).
[4] p., 28p. of plates : ill. ; 19cm.
(Small picture book ; no. 3)
At head of title: Victoria and Albert Museum. — Introduction signed "W.B.H." [i.e. W.B. Honey]. — Card wrappers, with colour photograph, printed on pink.

V.1957.011   *Printed books : a short introduction to fine typography* / T.M. MacRobert.
London : H.M.S.O., 1957 (Printed by W.S. Cowell Ltd., Ipswich).
7, [46] p. : ill. ; 31 cm.
Mainly reproductions of pages and title-pages of books in the Victoria and Albert Museum. — Bibliography: p. 7. — Grey wrappers with title decoration printed in brown.

V.1957.012   *Romanesque art.* New ed.
London : H.M.S.O., 1957 (Printed by W.S. Cowell Ltd., Ipswich).
[4] p., 28 p. Of plates : ill. ; 18 cm.
(Small picture book ; no. 15)
At head of title: Victoria and Albert Museum. — Introduction signed "J.B." [i.e. John Beckwith]. — Card wrappers with illustration and decorative border, chiefly black.

V.1957.013   *Tea-pots in pottery and porcelain.* 4th imp.
London : H.M.S.O., 1955 [i.e. 1957?] (Printed by W.S. Cowell Ltd., Ipswich, 1957).
[4] p., 28 p. of plates : ill. ; 13 x 19 cm.
(Small picture book ; no. 9)
At head of title: Victoria & Albert Museum. Cover title: Teapots. — Introduction signed A.L. [i.e. Arthur Lane]. — Card wrappers with ill.; decorated title in pink and green.

V.1957.014   *Victoria & Albert Museum guide.* Rev. ed.
London : H.M.S.O., 1957 (Printed by Cheltenham Press).
126 p. : plans ; 25 cm.
"Autumn 1957." — Index. — Printing: 9/57. — Wrappers coloured orange.
Copy note: Loosely inserted leaflet ([4] p.) concerning rearrangement of Rooms 1–3, and the new Paintings galleries, Rooms 103–106.

V.1957.015   *The Virgin with the laughing Child* / by John Pope-Hennessy. 2nd imp.
London : H.M.S.O., 1957.
10 p., 12 p. of plates : ill. ; 25 cm.
(Museum monograph ; no.2)
Bibliography: p. 10. — Unseen. Record from OCLC.

V.1957.016   *The Wellington Museum, Apsley House : a guide* / by C.H. Gibbs-Smith and H.V.T. Percival. 3rd (rev.) ed.
London : H.M.S.O., 1957 (Printed by W.S. Cowell Ltd., Ipswich).
55 p., [8] p. of plates : ill., facsims., plan, port ; 22 cm.
Cover title: Apsley House, a guide to the Wellington Museum. — Foreword / Trenchard Cox. — Bibliography: p. 55. Index of painters. — Stapled; cream wrappers with graphic illustration, printed black and in reverse, on red.

1958

V.1958.001   *The Andrews Diptych* / by John Beckwith.
London : H.M.S.O., 1958 (Printed by John Wright & Sons Ltd. at the Stonebridge Press, Bristol).
38 p., [5] leaves of plates : ill. ; 25 cm.
(Museum monograph ; no. 12)
At head of title: Victoria and Albert Museum. — Bibliography: p. 38. — Card wrappers with illustration, printed on red background.

V.1958.002   *Bottle-tickets.*
London : H.M.S.O., 1958 (Printed by W.S. Cowell Ltd., Ipswich).
[5] p., [13] leaves of plates : ill ; 12 x 18 cm.
(Small picture book ; no. 44)
At head of title: Victoria and Albert Museum. — Introduction signed "B.W.R." [i.e. Basil W. Robinson]. — Tan wrappers; illustration printed in brown, title in yellow.

V.1958.003   *Charles II domestic silver.* 2nd imp.
London : H.M.S.O., 1949, reprinted 1958 (Printed by John Wright & Sons at the Stonebridge Press, Bristol).
[5] p., [26] p. of plates : ill. ; 18 cm.
(Small picture book ; no. 17)
At head of title: Victoria and Albert Museum. — Introduction signed "C.C.O." [i.e. Charles Chichele Oman]. — Card wrappers, decorated title printed black and white on grey.

V.1958.004   *English furniture designs of the eighteenth century* / by Peter Ward-Jackson.
London : H.M.S.O., 1958 (Printed by W.S. Cowell Ltd., Ipswich).
viii, 68 p., [279] p. of plates : ill. ; 28 cm.
At head of title: Victoria & Albert Museum. — Preface / Trenchard Cox. — Bibliography: p. viii. Index of designers. — Boards covered in greenish-blue cloth. Grey dust jacket with decorated title, printed on green and black. — Illustrated with engravings and drawings from the collections of the Victoria and Albert Museum (Library and Dept. of Engraving, Illustration and Design), Sir John Soane's Museum and the Royal Institute of British Architects.

V.1958.005   *English prehistoric pottery.* 2nd imp.
London : H.M.S.O., 1952 (Printed by John Wright & Sons at the Stonebridge Press, Bristol, 1958).
[4] p., [28] p. of plates : ill. ; 19 cm.
(Small picture book ; no. 26)
At head of title: Victoria and Albert Museum. — Introduction signed "H.W." [i.e. Hugh Wakefield]. — Card wrappers with illustration, border and title in reverse on earth colour. "The pottery illustrated . . . is all from a collection which has been gathered together by the Circulation Department of the Museum . . . the bulk of the material has been lent . . . by . . . the British Museum"–foreword.

V.1958.006   *European firearms* / by J.F. Hayward. 2nd imp., rev.
London : H.M.S.O., 1955 (Printed by W.S. Cowell Ltd., Ipswich, 1958).
[4], 54 p., xxxiv p. of plates : ill. ; 25 cm.
At head of title: Victoria and Albert Museum. — Foreword / Trenchard Cox: "[T]his work is . . . a guide to the Museum collection of firearms". — Bibliography: p. 32. — Grey card wrappers with illustration, printed in black and red.

v.1958.007   *Exhibition of masterpieces of Byzantine art : sponsored by the Edinburgh Festival Society and arranged in association with the Royal Scottish Museum, Edinburgh, and the Victoria and Albert Museum, London : hand-list.*
[London : Victoria and Albert Museum, 1958] (Printed under the authority of H.M.S.O. by John Wright & Sons at the Stonebridge Press, Bristol).
14 p. ; 22 cm.
Stapled; no wrappers. — "Corrections" slip loosely inserted.
EXHIBITION: vx.1958.009

v.1958.008   *Fifty masterpieces of textiles.*
London : H.M.S.O., 1951, reprinted 1958 (Printed by John Wright & Sons at the Stonebridge Press, Bristol).
[104] p. : chiefly ill. ; 16 x 16 cm.
At head of title: Victoria & Albert Museum. Cover title: 50 masterpieces of textiles. — Card wrappers, with title and device printed on pink.

v.1958.009   *Georgian furniture* / introduction by Ralph Edwards. 2nd ed.
London : H.M.S.O., 1958 (Printed by W.S. Cowell Ltd., Ipswich).
23 p., [106] p. of plates : ill. ; 24 cm.
(Large picture book ; no. 1)
At head of title: Victoria & Albert Museum. — Ivory wrappers with design adapted from an 18th century trade card.

v.1958.010   *The Gloucester candlestick* / by Charles Oman.
London : H.M.S.O., 1958 (John Wright & Sons Ltd.).
14 p., 30 p. of plates : ill. ; 25 cm.
(Monograph ; no. 11)
Includes bibliography. — Wrappers in lilac with black and white ill. on front.

v.1958.011   *The history of the Victoria & Albert Museum.* Repr. with amendments
London : H.M.S.O., 1958 (Printed by W.S. Cowell Ltd., Ipswich).
32 p. : ill., plan, ports. ; 16 cm.
(Small picture book ; no. 31)
Prepared by C.H. Gibbs-Smith and Katharine Dougharty. Foreword / Trenchard Cox. — Stapled; wrappers, printed on orange.

v.1958.012   *An ordinary of British armorial bookbindings in the Clements collection, Victoria and Albert Museum* / by Denis Woodfield.
London : Victoria and Albert Museum, 1958.
191 p. ; 33 cm.
At head of cover: Victoria and Albert Museum. — Indexes of monograms and initials, mottoes and legends, names and titles. — Printed from typescript. Stapled in pink wrappers, spine taped.

v.1958.013   *Osterley Park : a guide* / by Peter Ward-Jackson. 2nd ed., 3rd imp. with amendments.
London : H.M.S.O., 1954 (Text [printed] by Cheltenham Press; cover by Sanders Phillips & Co., 1958).
19 p., [8] p. of plates : ill., plans ; 21 cm.

At head of title: Victoria & Albert Museum. Cover title: Guide to Osterley Park : illustrated. — Introductory note / Trenchard Cox. — Includes bibliographic references. — Printing: 3/58. — Stapled; grey card wrappers, printed in white and black.

V.1958.014   *The Raphael cartoons* / introduction by John Pope-Hennessy. 3rd imp. London : H.M.S.O., 1950, reprinted 1958 (Printed by John Wright & Sons at the Stonebridge Press, Bristol).
10 p., [30] p. of plates : ill. ; 18 x 25 cm.
(Large picture book ; no. 5)
At head of title: Victoria & Albert Museum. — Foreword / Trenchard Cox. — Buff wrappers. Reversed-out title in purple panel. Decorative border.

V.1958.015   *Roman lettering : a book of alphabets and inscriptions.*
London : H.M.S.O., 1958 (Printed by Jarrold & Sons, Norwich).
[38] p. : ill. ; 19 x 25 cm.
(Large picture book ; no. 12)
Cream card wrappers with title in reverse on tan panel; decorative border.

V.1958.016   *Twentieth century British water-colours : from the Tate Gallery and the Victoria & Albert Museum.*
London : H.M.S.O., 1958 (Printed by John Wright & Sons at the Stonebridge Press, Bristol).
9 p., 48 p. of plates : ill. ; 22 cm.
(Illustrated booklet ; no. 8)
At head of title: Victoria & Albert Museum. Cover title: Twentieth century water-colours. — Introduction signed "G.R." [i.e. Graham Reynolds]. — Yellow wrappers.
EXHIBITION: vx.1959.008

V.1958.017   *Wedgwood.*
London : H.M.S.O., 1958 (Printed by John Wright & Sons at the Stonebridge Press, Bristol).
[4] p., [28] p. of plates : ill. ; 19 cm.
(Small picture book ; no. 45)
Sized card wrappers with photograph; printed on blue.

V.1958.018   *William Morris.*
London : H.M.S.O., 1958 (Printed by John Wright & Sons, Bristol).
[2], [3] p., 27 p. of plates : ill. ; 18 cm.
(Small picture book ; no. 43)
At head of title: Victoria & Albert Museum. — Introduction signed "P.F." [i.e. Peter Floud]. — Includes technical notes. — Pale blue wrappers with William Morris design in green.

1959

V.1959.001   *17th and 18th century costume* / introduction by James Laver.
London : H.M.S.O., 1951, 1959 reprint (Printed by John Wright & Sons at the Stonebridge Press, Bristol).
10 p., [86] p. of plates : ill. ; 25 cm.
(Large picture book ; no. 9)
At head of title: Victoria and Albert Museum. Original title: Costume illustration: the seventeenth and eighteenth centuries. — Foreword / Trenchard Cox. — Card wrappers, with colour illustration, printed on tan.

v.1959.002   *Early keyboard instruments* / by Raymond Russell.
London : H.M.S.O., 1959 (Printed by John Wright & Sons at the Stonebridge Press, Bristol).
[4] p., 28 p. of plates : ill. ; 19 cm.
(Small picture book ; no. 48)
At head of title: Victoria and Albert Museum. — Sized wrappers, with illustration, printed on salmon.

v.1959.003   *Early Stuart silver.* 2nd imp.
London : H.M.S.O., 1950 (Printed by John Wright & Sons at the Stonebridge Press, Bristol, 1959).
[4] p., [14] leaves of plates : ill. ; 18 cm.
(Small picture book ; no. 24)
At head of title: Victoria & Albert Museum. — Introduction signed "C.C.O." [i.e. Charles Oman]. — Card wrapper; title and decorative border printed in reverse; black 'label' on grey.

v.1959.004   *Easter picture book.* 2nd imp.
London : H.M.S.O., 1952, reprinted 1959 (Printed by John Wright & Sons at the Stonebridge Press, Bristol).
29 p. : ill. ; 19 cm.
(Small picture book ; no. 30)
At head of title: Victoria and Albert Museum. — Cream wrappers, printed in black, green and gold.

v.1959.005   *Ham House : a guide* / by Ralph Edwards and Peter Ward-Jackson.
4th ed., rev. and enl.
London : H.M.S.O., 1959 (Printed by the Curwen Press).
60 p. : ill., plan ; 22 cm.
At head of title: Victoria and Albert Museum. — Introductory note / Trenchard Cox. — Bibliography: p. 60. — Cream card wrappers with illustration, partly coloured red.

v.1959.006   *Indian art.* 4th imp.
London : H.M.S.O., 1948 (1959 printing).
[4] p., 28p. of plates : ill. ; 19 cm.
(Small picture book ; no. 7)
At head of title: Victoria & Albert Museum. — Introduction signed by "J.C.I." [i.e. J.C. Irwin]. — Tan wrappers with illustrations. — 3rd imp. not traced.

v.1959.007   *Indian painting in Bundi and Kotah* / by W.G. Archer.
London : H.M.S.O., 1959 (Printed by John Wright & Sons Ltd., Stonebridge Press, Bristol).
v, 58 p., 56 p. of plates : ill., map ; 25 cm.
(Museum monograph ; no. 13)
At head of title: Victoria and Albert Museum. — Foreword / Trenchard Cox. — Includes a catalogue of Bundi and Kotah pictures in the Museum's collection. — Includes bibliographic references. — Sized wrappers, with illustration, printed on lime green.

v.1959.008   *Irish silver.*
London : H.M.S.O., 1959 (Printed by John Wright & Sons at the Stonebridge Press, Bristol).
[4] p., 28 p. of plates : ill. ; 18 cm.
(Small picture book ; no. 46)
At head of title: Victoria & Albert Museum. — Introduction signed "C.C.O." [i.e. Charles Chichele Oman]. — Green wrappers with illustration.

V.1959.009   *Mstislav V. Dobujinsky, 1875–1957 : memorial exhibition.*
              London : [Victoria and Albert Museum?], 1959.
              [24] p. : ill., port. ; 14 cm.
              At head of title: Victoria and Albert Museum. — Preface by James Laver. — Stapled;
              white wrappers.
              EXHIBITION: VX.1959.002

V.1959.010   *Norwegian art treasures : 900 years of textiles, sculpture and silver :
              hand list.*
              [London : Victoria and Albert Museum, 1959] (Printed under the
              authority of H.M.S.O. by John Wright & Sons at the Stonebridge
              Press, Bristol).
              15 p. ; 21 cm.
              At head of title: Victoria and Albert Museum. — Stapled; no cover.
              EXHIBITION: VX.1959.001

V.1959.011   *Notes on applied work and patchwork.* 3rd imp.
              London : H.M.S.O., 1959 (Printed by John Wright & Sons at the
              Stonebridge Press, Bristol).
              10 p., [1], 16 p. of plates : ill. ; 18 cm.
              At head of title: Victoria and Albert Museum. — Prefatory note / Trenchard Cox. —
              Select bibliography: p. [4]. — Printing: 1/60. — Cream wrappers; decorative border;
              title printed in purple.

V.1959.012   *Portrait miniatures.* 2nd imp.
              London : H.M.S.O., 1948 (Printed by John Wright & Sons Ltd. at the
              Stonebridge Press, Bristol, 1959).
              [4] p., xxviii p. of plates : ports. ; 18 cm.
              (Small picture book ; no. 11)
              At head of title: Victoria & Albert Museum. — Introduction signed "G.R."
              [i.e. Graham Reynolds]. — Buff wrappers with decorative title border printed in
              salmon.

V.1959.013   *Queen Anne domestic silver.* 2nd imp.
              London : H.M.S.O., 1951 (Printed by John Wright & Sons at the
              Stonebridge Press, Bristol, 1959).
              [4] p., [28] p. of plates : ill. ; 18 cm.
              (Small picture book ; no. 25)
              At head of title: Victoria and Albert Museum. — Introduction signed "C.C.O."
              [i.e. Charles Chichele Oman]. — Wrappers; title printed in decorative border; grey
              background.

V.1959.014   *Scandinavian silver.*
              London : H.M.S.O., 1959 (Printed by John Wright & Sons at the
              Stonebridge Press, Bristol).
              [4] p., 28 p. of plates : ill. ; 18 cm.
              (Small picture book ; no. 47)
              At head of title: Victoria & Albert Museum. — Introduction signed "C.C.O."
              [i.e. Charles Chichele Oman]. — Wrappers; design printed on turquoise.

V.1959.015   *A synopsis of 19th century women's fashions : a selection of 21
              drawings* / Victoria and Albert Museum.
              London : H.M.S.O., 1959 (Printed at the Curwen Press).
              1 sheet, folded ([4] p.) : chiefly ill. ; 23 cm.

Signed "C.H.G.-S." [i.e. Charles Gibbs-Smith]. — Drawings selected from those used in
V.1960.013.

V.1959.015A   [Another issue]
(Printed by John Wright & Sons at the Stonebridge Press, Bristol).
Unsigned — Printed on pink paper.

V.1959.016   *Tippoo's tiger* / Mildred Archer.
London : H.M.S.O., 1959 (Printed by John Wright & Sons at the
Stonebridge Press, Bristol).
30 p., [1], 22 p. of plates : ill., ports. ; 25 cm.
(Museum monograph ; no. 10)
At head of title: Victoria & Albert Museum. — Foreword / Trenchard Cox. Technical
aspects of Tipu's organ / Henry Willis. — Bibliography: p. 22–23. — Sized wrappers,
with photographic illustration.

V.1959.017   *Wedgwood bicentenary exhibition 1759–1959 : 23 June to 30 August
1959, Victoria and Albert Museum.*
[London : H.M.S.O.?, 1959] (Eyre and Spottiswoode, printers, at the
Thanet Press).
47 p., [12] p. of plates : ill. ; 22 cm.
Foreword / Trenchard Cox. Introduction / Arthur Lane. 'The tradition lives on', signed
"J.W., N.W.". — Errata slip pasted in at front. Additional catalogue entry (no. 318)
pasted in at end. — Stapled; white wrappers with title printed in grey; pink and grey
decorative border.
EXHIBITION: VX.1959.007

V.1959.018   *The Wellington Museum, Apsley House : a guide* / by C.H. Gibbs-
Smith and H.V.T. Percival. 3rd (rev.) ed., 2nd imp.
London : H.M.S.O., 1959 (Printed by John Wright and Sons, Bristol).
54, [1] p., [8] p. of plates : ill., plans ; 22 cm.
Cover title: Apsley House, a guide to the Wellington Museum. — Foreword / Trenchard
Cox. — Bibliography: p. [55]. Index of painters. — Loosely inserted: 1 sheet, 'Notes on
the rearrangement of the rooms'.

1960

V.1960.001   *The basic stitches of embroidery* / by N. Victoria Wade.
London : H.M.S.O., 1960 (Printed by John Wright and Sons, Bristol).
[27] p. : ill. ; 25 cm.
At head of title: Victoria & Albert Museum. — Foreword by Trenchard Cox. — Ivory
wrappers, with decoration, printed in red.

V.1960.002   *British pewter.*
London : H.M.S.O., 1960 (Printed by John Wright & Sons at the
Stonebridge Press, Bristol).
[4] p., 28 p. of plates : ill. ; 18 cm.
(Small picture book ; no. 54)
At head of title: Victoria and Albert Museum. — Introduction signed "C.B."
[i.e. Claude Blair]. — Sized wrappers; title and device printed on black.

V.1960.003   *Caskets from Cordoba* / by John Beckwith.
London : H.M.S.O., 1960 (Printed by John Wright & Sons at the
Stonebridge Press, Bristol).
72 p. : ill., map ; 25 cm.

([Museum monograph ; no. 14])
At head of title: Victoria and Albert Museum. — Bibliography: p. 36. — Sized
wrappers; all-over decoration in pink; title printed in green.

v.1960.004   *Catalogue of a loan exhibition of English chintz : English printed
furnishing fabrics from their origins until the present day : Victoria
and Albert Museum, London, May 18th to July 17th, 1960.*
London : H.M.S.O., 1960 (Printed by John Wright and Sons, Bristol).
[4], 75 p. ; 21 cm.
Introduction / Trenchard Cox. — Includes bibliographic references. Index of designers,
printers and merchants, and of lenders. — Stapled; illustrated wrappers printed in blue.
EXHIBITION: vx.1960.005

v.1960.005   *Catalogue of the Constable collection* / by Graham Reynolds.
London : H.M.S.O., 1960 (Printed by John Wright & Sons at the
Stonebridge Press, Bristol).
vii, 260 p., 310, [1] p. of plates : ill. (1 col.) ; 26 cm.
At head of title: Victoria and Albert Museum. Spine title: Catalogue of the Constable
collection in the Victoria and Albert Museum. — Foreword / Trenchard Cox. —
Bibliography: p. 242–243. Index, concordance of Museum numbers. — Green cloth
covered boards; dust-jacket with coloured illustration.

v.1960.006   *Catalogue of the Tiepolo drawings in the Victoria and Albert Museum*
/ by George Knox.
London : H.M.S.O., 1960 (Text printed by W.S. Cowell Ltd., litho
plates by Sanders Phillips & Co.).
xi, 111 p., [178] p. of plates : ill. ; 28 cm.
At head of title: Victoria and Albert Museum. — Foreword / Trenchard Cox. —
Bibliography: p. 100–102. Index, concordance of Museum numbers. — Red cloth
covered boards; white dust-jacket with ill.; title printed in red.

v.1960.007   *Chests of drawers and commodes in the Victoria and Albert Museum* /
by John F. Hayward.
London : H.M.S.O., 1960 (Printed by John Wright & Sons at the
Stonebridge Press, Bristol).
44 p. : ill. ; 22 cm.
(Illustrated booklet ; no. 9)
Stapled; sized wrappers with illustration printed in brown.

v.1960.008   *Cream-coloured earthenware.*
London : H.M.S.O., 1960 (Printed by John Wright & Sons Ltd. at the
Stonebridge Press, Bristol).
[4] p., [28] p. of plates : ill. ; 18 cm.
(Small picture book ; no. 53)
At head of title: Victoria & Albert Museum. — Text signed "J.E.L." [i.e. J.E. Lowy]. —
Cream wrappers with decorated title printed in tan and black.

v.1960.009   *Dolls.*
London : H.M.S.O., 1960 (Printed by John Wright & Sons at the
Stonebridge Press, Bristol).
[4] p., 28 p. of plates : ill. ; 18 cm.
(Small picture book ; no. 50)
At head of title: Victoria & Albert Museum. — Text signed "M.B." [i.e. Madeleine
Blumstein]. — Sized wrappers with photograph printed on patterned green
background.

V.1960.010   *Dolls' houses.*
                London : H.M.S.O., 1960 (Printed by John Wright & Sons at the
                Stonebridge Press, Bristol).
                [4] p., 28 p. of plates : ill. ; 12 x 19 cm.
                ([Small picture book ; no. 51])
                At head of title: Victoria and Albert Museum. — Introduction signed "C.M.W." [i.e.
                C.M. Weekley]. — Bibliography (2 items): p. [4]. — Sized wrappers with illustration.
                Title printed on pink.

V.1960.011   *English printed textiles, 1720–1836.*
                London : H.M.S.O., 1960 (Printed by John Wright & Sons, the
                Stonebridge Press, Bristol).
                76 p. : ill. ; 25 cm.
                (Large picture book ; no. 13)
                At head of title: Victoria and Albert Museum. — Foreword / Trenchard Cox. Compiled
                by Peter Floud.— Bibliography: p. 79. — Sized wrappers with floral pattern in salmon;
                title printed in black.

V.1960.012   *The engravings of Eric Gill : the gift of Mrs. Mary Gill.*
                London : H.M.S.O., 1960.
                v, 265 p. ; 22 cm.
                (Department of Engraving, Illustration and Design and Department of
                Paintings accessions, 1952, Vol. II)
                At head of title: Victoria and Albert Museum. — "The catalogue is the work of . . .
                J.F. Physick"–Foreword / Trenchard Cox.

V.1960.013   *The fashionable lady in the 19th century* / by Charles H. Gibbs-Smith.
                London, H.M.S.O., 1960 (Printed by John Wright & Sons at the
                Stonebridge Press, Bristol).
                184 p. : chiefly ill. ; 26 cm.
                At head of title: Victoria and Albert Museum. — Foreword / Trenchard Cox. —
                Bibliography: p. 181; Sources: p. 182–184. — Red cloth covered boards, with blind-
                stamped illustration; cream dust-jacket with coloured illustration.

V.1960.014   *French domestic silver.*
                London : H.M.S.O., 1960 (Printed by John Wright and Sons).
                [5] p., 27 p. of plates : ill. ; 18 cm.
                (Small picture book ; no. 52)
                At head of title: Victoria and Albert Museum. — Text signed "C.C.O."
                [i.e. Charles Chichele Oman]. — Yellow wrappers with illustrative title.

V.1960.015   *German and Swiss domestic silver of the Gothic period.*
                London : H.M.S.O., 1960 (Printed by John Wright & Sons at the
                Stonebridge Press, Bristol).
                [4] p., [27] p. of plates : ill. ; 18 cm.
                (Small picture book ; no. 55)
                At head of title: Victoria & Albert Museum. — Introduction signed "C.C.O."
                [i.e. Charles Chichele Oman]. — Sized wrappers with photograph on front, printed on
                red.

V.1960.016   *A guide to the collection of tiles* / by Arthur Lane. 2nd ed.
                London : H.M.S.O., 1960 (Printed by John Wright & Sons at the
                Stonebridge Press, Bristol).
                xi, 88 p., [1], 48 p. of plates : ill. ; 25 cm.

At head of title: Victoria and Albert Museum. — Foreword / Trenchard Cox. —
Bibliographies at end of each chapter. Subject and numerical indexes. — Black cloth
covered boards, illustrated dust-jacket.

V.1960.017   *Heraldry.*
London : H.M.S.O., 1960 (Printed by John Wright & Sons,
Bristol).
[3] p., [29] p. Of plates : ill., 18 cm.
(Small picture book ; no. 49)
At head of title: Victoria and Albert Museum. Cover title: Heraldry in the Victoria &
Albert Museum. — Text by John A. Goodall. — Sized wrappers with photographic
illustration, printed on orange.

V.1960.018   *A nonsense alphabet* / by Edward Lear. 4th imp. with
amendments.
London : H.M.S.O., 1952 (Printed by John Wright & Sons at the
Stonebridge Press, Bristol, 1960).
[36] p. : ill. ; 12 x 18 cm.
(Small picture books ; no. 32)
At head of title: Victoria & Albert Museum. — Foreword / Trenchard Cox.
Introduction / Brian Reade. — Stapled; salmon wrappers with illustrations.

V.1960.019   *Notes on quilting.* 3rd imp.
London : H.M.S.O., 1960 (Printed by John Wright & Sons at the
Stonebridge Press, Bristol).
8 p., [17] p. of plates ; 19 cm.
At head of title: Victoria and Albert Museum. — Prefatory note / Trenchard Cox. —
"Select bibliography": p. [4]. — Wrappers with blue and white overall decoration,
printed in black.

V.1960.020   *Regency domestic silver.*
London : H.M.S.O., 1952, reprinted 1960 (Printed by John Wright &
Sons at the Stonebridge Press, Bristol).
[4] p., 32 p. of plates : ill. ; 19 cm.
(Small picture book ; no. 33)
At head of title: Victoria & Albert Museum. — Wrappers, printed green, with
decoration.

V.1960.021   *Samplers* / by Donald King.
London : H.M.S.O., 1960 (Printed by John Wright & Sons at the
Stonebridge Press, Bristol).
15 p., [62] p. of plates : ill. ; 25 cm.
(Large picture book ; no. 14)
At head of title: Victoria and Albert Museum. — Foreword / Trenchard Cox. —
Bibliography: p. 11. — Sized wrappers with col. ill. on front.

V.1960.022   *Victoria & Albert Museum guide.* Rev. ed.
London : H.M.S.O., 1960 (Printed by Cheltenham Press).
128 p. : plans ; 25 cm.
"Spring 1960." — Edited by the Department of Museum Extension Services. — Index.
— Printing: 12/59. — Wrappers coloured orange.

V.1960.023   *The wood engravings of Robert Gibbings : an introduction by
Thomas Balston to the memorial exhibition at the Victoria and Albert
Museum . . . Spring 1960.*

[London : The Museum?, 1960] (Printed at the Aldine Press, Letchworth).
[5] p. : ill. ; 23 cm.
Stapled. No cover.
EXHIBITION: VX.1960.001

1961

V.1961.001   *Bookbindings* / by John P. Harthan. 2nd rev. ed.
London : H.M.S.O., 1961 (Printed by John Wright & Sons at the Stonebridge Press, Bristol).
33 p., [76] p. of plates : ill. ; 22 cm.
(Illustrated booklet ; no. 2)
At head of title: Victoria & Albert Museum. — Bibliography: p. 21–23. Glossary. — Green cloth covered boards.

V.1961.002   *Christmas picture book*. Repr.
London : H.M.S.O., 1961 (Printed by John Wright & Sons at the Stonebridge Press, Bristol).
[4] p., 28 leaves of plates : ill. ; 19 cm.
(Small picture book ; no. 18)
At head of title: Victoria and Albert Museum. — Printing: 5/61. — Cream wrappers with illustration, printed in red and black.

V.1961.003   *Elizabethan embroidery*. 4th imp. with amendments.
London : H.M.S.O., 1961 (Printed by John Wright & Sons at the Stonebridge Press, Bristol).
[6] p., 26 p. of plates : ill. ; 18cm.
(Small picture book ; no. 5)
At head of title: Victoria and Albert Museum. — Introduction signed "G.B." [i.e. Gerard Brett]. — Includes technical notes. — Cream decorated wrappers, printed in black and red.

V.1961.004   *English embroidery* / by Barbara J. Morris.
London : H.M.S.O., 1961 (Printed by John Wright & Sons, Stonebridge Press, Bristol).
15 p., [16] leaves of plates : ill. ; 22 cm.
(Illustrated booklet ; no. 1)
Cover title: The history of English embroidery. — Bibliography: p. 15. — Cover design by D.H. McKay. — Wrappers, sage and pink.

V.1961.005   *Finlandia : modern Finnish design.*
[London : Victoria and Albert Museum, 1961] (Printed by W.S. Cowell Ltd.).
[8] p., 28 p. of plates : ill. ; 26 cm. + 1 sheet, folded ([4] p.).
Introduction written by Hugh Wakefield. — Text printed brown on brown. Sized wrappers with photographic illustration. — List of manufacturers and designers on separate leaflet.
EXHIBITION: VX.1961.010

V.1961.006   *Kuniyoshi* / by B.W. Robinson.
London : H.M.S.O., 1961 (Printed by John Wright & Sons at the Stonebridge Press, Bristol).

xv, 71 p., [1], 98 p. of plates : ill. (1 col.) ; 26 cm.
([Museum monograph ; no. 16])

At head of title: Victoria and Albert Museum. — Foreword / Trenchard Cox. —
Bibliographic references included in "Notes" (p. 34–35). Glossary. Index. — Orange
cloth covered boards with illustration. Blue-green and grey dust-wrappers, with
illustration. Illustration printed in brown on grey end-papers.

EXHIBITION: VX.1961.006

V.1961.007   *The listening eye : teaching in an art museum* / by Renée Marcousé.
London : H.M.S.O., 1961 (Printed by John Wright & Sons at the
Stonebridge Press, Bristol).
14 p., 17 p. of plates : ill. ; 25 cm.

Cover: Victoria & Albert Museum. — Foreword / Trenchard Cox. — Includes
bibliographic references. — Blue sized wrappers with illustration.

V.1961.008   *Osterley Park : a guide* / by Peter Ward-Jackson. 2nd ed.,
5th imp.
London : H.M.S.O., 1954 (Printed by John Wright & Sons, 1961).
20 p., [8] p. of plates : ill., plans ; 22 cm.

At head of title: Victoria & Albert Museum. Cover title: Guide to Osterley Park. —
Introductory note / Trenchard Cox. — Includes bibliographic references. — Stapled,
grey wrappers, printed in white and black. — 4th imp. not traced.

V.1961.009   *Romanesque art.* New ed., 2nd imp.
London : H.M.S.O., 1957 (Printed by John Wright & Sons at the
Stonebridge Press, Bristol, 1961).
[4] p., 28 p. of plates : ill. ; 18 cm.
(Small picture book ; no. 15)

At head of title: Victoria and Albert Museum. — Introduction signed "J.B."
[i.e. John Beckwith]. — Decorated black wrappers printed in white.

V.1961.010   *Tables in the Victoria and Albert Museum* / by John F. Hayward.
London : H.M.S.O., 1961 (Printed by John Wright & Sons at the
Stonebridge Press, Bristol).
18 p., 53 p. of plates : ill. ; 22 cm.
(Illustrated booklet ; no. 10)

Includes bibliographic references. — Sized wrappers coloured green, with ill.

1962

V.1962.001   *100 things to see in the Victoria & Albert Museum.*
London : H.M.S.O., 1962.
[60] p. : ill., plans ; 24 cm.

At head of title: Victoria & Albert Museum. — Printing: 1/62. — Sized wrappers
with title and coat of arms printed on turqoise panel. — "Addenda" slip loosely
inserted.

V.1962.002   *Adam silver.* 2nd imp.
London : H.M.S.O., 1953 (Printed by the Curwen Press, 1962).
[4] p., [14] leaves of plates : ill. ; 19 cm.
(Small picture book ; no. 35)

At head of title: Victoria & Albert Museum. — Wrappers; title and design printed in
reverse on grey.

V.1962.003 *A brief guide to Indian art.*
London : H.M.S.O., 1962 (Printed by the Curwen Press).
[39] p. : ill. ; 25 x 12 cm.
At head of title: Victoria and Albert Museum. Cover title: Indian art, a brief guide. —
Preface signed "J.C.I." [i.e. J.C. Irwin]. — Bibliography : p. [37]. Chronological table
and glossary. — Printing: 11/62. — Wrappers, red and green with ill.

V.1962.004 *A brief guide to the Costume Court : with notes on related material
elsewhere in the Museum.*
[London : H.M.S.O.], 1962.
20 p. ; 25 cm.
At foot of title: Victoria and Albert Museum, London S.W.7. — Written by
Madeleine Blumstein. — Bibliography: p. 19–20.— Printing: 6/62. — Stapled,
no cover.
Copy note: One copy printed: 8/62.

V.1962.005 *Constable.* Repr. with amendments
London : H.M.S.O., 1962 (Printed by the Curwen Press).
[15] p., 33 p. of plates : ill. ; 18 cm.
(Small picture book ; no. 23)
Text signed "G.R." [i.e. Graham Reynolds]. — Dark green wrappers with illustration.

V.1962.006 *Early printers' marks.*
London : H.M.S.O., 1962 (Printed by the Curwen Press).
[4] p., 28 p. of plates : ill. ; 18 cm.
(Small picture book ; no. 56)
At head of title: Victoria & Albert Museum. — Bibliography. — Wrappers with device,
printed in red and white.

V.1962.007 *English medieval silver.* Repr. with amendments
London : H.M.S.O., 1952 (Printed by John Wright & Sons at the
Stonebridge Press, Bristol, 1962).
6 p., 25 p. of plates : ill. ; 18 cm.
(Small picture book ; no. 27)
At head of title: Victoria & Albert Museum. — Wrappers, printed in grey with
design.

V.1962.008 *English wrought-iron work.* 5th imp.
London : H.M.S.O., 1950 (Printed by the Curwen Press, 1962
printing).
[5] p., 27 p. of plates : ill. ; 18 cm.
(Small picture book ; no. 20)
At head of title: Victoria and Albert Museum. — Includes bibliography. — Cream
wrappers with black decoration and title printed label-style on orange. — 4th imp. not
traced.

V.1962.009 *The engraved work of Eric Gill.*
London : H.M.S.O., 1962 (Printed by the Curwen Press).
[8], 94 p. : chiefly ill. ; 25 cm.
(Large picture book ; no. 17)
At head of title: Victoria and Albert Museum. — Note by Trenchard Cox. —
"contains reproductions of 221 engravings on wood and metal by Eric Gill, chosen
almost entirely from the . . . collection given to the Department of Prints and Drawings
by his widow in 1952"–Introduction. — Grey wrappers with illustration:
"Approaching dawn."

V.1962.010   *Four masterpieces to see in 15 minutes (near the Exhibition Road Entrance).*
[London : H.M.S.O., 1962] (S.P.& S. [printer]).
1 sheet, folded ([4] p.) ; 18 cm.
Caption title. At head of title: Victoria and Albert Museum, London. — Printing: 6/62. — Printed in red.

V.1962.011   *Four masterpieces to see in 15 minutes (near the Main Entrance).*
[London : H.M.S.O., 1962] (S.P.& S. [printer]).
1 sheet, folded ([4] p.) ; 18 cm.
Caption title. At head of title: Victoria and Albert Museum, London. — Printing: 6/62. — Printed in blue.

V.1962.012   *Glass table-ware.*
London : H.M.S.O., 1947 (Curwen Press, 1962 printing).
[4] p., 28 p. of plates : ill. ; 18 cm.
(Small picture book ; no. 1)
Cover title: Glass. — Introductory text by "W.B.H." (i.e. W.B. Honey). — Grey wrappers with illustration.

V.1962.013   *The International Exhibition of 1862.*
London : H.M.S.O., 1962 (Printed by the Curwen Press).
[8] p., 28 p. of plates : ill. ; 19 cm.
(Small picture book ; no. 60)
At head of title: Victoria and Albert Museum. Caption title: The decorative arts at the International Exhibition of 1862. — Introduction signed "H.W." [i.e. Hugh Wakefield]. — Printing: 6/62. — Illustrative cover printed in purple; title in tan.
EXHIBITION: VX.1962.005

V.1962.014   *Italian secular silver.*
London : H.M.S.O., 1962 (John Wright & Sons).
[3] p., 28 p. of plates : ill. ; 18 cm.
(Small picture book ; no. 57)
Introduction signed "C.C.O." [i.e. Charles Oman]. — Pale blue wrappers with ill.

V.1962.015   *Modern American wall hangings : a loan exhibition arranged by the Victoria and Albert Museum.*
[London : The Museum, 1962.]
[4] p. : 1 col. ill. ; 22 cm.
EXHIBITION: VX.1962.001

V.1962.016   *A nonsense alphabet* / by Edward Lear. 5th imp. with amendments.
London : H.M.S.O., 1952 (Printed by John Wright & Sons at the Stonebridge Press, Bristol, 1962).
[36] p. : ill. ; 12 x 18 cm.
(Small picture book ; no. 32)
At head of title: Victoria & Albert Museum. — Introduction by Brian Reade. — Salmon wrappers with illustration.

V.1962.017   *A second Christmas picture book.* 3rd imp.
London : H.M.S.O., 1954 (Printed by the Curwen Press, 1962).
[4] p., 28 p. of plates : ill. ; 18 cm.
(Small picture book ; no. 38)
At head of title: Victoria and Albert Museum. — Wrappers with illustration in blue and border in red. — 2nd imp. not traced.

v.1962.018 *The Veroli casket* / by John Beckwith.
     London : H.M.S.O., 1962 (Printed by John Wright & Sons at the
     Stonebridge Press, Bristol).
     28 p., 16 p. of plates : ill. ; 25 cm.
     (Museum monograph ; no. 18)
     At head of title: Victoria and Albert Museum. — Foreword / Trenchard Cox. —
     Bibliography: p. 26. — Sized wrappers. Photograph on front, printed on grey-green.

v.1962.019 *Victorian furniture.*
     London : H.M.S.O., 1962 (Printed by the Curwen Press).
     [5] p., 27 p. of plates : ill. ; 18 cm.
     (Small picture book ; no. 59)
     At head of title: Victoria & Albert Museum. — Sized wrappers; partly patterned front
     cover.

v.1962.020 *Wedgwood.* 2nd imp.
     London : H.M.S.O., 1958 (Printed by the Curwen Press, 1962).
     [4] p., [28] p. of plates : ill. ; 19 cm.
     (Small picture book ; no. 45)
     Introduction signed "R.J.C." [i.e. R.J. Charleston]. — Sized wrappers with illustration
     on front, printed on blue.

1963

v.1963.001 *Arms and armour of old Japan* / by B.W. Robinson. Repr.
     London : H.M.S.O., 1951, reprinted 1963 (Printed by the Curwen
     Press).
     18 p., 26 p. of plates : ill. ; 22 cm.
     (Illustrated booklet ; no. 6)
     At head of title: Victoria & Albert Museum. Cover title: Arms & armour of old Japan.
     — Buff wrappers with illustration printed in tan.

v.1963.002 *Art nouveau and Alphonse Mucha* / by Brian Reade.
     London : H.M.S.O., 1963 (Printed by the Curwen Press).
     34 p., 36 p. of plates : 25 cm.
     (Large picture book ; no. 18)
     Pale blue wrappers printed in violet, with illustrations.
     EXHIBITION: vx.1963.006

v.1963.003 *The Basilewsky situla* / by John Beckwith.
     London : H.M.S.O., 1963 (Printed by the Curwen Press).
     17 p., xiv p. of plates : ill. ; 25 cm.
     (Monograph ; no. 21)
     At head of title: Victoria and Albert Museum. — Foreword / Trenchard Cox. —
     Bibliography: p. [18]. — Sized wrappers; illustration on front, printed in purple.

v.1963.004 *Brief guide to the Museum.*
     London : [H.M.S.O.?], 1963.
     28 p., [4] p. of plates : ill., plans ; 24 cm.
     At head of title: Victoria & Albert Museum. Cover title. — "Under revision." —
     Stapled, lime wrappers.

V.1963.005   *The engraved work of Eric Gill.*
London : H.M.S.O., 1963 (Printed by the Curwen Press).
[10], 94 p. : ill. ; 25 cm.
(Large picture book ; no. 17)

At head of title: Victoria and Albert Museum. — Note by Trenchard Cox. — Published
in conjunction with v.1963.006: "contains reproductions of 206 engravings on wood
and metal by Eric Gill, chosen almost entirely from the . . . collection given to the
Department of Prints and Drawings by his widow in 1952". — Introduction signed
"J.P." [i.e. John Physick]. — Grey wrappers with lion illustration.

V.1963.006   *The engraved work of Eric Gill* / by J.F. Physick.
London : H.M.S.O., 1963 (Printed by F. Mildner & Sons).
vii, 265 p. ; 22 cm.

At head of title: Victoria and Albert Museum. Spine title: Catalogue of the engraved
work of Eric Gill. — "It is an edition of the catalogue in the series of annual accessions
lists of the Department of Prints and Drawings"–Foreword / Trenchard Cox. Catalogue
by John Physick. — Includes bibliographic references; index. — Printing: 1/63. — Blue
cloth covered boards. Dust jacket coloured grey, printed on blue.

V.1963.007   *Fifty masterpieces of pottery, porcelain, glass vessels, stained glass,
painted enamels : selected and described by officers of the Department
of Ceramics.* 2nd ed.
London : H.M.S.O., 1963 (Printed by the Curwen Press).
102 p., [1] p. of plates : ill. ; 16 cm.

At head of title: Victoria & Albert Museum. Cover title: 50 masterpieces of pottery and
glass. — Wrappers, printed on turquoise.

V.1963.008   *Flowers in English embroidery.* 2nd ed.
London : H.M.S.O, 1963 (Printed by John Wright & Sons).
[6], 26 p. of plates : ill. ; 18 cm.
(Small picture books ; no. 2)

Wrappers; coloured ill. on front; printed on grey.

V.1963.009   *Gospel stories in English embroidery.*
London : H.M.S.O., 1963 (Printed by the Curwen Press).
[68] p. : chiefly ill. ; 16 cm.
([Large picture book ; no. 15])

At head of title: Victoria and Albert Museum. — Introduction signed "D.K."
[i.e. Donald King]. — Wrappers; front ill. printed red.

V.1963.010   *Late antique and Byzantine art.*
London : H.M.S.O., 1963 (Printed by the Curwen Press).
[6] p., 50 p. of plates. ; 22 cm.
(Illustrated booklet ; no. 12)

At head of title: Victoria and Albert Museum. — Sized wrappers, with photographic
illustration, printed on puce.

V.1963.011   *Loan exhibition of Polish puppetry and British puppets past and
present.*
[London : Bethnal Green Museum], 1963.
1 sheet, 24 cm.

At head of title: Bethnal Green Museum . . . . — Technical notes by Gerald Morice and
George Speaight.
EXHIBITION: VX.1963.BGM.001

v.1963.012   *Medieval silver nefs* / by Charles Oman.
                London : H.M.S.O., 1963 (London : Curwen Press).
                30p., xxiv p. of plates : ill. ; 25 cm.
                (Monograph ; no. 15)
                At head of title: Victoria and Albert Museum. — Sized wrappers in maroon and
                primrose; ill. on front cover printed in black.

v.1963.013   *Osterley Park : a guide* / by Peter Ward-Jackson. 2nd ed., 6th imp.
                with amendments.
                London : H.M.S.O., 1954 (Printed by the Curwen Press, 1963).
                20 p., [8] p. of plates : ill., plans ; 22 cm.
                At head of title: Victoria & Albert Museum. Cover title: Guide to Osterley Park. —
                Introductory note / Trenchard Cox. Includes bibliographic references. — Stapled, grey
                wrappers, printed in white and black.

v.1963.014   *Swords & daggers* / by J.F. Hayward. 2nd ed.
                London : H.M.S.O., 1963 (Printed by the Curwen Press).
                12 p., 46 p. of plates : ill. ; 22 cm.
                (Illustrated booklet ; no. 3)
                At head of title: Victoria and Albert Museum. — Cream wrappers with ill.; title printed
                in red.

v.1963.015   *Victorian paintings.* 2nd ed.
                London : H.M.S.O., 1963.
                [4] p., 28 p. of plates : ill. ; 18 cm.
                (Small picture book ; no. 10)
                Unseen. Record from OCLC.

1964

v.1964.001   *Bottle-tickets.* 2nd imp.
                London : H.M.S.O., 1958 (Printed by the Curwen Press, 1964).
                [6] p., 26 p. of plates : ill ; 12 x 18 cm.
                (Small picture book ; no. 44)
                At head of title: Victoria and Albert Museum. — Introduction signed "B.W.R."
                [i.e. Basil W. Robinson]. — Sized wrappers with illustration printed on red.

v.1964.002   *Brief guide to the Museum.* 2nd ed.
                London : [H.M.S.O.], 1964.
                28 p. : plans ; 24 cm.
                Cover title. At head of title: Victoria & Albert Museum. — Printing: 11/64. — Stapled,
                tan wrappers.

v.1964.003   *British ecclesiastical architecture : pages 1–28.*
                London : Victoria & Albert Museum [ca. 1964].
                28 leaves ; 33 cm.
                (Catalogue of 2 x 2 colour transparencies)
                Cover title. — Duplicated copy of typewritten and hand-lettered original. — Stapled in
                green paper covers.

v.1964.004   *British secular architecture : pages 1–36.*
                London : Victoria & Albert Museum [ca. 1964].
                36 leaves ; 33 cm.
                (Catalogue of 2 x 2 colour transparencies)

Cover title. — Duplicated copy of typewritten and hand-lettered original. — Stapled in green paper covers.

v.1964.005   *Catalogue of Italian sculpture in the Victoria and Albert Museum* /
John Pope-Hennessy ; assisted by Ronald Lightbown.
London : H.M.S.O., 1964 (Printed by Butler and Tanner; plates by the Curwen Press).
3 v. (xvi, v, 767 p., 426 p. of plates : ill. [Vol. 3] ; 29 cm.
Vol. I, Text : eighth to fifteenth century. Vol. II, Text : sixteenth to twentieth century. Vol. III, Plates. — Bibliographic references and abbreviations (p. 700–708). Artist, object, numerical and provenance indexes. — Red cloth covered boards. In slip-case.

v.1964.006   *English cabinets in the Victoria and Albert Museum* / by
J.F. Hayward.
London : H.M.S.O., 1964 (Printed by the Curwen Press).
21 p., 34 p. of plates : ill. ; 22cm.
(Illustrated booklet ; no. 11)
Includes bibliographic references. — Wrappers, with ill., printed on salmon pink.

v.1964.007   *Fifty masterpieces of sculpture.* 2nd ed.
London : H.M.S.O., 1964 (Printed by the Curwen Press).
50 leaves of plates : ill. ; 16 cm.
At head of title: Victoria and Albert Museum. — Grey wrappers, printed in black and white.

v.1964.008   *Four hundred years of English handwriting : an exhibition of manuscripts and copy books 1543–1943, held at the Victoria and Albert Museum, London, 1964.*
[London : The Museum, 1964].
iii, 15 leaves. ; 34 cm.
Exhibition and catalogue by Shirley Bury and Irene Whalley; introduction by John P. Harthan. — Items exhibited drawn from the holdings of the National Art Library, Victoria and Albert Museum. — Typescript, illustration on cover.
EXHIBITION: vx.1964.010

v.1964.009   *The Great Exhibition of 1851* / C.H. Gibbs-Smith. Amended repr.
London : H.M.S.O., 1964 (Printed by W.S. Cowell Ltd., Ipswich).
142 p. : ill. ; 22 cm.
At head of title: Victoria & Albert Museum. Cover title: The Great Exhibition of 1851 : a commemorative album. — Foreword / Leigh Ashton. — Bibliography: p. 40. — Wrappers with coloured illustration (salmon and magenta) on front and royal arms at back. — Originally published on the occasion of vx.1951.003.

v.1964.010   *Ham House : a guide* / by Ralph Edwards and Peter Ward-Jackson.
4th ed., 2nd imp.
London : H.M.S.O., 1959 (Printed by the Curwen Press, 1964).
[1], 60, [2] p. : ill., plans ; 22 cm.
At head of title: Victoria and Albert Museum. — Introductory note / Trenchard Cox. — Bibliography: p. 60. — Cream wrappers with illustration, with red.

v.1964.011   *Handbook to the Departments of Prints and Drawings, and Paintings.*
London : H.M.S.O., 1964 ("McC", printer).
viii, 116 p. ; 25 cm.
At head of title: Victoria and Albert Museum. — Foreword / Graham Reynolds. Edited by John Physick. — Includes bibliographic references. — Printing: 6/64. — Yellow wrappers.

V.1964.012   *The legend of Saint Ursula* / by C.M. Kauffmann.
London : H.M.S.O., 1964 (Printed by the Curwen Press).
34 p., 28 p. of plates : ill. ; 25 cm.
(Monograph ; no. 22)

At head of title: Victoria and Albert Museum. — Introduction. The legend of
St. Ursula. The expansion of the legend and the "Martyrdom of St. Ursula and the
eleven thousand virgins" in the Victoria and Albert Museum. The iconography of the
series. The Master of the St. Ursula Legend and the school of Cologne in the late
15th century. The provenance of the paintings and the pattern of patronage at Cologne.
Notes on the text (p. 30–33). — Sized wrappers with illustration, title printed on red
band.

V.1964.013   *The orange and the rose : Holland and Britain in the age of
observation, 1600–1750 : an exhibition of paintings, drawings,
graphic art, sculpture, silver, medals, furniture, ceramics, scientific
instruments, books and documents.*
[London : Victoria and Albert Museum?, 1964] (Shenval Press,
printer).
86 p., [32] p. of plates : ill., geneal. tables ; 26 cm.

Bibliography: p. 81. Indexes of sitters and lenders. — Wrappers, orange outside, lined in
red.
EXHIBITION: VX.1964.009

V.1964.014   *Sheffield plate.* 2nd imp.
London : H.M.S.O., 1955 (Printed by the Curwen Press, 1964).
[32] p. : ill. ; 18 cm.
(Small picture book ; no. 39)

At head of title: Victoria & Albert Museum. — Introduction signed "J.H." [i.e. John
Hayward]. — Wrappers; printed in reverse on grey, with illustration.

V.1964.015   *Signs of the zodiac.*
London : H.M.S.O., 1964 (Printed by the Curwen Press).
[25] p. : ill. ; 16 cm.
(Small picture book ; no. 61)

At head of title: Victoria & Albert Museum. — Foreword signed "C.H.G-S." [i.e.
Charles Gibbs-Smith]. — Printed on pink paper. Cream wrappers with ill. Title printed
in red.

V.1964.016   *The Wellington Museum, Apsley House : a guide* / by C.H. Gibbs-
Smith and H.V.T. Percival. 4th ed.
London : H.M.S.O., 1964.
54 p., [4] p. of plates : facsim., plan, port.; 24 cm.

Cover title: A guide to the Wellington Museum. — Foreword / Trenchard Cox. —
Bibliography at end. Index of painters. — Sized wrappers with ill., partly printed
in red.

1965

V.1965.001   *The Barbizon school* / by C.M. Kauffmann.
London : H.M.S.O., 1965 (Printed by the Curwen Press).
20, [20] p. : ill. ; 13 x 19 cm.
(Small picture book ; no. 4)

At head of title: Victoria and Albert Museum. — Wrappers, with ill; title printed in
brown.

v.1965.002   *Bohemian glass.*
London : H.M.S.O., 1965 (Printed by W.S. Cowell Ltd., Ipswich).
18 p., 45 p. of plates : ill. ; 25 cm.
(Large picture book ; no. 29)
At head of title: Victoria and Albert Museum. — Foreword / Trenchard Cox. Text by
Libuĕe Urešová. — Sized wrappers with photograph, printed white on black. —
"Addenda" on separate sheet.
EXHIBITION: vx.1965.003

v.1965.003   *Bohemian glass exhibition : 2nd April–27th June 1965.*
[London : H.M.S.O.?, 1965] (Printed by W.S. Cowell Ltd., Ipswich).
18 p. ; 24 cm.
Cover title. — Errata slip loosely inserted.
EXHIBITION: vx.1965.003

v.1965.004   *British painting.*
London : Victoria & Albert Museum Public Relations Dept., 1965.
206 p. ; 33 cm.
(Catalogue of 2 x 2 lantern slides)
Cover title.

v.1965.005   *Dolls.* 2nd imp.
London : H.M.S.O., 1960 (Printed by the Curwen Press, 1965).
[4] p., 28 p. of plates : ill. ; 18 cm.
(Small picture book ; no. 50)
At head of title: Victoria & Albert Museum. — Introduction signed "M.B."
[i.e. Madeleine Blumstein]. — Sized wrappers with photograph printed on patterned
green background.

v.1965.006   *The Duke of Wellington in caricature* / by John Physick.
London : H.M.S.O., 1965 (Printed by Eyre and Spottiswoode at
Grosvenor Press, Portsmouth).
[100] p. : ill. ; 22 cm.
(Large picture book ; no. 19)
At head of title: Victoria and Albert Museum. — Foreword / the Duke of Wellington. —
Bibliography. — Illustrated with a selection of works in the collection of the
Department of Prints and Drawings, Victoria and Albert Museum. — Sized wrappers
with illustration; title printed in red.

v.1965.007   *Dutch painting.*
London : Victoria & Albert Museum Public Relations Dept., 1965.
53 p. ; 33 cm.
(Catalogue of 2 x 2 lantern slides)
Cover title. — "This catalogue is for reference only." — Stapled in blue paper covers.

v.1965.008   *English chairs* / with an introduction by Ralph Edwards. 2nd ed.
London : H.M.S.O., 1965 (Printed by the Curwen Press).
26 p., 120 p. of plates : ill. ; 25 cm.
At head of title: Victoria and Albert Museum. — Foreword / Trenchard Cox. —
Includes bibliographic references. — Sized wrappers; black and white photographic
illustration printed on tan.

v.1965.009   *English silversmiths' work, civil and domestic : an introduction* / by
Charles Oman.
London : H.M.S.O., 1965 (Printed by the Curwen Press).

15 p., [193] p. of plates : ill. ; 26 cm.
([Large picture book ; no. 16])
At head of title: Victoria and Albert Museum. — Intended to provide an introduction to
the collection of English silver in the Department of Metalwork, Victoria and Albert
Museum, "as it was at the close of 1961"–Foreword / Trenchard Cox. — Red cloth
covered boards.

V.1965.010   *European armour* / by J.F. Hayward. [2nd ed.]
London : H.M.S.O., 1965 (Printed by the Curwen Press).
[32] p. : 14 x 22 cm.
(Illustrated booklet ; no. 5)
Includes bibliographic references. — Grey wrappers.

V.1965.011   *Flemish painting.*
London : Victoria & Albert Museum Public Relations Dept., 1965.
28 p. ; 33 cm.
(Catalogue of 2 x 2 lantern slides)
Cover title. — "This catalogue is for reference only." — Stapled in blue paper
covers.

V.1965.012   *German domestic silver of the eighteenth century.*
London : H.M.S.O., 1965 (Printed by the Curwen Press).
[4] p., [28] p. of plates : ill. ; 18 cm.
(Small picture book ; no. 58)
At head of title: Victoria and Albert Museum. — Introduction signed "C.C.O."
[i.e. Charles Chichele Oman]. — Wrappers; title printed over sepia illustration.

V.1965.013   *German painting : (including Austrian, Bohemian, Swiss),
Scandinavian painting.*
London : Victoria & Albert Museum Public Relations Dept.,
1965.
27 p. ; 33 cm.
(Catalogue of 2 x 2 lantern slides)
Cover title. — Stapled in blue paper covers.

V.1965.014   *Italian painting.*
London : Victoria & Albert Museum Public Relations Dept., 1965.
123 p. ; 33 cm.
(Catalogue of 2 x 2 lantern slides)
Cover title. — "This catalogue is for reference only." — Stapled in blue paper covers.

V.1965.015   *A nonsense alphabet* / by Edward Lear. 6th imp.
London : H.M.S.O., 1952 (Printed by John Wright & Sons at the
Stonebridge Press, Bristol, 1965).
[36] p. : ill. ; 12 x 18 cm.
(Small picture book ; no. 32)
At head of title: Victoria & Albert Museum. — Foreword / Trenchard Cox.
Introduction / Brian Reade. — Stapled, salmon wrappers with illustration.

V.1965.016   *Paintings at Apsley House* / by C.M. Kauffmann.
London : H.M.S.O., 1965 (Printed by the Curwen Press).
[8] p., 54 p. of plates : ill., ports. ; 25 cm.
(Large picture book ; no. 23)
At head of title: Wellington Museum. — Sized wrappers with portrait.

V.1965.017   *Persian paintings* / by B.W. Robinson. 2nd ed.
London, H.M.S.O., 1965 (Printed by the Curwen Press).
18 p., 36 p. of plates : ill. ; 25 cm.
(Large picture book ; no. 6)
At head of title: Victoria and Albert Museum. — Includes chronology. — Wrappers
coloured green, with ill. printed in blue.

V.1965.018   *Spanish painting.*
London : Victoria & Albert Museum Public Relations Dept., 1965.
15 p. ; 33 cm.
(Catalogue of 2 x 2 lantern slides)
Cover title. — "This catalogue is for reference only." — Stapled in blue paper covers.

V.1965.019   *The Waterloo despatch : the story of the Duke of Wellington's official
despatch on the Battle of Waterloo and its journey to London* / by
Reginald Colby ; with notes by Victor Percival.
London : H.M.S.O., 1965 (Printed by the Curwen Press).
43 p. : ill., ports., 22 cm.
(Monograph ; no. 24)
At head of title: Wellington Museum, Apsley House. — Foreword / Trenchard Cox. —
"Originally appeared in the July issue of the *Quarterly review*, 1962." — Sized
wrappers with illustration on front, and title printed on red.

V.1965.020   *Weaving for walls : modern British wall hangings and rugs : a loan
exhibition arranged by the Circulation Department of the Victoria and
Albert Museum with the co-operation of the Association of Guilds of
Weavers, Spinners and Dyers.*
[London : Victoria & Albert Museum, 1965?]
1 folded sheet ([5] p.) ; 24 x 11 cm.
Cover title. — Text by Hugh Wakefield.
EXHIBITION: vx.1965.002

V.1965.021   *William Morris.* 2nd imp.
London : H.M.S.O., 1958 (Printed by the Curwen Press Ltd., 1965).
[2], [3] p., 27 p. of plates : ill. ; 18 cm.
(Small picture book ; no. 43)
At head of title: Victoria & Albert Museum. — Introduction signed "P.F." [i.e. Peter
Floud]. — Includes technical notes. — Grey wrappers with William Morris design in
green.

1966

V.1966.001   *The Adoration of the Magi in whalebone* / by John Beckwith.
London : H.M.S.O., 1966 (Text [printed] by the Curwen Press, cover
by Multi-Machine Plates Ltd.).
[6], 40 p.. 1 leaf of plates : ill. : 25 cm.
(Museum monograph ; no. 28)
At head of title: Victoria & Albert Museum. — Foreword / Trenchard Cox. —
Bibliographic references included in "Notes" (p. 31–34). — Buff wrappers. Photograph
on front, printed on brown.

V.1966.002   *Art nouveau and Alphonse Mucha* / by Brian Reade. 2nd imp.
London : H.M.S.O., 1963 (Printed by the Curwen Press, 1966).

34 p., 36 p. of plates : 25 cm.
(Large picture book ; no. 18)
Originally published on the occasion of vx.1963.006. — Salmon pink wrappers printed in olive green, with illustration.

V.1966.003   *Aubrey Beardsley* / by Brian Reade.
London : H.M.S.O., 1966 (Printed by Jarrold & Sons, Norwich).
18 p., 50 p. of plates : ill. ; 25 cm.
(Large picture book ; no. 32)
Grey wrappers printed in orange, with illustration.
EXHIBITION: vx.1966.003

V.1966.004   *Aubrey Beardsley : exhibition at the Victoria and Albert Museum, 1966 : catalogue of the original drawings, letters, manuscripts, paintings, and of books, posters, photographs, documents, etc.* / by Brian Reade and Frank Dickinson.
[London : H.M.S.O., 1966] (Printed by Direct Design, Christchurch).
1 v. (unpaged: [10] p., 611 entries) ; 23 cm.
Includes bibliographic references. — Printing: 5/66. — Olive green wrappers.
Copy note: Slip pasted in: "The reader is asked to note that the catalogue was compiled, typed and lithographed in emergency conditions and that revision was not possible. The present copy is one of a limited number corrected by hand for lenders and others concerned with the exhibitions". Correction slips inserted.
EXHIBITION: vx.1966.003

V.1966.005   *The basic stitches of embroidery* / by N. Victoria Wade. 2nd ed.
London : H.M.S.O., 1966 (Norwich : Jarrold & Sons, printer).
[2], 26 p. : ill. ; 25 cm.
At head of title: Victoria & Albert Museum. — Ivory wrappers, printed in blue, with design.

V.1966.006   *Costume : a general bibliography* / by Pegaret Anthony and Janet Arnold.
London : The Costume Society c/o the Victoria & Albert Museum, 1966.
[1], 49 p. 28 cm.
(Bibliography ; no. 1)
At head of title: The Victoria & Albert Museum in association with the Costume Society. — Foreword / Charles H. Gibbs-Smith. — Yellow-green wrappers. Title printed in black and red.

V.1966.007   *The deterioration of art objects by light.*
London : Conservation Department of the Victoria and Albert Museum, 1966.
1 sheet, folded ([4] p.) ; 21 cm.
(Technical notes on the care of art objects ; no. 1)

V.1966.008   *Edgar Seligman gift.*
London : H.M.S.O., 1966.
vii, 992 p. ; 22 cm.
(Department of Prints and Drawings and Department of Paintings accessions ; 1960, Vol. 2)
At head of title: Victoria and Albert Museum. — Foreword by Graham Reynolds. — Bibliography: p. 909–914. Portrait index; artist index.

v.1966.009　　　*Fifty masterpieces of textiles.* 3rd imp.
London : H.M.S.O., 1951 (Printed by the Curwen Press, 1966).
[3] p., 50 leaves of plates : chiefly ill. ; 16 cm.
At head of title: Victoria & Albert Museum. — Sized wrappers, in pink, white and black, with illustration.

v.1966.010　　　*The house of David, his inheritance : a book of sample scripts, 1914 A.D.* / Edward Johnston.
London : Printed and published by H.M.S.O., 1966.
31 p. ; 26 cm.
(Facsimiles ; no. 1)
At head of title: Victoria and Albert Museum. Cover title: A book of sample scripts. — Facsimile of a manuscript."The first in a series of facsimile reproductions issued by the Victoria and Albert Museum"–dust-jacket. — Introduction / J.P. Harthan. — Boards covered in red cloth. Reversed-out facsims. on end-papers. Dust-jacket printed in black, white and red.

v.1966.011　　　*Medieval pottery : a travelling exhibition arranged by the Circulation Department of the Victoria and Albert Museum.*
[London : The Museum, 1966?]
1 sheet, folded ([5] p.) : 1 ill. ; 21 cm.
Printed on sized card.
EXHIBITION: vx.1968.012

v.1966.012　　　*Michelangelo : the Taddei tondo, lent by the Royal Academy of Arts.*
London : [s.n., 1966].
1 sheet folded ([3] p.) ; 23 cm.
At head of title: Victoria and Albert Museum.

v.1966.013　　　*Paintings by artists of all nationalities arranged alphabetically.*
2nd ed.
[London : Victoria & Albert Museum Public Relations Dept.?],
1966.
2 v. (111, 94 p.) ; 35 cm.
(Catalogue of 2 x 2 colour transparencies)
Cover title. — Previously Catalogue of 2 x 2 lantern slides? — "This catalogue is for reference only." — "Sept. 1966."— Part one, (1) Unattributed, (2), Artists A-L. Part two, Artists M-Z. — Printing: 8/66. — Stapled in orange paper covers.

v.1966.014　　　*Paintings of the Sikhs* / W.G. Archer.
London : H.M.S.O., 1966 (Printed by the Curwen Press).
xxiii, 284 p. : ill. (1 col.), map ; 25 cm.
(Monograph ; no. 31)
At head of title: Victoria and Albert Museum. — Includes: Catalogue of Sikh paintings in the Victoria and Albert Museum. — Bibliography: p. 76–103. Glossary. Index; concordance to Museum numbers. — Blue cloth boards, spine title in gold. Blue dust-jacket with illustration.

v.1966.015　　　*The Raphael cartoons* / introduction by John Pope-Hennessy.
London : H.M.S.O., 1966.
10 p., 30 p. of plates : ill. (some col.) ; 19 x 25 cm.
(Colour book ; no. 1)
At head of title: Victoria & Albert Museum. — Foreword / Trenchard Cox. — Sized wrappers, with colour illustration.

V.1966.016   *The Raphael cartoons : lent by Her Majesty the Queen.*
              [London : H.M.S.O., 1966.]
              10 p. ; 25 cm.
              Cover title. At foot of title: Victoria and Albert Museum, London S.W.7 . . . . — Text by
              Graham Reynolds. — Printing: 1/66. — Stapled.

V.1966.017   *A short history of English furniture.*
              London : H.M.S.O., 1966 (Printed by the Curwen Press).
              32 p., 100 p. of plates : ill. ; 26 cm.
              (Large picture book ; no. 20)
              At head of title: Victoria & Albert Museum. — Foreword / Trenchard Cox. —
              Bibliography: p. 19. — Boards covered in beige cloth; dust-jacket with illustration,
              printed on tan; illustrated wrappers in tan, printed in white.

1967

V.1967.001   *Art nouveau and Alphonse Mucha* / by Brian Reade. 2nd ed.
              London : H.M.S.O., 1967 (Printed by Butler & Tanner).
              34 p., [32] p. of plates : ill. ; 25 cm.
              (Large picture book ; no. 18)
              At head of cover: Victoria & Albert Museum. — First published on the occasion of
              VX.1963.006. — Blue wrappers with title and ills. printed in puce.

V.1967.002   *Ballet designs and illustrations, 1581–1940 : a catalogue raisonné* /
              by Brian Reade.
              London : H.M.S.O., 1967 (Text [printed] by the Curwen Press,
              monochrome plates by Clarke and Sherwell, colour plates by Jarrold
              & Sons, Norwich).
              [12], 58 p., [171] p. of plates : ill. (some col.) ; 32 cm.
              At head of title: Victoria and Albert Museum. — Foreword / Trenchard Cox. —
              Includes material held in the Dept. of Prints and Drawings, the Enthoven collection, and
              the National Art Library. — Bibliography: p. 57–58. — Blue cloth covered boards;
              mustard-coloured end-papers. White dust-jacket with coloured illustration.
              EXHIBITION: VX.1967.005

V.1967.003   *Brief guide to the Museum.* 2nd ed.
              London : [H.M.S.O.], 1964 (1967 printing).
              28 p. : plans ; 24 cm.
              Cover title. At head of title: Victoria & Albert Museum. — Printing: 2/67. — Stapled,
              tan wrappers.

V.1967.004   *Chinese porcelain of the Ch'ing dynasty.* 2nd imp.
              London : H.M.S.O., 1957 (Printed by Butler & Tanner, 1967).
              [4] p., 28 p. of plates : ill. ; 19 cm.
              (Small picture book ; no. 41)
              At head of title: Victoria & Albert Museum. — Introduction signed "A.L." [i.e. Arthur
              Lane]. — Sized wrappers; illustration and title printed on pale yellow.

V.1967.005   *Early keyboard instruments* / by Raymond Russell. 2nd imp.
              London : H.M.S.O., 1959 (Printed by Butler & Tanner, 1967).
              [6] p., [26] p. of plates : ill. ; 19 cm.
              (Small picture book ; no. 48)
              At head of title: Victoria and Albert Museum. — Sized wrappers, with illustration,
              printed on salmon.

V.1967.006   *Edward Gordon Craig, 1872–1966* / George Nash.
London : H.M.S.O., 1967 (Printed by Eyre and Spottiswoode at
Grosvenor Press, Portsmouth).
30 p., [18] p. of plates : ill., ports. ; 25 cm.
(Large picture book ; no. 35)
At head of title: Victoria and Albert Museum. — Grey wrappers, with illustration.
EXHIBITION: vx.1967.012

V.1967.007   *English chintz.* 2nd imp.
London : H.M.S.O., 1955 (Printed by Butler & Tanner, 1967).
[10] p., 32 p. of plates : ill. ; 18 cm.
(Small picture book ; no. 22)
At head of title: Victoria and Albert Museum. — Pink wrappers with decorated title
printed in pink and green. — Originally published on the occasion of
vx.1955.xxx.002.

V.1967.008   *The engravings of S.W. Hayter* / Graham Reynolds.
London : H.M.S.O., 1967 (Printed by Butler & Tanner).
13 p., [25] p. of plates : ill. (1 col.) ; 24 cm.
(Large picture book ; no. 34)
At head of title: Victoria and Albert Museum. — Sized wrappers. Title printed in white
on blue, with illustration in purple.
EXHIBITION: vx.1967.002

V.1967.009   *Figure drawings.* 6th imp.
London : H.M.S.O., 1949 (Printed by Butler & Tanner, 1967).
[4] p., 28 p. of plates : ill. ; 18 cm.
(Small picture book ; no. 13)
At head of title: Victoria and Albert Museum. — Introduction signed "B.E.R."
[i.e. Brian Reade]. — Tan wrappers, with illustration.

V.1967.010   *Flowers in English embroidery.* 2nd ed. 2nd imp.
London : H.M.S.O., 1963 (Printed by Butler & Tanner, 1967).
[6], 26 p. of plates : ill. ; 18 cm.
(Small picture book ; no. 2)
ISBN: 0112902413 (sd)
At head of title: Victoria & Albert Museum. — Wrappers; coloured ill. on front; printed
on grey.

V.1967.011   *German domestic silver 1618–1700.*
London : H.M.S.O., 1967 (Printed by Butler & Tanner).
[4] p., 27 p. of plates : ill. ; 19 cm.
(Small picture book ; no. 64)
At head of title: Victoria and Albert Museum. — Introduction signed "C.C.O."
[i.e. Charles Oman]. — Grey wrappers, with illustration.

V.1967.012   *German wood statuettes 1500–1800* / Michael Baxandall.
London : H.M.S.O., 1967 (Printed by Butler & Tanner).
14 p., 28 p. of plates : ill. ; 22 cm.
(Illustrated booklet ; no. 14)
At head of title: Victoria and Albert Museum. — Includes bibliographic references. —
Sized wrappers with illustration on front, printed on tan.

V.1967.013 *Hungarian art treasures : ninth to seventeenth centuries : 11 October 1967–14 January 1968, Victoria and Albert Museum, London.*
[London : The Museum?, 1967] (Designed and printed by Shenva [sic]).
101 p. : ill. ; 24 cm.
Foreword / John Pope-Hennessy. Introduction / Endre Rosta. Art of the 9th and 10th centuries : the era of the Magyar conquest / István Dienes. — Bibliography: p. 98–101. — Printed on sized paper; sized black wrappers with illustration.
EXHIBITION: VX.1967.010

V.1967.014 *Important finds of ancient Chinese ceramics since 1949* / by Fêng Hsien-Ming ; report translated by Hin-Cheung Lovell.
[London] : Victoria & Albert Museum in association with the Oriental Ceramic Society, 1967.
65 p., [7] p. of plates, 1 folded : ill., map ; 29 cm.
(Chinese translations ; no. 1)
Foreword / Basil Gray. — Translation of a report originally published in *Wen wu*, 1965, no. 9. — Stapled in grey covers.

V.1967.015 *Medieval Near Eastern pottery.* 2nd imp.
London : H.M.S.O., 1957 (Printed by Butler & Tanner, 1967).
[4] p., 28 p. of plates : ill. ; 18 cm.
(Small picture book ; no. 42)
At head of title: Victoria and Albert Museum. — Introduction signed "A.L." [i.e. Arthur Lane]. — Cream wrappers printed with design in russet and green.

V.1967.016 *Persian miniature painting from collections in the British Isles* / B.W. Robinson.
London : H.M.S.O., 1967 (Printed by Butler & Tanner).
120 p., 52 p. of plates : ill. (1 col.) ; 25 cm.
(Large picture book ; no. 33)
At head of title: Victoria and Albert Museum. — Preface / John Pope-Hennessy. — Includes bibliographic references. Indexes of artists, lenders and Museum numbers. — Plain wrappers; dust-jacket with coloured illustration.
EXHIBITION: VX.1967.008

V.1967.017 *Sketches by Thornhill in the Victoria and Albert Museum* / by Edgar de N. Mayhew.
London : H.M.S.O., 1967 (Printed by Butler & Tanner).
22 p., 41 leaves of plates : ill., facsims., plans ; 25 cm.
(Monograph ; no. 19)
Foreword / John Pope-Hennessy. — Wrappers; decorative border on front cover printed on puce.

V.1967.018 *S.W. Hayter's graphic work : a retrospective exhibition 1926–1966, February 17th to April 2nd 1967.*
[London : Victoria and Albert Museum, 1967.]
[4] p. ; 23 cm.
Cover title. At head of title: Victoria & Albert Museum Department of Prints and Drawings. — Text on inside wrappers. Stapled.
EXHIBITION: VX.1967.002

V.1967.019

Toys.
London : H.M.S.O., 1967 (Printed by Butler & Tanner).
28 p. : ill..; 12 x 19 cm.
(Small picture book ; no. 63)
At head of title: Victoria and Albert Museum, Bethnal Green Museum. — By Elizabeth Aslin. — Stapled, sized wrappers. Illustration on front cover, on pink.

V.1967.020

Victorian glass : a travelling exhibition mounted by the Circulation Department of the Victoria and Albert Museum.
[London : H.M.S.O., 1967] ("F.M. & S.", printer).
1 sheet, folded ([5] p.) : 1 ill. ; 21 cm.
EXHIBITION: vx.1968.014

1968

V.1968.001

An altar-piece of the Apocalypse from Master Bertram's workshop in Hamburg / by C.M. Kauffmann.
London : H.M.S.O., 1968 (Printed by Butler & Tanner).
[14], 50 p., 24 p. of plates : ill. ; 25 cm.
(Monograph ; no. 25)
At head of title: Victoria and Albert Museum. — Includes bibliographic references. — Gold wrappers with illustration.

V.1968.002

American studio pottery.
London : H.M.S.O., 1968 (Printed by Norman Brothers, Cheltenham).
[8] p. : [22] p. of plates ; 20 cm.
At head of title: Victoria and Albert Museum. — Introduction by Hugh Wakefield. — Selection from a Circulation Dept. exhibition. — Green wrappers with design in blue; first 8 pages printed on blue paper.
EXHIBITION: vx.1966.006

V.1968.003

Ballooning : a travelling exhibition arranged by the Circulation Department of the Victoria and Albert Museum from the collections of the Royal Aeronautical Society.
[London : H.M.S.O.?, 1968] (Printed by F. Mildner & Sons).
[10] p. ; 21 cm.
Cover title. — Stapled; illustration on cover.

V.1968.004

La belle époque : costume 1890–1914 : proceedings of the first Annual Conference of the Costume Society, April 1967.
London : Published for the Costume Society, Victoria and Albert Museum, 1968 (Printed by Baron Publishing, Woodbridge).
[2] 65 p. : ill. ; 26 cm.
Edited by Ann Saunders. — Includes: Introduction / James Laver. The sources for the study of Belle Epoque costume / Richard Ormond. The making and distribution of clothes / Madeleine Ginsburg. The film source for the age / Susan Crockford.
The cut and construction of women's dresses, 1890–1914 / Janet Arnold. Men's dress, 1890–1914 / A.A. Whife. Foundations of the active woman / Anne Buck. Accessories / Daphne Bullard. Lace in costume, 1890–1914 / Zillah Halls. The beaded dress / Joan Edwards.— Includes bibliographies. — Stapled; white sized wrappers with ill. in silhouette.

v.1968.005

Brief guide to the Museum. 2nd ed. 2nd imp.
London : [H.M.S.O.], 1964 (M.M.P. Ltd. [printer]).
28 p. : plans ; 24 cm.
Cover title. At head of title: Victoria & Albert Museum. — Printing: 5/68. — Stapled; tan wrappers.
Copy note: Loosely inserted: addenda sheet relating to Rooms 122 and 120.

v.1968.006

British water-colours / by Graham Reynolds. 2nd ed.
London : H.M.S.O., 1968 (Text [printed] by Butler & Tanner, cover by Norman Brothers).
68 p. : ill. ; 14 x 22 cm.
(Illustrated booklet ; no. 4)
At head of title: Victoria and Albert Museum. — Sized wrappers with coloured illustration on front.

v.1968.007

Catalogue of musical instruments. Vol. I, Keyboard instruments / Raymond Russell.
London : H.M.S.O., 1968 (Printed by the Curwen Press).
xvii, 94 p., [1] leaf, [60] p. of plates) : ill. (1 col.), music ; 26 cm.
At head of title: Victoria and Albert Museum. — Director's foreword / John Pope-Hennessy. — Bibliography: p. [83]–85. Index. — Tan cloth covered boards; brick red dust jacket with col. ill.; white and black lettering.

v.1968.008

Catalogue of musical instruments. Vol. II, Non-keyboard instruments / Anthony Baines.
London : H.M.S.O., 1968 (Printed by Jarrold & Sons, Norwich).
xiii, 121 p., [1] leaf, [95] p. of plates) : ill. (1 col.), music ; 26 cm.
At head of title: Victoria and Albert Museum. — Director's foreword / John Pope-Hennessy. — Bibliography: p. [107]–109. Index; numerical index. — Tan cloth covered boards; brick red dust jacket with col. ill.; white and black lettering.

v.1968.009

Catalogue of rubbings of brasses and incised slabs / by Muriel Clayton. 2nd ed., 2nd imp. (re-issue).
London : H.M.S.O., 1968 (Printed by A. Wheaton & Co., Exeter).
xiv, 251 p., 72 p. of plates : ill., facsims. ; 25 cm.
ISBN: 0112900879
At head of title: Victoria and Albert Museum. Cover title: Brass rubbings. — Bibliography: p. 32–33. Indexes of names and places. — White sized wrappers with illustrations; title in gold.

v.1968.010

Costume : a general bibliography / by Pegaret Anthony and Janet Arnold.
London : Victoria & Albert Museum in association with the Costume Society, 1966 (1968 reprint).
[1] 49 p. ; 28 cm.
(Costume Society bibliography ; no. 1)
Orange wrappers.

v.1968.011

Elizabethan art. 4th imp.
London : H.M.S.O., 1953 (Printed by W.S. Cowell, Ipswich, 1968 printing).
[4] p., 28 p. of plates : ill. ; 18 cm.
(Small picture book ; no. 8)

At head of title: Victoria and Albert Museum. — Introduction signed "G.R."
[i.e. Graham Reynolds].— Green decorated wrappers, printed in black and red. — 3rd
imp. not traced.

v.1968.012   *Elizabethan embroidery.* 5th imp.
London : H.M.S.O., 1948 (Printed by W. & J. Mackay & Co.,
Chatham, 1968).
[6] p., 26 p. of plates : ill. ; 18cm.
(Small picture book ; no. 5)
At head of title: Victoria and Albert Museum. — Introduction signed "G.B."
[i.e. Gerard Brett]. — Cream card decorated wrappers, printed in black and red.

v.1968.013   *English alabasters.*
[London : H.M.S.O.?, 1968?] (Printed by F. Mildner & Sons).
1 sheet, folded ([3] p.) : 1 ill. ; 21 cm.
Caption title: English alabaster carvings 1325–1550. — "A travelling exhibition
arranged by the Circulation Department of the Victoria and Albert Museum."–p. [4].

v.1968.014   *English creamware.*
[London : H.M.S.O., 1968] (Printed by McCorquodale & Co.).
7 p. : 1 ill. ; 25 cm.
Cover title. — "A travelling exhibition arranged by the Circulation Department of the
Victoria and Albert Museum."–p. 3. — Bibliography: p. 7. — Printing: 10/68. —
Stapled.
EXHIBITION: vx.1970.008

v.1968.015   *English desks and bureaux* / J.F. Hayward.
London : H.M.S.O., 1968 (Text [printed] by Butler & Tanner, cover
by Brown Knight & Truscott).
22 p., 40 p. of plates : ill. ; 25 cm.
(Large picture book ; no. 25)
At head of title: Victoria and Albert Museum. — Wrappers with col. ill.

v.1968.016   *English glass* / R.J. Charleston.
[London : H.M.S.O., 1968] (Printed by Norman Brothers Ltd).
15 p., [44] p. of plates : ill. ; 25 cm.
Back cover: Victoria and Albert Museum. — Foreword / John Pope-Hennessy. —
Printing: 7/68. — Sized wrappers; photograph printed on green.
EXHIBITION: vx.1968.015

v.1968.017   *"Englishmen in Italy" : an exhibition held in the Museum, July to
September 1968.*
[London : Printed by H.M.S.O. for the Victoria and Albert Museum,
1968.]
[22] leaves ; 30 cm.
Caption title. At head of title: Victoria & Albert Museum. — Printing: 9/68. — Printed
from typescript, stapled.
EXHIBITION: vx.1968.016

v.1968.018   *The etchings of Anthony Gross* / Graham Reynolds.
[London : H.M.S.O., 1968] (Printed by the Curwen Press).
23 p., 24 p. of plates : ill. ; 19 x 25 cm.
ISBN: 0901486035
Wrappers; ill. printed in black, title in white, on brown.
EXHIBITION: vx.1968.010

v.1968.019   *Exhibition of English glass: catalogue, 1968.*
                [London : Victoria and Albert Museum], 1968.
                [46] p. ; 23 cm.
                Cover title. At head of title: Victoria and Albert Museum. — Includes bibliographic
                references. — Stapled; wrappers with ill.
                Copy note: Some copies have inserted: Errata and addenda, Notes, Supplementary
                exhibits [3] p.
                EXHIBITION: vx.1968.015

v.1968.020   *Fifty masterpieces of metalwork.* 2nd imp.
                London : H.M.S.O., 1951 (Printed by Butler & Tanner, 1968).
                [3] p., 50 leaves of plates : ill. ; 16 cm.
                At head of title: Victoria & Albert Museum. Cover title: 50 masterpieces of metalwork.
                — Sized wrappers coloured green.

v.1968.021   *Fifty masterpieces of pottery, porcelain, glass vessels, stained glass,
                painted enamels : selected and described by officers of the Department
                of Ceramics.* 2nd ed., 2nd imp.
                London : H.M.S.O., 1963 (Printed by Butler & Tanner, 1968).
                102 p., [1] p. of plates : ill. ; 16 cm.
                At head of title: Victoria & Albert Museum. Cover title: 50 masterpieces of pottery and
                glass. — Wrappers; heraldic device and geometric border; printed on pale green.

v.1968.022   *The golden age of Hispanic silver, 1400–1665 /* Charles Oman.
                London : H.M.S.O., 1968 (Text [printed] by Eyre and Spottiswoode
                at Grosvenor Press, Portsmouth ; plates by Cotswold Collotype,
                Wootton-under-Edge).
                xlvii, 71 p., 179 p. of plates : ill., map ; 29 cm.
                At head of title: Victoria and Albert Museum. — Bibliography: p. 59–62. Indexes of
                town marks, goldsmiths and assayers, Museum numbers. — Map on endpapers. Dark
                blue cloth covered boards. — Catalogue of the collection in the Metalwork Department,
                Victoria and Albert Museum.

v.1968.023   *The graphic work of Anthony Gross : a retrospective exhibition,
                1921–1968 : 26 April–28 September 1968.*
                [London : Victoria and Albert Museum, Dept. of Prints and Drawings,
                1968.]
                [22] leaves ; 32 cm.
                At head of title: Victoria and Albert Museum, Department of Prints and Drawings. —
                Reproduced from typescript; stapled in yellow covers.
                EXHIBITION: vx.1968.010

v.1968.024   *Ham House : guide /* Victoria and Albert Museum. [New ed.]
                [London : H.M.S.O., 1968] (Printed by Swindon Press).
                79 p. : ill., plans ; 14 x 22 cm.
                Revised by Maurice Tomlin. Introductory note / John Pope-Hennessy, July 1968. —
                Bibliography: p. 75. — Sized wrappers with ill., coloured red.

v.1968.025   *Hispano Moresque pottery.* 2nd imp.
                London : H.M.S.O., 1957 (Printed by Norman Brothers, 1968).
                [4] p., 28 p. of plates : ill. ; 18 cm.
                (Small picture book ; no. 40)
                At head of title: Victoria and Albert Museum. — Introduction signed "A.L."
                [i.e. Arthur Lane]. — Buff wrappers with decorative design in ochre; title printed in
                blue.

V.1968.026   *Investigations of the Ting ware kiln-site at Chien-Tz'ŭ Ts'un, Hopei* / by Chih Pi-Chê and Lin Hung.
[London] : Victoria & Albert Museum in association with the Oriental Ceramic Society, 1968.
13 p., [8] p. of plates : ill., map ; 29 cm.
(Chinese translations ; no. 4)
Translation of an article first published in *K'ao ku*, no. 8 (1965). — Foreword / Basil Gray. Translator: Hin-Cheung Lovell.

V.1968.027   *Italian stage designs from the Museo teatrale alla Scala, Milan* / by Mario Monteverdi.
[London : H.M.S.O., 1968] (Printed by the Curwen Press).
31 p., [47] p. of plates : ill. ; 19 x 24 cm.
At head of title: Victoria and Albert Museum. — Preface / John Pope-Hennessy. — Printing: 10/68. — Wrappers with illustration in pink and green.
EXHIBITION: VX.1968.018

V.1968.028   *Library photograph collection : index to the principal "X" numbers.*
[London : National Art Library], 1968.
i, 43, i, 37 p. ; 33 cm.
At head of title: Victoria & Albert Museum. — Reproduced from typescript. — Includes corrigenda.

V.1968.029   *Musical instruments as works of art.*
London : H.M.S.O., 1968 (Printed by the Curwen Press).
[101] p. : ill. ; 21 x 30 cm.
(Large special miscellaneous publications ; no. 10)
At head of title: Victoria and Albert Museum. — Foreword / John Pope-Hennessy. — Printing: 6/68. — Preliminary pages printed in red on buff paper. Maroon wrappers with photographic illustration.

V.1968.030   *Nineteenth-century German drawings and water-colours* / by Dieter Graf.
London : Victoria and Albert Museum, 1968.
25 p., 52 p. of plates : ill. ; 19 x 25 cm.
Wrappers, with illustration, printed in red, grey and white on black background.
EXHIBITION: VX.1968.006

V.1968.031   *Nineteenth century German drawings from Düsseldorf : exhibition at the Victoria and Albert Museum, 1968* / a catalogue by Dieter Graf.
[London : Victoria and Albert Museum, 1968.]
37 p. ; 25 cm.
Cover title. — Introduction / John Pope-Hennessy. — Stapled, grey wrappers.
EXHIBITION: VX.1968.006

V.1968.032   *A nonsense alphabet* / by Edward Lear. 7th imp.
London : H.M.S.O., 1952 (Printed by Henry Ling Ltd., the Dorset Press, Dorchester, 1968).
[36] p. : ill. ; 12 x 18 cm.
(Small picture book ; no. 32)
At head of title: Victoria & Albert Museum. — Foreword / Trenchard Cox. Introduction / Brian Reade. — Stapled, salmon wrappers with illustration.

v.1968.033   *Osterley Park : a guide* / by Peter Ward-Jackson. 2nd ed. 8th imp.
              with amendments.
              London : H.M.S.O., 1954 (Printed by Butler & Tanner, 1968).
              19 p., [4] leaves of plates : ill. ; 22 cm.
              At head of title: Victoria & Albert Museum. Cover title: Guide to Osterley Park. —
              Introductory note / John Pope-Hennessy. — Includes bibliographic references. —
              Wrappers, printed in black and white on grey. — 7th imp. not traced.

v.1968.034   *Porcelain figures.* 2nd ed.
              London : H.M.S.O., 1968 (Text [printed] by Butler & Tanner, cover
              by Norman Brothers Ltd.).
              [4] p., 28 p. of plates : ill. ; 19 cm.
              (Small picture book ; no. 3.)
              At head of title: Victoria and Albert Museum. — Text signed "W.B.H." [i.e. W.B.
              Honey]. — Wrappers, coloured tan, with col. ill.

v.1968.035   *Raffaella of Master Alexander Piccolomini : or rather, A dialogue of
              the fair perfectioning of ladies: a worke very necessarie and profitable
              for all gentlewomen or other : first in the Italian tongue for the
              Academy of the Thunderstricken in Siena* / and now first done into
              English by J.N. [i.e. John Nevinson].
              [London : Costume Society c/o Victoria and Albert Museum Dept. of
              Textiles], 1968 (Glasgow : Imprinted . . . by Robert MacLehose and
              Company Limited at the University Press).
              105 p. : ill. ; 22 cm.
              (Costume Society extra series ; no. 1)
              Originally published as: *Dialogo; nel, Quale si ragiona della bella creanza delle donne*
              (1540).

v.1968.036   *Report on the excavation of Lung-ch'üan celadon kiln-sites in
              Chekiang* / by Chu Po-ch'ien.
              [London] : Victoria and Albert Museum in association with the
              Oriental Ceramic Society, 1968.
              13 p., [4] leaves of plates : ill., map ; 29 cm.
              (Chinese translations ; no. 2)
              Abbreviated abstract from a report originally published in *Wen wu*, no. 1, 1963,
              by Chu Po-ch'ien and Wang Shih-lun. — Foreword / Basil Gray. Translator:
              Hin-Cheung Lovell.

v.1968.037   *Report on the investigation of kiln-sites of Ju-type ware and Chün
              ware in Lin-ju Hsien, Honan* / by Fêng Hsien-ming.
              [London] : Victoria & Albert Museum in association with the Oriental
              Ceramic Society, 1968.
              18 p., [3] leaves of plates : ill. ; map ; 29 cm.
              (Chinese translations ; no. 3)
              An abstract translated from a report originally published in *Wen wu*, no. 8, 1964. —
              Foreword / Basil Gray. Translator: Hin-Cheung Lovell.

v.1968.038   *Samplers* / by Donald King. 2nd imp.
              London : H.M.S.O., 1960 (Printed by Balding and Mansell,
              1968).
              15 p., [62] p. of plates : ill. ; 25 cm.
              (Large picture book ; no. 14)

At head of title: Victoria and Albert Museum. — Foreword / Trenchard Cox. — Bibliography: p. 11. — Sized wrappers with col. ill. on front.

v.1968.039   *Signs of the zodiac.* 3rd imp.
London : H.M.S.O., 1964 (Printed by Eyre and Spottiswoode at Grosvenor Press, Portsmouth, 1968).
[28] p. : ill. ; 15 cm.
(Small picture book ; no. 61)
At head of title: Victoria & Albert Museum. — Foreword signed "C.H.G-S" [i.e. Charles Gibbs-Smith]. — Printed on pink paper. White wrappers with illustrations, and title printed in red. — 2nd imp. not traced.

v.1968.040   *A special brief guide for Sundays.*
London : Victoria & Albert Museum, 1968.
10, [1] p. : plans ; 24 cm.
Cover title. Added title: Galleries open on Sundays. — "First edition." — Stapled; blue wrappers.

v.1968.041   *Stage costume design in the twentieth century.*
[London : H.M.S.O.?, 1968] (Printed by F. Mildner & Sons).
1 sheet, folded ([7] p.) : 1 ill. ; 21 cm.
"A travelling exhibition arranged by the Circulation Department of the Victoria and Albert Museum"–p. [7].
EXHIBITION: vx.1970.015

v.1968.042   *Tables in the Victoria and Albert Museum* / by John F. Hayward. 2nd imp.
London : H.M.S.O., 1968 (Printed by Butler & Tanner, Frome).
18 p., 53 p. of plates : ill. ; 22 cm.
(Illustrated booklet ; no. 10)
Sized green wrappers with ornate design of a tabletop illustrated.

v.1968.043   *Tea-pots in pottery and porcelain.* 4th imp.
London : H.M.S.O., 1948 (1968 printing).
[4] p., 28 p. of plates : ill. ; 13 x 19 cm.
(Small picture book ; no. 9)
At head of title: Victoria & Albert Museum. Cover title: Teapots. — Introduction signed "A.L." [i.e. Arthur Lane]. —Sized wrappers; illustration on front printed on orange.

v.1968.044   *Victorian paintings.* 2nd ed., 2nd imp.
London : H.M.S.O., 1963 (Printed by Butler & Tanner Ltd., 1968).
[4] p., 28 p. of plates : ill. ; 18 cm.
(Small picture book ; no. 10)
At head of title: Victoria and Albert Museum. — Introduction signed "G.R." [i.e. Graham Reynolds]. — Sized wrappers with illustration; title reversed out on tan stripe.

v.1968.045   *Wedgwood.* 3rd imp.
London : H.M.S.O., 1958 (Printed by Norman Brothers Ltd., 1968).
[4] p., [28] p. of plates : ill. ; 19 cm.
(Small picture book ; no. 45)
At head of title: Victoria & Albert Museum. — Introduction signed "R.J.C." [i.e. R.J. Charleston]. — Sized wrappers with illustration on front, printed on blue.

v.1968.046   *Woodworm in furniture.*
London : Conservation Department of the Victoria and Albert Museum, 1968.

1 sheet, folded ([4] p.) ; 21 cm.
(Technical notes on the care of art objects ; no. 2)

1969

V.1969.001   *Adam silver*. Repr.
London : H.M.S.O., 1969.
(Small picture book ; no. 35)
ISBN: 0112900577
Unseen. Listed in *Government publications : Victoria and Albert Museum*. London :
H.M.S.O., 1972. (Sectional list ; 55).

V.1969.002   *Architecture, post Classical, British Isles*.
London : Victoria & Albert Museum, Slide Loan Service, 1969.
219 p. ; 33 cm.
(Catalogue of 2 x 2 lantern slides)
Cover title. — "This catalogue is for reference only." — Stapled in green paper covers.

V.1969.003   *Art nouveau pewter : a travelling exhibition arranged by the
Circulation Department of the Victoria and Albert Museum.*
[London : H.M.S.O.?, 1969?] ("F.M. & S.", printer).
1 sheet, folded (7 p.) : 1 ill. ; 20 cm.
EXHIBITION: VX.1970.016

V.1969.004   *An arts and crafts experiment : the silverwork of C.R. Ashbee* / by
Shirley Bury.
[London : Victoria and Albert Museum, 1969] (Printed for H.M.S.O.
by Eyre and Spottiswoode, Thanet Press, Margate).
9 p. : ill. ; 25 cm.
(Victoria and Albert Museum bulletin reprints ; 7)
"Reprinted from the *Bulletin*, Vol. III, no. l." — Includes bibliographic references. —
Stapled; wrappers coloured yellow.

V.1969.005   *Batiks.*
London : H.M.S.O., 1969 (Text [printed] by Norman Brothers, cover
by the Curwen Press.).
15 p., 32 p. of plates : ill. (some col.), map ; 30 cm.
(Large picture book ; no. 28)
ISBN: 0112900518
At head of title: Victoria and Albert Museum. — Foreword / John Pope-Hennessy.
Produced by John Irwin and Veronica Murphy. — Designed by H.M.S.O./Philip
Marriage. — Turquoise sized wrappers with illustration.

V.1969.006   *Canova's* Theseus and the Minotaur / Hugh Honour.
[London] : Victoria & Albert Museum, [1969?].
15 p. : ill. ; 28 cm.
Cover title. — "Reprinted from the *Victoria and Albert Museum* Yearbook I."

V.1969.007   *Cesare Borgia's sword-scabbard* / by Claude Blair.
London : Victoria and Albert Museum, 1969 (Printed for H.M.S.O.
by Eyre & Spottiswoode, Thanet Press, Margate).
14 p. : ill. ; 25 cm.
(Victoria and Albert Museum bulletin reprints ; 6)

"Reprinted from the *Bulletin*, Vol. II, no. 4." — Includes bibliographic references. — Stapled; wrappers coloured olive.

V.1969.008   *Claud Lovat Fraser* / by Grace Lovat Fraser.
London : H.M.S.O., 1969 (Printed at the Baynard Press).
29, 40 p. : ill. (some col.) ; 25 cm.
At head of title: Victoria and Albert Museum. — Foreword / Brian Reade. — Colour frontispiece tipped in.
EXHIBITION: VX.1969.010

V.1969.009   *Collingwood-Coper : rugs and wall-hangings by Peter Collingwood : pots by Hans Coper.*
[London : H.M.S.O., 1969] (Printed by the Curwen Press).
25 p. : ill., ports. ; 30 cm.
At head of title: Victoria and Albert Museum. — Foreword / John Pope-Hennessy. — Designed by HMSO-Alan Stephens. — Stapled, stone-coloured wrappers with illustration.
EXHIBITION: VX.1969.001

V.1969.010   *Collingwood Coper exhibition : catalogue.*
[London : Victoria and Albert Museum, 1969.]
1 sheet, folded ([6] p.) ; 24 cm.
Folded so that title forms cover.
EXHIBITION: VX.1969.001

V.1969.011   *Degas's ballet scene from* Robert le diable / *by Jonathan Mayne.*
London : Victoria and Albert Museum, 1969 (Dragon Press, Luton, printer).
10 p. : ill. ; 25 cm.
(Victoria and Albert Museum bulletin reprints ; 2)
"Reprinted from the *Bulletin*, Vol. II, No.4." — Includes bibliographic references. — Stapled, wrappers coloured purple.

V.1969.012   *Designs for English sculpture, 1680–1860* / John Physick.
London : H.M.S.O., 1969 (Printed by Butler and Tanner).
xiii, 205 p. : ill. (some col.) ; 29 cm.
ISBN: 0112900283
At head of title: Victoria and Albert Museum. — Foreword / John Pope-Hennessy: "a record of some of the material in that exhibition [i.e. VX.1966.009]." — Includes bibliographic references. Index. — Designed by HMSO/Alan Stephens. — Ill. on title page. Illustrated endpapers. Green cloth covered boards with brown pictorial endpapers printed in green. Pictorial dust-jacket; title printed in green.
EXHIBITION: VX.1966.009

V.1969.013   *Dolls.* 2nd ed.
London, H.M.S.O., 1968 [i.e. 1969] (Printed by Butler & Tanner).
[7] p., 28 p. of plates : ill. ; 19 cm.
(Small picture book ; no. 50)
Text signed "M.B.G." [i.e. Madeleine Ginsburg]. — Bibliography: p. [7]. — Green patterned wrappers with ills.

V.1969.014   *The Duke of Wellington : a pictorial survey of his life (1769–1852)* / by Victor Percival.
London : H.M.S.O., 1969 (Printed by Ebenezer Baylis and Son).
86 p. : ill., facsims., ports. ; 31 cm.
ISBN: 0112900224

At head of title: Victoria and Albert Museum. — Foreword / the Duke of Wellington. —
Bibliography: p. 85. — Designed by HMSO/Alan Stephens. — 1 col. ill. (port.) tipped-
in. — Grey wrappers printed inside and out, in red, with continuous illustration.

v.1969.015   *Early Victorian : costume 1830–1860 : proceedings of the third
                Annual Conference of the Costume Society, 1969.*
                London : Published for the Costume Society, Victoria and Albert
                Museum, 1969.
                [4] 46 p. : ill., ports. ; 27 cm.
                Includes: Men and angels : fashion 1830–1860 / Geoffrey Squire. Romantic to
                sentimental : the changing line of women's dress, 1830–1860 / Janet Arnold. Military
                costume / Daphne Edmonds. Hats, bonnets and hairstyles / Daphne Bullard. Boots and
                shoes / June Swann. Gloves / P.H. Rigden. Embroidering by machine / Joan Edwards.
                The early Victorian needlemakers / John G. Rollins. The young Queen and her clothes /
                Madeleine Ginsburg. — Includes bibliographies. — Stapled; white sized wrappers with
                ill. in silhouette.

v.1969.016   *Elizabethan embroidery.* Repr.
                London : H.M.S.O., 1969.
                (Small picture book ; no. 5)
                Unseen. Listed in *Government publications : Victoria and Albert Museum*. London :
                H.M.S.O., 1972. (Sectional list ; 55).

v.1969.017   *Embroidery today : 62 Group of the Embroiderers' Guild : a
                travelling exhibition arranged by the Circulation Department of the
                Victoria and Albert Museum.*
                [London : The Museum, 1969.]
                1 sheet, folded ([5] p.) ; 24 cm.
                EXHIBITION: vx.1969.007

v.1969.018   *English cutlery : sixteenth to eighteenth century* / J.F. Hayward. 2nd
                imp.
                London : H.M.S.O., 1957 (Printed by Butler & Tanner, 1969).
                44 p. : ill. ; 21 cm.
                At head of title: Victoria and Albert Museum. — Bibliography: p. 18. — Pale blue
                wrappers with illustrated title.

v.1969.019   *English handwriting, 1540–1853 : an illustrated survey based on
                material in the National Art Library, Victoria and Albert Museum* / by
                Joyce Irene Whalley.
                London : H.M.S.O., 1969 (Printed by Jarrold and Sons, Norwich).
                [1], xxiii, 92 p. : ill. (1 col.), facsims., ports. ; 29 x 38 cm.
                ISBN: 011290047X
                At head of title: Victoria and Albert Museum. — Foreword / John Pope-Hennessy: "Part
                of this material was shown in the exhibition [vx.1964.010]." — Bibliographies: p. xx-
                xxii. Glossary of hands. Index. — Designed by HMSO/Alan Stephens. — Green cloth
                covered boards. Lime-green end-papers with facsims. Green dust-jacket with facsim.

v.1969.020   *English watches* / by J.F. Hayward. 2nd ed.
                London : H.M.S.O., 1969 (Printed by Butler & Tanner).
                [4], 14, [64] p. : ill. ; 21 cm.
                ISBN: 0112903266
                At head of title: Victoria and Albert Museum. — Foreword / John Pope-Hennessy:
                "This handbook contains a brief survey of the history of watch-making in England
                followed by a catalogue raisonnée [sic] of the more important English watches in the
                Museum collection." — Bibliography: p. 13-14. — Wrappers, with line illustration
                printed on green.

v.1969.021   *European firearms* / by J.F. Hayward. 2nd ed.
London, H.M.S.O., 1969 (Printed by Butler & Tanner).
[4], 64 p., xliii p. of plates : ill. ; 25 cm.
ISBN: 0112900526
At head of title: Victoria and Albert Museum. — "A guide to the Museum collection of firearms"–Foreword / John Pope-Hennessy. — Bibliography: p. 37–38. — Grey wrappers, with illustrated title printed in purple and red.

v.1969.022   *The fashionable lady in the 19th century* / by Charles H. Gibbs-Smith. 2nd imp.
London : H.M.S.O., 1960 (Printed by Butler & Tanner, 1969).
[4], 184 p. : (chiefly ill.) ; 26 cm.
ISBN: 0112902294
At head of title: Victoria and Albert Museum. — Foreword / John Pope-Hennessy. — Bibliography: p. 181; Sources: p. 182–184. — Cream wrappers with coloured illustration; title printed in green. Or red cloth covered boards with illustration blind stamped; cream dust-jacket with coloured illustration.

v.1969.023   *Fine illustrations in Western European printed books* / by T.M. MacRobert.
London : H.M.S.O., 1969 (Printed by Butler & Tanner).
23 P., [106] p. of plates : ill. ; 25 cm.
(Large picture book ; no. 38)
At head of title: Victoria and Albert Museum. — Foreword / John Pope-Hennessy. — Selected from books in the National Art Library, Victoria and Albert Museum. — Bibliography: p. 15–17. — Wrappers, illustration printed in purple.

v.1969.024   *Four artists : reliefs, constructions and drawings : John Ernest, Anthony Hill, Malcolm Hughes, Gillian Wise.*
[London : Victoria and Albert Museum, 1969?].
[10] p. : ill., ports. ; 25 cm.
Cover title. — "A Victoria and Albert Museum loan exhibition."–Cover. — Stapled, wrappers.

v.1969.025   *Georgian furniture.* 3rd ed.
London : H.M.S.O., 1969 (Printed by Norman Brothers).
30 p., [288] leaves of plates : ill. (some col.) ; 29 cm.
(Large picture book ; no. 1)
ISBN: 0112900275
At head of title: Victoria & Albert Museum. — "A new edition revised and edited by Desmond Fitz-Gerald." Foreword / John Pope-Hennessy. — Bibliography: p. 21. — Blue cloth covered boards, with illustration on blue end-papers. Coloured pictorial dust-jacket.

v.1969.026   *Handel at Vauxhall* / by Terence Hodgkinson.
London : Victoria and Albert Museum, 1969 (Printed for H.M.S.O. by Butler & Tanner).
14 p. : ill. ; 25 cm. (Victoria and Albert Museum bulletin reprints ; 1)
"Reprinted from the *Bulletin*, Vol. I, no. 4 . . . with revisions." – Includes bibliographic references. — Stapled; wrappers coloured green. — Sculpture by Roubiliac.

v.1969.027   *The Harborne room* / by Barbara Morris.
London : Victoria and Albert Museum, 1969 (Printed for H.M.S.O. by Eyre & Spottiswoode).
15 p. : ill. ; 25 cm.
(Victoria and Albert Museum bulletin reprints ; 8)

"Reprinted from the *Bulletin*, Vol. IV, no. 3." — Includes bibliographic references. — Stapled; wrappers coloured green. — Room designed by John Henry Chamberlain.

v.1969.028   *High Victorian : costume 1860–1890 : proceedings of the second annual conference of the Costume Society, March 1968.*
London : Published for the Society, Victoria and Albert Museum, 1969.
[4], 53 p. : ill. ; 26 cm.
Edited by Ann Saunders. — Includes: Clothing manufacture, 1860–1890 / Madeleine Ginsburg. Pictorial sources for a study of costume, 1860–90 / Richard Ormond. Sartorial facts and fashions of the early 1890s / A.A. Whife. The cut and construction of women's dresses / Janet Arnold. Wedding dresses / Susan Mackenzie. The trap re-baited : mourning dress 1860–90 / Anne Buck. The foundations of fashion, 1860–1890 / Pegaret Anthony. Symingtons' corsets / C.E. Page. Machine lace in costume, 1860–1890 / Zillah Halls. — Stapled; white sized wrappers with ill. in silhouette.

v.1969.029   *The history of the Victoria & Albert Museum.* 3rd imp.
London : H.M.S.O., 1952 (Printed by Butler & Tanner, 1969).
32 p. : ill., ports. ; 16 cm.
(Small picture book ; no. 31)
ISBN: 0112900097
Revised by Shirley Bury. Foreword / John Pope-Hennessy. — Stapled; orange wrappers printed in black and white.

v.1969.030   *Indian art.*
London : H.M.S.O., 1969 (Cover [printed] by Multi-Machine Plates, text by Butler & Tanner).
vii, 62 p. of plates : ill. ; 25 cm.
(Large picture book ; no. 36)
ISBN: 0112900062
At head of title: Victoria and Albert Museum. — Preface signed "J.C.I." [i.e. J.C. Irwin]. — Includes list of guides to the Museum's collections of Indian art.— Designed by HMSO: Philip Marriage. — Green sized wrappers with illustration.

v.1969.031   *Italian Renaissance maiolica : a travelling exhibition mounted by the Circulation Department of the Victoria & Albert Museum.*
[London : The Museum, 1969] (Printed by Jarrold & Sons).
1 sheet ; 30 x 42 cm. folded to 30 x 11 cm.
Includes short bibliography. — Printing: 8/69. — Printed in brown on cream paper. illustrated title.

v.1969.032   *Lithographs by Honoré Daumier, 1808–1879 : a travelling exhibition arranged by the Circulation Department of the Victoria and Albert Museum.*
[London] : Printed for H.M.S.O. by the Curwen Press, [1969?].
1 sheet, folded (7 p.) : 1 ill. ; 30 x 11 cm.
Illustrated title. Display text printed in green.

v.1969.033   *Notes on carpet-knotting and weaving* / by C.E.C. Tattersall. 2nd [rev.] ed.
London : H.M.S.O., 1969.
[42 p., 14 plates : ill., 19 cm.]
ISBN: 0112900348
Unseen. Record from OCLC.

v.1969.034   *Opera in Victorian London : a travelling exhibition arranged by the Circulation Department of the Victoria and Albert Museum.*
[London] : H.M.S.O., [1969?] (Printed by the Curwen Press).
1 sheet (7 p.) ; 30 x 11 cm.
Printed on red paper. Illustrated title.

v.1969.035   *Paintings by artists of all nationalities arranged alphabetically.* 3rd ed., 1969/1970.
[London : Victoria & Albert Museum, Slide Loan Service, 1969?]
2 v. (188, 169 p.) ; 33 cm.
(Catalogue of 2" x 2" colour transparencies)
Cover title. At head of title: Victoria & Albert Museum Slide Loan Service. Part 1: Unattributed; Artists A–K. Part 2: Artists L–Z. — "This catalogue is for reference only."

v.1969.036   *Photographs by Henri Cartier-Bresson : Victoria & Albert Museum loan exhibition.*
[London : The Museum, 1969.]
1 sheet, folded : 1 ill. ; 29 x 44 cm. folded to 29 x 13 cm.
Foreword / Hugh Wakefield. Introduction signed "C.H." [i.e. Carol Hogben]. — Bibliography.
EXHIBITION: vx.1969.004

v.1969.037   *Queen Anne domestic silver.* Repr.
London : H.M.S.O., 1969.
(Small picture book ; no. 25)
ISBN: 0112900631
Unseen. Listed in *Government publications : Victoria and Albert Museum.* London : H.M.S.O., 1972. (Sectional list ; 55).

v.1969.038   *Recent acquisitions.*
[London] : Issued by the Dept. of Public Relations and Education, [Victoria and Albert Museum], 1969.
[9] leaves ; 30cm.
Caption title. At head of title: Victoria and Albert Museum press notice — Duplicated typescript.
EXHIBITION: vx.1969.003

v.1969.039   *The Rood-loft from Hertogenbosch* / Charles Avery.
London : Victoria and Albert Museum, 1969.
27 p. : ill. ; 28 cm.
"Reprinted from the *Victoria and Albert Museum yearbook* 1, 1969." — Includes bibliographic references.

v.1969.040   *The Shah Jahan cup* / by Robert Skelton.
London : Victoria and Albert Museum, 1969 (Printed for H.M.S.O. by Eyre & Spottiswoode Ltd., Thanet Press, Margate).
10 p. : ill. ; 25 cm.
(Victoria and Albert Museum bulletin reprints ; 5)
"Reprinted from the *Bulletin*, Vol. II, no. 3 . . . with revision." — Includes bibliographic references. — Stapled; wrappers coloured blue.

v.1969.041   *Some main streams and tributaries in European ornament from 1500 to 1750* / Peter Ward-Jackson.
London : Victoria and Albert Museum, 1969 (Printed for H.M.S.O. by Eyre & Spottiswoode, Thanet Press, Margate).

44 p. : ill. ; 25 cm.
(Victoria and Albert Museum bulletin reprints ; 3)
"Reprinted from the *Bulletin*, Vol. III, nos. 2–4." — Bibliography: p. 44. — Stapled; wrappers coloured turquoise.

V.1969.042   *A subject index for the visual arts* / compiled by Elizabeth Glass.
London : H.M.S.O., 1969.
2 v. (xix, 472 p.) : ill. ; 32 cm.
At head of title: Victoria and Albert Museum, Department of Prints and Drawings and Department of Paintings. — Foreword / Graham Reynolds. — Part I. Part II, Cross-references. — Printing: 12/68. — Printed from typescript, with typeset t.p. Printed transversely. Blue cloth covered boards. Printed paper label on spine. — "The present list . . . is the outcome of long experience in the Print Room of the Victoria and Albert Museum"–Foreword.

V.1969.043   *Tables.* Repr.
London : H.M.S.O., 1969.
(Illustrated booklet ; no. 10)
Unseen. Listed in *Government publications : Victoria and Albert Museum.* London : H.M.S.O., 1972. (Sectional list ; 55).

V.1969.044   *A tortoiseshell cabinet and its precursors* / by Simon Jervis.
London : Victoria and Albert Museum, 1969 (Printed for H.M.S.O. by Eyre & Spottiswoode, Thanet Press, Margate).
13 p. : ill. ; 25 cm.
(Victoria and Albert Museum bulletin reprints ; 9)
"Reprinted from the *Bulletin*, Vol. IV, no. 4 . . . with revision." — Includes bibliographic references. — Stapled; wrappers coloured mustard.

V.1969.045   *The Twenties : female fashion, 1920 to 1929 : a travelling exhibition arranged by the Circulation Department of the Victoria and Albert Museum.*
[London : H.M.S.O.?, 1969?]
1 sheet (6 p.) ; 30 x 11 cm.
Printed in blue on plum-coloured paper, with title illustration in pink. Title printed transversely.

V.1969.046   *Victoria and Albert Museum : brief guide.*
[London : H.M.S.O., 1969] (Printed by Butler & Tanner).
63 p. : ill., plans ; 30 x 12 cm.
Index to rooms. — Printing: 12/69. — Stapled; wrappers coloured red, with ill.; plans on turn-ins.

1970

V.1970.001   *Adolphe Appia.*
London : H.M.S.O., 1970 (Printed by St. Clements Fosh and Cross).
26 p., [15] p. of plates : ill., ports. ; 20 cm.
ISBN: 0901486221
At head of title: Victoria and Albert Museum. — Compiled by Edmund Stadler. Foreword / John Pope-Hennessy. — Stapled; wrappers coloured red.
EXHIBITION: VX.1970.018

V.1970.001A   2nd imp.

V.1970.002 *Arms and armour of old Japan* / by B.W. Robinson. 3rd imp.
London : H.M.S.O., 1951 (Printed by Butler & Tanner, 1970).
17 p., 26 p. of plates : ill. ; 21 cm.
(Illustrated booklet ; no. 6)
ISBN: 0112900747
At head of title: Victoria & Albert Museum. Cover title: Arms & armour of old Japan.
— Buff wrappers with illustration printed in tan.

V.1970.003 *Art & the East India trade.*
London : H.M.S.O., 1970 (Printed by Eyre & Spottiswoode,
Grosvenor Press, Portsmouth).
[36] p. : chiefly ill. ; 20 x 21 cm.
ISBN: 0901486272
At head of title: Victoria and Albert Museum. — Introduction signed: "J.C.I."
[i.e. John Irwin]. — Designed by HMSO: Philip Marriage. — Stapled. Red, black and
white illustrated wrappers. Map on inside back cover.
EXHIBITION: VX.1970.019

V.1970.004 *The basic stitches of embroidery* / by N. Victoria Wade. 2nd ed., 2nd
imp.
London : H.M.S.O., 1966 (Cover [printed] by Lonsdale &
Bartholomew Printing, Leicester, text by Product Support (Graphics)
Ltd., 1970).
[2], 26 p. : ill. ; 25 cm.
ISBN: 0112900860
At head of title: Victoria & Albert Museum. — Foreword / John Pope-Hennessy. —
Ivory wrappers, printed in blue.

V.1970.005 *The care of portrait miniatures.*
London : Issued by the Conservation Department of the Victoria and
Albert Museum, 1970.
1 sheet, folded ([3] p.) ; 21 cm.
(Technical notes on the care of art objects ; no. 3)

V.1970.006 *The care of wax objects.*
London : Issued by the Conservation Department of the Victoria and
Albert Museum, 1970.
1 sheet, folded ([3] p.) ; 21cm.
(Technical notes on the care of art objects ; no. 4)

V.1970.007 *Catalogue of rubbings of brasses and incised slabs* / by Muriel
Clayton. 2nd ed., 3rd imp.
London : H.M.S.O., 1968 (Printed by A. Wheaton & Co., Exeter,
1970).
xiv, 250 p., 72 p. of plates : ill. ; 25 cm.
At head of title: Victoria and Albert Museum. Cover title: Brass rubbings. —
Bibliography: p. 32–33. Place and name indexes. — White sized wrappers with
illustration. — 2nd imp. not traced.

V.1970.008 *Charles Dickens : an exhibition to commemorate the centenary of his
death, June-September 1970.*
London : H.M.S.O., 1970 (Text printed by Lonsdale & Bartholomew,
Leicester; illustrations by Curwen Press).
121 p., [60] p. of plates : ill., facsims., 1 plan, ports. ; 28 cm.

At head of title: Victoria and Albert Museum. — Foreword / John Pope-Hennessy. Introduction / Graham Reynolds. — Designed by HMSO: Philip Marriage. — Wrappers coloured red.

EXHIBITION: VX.1970.012

V.1970.009   *Chinese court robes in the Victoria and Albert Museum* / by Edmund Capon.
London : Victoria and Albert Museum, 1970 (Printed for H.M.S.O. by St Clements Fosh & Cross).
11 p. : ill. ; 25 cm.
(Victoria and Albert Museum bulletin reprints ; 14)
"Reprinted from the *Bulletin*, Vol. IV, no. 1." — Includes bibliographic references. — Stapled in wrappers coloured lime green.

V.1970.010   *Claud Lovat Fraser, 1890–1921 : a travelling exhibition arranged by the Circulation Department of the Victoria and Albert Museum.*
[London] : H.M.S.O., [1970] (Printed by Curwen Press).
1 sheet, folded (8 p.) : 1 ill. ; 30 x 11 cm.
Introduction printed on green background.

V.1970.011   *Design in glass : an exhibition of student work from three British art colleges 1969–1970 : a travelling exhibition arranged by the Circulation Department of the Victoria and Albert Museum.*
[London] : H.M.S.O., [1970?] (Printed by Curwen Press).
1 sheet, folded (5) ; p. 30 x 11 cm.
Printed in green on grey paper. Decorative title.
EXHIBITION: VX.1971.009

V.1970.012   *Dolls in the nineteenth century : a travelling exhibition arranged by the Circulation Department of the Victoria and Albert Museum.*
[London : H.M.S.O., 1970.]
1 sheet, folded ([6] p.) : ill. ; 30 x 11 cm.
Printed pink on purple (recto) and vice versa (verso). Title and captions in red.

V.1970.013   *Drawings from the Teyler Museum, Haarlem* / by I.Q. van Regteren Altena and P.W. Ward-Jackson.
[London : H.M.S.O., 1970] (Printed by Eyre & Spottiswoode, Thanet Press, Margate).
84 p., [1], 118 p. of plates : ill., port. ; 20 x 21 cm.
Foreword / John Pope-Hennessy. — Bibliographic references: p. 77–[79]. Index of artists. — Designed by HMSO / John Saville. — Silver card cover with illustration.
EXHIBITION: VX.1970.005

V.1970.014   *English chairs* / with an introduction by Ralph Edwards. 3rd ed.
London : H.M.S.O., 1970 (Printed by Butler & Tanner, Frome).
28 p., [1], 129 p. of plates : ill. (1 col.) ; 25 cm.
(Large picture book ; no. 10)
ISBN: 0112900313
At head of title: Victoria and Albert Museum. — Revised by Desmond Fitz-Gerald, assisted by Simon Jervis & J. Hardy. Foreword / John Pope-Hennessy. — Select bibliography: p. 17. — Sized card wrappers with photograph printed yellow on bright orange.

V.1970.015   *The engraved work of Eric Gill*. Repr.
London : H.M.S.O., 1970.

(Large picture book ; no. 17)
ISBN: 0112900402
Unseen. Listed in *Government publications : Victoria and Albert Museum.* London : H.M.S.O., 1972. (Sectional list ; 55).

V.1970.016 The exact dress of the head *by Bernard Lens, 1725.*
London : Costume Society c/o Victoria and Albert Museum, 1970.
9 p., 30 p. of plates : ill., facsims. ; 14 x 22 cm.
(Costume Society extra series ; no. 2)
First published 1726. — Introduction by John L. Nevinson.

V.1970.017 *The furniture designs of E.W. Godwin* / Elizabeth Aslin.
London : Victoria and Albert Museum, 1970 (Printed for H.M.S.O by St Clements Fosh & Cross).
12 p. : ill. ; 25 cm.
(Victoria and Albert Museum bulletin reprints ; 13)
"Reprinted from the *Bulletin*, Vol. III, no. 4." — Includes bibliographic references. — Stapled in wrappers coloured red. — The designs are in the collections of the Victoria and Albert Museum.

V.1970.018 *Guide to English embroidery* / by Patricia Wardle.
London : H.M.S.O., 1970 (Text [printed] by Butler & Tanner; cover by Swindon Press).
40 p., 57 p. of plates : ill. (1 col.) ; 19 x 25 cm.
ISBN: 0112900305
At head of title: Victoria and Albert Museum. — [Preface] by George Wingfield Digby. — Bibliography: p. 27-28. — Card cover with coloured illustration.

V.1970.019 *Illuminated manuscripts.*
[London : Victoria and Albert Museum], 1970.
25 p. ; 33 cm.
(Catalogue of 2 x 2 lantern slides)
Cover title. At head of title: Victoria & Albert Museum, Slide Loan Service. — About the Service / James C. Strand. — Printing: 12/68 [sic]. — Stapled in green paper covers.

V.1970.020 *Kiln-site investigations.*
London : Victoria & Albert Museum in association with the Oriental Ceramic Society, 1970.
20,18,19,p., [17] p. of plates : ill., maps ; 31 cm.
(Chinese translations ; no. 5)
Translations of articles first published in *Wen wu* (1964). — Foreword / Basil Gray. Tz'ŭ chou ware kiln-sites / by Li Hui-ping. Kiln-sites at Hao-Pi-Chi, Honan / by the staff of the Honan Culture Bureau. T'ang & Sung kiln-sites in Mi-hsien and Têng-fêng Hsien, Honan / by Fêng Hsien-ming. Translator: Hin-Cheung Lovell. — Stapled, in tan paper covers.

V.1970.021 *A masterpiece by Hubert Gerhard* / by Michael Baxandall.
London : Victoria and Albert Museum, 1970 (Printed for H.M.S.O. by St Clements Fosh & Cross).
19 p. : ill. ; 25 cm.
(Victoria and Albert Museum bulletin reprints ; 10)
"Reprinted, with revisions, from the *Bulletin*, Vol. I, no. 2." — "Bibliographical note": p. 18-19. — Stapled; card wrappers coloured orange. — Concerns the Christopher Fugger altar.

v.1970.022   *Modern Swedish ballet.*
London : H.M.S.O., 1970 (Printed by St. Clements Fosh & Cross, text and illustrations; Swindon Signcraft, cover).
[32] p. : ill., ports. ; 30 cm.
ISBN: 0901486337
At head of title: Victoria and Albert Museum. — Foreword / John Pope-Hennessy. The wise fools / Bent Häger. — Printing: 7/70. — Black card cover with illustration in black, title in pink.
EXHIBITION: vx.1970.014

v.1970.023   *Monti's allegory of the Risorgimento* / by Anthony Radcliffe.
London : Victoria and Albert Museum, 1970 (Printed for H.M.S.O. by Eyre & Spottiswoode, Thanet Press, Margate).
16 p. : ill. ; 25 cm.
(Victoria and Albert Museum bulletin reprints ; 4)
"Reprinted, with revisions, from the *Bulletin*, Vol. I". — Includes bibliographic references. — Stapled; card wrappers coloured puce.

v.1970.024   *The Mount Trust collection of Chinese art.*
London : Victoria and Albert Museum, 1970 (Printed by Eyre & Spottiswoode, Thanet Press, Margate).
[52] p. : ill. ; 25 cm.
At head of title: Victoria and Albert Museum. — Foreword / John Pope-Hennessy. Introduction signed "J.G.A." [i.e. John Ayers]. — Includes bibliographic references. — Wrappers, with ill. printed on front, on brown. — The collection was formed by Vivian Bulkeley-Johnson.
EXHIBITION: vx.1970.003

v.1970.025   *Origins of chintz : with a catalogue of Indo-European cotton-paintings in the Victoria and Albert Museum, London, and the Royal Ontario Museum, Toronto* / John Irwin and Katharine B. Brett.
London : H.M.S.O., 1970 (Printed by Butler & Tanner; colour plates by Dragon Press, Luton).
ii-viii, 132, [1] p., 166 plates. illus. (incl. 8 col.), maps. 31 cm.
ISBN: 0112900534
Bibliography: p. 59–63. Index. Concordance of Museum numbers. — Red cloth covered boards lettered in white. Ill. on dust-jacket.

v.1970.026   *Recent acquisitions 1969–70.*
[London] : Issued by the Department of Public Relations and Education, 1970.
[14] leaves ; 30 cm.
Caption title. At head of title: Victoria and Albert Museum press notice. — Reproduced typescript.
EXHIBITION: vx.1970.011

v.1970.027   *Swords & daggers* / by J.F. Hayward. 2nd ed. (2nd imp., amended)
London : H.M.S.O., 1963 (Text printed by Butler & Tanner, Frome ; cover by Product Support (Graphics) Ltd., Derby, 1970).
11 p. 46 p. of plates : chiefly ill. ; 22 cm.
(Illustrated booklet ; no. 3)
At head of title: Victoria and Albert Museum. — Cream card cover with ill.; title printed in red.

V.1970.028   *Tiepolo drawings : drawings by G.B. Tiepolo (1696–1770) from the*
Print Room of the Victoria and Albert Museum : a travelling
exhibition arranged by the Circulation Department of the Victoria and
Albert Museum.
[London : The Museum, 1970] (Printed by Lonsdale & Bartholomew
Printing, Leicester).
1 sheet, folded (7 p.) : 1 ill. ; 30 x 11 cm.
Text by Graham Reynolds. — Title printed in ochre and black.
EXHIBITION: VX.1969.BGM.001

V.1970.029   *Treasures from Althorp.*
[London : H.M.S.O.?, 1970.]
[4] p., 36 p. of plates : chiefly ill. ; 25 cm.
ISBN: 0901486019
At head of title: Victoria and Albert Museum. — Blue wrappers printed in violet.
EXHIBITION: VX.1970.007

V.1970.030   *Treasures from Althorp.*
[London : Victoria and Albert Museum, 1970] (Archer & Goodman,
Northampton, printer).
[10] p.; 25 cm.
Cover title. At foot of title: Victoria and Albert Museum. — Stapled exhibition
handlist.
EXHIBITION: VX.1970.007

V.1970.031   *Tudor domestic silver.*
London : H.M.S.O., 1970 (Printed by Butler & Tanner).
9 p., 30 p. of plates : ill. ; 22 cm.
(Illustrated booklet ; no. 15)
ISBN: 0112900429
Text signed "R.W.L." [i.e. Ronald Lightbown]. "Formerly Small picture book no.
6"–t.p. verso. — Silver wrappers with illustration.

V.1970.032   *Two garden sculptures by Antonio Corradini* / by Terence
Hodgkinson.
London : Victoria and Albert Museum, 1970 (Printed for H.M.S.O.
by Eyre & Spottiswoode, Thanet Press, Margate).
14 p. : ill. ; 25 cm.
(Victoria and Albert Museum bulletin reprints ; 11)
"Reprinted from the *Bulletin*, Vol. IV, no. 2 . . . with revisions and new photographs."
— Includes bibliographic references. — Stapled; card wrappers coloured orange.

V.1970.033   *A Venetian embroidered altar frontal* / by Donald King.
London : Victoria and Albert Museum, 1970 (Printed for H.M.S.O.
by Eyre & Spottiswoode, Thanet Press, Margate).
12 p. : ill. ; 27 cm.
(Victoria and Albert Museum bulletin reprints ; 12)
"Reprinted from the *Bulletin*, Vol. I, no. 4 . . . with revision." — Includes bibliographic
references. — Stapled; wrappers coloured orange.

V.1970.034   *The Wellington Monument* / by John Physick.
London : H.M.S.O., 1970 (Printed by Butler & Tanner).
xi, 176 p. : ill., ports. ; 25 cm.
ISBN: 0112900550

At head of title: Victoria and Albert Museum. — Includes: Catalogue of the models exhibited in Westminster Hall, 1857, with criticisms from contemporary sources. — Includes bibliographic references. Index. — Sized wrappers. Illustrated title, printed on orange. — Monument designed by Alfred Stevens.

V.1970.035   *"What the children like" : a selection of children's books, toys and games from the Renier Collection : exhibited at the Victoria and Albert Museum, December 1970–February 1971.*
[London : Victoria and Albert Museum, 1970.]
[28] p. ; 30 cm.
Catalogue based on labels compiled for the exhibition by Irene Whalley and Anne Hobbs.
EXHIBITION: VX.1970.021

V.1970.036   *Whistler : etchings and lithographs by J.A.McN. Whistler 1834–1903 : a travelling exhibition arranged by the Circulation Department of the Victoria and Albert Museum.*
[London : H.M.S.O., 1970] (McCorquodale Printers).
1 sheet, folded ([5] p.) : port. ; 30 x 11 cm.
Printed in sage green and gold on buff paper. Printed in columns. Illustrated title.
EXHIBITION: VX.1972.BGM.002

1971

V.1971.001   *The art of observation: a booklet for museum warders* / by Charles H. Gibbs-Smith.
[London] : H.M.S.O., 1971.
[16] p. ; 19 cm.
Cover title. At head of title: Victoria and Albert Museum. — "For official use." — Stapled; yellow wrappers.

V.1971.002   *Barnaba da Modena and the flagellants of Genoa* / by C.M. Kauffmann.
London : Victoria and Albert Museum, 1971 (Printed for H.M.S.O. by St. Clements Fosh & Cross).
11 p. : ill. ; 25 cm.
(Victoria and Albert Museum bulletin reprints ; 20)
ISBN: 090148623X
"Reprinted from the *Bulletin*, Vol. II, no. 1." — Includes bibliographic references. — Stapled; card wrappers coloured puce.

V.1971.003   *A bibliography of books on musical instruments in the Library of the Victoria and Albert Museum* / compiled by Michael I. Wilson.
London : H.M.S.O., [1971].
43 p. ; 30 cm + supplementary list (6 p. ; 30 cm.).
Cover title. At head of t.p. : Victoria and Albert Museum; Monthly list special supplement. — Printing: 1/71. — Supplementary six page bibliography loosely inserted. — Printed as typescript, stapled into green wrappers.

V.1971.004   *The care of ivory.*
London : Issued by the Conservation Department of the Victoria and Albert Museum, 1971.
1 sheet, folded ([3] p.) ; 21 cm.
(Technical notes on the care of art objects ; no. 6)

V.1971.005   *Contemporary theatre art in Poland . . . .*
[London : Victoria and Albert Museum, 1971.]
1 sheet ; 48 x 46 cm. folded to 24 x 23 cm.
Caption title. At head of title: Victoria and Albert Museum. — Factsheet.
EXHIBITION: VX.1971.004

V.1971.006   *The Costume Court : with notes on related material elsewhere in the
Museum* / by Madeleine Ginsburg.
London : [H.M.S.O.], 1971 (Printed by Headley Brothers).
19 p.; 25 cm.
ISBN: 0901486310
At head of title: Victoria and Albert Museum. — Bibliography: p. 19–20. — Printing :
7/71. — Wrappers with colour ill.

V.1971.007   *Covent Garden : 25 years of opera and ballet, Royal Opera House :
an exhibition organised by the Royal Opera House and the Victoria
and Albert Museum in co-operation with the Friends of Covent
Garden and the Arts Council of Great Britain. Victoria and Albert
Museum, 19 August–10 October, 1971.*
[London : The Organisers?, 1971] (Printed by the Shenval Press).
133 p., [19] p. of advertisements : ill. (some col.), ports. ; 26 cm.
Acknowledgements / John Pope-Hennessy, John Tooley. Foreword / Lord Goodman.
Introduction to the Royal Ballet / Peter Williams. Introduction to the Royal Opera /
Harold Rosenthal. — Designed by Gordon House. — White sized wrappers.
EXHIBITION: VX.1971.012

V.1971.008   *The decorated page : eight hundred years of illuminated manuscripts
and books : an exhibition held at the Victoria and Albert Museum,
London, May-October 1971.*
[London : The Museum, 1971.]
65 leaves ; 31 cm.
Catalogue based on labels compiled for the exhibition by Irene Whalley and Vera
Kaden. — Reproduced from typescript. Stapled in red covers with ill.
EXHIBITION: VX.1971.008

V.1971.009   *The Devonshire hunting tapestries* / by George Wingfield Digby ;
assisted by Wendy Hefford.
London : H.M.S.O., 1971 (Printed by Ebenezer Baylis & Son).
[10], 92, 47 p., 4 fold leaves : ill. (some col.) ; 31 x 31 cm.
ISBN: 0112900372
At head of title: Victoria & Albert Museum. — Includes: Notes on the costume / by
Madeleine Ginsburg. The Haarlem workshops' method of re-weaving / by Virginia Pow.
— Bibliography: p. 83–92. — Cloth covered boards with leather title label on spine;
illustrated dust-jacket.

V.1971.010   *Dolls.* Repr.
London : H.M.S.O., 1971.
(Small picture book ; no. 50)
ISBN: 0112901360
Unseen. Listed in *Government publications : Victoria and Albert Museum.* London :
H.M.S.O., 1972. (Sectional list ; 55).

V.1971.011   *dsh, dom sylvester houédard, visual poetries : a Victoria and Albert
Museum loan exhibition.*
[London : The Museum, 1971?]

1 sheet, folded ([9] p.) : 1 ill. ; 30 x 11 cm.
Cover title. — Acknowledgements / Hugh Wakefield. dsh : an introductory note /
Guy Brett. — Bibliography: p. [5].
EXHIBITION: vx.1971.017

v.1971.012   *English sculpture 1720–1830* / by Margaret Whinney.
London : H.M.S.O., 1971 (Text [printed] by Butler & Tanner; cover
by Product Support (Graphics) Ltd, Derby).
160 p., [1] leaf of plates : ill. ; 25 cm.
(Museum monograph ; no. 17)
ISBN: 0112900836
At head of title: Victoria and Albert Museum. — Foreword / John Pope-Hennessy. —
Includes bibliographic references. — Sized wrapper, lime-green and blue, with ill.

v.1971.013   *European armour* / by J.F. Hayward. 2nd ed., 2nd imp.,
amended.
London : H.M.S.O., 1965 (Printed by R. & R. Clark, Edinburgh,
1971).
[64 p.] : ill. ; 14 x 22 cm.
(Illustrated booklet ; no. 5)
ISBN: 0112901026
At head of title: Victoria & Albert Museum. — Includes bibliographic references. —
Wrappers, with ill.

v.1971.014   *Fashion : an anthology by Cecil Beaton* / catalogue compiled by
Madeleine Ginsburg. 2nd amended imp.
London : H.M.S.O., 1971 (Printed at the Baynard Press).
62 p., 15, [1] p. of plates : ill., ports. ; 25 cm.
ISBN: 090148640x
At head of title: Victoria and Albert Museum. — Foreword / John Pope-Hennessy. —
Bibliography: p. 61. — Designed by HMSO / Adrian Young. — Wrappers, with
photograph.
EXHIBITION: vx.1971.014

v.1971.015   *Flöckinger-Herman : jewellery by Gerda Flöckinger, glass by Sam
Herman.*
London : H.M.S.O., 1971 (Printed by St. Clements Fosh & Cross).
[8] p., 24 p. of plates : ill., ports. ; 30 cm.
ISBN: 0901486213
Introduction by Hugh Wakefield. — Designed by HMSO / Philip Marriage. — Printing:
2/71. — Stapled; wrappers.
EXHIBITION: vx.1971.003

v.1971.016   *The Franco-Prussian War and the Commune in caricature, 1870–71* /
Susan Lambert.
London : H.M.S.O., 1971 (Printed by Eyre & Spottiswoode, Thanet
Press, Margate).
119 p. : ill. ; 30 cm.
ISBN: 0901486302
At head of title: Victoria and Albert Museum. — Bibliography: p. 119. — Printing: 5/71
— Sized card wrappers with illustration; printed in red, blue and black.
EXHIBITION: vx.1971.010

V.1971.017   *French paintings.* Repr.
London : H.M.S.O., 1971.
(Large picture book ; no. 3)
ISBN: 0112900968
Unseen. Listed in *Government publications : Victoria and Albert Museum.* London :
H.M.S.O., 1972. (Sectional list ; 55).

V.1971.018   *Glass table-ware.* 5th imp.
London : H.M.S.O., 1947 (Text [printed] by Butler & Tanner; cover
by the Curwen Press, 1971).
[4] p., 28 p. of plates : ill. ; 18 cm.
(Small picture book ; no. 1)
ISBN: 01129000763
At head of title: Victoria and Albert Museum. Cover title: Glass. — Introduction signed
"W.B.H." [i.e. W.B. Honey]. — Grey wrappers with illustration. — 4th? imp. not
traced.

V.1971.019   *Hogarth's pug in porcelain* / by J.V.G. Mallet.
London : Victoria and Albert Museum, 1971 (Printed for H.M.S.O.
by Swindon Press).
14 p. : ill. ; 25 cm.
(Victoria and Albert Museum bulletin reprints ; 16)
ISBN: 0901486260
"Reprinted from the *Bulletin*, Vol. III, no. 2 . . . with revisions and an additional
figure." — Includes bibliographic references. — Stapled, wrappers coloured pink.

V.1971.020   *Homage to Senefelder : artists' lithographs from the Felix H. Man
collection.*
London : H.M.S.O., 1971 (Printed by St. Clements Fosh & Cross).
43 p., [56] p. of plates : ill. (some col.) ; 25 cm.
ISBN: 0901486388
At head of title: Victoria and Albert Museum. — Foreword / John Pope-Hennessy. —
Bibliographic references: p. 38–39. Index of artists. — Part printed in blue. Sized
wrappers with ill.
EXHIBITION: VX.1971.016

V.1971.021   *Indian sculpture : a travelling exhibition.*
London : H.M.S.O., 1971 (Printed by Eyre & Spottiswoode, Thanet
Press, Margate).
[32] p. : ill., map ; 25 cm.
ISBN: 0901486426
At head of title: Victoria and Albert Museum. — Foreword / Hugh Wakefield.
Introduction by Mark Haworth-Booth. — Bibliography: p. [9]. — Printing: 11/71. —
Map on inside back cover. Stapled; brown wrappers with ill.
EXHIBITION: VX.1972.XXX.002

V.1971.022   *An ivory by Giovanni Pisano* / by John Pope-Hennessy.
London : Victoria and Albert Museum, 1971 (Printed for H.M.S.O.
by St. Clements Fosh & Cross).
10 p. : ill. ; 25 cm.
(Victoria and Albert Museum bulletin reprints ; 19)
ISBN: 0901486175
"Reprinted from the *Bulletin*, Vol. I, No. 3." — Includes bibliographic references. —
Stapled; card wrappers coloured purple.

V.1971.023   *Kalighat paintings : a catalogue and introduction* / by
                W.G. Archer.
                London : H.M.S.O., 1971 (Printed by Butler & Tanner).
                xiv, 127 p., 65 plates : ill. (some col.) ; 26 cm.
                ISBN: 0112900291
                At head of title: Victoria & Albert Museum. — Bibliography: p. 29–40. Index. Glossary.
                Concordance of Museum numbers. — Tan cloth covered boards with illustration and
                spine title stamped in black; mustard dust-jacket with illustration.

V.1971.024   *Kokoschka : prints and drawings : lent by Reinhold Bethusy-Huc.*
                London : H.M.S.O., 1971 (Printed by Staples Printers).
                32 p., 31p. of plates : ill., (1 col.) ; 25 cm.
                ISBN: 090148637X
                Foreword / John Pope-Hennessy. Introduction / by E.H. Gombrich. Letters from Jan
                Tomeš, C.G. Heise. — Printing: 9/71.
                EXHIBITION: VX.1971.BGM.002

V.1971.025   *List of large size colour transparencies available on hire for colour
                printing.*
                London : Victoria and Albert Museum, [1971?].
                83 p. ; 30cm.
                Stapled in unlettered blue covers.

V.1971.026   *Martin ware : a travelling exhibition arranged by the Circulation
                Department of the Victoria and Albert Museum.*
                [London : H.M.S.O., 1971] (Printed by the Curwen Press).
                1 sheet, folded (6 p.) ; 30 cm.
                Written by D.R. Coachworth. — Printing: 9/71. — Printed in brown and cream.
                EXHIBITION: VX.1972.012

V.1971.027   *A Medici casket* / by R.W. Lightbown.
                London : Victoria and Albert Museum, 1971 (Printed by Swindon
                Press).
                12 p. : ill. ; 25 cm.
                (Victoria and Albert Museum bulletin reprints ; 15)
                ISBN: 0901486248
                "Reprinted from the *Bulletin*, Vol. III, no. 3." — Includes bibliographic references. —
                Stapled; tawny sized wrappers.

V.1971.028   *Modern chairs.*
                [London : H.M.S.O., 1971?] (Printed by McCorquodale Printers).
                1 sheet, folded ([9] p.) ; 30 x 11 cm.
                Cover title. — "A Victoria and Albert Museum travelling exhibition." — Written by
                Carol Hogben. — Printing: 9/71. — Part printed in red.
                EXHIBITION: VX.1970.XXX.001

V.1971.029   *The Mount Trust collection of Chinese art.* 2nd imp.
                London : Victoria and Albert Museum, 1970 (Printed by Eyre &
                Spottiswoode, Thanet Press, Margate, 1971).
                [52] p. : ill. ; 25 cm.
                At head of title: Victoria and Albert Museum. — Foreword / John Pope-Hennessy.
                Introduction signed "J.G.A." [i.e. John Ayers]. — Includes bibliographic references. —
                Wrappers, with ill. — The collection was formed by Vivian Bulkeley-Johnson.
                EXHIBITIONS: VX.1970.003; VX.1974.BGM.002

V.1971.030   *Nicholas Hilliard & Isaac Oliver* / by Graham Reynolds. 2nd ed.
London : H.M.S.O., 1971 (Printed by Eyre & Spottiswoode at
Grosvenor Press, Portsmouth).
115 p. : ill. (some col.) ; 30 cm.
ISBN: 0112900194
At head of title: Victoria and Albert Museum. — First published on the occasion of
vx.1947.005. — Indexes of portrait miniatures and collections. — Sized card wrappers.
Coloured illustration on front, printed on dark blue-green.

V.1971.031   *The picture postcard, 1870–1920 : a travelling exhibition arranged
by the Circulation Department of the Victoria and Albert
Museum.*
[London : The Museum, 1971.]
1 sheet, folded ([7] p.) : 1 ill. ; 30 x 11 cm.
Printed in columns in brown on buff paper. Illustrated cover adds turquoise. — Written
by P.N. Lawrence. Foreword / Barbara Morris.
EXHIBITION: vx.1970.020

V.1971.032   *Portrait drawings.* Repr.
London : H.M.S.O., 1971.
(Small picture book ; no. 12)
ISBN: 0112900925
Unseen. Listed in *Government publications : Victoria and Albert Museum.* London :
H.M.S.O., 1972. (Sectional list ; 55).

V.1971.033   *Printed books : a short introduction to fine typography* / T.M.
MacRobert. 2nd imp., amended.
London : H.M.S.O., 1957 (Printed by Butler & Tanner, 1971).
7 p., [46] p. of plates : ill. ; 31 cm.
ISBN: 0112901182
Grey wrappers. — Mainly reproductions of pages and title-pages of books in the
Victoria and Albert Museum.

V.1971.034   *Recent acquisitions 1970–71 : 25 March–19 September 1971.*
[London : Victoria and Albert Museum, 1971.]
16 p. ; 30 cm.
At head of title: Victoria and Albert Museum.
EXHIBITION: vx.1971.005

V.1971.035   *A rediscovered English reliquary cross* / by John Beckwith.
London : Victoria and Albert Museum, 1971 (Printed for H.M.S.O.
by St. Clements Fosh & Cross).
11 p. : ill. ; 25 cm.
(Victoria and Albert Museum bulletin reprints ; 17)
ISBN: 0901486094
"Reprinted from the *Bulletin*, Vol. II, no. 4." — Includes bibliographic references. —
Stapled; wrappers coloured yellow.

V.1971.036   *Regency domestic silver.* Repr.
London : H.M.S.O., 1971.
(Small picture book ; no. 33)
ISBN: 0112901042
Unseen. Listed in *Government publications : Victoria and Albert Museum.* London :
H.M.S.O., 1972. (Sectional list ; 55).

V.1971.037   *Season's greetings : an exhibition of British biscuit tins,*
              1868–1939 : Victoria and Albert Museum, December 1971–
              January 1972.
              [London : H.M.S.O., 1971.]
              1 sheet, folded ([3] p.) ; 30 x 11 cm.
              Printed in green and red.
              EXHIBITION: VX.1971.019

V.1971.038   *Signs of the zodiac.* Repr.
              London : H.M.S.O., 1971.
              (Small picture book ; no. 61)
              ISBN: 0112901077
              Unseen. Listed in *Government publications : Victoria and Albert Museum.* London :
              H.M.S.O., 1972. (Sectional list ; 55).

V.1971.039   *The Sketching Society : 1799–1851* / Jean Hamilton.
              London : H.M.S.O., 1971 (Printed by St. Clements Fosh & Cross).
              22 p., [25] leaves of plates : ill. ; 15 x 21 cm.
              ISBN: 9014686167
              At head of title: Victoria and Albert Museum. — Bibliography: p. 22. — Printing: 1/71.
              — Wrappers; ill., orange and black.
              EXHIBITION: VX.1971.001

V.1971.040   *The so-called age of elegance : costume 1785–1820 : proceedings*
              of the fourth Annual Conference of the Costume Society, 1970.
              London : Published for the Society, c/o the Department of Textiles,
              Victoria and Albert Museum, 1971.
              [6], 50 p. : ill. ; 26 cm.
              Includes: The beginning of the collection / Doris Langley Moore. Liberty, equality and
              antiquity / Geoffrey Squire. The classical influence on the cut, construction and
              decoration of women's dress, c.1785–1820 / Janet Arnold. Conservation / Karen Finch.
              The Royal Navy / P. Annis. The costume of Jane Austen and her characters / Anne
              Buck. Machine-made lace / Zillah Halls. — Includes bibliographies. — Stapled; white
              sized wrappers with ill. in silhouette.

V.1971.041   *Sports photographs by Gerry Cranham : a Victoria and Albert*
              Museum loan exhibition.
              [London : The Museum, 1971.]
              1 sheet, folded ([6] p.) : 1 ill. ; 11 cm.
              Texts by Geoffrey Nicholson, George Hughes. Acknowledgements / Hugh Wakefield. —
              "The 56 pictures shown in the present travelling version are still correctly described by
              their original catalogue numbers, but their sequence is no longer a complete one"–
              p. [7].
              EXHIBITION: VX.1971.006

V.1971.042   *Thomas Gainsborough's exhibition box* / by Jonathan Mayne.
              London : Victoria and Albert Museum, 1971 (Printed for H.M.S.O.
              by St. Clements Fosh & Cross).
              10 p. : ill. ; 25 cm.
              (Victoria and Albert Museum bulletin reprints ; 18)
              ISBN: 0901486108
              "Reprinted from the *Bulletin*, Vol. I, no. 3." — Includes bibliographic references. —
              Stapled in wrappers coloured yellow.

V.1971.043   *Turkish pottery.* Repr.
               London : H.M.S.O., 1971.
               (Small picture book ; no. 21)
               ISBN: 0112901034
               Unseen. Listed in *Government publications : Victoria and Albert Museum.* London :
               H.M.S.O., 1972. (Sectional list ; 55).

V.1971.044   *V & A Museum colour slides.*
               [London : The Museum, 1971.]
               i, 77 p. ; 21 cm.
               Cover title. — "All enquiries . . . should be made to: The Miniature Gallery . . ."–cover
               verso. — Printing: 4/71.

V.1971.045   *Victoria & Albert Museum : brief guide.* 2nd ed.
               London : H.M.S.O., 1971 (Printed by Butler & Tanner).
               63 p. : ill., 2 col. plans ; 30 x 13 cm.
               ISBN: 0901486256
               Index to rooms in the Primary Galleries.

V.1971.046   *Victoria & Albert Museum : guìa concisa.*
               London : H.M.S.O., 1971 (Printed by Eyre & Spottiswoode,
               Portsmouth).
               66 p. : ill., col. plans ; 30 x 13 cm.
               ISBN: 0901486140
               Tan wrappers, with turn-ins. — Printing: 2/71.

V.1971.047   *Victoria & Albert Museum : guida breve.*
               London : H.M.S.O., 1971 (Printed by Eyre & Spottiswoode,
               Portsmouth).
               66 p. : ill., col. plans ; 30 x 13 cm.
               ISBN: 0901486132
               Dark green wrappers, with turn-ins.

V.1971.048   *Victoria & Albert Museum : guide sommaire.*
               London : H.M.S.O., 1971.
               66 p. : ill., col. plans ; 30 x 13 cm.
               ISBN: 0901486124
               Printing: 2/71. — Kingfisher blue wrappers, with turn-ins.

V.1971.049   *Victoria & Albert Museum : kurzer Führer.*
               London : H.M.S.O., 1971 (Printed by Eyre & Spottiswoode,
               Portsmouth).
               66 p. : ill., col. plans ; 30 x 13 cm.
               ISBN: 0901486116
               Purple wrappers, with turn-ins.

V.1971.050   *Victorian church art.*
               London : H.M.S.O., 1971 (Printed by Headley Brothers).
               xxvi, 184 p. : ill. (1 col.), ports. ; 30 cm.
               ISBN: 0901486361
               At head of title: Victoria and Albert Museum. — Foreword / John Pope-Hennessy. —
               Bibliography: p. xxv. List of lenders and index. Glossary. — Printing: 11/71. — Sized
               wrappers with photograph; title printed orange.
               EXHIBITION: vx.1971.018

V.1971.051   *Victorian paintings.* 2nd ed. Repr.
London : H.M.S.O., 1971.
(Small picture book ; no. 10)
ISBN: 0112900119
Unseen. Listed in *Government publications : Victoria and Albert Museum.* London :
H.M.S.O., 1972. (Sectional list ; 55).

V.1971.052   *The Wellington Museum, Apsley House : a guide* / by C.H. Gibbs-
Smith and H.V.T. Percival. 5th ed.
London : H.M.S.O., 1971 (Printed by McCorquodale).
54, [5] p., [4] p. of plates : ill., facsims., plans ; 24 cm.
ISBN: 0901486183
Cover title: A guide to the Wellington Museum. — Foreword / John Pope-Hennessy. —
Bibliography: p. [59]. Index. — Printed on grey. Sized wrappers with ill.

V.1971.053   *Working class costume from* Sketches of characters *by William
Johnstone White ; edited by Pamela Clabburn.*
London : Costume Society c/o Department of Textiles, Victoria and
Albert Museum, 1971.
[9], 35 p : chiefly ill. ; 22 cm.
(Costume Society extra series ; no. 3)
Sketches of characters originally published 1818. — Bibliography: p. [35].

1972

V.1972.001   *Adolphe Appia.* [Repr.]
London : H.M.S.O., 1970 (Printed by St. Clements Fosh and Cross,
1972.
26 p., [15] p. of plates : ill., ports. ; 20cm.
ISBN: 0901486221
At head of title: Victoria and Albert Museum. — Compiled by Edmund Stadler.
Foreword / John Pope-Hennessy. — Stapled; wrappers coloured red.
EXHIBITION: vx.1970.018

V.1972.002   *Aspects of the book.*
[London : National Art Library, Victoria and Albert Museum, 1972?]
(Printed by the Victoria and Albert Museum Press).
1 sheet, folded ([7] p.) : ill. ; 22 x 11 cm.
Leaflet relating to a series of exhibitions in 1972–3, in the National Art Library's book
production gallery, Victoria and Albert Museum. Part printed in brown.
See note, vx.1972.017

V.1972.003   *Aubrey Beardsley* / by Brian Reade. 5th (amended) imp.
London : H.M.S.O., 1966 (Printed by Butler & Tanner, 1972).
18 p., 50 p. of plates : ill. ; 25 cm.
(Large picture book ; no. 32)
ISBN: 0112901409
First published on the occasion of vx.1966.003. — Printing: 5/72. — Grey wrappers; ill.
and title printed in orange.

V.1972.004   *Australian prints : exhibition July-November.*
London : H.M.S.O., 1972 (Printed by Eyre & Spottiswoode,
Portsmouth).

[57] p. : ill. (1 col.) ; 25 cm.
ISBN: 0901486507
At head of title: Victoria & Albert Museum. — Written by Margaret MacKean and
James Mollison. Foreword / John Pope-Hennessy. — Includes bibliographic references.
— Wrappers; col. ill. on front.
EXHIBITION: VX.1972.014

V.1972.005   *Beatrix Potter : a Christmas exhibition : Victoria & Albert Museum,*
              14 December 1972 to 28 January 1973, Bethnal Green Museum . . .
              14 February to 25 March 1973.
              [London : Victoria and Albert Museum, 1972] (Printed by the Victoria
              and Albert Museum Press).
              15 p. : ill. ; 18 cm.
              Prepared by Celia O'Malley and Irene Whalley. — Bibliography: p. [16]. — Stapled;
              sized wrappers with col. ills.
              EXHIBITION: VX.1972.028; VX.1973.BGM.002

V.1972.006   *Beatrix Potter children's competition.*
              [London] : Victoria and Albert Museum, [1972] (Printed by the
              Victoria and Albert Museum Press).
              15 p. : ill. ; 18 cm.
              EXHIBITION: VX.1972.028

V.1972.007   *The building erected in Hyde Park for the Great Exhibition of the*
              Works of Industry of All Nations, 1851 / illustrated by twenty-eight
              large plates, embracing plans, elevations, sections, and details, laid
              down to a large scale from the working drawings of the contractors,
              Messrs. Fox, Henderson, and Co. by Charles Downes ; with scientific
              description by Charles Cowper.
              [London : H.M.S.O., 1972] (Printed by Henry Hildesley Ltd.).
              iv, 45 p., 28 folded leaves of plates : ill., plans. ; 30 cm.
              ISBN: 0901486299
              Facsimile of original ed. published London: John Weale, 1852. — Foreword / Charles
              H. Gibbs-Smith. — Printing: 8/71. — Yellow card wrappers with illustration printed in
              grey and title in maroon.

V.1972.008   *Catalogue of Adam period furniture* / Maurice Tomlin.
              London : H.M.S.O., 1972 (Printed by Curwen Press).
              [xi], 211 p. : ill. ; 25 cm.
              ISBN: 0901486442
              At head of title: Victoria and Albert Museum. — Bibliography: p. 206–207. Index. —
              Printing: 0/72 [sic]. — Sized wrappers coloured dark green, with ill.

V.1972.009   *Catalogue of Japanese illustrated books in the Department of Prints*
              and Drawings / by Leonard G. Dawes.
              London : H.M.S.O., 1972.
              vi, 247 p. ; 31 cm.
              Cover title. At head: Victoria & Albert Museum. — Title and artist indexes. Glossary.
              — Printing: 4/71. — Stapled in pink card cover; spine taped. — Corrigenda on separate
              leaf.

V.1972.010   *Catalogue of rubbings of brasses and incised slabs* / by Muriel
              Clayton. 2nd ed., 4th imp.
              London : H.M.S.O., 1968 (A. Wheaton & Co., Exeter, printer, 1972).
              xiv, 250 p., 72 p. of plates : ill. 25 cm.

ISBN: 0112900879

At head of title: Victoria and Albert Museum. Cover title: Brass rubbings. — Bibliography: p. 32–33. Place and name indexes.

V.1972.011   *Catalogue of Russian drawings* / Larissa Salmina-Haskell.
London : H.M.S.O., 1972 (Printed at the University Press, Oxford).
54 p., xlviii p. of plates : ill., facsims. ; 24 cm.
At head of title: Victoria and Albert Museum. — Foreword / Graham Reynolds.
Includes texts in Russian and French. — Printing: 12/72.

V.1972.012   *Chinese cloisonné enamels* / B.W. Robinson.
London : H.M.S.O., 1972 (Printed by Wells KPL Swindon Press).
[12] p. : col. ill. ; 16 cm.
(Small colour book ; 1)
ISBN: 0112901301
At head of title: Victoria & Albert Museum. — Printing: 8/72. — Sized wrappers with col. ill.

V.1972.013   *Colour postcards : Victoria and Albert Museum, including out-stations: Bethnal Green Museum, Wellington Museum, Ham House, Osterley Park House.*
[London : Victoria and Albert Museum, 1972.]
38 p. ; 21 cm.
Caption title. — Printing: 5/72. — Stapled; wrappers.

V.1972.014   *Constable.* 6th imp., "in landscape format, with amendments".
London : H.M.S.O., 1950 (Text [printed] by Butler & Tanner, cover by Headley Brothers, 1972).
[10], 33, [5] p. : ill. ; 13 x 19 cm.
(Small picture book ; no. 23)
ISBN: 0112900941
Introduction signed "G.R." [i.e. Graham Reynolds]. — Sized olive green wrappers, with col. ill.

V.1972.015   *Crafts of Ecuador : a travelling exhibition arranged by the Circulation Department of the Victoria and Albert Museum.*
[London : The Museum, 1972.]
1 sheet, folded ([5] p.) : 1 ill. ; 30 x 11 cm.
Introduction Hugh Wakefield. — Printed in grey on grey card; title in grey and orange.
EXHIBITION: VX.1972.007

V.1972.016   *David Hockney : Grimm's fairy tales, a suite of etchings : a Victoria and Albert Museum loan exhibition.*
[London : The Museum, 1972.]
1 sheet, folded ([7] p.) : 1 ill. ; 30 x 11 cm.
Includes: David Hockney on print making: p. [5–7].
EXHIBITION: VX.1972.018

V.1972.017   *Dolls' houses.* Repr.
London : H.M.S.O., 1972.
(Small picture book ; no. 51)
ISBN: 0112901271
Unseen. Listed in *Government publications : Victoria and Albert Museum.* London : H.M.S.O., 1972. (Sectional list ; 55).

V.1972.018   *Drawings by William Mulready* / Anne Rorimer.
London : H.M.S.O., 1972 (Printed by R. & R. Clark).
173 p. : ill. (1 col.), ports. ; 25 cm.
ISBN: 0901486264
At head of title: Victoria and Albert Museum. — Bibliography: p. [174]. — Printing:
2/72. — Sized wrappers, with ills. — Catalogue of drawings in the Department of Prints
and Drawings.
EXHIBITION: VX.1972.003

V.1972.019   *English cabinets.*
London : H.M.S.O., 1972 (Text [printed] by Butler & Tanner ; cover
by Headley Brothers).
8, [40] p. : ill. ; 30 cm.
ISBN: 0112901263
At head of title: Victoria and Albert Museum. Original title: English cabinets in the
Victoria and Albert Museum. — Foreword / Peter Thornton. — Printing: 9/72. — Sized
wrappers with colour photographic illustration on front, printed on blue.

V.1972.020   *The graphic work of Merlyn Evans : a retrospective exhibition :
November, 1972–February, 1973, Victoria and Albert
Museum.*
London : H.M.S.O., 1972 (Printed at the Baynard Press).
[14] p., [33] leaves of plates : chiefly ill. ; 20 cm.
ISBN: 0901486558
Foreword / John Pope-Hennessy. Introduction / Robert Erskine. The abstract images of
Merlyn Evans / Bryan Robertson. — Sized card wrappers, white outside, green inside;
col. ill. on front.
EXHIBITION: VX.1972.025

V.1972.021   *A guide to Greek island embroidery* / Pauline Johnstone.
London : H.M.S.O., 1972 (Printed by Eyre & Spottiswoode, Thanet
Press, Margate).
111 p. : chiefly ill. (1 col.), 1 map ; 30 cm.
ISBN: 0112901204
At head of title: Victoria & Albert Museum. — Bibliography: p. 32.

V.1972.022   *International ceramics 1972 : exhibition, June-July.*
London : H.M.S.O., 1972 (Printed at the Baynard Press).
122 p. : ill. ; 25 cm.
ISBN: 0901486477
Foreword / John Pope-Hennessy. Introduction / Hugh Wakefield. — Design by
H.M.S.O.: Vera Brice. — Photography by Geremy Butler and Roger Hart. — Tan
wrappers.
Copy note: 2nd imp. seen.
EXHIBITION: VX.1972.011

V.1972.023   *Japanese illustrated books* / by Leonard G. Dawes.
London : H.M.S.O., 1972 (Printed by Butler and Tanner).
15 p., 60 p. of plates : ill. ; 19 x 24 cm.
(Large picture book ; no. 24)
ISBN: 011290100X
At head of title: Victoria and Albert Museum. — Printing: 7/72. — Sized card wrappers;
illustration on front, printed on salmon.

V.1972.024 *Jewellery* / Shirley Bury.
London : H.M.S.O., 1972 (Printed by Ebenezer Baylis & Son).
[19] p. : col. ill. ; 16 cm.
(Small colour book ; 3)
ISBN: 011290159X
At head of title: Victoria & Albert Museum. — Bibliography: p. [6]. — Stapled; sized wrappers with col. ill.

V.1972.025 *Jewellery Gallery handlist* / Victoria and Albert Museum.
[London : The Museum, 1972] (Printed by Raithby, Lawrence & Company, Ltd, at the De Montfort Press, Leicester).
[140] p. ; 30 cm.
Cover title. At head of title: Victoria & Albert Museum. — "Not to be taken away:"– p. [1] of cover. — Sized white wrappers with plastic bolts.

V.1972.026 *Looking at the Tudor period.*
[London : H.M.S.O., 1972] (Printed by the Curwen Press).
[12] p. : ill., geneal. table, ports. ; 24 cm.
ISBN: 0901486337
Cover title. At head of title: Victoria & Albert Museum. — Introduction to the Primary Galleries. "Written by members of the Education Department"–preface. Preface by Madeleine Mainstone & Arete Swartz. — Bibliography: inside back cover. — Designed by HMSO: Philip Marriage. — Stapled; card wrappers coloured red with ill. Large turn-in at front.

V.1972.027 *Louis Wain* / Brian Reade.
London : H.M.S.O., 1972.
27 p. : ill. (some col.) ; 19 x 25 cm.
ISBN: 090148654X
At head of title: Victoria and Albert Museum. — Stapled; wrappers coloured pink and purple.
EXHIBITION: VX.1972.027

V.1972.028 *The Marlborough tapestries at Blenheim Palace : and their relation to other military tapestries of the War of the Spanish Succession* / by Alan Wace.
London ; New York : Phaidon, 1968.
145 p. : ill. ; 32 cm.
ISBN: 0714813222
Bibliography: p. 137–138. — Wrappers, with ill. on front. Title printed in red. — Posthumously published work written in the 1930s by the then Keeper of the Dept. of Textiles, Victoria and Albert Museum. "Re-issued in 1972 for the Victoria & Albert Museum on the occasion of the presentation of seven military tapestries of this series by Mrs Oswald Finney in memory of her late husband"–wrappers.

V.1972.029 *Matisse : lithographs* / Susan Lambert.
London : H.M.S.O., 1972 (Printed by the Curwen Press).
75 p. : ill. ; 20 x 22 cm.
ISBN: 0901486531
At head of title: Victoria & Albert Museum. — Foreword / Hugh Wakefield. — Includes bibliographic references. — Designed by HMSO Graphic Design. — Card wrappers; buff dust-jacket with design pasted at spine.
EXHIBITIONS: VX.1972.BGM.006; VX.1975.014

V.1972.030 *A nonsense alphabet* / by Edward Lear. Repr.
London : H.M.S.O., 1972.

(Small picture book ; no. 32)
ISBN: 0112901565
Unseen. Listed in *Government publications : Victoria and Albert Museum*. London : H.M.S.O., 1974. (Sectional list ; 55).

V.1972.031   *Osterley Park.*
London : H.M.S.O., 1972 (Printed at the Baynard Press).
61 p. : ill. (1 col.), plans ; 14 x 22 cm.
At head of title: Victoria and Albert Museum. — Compiled by Maurice Tomlin. — Card wrappers with coloured photograph.

V.1972.032   *The Raphael cartoons* / introduction by John White.
London : H.M.S.O., 1972 (Printed by Ben Johnson & Co., York).
9 p., 40 p. of plates : ill. (some col.), plan ; 21 x 30 cm.
(Large colour book ; no. 1)
ISBN: 0112901352
At head of title: Victoria & Albert Museum. — Bibliography: p. [48]. — Typographic design by HMSO. — Card wrappers with col. ill.

V.1972.033   *Samplers* / by Donald King. 3rd imp.
London : H.M.S.O., 1960 (Printed by Balding and Mansell, 1972).
15 p., [62] p. of plates : ill. ; 25 cm.
(Large picture book ; no. 14)
ISBN: 00112901492
At head of title: Victoria and Albert Museum. — Foreword / John Pope-Hennessy. — Bibliography: p. 11. — Sized wrappers with col. ill. on front.

V.1972.034   *Sickert : etchings and dry-points : Walter Richard Sickert 1860–1942 : a travelling exhibition arranged by the Circulation Department of the Victoria and Albert Museum.*
[London : The Museum, 1972.]
1 sheet, folded (9 p.) : port. ; to 30 x 10 cm.
Includes short bibliography. — Printed in black and brown on cream paper.
EXHIBITIONS: VX.1972.BGM.003; VX.1975.005

V.1972.035   *A state bed from Erthig* / John Hardy, Sheila Landi & Charles D. Wright.
London : [H.M.S.O.], 1972 (Printed by Eyre & Spottiswoode, Thanet Press, Margate).
22 p. : ill. (1 col.) ; 20 x 21cm.
(Victoria and Albert Museum brochure ; 2)
ISBN: 901486515
At head of title: Victoria and Albert Museum. — Includes bibliographic references. — Printing: 1/73. — Stapled; wrappers coloured silver, printed in orange. — Established Welsh spelling of the house is Erddig. Spelt throughout item as "Erthig".

V.1972.036   *Three presentation swords in the Victoria and Albert Museum, and a group of English enamels* / Claude Blair.
London : H.M.S.O., 1972 (Printed by R & R Clark, Scotland).
53 p. : ill. (1 col.) ; 20 x 21 cm.
(Victoria and Albert Museum brochure ; 1)
ISBN: 0901486396
At head of title: Victoria and Albert Museum. — Includes bibliographic references. — "Appendix II: list of surviving work by James Morrisset and by John Ray and James Montague." — Printing: 8/72. — Wrappers, coloured silver, printed in blue.

V.1972.037   *Victoria & Albert Museum, recent acquisitions 1971–2 : exhibited in Room 49, 28 April to 23 July 1972.*
[London : The Museum], 1972.
21 p. ; 30 cm.
Stapled in brown paper covers.
EXHIBITION: VX.1972.009

V.1972.038   *Victorian glass* / by Betty O'Looney.
London : H.M.S.O., 1972 (Printed by Butler & Tanner).
[46] p. : ill. ; 21 cm.
ISBN: 0112901336
At head of title: Victoria & Albert Museum. — Includes bibliographic references. — Printing: 6/72. — Stapled; sized wrappers with illustration, printed on red.

V.1972.039   *The Virgin with the laughing Child* / by John Pope-Hennessy. 3rd imp.
London : H.M.S.O., 1949 (Printed by Butler & Tanner, 1972).
10 p., [1], 12 p. of plates : ill. ; 25 cm.
(Museum monograph ; no. 2)
ISBN: 0901486450
Bibliography: p. 10. — Sized card wrappers coloured tan, with photograph.

V.1972.040   *William Moorcroft, 1872–1945 : a travelling exhibition arranged by the Circulation Department of the Victoria and Albert Museum.*
[London : The Museum, 1972.]
1 sheet, folded ([7] p.) : 1 ill. ; 30 x 11 cm.
Text by Beatrix Moorcroft.
EXHIBITIONS: VX.1972.004; VX.1974.BGM.001

1973

V.1973.001   *19th century papier-mâché* / Simon Jervis.
London : H.M.S.O., 1973 (Printed by W.S. Cowell Ltd., Ipswich).
[12] p. : col. ill. ; 16 cm.
(Small colour book ; 4)
ISBN: 0112901859
At head of title: Victoria & Albert Museum. — Stapled ; sized card wrappers with col. ill.

V.1973.002   *Aspects of the book.*
[London : National Art Library, 1973?] (Printed by the Victoria and Albert Museum Press).
1 sheet, folded : ill. ; 22 cm.
At head of title: Victoria & Albert Museum. — Part printed in blue.
See note, VX.1973.032

V.1973.003   *A bibliography of books in the National Art Library for the exhibition "The floating world – Japanese popular prints, 1700–1900", 19 September–25 November 1973* / by Bruce D. Galbraith.
London : [The Library?], 1973.
25 leaves ; 30 cm.
At head of title: Victoria and Albert Museum. Cover title: The floating world . . . bibliography. — Stapled in blue paper covers.
EXHIBITION: VX.1973.024

V.1973.004　　*Catalogue of foreign paintings* / C.M. Kauffmann.
London : H.M.S.O., 1973 (Printed for H.M.S.O. by Eyre &
Spottiswoode, Thanet Press, Margate).
2 v. (xiii, 317 p., xiii, 115 p.) : ill. ; 25 cm.
ISBN: v.1 0901486728; v.2 0901486485
At head of title: Victoria and Albert Museum. — I, Before 1800. II, 1800–1900. —
Includes bibliographic references. Artist, subject and numerical indexes. — Wrappers
coloured black, with col. ill.

V.1973.005　　*A catalogue of oriental periodicals in the National Art Library* / by
Bruce D. Galbraith.
London : [H.M.S.O.], 1973.
93 p. ; 30 cm.
At head of title: Victoria & Albert Museum. — Printing: 8/73.

V.1973.006　　*Catalogue of pottery by William de Morgan* / Roger Pinkham.
London : H.M.S.O., 1973 (Printed by Staples Printers, St. Albans).
115 p. : ill. (some col.) ; 25 cm.
ISBN: 0901486469
At head of title: Victoria and Albert Museum. — Bibliography: p. 110. General and
numerical indexes. — White sized wrappers with col. ill. — Catalogue of De Morgan
ceramics and designs in the Victoria and Albert Museum.

V.1973.007　　*Catalogue of the Constable collection* / by Graham Reynolds. 2nd ed.
London : H.M.S.O., 1973 (Printed by Butler & Tanner).
viii, 263 p., 310, [1] p. of plates : ill. (1 col.) ; 26 cm.
ISBN: 0112901123
At head of title: Victoria and Albert Museum. Spine title: Catalogue of the Constable
collection in the Victoria and Albert Museum. — Bibliography: p. 248–249. Index.
Concordance of Museum numbers. — Green cloth covered boards; dust-jacket with
coloured ill.

V.1973.008　　*The compassionate camera : dustbowl pictures.*
[London : Victoria and Albert Museum, 1973.]
1 sheet, folded ([7] p.) : 1 ill. ; 30 x 11 cm.
Introduction / Mark Haworth-Booth. — Includes bibliography.
EXHIBITION: VX.1973.005

V.1973.009　　*Designs of modern costume engraved for Thomas Hope of Deepdene
by Henry Moses* / [with a new introduction by John Nevinson].
London : Costume Society c/o Department of Textiles, Victoria and
Albert Museum, 1973.
[4], 7 p., 20 leaves : chiefly ill. ; 14 x 22 cm.
(Costume Society extra series ; no. 4)
Originally published 1812. — Bibliography: p. 7.

V.1973.010　　*Dolls : a study of their history and development, 1750–1970.*
[London : H.M.S.O.], 1973 ("McC", printer).
1 sheet, folded ([9] p.) : 1 ill. ; 30 x 11 cm.
Introduction by Barbara Morris. — Bibliography: p. [9]. — Printing: 10/73. — Printed
on sized paper. Concertina-folded. — Catalogue of the newly-displayed collection of
dolls at the Bethnal Green Museum.

V.1973.011　　*E. McKnight Kauffer, poster art 1915–1940 : a travelling exhibition* /
arranged by the Circulation Department of the Victoria and Albert
Museum.

[London] : H.M.S.O., 1973 (Printed by the Millbrook Press, Southampton).
1 sheet, folded ([8] p.) : 1 ill. ; 30 x 11 cm.
Introduction / Mark Haworth-Booth. — Includes bibliography.

V.1973.012   *Eduardo Paolozzi : bunk : a box-file of images in print : Victoria and Albert Museum loan exhibition.*
[London] : H.M.S.O., 1973] (Printed by Wells KPL, Swindon Press).
1 sheet, folded ([10] p.) : 1 ill. ; 30 x 11 cm.
Includes transcript of an interview with the artist by Carol Hogben and Elizabeth Bailey. Paolozzi and the Independent Group / Frank Whitford. — Printing: 12/73.

V.1973.013   *Edward Ardizzone : a retrospective exhibition : Victoria & Albert Museum, 15 December 1973 to 13 January 1974.*
[London : The Museum, 1974] (Printed by the Victoria and Albert Museum Press).
32 p. : ill. ; 14 x 18 cm.
Introduction / by Gabriel White. — Bibliography: p. 15. — Stapled; sized wrappers with col. ill.
EXHIBITION: VX.1973.031

V.1973.014   *Eighteenth century musical instruments, France and Britain = Les instruments de musique au XVIIIe siècle, France et Grande-Bretagne* / G. Thibault (Mme de Chambure), Jean Jenkins, Josiane Bran-Ricci.
London : [H.M.S.O.], 1973 (Printed by Eyre & Spottiswoode, Thanet).
[xxx], 225 p. : ill. (some col.) ; 28 cm.
ISBN: 090148671X
At head of title: Victoria & Albert Museum. — English and French. — Includes index of manufacturers in Paris and London. — Wrappers with col. ill. City plans on end-papers.
EXHIBITION: VX.1974.004

V.1973.015   *European folk dress : a guide to 555 books and other sources of illustrations and information* / by James Snowden.
London : Published for the Costume Society, c/o Department of Textiles, Victoria and Albert Museum, 1973 (Printed by Parkside Business Services, Nottingham).
60 leaves ; 30 cm.
(Costume Society bibliography ; no. 2)
Pink card wrappers.

V.1973.016   *Five monuments from Eastwell* / John Physick. 2nd ed.
London, H.M.S.O., 1973 (Printed by Eyre & Spottiswoode, Thanet Press, Margate).
[3], 42 p. : ill., geneal. table, map, ports. ; 20 x 21 cm.
(Victoria and Albert Museum brochure ; 3)
ISBN: 0901486620
At head of title: Victoria and Albert Museum. — First published in *Victoria and Albert Museum yearbook*, 2, 1970. — Includes bibliographic references. — Stapled; wrappers coloured silver, printed in green.

V.1973.017   *The floating world : Japanese popular prints, 1700–1900* / R.A. Crighton.
London : H.M.S.O., 1973 (Text [printed] by Sir Joseph Causton & Sons; colour section by Product Support (Graphics) Ltd.; cover by Balding & Mansell).
[217] p. : ill. (some col.) ; 30 cm.
ISBN: 0112901905
At head of title: Victoria and Albert Museum. — Bibliography at end. — Card wrappers; coloured illustrated dust-jacket.
EXHIBITION: vx.1973.024

V.1973.018   *French exhibition pieces, 1844–78* / Elizabeth Aslin.
London : H.M.S.O., 1973 (Printed by the Curwen Press).
[36] p. : ill. ; 20 cm.
ISBN: 0901486523
At head of title: Victoria and Albert Museum. — "All the pieces illustrated are on exhibition in the Bethnal Green Museum." — Printing: 6/73. — Sized wrapper coloured tan; col. ill.

V.1973.019   *Ham House.* 3rd ed.
London : [H.M.S.O.], 1973 (Printed at the Baynard Press).
78 p. : ill. (1 col.), plans ; 14 x 22 cm.
ISBN: 0901486590
At head of title: Victoria & Albert Museum. — Revised by Maurice Tomlin. Introductory note / Peter Thornton. — Bibliography: p. 76. — Sized wrappers, with col. ills.

V.1973.020   *The Hennells : silversmiths and jewellers 1735–1973 : 29 March to 29 April 1973, Room 38a, Victoria and Albert Museum, South Kensington SW7.*
[London : The Museum, 1973] (Printed by the Victoria and Albert Museum Press).
1 sheet, folded : ill., geneal. table, ports. ; 30 cm.
EXHIBITION: vx.1973.012

V.1973.021   *International ceramics : a travelling exhibition arranged by the Circulation Department of the Victoria and Albert Museum.*
[London : The Museum, 1973.]
1 sheet, folded (7 p.) : 1 ill. ; 30 x 11 cm.
Based on acquisitions from vx.1972.011.

V.1973.022   *Jazz seen : the face of black music.*
[London : The Museum, 1973] (Printed by the Victoria and Albert Museum Press).
1 sheet, folded (6 p.) : 1 ill. ; 28 x 11 cm.
Foreword / Humphrey Lyttleton. Introduction / Val Wilmer.
EXHIBITION: vx.1973.019

V.1973.023   *John Constable's sketch-books of 1813 and 1814 : reproduced in facsimile* / introduction by Graham Reynolds.
London : H.M.S.O., 1973 (Printed and bound at the University Press, Oxford).
3 v. (78, [90], [80] p.) : ill., facsims. ; 19 cm.
(Facsimile ; no. 2)

ISBN: 0112900542

At head of title: Victoria & Albert Museum. — [1]. Introduction [and catalogue] by Graham Reynolds. [2]. Sketch-book 1813 (10 x 13 cm.). [3]. Sketch-book 1814 (9 x 12 cm.). — Includes bibliographic references. — Boards and case covered in green cloth; facsimile of the artist's signature stamped in gold on sketch-book vols. and case.

V.1973.024   *The Kashmir shawl* / by John Irwin. Rev. ed.
London : H.M.S.O., 1973 (Printed by William Clowes & Sons).
vii, 60 p., [52] p. of plates : ill. (some col.) ; 26 cm.
(Monograph ; 29)
ISBN: 0112901646

At head of title: Victoria & Albert Museum. Original title: Shawls: a study in Indo-European influences. — Bibliography: p. 43–47. Glossary of terms, and index. — Wrappers, with col. ill., on dark blue.

V.1973.025   *'Marble halls' : drawings and models for Victorian secular buildings : exhibition August-October 1973* / John Physick and Michael Darby.
London : H.M.S.O., 1973 (Design/printing by Eyre and Spottiswoode, Thanet Press, Margate).
220 p., [4] p. of plates : ill. (some col.), plans ; 28 cm.
ISBN: 090148668x

At head of title: Victoria and Albert Museum. — Foreword Graham Reynolds. — Includes bibliographic references. Index of lenders, people and places. — Wrappers with col. ill.

EXHIBITION: VX.1973.021

V.1973.026   *Master drawings of the Roman baroque from the Kunstmuseum Düsseldorf : a selection from the Lambert Krahe collection* / catalogue and introduction by Dieter Graf.
London ; Edinburgh : H.M.S.O., 1973 (Printed by Eyre and Spottiswoode, Thanet Press, Margate).
140, [162] p. : ill., port. ; 28 cm.
ISBN: 0901486566

At head of title: Victoria & Albert Museum and Scottish Arts Council. — Foreword / John Pope-Hennessy, Alexander Dunbar. — Bibliography: p. [157–160]. — Cream sized card wrappers with illustration. Orange title and end-papers.

EXHIBITION: VX.1973.010

V.1973.027   *The Mortons : three generations of textile creation : Alexander Morton & Company, Morton Sundour Fabrics, Edinburgh Weavers : 7 June to 15 July 1973 . . . .*
[London : Victoria and Albert Museum, 1973.]
[14] leaves ; 30 cm.
Cover title. At head of title: Victoria & Albert Museum . . . . — Foreword / Barbara Morris. Introduction / Jocelyn Morton. — Stapled in blue paper covers printed in green.

EXHIBITION: VX.1973.017

V.1973.028   *Musical instruments : a list of books and articles in the National Art Library* / compiled by M.I. Wilson. [Rev., enl. and updated ed.]
[London : Victoria and Albert Museum], 1973.
iv, 56 p. ; 30 cm.
Original title: A bibliography of books on musical instruments in the Library of the Victoria and Albert Museum.

V.1973.029   *The needle's excellency: a travelling exhibition.*
London : [H.M.S.O.], 1973 (Printed for by W.S. Cowell Ltd., Ipswich).
[56] p. : ill. ; 20 cm.
ISBN: 0901486604
At head of title: Victoria & Albert Museum. — Foreword / Hugh Wakefield. — Bibliography: p. [11]. — Typographic design by HMSO. — Printing: 4/73. — Buff wrappers with ill.
EXHIBITION: VX.1973.002

V.1973.030   *The Norfolk House music room* / Desmond Fitz-Gerald.
London : H.M.S.O., 1973 (Printed by Eyre & Spottiswoode, Thanet Press, Margate).
56 p. : ill. (1 col.), facsims., plan, port. ; 28 cm.
ISBN: 0901486434
At head of title: Victoria & Albert Museum. — Room designed by Matthew Brettingham.

V.1973.031   *Old master drawings from Chatsworth : a loan exhibition from the Devonshire collection : Victoria and Albert Museum, London, 1973 /* introduction and catalogue by James Byam Shaw ; foreword by Thomas S. Wragg.
London : Produced by the Meriden Gravure Company and the Stinehour Press for H.M.S.O., 1973.
50 p., 120 p. of plates : ill. ; 26 cm.
Foreword / John Pope-Hennessy. — Wrappers coloured tan, with ill. — Re-issue of the catalogue produced for the tour of the exhibition in the U.S.A. "Copyright 1969 by International Exhibitions Foundation."
EXHIBITION: VX.1973.029

V.1973.032   *Posters of a lifetime.*
[London : Victoria and Albert Museum, 1973] (Printed by the Victoria and Albert Museum Press).
1 sheet, folded ([7] p.) : ill. ; 30 cm.
Written by Mark Haworth-Booth, preface by Graham Reynolds.
EXHIBITION: VX.1973.BGM.003

V.1973.033   *The rural chair : a travelling exhibition arranged by the Circulation Department of the Victoria and Albert Museum.*
[London]: H.M.S.O., [1973] (Printed by St Clements Fosh & Cross).
1 sheet, folded ([7] p.) : 1 ill. ; 30 x 11 cm.
Introduction / M. Haworth-Booth. — Includes bibliography. — Printed in brown.
EXHIBITION: VX.1974.008

V.1973.034   *The Sanchi torso* / John Irwin.
[London : The Museum, 1973?]
22 p., [1] p. of plates : ill. (1 col.), 1 map, 1 plan ; 28 cm.
At head of title: Victoria and Albert Museum. — "Reprinted from the *Victoria and Albert Museum yearbook* 3, 1972"–cover. — Includes bibliographic references. — Stapled; orange wrappers.

V.1973.035   *Secrets of the stage : a Christmas exhibition, December 1973– January 1974.*
London : [Victoria and Albert Museum], 1973 (Curwen Press, printer).

At head of title: Victoria and Albert Museum. — Bibliography : p. [11]. — Stapled; cream wrappers with col. ill.

EXHIBITION: VX.1973.032

V.1973.036   *Some materials and commercial products used in the conservation of art objects.*
[London] : Victoria and Albert Museum Conservation Dept., 1973.
21 leaves ; 30 cm.
Duplicated; stapled.

V.1973.037   *Summary catalogue of British paintings.*
[London : H.M.S.O., 1973.]
ii, 164 p. ; 22 cm.
Cover title. At head of title: Victoria & Albert Museum. — Preface / Graham Reynolds. — Printing: 1/73. — Blue wrappers. Stapled.

V.1973.038   *Tibetan art* / John Lowry.
London : H.M.S.O., 1973. (Text [printed] by Butler and Tanner ; cover by Headley Brothers).
118 p. : ill. ; 22 cm.
ISBN: 0112901093
At head of title: Victoria and Albert Museum. — Bibliography: p. 10. Index. — Wrappers coloured dark green with col. ill.

V.1973.039   *Treasures from the European Community : Victoria & Albert Museum, 4 January–11 February 1973.*
[London : The Museum?, 1973] (Lund Humphries, printer).
[20] p. : col. ill. ; 21 cm.
Cover title. — Forewood / Alec Douglas-Home. — Designed by Graham Johnson. — Stapled; buff wrappers printed in black and gold.

EXHIBITION: VX.1973.001

V.1973.040   *Tudor & Jacobean miniatures* / Graham Reynolds.
London : H.M.S.O., 1973 (Printed by W. Heffer & Sons, Cambridge).
[16] p. : col. ill. ; 16 cm.
(Small colour book ; 2)
ISBN: 0112901174
At head of title: Victoria & Albert Museum. — Stapled; sized card wrappers with col. ill.

V.1973.041   *Victoria & Albert Museum, recent acquisitions 1972–3 : exhibited in Room 49, March to June 1973.*
[London : The Museum], 1973.
20 leaves ; 30 cm.
Stapled in tan paper covers.

EXHIBITION: VX.1973.008

V.1973.042   *Victorian architectural source books displayed in the exhibition 'Marble halls', 2 August to 28 October 1973 : Victoria & Albert Museum.*
[London : The Museum, 1973.]
82 p. ; 30 cm.
Stapled in red paper covers. — Books from the collection of the National Art Library, Victoria and Albert Museum.

EXHIBITION: VX.1973.021

V.1973.043   *Victorian engravings* / Hilary Beck.
London : H.M.S.O., 1973 (Printed by R. & R. Clark, Edinburgh).
75 p., [109] p. of plates : ill. ; 25 cm.
ISBN: 0901486647
At head of title: Victoria and Albert Museum. — Foreword / Graham Reynolds. — Bibliography: p. 71–72. Index of painters and engravers. — Photography by Richard Meredith. Typographic design by HMSO. — White sized wrappers with ill.
EXHIBITION: VX.1973.BGM.004

1974

V.1974.001   *Art deco : French decorative arts in the twenties : a Victoria and Albert Museum loan exhibition.*
[London : H.M.S.O., 1974] (Impress, printer, Acton).
1 sheet, folded (7 p.) : 1 ill. ; 30 cm.
Introduction / Carol Hogben. — Coloured title.
EXHIBITION: VX.1975.018

V.1974.001A   [Another issue]
1 sheet, folded ([15] p.) : 1 ill. ; 30 × 11 cm.
[Different format, otherwise the same.]

V.1974.002   *The art of Onisaburō : modern Japanese ceramics, calligraphy & painting : Victoria and Albert Museum.*
[London : H.M.S.O., 1974.]
1 sheet, folded ([9] p.) 1 ill. ; 30 cm.
Foreword / Hugh Wakefield. Introduction / Torao Deguchi. — Printed on grey paper.
EXHIBITION: VX.1974.001

V.1974.003   *Automobile art : catalogue of the James Barron collection.*
London : [H.M.S.O.], 1974 (Printed by Vivian Ridler at the University Press, Oxford).
40 p. : ill. ; 15 × 22 cm.
ISBN: 0901486779
At head of title: Bethnal Green Museum. — Foreword / Roy Strong. — Printing: 9/74. — Stapled; sized wrappers with col. ill.
EXHIBITION: VX.1974.BGM.003

V.1974.004   *The Bodhgayā pillar* / O.M. Starza.
[London : H.M.S.O.?], 1974 (Printed by the Cavendish Press, Leicester).
8 p. : ill., 1 plan ; 28 cm.
ISBN: 0901486841
Cover title. At head of title: Victoria and Albert Museum. — Includes bibliographic references. — Stapled in salmon wrappers.

V.1974.005   *Bodybox : an exhibition by the Education Department, Victoria & Albert Museum, 14 December 1974 to 26 January 1975* / devised by Eileen Graham and James Heard.
[London : H.M.S.O., 1974.]
1 sheet : ill. ; 60 × 84 cm. folded to 30 × 21 cm.
Broadsheet on the subject of the human figure in art. — Printed in blue, black and red.
EXHIBITION: VX.1974.032

V.1974.006   *Burmese art* / John Lowry.
London : H.M.S.O., 1974 (Printed by W.S. Cowell Ltd., Ipswich).
vii, [107] p., 1 folded : ill. ; 22 cm.
ISBN: 0112901794
At head of title: Victoria and Albert Museum. — Index. — Sized wrappers; col. ill. on dark tan.

V.1974.007   *Byron : an exhibition to commemorate the 150th anniversary of his death in the Greek War of Liberation, 19 April 1824 : 30 May–25 August 1974* / catalogue by Anthony Burton and John Murdoch.
London : H.M.S.O., 1974 (Printed by McCorquodale Printers).
xxx, 149 p., [24] leaves of plates : ill., facsims., plan, ports. ; 28 cm. + 1 booklet ([7] p. ; 26 cm.)
ISBN: 0901486760
At head of title: Victoria and Albert Museum. — Foreword / Roy Strong. — Catalogue design by HMSO: Joe Burns. — Brown wrappers. — Seven page booklet loosely inserted, entitled Byron: Additions and corrections to the catalogue of the exhibition, 30th May–25 August 1974.
EXHIBITION: VX.1974.016

V.1974.008   *Byron : exhibition guide.*
London : [H.M.S.O.], 1974. (Printed by W. & J. Mackay Ltd., Chatham).
[14] p., 8 p. of plates : ill., plan, ports. ; 21 cm.
ISBN: 0901486752
At head of title: Victoria & Albert Museum. — Text signed "J.H.M." [i.e. John Murdoch]. — Printing: 5/74. — Stapled; royal blue wrappers printed in white.
EXHIBITION: VX.1974.016

V.1974.009   *Canal boat art : a travelling exhibition arranged by the Circulation Department of the Victoria and Albert Museum.*
[London : The Museum, 1974?]
1 folded sheet ([11] p.) : 1 ill. ; 30 x 11 cm.
Foreword / Hugh Wakefield. — Includes bibliography. — Printed in brown on buff paper; title in red.
EXHIBITION: VX.1974.031

V.1974.010   *Children and their toys in English art : exhibition, December 1974–February 1975, Bethnal Green Museum.*
[London : Victoria and Albert Museum, 1974.]
1 sheet ([12] p. : ill. ; 30 x 63 cm. folded to 30 x 11 cm.
Introduction / Elizabeth Aslin. — Printed in dark green, with red decorations, on dull yellow-green.
EXHIBITION: VX.1974.BGM.004

V.1974.011   *Costume : a general bibliography* / by Pegaret Anthony and Janet Arnold [for the Victoria and Albert Museum and the Costume Society]. Rev. and enl. ed. / prepared by Janet Arnold.
London : Costume Society, 1974.
[6], 42 p. ; 22 cm.
(Costume Society bibliography ; no. 1)
ISBN: 090340706X

V.1974.012   *The destruction of the country house, 1875–1975.*
               [London : Victoria and Albert Museum, 1974] (Printed by the Victoria
               and Albert Museum Press).
               1 sheet, folded : ill., plan ; 22 cm.
               "Exhibition synopsis".
               EXHIBITION: VX.1974.026

V.1974.013   *The Devonshire hunting tapestries* / Eileen Graham.
               [London : Victoria and Albert Museum, between 1973 and 1975.]
               1 sheet : ill. (some col.). ; 59 x 84 cm. folded to 30 x 21 cm.
               Educational broadsheet. — Includes bibliography.

V.1974.014   *Drawings by Victor Hugo* / catalogue by Pierre Georgel.
               London : H.M.S.O., 1974 (Printed by the Curwen Press).
               [119] p. : ill. ; 25 cm.
               ISBN: 0901486736
               At head of title: Victoria and Albert Museum. — Foreword / Graham Reynolds. —
               Bibliography: p. [10–12]. — Maroon wrappers with col. ill.
               EXHIBITION: VX.1974.002

V.1974.015   *Early railway prints : from the collection of Mr. and Mrs. M.G.
               Powell* / Michael Darby.
               London : H.M.S.O., 1974 (Printed by Product Support (Graphics)
               Ltd., Derby).
               [10], 72 p. : ill. ; 14 x 22 cm.
               ISBN: 0901486744
               At head of title: Victoria and Albert Museum. Foreword / Graham Reynolds. —
               Wrappers; col. ill.
               EXHIBITION: VX.1974.014

V.1974.016   *The fabric of Pop : a travelling exhibition arranged by the Circulation
               Department of the Victoria and Albert Museum.*
               [London : H.M.S.O., 1974] (UDO (Litho) Ltd., printer).
               1 sheet, folded ([7] p.) : 1 col. ill. ; 30 cm.
               Introduction / Michael Regan. — Designed by HMSO/John Hughes.
               EXHIBITION: VX.1974.018

V.1974.017   *The glass drawing room from Northumberland House* / David
               Owsley, William Rieder.
               London : H.M.S.O., 1974 (Printed by Eyre & Spottiswoode, Thanet
               Press, Margate).
               31 p., [1] leaf of plates : ill. (some col.) ; 28 cm.
               ISBN: 0901486671
               At head of title: Victoria & Albert Museum. — Bibliography: p. 29–31. — Stapled;
               wrappers red inside, grey out, with col. ill. — Room designed by Robert Adam.

V.1974.018   *Hollywood still photography, 1927–1941, from the collection of
               John Kobal : a travelling exhibition arranged by the Circulation
               Department of the Victoria and Albert Museum.*
               [London : H.M.S.O., 1974] (Printed by Moore & Matthes).
               1 sheet, folded (16 p.) : ports. ; 30 cm.
               Acknowledgements / Elizabeth Bailey. Includes an interview with John Kobal. —
               Designed by Dennis Greeno. — Printing 10/74.
               EXHIBITION: VX.1974.028

V.1974.019   *Limoges painted enamels* / Roger Pinkham.
              London : H.M.S.O., 1974 (Printed by Wells KPL Swindon Press).
              [12] p. : col. ill. ; 16 cm.
              (Small colour book ; 5)
              At head of title: Victoria & Albert Museum. — Stapled; sized wrappers with col. ill.

V.1974.020   *Pierre Culot : ceramics : Victoria and Albert Museum . . . June 6 to
              July 14, 1974.*
              [London? : The Museum?, 1974] (Delpire Advico [printer], France).
              1 sheet : ill. ; 64 x 48 cm. folded to 16 x 24 cm.
              Poster.
              EXHIBITION: VX.1974.017

V.1974.021   *The Raphael cartoons : lent by Her Majesty the Queen.*
              London : Victoria and Albert Museum, 1974.
              9 p. ; 25 cm.
              Printing : 6/74.

V.1974.022   *Sculpture from Troyes in the Victoria and Albert Museum* / Charles
              Avery.
              London : [H.M.S.O.], 1974 (Printed by W.S. Cowell Ltd., Ipswich).
              [5], 66, [4] p., 1 folded : ill. (2 col.), map ; 20 cm.
              (Victoria and Albert Museum brochure ; 4)
              ISBN: 0901486795
              At head of title: Victoria and Albert Museum. — Includes bibliographic references. —
              Stapled; wrappers coloured silver, printed in brown.

V.1974.023   *South German sculpture 1480–1530* / by Michael Baxandall.
              London : H.M.S.O., 1974 (Printed by Butler & Tanner).
              74 p. : ill., map ; 25 cm.
              (Museum monograph ; no. 26)
              ISBN: 0112901638
              At head of title: Victoria and Albert Museum. — Foreword / Terence Hodgkinson. —
              Bibliography: p. 23. — Wrappers coloured brown, with ill.

V.1974.024   *Strata of society : proceedings of the seventh Annual Conference of the
              Costume Society, April 6–8, 1973.*
              London : Published for the Costume Society, c/o the Department of
              Textiles, Victoria and Albert Museum, 1974.
              56 p. : ill. ; 30 cm.
              Includes: Rural dress in Norfolk / Bridget Yates. The dress of domestic servants in the
              eighteenth century / Anne Buck. Victorian respectability and the etiquette of dress /
              Jane Grove. Some aspects of the use of non-fashionable stays / P. and R.A. Mactaggart.
              The dressmaker's craft / Janet Arnold. A guide to the study of occupational costume in
              the museums of England and Wales / Avril Lansdell. — Includes bibliographic
              references. — Stapled; white sized wrappers with decoration.

V.1974.025   *Three photographers : Nick Hedges, Christóbal Melián, Sylvester
              Jacobs : a travelling exhibition arranged by the Circulation
              Department of the Victoria and Albert Museum.*
              [London : H.M.S.O., 1974?] (Printed by PSG, Derby).
              1 sheet, folded : ill. ; 30 x 11 cm.
              Introduction signed "E.B." [i.e. Elizabeth Bailey]. — Part printed white on black.

v.1974.026   *The Wellington Museum, Apsley House : a guide* / by C.H. Gibbs-
               Smith and H.V.T. Percival. 6th ed.
               London : [H.M.S.O.], 1974 (Printed by McCorquodale Printers).
               54, [5] p., [4] p. of plates : ill., facsims., plans ; 24 x 12 cm.
               ISBN: 0901486760
               Cover title: A guide to the Wellington Museum. — Foreword / Roy Strong. —
               Bibliography: p. [59]. Index of painters. — Printing: 8/74. — Printed on grey paper.
               Sized wrappers with ill. in red.

v.1974.027   *Winnie-the-Pooh : original drawings by Ernest H. Shepard for the
               books by A.A. Milne.*
               [London : Victoria and Albert Museum, 1974.]
               1 sheet, folded ([2] p.) : 1 ill. ; 30 x 11 cm.
               "A travelling exhibition arranged by the Circulation Department . . . ." Sheet coloured
               green on one side.

1975

v.1975.001   *Alfred Stevens : centenary exhibition, 14 May–14 September 1975 :
               handlist.*
               [London] : Victoria and Albert Museum, 1975.
               38 p. ; 30 cm.
               Cover title: Alfred Stevens, 1817–1875. — "This handlist has been prepared from the
               labels used in the exhibition. They, in turn, have been compiled using a proof copy of
               Susan Beattie's forthcoming copy of the Stevens material in the Drawings Collection of
               the Royal Institute of British Architects". — Includes bibliographic references.
               EXHIBITION: vx.1975.012

v.1975.002   *Alfred Stevens, 1817–75* / Susan Beattie.
               London : Victoria & Albert Museum, 1975 (Printed by W.S. Cowell
               Ltd., Ipswich).
               48 p. : ill. ; 25 cm.
               ISBN: 0901486884
               Bibliography: p. 16. — Designed by HMSO Graphic Design. — Khaki and gold
               wrappers with portrait.
               EXHIBITION: vx.1975.012

v.1975.003   *Arthur Boyd Houghton : introduction and check-list of the artist's
               work* / by Paul Hogarth.
               London : [H.M.S.O.], 1975 (Printed by W & J Mackay Ltd.,
               Chatham).
               48 p., [16] p. of plates : ill. ; 21 cm.
               ISBN: 0901486914
               Foreword / Roy Strong. — Bibliography: p. 17. — Illustrated wrappers, printed on grey.
               EXHIBITION: vx.1975.031

v.1975.004   *Ben Nicholson : the graphic art : a Victoria and Albert Museum
               travelling exhibition.*
               [London : H.M.S.O.?, 1975.]
               1 sheet, folded (15 p.) : 1 ill. ; 30 x 11 cm.
               Introduction / Carol Hogben.
               EXHIBITION: vx.1975.015

V.1975.005   *Bibliography of Indian textiles.*
[London : Victoria and Albert Museum, 1975?]
31 p. ; 30 cm.
Caption title. At head of title: Victoria and Albert Museum, Indian Section. —
Duplicated typescript.

V.1975.006   *Catalogue of English non-illuminated manuscripts in the National Art Library up to December 1973* / compiled by Joyce Irene Whalley ; with the assistance of Alan T. Richmond.
[London : H.M.S.O.?], 1975.
i, iii, 130 p. : facsims. ; 30 cm.
At head of title: Victoria and Albert Museum. — Index of names. — Printing: 9/75. —
Stapled in grey paper covers with ill.; spine taped.

V.1975.007   *Catalogue of Scandinavian and Baltic silver* / R.W. Lightbown.
London : H.M.S.O., 1975 (Printed by William Clowes & Sons).
255 p. : ill. ; 25 cm.
ISBN: 0901486655
At head of title: Victoria and Albert Museum. — Bibliography: p. [24]–28. Indexes of
places of origin, makers and artists. Concordance of Museum numbers. — Printing:
12/75. — Wrappers coloured grey, with ill.

V.1975.008   *Catalogue of the Tiepolo drawings in the Victoria and Albert Museum* / by George Knox. 2nd ed.
London : H.M.S.O., 1975 (Printed by Eyre and Spottiswoode, Thanet Press, Margate).
xii, 121 p., [174] p. of plates : ill., 1 geneal. table ; 29 cm.
ISBN: 0901486639
Cover title: Tiepolo drawings. At head of cover: Victoria and Albert Museum
catalogues, Department of Prints and Drawings. — Foreword / Roy Strong. —
Bibliography: p. 106–110. Index. Concordance of Museum numbers. — Sized card
wrappers with illustration, printed on tan.

V.1975.009   *Chinese blue and white : a travelling exhibition arranged by the Circulation Department of the Victoria and Albert Museum.*
[London] : H.M.S.O., 1975 (Printed by Product Support (Graphics) Ltd., Derby).
1 sheet, folded (11 p.) : 1 ill. ; 30 cm.
Short bibliography. — Designed by HMSO / John Hughes. — Printing: 8/75. Printed in
blue.
EXHIBITION: VX.1977.003

V.1975.010   *Constable's Stonehenge* / Louis Hawes.
London : H.M.S.O., 1975 (Printed by W & J Mackay Ltd., Chatham).
22 p. : ill. ; 20 cm.
ISBN: 0112902235
At head of title: Victoria and Albert Museum. — Includes bibliographic references. —
White wrappers with col. ill.
EXHIBITION: VX.1975.021

V.1975.011   *Corn dollies : exhibition, July-September 1975, Bethnal Green Museum.*
[London : H.M.S.O., 1975.]
1 sheet, folded ([2] p.). : 1 ill. ; 30 cm.
Signed "P.J.G." [i.e. P.J. Glenn].
EXHIBITION: VX.1975.BGM.003

V.1975.012   *Design review : an international anthology of design-award-winning consumer products : a Victoria and Albert Museum loan exhibition.*
[London : H.M.S.O., 1975] (Printed by UDO (Litho) Ltd.).
1 sheet, folded ([13] p.) : 1 ill. ; 30 cm.
Introduction / Carol Hogben. — Designed by HMSO / John Hughes.
EXHIBITION: VX.1975.008

V.1975.013   *The destruction of the country house : a Victoria and Albert Museum travelling exhibition.*
[London : The Museum?, 1975.]
1 sheet, folded (13 p.) : 1 ill. ; 30 x 11 cm.
The country house dilemma / Roy Strong. — Based on VX.1974.026.

V.1975.014   *Dolls* / Caroline Goodfellow.
London : H.M.S.O., 1975 (Printed by W.S. Cowell Ltd., Ipswich).
[12] p. : col. ill. ; 16 cm.
(Small colour book ; 9)
ISBN: 0112902243
At head of title: Victoria & Albert Museum and Bethnal Green Museum. — Stapled; sized wrappers with col. ill.

V.1975.015   *Donatello's relief of the Ascension with Christ giving the keys to St. Peter* / by John Pope-Hennessy. 2nd imp.
London : H.M.S.O., 1949 (Printed by W & J Mackay Ltd, Chatham, 1975).
12 p., [1], 12 p. of plates (1 folded) : ill. ; 25 cm.
(Museum monograph ; no. 1)
ISBN: 0112901670
At head of title: Victoria and Albert Museum. — Stapled; grey wrappers.

V.1975.016   *Eighteenth century musical instruments, France and Britain = Les instruments de musique au XVIIIe siècle, France et Grande-Bretagne* / G. Thibault (Mme de Chambure), Jean Jenkins, Josiane Bran-Ricci. 2nd imp. with amendments.
London : [H.M.S.O.], 1973 (Printed by Eyre & Spottiswoode, Thanet, 1975).
[xxx], 225 p. : ill. (some col.) ; 28 cm.
ISBN: 090148671X
At head of title: Victoria & Albert Museum. — Foreword / John Pope-Hennessy. Acknowledgements / Hugh Wakefield. — English and French. — Index of manufacturers in Paris and London. — Grey wrappers with col. ill. City plans on end-papers.
EXHIBITION: VX.1974.004

V.1975.017   *Etchings by Seymour Haden : a travelling exhibition arranged by the Victoria and Albert Museum.*
[London : H.M.S.O., 1975] (Printed by UDO (Litho) Ltd.).
1 sheet, folded ([5] p.) : ill. ; 30 x 11 cm.
Printed in brown on brown.

v.1975.018   *Fashion, 1900–1939 : a Scottish Arts Council exhibition with the support of the Victoria and Albert Museum.*
London : Idea Books International in association with the Scottish Arts Council and the Victoria and Albert Museum, 1975 (Printed by CTD Printers).
79 p. : ill. (some col.) ; 30 cm.
[Preface] / Alexander Dunbar, Roy Strong. Acknowledgements / Robert Breen, Frances Hamilton. Fashion 1900–1939 / Madge Garland. Fashion: an art 1900–1939 / M.B. Ginsburg. Fashion photography 1900–1939 / Valerie Lloyd. Fashion illustration 1900–1939 / Martin Battersby. Textiles 1900–1939 / Martin Battersby. Corresponding styles in costume and the arts / 1975. — Includes bibliographic references. — Typography and catalogue design by Roy Walker MSIA. — Sized wrappers with turn-ins, col. ills.
EXHIBITION: vx.1976.005

v.1975.019   *The fine Crystal Palace the Prince built.*
[London : H.M.S.O., 1975] (Printed at the University Press, Oxford).
[8] p. : col. ill. ; 25 cm.
ISBN: 0901486787
Cover title. — Text signed "J.I.W." [i.e. Joyce Irene Whalley]. — Facsimile of ed. published: London: Dean and Son, [1851 or 1852] (Aunt Busy-Bee's new series). — Blue illustrated wrappers. — "This children's 'toy book' took advantage of the widespread interest shown in the Great Exhibition of 1851."

v.1975.020   *The Frank Lloyd Wright room.*
[London : Victoria and Albert Museum, 1975?]
1 sheet : ill., port. ; 30 cm.
Written by Simon Jervis and Valerie Mendes. — Includes bibliographic references. — Office designed for Edgar J. Kaufmann, acquired by the Museum.

v.1975.021   *Funeral decorations in early eighteenth century Rome* / Allan Braham.
London : [H.M.S.O.], 1975 (Printed by Albert Gait Ltd., Grimsby).
[3], 30 p. : ill. ; 20 x 21 cm.
(Victoria and Albert Museum brochure ; 7)
ISBN: 0901486833
At head of title: Victoria and Albert Museum. — Printing: 1/75. — Wrappers coloured silver, printed in black. — Concerns an album of drawings recording the decorations carried out by Carlo Fontana in Rome for the memorial services to Leopold I and Joseph I.

v.1975.022   *A gallery of children : the work of Henriette Willebeek le Mair : exhibition October-November 1975 : Bethnal Green Museum.*
[London : H.M.S.O.] 1975 (Printed by UDO (Litho) Ltd.).
1 sheet (7 p.) : 1 col. ill. ; 30 x 11 cm.
Text written by Riet Neerincx. — Printed in sage green on cream paper.
EXHIBITION: vx.1975.BGM.004

v.1975.023   *Handlist of the church plate study collections and the collection of monumental brasses in Rooms 83 & 84. Part 1, Room 84, Church plate of the British Isles, English monumental brasses.*
[London : Victoria and Albert Museum, ca. 1975.]
31 leaves ; 30 cm.
At head of title: Victoria and Albert Museum. Department of Metalwork. — Stapled into purple covers; title printed in violet and black.

V.1975.024   *Handlist of the church plate study collections and the collection of monumental brasses in Rooms 83 & 84. Part 2, Room 83, Church plate of Europe, and of the Eastern rite, Judaica and European monumental brasses.*
[London : Victoria and Albert Museum, ca. 1975.]
37 leaves ; 30 cm.
At head of title: Victoria and Albert Museum. Department of Metalwork. — Stapled into purple covers; title printed in violet and black.

V.1975.025   *The Ionides collection : Victoria & Albert Museum.*
[London : The Museum?, ca.1975?] (Printed by the Victoria and Albert Museum Press).
1 sheet, folded ([3] p.) : ill., ports ; 30 cm.
Caption title: The Constantine Alexander Ionides bequest : Victoria and Albert Museum, Room 105. — Written by C.M. Kauffmann. — Includes bibliographic references.

V.1975.026   *Joshua Cristall, (1768–1847)* / Basil Taylor.
London : [H.M.S.O.], 1975 (Printed by Product Support (Graphics) Ltd., Derby).
126 p. : ill. (2 col.) ; 25 cm.
ISBN: 090148685X
At head of title: Victoria and Albert Museum. — Foreword / Roy Strong. — Bibliography: p. 31. — Includes errata. — Wrappers coloured grey, with portrait.
EXHIBITION: VX.1975.003

V.1975.027   *The land : 20th century landscape photographs* / selected by Bill Brandt.
[London : H.M.S.O.], 1975 (Printed by UDO (Litho) Ltd.).
1 sheet, folded [(7) p.] : 1 ill., plan ; 21 cm.
Cover title. — Acknowledgements / Carol Hogben. Introduction / Mark Haworth-Booth, Elizabeth Bailey.
EXHIBITION: VX.1975.030

V.1975.028   *Leighton's frescoes in the Victoria and Albert Museum* / Richard Ormond.
London : [H.M.S.O.], 1975 (W & J Mackay Ltd., Chatham, printer).
[3], 43 p. : ill. ; 20 x 21 cm.
(Victoria and Albert Museum brochure ; 6)
ISBN: 0901486825
At head of title: Victoria and Albert Museum. — Includes bibliographic references. — Stapled; wrappers coloured silver, printed in red.

V.1975.029   *Liberty's, 1875–1975 : an exhibition to mark the firm's centenary, July-October 1975.*
London : [H.M.S.O.], 1975 (Printed by McCorquodale Printers).
128 p. : ill. ; 25 cm.
ISBN: 0901486892
Foreword / Roy Strong. Arthur Lasenby Liberty and the shop's first 40 years / Alison Adburgham. THE EASTERN BAZAAR: 1, The Japanese vogue / Edmund Capon. 2, A note on the metalwork / A.R.E. North. 3, A note on Indian handicrafts / Veronica Murphy. Furniture / Elizabeth Aslin. TEXTILES, EMBROIDERIES AND CARPETS: 1, Textiles. 2, Embroideries. 3, Carpets / Barbara Morris and Valerie Mendes. Costume / Madeleine Ginsburg. THE CYMRIC AND TUDRIC SCHEMES: 1, Cymric silver and jewellery / Shirley Bury. 2, Tudric Power / David Coachworth. Ceramics and glass /

David Coachworth. — Includes bibliographic references. List of Liberty catalogues in the Victoria and Albert Museum. Index of manufacturers and designers. — Card wrappers with title printed in cream and orange.
Copy note: one copy has title printed in cream only.
EXHIBITION: vx.1975.017

v.1975.030   *Liberty's, 1875–1975 : exhibition guide.*
London : H.M.S.O., 1975 (Printed by W.S. Cowell Ltd.).
14 p. : ill. ; 21 cm.
ISBN: 0901486906
At head of title: Victoria and Albert Museum. — Stapled; wrappers cream and dun.
EXHIBITION: vx.1975.017

v.1975.031   *Modern British watercolours : a travelling exhibition arranged by the Circulation Department, Victoria and Albert Museum.*
[London : H.M.S.O.], 1975 ("PSG", printer, Derby).
1 sheet, folded ([11] p.) ; 30 x 11 cm.
Printed in gold and purple on grey.
EXHIBITION: vx.1975.001

v.1975.032   *Mosaics from the Gilbert collection: summary catalogue* / by Charles Avery ; assisted by Arthur Emperatori.
[London : H.M.S.O.], 1975 (Printed by Jayprint of Leicester).
1 sheet, folded (11 p.) ; 21 cm.
Cover title. At head of title: Victoria & Albert Museum. — Col. ill. on cover.
EXHIBITION: vx.1975.016

v.1975.033   *Notes on carpet-knotting and weaving* / by C.E.C. Tattersall. 2nd ed., 2nd imp.
London : H.M.S.O., 1975 (Printed by Butler & Tanner).
42 p., xii p. of plates : ill., 19 cm.
ISBN: 0112900348
"This pamphlet is substantially the work of the late Mr. C.E.C. Tattersall but has been revised in the Department of Textiles in the light of more recent information"– p. 5. — Bibliography: p. 38. — Cream card wrappers with ill., printed in blue and black.

v.1975.034   *The pack age : a century of wrapping it up : Victoria and Albert Museum.*
[London : H.M.S.O., 1975] (Printed by UDO (Litho) Ltd.).
1 sheet (8 p.) : ill. ; 30 x 11 cm.
Written by Robert Opie. — Index of brands and products. — Printed in blue on blue paper.
EXHIBITION: vx.1975.032

v.1975.035   *Paul Nash as designer* / Susan Lambert.
London : [H.M.S.O.], 1975 (Printed by W.S. Cowell Ltd., Ipswich).
19 p. : ill. ; 21 x 30 cm. + 1 sheet.
ISBN: 0901486922
Acknowledgements / Carol Hogben. — Includes bibliographic references. — Designed by HMSO / John Hughes. — Stapled; decorated wrappers; buff free end-papers. — "Ex-catalogue list for showing at the Victoria and Albert Museum" on separate sheet.
EXHIBITION: vx.1975.029

V.1975.036   *Photography and the South Kensington Museum* / John Physick.
London : [H.M.S.O.], 1975 (Printed by Albert Gait Ltd., Grimsby).
19 p. : ill. ; 20 x 21 cm.
(Victoria and Albert Museum brochure ; 5)
ISBN: 0901486817
At head of title: Victoria and Albert Museum. — Bibliography: p. [19]. — Printing:
12/74. — Stapled; wrappers coloured silver, printed in brown.

V.1975.037   *Rodin sculptures* / Jennifer Hawkins.
London : H.M.S.O., 1975 (Printed at the University Press, Oxford).
34 p., [2] leaves of plates, [38] p. of plates : ill., facsim., ports. ; 25 cm.
(Museum monograph ; no. 30)
ISBN: 0112902103
At head of title: Victoria and Albert Museum. — Bibliography: p. 33–34. — Sized white
wrappers, ill.

V.1975.038   *Ruskin pottery : a Victoria and Albert Museum travelling exhibition.*
[London : H.M.S.O.], 1975 (Printed by UDO (Litho) Ltd.).
1 sheet, folded ([11] p.) : 1 col. ill. ; 30 x 11 cm. + 1 sheet
Introduction signed "D.R.C." [i.e. David Coachworth]. — "Additional items exhibited
at the Victoria and Albert Museum, 9 October–2 November 1975" (vx.1975.026) on
separate sheet.

V.1975.039   *Samuel Cooper's pocket-book* / Graham Reynolds.
London : H.M.S.O., 1975 (Printed by W.S. Cowell Ltd.).
21 p. : ill., ports. ; 20 x 22 cm.
(Victoria and Albert Museum brochure ; 8)
ISBN: 0901486876
At head of title: Victoria and Albert Museum. — Includes bibliographic references. —
Printing: 12/75. — Stapled; wrappers coloured silver, printed in grey.

V.1975.040   *Spitalfields silks* / Natalie Rothstein.
London : H.M.S.O., 1975 (Raithby, Lawrence & Co., Leicester).
[12] p. : col. ill. ; 16 cm.
(Small colour book ; 6)
ISBN: 0112902081
At head of title: Victoria & Albert Museum. — Sized wrappers with col. ill.

V.1975.041   *The thirties : progressive design in ceramics, glass, textiles and
wallpapers : a travelling exhibition arranged by the Circulation
Department of the Victoria and Albert Museum.*
[London : H.M.S.O., 1975?] (Printed by UDO (Litho) Ltd.).
1 sheet, folded ([11] p.) : 1 ill. ; 30 x 11 cm.
Introduction signed "J.H." [i.e. Jennifer Hawkins]. — Designed by HMSO /
John Hughes. — Printed in brown, with green, on cream.
EXHIBITIONS: VX.1975.BGM.002; VX.1976.007

V.1975.042   *Toys* / Caroline Goodfellow.
London : H.M.S.O., 1975 (Printed by W.S. Cowell Ltd., Ipswich).
[12] p. : col. ill. ; 15 cm.
(Small colour book ; 8)
ISBN: 0112902200
At head of title: Victoria & Albert Museum and Bethnal Green Museum. — Stapled;
sized wrappers with col. ill. — From the toy collection of Bethnal Green Museum.

V.1975.043   *Victoria & Albert Museum : brief guide.* 4th ed.
[London : H.M.S.O.], 1975 (Printed by McCorquodale Printers).
70 p. : ill., col. plans ; 30 x 13 cm.
ISBN: 0901486809
Index to rooms in the Primary Galleries. — Wrappers coloured red, with ill.; turn-ins.

V.1975.044   *Wallpaper designs from the Westfries Museum, Hoorn.*
[London : H.M.S.O., 1975.]
4 p.
Unseen. Record from *Review of the years 1974–1978* (1981), p. 131.
EXHIBITION: VX.1975.025

V.1975.045   *Your guide to 'The makers', Victoria & Albert Museum, 1976 :
artist-craftsmen at work : who they are and where they are, 11.00 to
16.00 from 29 December 1975 to 3 January 1976 (except New Year's
Day).*
[London : The Museum, 1975?] (Printed by the Victoria and Albert
Museum Press).
1 sheet, folded : plan ; 60 x 42 cm. folded to 30 cm.
Part printed in red.
EXHIBITION: VX.1975.033

1976

V.1976.001   *200th anniversary, Burgtheater, Vienna 1776–1976 : Victoria and
Albert Museum, 11th March–19th April 1976 : an exhibition arranged
by the Austrian Institute in co-operation with the Theatre Museum.*
[London : Victoria and Albert Museum?, 1976.]
1 sheet, folded (6 p.) : 1 ill. ; 21 cm.
EXHIBITION: VX.1976.THM.001

V.1976.002   *American art 1750–1800 : towards independence* / Charles F.
Montgomery and Patricia E. Kane, general editors ; with essays on
American art and culture by J.H. Plumb . . . [et al.].
Boston : Published for Yale University Art Gallery, New Haven, and
the Victoria and Albert Museum, London, by the New York Graphic
Society, 1976.
320 p. : ill. (some col.) ; 30 cm.
ISBN: 0821206923
Prefaces by Roy Strong, Alan Shestack. Essays: America and England, 1720–1820: the
fusion of cultures / J.H. Plumb. The making of an American culture: 1750–1800 / Neil
Harris. Style in American art: 1750–1800 / Jules David Prown. The metamorphoses of
Britannia / Frank H. Sommer. Regional preferences and characteristics in American
decorative arts: 1750–1800 / Charles F. Montgomery. — Bibliography: p. [268]–271.
Index. — Stone-coloured cloth covered boards; red end-papers; dust-jacket with col. ills.
EXHIBITION: VX.1976.013

V.1976.003   *American art 1750–1800 : towards independence : exhibition guide.*
London : H.M.S.O., 1976 (Printed by UDO (Litho) Ltd.).
15 p. : ill., map, plan ; 21 cm.
Cover title. At head of title: Victoria and Albert Museum. — Stapled; ill. and plan on
wrappers.
EXHIBITION: VX.1976.013

V.1976.004   *Ansel Adams photographs : 100 works : Victoria and Albert Museum,*
              16 July–29 August 1976.
              [London : The Museum, 1976.]
              1 sheet, folded ([3] p.) ; 30 cm.
              Caption title. — Foreword / Roy Strong. — Exhibition handlist.
              EXHIBITION: vx.1976.014

V.1976.005   *Ansel Adams photographs : a Victoria & Albert Museum travelling*
              exhibition.
              London : H.M.S.O., 1976 (Printed by McCorquodale Printers).
              8 p. : 1 ill. ; 30 cm.
              Introduction / Mark Haworth-Booth; interview with Ansel Adams: Mark Haworth-
              Booth and Diane Lyon. — Bibliography: p. 4. — Printing: 7/76. — Stapled; ill.
              on front.
              EXHIBITION: vx.1976.014

V.1976.006   *The Ardabil carpet.*
              [London : H.M.S.O.?, 1976] ("PSG", printer, Derby).
              1 sheet, folded ([3] p.) : ill. (1 col.) ; 30 cm.
              (Masterpieces ; sheet 5)
              By Natalie Rothstein. Printing: 9/76.

V.1976.007   *Art nouveau and Alphonse Mucha* / by Brian Reade. 2nd ed.,
              4th imp.
              London : H.M.S.O., 1967 (Printed by Butler & Tanner, 1976).
              34 p., [32] p. of plates : ill. ; 25 cm.
              (Large picture book ; no. 18)
              "First published on the occasion of vx.1963.006." — Blue wrappers with title and ills.
              printed in puce.

V.1976.008   *The art press : two centuries of art magazines : essays published for*
              the Art Libraries Society on the occasion of the international
              conference on art periodicals and the exhibition 'The Art Press' at the
              Victoria and Albert Museum, London / edited by Trevor Fawcett &
              Clive Phillpot.
              London : Published by the Art Book Company for the Art Libraries
              Society and the Victoria & Albert Museum, 1976 (Printed by CTD,
              Twickenham).
              63 p. : ill. ; 30 cm.
              (Art documents ; no. 1)
              Includes bibliographic references and index. — Designed by Hugh Pilkington and Roy
              Walker. — Wrappers, coloured brick red.

V.1976.009   *The artists of Disney : material from the Walt Disney Archive :*
              a travelling exhibition arranged by the Victoria and Albert
              Museum.
              [London : H.M.S.O.] 1976 (Printed by UDO (Litho) Ltd.).
              1 sheet, folded (12 p.) : 1 ill. ; 30 cm.
              Foreword / Roy Strong. Introduction John Russell Taylor. — Selected bibliography.
              Printed in brown.
              EXHIBITION: vx.1976.025

V.1976.010   *Aubrey Beardsley* / by Brian Reade. 6th imp.
              London : H.M.S.O., 1966 (Printed by Butler & Tanner, 1976).

18 p., 50 p. of plates : ill. ; 25 cm.
(Large picture book ; no. 32)
ISBN: 0112901409
First published on the occasion of vx.1966.003. — Printing: 2/76. — Grey wrappers with ill. printed in orange.

V.1976.011   *Bernini's* Neptune and Triton.
[London : H.M.S.O.], 1976 (Printed by Product Support (Graphics) Ltd., Derby).
1 sheet, folded ([3] p.) : ill. (1 col.) ; 30 cm.
(Masterpieces ; sheet 1)
Title from cover (i.e. p. [1]). — By Ronald Parkinson. — Includes bibliographic references. — Printing: 6/76.

V.1976.012   *British water-colours* / by Graham Reynolds. 2nd ed., 2nd imp. with amendments
London : H.M.S.O., 1969 (Text [printed] by Butler & Tanner, cover by Headley Brothers, 1976).
68 p. : ill. ; 14 x 22 cm.
(Illustrated booklet ; no. 4)
ISBN: 0112902510
At head of title: Victoria and Albert Museum. — Printing: 10/76. — Wrappers with col. ill.

V.1976.013   *Chinese tomb figures* / Edmund Capon.
London : H.M.S.O., 1976 (Printed by W.S. Cowell Ltd., Ipswich).
[12] p. : col. ill. ; 16 cm.
(Small colour book ; 11)
ISBN: 0112902332
At head of title: Victoria & Albert Museum. — Stapled; card wrappers with col. ill.

V.1976.014   *Constable's Stonehenge : a travelling exhibition from the Victoria and Albert Museum.*
[London] : Issued by the Dept. of Regional Services, [Victoria and Albert Museum], 1976.
1 sheet : ill. ; 15 x 21 cm.
Caption title.

V.1976.015   *Constable's studies for* The hay-wain.
[London : H.M.S.O.?, 1976] (Printed by the Victoria & Albert Museum Press).
1 sheet, folded ([3] p.) : ill. (1 col.) ; 30 cm.
(Masterpieces ; sheet 2)
By C.M. Kauffmann. — Includes bibliographic references.

V.1976.016   *Daumier : eyewitness of an epoch* / J.R. Kist.
London : H.M.S.O., 1976 (Printed by the Hillingdon Press, Uxbridge).
26, 96 p. : ill. ; 18 cm.
ISBN: 0901486930
At head of title: Victoria and Albert Museum. — Translation of: Daumier: verslaggever van zijn tijd, 1832–1872. — Bibliography: p. 23. — Printing: 5/76. — Sized wrappers with ills. printed on blue.
EXHIBITION: vx.1976.010

V.1976.017　　　*David Garrick (1717–79)* / by Howard Burnham.
[s.l. : s.n.], 1976 (Printed for H.M.S.O. by Product Support (Graphics) Ltd., Derby).
1 sheet : ill., port. ; 30 cm.
(Theatre Museum card ; 3)
Includes bibliography. — Designed by H.M.S.O. Graphic Design. — Printed in brown on cream card.

V.1976.018　　　*The Devonshire hunting tapestries.*
[London : Victoria and Albert Museum?, 1976?] (Printed by the Victoria & Albert Museum Press).
1 sheet, folded ([3] p.) : ill. (1 col.) ; 30 cm.
(Masterpieces ; sheet 3)
[By Wendy Hefford.]

V.1976.019　　　*Dolls' houses* / Caroline Goodfellow.
London : H.M.S.O., 1976 (Printed by W.S. Cowell Ltd., Ipswich).
[12] p. : col. ill. ; 16 cm.
(Small colour book ; 10)
ISBN: 0112902324
At head of title: Victoria & Albert Museum and Bethnal Green Museum. — Stapled; sized wrappers with col. ill.

V.1976.020　　　*Dr Thomas Monro (1759–1833) and the Monro Academy : Victoria & Albert Museum, Prints and Drawings Gallery, February–May 1976.*
[London : H.M.S.O.], 1976.
[16] p. : ill., ports. ; 21 cm.
Cover title. — Text by F.J.G. Jefferiss; foreword by C.M. Kauffmann. — Part printed in brown, on brown paper. Stapled; port. on cover.
EXHIBITION: vx.1976.002

V.1976.021　　　*Early keyboard instruments* / by Raymond Russell. 3rd imp.
London : H.M.S.O., 1959 (Printed by W. & J. Mackay Ltd., Chatham, 1976).
[6] p., [26] p. of plates : ill. ; 19 cm.
(Small picture books ; 48)
ISBN: 0112902405
At head of title: Victoria and Albert Museum. — Sized wrappers, with ill., printed on salmon.

V.1976.022　　　*Ellen Terry* / by Hazel Holt.
[s.l. : s.n.], 1976 (Printed for H.M.S.O. by Product Support (Graphics) Ltd., Derby).
1 sheet : ports. ; 30 cm.
(Theatre Museum card ; 2)
Includes bibliography. — Designed by H.M.S.O. Graphic Design. — Printed in brown on cream card.

V.1976.023　　　*English medieval alabasters* / Terence Hodgkinson.
London : H.M.S.O., 1976 (Printed by W.S. Cowell Ltd., Ipswich).
[12] p. : col. ill. ; 16 cm.
(Small colour book ; 7)
ISBN: 0112902138
At head of title: Victoria & Albert Museum. — Stapled; sized wrappers with col. ill.

v.1976.024   *Fashion, 1900–1939 : a Scottish Arts Council exhibition with the support of the Victoria and Albert Museum.*
[London] : Printed for H.M.S.O. by UDO (Litho) Ltd., 1976.
[8] p. : ill. ; 21 cm.
ISBN: 0905093011
Cover title. — Written by Madeleine Ginsburg. — Bibliography: p. [8]. — Stapled; ill. on cover.
EXHIBITION: vx.1976.005

v.1976.025   *Flowers in English embroidery.* 2nd ed., 3rd imp.
London : H.M.S.O, 1963 (Printed by W & J Mackay Ltd., Chatham, 1976).
[6] p., 26 p. of plates : ill. ; 18 cm.
(Small picture books ; no. 2)
ISBN: 0112902413
At head of title: Victoria & Albert Museum. — Wrappers; col. ill. printed on grey.

v.1976.026   *Garrick's contemporaries* / by Howard Burnham.
[s.l. : s.n.], 1976 (Printed for H.M.S.O. by Product Support (Graphics) Ltd., Derby).
1 sheet : ill., port. ; 30 cm.
(Theatre Museum card ; 8)
Includes bibliography. — Designed by H.M.S.O. Graphic Design. — Printed in brown on cream card.

v.1976.027   *The Globe Theatre* / by Hazel Holt.
[s.l. : s.n.], 1976 (Printed for H.M.S.O. by Product Support (Graphics) Ltd., Derby).
1 sheet : ill., ports. ; 30 cm.
(Theatre Museum card ; 6)
Includes bibliography. — Designed by H.M.S.O. Graphic Design. — Printed on buff card.

v.1976.028   *Ham House.* 4th ed.
London : [H.M.S.O.], 1976 (Printed by W & J Mackay Ltd.).
75 p. : ill., plans ; 14 x 22 cm.
ISBN: 0901486957
At head of title: Victoria & Albert Museum. — Compiled by Maurice Tomlin. Introduction / Peter Thornton. — Bibliography: p. 72–3. — Printing: 1/77. — Wrappers, with 2 col. ills.

v.1976.029   *The history of the Victoria & Albert Museum.* 2nd ed.
London : H.M.S.O., 1976 (Printed by W & J Mackay Ltd., Chatham).
32 p. : ill., plan, ports. ; 16 cm.
(Small picture book ; no. 31)
ISBN: 0112902189
Revised by John Physick. Foreword / Roy Strong. — Stapled; sized wrappers, with ill. printed on brown.

v.1976.030   *Homage to Kokoschka : prints and drawings lent by Reinhold, Count Bethusy-Huc.*
London : [H.M.S.O.], 1976 (Printed by McCorquodale Printers).
64 p. : ill. (some col.) ; 21 cm.
ISBN: 0901486949

At head of title: Victoria and Albert Museum. — Foreword / Roy Strong. Introduction / E.H. Gombrich. The birth of a collection / Reinhold, Count Bethusy-Huc. The Symbolist legacy in the work of Kokoschka / Edith Hoffmann. On Oskar Kokoschka's portrait of Yvette Guilbert / Fritz Novotny. *Der Sturm* / Hans Bolliger. Kokoschka's 'Agony in the garden' / Jan Tomeš. Kokoschka's late graphic work: a publisher's view / Bernhard Baer. Catalogue / Reinhold, Count Bethusy-Huc and Susan Lambert. — Includes bibliographic references. — Printing: 4/76. — Stapled; wrappers; col. ill.
EXHIBITION: vx.1976.009

V.1976.031   *The House of David, his inheritance : a book of sample scripts, 1914 A.D.* / Edward Johnston. 2nd imp., with amendments.
London : H.M.S.O., 1966 (Printed by Ebenezer Baylis & Son, 1976).
32 p. ; 26 cm.
(Facsimiles ; no. 1)
ISBN: 0112902367
At head of title: Victoria and Albert Museum. Cover title: A book of sample scripts. — Introduction / J.P. Harthan. — Sized wrappers, part printed in red; facsims. on end-papers.

V.1976.032   *Islamic metalwork from Iranian lands (8th–18th centuries) : Victoria and Albert Museum exhibition, April-May 1976* / A.S. Melikian-Chirvani.
[London : H.M.S.O.], 1976 (Printed by UDO (Litho) Ltd.).
19 p. : ill. ; 21 cm.
Cover title. — Includes bibliographic references. — Stapled; wrappers with ill.
EXHIBITION: vx.1976.006

V.1976.033   *Italian Renaissance bronzes* / Anthony Radcliffe.
London : H.M.S.O., 1976 (Printed by W.S. Cowell Ltd., Ipswich).
[12] p. : col. ill. ; 16 cm.
(Small colour book ; 14)
ISBN: 011290243X
At head of title: Victoria & Albert Museum. — Stapled, sized wrappers with col. ill.

V.1976.034   *Jean Hugo designs for the theatre : Theatre Museum, Victoria and Albert Museum Room 132, 23 October to 5 December 1976.*
[London : H.M.S.O.], 1976 (Printed by UDO (Litho) Ltd.).
1 sheet, folded (7 p.) : ill. ; 30 cm.
EXHIBITION: vx.1976.THM.004

V.1976.035   *Jumbo and some other elephants : Bethnal Green Museum of Childhood, exhibition November 1976–January 1977*
[London : H.M.S.O.], 1976 (UDO (Litho) Ltd.).
6, [1] p. : ill. ; 21 cm.
Cover title. — Written by P.J. Glenn. — Stapled; wrappers coloured grey, with ill.
EXHIBITION: vx.1976.BGM.002

V.1976.036   *Landscape photography : 50 pictures chosen by Bill Brandt : a Victoria & Albert Museum travelling exhibition.*
[London : H.M.S.O.], 1976 (Printed by UDO (Litho) Ltd.).
1 folded sheet ([5] p.) : 1 ill. ; 30 cm.
Introduction / Mark Haworth-Booth. — Bibliography: p. [5].

v.1976.037   *The makers : Victoria & Albert Museum, 1976.*
London : The World's End Press, in collaboration with the Victoria
and Albert Museum, 1976 (Printed by the Victoria and Albert
Museum Press).
1 box ([6] folded leaves, [4] leaves of plates) : ill. ; 23 cm.
Cover title. — "Poems by Edward Lucie-Smith; calligraphy by Ann Hechle; etching by
Ann Brunskill; wood-engraving by John Lawrence; embroidery by Diana Springall;
boxes made by Adrian Pasotti; engraving of a ewer by Georg Wechter, c. 1526–1586 ..
. ; Walter Keeler, potter at work."
Box covered with Laura Ashley pink and white paper, quarter bound in maroon leather.
"A limited edition of 140 copies of this book has been published ... with two original
prints and two original photographs. 14 copies ... are hors concours ... 26 copies are
lettered A to Z. 100 copies are numbered 1 to 100. All copies are signed by Edward
Lucie-Smith."
EXHIBITION: vx.1976.023

v.1976.038   *The makers : Victoria & Albert Museum, 1976–7.*
London : Victoria and Albert Museum, 1976 (Printed by UDO (Litho)
Ltd.).
[12] p. : ill. ; 21 cm.
Cover title. — Stapled; wrappers. — Printed edition of v.1976.037.
EXHIBITION: vx.1976.023

v.1976.039   *Mid-Georgian domestic silver.* 4th imp.
London : H.M.S.O., 1952 (Printed by W.S. Cowell Ltd., Ipswich,
1976).
[3] p., 30 p. of plates : ill. ; 18 cm.
(Small picture book ; no. 28)
ISBN: 0112902545
At head of title: Victoria and Albert Museum. — Wrappers; decorated title, printed on
grey.

v.1976.040   *Minton, 1798–1910 : exhibition August-October 1976* / Elizabeth
Aslin and Paul Atterbury.
London : H.M.S.O., 1976 (Printed by McCorquodale Printers).
111, 4 p. of plates : ill. (some col.) ; 20 x 21 cm.
ISBN: 0901486965
At head of title: Victoria and Albert Museum, Thomas Goode & Company Limited. —
Foreword / Roy Strong. — Bibliography: p. 14–15. Index. Marks. List of lenders. —
Sized white wrappers with ills.
EXHIBITION: vx.1976.015

v.1976.041   *The music hall* / by Hazel Holt.
[s.l. : s.n.], 1976 (Printed for H.M.S.O. by Product Support (Graphics)
Ltd., Derby).
1 sheet : ill. ; 30 cm.
(Theatre Museum card ; 1)
Includes bibliography. — Designed by H.M.S.O. Graphic Design. — Printed in blue on
red card.

v.1976.042   *Music hall portraits.*
[s.l. : s.n.], 1976 (Printed for H.M.S.O. by Product Support (Graphics)
Ltd., Derby).
1 sheet, folded ([4] p.) : ports. ; 30 cm.
(Theatre Museum card ; 7)
Designed by H.M.S.O. Graphic Design. — Printed on red card.

V.1976.043 *Musical instruments : a list of books and articles in the National Art Library, Victoria and Albert Museum* / compiled by M.I. Wilson.
[Rev. & enl. ed.]
[London : The Library], 1976 (Printed by HMSO Reprographic Services, Manchester).
126 p. : ill. ; 30 cm.
At head of title: Victoria and Albert Museum. Original title: A bibliography of books on musical instruments in the Library of the Victoria and Albert Museum. — Printing: 8/76. — Stapled in grey paper covers with ill.; spine taped.

V.1976.044 *Playing cards* / Frances Hicklin.
London : H.M.S.O., 1976 (Printed by W.S. Cowell Ltd., Ipswich).
[12] p. : col. ill. ; 16 cm.
(Small colour book ; 12)
At head of title: Victoria & Albert Museum. — Bibliography: p. [3]. — Printing: 5/76. — Stapled; sized wrappers with col. ill.

V.1976.045 *Pop art* / Elizabeth Bailey.
London : H.M.S.O., 1976 (Printed by W.S. Cowell Ltd., Ipswich).
9 p. : col. ill. ; 16 cm.
(Small colour book ; 13)
ISBN: 0112902350
At head of title: Victoria & Albert Museum. — Stapled; sized wrappers with col. ill.

V.1976.046 *Puppets* / Caroline Goodfellow.
London : H.M.S.O., 1976 (Printed by W.S. Cowell Ltd., Ipswich).
[12] p. : col. ill. ; 16 cm.
(Small colour book ; 15)
ISBN: 0112902561
At head of title: Victoria and Albert Museum and Bethnal Green Museum. — Photography: Ken Jackson. — Stapled; sized wrappers with col. ills.

V.1976.047 *Rachel* / by Norman Aarons.
[s.l. : s.n.], 1976 (Printed for H.M.S.O. by Product Support (Graphics) Ltd., Derby).
1 sheet : ill., port. ; 30 cm.
(Theatre Museum card ; 5)
Includes bibliography. — Designed by H.M.S.O. Graphic Design. — Printed in brown on cream card.

V.1976.048 *The rediscovery of an artist : the drawings of James Jefferys (1751–1784) : exhibition February–May 1976.*
[London : H.M.S.O.?, 1976] (Printed by W.S. Cowell Ltd., Ipswich).
15 p. : ill. ; 21 cm.
Cover title. At head of title: Victoria & Albert Museum. — Written by Timothy Clifford and Susan Legouix. Acknowledgements / C.M. Kaufmann. — Includes bibliographic references. — Stapled; portrait on cover.
EXHIBITION: VX.1976.003

V.1976.049 *Restoration drama* / by Howard Burnham.
[s.l. : s.n.], 1976 (Printed for H.M.S.O. by Product Support (Graphics) Ltd., Derby).
1 sheet, folded ([4] p.) : ill., ports. ; 30 cm.
(Theatre Museum card ; 9)
Includes bibliography. — Designed by H.M.S.O. Graphic Design. — Printed in green on yellow card.

v.1976.050   *The Richard Wagner non stop 'Ring' show.*
                [London : H.M.S.O.], 1976 (Printed by McCorquodale Printers).
                4 p. : ill. ; 56 cm.
                "The Theatre Museum presents the Richard Wagner non stop Ring show at the Theatre
                Museum, Room 132, Victoria and Albert Museum . . . A continuous performance of the
                Decca recording and an exhibition of the Ring in England and Scotland, Monday
                August 2 to Sunday October 3, 1976 . . . ." Printed in the format of a broadsheet
                newspaper, containing articles reproduced from British newspapers, 1876–1908.
                EXHIBITION: vx.1976.THM.003

v.1976.051   *Samuel Beckett by Avigdor Arikha : a tribute to Samuel Beckett on his
                70th birthday : Victoria and Albert Museum, February–May 1976.*
                [London : H.M.S.O., 1976] (Printed by UDO Litho).
                11, [1] p. : ill. ; 21 cm.
                Cover title. — Catalogue by Mordechai Omer, foreword by C.M. Kauffmann. —
                Printed on buff paper; stapled.
                EXHIBITION: vx.1976.004

v.1976.052   *The Sanchi torso.*
                [London : H.M.S.O., 1976] ("PSG", printer, Derby).
                1 sheet, folded ([5] p.) : ill. (1 col.) ; 30 cm.
                (Masterpieces ; sheet 7)
                By John Irwin. — Includes references for "Further reading". — Printing: 9/76.

v.1976.053   The seasons : *illustrations to James Thomson's poem, 1730–1830,
                lent from the collection of Dr Mordechai Omer : a Victoria and Albert
                Museum travelling exhibition.*
                [London : H.M.S.O.], 1976 (Printed by W.S. Cowell Ltd., Ipswich).
                1 folded sheet ([8] p.) : 1 ill. ; 30 x 11 cm.
                Introduction and catalogue entries by Mordechai Omer. Acknowledgements / Barbara
                Morris. — Includes bibliographic references.
                EXHIBITION: vx.1976.016

v.1976.054   *Sir Henry Irving* / by Howard Burnham.
                [s.l. : s.n.], 1976 (Printed for H.M.S.O. by Product Support (Graphics)
                Ltd., Derby).
                1 sheet : ports. ; 30 cm.
                (Theatre Museum card ; 4)
                Includes bibliography. — Designed by H.M.S.O. Graphic Design. — Printed in brown
                on cream card.

v.1976.055   *Staffordshire blue & white : a Victoria & Albert Museum travelling
                exhibition.*
                [London : H.M.S.O., 1976] (Printed by PSG Ltd., Derby).
                1 sheet, folded (11 p.) : 1 ill. ; 30 x 11 cm.
                Brief bibliography: p. 3. — Printed in blue.

v.1976.056   *Stanbrook Abbey Press and Sir Sydney Cockerell : a centenary
                exhibition, 10 November 1976 to 13 February 1977* / exhibition
                arranged and catalogue compiled by G.D.A. McPherson and J.I.
                Whalley.
                [London : National Art Library, 1976].
                [1], iii, 23 p. ; 30 cm.
                Foreword R.W. Lightbown. — Printing: 11/76. — Stapled in blue paper covers.
                EXHIBITION: vx.1976.020

V.1976.057   *Supplement to the catalogue of English non-illuminated manuscripts in the National Art Library : accessions and re-catalogued items for 1974.*
[London : H.M.S.O.], 1975 [i.e. 1976?].
7 p. ; 30 cm.
At head of title: Victoria and Albert Museum. Cover title: Catalogue of English non-illuminated manuscripts. — Index. — Printing: 3/76. — Stapled in grey covers with ill.

V.1976.058   *Supplement to the catalogue of English non-illuminated manuscripts in the National Art Library : accessions and re-catalogued items for 1975.*
[London : H.M.S.O.], 1975 [i.e. 1976?].
12 p. ; 30 cm.
At head of title: Victoria and Albert Museum. Cover title: Catalogue of English non-illuminated manuscripts. — Index. — Printing: 3/76. — Stapled in grey covers with ill.

V.1976.059   *Tea-pots in pottery and porcelain.* 5th imp.
London : H.M.S.O., 1948 (Printed by W & J Mackay Ltd., Chatham, 1976).
[4] p., 28 p. of plates : ill. ; 13 x 19 cm.
(Small picture book ; no. 9)
ISBN: 0112902421
At head of title: Victoria & Albert Museum. Cover title: Teapots. — Introduction signed "A.L." [i.e. Arthur Lane]. — Printing: 6/76. — Sized wrappers; title and ill. printed on orange.

V.1976.060   *The Theatre Museum presents Hoffnung's world of music : 21st December 1976 to 27th March 1977 : Victoria and Albert Museum, Room 132.*
[London : H.M.S.O.], 1976 (Printed by UDO (Litho) Ltd.).
1 sheet : ill. ; 25 x 31 cm.
Caption title. — Gerard Hoffnung / Annetta Hoffnung.
EXHIBITION: VX.1976.THM.005

V.1976.061   *Theatre peepshow : a dip into the Theatre Museum's collections exhibited at the National Theatre from March 1976.*
[London : The Museum, 1976.]
1 sheet, folded ; 26 cm.
EXHIBITION: VX.1976.XXX.002

V.1976.062   *Tibetan art* / John Lowry. 2nd imp. with amendments.
London : H.M.S.O., 1973 (Text [printed] by Butler and Tanner ; cover by Headley Brothers, 1976).
118 p. : ill. ; 22 cm.
ISBN: 0112901093
At head of title: Victoria and Albert Museum. — Bibliography: p. 10. Index. — Printing: 9/76. — Wrappers with col. ill. on green.

V.1976.063   *A tonic to the nation.*
[London : H.M.S.O., 1976] (Printed by U.D.O. (Litho) Ltd.).
[7] p. : ill. ; 21 cm.
ISBN: 0901486973
Cover title. — By Mary Banham, Christopher Firmstone, Bevis Hillier. — Stapled; photograph on wrappers.
EXHIBITION: VX.1976.022

V.1976.064   *Unknown dolls from the Gauder-Auka-Stuttgart collection :*
               exhibition September-October 1976.
               [London : H.M.S.O.], 1976 (Printed by UDO (Litho) Ltd.).
               11 p. : ill. ; 21 cm.
               Cover title. — Written by Caroline Goodfellow. Foreword / Roy Strong. — Printed in
               sepia on cream. Stapled.
               EXHIBITION: VX.1976.BGM.001

V.1976.065   *[V&A masterpieces]*
               [London : Victoria and Albert Museum, 1976.]
               13 cards : ill. ; 18 x 22 cm.
               A series of cards produced to accompany Man-made, a residency at the Victoria and
               Albert Museum for a group of craftspeople, 29–31 December 1976. Each card
               illustrates an object in the Museum selected by one of the participants, relating it to
               their own work, with emphasis on technical aspects. Includes bibliographic references.
               Flemish mitre [Inv. no. 203–1881] / Jennifer Boyd-Carpenter. – Devonshire hunting
               tapestries [Inv. no. T.203–1957] / Archie Brennan. – Indian miniature [Inv. no.
               I.S.99–1965] / Ann Brunskill [Brunskill's object is a painting but she describes the
               technique of etching]. – Archlute by Christoforo Choco [Inv. no. 7756–1862] / Stephen
               Gottlieb. – English psalter [Inv. no. 816–1894] / Ann Hechle. – Italian amethyst cameo
               [A Flemish ivory is also illustrated. Inv. nos. A.5–1959; 2149–1855] / Nik Lambrinides.
               – Wood-engraving: *The lady of Shalott* [Dalziel Brothers, after D.G. Rossetti, Inv. no.
               E.2922–1904] / John Lawrence ['The chamber idyll', a wood-engraving by Edward
               Calvert, Inv. no. E.511–1926, is also illustrated]. – Book binding by Roger Payne
               [Inv. no. L.1791–1934] / Adrian Pasotti. – The 'Three Fates' tapestry [Inv. no. 65–1886]
               / Barbara Mullins. – Buckinghamshire bobbin lace [Inv. nos. T.166–1925; T.219–1923]
               / Kathleen Riley & Margaret Susans. – Chinese stem cup [Inv. nos.
               168–1905; C.30–1953; C.893–1936] / Ray Silverman. – Embroidered workbox, 1692
               [Inv. no. T.6–1926] / Diana Springall. – The Shannongrove gorget [Inv. no. M.35–1948]
               / Matthew Tomalin.
               EXHIBITION: VX.1976.023

V.1976.066   *Victorian and Edwardian decorative arts.* 3rd imp.
               London : H.M.S.O., 1952 (Printed by Butler & Tanner, 1976).
               39 p. : ill. ; 18 cm.
               (Small picture book ; no. 34)
               At head of title: Victoria & Albert Museum. — Introduction signed "P.F."
               [i.e. Peter Floud]. — Sized wrappers; title and illustration printed on green. —
               First issued in conjunction with VX.1952.005.

V.1976.067   *William Morris.* 4th imp.
               London : H.M.S.O., 1958 (Printed by Butler & Tanner, 1976).
               [2], [3] p., 27 p. of plates : ill. ; 18 cm.
               (Small picture book ; no. 43)
               ISBN: 0112900887
               At head of title: Victoria & Albert Museum. — Introduction signed "P.F."
               [i.e. Peter Floud]. — Pale blue wrappers with William Morris design in green.

V.1976.068   *Your guide to* Man-made : *artist-craftsmen at work : who they are*
               and where they are : Victoria & Albert Museum 29 to 31 December
               1976.
               [London : The Museum, 1976] (Printed by the Soman-Wherry Press,
               Norwich).
               1 sheet, folded : 1 ill., plan ; 18 x 21 cm.
               Designed by Michael Martin.
               EXHIBITION: VX.1976.023

1977

V.1977.001   *Arms and armour of old Japan* / by B.W. Robinson. 4th imp.
London : H.M.S.O., 1951 (Printed at the University Press, Oxford, 1977).
17 p., 26 p. of plates : ill. ; 22 cm.
(Illustrated booklet ; no. 6)
ISBN: 0112900747
At head of title: Victoria & Albert Museum. Cover title: Arms & armour of old Japan. — Printing: 6/77. — Buff wrappers with ill. printed in tan.

V.1977.002   *The art of Bernard Leach : a loan retrospective exhibition, March to May 1977.*
London : [H.M.S.O.], 1977 (Printed by Balding + Mansell, Wisbech).
29 p. : ill. ; 21 cm.
Cover title. At head of title: Victoria and Albert Museum. — Introduction by John Houston. Foreword / Roy Strong. — Bibliography: p. 28. Index of lenders. — Printing: 4/77. — Stapled; potter's mark illustrated on wrappers.
EXHIBITION: VX.1977.005

V.1977.003   *The Bible in British art, 10th to 20th centuries : Victoria and Albert Museum, exhibition September 1977–January 1978* / C.M. Kauffmann.
[London : H.M.S.O., 1977] (Printed by PSG Ltd.).
40 p. : ill. ; 21 cm.
Cover title. — Bibliography: p. 3. Index of lenders. — Stapled; wrappers with ills.
EXHIBITION: VX.1977.015

V.1977.004   *A bibliography of pre–19th century topographical works, including facsimile editions, relating chiefly to England, Scotland, and Wales in the National Art Library, Victoria and Albert Museum* / compiled by M.I. Wilson.
[London : The Library], 1977 (Printed by HMSO Reprographic Services, Manchester).
ii, 88 p. : ill. ; 30 cm.
Cover title: Early British topography: a list of books and articles . . . . — Index of names. Blue wrappers with ills.

V.1977.005   *Catalogue of Italian maiolica* / by Bernard Rackham ; with emendations and additional bibliography by J.V.G. Mallet. 2nd imp., with amendments.
London : H.M.S.O., 1977 (Printed by Billing & Sons).
2 v. (xl, 485 p., [1] leaf of plates; xxvii p., [1] leaf, 222 p. of plates) : ill. ; 26 cm.
ISBN: 011290095X (set).
At head of title: Victoria and Albert Museum. Title on spine: Italian maiolica. — Vol. I, Text. Vol. II, Plates. — Bibliography: p. xxi-xl. General and numerical indexes. — Blue cloth covered boards. In slip-case.

V.1977.006   *Change & decay : the future of our churches.*
[London : H.M.S.O., 1977.]
12, [2] p. : ill. ; 21 cm.
ISBN: 0905209087

Cover title. At head of title: Victoria and Albert Museum. — Signed "M.B.", "J.P." [i.e. Marcus Binney, John Physick]. — Stapled; ills. on wrappers.
EXHIBITION: VX.1977.013

V.1977.007   *Cibber's figures from the gates of Bedlam.*
[London : H.M.S.O.?], 1977.
1 sheet, folded ([5] p.) : ill., 1 col. ; 30 cm.
(Masterpieces ; sheet 14)
Title from cover (i.e. p. [1]). — By Patricia Allderidge. — Includes bibliographic references.

V.1977.008   *The complete prints of Eduardo Paolozzi : prints, drawings, collages 1944–77* / Rosemary Miles.
London : [H.M.S.O.], 1977 (Printed by Ebenezer Baylis & Son).
79 p. : ill. ; 19 cm.
ISBN: 0905209036
At head of title: Victoria & Albert Museum. — Foreword / C.M. Kauffmann. — Bibliography: p. 61–64. — Sized wrappers with ills., 1 col.
EXHIBITION: VX.1977.010

V.1977.009   *Costume : a general bibliography* / by Pegaret Anthony and Janet Arnold ; rev. and enl. ed. prepared by Janet Arnold. Repr.
London : Costume Society c/o Dept. of Textiles, Victoria & Albert Museum, 1974, 1977 (Daedalus Press, printer, King's Lynn).
[6], 42 p. ; 22 cm.
(Costume Society bibliography ; no.1)
Stapled; brown wrappers.

V.1977.010   *Donatello's* Chellini Madonna.
[London : H.M.S.O.], 1976 [i.e. 1977?] ("PSG", printer).
1 sheet, folded ([3] p.) : ill. (1 col.) ; 30 cm.
(Masterpieces ; sheet 9)
By Charles Avery. — Includes bibliographic references. — Printing: 3/77.

V.1977.011   *English chairs.* 3rd ed. [rev. Desmond Fitz-Gerald], 2nd imp.
London : H.M.S.O., 1970 (Printed by W & J Mackay Ltd, Chatham, 1977).
28 p., [1], 129 p. of plates : ill. (1 col.) ; 25 cm.
(Large picture book ; no. 10)
ISBN: 0112900313
At head of title: Victoria and Albert Museum. — Sized wrappers with photograph, printed on blue.

V.1977.012   *The engraved work of Eric Gill.* 2nd ed.
London : H.M.S.O., 1977 (Printed by W & J Mackay Ltd., Chatham).
82 p. : ill. ; 25 cm.
(Large picture book ; no. 17)
ISBN: 0112902715
At head of title: Victoria and Albert Museum. — Cream wrappers with ill.

V.1977.013   *European puppets in history* / by George Speaight.
[s.l. : s.n.], 1977 (Printed for H.M.S.O. by W. & J. Linney Ltd.).
1 sheet : ill. ; 30 cm.

(Theatre Museum card ; 12)
Includes bibliography. — Designed by H.M.S.O. Graphic Design. — Printed on buff
card.

V.1977.014   *Experimental theatre I : Russia, land of giants* / by James Roose-
Evans.
[s.l. : s.n.], 1977 (Printed for H.M.S.O. by W. & J. Linney Ltd.).
1 sheet : ill., ports. ; 30 cm.
(Theatre Museum card ; 21)
Includes bibliography. — Designed by HMSO Graphic Design. — Printed in blue on
mustard card.

V.1977.015   *Fabergé (1846–1920) : goldsmith to the imperial court of Russia.*
[London] : H.M.S.O., 1977 (Printed by McCorquodale Printers).
[12] p. : ill. ; 21 cm.
ISBN: 0905209079
Caption title. Cover title: Fabergé. — Stapled; wrappers with ills.
Copy notes : Printing: 6/77; 9/77.
EXHIBITION: VX.1977.012

V.1977.015A   [2nd imp.]
Printing: 9/77.

V.1977.016   *Fabergé 1846–1920 : goldsmith to the imperial court of Russia :
an international loan exhibition assembled on the occasion of the
Queen's Silver Jubilee and including objects from the royal collection
at Sandringham, 23 June–25 September 1977.*
London : Debrett's Peerage, for the Victoria and Albert Museum,
1977 (Produced by the Compton Press, Salisbury ; colour printing by
Harrison & Sons (London).
131 p. : ill. (some col.) ; 19 x 25 cm.
ISBN: 0905649036; 0905649028 (pbk.)
Catalogue by A. Kenneth Snowman. — Designed by Humphrey Stone. — Black cloth
covered boards stamped with crest in gold; dust-jacket with col. ills.; or wrappers.
EXHIBITION: VX.1977.012

V.1977.017   *For Her Majesty's Silver Jubilee the Theatre Museum respectfully
presents Royal box : a souvenir portfolio of an exhibition* / with an
introduction by Ian Bevan . . . .
[London : H.M.S.O.], 1977 (Printed by UDO (Litho) Ltd.).
1 portfolio ([13] leaves, one folded) : chiefly ill. (some col.) ; 30 cm.
EXHIBITION: VX.1977.THM.001

V.1977.018   *Forty two British watercolours from the Victoria and Albert Museum* /
John Murdoch.
London : H.M.S.O., 1977 (Printed by E. Baylis & Son).
[86] p. : ill. ; 20 x 21 cm.
ISBN: 090148699X
Includes bibliographic references. — Wrappers, with ill., printed on burgundy.
EXHIBITION: VX.1977.XXX.004

V.1977.019   *French gold boxes* / Charles Truman.
London : H.M.S.O., 1977 (Printed by W.S. Cowell Ltd., Ipswich).
[12] p. : col. ill. ; 16 cm.

(Small colour book ; 16)
ISBN: 0112902596
At head of title: Victoria & Albert Museum. — Stapled; sized wrappers with col. ill.

V.1977.020   *The Gamble Room* / John Physick.
[London : H.M.S.O.], 1977 (Printed by W.S. Cowell Ltd., Ipswich).
1 sheet, folded ([3] p.) : ill. (1 col.), plans ; 30 cm.
At head of title: Victoria & Albert Museum. — Printing: 7/77.

V.1977.021   *The great bed of Ware.*
[London : H.M.S.O.], 1976 [i.e. 1977?].
1 sheet, folded ([3] p.) : ill. ; 30 cm.
(Masterpieces ; sheet 8)
Written by P.K. Thornton. — Printing: 2/77.

V.1977.022   *A guide to the Wellington Museum : Apsley House.* 7th ed.
London : [H.M.S.O.], 1977 (Printed by McCorquodale, Printers).
54, [5] p., [4] p. of plates : ill., plans ; 24 cm.
ISBN: 0905209060
Previously titled: The Wellington Museum, Apsley House. — Prepared by Victor
Percival in conjunction with C.H. Gibbs-Smith. Foreword / John Pope-Hennessy. —
Bibliography: p. [58–59]. Includes lists of paintings on display and index to painters. —
Printing: 5/77. — Text printed on grey paper. Card wrappers with illustration printed
on red.

V.1977.023   *Indian art.* 2nd imp. with amendments.
London : H.M.S.O., 1977 (Printed at the University Press, Oxford).
vi, [70] p. : chiefly ill., ports. ; 25 cm.
(Large picture books ; no. 36)
ISBN: 0112900062 (pbk.)
At head of title: Victoria and Albert Museum. — Preface signed "J.C.I." [i.e. John
Irwin]. — Designed by HMSO: Philip Marriage. — Green sized wrappers with ill.

V.1977.024   *Isadora Duncan* / by James Roose-Evans.
[s.l. : s.n.], 1977 (Printed for H.M.S.O. by W. & J. Linney Ltd.).
1 sheet : ports. ; 30 cm.
(Theatre Museum card ; 20)
Includes bibliography. — Designed by H.M.S.O. Graphic Design. — Printed in blue on
cream card.

V.1977.025   *Jasper Johns : etchings, the pages of* Fizzles/Foirades : *lithograph, four
panels from* Untitled 1972.
[London : Victoria and Albert Museum, 1977 or 1978?]
1 sheet ; 30 cm.
Caption title. At head of title: A Victoria and Albert Museum travelling exhibition. —
Written by Roberta Bernstein. — Includes bibliographic references.

V.1977.026   *Jubilation : royal commemorative pottery from the collection of James
Blewitt : exhibition May to September 1977.*
London : [H.M.S.O.], 1977 (Printed by W.S. Cowell Ltd., Ipswich).
26 p., [32] p. of plates : ill. ; 15 x 21 cm.
ISBN: 0905209044
At head of title: Bethnal Green Museum of Childhood. — Foreword / Elizabeth Aslin.
Compiled by John May. — Stapled; sized wrappers with col. photograph, printed on
black.
EXHIBITION: VX.1977.BGM.002

V.1977.027   *Keith Murray : a travelling exhibition arranged by the Circulation Department of the Victoria and Albert Museum.*
[London : H.M.S.O.], 1977 (Printed by "PSG Ltd.", Derby).
1 folded sheet ([11] p.) : 2 ill. ; 30 x 11 cm.
Introduction signed "J.H." [i.e. Jennifer Hawkins].
EXHIBITION: vx.1977.009

V.1977.028   *Look-out for churches.*
[London] : Victoria & Albert Museum, [1977].
[14] p. : ill. ; 15 x 21 cm.
Cover title. — Written and compiled by Celia O'Malley, drawings by Moira Shippard. — Printed in brown. Original text hand-written. Stapled. — Educational booklet for children.
EXHIBITION: vx.1977.013

V.1977.029   *The Luck of Edenhall.*
[London : H.M.S.O.], 1976 [i.e. 1977?] ("PSG", printer, Derby).
1 sheet, folded ([3])p. : ill. (1 col.) ; 30 cm.
(Masterpieces ; sheet 6)
Written by R.J. Charleston. — Printing: 2/77.

V.1977.030   *The Mandalay shrine.*
[London : H.M.S.O.], 1976 ("PSG", printer, Derby).
1 sheet, folded ([3] p.) : ill. (1 col.) ; 30 cm.
(Masterpieces ; sheet 12)
Written by John Lowry. — Printing: 2/77.

V.1977.031   *Ming porcelains* / John Ayers.
London : H.M.S.O., 1977 (Printed by W.S. Cowell Ltd., Ipswich).
[12] p. : col. ill. ; 16 cm.
(Small colour book ; 17)
ISBN: 011290260X
At head of title: Victoria & Albert Museum. — Stapled; sized wrappers with col. ill.

V.1977.032   *A Morris and De Morgan tile-panel.*
[London : H.M.S.O.], 1977 ("PSG", printer).
1 sheet, folded ([3] p.) : ill., 1 col. ; 30 cm.
(Masterpieces ; sheet 13)
By Roger Pinkham. — Includes "Further reading". — Printing: 7/77.

V.1977.033   *Nicholas Hilliard's* Young man among roses.
[London : H.M.S.O.], 1976 [i.e. 1977?] ("PSG", printer, Derby).
1 sheet, folded ([3] p.) : ill. (1 col.), ports. ; 30 cm.
(Masterpieces ; sheet 10)
By Roy Strong. — Printing: 2/77.

V.1977.034   *Oriental puppets* / by George Speaight.
[s.l. : s.n.], 1977 (Printed for H.M.S.O. by W. & J. Linney Ltd.).
1 sheet : ill. ; 30 cm.
(Theatre Museum card ; 14)
Includes bibliography. — Designed by H.M.S.O. Graphic Design. — Printed on buff card.

V.1977.035　　　*Osterley Park.* 2nd ed.
London : [H.M.S.O.], 1977 (Printed by Staples Printers).
58 p. : ill., map, plan ; 14 x 22 cm.
ISBN: 0905209052
At head of title: Victoria & Albert Museum. — Written by Maurice Tomlin.
Introduction / Peter Thornton. — Includes bibliographic references. — Sized card
wrappers with colour photographs.

V.1977.036　　　*Persian oil paintings* / B.W. Robinson.
London : H.M.S.O., 1977 (Printed by Raithby, Lawrence & Co.).
[12] p. : col. ill. ; 16 cm.
(Small colour books ; 20)
ISBN: 0112902685
At head of title: Victoria & Albert Museum. — Stapled; sized wrappers with col. ill.

V.1977.037　　　*Punch and Judy* / by George Speaight.
[s.l. : s.n.], 1977 (Printed for H.M.S.O. by W. & J. Linney Ltd.).
1 sheet : ill. ; 30 cm.
(Theatre Museum card ; 13)
Includes bibliography. — Designed by H.M.S.O. Graphic Design. — Printed on buff
card.

V.1977.038　　　*The puppet revival* / by George Speaight.
[s.l. : s.n.], 1977 (Printed for H.M.S.O. by W. & J. Linney Ltd.).
1 sheet : ill. ; 30 cm.
(Theatre Museum card ; 15)
Includes bibliography. — Designed by H.M.S.O. Graphic Design. — Printed on buff
card.

V.1977.039　　　*Puppets* / by George Speaight.
[s.l. : s.n.], 1977 (Printed for H.M.S.O. by W. & J. Linney Ltd.).
1 sheet : ill., port. ; 30 cm.
(Theatre Museum card ; 11)
Includes bibliography. — Designed by H.M.S.O. Graphic Design. — Printed on buff
card.

V.1977.040　　　*Report of the Sepulchral Monuments Committee, preceded by copies
of a letter from the Office of Works, &c., and of Resolutions of the
Council : presented to both Houses of Parliament by command of Her
Majesty* / Society of Antiquaries of London. Repr.
[London] : H.M.S.O. 1977 (Printed by UDO (Litho) Ltd.).
57 p. ; 33 cm.
Cover title: National monuments. — Originally published 1872, reprinted in connection
with vx.1977.013. — Foreword / Roy Strong. — Stapled; sized wrappers coloured
green, with ill.

V.1977.041　　　*Revue* / by Sandy Wilson.
[s.l. : s.n.], 1977 (Printed for H.M.S.O. by W. & J. Linney Ltd.).
1 sheet : ill. ; 30 cm.
(Theatre Museum card ; 19)
Designed by H.M.S.O. Graphic Design. — Printed on red card.

V.1977.042　　　*The romantic ballet* / by Ivor Guest.
[s.l. : s.n.], 1977 (Printed for H.M.S.O. by W. & J. Linney Ltd.).
1 sheet, folded ([4] p.) : ill., ports. ; 30 cm.

(Theatre Museum card ; 10)

Includes bibliography. — Designed by H.M.S.O. Graphic Design. — Printed on blue card.

V.1977.043   *Roubiliac's* Handel.
[London : H.M.S.O.], 1976 [i.e. 1977?] ("PSG", printer).
1 sheet, folded ([3] p.) : ill. ; 30 cm.
(Masterpieces ; sheet 4)

By Madeleine Mainstone. — Includes bibliographic references. — Printing: 3/77.

V.1977.044   *Royal Shakespeare Theatre, Stratford-upon-Avon* / by R.B. Marriott.
[s.l. : s.n.], 1977 (Printed for H.M.S.O. by W. & J. Linney Ltd.).
1 sheet : ill. ; 30 cm.
(Theatre Museum card ; 24)

Includes bibliography. — Designed by H.M.S.O. Graphic Design. — Printed on buff card.

V.1977.045   *Samplers* / by Donald King. 4th imp.
London : H.M.S.O., 1960 (Printed by W & J Mackay Ltd., Chatham).
15 p., [62] p. of plates : ill. ; 25 cm.
(Large picture book ; no. 14)

ISBN: 0112901492

At head of title: Victoria and Albert Museum. — Bibliography: p. 11. — Printing: 12/77. — Sized wrappers with col. ill.

V.1977.046   *Scraps : one hundred and fifty years of stamped, embossed reliefs : exhibition February-April 1977* / Alistair Allen.
[London] : H.M.S.O., 1977 (Printed by Balding + Mansell, Wisbech).
50 p. ; 21 cm.

ISBN: 0901486981

At head of title: Bethnal Green Museum of Childhood. — Bibliography: p. 30. Subject index. List of scrap producers, 1825–1975. — Printing: 2/77. — Stapled; col. ills. on wrappers.
EXHIBITION: VX.1977.BGM.001

V.1977.047   *Six studio potters : a Victoria and Albert Museum travelling exhibition.*
[London : The Museum], 1977 (Printed by UDO (Litho) Ltd.).
1 folded sheet (10 p.) : ports. ; 30 x 11 cm.

Gordon Baldwin, Michael Casson, Hans Coper, Ian Godfrey, Jacqueline Poncelet, Peter Simpson.
EXHIBITION: VX.1976.017

V.1977.048   *The Theatre Museum at the National Theatre presents Harley Granville Barker* / exhibition arranged by Margery Morgan ; designed by John Ronayne.
[London : H.M.S.O.], 1977 (UDO (Litho) Ltd., printer).
1 sheet, folded ([9] p.) ; 30 cm.
Includes bibliography. — Printed on cream paper.
EXHIBITION: VX.1977.XXX.001

V.1977.049   *Third supplement to the catalogue of English non-illuminated manuscripts in the National Art Library : accessions and re-catalogued items for 1976* / compiled by J.I. Whalley, with the assistance of Vera Kaden and Michael Keen.

London : H.M.S.O., 1977.
14 p. ; 30 cm.
At head of title: Victoria and Albert Museum. Cover title: Catalogue of English
non-illuminated manuscripts. — Name and subject indexes. — Printing: 5/77. —
Stapled in orange paper covers with ill.

V.1977.050   *Tibetan tangkas* / John Lowry.
London : H.M.S.O., 1977 (Printed by Raithby, Lawrence & Co.).
[12] p. : col. ill. ; 16 cm.
(Small colour book ; 18)
ISBN: 0112902642
At head of title: Victoria & Albert Museum. — List of plates inside front cover. —
Stapled; sized wrappers with col. ill.

V.1977.051   *Tippoo's tiger.*
[London : H.M.S.O.], 1976 [i.e. 1977?] ("PSG", printer, Derby).
1 sheet, folded ([3] p.) : ill. (1 col.) ; 30 cm.
(Masterpieces ; sheet 11)
Written by Veronica Murphy. — Includes bibliographic references — Printing: 2/77.

V.1977.052   *The toy theatre in England* / by George Speaight.
[s.l. : s.n.], 1977 (Printed for H.M.S.O. by W. & J. Linney Ltd.).
1 sheet : ill. ; 30 cm.
(Theatre Museum card ; 16)
Includes bibliography. — Designed by H.M.S.O. Graphic Design. — Printed on buff
card.

V.1977.053   *The toy theatre in Europe* / by George Speaight.
[s.l. : s.n.], 1977 (Printed for H.M.S.O. by W. & J. Linney Ltd.).
1 sheet : ill. ; 30 cm.
(Theatre Museum card ; 17)
Includes bibliography. — Designed by H.M.S.O. Graphic Design. — Printed on buff
card.

V.1977.054   *Treasures of the Print Room : acquisitions 1975–6 : Victoria & Albert
Museum, 6 January until 17 April . . . .*
[London : The Museum, 1977.]
1 sheet, folded ([5] p.) : ill. ; 21 x 10 cm.
Text by C.M Kauffmann.
EXHIBITION: VX.1977.001

V.1977.055   *The wireless show! : 130 classic radio receivers, 1920s to 1950s : a
loan exhibition presented by the Museum in association with the
British Vintage Wireless Society, October to December 1977.*
[London : H.M.S.O.], 1977 (Printed by McCorquodale Printers).
15 p. : ill. ; 30 cm.
Cover title. At head of title: Victoria & Albert Museum. — Introduction by Carol
Hogben. — Bibliography: p. 8. Index of lenders. — Printing: 10/77. — Stapled.
EXHIBITION: VX.1977.019

1978

V.1978.001   *Adeline Genée* / by Ivor Guest.
[s.l. : s.n.], 1978 (Printed for H.M.S.O. by W. & J. Linney Ltd.).
1 sheet : ports. ; 30 cm.
(Theatre Museum card ; 44)
Includes bibliography. — Designed by H.M.S.O. Graphic Design. — Printed in blue on cream card.

V.1978.002   *The American musical* / by Sandy Wilson.
[s.l. : s.n.], 1978 (Printed for H.M.S.O. by W. & J. Linney Ltd.).
1 sheet : ill. ; 30 cm.
(Theatre Museum card ; 89)
Designed by H.M.S.O. Graphic Design. — Printed in blue on mustard-coloured card.

V.1978.003   *Anglo-Jewish silver : an exhibition of Jewish ritual silver and plate associated with the Jewish community in England* / organised under the auspices of the Jewish Historical Society of England and the V & A.
[London? : The Organisers?, 1978.]
21 p. ; 21 cm.
Cover title. At head of title: Victoria and Albert Museum, 10 May–9 July 1978. — Reproduced from typescript. Stapled; blue wrappers, with ill.
EXHIBITION: VX.1978.012

V.1978.004   *Anti-theatre 1948–1971* / by Ronald Hayman.
[s.l. : s.n.], 1978 (Printed for H.M.S.O. by W. & J. Linney Ltd.).
1 sheet : ill., port. ; 30 cm.
(Theatre Museum card ; 54)
Includes bibliography. — Designed by H.M.S.O. Graphic Design. — Printed in blue on mustard-coloured card.

V.1978.005   *Antonin Artaud (1896–1948)* / by Ronald Hayman.
[s.l. : s.n.], 1978 (Printed for H.M.S.O. by W. & J. Linney Ltd.).
1 sheet : ports. ; 30 cm.
(Theatre Museum card ; 64)
Includes bibliography. — Designed by H.M.S.O. Graphic Design. — Printed on cream card.

V.1978.006   *The art of fashion, 1600–1939* / Madeleine Ginsburg.
London : H.M.S.O., 1978 (Printed by Raithby, Lawrence & Co. at the De Montfort Press).
[16] p. : col. ill. ; 16 cm.
(Small colour book ; 19)
ISBN: 0112902669
At head of title: Victoria & Albert Museum. — Stapled; sized wrappers with col. ill.

V.1978.007   *Arthur Wing Pinero* / by R.B. Marriott.
[s.l. : s.n.], 1978 (Printed for H.M.S.O. by W. & J. Linney Ltd.).
1 sheet : ill., ports. ; 30 cm.
(Theatre Museum card ; 37)
Includes bibliography. — Designed by H.M.S.O. Graphic Design. — Printed in purple on cream card.

V.1978.008   *August Strindberg (1849–1912)* / by Ronald Hayman.
[s.l. : s.n.], 1978 (Printed for H.M.S.O. by W. & J. Linney Ltd.).
1 sheet : ill., port. ; 30 cm.
(Theatre Museum card ; 42)
Includes bibliography. — Designed by H.M.S.O. Graphic Design. — Printed in purple on cream card.

V.1978.009   *Barry Jackson* / by R.B. Marriott.
[s.l. : s.n.], 1978 (Printed for H.M.S.O. by W. & J. Linney Ltd.).
1 sheet : ill., port. ; 30 cm.
(Theatre Museum card ; 29)
Includes bibliography. — Designed by H.M.S.O. Graphic Design. — Printed in brown on cream card.

V.1978.010   *Ben Jonson (ca 1572–1637)* / by Ronald Hayman.
[s.l. : s.n.], 1978 (Printed for H.M.S.O. by W. & J. Linney Ltd.).
1 sheet : ill. ; 30 cm.
(Theatre Museum card ; 73)
Includes bibliography. — Designed by H.M.S.O. Graphic Design. — Printed on cream card.

V.1978.011   *Bertolt Brecht 1898–1956* / by Ronald Hayman.
[s.l. : s.n.], 1978 (Printed for H.M.S.O. by W. & J. Linney Ltd.).
1 sheet : ill., port. ; 30 cm.
(Theatre Museum card ; 63)
Includes bibliography. — Designed by H.M.S.O. Graphic Design. — Printed on cream card.

V.1978.012   *Bewick : wood engravings* / Frances Hicklin.
London : H.M.S.O., 1978 (Printed at the University Press, Oxford).
32 p. : ill. ; 19 cm.
ISBN: 0112902901
At head of title: Victoria and Albert Museum. — Bibliography: p. 32. — White wrappers with ills., part printed in sage green. — "The illustrations in this booklet have been reproduced from four albums of proofs of Bewick's wood-engravings in the Museum's Department of Prints and Drawings"–t.p. verso.

V.1978.013   *Bulls fighting, with a view of St Donatt's Castle, Glamorganshire.*
[London : H.M.S.O.], 1978 (Printed by UDO Litho Ltd).
1 sheet, folded ([3] p.) : ill., some col. ; 30 cm.
(Masterpieces ; 20)
By Lionel Lambourne. — Includes bibliographic references. — Concerns a painting by James Watt.

V.1978.014   *C. Wilhelm* / by Ivor Guest.
[s.l. : s.n.], 1978 (Printed for H.M.S.O. by W. & J. Linney Ltd.).
1 sheet : ill. ; 30 cm.
(Theatre Museum card ; 35)
Includes bibliography. — Designed by H.M.S.O. Graphic Design. — Printed on cream card. — C. Wilhelm was the stage name of William J.C. Pitcher, stage costume designer.

V.1978.015   *Cars : photographs by Langdon Clay.*
[London : Victoria and Albert Museum, 1978.]
1 sheet, folded ([2] p.) : 1 col. ill. ; 21 cm.
Written by Mark Haworth-Booth.
EXHIBITION: VX.1978.018

v.1978.016 *Catalogue of musical instruments. Vol II, Non-keyboard instruments /*
Anthony Baines. 2nd ed.
London : H.M.S.O., 1978 (Printed by W & J Mackay Ltd., Chatham).
xi, 123 p., [95] p. of plates : ill. ; 25 cm.
ISBN: 0112903991
At head of title: Victoria and Albert Museum. — Foreword / Peter Thornton. —
Bibliography: p. 109–111. General and numerical indexes. — Wrappers. Coloured ill.
on tan background.

v.1978.017 *Charles B. Cochran (1872–1951).*
[s.l. : s.n.], 1978 (Printed for H.M.S.O. by W. & J. Linney Ltd.).
1 sheet, folded ([4] p.) : ill. ; 30 cm.
(Theatre Museum card ; 26)
Includes bibliography. — Designed by H.M.S.O. Graphic Design. — Printed in blue on
mustard coloured card.

v.1978.018 *Charles Kean (1811–68) /* by Ronald Hayman.
[s.l. : s.n.], 1978 (Printed for H.M.S.O. by W. & J. Linney Ltd.).
1 sheet : ill. ; 30 cm.
(Theatre Museum card ; 80)
Includes bibliography. — Designed by H.M.S.O. Graphic Design. — Printed in brown
on cream card.

v.1978.019 *Christopher Marlowe (1564–95) /* by Ronald Hayman.
[s.l. : s.n.], 1978 (Printed for H.M.S.O. by W. & J. Linney Ltd.).
1 sheet : ill., port. ; 30 cm.
(Theatre Museum card ; 75)
Includes bibliography. — Designed by H.M.S.O. Graphic Design. — Printed on cream
card.

v.1978.020 *The circus /* by George Speaight.
[s.l. : s.n.], 1978 (Printed for H.M.S.O. by W. & J. Linney Ltd.).
1 sheet : ill. ; 30 cm.
(Theatre Museum card ; 33)
Includes bibliography. — Designed by H.M.S.O. Graphic Design. — Printed on mustard
coloured card.

v.1978.021 *The circus /* by George Speaight.
[s.l. : s.n.], 1978 (Printed for H.M.S.O. by W. & J. Linney Ltd.).
1 sheet : ill. ; 30 cm.
(Theatre Museum card ; 83)
Text as v.1978.020, with different illustrations. — Bibliography. — Designed by
H.M.S.O. Graphic Design. — Printed in brown on mustard coloured card.

v.1978.022 *The circus 2 : liberty acts /* by Antony D. Hippisley Coxe.
[s.l. : s.n.], 1978 (Printed for H.M.S.O. by W. & J. Linney Ltd.).
1 sheet : ill. ; 30 cm.
(Theatre Museum card ; 90)
Includes bibliography. — Designed by H.M.S.O. Graphic Design. — Printed in brown
on mustard coloured card.

v.1978.023 *The circus 3 : High School riding acts /* by Antony D. Hippisley
Coxe.
[s.l. : s.n.], 1978 (Printed for H.M.S.O. by W. & J. Linney Ltd.).
1 sheet : ill. ; 30 cm.

(Theatre Museum card ; 91)

Includes bibliography. — Designed by H.M.S.O. Graphic Design. — Printed in brown on mustard coloured card.

V.1978.024   *Decorative sculpture* / John Physick.
[London : H.M.S.O.], 1978.
1 sheet, folded ([5] p.) : ill. ; 30 cm.

At head of title: Victoria & Albert Museum. — Describes the sculpture on the V&A building. — Col. ill. on front.

V.1978.025   *Designs for the dream king : the castles and palaces of Ludwig II of Bavaria.*
London : Debrett's Peerage in association with Victoria and Albert Museum, London, and Cooper-Hewitt Museum, New York, 1978 (Produced by the Compton Press, Salisbury; colour printing by Harrison & Sons).
76, [4] p. : ill. (some col.), ports. ; 26 cm.
ISBN: 0905649141; 090564915x (pbk.)

At head of title: Debrett, Cooper-Hewitt, V&A. — Introduction / Roy Strong, Lisa Taylor. Essays by Simon Jervis, Gerhard Hojer; catalogue by Simon Jervis. — Bibliography: p. [79]. — Designed by Humphrey Stone.
EXHIBITION: VX.1978.020

V.1978.026   *Experimental theatre : Germany* / by James Roose-Evans.
[s.l. : s.n.], 1978 (Printed for H.M.S.O. by W. & J. Linney Ltd.).
1 sheet : ill. ; 30 cm.
(Theatre Museum card ; 70)

Includes bibliography. — Designed by H.M.S.O. Graphic Design. — Printed in blue on mustard-coloured card.

V.1978.027   *Fans from the East.*
London : Debrett's Peerage, for the Birmingham City Museum and Art Gallery, the Victoria and Albert Museum and the Fan Circle, 1978 (Printed by Raithby Lawrence and Co.).
[4], 87 p. : ill. (some col.) ; 26 cm.
ISBN: 0905649222; 0905649214 (pbk.)

Foreword / Roy Strong, Dennis Farr. Introduction by the Countess of Rosse. Fans from the east / Madeleine Ginsburg. Chinese fans and fans from China / Julia Hutt. The fan in Japan / Joe Earle. Chinoiserie / The Fan Circle and the Victoria & Albert Museum. From India to the Philippines / Nancy Armstrong. Chapter 5 / Katy Talati. — Bibliography: p. 85. — Green cloth covered boards; dust-jacket with col. ill.
EXHIBITION: VX.1979.004

V.1978.028   *Federico Garcia Lorca (1898–1936)* / by Ronald Hayman.
[s.l. : s.n.], 1978 (Printed for H.M.S.O. by W. & J. Linney Ltd.).
1 sheet : port. ; 30 cm.
(Theatre Museum card ; 49)

Includes bibliography. — Designed by H.M.S.O. Graphic Design. — Printed on cream card.

V.1978.029   *Fourth supplement to the catalogue of English non-illuminated manuscripts in the National Art Library : accessions for 1977* / compiled by J.I. Whalley ; with the assistance of Peter Castle.
London : [H.M.S.O.], 1978.
12 p. ; 30 cm.

At head of title: Victoria and Albert Museum. Cover title: Catalogue of English non-illuminated manuscripts. — Name and subject indexes. — Printing: 4/78. — Stapled in olive covers with ill.

V.1978.030   *Frank Benson* / by R.B. Marriott.
[s.l. : s.n.], 1978 (Printed for H.M.S.O. by W. & J. Linney Ltd.).
1 sheet : ill. ; 30 cm.
(Theatre Museum card ; 53)
Includes bibliography. — Designed by H.M.S.O. Graphic Design. — Printed in brown on cream card.

V.1978.031   *French silver* / R.W. Lightbown.
London : H.M.S.O., 1978 (Printed by W. & J. Mackay Ltd).
ix, 117 p. : ill. ; 29 cm.
ISBN: 0112902502
Bibliography: p. [viii]–ix. Indexes of places, makers' names and marks, and Museum numbers. — Blue cloth covered boards; title and device stamped in silver; grey dust-jacket with col. ill.

V.1978.032   *George Alexander* / by R.B. Marriott.
[s.l. : s.n.], 1978 (Printed for H.M.S.O. by W. & J. Linney Ltd.).
1 sheet : ill. ; 30 cm.
(Theatre Museum card ; 40)
Includes bibliography. — Designed by H.M.S.O. Graphic Design. — Printed in brown on cream card.

V.1978.033   *George Bernard Shaw (1856–1950)* / by Ronald Hayman.
[s.l. : s.n.], 1978 (Printed for H.M.S.O. by W. & J. Linney Ltd.).
1 sheet : ill. ; 30 cm.
(Theatre Museum card ; 74)
Includes bibliography. — Designed by H.M.S.O. Graphic Design. — Printed on cream card.

V.1978.034   *George Robey* / by R.B. Marriott.
[s.l. : s.n.], 1978 (Printed for H.M.S.O. by W. & J. Linney Ltd.).
1 sheet : ill. ; 30 cm.
(Theatre Museum card ; 46)
Includes bibliography. — Designed by H.M.S.O. Graphic Design. — Printed on red card.

V.1978.035   *Gerald du Maurier* / by R.B. Marriott.
[s.l. : s.n.], 1978 (Printed for H.M.S.O. by W. & J. Linney Ltd.).
1 sheet : ill. ; 30 cm.
(Theatre Museum card ; 43)
Includes bibliography. — Designed by H.M.S.O. Graphic Design. — Printed in brown on cream card.

V.1978.036   *German Expressionist drama 1910–24* / by Ronald Hayman.
[s.l. : s.n.], 1978 (Printed for H.M.S.O. by W. & J. Linney Ltd.).
1 sheet : ill. ; 30 cm.
(Theatre Museum card ; 51)
Includes bibliography. — Designed by H.M.S.O. Graphic Design. — Printed in blue on mustard coloured card.

V.1978.037   *Giambologna's* Samson and a Philistine.
[London : H.M.S.O.], 1978 (Printed by UDO Litho Ltd.).

1 sheet ([5] p.) : ill. (1 col.) ; 30 cm.
(Masterpieces ; sheet 18)
By Charles Avery. — Bibliography.

V.1978.038   *The graphic work of William Nicholson : catalogue of an exhibition held at the Victoria & Albert Museum, 1st March–9th April 1978.*
[London : National Art Library, 1978.]
8 p. ; 30 cm.
Compiled from labels prepared by J.I. Whalley. — Duplicated sheets, stapled.
EXHIBITION: VX.1978.008

V.1978.039   *Grimaldi or Joey the clown* / by James Roose-Evans.
[s.l. : s.n.], 1978 (Printed for H.M.S.O. by W. & J. Linney Ltd.).
1 sheet : ill., port. ; 30 cm.
(Theatre Museum card ; 30)
Includes bibliography. — Designed by H.M.S.O. Graphic Design. — Printed in brown on cream card.

V.1978.040   *Harley Granville Barker* / by Margery M. Morgan.
[s.l. : s.n.], 1978 (Printed for H.M.S.O. by W. & J. Linney Ltd.).
1 sheet : ill. ; 30 cm.
(Theatre Museum card ; 52)
Includes bibliography. — Designed by H.M.S.O. Graphic Design. — Printed in purple on cream card.

V.1978.041   *Harry Lauder* / by R.B. Marriott.
[s.l. : s.n.], 1978 (Printed for H.M.S.O. by W. & J. Linney Ltd.).
1 sheet : ports. ; 30 cm.
(Theatre Museum card ; 66)
Includes bibliography. — Designed by H.M.S.O. Graphic Design. — Printed in blue on red card.

V.1978.042   *Herbert Beerbohm Tree* / by R.B. Marriott.
[s.l. : s.n.], 1978 (Printed for H.M.S.O. by W. & J. Linney Ltd.).
1 sheet : ill. ; 30 cm.
(Theatre Museum card ; 93)
Includes bibliography. — Designed by H.M.S.O. Graphic Design. — Printed in brown on cream card.

V.1978.043   *Indian art.*
London : [H.M.S.O.], 1978 (Printed by Oxford University Press).
28 p. : ill. ; 15 x 21 cm.
(Victoria & Albert Museum departmental guides)
ISBN: 0905209117
Preface signed "J.C.I." [i.e. John Irwin]. — Stapled; white sized wrappers with col. ills.

V.1978.044   *Ironwork. Part I, From the earliest times to the end of the mediaeval period* / by J. Starkie Gardner ; revised by W.W. Watts. Photolitho impression of 4th ed. with supplementary bibliography compiled by Marian Campbell.
London : Printed under the authority of the Board of Education, 1927 (Printed for H.M.S.O. by Balding + Mansell, Wisbech, 1978).
xi, 146 p., 63 p. of plates : ill. ; 22 cm.
ISBN: 0905209001

At head of title: Victoria and Albert Museum. — Prefaces by Cecil Smith, Eric
Maclagan. — Bibliography: p. 147–148. General and topographical indexes. —
Printing: 4/78. — Sized white wrappers with ills.

v.1978.045   *Ironwork. Part II, Continental ironwork of the Renaissance and later
periods* / by J. Starkie Gardner ; revised and enlarged by W.W. Watts.
Photolitho impression of the 2nd ed. with supplementary bibliography
compiled by Marian Campbell.
London : Published under the authority of the Board of Education,
1930 (Printed for H.M.S.O. by Balding + Mansell, Wisbech, 1978).
xii, 126 p., 44 p. of plates : ill. ; 23 cm.
ISBN: 090520901X
At head of title: Victoria and Albert Museum. — Preface / Eric Maclagan. — "List of
books in the Library of the Victoria and Albert Museum . . .": p. 112–114.
Supplementary bibliography: p. 125–126. General and topographical indexes, and index
of designers and craftsmen. — Printing: 4/78. — Sized white wrappers, with ills.

v.1978.046   *Ironwork. Part III, A complete survey of the artistic working of iron
in Great Britain from the earliest times* / J. Starkie Gardner. Photolitho
impression with supplementary bibliography compiled by Marian
Campbell.
London : Published under the authority of H.M.S.O., 1922 (Printed
for H.M.S.O. by Balding + Mansell, Wisbech, 1978).
198 p., [46] p. of plates : ill. ; 23 cm.
ISBN: 0905209028
At head of title: Victoria and Albert Museum. — Prefatory note / Cecil H. Smith. —
General and topographical indexes. — Printing: 4/78. — Sized white wrappers, with ills.

v.1978.047   *Ivor Novello (1893–1951)* / by Sandy Wilson.
[s.l. : s.n.], 1978 (Printed for H.M.S.O. by W. & J. Linney Ltd.).
1 sheet : ill. ; 30 cm.
(Theatre Museum card ; 25)
Includes bibliography. — Designed by H.M.S.O. Graphic Design. — Printed on buff
card.

v.1978.048   *John Martin-Harvey* / by R.B. Marriott.
[s.l. : s.n.], 1978 (Printed for H.M.S.O. by W. & J. Linney Ltd.).
1 sheet : ill., port. ; 30 cm.
(Theatre Museum card ; 65)
Designed by H.M.S.O. Graphic Design. — Printed in brown on cream card.

v.1978.049   *John Millington Synge (1871–1909)* / by Ronald Hayman.
[s.l. : s.n.], 1978 (Printed for H.M.S.O. by W. & J. Linney Ltd.).
1 sheet : ill. ; 30 cm.
(Theatre Museum card ; 87)
Includes bibliography. — Designed by H.M.S.O. Graphic Design. — Printed in blue on
cream card.

v.1978.050   *Johnston Forbes-Robertson* / by R.B. Marriott.
[s.l. : s.n.], 1978 (Printed for H.M.S.O. by W. & J. Linney Ltd.).
1 sheet : ill. ; 30 cm.
(Theatre Museum card ; 57)
Includes bibliography. — Designed by H.M.S.O. Graphic Design. — Printed in brown
on cream card.

v.1978.051   *Julia Neilson and Fred Terry* / by R.B. Marriott.
                [s.l. : s.n.], 1978 (Printed for H.M.S.O. by W. & J. Linney Ltd.).
                1 sheet : ill. ; 30 cm.
                (Theatre Museum card ; 61)
                Includes bibliography. — Designed by H.M.S.O. Graphic Design. — Printed in brown
                on cream card.

v.1978.052   *Konstantin Stanislavski (1863–1938)* / by Ronald Hayman.
                [s.l. : s.n.], 1978 (Printed for H.M.S.O. by W. & J. Linney Ltd.).
                1 sheet : ill. ; 30 cm.
                (Theatre Museum card ; 85)
                Includes bibliography. — Designed by H.M.S.O. Graphic Design. — Printed in brown
                on cream card.

v.1978.053   *Lilian Baylis* / by R.B. Marriott.
                [s.l. : s.n.], 1978 (Printed for H.M.S.O. by W. & J. Linney Ltd.).
                1 sheet : ill., port. ; 30 cm.
                (Theatre Museum card ; 86)
                Includes bibliography. — Designed by H.M.S.O. Graphic Design. — Printed in blue on
                magenta card.

v.1978.054   *The Louis XII triptych.*
                [London : H.M.S.O.], 1978 (Printed by UDO (Litho) Ltd.).
                1 sheet, folded ([4] p.) : ill., 1 col. ; 30 cm.
                (Masterpieces ; sheet 19)
                At head of title: Victoria & Albert Museum. — By Roger Pinkham. — Includes "Further
                reading".

v.1978.055   *Luigi Pirandello (1867–1936)* / by Ronald Hayman.
                [s.l. : s.n.], 1978 (Printed for H.M.S.O. by W. & J. Linney Ltd.).
                1 sheet : ill., port. ; 30 cm.
                (Theatre Museum card ; 67)
                Includes bibliography. — Designed by H.M.S.O. Graphic Design. — Printed on cream
                card.

v.1978.056   *The Lyceum* / by Anthony S. Latham.
                [s.l. : s.n.], 1978 (Printed for H.M.S.O. by W. & J. Linney Ltd.).
                1 sheet, folded ([4] p.) : ill. ; 30 cm.
                (Theatre Museum card ; 18)
                Includes bibliography. — Designed by H.M.S.O. Graphic Design. — Printed on buff
                card.

v.1978.057   *Madge Kendal* / by R.B. Marriott.
                [s.l. : s.n.], 1978 (Printed for H.M.S.O. by W. & J. Linney Ltd.).
                1 sheet : ports. ; 30 cm.
                (Theatre Museum card ; 60)
                Includes bibliography. — Designed by H.M.S.O. Graphic Design. — Printed in brown
                on cream card.

v.1978.058   *Marie Lloyd* / by R.B. Marriott.
                [s.l. : s.n.], 1978 (Printed for H.M.S.O. by W. & J. Linney Ltd.).
                1 sheet : ill., ports. ; 30 cm.
                (Theatre Museum card ; 38)
                Includes bibliography. — Designed by H.M.S.O. Graphic Design. — Printed in brown
                on cream card.

v.1978.059   *Marie Tempest* / by R.B. Marriott.
[s.l. : s.n.], 1978 (Printed for H.M.S.O. by W. & J. Linney Ltd.).
1 sheet : ill. ; 30 cm.
(Theatre Museum card ; 41)
Includes bibliography. — Designed by H.M.S.O. Graphic Design. — Printed in brown on cream card.

v.1978.060   *Master Betty : the infant phenomemon* / by James Roose-Evans.
[s.l. : s.n.], 1978 (Printed for H.M.S.O. by W. & J. Linney Ltd.).
1 sheet : ill. ; 30 cm.
(Theatre Museum card ; 28)
Includes bibliography. — Designed by H.M.S.O. Graphic Design. — Printed in brown on cream card.

v.1978.061   *Miss Horniman and the Gaiety Theatre, Manchester* / by R.B. Marriott.
[s.l. : s.n.], 1978 (Printed for H.M.S.O. by W. & J. Linney Ltd.).
1 sheet : ill., port. ; 30 cm.
(Theatre Museum card ; 32)
Includes bibliography. — Designed by H.M.S.O. Graphic Design. — Printed on buff card.

v.1978.062   *Mrs Patrick Campbell* / by R.B. Marriott.
[s.l. : s.n.], 1978 (Printed for H.M.S.O. by W. & J. Linney Ltd.).
1 sheet : ill., port. ; 30 cm.
(Theatre Museum card ; 62)
Includes bibliography. — Designed by H.M.S.O. Graphic Design. — Printed in brown on cream card.

v.1978.063   *Musical instruments at the Victoria & Albert Museum* / photography by Moira Hulse ; written and narrated by Carole Patey ; producer, Ritchie Cogan.
London : H.M.S.O., 1978.
53 slides : col. ; 2x2 in. & 1 cassette (2–track. mono. ca. 80 min.), documentary booklet, guide to cassette, and cue sheet for slides.
"A V & A Education Department presentation." — In blue cardboard box.

v.1978.064   *Musical instruments at the Victoria & Albert Museum : an introduction* / Carole Patey.
London : H.M.S.O., 1978. (Printed by Raithby, Lawrence & Co., Leicester).
30 p. : ill. ; 15 x 21 cm.
ISBN: 011290274X
At head of title: Victoria & Albert Museum Education Department. — Bibliography: p. 30. — Wrappers with col. ill.

v.1978.065   *Objects : the V & A collects, 1974–1978 : 31 May–13 August.*
[s.l. : s.n., 1978] (Printed by C.P. Ltd.).
1 sheet, folded ([5] p.) : ill. (1 col.), port. ; 21 cm.
Printing: 5/78.
EXHIBITION: vx.1978.013

v.1978.066   *The old price riots* / by James Roose-Evans.
[s.l. : s.n.], 1978 (Printed for H.M.S.O. by W. & J. Linney Ltd.).

1 sheet : ill. ; 30 cm.
(Theatre Museum card ; 27)
Includes bibliography. — Designed by H.M.S.O. Graphic Design. — Printed on blue on mustard coloured card.

v.1978.067   *The Old Vic* / by R.B. Marriott.
[s.l. : s.n.], 1978 (Printed for H.M.S.O. by W. & J. Linney Ltd.).
1 sheet : ill., port. ; 30 cm.
(Theatre Museum card ; 31)
Includes bibliography. — Designed by H.M.S.O. Graphic Design. — Printed on buff card.

v.1978.068   *Oliver Goldsmith (1730(?)–1774)* / by Ronald Hayman.
[s.l. : s.n.], 1978 (Printed for H.M.S.O. by W. & J. Linney Ltd.).
1 sheet : ill. ; 30 cm.
(Theatre Museum card ; 72)
Includes bibliography. — Designed by H.M.S.O. Graphic Design. — Printed on cream card.

v.1978.069   *Oscar Wilde (1856–1900)* / by Ronald Hayman.
[s.l. : s.n.], 1978 (Printed for H.M.S.O. by W. & J. Linney Ltd.).
1 sheet : ill. ; 30 cm.
(Theatre Museum card ; 84)
Includes bibliography. — Designed by H.M.S.O. Graphic Design. — Printed in blue on cream card.

v.1978.070   *Paintings, water-colours and miniatures* / C.M. Kauffmann.
London : [H.M.S.O.], 1978 (Printed by W.S. Cowell Ltd., Ipswich).
24 p. : ill., ports. ; 15 x 21 cm.
(Victoria & Albert Museum departmental guides)
ISBN: 0905209109
Stapled; sized white wrappers with ills., 1 col.

v.1978.071   *Photographs by W. Eugene Smith : Victoria and Albert Museum, June 28–September 3 1978.*
London : H.M.S.O., 1978 (Printed by UDO (Litho) Ltd.).
1 sheet, folded (10 p.) : ill. ; 19 cm.
Introduction by Elizabeth Underhill. Foreword by Roy Strong. — Includes bibliographic references. — Designed by HMSO.
EXHIBITION: vx.1978.015

v.1978.072   *Photography in book illustration, 1840–1900 : an exhibition in the Library Gallery at the Victoria & Albert Museum, London, 4 February until 26 February 1978.*
[London : National Art Library, 1978.]
[2] leaves ; 29 cm.
Duplicated typescript.
EXHIBITION: vx.1978.001

v.1978.073   *The plays of T.S. Eliot* / by Ronald Hayman.
[s.l. : s.n.], 1978 (Printed for H.M.S.O. by W. & J. Linney Ltd.).
1 sheet : ill., port. ; 30 cm.
(Theatre Museum card ; 69)
Includes bibliography. — Designed by H.M.S.O. Graphic Design. — Printed on cream card.

v.1978.074   *The Poole potteries : February to April 1978.*
               [London : H.M.S.O., 1978] (Printed by Brightman & Stratton Ltd).
               32 p. : ill. ; 3 cm.
               Cover title. At head of title: Victoria & Albert Museum. — Written by Jennifer
               Hawkins. — Bibliography: p. 6. — Stapled; col. ill. on cover.
               EXHIBITION: VX.1978.002

v.1978.075   *Postcards from the nursery 1900–1914, from the collection of Dawn
               and Peter Cope : 1 November 1978–21 January 1979.*
               [London : H.M.S.O., 1978] (Printed by U.D.O. (Litho) Ltd.).
               1 sheet, folded ([11] p.) : ill. (1 col.), 30 cm.
               At head of title: The Museum of Childhood, Bethnal Green. — Designed by HMSO. —
               Ill. on cover designed by Peter Cope.
               EXHIBITION: VX.1978.BGM.002

v.1978.076   *Reading list 1 : theatre* / compiled by Anthony S. Latham.
               [s.l. : s.n.], 1978 (Printed for H.M.S.O. by W. & J. Linney Ltd.).
               [12] p. ; 30 cm.
               (Theatre Museum card ; 34)
               Designed by H.M.S.O. Graphic Design.

v.1978.077   *The Reichenau crozier.*
               [London : H.M.S.O.], 1978 ("PSG", printer, Derby).
               1 sheet, folded ([3] p.) : ill., (some col.) ; 30 cm.
               (Masterpieces ; sheet 15)
               By Anna Somers Cocks. — Printing: 7/78.

v.1978.078   *Richard Brinsley Sheridan (1751–1816)* / by Ronald Hayman.
               [s.l. : s.n.], 1978 (Printed for H.M.S.O. by W. & J. Linney Ltd.).
               1 sheet : ill. ; 30 cm.
               (Theatre Museum card ; 82)
               Includes bibliography. — Designed by H.M.S.O. Graphic Design. — Printed in blue
               on cream card.

v.1978.079   *The Royal Academy of Dancing* / by Ivor Guest.
               [s.l. : s.n.], 1978 (Printed for H.M.S.O. by W. & J. Linney Ltd.).
               1 sheet : ill. ; 30 cm.
               (Theatre Museum card ; 45)
               Designed by H.M.S.O. Graphic Design. — Printed on blue card.

v.1978.080   *The Royal Court Theatre* / by R.B. Marriott.
               [s.l. : s.n.], 1978 (Printed for H.M.S.O. by W. & J. Linney Ltd.).
               1 sheet : ill. ; 30 cm.
               (Theatre Museum card ; 55)
               Includes bibliography. — Designed by H.M.S.O. Graphic Design. — Printed on buff
               card.

v.1978.081   *Sarah Siddons* / by Sarah C. Woodcock.
               [s.l. : s.n.], 1978 (Printed for H.M.S.O. by W. & J. Linney Ltd.).
               1 sheet : ill., port. ; 30 cm.
               (Theatre Museum card ; 71)
               Includes bibliography. — Designed by H.M.S.O. Graphic Design. — Printed in brown
               on cream card.

v.1978.082   *Shah Jahan's jade cup.*
              [London : H.M.S.O.], 1978 (Printed by UDO (Litho) Ltd.).
              1 folded sheet ([3] p.) : ill. (1 col.) ; 30 cm.
              (Masterpieces ; sheet 16)
              Written by Robert Skelton. — "Further reading."

v.1978.083   *Shakespearian production. I, Until 1642* / by Ronald Hayman.
              [s.l. : s.n.], 1978 (Printed for H.M.S.O. by W. & J. Linney Ltd.).
              1 sheet : ill. ; 30 cm.
              (Theatre Museum card ; 76)
              Includes bibliography. — Designed by H.M.S.O. Graphic Design. — Printed in green on
              mustard coloured card.

v.1978.084   *Shakespearian production. II, 1660–1776* / by Ronald Hayman.
              [s.l. : s.n.], 1978 (Printed for H.M.S.O. by W. & J. Linney Ltd.).
              1 sheet : ill., port. ; 30 cm.
              (Theatre Museum card ; 77)
              Includes bibliography. — Designed by H.M.S.O. Graphic Design. — Printed in green on
              mustard coloured card.

v.1978.085   *Shakespearian production. III, 1776–1898* / by Ronald Hayman.
              [s.l. : s.n.], 1978 (Printed for H.M.S.O. by W. & J. Linney Ltd.).
              1 sheet : ill. ; 30 cm.
              (Theatre Museum card ; 78)
              Includes bibliography. — Designed by H.M.S.O. Graphic Design. — Printed in green on
              mustard coloured card.

v.1978.086   *Shakespearian production. IV, 1898–1964* / by Ronald Hayman.
              [s.l. : s.n.], 1978 (Printed for H.M.S.O. by W. & J. Linney Ltd.).
              1 sheet : ill. ; 30 cm.
              (Theatre Museum card ; 79)
              Includes bibliography. — Designed by H.M.S.O. Graphic Design. — Printed in green on
              mustard coloured card.

v.1978.087   *Sir Gilbert Scott (1811–1878), architect of the Gothic Revival :
              Victoria and Albert Museum, 31 May–10 September 1978.*
              [London : H.M.S.O., 1978.]
              [32] p. : ill. ; 21 cm.
              Cover title. — Foreword / C. M. Kauffmann. — Bibliography: p. [4]. Index. — Stapled;
              sized white wrappers with ill.
              EXHIBITION: vx.1978.014

v.1978.088   *Sir Tyrone Guthrie : British theatre director 1900–1971* / by James
              Roose-Evans.
              [s.l. : s.n.], 1978 (Printed for H.M.S.O. by W. & J. Linney Ltd.).
              1 sheet : ill. ; 30 cm.
              (Theatre Museum card ; 68)
              Includes bibliography. — Designed by H.M.S.O. Graphic Design. — Printed in brown
              on cream card.

v.1978.089   *Sybil Thorndike (1882–1976) and Lewis Casson (1875–1970)* / by
              Ronald Hayman.
              [s.l. : s.n.], 1978 (Printed for H.M.S.O. by W. & J. Linney Ltd.).
              1 sheet : ill., port. ; 30 cm.

(Theatre Museum card ; 56)
Includes bibliography. — Designed by H.M.S.O. Graphic Design. — Printed in brown on cream card.

v.1978.090   *Teaspoons to trains : the work of Frank Pick, 1878–1941 . . . /* text by Jennifer Hawkins and Michael F. Levey.
[London : H.M.S.O., 1978] (Printed by UDO Litho Ltd.).
1 sheet, folded (13 p.) : ill., 1 col. ; 30 cm.
Introduction / Roy Strong. Frank Pick and London Transport / R.M. Robbins.
EXHIBITION: VX.1978.022

v.1978.091   *Textiles and dress.*
London : H.M.S.O., 1978 (Oxford University Press, printer).
24 p. : ill. ; 15 x 21 cm.
(Victoria & Albert Museum departmental guides)
ISBN: 0905209095
Stapled; sized white wrappers with col. ills.

v.1978.092   *Theatre Royal, Drury Lane /* by R.B. Marriott.
[s.l. : s.n.], 1978 (Printed for H.M.S.O. by W. & J. Linney Ltd.).
1 sheet, folded ([4] p.) : ill. ; 30 cm.
(Theatre Museum card ; 48)
Includes bibliography. — Designed by H.M.S.O. Graphic Design. — Printed on buff card.

v.1978.093   *Theatre Royal, Haymarket /* by R.B. Marriott.
[s.l. : s.n.], 1978 (Printed for H.M.S.O. by W. & J. Linney Ltd.).
1 sheet : ill. ; 30 cm.
(Theatre Museum card ; 39)
Includes bibliography. — Designed by H.M.S.O. Graphic Design. — Printed on buff card.

v.1978.094   *Toys : a selection from the Museum of Sonneberg, German Democratic Republic : March until September 1978.*
[London : H.M.S.O.], 1978 (Printed by UDO (Litho) Ltd.).
1 sheet, folded (9 p.) : ill. (1 col.) ; 30 x 11 cm.
At head of title: Bethnal Green Museum of Childhood. — Foreword / Elizabeth Aslin. — Bibliography: p. 9.
EXHIBITION: VX.1978.BGM.001

v.1978.095   *Vesta Tilley /* by R.B. Marriott.
[s.l. : s.n.], 1978 (Printed for H.M.S.O. by W. & J. Linney Ltd.).
1 sheet : ill., ports. ; 30 cm.
(Theatre Museum card ; 36)
Includes bibliography. — Designed by H.M.S.O. Graphic Design. — Printed in brown on cream card. — The music hall performer was known especially for cross-dressing roles.

v.1978.096   *Victorian melodrama /* by Ronald Hayman.
[s.l. : s.n.], 1978 (Printed for H.M.S.O. by W. & J. Linney Ltd.).
1 sheet : ill. ; 30 cm.
(Theatre Museum card ; 47)
Includes bibliography. — Designed by H.M.S.O. Graphic Design. — Printed in blue on mustard coloured card.

V.1978.097   *The way we live now : designs for interiors, 1950 to the present day* /
                Margaret Timmers.
                [London : H.M.S.O. for the Victoria and Albert Museum?, 1978]
                (Printed by Staples Printers at the Priory Press, St Albans).
                38 p. : ill. ; 21 cm.
                Card cover with coloured illustrations.
                EXHIBITION: VX.1978.023

V.1978.098   *William Congreve (1670–1729)* / by Ronald Hayman.
                [s.l. : s.n.], 1978 (Printed for H.M.S.O. by W. & J. Linney Ltd.).
                1 sheet : ill., port. ; 30 cm.
                (Theatre Museum card ; 88)
                Includes bibliography. — Designed by H.M.S.O. Graphic Design. — Printed on cream
                card.

V.1978.099   *William Morris : designs for printed textiles* / Linda Parry.
                [London : H.M.S.O., 1987] (Printed by SPS Ltd.).
                1 sheet, folded ([3] p.) : ill. (some col.) ; 30 cm.
                At head of title: Victoria & Albert Museum.
                EXHIBITION: VX.1978.007

V.1978.100   *William Poel* / by R.B. Marriott.
                [s.l. : s.n.], 1978 (Printed for H.M.S.O. by W. & J. Linney Ltd.).
                1 sheet : ill. ; 30 cm.
                (Theatre Museum card ; 50)
                Includes bibliography. — Designed by H.M.S.O. Graphic Design. — Printed in purple
                on cream card.

V.1978.101   *Yankee Doodle comes to town* / by James Roose-Evans.
                [s.l. : s.n.], 1978 (Printed for H.M.S.O. by W. & J. Linney Ltd.).
                1 sheet : ill., port. ; 30 cm.
                (Theatre Museum card ; 92)
                Includes bibliography. — Designed by H.M.S.O. Graphic Design. — Printed on mauve
                card. — Concerns the showman P.T. Barnum, and the dwarf Tom Thumb.

1979

V.1979.001   *The art of Islam : Galleries 42–47B.*
                [London : V & A Associates, 1979] (Printed by Penshurst Press).
                1 sheet : ill., plans ; 64 x 30 cm. folded to 21 x 15 cm.
                (Broadsheets)
                Written by Yolande Crowe. — Printed on buff.

V.1979.002   *A bibliography of the trade directories of the British Isles in the
                National Art Library* / compiled by Michael E. Keen.
                [London : H.M.S.O.], 1979 (Printed by HMSO Reprographic Services,
                Manchester).
                iii, 121 p. : ill. ; 30 cm.
                At head of title: Victoria & Albert Museum. — Index of names. — Blue wrappers with
                ill.

V.1979.003   *A brief history of bookplates in Britain : with reference to examples at
              the Victoria & Albert Museum* / the Bookplate Society and the
              Victoria & Albert Museum.
              London : H.M.S.O., 1979.
              24 p. : ill. ; 19 x 25 cm.
              Cover title: Bookplates in Britain. — Bibliography: p. 24. — Stapled; decorated and
              illustrated wrappers, part printed in green.
              EXHIBITION: vx.1979.015

V.1979.004   *The Doulton story : a catalogue of the exhibition held at the Victoria
              and Albert Museum, London, 30 May–12 August 1979.*
              [London : The Museum, 1979.]
              31 p. ; 18 cm.
              With: The world of Doulton, and several press releases. — In portfolio with cover title :
              Royal Doulton tableware.
              EXHIBITION: vx.1979.014

V.1979.005   *Early medieval art : Gallery 43.*
              [London : V & A Associates, 1979] (Printed by Penshurst Press).
              1 sheet : ill., plans ; 64 x 30 cm. folded to 21 x 15 cm.
              (Broadsheets)
              Written by Paul Williamson. — Printed on pale green.

V.1979.006   *Early railway prints : from the collection of Mr. and Mrs. M.G.
              Powell* / Michael Darby.
              London : H.M.S.O., 1974 (Printed by Product Support (Graphics)
              Ltd., Derby, 1979).
              [12], 72 p., [2] p. : ill. ; 14 x 22 cm.
              ISBN: 0901486744
              At head of title: Victoria and Albert Museum.
              EXHIBITION: vx.1974.014

V.1979.007   *The Edward Henry and Eva Pinto bequest : a hand-list of the
              collection in the National Art Library* / catalogued and compiled by
              Michael E. Keen.
              [London] : Victoria & Albert Museum, 1979.
              24 p. ; 30 cm.
              Collection of London directories.

V.1979.008   *English watches* / by J.F. Hayward. 2nd ed., 2nd imp.
              London : H.M.S.O., 1969 (Printed by the Campfield Press, St Albans,
              1979).
              [5], 14, [64] p. : ill. ; 21 cm.
              ISBN: 0112903266
              At head of title: Victoria and Albert Museum. — Bibliography: p. 13–14. — Wrappers,
              with line ill. printed on green. — "Includes a catalogue raisonnée [sic] of the more
              important English watches in the Museum collection"–foreword.

V.1979.009   *Fans : a V & A study guide.*
              [London : The Museum, 1979] (Printed by UDO Litho Ltd.).
              1 sheet : col. ill. ; 30 x 21 cm. folded to 10 x 21 cm.
              Written by Madeleine Ginsburg. — Includes bibliography. — Printing: 1/79. — Printed
              in white and yellow on black.

V.1979.010   *Far Eastern art : Galleries 44–47D.*
                  [London : V & A Associates, 1979] (Printed by Penshurst Press).
                  1 sheet : ill., plans ; 64 x 30 cm. folded to 21 x 15 cm.
                  (Broadsheets)
                  Written by Edmund Capon. — Printed on wheat colour.

V.1979.011   *Fifth supplement to the catalogue of English non-illuminated*
                  manuscripts in the National Art Library : accessions for 1978 /
                  compiled by J.I. Whalley ; with the assistance of Robert Howell.
                  London : H.M.S.O., 1979.
                  9 p. ; 30 cm.
                  At head of title: Victoria and Albert Museum. Cover title: Catalogue of English non-
                  illuminated manuscripts. — Name and subject indexes. — Stapled in blue covers with
                  ill.

V.1979.012   *Hollar to Heideloff : an exhibition of fashion prints drawn from*
                  the collection of members of the Costume Society and held at the
                  Victoria and Albert Museum, 5 December 1979 to 18 February
                  1980.
                  London : Costume Society c/o Victoria and Albert Museum, 1979
                  (Printed at Daedalus Press, Wisbech).
                  46 p. ; 22 cm.
                  Acknowledgments / Anne Buck. — Bibliography: p. 45–46. — Stapled, in red
                  wrappers.
                  EXHIBITION: VX.1979.025

V.1979.013   *Illustrations to Ted Hughes' poems : the Library, Victoria and Albert*
                  Museum.
                  [London : National Art Library, 1979.]
                  9 p. ; 30 cm.
                  Duplicated; stapled; ill. on cover.
                  EXHIBITION: VX.1979.020

V.1979.014   *Italian drawings. Vol. 1, 14th–16th century* / Peter Ward-Jackson.
                  London : H.M.S.O., 1979 (Printed by W.S. Cowell).
                  275 p. : ill. ; 29 cm.
                  ISBN: 0112902316
                  At head of title: Victoria and Albert Museum catalogues. — Bibliographic references:
                  p. 257–260. Owner, location, subject and numerical indexes, and index to artists in
                  both vols. — Designed by H.M.S.O. Graphic Design: David Napthine. — Blue cloth
                  covered boards with title and design in silver; illustrated dust-jackets. — Errata slip
                  inserted, p. 204, concerning a reattribution.

V.1979.015   *John Constable's sketch-books of 1813 and 1814 : reproduced in*
                  facsimile / introduction by Graham Reynolds. 2nd ed.
                  London : H.M.S.O., 1979 (Printed and bound at the University Press,
                  Oxford).
                  3 v. in case : ill., facsims. ; 19 cm.
                  ISBN: 0112902960 (set)
                  At head of title: Victoria & Albert Museum. — [1]. Introduction [and catalogue] by
                  Graham Reynolds. – [2]. Sketch-book 1813 (10 x 13 cm.). – [3]. Sketch-book 1814
                  (9 x 12 cm.). — Boards and case covered in blue cloth; facsimile of the artist's signature
                  stamped in gold on sketch-book vols. and case.

V.1979.016   *Masterpieces of cutlery and the art of eating* / an exhibition organised
              by the Victoria and Albert Museum in conjunction with the
              Worshipful Company of Cutlers of London, 11 July to 26 August
              1979.
              London : [H.M.S.O.], 1979.
              xxii, 55 p. : ill. (some col.) ; 20 cm.
              At head of title: Victoria and Albert Museum, 1979. — Director's foreword / Roy
              Strong. Includes: The Worshipful Company of Cutlers: a brief history / by K.S.G. Hinde.
              Introduction to the history of cutlery / by C. Blair. The art of eating / by A. Somers
              Cocks. — Bibliography: p. xii. Glossary. — Design by HMSO Graphic Design.
              EXHIBITION: VX.1979.018

V.1979.017   *The open & closed book : contemporary book arts: 12 September–18*
              November 1979.
              [London : H.M.S.O., 1979] (Printed by W.J. Linney Ltd., Mansfield).
              [10], 137 p. : ill. (1 col.) ; 22 cm.
              At foot of title: Victoria and Albert Museum. — Preface / R.C. Kenedy. — A, Private
              presses. B, Illustration. C, Fine binding. D, Concrete poetry. E, Typography. F,
              Conceptual art. G, Commercial publishers. g [sic], Children's books. H, Calendars. K,
              Ex-libris designs. L, Literature. M, Models, maquettes (three-dimensional objects). V,
              Audio-visual aids. — Index. — Wrappers with col. ills.
              EXHIBITION: VX.1979.021

V.1979.018   *Parade : dance costumes of three centuries : 20 August–14 September*
              1979 / presented by the Theatre Museum, Victoria & Albert Museum,
              and the Edinburgh Festival Society.
              [London] : H.M.S.O., 1979 (Printed by the Soman-Wherry Press,
              Norwich).
              1 sheet, folded (15 p.) : ill. (some col.) ; 30 cm.
              EXHIBITION: VX.1979.XXX.002

V.1979.019   *Photography in printmaking* / Charles Newton.
              [London] : Published for the Victoria and Albert Museum exhibition .
              . . by the Compton Press, Tisbury, and Pitman, 1979 (Printed by the
              Hillingdon Press).
              64 p. : ill. (some col.), 1 map, ports. ; 25 cm.
              ISBN: 0273014706 (pbk.)
              Foreword / C.M. Kauffmann. — Bibliography: p. 32. Glossary. — Designed by
              Humphrey Stone. — Sized white wrappers with col. ill.
              EXHIBITION: VX.1979.022

V.1979.020   *The state bed from Melville House.*
              [London : H.M.S.O.], 1979 (Printed by UDO Litho Ltd.)
              1 sheet, folded ([6] p.) : ill. ; 30 cm.
              (Masterpieces ; sheet 21)
              By Lisa Clinton. — Includes bibliographic references.

V.1979.021   *Vienna in the age of Schubert : the Biedermeier interior 1815–1848* /
              with contributions by Gerhart Egger . . . [et al.].
              London : Elron Press in association with the Victoria and Albert
              Museum, 1979 (Printed and bound by the Hillingdon Press,
              Uxbridge).
              111 p. : ill. (some col.), 2 maps, 2 ports. ; 25 cm.
              ISBN: 0904499073

Preface / Dr Roy Strong. Foreword / Professor Dr Wilhelm Mrazek, Minister Herta
Firnberg. Introduction / Wilhelm Mrazek. Domestic life / Christian Witt-Dörring.
Furniture / Franz Windisch-Graetz. Silver / Gerhart Egger. Porcelain / Waltraud
Neuwirth. Glass / Wilhelm Mrazek, Waltraud Neuwirth. Textiles and fashion /
Angela Volker. Clocks / Erika Hellich. Water-colours / Walter Koschatzky. Painting /
Gerbert Frodl. — Bibliography: p. 105–107. — Book design: Gerald Cinamon. —
Sized wrappers; col. ills.
EXHIBITION: VX.1979.003

V.1979.022   *Vienna in the age of Schubert : the Biedermeier interior 1815–1848 :
exhibition catalogue.*
London : [Victoria and Albert Museum?, 1979] (Printed and bound by
the Hillingdon Press, Uxbridge).
[17] p. ; 25 cm.
Cover title. At head of title: Victoria and Albert Museum. — Design and production by
Elron Press. — Stapled in wrappers.
EXHIBITION: VX.1979.003

V.1979.023   *Vienna in the age of Schubert : the Biedermeier interior 1815–1848 :
Victoria & Albert Museum, Room 45, January 31–April 1, 1979* . . . .
[London] : H.M.S.O., 1979 (Printed by UDO Litho Ltd.).
1 sheet, folded ([7] p.) : ill. (some col.) ; 21 cm.
By Simon Jervis.
EXHIBITION: VX.1979.003

1980

V.1980.001   *The art of India : Gallery 41.*
[London : V & A Associates, between 1979 and 1981] (Printed by
Penshurst Press).
1 sheet : ill., plans ; 64 x 30 cm. folded to 21 x 15 cm.
(Broadsheets)
Written by Robert Skelton. — Printed on salmon pink.

V.1980.002   *Berthold Wolpe : a retrospective survey.*
London : Victoria and Albert Museum and Faber & Faber, 1980
(Printed by the Westerham Press).
[90 p.] 8 p. of plates : ill. (some col.), port., facsims. ; 26 cm.
ISBN: 0571116558; 090520915X (pbk.)
Preface / Peter Castle. Introduction / A.S. Osley. — Includes bibliography. Index. —
Green wrappers; title with border and device printed in tan and black.
EXHIBITION: VX.1980.019

V.1980.003   *A bibliography of the microfilms in the National Art Library,
Victoria and Albert Museum* / compiled and catalogued by
Michael E. Keen.
[London : The Library], 1980.
42 p. ; 30 cm.
Cover title: Microfilms in the National Art Library.

V.1980.004   *British watercolours in the Victoria and Albert Museum : an
illustrated summary catalogue of the national collection* / compiled by
Lionel Lambourne and Jean Hamilton.

London : Sotheby Parke Bernet in association with the Victoria and
Albert Museum, 1980 (Printed by Jolly & Barber, Rugby; bound by
Weatherby Woolnough, Wellingborough).
xxi, 455 p., [16] p. of plates : ill. (some col.) ; 29 cm.
ISBN: 0856671118
Foreword / C.M. Kauffmann. — Bibliography: p. 435. Index of places, sitters, subjects,
authors illustrated and donors. — Ginger cloth covered boards; ill. on end-papers. —
"Published by Philip Wilson Publishers and . . . Biblio Distribution Centre [sic], Totowa,
N.J."

v.1980.005   *Catalogue of colour transparencies. Paintings by artists of all
               nationalities arranged alphabetically.*
               [London : National Art Slide Library?], 1980
               2 v. (260, [?] p.) ; 30 cm.
               Cover title. At head of title: Victoria and Albert Museum, National Art Slide Library. —
               Part 1, A to K. Part 2, L to Z [unseen]. — Red wrappers.

v.1980.006   *Charles Wyndham* / by R.B. Marriott.
               [s.l. : s.n.], 1980 (Printed for H.M.S.O. by W. & J. Linney Ltd.).
               1 sheet : ill. ; 30 cm.
               (Theatre Museum card ; 81)
               Includes bibliography. — Designed by H.M.S.O. Graphic Design. — Printed in brown
               on cream card.

v.1980.007   *The circus 1 : trick-riding* / by Antony D. Hippisley Coxe.
               [s.l. : s.n.], 1980 (Printed for H.M.S.O. by W. & J. Linney Ltd.).
               1 sheet : ill. ; 30 cm.
               (Theatre Museum card ; 22)
               Includes bibliography. — Printed in brown on mustard coloured card.

v.1980.008   *Department of Prints, Drawings & Photographs and Paintings
               acquisitions : objects added to the collection in the years 1977 to
               1980.*
               [London : The Museum, 1980.]
               1 sheet : ill. ; 59 x 42 cm. folded to 30 x 21 cm.
               Poster. — Text by C.M. Kauffmann.
               EXHIBITION: vx.1980.006

v.1980.009   *Early keyboard instruments at the Victoria and Albert Museum :
               an introduction in words, music and pictures to the collection of
               virginals, harpsichords and clavichords in the V & A.*
               London : H.M.S.O., 1980.
               26 slides : col. + 1 sound cassette (60 min., stereo.) + 1 guide (7 p.) + 1
               cue card.
               ISBN: 0112903339
               Title from container. — Commentary by Carole Patey. Producer / Ritchie Cogan. —
               "A Victoria & Albert Museum Education Department presentation".

v.1980.010   *Edmund Kean (ca. 1789–1833)* / by Ronald Hayman.
               [s.l. : s.n.], 1980 (Printed for H.M.S.O. by W. & J. Linney Ltd.).
               1 sheet : ports. ; 30 cm.
               (Theatre Museum card ; 58)
               Includes bibliography. — Printed in brown on cream card.

v.1980.011   *Eleonora Duse (1858–1924)* / by Ronald Hayman.
                [s.l. : s.n.], 1980 (Printed for H.M.S.O. by W. & J. Linney Ltd.).
                1 sheet : ports. ; 30 cm.
                (Theatre Museum card ; 59)
                Includes bibliography. — Printed in brown on cream card.

v.1980.012   *English sculpture : Gallery 50 (West).*
                [London : V & A Associates, 1980 or 1981] (Printed by Penshurst
                Press).
                1 sheet : ill., plans ; 64 x 30 cm. folded to 21 x 15 cm.
                (Broadsheets)
                Written by Malcolm Baker. — Printed on salmon pink.

v.1980.013   *European art, 1700–1800 : Galleries 4–5–6–7.*
                [London : V & A Associates, 1980 or 1981] (Printed by Penshurst
                Press).
                1 sheet : ill., plans ; 64 x 30 cm. folded to 21 x 15 cm.
                (Broadsheets)
                Printed on blue.

v.1980.014   *European baroque : Galleries 1–2.*
                [London : V & A Associates, 1980 or 1981] (Printed by Penshurst
                Press).
                1 sheet : ill., plans ; 64 x 30 cm. folded to 21 x 15 cm.
                (Broadsheets)
                Printed on green.

v.1980.015   *European baroque : Gallery 3.*
                [London : V & A Associates, 1980 or 1981.]
                1 sheet : ill., plans ; 64 x 30 cm. folded to 21 x 15 cm.
                (Broadsheets)
                Printed on green.

v.1980.016   *European sculpture : Gallery 50 (East).*
                [London : V & A Associates, between 1979 and 1981] (Printed by
                Penshurst Press).
                1 sheet : ill., plans ; 64 x 30 cm. folded to 21 x 15 cm.
                (Broadsheets)
                Written by Paul Williamson. — Printed on blue.

v.1980.017   *Far Eastern ceramics in the Victoria and Albert Museum* / John Ayers.
                London : Sotheby Parke Bernet, in association with the Victoria and
                Albert Museum, 1980.
                174 p. : ill. ; 38 cm.
                (Oriental ceramics : the world's greatest collections ; v. 6)
                ISBN: 0856670766
                English language ed. of VR.1975.009. — "Reprinted from original blocks and bound in
                Japan." — Published for Sotheby Parke Bernet Publications by Philip Wilson Publishers
                Ltd. and Biblio Distribution Centre, New Jersey.

v.1980.018   *French art, 1700–1800 : Galleries 5–6–7 (Jones Collection).*
                [London : V & A Associates, 1980 or 1981] (Printed by Penshurst
                Press).

1 sheet : ill., plans ; 64 x 30 cm. folded to 21 x 15 cm.
(Broadsheets)
Printed on buff.

V.1980.019   *Ganymed : printing, publishing, design : Victoria and Albert Museum,
19 November 1980–31 January, 1981.*
London : Victoria and Albert Museum, [1980] (Designed and printed
by Harrison & Sons).
43 p., [1] leaf of plates, [15] p. of plates : ill. (1 col.) ; 25 cm.
ISBN: 0905209141
Introduction by Bernhard Baer. Preface by Duncan Haldane. — Sized wrappers, ill.
EXHIBITION: VX.1980.018

V.1980.020   *The gold reliquary of Charles the Bold: Victoria and Albert Museum
exhibition, March 26–June 1, 1980.*
[London : Victoria and Albert Museum, 1980] (printed by U.D.O.
Litho).
[10] p. : ill., 1 geneal. table, 1 port., 1 map ; 21 cm.
Cover title. — Text by Marian Campbell. — Bibliography: p. [10]. — Stapled; col. ill.
on wrappers.
EXHIBITION: VX.1980.005

V.1980.021   *Ham House inventories 1654, 1677, 1679, 1683, 1728, 1844, 1884 :
[and selected bills dating from 1729–1741].*
London : Victoria and Albert Museum, Dept. of Furniture and
Woodwork, 1980.
8 microfiches ; 10 x 15 cm.
Issued in conjunction with VR.1980.004.

V.1980.022   *Harpsichords and virginals at the Victoria and Albert Museum.*
[London] : H.M.S.O., 1980 (Produced by CBS Manufacturing,
Aylesbury).
1 sound cassette.
ISBN: 011290338X
"A V & A Education Department Presentation."

V.1980.023   *An introduction to courtly jewellery* / Anna Somers Cocks.
Warminster ; London : Compton Press and Pitman House, 1980
(Printed and bound by New Interlitho Milan).
48 p. : ill. (chiefly col.), ports. ; 26 cm.
(V & A introductions to the decorative arts)
ISBN: 0273014552
Edited by Anthony Burton. — Bibliography: p. 48. Glossary. — Designed by Humphrey
Stone. — Black paper covered boards with col. ill.
Copy note: Bears labels with re-assigned ISBN: 0112903908.

V.1980.024   *An introduction to fashion illustration* / Madeleine Ginsburg.
Warminster ; London : Compton Press and Pitman, 1980 (Printed by
W.S. Cowell Ltd., Ipswich).
48 p. : ill. (some col.) ; 26 cm.
(V & A introductions to the decorative arts)
ISBN: 0273014714
Edited by Anthony Burton. — Bibliography: p. 47–48. — Designed by Humphrey Stone.
— Black paper covered boards with col. ill.

v.1980.025　　　*An introduction to Japanese prints* / Joe Earle.
Warminster ; London : Compton Press and Pitman House, 1980
(Printed and bound by New Interlitho, Milan).
47 p. : chiefly col. ill. ; 26 cm.
(V & A introductions to the decorative arts)
ISBN: 0273014544
Edited by Anthony Burton. — Bibliography: p. 46. — Designed by Humphrey Stone. —
Photography by Ian Thomas. — Black paper covered boards with col. ill.

v.1980.026　　　*An introduction to netsuke* / Joe Earle.
Warminster ; London : Compton Press and Pitman House, 1980
(Printed and bound by New Interlitho, Milan).
47 p. : col. ill. ; 26 cm.
(V & A introductions to the decorative arts)
ISBN: 0273014536
Edited by Anthony Burton. — Bibliography: p. 45. — Designed by Humphrey Stone. —
Photography by Ian Thomas. — Black paper covered boards with col. ill.

v.1980.027　　　*Italian drawings. Vol. 2, 17th–18th century* / Peter Ward-Jackson.
London : H.M.S.O., 1980 (Printed by W.S. Cowell).
229 p. : ill. ; 29 cm.
ISBN: 0112902588
At head of title: Victoria and Albert Museum catalogues. — Bibliographic
abbreviations: p. 211–214. — Owner, location, subject and numerical indexes, and
index to artists in both vols. — Designed by H.M.S.O. Graphic Design: David
Napthine. — Blue cloth covered boards with title and design in silver; ill.
dust-jacket.

v.1980.028　　　*Italian sculpture 1400–1500 : Galleries 16–12.*
[London : V & A Associates, between 1979 and 1981] (Printed by
Penshurst Press).
1 sheet : ill., plans ; 64 x 30 cm. folded to 21 x 15 cm.
(Broadsheets)
Written by Anthony Radcliffe. — Printed on pale yellow.

v.1980.029　　　*Japan style : an exhibition organised by the Victoria and Albert
Museum and the Japan Foundation, 1980.*
Tokyo : Kodansha International in collaboration with the Japan
Foundation and the Victoria and Albert Museum, 1980.
148 p. : ill. (chiefly col.) ; 25 x 26 cm.
ISBN: 087011400X
Includes: Japan style – yesterday, today and tomorrow / Masuru Katzumie.
Why Japan? / J.V. Earle. Japanese aesthetic ideals / Mitsukuni Yoshida. Madame
Butterfly in a rabbit-hutch: Western perceptions and stereotypes of the Japanese /
Jean-Pierre Lehmann. — Catalogue design: Ken'ichi Samura.
EXHIBITION: vx.1980.003

v.1980.030　　　*Martha Graham* / by James Roose-Evans.
[s.l. : s.n.], 1980 (Printed for H.M.S.O. by W. & J. Linney Ltd.).
1 sheet : ill. ; 30 cm.
(Theatre Museum card ; 23)
Includes bibliography. — Printed in brown on mustard coloured card.

V.1980.031   *Metalwork.*
London : H.M.S.O., 1980 (Printed by W.S. Cowell Ltd., Ipswich).
28 p. : ill. ; 15 x 21 cm.
(Victoria & Albert Museum departmental guides.)
ISBN: 0905209125
Stapled; sized white wrappers with col. ills.

V.1980.032   *Music gallery.*
[London : V & A Associates, between 1979 and 1981] (Printed by
Penshurst Press).
1 sheet : ill., plans ; 64 x 30 cm. folded to 21 x 15 cm.
Written by Carole Patey. — Printed on blue.

V.1980.033   *Musical-boxes at the Victoria & Albert Museum : an introduction* /
Carole Patey.
London : H.M.S.O., 1980 (Printed by Ebenezer Baylis & Son, Trinity
Press).
36 p. : ill. (some col.) ; 15 x 21 cm. + 1 sound cassette.
ISBN: 0112903495; 0112903509 (cassette)
At head of title: Victoria & Albert Museum. — Bibliography: p. 36. — Stapled;
wrappers coloured tan with col. ill.

V.1980.034   *Princely magnificence : court jewels of the Renaissance, 1500–1630 :
15th October 1980–1st February 1981.*
London: Debrett's Peerage in association with the Victoria and Albert
Museum, 1980.
140, [1] p. : ill. (some col.) ; 27 cm.
ISBN: 0905649427
Bibliography : p. [141].
EXHIBITION: vx.1980.013

V.1980.035   *Roger Doyle : Victoria and Albert Museum, 23 July–3 September
1980.*
[London : The Museum, 1980.]
1 sheet, folded ([3] p.) : 1 col. ill. ; 19 cm.
EXHIBITION: vx.1980.011

V.1980.036   *The Symmachi panel.*
[London : H.M.S.O.], 1980 (Printed by UDO Litho Ltd.).
1 sheet, folded ([5] p.) : ill., 1 col ; 30 cm.
(Masterpieces ; sheet 22)
By Paul Williamson. — Bibliography.

V.1980.037   *The tapestry collection : medieval and renaissance* / George Wingfield
Digby ; assisted by Wendy Hefford.
London : H.M.S.O., 1980 (Printed by W.S. Cowell Ltd., Ipswich).
83 p., [110] p. of plates : ill. ; 23 x 29 cm.
ISBN: 0112902464
At head of title: Victoria and Albert Museum. — Bibliography: p. 83. — Designed by
HMSO Graphic Design. — Tweed-effect cloth covered boards. Dust-jacket with
col. ill.

v.1980.038   *The universal penman : a survey of western calligraphy from the Roman period to 1980 : catalogue of an exhibition held at the Victoria and Albert Museum, London, July-September 1980* / Joyce Irene Whalley and Vera C. Kaden.
London : H.M.S.O., 1980 (Printed by Raithby, Lawrence & Co. at the De Montfort Press).
ix, 152 p. : ill., facsims. ; 21 x 30 cm.
ISBN: 0112903398
At head of title: Victoria and Albert Museum. — Includes bibliographic references. Index. — Design by HMSO Graphic Design. — Sized wrappers coloured brown with col. ills.
EXHIBITION: vx.1980.008

1981

v.1981.001   *America at play, 1870–1955 : the Lawrence Scripps Wilkinson collection of toys : an exhibition at the Bethnal Green Museum of Childhood . . . 2 December 1981–28 February 1982. . . .*
[London : The Museum, 1981.]
1 sheet, folded ([4] p.) ; 30 cm.
Includes annotated list of American toy makers. — Printed in red. Decorated title.
EXHIBITION: vx.1981.BGM.003

v.1981.002   *Catalogue of rubbings of brasses and incised slabs* / by Muriel Clayton. Repr.
London : H.M.S.O., 1981.
ISBN: 0112900879
Unseen. Listed in *Government publications : Victoria and Albert Museum*. London : H.M.S.O., 1985. (Sectional list ; 55).

v.1981.003   *The Chalon brothers : landscape, the theatre and caricature in the work of Alfred-Edouard Chalon (1781–1860) and Jean-Jacques called John James Chalon (1778–1845)* / Lionel Lambourne.
[London : H.M.S.O., 1981] (Printed by UDO Litho Ltd.).
1 sheet : ill. (1 col.) ; 59 x 42 cm. folded to 30 x 21 cm.
Poster. — Written by Lionel Lambourne. — Designed by HMSO Graphic Design.
EXHIBITION: vx.1981.006

v.1981.004   *Drawing : technique & purpose : Victoria & Albert Museum, 28 January–26 April, 1981.*
[London : H.M.S.O., 1981] (Printed by Hobbs the Printers, Southampton).
69 p. : ill. ; 21 cm.
Cover title. Foreword / C.M. Kauffmann. — Exhibition and catalogue by Susan Lambert. — Bibliography: p. 5. Index of lenders. — Printing: 1/81. — Stapled; white wrappers with ill.
EXHIBITION: vx.1981.001

v.1981.005   *The Duke of Wellington : a pictorial survey of his life (1769–1852)* / by Victor Percival. Reissue.
London : H.M.S.O., 1969 (Printed by Brown, Knight & Truscott, 1981).

86 p. : ill., coat of arms, facsims., ports. (1 col.) ; 31 cm.
ISBN: 0112903606
At head of title: Victoria and Albert Museum. — Foreword by the Duke of Wellington. — Bibliography: p. 85. — Designed by HMSO / Alan Stephens. — Coloured portrait tipped in as frontispiece — Grey card wrappers printed inside and out, in red, with continuous illustration.

V.1981.006   *The engraved work of Eric Gill.* Repr.
London : H.M.S.O., 1981.
(Large picture book ; no. 17)
ISBN: 0112902715
Unseen. Listed in *Government publications : Victoria and Albert Museum.* London : H.M.S.O., 1985. (Sectional list ; 55).

V.1981.007   *Getting dressed* / Edward T. Joy.
London : H.M.S.O., 1981 (Printed by Balding + Mansell, Wisbech).
64 p. : ill. (some col.) ; 19 cm.
(The arts and living)
ISBN: 0112902855
At head of title: Victoria and Albert Museum. — General editors : John Fleming and Hugh Honour. — Bibliography: p. 63. Index. — Design by HMSO Graphic Design. — Sized wrappers coloured blue, with col. ill.

V.1981.008   *Going to bed* / Eileen Harris.
London : H.M.S.O., 1981 (Printed by Balding + Mansell, Wisbech).
72 p. : ill. (some col.) ; 19 cm.
(The arts and living)
ISBN: 0112902871
At head of title: Victoria and Albert Museum. — General editors: John Fleming and Hugh Honour. — Bibliography: p. 70–71. Index. — Design by HMSO Graphic Design. — Sized wrappers coloured blue, with col. ill.

V.1981.009   *The Great Exhibition of 1851* / C.H. Gibbs-Smith. 2nd ed.
London : H.M.S.O., 1981 (Printed by Raithby, Lawrence & Co.).
96 p. : ill. ; 20 cm.
ISBN: 0112903444
At head of title: Victoria & Albert Museum. — Foreword / Roy Strong. Edited by John Physick. — Beige wrappers with ills. — Reduced ed. of v.1964.009.

V.1981.010   *Hille : 75 years of British furniture* / Sutherland Lyall.
London : Elron Press in association with the Victoria & Albert Museum, 1981.
95 p. : ill. (some col.) ; 24 cm.
ISBN: 0904499103
Sized card wrappers.
EXHIBITION: VX.1981.003

V.1981.011   *The Kashmir shawl* / John Irwin. 2nd imp.
London : H.M.S.O., 1973 (Printed by Albert Gait Ltd., Grimsby, 1981).
vii, 60 p., [52] p. of plates : ill. (some col.) ; 26 cm.
(Museum monograph ; 29)
ISBN: 0112901646
At head of title: Victoria & Albert Museum. — Bibliography: p. 43–47. Glossary of terms, and index. — Wrappers coloured navy, with col. ill.

V.1981.012　　　*Masterpieces of Serbian goldsmiths' work, 13th–18th century : 1 July–2 August 1981.*
London : H.M.S.O., 1981 (Printed by Balding + Mansell).
68 p. : ill. ; 20 x 21 cm.
ISBN: 0905209168 (pbk.)
At head of title: Victoria and Albert Museum. — Foreword / Roy Strong. Introduction / by Bojana Radojković. Catalogue by Dušan Milovanović. — Bibliography: p. 67. Glossary. — Design by HMSO Graphic Design. — Wrappers coloured dark blue with col. ills.
EXHIBITION: VX.1981.008

V.1981.013　　　*Mourning* / Nicholas Penny.
London : H.M.S.O., 1981 (Printed by Balding + Mansell, Wisbech).
64 p. : ill. (some col.) ; 19 cm.
(The arts and living)
ISBN: 011290288x (pbk.)
At head of title: Victoria and Albert Museum. — General editors : John Fleming and Hugh Honour. — Bibliography: p. 62–63. Index. — Design by HMSO Graphic Design. — Sized wrappers coloured blue, with col. ill.

V.1981.014　　　*A nonsense alphabet* / by Edward Lear. Repr.
London : H.M.S.O., 1981.
(Small picture book ; no. 32)
ISBN: 0112901565
Unseen. Listed in *Government publications : Victoria and Albert Museum*. London : H.M.S.O., 1985. (Sectional list ; 55).

V.1981.015　　　*Old and modern masters of photography* / selected and introduced by Mark Haworth-Booth ; foreword by Roy Strong.
London : H.M.S.O., 1981 (Printed by W.S. Cowell Ltd., Ipswich).
6 p., 59 p. of plates : chiefly ill. ; 32 cm.
ISBN: 0112903622; 0112903614
At head of title: Victoria and Albert Museum. — Cream wrappers with ill.; beige end papers.
EXHIBITIONS: VX.1978.006; VX.1981.005

V.1981.016　　　*Six things to make* / Imogen Stewart.
London : H.M.S.O., 1981 (Printed by Sackville Press, Billericay).
23 p. : ill. (some col.) ; 20 cm.
ISBN: 0112903703
At head of title: Bethnal Green Museum of Childhood. — Stapled; wrappers with col. ills.

V.1981.017　　　*Sketches by John Constable in the Victoria and Albert Museum* / C.M. Kauffmann.
London : H.M.S.O., 1981 (Printed by Ebenezer Baylis & Son, Trinity Press).
48 p. : ill. ; 19 x 21 cm.
ISBN: 0112903436
At head of title: Victoria and Albert Museum. — Bibliography: p. 47–48. — Wrappers with col. ill.

V.1981.018　　　*Splendours of the Gonzaga : catalogue* / edited by David Chambers & Jane Martineau.
London : Victoria & Albert Museum, Amilcare Pizzi, 1981.

xxiii, 248 p. : ill. (some col.), geneal. table, plans, ports. ; 27 cm.

Foreword by Dr. Roy Strong. Introduction : the Gonzagas and Mantua / by D.S. Chambers. Essays: Lancaster and Gonzaga : the collar of SS / by Ilaria Toesca. Gonzaga tombs and catafalques / by Rodolfo Signorini. Mantegna and Mantua / by Caroline Elam. The Gonzaga and Renaissance architecture / by Howard Burns. The Gonzaga and ceramics / by J.V.G. Mallet. Ceramic tiles for the Gonzaga / by Mariarosa Palvarini Gobio Casali. Antico and the Mantuan bronze / by Anthony Radcliffe. Isabella d'Este, patron and collector / by J.M. Fletcher. The Gonzaga devices / by Mario Praz. Federico II Gonzaga as a patron of painting / by Charles Hope. "That rare Italian master . . ." : Giulio Romano, court architect, painter and impresario / by E.H. Gombrich. The Gonzaga and music / by Iain Fenlon. Charles I and the Gonzaga collections / by David Howarth. — Bibliography: p. ix–[xvi]. — Sized wrappers with col. ills. — Errata inserted ([4] p.).

EXHIBITION: VX.1981.013

V.1981.019   *Spotlight : four centuries of ballet costume : a tribute to the Royal Ballet, Victoria and Albert Museum, 8 April to 26 July 1981.*
[London : The Museum, 1981.]
104 p. : ill. ; 21 cm.

"Part 1 by Roy Strong; part 2 by Ivor Guest; part 3 by Richard Buckle; part 4 by Sarah C. Woodcock and Philip Dyer"–p. 2.

EXHIBITION: VX.1981.THM.001

V.1981.020   *The stemma of René of Anjou.*
[London : H.M.S.O., 1981?]
1 sheet, folded ([5] p.) : ill. (1 col.) ; 30 cm.
(Masterpieces ; sheet 23)

By Mark Evans. — Bibliography: p. [5]. — Object by Della Robbia.

V.1981.021   *Victorian illustrated music sheets* / Catherine Haill.
London : H.M.S.O., 1981 (Printed by Colorgraphic Ltd., Leicester).
32 p. : col. ill. ; 25 cm.
ISBN: 011290355X (pbk.)

At head of title: Victoria & Albert Museum. — Illustrated from the collections of the Theatre Museum, Victoria and Albert Museum. — Sized wrappers; coloured maroon, with col. ill.

V.1981.022   *Wedding dress, 1740–1970* / Madeleine Ginsburg.
London : H.M.S.O., 1981 (Printed by Balding + Mansell, Wisbech).
[6], 53 p. : chiefly ill. ; 21 x 22 cm.
ISBN: 0112903282

At head of title: Victoria and Albert Museum. — Includes bibliographic references. — Printed in brown; ills on end-papers and paper covered boards. — Errata slip loosely inserted. — "This book illustrates and comments on a selection only of the wedding dress collection of the Victoria and Albert Museum, of which a number are currently (1981) on display at the Bethnal Green Museum of Childhood."

V.1981.023   *Writing* / Leonee Ormond.
London : H.M.S.O., 1981 (Printed by Balding + Mansell, Wisbech).
72 p. : ill. (some col.) ; 19 cm.
(The arts and living)
ISBN: 0112902820

At head of title: Victoria & Albert Museum. — General editors: John Fleming and Hugh Honour. — Bibliography: p. 71. Index. — Design by HMSO Graphic Design. — Sized wrappers coloured blue, with col. ill.

1982

V.1982.001   *Bernard Moore, master potter 1850–1935 : 15 December–6 February 1983 : exhibition organised by Aileen Dawson and Richard Dennis.*
[London] : Victoria & Albert Museum, 1982 (Printed by Lund Humphries).
27 p. : ill. ; 25 cm.
Foreword / Roy Strong. — Stapled; wrappers with col. ills.

V.1982.002   *The cast courts* / Malcolm Baker.
[London] : H.M.S.O., [1982] (Printed by Witley Press, Hunstanton).
1 sheet, folded (5 p.) : ill., 1 col. ; 30 cm.
At foot of title: Victoria & Albert Museum. — Includes bibliographic references. — Designed by Richard Cottingham, Design Section, V&A.

V.1982.003   *Catalogue of Adam period furniture* / Maurice Tomlin. [2nd ed.]
London : [H.M.S.O.], 1982 (Printed by McCorquodale Printers).
vii, 207 p. : ill. ; 25 cm.
ISBN: 0901486442
At head of title: Victoria and Albert Museum. — Bibliography: p. 202–203. Index. — Sized wrappers coloured dark green, with ill.

V.1982.004   *Catalogue of paintings in the Wellington Museum* / C.M. Kauffmann.
London : H.M.S.O., 1982 (Printed by Jolly & Barber, Rugby).
176 p. : ill., ports. ; 26 cm.
ISBN: 0112903800: 0112903738 (pbk.)
At head of title: Victoria and Albert Museum. — Includes: Picture frames and picture hanging at Apsley House / Simon Jervis. — Includes bibliographic references. Indexes of artists and subjects, and museum numbers. — Sized wrappers coloured dark tan; col. ill.

V.1982.005   *Early stringed instruments at the Victoria & Albert Museum : an introduction in words, music and pictures to the collection of early stringed instruments in the V & A.*
London : H.M.S.O., 1982.
30 slides : col. + 1 sound cassette (60 min) + 1 guide + 1 cue card for slides (in container 25 x 19 cm.)
ISBN: 011290369X
Title from container. — Commentary by Carole Patey. — Includes v.1982.029.

V.1982.006   *Gaming* / Edward T. Joy.
London : H.M.S.O., 1982 (Printed by McCorquodale Printers).
63 p. : ill. (some col.) ; 19 cm.
(The arts and living)
ISBN: 0112903010
At head of title: Victoria and Albert Museum. — Bibliography: p. 63. Index. — Design by HMSO Graphic Design. — Sized wrappers coloured blue, with col. ill.

V.1982.007   *Ganjifa, the playing cards of India : a general survey with a catalogue of the Victoria and Albert Museum collection* / by Rudolf von Leyden ; with contributions by Michael Dummett.
London : Victoria and Albert Museum, [1982] (Printed by Penshurst Press, Tunbridge Wells).
xiv, 128 p., [8] p. of plates : ill. (some col.) ; 19 x 25 cm.
ISBN: 0905209176

Foreword / Roy Strong. — Bibliography: p.126–128. Glossary. Concordance of Museum numbers. — Design by HMSO Graphic Design / Ian B. Dobson. — Printing: 2/82. — Sized wrappers with col. ills. — Published to coincide with VX.1982.BGM.001.

V.1982.008   *Handbook to the Departments of Prints, Drawings & Photographs and Paintings* / edited by H. Barkley. 2nd ed.
London : H.M.S.O., 1982 (Printed by McCorquodale Printers).
vii, 130 p. : ill. ; 25 cm.
ISBN: 0905209370
At head of title: Victoria and Albert Museum. — Foreword / C.M. Kauffmann. — Bibliography: p. 124–130.

V.1982.009   *Hindu gods and goddesses* / A.G. Mitchell.
London : H.M.S.O., 1982 (Printed by Biddles Ltd., Guildford and King's Lynn).
xv, 120 p. : ill. ; 22 cm.
ISBN: 011290372X
At head of title: Victoria and Albert Museum. — Completed by John Lowry after the author's death. — Bibliography: p. xv. Index. — Design by HMSO Graphic Design. — Sized wrappers with col. ill.

V.1982.010   *Historia naturalis : Pliny the Elder* / Joyce Irene Whalley.
London : Victoria and Albert Museum, 1982 (Printed and bound by Amilcare Pizzi, Milan.).
48 p. : col. ill. ; 31 cm.
ISBN: 0905209214
Reproduces miniatures probably painted by Giuliano Amadei. — Bibliography: p. 48. — Designed and produced by Oregon Press. — Photography by Graham Brandon. — Olive cloth covered boards; dust jacket with col. ills.

V.1982.011   *The illustration of plants and gardens, 1500–1850* / Vera Kaden.
[London] : H.M.S.O., 1982 (Printed by W.S. Cowell Ltd., Ipswich).
vii, 48 p., 103 plates (some col.) : ill. ; 28 cm.
ISBN: 0112903754; 0112903312 (pbk.)
At head of title: Victoria and Albert Museum. — Select bibliography: p. 45–48. Index. — Illustrated from works held in the National Art Library.

V.1982.012   *India observed : India as viewed by British artists 1760–1860* / by Mildred Archer and Ronald Lightbown.
London : Victoria and Albert Museum, 1982 (Printed by Lund Humphries).
160 p., [4] p. of plates : ill. (some col.) ; 24 cm.
ISBN: 0905209184; 0862940249 (Trade ed.)
Bibliography: p. 157–158. Indexes of artists, places, people, "miscellaneous". — Designed by Graham Johnson and Cathy O'Neill/Lund Humphries. — Sized white wrappers with col. ills. — Trade ed. distributed by Trefoil Books.
EXHIBITION: VX.1982.003

V.1982.013   *The Indian heritage : court life & arts under Mughal rule : Victoria & Albert Museum, 21 April–22 August 1982.*
[London : The Museum, 1982] (Printed by Balding + Mansell).
176 p. : ill. (some col.), 1 map, ports. ; 27 cm.
ISBN: 0905209206
Foreword / John Pope-Hennessy. Acknowledgements / Robert Skelton. — Bibliography: p. 172–176. Glossary. — Design by HMSO Graphic Design. — Sized wrappers coloured blue, with col. ill.
EXHIBITION: VX.1982.002

V.1982.014   *Indian playing cards : the Victoria & Albert Museum's collection*
                  exhibited for the first time.
                  [London : The Museum, 1982] (Printed by the V & A Press).
                  1 folded sheet ([4] p.) : ill. ; 30 cm.
                  EXHIBITION: VX.1982.BGM.001

V.1982.015   *An introduction to brass* / Eric Turner.
                  London : H.M.S.O., 1982 (Printed by W.S. Cowell Ltd., Ipswich).
                  48 p. : col. ill. ; 26 cm.
                  (V & A introductions to the decorative arts)
                  ISBN: 0112903762
                  Cover title: Brass. — Edited by Anthony Burton. — Bibliography: p. 48. — Designed by
                  Andrew Shoolbred to a series design by Humphrey Stone. — Black paper covered
                  boards with col. ill.

V.1982.016   *An introduction to European swords* / Anthony North.
                  London : H.M.S.O., 1982 (Printed by W.S. Cowell Ltd., Ipswich).
                  48 p. : ill. ; 26 cm.
                  (V & A introductions to the decorative arts)
                  ISBN: 0112903789
                  Cover title: European swords. — Edited by Anthony Burton. — Bibliography: p. 47–48.
                  — Designed by Andrew Shoolbred to a series design by Humphrey Stone. — Black
                  paper covered boards with col. ill.

V.1982.017   *An introduction to medieval ivory carvings* / Paul Williamson.
                  London : H.M.S.O., 1982 (Printed by W.S. Cowell Ltd., Ipswich).
                  47 p. : ill. (some col.) ; 26 cm.
                  (V & A introductions to the decorative arts)
                  ISBN: 0112903770
                  Cover title: Medieval ivory carvings. — Edited by Anthony Burton. — Bibliography: p.
                  47. — Designed by Andrew Shoolbred to a series design by Humphrey Stone. — Black
                  paper covered boards with col. ill.

V.1982.018   *An introduction to "Victorian" genre painting : from Wilkie to Frith* /
                  Lionel Lambourne.
                  London : H.M.S.O., 1982 (Printed by W.S. Cowell Ltd., Ipswich).
                  48 p. : ill. (some col.) ; 26 cm.
                  (V & A introductions to the decorative arts)
                  ISBN: 0112903797
                  Cover title: "Victorian" genre painting. — Edited by Anthony Burton. — Design by
                  Andrew Shoolbred to a series design by Humphrey Stone. — Black paper covered
                  boards with col. ill.

V.1982.019   *Islamic metalwork from the Iranian world, 8–18th centuries* /
                  Asadullah Souren Melikian-Chirvani.
                  London : H.M.S.O., 1982 (Printed by the Oxford University Press).
                  445 p. : ill., map ; 29 cm.
                  ISBN: 0112902529
                  At head of title: Victoria and Albert Museum catalogue. — Foreword / C. Blair. —
                  Bibliographies: p. 369–380. General, object, name and provenance indexes. — Design
                  by HMSO Graphic Design. — Blue cloth covered boards.

V.1982.020   *Jewellery Gallery : summary catalogue* / Shirley Bury. [2nd ed.]
                  London : Victoria and Albert Museum, 1982 (Printed and bound by
                  Four Winds Press, Hampton).

252 p. : ill. ; 30 cm.
ISBN: 090520929X
Rev. ed. of v.1972.024. — Designed by Leonard Lawrance. — Sized wrappers with col. ill.

V.1982.021   *Keeping warm* / Eileen Harris.
London : H.M.S.O., 1982 (Printed by McCorquodale Printers).
71 p. : ill. (some col.) ; 19 cm.
(The arts and living)
ISBN: 0112902936
At head of title: Victoria and Albert Museum. — Bibliography: p. 70–71. Index. — Design by HMSO Graphic Design. — Sized wrappers coloured blue, with col. ill.

V.1982.022   *King Cole : a picture portrait of Sir Henry Cole, KCB 1808–1882* / Elizabeth Bonython.
[London] : Victoria and Albert Museum, [1982] (Printed for H.M.S.O. by Balding & Mansell, Wisbech).
70 p. : ill. (some col.), ports. ; 25 cm.
ISBN: 0905209192
Foreword / Roy Strong. — Bibliography: p. 66. Index. — Sized wrappers coloured grey, with col. ill.

V.1982.023   *Lighting* / Alastair Laing.
London : H.M.S.O., 1982 (Printed by McCorquodale Printers).
71 p. : ill. (some col.) ; 19 cm.
(The arts and living)
ISBN: 0112902847
At head of title: Victoria & Albert Museum. — Bibliography: p. 69–71. Index. — Design by HMSO Graphic Design. — Sized wrappers coloured blue, with col. ill.

V.1982.024   *Likenesses in line : an anthology of Tudor and Stuart engraved portraits* / Harold Barkley.
London : H.M.S.O., 1982 (Printed by Swindon Press).
87 p. : ill. ; 19 x 24 cm.
ISBN: 0112903525
At head of title: Victoria and Albert Museum. — Includes bibliographic references. — Design by HMSO Graphic Design. — Sized wrappers coloured blue, with ill.

V.1982.025   *Lucie Rie.*
[London : Victoria and Albert Museum, 1982.]
1 sheet, folded (7 p.) : ill. ; 21 cm.
Text by John Houston. Foreword by Roy Strong. — Bibliography. — Designed by Leonard Lawrance.
EXHIBITION: VX.1982.001

V.1982.026   *Musical instruments as works of art* / Peter Thornton. 2nd ed.
[London] : H.M.S.O., [1982] (Printed by Staples Printers, Priory Press, St Albans).
52 p. : ill. (some col.) ; 20 cm.
ISBN: 0112903258
At head of title: Victoria and Albert Museum. — Stapled; sized wrappers coloured green, with col. ill.

V.1982.027   *Reynolds Stone, 1909–1979 : an exhibition held in the Library of the Victoria and Albert Museum from 21 July to 31 October 1982.*

London : The Library of the Victoria and Albert Museum, 1982
(Printed by Skelton's Press).
84 p. : ill., port. ; 22 cm.
ISBN: 0905209222
Introduction / Ruari McLean. Foreword / Roy Strong, Roger Peers, Duncan Haldane,
Emma Beck. — Bibliography: p. 82–84. — Designed by Humphrey Stone. — Part
printed in brown. Cream wrappers with vignettes.
EXHIBITION: VX.1982.007

V.1982.028   *The Sèvres Egyptian service, 1810–12* / Charles Truman.
[London] : Victoria & Albert Museum, 1982 (Printed by Penshurst
Press, Tunbridge Wells).
72 p., [1] folded leaf of plates : ill. (some col.) ; 20 x 21 cm.
ISBN: 0905209249
Foreword / Roy Strong. — Bibliography: p. 30. Marks. — Design by HMSO Graphic
Design. — Sized wrappers with col. ills.

V.1982.029   *Solemn and sweet airs sound recording : a recital of historic music for
strings.*
[London] : Produced for H.M.S.O. and the Victoria and Albert
Museum by AAV Productions, 1982.
1 sound cassette.
ISBN: 0112903630
Description of instruments played in the recordings on container insert. — Also issued
as part of V.1982.005.

V.1982.030   *Stravinsky rehearses Stravinsky* / photographs by Laelia Goehr.
London : Theatre Museum, Victoria and Albert Museum, 1982
(Printed by Harrison & Sons).
[24] p. : chiefly ports. ; 28 cm.
ISBN: 0905209265
Cover title. — Designed and produced by Wurr & Wurr. — Stapled; black wrappers
with portrait.
EXHIBITION: VX.1982.THM.001

V.1982.031   *Towards a new iron age : May 12th-July 10th 1982.*
[London : H.M.S.O.], 1982 (Printed by Commercial Colour
Press).
100 p. : ill. (some col.), ports ; 20 X 21 cm.
ISBN: 0905209230
Bibliography: p. 97–100. — At foot of title: Victoria & Albert Museum. — Preface /
Roy Strong. Foreword / Victor Margrie. On ironwork / Antonio Benetton. Forged
ironwork today / Caroline Pearce-Higgins. Blacksmithing in the twentieth century /
Dorothy Bosomworth. Iron: the metal and the smiths / Claude Blair, Richard Quinnell.
— Black sized wrappers.
EXHIBITION: VX.1982.004

V.1982.032   *The Victoria and Albert Museum : the history of its building* / John
Physick.
London : [The Museum], 1982 (Printed by Westerham Press).
288 p., [22] p. of plates : ill. ; 25 cm.
ISBN: 0905209257
Foreword / Roy Strong. — Includes bibliographic references. Index. — Designer:
Gail Engert. — Designed and produced by Oregon Press. — Olive cloth covered boards;
illustrated dust-jacket.

V.1982.033   *Wallpapers : a history and illustrated catalogue of the collection of the Victoria and Albert Museum* / Charles C. Oman and Jean Hamilton ; bibliography by E.A. Entwisle.
[London] : Sotheby in association with the Victoria and Albert Museum, 1982 (Printed by BAS Printers, Over Wallop; bound by Webb Son & Co., Glamorgan).
486 p. : ill. (some col.) ; 29 cm.
ISBN: 0856670960
Foreword / C.M. Kauffmann. — Bibliography: p. 457–466. — Designers. General index. Index of titles and pictorial subjects. — Designed by the staff of Philip Wilson Publishers. — Red cloth covered boards; decorated end-papers; illustrated dust-jacket.

V.1982.034   *Wendy Ramshaw : 6 October 1982–16 January 1983*.
[London : The Museum, 1983] (Printed by Harrison & Sons).
[60] p. : chiefly ill. (some col.) ; 21 cm.
ISBN: 0905209273
At head of title: Victoria and Albert Museum. — Foreword / Roy Strong. Includes texts by Shirley Bury and Edward Lucie-Smith. — Designed and produced by Wurr & Wurr. — Sized wrappers, col. photographs.
EXHIBITION: VX.1982.009

V.1982.035   *Wire toys from Zimbabwe : an exhibition at the Bethnal Green Museum of Childhood, London E2, 1 December 1982 to 16 January 1983*.
London : Bethnal Green Museum, [1982].
1 folded sheet : ill. ; 42 x 60 cm. folded to 21 x 10 cm.
Cover title. — Includes bibliographic references. — Designed by The Partnership. — Printed on buff.
EXHIBITION: VX.1982.BGM.007

1983

V.1983.001   *20th century : an introduction to women's fashionable dress, 1900–1980* / Valerie D. Mendes.
London : Victoria & Albert Museum, [1983] (Printed by the V&A Press).
12 p. : ill. ; 22 cm.
(Leaflet / Department of Textiles and Dress ; no. 1)
Cover title. — "Short reading list": p. 12. — Designed by V&A Design Section. — Stapled. Col. ills. on wrappers.

V.1983.002   *Artists of the Tudor court : the portrait miniature rediscovered, 1520–1620* / Roy Strong ; with contributions from V.J. Murrell.
[London] : Victoria & Albert Museum, 1983 (Monochrome section printed . . . by BAS Printers, Over Wallop ; colour section . . . by Balding and Mansell).
168 p. : ill. (some col.), ports. ; 27 cm.
ISBN: 0905209346
Bibliography: p. 26–27. Index. — Designed and produced by Thames and Hudson. — Sized wrappers, with col. ill.
EXHIBITION: VX.1983.015

V.1983.003   *British art and design, 1900–1960 : a collection in the making.*
[London] : Victoria and Albert Museum, 1983 (Printed by Robert
Stockwell Ltd.).
xxiii, 222 p. : ill. (some col.) ; 24 cm.
ISBN: 0905209575 (pbk.)
Introduction by Carol Hogben. Compiled by Garth Hall and Andrew Hiskens in
collaboration with Michael Darby, Carol Hogben, Simon Jervis and Clive Wainwright.
Foreword by Roy Strong. — Designed by Paul Sharp. — Spiral bound. Ill. on front
cover. — "Published by the V & A in 1983 for the opening of the gallery of British Art
and Design 1900–1960"–t.p. verso.

V.1983.004   *British art in the Victoria and Albert Museum* / Michael Darby.
London : Philip Wilson and Summerfield Press, 1983 (Produced by
Scala Istituto Fotografico Editoriale, Firenze).
128 p. : col. ill. ; 28 cm.
ISBN: 0856671126
Index. — Sized wrappers with col. ills. — "Published in association with the Victoria
and Albert Museum."

V.1983.005   *Catalogue of Romanesque sculpture* / Paul Williamson.
[London] : Victoria and Albert Museum, 1983 (Printed by Drukkerij
de Lange/van Leer, the Netherlands).
118 p. : ill. ; 25 cm.
ISBN: 0905209303
At foot of title: Victoria and Albert Museum. — Includes bibliographic references.
Numerical index. — Designed by Roger Huggett and Sharon Ellis Davies/Sinc. —
Maroon cloth covered boards; dust-jacket with ill.

V.1983.006   *The common chronicle : an exhibition of archive treasures from the
County Record Offices of England and Wales, 15 June–11 September
1983* / the Association of County Archivists with the Victoria and
Albert Museum.
London : Victoria and Albert Museum, 1983 (Printed by Gavin
Martin Limited).
84 p., 4 p. of plates : ill. (some col.), facsims., plans ; 25 cm.
ISBN: 0905209427
At foot of title: Victoria and Albert Museum. — Foreword Roy Strong. — List of
donors and depositories. — Designed by Graham Johnson. — Sized wrappers with
col. ill.
EXHIBITION: VX.1983.012

V.1983.007   *David Bailey : black and white memories : an exhibition held in the
Galleries of the Art of Photography, Henry Cole Wing, 28
September–27 November 1983.*
[London] : Victoria and Albert Museum, 1983 (Printed by Four Winds
Press, Hampton).
24 p. : ill., ports. ; 30 cm.
ISBN: 0905209559
Foreword / Roy Strong. Texts by David Mellor, Martin Harrison. — Includes
bibliographic references. — Designed by Gail Engert and Martin Newton. — Stapled;
white wrappers with ill.
EXHIBITION: VX.1983.021

v.1983.008 *Dear Peter Pan* — / Catherine Haill ; foreword by Nanette Newman.
London : Victoria and Albert Museum, 1983 (Printed by Drukkerij de
Lange/van Leer, the Netherlands).
25 p., [55] p. : ill., facsims., ports. ; 23 cm.
ISBN: 0905209516
At foot of title: Theatre Museum; Victoria and Albert Museum. — Includes letters
written to 'Peter Pan' (as played by Eva Embury, 1918) by children. — Design by
Patrick Yapp. — Photography by Hugh Sainsbury. — Black paper covered boards with
col. ills.

v.1983.009 *Drawing in the Italian Renaissance workshop* / Francis Ames-Lewis
and Joanne Wright.
London : Victoria and Albert Museum, 1983 (Printed by Westerham
Press).
328 p. : ill. (some col.) 27 cm.
ISBN: 0905209311; 090369223 hbk trade ed., Hurtwood
Foreword / Roy Strong, Richard Schofield. — Bibliography: p. [327]–328. Glossary,
and biographical details of artists. — Designed by Patrick Yapp. — Sized wrappers with
col. ills.
EXHIBITION: vx.1983.008

v.1983.010 *English men's fashionable dress 1600–1799* / Avril D. Hart.
London : Victoria and Albert Museum, [1983] (Printed by the V&A
Press).
12 p. : ill. ; 22 cm.
(Leaflet / Department of Textiles and Dress ; no. 2)
Cover title. — Designed by V&A Design Section. — Stapled; sized card wrappers with
col. ills.

v.1983.011 *European art in the Victoria and Albert Museum* / text by Anthony
Burton ; captions by Susan Haskins.
London : Philip Wilson and Summerfield Press, 1983 (Produced by
Scala Istituto Fotografico Editoriale, Firenze).
128 p. : col. ill. ; 28 cm.
ISBN: 0856671215
Index. — Designed by Paul Sharp. — Sized wrappers with col. ills. — "Published in
association with the Victoria and Albert Museum."

v.1983.012 *Felix H. Man : 60 years of photography.*
[London : Victoria and Albert Museum, 1983.]
23 p. : ill. ; 21 cm.
At foot of title: Victoria and Albert Museum. — [Preface] / C.M. Kauffmann. —
Bibliography: p. 19. — Designed by Leonard Lawrance. — Stapled; wrappers coloured
black, with ills.
EXHIBITION: vx.1983.010

v.1983.013 *Georgina Follett : Victoria and Albert Museum.*
[London : The Museum, 1983.]
1 sheet, folded ([3] p.) : ill. ; 21 cm.
Text signed "A.S.C." [i.e. Anna Somers Cocks]. — Includes bibliographic references. —
Designed by Leonard Lawrance.
EXHIBITION: vx.1983.001

V.1983.014   *A guide to early photographic processes* / Brian Coe, Mark Haworth-Booth.
[London] : Victoria and Albert Museum in association with Hurtwood Press, 1983 (Printed by the Westerham Press).
112 p. : ill. (some col.), ports. (some col.), facsims. ; 31 cm.
ISBN: 0905209400
Foreword / Roy Strong. Includes: The care of photographs / Elizabeth Martin. — Bibliography: p. 111–112. — Designed by Roger Huggett and Sharon Ellis Davies/Sinc. — Sized card wrappers with illustrations on back and front, printed on black.
EXHIBITION: VX.1983.005

V.1983.014A   [Another issue]
Hurtwood in association with the Victoria and Albert Museum, 1983.
32 cm.
ISBN: 0903696231

V.1983.015   *The House of David, his inheritance : a book of sample scripts, 1914 A.D.* / Edward Johnston. 4th imp.
London : H.M.S.O., 1966 (1983 printing).
32 p. ; 26 cm.
(Facsimiles ; no. 1)
ISBN: 0112902367
At foot of title: Victoria and Albert Museum. Cover title: A book of sample scripts. — Introduction / J.P. Harthan. — Part printed in red. Sized wrappers. — 3rd imp. not traced.

V.1983.016   *An introduction to caricature* / Lionel Lambourne.
London : H.M.S.O., 1983.
48 p. : ill. (some col.), ports. ; 26 cm.
(V & A introductions to the decorative arts)
ISBN: 0112903975
Cover title: Caricature. — Series editor: Julian Berry. — Bibliography: p. 48. — Design by HMSO Graphic Design. — Black paper covered boards with col. ill.

V.1983.017   *An introduction to illuminated manuscripts* / John Harthan.
London : H.M.S.O., 1983.
48 p. : ill. (some col.) ; 26 cm.
(V & A introductions to the decorative arts)
ISBN: 0880450193
Cover title: Illuminated manuscripts. — Series editor: Julian Berry. — Bibliography: p. 48. — Design by HMSO Graphic Design. — Black paper covered boards with col. ill.

V.1983.018   *An introduction to medieval enamels* / Marian Campbell.
London : H.M.S.O., 1983.
48 p. : ill. (some col.) ; 26 cm.
(V & A introductions to the decorative arts)
ISBN: 0112903851
Cover title: Medieval enamels. — Series editor: Julian Berry. — Bibliography: p. 47–48. — Design by HMSO Graphic Design. — Black paper covered boards with col. ill.

V.1983.019   *An introduction to wallpaper* / Jean Hamilton.
London : H.M.S.O., 1983.
48 p. : ill. ; 26 cm.
(V & A introductions to the decorative arts)
ISBN: 011290386X

Cover title: Wallpaper. — Series editor: Julian Berry. — Includes bibliographic references. — Design by HMSO Graphic Design. — Black paper covered boards with col. ill.

V.1983.020   *Islamic bookbindings in the Victoria and Albert Museum* / Duncan Haldane.
London : World of Islam Festival Trust in association with the Victoria and Albert Museum, 1983 (Printed by Penshurst Press).
205 p. : ill. (some col.) ; 31 cm.
ISBN: 0905035322
Spine title: Islamic bookbindings. — Bibliography: p. 201–202. Index. — Design and art direction: Colin Larkin. — Brown imitation leather covered boards; imitation marbled end-papers; dust-jacket with col. ills. and port. of author.
EXHIBITION: VX.1983.026

V.1983.021   *John Pollard Seddon* / by Michael Darby.
London : Victoria and Albert Museum, 1983 (Printed by Lund Humphries).
120 p. : ill., plans, 1 port. ; 31 cm.
(Catalogues of architectural drawings in the Victoria and Albert Museum)
ISBN: 0905209419
Foreword / C.M. Kauffmann. — Includes bibliographic references. Index of names and places. — Designed by Graham Johnson. — Brown cloth covered boards; dust jacket with col. ills. and port. of author.

V.1983.022   *Joseph Beuys, drawings : City Art Gallery, Leeds, Kettle's Yard Gallery, Cambridge, Victoria and Albert Museum, London.*
[London] : Victoria & Albert Museum, 1983 (Printed by Westerham Press).
25, 150 p. : ill. (some col.), ports. ; 30 cm.
ISBN: 0905209451; 0905209435 (pbk.)
Foreword / Robert Rowe, Jeremy Lewison, Roy Strong. The drawings of Joseph Beuys / Anne Seymour. — White wrappers with col. ill. — "6000 copies printed . . . of which 500 have been bound and signed by the artist."–t.p. verso.
EXHIBITION: VX.1983.016

V.1983.023   *Lace : a history* / Santina M. Levey.
[London] : Victoria & Albert Museum in association with W.S. Maney & Son, 1983.
140 p., [360] p. of plates : ill. ; 34 cm.
ISBN: 090128615X
Bibliography: p. [128]–131. Glossary. Index. — Grey cloth covered boards; red end-papers. Col. ill. on dust-jacket.

V.1983.024   *A month in the country : an exhibition presented by the Theatre Museum, Victoria and Albert Museum, and arranged in conjunction with April FitzLyon* / catalogue by April FitzLyon and Alexander Schouvaloff.
[London] : Victoria and Albert Museum, 1983 (Printed by Balding + Mansell).
79 p. : ill. ; 25 cm.
ISBN: 0905209443
Bibliography: p. 33. Index. — Designed by Roger Huggett and Sharon Ellis Davies/Sinc. — Plain wrappers, white dust-jacket, fixed, with ill.
EXHIBITION: VX.1983.THM.001

v.1983.025   *National Art Library microforms : microfilms and fiches in the*
              National Art Library / compiled by Michael Keen. [2nd ed.]
              [London : The Library?], 1983 (Microfi, Royston).
              2 microfiches (36 frames).

v.1983.026   *Notes on carpet-knotting and weaving* / by C.E.C. Tattersall. 2nd ed.,
              3rd imp.
              [London] : Victoria and Albert Museum, 1983.
              42, xii p. of plates : ill. ; 19 cm.
              ISBN: 0112900348
              Bibliography: p. 38.— Printing: 5/83. — Cream wrappers with ill. in blue and black.

v.1983.027   *Oliver Messel : an exhibition held at the Theatre Museum, Victoria*
              and Albert Museum, 22 June–30 October 1983 / edited by Roger
              Pinkham.
              London : Victoria & Albert Museum, 1983 (Printed by Robert
              Stockwell Ltd.).
              200 p. : ill. (some col.), port. ; 28 cm.
              ISBN: 0905209508
              A tribute / Roy Strong. Foreword / Alexander Schouvaloff. Acknowledgements / Roger
              Pinkham. Oliver Messel and the theatre / Cecil Beaton, Christopher Fry, Peter Glenville,
              Stanley Hall, R. Myerscough-Walker, Roger Pinkham, Sybil Rosenfeld, Carl Toms,
              Rosemary Vercoe. Messel's *Sleeping beauty* / Richard Buckle. Outside the theatre /
              Thorold Dickinson, Roger Pinkham, Agi Sekers. Catalogue / Philip Dyer, Leela
              Meinertas, Roger Pinkham, Sarah C. Woodcock. — Bibliography: p. [196]–197. Index.
              — Designed by Patrick Yapp. — Sized wrappers coloured grey with col. ill.
              EXHIBITION: VX.1983.THM.002

v.1983.028   *Oriental art in the Victoria and Albert Museum* / John Ayers ; with
              contributions by Andrew Topsfield and John Lowry.
              London : Philip Wilson and Summerfield Press, 1983 (Produced by
              Scala Istituto Fotografico Editoriale, Firenze).
              128 p. : col. ill. ; 28 cm.
              ISBN: 0856671207
              Index. — Designed by Paul Sharp. — Sized wrappers with col. ill. — "Published in
              association with the Victoria and Albert Museum."

v.1983.029   *Pattern and design : designs for the decorative arts, 1480–1980 : with*
              an index to designers' drawings in the Victoria and Albert Museum /
              edited by Susan Lambert.
              London : Victoria and Albert Museum, 1983 (Printed and bound by
              Four Winds Press, Hampton).
              xi, 196 p. : ill. (some col.) ; 24 cm.
              ISBN: 0905209354
              Foreword / C.M. Kauffmann. — Includes bibliographic references. — Designed by
              Leonard Lawrance. — Sized wrappers coloured blue, with col. ill.
              EXHIBITION: VX.1983.004

v.1983.030   *Penny dreadfuls and comics : English periodicals for children from*
              Victorian times to the present day : a loan exhibition from the Library
              of Oldenburg University, West Germany at the Bethnal Green
              Museum of Childhood, 2 June–2 October 1983.
              [London] : Victoria and Albert Museum, 1983 (Printed by Royle
              Print).

124 p. : ill. (some col.) ; 27 cm.
ISBN: 0905209478
Catalogue by Kevin Carpenter. Foreword / Sir Roy Strong. — Includes bibliographic references. Index. — Designed by Richard Sage. — Sized wrappers with col. ill.
EXHIBITION: VX.1983.BGM.002

V.1983.031 *Personal choice : a celebration of twentieth century photographs selected and introduced by photographers, painters, and writers, 23 March–22 May 1983.*
London : Victoria and Albert Museum, 1983 (Printed by Westerham Press).
130 p., [1] leaf of plates : ill. ; 31 cm.
ISBN: 0905209389
Introduction / Mark Haworth-Booth. — Index. — Designed by Patrick Yapp. — Sized card wrappers coloured grey with ill.
EXHIBITION: VX.1983.003

V.1983.032 *Pilgrims* / Markéta Luskáčova.
London : Victoria & Albert Museum, 1983 (Printed by Precision Press).
[64] p. : ill. ; 25 x 27 cm.
ISBN: 0905209605
[Foreword] / Roy Strong. Introduction / Mark Haworth-Booth. — Bibliography. — Designed by Simon Rendall. — Sized wrappers; ill. printed on black.
EXHIBITION: VX.1983.025

V.1983.033 *Printmaking* / Susan Lambert.
London : H.M.S.O., 1983.
47 p. : ill. ; 21 cm.
ISBN: 0112903819
At head of cover: Victoria and Albert Museum. — Bibliography: p. 43–44. Index. — Stapled; wrappers coloured blue, with ill.

V.1983.034 *Richard Doyle and his family : an exhibition . . . held at the Victoria and Albert Museum, 30th November 1983 to 26th February 1984.*
London : Victoria and Albert Museum, 1983 (Printed by Royle Print).
73 p. : ill. (some col.), geneal. table, ports. ; 25 cm.
ISBN: 0905209583
Texts by Rodney Engen, Michael Heseltine, Lionel Lambourne. — Bibliography: p. 72. — Designed by Richard Sage and Ray Kyte. — Col. ills. on wrappers and end-papers.
EXHIBITION: VX.1983.024

V.1983.035 *The school of manners, or, Rules for childrens behaviour : at church, at home, at table, in company, in discourse, at school, abroad, and among boys, with some other short and mixt precepts* / by the author of the English exercises.
London : Victoria and Albert Museum, 1983 (Printed and bound by Butler and Tanner, Frome).
64 p. : ill. ; 15 cm.
ISBN: 0905209362
Author: John Garretson. Introduction / Joyce Irene Whalley. — Designed and produced by Oregon Press. — Design by Laurence Bradbury. — Pale blue paper covered boards and dust-jacket, ill. — Facsim of: 4th ed. London : Printed for Tho. Cockerill, at the Three Legs and Bible against Grocers-Hall in the Poultrey, 1701.

V.1983.036   *Theatre posters* / Catherine Haill.
London : H.M.S.O., 1983.
48 p. : ill. (some col.) ; 25 cm.
ISBN: 0112904181
At head of title: Victoria & Albert Museum. — Photography by Graham Brandon. —
Stapled; sized wrappers coloured yellow, with ills.

V.1983.037   *Tippoo's tiger* / Mildred Archer. [Repr.]
London : Victoria and Albert Museum, 1959 (1983 printing).
30 p., [22] p., [1] leaf of plates : ill., 1 map, ports. ; 25 cm.
(Monograph / Victoria and Albert Museum ; no. 10)
ISBN: 0905209532
Foreword / Trenchard Cox. — Bibliography: p. 22–23. — Sized wrappers coloured red,
with ill.

V.1983.038   *Toys and games from the Bethnal Green Museum = Jouets et jeux du
Bethnal Green Museum = Spielzeug und Spiele aus dem Bethnal Green
Museum = Giocattoli e giuochi dal Bethnal Green Museum* /
introduction and text, Peter Glenn.
[Italy] : Scala, Istituto Fotografico Editoriale, 1983.
36 slides : col. ; + 1 booklet (31 p.).
Text in English, French, German and Italian. — "Published in association with the
Victoria and Albert Museum."

V.1983.039   *The twentieth century primary galleries : British art and design
1900–1960 : summary catalogue.*
[London : Victoria and Albert Museum, 1983?] (Printed by the V & A
Press).
26 p. ; 20 x 23 cm.
Cover title. At head of title: Victoria & Albert Museum. — Stapled.

V.1983.040   *Twentieth century : water colours* / Victoria & Albert Museum.
[London : H.M.S.O.], 1983.
1 sheet, folded ([5] p.) : ill. (some col.) ; 30 cm.
(Twentieth century V & A)
Written by Michael Kauffmann. — Includes bibliographic references.

V.1983.041   *Le Victoria & Albert Museum.*
Paris : Editions Scala, publié en association avec le Victoria and Albert
Museum, 1983.
384 p. : ill. (chiefly col.) ; 28 cm.
ISBN: 2866560124
French translation of v.1983.042.

V.1983.042   *The Victoria & Albert Museum* / Michael Darby ; Anthony Burton
and Susan Haskins ; John Ayers.
London : Philip Wilson, Publishers and Summerfield Press, 1983
(Printers: Scala Istituto Fotografico Editoriale, Florence; Tradespools,
Frome).
384 p. : ill. (some col.), 2 plans, ports. ; 29 cm.
ISBN: 0856671290
Contents: v.1983.004, v.1983.011 and v.1983.028. — Index. — Designed by Paul
Sharp. — Green cloth covered boards; dust jacket with col. ills.

V.1983.043   *The way howe to lymne : Tudor miniatures observed* / by Jim Murrell.
London : Victoria and Albert Museum, 1983 (Printed by BAS Printers,
Over Wallop).
xv, 100 p., [34] p. of plates : ill. (some col.), ports. ; 25 cm.
ISBN: 0905209397
Foreword / by Roy Strong. — Includes bibliographic references. Index. — Designed by
John Mitchell. — Blue cloth covered boards; dust-jacket coloured blue, with col. ports.
— Published to accompany vx.1983.015.

V.1983.044   *Wedgwood.* 5th imp.
London : H.M.S.O., 1958 (1983 printing).
[4] p., [28] p. of plates : chiefly ill. ; 19 cm.
(Small picture book ; no. 45)
ISBN: 011290131X
At head of title: Victoria & Albert Museum. — Introduction signed "R.J.C."
[i.e. Robert Charleston]. — Printing: 5/83. Wrappers coloured blue, with ill. — 4th imp.
not traced.

V.1983.045   *The Wedgwood copies of the Portland Vase.*
[London : H.M.S.O., 1983.]
1 sheet, folded, ([5] p.) : ill., some col. ; 30 cm.
(Masterpieces ; sheet 26)
By Ann Eatwell. — Bibliography: p. [5]. — Printing: 4/83.

V.1983.046   *William Eggleston : colour photographs from the American South.*
[London : Victoria and Albert Museum, 1983] (Printed by Royle
Print).
1 sheet, folded ([5] p.) : col. ill. ; 31 x 31 cm.
At head of title: Victoria and Albert Museum. — Written by Mark Haworth-Booth. —
Designed by Gail Engert.
EXHIBITION: vx.1983.020

1984

V.1984.001   *100 things to see in the Victoria & Albert Museum.* 2nd ed.
London : H.M.S.O., 1984.
[67] p. (some folded) : ill., col. plans, ports. ; 21 cm.
ISBN: 0112904149
At head of title: Victoria and Albert Museum. — Foreword / Roy Strong. — Design by
HMSO Graphic Design. — Cover ill. by R. Cottingham. — Sized wrappers.

V.1984.002   *Apsley House, Wellington Museum* / Simon Jervis & Maurice Tomlin.
London : Victoria & Albert Museum, 1984 (Printed and bound by
Four Winds Press).
85 p. : col. ill., map, plans, ports. ; 25 cm.
ISBN: 0905209680
Foreword / Peter Thornton. — Designed by Leonard Lawrance. — Photography by Ken
Jackson, Jeremy Whitaker, Richard Bryant. — Sized wrappers with col. ills.

V.1984.003   *British art and design 1900–1960 : a collection in the making.*
2nd ed.
[London] : Victoria and Albert Museum, 1983 (Printed by Robert
Stockwell Ltd., 1984).

xxiii, 222 p. : ill. (some col.) ; 24 cm.
ISBN: 0905209575

Introduction / Carol Hogben. Compiled by Garth Hall and Andrew Hiskens in collaboration with Michael Darby, Carol Hogben, Simon Jervis and Clive Wainwright. Foreword / Roy Strong. — Designed by Paul Sharp. — Wrappers coloured black; ill. on front.

V.1984.004   *British biscuit tins* / M.J. Franklin.
[London] : Victoria & Albert Museum, 1984 (Designed and printed by Robert Stockwell Ltd., Southwark Press).
59 p. : ill. ; 26 cm.
ISBN: 0905209621

Bibliography: p. 37. — Designer: Bernard Roberts. — Photography by Geoffrey Shakerley, Sally Chappell, Richard Davis. — Green sized paper covered boards with col. ills. — Includes catalogue of items from the M.J. Franklin gift of tins to the Victoria and Albert Museum, by Elisabeth Darby.
EXHIBITION: VX.1984.026

V.1984.005   *Chinese export watercolours* / Craig Clunas ; photography by Ian Thomas.
[London] : Victoria and Albert Museum, 1984 (Printed by Drukkerij de Lange/van Leer, the Netherlands).
111 p. : ill. (some col.), maps ; 26 cm.
(Far Eastern series)
ISBN: 0905209613

Bibliography: p. 106. Index. — Designed by Sharon Ellis-Davies/Sinc. — Boards covered in sized decorated paper. Dust-jacket with col. ills.
EXHIBITION: VX.1984.007

V.1984.006   *The discovery of the Lake District : a northern Arcadia and its uses.*
[London] : Victoria and Albert Museum, 1984 (Printed by Precision Press).
174 p. : ill. (some col.) ; 25 cm.
ISBN: 0905209966

Foreword / Roy Strong. Preface / John Murdoch. — Includes list of lenders. — Designed by Grant Merrison. — Sized wrappers with col. ills.
EXHIBITION: VX.1984.018

V.1984.007   *Drawings by William Kent (1685–1748) from the Print Room collection : Henry Cole Wing, 6 June–2 September 1984.*
[London] : Victoria and Albert Museum, [1984] (Designed and printed by the V&A Press).
11 p. : 30 cm.

Cover title. — Introduction / Harold Barkley. — Bibliography: p. 11. — Stapled; cream wrappers with ill. — Includes: Book illustrations and decorations, architectural drawings, sculpture designs.
EXHIBITION: VX.1984.015

V.1984.008   *English caricature : 1620 to the present : caricaturists and satirists, their art, their purpose and influence.*
London : Victoria and Albert Museum, 1984 (Printed by the St Edmundsbury Press, Bury St. Edmunds).
144 p., [16] p. of plates : ill. (some col.), ports. ; 24 cm.
ISBN: 0905209958

Introduction by Richard Godfrey. — Bibliography: p. 138–141. — Sized white wrappers with col. ills. — Produced by the South Leigh Press, Haslemere.
EXHIBITION: vx.1985.013

V.1984.009   *English furniture designs of the eighteenth century* / by Peter Ward-Jackson. [New ed.]
London : Victoria & Albert Museum, 1984.
viii, 68 p., [ca. 300] p. of plates : ill. ; 28 cm.
ISBN: 0905209486
Includes bibliographic references. Index of designers. — Addenda and corrigenda / compiled by Michael Snodin. — Sized white wrappers; decorated title.

V.1984.010   *Four hundred years of fashion* / foreword by Sir Roy Strong ; editor, Natalie Rothstein ; text by Madeleine Ginsburg, Avril Hart, Valerie D. Mendes, with other members of the Department of Textiles and Dress ; photography by Philip Barnard.
London : Victoria and Albert Museum in association with William Collins, 1984 (Made and printed by New Interlitho, Milan).
176 p. : ill. ; 29 cm.
ISBN: 0002171899; 0002171902 (pbk.)
Includes glossary. — Sized wrappers with col. ills.

V.1984.011   *The golden age of British photography, 1839–1900 : photographs from the Victoria and Albert Museum, London, with selections from the Philadelphia Museum of Art, Royal Archives, Windsor Castle, the Royal Photographic Society, Bath, Science Museum, London, Scottish National Portrait Gallery, Edinburgh* / edited and introduced by Mark Haworth-Booth.
[Millerton : Aperture in association with the Philadelphia Museum of Art and the Victoria and Albert Museum, 1984.]
189 p. : ill. ; 30 cm.
ISBN: 0905209672 (0893811440 "An Aperture book"; 0893811459 "An Aperture book in association with the Philadelphia Museum of Art")
Preface / Anne d'Harnoncourt, Roy Strong. Includes essays: The dawning of an age : Chauncy Hare Townshend, eyewitness / Mark Haworth-Booth. The circle of William Henry Fox Talbot / Carolyn Bloore. Roger Fenton and the making of a photographic establishment / Valerie Lloyd. Julia Margaret Cameron : Christian pictorialist / Mike Weaver. Peter Henry Emerson : art and solitude / Ian Jeffrey. James Craig Annan : brave days in Glasgow / William Buchanan. — Bibliographic references: p. 189. Index. — Sized wrappers coloured grey, with ills.
EXHIBITION: vx.1984.014

V.1984.012   *An introduction to English glassware to 1900* / Charles Truman.
London : H.M.S.O., 1984.
47 p. : ill. (some col.) ; 26 cm.
(V & A introductions to the decorative arts)
ISBN: 0112904114
Cover title: English glassware to 1900. — Series editor: Julian Berry. — Bibliography: p. 47. — Designed by HMSO Graphic Design. — Black sized paper covered boards with col. ills. Ills on end-papers.

V.1984.013   *An introduction to Indian court painting* / Andrew Topsfield.
London : H.M.S.O., 1984.
47, [1] p. : ill. (some col.), maps ; 26 cm.
(V & A introductions to the decorative arts)

ISBN: 0112903835
Cover title: Indian court painting. — Series editor: Julian Berry. — Bibliography: p. 47–[48]. — Designed by HMSO/Graphic Design. — Black sized paper covered boards with col. ills. Map on end-papers.

v.1984.014   *An introduction to rings* / Shirley Bury.
London : H.M.S.O., 1984.
47 p. : ill. (some col.) ; 26 cm.
(V & A introductions to the decorative arts)
ISBN: 0112904106
Cover title: Rings. — Series editor: Julian Berry. — Bibliography: p. 47. — Designed by HMSO Graphic Design. — Black sized paper covered boards with col. ills. Ills on end-papers.

v.1984.015   *John Deakin : the salvage of a photographer* / an exhibition held in the Photo Gallery of the Henry Cole Wing from 26 September 1984 to 20 January 1985.
[London] : Victoria and Albert Museum, 1984 (Printed by Foister & Jagg, Cambridge).
47 p. : ill., ports. ; 28 cm.
ISBN: 0905209877
Preface / C.M. Kauffmann, Mark Haworth-Booth. Introduction / Bruce Bernard. Essay by Alex Noble. — Designed by Grant Morrison. — Sized white wrappers with ill.
EXHIBITION: VX.1984.020

v.1984.016   *John French : fashion photographer* / compiled and edited by Valerie D. Mendes with the assistance of Lynn Szygenda ; in collaboration with Vere French.
[London] : Victoria and Albert Museum, 1984 (Printed by Jolly & Barber, Rugby).
173 p. : ill., ports. ; 28 cm.
ISBN: 0905209974
Foreword / Roy Strong. Introduction by Lord Snowdon. John French remembered / Vere French, David Bailey, Terence Donovan, Charles Fielder, Brigid Keenan, Tania Radcliffe. — Bibliography: p. 175. — Designed by Patrick Yapp. — Sized grey wrappers with ills.
EXHIBITION: VX.1984.025

v.1984.017   *John Varley, 1778–1842* / C.M. Kauffmann.
London : B.T. Batsford in association with the Victoria & Albert Museum, 1984 (Typeset and printed by Butler & Tanner).
190 p., [8] p. of plates : ill. (some col.), ports. ; 26 cm.
ISBN: 0713434023; 0713434031 (pbk.)
Includes: Catalogue of Varley's watercolours in the collection of the Victoria & Albert Museum. — Bibliography: p. 180–181. Place, name and number indexes. — Sized wrappers coloured olive with col. ills.
EXHIBITION: VX.1984.027

v.1984.018   *Literary Britain photographed by Bill Brandt* / with an introduction by John Hayward ; edited with an afterword by Mark Haworth-Booth.
London : Victoria and Albert Museum in association with Hurtwood Press, 1984 (Printed by Westerham Press).
[184] p. : ill., ports. ; 25 cm.
ISBN: 0905209664; 0903696274 (Hurtwood Press)

Foreword / Roy Strong. — Designed by Simon Rendall. — Sized wrappers coloured black, with ill.
EXHIBITION: vx.1984.006

v.1984.019　　　*Marilynn Nicholson : jeweller : 3 November until 3 January 1985.*
[London] : Victoria and Albert Museum, [1984] (Printed by V & A Press).
1 sheet, folded ([7] p.) : ill. (1 col.) ; 25 cm.
By Jane Stancliffe. — Designed by V&A Design Section.
EXHIBITION: vx.1984.023

v.1984.020　　　*Michael Angelo Rooker, 1746–1801* / Patrick Conner.
London : B.T. Batsford in association with the Victoria & Albert Museum, 1984 (Printed by Butler & Tanner).
189 p., [8] p. of plates : ill. (some col.) ; 26 cm.
ISBN: 0713437561; 071343757x (pbk.)
Bibliography: p. [183]. Index. — Sized wrappers coloured grey, with col. ills. — Includes a catalogue of works by the artist in the collection of the Victoria and Albert Museum Department of Prints & Drawings and Paintings.
EXHIBITION: vx.1984.027

v.1984.021　　　*Modern artists' jewels : an exhibition held in the Jewellery Gallery of the Victoria and Albert Museum, 11 September to 1 November 1984.*
[London] : Victoria and Albert Museum, 1984 (Printing: Graphis Press).
[8] p. : ill. (some col.) ; 25 cm.
Introduction / Carol Hogben. Preface / Shirley Bury. — Design: Harrison Zulver. — Stapled; col. ills on wrappers.
EXHIBITION: vx.1984.017

v.1984.022　　　*Patricia Meyerowitz: Victoria and Albert Museum.*
[London : The Museum, 1984.]
19 p. : ill. ; 24 cm.
Cover title. — Introduction / Anna Somers Cocks. — Stapled; col. ill. on wrappers.
EXHIBITION: vx.1984.005

v.1984.023　　　*The Playfair Hours : a late fifteenth century illuminated manuscript from Rouen (V&A, L.475–1918)* / Rowan Watson.
[London] : Victoria and Albert Museum, with the Folio Society and the Readers' Union, 1984 (Printed by Westerham Press).
126, [1] p. : ill. (some col.) ; 23 cm.
ISBN: 0905209982
Bibliographic references: p. 121–[127] — Designed by Patrick Yapp. — Includes 32 colour plates, reproduced from the Playfair hours. — Boards and case covered in blue cloth; ill. pasted on front.

v.1984.024　　　*Portraits of plants* / Jacques le Moyne de Morgues (1533–1588).
London : Victoria and Albert Museum, [1984?] (Printed and bound by Springbourne Press, Basildon).
[48] p. : chiefly ill. (some col.) ; 28 cm.
ISBN: 0905209524
Introduction signed "L.L."[i.e. Lionel Lambourne]. — Designed and produced by Oregon Press. — Sized illustrated paper covered boards; dust-jacket coloured pale green with col. ills.

V.1984.025   *The Raphael cartoons : Victoria and Albert Museum.* 2nd imp.
London : H.M.S.O., 1972 (1984 printing).
9 p., 42 p. of plates : ill. (some col.), plan ; 21 x 30 cm.
ISBN: 0112901352
Cover title. — Note signed "J.W." [i.e. John White] — "Short bibliography" at end. —
Photography: Geoffrey Shakerley. — Sized wrappers with col. ills.

V.1984.026   *Rococo : art and design in Hogarth's England : 16 May –30
September 1984, the Victoria and Albert Museum.*
London : Trefoil Books, Victoria & Albert Museum, [1984]
(Printed by BAS Printers, Over Wallop).
333 p., [24] p. of plates : ill. (some col.) ; 26 cm.
ISBN: 086294046X
Edited by Michael Snodin, assisted by Elspeth Moncrieff. — Foreword / Roy Strong.
Contents: The English rococo : historical background / [Linda Colley]. What is rococo?
English rococo and its continental origins / [Michael Snodin]. Italy in England. France in
England. Gravelot and printmaking. Hogarth and St Martin's Lane. Vauxhall Gardens
[David Coke]. Silver [Design / Elaine Barr. Patrons and craftsmen / Philippa Glanville].
Gold chasing / [Richard Edgcumbe]. Objets der vertue. Arms and armour. Base metal.
Furniture and carving / [John Hardy]. Architecture and interiors / [Gervase Jackson-
Stops]. Textiles and dress [Rococo in textile design / Natalie Rothstein. Tapestries and
carpets / Wendy Hefford. Silk design / [Natalie Rothstein. Embroidery. Printed textiles].
[Rococo in English ceramics / J.V.G. Mallet.] Porcelain. Earthenware. Enamels and
glass. Chinoiserie and Gothic. Sculpture / [Malcolm Baker]. — Bibliography: p.
310–322. Index and list of lenders. — Sized wrappers with col. ills.
EXHIBITION: VX.1984.012.

V.1984.027   *Rococo ornament : a history in pictures.*
London : Victoria and Albert Museum, 1984 (Printed by Precision
Press).
32 p. : ill. ; 30 cm.
By Peter Ward-Jackson; edited, with further contributions, by Michael Snodin.
Foreword / C.M. Kauffmann. — Includes bibliographic references. Index of artists and
engravers. — Designed by Patrick Yapp. — Stapled, white wrappers with ill. —
Published to coincide with VX.1984.012.

V.1984.028   *Ros Conway : exhibition of jewellery in the Jewellery Gallery, Victoria
and Albert Museum, 5 May–28 June 1984.*
[London : Victoria and Albert Museum, 1984] (Printed by the
Hillingdon Press).
16 p. : chiefly ill. (some col.) ; 27 cm.
Introduction / Anna Somers Cocks. Includes statement by Hugh O'Donnell. — Designed
by Tim Harvey. — Photographs by David Cripps, Prudence Cuming and Elizabeth
Holder. — Stapled; col. ill. on wrappers.
EXHIBITION: VX.1984.009

V.1984.029   *Rosenthal: a century of porcelain.*
[London? : Victoria and Albert Museum, 1984.]
26 p. ; 23 x 22 cm.
Foreword by Roy Strong. — Translated from German. — Printed on grey paper.
EXHIBITION: VX.1984.008

V.1984.030   *Surprise pantomime spectacular.*
[London] : Theatre Museum, Victoria and Albert Museum, [1984]
(Printed by Gavin Martin Ltd.).
1 sheet : col. ill. ; 25 cm.

Adapted from the programme for the performance of *Mother Goose* at Drury Lane Theatre, 2 Dec. 1984, in aid of the Theatre Museum. — Text by Catherine Haill. — Designed by Patrick Yapp.

V.1984.031   *Tea-pots in pottery and porcelain.* 6th imp.
London : H.M.S.O., 1948 (1984 printing).
[30] p. : ill. ; 13 x 19 cm.
(Small picture book ; no. 9)
ISBN: 0905209885
At foot of title: Victoria & Albert Museum. Cover title: Teapots. — Introduction signed: "A.L." [i.e. Arthur Lane]. — Stapled; wrappers coloured orange with ill.

V.1984.032   *Twentieth century : prints* / Victoria & Albert Museum.
[London : H.M.S.O., 1984?]
1 sheet, folded ([5] p.) : ill. (1 col.) ; 30 cm.
(Twentieth century V and A ; 2)
Written by Rosemary Miles. — Includes bibliography.

V.1984.033   *Willie Rushton's great moments of history : 24 illustrations in glorious colour.*
[London] : Victoria and Albert Museum, 1984 (Printed by Alan Pooley Ltd.).
[55] p. : chiefly col. ill. ; 43 cm.
ISBN: 0905209893
Foreword / Nicky Bird. — Designed by The Partners. — Wrappers coloured blue with col. ills. — "V & A special edition of 1000."

V.1984.034   *Working day on the late Ming period.*
[London] : Victoria & Albert Museum Far Eastern Dept. [1984?].
10, 10, 5, 6, 11 p. ; 30 cm.
— Cover title. — "Papers . . . originally given at a Working Day on the late Ming period, organised by the Far Eastern Department of the Victoria and Albert Museum and held in the Museum on 21st March 1984"–foreword. 1580–1640 / Glen Dudbridge. Art and the artisan in the late Ming / Anne Farrer. The taste for Japanese lacquer in the late Ming : the textual evidence / Craig Clunas. The taste for Japanese lacquer in the late Ming : the evidence from Japanese lacquer for other markets / J.V. Earle. Ming cast-iron : a Chinese industrial revolution / Clayton Bredt. — Includes bibliographic references. — Stapled in blue paper covers. — Errata slip inserted. — "For private circulation only."

1985

V.1985.001   *100 great paintings in the Victoria & Albert Museum.*
[London] : Victoria and Albert Museum, 1985 (Printed by Penshurst Press).
220 p. : col. ill. ; 25 cm.
ISBN: 094810769X; 0905209370 (pbk.)
[Preface] / Roy Strong. Introduction / Michael Kauffmann. — Index. — Designed by Derek Birdsall. — Ivory cloth covered boards; red end-papers; illustrated dust-jacket.

V.1985.002   *A.W.N. Pugin and the Pugin family* / by Alexandra Wedgwood.
London : Victoria and Albert Museum, 1985 (Printed by Jolly & Barber, Rugby).
360 p. : ill. ; 31 cm.

(Catalogues of architectural drawings in the Victoria and Albert Museum)
ISBN: 0948107014
Foreword / C.M. Kauffmann. — Bibliography: p. 327–331. Index of names and places; 'diaries'. Concordance of Museum numbers. — Designed by Graham Johnson. — Red paper covered boards; dust-jacket with col. ills. and photograph of author.

v.1985.003   *Alan Craxford : jeweller : 12 January until 7 March 1985.*
[London : Victoria and Albert Museum, 1985] (Printed by V & A Press).
1 sheet, folded ([7] p.) : ill. (1 col.) ; 25 cm.
By Jane Stancliffe. — Designed by V&A Design Section.
EXHIBITION: vx.1985.001

v.1985.004   *Artist's* [sic] *graphic design before World War II.*
[London : National Art Library, Victoria and Albert Museum, 1985.]
9 p. ; 30 cm. + [2] p.
Title contains error: Artist's [sic] . . . . — By A.S. Hobbs, with the assistance of J. Bigham. — Includes bibliography. — Duplicated; stapled.
EXHIBITION: vx.1985.007

v.1985.005   *Beatrix Potter, the V & A collection : Library landing, 6 November 1985–2 February 1986 : a small exhibition of material from the Linder Bequest to celebrate the re-opening of the National Art Library and the publication of the catalogue* Beatrix Potter : the V & A collection / *organised by Anne Stevenson Hobbs.*
[London : National Art Library, Victoria & Albert Museum, 1985.]
[19] p. ; 30 cm.
Duplicated typescript, stapled in blue covers, with ill.
EXHIBITION: vx.1985.024

v.1985.006   *Beatrix Potter : the V & A collection : the Leslie Linder bequest of Beatrix Potter material : watercolours, drawings, manuscripts, books, photographs and memorabilia /* catalogue compiled by Anne Stevenson Hobbs & Joyce Irene Whalley with the assistance of Emma Stone & Celia O'Malley ; under the general editorship of Joyce Irene Whalley.
London : Victoria and Albert Museum and Frederick Warne, 1985 (Printed and bound by William Clowes Ltd.).
240 p., [36] p. of plates : ill. (some col.), facsims., ports. ; 26 cm.
ISBN: 0723232601
— Bibliography: p. 230–233. Index. — Designed by Gail Engert. — Blue cloth covered boards; illustrated end-papers and dust-jacket.
EXHIBITION: vx.1985.024

v.1985.007   *Bewick : wood engravings /* Frances Hicklin. 2nd imp.
London : H.M.S.O., 1978 (1985 printing).
32 p. : ill. ; 19 cm.
ISBN: 0112902901
At head of title: Victoria and Albert Museum. — Printing: 2/85. — Stapled; buff wrappers with ills.

V.1985.008   *Bidri ware : inlaid metalwork from India* / Susan Stronge.
                [London] : Victoria and Albert Museum, 1985 (Printed by Butler &
                Tanner).
                96 p. : ill. (some col.), map ; 26 cm.
                ISBN: 090520963X
                Bibliography: p. 92–93. Glossary. Index of Museum numbers. — Designed by Tim
                Harvey. — Brown cloth covered boards; decorated end-papers; illustrated dust-jacket.
                — Catalogue of the Victoria and Albert Museum collection.

V.1985.009   *Bonington, Francia & Wyld* / Marcia Pointon.
                London : B.T. Batsford in association with the Victoria & Albert
                Museum, 1985 (Typeset and printed by Butler & Tanner).
                191 p., [8] p. of plates : ill. (some col., port.) ; 26 cm.
                ISBN: 0713418176: 0713418184 (pbk.)
                Series general editor: John Murdoch. — Bibliography: p. 187–188. Index. — Sized
                wrappers coloured camel with col. ills.
                EXHIBITION: VX.1985.012

V.1985.010   *Bookbindings* / John P. Harthan. 3rd ed.
                London : H.M.S.O., 1985.
                152 p. : ill. (some col.). ; 22 cm.
                ISBN: 011290226X
                At head of title: Victoria and Albert Museum. — Bibliography: p. 38–40. Glossary. —
                Printing: 2/85. — Sized wrappers with turn-ins; col. ills. — "Though based on the 1961
                edition it contains much new material, examples of bindings acquired by the V & A in
                recent years together with new and more up-to-date information on developments in the
                British bookbinding world"–p. [4].

V.1985.011   *Browne muggs : English brown stoneware* / Robin Hildyard.
                [London] : Victoria and Albert Museum, 1985 (Printed by Jolly &
                Barber).
                127 p. : ill. ; 25 cm.
                (V & A ceramic series)
                ISBN: 0948107243
                Foreword / Roy Strong. — Bibliography: p. 126–127. — Designed by Grundy &
                Northedge. — Sized wrappers with col. ills.
                EXHIBITION: VX.1985.019

V.1985.012   *Catalogue of European ambers in the Victoria and Albert Museum* /
                Marjorie Trusted.
                [London : Victoria and Albert Museum], 1985 (Printed by Balding +
                Mansell, Wisbech).
                119 p. : ill. (some col.) ; 25 cm.
                ISBN: 0948107138
                Foreword / Anthony Radcliffe. — Bibliography: p. 22–23. Index. Index of museum
                numbers. — Designed by Paul Sharp. — Tan paper covered boards and end-papers;
                dust-jacket with col. ill.

V.1985.013   *Catalogue of musical instruments. Vol. I, Keyboard instruments* /
                Howard Schott. 2nd ed.
                London : H.M.S.O., 1985.
                148 p. : ill. ; 25 cm.
                ISBN: 0112903991.
                At head of title: Victoria and Albert Museum. — Foreword / Peter Thornton. —
                Bibliography: p. 142–144. — Sized wrappers with col. ills.

V.1985.014   *Decorative endpapers.*
Exeter : Webb & Bower in association with the Victoria and Albert
Museum, 1985 (Printed and bound by Mandarin Offset International,
Hong Kong).
13, [2] p., 32 p. of plates : col. ill. ; 21 cm.
(The Victoria and Albert colour books)
ISBN: 0863500862
Written by Jean Hamilton. — Bibliography: p. [4]. — Book, cover and slip case design
by Cooper Thirkell Ltd. — Decorated cover and lining paper. — Published in the U.S.A.
by H.N. Abrams.

V.1985.015   *Department of Prints, Drawings & Photographs and Paintings :
acquisitions 1981–85.*
[London : Victoria and Albert Museum, 1985.]
1 sheet : ill. ; 42 x 60 cm folded to 21 x 20 cm.
Poster. — Text by C.M. Kauffmann. — Part printed in orange.
EXHIBITION: VX.1985.025

V.1985.016   *Frances Bendixson : jeweller : 16 March until 9 May 1985.*
[London : Victoria and Albert Museum, 1985] (Printed by V & A
Press).
1 sheet, folded ([7] p.) : ill. (1 col.) ; 25 cm.
By Jane Stancliffe. — Designed by V&A Design Section.
EXHIBITION: VX.1985.005

V.1985.017   *From Manet to Hockney : modern artists' illustrated books* / edited by
Carol Hogben & Rowan Watson ; introduction by Carol Hogben.
[London] : Victoria & Albert Museum, 1985 (Printed by Royle Print).
379 p. : ill. (some col.), facsims., music, ports. ; 28 cm.
ISBN: 0948107081; 0948107073 (pbk.)
Preface / Duncan Haldane. — Bibliography: p. 375–376. Indexes of artists, authors and
publishers. — Designed by Grundy & Northedge. — Beige cloth covered boards; paper
labels with col. ills. on back and front; title stamped in blue on spine, illustrated dust-
jacket; or illustrated wrappers.
EXHIBITION: VX.1985.006

V.1985.018   *Guanyin : a masterpiece revealed* / John Larson & Rose Kerr.
[London] : Victoria and Albert Museum, 1985 (Printed by Lund
Humphries).
76 p. : ill. (some col.) ; 25 cm.
ISBN: 0905209915
Bibliography: p. 73. Index. — Designed by Paul Sharp. — Photography by John
Hammond, Ian Thomas, Steve Williams, Hugh Sainsbury. — Blue paper covered
boards, green end-papers, dust-jacket with col. ills.

V.1985.019   *A guide to the print rooms in the United Kingdom and Eire.*
London : Victoria & Albert Museum, June 1985.
[74] p. ; 15 x 21 cm.
Cover title. — Prepared by the Department of Prints, Drawings & Photographs, and
Paintings. — Includes bibliographic references. — Stapled in lime covers.

V.1985.020   *The Ham House kitchen* / by Caroline Davidson.
[London] : Victoria and Albert Museum, [1985] (Printed by Royle
Print).
47 p. : ill. (some col.) ; 25 cm.

ISBN: 0905209931
Bibliography: p. 47. — Designed by Grundy & Northedge. — Photography by Geoffrey Shakerley. — Sized wrappers with col. ills.

v.1985.021 *Hats from India* / Rosemary Crill.
[London : Victoria and Albert Museum, 1985] (Printed by Henry Stones & Son).
64 p. : ill. (some col.), 1 map, ports. ; 22 cm.
ISBN: 0948107308
Bibliography: p. 24. — Designed by Laurence Bradbury assisted by Sarah Collins. — Stapled; col. ill. on wrappers.
EXHIBITION: VX.1985.021

v.1985.022 *Indian floral patterns.*
Exeter : Webb & Bower in association with the Victoria and Albert Museum, 1985 (Printed and bound by Mandarin Offset International).
13, [2] p., 32 p. of plates : col. ill. ; 21 cm.
(The Victoria and Albert colour books)
ISBN: 0863500854
Written by Susan Stronge and Rosemary Crill. — Bibliography: p. [14]. — Book, cover and slip case design by Cooper Thirkell Ltd. — Decorated cover and lining paper. — Published in the U.S.A. by H.N. Abrams.

v.1985.023 *An introduction to English silver from 1660* / Eric Turner.
London : H.M.S.O., 1985.
48 p. : ill. (some col.) ; 26 cm.
(V & A introductions to the decorative arts)
ISBN: 0112904122
Cover title: English silver from 1660. — Series editor: Julian Berry. — Bibliography: p. 47–48. — Designed by HMSO Graphic Design. — Black sized paper covered boards with col. ill. Ills on end-papers.

v.1985.024 *An introduction to English stained glass* / Michael Archer.
London : H.M.S.O., 1985.
48 p. : ill. (some col.) ; 26 cm.
(V & A introductions to the decorative arts)
ISBN: 0112904165
Cover title: English stained glass. — Series editor Julian Berry. — Bibliography: p. 48. — Designed by HMSO Graphic Design. — Black sized paper covered boards with col. ill. Ills. on end-papers.

v.1985.025 *An introduction to ironwork* / Marian Campbell.
London : H.M.S.O., 1985.
48 p. : ill. (some col.) ; 26 cm.
(V & A introductions to the decorative arts)
ISBN: 0112904157
Cover title: Ironwork. — Series editor: Julian Berry. — Bibliography: p. 16–18. — Designed by HMSO Graphic Design. — Black sized paper covered boards with col. ills. Ills on end-papers.

v.1985.026 *An introduction to Islamic arms* / Anthony North.
London : H.M.S.O., 1985.
48 p. : ill. (some col.) ; 26 cm.
(V & A introductions to the decorative arts)
ISBN: 0112903843

Cover title : Islamic arms. — Series editor: Julian Berry. — Bibliography: p. 47–48.
Glossary. — Designed by HMSO Graphic Design. — Black sized paper covered boards
with col. ills.

v.1985.027   *An introduction to sentimental jewellery* / Shirley Bury.
London : H.M.S.O., 1985.
48 p. : ill. (some col.) ; 26 cm.
(V & A introductions to the decorative arts)
ISBN: 0112904173
Cover title: Sentimental jewellery. — Series editor: Julian Berry. — Bibliography:
p. 47–48. — Designed by HMSO Graphic Design. — Black sized paper covered boards
with col. ill. Ills. on end-papers.

v.1985.028   *Jacqueline Mina : jewellery 1973–1985 . . . .*
[London : Victoria and Albert Museum, 1985] (Printed by Instep
(Print & Design) Ltd.).
[8] p. : col. ill., port. ; 20 cm.
ISBN: 0948107251
Cover title. — By Richard Edgcumbe and Jane Stancliffe. — Bibliography. —
Photographs by David Cripps, Joël Degen, Michael Minas, Dominic Naish. — Stapled;
col. ills on wrappers.
EXHIBITION: vx.1985.018

v.1985.029   *John Constable's sketch-books of 1813 and 1814 : reproduced in
facsimile* / introduction by Graham Reynolds. 3rd ed.
London : H.M.S.O., 1985 (Printed by UPS Blackpool ; bound by
Smith Settle).
3 v. in case : ill., facsims. ; 19 cm.
ISBN: 0112902960 (set); 0948107154
At foot of title: Victoria & Albert Museum. — [1]. Introduction [and catalogue] by
Graham Reynolds. [2]. Sketch-book 1813 (10 x 13 cm.). [3]. Sketch-book 1814
(9 x 12 cm.). — Boards and case covered in red cloth; facsimile of the artist's signature
stamped in gold on each.

v.1985.030   *Kevin Coates : 16 November–9 January 1986.*
[London : Victoria and Albert Museum, 1985] (Printed by Instep
Ltd.).
[20] p. : ill. (chiefly col.), port. ; 20 cm.
ISBN: 1851770569
Cover title. — By Richard Edgcumbe and Jane Stancliffe. — Bibliography. — Designed
by V&A Design Section. — Stapled; col. ill. on wrappers.
EXHIBITION: vx.1985.026

v.1985.031   *Knit one, purl one : historic and contemporary knitting from the
V & A's collection* / Frances Hinchcliffe.
[London : The Museum, 1985] (Printed by Precision Press).
30 p. : ill. (some col.) ; 22 cm.
ISBN: 1851770216
Cover title. — Bibliography: p. [2]. — Photography and design by David Cripps. —
Stapled; col. ill. on wrappers.
EXHIBITION: vx.1985.023

v.1985.032   *Luggage labels from the great age of shipping : twelve decorative,
sticky labels to adorn your luggage, with an introduction on the era of
the liner.*

[London] : Victoria and Albert Museum, 1985 (Printed by Precision Press).
8 p., 12 leaves of plates : ill. (some col.) ; 28 cm.
ISBN: 0905209281
Text by Nicky Bird. — Designed by The Partners. — Sized wrappers with col. ills.

V.1985.033 *Oranges & lemons : fruit wrappers from the Victoria & Albert Museum : a selection of twenty one original designs faithfully reproduced in full colour.*
[London] : Victoria and Albert Museum, 1985.
21 [i.e. 42] leaves : col. ill. ; 19 cm.
Cover title.

V.1985.034 *Ornate wallpapers.*
Exeter : Webb & Bower in association with the Victoria and Albert Museum, 1985 (Printed and bound by Mandarin Offset International).
9, [2] p., 36 p. of plates : chiefly col. ill. ; 21 cm.
(The Victoria and Albert colour books)
ISBN: 0863500870
Written by Gill Saunders. — Book, cover and slip case design by Cooper Thirkell Ltd. — Decorated cover and lining paper. — Published in the U.S.A. by H.N. Abrams.

V.1985.035 *Osterley Park House* / John Hardy, Maurice Tomlin.
[London] : Victoria and Albert Museum, 1985 (Printed by Balding + Mansell, Wisbech).
110 p. : col. ill., plans ; 25 cm.
ISBN: 0948107146
Introduction / Simon Jervis. — Bibliography: p. 112. — Design by Patrick Yapp. — Photography by Ken Jackson, Jeremy Whitaker and Fritz von der Schulenberg. — Sized wrappers with col. ills., decorated end-papers.

V.1985.036 *The people & places of Constantinople : watercolours by Amadeo Count Preziosi, 1816–1882* / Briony Llewellyn and Charles Newton.
[London] : Victoria & Albert Museum, 1985 (Printed by Precision Press).
54 p. : ill. (some col.) ; 27 cm.
ISBN: 0948107030
Preface / C.M. Kauffmann. — Bibliography: p. [56] — Designed by Grant Morrison. — Plain wrappers; decorated sized dust-jacket with col. ill.).
EXHIBITION: VX.1985.003

V.1985.037 *Rococo silks.*
Exeter : Webb & Bower in association with the Victoria and Albert Museum, 1985 (Printed and bound by Mandarin Offset International).
11, [2] p., 34 p. of plates : col. ill. ; 21 cm.
(The Victoria and Albert colour books)
ISBN: 0863500846
Written by Gill Saunders. — Illustrated with designs from an album by William Kilburn. — Book, cover and slip case design by Cooper Thirkell Ltd. — Bibliography: p. 14. — Decorated cover and lining paper. — Published in the U.S.A. by H.N. Abrams.

v.1985.038   *Samuel Prout, 1783–1852* / Richard Lockett.
London : B.T. Batsford in association with the Victoria & Albert
Museum, 1985 (Typeset and printed by Butler & Tanner).
192 p., [8] p. of plates : ill. (some col.) ; 26 cm.
ISBN: 0713434902; 0713434910 (pbk.)
Series general editor: John Murdoch. — Bibliography: p. 190. Index. — Sized wrappers
coloured orange with col. ills. — Includes: Catalogue of watercolours and drawings by
Samuel Prout in the Victoria & Albert Museum.

v.1985.039   *Shots of style : great fashion photographs* / chosen by David Bailey ;
introduction by Martin Harrison.
London : Victoria and Albert Museum, 1985 (Printed by Alan Pooley
Ltd.).
256 p. : ill. ; 33 cm.
ISBN: 094810726X; 185177081X
Foreword / Roy Strong. Acknowledgements / Mark Haworth-Booth. — Bibliography:
p. [254]. — Designed by Patrick Yapp. — Sized card wrappers with black and white
photographs; beige cloth covered boards; dust-jacket with black and white photographs.
Copy note: Reprinted in the year of publication.
EXHIBITION: vx.1985.020

v.1985.040   *Sir John Soane* / by Pierre de la Ruffinière du Prey.
London : Victoria and Albert Museum, 1985 (Printed by Drukkerij
de Lange/van Leer, the Netherlands).
126 p. : ill. ; 31 cm.
(Catalogues of architectural drawings in the Victoria and Albert
Museum)
ISBN: 0948107006
Foreword / C.M. Kauffmann. — Bibliography: p. 115–118. Index of names and places.
Concordance of Museum numbers. — Designed by Graham Johnson. — Blue paper
covered boards; dust-jacket with col. ills. and photograph of author.

v.1985.041   *A sketchbook by Richard Doyle, 1824–1883 : a facsimile* / with an
introduction by Lionel Lambourne and a memoir of Arnold Fawcus
by Nicolas Barker.
[London] : Victoria and Albert Museum, 1985 (September Press,
Wellingborough).
xv, 22 p. : ill. ; 30 cm.
ISBN: 0905209567
"This edition is limited to 225 copies"–p. [iv]. The facsimile was made and printed by
Arnold Fawcus for publication by the Trianon Press. At his death in 1979, about 200
copies had been printed. They were taken over by the Museum to form the basis of this
edition. — Designed by Christopher Skelton. — Dark brown cloth covered boards; title
stamped in gold. — The original sketchbook, dating from about 1842, is in the Victoria
and Albert Museum.

v.1985.042   *Stage by stage : the making of the Theatre Museum* / Jean Scott
Rogers ; with a foreword by Donald Sinden.
London : H.M.S.O., 1985.
xvi, 72 p. : ill. (some col.) ; 25 cm.
ISBN: 011290419X
Bibliography: p. 68. Index. — Design by HMSO Graphic Design. — Sized wrappers
with col. ill.

v.1985.043   *Tall stories of Baron Munchausen : a book accompanying the exhibition at the Bethnal Green Museum of Childhood, 18 September to 10 November 1985, to celebrate the bicentenary of the publication of* The adventures of Baron Munchausen : *twelve illustrated tales with two essays and a checklist of illustrators.*
[London] : Published by the Victoria & Albert Museum for the Bethnal Green Museum of Childhood, 1985.
32 p. : ill. ; 25 cm.
ISBN: 1851770615
Includes: R.E. Raspe, the author / Maurice Richardson. Tall stories / Brian Alderson. Illustrators of Munchausen / Tessa Chester. — Bibliography. — Designed by Julien & Weldon.
EXHIBITION: VX.1985.BGM.003

v.1985.044   *Tea caddies : an illustrated history* / written by Gillian Walkling.
[London] : Victoria and Albert Museum, 1985 (Printed by CTD).
[24] p., [55] p. of plates : ill. (some col.) ; 24 cm.
ISBN: 0905209540
Designed by The Partners. — Plain wrappers; dust-jacket coloured grey with ills.; title in gold.

v.1985.045   *The Triumph of the Archduchess Isabella, 31st May, 1615.*
[London : H.M.S.O., ca. 1985?]
1 sheet, folded ([7] p.) : ill. (chiefly col.) ; 30 cm.
(Masterpieces ; sheet 23)
By Lionel Lambourne. — Concerns a painting by Denis van Asloot.

v.1985.046   *Turkish embroidery* / Pauline Johnstone.
[London] : Victoria and Albert Museum, 1985 (Printed by Van Leer, the Netherlands).
96 p. : ill. (some col.) ; 28 cm.
ISBN: 0948107022
Bibliography: p. 22. — Designed by Tim Harvey. — Photography by Jeremy Whitaker. — Sized wrappers, with col. ills.

v.1985.047   *Twentieth-century : silver and jewellery designs* / Victoria & Albert Museum.
[London : H.M.S.O., 1985?] (Printed by UDO Litho Ltd.).
1 sheet, folded ([3] p.) : ill. (1 col.) ; 30 cm.
(Twentieth century V and A ; 4)
By Michael Snodin. — Bibliography.

v.1985.048   *Twentieth-century : wallpaper* / Victoria & Albert Museum.
[London : H.M.S.O., 1985?] (Printed by UDO Litho Ltd.).
1 sheet, folded ([3] p.) : ill. (1 col.) ; 30 cm.
(Twentieth century V and A ; 3)
By Jean Hamilton. — Bibliography.

v.1985.049   *A vision exchanged : an exhibition held at the Victoria & Albert Museum from 6 February until 8 April 1985, and at the National Museum of Photography, Film and Television at Bradford from 23 April until 23 June 1985.*
[London] : Victoria & Albert Museum, [1985] (Printed by Royle Print).

48 p. : ill., 1 facsim. ; 25 cm.
ISBN: 0948107057
Sub-title on cover: Amateurs & photography in mid-Victorian England. — Preface /
C.M. Kauffmann, Mark Haworth-Booth. Authors named on cover: Carolyn Bloore &
Grace Seiberling. — Designed by Grundy & Northedge Designers. — Sized white
wrappers with ills.
EXHIBITION: VX.1985.002

1986

V.1986.001   *Additions to catalogue of colour transparencies.*
[London : National Art Slide Library, Victoria and Albert Museum],
1986.
Supplement to V.1980.005.

V.1986.002   *Alexander Cozens : Victoria and Albert Museum, 5 November 1986
to 4 January 1987.*
[London : The Museum?, 1986.]
[4] p. ; 26 cm.
EXHIBITION: VX.1986.021

V.1986.003   *American potters today : an exhibition of American studio pottery
organised by the Ceramics Department, Victoria and Albert Museum,
in conjunction with Garth Clark, Los Angeles, May 14th-August 31st
1986* / Garth Clark and Oliver Watson.
Victoria and Albert Museum, 1986 (Printed by Precision Press).
87 p. : ill. (some col.) ; 25 cm.
(V & A ceramic series)
Includes bibliographic references and index of donors. — Designed by Grundy &
Northedge Designers.
EXHIBITION: VX.1986.008

V.1986.004   *Bethnal Green Museum of Childhood.*
[London] : Victoria and Albert Museum, 1986.
Written by Anthony Burton. — Reprint only seen: V.1993.004.

V.1986.005   *Bottle tickets* / Jane Stancliffe.
[London] : Victoria & Albert Museum, [1986] (Printed and bound by
Drukkerij de Lange/van Leer, the Netherlands).
48 p. : ill. (some col.) ; 20 cm.
ISBN: 0905209907
Bibliography: p. 48. — Grey cloth covered boards; paper labels with col. ills.

V.1986.006   *Boydell and the foundation of the British school of painting* /
exhibition arranged by Jim Fowler and Lionel Lambourne with
Sarah Postgate ; catalogue by Jim Fowler.
London : V & A, 1986.
[14] leaves ; 30 cm.
Typescript. Photocopied cover.
EXHIBITION: VX.1986.026

v.1986.007   *Boyhood heroes : to accompany the* World of adventure *exhibition at the Bethnal Green Museum of Childhood, 9 July to 21 September 1986.*
[London : The Museum, 1986.]
[20] p. : ill. ; 30 cm.
Cover title. — "compiled on behalf of the . . . Museum by Kevin Carpenter" (cover, verso). — Bibliography: back cover. — Stapled; wrappers coloured green, with ill.
EXHIBITION: VX.1986.BGM.002

v.1986.008   *Chess in art & society.*
London : Victoria and Albert Museum, [1986?]
1 sheet, folded ([6] p.) : ill. ; 30 cm.
Caption title. At head of title: Victoria & Albert Museum.
EXHIBITION: VX.1986.007

v.1986.009   *Chinese ceramics : porcelain of the Qing dynasty, 1644–1911* / Rose Kerr ; photography by Ian Thomas.
[London] : Victoria and Albert Museum, 1986 (Printed by Precision Press).
142 p. : ill. (some col.) ; 26 cm.
(Far Eastern series)
ISBN: 0948107170
Bibliography: p. 136. Index. — Designed by Morrison Dalley Design Partnership. — Line ills by Paul Sharp. — Black end papers and cloth covered boards; title in white. Dust-jacket coloured green with col. ills.

v.1986.010   *Chinese dress* / Verity Wilson ; photography by Ian Thomas.
[London] : Victoria and Albert Museum, 1986 (Printed by CTD Printers, Twickenham).
135 p. : ill.(some col.), ports ; 26 cm.
(Far Eastern series)
ISBN: 0948107189
Bibliography: p. 13. Index. — Black cloth covered boards lettered in white. Dust-jacket chiefly red and black, with col. ill.

v.1986.011   *The country house described : an index to the country houses of Great Britain and Ireland* / Michael Holmes.
Winchester : Saint Paul's Bibliographies in association with Victoria & Albert Museum, 1986 (Printed by St Edmundsbury Press, Bury St. Edmunds).
viii, 328 p. : ill. ; 29 cm.
ISBN: 0906795397
"Literature on individual country houses. . .held in the National Art Library at the Victoria and Albert Museum"–p. 1. — Bibliography: p. 326–328. — Grey paper covered boards; dust-jacket with col. ill.
EXHIBITION: VX.1986.020

v.1986.012   *The court ballet of Louis XIII : a collection of working designs for costumes 1615–33* / text by Margaret M. McGowan.
London : Victoria and Albert Museum in association with Hobhouse and Morton Morris, [1986?] (Printed by Balding + Mansell, Wisbech).
[98] p. : ill. (some col.) ; 31 cm.
ISBN: 1851770135

Bibliography: p. [21–22]. — Designed by Graham Johnson. — Red cloth covered boards; dust-jacket with col. ills. — Includes works owned by the Theatre Museum.
EXHIBITION: vx.1987.THM.002

v.1986.013   *Designs for British dress and furnishing fabrics : 18th century to the present.*
[London] : Victoria and Albert Museum, 1986 (Printed by Yale Press).
51 p. : ill. ; 22 cm.
ISBN: 185177047X
Foreword / Roy Strong. Introduction / John Murdoch. Texts by Charles Newton and Hilary Young, Nathalie Rothstein. — Bibliography: p. 51. — Designed by Laurence Bradbury Design Associates. — Stapled; sized wrappers, coloured.
EXHIBITION: vx.1986.027

v.1986.014   *Designs for interiors.*
[London] : Victoria & Albert Museum, 1986 (Designed and printed by the V&A Press).
40 p. : ill. (some col.) ; 22 cm.
ISBN: 1851770089
Cover title. — By Stephen Calloway. — Stapled; sized wrappers with col. ill.
EXHIBITION: vx.1986.015

v.1986.015   *Fables* / edited by Anne Stevenson Hobbs.
[London] : Victoria and Albert Museum, 1986 (Printed by Butler & Tanner).
144 p. : ill. (some col.) ; 26 cm.
ISBN: 094810712
Bibliography: p.137–139. General and thematic indexes. — Designed and produced by Patrick Yapp. — Red cloth covered boards; illustrated end-papers; dust-jacket coloured red, with ill. — "A cross-section of fable illustration in printed books from the collections of the National Art Library"–Apologia.
EXHIBITION: vx.1986.023

v.1986.016   *Facets of Indian art : a symposium held at the Victoria and Albert Museum on 26, 27, 28 April and 1 May, 1982* / edited by Robert Skelton, Andrew Topsfield, Susan Stronge and Rosemary Crill ; editorial assistant, Graham Parlett.
London : Victoria & Albert Museum, 1986 (Printed by Jolly & Barber, Rugby).
269 p. : ill. ; 29 cm.
ISBN: 0948107421
Preface / Robert Skelton. — Includes bibliographies. — Designed by John Mitchell. — Blue cloth covered boards; decorated end-papers; dust-jacket coloured blue. — A symposium adjunct to vx.1982.002.

v.1986.017   *Frank Bauer : 18 January–13 March.*
[London : Victoria and Albert Museum, 1986] (Printed by V & A Press).
[12] p. : ill. (some col.), port. ; 20 x 20 cm.
ISBN: 1857177086
Cover title. — Text by Dick Richards. Acknowledgements / Jane Stancliffe, Richard Edgcumbe. — Bibliography: p. [8]. — Designed by V & A Design Section. — Photography by Robert Pilcher, Frank Bauer, Phil Sayer. — Stapled; col. ills. on wrappers.
EXHIBITION: vx.1986.001

V.1986.018   *Furniture of about 1900 from Austria & Hungary in the Victoria & Albert Museum* / Simon Jervis.
London : Victoria and Albert Museum, 1986 (Printed by Jolly & Barber, Rugby).
93 p. : ill. ; 28 cm.
ISBN: 0948107480
Combined subject/name index, concordance of Museum numbers. — Designed by Graham Johnson. — Ginger cloth covered boards and end-papers; dust-jacket with col. ill.

V.1986.019   *Gerda Flöckinger : 15 October–30 November 1986.*
[London] : Victoria and Albert Museum, [1986].
20 p. : ill. (chiefly col.) ; 20 x 20 cm.
ISBN: 0948107405
Introduction / Barbara Cartlidge. Acknowledgements / Richard Edgcumbe, Jane Stancliffe. — Designed by Michael Martin. — Photography by Dominic Naish. — Stapled; sized wrappers with col. ill.
EXHIBITION: vx.1986.019

V.1986.020   *The ghosts of Ham House.*
[London] : Victoria and Albert Museum, 1986 (Printed by J.E.C. Potter & Son).
14 p. : ill. ; 22 cm.
ISBN: 1851770070
Written by Maurice Tomlin. — Designed by Grundy & Northedge. — Photographed by Ken Jackson. Illustrated by Gerald Mynott. — Stapled; black wrappers, dust-jacket with col. ill.

V.1986.021   *Ham House* / Maurice Tomlin.
[London] : Victoria and Albert Museum, 1986 (Printed by Jolly & Barber, Rugby).
109 p. : ill. (chiefly col.), plans, ports. ; 25 cm.
ISBN: 0948107499
Foreword / John Morley. — Includes bibliographic references (p. 109). — Design by Laurence Bradbury Design Associates. — Coloured wrappers with photographic ills; illustrated end-papers.

V.1986.022   *Heraldic symbols : Islamic insignia and western heraldry* / William Leaf, Sally Purcell.
London : Victoria and Albert Museum, 1986 (Printed by R.J. Acford Ltd., Chichester).
126 p., [16] p. of plates : ill. (some col.) ; 26 cm.
ISBN: 0905209923
Foreword / Michael Maclagan. — Bibliography: p. 122. Glossary. — Designed by Tim Harvey. — Blue paper covered boards; dust-jacket coloured black with col. ills. — Produced by the South Leigh Press, Haslemere.

V.1986.023   *Inspiration for design : the influence of the Victoria and Albert Museum* / Barbara Morris.
London : Victoria and Albert Museum, 1986 (Produced by the South Leigh Press; printed by R.J. Acford, Chichester).
224 p., [16] p. of plates : ill. (some col.) ; 26 cm.
ISBN: 0948107391
Bibliography: p. 218–220. Index — Designed by Peter Campbell. — Grey paper covered boards; dust-jacket with ills.

v.1986.024   *An introduction to the Beaumont Press : illustrated from material in
                the National Art Library* / Eva White.
                [London : Victoria and Albert Museum], 1986 (Printed by V & A
                Press).
                23 p. : ill. ; 22 cm.
                ISBN: 1851770976
                Bibliography: p. 20. — Stapled; buff wrappers with turn-ins; device.
                EXHIBITION: vx.1986.028

v.1986.025   *An introduction to the Doves and Ashendene Presses : illustrated from
                material in the National Art Library* / Janet Skidmore.
                [London : Victoria and Albert Museum], 1986 (Printed by V & A
                Press).
                24 p. : ill., facsims., port. ; 22 cm.
                ISBN: 1851770038
                "Books, specimen and proof sheets of the Doves and Ashendene Presses held in the
                National Art Library": p. 20–24. Bibliography: p. 19. — Grey wrappers.
                EXHIBITION: vx.1986.029

v.1986.026   *An introduction to the Essex House Press : illustrated from material in
                the National Art Library* / Susanna Robson.
                [London : Victoria and Albert Museum], 1986 (Printed by V & A
                Press).
                24 p. : ill., facsims. ; 22 cm.
                ISBN: 1851770429
                "Books of the Essex House Press held in the National Art Library": p. 19–24.
                Bibliography: p. 16–17 — Ivory wrappers.
                EXHIBITION: vx.1985.029

v.1986.027   *An introduction to the Kelmscott Press : illustrated from material in
                the National Art Library* / Andrew Isherwood.
                [London : Victoria and Albert Museum], 1986 (Printed by V & A
                Press).
                28 p. : ill., facsims. ; 22 cm.
                ISBN: 1851770186
                Bibliography: p. 22. — Brownish wrappers.
                EXHIBITION: vx.1986.030

v.1986.028   *An introduction to the Nonesuch Press : illustrated from material in
                the National Art Library* / Judith Bradfield.
                [London : Victoria and Albert Museum], 1986 (Printed by V & A
                Press).
                23 p. : ill. ; 22 cm.
                ISBN: 1851770283
                Greyish wrappers.
                EXHIBITION: vx.1987.002

v.1986.029   *Japanese art and design* / editor, Joe Earle ; texts, Joe Earle, Rupert
                Faulkner, Verity Wilson, Rose Kerr, Craig Clunas ; photography, Ian
                Thomas ; design, Patrick Yapp.
                [London] : Victoria & Albert Museum, 1986 (Printed by Balding &
                Mansell, Wisbech).
                222 p. : col. ill., map ; 28 cm.

ISBN: 0948107650
At head of title: The Toshiba Gallery. — Prefaces by Shoichi Saba, Lord Carrington, Toshio Yamazaki, Sydney Giffard. — Glossary. — Sized wrappers; col. ills; illustrated end-papers.

v.1986.030   *Keyboard instruments at the Victoria and Albert Museum* / James Yorke.
London : Victoria and Albert Museum, 1986 (Printed by Butler & Tanner).
63 p. : ill. (some col.) ; 21 x 24 cm.
ISBN: 0948107049 (pbk.)
Spine title: Keyboard instruments. — Foreword / Peter Thornton. — Designed by Patrick Yapp. — Sized wrappers with col. ills.; music on end-papers.

v.1986.031   *The Lake District, a sort of national property : papers presented to a symposium held at the Victoria & Albert Museum, 20–22 October 1984.*
Cheltenham ; London : Published jointly by Countryside Commission, Victoria & Albert Museum, 1986 (Produced by CGS Studios, Cheltenham ; Printed by Wembley Press, Reading).
124 p. : ill., facsims., ports.
ISBN: 086170133X
Preface / John Murdoch. The matter of fact Paradise / Robert Woof. Et in Arcadia ego: the ruin in the landscape and Wordsworth's *Michael* / Malcolm Kelsall. Wordsworth and the ideal of nature in 1800 / Jonathan Wordsworth. Foregrounds and focus: changes in the perception of landscape, c.1800 / John Murdoch. The drawing of mountains: Constable's 1806 Lake District tour / Charles Rhyne. The cult of the cottage / John Dixon Hunt. Lakeland trails: Beatrix Potter to Schwitters / William Feaver. The art and sport of rock climbing in the English Lake District / Douglas Milner. A sort of national property: the growth of the National Parks movement in Britain / Jay Appleton. In conclusion / Adrian Phillips.

v.1986.032   *The Medieval Treasury : the art of the Middle Ages in the Victoria and Albert Museum* / edited by Paul Williamson.
[London] : Victoria and Albert Museum, 1986 (Printed by Balding + Mansell, Wisbech).
248 p. : ill. (some col.) ; 24 cm.
ISBN: 0948107383
Foreword / Roy Strong. — Bibliography: p. 244–246. Glossary. — Designed by Paul Sharp. — Sized wrappers, col. ill. on front cover.

v.1986.033   *Mulready : a book with catalogue, published to accompany the exhibition* William Mulready, 1786–1863 : *organised to celebrate the bicentenary of the artist's birth, at the Victoria and Albert Museum, London, 1 July–12 October 1986, continuing at the National Gallery of Ireland, Dublin, and at the Ulster Museum, Belfast, Autumn/Winter 1986–87* / by Marcia Pointon.
London : Victoria and Albert Museum, 1986 (Printed by Jolly & Barber, Rugby).
184 p. : ill. (some col.) ; 25 cm.
ISBN: 1851770577
Foreword / Roy Strong. — Bibliography: p. 177–180. Index. — Designed by Tim Harvey. — Photography by Ian Jones. — Sized wrappers with col. ill.
EXHIBITION: VX.1986.011

v.1986.034   *Paul and Thomas Sandby* / Luke Herrmann.
London : B.T. Batsford in association with the Victoria & Albert
Museum, 1986 (Printed by Butler & Tanner).
175 p., [8] p. of plates : ill. (some col.) ; 26 cm.
ISBN: 0713447885; 0713447893 (pbk.)
Bibliography: p. [169]–170. Index. — Wrappers coloured blue with col. ills. — Includes
catalogue of the artists' works at the V&A.
EXHIBITION: vx.1986.013

v.1986.035   *The Renier Collection of Historic and Contemporary Children's
Books : introduction to occasional lists* / [by T.R. Chester].
[London : Bethnal Green Museum, 1986.]
4 p.
Duplicated typescript; stapled.

v.1986.036   *The Rococo in England : a symposium* / edited by Charles Hind.
London : Victoria & Albert Museum, 1986 (Printed by Butler &
Tanner).
192 p. : ill. ; 23 cm.
ISBN: 0948107375
Symposium held 17–19 May at the V&A under the auspices of the Georgian Group, the
Museum and the Association of Art Historians, on the occasion of vx.1984.012. —
Introduction / Michael Snodin. The artinatural style / John Harris. Foreign decorators
and plasterers in England / Alastair Laing. Watteau and England / Marianne Roland
Michel. The Huguenots and English rococo / Tessa Murdoch. Trade cards and English
rococo / Michael Snodin. Book illustrators, mainly Gravelot and Bentley / Robert
Halsband. Frederick, Prince of Wales : a patron of the rococo / Stephen Jones. Francis
Hayman and the supper-box paintings for Vauxhall Gardens / Brian Allen. Roubiliac ;
some problems / David Bindman. Sir Henry Cheere and the response to rococo in
English sculpture / Malcolm Baker. Nicolas Gauron : a virtuoso modeller at Tournai
and Chelsea / Timothy Clifford. Isaac Ware and Chesterfield House / Roger White. —
Includes bibliographic references. — Sized wrappers with ills.

v.1986.037   *Royal gifts & Princess Daisy* / Vera Kaden and Imogen Stewart.
[London] : Victoria and Albert Museum, 1986 (Printed by J.E.C.
Potter, Stamford, Lincs.).
16 p. : ill. (some col.) ; 22 cm.
ISBN: 1851770313
Photographs by Mike Kitcatt. — Designed by V&A Design Section. — Stapled; sized
wrappers with col. ills.

v.1986.038   *Silver toys & miniatures* / Miranda Poliakoff.
[London] : Victoria & Albert Museum, [1986] (Printed and bound by
Drukkerij de Lange/van Leer, the Netherlands).
48 p. : ill. (some col.) ; 20 cm.
ISBN: 090520994X
Edited by Philippa Glanville. — Bibliography: p. 48. — Designed by Aitken Blakely. —
Photography by Geoffrey Shakerley. — Grey cloth covered boards; illustrated end-
papers; paper labels with col. ills.

v.1986.039   *The street photographs of Roger Mayne.*
[London] : Victoria & Albert Museum, 1986 (Printed by Lund
Humphries).
88 p. : chiefly ill. ; 28 cm.
ISBN: 185177002X

Text by Mark Haworth-Booth. — Bibliography: p. 83–88. — Designed by Morrison
Dalley Design Partnership. — White wrappers with ill.
EXHIBITION: VX.1986.006

v.1986.040   *Swiss stained glass designs of the Reformation.*
                [London : Victoria and Albert Museum, 1986] (Printed by the V&A
                Press).
                [12] p. : ill. ; 30 cm.
                Caption title. At head of title: Victoria & Albert Museum. — Written by
                C.M. Kauffmann. — Bibliography: p. [5]. — Stapled; no cover.
                EXHIBITION: VX.1986.005

v.1986.041   *The Ted Tinling tennis collection.*
                [London : Victoria and Albert Museum], 1986.
                23 postcards : ill., port. ; 15 cm.
                Title from box. At foot of title: Victoria & Albert Museum. — "Published to
                accompany the Ted Tinling study day held on June 17, 1986 at the Victoria and Albert
                Museum." — In white paper box, pierced with circular hole.
                EXHIBITION: VX.1986.009

v.1986.042   *Two railway alphabets* / introduction by Irene Whalley.
                [London] : Victoria and Albert Museum, 1986 (Printed by Henry
                Stone & Son, Banbury).
                [23] p. : col. ill. ; 24 cm.
                ISBN: 090520946x (pbk.)
                "A colour facsimile of two Victorian railway alphabets"–cover. — Railway alphabet.
                London: Thomas Dean and Son, 1852. The railroad alphabet. London: George
                Routledge & Sons, 188?. — Designed by Grundy & Northedge. — Stapled; sized yellow
                wrappers with col. ill.

v.1986.043   *Victoria & Albert Museum : Führer* / Julius Bryant.
                [London] : Victoria and Museum, 1986 (Gedruckt in England von
                Raithby, Lawrence and Co., De Montfort Press).
                136 p. : ill. (some col.), plans ; 22 cm.
                ISBN: 0905209494 [sic]
                German version of v.1986.046, produced by Lesley Bernstein Editorial and Translation
                Services. — Red wrappers.

v.1986.044   *Victoria & Albert Museum : guía* / Julius Bryant.
                Spanish version of v.1986.046, produced by Lesley Bernstein Editorial and Translation
                Services. — Unseen. Information from V&A Publications Department catalogue.

v.1986.045   *Victoria & Albert Museum : guida* / Julius Bryant.
                [London] : Victoria and Albert Museum, 1986 (Stampato dalla
                Raithby, Lawrence and Co. alla De Montfort Press).
                136 p. : ill. (some col.), plans ; 22 cm.
                ISBN: 0905209494 [sic]
                Italian version of v.1986.046, produced by Lesley Bernstein Editorial and Translation
                Services. — Red wrappers.

v.1986.046   *Victoria & Albert Museum : guide* / Julius Bryant.
                [London] : Victoria and Albert Museum, 1986 (Printed by Raithby,
                Lawrence and Co. at the De Montfort Press).
                136 p. : ill. (some col.), plans ; 22 cm.
                ISBN: 0905209494 [sic]
                Introduction by Roy Strong. — Includes index. — Designed by Howard Brown. — Red
                wrappers.

v.1986.047   *Victoria & Albert Museum : guide* / Julius Bryant.
French version of v.1986.046, produced by Lesley Bernstein Editorial and Translation
Services. — Unseen. Information from V&A Publications Department catalogue.

1987

v.1987.001   *Ascher : Zika and Lida Ascher ; fabric, art, fashion* / text Valerie D.
Mendes and Frances M. Hinchcliffe ; design Patrick Yapp.
London : Victoria & Albert Museum, 1987 (Printed by Balding +
Mansell).
260 p. : ill. (some col.) ; 27 cm.
Foreword / Roy Strong. — Sized wrappers with ills: illustrated end-papers.
EXHIBITION: VX.1987.007

v.1987.002   *Catalogue of the W.H. Smith Illustration Awards 1987 : Wednesday
15th July 1987 to Sunday 1st November 1987.*
[London] : Victoria and Albert Museum, 1987 (Printed by V & A
Press).
[30] p. : ill. ; 21 cm.
ISBN: 1851770259
Cover title: W.H. Smith illustration awards. — Designed by Splash of Paint. — Stapled;
col. ill. on white wrappers.
EXHIBITION: VX.1987.012

v.1987.003   *Chinese export art and design* / editor, Craig Clunas ; texts, Craig
Clunas, Verity Wilson, Rose Kerr, Nick Pearce ; photography, Ian
Thomas ; design, Patrick Yapp.
[London] : Victoria and Albert Museum, 1987 (Printed by Westerham
Press).
120 p., [7] p. of plates : col.ill. ; 25 cm.
ISBN: 1851770003
Preface by Gerald Godfrey and Lord Carrington. — Sized wrappers with col. ills. and
decorated end-papers.

v.1987.004   *Ehret's flowering plants.*
Exeter ; London : Webb & Bower and Michael Joseph Ltd. in
association with the Victoria and Albert Museum, 1987 (Printed by
AGT, Toledo).
63 p. : ill. (some col.), port. ; 25 cm.
(The Victoria and Albert natural history illustrators)
ISBN: 0863501761
Author: Gill Saunders. — Designed by Williams and Phoa. — Paper covered boards
with col. ills.

v.1987.005   *Floral borders* / introduction by Hilary Young.
Exeter ; London : Webb and Bower and Michael Joseph in association
with the Victoria and Albert Museum, 1987 (Printed and bound by
Mandarin Offset International, Hong Kong).
13 p., 32 p. of plates : col. ill. ; 21 cm.
(The Victoria and Albert colour books)
ISBN: 0863501494
Bibliography: p. 13. — Book, cover and slip case design by Carroll, Dempsey & Thirkell
Ltd. — Decorated cover and lining paper. — Published in the U.S.A. by H.N. Abrams.

v.1987.006   *Fritz Maierhofer : 9 December 1987–6 March 1988.*
                  [London : Victoria and Albert Museum, 1987] (Typeset and printed
                  by V & A Press).
                  [16] p. : ill. (some col.), port. ; 20 cm.
                  ISBN: 1851770909
                  By Jane Stancliffe and Richard Edgcumbe. Introduction / Tony Laws. — Designed by
                  Michael Martin, V&A Design Studio. — Photography by Dominic Naish. — Stapled;
                  ill. on wrappers.
                  EXHIBITION: vx.1987.018

v.1987.007   *Gould's exotic birds.*
                  Exeter ; London : Webb & Bower and Michael Joseph Ltd. in
                  association with the Victoria and Albert Museum, 1987 (Printed by
                  AGT, Toledo).
                  63 p. : chiefly ill. (some col.), ports. ; 25 cm.
                  (The Victoria and Albert natural history illustrators)
                  ISBN: 0863501753
                  Author: Maureen Lambourne. — Designed by Williams and Phoa. — Paper covered
                  boards with col. ills.

v.1987.008   *Hand-coloured British prints : 18th March to 5th July 1987 /*
                  Elizabeth Miller.
                  [London : Victoria and Albert Museum] 1987 (Printing and
                  origination by S. Straker and Sons).
                  48 p. : ill. (chiefly col.), ports. ; 20 cm.
                  ISBN: 0948107936
                  Includes bibliographic references. — Design: John Bloxham. — Wrappers coloured blue
                  with col. ill.
                  EXHIBITION: vx.1987.005

v.1987.009   *An introduction to the Golden Cockerel Press : illustrated from*
                  material in the National Art Library / Julia Bigham.
                  [London : Victoria and Albert Museum], 1987 (Printed by V & A
                  Press).
                  28 p. : ill. ; 22 cm.
                  ISBN: 1851770356
                  Bibliography: p. 21. — Dark green wrappers.
                  EXHIBITION: vx.1987.020

v.1987.010   *An introduction to the Gregynog Press : illustrated from material in*
                  the National Art Library / Wendy Fish.
                  [London : Victoria and Albert Museum], 1987.
                  22 p. : ill. ; 21 cm.
                  ISBN: 1851770054
                  Bibliography: p.18.
                  EXHIBITION: vx.1987.021

v.1987.011   *Patterns for papers /* introduction by Sarah Postgate.
                  Exeter ; London : Webb and Bower and Michael Joseph in association
                  with the Victoria and Albert Museum, 1987 (Printed and bound by
                  Mandarin Offset International, Hong Kong).
                  13 p., 32 p. of plates : col. ill. ; 21 cm.
                  (The Victoria and Albert colour books)

ISBN: 086350148
Bibliography: p. 13. — Book, cover and slip case design by Carroll, Dempsey & Thirkell
Ltd. — Decorated cover and lining paper. — Published in the U.S.A. by H.N. Abrams.
— Illustrated with examples from the Curwen Press.

v.1987.012   *Patterns for textiles* / introduction by Hilary Young.
Exeter ; London : Webb and Bower and Michael Joseph in association
with the Victoria and Albert Museum, 1987 (Printed and bound by
Mandarin Offset International, Hong Kong).
13 p., 32 p. of plates : col. ill. ; 21 cm.
(The Victoria and Albert colour books)
ISBN: 0863501508
Bibliography: p. 13. — Book, cover and slip case design by Carroll, Dempsey & Thirkell
Ltd. — Decorated cover and lining paper. — Published in the U.S.A. by H.N. Abrams.
— Based on albums of designs in the Victoria and Albert Museum.

v.1987.013   *Penguin publications for children.*
London : Bethnal Green Museum of Childhood, 1987.
24 p. : ill., facsims. ; 21 cm.
(Occasional list / Renier Collection of Historic and Contemporary
Children's Books ; no. 2)
Cover title. — Compiled by Tessa Rose Chester. — "Autumn 1987"–cover. —
Reproduced typescript, stapled. Yellow wrappers.

v.1987.014   *The royal photographs by Sir Cecil Beaton : an exhibition in the
Photography Galleries, Henry Cole Wing, Victoria and Albert
Museum, 17 September 1987–1 February 1988.*
London : Victoria & Albert Museum, [1987] (Printed by the V&A
Press).
16 p. : ports. ; 30 cm.
ISBN: 1851770607
Foreword / Roy Strong. — Bibliography: p. 16. — Designed by Michael Martin,
V & A Design Section. — Stapled; grey wrappers; white dust-jacket with col. port.
EXHIBITION: vx.1987.015

v.1987.015   *Spirit of Christmas : Christmas around the world : a booklet to
accompany the seventh "Spirit of Christmas" exhibition at Bethnal
Green Museum of Childhood* / compiled by Halina Pasierbska.
[London : Bethnal Green Museum of Childhood, 1987.]
[46] p. : ill., maps ; 30 cm.
Cover title: Spirit of Christmas round [sic] the world. — Bibliography: p. [46]. —
Stapled sheets.
EXHIBITION: vx.1987.bgm.006

v.1987.016   Struwwelpeter : *editions, translations and imitations in the Renier
Collection.*
London : Bethnal Green Museum of Childhood, 1987.
20 p. : ill., 21 cm.
(Occasional list / Renier Collection of Historic and Contemporary
Children's Books ; no. 1)
Cover title. — Compiled by Tessa Rose Chester. — Reproduced typescript. Stapled; blue
wrappers. — On Heinrich Hoffmann.

v.1987.017   *Susie Cooper productions* / by Ann Eatwell.
[London : Victoria and Albert Museum, 1987] (Printed by CTD
Printers).
107 p. : ill. (some col.) ; 25 cm.
(V & A ceramic series)
Foreword / Roy Strong. — Bibliography: p. 106–107. — Designed by Ian Logan Design
Co. — Sized wrappers coloured green with col. ills.; decorated end-papers.
EXHIBITION: vx.1987.009

v.1987.018   *The Theatre Museum unpacks : treasures from the costume collection.*
[London : The Museum, 1987.]
[28] p. : ill. (some col.), ports ; 26 cm.
Text by Sarah C. Woodcock, Philip Dyer. — 14 loose leaves in a red folder.
EXHIBITION: vx.1987.THM.003

v.1987.019   *Tile paintings* / introduction by Gill Saunders.
Exeter ; London : Webb and Bower and Michael Joseph in association
with the Victoria and Albert Museum, 1987.
(The Victoria and Albert colour books)
ISBN: 0863501478
Published in the U.S.A. by H.N. Abrams. — Unseen. Record from OCLC.

v.1987.020   *Turkish velvet cushion covers* / Jennifer M. Wearden.
London : Victoria & Albert Museum, [ca. 1987].
(Leaflet / Victoria and Albert Museum, Department of Textiles and
Dress ; no. 5)
Cover title. — Includes bibliographic references. — Designed by the V&A Design
Section. — Stapled; col. ills. on wrappers.

v.1987.021   *Wally Gilbert, Thomas Gentille : 17 June–20 September.*
[London : Victoria & Albert Museum], 1987 (Printed by Gaffyne &
Brown).
[16] p. : ill. (some col.), ports. ; 20 x 20 cm.
ISBN: 1851770100
Cover title. At foot of title: Victoria & Albert Museum. — Includes bibliographic
references. — Designed by V&A Design Studio. — Photography by Dominic Naish. —
Stapled; col. ill. on wrappers.
EXHIBITION: vx.1987.010

v.1987.022   *Witness in brass.*
[London : Victoria & Albert Museum, 1987] (Designed and printed
by the V & A Press).
43 p. : ill. ; 26 cm.
Cover title. — Prepared by John Page-Phillips. Introduction / John Murdoch.. —
Bibliography: p. 42. — Stapled; cover ills. printed on black.
EXHIBITION: vx.1987.014

1988

v.1988.001   *The Burberry story : until 20th August 1989*
London : Victoria & Albert Museum, [1988?].
1 sheet : ill. ; 22 x 68 cm. folded to 22 x 9 cm.
By Margot Coatts.
EXHIBITION: vx.1988.024

v.1988.002   *Chinese furniture* / Craig Clunas ; photography by Ian Thomas.
                London : Bamboo, 1988 (Printed by Springbourne Press, Basildon).
                119 p. : ill.(some col.), maps ; 26 cm.
                (Far Eastern series).
                ISBN: 1870076060
                At foot of title: Victoria and Albert Museum. — Includes bibliographic references.
                Index. — Dark brown cloth covered boards; dust-jacket with ills.

v.1988.003   *Circus! circus! : catalogue of an exhibition at the Theatre Museum, 15
                December 1988 until 2 April 1989.*
                [London : The Museum, 1988.]
                [12] p. : ill. ; 30 cm.
                Cover title. — Exhibition selected and catalogued by Catherine Haill and Jane
                Broughton-Perry. — Catalogue design by David Driver. — Stapled; ills. on wrappers.
                EXHIBITION: vx.1988.THM.005

v.1988.004   *Designs for shawls* / introduction by Hilary Young.
                Exeter ; London : Webb and Bower and Michael Joseph in association
                with the Victoria and Albert Museum, 1988 (Printed and bound by
                Mandarin Offset International, Hong Kong).
                13 p., 32 p. of plates : col. ill. ; 21 cm.
                (The Victoria and Albert colour books)
                Bibliography: p. 13. — Design by Carroll, Dempsey & Thirkell. — Decorated cover and
                lining paper. — Published in the U.S.A. by H.N. Abrams.

v.1988.005   *English country traditions* / written by Ian Niall ; wood engravings by
                Christopher Wormell.
                [London] : Victoria & Albert Museum, 1988 (Printed at the Hand
                Press, Westerham).
                74 p. : ill. ; 24 cm.
                ISBN: 094810743X
                Designed by John Gorham. — Dark green cloth covered boards and slip-case; decorated
                end-papers. Title label pasted on. — Limited ed. of 500 copies.

v.1988.006   *English medieval furniture and woodwork* / by Charles Tracy.
                [London] : Victoria and Albert Museum, 1988 (Printed by Napier,
                Jones Ltd.).
                xxviii, 29–216 p. : ill. (some col.) ; 29 cm.
                Foreword / Simon Jervis. — Bibliography: p. 208–215. Index of places. Concordance of
                Museum numbers. — Designed by Tim Harvey. — Dark green cloth covered boards,
                title stamped in gold. Illustrative coloured label on front cover. — Catalogue of the
                V&A's collection.

v.1988.007   *Fashion magazines from the 1890s to the 1980s : an account based on
                the holdings of the National Art Library* / by Alice Grant.
                [London : National Art Library, 1988.]
                16 p. : ill., facsims. ; 30 cm.
                ISBN: 1851770704
                Bibliography: p. 16. — Stapled; ills. on wrappers.
                EXHIBITION: vx.1987.019

v.1988.008   *G.A. Henty.*
                London : Bethnal Green Museum of Childhood, 1988.
                28 p. : ill., facsims. ; 21 cm.

(Occasional list / Renier Collection of Historic and Contemporary Children's Books ; no. 4)

Cover title. — Compiled by Tessa Rose Chester — "Autumn 1988"–Cover. — Includes indexes. Reproduced typescript, stapled. Grey wrappers.

V.1988.009   *A golden treasury : jewellery from the Indian subcontinent* / Susan Stronge, Nima Smith and J.C. Harle.
London : Victoria and Albert Museum in association with Mapin Publishing, Ahmedabad, 1988 (Printed and bound by Mandarin Offset, Hong Kong).
144 p. : ill. (chiefly col.), map ; 29 cm.
(Indian art series)
ISBN: 0944142168
Series editor: John Guy. — Bibliography: p. 140–142. Glossary. Index. — Designer: Yvonne Dedman. — Green paper covered boards; decorated end-papers; dust-jacket with col. ills. — Published in the USA by Grantha Corp., Middleton, NJ.
EXHIBITION: VX.1988.XXX.001

V.1988.010   *A history of children's book illustration* / Joyce Irene Whalley and Tessa Rose Chester.
London : John Murray with the Victoria and Albert Museum, 1988 (Produced by the South Leigh Press, Haslemere; printed by BAS Printers, Over Wallop).
268 p., [32] p. of plates : ill. (some col.) ; 26 cm.
ISBN: 0719545846
Bibliography: p. 249–252. Index. — Designed by Peter Campbell. — Blue paper covered boards; pictorial dust jacket.

V.1988.011   *Japanese stencils* / introduction by Rupert Faulkner.
Exeter ; London : Webb and Bower and Michael Joseph in association with the Victoria and Albert Museum, 1988 (Printed and bound by Mandarin Offset International, Hong Kong).
10, [5] p., 32 p. of plates : col. ill. ; 21 cm.
(The Victoria and Albert colour books)
Bibliography: p. [12]. — Design by Carroll, Dempsey & Thirkell. — Decorated cover and lining paper. — Published in the U.S.A. by H.N. Abrams.

V.1988.012   *Moveable books.*
London : Bethnal Green Museum of Childhood, 1988.
40 p. : ill. ; 21 cm.
(Occasional list / Renier Collection of Historic and Contemporary Children's Books ; 3)
Cover title. — Compiled by Tessa Rose Chester. — Includes index. — "Spring 1988"–Cover. — Reproduced typescript, stapled. Green wrappers.

V.1988.013   *Northern Gothic sculpture 1200–1450* / Paul Williamson ; assisted by Peta Evelyn.
[London] : Victoria and Albert Museum, 1988 (Printed by Jolly & Barber, Rugby).
211 p. : ill., 1 map ; 31 cm.
ISBN: 0948107464
Bibliography: p. 201–209. Index of collectors and dealers. Concordance of Museum numbers. — Designed by Sharon Ellis. — Black paper-covered boards. Illustrative dust-wrapper. — Catalogue of the V&A's holdings.

v.1988.014   *Novelty fabrics* / introduction by Valerie Mendes.
Exeter ; London : Webb and Bower and Michael Joseph in association
with the Victoria and Albert Museum, 1988 (Printed and bound by
Mandarin Offset International, Hong Kong).
10, [5] p., 32 p. of plates : col. ill. ; 21 cm.
(The Victoria and Albert colour books)
Design by Carroll, Dempsey & Thirkell. — Decorated cover and lining paper. —
Published in the U.S.A. by H.N. Abrams.

v.1988.015   *Playing cards in the Victoria and Albert Museum* / Jean Hamilton.
London : H.M.S.O., 1988.
79 p. : ill. (some col.) ; 25 cm.
ISBN: 0112904610
At head of title: Victoria and Albert Museum. — Bibliography: p. 75.

v.1988.016   *A record of pop : images of a decade : photographs by Harry
Hammond.* [New ed.]
London : Victoria and Albert Museum, 1988 (Printed by BAS
Printers).
160 p. : chiefly ill., ports. ; 28 cm.
ISBN: 1851770062
Cover title. — Designed by David Fuller. — Sized wrappers coloured black, with ill. —
First published : Sidgwick and Jackson, 1984.
EXHIBITION: VX.1988.THM.001

v.1988.017   *Richard Redgrave, 1804–1888* / edited by Susan P. Casteras and
Ronald Parkinson ; with essays by Elizabeth Bonython . . . [et al.].
New Haven ; London : Published in association with the Victoria and
Albert Museum and the Yale Center for British Art by Yale University
Press, 1988 (Printed by the Bath Press, Avon).
175 p. ; ill. (some col.) ; 26 cm.
ISBN: 0300043058
Preface / Elizabeth Esteve-Coll, Duncan Robinson. Introduction / John Murdoch.
Richard and Samuel Redgrave and their family / Elizabeth Bonython. 'Social wrongs' :
the painted sermons of Richard Redgrave / Susan P. Casteras. Richard Redgrave the
draughtsman / Robert Twyman-Heaven. Redgrave and Felix Summerly's art-
manufactures / Shirley Bury. Redgrave as art educator, museum official and design
theorist / Anthony Burton. 'Green lanes and chequered shade' : the landscapes of
Richard Redgrave / Susan P. Casteras. Redgrave and the Royal collection / Oliver
Millar. Richard Redgrave today / Lionel Lambourne. — Includes bibliographic
references. Index. — Designed by Faith Glasgow. — Sized wrappers, with col. ill. —
"The softback version is a V&A Museum book . . ."–label pasted in.
EXHIBITION: VX.1988.003

v.1988.018   *Robert Adam* / by Alistair Rowan.
London : Victoria and Albert Museum, 1988 (Printed by Jolly &
Barber, Rugby).
122 p. : ill., plans ; 31 cm.
(Catalogues of architectural drawings in the Victoria and Albert
Museum)
ISBN: 1851770704
Foreword / John Murdoch. — Bibliography: p. 113–116. Index. Concordance of
Museum numbers. — Designed by Simon Rendall. — Orange paper covered boards;
dust-jacket with col. ills. and author photograph.

V.1988.019 *Thirties floral fabrics* / introduction by Frances Hinchcliffe.
Exeter ; London : Webb and Bower and Michael Joseph in association
with the Victoria and Albert Museum, 1988 (Printed and bound by
Mandarin Offset International, Hong Kong).
11, [4] p., 32 p. of plates : col. ill. ; 21 cm.
(The Victoria and Albert colour books)
Bibliography: p. [13]. — Design by Carroll, Dempsey & Thirkell. — Decorated cover
and lining paper. — Published in the U.S.A. by H.N. Abrams. — Unseen. Record from
OCLC.

1989

V.1989.001 *Book art : a selection of 1988 acquisitions in the National Art
Library.*
[London : The Library, 1989.]
1 sheet ; 30 cm.
Photocopied typescript.
EXHIBITION: VX.1989.006

V.1989.002 *Doll and toy stories. 1.*
London : Bethnal Green Museum of Childhood, 1989.
24 p. : ill., facsims. ; 21 cm.
(Occasional list / Renier Collection of Historic and Contemporary
Children's Books ; 5)
Cover title: — Designed and compiled by Tessa Rose Chester. — "Spring 1989"–cover.
— Includes indexes. — Duplicated typescript; stapled. Orange wrappers.

V.1989.003 *Doll and toy stories. 2.*
London : Bethnal Green Museum of Childhood, 1989.
24 p. : ill., facsims. ; 21 cm.
(Occasional list / Renier Collection of Historic and Contemporary
Children's Books ; no. 6)
Cover title. — Designed and compiled by Tessa Rose Chester. — "Autumn
1989"–cover. — Includes indexes. — Duplicated typescript; stapled. Orange
wrappers.

V.1989.004 *Fifties furnishing fabrics* / introduction by Frances Hinchcliffe.
Exeter ; London : Webb & Bower in association with Michael Joseph
[and] the Victoria and Albert Museum, 1989 (Printed and bound in
Hong Kong).
12, [3] p., 32 p. of plates : col. ill. ; 21 cm.
(The Victoria and Albert colour books. Series 4)
ISBN: 0863502997
Book, cover and slipcase design by Carroll, Dempsey & Thirkell. — Decorated cover
and lining paper. — Published in the U.S.A. by H.N. Abrams.

V.1989.005 *Going Dutch : decorative arts from the age of William & Mary.*
[London : Trustees of the Victoria and Albert Museum : Governor and
Company of the Bank of England, 1989.]
[12] p. : ill. (chiefly col.) ; 21 x 10 cm.
Cover title. — Stapled in illustrated wrappers.
EXHIBITION: VX.1989.XXX.002

V.1989.006   *Ikats* / introduction by Clare Woodthorpe Browne.
Exeter ; London : Webb & Bower in association with Michael Joseph
[and] the Victoria and Albert Museum, 1989 (Printed and bound in
Hong Kong).
12, [3] p., 32 p. of plates : col. ill. ; 21 cm.
(The Victoria and Albert colour books. Series 4)
ISBN: 0863502989
Bibliography: p. [13]. — Book, cover and slipcase design by Carroll, Dempsey &
Thirkell. — Decorated cover and lining paper. — Published in the U.S.A. by
H.N. Abrams.

V.1989.007   *Indian architectural designs* / introduction by Susan Stronge.
Exeter ; London : Webb & Bower in association with Michael Joseph
[and] the Victoria and Albert Museum, 1989 (Printed and bound in
Hong Kong).
12, [3] p., 30 p. of plates : col. ill. ; 21 cm.
(The Victoria and Albert colour books. Series 4)
ISBN: 0863503012
Bibliography: p. [13]. — Book, cover and slipcase design by Carroll, Dempsey &
Thirkell. — Decorated cover and lining paper. — Published in the U.S.A. by H.N.
Abrams.

V.1989.008   *National Art Library : periodicals from the 1890s to the 1980s.*
[London] : National Art Library, Victoria & Albert Museum, 1989.
1 sheet ; 30 cm.
Photocopied typescript.
EXHIBITION: VX.1989.011

V.1989.009   *The Orient observed : images of the Middle East from the Searight
collection* / by Briony Llewellyn.
London : Victoria and Albert Museum in association with Shell
International Petroleum Co., 1989 (Printed by the Roundwood Press).
147 p. : ill. (some col.) ; 28 cm.
ISBN: 1851770038
Bibliography: p. 45. Index of artists. — Designed by Bryan Denyer. — Sized wrappers
with col. ills.
EXHIBITION: VX.1989.025

V.1989.010   *Oxtoby's rockers : twelve great rockers : from Bill Haley to Little
Richard : from a collection of paintings destroyed by fire in 1979.*
[London] : Theatre Museum, Victoria and Albert Museum, [1989].
[12] leaves of plates : ports. ; 41 cm.
In slip case. — Bears label: The artist forbade sale of this publication because of poor
colour reproduction.

V.1989.011   *Persian printed cottons* / introduction by Jennifer Mary Wearden.
Exeter ; London : Webb and Bower in association with Michael
Joseph [and] the Victoria and Albert Museum, 1989 (Printed and
bound in Hong Kong).
12, [3] p., 32 p. of plates : chiefly col. ill. ; 20 cm.
(The Victoria and Albert colour books. Series 4)
ISBN: 0863503004
Bibliography: p. [13]. — Book, cover and slipcase design by Carroll, Dempsey &
Thirkell. — Decorated cover and lining paper. — Published in the U.S.A. by
H.N. Abrams.

v.1989.012   *Photography now* / Mark Haworth-Booth.
                London : Dirk Nishen, in association with the Victoria & Albert
                Museum, 1989 (Printing: H. Heenemann, D-Berlin).
                143 p. : ill. (some col.), 30 cm.
                ISBN: 185378012X
                Preface / Elizabeth Esteve-Coll. — Wrappers coloured black with col. ill.
                EXHIBITION: vx.1989.002

v.1989.013   *Scandinavia : ceramics & glass in the twentieth century : the
                collections of the Victoria & Albert Museum* / by Jennifer Hawkins
                Opie.
                London : Victoria & Albert Museum, 1989 (Printed by Arti Graphice
                Motta, Milan).
                183 p. : ill. (some col.), map ; 25 cm.
                ISBN: 1851770712
                Foreword / Elizabeth Esteve-Coll. Prelude : a personal view / J.G.V. Mallet. — Index.
                Concordance of Museum numbers. — Designed by Morrison Dalley Design Partnership.
                — Sized wrappers coloured black, with ills.
                EXHIBITION: vx.1989.019

v.1989.014   *Shooting stars! : the theatre photography of Houston Rogers.*
                [London : Theatre Museum?, 1989.]
                1 sheet, folded : 1 ill. ; 30 cm.
                EXHIBITION: vx.1989.THM.002

v.1989.015   *V&A cats* / with an introduction by Beryl Reid.
                London : Victoria and Albert Museum, 1989.
                96 p. : ill. (some col.) ; 21 cm.
                ISBN: 1851770569
                Compiled by Michael Wilson. — Bibliography: p. 96. — Designed by Chrissie Charlton
                & Co. — Black cloth covered boards; dust-jacket with col. ills.

1990

v.1990.001   *Apsley House, Wellington Museum* / Simon Jervis & Maurice Tomlin.
                [Rev.]
                London : Victoria and Albert Museum, 1990.
                85 p. : col. ill. ; 25 cm.
                ISBN: 0905209680
                Unseen. Record from OCLC.

v.1990.002   *Artifacts at the end of a decade : National Art Library, 7 March–29
                April 1990.*
                [London : The Library, 1990.]
                [8] leaves ; 30 cm.
                Introduction and handlist. — Photocopy.
                EXHIBITION: vx.1990.006

v.1990.003   *Arts of India : 1550–1900* / Rosemary Crill, John Guy, Veronica
                Murphy, Susan Stronge and Deborah Swallow ; edited by John Guy
                and Deborah Swallow.
                London : Victoria & Albert Museum, 1990 (Printed by Amilcare
                Pizzi).

240 p. : ill. (some col.) ; 29 cm.
ISBN: 1851770224
Published on the occasion of the opening of the Nehru Gallery of Indian Art. Prefaces:
Lord Armstrong of Ilminster, Elizabeth Esteve-Coll. — Bibliography: p. 230–237.
Glossary. Index. — Illustrated endpapers. Blue cloth covered boards; dust-jacket
coloured buff with col. ills. Or sized wrappers.

V.1990.004   *British design, 1790–1990* / V&A.
[U.S.A.? : Victoria & Albert Museum?, 1990.]
[8] p. : col. ill. ; 28 cm.
Cover title. — Foreword / Antony Acland (British Ambassador to the U.S.A.). Preface
by Elizabeth Esteve-Coll. Text by Catherine McDermott. — Stapled. — Published to
promote an exhibition from the collections of the Victoria and Albert Museum at the
South Coast Plaza Retail Center, Orange County, California.
EXHIBITION: VX.1990.XXX.004

V.1990.005   *British studio pottery : the Victoria and Albert Museum collection* /
Oliver Watson ; photography by Ian Thomas and Mike Kitcatt.
Oxford : Phaidon, Christie's, in association with the Victoria and
Albert Museum, 1990 (Printed and bound by Butler & Tanner).
287 p. : ill. (some col.) ; 29 cm.
ISBN: 0714880671
Preface / J.V.G. Mallet. — Bibliography: p. 286–287. Concordance of Museum
numbers. Index. Potters' marks. — Designed by Andrew Shoolbred. — Tan cloth-style
paper covered boards; dust jacket with col. ills.
EXHIBITION: VX.1990.019

V.1990.006   *Catalogue of British oil paintings, 1820–1860* / Ronald Parkinson.
London : H.M.S.O., 1990.
xx, 314 p. : ill. (some col.) ; 30 cm.
ISBN: 0112904637
At head of title: Victoria & Albert Museum. — Preface / John Murdoch. — Includes
bibliographic references. Indexes of titles, sitters, places, literary sources, donors. —
Green leather-style boards; green end-papers; dust-jacket with col. ills.

V.1990.007   *Chinese dress* / Verity Wilson ; photography by Ian Thomas. [Repr.]
Hong Kong : [London?] : Oxford University Press, in association with
the Victoria and Albert Museum ; Bamboo Publishing, 1990.
135 p. : ill.(some col.), ports ; 26 cm.
(Far Eastern series)
ISBN: 0195851676
Bibliography: p.131. Index. — Sized wrappers, chiefly red and black, with col. ill.

V.1990.008   *Ernest Nister.*
London : Bethnal Green Museum of Childhood, 1990.
52 p. : ill. ; 21 cm.
(Occasional list / Renier Collection of Historic and Contemporary
Children's Books ; no. 8)
"Ernest Nister: publications in the Renier Collection" – p.[1]. — Compiled by Tessa
Chester. — Errata slip inserted.

V.1990.009   *German Renaissance medals : a catalogue of the collection in the
Victoria and Albert Museum* / by Marjorie Trusted.
London : Victoria & Albert Museum, 1990 (Produced by Alan Sutton
Publishing, Gloucester).
128 p. : ill., ports. ; 31 cm.

ISBN: 1851770135
Includes bibliographic references. Indexes of subjects and Museum numbers. — Green
cloth covered boards; dust-jacket.

V.1990.010   *Kate Greenaway.*
London : Bethnal Green Museum of Childhood, 1990.
36 p. : ill., facsims. ; 21 cm.
(Occasional list / Renier Collection of Historic and Contemporary
Children's Books ; no. 7)
Caption title. — "Designed and compiled by Tessa Rose Chester"–p. 36. — "Autumn
1989"–cover. — Includes indexes.

V.1990.011   *Later Chinese bronzes* / Rose Kerr ; photography by Ian Thomas.
London : Bamboo Publishing in association with the Victoria and
Albert Museum, 1990 (Printed by Toppan Printing Co.,
Singapore).
115 p. : ill. (some col.), map ; 26 x 26 cm.
(Far Eastern series)
ISBN: 1870076117
Bibliography: p. 111. Index. — Designed by Denyer Design Associates. — Dark blue
cloth covered boards; dust-jacket with col. ills.

V.1990.012   *Miss Jones and her fairyland : Wedgwood fairyland lustre : the work
of Daisy Makeig-Jones* / by Una des Fontaines, Lionel Lambourne and
Ann Eatwell (editor).
[London] : Victoria & Albert Museum, [1990] (Printed by Napier,
Jones).
47 p. : ill. (some col.), 1 port. ; 25 cm.
ISBN: 1851770348
At foot of title: The Weinstein gift to the Victoria and Albert Museum. — Foreword /
Elizabeth Esteve-Coll. Preface / J.G.V. Mallet, Suzanne and Frederic Weinstein. —
Bibliography: p. [48]. — Designed by Richard Cottingham, V&A Design Studio. —
Sized wrappers with col. photographs.
EXHIBITION: VX.1990.021

V.1990.013   *The Nehru Gallery of Indian Art, 1550–1900 : a guide for schools.*
London : Victoria & Albert Museum, 1990.
16 p. : ill., maps ; 30 cm.
Cover title. — Stapled; wrappers printed in yellow on dark blue.

V.1990.014   *The plastics age : from modernity to post-modernity* / edited by
Penny Sparke.
[London] : Victoria & Albert Museum, 1990 (Printed by BAS
Printers).
159 p. : ill. (some col.) ; 28 cm.
ISBN: 1851770666
PLASTICS PRE-HISTORY 1860–1918: Introduction. The technology of early plastics /
Susan Mossman. The first plastic / Robert Friedel. PLASTICS AND MODERNITY
1915–1960: Introduction. Plastics in the American machine age 1920–1950 / Jeffrey L.
Meikle. Plastics and the future. V.E. Yarsley and E.G. Couzens. Industrial design and
commercial art / John Gloag. Perceptions of plastics : a study of plastics in Britain
1945–1956 / Claire Catterall. The Italian way to plastics / Giampiero Bosoni. PLASTICS
AND POST-MODERNITY 1961–1990: Introduction. Plastics and pop culture / Penny
Sparke. Triumph of software / Reyner Banham. Plastic / Roland Barthes. Natural wood,
cultural wood / Jean Baudrillard. Objects and their skin / Ezio Manzini. Plastic laminate.

Barbara Radice. And of plastics? / Ezio Manzini. Plastics in the '80s / Sylvia Katz. — Bibliography: p.154–5. Index. — Designed by Bernard Higton. — Sized wrappers with col. ills.
EXHIBITION: VX.1990.003

V.1990.015   *Recording Britain : a pictorial Domesday of pre-war Britain* / David Mellor, Gill Saunders and Patrick Wright.
London : David & Charles in association with Victoria & Albert Museum, 1990 (Printed by C.S. Graphics, Singapore).
160 p. : ill. (chiefly col.) ; 25 x 28 cm.
ISBN: 0715397982
Includes index. — Typeset and designed by John Youé. — Green paper covered boards; dust-jacket with col. ills.
EXHIBITION: VX.1990.017

V.1990.016   *Silver in Tudor and early Stuart England : a social history and catalogue of the national collection, 1480–1660* / Philippa Glanville.
[London] : Victoria and Albert Museum, 1990 (Printed by BAS Printers, Over Wallop).
528 p. : ill. (some col). ; 29 cm.
ISBN: 1851770305
Foreword / Elizabeth Esteve-Coll. — Bibliography: p. [506]–514. Index. Concordance of Museum numbers. — Designed and produced by Patrick Yapp. — Decorated endpapers. Black cloth covered boards. Black dust-jacket with ills.

V.1990.017   *Theatre caricatures by Al Frueh : West end meets Broadway* / introduction by Mike & Nancy Frueh.
London : Theatre Museum, [1990] (Printed by the V&A Press).
1 v. : ill. ; 30 cm.
EXHIBITION: VX.1990.THM.001

V.1990.018   *Victoria & Albert Museum : a guide for schools.*
London : V&A, [1990].
24 p. : ill. ; 30 cm.
Introduction from the Director / Elizabeth Esteve-Coll. — Stapled; wrappers printed in blue and red, with ills. Outside and lower edges of back cover extended into flaps.

V.1990.019   *Wooden toys 1990 : Bethnal Green Museum of Childhood, 14 March–29 April : handlist* / organised in conjunction with John Gould of the London College of Furniture, City Poly.
[London : The Museum, 1990.]
12 p. ; 30 cm.
Cover title. — Typescript reproduced on grey paper; stapled.
EXHIBITION: VX.1990.BGM.002

V.1990.020   *The world of William : Richmal Crompton's schoolboy hero : 10 August–4 November 1990, Bethnal Green Museum of Childhood, London.*
[London : The Museum, 1990.]
19 p. ; 30 cm.
Caption title. Cover title: The world of William : handlist of exhibits in the exhibition. — Photocopy.
EXHIBITION: VX.1990.BGM.004

1991

V.1991.001   *The art of death : visual culture in the English death ritual*
c.1500–c.1800 / Nigel Llewellyn.
London : Reaktion, in association with the Victoria and Albert
Museum, 1991 (Printed and bound by BAS Printers, Over Wallop).
160 p. : ill. (some col.), ports. ; 24 cm.
ISBN: 0948462167
Bibliography: p. 146–50. Index. — Designed by Humphrey Stone. Jacket design
by Ron Costley. — Sized wrappers with col. ill.
EXHIBITION: VX.1992.001

V.1991.002   *Chinese art and design : the T.T. Tsui Gallery of Chinese Art* /
editor Rose Kerr ; texts, Rose Kerr, Verity Wilson, Craig Clunas ;
photography, Ian Thomas ; design, Patrick Yapp.
London : Victoria and Albert Museum, 1991 (Origination and
printing by Arnoldo Mondadori, Verona).
255 p. : ill. (chiefly col.), maps ; 28 cm.
ISBN: 1851770399; 1851770178 (pbk.)
Prefaces by T.T. Tsui, Lord Armstrong of Ilminster. — Index. — Illustrated end-papers;
wrappers coloured black with col. ills.

V.1991.003   *Einführung in das Victoria und Albert Museum.*
ISBN: 1851771077
German translation of V.1991.004.

V.1991.004   *Introducing the Victoria and Albert Museum.*
London : Victoria and Albert Museum, 1991.
40 p. : col. ill. ; 20 cm.
ISBN: 1851770097
Cover title. — Compiled and edited by Michael Wilson and Charles Saumarez-Smith.
Introduction / Elizabeth Esteve-Coll. — Stapled; sized wrappers with col. ills., and plans
on turn-ins.

V.1991.005   *Introduction au Musée Victoria et Albert.*
ISBN: 1851771069
French translation of V.1991.004.

V.1991.006   *Jewish ritual art in the Victoria & Albert Museum* / Michael E. Keen.
London : H.M.S.O., 1991.
vi, 126 p. : ill. (some col.) ; 29 cm.
ISBN: 0112904491
At head of title: Victoria & Albert Museum. — Bibliography: p. 123–124. Glossary.
Index. — Blue cloth covered boards; blue end-papers; dust-jacket coloured purple with
col. ills.

V.1991.007   *Karl Friedrich Schinkel : a universal man* / edited by Michael Snodin.
New Haven ; London : Yale University Press in association with the
Victoria and Albert Museum, 1991 (Printed by Amilcare Pizzi, Milan).
xii, 218 p. : ill. (some col.), facsims, map, plans ; 28 cm.
ISBN: 0300051654; 0300051662 (pbk.)
Prefaces by Tom Purves (Managing Director, BMW (GB) Ltd.), Baron Hermann von
Richthofen, Werner Knopp, Elizabeth Esteve-Coll. Karl Friedrich Schinkel : a universal
man / Peter Betthausen. Schinkel the artist / Helmut Börsch-Supan. Schinkel's buildings
and plans for Berlin / Gottfried Riemann. Schinkel and Durand : the case of the Altes
Museum / Martin Goalen. Royal residences on the Havel / Hans-Joachim Giersberg.

Schinkel's architectural theory / Alex Potts. Art and industry / Angelika Wesenberg. — Bibliography: p. 214–218. — Designed by John Nicoll. — Blue cloth covered boards; dust-jacket with col. ills.
EXHIBITION: vx.1991.013

v.1991.008　　*Landscape prints by Francis Vivares (1709–1780).*
[London : Victoria and Albert Museum Dept. of Prints, Drawings and Paintings], 1991.
[9] leaves ; 30 cm.
Written by Elizabeth Miller. — Photocopied typescript.
EXHIBITION: vx.1991.018

v.1991.009　　*Masterpieces of Japanese prints : the European collections : Ukiyo-e from the Victoria and Albert Museum* / Rupert Faulkner in consultation with B.W. Robinson.
[London] : Victoria and Albert Museum, 1991 (Printed in Japan).
152 p. : ill. (some col.) ; 30 cm.
ISBN: 1851771018
Includes essay by Richard Lane. — Bibliography: p. 152. — Adapted in part from vr.1989.017–018. — Dark green cloth covered boards; tan end-papers; dust-jacket coloured silver with col. ills.

v.1991.010　　*Modern fashion in detail* / by Claire Wilcox & Valerie Mendes ; photography by Richard Davis ; line drawings by Leonie Davis.
[London] : Victoria and Albert Museum, 1991 (Printed in Hong Kong).
143 p. : ill. (chiefly col.) ; 30 cm.
ISBN: 1851770321
　"Histories of 20th century dress . . . usually include a few details of fabric, construction and trimming but this is the first time a whole volume has been devoted entirely to close-ups illustrating in detail the intricate skills of high fashion . . . To illustrate the clothes in their entirety, each colour plate is accompanied by . . . line drawings which resemble those featured on the reverse of paper patterns"–Foreword. — Bibliography: p. 142–3. Glossary. — Designed by Area. — Sized wrappers with col. ill.

v.1991.011　　*Nicholas Rea : the art of making the book, 13 March–2 June 1991, National Art Library, Victoria & Albert Museum.*
[London] : National Art Library, 1991.
1 folded sheet ([3] p.) ; 30 cm.
Introduction by R.K. Francis.
EXHIBITION: vx.1991.004

v.1991.012　　*Periodicals and annuals before 1900 in the Renier Collection.*
London : Bethnal Green Museum of Childhood, 1991.
52 p. : ill., facsims. ; 21 cm.
(Occasional list / Renier Collection of Historic and Contemporary Children's Books ; no. 9)
Cover title: Periodicals and annuals before 1900. — "Designed and compiled by Tessa Rose Chester."–p. 52.

v.1991.013　　*Publishing interventions : Stephen Willats, 1965–1991 : National Art Library, Victoria and Albert Museum.*
[London : The Library, 1991.]
11 p. ; 21 cm.

Texts by Stephen Willats. Bibliographies compiled by Simon Ford. — Reproduced from typescript. Stapled; white wrappers with photograph. — The works in the display form part of Stephen Willats Printed Archive at the National Art Library.
EXHIBITION: VX.1991.009

V.1991.014   *Spirit of Christmas round the world.* [Repr.]
[London : Bethnal Green Museum of Childhood, 1991.]
[40] p. : ill. ; 21 cm.
Written by Anthony Burton, Pauline Cockrill, Caroline Goodfellow, Vera Kaden, Halina Pasierbska, Jennifer Turnbull. — Includes recipes. — Typescript reproduced on green paper; stapled. Green decorated wrappers. Reprint of v.1987.017.
EXHIBITION: VX.1991.BGM.006

V.1991.015   *Telling tales : a Museum trail for 7–11s.*
[London : Victoria and Albert Museum Education Dept., 1991.]
1 sheet, folded ([6] p.) : ill., plan ; 30 cm.
At head of title: V&A. — "In connection with Puffin's 50th birthday exhibition."
EXHIBITION: VX.1991.007

V.1991.016   *Tie-dyed textiles of India : tradition and trade* / Veronica Murphy and Rosemary Crill.
London : Victoria and Albert Museum : in association with Mapin Publishing, 1991 (Printed and bound by Toppan Printing Co., Singapore).
206 p. : ill. (chiefly col.), map ; 29 cm.
(Indian art series)
ISBN: 0944142303
Bibliography: p. 201–3. Glossary. Index. — Designer: Yvonne Dedman. — Decorated endpapers. Tan cloth covered boards; dust-jackets with col. ills.

V.1991.017   *Das Victoria and Albert Museum* / Einführung von der Direktorin ; Beiträgen der Konservatoren.
ISBN: 1870248686 [sic]
German translation of v.1991.019.

V.1991.018   *Le Victoria & Albert Museum* / préface de la Directrice ; texte rédigé par les conservateurs.
ISBN: 1870248686 [sic]
French translation of v.1991.019.

V.1991.019   *The Victoria and Albert Museum* / introduction by the Director ; text by the curators.
London : Scala Books in association with the Victoria and Albert Museum, 1991 (Printed by Graphicom, Vicenza).
160 p. : col. ill. ; 28 cm.
ISBN: 1870248686 [sic]
Edited by Paul Holberton. Texts by: Philippa Glanville, John Guy, Robin Hildyard, Rose Kerr, Lionel Lambourne, Clive Wainwright, Oliver Watson, Paul Williamson. — Designed by Alan Bartram. — Index. — Sized wrappers, with col. ills.

V.1991.020   *Victoria and Albert Museum collections management policy.*
[London : The Museum], 1991.
41 p. ; 30 cm.
ISBN: 1851771026
Caption title. — Date on cover: March 1991. Text dated April 1991. — Comb-bound, blue covers.

V.1991.021   *Visions of Japan, 17 September 1991–5 January 1992 : information for teachers and group leaders : technology, design, arts, history, geography, English, R.E.*
[London : Victoria and Albert Museum Education Dept., 1991?]
1 sheet, folded (3 p.) : col. ill. ; 20 cm.
1 sheet, 40 cm.² with central panel (20 cm.²) removed. Printed in 10 cm.² sections; cut, twisted and folded to result in booklet with 3 faces.
EXHIBITION: VX.1991.015

1992

V.1992.001   *The art of death : objects from the English death ritual 1500–1800 : 8 January–22 March 1992 : Victoria and Albert Museum.*
[London : The Museum, 1992.]
1 sheet, folded ([5] p.) ; 30 cm.
Note by Elizabeth Esteve-Coll. — Decorated caption title. — Exhibition handlist.
EXHIBITION: VX.1992.001

V.1992.002   *The art of death : objects from the English death ritual 1500–1800 : Victoria and Albert Museum, 8 January to 22 March 1992 : information for teachers.*
London : Victoria and Albert Museum Education Dept., 1992.
[6] p. : ill. ; 30 cm.
Written by Caroline Lang. — Includes bibliography. — Designed by Linda Reed. — Stapled.
EXHIBITION: VX.1992.001

V.1992.003   *A book of birds* / introduction by Charles Newton.
[London] : Victoria and Albert Museum, 1992 (Printed in Singapore).
[48] p. : col. ill. ; 16 x 16 cm.
ISBN: 1851771093
Designed by Bernard Higton. — Sized paper covered boards, with col. ills. printed on blue.

V.1992.004   *A book of dragons & monsters* / introduction by Susan Stronge.
[London] : Victoria and Albert Museum, 1992 (Printed in Singapore).
[48] p. : col. ill. ; 16 x 16 cm.
ISBN: 1851771107
Designed by Bernard Higton. — Sized paper covered boards with col. ills. printed on red.

V.1992.005   *A book of sea creatures* / introduction by Gill Saunders.
[London] : Victoria and Albert Museum, 1992 (Printed in Singapore).
[48] p. : col. ill. ; 16 x 16 cm.
ISBN: 1851771115
Designed by Bernard Higton. — Sized paper covered boards with col. ills. printed on grey-green.

V.1992.006   *Catalogue of paintings at the Theatre Museum, London* / by Geoffrey Ashton ; edited by James Fowler.
[London] : Victoria and Albert Museum in association with the Society for Theatre Research, 1992 (Produced by Alan Sutton Publishing, Stroud).

xi, 211 p. : ill., ports. ; 29 cm.
ISBN: 1851771026
Foreword / Jack Reading, James Fowler. — Indexes of artists, plays, previous owners. — Black cloth covered boards; dust-jacket with col. ills. and author's photograph.

V.1992.007   *Company paintings : Indian paintings of the British period* / Mildred Archer ; assisted by Graham Parlett.
London : Ahmedabad : Victoria and Albert Museum in association with Mapin Publishing, 1992 (Printed and bound by Tien Wah Press, Singapore).
240 p. : ill. (chiefly col.), map, ports. ; 29 cm.
(Indian art series)
ISBN: 0944142176
Catalogue of the collection in the Victoria and Albert Museum Indian Collection. — Bibliography: p. 230–233. Index, concordance of Museum numbers. — Orange cloth covered boards; decorated end-papers. Dust-jacket coloured dark blue, with col. ills.

V.1992.008   *Costumes from* The House of Eliott, *a BBC television drama series : Dress Gallery, Victoria and Albert Museum, 25th September [1992]–31st January 1993.*
[London : The Museum, 1992.]
1 sheet, folded ([6] p.) : ill. ; 21 x 10 cm.
Written by Amy de la Haye.
EXHIBITION: vx.1992.021

V.1992.009   *Four hundred years of fashion* / editor: Natalie Rothstein ; text by Madeleine Ginsburg, Avril Hart, Valerie D. Mendes and with other members of the Department of Textiles & Dress ; photography by Philip Barnard. Repr.
[London] : Victoria & Albert Museum, [1984] (Made and printed by New Interlitho S.p.a, Milan, 1992).
176 p. : ill. (some col.) ; 29 cm.
ISBN: 1851771166
With a new introduction. — Includes bibliographic references. Glossary. — Cover photography by Daniel McGrath. — Sized wrappers, with col. ills.

V.1992.010   *Green images : posters and printed ephemera . . . : information for teachers.*
[London] : Victoria and Albert Museum, 1992.
1 sheet ([4] p.) : ill. ; 30 cm.
Written by Colin Mulberg. — Designed by Richard Malt. — Part printed in green on Sylvancoat recycled paper from Silverton Mill.
EXHIBITION: vx.1992.002

V.1992.011   *A guide for blind and partially sighted visitors to the Victoria and Albert Museum.* [Braille ed.]
[London : The Museum, 1992.]
20 p. of braille ; 30 cm.
Title from printed label on cover. — Produced by the Museum's Education Department; written by Imogen Stewart. — Brailled by the Royal National Institute for the Blind. — "Archive ref. 507517". — First and last leaves do not contain text.

V.1992.012   *A guide for partially sighted visitors to the Victoria and Albert Museum.* [Large print ed.]
[London : The Museum, 1992.]

10 p. (large print) : 1 ill. ; 30 cm.
Cover title. — Produced by the Museum's Education Department; written by Imogen Stewart. Stapled; yellow wrappers.

V.1992.013   *Korea : the Samsung gallery of Korean art.*
[London] : Victoria and Albert Museum, 1992.
1 sheet, folded ([8] p.) : ill. ; 30 cm.
Gallery trail for children. — Produced by the Education Dept. – Written by Elizabeth Newbery; design and illustration by Linda Francis.

V.1992.014   *Korean art and design : the Samsung gallery of Korean art* / text, Beth McKillop ; photography, Ian Thomas ; design and production, Patrick Yapp.
[London] : Victoria and Albert Museum, 1992 (Printed by the University Press, Cambridge).
191 p. : ill. (chiefly col.), maps ; 28 cm.
ISBN: 1851771042
Prefaces by Kun Hee Lee (Chairman, Samsung Group), Lord Armstrong of Ilminster. — Bibliography: p. 189. Index. — Pale green wrappers with col. ills. Ill. on end-papers.

V.1992.015   *Mediaeval European jewellery : with a catalogue of the collection in the Victoria & Albert Museum* / Ronald W. Lightbown.
[London] : Victoria & Albert Museum, 1992 (Printed in Hong Kong).
i-vi, 7–589 p. : ill. (some col.), ports. ; 31 cm.
ISBN: 0948107871
Bibliography: p. 537–550. Index. — Designed by Tim Harvey. — "With the assistance of the Getty grant programme." — Black cloth covered boards; black end-papers; dust-jacket coloured black, with col. ills. and author's photograph.

V.1992.016   *"More than funny" – comics in the National Art Library : a display to mark the acquisition of the Ian Rakoff collection of comics and graphic novels, 11 March–24 May 1992* / curator: M.A. Bradley.
[London : The Library, 1992.]
[4] p. ; 30 cm.
Photocopied typescript.
EXHIBITION: VX.1992.005

V.1992.017   *Plant motifs : information and ideas for secondary art and textiles teachers.*
[London : Victoria and Albert Museum Education Dept.], 1992.
[8] p. : ill. ; 30 cm.
Cover title. — Produced by Morna Hinton, with contributions from Shireen Akbar and Imogen Stewart. — Includes bibliography. — Part printed in blue. Stapled.

V.1992.018   *Portugal's silver service : a victory gift to the Duke of Wellington* / Angela Delaforce, James Yorke ; with a contribution from Jonathan Voak.
[London] : Victoria & Albert Museum, 1992 (Printed by BAS Printers).
143 p. : ill. (chiefly col.), ports. ; 29 cm.
ISBN: 1851771034
Prefaces by Antonio Vaz-Pereira, Ambassador of Portugal (to the U.K.) and by Elizabeth Esteve-Coll. — Bibliography: p. 143. — Cream cloth covered boards, stamped in gold; dust-jacket colour royal blue with col. ills.

V.1992.019   *Smile classified* / by Simon Ford.
               [London] : National Art Library, [1992].
               8 p. ; 21 cm.
               Cover title. — Includes a checklist of published issues of *Smile*, and bibliographic
               references. — Stapled; white wrappers with skull & crossbones.
               EXHIBITION: VX.1992.007

V.1992.020   *Snuff boxes from China : the Victoria and Albert Museum collection* /
               Helen White ; photography by Ian Thomas.
               London : Bamboo Publishing in association with the Victoria and
               Albert Museum, 1992 (Printed and bound in Singapore by Toppan).
               291 p. : col. ill. ; 37 cm.
               ISBN: 1870076109
               Bibliographic references: p. 291. Concordance of Museum numbers. — Designed by
               Denyer Design Associates. — Green silk covered boards, stamped in gold; textured end-
               papers. Dark green dust-jacket with col. ill. In slip-case bound in green silk.

V.1992.021   *Sovereign family pack : things to do for parents and children.*
               London : Victoria and Albert Museum, 1992.
               1 folder (24 items) : ill., coat of arms, genealogical table, map, music ;
               23 x 31 cm.
               ISBN: 1851771123
               Title from contents sheet. — Devised and written by Carole Mahoney and Mary
               Mellors. — Designed and illustrated by S. Clark. — Folder of sized card with col. ill. —
               Includes plastic bag containing balloons and streamers.
               EXHIBITION: VX.1992.008

V.1992.022   *Sovereign teacher's pack : a guide for teachers on making educational
               use of the Sovereign exhibition.*
               London : Victoria and Albert Museum, 1992.
               1 folder (10 pamphlets) : ill., genealogical table, plans, ports. ;
               23 x 31 cm.
               ISBN: 1851771131
               Authors: Gill Corbishley, Susan Morris, Joanna Marschner, Imogen Stewart, Jill Slaney,
               Sheila Whitaker.— Contents: [Introductory]. What's in the exhibition? The status and
               image of monarchy. Dress for special occasions. Forty years of fashion. Jewellery, hair
               ornaments and head gear. Looking at thrones. Craftsmanship: monarchs as patrons.
               Royal animals and symbolic animals. Exhibitions as evidence. — Bibliography. —
               Produced by Carole Mahoney. Designed by Linda Reed, Joss Nizan. — Folder of sized
               card with coloured illustration.
               EXHIBITION: VX.1992.008

V.1992.023   *Studying the Tudors and Stuarts at the V & A.*
               [London : Victoria and Albert Museum], 1992.
               [8] p. : ill. ; 30 cm.
               Cover title. — "Designed for teachers, to support the National History Curriculum Key
               Stage 2". — Written by Carole Mahoney. — "Suggestions for further reading": back
               cover. — Illustrated by Richard Cottingham. Designed by Bruce Grove, Designers Ink.
               — Part printed in grey green. Stapled; ill. on wrappers.

V.1992.024   *Theatre works : a guide to working in the theatre* / written by Norma
               Cohen ; assisted by Joseph Smith.
               [London] : Royal National Theatre Education : Theatre Museum,
               1992.
               55 p. : ill. ; 24 cm.

"Some of the exerpts in this booklet have been taken from . . . an exhibition showing at the Theatre Museum."
EXHIBITION: VX.1991.THM.002

v.1992.025   *Trash or treasure : a dip into 400 years of children's books :*
Bethnal Green Museum of Childhood, London : opening July 28th
1992.
[London : Bethnal Green Museum of Childhood, 1992].
52 p. : 1 ill. ; 30 cm.
Caption title. On cover: List of exhibits. — Edited by Tessa Rose Chester. — "Further reading": p. 51–52.
EXHIBITION: VX.1992.BGM.001

v.1992.026   *V & A : education for all.*
London : Victoria and Albert Museum, 1992 (Printed by Haynes Cannon).
22 p. : ill. (chiefly col.) ; 31 cm.
Introduction / Elizabeth Esteve-Coll. — Designed by Touchpaper. — Photography by Barry Lewis. — Printed on cream; stapled in cream wrappers with turn-in at rear (for enclosures?) and col. ill.

v.1992.027   *V&A needlepoint collection* / Karen Elder ; in association with the Victoria and Albert Museum.
London : Anaya Publishers, 1992 (Printed by Dai Nippon, Hong Kong).
143 p. : col. ill. ; 32 cm.
ISBN: 185470124X
Includes index. — Designer: Edwin Belchamber. — Blue cloth covered boards; dust-jacket with col. ills.

v.1992.028   *V & A patrons.*
[London : The Museum, 1992.]
[16] p. : col. ill. ; 30 cm.
Cover title. — Promotional booklet to encourage benefactors. — Designed by Saatchi & Saatchi Design. — Envelope at back contains 2 sheets: V & A financial breakdown ; membership application form.

v.1992.029   *The Victoria & Albert Museum's textile collection : British textiles*
from 1900 to 1937 / by Valerie Mendes.
[London] : Victoria and Albert Museum, 1992 (Printed in Singapore).
95 p. : col. ill. ; 30 cm.
(The Victoria & Albert Museum's textile collection)
ISBN: 185177114X
Bibliography: p. 95. Glossary. — Designed by Area. — Sized wrappers with col. ill. — Contents adapted from VR.1980.002.

v.1992.030   *The Victoria & Albert Museum's textile collection : design for printed*
textiles in England from 1750–1850 / by Wendy Hefford.
[London] : Victoria and Albert Museum, 1992 (Printed in Singapore).
159 p. : col. ill. ; 30 cm.
(The Victoria & Albert Museum's textile collection)
ISBN: 1851771158
Includes bibliographic references. Glossary. — Designed by Area. — Sized wrappers with col. ill. — Contents adapted from VR.1980.002.

V.1992.031 *Vikutoria to Arubāto Bijutsukan ten* / kaisetsu: Vikutoria to Arubāto Bijutsukan Kanchō gakugeiin ; Tanabe Tōru yaku.
Tokyo : Misuzu Shobo Publishing Co. and Scala Publications, 1992 (Printed and bound by Graphicom, Vicenza).
160 p. : col. ill. ; 28 cm.
Japanese translation of v.1991.019. — "Scala Books, published in association with the Victoria and Albert Museum"–t.p. — Edited by Paul Holberton. — Designed by Alan Bartram — Sized wrappers with col. ills.

V.1992.032 *Yuki : 20 years.*
London : Victoria & Albert Museum, 1992 (Origination, printing and binding, Balding + Mansell).
30, [2] p. : ill. (chiefly col.) ; 29 cm.
ISBN: 1851771174
Text by Amy de la Haye. Foreword / Valerie D. Mendes. — Art direction, design and production: David Milbank Challis. — Photography: Trevor Hurst. — Plain grey wrappers; sized black dust-jacket with col. ills. Issued in grey envelope.
EXHIBITION: VX.1992.014

1993

V.1993.001 *20th Century Gallery : ideas and information for teachers.*
[London] : Victoria and Albert Museum, 1993 (Reprographics and printing by V&A Print Section).
[8] p. : ill., plan ; 30 cm.
Cover title. — Written by Colin Mulberg and Margaret Knight. — Includes bibliography. — Designed by Malcolm Frost. — Part printed in red. Stapled; ill. and plans on wrappers.

V.1993.002 *5000 years of textiles* / edited by Jennifer Harris.
London : British Museum Press in association with the Whitworth Art Gallery and the Victoria and Albert Museum, 1993 (Printed and bound in Hong Kong).
320 p. : ill. (chiefly col.), maps ; 29 cm.
ISBN: 0714117153
Preface; Introduction / Jennifer Harris. I, A SURVEY OF TEXTILE TECHNIQUES / Jennifer Harris. 1, Weaving. 2, Tapestry. 3, Rug weaving. 4, Embroidery. 5, Lace. 6, Dyeing and printing. 7, Knitting. 8, Netting, knotting and crochet. 9, Felt and bark cloth. II, A SURVEY OF WORLD TEXTILES. THE ANCIENT WORLD: 1, Introduction; 2, The Mediterranean / Joan Allgrove McDowell. 3, Central and northern Europe / John-Peter Wild. THE NEAR AND MIDDLE EAST: 4, Sassanian textiles; 5, Early Islamic textiles / Joan Allgrove McDowell. 6, Byzantine silks / Anna Muthesius. 7, Safavid Iran (1499–1722); 8, The Ottoman Empire / Joan Allgrove McDowell. 9, Central Asian textiles / Jennifer Wearden. 10, Palestinian embroidery / Shelagh Weir. INDIA AND PAKISTAN: 11, Historical development and trade; 12, Tribal textiles / Margaret Hall. CARPETS: 13, Carpets of the Middle and Far East / Patricia L. Baker. THE FAR EAST: 14, China / Verity Wilson. 15, Japan / Susan-Marie Best. 16, South-East Asia / Sylvia Fraser-Lu. WESTERN EUROPE: 17, Sicilian silks / Anna Muthesius. 18, Italian silks (1300–1500) / Lisa Monnas. 19, Italian silks (1500–1900); 20, Spanish silks / Jacqueline Herald. 21, French silks (1650–1800) / Lesley Miller. 22, Figured linen damasks / Jacqueline Herald. 23, Tapestry / Thomas Campbell. 24, Embroidery; 25, Lace / Santina M. Levey. 26, Printed textiles / Jennifer Harris. CENTRAL AND EASTERN EUROPE: 27, Eastern Europe / Jennifer Wearden. 28, Greece, the Greek Islands and Albania / Roderick R. Taylor. THE AMERICAS: 29, Colonial North America (1700–1990s) / Mary Schoeser. 30, Native North America / Colin and Betty Taylor. 31, Latin America / Chloë Sayer and Penny Bateman. AFRICA: 32, North Africa / Caroline Stone. 33, Sub-Saharan Africa and the offshore islands / John Mack.

— Bibliography: p. 306–311. Glossary. Index. — Designed by Harry Green. — Mulberry coloured cloth covered boards; decorated end-papers; dust-jacket with col. ill.

v.1993.003   *Beatrix Potter and* The tailor of Gloucester : *handlist of the exhibition, 2 October 1993–9 January 1994, Twentieth Century Exhibition Gallery, Victoria and Albert Museum.*
[London : The Museum, 1993.]
[11] p. ; 30 cm.
Cover title. — Written by Avril Hart. — Stapled; red front cover.
EXHIBITION: vx.1993.026

v.1993.004   *Bethnal Green Museum of Childhood.* [Repr.]
[London] : Victoria and Albert Museum, 1986 (Printed by Balding + Mansell, Wisbech, 1993).
48 p. : ill. (some col.) ; 25 cm.
ISBN: 1851771328
Written by Anthony Burton. — Stapled; sized wrappers, with col. ills.

v.1993.005   *China : a teacher's pack.*
[London] : Victoria and Albert Museum, 1993 (Printed by Battley Brothers).
1 folder (8 items) : ill. (some col.), plans ; 31 cm.
ISBN: 1851771344
Title from folder. — Written by Verity Wilson with Gail Durbin, Judith Everington, Morna Hinton, Amy Lai, Susan Morris, Colin Mulberg, Roy Richards, Tony Wheeler. — Contains 5 wall charts and 3 booklets. — Based on the T.T. Tsui Gallery of Chinese Art. — Contents: Making use of this pack (9 p.). The Tsui Gallery : information for teachers (52 p.). The wallcharts (12 p.). China : a timeline. What is it made of? What is the decoration about? Dragons. Stories. — Bibliographies. — Designed by Tony Garrett.

v.1993.006   *European Ornament Gallery : information and ideas for teachers.*
[London] : Victoria and Albert Museum, 1993.
[8] p. : ill. ; 30 cm.
Cover title. — Written by Colin Mulberg and Anna Parker. — Includes bibliography. — Designed by Bruce Grove, Designers Ink. — Part printed in pale salmon and tan; stapled.

v.1993.007   *Form follows function?* / Susan Lambert.
[London] : Victoria & Albert Museum, 1993 (Printed by BAS Printers).
72 p. : ill. ; 23 cm.
(Design in the 20th century ; 2)
ISBN: 1851771220
"a series related to the the 20th Century Gallery at the Victoria & Albert Museum"–back cover. — Bibliography: p. 67–70. Index— Designer: Karen Wilks. — Sized wrappers with ills. part printed in blue.

v.1993.008   *Frank Lloyd Wright : the Kaufmann office* / Christopher Wilk.
London : Victoria & Albert Museum, 1993 (Printed by BAS Printers).
86, [1] p. : ill. (some col.), plans, ports. ; 24 cm.
ISBN: 1851771050
Preface / Elizabeth Esteve-Coll. — Bibliography: p. 86. Index. — Designed by Area. — Red paper covered boards; cream dust-jacket with ills.

V.1993.009   *Free range : a selection of his published works* / Ian Breakwell.
[London : National Art Library, Victoria and Albert Museum,
1993.]
[22] p. ; 21 cm.
Edited by Ian Breakwell. Catalogue list of works by William Greenwood. Interview with
the artist, by Stefan Szczelkun. — Bibliography: p. [15–18]. — Cover photograph by
Felicity Sparrow. — White wrappers; stapled.
EXHIBITION: vx.1993.008

V.1993.010   *John Channon and brass-inlaid furniture, 1730–1760* / Christopher
Gilbert and Tessa Murdoch.
London ; New Haven : Yale University Press in association with Leeds
City Art Galleries and the Victoria and Albert Museum, 1993.
viii, 164 p., [16] p. of plates : ill. (some col.), geneal. tables, plans ;
28 cm.
ISBN: 0300058128
Includes contributions by Josephine Darrah, Sarah Medlam, Anthony North and Kevin
Rogers, Helen Hayward and Sarah Medlam, Carolyn Sargentson. — Bibliography: p.
152. Name index. — Designed by John Trevitt. — Black cloth covered boards; brown
end-papers; dust-jacket coloured green with col. ills.
EXHIBITION: vx.1994.005

V.1993.011   *The National Art Library : a policy for the development of the
collections* / edited by Jan van der Wateren & Rowan Watson.
London : National Art Library, Victoria and Albert Museum, 1993.
67, 8, [14] p. ; 30 cm.
ISBN: 0952120909
Bibliography: p. 57–58. — Includes: Notes on the National Art Library, South
Kensington Museum. No 1, (1869) (Appendix 1). — Printed typescript. — Wire comb
bound.

V.1993.012   *Nationalism and internationalism* / Jeremy Aynsley.
[London] : Victoria & Albert Museum, 1993 (Printed by BAS
Printers).
72 p. : ill. ; 23 cm.
(Design in the 20th century ; 1)
ISBN: 1851771212
Bibliography: p. 67–70. Index. — "a series related to the the 20th Century Gallery at
the Victoria & Albert Museum"–back cover. — Designer: Karen Wilks. — Sized
wrappers with ills. part printed in red.

V.1993.013   *Painting and colouring books in the Renier Collection.*
[London : Bethnal Green Museum of Childhood], 1993.
52 p. : ill.; 30 cm.
(Occasional list / Renier Collection of Historic and Contemporary
Children's Books ; no. 10)
Caption title. — Designed and compiled by Tessa Rose Chester. — Stapled in cream
covers with ill.

V.1993.014   *Peter Rabbit, 1893–1993 : handlist of the exhibition* / by Anne
Stevenson Hobbs.
[London : Victoria and Albert Museum, 1993.]
[24] leaves ; 30 cm.
Stapled; blue front cover with ill.
EXHIBITION: vx.1993.027

V.1993.015   *The research policy of the Victoria and Albert Museum.*
                    [London : The Museum], 1993 (Designed and printed by the Libanus
                    Press, Marlborough).
                    [16] p. ; 27 cm.
                    Grey wrappers, printed in blue.

V.1993.016   *Studio pottery : twentieth century British ceramics in the Victoria and*
                    Albert Museum collection / Oliver Watson ; photography by Ian
                    Thomas and Mike Kitcatt. 1st paperback ed.
                    Oxford : Phaidon Press in association with the Victoria and Albert
                    Museum, 1993 (Printed in Singapore).
                    287 p. : ill. (some col.) ; 29 cm.
                    ISBN: 071482948X
                    Original title: British studio pottery. Preface / J.G.V. Mallet. — "some attribution dates
                    have been revised"– t.p. verso. — Bibliography: p. 286–287. Index. Concordance of
                    Museum numbers. Marks. — Wrappers with turn-ins; col. ills. on black and red.

V.1993.017   *Teaching maths through Islamic art : information and ideas for*
                    teachers.
                    [London : Victoria and Albert Museum], 1993.
                    12 p. : ill. ; 30 cm.
                    Cover title. — Written by Lydia Sharman. Edited by Gail Durbin. — Bibliography:
                    p. 12. — Designed by Bruce Grove, Designers Ink. — Part printed in green. Stapled.

V.1993.018   *Trash or treasure : a dip into 400 years of children's books : Bethnal*
                    Green Museum of Childhood, London : opening July 28th 1992.
                    [Repr. with corrections]
                    [London : Bethnal Green Museum of Childhood, 1992 (1993
                    printing).]
                    52 p. : 1 ill. ; 30 cm.
                    Caption title. On cover: List of exhibits. — Edited by Tessa Rose Chester. — "Further
                    reading": p. 51–52. — Stapled; grey covers with ill.
                    EXHIBITION: VX.1992.BGM.001

V.1993.019   *Using the V & A for GCSE and A-level coursework.*
                    [London : V & A Education Dept.], 1993.
                    [12] p. : ill. ; 21 x 10 cm.
                    Written by Carole Mahoney. — Designed by Bruce Grove, Designers Ink. — Printed in
                    black, white, blue and yellow. Stapled.

V.1993.020   *Victoria and Albert Museum : information for teachers.*
                    London : Victoria and Albert Museum, 1993 (Reprographics and
                    printing by V&A Printing Section).
                    16 p. : ill., plans ; 30 cm.
                    ISBN: 1851771352
                    Cover title. — Written by Colin Mulberg. — Designed by Linda Reed. — Stapled;
                    wrappers with ills., part printed in plum-colour.

V.1993.021   *The Victoria & Albert Museum's textile collection : British textiles*
                    from 1850 to 1900 / by Linda Parry.
                    [London] : Victoria and Albert Museum, 1993 (Printed by Grafiche
                    Milani).
                    146 p. : col. ill. ; 30 cm.
                    (The Victoria & Albert Museum's textile collection)

ISBN: 1851771271
Bibliography: p. 147. Glossary, biographies and notes on firms. — Designed by Area. —
Sized wrappers with col. ill. — Contents adapted from VR.1980.002.

V.1993.022   *The Victoria & Albert Museum's textile collection : embroidery in
              Britain from 1200 to 1750* / by Donald King & Santina Levey.
              [London] : Victoria & Albert Museum, 1993 (Printed by Grafiche
              Milani).
              112 p. : ill. (chiefly col.) ; 30 cm.
              (The Victoria & Albert Museum's textile collection)
              ISBN: 1851771263
              Includes glossary. — Designed by Area. — Sized wrappers with col. ill. — Contents
              adapted from VR.1980.002.

V.1993.023   *Vikutoria & Arubāto Bijutsukan gaido bukku.*
              [London : Victoria and Albert Museum], 1993 (Printed in Italy).
              40 p. : col. ill., plans ; 20 cm.
              ISBN: 1851770097
              Cover title. — Compiled and edited by Michael Wilson and Charles Saumarez-Smith. —
              Japanese translation of V.1991.004.

V.1993.024   *Wing your way around the V&A : a Christmas trail.*
              [London] : Victoria and Albert Museum, 1993 (Printed by the Victoria
              and Albert Museum Printing Section).
              1 sheet ([5] p.) : ill. ; 30 x 14 cm.
              Written by Jill Slaney. — Designed and illustrated by Linda Francis. — Printed in blue
              and red.

1994

V.1994.001   *Ceremonial and commemorative chairs in Great Britain* / Clare
              Graham.
              [London] : Victoria & Albert Museum, 1994 (Produced by Alan
              Sutton Publishing; printed by the Bath Press, Avon).
              viii, 134 p. : ill. ; 31 cm.
              ISBN: 1851771360
              Bibliography: p. 126–129. Index. — Blue cloth covered boards; col. ills. on dust-jacket.

V.1994.002   *Chanel : the couturière at work* / Amy de la Haye, Shelley Tobin.
              [London] : Victoria & Albert Museum, 1994 (Printed by Grafiche
              Milani).
              136 p. : ill. (some col.), ports. ; 30 cm.
              ISBN: 1851771190
              Bibliography: p. 131. Index. — Designed by Area, London. — Sized wrappers, with ills.
              Corrigenda slip loosely inserted. — Also published: Woodstock, N.Y. : Overlook Press,
              1994.

V.1994.003   *Experimenting with the book : Janus Press.*
              [London : National Art Library, 1994] (Produced by Victoria and
              Albert Museum Printing Section).
              [16] p. ; 21 cm.
              Introduction / Jan van der Wateren. Catalogue entries by Eoin Shalloo. — Includes
              select bibliography. — Text typeset by Claire Van Vliet. — Stapled; red wrappers.
              EXHIBITION: VX.1994.019

v.1994.004   *A fine line : commercial wood engraving in Britain.*
London : Victoria and Albert Museum, [1994].
1 sheet, folded ([6] p.) ; 21 cm.
Caption title. At head of title, in blue: Prints, Drawings and Paintings Collection temporary display.
EXHIBITION: vx.1994.022

v.1994.005   *The first years of the National Art Library: from the School of Design to the Department of Practical Art* / Eva White.
[London : The Library, 1994] (Printed by V&A Printers).
28 p. : ill. ; 21 cm.
Bibliography: p. 28. — Stapled; white wrappers with ill.
EXHIBITION: vx.1994.020

v.1994.006   *Gothic : gallery trail : Gallery 23.*
[London] : V&A Education, 1994 (Printed by the V&A Printing Section).
1 sheet, folded ([6] p.) : ill. ; 30 cm. + 1 sheet.
Written by Anthea Peppin; edited by Clio Whittaker. — Designed by Nicole Griffin; illustrated by Danuta Mayer. — "Notes for adults" on separate sheet. — Part printed in purple.

v.1994.007   *Hidden pleasures : 400 years of decorative book end-papers in the National Art Library . . . .*
[London : The Library, 1994.]
1 sheet, folded ([5] p.) ; 30 cm.
Written by Marian Keyes. — Includes select bibliography. — Decorated with marbling design.
EXHIBITION: vx.1994.001

v.1994.008   *India : the Nehru Gallery of Indian Art : gallery trail : the great Mughals.* 2nd ed.
[London] : V&A Education, 1994 (Printed by the V&A Printing Section).
1 sheet, folded ([6] p.) : ill. ; 30 cm. + 1 sheet.
Written by Elizabeth Newbery and Susan Stronge; edited by Clio Whittaker. — Designed by Nicole Griffin; illustrated by Danuta Mayer and Pippa Palmer. — "Notes for adults" on separate sheet. — Partly printed in turquoise. — Also issued in Arabic, Bengali, Gujurati, Hindi, Punjabi and Urdu.

v.1994.009   *Josef Albers prints.*
London : Victoria and Albert Museum, [1994].
1 sheet, folded ([6] p.) ; 21 cm.
Caption title. At head of title, in blue: Prints, Drawings and Paintings Collection temporary display.
EXHIBITION: vx.1994.008

v.1994.010   *Morris Cox and the Gogmagog Press . . . .*
[London : National Art Library, 1994] (Produced by the V&A Printing Section).
[16] p. ; 21 cm.
Cover title. — Preface / Jan van der Wateren. — Bibliography at end. — Stapled; white wrappers, with ills. — Errata slip loosely inserted.
EXHIBITION: vx.1994.006

V.1994.011 *Motifs in art : a guide for visually impaired visitors to the Victoria and Albert Museum.*
[London : Victoria and Albert Museum Education Dept., 1994] (Produced by V&A Printing Section).
7 p. ; 30 cm.
Cover title. — Large print. — Stapled; buff wrappers, with line drawing.

V.1994.012 *Motifs in art : a guide for visually impaired visitors to the Victoria and Albert Museum.*
[Braille ed.]
[London : V&A Education Dept., 1994] (Brailled by the Royal National Institute for the Blind).
[16] p. ; 33 cm.
[Title from v.1994.011. Printed label omits main title.] — "Archive ref. 517392". — Text on brown paper. White card wrappers.

V.1994.013 *Museum conservation : science and technology projects for Key Stage 2.*
[London : Victoria and Albert Museum], 1994 (Printed by V&A Printing Section).
11 p. : ill. ; 30 cm.
ISBN: 1851771530
Cover title. — Written by John Yorath. Edited and produced by Clio Whittaker. Series editor Gail Durbin. — Bibliography: back cover. — Designed by Susan England. — Stapled, in wrappers. Part printed in yellow.

V.1994.014 *Policy and procedures for studentships, internships and placements in the Conservation Department of the V&A* / Alan Cummings.
[London : The Department], 1994.
23, 1 p. ; 30 cm.
Cover title. — "Amended version"–cover. — Includes application form.

V.1994.015 *Prospects, thresholds, interiors : watercolours from the national collection at the Victoria and Albert Museum* / Lewis Johnson.
Cambridge : Cambridge University Press in association with the Victoria and Albert Museum, 1994.
xx, 250 p. : ill. (some col.) ; 28 cm.
ISBN: 0521444888; 0521449287 (pbk.)
Bibliography: p. 243–248. Index of artists. — Sized wrappers coloured pink with col. ills.
EXHIBITION: vx.1994.003

V.1994.016 *Pugin : a Gothic passion* / edited by Paul Atterbury & Clive Wainwright.
New Haven ; London : Yale University Press, in association with the Victoria & Albert Museum, 1994 (Printed by Amilcare Pizzi, Milan).
xiii, 310 p. : ill. (some col.), plans, ports. ; 29 cm.
ISBN: 0300060122; 0300060149 (pbk.)
Sponsor's preface / Michael Blakenham (chairman Pearson plc). 'Not a style but a principle' : Pugin & his influence / Clive Wainwright. The early years / Alexandra Wedgwood. Pugin and the theatre / Lionel Lambourne. Domestic architecture / Alexandra Wedgwood. Pugin as a church architect / Roderick O'Donnell. The antiquary and collector / Clive Wainwright. Pugin writing / Margaret Belcher. Wallpaper / Joanna

Banham. Furniture / Clive Wainwright. Ceramics / Paul Atterbury. Book design and production / Clive Wainwright. Jewellery / Shirley Bury. Metalwork / Ann Eatwell and Anthony North. Monuments and brasses / David Meara. Stained glass / Stanley A. Shepherd. Textiles: I, Ecclesiastical textiles / Dom Bede Millard. II, Domestic textiles / Linda Parry. III, Woven braids / Paul Harrison. The new Palace of Westminster / Alexandra Wedgwood. The mediaeval court / Alexandra Wedgwood. Pugin in Australia / Brian Andrews. The later Pugins / Roderick O'Donnell. The fate of Pugin's *True principles* / Andrew Saint. The opening of the Pugin burial vault / David Meara. — Includes bibliographic references and indexes. — Black cloth covered boards with col. ills. on end-papers and dust-jacket. Or sized wrappers.
EXHIBITION: VX.1994.016

V.1994.017   *Studying the Victorians at the Victoria and Albert Museum : a handbook for teachers.*
[London : The Museum], 1994 (Printed by V&A Print Section).
48 p. : ill. ; 30 cm.
ISBN: 1851771468
Cover title. — Contributing editor Gail Durbin. Additional contributions from Geoff Opie, Imogen Stewart and Sue Wilkinson. Edited and produced by Clio Whittaker. — Includes bibliographic references. — Designed by Tony Garrett, Fathom Graphics. — Stapled; sized wrappers with ills, 1 col.

V.1994.018   *Vicky and Albo and the holiday topic!*
[London : Victoria and Albert Museum], 1994.
1 sheet, folded ([6] p.) : col. ill. ; 30 cm.
ISBN: 1851771476
Edited by Gail Durbin. "Original concept by Jonathan Barnes." — Comic strip format. Drawn by Tom Paterson.

V.1994.019   *Das Victoria and Albert Museum* / Einführung von der Direktorin ; Beiträgen der Konservatoren. Neue Aufl.
London : Scala Books . . . in Zusammenarbeit mit dem Victoria and Albert Museum, 1994 (Druck und Binding: Graphische Milani, Milan).
160 p. : col. ill. ; 28 cm.
ISBN: 1870248694
Herausgeber: Paul Holberton. [Authors' names omitted.] — Layout: Alan Bartram. — Sized wrappers with col. ills. — German version of v.1995.031.

V.1994.020   *Le Victoria & Albert Museum* / préface de la Directrice ; texte rédigé par les conservateurs. 2e imp.
London : Scala Books en association avec le Victoria & Albert Museum, 1991 (1994 printing).
160 p. : col. ill. ; 28 cm.
ISBN: 1870248708
Conception éditoriale : Paul Holberton. [Authors' names omitted.] — Maquette: Alan Bartram. — Sized wrappers with col. ills. — French version of v.1995.031.

V.1994.021   *The Victoria & Albert Museum's textile collection : woven textile design in Britain from 1750 to 1850* / by Natalie Rothstein.
London : Victoria & Albert Museum, 1994 (Printed by Grafiche Milani).
112 p. : col. ill. ; 30 cm.
(The Victoria & Albert Museum's textile collection)
ISBN: 1851771298

Acknowledgements / Valerie Mendes. — Includes bibliographic references. Glossary. — Designed by Area. — Sized wrappers with col. ill. — Contents adapted from VR.1980.002.

V.1994.022   *The Victoria & Albert Museum's textile collection : woven textile design in Britain to 1750* / by Natalie Rothstein.
[London] : Victoria & Albert Museum, 1994 (Printed by Grafiche Milani).
128 p. : col. ill. ; 30 cm.
(The Victoria & Albert Museum's textile collection)
ISBN: 185177128X
Acknowledgements / Valerie Mendes. — Includes bibliographic references. Glossary. — Designed by Area. — Sized wrappers with col. ill. — Contents adapted from VR.1980.002.

V.1994.023   *Victorian social life : working from paintings.*
[London : Victoria and Albert Museum Education Dept.], 1994 (Printed by the V&A Printing Section).
8 p. : ill. ; 30 cm.
ISBN: 1851771549
Cover title. — Written by Carole Mahoney. Edited and produced by Clio Whittaker. Series edited by Gail Durbin. Bibliography: inside back cover. — Part printed in purple. Stapled. Ill. on wrappers.

V.1994.024   *Walter Strachan : defender in England of the livre d'artiste, Three masters of copper engraving : Roger Vieillard, Albert Flocon & Abram Krol . . . .*
[London : National Art Library, 1994] (Produced by V&A Printing Section).
[12] p. : ill. ; 21 cm.
Cover title. — Text by Walter Strachan. Includes: Walter Strachan : an appreciation / Elizabeth Esteve-Coll. — Stapled; white wrappers with portrait and ill.
EXHIBITION: VX.1994.007

1995

V.1995.001   *Accessories : information and ideas for teachers.*
[London : V&A Education], 1995 (Printed by the Local Press Printers, Totnes).
8 p. : ill. ; 30 cm.
Cover title. — Written by Morna Hinton with contributions from Avril Hart and Diane Symons. Edited and produced by Clio Whittaker. Series editor Gail Durbin. — Bibliography: back cover. — Designed by Tony Garrett, Fathom Graphics. — Partly printed in pink. Stapled. Ills. and text on wrappers.

V.1995.002   *Africa 95 : prints and photographs by artists of African descent.*
London : Victoria and Albert Museum, [1995].
1 sheet, folded ([6] p.) ; 21 cm.
Caption title. At head of title, in blue: Prints, Drawings and Paintings Collection temporary display. — Written by Rosemary Miles.
EXHIBITION: VX.1995.029

v.1995.003   *Apsley House, Wellington Museum* / Simon Jervis & Maurice
              Tomlin ; revised by Jonathan Voak.
              London : Victoria & Albert Museum, 1995 (Printed in Italy).
              79 p. : col. ill., plans ; 25 cm.
              ISBN: 1851771611
              Foreword / Elizabeth Esteve-Coll. — Photography by Ken Jackson, Jeremy Whitaker,
              Richard Bryant. — First ed. designed by Leonard Lawrance. — Sized wrappers with
              col. ills.
              Copy note: some copies issued with Foreword signed Alan Borg.

v.1995.004   *At home in the thirties : the EKCo collection of trade catalogues* /
              Elizabeth McMurray.
              London : National Art Library, Victoria and Albert Museum, 1995
              (Produced by the V&A Printing Section).
              21 p. : ill. ; 21 cm.
              Bibliography: p. 20–21. — Stapled; white wrappers with ill.
              EXHIBITION: vx.1995.025

v.1995.005   *The back of the envelope : first thoughts in design.*
              London : Victoria and Albert Museum, [1995].
              1 sheet, folded ([4] p.) : 1 ill. ; 21 cm.
              Caption title. At head of title, in blue: Prints, Drawings and Paintings Collection
              temporary display.
              EXHIBITION: vx.1995.031

v.1995.006   *Bikt'olia Aelbŏtŭ Pangmulgwan annae sŏ.*
              [London] : Victoria and Albert Museum, 1995 (Produced by Hexacom
              Ltd. and Accent on Type).
              40 p. : col. ill. ; 20 cm.
              ISBN: 1851771660
              Cover title. — Compiled and edited by Michael Wilson and Charles Saumarez-Smith. —
              Designed by Area. — Stapled; sized wrappers with col. ills., and plans on turn-ins. —
              Korean language ed. of v.1991.004. "First published 1991", but this is believed to be
              the first Korean edition.

v.1995.007   *The book and beyond : electronic publishing and the art of the
              book . . . .*
              [London : Victoria and Albert Museum, 1995.]
              [26] p. ; 21 cm.
              Cover title. — By Douglas Dodds. — Stapled; white wrappers with ill.
              EXHIBITION: vx.1995.011

v.1995.008   *Constable and Hampstead : a new display of drawings and
              watercolours . . . .*
              London : Victoria and Albert Museum, [1995].
              1 sheet, folded ([5] p.) ; 21 cm.
              Caption title. At head of title, in blue: Prints, Drawings and Paintings Collection
              temporary display.
              EXHIBITION: vx.1995.016

v.1995.009   *A diversity of gifts : four benefactors of the National Art Library :
              Chauncy Hare Townshend, Austen Henry Layard, Emilia Francis
              Strong Pattison (Lady Dilke) and Francis William Baxter . . . .*

London : National Art Library, Victoria and Albert Museum, 1995.
[6], 38, [2] p. : ill., ports. ; 21 cm.
ISBN: 1851771638
Chauncy Hare Townshend (1798–1868) / by Eoin Shalloo. Sir Austen Henry Layard
(1817–1894) / by Rebecca Coombes. Emilia Francis Strong Pattison, Lady Dilke
(1840–1904) / by Susanna Robson. — Francis William Baxter (1876–1932) / by
Jonathan Hopson. — Includes bibliographies. — Stapled; white wrappers with
decorated title.
EXHIBITION: VX.1995.012

V.1995.010   *Expressionist prints : cultural border-crossing in the early 20th
century.*
London : Victoria and Albert Museum, [1995].
1 sheet, folded ([6] p.) ; 21 cm.
Caption title. At head of title, in blue: Prints, Drawings and Paintings Collection
temporary display. — Written by Rosemary Miles.
EXHIBITION: VX.1995.026

V.1995.011   *Four hundred years of fashion* / editor Natalie Rothstein ; text by
Madeleine Ginsburg, Avril Hart, Valerie D. Mendes and with other
members of the Department of Textiles and Dress ; photography by
Philip Barnard. [Repr.]
Unseen. Recorded in v.1996.017.

V.1995.012   *From Marcantonio Raimondi to the postcard : prints of the Raphael
cartoons.*
London : Victoria and Albert Museum, [1995].
1 sheet, folded ([6] p.) ; 21 cm.
Caption title. At head of title, in blue: Prints, Drawings and Paintings Collection
temporary display. — Written by Elizabeth Miller. — Includes bibliography.
EXHIBITION: VX.1995.010

V.1995.013   *The genius of Wedgwood* / edited by Hilary Young.
London : Victoria and Albert Museum, 1995 (Printed and bound by
Butler and Tanner).
239 p. : ill. (some col.), ports. ; 25 cm.
Foreword / Elizabeth Esteve-Coll, A.J.F. O'Reilly (Chairman, Waterford Wedgwood
plc). Introduction; From the Potteries to St Petersburg : Wedgwood and the making and
selling of ceramics / Hilary Young. Josiah Wedgwood, a lifetime of achievement / Robin
Reilly. The London decorating studio / Gaye Blake Roberts. A rage for exhibitions : the
display and viewing of Wedgwood's frog service / Malcolm Baker. The frog service and
its sources / Michael Raeburn. By imperial command / Michael Raeburn. The frog
service in Russia / Lydia Liackhova. Josiah Wedgwood's trade with Russia / Gaye Blake
Roberts. — Bibliography: p. 222–227. Index. — Designed by Bernard Higton. —
Sized white wrappers with col. ills.
EXHIBITION: VX.1995.020

V.1995.014   *The Glass Gallery : information and ideas for teachers.*
[London] : V&A Education, 1995.
11 p. : ill. ; 30 cm.
ISBN: 1851771719
Cover title. Caption title: Glass. — Written by Jenny Kershaw and Morna Hinton.
Edited by Clio Whittaker and Susan Morris. Series editor Gail Durbin. — Bibliography:
p. 11. — Designed by Tony Garrett. — Stapled; wrappers with ills. part printed in
blue.

V.1995.015   *Japanese studio crafts : tradition and the avant-garde /* Rupert
Faulkner.
London : Laurence King, 1995 (Printed in Singapore).
192 p. : col. ill., map ; 29 cm.
ISBN: 1856690628; 1856690652 (pbk.)
"Published in association with the Trustees of the Victoria and Albert Museum"–
dust-jacket. Bibliography: p. 180–185. Index. — Designed by David Fordham. — Black
cloth covered boards; dust-jacket with col. ills. Or sized wrappers. — Published in the
U.S.A. by the University of Pennsylvania Press, 1995.
EXHIBITION: VX.1995.019

V.1995.016   *Japanese studio crafts, tradition and the avant-garde : 25 May–
3 September 1995, demonstrations, masterclasses, gallery talks,
symposium, educational activities.*
[London] : Victoria and Albert Museum [Education Dept., 1995].
1 sheet, folded ([11] p.) : ill. ; 21 cm.
Includes information about Japanese artists working in the Museum.
EXHIBITION: VX.1995.019

V.1995.017   *Korea : the Samsung Gallery of Korean Art : gallery trail.* [2nd ed.]
[London] : V&A Education, 1995.
1 sheet, folded ([6] p.) : ill. ; 30 cm. + 1 sheet.
Written by Elizabeth Newbery; edited by Clio Whittaker. — Designed and illustrated by
Linda Francis. — Part printed in green. — Notes for adults on separate sheet.

V.1995.018   *The National Art Library : a policy for cataloguing the collections /*
compiled and edited by Jane Savidge and Douglas Dodds for the
National Art Library Cataloguing Policy Group.
London : National Art Library, Victoria and Albert Museum, 1995.
26 p. ; 21 cm.
ISBN: 1851771816
Bibliography: p. 16–18. — Stapled; yellow wrappers.

V.1995.019   *The National Art Library and its buildings : from Somerset House to
South Kensington /* Chiara Barontini.
[London : The Library, 1995] (Printed by V&A Printers).
47 p. : 1 ill. ; 21 cm.
Select bibliography: p. 46–47. — Stapled; white wrappers with plans.
EXHIBITION: VX.1995.006

V.1995.020   *The origins of British watercolour painting : a new display . . . .*
London : Victoria and Albert Museum, [1995].
1 sheet, folded ([6] p.) ; 21 cm.
Caption title. At head of title, in blue: Prints, Drawings and Paintings Collection
temporary display.
EXHIBITION: VX.1995.002

V.1995.021   *Photographs of African sculpture by Walker Evans.*
London : Victoria and Albert Museum, [1995].
1 sheet, folded ([6] p.) ; 21 cm.
Caption title. At head of title, in blue: Prints, Drawings and Paintings Collection
temporary display. — Written by Mark Haworth-Booth.
EXHIBITION: VX.1995.028

V.1995.022 *Picturing plants : an analytical history of botanical illustration* / by
Gill Saunders.
London : Zwemmer in association with the Victoria and Albert
Museum, 1995 (Printed and bound in Singapore).
152 p. : ill. (some col.) ; 23 cm.
ISBN: 0302006524
Bibliography: p. 149. Index. — Designed and typeset by Christopher Matthews and Ian
Muggeridge. — Sized wrappers with col. ills. — Published in the U.S.A. by University of
California Press, 1995.
EXHIBITION: vx.1995.017

V.1995.023 *Recent acquisitions for the photography collection ... & The early
years of the photography collection, 1856–69.*
London : Victoria and Albert Museum, [1995].
1 sheet, folded ([6] p.) ; 21 cm.
Caption title. At head of title: Prints, Drawings and Paintings Collection temporary
display. — Includes glossary.
EXHIBITION: vx.1995.003

V.1995.024 *The rule of taste : designs for Georgian architecture.*
London : Victoria and Albert Museum, [1995].
1 sheet, folded ([6] p.) ; 21 cm.
Caption title. At head of title: Prints, Drawings and Paintings Collection temporary
display.
EXHIBITION: vx.1995.013

V.1995.025 *The silversmith's studio, San Lorenzo : Victoria and Albert Museum,
Gallery 70 Design Now, October '95–April '96.*
[London : The Museum, 1995.]
1 sheet, folded ([10] p.) : chiefly ill. ; 21 cm.
Caption title.
EXHIBITION: vx.1995.027

V.1995.026 *A teacher's guide to using the Print Room.*
[London] : V&A Education, 1995 (Printed by Able Printing).
36 p. : ill. ; 30 cm.
ISBN: 1851771557
Cover title. — Written by Colin Mulberg with contributions from Jean Burns, Pauline
Cameron, Anthony Dyson, Brian Gee, Susan Morris. Edited by Clio Whittaker, series
editor Gail Durbin. — Bibliography: p. 36. — Designed by Oblique Design. — Stapled
with ills. (1 col.); wrappers; sized.

V.1995.027 *Twenty British works on paper 1980–1995, from the permanent
collection : a new display in the Watercolours Gallery ....*
London : Victoria and Albert Museum, [1995].
1 sheet, folded ([6] p.) ; 21 cm.
Caption title. At head of title, in blue: Prints, Drawings and Paintings Collection
temporary display. – Written by Susan Lambert.
EXHIBITION: vx.1995.023

V.1995.028 *Twenty great watercolours and drawings by John Constable
(1776–1837) : a new display of drawings and watercolours ....*
London : Victoria and Albert Museum, 1995.
1 sheet, folded ([6] p.) ; 21 cm.

Caption title. At head of title, in blue: Prints, Drawings and Paintings Collection temporary display. – Written by Ronald Parkinson.
EXHIBITION: VX.1995.030

V.1995.029　　　*Using the dress collection at the V&A : a handbook for teachers.*
London : Victoria and Albert Museum, 1995 (Printed by Able Printing).
36 p. : ill. ; 30 cm.
ISBN: 1851771492
Written by Morna Hinton with contributions from Amy de la Haye, Valerie Mendes, Susan Morris, Charles Newton, Nancy Osborn, Imogen Stewart, Diane Symons, Verity Wilson. Edited by Clio Whittaker, series editor Gail Durbin. — Bibliography: p. 35. — Designed by Bruce Grove, Designers Ink. — Stapled; sized wrappers with col. ills.

V.1995.030　　　*Vandals and enthusiasts : views of illumination in the nineteenth century* / Rowan Watson.
[London : Victoria and Albert Museum, 1995.]
46 p. : 1 ill. ; 30 cm.
[ISBN: 1851771670]
Cover title. At head of title: Victoria and Albert Museum. — "Contains the texts of labels and graphic panels made for the exhibition"–[preface]. — Includes indexes of illuminators, provenance, publishers, and manuscript names, and concordance of museum inventory numbers. — Comb bound.
EXHIBITION: VX.1995.005

V.1995.031　　　*The Victoria and Albert Museum* / introduction by the Director ; text by the curators. [Corrected reprint]
London : Scala Books in association with the Victoria and Albert Museum, 1991 (Printed and bound by Grafiche Milani, 1995).
160 p. : col. ill. ; 28 cm.
ISBN: 1870248686
Editor's and authors' names omitted. — Index. — Designed by Alan Bartram. — Sized wrappers, with new ills.

V.1995.032　　　*Vikutoria & Arubāto Bijutsukan ten* / kaisetsu Vikutoria & Arubāto Bijutsukan kanchō gakugeiin ; Tanabe Tōru yaku. [Repr.]
Tokyo : Misuzu Shobō Publishing Co. and Scala Publications, 1992 (Printed and bound by Grafiche Milani, 1995).
160 p. : col. ill. ; 28 cm.
"Scala Books, published in association with the Victoria and Albert Museum"–t.p.
— Japanese translation of v.1995.031.

V.1995.033　　　*Voyages & visions : nineteenth-century European images of the Middle East from the Victoria and Albert Museum* / Esin Atil, Charles Newton, Sarah Searight.
Washington, D.C. ; London : Smithsonian Institution Traveling Exhibition Service and the Victoria and Albert Museum in association with University of Washington Press, 1995.
127 p. : col. ill., map ; 30 cm.
ISBN 0295974907; 0865280428 (pbk.)
Bibliography: p. 126. Index of artists.
EXHIBITION: VX.1995.XXX.005

1996

V.1996.001   *The 20th Century Gallery : a teachers [sic] guide.*
[London : Victoria and Albert Museum Education Dept.], 1996.
38 p. : ill., plan ; 30 cm.
ISBN: 1851771913
Cover title. — Written by Colin Mulberg with contributions from Susan Royale and
Jill Slaney, edited by Clio Whittaker, series editor Gail Durbin. — Bibliography: p. 37.
— Designed by In One Design. — Stapled; sized wrappers coloured black with
col. ills.

V.1996.002   *Alphabet of a century : style, taste & society in 18th century
London . . . .*
London : Victoria & Albert Museum, [1996].
1 sheet, folded ([5] p.) : ill. ; 21 cm.
Cover title.
EXHIBITION: vx.1996.039

V.1996.003   *American photography 1890–1965 from the Museum of Modern Art,
New York : exhibition guide . . . .*
[London] : Victoria and Albert Museum, [1996].
1 sheet, folded ([11] p.) : ill. ; 21 cm.
Text compiled by Mark Haworth-Booth, based on VR.1995.002. — Partly printed in
orange.
EXHIBITION: vx.1996.036

V.1996.004   *Apsley House, Wellington Museum* / Simon Jervis & Maurice Tomlin ;
revised by Jonathan Voak. [Repr. with new photography]
London : Victoria and Albert Museum, 1996 (Printed in Italy).
79 p. : col. ill., plans ; 25 cm.
ISBN: 1851771611
Foreword / Alan Borg. — Photography by Ken Jackson, Daniel McGrath, Sara Hodges,
James Stevenson, V&A Photographic Studio. — First ed. designed by Leonard
Lawrance. — Sized wrappers with col. ills.

V.1996.005   *The Arundel Society 1848–1897.*
London : Victoria and Albert Museum, [1996].
1 sheet, folded ([5] p.) : 1 ill. ; 21 cm.
Caption title. At head of title, in blue: Prints, Drawings and Paintings Collection
temporary display. — Written by Frances Rankine.
EXHIBITION: vx.1996.029

V.1996.006   *The Bettine, Lady Abingdon collection : the bequest of Mrs T.R.P.
Hole : a handbook* / Sarah Medlam.
London : Victoria and Albert Museum, 1996 (Printed in Italy).
104 p. : ill. (some col.), plans, ports. ; 28 cm.
ISBN: 1851771794
Bibliography: p. 102–103. — Designed by Area. — Black paper covered boards; dust-
jacket. — Collection mainly assembled by Lord Stuart de Rothesay.

V.1996.007   *Children's pleasures : books, toys and games from the Bethnal Green
Museum of Childhood* / Anthony Burton.
London : V&A Publications, 1996 (Printed in Italy).
186 p. : ill. (chiefly col.), 28 cm.
ISBN: 1851771743

Designed by the Bridgewater Book Company. — Red paper covered boards and end-papers; dust-jacket with col. ills.

v.1996.008   *Chinese carving* / Craig Clunas.
[London] : Co-published by the Victoria & Albert Museum, Sun Tree Publishing, 1996.
103 p. : ill. (some col.) ; 30 cm.
ISBN: 085667463X
Includes bibliographic references and index. — Photography by Ian Thomas. — White paper covered boards; title blocked in gold; col. ills. on dust-jacket and end-papers.

v.1996.009   *Chinese dress* / Verity Wilson ; photographs by Ian Thomas.
London : Victoria and Albert Museum, 1986 (Printed by Toppan Printing Co. Singapore, 1996.)
135 p. : ill. (some col.), map, ports. ; 26 cm.
(Far Eastern series)
ISBN: 1851771840
Bibliography: p. 131. Index. — Book design by Morrison Dalley Design Partnership, cover design by Mariana Canelo. — Sized wrappers, with col. ills. on black.

v.1996.010   *Collecting Constable : a new display . . . .*
London : Victoria and Albert Museum, 1996.
1 sheet, folded ([6] p.) ; 21 cm.
Caption title. At head of title, in blue: Prints, Drawings and Paintings Collection temporary display. – Written by Ronald Parkinson.
EXHIBITION: vx.1996.032

v.1996.011   *Constable : information and ideas for teachers.*
[London] : V&A Education, 1996.
6 p. : ill. ; 30 cm.
Cover title. — Written by Morna Hinton and Ronald Parkinson. Series editor: Susan Morris. — Includes brief bibliography. — Designed by Oblique Design.

v.1996.012   *Designs for goldsmiths : drawings for English gold and silver.*
London : Victoria and Albert Museum, [1996].
1 sheet, folded ([6] p.) : 1 ill. ; 21 cm.
Caption title. At head of title, in blue: Prints, Drawings and Paintings Collection temporary display. — Written by Michael Snodin.
EXHIBITION: vx.1996.030

v.1996.013   *Drawing in museums : information and ideas for teachers.*
[London] : V&A Education, 1996.
6 p. : ill. ; 30 cm.
Cover title. — Written by Morna Hinton, edited by Clio Whittaker, series editor Gail Durbin. — Includes brief bibliography. — Designed by Bruce Grove, Designers Ink. Part printed in pink; stapled.

v.1996.014   *European sculpture at the Victoria and Albert Museum* / edited by Paul Williamson.
London : Victoria and Albert Museum, 1996 (South Sea International Press, Hong Kong, printer).
191 p. : ill. (some col.), ports. ; 28 cm.
ISBN: 1851771735
Written by members of the Sculpture Collection. — Bibliography: p. 186–188. Index. — Designed by Bernard Higton. — Black paper covered boards; dust-jacket with col. ills.

V.1996.015   *The 'exhibition' watercolour : a new display . . . .*
London : Victoria and Albert Museum, [1996].
1 sheet, folded ([6] p.) ; 21 cm.
Caption title. At head of title, in blue: Prints, Drawings and Paintings Collection
temporary display. – Written by Ronald Parkinson.
EXHIBITION: VX.1996.002

V.1996.016   *First impressions : school work and the Print Room.*
London : Victoria and Albert Museum, [1996].
1 sheet, folded ([6] p.) ; 21 cm.
Caption title. At head of title, in blue: Prints, Drawings and Paintings Collection
temporary display. – Written by Colin Mulberg, Moira Thunder.
EXHIBITION: VX.1996.033

V.1996.017   *Four hundred years of fashion* / editor Natalie Rothstein ; text by
Madeleine Ginsburg, Avril Hart, Valerie D. Mendes and with other
members of the Department of Textiles and Dress ; photography by
Philip Barnard. [Repr.]
[London] : Victoria & Albert Museum, 1996 (Made and printed
by Grafiche Milani).
176 p. : ill. (some col.) ; 29 cm.
ISBN: 1851771166
Includes glossary; bibliographic references. — Cover photography by Daniel McGrath.
— Wrappers, with col. ills.

V.1996.018   *Graphic responses to AIDS.*
London : Victoria and Albert Museum, [1996].
1 sheet, folded ([6] p.) ; 21 cm.
Caption title. At head of title, in blue: Prints, Drawings and Paintings Collection
temporary display. — Written by Shaun Cole.
EXHIBITION: VX.1996.017

V.1996.019   *Introducing the V&A : a guide to the collections for teachers.*
London : Victoria and Albert Museum, 1996.
11 p. : ill., plans ; 30 cm.
ISBN: 185177212X
Cover title. — Authors Colin Mulberg and Sharon Trotter; contributing editor
Susan Morris. — Designer: Oblique Design. — Stapled. Part printed in purple.

V.1996.020   *Jewellery and adornment : information and ideas for teachers.*
[London] : V&A Education, 1996.
10 p. : ill. ; 30 cm.
Cover title. — Written by Colin Mulberg, with contributions from Liz Cosslett and
Julia Mannheim; edited by Clio Whittaker. Series editor: Gail Durbin. — Brief
bibliography. — Designed by Bruce Grove, Designers Ink. — Part printed in green,
stapled.

V.1996.021   *The Medieval Treasury : the art of the Middle Ages in the Victoria
and Albert Museum* / edited by Paul Williamson. Repr.
London : Victoria and Albert Museum, 1986, reprinted 1996.
247 p. : ill. (some col.) ; 24 cm.
Foreword / Alan Borg. — With "a few emendations to the text in the light of recent
scholarship" and an extended bibliography. — Bibliography: p. 244–247. Glossary. —
Designed by Paul Sharp. — Sized wrappers; col. ill. on front cover.

v.1996.022   *Merchants and luxury markets : the marchands merciers of eighteenth-century Paris* / Carolyn Sargentson.
London ; Malibu : Victoria and Albert Museum in association with the J. Paul Getty Museum, 1996 (Printed by Butler and Tanner, Frome).
xi, 224 p., [16] p. of plates : ill. (some col.), plan ; 29 cm.
(Victoria and Albert Museum studies in the history of art and design)
ISBN: 185177176X; 0892362952 (J. Paul Getty Museum)
Bibliography: p. 193–209. Index. — Produced by Alan Sutton Publishing Ltd. — Blue paper covered boards; ill. on dust-jacket.

v.1996.023   *Ornament : a social history since 1450* / Michael Snodin & Maurice Howard.
New Haven ; London : Yale University Press in association with the Victoria and Albert Museum, 1996 (Printed and bound in Hong Kong).
232 p. : ill. (some col.), ports. ; 27 cm.
ISBN: 030064551
Bibliography: p. 218–226. Index. — Designed by Derek Birdsall. — Black paper covered boards; dust-jacket with col. ills.

v.1996.024   *The photography of art and the South Kensington Museum.*
London : Victoria and Albert Museum, [1996].
1 sheet, folded ([5] p.) ; 21 cm.
Caption title. At head of title: Prints, Drawings and Paintings Collection temporary display. — Written by Anthony Hamber. — Includes bibliography.
EXHIBITION: vx.1996.003

v.1996.025   *The Pre-Raphaelites and early British photography : a new display . . . .*
London : Victoria and Albert Museum, [1996].
1 sheet, folded ([5] p.) ; 21 cm.
Caption title. At head of title, in blue: Prints, Drawings and Paintings Collection temporary display. – Written by Ronald Parkinson.
EXHIBITION: vx.1996.016

v.1996.026   *The Raphael tapestry cartoons : narrative, decoration, design* / Sharon Fermor.
London : Scala Books in association with the Victoria and Albert Museum, 1996 (Printed and bound by Sfera International, Milan).
96 p. : ill. (chiefly col.) ; 28 cm.
ISBN: 1857591518
Bibliography: p. 95. Index. — Designed and typeset by Malcolm Preskett. —Black paper covered boards; col. ills. on dust-jacket. Or wrappers.

v.1996.027   *RCA—V&A conservation 1996 : a display of conservation work by graduates of the Royal College of Art/Victoria & Albert Museum Joint Course in Conservation . . . .*
[London : The Course, 1996] (Printed at the V&A).
1 sheet, folded ([11] p.) : ill. ; 21 cm.
Designed by Amelia Noble.
EXHIBITION: vx.1996.018

V.1996.028　　　*Sculpture at the V&A : a handbook for teachers.*
[London] : Victoria and Albert Museum, 1996 (Printed by the Printing Workshop).
36 p. : ill. ; 30 cm.
ISBN: 1851771905
Written by Morna Hinton with contributions from Andrew Bolton and Peta Evelyn. Edited by Clio Whittaker; series editor Gail Durbin. — Further reading and resources: p. 35–36. — Designed by Oblique Design. — Stapled; sized wrappers with col. ills.

V.1996.029　　　*Silver* / edited by Philippa Glanville.
London : Victoria and Albert Museum, 1996 (South Sea International, Hong Kong, printer).
143 p. 1 p. : ill. (some col.) ; 28 cm.
ISBN: 1851771727; 1851771891 (pbk.)
Introduction / Philippa Glanville. I, DESIGN AND CONTEXT: The Middle Ages. Plate and piety. Renaissance. Spoons : the universal luxury. Mannerism. Charles I as patron. Welcome and Bath cups. Baroque. The new hot drinks. The arrival of the dinner service. Laying the table. Rediscovery of the antique. Arms. Regency and Empire. The dispersal of historic plate. Eclecticism. Elkington's the innovators. Design reform in England. The dilemma of the 1890s : old or new? Novelties. The emergence of modernism. The impact of modernism. The post-war revival. International highlights of the past ten years. II, THE CRAFT: What is a goldsmith? What is a hallmark? Working and decorating silver. How to cast. Care and cleaning. Design. Imitations and substitutes. Selling silver. A London business. III, ATTITUDES TO SILVER: Gifts, prizes and rewards. The Goldsmiths' Company of London. Collecting. Fakes, forgeries and confections. Small silver for collectors. Ceremony and authority. Women and silver. Silver in paintings. Authors: Marian Campbell, Helen Clifford, Matthew Cock, Ann Eatwell, Amelia Fearn, Celina Fox, Philippa Glanville, Anthony North, Clare Phillips, Rosemary Ransome-Wallis, Pippa Shirley, Andrew Spira, Eric Turner, James Yorke. — Bibliography: p. 137–138. Index. — Designed by Bernard Higton. — Black paper covered boards; col. photograph on dust-jacket; Sized wappers coloured black with col. photograph.

V.1996.030　　　*Sir William Chambers* / edited by Michael Snodin ; essays by John Harris . . . [et al.].
London : V&A Publications, 1996 (Printed by Grafiche Milani).
224 p., viii p. of plates : ill. (some col.), plans ; 31 cm.
(Catalogues of architectural drawings in the Victoria and Albert Museum)
ISBN: 1851771824
Foreword / Susan Lambert. The drawings of Sir William Chambers and the V&A collection / John Harris, Michael Snodin and Stephen Astley. The Franco-Italian album and its significance / Janine Barrier. Chambers's catalogue of casts of engraved gems / Gertrud Seidmann. Catalogue / Stephen Astley, Michael Snodin, Janine Barrier and Rosemary Battles Foy. — Bibliography: p. 216–217. Index. Concordance of Museum numbers. — Grey paper covered boards; white dust jacket with col. ills.

V.1996.031　　　*Spanish sculpture : catalogue of the post-medieval Spanish sculpture in wood, terracotta, alabaster, marble, stone, lead and jet in the Victoria and Albert Museum* / Marjorie Trusted.
London : Victoria and Albert Museum, 1996 (Printed by Butler and Tanner, Frome).
x, 172 p : ill. (some col.), map ; 29 cm.
ISBN: 1851771778
Dust-jacket subtitle: A catalogue of the collections in the Victoria and Albert Museum. — Bibliography: p. 157–168. Indexes of artists, subjects and inventory numbers. — Produced by Sutton Publishing Ltd. — Red paper boards, dust-jacket with illustrations.

v.1996.032　　　*Surfers soulies skinheads & skaters : subcultural style from the forties to the nineties* / Amy de la Haye and Cathie Dingwall ; photography by Daniel McGrath.
London : Victoria and Albert Museum, 1996 (Printed by C.S. Graphics, Singapore).
[160] p. : col. ill., ports. ; 30 cm.
ISBN: 1851771751
Brief bibliography. — Designed by Johnson Banks. — Wrappers with col. ills.
EXHIBITION: vx.1994.027

v.1996.033　　　*Using the V&A at Key Stage 1 : information and ideas for teachers.*
[London] : Victoria and Albert Museum Education Dept., 1996.
7 p. : ill. ; 30 cm.
ISBN: 1851772022
Cover title. — Written by Carole Mahoney; series editor Gail Durbin. — Designed by In One Design. — Partly printed in blue; stapled.

v.1996.034　　　*V&A : a hundred highlights* / edited by Anna Jackson.
[London] : Victoria and Albert Museum, 1996 (Printed in Italy).
79 p. : ill. (chiefly col.), plan ; 24 cm.
ISBN: 1851771832
Foreword / Alan Borg. — Designed by Harry Green. — Sized wrappers with col. ills.

v.1996.035　　　*V&A : cent chefs d'oeuvre* / sous la direction d'Anna Jackson.
[London] : Victoria and Albert Museum, 1996 (Imprimé en Italie).
79 p. : ill. (chiefly col.), plan ; 24 cm.
ISBN: 1851771859
Introduction / Alan Borg. — Maquette: Harry Green. — Sized wrappers with col. ills. — French translation of v.1996.034.

v.1996.036　　　*V&A : einhundert Glanzstücke* / redaktion Anna Jackson.
[London] : Victoria and Albert Museum, 1996 (Printed in Italy).
79 p. : ill. (chiefly col.), plan ; 24 cm.
ISBN: 1851771867
German translation of v.1996.034.

v.1996.037　　　*V&A : Vikutoria & Arubāto hyaku sen* [edited by Anna Jackson].
[London] : Victoria and Albert Museum, 1996.
ISBN: 1851771875
Japanese translation of v.1996.034.

v.1996.038　　　*Visiting the V&A : essential information for teachers, 1996–97.*
London : Victoria and Albert Museum, 1996.
11 p. : ill., plans ; 30 cm.
ISBN: 1851772111
Cover title. — Authors Colin Mulberg and Sharon Trotter; contributing editor Susan Morris. — List of publications available from the V&A Education Dept.: p. 6. — Designer: Oblique Design. — Stapled. Partly printed in red.

v.1996.039　　　*Western furniture, 1350 to the present day, in the Victoria and Albert Museum, London* / edited by Christopher Wilk.
London : Philip Wilson in association with the Victoria and Albert Museum, 1996 (Printed and bound by Società editoriale libraria p.a., Trieste).
231 p. : ill. (some col.) ; 28 cm.

ISBN: 1856674435; 085667463x (pbk.)

Includes bibliographic references. General and numerical indexes. — Designed and typeset by Christopher Matthews and Malcolm Preskett. — Brown paper covered boards, col. ill on dust-jackets. Or sized wrappers.

v.1996.040   *William Morris* / edited by Linda Parry.
London : Philip Wilson in association with the Victoria and Albert Museum, 1996 (Printed and bound by Società editoriale libraria, Trieste).
384 p. : ill. (some col.), ports. ; 29 cm.
ISBN: 856674419; 856674427 (pbk.)

Preface / Alan Borg. Sponsor's preface / Michael Blakenham (Chairman, Pearson plc). Catalogue. THE MAN: A, Introduction / Linda Parry. B, The designer / Fiona MacCarthy. C, The writer / Peter Faulkner. D, The businessman / Charles Harvey and Jon Press. E, The political activist / Nicholas Salmon. F, The conservationist / Chris Miele. THE ART: G, Painting / Ray Watkinson. H, Church decoration and stained glass / Martin Harrison. I, Domestic decoration / Linda Parry. Furniture / Frances Collard. K, Tiles and tableware / Jennifer Hawkins Opie. L, Wallpaper / Lesley Hoskins. M, Textiles / Linda Parry. N, Calligraphy / John Nash. O, The Kelmscott Press / John Dreyfus. THE LEGACY: P, The Morris who reads us / Norman Kelvin. Q, Morris in context / Clive Wainwright. R, Morris after Morris / Paul Greenhalgh. List of Morris objects in the V&A by Howard Batho. — Bibliography: p. 376–377. Index. List of lenders. — Designed by Gillian Greenwood. — Green paper covered boards, decorated end-papers, dust-jacket. Or sized wrappers.
EXHIBITION: vx.1996.013

v.1996.041   *William Morris pack* / Norman Birch, Colin Mulberg.
London : Victoria and Albert Museum : Pictorial Charts Educational Trust, 1996.
8 posters : col. ill. ; 42 cm. + leaflet (4 p.).
(PCET wallcharts. A ; 108)
In plastic wallet.
EXHIBITION: vx.1996.013

PERIODICAL PUBLICATIONS
OF THE
VICTORIA AND ALBERT MUSEUM

Titles are listed in chronological order by publication of first issue.

Explanation of entries
(See also notes at head of main bibliography, p. 3):

Citation number	VP.1986.001
Title	*Victoria and Albert Museum : report of the Board of Trustees.*
Publication details	London : Victoria and Albert Museum (Printed by Gavin Martin Ltd.).
Frequency, designation, dates	Triennial[a], October 1983/March 1986[b] (1986[c])–<October 1993/March 1996 (1996)>[d]
Physical description	<4>[e] v. : ill.(some col.), ports; 30 cm.
	ISBN: 1851770232; 1851770186; 1851771182; 1851771646
Notes	First two reports edited by Jonathan Voak, second two by Susan Laurence.

[a] Frequency
[b] Volume/issue designation, number or date.
[c] Publication date (included unless identical with date of designation).
[d] Diamond brackets denote the last issue published up to and including 1996, and that the title continued publication.
[e] Diamond brackets denote the number of issues published up to and including 1996, and that the title continued publication.

Where a periodical has changed its name but otherwise remains substantially the same, the entries are grouped together under a gathering entry:

VP.1950.001
1950?–1975[f]

Gathering title[g]	[Circulation Department loan collections]

VP.1950.001A

Title proper	*School loans : loans available to art schools and training colleges.* [etc.]

[f] Publication date span is included where the journal has multiple entries and is defunct.
[g] Square brackets indicate a supplied title.

For abbreviations and usages see p. 4.

VP.1868.001   [Acquisitions]
1868–1912

VP.1868.001A   *List of objects in the Art Division, South Kensington Museum,*
                 acquired during the year . . . : arranged according to the dates of
                 acquisition.
                 London : Printed by George E. Eyre and William Spottiswoode for
                 H.M.S.O.
                 Annual, 1852 to the end of 1867 (1868)–1891 (1892).
                 25 v. ; 25 cm.
                 At head of title (to 1885 (1886)): Science and Art Department of the Committee of
                 Council on Education. From 1886 (1887): Department of Science and Art of the
                 Committee of Council on Education. Caption title: Inventory of art objects acquired in
                 the year . . . Added title for "Vol. I" : Inventory of the objects in the Art Division of the
                 Museum at South Kensington. — Copies bear note: "Under revision" or "Proof under
                 revision". — From 1872 (1873): "With index". From 1874 (1875): "With index and
                 appendix". — Blue wrappers. — Issues for 1852–1867 published together, though
                 individually paginated, as "Vol. I" (1868). All other years regular.

VP.1868.001B   *List of works of art acquired by the South Kensington Museum during*
                 the year . . . : arranged according to the dates of acquisition, with
                 appendix and indices.
                 London : Printed for H.M.S.O. by Eyre and Spottiswoode.
                 Annual, 1892 ("1893", printed 1894)–1895 (1897), all 2 years in
                 arrears.
                 4 v. ; 25 cm.
                 At head of title: Department of Science and Art of the Committee of Council on
                 Education. — Caption title: Works of art acquired by the South Kensington Museum
                 during the year . . . . — Caption title for 1895: Acquisitions, South Kensington Museum,
                 . . . . — Copies bear note: "Proof under revision". — Issue for 1895: Printed for Her
                 Majesty's Stationery Office by Wyman and Sons, Limited. — Blue paper wrappers.

VP.1868.001C   *List of works of art acquired by the Victoria and Albert Museum*
                 during the year . . . : arranged according to the dates of acquisition,
                 with appendix and indices.
                 London : Printed for H.M.S.O. by Wyman and Sons.
                 Annual, 1896 (1900)–1908 (1912), all 4 years in arrears except 1900
                 (1903), 1907 (1912).
                 13 v. ; 25 cm.
                 At head of title: Board of Education, South Kensington. — Caption title: Acquisitions,
                 Victoria and Albert Museum, ... — Copies bear note: "Proof under revision".
                 From 1905 (1909) printed by Eyre and Spottiswoode. — Blue paper wrappers. Issue for
                 1905 (1909) has cream paper wrapper.

VP.1868.001D   *List of works of art acquired by the Victoria and Albert Museum*
                 during the year 1901 : (Jermyn Street collection).
                 London : Printed for H.M.S.O. by Wyman and Sons, 1907–1909.
                 4 v. (265, 113, 188?, 183 p.) ; 24 cm.
                 At head of title: Board of Education, South Kensington. "Proof under revision". — Part
                 I, Part II (1907); Part III (1908); Part IV (1909). — Index. Marks. — Comprises the
                 bulk of the collection of the Museum of Practical Geology.

1. *The treasury of ornamental art* (VR. 1857.002). The Museum cooperated with specialist printers to obtain and publish high quality reproductions of its collections.

CAFFAGGIOLO.

HOSE who may have travelled by the old poft road from Bologna to Florence will probably recollect a ftern but picturefque machicolated building, ftanding not far from the laft poft-houfe before reaching the Tufcan capital. Built by Cofmo, this villa was one of the favourite reforts of Lorenzo dei Medici; and at Caffaggiolo the young Giovanni, afterwards Leo X., was educated by Politian. Within thofe walls alfo the beautiful Eleonora di Toledo was murdered by her hufband, Pietro de' Medici, in 1576.

It is probable that were the archives of Florence thoroughly fearched fome record might be found of the eftablifhment or exiftence at Caffaggiolo, of an artiftic pottery encouraged and patronized by that family, but at prefent we have no fuch recorded hiftory. Here again the objects themfelves have been their beft and only hiftorians. It was but a few years fince that the ill indited name of this "*botega*," noticed upon the back of a plate, was read as that of the artift who had painted it, until the difcovery of others, more legibly written, proved that at this fpot important and highly artiftic works had been produced. The occurrence of a monogram upon feveral, and the comparifon of their technical details, has lead to the recognition of many others, and revealed the fact that this fabrique had exifted from an early period, and was productive of a large number of pieces of varying quality.

M. Jacquemart[1] furmifes that at Caffaggiolo Luca della Robbia earnt the nature of the enamel glaze, which he applied to his relievos

---

[1] "Les Merveilles de la Céramique." 2ᵉ pt. Paris, 1868. p. 122.

PLASTICS AND THE FUTURE

V.E.Yarsley and E.G.Couzens

SOME DAY YOU'LL BATHE IN A MOLDED TUB

BUT NOT YET, BROTHER, NOT YET!

BOONTON MOLDING COMPANY
BOONTON · NEW JERSEY

An advertisement for a moulded plastic baby bath. *Modern Plastics*, February 1938.

Let us try to imagine a dweller in the 'Plastic Age' that is already upon us. This creature of our imagination, this 'Plastic Man', will come into a world of colour and bright shining surfaces, where childish hands find nothing to break, no sharp edges or corners to cut or graze, no crevices to harbour dirt or germs, because, being a child, his parents will see to it that he is surrounded on every side by this tough, safe, clean material which human thought has created. The walls of his nursery, all the articles of his toilet, his bath and certain other necessities of his small life, all his toys, his cot, the moulded light perambulator in which he takes the air, the teething ring he bites, the unbreakable bottle he feeds from, later all the equipment for his more mature daily meals, the trays, the spoons and mugs, all will be plastic, brightly self-coloured and patterned with every design likely to please his childish mind. As he grows up he cleans his teeth and brushes his hair with plastic bristles, clothes himself in plastic clothes of synthetic silk and wool fastened with plastic zip-fasteners, wears shoes of plastic and textiles covered with a plastic finish, writes his lessons with a plastic pen and does his lessons with books bound in plastic. He sits in a new kind of schoolroom with shining unscuffable walls at a moulded desk, warm and smooth and clean to the touch, unsplinterable, without angles or projections.

Baby's rattle made of bakelite. 1940s.

55

Page design of V&A publications.

2. (*facing page*) Fortnum, C. Drury, *A descriptive catalogue of the maiolica ... in the South Kensington Museum* (v. 1873.009) illustrates the historicist approach to typography and ornament found in the Museum's first major publications.

3. (*above*) Sparke, Penny, ed., *The plastics age* (v. 1990.014) won awards from the British Printing Industries Federation, including a Redwood award for design and production.

In both books, the concern for style extends to the prose.

VICTORIA
& ALBERT
MUSEUM

A PICTURE BOOK
OF BYZANTINE ART

PRICE SIXPENCE NET

VICTORIA
& ALBERT
MUSEUM

A PICTURE BOOK OF
GERMAN PORCELAIN
FIGURES

PRICE SIXPENCE NET

VICTORIA
& ALBERT
MUSEUM

A PICTURE BOOK
OF ENGLISH
LACE

PRICE SIXPENCE

THE MINNEAPOLIS
INSTITUTE OF ARTS

A PICTURE BOOK OF
TAPESTRIES

MINNEAPOLIS, 1939

4. The popular series of small-format *Picture books* was produced from 1925 to 1938. The odd-man-out here shows the influence of their design. The illustrations were black-and-white photographs.

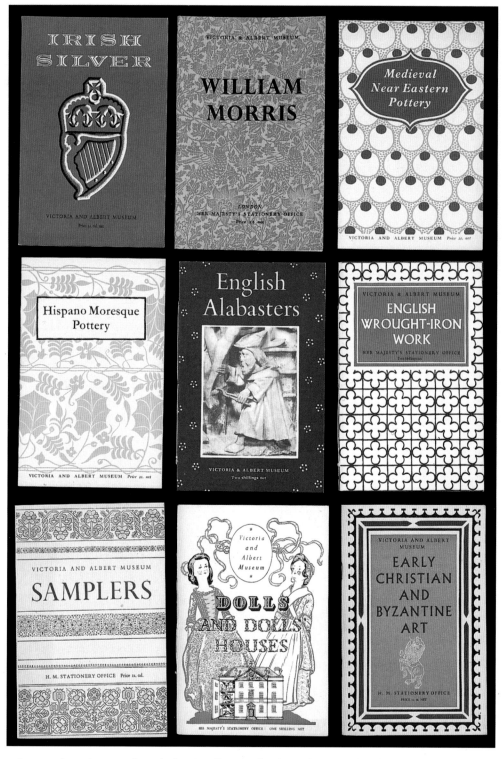

5. In 1947 the series was relaunched as *Small picture books*, with more colourful, variegated wrappers, and the photographs printed on coated paper.

6. *Log Book*, a sculpture by Helene Fesenmaier, commissioned for 'The open & closed book' (VX. 1979.021), stood on the pavement in front of the main entrance of the V&A for the duration of the exhibition.

7. Leaflets to accompany the travelling exhibitions of the V&A Circulation Department. The distinctive tall folded format was adopted in 1969.

8. A selection of books published by the Museum in 1996, the year the V&A Publications imprint was relaunched. The 'house style' is adaptable to the different subjects and intentions of the publications.

VP.1871.001   [Loans]
1871–1892

VP.1871.001A   *List of objects in the Art Division, South Kensington Museum, lent*
                     during the year . . . .
                     London : Printed by George E. Eyre and William Spottiswoode for
                     H.M.S.O.
                     Annual, 1870 (1871)–1876 (1877).
                     4 v. ; 21 cm.
                     At head of title: Science and Art Department of the Committee of Council on Education.
                     — "Arranged according to the dates of loan, with alphabetical index of lenders."

VP.1871.001B   *List of art objects in the South Kensington Museum and in the Branch*
                     Museum, Bethnal Green, lent during the year . . . .
                     London : Printed by George E. Eyre and William Spottiswoode for
                     H.M.S.O.
                     Annual, 1875 (1876)–1886/7 (1888). 1888/1891 (1892).
                     14 v. ; 21 cm.
                     At head of title: Science and Art Department of the Committee of Council on Education.
                     — "Arranged according to the dates of loan, with alphabetical index of lenders."

VP.1871.002   *A list of reproductions . . . acquired by the South Kensington Museum*
1871?–1911?   *[Victoria and Albert Museum] in the year[s]* . . .
                     London : Printed by George E. Eyre and William Spottiswoode
                     [Wyman and Sons] for H.M.S.O.
                     Mainly annual.

VP.1871.002A   *A list of reproductions in metal casting, electrotype and plaster* . . . .
                     Known copies: 1869 and 1870 (1871), 1874 and 1875 (1876).

VP.1871.002B   *A list of reproductions in electrotype, fictile ivory and plaster acquired*
                     by the South Kensington Museum during the years 1871, 1872 and
                     1873 (1874).
                     "With indexes."

VP.1871.002C   *List of reproductions in electrotype and plaster* . . . .
                     Known copies: 1876 (1877), 1877, 1878, 1879 (1880), 1880–1888
                     (1881–1889), 1889 and 1890 (1891), 1891–1894 (1892–1895). Some
                     or all reprinted in 1906.
                     At head of title: Science and Art Department of the Committee of Council on Education,
                     South Kensington Museum. — "For official use only." — Indexes to names, subjects
                     and objects, and chronological index.

VP.1871.002D   *A list of reproductions in casts from the antique acquired by the South*
                     Kensington Museum in the years 1882 to 1884 (1885).
                     "For official use only." — Index, chronological index, index to Museum numbers.

VP.1871.002E   *List of reproductions in metal and plaster* . . . .
                     Known copies: 1893 (1895, 1900), 1894, 1895 (1896, 1903), 1896,
                     1897 (1901), 1898 (1902), 1899 (1903), 1900 (1904), 1901, 1902
                     (1904), 1903 (1906), 1904, 1905 (1908), 1906 (1909), 1907 and
                     1908 (1911).
                     At head of title: Board of Education, South Kensington. — "For official use only." —
                     Indexes to subjects, names, artists, and chronological index.

VP.1910.001   [Prints, drawings and paintings : accessions]
1910–1969

VP.1910.001A   *Department of Engraving, Illustration and Design : accessions.*
                     London : Printed for H.M.S.O. ("E & S", printer).
                     Annual. 1909 (1910)–1913 (1914), 1915 (1916).
                     6 v. ; 22 cm.
                     At head of title: Victoria & Albert Museum. — In brown card wrappers.

VP.1910.001B   *Department of Engraving, Illustration and Design & Department of*
                     Paintings : accessions.
                     London : Published under the authority of H.M.S.O.
                     Annual, 1914 (1915), 1916/1918 (1920)–1948 (1957). After 1939
                     (1950), publication up to a decade in arrears.
                     33 v. ; 22 cm.
                     At head of title: Victoria & Albert Museum. — Publication varies: Published under the
                     authority of the Board [or Ministry] of Education. — From 1939 (1950) includes
                     bibliographic references. List of donors. — Accessions 1916–1918 issued in 1 v. —
                     Redesigned after 1939 (1950): rule round title page, "and" for &; coloured card
                     wrappers, different each year. — Vol. II of 1948 (1957) wholly comprises the Henry
                     Herbert Harrod Bequest (see v.1957.007).

VP.1910.001C   *Department of Prints, Drawings and Paintings : accessions.*
                     London : H.M.S.O. ("F M & S", printer).
                     Annual, 1949 (1961)–1968 (1969). 1955/1956 (1963), 1957/1958
                     (1964), 1960/1961 (1964) are combined issues.
                     19 v. ; 22 cm.
                     At head of title: Victoria and Albert Museum. — From 1952 (1963): Foreword /
                     Graham Reynolds. — Includes bibliographic references. List of donors. — Coloured
                     card wrappers. — Vol. II of 1952 (1960) wholly comprises the engravings of Eric Gill,
                     the gift of Mrs. Mary Gill (see v.1960.012). Vol. II of 1960 (1966) wholly comprises the
                     Edgar Seligman gift (see v.1966.008).

VP.1912.001   *Review of the principal acquisitions.*
                     London : H.M.S.O.
                     Annual, 1911 (1912)–1938 (1939).
                     28 v. : ill. ; 25 cm.
                     At head of title: Victoria and Albert Museum. — The Reviews for 1919 and subsequent
                     years contain also the Annual report, previously issued as a separate publication
                     (VRP.1922.001 etc.).
                     Printers vary. — 1911 (1912)–1928 (1929) issued in blue paper wrappers. 1929
                     (1930)–1932 (1933) in cream card wrapper with all-over pattern. Thereafter, in cream
                     or buff card wrapper, with decorative title or border. After publication ceased in
                     1939, no further reports for the Museum as a whole were published until
                     VP.1981.001.

VP.1933.001   [National Art Library acquisitions]
1933–1985

VP.1933.001A   *List of accessions to the catalogue of the Library . . . .*
                     [London : National Art Library.]
                     Monthly, Jan. 1933 (1933)–Oct. 1976 (1977).
                     33 cm.
                     At head of title: Victoria and Albert Museum.

Title varies. 1933–1935, Library : accessions to the catalogue; 1935–1963, A list of the accessions made by the Library during the month . . .; 1964–1969, List of additions to the catalogue of the Library : for the month of . . .; 1970–1972, Victoria and Albert Museum Library monthly list; 1972–1976, Library catalogue list : for the month of . . . . Caption title: Victoria and Albert Museum Library accessions.
Journal articles, recatalogued items and exhibition catalogues are listed separately. — Duplicated typescript, mainly printed on one side of the sheet only.

Combined issues: 1934 Nov.–Dec.; 1937 May–June; 1938 Sept.–Oct.; 1940 Aug.–Sept.; 1941 Nov.–Dec.; 1943 Jan.–Feb., Oct.–Dec.; 1944 June–July, Aug.–Sept., Oct.–Dec.; 1945 Mar.–May, June–Aug., Sept.–Dec.; 1946 Jan.–Mar., Apr.–June, July–Sept., Oct.–Dec.; 1947 Jan.–Feb., Apr.–May, Sept.–Oct., Nov.–Dec.; 1948 Mar.–Apr., May–June, July–Aug.; 1949 Jan.–Feb., July–Aug., Oct.–Nov.; 1950 Jan.–Feb., Apr.–May, July–Aug.; 1952 Mar.–Apr., Aug.–Sept.; 1953 June–July, Oct.–Nov.; 1954 July–Aug.; 1957 Nov.–Dec.; 1958 Nov.–Dec.; 1960 Mar.–Apr., May–June, Nov.–Dec.; 1961 Jan.–Feb.; 1962 June–July; 1963 Nov.–Dec.; 1968 June–July; 1974 Jan.–Feb. 1975 and 1976 issues all bimonthly.

"Special supplements"
> [1967]: Victorian books exhibition : Illustrated books, Children's books, Index. EXHIBITION: vx.1965.013
> Mar. 1968: Church guides : new ed.
> [1969]: The remaining uncatalogued portion of the Harrod bequest of illustrated books.
> Dec. 1969: A collection of catalogues issued in the 19th century by dealers in photographic prints.
> Jan. 1970: Contributions to a "Bartsch corpus".
> Dec. 1970: Recently acquired manuscript material on the Pugin family and others, and items acquired pre–1890 now re-catalogued.
> 1971: A bibliography of books on musical instruments in the Library of the Victoria and Albert Museum / compiled by M.I. Wilson. (See also v.1971.001)
> A bibliography of 120 pattern books and trade catalogues in the Library of the Victoria and Albert Museum / compiled by J. Bunston.
> Jan. 1971: 3 recent gifts of children's books.
> Feb. 1971: Catalogue of miniature books in the Library, including royal loans / compiled by A.J. Sloggett.
> Aug. 1971: Illustrators of La Fontaine . . . / compiled by Anne Stevenson Hobbs.
> Sept. 1971: Recently acquired manuscripts together with some acquired before 1890 and now re-catalogued / compiled by J.I. Whalley.
> Jan. 1972: Illustrated fables . . . Part I, Other than Aesop / by A.S. Hobbs.
> Apr. 1972: Illustrated fables . . . Part II, Aesop, Addenda & corrigenda to Part I.
> Dec. 1972: Recently acquired or recatalogued manuscript material.
> Jan. 1973: A folder of "miscellaneous exhibitions", mostly one-man shows at once-only galleries in London / extracted, identified and catalogued by B. Simmons.
> The personal papers, manuscripts, pamphlets and other documents left by Sir Henry Cole . . . / catalogued by Vera Kaden.
> Feb. 1973: 74 children's books from the Guy Little bequest / catalogued by M.J.A. Holmes.
> Nov. 1973: Manuscripts received and catalogued during 1973 / . . . prepared by J.I. Whalley.
> Children's books to the end of the Newbery period (1802), Part I.
> Jan.–Feb. 1976: Chapbooks.

VP.1933.001B *List of acquisitions.*
[London : National Art Library, Victoria and Albert Museum]
(Printed by HMSO Reprographic Services, Manchester).
Quarterly, no. 1 (1978)–no. 26 (1985).
26 issues ; 30 cm.
Cover title. At head of title: Victoria and Albert Museum, Library. — Green wrappers. — 2 issues in 1978; 3 issues only in 1983.

VP.1950.001   [Circulation Department loan collections]
1950?–1975

VP.1950.001A   *School loans : loans available to art schools and training colleges.*
                   [London] : H.M.S.O. (Printed by Benham & Co., Colchester).
                   Annual, [1950/1951 (1950)?]–1965/66 (1965), 1966/68 (1966).
                   [13?] v.: ill.; 18 cm. ; 24 cm.
                   At head of title, 1966/68: National Museum Loan Service. Produced by the Circulation
                   Department. — Printers: W.S. Cowell Ltd. (1965/66), Grosvenor Press (1966/68). —
                   "Designed at the Royal College of Art by Peter Pickard"–1954/55. — Wrappers: grey
                   (to issue for 1958), white (to 1964), orange (1965), brown (1966); sized paper from
                   1960. Printed in different colours. — Earliest issue seen: 1954/55 (1954).

VP.1950.001B   *Loan collections : available to colleges and schools of art, colleges of
                   education, university departments, and other further education
                   institutions.*
                   [London] : Victoria and Albert Museum Circulation Department
                   (Printed for H.M.S.O. by Butler & Tanner).
                   Annual, 1968/70 (1968?)–1975/77 (1975).
                   5 v.: ill.; 22 cm.
                   At head of title: National Museum Loan Service. — Printers: McCorquodale Printers
                   (1972/74–1974/76); W.S. Cowell (1975/77). — Sized paper wrappers: red, black, green,
                   yellow, navy blue.

VP.1950.002   [Circulation Department travelling exhibitions]
1950?–1976

VP.1950.002A   *Travelling exhibitions available for loan to public museums, art
                   galleries and libraries.*
                   [London : V&A, Circulation Department.]
                   Annual, [1951 ([1950])?]–1954 ([1953]).
                   At head of title: Victoria & Albert Museum Circulation Department. — Text by Peter
                   Floud. — Issues seen: 1951 ([1950]), 1953 ([1952]), 1954 ([1953]).

VP.1950.002B   *Exhibitions : exhibitions for loan to museums, art galleries and
                   libraries.*
                   [London] : H.M.S.O. (Printed by W.S. Cowell at the Butter Market,
                   Ipswich).
                   Annual, 1955 (1954)–1969/70 (1968).
                   [15?] v. : ill., 19 cm.–24 cm.
                   At head of title from issue for 1966/67: National Museum Loan Service. — Produced by
                   the Circulation Department.
                   Printers: John Wright & Sons, (1959–1962/63); Curwen Press (1963/64–1966/67);
                   Swindon Press (1967/68–1969/70).
                   "Originally designed at the Royal College of Art by Peter Pickard"–1956. — Illustrated
                   from issue for 1965/66. — Wrappers: plain in different colours, until issue for 1958;
                   printed over design on sized card, to 1964/65; then lettered in white on plain colours.

VP.1950.002C   *Travelling exhibitions : exhibitions for loan to museums, art galleries
                   and libraries.*
                   [London] : Circulation Department, Victoria and Albert Museum
                   (Printed by Eyre & Spottiswoode at Grosvenor Press, Portsmouth).
                   Annual, 1970/71 (1969)–1977/78 (1976).
                   8 v. : ill., 21 cm.

At head of title: National Museum Loan Service. — Printers: McCorquodale
(1975/76–1977/78). — Plain card wrappers, in different colours.

VP.1965.001   *Bulletin* / Victoria and Albert Museum.
London : Published for the Victoria and Albert Museum by
H.M.S.O.
Quarterly, Vol. I, no. 1 (Jan. 1965)–vol. IV, no. 4 (Oct. 1968).
16 issues : ill. ; 25 cm.
ISSN: 0506–8630
Includes bibliographic references. — Printers: Jarrold & Sons, Eyre and Spottiswoode,
George Pulman and Sons. — Sized card wrappers, illustrated.

Vol. I

1. The Museum in a changing world / Trenchard Cox. A sketch-model by Benvenuto
    Cellini [head of Medusa] / John Pope-Hennessy. English brass-inlaid furniture /
    John Hayward. A Laudian embroidery / Patricia Wardle. Two documented Chelsea
    gold-anchor vases / J.V.G. Mallet. A gift from William Morris [Indian bronze
    figure of the monkey god Hanumān] / John Irwin.

2. A masterpiece [altar] by Hubert Gerhard / Michael Baxandall. A hundred years of
    English silver [1. The Victorian period] / Charles Oman. An ingenious man for
    carving in ivory [David Le Marchand] / Terence Hodgkinson. Portrait sculptures
    by Ridolfo Sirigatti / John Pope-Hennessy. A Sung lacquer cup-stand / John Ayers.
    A relief of the Jain goddess Ambikā / Robert Skelton.

3. The glass of Maurice Marinot / R.J. Charleston. An ivory by Giovanni Pisano /
    John Pope-Hennessy. Thomas Gainsborough's exhibition box / Jonathan Mayne.
    Monti's allegory of the Risorgimento / Anthony Radcliffe.
    A Louis XIV chalice [maker, Jean-Baptiste Loir] / Ronald Lightbown. An Indian
    tree spirit / Robert Skelton.

4. Handel at Vauxhall / Terence Hodgkinson. A Venetian embroidered altar
    frontal / Donald King. The Vile Problem [medal cabinets] / Derek Shrub. A
    grand chivalric entertainment [stage designs by Clarkson Stanfield] / George
    Nash.

Vol. II

1. The Norfolk House music room / Desmond Fitz-Gerald. Barnaba da Modena
    [banner] and the flagellants of Genoa / C. M. Kauffmann. Early Ming taste in
    porcelain / John Ayers. The Coventry ribbon [silk] / Michael Darby.

2. A hundred years of [English] silver [2. The twentieth century] / Charles Oman.
    A lost Persian miniature [ms. of a tale by Nizāmī Ganjavī, 1141–1203, painted by
    Rizā-i 'Abbasī?] / B.W. Robinson. The Channon family of Exeter and London,
    chair and cabinet makers / John Hayward. An allegory of propaganda by Paul
    Klee / C.M. Kauffmann. A new work by Giovanni Bologna / John Pope-Hennessy.
    A Florentine embroidery / Donald King.

3. The restoration of the Devonshire hunting tapestries / George Wingfield Digby.
    Two travel diaries by Sir James Thornhill / John Harthan. Was Samuel Cooper
    influenced by Rembrandt? / Graham Reynolds. The Shah Jahan [jade] cup / Robert
    Skelton. A Rhenish ivory *Noli me tangere* / John Beckwith.

4. A rediscovered English reliquary cross [ivory] / John Beckwith. Cesare Borgia's
    sword-scabbard [leather] / Claude Blair. Abraham Roentgen 'englische
    Kabinettmacher' and some further reflections on the work of John Channon / Peter
    Thornton & Desmond Fitz-Gerald. Degas's ballet scene from *Robert le diable* /
    Jonathan Mayne. Jacobite garters / Michael Darby.

Vol. III

1. Battersea, Bilston – or Birmingham? [painted enamels] / R.J. Charleston. Antonio
    Calcagni's bust of Annibale Caro / John Pope-Hennessy. An arts and crafts
    experiment : the silverwork of C.R. Ashbee / Shirley Bury. Some eighteenth-century
    designs for monuments in Westminster Abbey / J.F. Physick. *Time and death* : a
    new [wax] relief by Zumbo / R.W. Lightbown.

2. Hogarth's pug in porcelain [Chelsea figure, after Roubiliac] / J.V.G. Mallet. Siva
    the Great Teacher / John Irwin. Some main streams and tributaries in European
    ornament from 1500 to 1750 : Part 1 [the grotesque] / Peter Ward-Jackson. Joseph
    Wilton and Doctor Cocchi [portrait bust] / Terence Hodgkinson.

3. A Medici casket [in steel] / R.W. Lightbown. Some main streams and tributaries in European ornament from 1500 to 1750 : Part 2 : The arabesque / Peter Ward-Jackson. Persian miniature painting from collections in the British Isles / B.W. Robinson. A Poussin tapestry from the Gobelins / George Wingfield Digby & Wendy Hefford. Some recent acquisitions.

4. Some main streams and tributaries in European ornament from 1500 to 1750 : Part 3 [Ornaments of the grotto. The cartouche] / Peter Ward-Jackson. Foggini and Soldani : some recent acquisitions / John Pope-Hennessy. The furniture designs of E.W. Godwin / Elizabeth Aslin. Metalwork acquisitions.

Vol. IV

1. An English Delftware charger of General Monck / Michael Archer. A Sheraton designed bookcase and the Giannellis / Desmond Fitz-Gerald. Chinese court robes in the Victoria and Albert Museum / Edmund Capon. Three Spanish cloaks / Donald King. Some recent acquisitions by the Department of Circulation.

2. Two garden sculptures by Antonio Corradini / Terence Hodgkinson. An Islamic crystal mounted as a pendant in the West / R. W. Lightbown. A relic of 'Noble Erpingham' [ecclesiastical vestments] / Donald King. A Langlois commode / Theodore Dell. Ceramic acquisitions.

3. Rowlandson at Vauxhall / Jonathan Mayne. The Harborne room [by John Henry Chamberlain] / Barbara Morris. A panel of stained glass from Erfurt Cathedral / Hans Wentzel. An Italian embroidered picture / Patricia Wardle. Three seventeenth-century Tibetan t'ankas / John Lowry. A Mendelssohn manuscript / Michael Wilson.

4. The earliest Vienna porcelain figures / J.V.G.Mallet. The *Descent from the Cross* by Charles Le Brun / Jennifer Montagu. A tortoiseshell cabinet and its precursors / Simon Jervis. Paris in the cellars [caricatures of the Franco-Prussian War and the Commune] / Brian Gould. Illustrations for Isaac Watts's *Divine and moral songs* / J. Irene Whalley. A woven address [ribbon designed by Richard Rivington Holmes for the wedding of the Prince of Wales, 1863] / Michael Darby. Sculpture acquisitions.

Indexes to Vols. I & II; III & IV.

VP.1966.001   *The National Museum Loan Service : the year's work.*
London : Victoria & Albert Museum.
Annual, 1964/5 (1966)–1975/7 (1978?).
12 v. ; 25 cm.
Cover title. At head of title: Victoria and Albert Museum Department of Circulation. At foot of title: "Including the Purchase Grant for assisting museums, galleries and libraries in the acquisition of works of art, science and literature." — Introduction / Hugh Wakefield. (1964/65: Preface / Trenchard Cox.)

VP.1968.001   *Costume : the journal of the Costume Society.*
London : Published for the Society, Victoria and Albert Museum.
Annual, no. 1/2 (1968)– <no. 7 (1973)>
7 v. : ill., ports. ; 26–29 cm.
ISSN: 0590-8876
Nos. 4–7: Published for the Society c/o the Department of Textiles, Victoria and Albert Museum. — A Newsletter preceded this title: Vol. 1, no. i (1965), no. 2 (Winter 1965–66), no. 3 (Winter 1966–67). — The journal continues, published independently.

1. François Boucher, a tribute / James Laver. The National Film Archive / Colin Ford. The Worcestershire County Museum costume collection / Daphne Bullard. Straw hats, a bibliography / John G. Dony. A wedding dress worn by the Danish Princess Sophia Magdalena in 1766 / Janet Arnold.

2. Exhibition of legal costume : letter from Mr. Julian Baughan. Prince Edward's clothes / J.L. Nevinson. Manuscript sources for the history of medieval costume / Janet Backhouse. Jinbaori, the Japanese military overcoat / H. Russell Robinson. "Warriors for the working day": territorial artillery costume 1961–67 / A.T. Heathcote. Dyeing and cleaning clothes in the late eighteenth and early

nineteenth centuries / Alan Mansfield. Castle Howard : a costume museum in a stately home / Cecile Hummel. Female costume in the aesthetic movement of the 1870s and 1880s / Leonée Ormond. Hosiery : a bibliography / Madeleine Ginsburg. Fashion foibles of 1967 / Ivy Sharp. Notes and pattern of a caftan / Janet Arnold.

3. Conversation at Castle Howard : Miss Annie Wilkinson interviewed / Cecile Hummel. Tailors' masterpiece-books / Ingeborg Petrascheck-Heim. The medieval 'corset' / Kay Staniland. Marriage trousseaux of the common people in the eighteenth century / Henriette Vanier. The first British naval uniform / P.G.W. Annis. The costume collection in Strangers' Hall, Norwich / Pamela Clabburn. A pink silk domino c.1760–70 / Janet Arnold. The costume styles of the classical Maori in New Zealand, 1642–1800 A.D. / Sidney M. Mead. The traditional costumes of the Arab women of Palestine / Shelagh Weir. The development of riding costume, c.1880–1920 / Irene Foster. Tambour beading / Joan Edwards.

4. Daphne Bullard: obituary. The rates of the London Custom House in 1550 / Joan Edwards and J.L. Nevinson. The Polish nobleman's attire / George E. Borchard. Conservation of corps de ballet costume designed by Diaghilev for the Firebird ballet / Karen Finch and Joyce Plester. A mantua, c.1708–9 / Janet Arnold. Paisley shawls, and others / Dorothy Whyte. Bejewelled fur tippets – and the Palatine fashion / Francis Weiss. Church vestments and embroidery / Gilbert Cope. A costume display case for a museum loan service / Daphne Bullard, Brian Blench, and Brian Harper. Old Deerfield / Adèle Jay-Filene. Play it cool / Ivy Sharp. Clothes from Scottish country houses / Janet Arnold.

5. Byronic dress / Doris Langley Moore. Burgundian court costume from a Norwich tapestry / Lesley Parker. Parson Woodforde's view of fashion / Pamela Clabburn. Our predecessors / J.L. Nevinson. Blazers / Alan Mansfield. Current costume, 1970–71 / Alison Adburgham. The reliability of sources / Ruth Green. New books / Anne Buck. A study of three jerkins / Janet Arnold.

6. Japanese court ladies' formal costume – Junihitoe / Fusako Kubo. Nightgown into dressing gown / Margaret H. Swain. Sumptuary legislation and English costume / Clifford R. Bell and Evelyn Rose. Conscience and costume in seventeenth century Scotland / Rosalind K. Marshall. The expectant Victorian / Zuzanna Schonfield. Cycling in the 1890's / Nancy Bradfield. A court mantua of c.1740 / Janet Arnold. Wedding bouquets / Audrey Baker. Otto Haas-Haye / Adèle Jay-Filene. Costume on postage stamps / Ian F. Finlay. The tailoring and dressmaking trades, 1700–1850 / Madeleine Ginsburg. The Gallery of English Costume, Platt Hall, Manchester / Anne Buck. Vestments from the Robinson Collection at the Whitworth Gallery, Manchester / Joan Allgrove. Why a Museum of Religious Dress? / Pamela Clabburn. The Sisters of Charity of St. Vincent de Paul / Bridget Goshawk. A fifteenth century pattern for 'Chausses' / Christina Hawkins. The development of the religious habits of the Faithful Companions of Jesus / Irene V. Duchenne. New books / Anne Buck.

7. A Byzantine imperial coronation of the sixth century A.D. / Averil Cameron. White lace in the seventeenth century / A.M. Louise Mulder-Erkelens. Deer skin leathers and their use for costume / C.H. Spiers. The Warner collection / Nathalie Rothstein. Bonnard's *Costume historique* – a Pre-Raphaelite source book / Roger Smith. An eighteenth century boy's suit / Lou Taylor. A court mantua of c.1760–5 / Janet Arnold. Furred serpents, snuffkins and stomachers / Francis Weiss. The costume of the cricketer / Diana Rait-Kerr. The 'heavy' and 'light' clothing industries, 1850 to 1970 / Alison Beazley. Studies of an 1814 pelisse and bonnet / Nancy Bradfield. Eighteenth century hats in Exeter museums / P.M. Inder. Eaton's and its catalogues / M. Batts. Costume in a local history museum, Weybridge, Surrey / Averil Lansdell. Painters of folk dress / James Snowden. New books, 1972–73 / Kay Staniland.

VP.1969.001

Victoria and Albert Museum yearbook.
London : Phaidon Press (Leicester : Printed by the Cavendish Press).
Annual, no. 1 (1969), no. 2 (1970), no. 3 (1972), no. 4 (1974).
4 v. : ill. (some col.) ; 29 cm.
ISSN: 0083–5927
ISBN: 0714813842; 0714814512; 0714815098; 0714815594
Includes bibliographic references and index. — Cloth covered boards, illustrated dust-jackets.

1. Foreword / John Pope-Hennessy. Canova's *Theseus and the Minotaur* / Hugh Honour. A masterpiece by Girolamo dai Libri [illuminated manuscript leaf] / Mirella Levi D'Ancona. A design for a candlestick by George Michael Moser, R.A. / Shirley Bury and Desmond Fitz-Gerald. A Windsor tapestry portrait [of Queen Victoria] / Wendy Hefford. Two Mughal lion hunts / Robert Skelton. Notes on two paintings [a 15th century Sicilian crucifix, by Antonio de Saliba?; a 'Saturday painting' by Johann Melchior Roos] / C.M. Kauffmann. Some unrecognized Venetian woven fabrics ['half-silks'] / Donald King. An early seventeenth-century master goldsmith / Shirley Bury. Turner at East Cowes Castle / Graham Reynolds. Charles VIII's Trojan War tapestry / J.P. Asselberghs. Pugin's marriage jewellery / Shirley Bury. Buddhist porcelain figures of the Yüan Dynasty / John Ayers. The rood-loft from Hertogenbosch / Charles Avery. Some lithographs by Odilon Redon / Frank Dickinson. The mural from 44 Grosvenor Square / Desmond Fitz-Gerald. John Lochée, portrait sculptor / Terence Hodgkinson.

2. The Gherardini collection of Italian sculpture / John Pope-Hennessy. A manuscript of Petrarch's Rime and Trionfi / J.J.G. Alexander. Mughal paintings from the Harivamśa manuscript / Robert Skelton. Medieval and Renaissance embroidery from Spain / Donald King. The altar-piece of St. George from Valencia [by Andrés Marzal de Sas] / C.M. Kauffmann. The glass drawing room from Northumberland House [designed by Robert Adam] / D. Owsley and W. Rieder. Five monuments from Eastwell / John Physick. English silver: new pieces and new facts / S. Bury and R.W. Lightbown.

3. The Sanchi torso / John Irwin. Bronze oil lamps by Riccio / Anthony Radcliffe. Some fifteenth-century hexagonal tiles from the Near East / John Carswell. An Elizabethan embroidered cover [with inscriptions] / Santina M. Levey. Antler and horn furniture / Simon Jervis. French eighteenth-century portrait sculptures in the Victoria and Albert Museum / Terence Hodgkinson. A Burmese Buddhist shrine / John Lowry. The case of the Victorian piano [includes painted cases] / Michael I. Wilson.

4. A masterpiece by Isaac Oliver / Graham Reynolds. Some newly acquired Italian sculptures: a relief of the Rape of Europa [by or after Verrocchio], a fountain by Rustici, a portrait sketch by Algardi / John Pope-Hennessy. A cupboard by Jacob Frères / Desmond Fitz-Gerald. François Dieussart, portrait sculptor to the courts of Northern Europe / Charles Avery. Acquisitions by the Far Eastern Section: Chinese Buddhist sculpture / Edmund Capon. Chinese painting / R.A. Crighton. Two Ming lacquers / John Ayers. A Viennese Gothic bookcase / Elizabeth Aslin.

VP.1978.001 *Conservation Department newsletter.*
[London : The Department.]
Quarterly, 1978–1980 and 1984–Summer 1985. Three issues yearly, 1981–1983.
[no. 1 (Sept. 1978)]–no. 24 (Summer 1985).
24 issues ; 30 cm.
Departmental newsletter, also circulated informally outside the Museum. — Issues 1–7 edited by M. Goodwin and K. Marko.

VP.1981.001 *Review of the years 1974–1978.*
London : H.M.S.O., 1981 (Printed by Linneys, Mansfield).
180 p., [8] p. of plates : ill. ; 25 cm.
ISBN: 0112903592
At head of title: Victoria & Albert Museum. — Edited by A.P. Burton. Introduction / Alexander Glen. — Bibliography of staff publications: p. 143–168. — Black sized card wrappers with illustration.

A *Review of the years 1979–1983* was prepared by the same editor, but never published.

VP.1982.001   *The V & A album.*
[London] : Templegate Publishing in association with the Friends of
the V&A.
Annual, 1 (1982)–5 (1986); "Gold" ([1986]); Quarterly, Summer
1988–Spring 1989.
8 v. : ill. (some col.) ; 30 cm.
ISSN: 0950-7981
ISBN: 0946345015; 0946345031; 0905209990; 0948107162; 1851770771;
0947991034
Editors: Stephen Calloway (1), John Physick (2), Anna Somers Cocks (3, 4), John Guy
(5), Sir Hugh Casson ([6] "Gold edition"), Miriam Kramer (Summer 1988–). Published
by the Associates of the V&A, distributed by De Montfort Publishing. "Gold" ed.,
Summer 1988–Spring 1989 published by De Montfort Publishing.

1.   Sir Henry Cole : first Director of the V&A / Elizabeth Bonython. Vivant Denon
     and the service égyptien / Charles Truman. Gilding the lily : French ormolu
     1690–1790 / Martin Chapman. Homage to the Queen : Hilliard and the cult of
     Queen Elizabeth / Roy Strong. Oliver Messel in the theatre / John Barber. A glory
     to the Museum : the casting of the Pórtico de la Gloria / Malcolm Baker. The
     image sellers [small plaster casts] / Lionel Lambourne. The picturesque eye :
     Benjamin Brecknell Turner's album / Mark Haworth-Booth. Horace Walpole and
     Strawberry Hill / Stephen Calloway. Igor Stravinsky on the stage : a centenary
     toast to the future / Alexander Schouvaloff. The court painters of Udaipur /
     Andrew Topsfield. The liberal connoisseur : Constantine Alexander Ionides and his
     collection / Stephen Jones. Second thoughts on *My second sermon* by Millais /
     Lionel Lambourne. Contemporary prints : the V&A collects / Susan Lambert.
     Royal babies / Henrietta Front. The great bed of Ware : holotype or syntype? /
     Michael Darby. The king of the hoardings : the posters of Tom Purvis / Bevis
     Hillier. Royal French firearms : a collection made for Louis XIII / A.R.E. North.
     The public face of private mourning : the London funeral 1695–1945 / Julian W.S.
     Litten. Karsavina and friends : an autochrome by Baron de Meyer / Richard Buckle
     and Mark Haworth-Booth. Attic or treasure house? / Simon Tait. The V&A
     Houses. The London streets at Christmas / Anthony Burton.

2.   The Advisory Council: 1913–1983 / Sir Alexander Glen. Apsley House and the
     battle of the Waterloo banquets / The Countess of Longford. The small-scale arts
     of Romanesque England / Paul Williamson. The Margaret de Foix book of hours /
     Rowan Watson. Two early Company albums / Andrew Topsfield. The Speaker's
     state bed [Westminster Palace] / Clive Wainwright. Theatre models / James Fowler.
     Travels with the V&A / Charles and Anne Foster. Pictures by potters [tiles] /
     Michael Archer. Richard Redgrave, RA : artist and administrator / Lionel
     Lambourne. Queen Mab's chariot among the steam engines : the V&A, the RCA
     and the reform of design / Christopher Frayling. The seventeenth-century kitchen
     at Ham House / Caroline Davidson. Nature, the only teacher : a nautilus cup from
     a noble Polish collection / Anna Somers Cocks. Tales of the unexpected : the
     decoration of Japanese export lacquer / Joe Earle. Someone's behind us / Simon
     Tait. The Queen opens the Henry Cole Wing. An ill-arranged affair / John Physick.
     Trophies from the Great Exhibition of 1851 [gold- and silversmiths' work] /
     Shirley Bury. Royal jewels in the V&A / Shirley Bury and Anna Somers Cocks.
     Saving stained glass / June Lennox. Twenty years of ceramic and glass design : the
     collections of the British Institute of Industrial Art and Industry / Jennifer Hawkins
     Opie. Looking at dolls' houses / Anthony Burton. A collection grows : the gift of
     British fashions for Winter 1979 / Valerie Mendes. Persian carpets of the Safavid
     period / Donald King. Painted paper of Pekin : Chinese wallpapers in England /
     Gillian Saunders. Aston Webb / Gavin Stamp. The files of Francis Frith [postcard
     photography] / Valerie Lloyd. George Bickham Junior : master of the rococo
     [engravings] / Michael Snodin. A quartier latin of a dignified and popular sort :
     Prince Albert's own contribution to South Kensington / Hermione Hobhouse.
     Noble works or base deceptions? some Victorian fakes and forgeries / Malcolm
     Baker.

3.   'Triumphs and tribulations' : The Chairman of the Trustees looks to the future /
     Lord Carrington. English hunting swords / A.R.E. North. Remembering Bill Brandt
     / Mark Haworth-Booth. 'Moulding a physiognomy' : a Chinese portrait figure /
     Craig Clunas. Carved ambers : Baltic gold : Prussian silver / Marjorie Trusted.

Stratford Canning's pictures of Turkey / Charles Newton. John Constable in the Lake District, September-October 1806 / John Murdoch. Desert island objects / Stephen Bayley. On toy-shops and toy-sellers / Anthony Burton. Apsley House in 1853 / Simon Jervis. Osterley Park House : a temple of Flora / J. Hardy. Art applied to the home : the household taste of Henry Cole and his circle / Elizabeth Bonython. The V&A and another Cole [Cole & Son (Wallpapers) Ltd.] / Jean Hamilton. An heraldic walk round the V&A / Michael Maclagen [i.e. Maclagan]. Türkmen in Victorian Kensington / Donald King. Three Japanese lacquers / Joe Earle. A group of Chinese porcelains of the Daoguang period (1821–1850) / Rose Kerr. Chinese porcelain and English goldsmiths c.1560 to c.1660 / Philippa Glanville. The collection of post–1920 jewellery in the V&A / Anna Somers Cocks. Some fine watches in the V&A / A.R.E. North. The taste for Regency and Empire furniture in the later nineteenth century / Frances Collard. The conservation of six of the dolphin chairs, Ham House / Nicola Gentle. Gothic rampant : designs by L.N. Cottingham for Snelston Hall / Simon Jervis. Spain and South Kensington : John Charles Robinson and the collecting of Spanish sculpture in the 1860s / Malcolm Baker.

4. Give to the Museum that gives / Sir Roy Strong. Supporting the V&A : from charity to sponsorship / Julie Laird. Fakes & forgeries of Islamic pottery / Oliver Watson. An ebony and ivory cabinet [from Naples] / Simon Jervis and Reinier Baarsen. The grand Jersey ball at Osterley / The Friends of the V&A. In search of 'the little black dress' / Valerie Mendes. David Bailey and great fashion photographers / Martin Harrison. Costume and fashion jewellery of the twentieth century / Jane Stancliffe. Llewelyn and instantaneity / Christopher Titterington. Some designs for English gold and silver / Michael Snodin. Silver toys / Miranda Poliakoff. Souvenirs of Italy (for nineteenth century travellers) / R.W. Lightbown. The Serilly cabinet : Anne-Marie De Serilly and the story of the 'boudoir' / Margaret English and Lucia Scalisi. Thomas Hope's vase and Alexis Decaix / Martin Chapman. Desert island objects : Sir Ernst Gombrich chooses / Jill Tilden. Fragments and questions unanswered [Caucasian carpets] / Jennifer Wearden. A new Japanese gallery / Joe Earle. Japanese tea ceramics in the V&A : acquisitions of 1877 / Rupert Faulkner. Chinese children's dress / Verity Wilson. An imperial gift : a jade ruyi in the V&A / Nick Pearce. The Chinese chair and the Danish designer [Hans Wegner] / Craig Clunas. Contemporary Chinese crafts / Rose Kerr. A lost Mughal miniature rediscovered / Rosemary Crill. Art and deco : the problems of British ceramics in the International Exhibition, Paris 1925 / Jennifer Hawkins Opie. Arthur Sabin, Mrs Greg and the Queen ["directing the (Bethnal Green) Museum . . . towards children"] / Anthony Burton and Caroline Goodfellow. The image of the curator / Anthony Burton. Posters now . . . and then / Margaret Timmers.

5. Foreword, forward, foreward / Jean Muir. The philosophy of museum display : the continuing debate / Charles Saumarez Smith. Paintings on copper at Apsley House / David Scrase. Trompe l'oeil : visual deception in European art / Gillian Saunders. Gothic interiors of the 19th century : John Gregory Crace at Abney Hall / Megan Aldrich. Twentieth century sitting / Geoffrey Opie. Biscuit tins : a lost Christmas tradition / M.J. Franklin. Flower carpets of the great Mughals / Rosemary Crill. Ladies' court dress : economy and magnificence / Madeleine Ginsburg. A singular substitute : batiks of the north coast of Java / Deborah Swallow. Reflections upon Gianni Versace's work : tradition and innovation 1980 to 1984 / Rosa Maria Letts and Valerie Mendes. Roger Mayne : Southam Street revisited / Mark Haworth-Booth. From today 'modernism' is dead! : functionalism as style? / Susan Lambert and John Murdoch. Susie Cooper : her pre-war productions : 1922–1939 / Ann Eatwell. Modernism and English silver / Eric Turner. Desert island objects : Howard Hodgkin selects / John Guy. Objects from a medieval treasury / Paul Williamson. The secular tradition in medieval metalwork / Marian Campbell. Jewels for the Mughal court / Susan Stronge. Chinese taste and eighteenth century porcelain / Rose Kerr. Sèvres porcelain in the V&A : new light on some eighteenth century hard-paste rarities / Aileen Dawson. Dolls old and new : the doll gallery at the Bethnal Green Museum of Childhood / Caroline G. Goodfellow. The dandy as social revolutionary / Stephen Jones.

'Gold' edition
Introduction / Sir Hugh Casson. A tribute to Sir Roy Strong / Lord Carrington. Directorship of Sir Roy Strong : a chronology of major events, acquisitions and exhibitions 1974–1987 / Jonathan Voak. Art and design of the Far East / Sir John

Figgess. "Accidents and sagacity" in the Indian Department / Bamber Gascoigne. "A multitude of reference" : a textile designer and the V&A / Eddie Squires. Ceramics and glass in 1987 : a personal view on the importance of the Museum's collection / Lord Queensberry. Elizabethan miniatures and society / A.L. Rowse. Cole to Constable : an appreciation of the Henry Cole Wing at the V&A / Roger de Grey. Photography : addressing the bogey of the art world / David Brittain. Fashion : a purist approach to the romance of dress / Suzy Menkes. Back to the roots of arts and craft : the Metalwork collection at the V&A / Suzy Menkes. Through a sculptor's eye / Eduardo Paolozzi. Everything the public should least predict : 14 years of the Furniture and Interior Design Department / Clive Aslet. Restoring a great museum (1974–1987) / Colin Amery. The "delightful luxury" that defied extinction : the Theatre Museum in Covent Garden / Milton Shulman. Toys and reasons : the development of Bethnal Green Museum of Childhood / Christina Hardyment.

Summer 1988
The rise and rise of Chinese export porcelain / Vanessa Clewes Salmon. Desert island objects / Cynthia Harvey. Miniature weapons / Anthony North. Georgian furniture and its uses / David Harvey. Interior design at Lloyds / Iain Gale. Profile : Elizabeth Esteve-Coll / Miriam Kramer. Fashion and surrealism / Richard Martin. Georgian public life chronicled in enamels / Susan Benjamin. Three American painters in London [John Singleton Copley, Benjamin West, Gilbert Stuart] / Stuart Greenspan. American potters today / Oliver Watson. Peking at Osterley Park House / Susan Moore. The V&A masterplan / Michael Hopkins Partnership. What's on at the V&A.

Autumn 1988
High craft or tourist art? [20th century Chinese lacquer[/ Craig Clunas. Serious style / Lewis Biggs. Profile : Willard C. Butcher [chairman, Chase Manhattan Bank] / Stuart Greenspan. Henry Cole as photographer / Mark Haworth-Booth. Abstraction, art and design / Colin Gleadell. Emperor of fashion [Charles Frederick Worth] / Vivienne Couldrey. Adam period household silver / Myrtle Ellis. Early American folk interiors / Gilbert T. Vincent. Derby figures : the first 50 years / Pamela Rowan. Aspects of Italian baroque and rococo furniture / William Lorimer. Desert island objects / Clement Freud. Doll's house and miniature kitchens / Halina Pasierbska.

Spring 1989
The new designers [Duncan Chorley, Louisa Pryor, Susan Wilkinson] / Judy Spours. 1992 / Ivor Turnbull. Rossetti's The day-dream / Julia Atkins. Profile : Jacques Tajan / Simon Hewitt. Jewellery and the French Revolution / Martin Chapman. Hats as art / Valerie D. Mendes. Desert island objects / Anita Roddick. Architect-designed furniture / Victoria Geibel. Chinese snuff bottles / Helen White. A rose by any other name . . . [E. Gordon Craig] Arnold Rood. William De Morgan / Hilary Young. Dining glass in the 19th century / Kate Dyson. What's on at the V&A.

VP.1986.001   *Victoria and Albert Museum : report of the Board of Trustees.*
London : Victoria and Albert Museum (Printed by Gavin Martin Ltd.).
Triennial, October 1983/March 1986 (1986)–<October 1993/March 1996 (1996)>
<4> v. : ill.(some col.), ports ; 30 cm.
ISBN: 1851770232; 1851770186; 1851771182; 1851771646
First two reports edited by Jonathan Voak, second two by Susan Laurence.

VP.1986.002   *National Art Library staff newsletter.*
[London : The Library.]
Monthly, Oct. 1986–<Dec. 1996>
<105> issues : ill. ; 30 cm.
1986: No 1., Oct.; 1987: Nos. 2–5, Feb., May, July, Nov.; 1988: New series, Nos. 1–3, Mar., Apr., May; monthly July–Nov.; 1989: Jan., Apr., June, [July], [Aug.], Sept., Nov., Dec. Thereafter, regular.
Alternative title: NAL newsletter. — From Nov. 1989 "Edited by Elizabeth James". Internal Departmental newsletter, also circulated informally outside the Museum.

VP.1988.001   [Events]

VP.1988.001A   *What's on : forthcoming events at the Victoria and Albert Museum.*
                  [London : The Museum.]
                  3 issues yearly, June/Sept. 1988, Oct. 1988/Jan. 1989, Feb./June 1989,
                  May/Sept. 1989, Oct./Dec. 1989, Jan./Apr. 1990, then regular to
                  May/Aug. 1992.
                  13 issues : ill. (chiefly col.), ports. ; 30 cm.
                  Title of first issue: What's on at the V&A. — Jan./Apr. 1992: "Now incorporating
                  Friends of the V&A newsletter". — Printed on sized paper. Stapled.

VP.1988.001B   *In-view : news and events at the Victoria and Albert Museum.*
                  [London : The Museum.]
                  3 issues yearly, Sept./Dec. 1992–<Sept./Dec. 1996>
                  <13> issues : ill. (chiefly col.), ports. ; 30 cm.
                  Includes Friends of the V&A (to Sept./Dec. 1993). — From Jan./Apr. 1994, produced
                  by Wordsearch Ltd. — Title ceased after Sept./Dec. 1997. — Printed on sized paper.
                  Stapled.

VP.1989.001   *The National Art Library : annual report.*
                  [London : The Library.]
                  1988–1989 (1989)–<1995–1996 (1996)>
                  <7> v. ; 30 cm.
                  Cover title. At foot of title: Victoria and Albert Museum. Title of first issue:
                  The National Art Library at the Victoria & Albert Museum : annual report. —
                  Printed typescript. Comb bound in coloured covers. — Report for 1991–1992
                  unpublished.

VP.1990.001   [Research]

VP.1990.001A   *Research register.*
                  [London] : Victoria & Albert Museum.
                  Annual, 1990 (1991)–1993 (1994).
                  4 v. ; 30 cm.
                  Cover title. — Includes: Message from the Director. — Index. — Comb bound, in green
                  covers (last issue in white, title printed red).

VP.1990.001B   *The Victoria & Albert Museum research report.*
                  [London] : Victoria and Albert Museum (Printed by J.W. Arrowsmith,
                  Bristol).
                  Biennial, 1994 (1995)–
                  <1> v. (84 p) ; 30 cm.
                  ISBN: 1851771697
                  Compiled and edited by Malcolm Baker, Jane Savidge, Gerry White, Ghislaine
                  Wood. Introduction / Elizabeth Esteve-Coll. — Designed by Ruth Levy. — Wrappers
                  with ills.

VP.1991.001   *V & A conservation journal : the quarterly publication of the Victoria
                  and Albert Museum Conservation Department.*
                  [London : The Museum.]
                  Quarterly, no. 1 (Oct. 1991)–<no. 21 (Oct. 1996)>
                  <21> issues : ill. ; 26 cm.
                  Cover title. — Editorials by Jonathan Ashley-Smith. Reports on the Royal College of
                  Art / V&A MA Conservation Course by Alan Cummings. Conservation staff charts on
                  back cover.

1.   'It'll be alright on the night. . .' [Tsui Gallery] / Amanda Ward. The conservation of
      a rare metal head of Buddha / John Larson. The conservation of oriental lacquer /
      Stephen Sheasby. UV-VIS-NIR spectroscopy / Graham Martin & Boris Pretzel.
      Frank Lloyd Wright in Japan / Lynda Hillyer. Review: Evaluation of cellulose
      ethers for conservation / Alan Derbyshire, Jane Rutherston.

2.   An assessment of the conservation of a unicorn tapestry / Val Blyth. Study tour of
      Swedish textile conservation studios / Nicola Gentle. Report on a summer
      placement at the National Museum of Natural History, Washington DC / Diana
      Drummond. A fibre optic video microscope / Graham Martin. Upholstery
      conservation / Derek Balfour. Introducing 'New methods in cleaning objects' to the
      V&A / Lucia Scalisi. RAIdiation sickness? / Alan Cummings. Review: Paper and
      textiles : the common ground / Vicky Oakley. Report on the International
      Symposium on the Conservation of Ceramics and Glass, Amsterdam / Vicky
      Oakley.

3.   The resurrection of *Death on a pale horse* [stained glass] / Drew Anderson and
      Samantha Whitney. Vessel glass deterioration in the museum environment : a
      quantitative study by surface analysis / Victoria Oakley . . . [et al.]. The mounting
      and framing of a large work of art on paper : a case study / Nicki Edwards Smith.
      Graphic descriptions : side-lights from manuscript sources on English drawing
      materials / Jim Murrell. Conservation study day at the V&A, 1991 / Lucia Scalisi.

4.   Furniture timbers / Josephine A. Darrah. Data from the ether! [radio telemetry] /
      Graham Martin and David Ford. Corrosion of metals associated with wood / Nick
      Umney. The technical examination and conservation of painted furniture / Stephen
      Sheasby. Interim meeting of the ICOM 'Graphic documents' Working Group held
      at the V&A / Gerhard Banik. A review of the Institute of Paper Conservation
      Conference, Manchester . . . 1992 / Barry Danby. A review of 'The imperfect
      image' / Megan Gent. Disaster reaction planning progress / Susannah Edmunds.
      A question of research / Christopher Frayling.

5.   Working with students on collection condition surveys at Blythe House / Alison
      Richmond. The AMECP Project : prevention is better than cure [environment
      monitoring] / Agnes Holden. Conservation and rotating displays in the Nehru
      Gallery of Indian Art / Deborah Swallow. The Raphael cartoons : conservation
      treatments, past and present / John Wagstaff. Exchange visit to the National Palace
      Museum, Taipei, Taiwan / Pauline Webber. A review of the Interim Symposium of
      the ICOM Leather and Related Materials Group / Annette Low. Closed for
      summer or shuttered for good? : the RCA/V&A Conservation Course study trip
      1992 [Venice] / Janet Gilburt.

6.   The conservation of Roger Fenton's album of Crimean photographs / Helen
      Shenton. A question of principle [conservation ethics] / Nick Umney. A survey of
      plastics objects at the Victoria & Albert Museum / Edward Then, Victoria Oakley.
      Preventive conservation in practice / Graham Martin, Boris Pretzel and Nick
      Umney. Textile conservation in Russia / Lynda Hillyer.

7.   Conservation liaison : a case study / Elizabeth Miller and Alison Richmond.
      Alabaster conservation / Charlotte Hubbard. Mind the gap : conservation of a
      Delftware bowl / Lorna Barnes. Accessories for the UV-VIS-NIR
      spectrophotometer : the external integrating head / Boris Pretzel. Frank Lloyd
      Wright stained glass / Drew Anderson. 'It was the least unethical thing we could
      do' [conservation of a clock] / Albert Neher. Successful double act : Paintings
      Conservation and PDP . . . Collection / Ronald Parkinson and Lucia Scalisi.

8.   Polychrome and petrographical analysis of the De Lucy effigy / Sarah Jane Boulter.
      Protecting Tutankhamun / Christopher Frayling. Hankyu, the final analysis? : a
      new approach to condition reporting for loans / Lea Jones. Camille Silvy, River
      scene, France / Elizabeth Martin. An investigation of a practical treatment for
      removing iron stains in platinum prints / Jacqueline Rees and Megan Gent. Film
      '93 : a visit to BFI-NFTVA J. Paul Getty Jr. Conservation Centre, Berkhamsted /
      Helen Jones.

9.   The conservation of Charles Dickens' manuscripts / Annette Low. The Wooden
      Artefacts Rheology Project [environmental control] / Nick Umney. What is
      3–carene? / Nigel Blades. The mounting of single leaf parchment and vellum
      objects for display and storage / Daniel Norman. The use of vacuum packing in
      Australia / Helen Shenton. Conservation Course study trip, Rome 1993 / Jane
      Davies. RCA/V&A Conservation Course abstracts : final year projects / Alan
      Cummings.

10. Conservation ethics workshop / Alison Richmond, Susan Lambert. The flattening of large rolled paper objects / Carol Barker. Beating unwanted guests [insect pest control] / Lynda Hillyer, Valerie Blyth. Stained glass in Eastern Europe / Samantha Whitney and Drew Anderson. The Sherman Fairchild Center for Objects Conservation, the Metropolitan Museum of Art, New York / Leesa Vere-Stevens. RCA/V&A Conservation Course abstracts : materials and techniques essays 1992–3 & M.Phil theses 1993 / Helen Jones.

11. A saint unveiled [mosaic] / Marie-Thérèse Weech. 17th century Chinese canopied bed / John Bornhoft. Recording the changes : V&A Conservation Departmental archive / Dorothy Rogers. The ageing and stabilisation of shellac varnish resin / Stephen Copestake. Treatment of an early 18th century Indian chintz qanat / Nicola Gentle. ICCROM Japanese paper conservation course : an introduction to the ancient skills of scroll mounting for the modern conservator / Alison Richmond. Sand cast aluminium / Vivienne Farmer.

12. Conservation of a pang khebs ["portion of a masker's costume from . . . Sikkim"] / Anne Godden Amos. Now you see it, down you don't : the conservation of a Turkey work chair / Gill Owens. The inaugural meeting of the Infrared Users Group / Boris Pretzel. The Angel of the Annunciation [French 15th century] / Alexandra Kosinova. South Kensington Forum / Alan Cummings. A broader view [Calcutta Tercentenary Trust project at the Victoria Memorial Museum, Calcutta] / Lucia Scalisi. Review : IPC 'Modern works, modern problems? conference' / Jane Rutherston.

13. The Science Group : the way forward / Graham Martin. The Inorganics Group : a wider perspective / Agnes Holden. The Training and Research Group : SIP code / Alan Cummings. 'Of making many books there is no end' : the Paper and Book Group / Helen Shenton. The Organics Group : from the top down & the bottom up / Nick Umney. Management services / Sarah Graham-Campbell.

14. Editorial / Graham Martin. T168–1993 ceremonial hat for eating bouillabaisse, Eileen Agar 1936 / Marion Kite. Measuring pollution in the museum environment / Nigel Blades. The tail of the tiger : conservation of a pichwai fragment [Indian textile] / Jenny Potter. The role of the 'barefoot' Conservator / Jane Rutherston. Polymers in museums : 208th meeting of the American Chemical Society, Historical Plastics Research Scientists meeting / Brenda Keneghan. 'New horizons': the Designer Bookbinders' Conference / Annette Low. The annual conference of the Association for Historical and Fine Art Photographers / Magdalena Kozera, Arjan van den Oudenrijn.

15. Editorial / Helen Shenton. The Parkes collection of Japanese paper / Pauline Webber. Restoration – is it acceptable? : review of the conference held at the British Museum, 24–25 November 1994 / Alison Richmond. To play or not to play : the ethics of musical instrument conservation / Andrew Lamb. The conservation and rehousing of a collection of photographs and photomechanical prints / Jeanette C. Kay. Book review / Jonathan Ashley-Smith. RCA/V&A Conservation Course abstracts.

16. Editorial / Nick Umney. Glass Gallery fragments : mounting & display / Juanita Navarro. Chemical stabilisation of weathered glass : a new approach to glass conservation? / Jason Ryan. 'The stupendous chandelier' / Rachel Oliver. A condition survey of the ceramics collection at the Ulster Museum / Victoria Oakley, Jim McGreevy. Placement at the Theatre Museum / Dottie Rogers. Those who can . . . [conservation teaching] / Helen Jones. Study trip to Australia / Victoria Button.

17. Editorial / Agnes Holden. Conservation of the Portuguese centrepiece [Apsley House] / Diana Heath. Leighton centenary 1996 / Tim Barringer. The conservation of Lord Leighton's spirit frescoes 'War' & 'Peace' / Stephen Rickerby. The conservation of a fourteenth century chasuble / Albertina Cogram. The conservation of the portrait bust of Giovanni de'Medici / Alexandra Kosinova. Ethics in America 23rd annual meeting of the American Institute for Conservation (AIC) / Alison Richmond. Conservation of leathercraft and related objects : interim meeting, ICON-CC Working Group / Timothy Hayes. Conservation course study trip, Berlin 1995 / Andrew Lamb and Hannah Eastwood.

18. The examination and conservation of the Raphael cartoons : an interim report / Alan Derbyshire. Tarnishing of silver : a short review / Masamitsu Inaba. The Xmas cake dress / Marion Kite. Lining and backing : the support of paintings,

paper and textiles, UKIC Conference / Lynda Hillyer. Summer placement at the Canadian Museum of Civilisation / Sonja Müller. Summer placement at the Asian Art Museum of San Francisco / Rachel Oliver. Summer placement at the Metropolitan Museum of Art of New York / Merete Winness.

19. Preparing for Morris : the treatment of a Philip Webb chest / John Courtney. Conservation Liaison : stained glass for the William Morris exhibition / Agnes Holden. Digital imaging and stained glass conservation / Ariana Makau. The restoration of the east staircase ceiling and the Leighton Corridor / Lisa Oestreicher. The 'Leighton project' : backstage / Olivia Levental. RCA/V&A conservation course abstracts.

20. Introduction / Helen Shenton. The Research and Conservation of Art Centre / Gwyn Miles. The Victoria and Albert Museum, Royal College of Art building project / Peter Lyon. Designing the interior / Elaine Clerici. Textile Conservation studio / Lynda Hillyer. The Michael Snow Laboratory / Graham Martin. The hole in the ground : Sculpture Conservation's new studio / Richard Cook. New working practices : could we do it like that? / Matthew Smith. Time for a change : the new Paper Conservation studios. Book Conservation studio / Helen Shenton.

21. Plastics? – not in my collection / Brenda Keneghan. Plastic, pop and mass-produced design in the V&A's collections / Gareth Williams. Two pooped-out chairs : what is the future for our plastic collections? / Roger Griffith. An object media enigma / Jane Rutherston. Milk and modernism : conservation of a smoker's cabinet designed by Charles Rennie Mackintosh / Shayne Lang. 'Sham columns in a casing of crockery' / Charlotte Hubbard.

VP.1991.002   [Planning]

VP.1991.002A   *Strategic plan.*
London : Victoria and Albert Museum.
Annual, 1991/1996 (1991)–1992/1997 (1992).
2 v. ; 30 cm.
Cover title. At head of title of 1991/1996: Quo V&Adis? — Introduction / Elizabeth Esteve-Coll. — Comb bound between card covers with ill. (by Christopher Wormell, 1992/1997).

VP.1991.002B   *Corporate plan.*
London : Victoria and Albert Museum.
Annual, 1994–1997 ([1993?])–<1996–2000 (1996)>
4 v. ; 30 cm.
Cover title. — Typeset and printed by V&A Printing Section (1995/1999). — Stapled; sized wrappers with col. ill., except 1994–1997 comb bound, ill. on covers. Photographs by Barry Lewis, Richard Davis.

VP.1992.001   *Account of the Victoria and Albert Museum for the year ended 31 March ... : together with the report of the Comptroller and Auditor General thereon.*
London : H.M.S.O.
Annual, 1991/92 (1992)–<1995/96 (1996)>
<5> v. ; 30 cm.
At head of title: Museums and Galleries Act 1992. — Ordered by the House of Commons to be printed ....

VP.1994.001   *Friends news.*
London : Friends of the V&A.
3 issues yearly, Spring 1994–<Autumn 1996>
<9> issues : col. ill. ; 30 cm.
'From the Chairman ...' / Jane Gordon Clark. — Newsletter previously incorporated in VP.1988.001.

VP.1994.002   [Purchase Grant Fund report]

VP.1994.002A   *Report 1994/95 : Museums & Galleries Commission/Victoria and*
                   Albert Museum Purchase Grant Fund.
                   London : MGC/V&A Purchase Grant Fund, 1995.
                   15 p. : ill. (some col.) ; 30 cm.
                   Wrappers, stapled, with col. ills.

VP.1994.002B   *Review : Museums & Galleries Commission/Victoria and Albert*
                   Museum Purchase Grant Fund.
                   London : MGC/V&A Purchase Grant Fund.
                   Annual, 1995/96 (1996)–
                   <1> v. : col. charts ; 30 cm.
                   Stapled in purple covers with ills.

VP.1994.003   *Things.*
                   London : Published . . . by students on the Victoria & Albert
                   Museum/Royal College of Art MA Course in the History of Design.
                   Bi-annual, 1 (Winter 1994)–3 (Summer 1995).
                   3 issues : ill. ; 21 cm.
                   ISSN: 1356-921X
                   Editor (2–) Hildi Hawkins. Co-editors (2): Sarah Foster, Eleanor John, Victoria Kelley;
                   (3): Eleanor John, Victoria Kelley, Katherine Sharp, Alice Twemlow. 'Other things'
                   editor (2–) Hannah Andrassy. — Includes: 'Other things : texts, exhibitions, ideas,
                   debate', an anthology of short pieces, reviews and extracts. — Design (1–2) Ruth Levy;
                   (3) Alastair O'Neill. — Wrappers with ill. — The journal subsequently continued
                   independently.
                   1.   The Chesterfield ice-pails [silver plate] / Isabelle Cartier. The comb as type-object /
                        Lisa Hirst. The rise and fall of fitted carpets : carpet production and design in the
                        19th century / Katharine Sharp. The use of personality : Allan Walton Textiles and
                        screen-printing in the 1930s / Sarah Foster. The shop as shop floor : a short history
                        of the cash register 1878–1939 / Victoria Kelley. Who are the public? : design for
                        the common good / Stephen Escritt. What is a museum object? : natural history
                        and the 'new' museology / Ann Kelly. 'Other things.' Letter from Cracow / Jeremy
                        Aynsley.
                   2.   The makers of old silver : goldsmiths, their marks and methods of manufacture /
                        Helen Clifford. A taste for the oriental : a tea tub by Parker & Wakelin / Sarah
                        Foster. Lord Exeter's liking for cheese : a cheese plate by Parker & Wakelin /
                        Katharine Sharp. Ponds in the parlour : the Victorian aquarium / Ann Kelly. Little
                        English landscapes : developing suburban gardens between the wars / Rebecca
                        Preston. The story of Matti & Maija [pottery figures] : beyond 'good taste' in
                        Finnish design / Harri Kalha. 'Other things.' Letter from Helsinki.
                   3.   Dandies and servants of the crown : sailors' uniforms in the early 19th century /
                        Jacqueline Durran. 'How shall we get beds?' : furniture in early colonial India
                        1750–1830 / Amin Jaffer. Taking the silk : rayon stockings and the democratic
                        spirit / Lisa Hirst. The aesthetics of rationality : Braun in 1950s West Germany /
                        Erica Carter. Thinking things differently / Steve Baker. 'Other things.' Wash-day
                        blues : the rotary clothes dryer in south London / Jean Macintyre.

VP.1995.001   *The reading room : a newsletter for National Art Library users.*
                   [London] : National Art Library.
                   Bi-annual, no.1, Spring 1995–<no. 4, Autumn 1996>
                   <4> issues ; 30 cm.
                   ISSN: 1359-4818

VP.1996.001   *Annual reports : V&A Enterprises.*
                 [London : V&A Enterprises.]
                 <1> v. : ill. ; 43 cm.
                 Annual, 1996–
                 Cover title. "V & A Enterprises"–cover. — Texts by Michael Cass, Keith Folley,
                 Michelle Alfandari, Nicole Swengley, Mary Butler, Robert Clark, Ken Mannering, Rhys
                 David, Alan Borg.

PUBLICATIONS RELATED TO, BUT NOT PUBLISHED BY, THE VICTORIA AND ALBERT MUSEUM

Related publications are described in slightly less detail than V&A publications proper. Details of printing and binding are omitted. For explanation of entries, abbreviations and usages, see head of main bibliography, p. 3.

1854

VR.1854.001 *Catalogue of a collection of models in wax and terra cotta by various Italian masters known as the Gherardini collection : now being exhibited at the Museum of Ornamental Art at Marlborough House, March 1854.*
London : Printed by George E. Eyre and William Spottiswoode for H.M.S.O., 1854.
15 p. ; 22 cm.
At head of title: Board of Trade, Department of Science and Art. — Contents: Introduction / J.C. Robinson. Catalogue. Extracts from a report made to the Chancellor of the Exchequer . . . by Mr Dyce and Mr Herbert.

VR.1854.002 *An introductory lecture on the Museum of Ornamental Art of the Department* / by J.C. Robinson.
London : Chapman and Hall, 1854.
31 p. ; 20 cm.
At head of title: Board of Trade, Department of Science and Art.

1855

VR.1855.001 *Lectures on the articles in the Museum of the Department* / by Owen Jones.
London : Printed by George E. Eyre and William Spottiswoode for H.M.S.O., 1855.
14 p. ; 21 cm.
At head of title: Department of Practical Art.

1856

VR.1856.001 *Catalogue of the Soulages collection : being a descriptive inventory of a collection of works of decorative art, formerly in the possession of M. Jules Soulages of Toulouse; now, by permission of the Committee*

of *Privy Council for Trade, exhibited to the public at the Museum of Ornamental Art, Marlborough House* / by J.C. Robinson.
London : Chapman & Hall, 1856.
xiii, 200 p. ; 25 cm.

VR.1856.001A   [Another issue]
As above, with 10 leaves of plates: photographs pasted on to blank leaves.

1857

VR.1857.001   *Catalogue of the collection of animal products belonging to Her Majesty's Commissioners for the Exhibition of 1851 : exhibited in the South Kensington Museum.*
London : Printed for Her Majesty's Commissioners by W. Clowes and Sons, 1857.
iv, 117 p. ; 20 cm.
Preface / Edgar A. Bowring. Compiled by P.L. Simmonds.

VR.1857.002   *The treasury of ornamental art : illustrations of objects of art and vertù* / photographed from the originals and drawn on stone by F. Bedford ; with descriptive notices by I. [sic] C. Robinson.
London : Day & Son, [1857 or 1858].
[76] p., [71] leaves of plates (1 folded) : col. ill. ; 26 cm.
The majority of objects illustrated are from the Museum of Ornamental Art at Marlborough House.

1858

VR.1858.001   *Catalogue of the exhibition of works of art-manufacture designed or executed by students of the Schools of Art, in connexion with the Science and Art Department of the Committee of Council on Education, South Kensington, London* / with an introduction by George Wallis.
[London] : Printed by George E. Eyre and William Spottiswoode for H.M.S.O., 1858.
127 p. ; 25 cm.
Introduction dated June 1858. — Indexes of manufacturers, schools and student exhibitors.
EXHIBITION: VX.1858.002

VR.1858.002   *Exhibition of photographs and daguerreotypes at the South Kensington Museum : fifth year.*
London : Printed by Taylor and Francis [for the Photographic Society], 1858.
35 p. ; 24 cm.
At head of title: Photographic Society. — Includes: Exposition de la Société française de photographie, p. 27–35.
EXHIBITION: VX.1858.001

VR.1858.003   *Illustrations to be employed in practical lessons on botany : adapted*
to beginners of all classes : prepared for the South Kensington
Museum.
London : Chapman and Hall, 1858.
32 p. : ill. ; 19 x 12 cm.
Cover title.

1859

VR.1859.001   *Waterford art exhibition in connection with the School of Practical*
Art and Design, containing selections from the Queen's and the South
Kensington Museums; also paintings, statuary and objects of vertu,
contributed by the neighbouring nobility and gentry, now being
exhibited at the Town Hall, Waterford : official catalogue.
Waterford : By authority of the Committee, 1858 (Thomas S. Harvey,
printer).
15 p. ; 22 cm.

1860

VR.1860.001   *Report from the Select Committee on the South Kensington Museum :*
together with the proceedings of the Committee, minutes of evidence,
and appendix.
1860.
xx, 182 p. (some folded) 29 p., [3] folded leaves of plates : ill., plans
(1 col.) ; 34 cm.
"Ordered by the House of Commons to be printed, 1 August 1860." — Witnesses to the
Committee include: Henry Cole, Richard Redgrave, J.C. Robinson, Francis Fowke,
George Gilbert Scott, Charles Thurston Thompson. — The work of the Photographic
Department is emphasised. — Index.

1861

VR.1861.001   *Some account of the buildings designed by Francis Fowke, Capt. R.E.,*
for the International Exhibition of 1862, and future decennial
exhibitions of the works of art and industry.
London : Chapman and Hall, 1861.
35 p., [5] leaves of plates (1 folded) : ill., col. map ; 26 cm.
Added t.p.: Some account of the buildings for the International Exhibition of 1862.
EXHIBITION: vx.1862

1862

VR.1862.001   *The art wealth of England : a series of photographs representing fifty*
of the most remarkable works of art contributed on loan to the special
exhibition at the South Kensington Museum, 1862 / selected and
described by J.C. Robinson ; the photographs by C. Thurston
Thompson.

[London] : Published by authority of the Science and Art Department of the Committee of Council on Education by P. and D. Colnaghi, Scott and Co., 1862.
[28] p., 50 leaves of plates : ill. ; 60 cm.
Photographs pasted on to leaves.
EXHIBITION: VX.1862.001

1863

VR.1863.001   *A descriptive catalogue of the wedding presents accepted by Their Royal Highnesses the Prince and Princess of Wales : now on view at the South Kensington Museum.*
London : H.G. Clarke & Co., 1863.
16 p. ; 19 cm.
Notice / Henry Cole.
EXHIBITION: VX.1863.001

VR.1863.002   *Gold and silver plate lent to the South Kensington Museum for public instruction : July 1863.*
[London? : The Lender?, 1863.]
1 sheet, folded ([3] p.) ; 22 cm.
All items lent by G. Moffatt.

1865

VR.1865.001   *A guide to the South Kensington Museum : illustrated with ground plans and wood engravings.*
[London] : Printed by William Clowes and Sons, and sold with the sanction of the Department of Science and Art, in the South Kensington Museum, 1865.
64 p. : ill., plans ; 21 cm.
At head of title: Sanctioned by the Department of Science and Art. — Science Division, in the temporary iron buildings: The Museum of Building Materials. The Educational Museum and reading room. The collection of naval models. The Food Museum. Art Division, in the permanent buildings: The Art Library. The Museum of Ornamental Art. The architectural collection. The picture galleries. — Cab fares from 'Bell and Horns' cab stands: p. 63. — Purple wrappers.

VR.1865.002   *Local metropolitan museums : report of the proceedings held in the Lecture Theatre, South Kensington Museum, on Saturday 6th May 1865.*
London : Printed by George E. Eyre and William Spottiswoode for H.M.S.O., [1865].
31 p., 1 leaf of plates : plan : 22 cm.
Cover title. At head of title: South Kensington Museum (Science and Art Department). – "considering how the Iron Building of the South Kensington Museum may be made useful [in establishing] Suburban Museums of Science and Art."

1866

VR.1866.001   *Catalogue of the first special exhibition of national portraits ending with the reign of King James the Second : on loan to the South Kensington Museum, April 1866.*
London : Arundel Society for Promoting the Knowledge of Art, [1866?].
xi, [i], 202 p. ; 22 cm.

At head of title: Science and Art Department of the Committee of Council on Education. — Introductory notice by Samuel Redgrave. — Statistical table, p. 192. Indexes of lenders, painters and portraits. — Appendix: p. [193]–202 consists of notes on the pictures, mainly relating to attributions.

Copy note: VR.1866.002 bound in; also advertisements for photographs of exhibits in VX.1865.001.

EXHIBITION: VX.1866.001

VR.1866.002   *A guide to the South Kensington Museum : illustrated with ground plans and wood engravings.* 2nd ed.
[London] : Printed by William Clowes and Sons, and sold with the sanction of the Department of Science and Art, in the South Kensington Museum, 1865.
64? p. : ill., plans ; 21 cm.

At head of title: Sanctioned by the Department of Science and Art. — Contents as VR.1865.001. — Incomplete copy seen.

VR.1866.003   *Photographs of portrait miniatures in the loan exhibition at the South Kensington Museum in 1865.*
London : Arundel Society for Promoting the Knowledge of Art, [1866?].
8 p. ; 21 cm.

At head of title: With the sanction of the Science and Art Department of the Committee of Council on Education. — Lists the photographs available for purchase.

EXHIBITION: VX.1865.001

VR.1866.004   *[Photographs of portrait miniatures in the loan exhibition at the South Kensington Museum]*

Unseen. "The set of two hundred photographs, together with a copy of the official catalogue, bound in three volumes in half-morocco, may be had for ten guineas"–VR.1866.003 p. 2.

EXHIBITION: VX.1865.001

VR.1866.005   *Photographs of terra cotta columns modelled for the lecture theatre at the South Kensington Museum by Godfrey Sykes : with descriptions and a brief memoir of the artist's life.*
London : Arundel Society for Promoting the Knowledge of Art, 1866.
9 p., 15 leaves of plates : ill. ; 38 cm.

At head of title: By authority of the Science and Art Department of the Committee of Council on Education. — Text by J.H. Pollen.

VR.1866.006   *A series of historical portraits selected from the national portrait exhibition of 1866 : photographed from the original paintings.*
London : Arundel Society for Promoting the Knowledge of Art, [1866?].
10 v. : ports. ; 26 cm.

At head of title: With the sanction of the Science and Art Department of the Committee of Council on Education. — "Or any purchaser may select for himself one hundred portraits, which will be half-bound in morocco . . ." [advertisement bound in VR.1866.001].

EXHIBITION: VX.1866.001

1867

VR.1867.001   *Classified list of photographs of drawings, paintings, and sculpture. Etchings of objects of art.*
London : Arundel Society for Promoting the Knowledge of Art, [1867?].
4, 104, 8 p. ; 21 cm.
Cover: Classified list of photographs taken for the Department of Science and Art. "Specimens of the photographs . . . may be seen in the Arundel Society's sale-rooms at the South Kensington Museum . . . A complete collection may be consulted in the National Art Library." — Includes catalogues of works in VX.1865.001, VX.1866.001. — Cover partly printed in red.

VR.1867.002   *A classified list of photographs of drawings, paintings and sculpture, precious metals and enamels, carvings in ivory and wood, pottery, porcelain and glass : taken for the Department of Science and Art.*
London : Arundel Society for Promoting the Knowledge of Art, 1867.
22 cm.
At head of title: With the sanction of the Science and Art Department of the Committee of Council on Education. — Comprises VR.1867.001 and 003–004 bound together, with collective title page.

VR.1867.003   *Classified list of photographs taken for the Department of Science and Art : precious metals and enamels : carvings in ivory and wood.*
London : Arundel Society for Promoting the Knowledge of Art, [1867?].
99 p. ; 22 cm.
Cover: Classified list of photographs taken for the Department of Science and Art. — "Specimens of the photographs . . . may be seen in the Arundel Society's sale-rooms at the South Kensington Museum . . . A complete collection may be consulted in the National Art Library." — Printing: 1/67.

VR.1867.004   *Classified list of photographs : works of decorative art in pottery, porcelain and glass.*
London : Arundel Society for Promoting the Knowledge of Art, [1867?].
101 p. ; 21 cm.
Cover: Classified list of photographs taken for the Department of Science and Art. — "Specimens of the photographs . . . may be seen in the Arundel Society's sale-rooms at the South Kensington Museum . . . A complete collection may be consulted in the National Art Library."

VR.1867.005   *A guide to the art collections of the South Kensington Museum : illustrated with plans and wood engravings.*
London : Spottiswoode & Co., printers, and sold in the South Kensington Museum, 1867.
56 p., [8] leaves of plates : ill., ; 21 cm.
At head of title: Sanctioned by the Department of Science and Art. Cover title: A guide to the South Kensington Museum. — "In former editions brief notices have been

included of the various interesting and valuable collections comprised in the Science Division. Owing, however, to the projected removal of the temporary iron buildings, the position and arrangement of these collections has been rendered so uncertain that it has been judged inexpedient to print any extended notice which, in the lapse of a few weeks, may become inapplicable."–t.p. verso. — Part II: Guide to the picture galleries in the South Kensington Museum. — Red wrappers.

VR.1867.006   *Special exhibition of national portraits on loan to the South Kensington Museum : galleries and bays of the national portrait exhibition, 1866, shown in seventy-seven photographs.*
Unseen. Record from British Library catalogue.
EXHIBITION: vx.1866.001

1868

VR.1868.001   *Ecclesiastical metal work of the Middle Ages : with an introductory notice of the vessels, etc. used in the services of the mediaeval Church.*
London : Arundel Society for Promoting the Knowledge of Art, 1868.
14 p., 20 leaves of plates : ill. ; 38 cm.
(Examples of art workmanship of various ages and countries)
"Under the sanction of the Science and Art Department, for the use of Schools of Art and amateurs." — Text by A.C. King. — Illustrated from works in the South Kensington Museum and private collections.

VR.1868.002   *A guide to the art collections of the South Kensington Museum : illustrated with plans and wood engravings.*
London : Printed by Spottiswoode & Co. and sold in the South Kensington Museum, 1868.
[6], 64 p., [5] leaves of plates (some folded), [9] p. of advertisements : ill., plans ; 21 cm.
At head of title: Sanctioned by the Department of Science and Art. Cover title: A guide to the South Kensington Museum. — Part II: Guide to the picture galleries in the South Kensington Museum. — Red wrappers, with advertisements.

VR.1868.003   *Henri Deux ware : photographs of twenty examples of this ware chiefly in English collections : with an introductory notice.*
London : Arundel Society for Promoting the Knowledge of Art, 1868.
8 p., 20 leaves of plates : ill. ; 38 cm.
(Examples of art workmanship of various ages and countries)
"Under the sanction of the Science and Art Department, for the use of Schools of Art and amateurs." — Text by A.C. King. — Illustrated from works in the South Kensington Museum and private collections.

VR.1868.004   *Italian jewellery as worn by the peasants of Italy : collected by Signor Castellani, and purchased from the Paris Universal Exhibition for the South Kensington Museum.*
London : Arundel Society for Promoting the Knowledge of Art, 1868.
8 p., 12 leaves of plates : ill. ; 38 cm.
(Examples of art workmanship of various ages and countries.)
"Under the sanction of the Science and Art Department, for the use of Schools of Art and amateurs."

VR.1868.005   *List of photographs of national historical portraits : exhibitions of 1867 and 1868.*
London : Arundel Society for Promoting the Knowledge of Art, [1868].
96 p. ; 21 cm.
Cover title: Classified list of photographs taken for the Department of Science and Art.
EXHIBITIONS: VX.1867.001, VX.1868.001

VR.1868.006   *A series of historical portraits selected from the national portrait exhibitions : photographed from the original paintings.*
London : Arundel Society for Promoting the Knowledge of Art, [1868?].
9 v. : ports. ; 26 cm.
At head of title: With the sanction of the Science and Art Department of the Committee of Council on Education.
EXHIBITIONS: VX.1867.001, VX.1868.001

1869

VR.1869.001   *Choice treasures of art of the South Kensington Museum : eight illustrations printed by Leighton brothers' chromatic process* / described by C.C. Black.
London : Leighton Brothers, 1869.
1 leaf, [16] p., [8] leaves of plates : col. ill. ; 27 cm.
At head of title: With the sanction of the Science and Art Department of the Committee of Council on Education.

VR.1869.002   *A guide to the art collections of the South Kensington Museum : illustrated with plans and wood engravings.*
London : Printed by Spottiswoode & Co., sold in the South Kensington Museum, February 1869.
[6], 64 p., [5] leaves of plates, some folded, [2], [10] p. of advertisements : ill. (1 col.), plans (1 col.) ; 21 cm.
At head of title: Sanctioned by the Science and Art Department. Cover title: A guide to the South Kensington Museum. — Part II: Guide to the picture galleries in the South Kensington Museum. — Red wrappers, with advertisements.

VR.1869.002A   July 1869.
65 p., [5] leaves of plates, some folded, [2], [11] p. of advertisements

VR.1869.003   *Italian sculpture of the Middle Ages and period of the revival of art.*
London : Arundel Society for Promoting the Knowledge of Art, 1869.
4 p., 20 leaves of plates : ill. ; 38 cm.
(Examples of art workmanship of various ages and countries)
"Under the sanction of the Science and Art Department, for use of Schools of Art and amateurs." — Illustrated from works in the South Kensington Museum.

VR.1869.004   *Musical instruments in the South Kensington Museum* / with descriptions by Carl Engel.
London : Arundel Society for Promoting the Knowledge of Art, 1869.

8 p., xx leaves of plates : ill. ; 38 cm.
(Examples of art workmanship of various ages and countries)
"Under the sanction of the Science and Art Department, for the use of Schools of Art and amateurs."

VR.1869.005   *Report of the Commission on the heating, lighting and ventilation of the South Kensington Museum : together with minutes of evidence and appendix.*
London : H.M.S.O., 1869.
v, 102 p. ; 25 cm.
"Presented to both Houses of Parliament by command of Her Majesty."

1870

VR.1870.001   *Explanatory catalogue of engravings, prints and photographs collected by S.T. Davenport to illustrate his paper on 'Prints and their production' read before the Society of Arts on the 8th December 1869 : now exhibiting at the South Kensington Museum.*
London : Printed [for the author?] by W. Trounce, 1870.
16 p. ; 22 cm.

1871

VR.1871.001   *Decorative furniture, French.*
London : Arundel Society for Promoting the Knowledge of Art, 1871.
8 p., xx leaves of plates : ill. ; 37 cm.
(Examples of art workmanship of various ages and countries)
"Under the sanction of the Science and Art Department, for the use of Schools of Art and amateurs." — Illustrations chiefly of objects from vx.1853.xxx.001.

VR.1871.002   *A guide to the art collections of the South Kensington Museum : illustrated with plans and wood engravings.*
London : Printed by Spottiswoode & Co., sold in the South Kensington Museum, May 1871.
[8], 64 p., [5] leaves of plates, [4], [24] p. of advertisements : ill. (some col.), plans ; 21 cm.
At head of title: Sanctioned by the Science and Art Department. Cover title: A guide to the South Kensington Museum. — Part II: Guide to the picture galleries in the South Kensington Museum. — Red wrappers, with advertisements.

1872

VR.1872.001   *A guide to the Bethnal Green Branch of the South Kensington Museum.*
London, 1872. (Spottiswoode & Co., printers).
32 p. : ill. ; 22 cm.
At head of title: Sanctioned by the Science and Art Department. — Text signed "C.C.B" [i.e. Charles Christopher Black].

1873

VR.1873.001   *A guide to the art collections of the South Kensington Museum :*
               illustrated with plans and wood engravings.
               London : Printed by Spottiswoode & Co., sold in the South
               Kensington Museum, [1873?].
               [6], 64 p., [5] leaves of plates (some folded) : ill. (1 col.), plans ;
               21 cm.

               At head of title: Sanctioned by the Science and Art Department. Cover title: A guide to
               the South Kensington Museum. — Part II: Guide to the picture galleries in the South
               Kensington Museum. — Red wrappers, with advertisements.

1875

VR.1875.001   *A catalogue of books illustrated with photographs, published under*
               the sanction of the Science and Art Department.
               [London : Arundel Society?], [1875] (Chiswick Press: C. Whittingham,
               printer).
               [20] p. ; 26 cm.

               "Negatives the property of the South Kensington Museum . . . Any of these works can
               be obtained on application to the Director, South Kensington Museum; or of the
               Secretary of the Arundel Society . . ."–p. [3].

1879

VR.1879.001   *A guide to the art collections of the South Kensington Museum :*
               illustrated with plans and wood engravings.
               London : Printed by Spottiswoode & Co., sold in the South
               Kensington Museum, [1879?].
               [12], 64 p., [3] folded leaves of plates, [14] p. of advertisements : ill.
               (some col.), plans ; 21 cm.

               At head of title: Sanctioned by the Science and Art Department. Cover title: A guide to
               the South Kensington Museum. — Part II: Guide to the picture galleries in the South
               Kensington Museum. — Red wrappers, with advertisements.

1881

VR.1881.001   *Report on the system of circulation of art objects on loan from the*
               South Kensington Museum for exhibition : as carried on by the
               Department from its first establishment to the present time.
               London : Printed by George Edward Eyre and William Spottiswoode
               for H.M.S.O., 1881.
               21 p. ; 33 cm.
               (C. ; 2836)

               At head of title: Science and Art Department of the Committee of Council on Education,
               South Kensington. — "Presented to both Houses of Parliament by command of Her
               Majesty."

1882

VR.1882.001   *A guide to the art collections of the South Kensington Museum :*
               illustrated with plans and wood engravings.
               London : Printed by Spottiswoode & Co., sold in the South
               Kensington Museum, [1882?].

[6], 66 p., [2] folded leaves of plates, [16] p. of advertisements : ill.
(some col.), plans, 1 col. ; 21 cm.

At head of title: Sanctioned by the Science and Art Department. Cover title: A guide to
the South Kensington Museum. — Part II: Guide to the picture galleries in the South
Kensington Museum. — Red wrappers, with advertisements.

1883

VR.1883.001   *Catalogue of a collection of precious stones mounted as rings : lent by
Professor A.H. Church.*
[London? : The Collector?, 1883?]
[6] p. ; 20 cm.

Caption title.

1884

VR.1884.001   *An illustrated catalogue of silver plate of the time of Queen Anne and
the early Georges, on loan at the Bethnal Green Museum : prepared
for the use of visitors to that museum, and to the Bethnal Green Free
Library.*
(London : Printed by J.S. Virtue and Co.) [1884].
30 p. : ill ; 19 cm.

At head of title: From the collection of Joseph Bond, Esq. — Introduction signed "E.C.".

1885

VR.1885.001   *A guide to the art collections of the South Kensington Museum :
illustrated with plans and wood engravings.*
London : Printed by Spottiswoode & Co., sold in the South
Kensington Museum, [1885?].
[2], 66 p., [2] folded leaves of plates, [16] p. of advertisements : ill.
(some col.), plans, 1 col. ; 21 cm.

At head of title: Sanctioned by the Science and Art Department. Cover title: A guide to
the South Kensington Museum. — Part II: Guide to the picture galleries in the South
Kensington Museum. — Red wrappers, with advertisements.

1888

VR.1888.001   *Figures from the cartoons of Raphael, drawn from the originals in the
South Kensington Museum : with a sketch of the history of the
cartoons and full instructions for copying.*
London : Blackie & Son, [1888].
[4], 16 p., 12 leaves of plates : ill. ; 40 cm.
(Poynter's South Kensington drawing-book)

At head of title: Under the sanction of the Lords of the Committee of Council on
Education. "The original drawings have been made by pupils of the National Art
Training School, under the personal superintendence of Mr. Poynter"–p. [3]. —
Cased in boards imitating the livery of the South Kensington Museum art handbooks
(see Series index, p. 743).[2]

---

[2] P. [3] explains that Poynter's South Kensington drawing-books are intended to replace *The drawing book
of the Government School of Design* of William Dyce (1842) by "a new series of examples . . . so as to meet

VR.1888.002   *A guide to the collections of the South Kensington Museum :
illustrated with plans and wood engravings.*
London : Printed by Spottiswoode & Co., sold in the South
Kensington Museum, [1888?].
vi, 66 p., [2] folded leaves of plates, [16] p. of advertisements. ill.
(1 col.), plans (1 col.) ; 22 cm.
At head of title: Sanctioned by the Department of Science and Art. Cover title: A guide
to the South Kensington Museum. — Red wrappers, with advertisements.

VR.1888.003   *Historical and descriptive catalogue of the pictures, busts, &c in the
National Portrait Gallery, on loan at the Bethnal Green Museum* / by
George Scharf. New enl. ed.
London : Printed by Eyre and Spottiswoode for H.M.S.O., 1888.
608 p. ; 22 cm.
Includes indexes.

1889

VR.1889.001   *Embroidery from the South Kensington Museum* / edited by Alan S.
Cole.
London : R. Sutton & Co., [1889].
[4] p., [1], xv leaves of plates : chiefly ill. ; 49 cm.
(Studies from the museums)
At head of title: Published under the sanction of the Science and Art Department. —
Photographic plates.

VR.1889.002   *Reproduction of illustrations of ornamental metal-work, forming*
L'art du serrurier, *par Mathurin Jousse, 1627.*
[London] : Reproduced for the Department of Science and Art in
photo-lithography by W. Griggs, 1889.
[8] parts : facsims. ; 27 cm.
(Portfolio of French art)
Parts 2–10 of VRP.1881.002F

1890

VR.1890.001   *[A guide to the collections of the South Kensington Museum :
illustrated with plans and wood engravings.*
London : Printed by Spottiswoode & Co., sold in the South
Kensington Museum, 1890?]
vi, 68 p., [2] folded leaves of plates, [10] p. of advertisements : ill.
(1 col.), plans (1 col.) ; 21 cm.
At head of cover: Sanctioned by the Department of Science and Art. Cover title: A guide
to the South Kensington Museum. — Red wrappers, with advertisements. — Incomplete
copy seen.

VR.1890.002   *Hand-made laces from the South Kensington Museum* / edited by Alan
S. Cole.
London : R. Sutton & Co., [1890].

the wants of the numerous elementary schools and art classes under the Department [of Science and Art] . . .
all over the United Kingdom." These drawing-books were the basis of the 'South Kensington system' of design
training (discussed in Bell, Quentin, *The schools of design* (Routledge & Kegan Paul, 1963), e.g. p. 261).

[5] p., [1], xxx leaves of plates : chiefly ill. ; 49 cm.
(Studies from the museums)

At head of title: Published under the sanction of the Science and Art Department. —
Photographic plates.

1892

VR.1892.001   *Report of the Commission appointed to enquire into the question of
the housing of the Raffaelle cartoons : together with minutes of
evidence and appendix.*
London : H.M.S.O., 1892.
xi, 22 p. ; 34 cm.

1894

VR.1894.001   *A guide to the collections of the South Kensington Museum :
illustrated with plans and wood engravings.*
London : Printed by Spottiswoode & Co., sold in the South
Kensington Museum, [1894?].
vi, 72 p., [8] leaves of plates (2 folded), [12] p. of advertisements :
ill. (some col.), plans (1 col.) ; 22 cm.

At head of title: Sanctioned by the Department of Science and Art. Cover title: A guide
to the South Kensington Museum. — Red wrappers, with advertisements.

VR.1894.001A   [Another issue]

"With 8 coloured plates"–cover, VR.1894.001. — Unseen.

1897

VR.1897.001   *First report from the Select Committee on Museums of the Science and
Art Department : with the proceedings of the Committee.*
London : H.M.S.O., 1897.
x p. ; 33 cm.

"Ordered by the House of Commons to be printed, 21 May 1897" (no. 223).

VR.1897.002   *A guide to the collections of the South Kensington Museum :
illustrated with plans and wood engravings.*
London : Printed by Spottiswoode & Co., sold in the South
Kensington Museum, "1897–98".
vi, 76 p. : ill., (some col.) ; 22 cm.

At head of title: Sanctioned by the Department of Science and Art. Cover title: A guide
to the South Kensington Museum. — Unseen. Record from OCLC.

VR.1897.003   *An illustrated record of the retrospective exhibition held at South
Kensington, 1896* / compiled and edited by John Fisher.
London : Chapman & Hall, 1897.
xii p., 156 leaves of plates : chiefly ill. ; 29 cm.

Photographs of designs, models, paintings, life drawings etc. for which medals had been
awarded to students by the Department of Science and Art.

EXHIBITION: VX.1896.003

VR.1897.004   *Second report from the Select Committee on Museums of the Science and Art Department : with the proceedings of the Committee, minutes of evidence, appendix and index.*
London : H.M.S.O., 1897.
x, 660 p. ; 33 cm.
"Ordered by the House of Commons to be printed, 23 July 1897" (no. 341). — "Your Committee . . . have been unable to complete the inquiry in the course of the present session . . . have agreed to report the minutes of evidence taken before them . . . and . . . recommend that the Committee be re-appointed . . ."–p. iii.

1898

VR.1898.001   *First report from the Select Committee on Museums of the Science and Art Department : with the proceedings of the Committee.*
London : H.M.S.O., 1898.
vii p. ; 33 cm.
("175")
"Ordered by the House of Commons to be printed, 26 April 1898" (no. 175).

VR.1898.002   *A guide to the collections of the South Kensington Museum : illustrated with plans and wood engravings.*
London : Printed by Spottiswoode & Co., sold in the South Kensington Museum, "1898–99".
iii, 74 p., iii leaves of plates, [8] p. of advertisements : ill., col. plans ; 22 cm.
At head of title: Sanctioned by the Department of Science and Art. Cover title: A guide to the South Kensington Museum. — Red wrappers with advertisements.
Copy note: Slip pasted in: "By command of Her Majesty the Queen this Institution is now styled: The Victoria and Albert Museum".

VR.1898.002A   [Another issue]
" With six coloured plates"–cover, VR.1898.002. — Unseen.

VR.1898.003   *Second report from the Select Committee on Museums of the Science and Art Department : with the proceedings of the Committee, minutes of evidence, appendix and index.*
London : H.M.S.O., 1898.
cviii, 275 p. : col. plans ; 33 cm.
"Ordered by the House of Commons to be printed, 29 July 1898" (no. 327).

1899

VR.1899.001   *Measured drawings of French furniture from the collection in South Kensington Museum* / by W.G. Paulson Townsend.
London : Truslove, Hanson & Comba, 1899.
ca. 150 leaves : chiefly ill., plans ; 38 cm.

VR.1899.002   *Minute by the Right Honourable the Lords of the Committee of the Privy Council on Education on the Second report from the Select Committee (1898) on the Museums of the Science & Art Department : with appendix.*
London : H.M.S.O., 1899.

23 p. ; 33 cm.
(C. ; 9163)
At head of title: Museums of the Science and Art Department. — "Presented to both
Houses of Parliament by command of Her Majesty."

1901

VR.1901.001   *Catalogue of the loan exhibition of modern illustration : held at the
Museum of Science and Art, Edinburgh, June to September, 1901.*
London : William Clowes and Sons, [1901].
108 p., viii p. of advertisements, 1 leaf of plates : 1 port. ; 22 cm.
At head of title: Scotch Education Department. — [Foreword] by F. Grant Ogilvie.
Introduction by Henry B. Wheatley.
EXHIBITION: VX.1901.001

VR.1901.002   *Food grains of India : supplement (1901) containing analyses made
since the year 1866* / by A.H. Church.
[s.l.] : Printed for the author with the sanction of the Board of
Education, 1901 (printed by John Bellows, Gloucester).
23 p. ; 27 cm.
Includes bibliographic references and index. — Bound uniform with v.1886.002.

VR.1901.003   *Problèmes de géométrie et d'hydraulique . . . : manuscrits inédites,
reproduits d'après les originaux conservés à la "Forster Library,
South Kensington Museum, London"* / Léonard de Vinci.
Paris : Edouard Rouveyre, 1901.
3 v. : facsims. ; 26 cm.
(Manuscrits inédits de Léonard de Vinci)
111 mounted facsimiles (text and diagrams) each preceded by a leaf with a mounted
label. — [t.1–2] Les solides d'égal volume. [t. 3] Machines hydrauliques : application du
principe de la vis d'Archimède; Pompes; Machines d'épuisement et de dragage. —
Edition of 100.

1902

VR.1902.001   *Catalogue of the important collection of early English & foreign silver
and silver-gilt plate, bijouterie & objects of art of J. Dunn-Gardner,
Esq. which has been for many years past exhibited at the Victoria and
Albert Museum, South Kensington : which will be sold by auction by
Messrs. Christie, Manson & Woods . . . .*
56 p., [19] leaves of plates : ill. ; 26 cm.
Sale date: 29, 30 Apr. 1902. — Lugt 60118.

VR.1902.002   *The Constantine Alexander Ionides collection : (a first selection of
fifty-two subjects) : photographed and published by permission.*
London : W.A. Mansell & Co. [1902?].
[8] p. : ill. ; 15 x 25 cm.

1904

VR.1904.001   *A catalogue of the large and magnificent collection of objets d'art*
commenced by the late C.B. Lee-Mainwaring, Esq. in the year 1820,
and from 1874 largely added to by the Hon. W.F.B. Massey-
Mainwaring M.P. and the Hon. Mrs. Massey-Mainwaring :
comprising specimens from all the most important art sales dispersed
during the above periods . . . : which will be sold at auction by Messrs.
Robinson & Fisher . . . .
[4], 99 p., [35] leaves of plates : ill. ; 29 cm.
At head of title: Willis's Rooms. — Sale date: 6–11 June 1904. — "Since 1874 exhibited
at the Victoria and Albert and Bethnal Green Museums." — "This catalogue is copied
from the official catalogue of the Bethnal Green Museum [i.e. v.1888.002], to which
some additional notes have been added"–Preface. — Lugt 62390.

1905

VR.1905.001   *An Almain armourer's album : selections from an original ms. in the*
Victoria and Albert Museum, South Kensington / with introduction
and notes by Viscount Dillon.
London : Reproduced and printed by W. Griggs, 1905.
3 p., xxx, [3] leaves of plates, 1 folded : col. ill. ; 51 cm.
Jacob Topf is the presumed author of the manuscript. — Captions are interleaved.

VR.1905.002   *The guide to the Victoria and Albert Museum, South Kensington :*
with plans and illustrations.
London : Printed by Spottiswoode & Co. Ltd., sold by permission in
the Victoria and Albert Museum, "1905–6".
76 p., [5?] leaves of plates, some folded : ill., plans ; 22 cm.
Includes index. — Incomplete copy seen.

1906

VR.1906.001   *The Red Line guide to the Victoria and Albert Museum, South*
Kensington : (art collections, main building).
London : J.J. Keliher & Co., [1906].
[4], 60p., [2] leaves, folded : ill., plans ; 25 cm.
Written by H.P. Mitchell.

1907

VR.1907.001   *Japanese educational exhibition : notes on the organisation of*
Japanese education.
London : H.M.S.O., 1907.
20 p. ; 22 cm.
At head of title: Board of Education. — Text revised by Baron Kikuchi.
EXHIBITION: vx.1907.001

1908

VR.1908.001   *The guide to the Victoria and Albert Museum, South Kensington :*
               with plans and illustrations.
               London : Printed by Spottiswoode & Co., sold by permission in the
               Victoria and Albert Museum, "1908–9".
               iii, 76 p., 4 p., [5] leaves, of plates, some folded, [12?] p. of
               advertisements : ill., plans ; 22 cm.
               Red wrappers, with advertisements.

VR.1908.001A   [Another issue]
               " With six coloured plates"–cover, VR.1908.001. — Unseen.

VR.1908.002   *The Victoria and Albert Museum (Art Division) : report of the*
               Committee of Re-arrangement : (adopted July 29th, 1908) : presented
               to Parliament by command of His Majesty.
               London : H.M.S.O., 1908.
               36 p., [4] leaves, folded : plans, 33 cm.
               (Cd. 4389)
               At head of title: Board of Education. — Report signed Cecil H. Smith, W.A.S. Benson,
               Lewis Day, H. Powell, J.C. Wedgwood. — Includes: Report on foreign museums.

1910

VR.1910.001   *A book of porcelain : fine examples in the Victoria & Albert Museum*
               / painted by William Gibb ; with text by Bernard Rackham.
               London : Adam and Charles Black, 1910.
               xv, 95 p., 1, 28 leaves of plates : col. ill. ; 26 cm.
               Colour photographs, pasted on to grey leaves, interleaved with captions.

VR.1910.002   *Nation's treasures : measured drawings of fine old furniture in the*
               Victoria & Albert Museum / by H.P. Benn and H.P. Shapland.
               London : Published by Simpkin, Marshall, Hamilton, Kent, and Benn
               Bros., [1910].
               71 p. : ill. ; 31 cm.

1912

VR.1912.001   *Capetown [sic] Cathedral memorial of the South African war, 1899,*
               1900, 1901, 1902 : exhibition of the book (unbound in framed sheets)
               containing the names of those who died in the war on behalf of the
               Empire : 23rd May and three following weeks, Victoria and Albert
               Museum, South Kensington.
               [London? : Memorial Fund?, 1912] (Chiswick Press, printer).
               13 p. ; 23 cm.
               Text signed Graily Hewitt, Allan F. Vigers.
               EXHIBITION: VX.1912.003

1913

VR.1913.001 *Catalogue of the choice collection of English and foreign silver formed by J.H. Fitzhenry Esq. . . . : which will be sold at auction by Messrs. Christie, Manson & Woods at their great rooms . . . .*
35 p. ; 25 cm.
Sale date: 17, 20 Nov. 1913. — "The greater part of the collection has for several years been on loan at the Victoria and Albert Museum." — Lugt 73335.

VR.1913.002 *Catalogue of the collection of works of art chiefly of the mediaeval and Renaissance periods formed by J.H. Fitzhenry, Esq. . . . : which will be sold at auction by Messrs. Christie, Manson & Woods at their great rooms . . . .*
97 p., [8] leaves of plates : ill. ; 25 cm.
Sale date: 18–26 Nov. 1913. — "The greater part of the collection has for several years been on loan at the Victoria and Albert Museum." — Lugt 73350.

VR.1913.003 *Old English costumes selected from the collection formed by Mr Talbot Hughes.*
[London : s.n., 1913.]
79 p. : ill. (some col.) ; 31 cm.
Introductory text by Philip Gibbs, reprinted from the *Connoisseur* (Nov. 1913). Preface by Cecil Harcourt Smith.
EXHIBITION: VX.1913.XXX.001

1914

VR.1914.001 *Catalogue of the exhibition of students' work, sessions 1913–14 : Royal College of Art.*
London : Printed by Eyre and Spottiswoode, 1914.
22 p. ; 25 cm.
Cover title. At head of title: Board of Education.
EXHIBITION: VX.1914.006

1915

VR.1915.001 *Exhibition of the works of Ivan Meštrović : Victoria & Albert Museum, summer 1915.*
[London : Exhibition Committee?, 1915.]
[16] p., [8] leaves of plates : ill. ; 24 cm.
Meštrović and his art / James Bone. Meštrović and the Jugoslav idea / R.W. Seton-Watson.
EXHIBITION: VX.1915.001

1916

VR.1916.001 *British Industries Fair : Victoria and Albert Museum, South Kensington, London S.W., Feb. 21st–March 3rd, 1916.*
London : Board of Trade (Commercial Intelligence Branch), [1916].
viii, 156 p., [2] folded leaves of plates : plans ; 18 cm.

Alphabetical and classified list of exhibitors, British manufacturers in the following trades: toys and games, earthenware, porcelain and china, glass, fancy goods, stationery and printing.
EXHIBITION: VX.1916.001

1917

VR.1917.001 *British Industries Fair : Victoria and Albert Museum, South Kensington, London S.W., Feb. 26th-March 9th, 1917.*
London : Board of Trade (Commercial Intelligence Branch), [1917].
viii, 208 p., [2] folded leaves of plates : plans ; 18 cm.
Alphabetical and classified list of exhibitors, British manufacturers in the following trades: toys and games, earthenware, porcelain and china, glass, fancy goods, stationery and printing.
EXHIBITION: VX.1917.001

1918

VR.1918.001 *Memorials of London. No 2, Artists and craftsmen.*
London : Underground Railways & London General Omnibus Co., [1918].
12 p. : ill. ; 23 cm.
Written by Charles White. — Concerns the statues on the façade of the V&A.

1919

VR.1919.001 *Inscriptions suggested for war memorials.*
[London?] : Privately printed, 1919.
44 p. ; 20 cm.
Prefatory note signed: Cecil Harcourt Smith.
EXHIBITION: VX.1919.001

1922

VR.1922.001 *British Institute of Industrial Art : exhibition of present day industrial art : Victoria and Albert Museum, South Kensington, 16th January to 25th February 1922.*
[London : The Institute, 1922.]
42 p., xviii p. of advertisements : plan ; 22 cm.
Cover title. At head of title: Board of Trade, Board of Education. — "Under revision"–cover. — Advertisements on wrappers.
EXHIBITION: VX.1922.001

VR.1922.001A [Rev. ed.]
48 p.
Lacks "Under revision" note. — Includes index of craftsmen, designers and manufacturers.

VR.1922.002 *International theatre exhibition : designs and models for the modern stage : Victoria & Albert Museum, June 3–July 16, 1922.*
[London : Exhibition Committee?, 1922.]
54 p. ; 24 cm.

"Catalogue"–cover. — Ivory wrappers with heraldic device printed in blue. — Loosely
inserted: International theatre exhibition: supplement to catalogue (6 p. ; 23 cm.)
EXHIBITION: VX.1922.002

VR.1922.003   *International theatre exhibition : designs and models for the modern*
stage : Victoria & Albert Museum, June 3–July 31, 1922.
[London : Exhibition Committee?, 1922.]
60 p. ; 24 cm.
"Catalogue"–cover. — Index of artists.
EXHIBITION: VX.1922.002

VR.1922.004   *International theatre exhibition : designs and models for the modern*
stage : Victoria & Albert Museum, June 3–July 31, 1922.
[London : Exhibition Committee?, 1922.]
110 p., [16] p. of plates : ill. ; 24 cm.
"Catalogue and bibliography"–cover. — Foreword by Gordon Craig. Introduction by
Cecil Harcourt Smith. — "List of works on the art of the theatre in the Victoria and
Albert Museum Library": p. 66–110. — Ivory paper covered boards with heraldic
device printed in blue; quarter bound in ivory cloth.
EXHIBITION: VX.1922.002

1923

VR.1923.001   *Association of Old Students of the Royal College of Art : first*
exhibition, North Court, Victoria and Albert Museum, South
Kensington, S.W.7 : 15th December 1923 to 19th January 1924.
[London : The Association, 1923.]
36, [6] p. ; 22 cm.
Foreword by Alexander Fisher.
EXHIBITION: VX.1923.007

VR.1923.002   *British Institute of Industrial Art : exhibition of industrial art today :*
North Court, Victoria and Albert Museum, South Kensington,
September-October 1923.
[London : The Institute, 1923.]
58 p., [iv?] p. of advertisements ; 22 cm.
EXHIBITION: VX.1923.006

VR.1923.002A   [Rev. ed.]
62 p., [vi] p. of advertisements ; 22 cm.
Includes index of exhibitors and designers. — Printed in brown.

1924

VR.1924.001   *Bethnal Green Men's Institute : catalogue of an exhibition of drawings*
& paintings held at the Bethnal Green Museum, spring 1924.
[London : The Institute, 1924.]
8 p. ; 17 cm.
Cover title. — Foreword by A.K. Sabin.
EXHIBITION: VX.1924.BGM.001

VR.1924.002 *Fine carpets in the Victoria & Albert Museum : twenty examples, reproduced for the first time in colour, of old carpets from Persia, India, Caucasia, Armenia, Turkey, China, Spain and England* / with an introduction and descriptive notes by A.F. Kendrick and C.E.C. Tattersall.
London : Ernest Benn, 1924.
26 p., 20 leaves of plates : ill. ; 41 cm.
"This edition . . . is strictly limited to 450 copies only for sale, of which 100 are reserved for the United States of America." — Issued in the U.S.A. by Scribner's.

1925

VR.1925.001 *Arts & crafts exhibition in the North Court, Victoria and Albert Museum, May 16 to June 1, 1925 : catalogue and programme of music.*
[London : Civil Service Arts Council, 1925.]
52 p. : maps ; 19 cm.
At head of title: Civil Service Arts Council. — Index of exhibitors.
EXHIBITION: VX.1925.002

1926

VR.1926.001 *Arts and crafts exhibition in the North Court, Victoria and Albert Museum, March 20 to April 5, 1926 : catalogue and programme of music.*
[London : Civil Service Arts Council, 1926.]
55 p. : maps ; 19 cm.
At head of title: Civil Service Arts Council. — Index of exhibitors.
EXHIBITION: VX.1926.001

VR.1926.002 *Bethnal Green Men's Institute : catalogue of an exhibition of drawings and paintings held at the Bethnal Green Museum, spring 1926.*
[London : The Institute, 1926.]
8 p. ; 17 cm.
Cover title. — Foreword by A.K. Sabin.
EXHIBITION: VX.1926.BGM.001

1927

VR.1927.001 *Bethnal Green Men's Institute : catalogue of an exhibition of drawings and paintings held at the Bethnal Green Museum, spring 1927.*
[London : The Institute, 1927.]
8 p. ; 19 cm.
Cover title. — Foreword by A.K. Sabin.
EXHIBITION: VX.1927.BGM.001

VR.1927.002 *Exhibition of arts in the North Court, Victoria and Albert Museum, March 19 to April 2, 1927 : catalogue and programme of music.*
[London : Civil Service Arts Council, 1927.]

45 p. : map ; 19 cm.
At head of title: Civil Service Arts Council. — Index of exhibitors.
EXHIBITION: VX.1927.001

VR.1927.003   *Exhibition of contemporary French prints . . . under the auspices of
l'Association française d'expansion et d'échanges artistiques : Victoria
and Albert Museum, South Kensington, from May 10th to June 20th,
1927.*
[s.l. : s.n., 1927] (Le Vesinet : Ch. Brande, Imprimeur).
40 p., [44] p. of plates : ill. ; 22 cm.
Preface by P.A. Lemoisne. — Index.
EXHIBITION: VX.1927.004

1928

VR.1928.001   *Bethnal Green Men's Institute : catalogue of an exhibition of drawings
and paintings held at the Bethnal Green Museum, spring 1928.*
[London : The Institute, 1928.]
8 p. ; 19 cm.
Cover title. — Foreword by Arthur K. Sabin.
EXHIBITION: VX.1928.BGM.001

VR.1928.002   *Exhibition of arts in the North Court, Victoria and Albert Museum,
March 17 to 31 : catalogue.*
[London : Civil Service Arts Council, 1928.]
36 p., [4] p. of advertisements : map ; 19 cm.
At head of title: Civil Service Arts Council. — Index of exhibitors.
EXHIBITION: VX.1928.001

VR.1928.003   *Interim report : dated 1st September 1928* / presented by the Secretary
of State for the Home Department to Parliament by command of His
Majesty.
London : Printed and published by H.M.S.O., 1928.
64 p., [3] folded leaves of plates : plans. ; 25 cm.
(Cmd. 3192)
At head of title: Royal Commission on National Museums & Galleries. — [Preface] /
W. Joynson-Hicks. — Includes reports on the V&A, Bethnal Green Museum and
Science Museum. — Index.

1929

VR.1929.001   *Ancient Russian icons : from the XIIth to XIXth centuries : lent by the
Government of the U.S.S.R. to a British Committee and exhibited by
permission at the Victoria and Albert Museum, South Kensington,
18th November to 28th December, 1929.*
London : [Russian Icon Exhibition Committee], 1929.
40 p. : ill. ; 22 cm.
Introduction by Martin Conway. Text by Igor Grabar. — Bibliography: p. 32.
EXHIBITION: VX.1929.006

VR.1929.001A   "2nd ed."

VR.1929.002   *Bethnal Green Men's Institute : catalogue of an exhibition of
               drawings, paintings and other objects by members of the Institute,
               held at the Bethnal Green Museum, spring 1929.*
               [London : The Institute, 1929.]
               8 p. ; 19 cm.
               Cover title. — Foreword by A.K. Sabin.
               EXHIBITION: VX.1929.BGM.001

VR.1929.003   *Catalogue of the British Institute of Industrial Art autumn exhibition
               illustrating British industrial art for the slender purse : . . . North
               Court, Victoria and Albert Museum, South Kensington, 9th November
               to 18th December 1929.*
               [London : The Institute], 1929.
               99 p. ; 22 cm.
               The British Institute of Industrial Art permanent collection of work by modern British
               artists, manufacturers and craftsmen: p. 77–93. — The Margaret Bulley collection
               illustrating certain modern tendencies in European industrial art: p. 95–99.
               EXHIBITION: VX.1929.005

VR.1929.003A   [Rev.]
               105 p., [10?] p. of advertisements ; 22 cm.
               The British Institute of Industrial Art permanent collection of work by modern British
               artists, manufacturers and craftsmen: p. 83–99. — The Margaret Bulley collection
               illustrating certain modern tendencies in European industrial art: p. 100–105 (includes
               index). — Index to exhibition: p. 79.

VR.1929.004   *Exhibition of arts in the North Court, Victoria and Albert Museum,
               March 16 to April 1, 1929 : catalogue.*
               [London : Civil Service Arts Council, 1929.]
               46 p. : map ; 19 cm.
               At head of title: Civil Service Arts Council. — Index of exhibitors. — Correction slip
               loosely inserted for p. 45.
               EXHIBITION: VX.1929.002

VR.1929.005   *Exhibition of contemporary American prints : Victoria and Albert
               Museum, South Kensington, May 14–June 22, 1929 . . . under the
               auspices of the American Federation of Arts.*
               [s.l. : s.n., 1929] (Washington, D.C. : B.S. Adams, printer).
               32 p., [23] p. of plates : ill. ; 21 cm.
               Introduction by Leila Mechlin.
               EXHIBITION: VX.1929.003

VR.1929.006   *Final report. Part I, General conclusions and recommendations : dated
               20th September 1929.*
               London : Printed and published by H.M.S.O., 1929.
               93 p. ; 25 cm.
               (Cmd. 3401)
               At head of title: Royal Commission on National Museums & Galleries. — "Presented
               by the Secretary of State for the Home Department to Parliament by command of His
               Majesty . . ."–t.p.

VR.1929.007   *Oral evidence, memoranda and appendices to the final report.*
               London : Printed and published by H.M.S.O., 1929.
               viii, 211 p. ; 34 cm.
               At head of title: Royal Commission on National Museums and Galleries. — Indexes to
               witnesses and subjects.

1930

VR.1930.001   *Bethnal Green Men's Institute : catalogue of an exhibition of
               drawings, paintings and other objects by members of the Institute,
               held at the Bethnal Green Museum, spring 1930.*
               [London : The Institute, 1930.]
               8 p. ; 19 cm.
               Cover title. — Foreword by Arthur K. Sabin.
               EXHIBITION: VX.1930.BGM.001

VR.1930.002   *Final report. Part II, Conclusions and recommendations relating to
               individual institutions : dated 1st January 1930.*
               London : Printed and published by H.M.S.O., 1930.
               104 p., 1 folded p. of plates : plan ; 25 cm.
               (Cmd. 3463)
               At head of title: Royal Commission on National Museums & Galleries. — "Presented
               by the Secretary of State for the Home Department to Parliament by command of His
               Majesty . . ."–t.p. — Includes reports on the V&A, Bethnal Green Museum, Science
               Museum and the South Kensington Site.

VR.1930.003   *I manoscritti e i disegni di Leonardo da Vinci* / pubblicati dalla Reale
               commissione vinciana sotto gli auspici del Ministero dell'educazione
               nazionale. Serie minore, Il codice Forster . . . nel "Victoria and Albert
               Museum".
               Roma : Danesi, 1930–1936.
               5 v. : ill., facsims. (some col.) ; 28 cm.
               Facsimiles and transcriptions in print on opposite pages. — I: I (1930). II: II,1 (1934).
               III: II,2 (1934). IV: III (1934). V: Prefazione, Indice (1936). — "Edizione di 300
               esemplari numerati".

1931

VR.1931.001   *Bethnal Green Men's Institute : catalogue of an exhibition of drawings
               and paintings by members of the Institute, held at the Bethnal Green
               Museum, spring 1931.*
               [London : The Institute, 1931.]
               8 p. ; 19 cm.
               Cover title. — Foreword by Arthur K. Sabin.
               EXHIBITION: VX.1931.BGM.001

VR.1931.002   *Measured drawings of English furniture (the oak period)* / by
               P.E. Marx and M.S. Taylor.
               London : Ernest Benn Ltd., 1931.
               xii, [13]–85 p. : ill., plans ; 32 cm.

"In the following pages will be found a number of measured drawings of English furniture dating from 1500 to 1680; all are present in the Victoria and Albert Museum, South Kensington . . ."–p. ix.

1932

VR.1932.001   *Bethnal Green Men's Institute : catalogue of an exhibition of drawings, paintings and lithographs by members of the Institute, held at the Bethnal Green Museum, spring 1932.*
[London : The Institute, 1932.]
12 p. ; 19 cm.
Cover title. — Foreword by Arthur K. Sabin.
EXHIBITION: VX.1932.BGM.001

VR.1932.002   *Catalogue : exhibition of modern British embroidery : Victoria and Albert Museum, 1st to 30th July, 1932.*
[London : British Institute of Industrial Art, 1932.]
xv, 14 p. ; 22 cm.
Cover title. — Includes advertisements.
EXHIBITION: VX.1932.004

VR.1932.003   *Exhibition of illustrated books for children : historical section : catalogue.*
London : National Book Council, 1932.
55 p. ; 22 cm.
At head of title: Victoria and Albert Museum. Cover title: Catalogue of the exhibition of illustrated books for children : (historical section). — Prefatory note by Eric Maclagan. Introduction by E.V. Lucas.
EXHIBITION: VX.1932.005

VR.1932.003A   2nd ed.
One additional entry.

1934

VR.1934.001   *Bethnal Green Men's Institute : catalogue of an exhibition of drawings and paintings held at the Bethnal Green Museum, 1934.*
[London : The Institute, 1934.]
8 p. ; 19 cm.
Cover title. — Foreword by A.K. Sabin.
EXHIBITION: VX.1934.BGM.001

1936

VR.1936.001   *Bethnal Green Men's Institute : catalogue of an exhibition of drawings and paintings held at the Bethnal Green Museum, 1936.*
[London : The Institute, 1936.]
7 p. ; 19 cm.
Cover title. — Foreword by A.K. Sabin.
EXHIBITION: VX.1936.BGM.001

VR.1936.002   *Polish art : graphic art, textiles.*
[Poland? : s.n., 1936] (Kraków : Drukarnia Narodowa, printer).
52 p., [16] p. of plates : ill. ; 21 cm.
Introduction by Mieczysław Treter.
EXHIBITION: VX.1936.004

1937

VR.1937.001   *Bethnal Green Men's Institute : catalogue of an exhibition of drawings
and paintings held at the Bethnal Green Museum, 1937.*
[London : The Institute, 1937.]
8 p. ; 19 cm.
Cover title. — Foreword by Arthur K. Sabin.
EXHIBITION: VX.1937.BGM.001

VR.1937.002   *Coronation exhibition (thirteenth annual Civil Service exhibition of
arts) : North Court, Victoria and Albert Museum. London S.W.7 :
March 24 to April 28, 1937 : catalogue.*
[London : Civil Service Arts Council, 1937.]
36 p. ; 19 cm.
At head of title: Civil Service Arts Council. — Includes a section of books, organized by
the Civil Service Society of Authors. — Index of exhibitors.
EXHIBITION: VX.1937.001

VR.1937.003   *Hungarian graphic art : London, 1937, Victoria and Albert Museum.*
Budapest : Printed by Officina [for the Society of Hungarian Painter-
Etchers, 1937].
39 p., [32] p. of plates : ill. ; 17 cm.
Introduction / Edith Hoffmann. Graphic art in Hungary / Charles Rosner. — "This
catalogue is also being published in Hungarian, as the second volume of the Officina
picture-books . . ."–p. 39 verso.
EXHIBITION: VX.1937.002

1938

VR.1938.001   *Bethnal Green Men's Institute : catalogue of an exhibition of drawings
and paintings held at the Bethnal Green Museum, 1938.*
[London : The Institute, 1938.]
8 p. ; 19 cm.
Cover title. — Foreword by A.K. Sabin.
EXHIBITION: VX.1938.BGM.001

VR.1938.002   *Exhibition of graphic art NGU : Northern Graphic Union comprising
Denmark, Finland, Iceland, Norway, Sweden : Victoria & Albert
Museum, London, April 1938.*
[s.l. : Northern Graphic Union?], 1938 (Helsingfors : Frenckellska
Tryckeri Aktiebolaget).
110 p. : ill. ; 22 cm.
Cover title: NGU exhibition of graphic art. — Foreword by Lennart Segerstråle. Texts
by Andreas Friis (Denmark), Onni Okkonen (Finland), Kristofer Eriksen (Norway), L.S.
[i.e. Louis Sparre] (Sweden).
EXHIBITION: VX.1938.001

1939

VR.1939.001   *The art of glass : illustrated from the Wilfred Buckley collection in the Victoria and Albert Museum, London* / by Wilfred Buckley.
London : Phaidon Press : George Allen & Unwin, 1939.
285 [i.e. 281], 1 p. : ill. ; 30 cm.
After the author's death, the work was completed by B.T. Buckley. — "Catalogue of the Wilfred Buckley collection of glass": p. [235]–[286]. — Bibliography: p. 10.

1942

VR.1942.001   *An exhibition of British landscapes in oils, from George II to Queen Victoria : C.E.M.A. 1942–43.*
London : Council for the Encouragement of Music and the Arts, [1942].
15 p. ; 23 cm.
Cover title. — Foreword by Ralph Edwards. — Index.
EXHIBITION: VX.1942.003

1943

VR.1943.001   *Design in the home : an exhibition arranged by the Victoria and Albert Museum for C.E.M.A., 1943.*
London : Council for the Encouragement of Music and the Arts, [1943].
1 sheet, folded ([3] p.) ; 14 cm.
Catalogue of a touring exhibition. — Text by W.B. Honey.

1944

VR.1944.001   *Holbein (1497–1543) : a commemorative exhibition of reproductions.*
London : Council for the Encouragement of Music and the Arts, 1944.
19 p. ; 19 cm.
Catalogue by Carl Winter.
EXHIBITION: VX.1943.002

VR.1944.002   *A selection from* Recording Britain : *an exhibition of water-colours & drawings.*
London : Arts Council of Great Britain, [1944].
1 sheet, folded ([4] p.) ; 19 cm.
EXHIBITION: VX.1944.001

1945

VR.1945.001   *Exhibition of paintings by Picasso and Matisse = Exposition Picasso Matisse : December 1945.*
[Paris?] : Publidis, for L'Association française d'action artistique, 1945.
[34] p. : ill., ports. ; 26 cm.

At head of title: Victoria and Albert Museum. — Includes: Pablo Picasso / Christian
Zervos. Henri Matisse / Jean Cassou. — In English and French.
EXHIBITION: VX.1945.003

VR.1945.002   *An exhibition of the royal effigies, sculpture & other works of art :
prior to their being re-installed in Westminster Abbey : November
1945.*
London : Society of Antiquaries of London, 1945.
24 p., 2 leaves of plates : ill. ; 22 cm.
At head of title: Victoria and Albert Museum. — Cover title: The royal effigies,
sculpture & other works of art from Westminster Abbey. — Foreword by Paul de
Labilliere. Texts signed J.G.M., E.M. [i.e. J.G. Mann, Eric Maclagan].
EXHIBITION: VX.1945.004

1946

VR.1946.001   *American colonial architecture : an exhibition of photographs of
eighteenth and early nineteenth century American buildings /*
presented by the Georgian Group, 1946.
[London : Georgian Group, 1946.]
15 p., [2] leaves of plates : ill. ; 21 cm.
EXHIBITION: VX.1946.002

VR.1946.002   *Britain can make it exhibition : organised by the Council of Industrial
Design at the Victoria and Albert Museum, London, opening 24th
September, 1946.*
[London : The Council, 1946.]
160 p. : ill. ; 21 cm.
EXHIBITION: VX.1946.004

VR.1946.002A   *The Council of Industrial Design presents Britain can make it
exhibition at the V & A : catalogue supplement.*
[London] : Published for the Council of Industrial Design by
H.M.S.O., 1946.
p. 162–242 : plan ; 20 cm.
Cover title. — Printing: 10/46.

VR.1946.002B   *"Britain can make it" exhibition . . . catalogue amendments.*
p. [245]–[256] ; 20 cm.
Caption title. — Printing: 12/46.

VR.1946.003   *Picasso, Matisse exhibition.*
[London : Arts Council of Great Britain, 1946?]
12 p., 1, 4 p. of plates : ill. ; 21 cm.
Cover title. — Includes: Picasso: between two charnel houses / Christian Zervos.
Matisse / Jean Cassou. Picasso and Matisse / Philip James. — Published to accompany
touring version of VX.1945.003.

VR.1946.004   *Recording Britain /* edited, with notes, by Arnold Palmer.
[London] : Oxford University Press, 1946–1949.
4 v. : ill. (some col.) ; 26 cm.
"Drawings of places and buildings of characteristic national interest, particularly
those exposed to the danger of destruction by the operations of war." — V. 1. London
and Middlesex, Surrey, Berkshire, Buckinghamshire, Hertfordshire, Bedfordshire.

V. 2. Essex, Suffolk, Cambridgeshire and Huntingdonshire, Northamptonshire and
Rutlandshire, Norfolk, Yorkshire. V. 3. Lancashire and Westmoreland, Derbyshire,
Cheshire and Shropshire, Staffordshire, Welsh Counties, Worcestershire, Herefordshire,
Oxfordshire, Gloucestershire. V. 4. Wiltshire, Somerset, Cornwall, Devon, Dorset,
Hampshire, Sussex, Kent. — The collection was given to the V&A by the Pilgrim Trust.

1947

VR.1947.001   *Contemporary British prints and drawings from the Wakefield*
                 collection of the British Council : Victoria and Albert Museum, March
                 12th-April 12th, 1947.
                 [London : British Council, 1947.]
                 [16] p. ; 22 cm.
                 Cover title. — Preface / A.A. Longden. — Index.
                 EXHIBITION: vx.1947.002

VR.1947.002   *Masterpieces of French tapestry : an exhibition held at the Victoria*
                 and Albert Museum, March 29 to May 31.
                 [London] : Arts Council of Great Britain, 1947.
                 [32] p. : chiefly ill. (some col.) ; 30 cm.
                 Picture book. — Bibliography: p. v-viii.
                 EXHIBITION: vx.1947.003

VR.1947.003   *Masterpieces of French tapestry : catalogue : an exhibition arranged*
                 by the Victoria and Albert Museum and the Arts Council of Great
                 Britain under the auspices of the French Government : March 29 to
                 May 31.
                 [London] : Arts Council of Great Britain, 1947.
                 viii, 32 p. ; 23 cm.
                 Cover title: French tapestry. — Foreword / Leigh Ashton, Philip James. — Bibliography:
                 p. v-viii.
                 EXHIBITION: vx.1947.003

VR.1947.003A   [Small ed.]
                 19 cm.

VR.1947.004   *Pictures for schools : an exhibition organised by the Society for*
                 Education in Art, with the support of the Arts Council of Great
                 Britain : May 22nd-June 14th 1947 : Victoria and Albert Museum,
                 South Kensington.
                 [London : The Society, 1947.]
                 1 sheet, folded ([6] p.) ; 22 cm.
                 Introduction by Herbert Read. — Printed in brown.
                 EXHIBITION: vx.1947.004

VR.1947.005   *Style in sculpture* / edited by Leigh Ashton.
                 London : Geoffrey Cumberlege, Oxford University Press, 1947.
                 64 p. : ill. ; 20 cm.
                 "The book is one which in normal times the Museum would have probably published
                 itself . . . The fees paid by the Oxford University Press will be devoted to the purchase of
                 a work of art for [the] Department"–Preface, p. 4.
                 EXHIBITION: vx.1946.003

1948

VR.1948.001   *The Albertina collection of old master drawings : an illustrated*
              supplement to the exhibition catalogue.
              [London] : Arts Council of Great Britain, 1948.
              [32] p. of plates, [4] p. : ill. ; 28 cm.
              Includes: A short history of the Albertina Collection / Otto Benesch.
              EXHIBITION: vx.1948.002

VR.1948.002   *Catalogue of the 'Sport in art' exhibition, together with a list of*
              awards in the international competition : 15 July to 14 August, held at
              the Victoria and Albert Museum.
              [London : XIVth Olympiad, 1948] (Oliver Burridge & Co., printer).
              51 p. ; 22 cm.
              At head of title: The XIVth Olympiad, London 1948. — Index of artists.
              EXHIBITION: vx.1948.007

VR.1948.003   *Danish art treasures through the ages : catalogue illustrated [sic] : an*
              exhibition arranged by the Danish government and the Victoria &
              Albert Museum : 28th October 1948–2nd January 1949.
              [London?] : Exhibition Committee, 1948 (Copenhagen : Berlingske
              Bogtrykkeri).
              154 p. : ill. ; 21 cm.
              Preface by K. Paludan-Müller.
              EXHIBITION: vx.1948.009

VR.1948.004   *Danish folk costumes* / by Ellen Anderson.
              London : Committee of the Exhibition, 1948 (Copenhagen :
              Gyldendalske Boghandel, Nordisk Verlag).
              35 p. : ill. ; 19 cm.
              Translated from the Danish.
              EXHIBITION: vx.1948.009

VR.1948.005   *English pottery and porcelain : coming-of-age exhibition : held at the*
              Victoria & Albert Museum, May 5–June 2, 1948.
              [London : English Ceramic Circle, 1948.]
              [ii], 56 p., [8] p. of plates : ill. ; 18 cm.
              At head of title: The English Ceramic Circle 1927–1948. — Preface by Aubrey J.
              Toppin. — Index of lenders.
              EXHIBITION: vx.1948.003

VR.1948.006   *The exhibition of Danish art treasures through the ages : a short*
              guide.
              [London] : Exhibition Committee, 1948.
              14 p. ; 22 cm.
              Cover title. — Translated from the Danish.
              EXHIBITION: vx.1948.009

VR.1948.007   *An exhibition of old master drawings from the Albertina Collection,*
              Vienna.
              [London] : Arts Council of Great Britain, 1948.
              40 p. ; 18 cm.

Cover title: Old master drawings from the Albertina. — Foreword signed "P.J." [i.e. Philip James]. Introduction by A.E. Popham. — Bibliographic references: p. 8. Index of artists. — Errata slip pasted in.
EXHIBITION: vx.1948.002

VR.1948.007A   2nd imp. [corrected]

VR.1948.008   *Illustrations from the XIVth Olympiad 'Sport in art' exhibition, London, 1948 : held at the Victoria and Albert Museum.*
[London : XIVth Olympiad, 1948] (Oliver Burridge & Co., printer).
48 p. : chiefly ill. ; 25 cm.
Cover title.
EXHIBITION: vx.1948.007

1949

VR.1949.001   *Art for all : an exhibition of original paintings for posters produced by London Transport 1908–1949 : April 6 to June 30, 1949.*
[London : London Transport], 1949 (Shenval Press, printer).
14 p. ; 18 cm.
Cover title. — Index.
EXHIBITION: vx.1949.002

VR.1949.002   *Eighteen paintings from the Wellington Gift.*
[London] : Arts Council of Great Britain, 1949.
15, 1 p., [4] p. of plates : ill., ports. ; 23 cm.
Introduction by E.K. Waterhouse. — Errata slip pasted in.
EXHIBITION: vx.1950.011

VR.1949.003   *English pottery and porcelain : commemorative catalogue of an exhibition held at the Victoria & Albert Museum, May 5–June 2, 1948.*
London : Routledge and Kegan Paul, [1949].
xv, 94 p., 1, 123 p. of plates : ill. (1 col.) ; 29 cm.
At head of title: The English Ceramic Circle 1927–1948. — Preface by Aubrey J. Toppin. Foreword by Bernard Rackham. — Index of lenders. — Limited edition of 1,000 copies.
EXHIBITION: vx.1948.003

1950

VR.1950.001   *The Arts & Crafts Exhibition Society : a catalogue of the twenty-second exhibition, at the Victoria & Albert Museum : 1st November to 3rd December 1950 ....*
[London : The Society, 1950.]
62 p. ; 19 cm.
Foreword by Leigh Ashton. — Includes lists of members and exhibitors. Published to accompany touring version of vx.1945.003.

VR.1950.002   *Exhibition of British stage design : Victoria and Albert Museum, 1950.*
[London : Association of Theatrical Designers and Craftsmen, 1950.]
[8] p. ; 22 cm.

Caption title. — At head of title: Association of Theatrical Designers and Craftsmen.
EXHIBITION: VX.1950.004

VR.1950.003　　　　*Exhibition of Polish book illustration and book covers : catalogue.*
[London? : s.n., 1950.]
13 p. : ill. ; 21 cm.
Introduction by Ignacy Witz.
EXHIBITION: VX.1950.012

VR.1950.004　　　　*The public house of tomorrow : Victoria and Albert Museum, April 4
to 29, 1950.*
[London? : s.n., 1950] (Kingston-on-Thames : Knapp, Drewett & Sons
Ltd., printers).
[5] p. : ill. ; 22 cm.
EXHIBITION: VX.1950.002

VR.1950.005　　　　*The Rural Industries Bureau presents an exhibition of handmade
furniture : including the winning pieces of the Bureau's furniture
competition for rural craftsmen : from the 5th to the 30th April
1950.*
London : Rural Industries Bureau, [1950].
[8] p. ; 21 cm.
Cover title. — At head of title: Victoria & Albert Museum. — Introduction by Cosmo
Clark. — Includes names and addresses of rural craftsmen.
EXHIBITION: VX.1950.003

VR.1950.006　　　　*William & Mary and their time : an exhibition held at the Victoria &
Albert Museum, London, 21 June to 20 August.*
[London] : Arts Council of Great Britain, 1950.
76 p., xvi leaves of plates : ill., geneal. tables ; 24 cm.
Foreword / Philip James. A note on the arts of England in the time of William and
Mary by Oliver Millar. Introduction G.N. Clark. — Indexes of lenders, artists and
craftsmen.
EXHIBITION: VX.1950.005

1951

VR.1951.001　　　　*Der Buchumschlag : veranstaltet vom Victoria & Albert Museum,
London : Kunstgewerbemuseum Zürich, 3. Februar bis 4 März
1951.*
Zürich : Das Kunstgewerbemuseum, [1951].
55 p., [16] p. of plates : ill. ; 21 cm.
(Wegleitung ; 189)
At head of title: Internationale Ausstellung. Cover title: Die Kunst des Buch-Umschlages.
— Introduction by Charles Rosner. — Selected from VX.1949.006.

Addendum [VR.1950.007] *Hindu medieval sculpture : 79 original photographs* / Raymond Burnier. — Paris:
La Palme, [1950]. — [188] p. : ill.; 37 cm. — "conceived and produced by Pierre Berès." "exhibited for the
first time in Europe by Pierre Berès, in Paris, in June 1948 and in America at the Metropolitan Museum, New-
York, in November 1949."
EXHIBITION: VX.1952.IND.001

VR.1951.001A   Also issued in illustrated wrappers, for the Stedelijk Museum, Amsterdam.
                Cover title: Boekomslagen. — "Cat. 86"–cover.

VR.1951.002   *Exhibition of books : arranged by the National Book League at the
               Victoria & Albert Museum.*
               London : Published for the National Book League by the Cambridge
               University Press, 1951.
               224 p. ; 22 cm.
               At head of title: The Festival of Britain. — Catalogue compiled by John Hadfield.
               Foreword / Norman Birkett. — List of lenders. Index of authors. — Advertisements,
               p. 193–224.
               EXHIBITION: VX.1951.004

VR.1951.003   *Internationell utställning av bokomslag : Nationalmusei
               utställningskatalog nr. 186.*
               Stockholm : Esselte AB, 1951.
               [36] p. ; 22 cm.
               Introduction by Charles Rosner. — Selected from VX.1949.006.

VR.1951.004   *Masterpieces of Victorian photography, 1840–1900, from the
               Gernsheim collection : published by the Arts Council of Great Britain
               on the occasion of the Festival of Britain.*
               [London] : Arts Council of Great Britain, 1951.
               35 p., 1 leaf, 15 p. of plates : ill., port. ; 23 cm. + 1 sheet.
               Foreword / Philip James. Note to the reader / Helmut Gernsheim. — Frontispiece pasted
               in. Coloured drawing on cover by Edward Ardizzone. — On separate sheet: list of
               photographs selected for a travelling exhibition.
               EXHIBITION: VX.1951.002

1952

VR.1952.001   *Exhibition illustrated : Women's Institutes exhibition of handicrafts :
               Victoria and Albert Museum, London, S.W.7, 13 to 26 March 1952
               . . . .*
               London : National Federation of Women's Institutes, [1952].
               16 p. : chiefly ill. ; 24 cm.
               EXHIBITION: VX.1952.001

VR.1952.002   *An exhibition of handmade furniture from the permanent collections
               of the Rural Industries Bureau : lent by the Victoria & Albert
               Museum, London.*
               [London : The Bureau, 1952.]
               15p ; 21 cm.
               Cover title. — Unsigned introduction dated 1952.

VR.1952.003   *Women's Institutes exhibition of handicrafts : Victoria and Albert
               Museum, London S.W.7, 13 to 26 March 1952 . . . .*
               [London : National Federation of Women's Institutes, 1952.]
               64 p. ; 22 cm.
               Includes bibliographic references. — Advertisements, p. 1–4, 58–64, and on wrappers.
               EXHIBITION: VX.1952.001

1953

VR.1953.001   *Coronation year exhibition : Victoria and Albert Museum.*
                  [London : Royal College of Art], 1953.
                  24 p. ; 34 cm.
                  [Foreword] / Robin Darwin. — List of artists and titles.
                  EXHIBITION: VX.1953.005

VR.1953.002   *Exhibition of Gothic art from the Victoria and Albert Museum:*
                  Peterborough Cathedral (north transept), 11th July–1st September
                  1953.
                  [Peterborough : Coronation Arts Festival, 1953.]
                  [8] p. ; 21 cm.
                  At head of title: Coronation Arts Festival, 1953.
                  EXHIBITION: VX.1953.XXX.001

1954

VR.1954.001   *An exhibition of handmade furniture from the permanent collections*
                  of the Rural Industries Bureau : lent by the Victoria & Albert
                  Museum, London.
                  [London : The Bureau, 1954.]
                  15p ; 21cm.
                  Cover title. — Unsigned introduction dated 1954.

1955

VR.1955.001   *E. McKnight Kauffer : memorial exhibition . . . presented by the*
                  Society of Industrial Artists, with the support of the Royal Society of
                  Arts, at the Victoria and Albert Museum, London, October to
                  November 1955.
                  [London : Society of Industrial Artists, 1955.]
                  [32] p. : ill. (some col.), plans, port. ; 28 cm.
                  Introduction by Ashley Havinden. An appreciation by Sir Francis Meynell. A tribute by
                  Thomas Eckersley.
                  EXHIBITION: VX.1955.006

VR.1955.002   *French theatre art (1935–1955) : Victoria and Albert Museum : avril*
                  [sic] 1955.
                  [s.l. : s.n., 1955] (Paris : Presses artistiques).
                  [20] p. : ill. ; 21 cm.
                  At head of title: Victoria and Albert Museum. — Prefaces by Leigh Ashton, René L.
                  Varin.
                  EXHIBITION: VX.1955.002

VR.1955.003   *Indian paintings from the Victoria & Albert Museum.*
                  [London] : Arts Council of Great Britain, 1955.
                  [12] p. ; 22 cm.
                  Cover title. — "To this exhibition have been added an additional fifteen works selected
                  by Mr. W.G. Archer." — Foreword by John Commander. — 'Short bibliography' on
                  rear turn-in of wrappers.
                  EXHIBITION: VX.1955.XXX.001

1956

VR.1956.001   *Catalogue of an exhibition of Anglo-Jewish art and history : in*
                commemoration of the tercentenary of the resettlement of the Jews in
                the British Isles . . . Anglo-Jewish art and history.
                [London? : East and West Library for the Tercentenary Council,
                1956.]
                106 p. ; 23 cm. + 1 sheet
                Introduction signed "C.R." [i.e. Cecil Roth?]. — List of exhibitors. — On separate
                sheet: diagram of exhibition and corrigenda. — Accompanied by advertisement for a
                commemorative medallion.
                EXHIBITION: VX.1956.001

VR.1956.001A   [Illustrated ed.]
                106 p., [32] p. of plates : ill., ports. ; 23 cm. + 2 leaves.
                On cover: "Illustrated catalogue".

VR.1956.002   *Windows for Coventry : the ten stained glass windows for the nave of*
                Coventry Cathedral.
                [London] : Royal College of Art, 1956.
                10 p., 4 leaves of plates (some col.) : fold. plan ; 23 cm.
                Texts by Basil Spence, Robin Darwin, Lawrence Lee, Keith New, Basil Taylor.
                EXHIBITION: VX.1956.007

1957

VR.1957.001   *Argenti inglesi, 1660–1830 : mostra organizzata dal Victoria and*
                Albert Museum in collaborazione con il British Council : Roma –
                Palazzo Venezia, 23 novembre 1957–12 gennaio 1958.
                Roma : De Luca, 1957.
                56 [2, 4] p., [32] p. of plates : ill. ; 21 cm.
                Introduction by Charles Oman.
                EXHIBITION: VX.1957.003

VR.1957.002   *The crafts 1957 : a catalogue of the twenty-fifth exhibition, at the*
                Victoria & Albert Museum, Cromwell Road, S.W.7, 6th November to
                8th December 1957 . . . .
                [London : Arts & Crafts Exhibition Society, 1957.]
                83 p. ; 19 cm.
                At head of title: The Arts & Crafts Exhibition Society. — Foreword by Trenchard Cox.
                — Includes lists of members and exhibitors.
                EXHIBITION: VX.1957.004

1958

VR.1958.001   *Art treasures from Japan : an exhibition of paintings and sculpture :*
                the Victoria and Albert Museum, 2 July to 17 August.
                [London] : Arts Council of Great Britain, 1958.
                62 p., [69] p. of plates : ill. (2 col.) ; 21 cm.

Addendum [VR.1956.003] *Rococo art from Bavaria.* — London : Lund Humphries, [1956]. — [34] p., 1, [100]
leaves of plates: ill. (some on col. leaves); 30 cm. — Preface / Hans Heinrich Herwarth von Bittenfeld.
Introduction / David Eccles. Bavarian rococo – or the eloquent in art / Nikolaus Pevsner. "illustrates almost
every piece"–Acknowledgments.
EXHIBITION: VX.1954.004

Forewords by Philip James, Yahachi Kawai. Preface by William Watson.
EXHIBITION: VX.1958.006

VR.1958.002   *Engelsk sølv, 1660–1830 : organiseret af Victoria and Albert Museum*
                i samarbejde med British Council.
                [København : Danske kunstindustrimuseum, 1958.]
                59 p., 20 leaves of plates : ill. ; 21 cm.
                (Udstilling ; nr. 497)
                Introduction by Charles Oman.
                EXHIBITION: VX.1957.003

VR.1958.003   *Engelskt silver, 1660–1830 : an utställning ordnad av Victoria &*
                Albert Museum i samarbete med British Council.
                [Stockholm : Victor Pettersons Bokindustri Aktiebolag, 1958.]
                59 p., 19 leaves of plates : ill. ; 21 cm.
                (Nationalmusei utställningskatalog ; nr. 244)
                Introduction by Charles Oman.
                EXHIBITION: VX.1957.003

VR.1958.004   *Finnish rugs : an exhibition arranged by the Finnish Society of Crafts*
                and Design, and held in the Victoria and Albert Museum, London,
                from 7th March to 4th May, 1958.
                [London? : The Society?, 1958.]
                13 p. : ill. ; 21 cm + 1 sheet.
                Foreword / Trenchard Cox. Text by Eila Pajastie. — Separate sheet: Catalogue loose-
                leaf.
                EXHIBITION: VX.1958.003

VR.1958.005   *Masterpieces of Byzantine art : sponsored by the Edinburgh Festival*
                Society in association with the Royal Scottish Museum and the
                Victoria and Albert Museum.
                [Edinburgh] : Edinburgh Festival Society, 1958.
                96 p., 16 p. of plates : ill. ; 22 cm.
                Foreword / Trenchard Cox. Text signed "D.T.R." [i.e. David Talbot Rice]. —
                Bibliography: p. 96.
                EXHIBITION: VX.1958.009

VR.1958.005A   2nd ed.
                93 p., [15] p. of plates.
                "London, October 1 to November 9"–t.p.

VR.1958.006   *Norwegian art treasures : 900 years of textiles, sculpture and silver :*
                Royal Scottish Museum, Edinburgh, October-November 1958,
                Victoria and Albert Museum, London, January-March 1959.
                [Edinburgh? : Exhibition Committee?, 1958] (Oslo : Printed by
                Grøndahl & Søn).
                55 p., [42] p. of plates : ill., map ; 22 cm.
                Edited by Guthorm Kavli; text by Alf Bøe. — Bibliography: p. 55-[56].
                EXHIBITION: VX.1959.001

VR.1958.007   *Orfèvrerie anglaise, 1660–1830 : exposition organisée par le Victoria*
                and Albert Museum et le British Council : Musée d'art et d'histoire,
                Genève, 19 janvier–23 février 1958.
                [Genève : Le Musée, 1958.]

63 p. : ill. ; 21 cm.
Introduction by Charles Oman.
EXHIBITION: vx.1957.003

1959

VR.1959.001 *Catalogue of an exhibition of three centuries of Swedish pottery :
Rörstrand 1726–1959, and Marieberg 1758–1788.*
[s.l. : s.n., 1959] (Stockholm : Printed by Nordisk Rotogravyr).
83, 1 p. : ill. (some col.) ; 22 cm.
At head of title: Victoria and Albert Museum. — [Preface] / Trenchard Cox. Texts by
R.J. Charleston, Ulf Hård af Segerstad. — Bibliography: p. [84]. Marks.
EXHIBITION: vx.1959.003

VR.1959.002 *Graphic design.*
[Birmingham : West Midlands Advisory Council for Technical,
Commercial and Art Education, 1959.]
1 sheet (5 p.) ; 21 cm.
Foreword signed Hugh Chance.
EXHIBITION: vx.1959.004

1960

VR.1960.001 *The country year : Women's Institutes exhibition of handicrafts :
Victoria and Albert Museum, London S.W.7, 9–29 March 1960 ....*
[London? : National Federation of Women's Institutes, 1960.]
64 p. ; 22 cm.
Index by county.
EXHIBITION: vx.1960.002

VR.1960.002 *The country year, exhibition illustrated : Women's Institutes
exhibition of handicrafts : Victoria & Albert Museum, 9–29 March
1960.*
[London] : National Federation of Women's Institutes, [1960].
[16] p. : chiefly ill. ; 18 x 23 cm.
Cover title: Exhibition illustrated.
EXHIBITION: vx.1960.002

VR.1960.003 *Modern French tapestries : Victoria and Albert Museum, 26th
April–22nd May 1960, in connection with the French season.*
[London : s.n., 1960] (Imprimerie Franco-Britannique, Ready Press).
[4] p. : ill. ; 24 cm.
Foreword / Henri Gleizes.
EXHIBITION: vx.1960.004

VR.1960.004 *Mural art today : an exhibition organized by the Society of Mural
Painters, at the Victoria and Albert Museum.*
[London? : The Society, 1960.]
[56] p. : ill. ; 19 cm.
Foreword / Trenchard Cox. — Accompanied by handlist of exhibits.
EXHIBITION: vx.1960.008

VR.1960.005   *Rex Whistler: 1905–1944 : a memorial exhibition.*
[London] : Arts Council of Great Britain, 1960.
31, 1 p., [12] p. of plates : ill. ; 22 cm.
Foreword signed "G.W." [i.e. Gabriel White]. Introduction Laurence Whistler.
EXHIBITION: VX.1960.007

1961

VR.1961.001   *An exhibition of national art treasures of Korea : lent by the*
Government of the Republic of Korea : Victoria & Albert Museum,
23 March to 7 May.
[London] : Arts Council of Great Britain, 1961.
[90] p. : ill. (1 col.), map ; 24 cm.
Foreword signed "G.W." [i.e. Gabriel White]. — Introduction by G.StG.M. Gompertz.
EXHIBITION: VX.1961.002

VR.1961.002   *International exhibition of modern jewellery, 1890–1961 : exhibition*
organised by the Worshipful Company of Goldsmiths in association
with the Victoria and Albert Museum, 26th October till 2nd
December 1961 at Goldsmiths Hall, Foster Lane, Cheapside, London
E.C.2.
[London] : Goldsmiths' Company, 1961.
2 v. ([118] p.), [56] p. of plates : ill. ; 21 cm.
Foreword / C.S. Padgett. Introduction signed "G.H." [i.e. Graham Hughes]. — v.1.
Catalogue. v.2. Illustrations.
EXHIBITION: VX.1961.XXX.001

VR.1961.003   *Italian bronze statuettes : an exhibition organized by the Arts Council*
of Great Britain with the Italian Ministry of Education and the
Rijksmuseum, Amsterdam : the Victoria and Albert Museum, London
27th July to 1st October 1961.
[London] : Arts Council of Great Britain, 1961.
[48] p., 32 p. of plates : ill. ; 25 cm.
Foreword / Gabriel White. — Includes bibliographic references. Indexes to artists and
lenders.
EXHIBITION: VX.1961.007

VR.1961.004   *Italian bronze statuettes : an exhibition organized by the Arts Council*
of Great Britain with the Italian Ministry of Education and the
Rijksmuseum, Amsterdam : the Victoria and Albert Museum, London
27th July to 1st October 1961 : handlist.
[London] : Arts Council of Great Britain, 1961.
11 p. ; 25 cm.
EXHIBITION: VX.1961.007

VR.1961.005   *Morris and Company, 1861–1940 : a commemorative centenary*
exhibition.
[London] : Arts Council of Great Britain, 1961.
32 p., 8 p. of plates : ill. ; 27 cm.
Foreword signed "G.W." [i.e. Gabriel White]. Introduction / Barbara J. Morris. —
Includes bibliographic references.
EXHIBITION: VX.1961.003

VR.1961.006   *Tiepolo drawings from the Victoria and Albert Museum, London.*
                 [Washington, D.C.? : Smithsonian Institution?, 1961?]
                 32 p., [16] leaves of plates : ill., ports. ; 26 cm.
                 Foreword by Trenchard Cox. Introduction by Graham Reynolds. — Bibliography:
                 p. 32.
                 EXHIBITION: VX.1961.XXX.002

1962

VR.1962.001   *Bookbindings and rubbings of bindings in the Victoria and Albert
                 Museum* / by W.H. James Weale.
                 London : Holland Press, 1962.
                 cl, iii, 329 p. : ill. ; 22 cm.
                 Facsimile reprint of v.1894.001 and v.1898.001.

VR.1962.002   *Circle of Glass Collectors commemorative exhibition, 1937–1962 :
                 catalogue : Victoria and Albert Museum, London, 16th May–8th July
                 1962.*
                 [London? : The Circle, 1962.]
                 72 p., xvi p. of plates : ill. ; 25 cm. + 1 sheet.
                 Foreword / Trenchard Cox. Introduction / R.J. Charleston. Text by W.A. Thorpe. —
                 Index of lenders. — Accompanied by: Supplementary exhibits not in the catalogue
                 [duplicated typescript].
                 EXHIBITION: VX.1962.004

VR.1962.003   *Third international art treasures exhibition : presented by C.I.N.O.A.
                 (the International Confederation of Art Dealers) : 2nd March until
                 29th April 1962.*
                 [s.l. : C.I.N.O.A., 1962.]
                 [16], 80 p. ; 25 cm.
                 At head of title: Victoria and Albert Museum. Cover title: International art treasures
                 exhibition. — Foreword / Henry R. Ruben. — Index.
                 EXHIBITION: VX.1962.002

VR.1962.003A   [Illustrated ed.]
                 [16], 80 p., 332 p. of plates : ill. ; 25 cm.

1963

VR.1963.001   *The art of the armourer : an exhibition of armour, swords and
                 firearms : catalogue : Victoria and Albert Museum, London, 19th
                 April–5th May.*
                 [London? : Arms and Armour Society, 1963.]
                 100 p., [28] p. of plates : ill. ; 25 cm.
                 At head of title: Arms and Armour Society. — Foreword / Howard L. Blackmore.
                 EXHIBITION: VX.1963.003

VR.1963.002   *Drawings, Eisenstein : catalogue : an exhibition at the Victoria and
                 Albert Museum, Sept. 26th–Nov. 10th : presented by the Friends of
                 the National Film Archive.*
                 [Ipswich] : Friends of the National Film Archive, [1963].

[18] p. ; 26 cm.
Introduction / Ivor Montague. Text / David Robinson. — Bibliography: p. [14–18].
EXHIBITION: VX.1963.010

VR.1963.003   *Opus anglicanum : English medieval embroidery : the Victoria and Albert Museum, 26 September to 24 November 1963.*
[London] : Arts Council of Great Britain, 1963.
64 p., [3], 24 p. of plates : ill. (some col.) ; 25 cm.
Foreword signed "G.W." [i.e. Gabriel White]. Written by Donald King. — Glossary.
EXHIBITION: VX.1963.011

VR.1963.004   *Swedish silver 1650–1800.*
[s.l. : Swedish Institute for Cultural Relations?], 1963 (Printed by Esselte AB).
29 p., 21 p. of plates : ill. ; 21 cm.
Preface / Trenchard Cox. Introduction / Carl Hernmarck. — Marks.
EXHIBITION: VX.1963.008

1964

VR.1964.001   *The arts of Thailand : the Victoria and Albert Museum, 6 March–12 April 1964.*
[London : Arts Council of Great Britain, 1964.]
[48] p., [2] leaves, 24 p. of plates : ill. (some col.), map ; 25 cm.
Preface by Prince Plerng Nobadol Rabibhadana. Foreword signed "G.W." [i.e. Gabriel White]. Introduction by John Irwin. — Includes bibliography. Glossary.
EXHIBITION: VX.1964.001

VR.1964.002   *Eikoku ginkī bījutsuten : gōka tenrei Eikoku-chō geijutsu no sui : Eikokuritsu Vikutoria & Arubāto Hakubutsukan hizō : 1964.*
[Tokyo?] : Nihon Keizai Shinbunsha, Kikakubu, [1964].
73 p. : ill., 1 col. ; 26 cm.
Cover title: Victoria and Albert Museum exhibition of fine English silver. — Message from E.W.F. Tomlin (also in English). Foreword by Nihon Keizai Shinbunsha. Text: Igirisu no ginkī [English silver] 1660–1910 / John Hayward, Shirley Bury.
EXHIBITION: VX.1964.XXX.001

VR.1964.003   *The growth of London, A.D. 43–1964 : catalogue of an exhibition at the Victoria & Albert Museum, 17 July–30 August 1964.*
London : 20th International Geographical Congress, [1964].
x, 102 p. : ill. ; 25 cm.
Foreword / R.A. Shelton. Introduction by T.F. Reddaway. — Index of owners. — Coloured plate pasted in as frontispiece.
EXHIBITION: VX.1964.005

VR.1964.004   *Townswomen at home : May 26th to June 7th 1964.*
[London? : National Union of Townswomen's Guilds, 1964.]
22 p. ; 22 cm.
At head of title: National art and crafts exhibition 1964. — [Foreword] / H.L. Morgan.
EXHIBITION: VX.1964.003

1965

VR.1965.001   *Bugholzmöbel : das Werk Michael Thonets : ein Wiener Sessel erobert
die Welt.*
Wien : Österreichisches Bauzentrum, [1965?].
[16] p. : ill., port. ; 21 x 30 cm.
Cover title.
EXHIBITION: VX.1968.BGM.001

VR.1965.002   *Chinese painting and calligraphy from the collection of John M.
Crawford Jr. : at the Victoria and Albert Museum, 17 June to 1
August 1965.*
London : Arts Council of Great Britain, 1965.
40 p., [24] leaves of plates : ill. ; 24 cm.
Foreword signed "G.W." [i.e. Gabriel White]. Includes texts by Laurence Sickman, Max
Loehr and Lien-Sheng Yang, originally written for the catalogue of an exhibition of the
collection held in 1962 at the Pierpont Morgan Library. — Bibliographies.
EXHIBITION: VX.1965.008

VR.1965.003   *World of the Bible : centenary exhibition of the Palestine Exploration
Fund in co-operation with the British School of Archaeology in
Jerusalem.*
[London : Palestine Exploration Fund, 1965] (Shenval Press, printer).
xii, 73 p., viii p. of plates : ill., map ; 23 cm.
Foreword / C.B. Mortlock. INTRODUCTION: Palestine in the Middle Ages, AD
638–1516 / C.N. Johns. Pilgrims to archaeologists, AD 1516–1865 / D.R. Howell.
PALESTINE EXPLORATION FUND, AD 1865–1965: Foundation and growth /
C.M. Watson. Surveys of Palestine / I.D. Hart. Second half-century / D.R. Howell.
PROGRESS REPORT ON THE CENTURY: NATURAL ENVIRONMENT:
Geology / C.H. Brunton. Position and climate / J.M. Sheldon. Vegetation / G.W.
Dimbleby. Vertebrate fauna / I.W. Cornwall. Early cereals / J.K. Jones. PREHISTORY:
Mount Carmel people, Palaeolithic-Mesolithic, c. 50000–8000 BC / K.P. Oakley and
G. Sieveking. Jericho, Neolithic-Chalcolithic c. 8000–3000 BC / K.M. Kenyon and
J.C. Payne. HISTORY: Villagers to townsmen / P.J. Parr (Early Bronze Age
c. 3000–2100 BC). Intermediate invaders / O. Tufnell (Between Early and Middle
Bronze Ages c. 2100–1900 BC). The Patriarchs / D.J. Wiseman (Middle Bronze Age
c. 1900–1550 BC). Egyptian empire / J.A. Kitchen (Late Bronze Age c. 1550–1200 BC).
Kingdoms and conquests / P.R. Ackroyd (Iron Age c. 1200–600 BC). Between two
powers / S. Perowne (Persian-Hellenistic c. 600–63 BC). Pax Romana / S. Perowne and
P.J. Parr. Roman period c. 63 BC-AD 330 / P.J. Parr. Cross and Crescent / S. Perowne
(Byzantine and Arab c. AD 330–638). Jerusalem / K.M. Kenyon. Writing and the
alphabet / D. Diringer.
EXHIBITION: VX.1965.011

1966

VR.1966.001   *British watercolours, 1750–1850 : a loan exhibition from the Victoria
and Albert Museum, circulated by the International Exhibitions
Foundation, 1966–67.*
[Washington, D.C.] : International Exhibitions Foundation, 1966.
24, [2] p., [58] p. of plates : ill. ; 27 cm.
Acknowledgments / Annemarie H. Pope. Introduction / Jonathan Mayne. —
Bibliography: p. 24.
EXHIBITION: VX.1966.XXX.001

VR.1966.002   *English domestic silver, 1660–1910 : from the Victoria and Albert Museum, London : 4th March–24 April 1966, the City Hall Art Gallery, Hong Kong* / presented in association with the British Council.
[Hong Kong : s.n., 1966.]
[40] p. : ill. ; 26 cm.
Text signed John Hayward, Shirley Bury. Introduction by Jonathan Mayne. — Text in English, summary and captions also in Chinese.
EXHIBITION: VX.1966.XXX.002

VR.1966.003   *Old Sheffield plate 1750–1850.*
[Barnard Castle : Bowes Museum, 1966.]
[24] p., [8] p. of plates : ill. ; 19 cm.
Introduction / Frank Atkinson.
EXHIBITION: VX.1966.008

1967

VR.1967.001   *Great Britain, USSR : an historical exhibition organized by the British Foreign Office and the Soviet Ministry of Foreign Affairs through the Arts Council of Great Britain and the Victoria and Albert Museum, and through the Soviet Ministry of Culture and the Soviet State Archives : Victoria and Albert Museum, February 9 to April 2, 1967.*
London : Arts Council of Great Britain, 1967.
32 p. ; 25 cm.
Acknowledgments / John Pope-Hennessy, Gabriel White. Introduction / Rohan Butler.
EXHIBITION: VX.1967.001

VR.1967.002   *Käthe Kollwitz : engravings, drawings, sculpture : a German Art Council exhibition.*
[London : German Art Council?, 1967] (Berlin : Printer: Brüder Hartmann).
[48] p. : ill. (1 col.), facsim., port. ; 20 cm.
Foreword by Gabriel White. Text by Kurt Martin.
EXHIBITION: VX.1967.BGM.002

VR.1967.003   *Turkish art of the Seljuk and Ottoman periods : an exhibition organized in honour of the State Visit of His Excellency the President of the Republic of Turkey : Victoria and Albert Museum, 7 November to 3 December.*
[London] : Arts Council of Great Britain, 1967.
[24] p. ; 24 cm.
Cover title: Turkish art. — Messages from I.S. Caglayangil, George Brown. Foreword by Ü. Haluk Bayüllien. Acknowledgments / John Pope-Hennessy, Gabriel White.
EXHIBITION: VX.1967.013

1968

VR.1968.001   *Bentwood furniture : the work of Michael Thonet : an exhibition designed by the architects Karl and Eva Mang, originally held at the Austrian Building Centre, Liechtenstein Palace, Vienna.*

[s.l. : s.n., 1968.]
[11] p. ; 21 cm.
Texts by Wilhelm Mrazek, Karl Mang, Herman Heller, Wilhelm Franz Exner.
EXHIBITION: VX.1968.BGM.001

VR.1968.002   *The British Antique Dealers' Association Golden Jubilee exhibition :*
Victoria & Albert Museum, London, May 1968.
[London? : B.A.D.A., 1968.]
[42] p., 96 p. of plates : ill. ; 31 cm.
Foreword / C-L. De Beaumont — Includes a list of members.
EXHIBITION: VX.1968.011

VR.1968.003   *Charles Rennie Mackintosh, 1868–1928 : architecture, design and*
painting : an exhibition arranged by the Scottish Arts Council in
association with the Edinburgh Festival Society / introduction, notes
and catalogue by Andrew McLaren Young.
[Scotland? : Exhibition Arrangers?, 1968.]
71 p., 32 p. of plates : ill., ports. ; 26 cm.
At head of title: A centenary exhibition. — Foreword / John Pope-Hennessy, Gabriel
White. — "Bibliographical notes": p. 11.
EXHIBITION: VX.1968.019

VR.1968.004   *Two centuries of Danish design : London, April 18–June 3, 1968.*
[s.l. : Danish Society of Arts and Crafts and Industrial Design, 1968.]
100, [4] p., [32] p. of plates : ill. ; 23 cm.
At head of title: Victoria & Albert Museum. — Forewords by John Pope-Hennessy,
Anders Hostrup-Pedersen. — Index of exhibitors.
EXHIBITION: VX.1968.009

1969

VR.1969.001   *Annotated proofs of the works of Charles Dickens from the Forster*
collection in the Victoria & Albert Museum, London.
East Ardsley, Wakefield : Micro Methods, 1969.
3 microfilm reels.
Bleak House; Dombey and Son; Little Dorrit; Hard times; The chimes; David
Copperfield.

VR.1969.002   *Baroque in Bohemia : an exhibition of Czech art organized by the*
National Gallery, Prague : Victoria & Albert Museum, London, SW7,
10 July–14 September, City Museum & Art Gallery, Birmingham 3, 3
October–30 November.
London : Arts Council of Great Britain, 1969.
1 leaf, [118] p. : ill. (some col.) ; 25 cm.
Foreword / Gabriel White. The Baroque period in Bohemia; Architecture; Sculpture /
Oldřich J. Blažíček. Painting / Pavel Preiss. Applied arts / Dagmar Hejdová.
EXHIBITION: VX.1969.008

VR.1969.003   *Berlioz and the romantic imagination : an exhibition organized by the*
Arts Council and the Victoria and Albert Museum on behalf of the
Berlioz Centenary Committee in cooperation with the French
Government, 17 October to 14 December.

London : Arts Council of Great Britain, 1969.
xxiv, 147 p. : ill. (some col.), facsims., plan, ports. ; 26 cm.
ISBN: 0900085126
Edited by Elizabeth Davison. Acknowledgments / John Pope-Hennessy, Gabriel White.
Introduction David Cairns. Berlioz in perspective / Edward Lockspeiser. —
Bibliography: p. xxii-xxiv. General and lenders' indexes.
EXHIBITION: VX.1969.013

VR.1969.004   *Correspondence and papers of David Garrick, 1717–1779.*
East Ardsley, Wakefield : Micro Methods, [ca. 1969?].
6 microfilm reels.
Papers from the Forster collection, National Art Library.

VR.1969.005   *Correspondence of James Butler, first Duke of Ormonde, 1610–1688,*
and James Butler, second Duke of Ormonde, 1655–1745.
[Wakefield] : Micro Methods, 1969.
2 microfilm reels.
Papers from the Forster collection, National Art Library.

VR.1969.006   *Correspondence of Roger Boyle, the first Earle of Orrery, 1621–1679.*
East Ardsley, Wakefield : Micro Methods, 1969.
1 microfilm reel.
Papers from the Forster collection, National Art Library.

VR.1969.007   *A decade of English naturalism 1810–1820.*
[Norwich? : University of East Anglia School of Fine Arts and Music?,
1969.]
41 p. : ill. ; 25 cm.
By John Gage. Foreword / P. Lasko. — Includes bibliographic references.
EXHIBITION: VX.1970.002

VR.1969.008   *Festival designs by Inigo Jones : an exhibition of drawings for scenery*
and costumes for the court masques of James I and Charles I /
introduction and catalogue by Roy Strong ; foreword by Thomas S.
Wragg.
[s.l. : s.n.], 1969 printing.
1 v. (unpaged) : ill. ; 22 x 26 cm.
"From the Devonshire collection, Chatsworth"–cover. — Director's foreword / John
Pope-Hennessy. — Includes bibliographic references. — First published, U.S.A.:
International Exhibitions Foundation, 1966.
EXHIBITION: VX.1969.006

VR.1969.009   *Islamic pottery, 800–1400 AD : an exhibition arranged by the Islamic*
Art Circle and held at the Victoria and Albert Museum, 1 Oct. to 30
Nov. 1969.
[s.l. : Islamic Art Circle, 1969.]
55 p. : ill. ; 30 cm.
Foreword / John Pope-Hennessy. Preface / Edmund de Unger. Introduction / R.H.
Pinder-Wilson. — Includes bibliographic references. Index of lenders.
EXHIBITION: VX.1969.012

VR.1969.010   *Manuscripts of the works of Charles Dickens : from the Forster*
collection in the Victoria and Albert Museum, London.
London : Micro Methods, 1969.

10 microfilm reels.

Oliver Twist; The old curiosity shop; Barnaby Rudge; Martin Chuzzlewit; Dombey and Son; David Copperfield; Bleak House; Hard times; Little Dorrit; A tale of two cities; The mystery of Edwin Drood; The chimes.

VR.1969.011   *Papers on the conservation and technology of wood : deterioration and treatment of wood : joint meeting of the ICOM Committee for Scientific Museum Laboratories and the ICOM Sub-committee for the Care of Paintings, Amsterdam, September 1969* / N.S. Brommelle, A.J. Moncrieff.
[s.l. : International Council of Museums, 1969?]
[2], 27, 26, 17, 1, 3 p. ; 30 cm.
Cover title. — Produced and printed in the V&A Conservation Department by members of staff of the Department.

VR.1969.012   *The prints of George Stubbs* / Basil Taylor.
London : Paul Mellon Foundation for British Art, 1969.
60 p. : ill. ; 22 x 25 cm.
EXHIBITION: VX.1969.009

VR.1969.013   *The prints of George Stubbs . . . .*
[London : Paul Mellon Foundation, 1969.]
1 sheet, folded ([4] p.) 22 cm.
Exhibition handlist. — Printed on buff paper. — Includes list of Paul Mellon Foundation publications.

VR.1969.014   *William Holman Hunt : an exhibition arranged by the Walker Art Gallery : Walker Art Gallery, Liverpool, March-April 1969, Victoria and Albert Museum, May-June 1969.*
Liverpool : Walker Art Gallery, 1969.
95 p., [1, 56] p. of plates : ill., 1 col. ; 25 cm.
ISBN: 0950033901
Foreword / Gabriel White, Hugh Scrutton. Introduction / Mary Bennett. — Bibliographic references: p. 17–18. Index of lenders.
EXHIBITION: VX.1969.005

1970

VR.1970.001   *Architectural drawings in the Victoria and Albert Museum.*
Wakefield : Micro Methods, 1970.
23 microfilm reels.

VR.1970.002   *Europe and the Indies : the era of the Companies, 1600–1824.*
[London] : BBC, 1970.
38, [2] p., [16] p. of plates : ill., maps, plan, ports. ; 23 cm.
ISBN: 0543102063
The era of the Companies / John Harrison. Art as merchandise / John C. Irwin. Indo-European architecture / John Lowry. British painting in India / Mildred Archer. The European impact on Mughal art / Robert Skelton. — Bibliography: p. 36–38. — Published to accompany both the exhibition and a series of broadcasts on BBC Radio 3.
EXHIBITION: VX.1970.019

VR.1970.003   *The Harari collection of Japanese paintings and drawings : an exhibition organized by the Arts Council at the Victoria and Albert Museum, 14 January–22 February 1970.*
[London : Arts Council of Great Britain, 1970.]
64 p., [8] leaves of plates : ill. (some col.) ; 31 cm.
ISBN: 0900085169
Catalogue introduction by J. Hillier. — Bibliography: p. 63. Glossary.
EXHIBITION: VX.1970.001

VR.1970.004   *Modern chairs, 1918–1970 : an international exhibition presented by the Whitechapel Art Gallery in association with the Observer /* arranged by the Circulation Department, Victoria and Albert Museum.
London : Whitechapel Gallery, 1970.
32 p., 120 p. of plates : ill., ports. ; 24 cm.
Foreword / Mark Glazebrook. Acknowledgments / Hugh Wakefield. Introduction / Carol Hogben. New developments in chair manufacture / Dennis Young. The chair as art / Reyner Banham. The chair: today and tomorrow / Sherban Cantacuzino. Has the chair a future? / Joseph Rykwert. — Indexes of lenders, manufacturers, designers.
EXHIBITION: VX.1970.XXX.001

1971

VR.1971.001   *Catalogue of an exhibition of the ceramic art of China : organized by the Arts Council of Great Britain and the Oriental Ceramic Society to commemorate the founding of the Society in 1921 : June 9th to July 25th 1971, the Victoria and Albert Museum.*
London : Oriental Ceramic Society, 1971.
[61] p., 66 plates : ill. (some col.), map ; 25 cm.
ISBN: 095002841X
Cover title: The ceramic art of China. — Foreword / Harry M. Garner. Introduction / Basil Gray. — Index of lenders. — Catalogued from 2nd ed.
EXHIBITION: VX.1971.011

VR.1971.002   *Modern British bookbindings : an exhibition of modern British bookbinding by members of Designer Bookbinders.*
London : Designer Bookbinders, 1971.
63 p. : ill. ; 24 cm.
ISBN: 0950076511
Edited by Ivor Robinson and Bernard Middleton. — Designed by Philip Smith.
EXHIBITION: VX.1972.013

VR.1971.003   *Modern chairs, 1918–1970*
London : Lund Humphries, 1971.
ISBN: 0853312840
Hardcover ed. of VR.1970.004.
EXHIBITION: VX.1970.XXX.001

VR.1971.004   *Victorian glass : an exhibition of British glass of the Victorian period from the Circulation Department of the Victoria and Albert Museum, London, to be circulated by the Smithsonian Institution, Washington, D.C.*

Corning, N.Y. : Corning Museum of Glass, 1971.
15 p. : ill. ; 21 x 26 cm.
Text and catalogue by Betty O'Looney.
EXHIBITION: VX.1971.XXX.001

VR.1971.005   *Watercolours by John Robert Cozens.*
[Manchester? : Whitworth Art Gallery?, 1971.]
77 p. : ill. ; 26 cm.
By Francis W. Hawcroft. Foreword / Reginald Dodwell. — Bibliography: p. 38.
EXHIBITION: VX.1971.007

1972

VR.1972.001   *The age of neo-classicism : a handlist to the fourteenth exhibition of the Council of Europe : the Royal Academy and the Victoria and Albert Museum, London, 9 September–19 November 1972.*
London : Arts Council of Great Britain, 1972.
85 p. ; 22 cm.
Introduction: Neo-classicism / Hugh Honor [sic].
EXHIBITION: VX.1972.019

VR.1972.002   *The age of neo-classicism : the fourteenth exhibition of the Council of Europe : the Royal Academy and the Victoria and Albert Museum, London, 9 September–19 November 1972.*
London : Arts Council of Great Britain, 1972.
ciii, 1037 p., xvi, 160 p. of plates : ill. (some col.), plan ; 22 cm.
Foreword / John Pope-Hennessy. Neo-classicism / Hugh Honour. Winckelmann / L.D. Ettlinger. Goethe and the contemporary fine arts / Herbert von Einem. Archaeological excavations in Italy 1750–1850 / Carlo Pietrangeli. Architecture in the age of neo-classicism / Wend von Kalnein. Louis David, reform and revolution / Michel Laclotte. Neo-classicism in the French Revolution / Robert Herbert. Early neo-classical sculpture in France and Italy / Gerard Hubert. Sergel and Thorvaldsen / Dyveke Helsted. The meaning and diffusion of the Empire style / Mario Praz. Themes and aspects of neo-classical stage design / Mario Monteverdi. — Includes bibliographic references. Indexes.
Copy note: "Press copy" in grey card wrapper.
EXHIBITION: VX.1972.019

VR.1972.003   *Eighteenth century stage, Britain : exhibition organized jointly by the Theatre Section, Department of Prints and Drawings, of the Victoria and Albert Museum and the Saskatoon Gallery and Conservatory Corporation, with the assistance of the British Council, for the Second Bi-Annual Conference of the Canadian Society for Eighteenth-century Studies.*
Saskatoon : Mendel Art Gallery, [1972].
32 p. : ill. ; 21 x 28 cm.
Exhibition organized and catalogue written by George W. Nash.
EXHIBITION: VX.1972.XXX.003

VR.1972.004   *Flemish drawings of the seventeenth century from the collection of Frits Lugt, Institut néerlandais, Paris.*
[s.l. : s.n., 1972] (Printed by Erasmus Ltd., Ghent).
xlvii, 185 p., [128] p. of plates : ill. ; 26 cm.

Preface / Carlos van Hasselt. 'In memoriam Fritz Lugt' / J.G. van Gelder. Introduction / R.-A. d'Hulst. — Bibliographic references: p. 179. Indexes of artists, former owners. — First published in French: Dessins flamands du dix-septième siècle : Collection Frits Lugt . . . .
EXHIBITION: VX.1972.002

VR.1972.005   *The Francis Williams Bequest : an exhibition of illustrated books /* selected by John Harthan, David Hockney, Ruari McLean, Clifford Simmons.
London : National Book League, [1972].
51 p. : ill. ; 21 cm.
ISBN: 0853531439
Introduction / John Pope-Hennessy. — Index of publishers. — Designed by Ruari McLean.
EXHIBITION: VX.1972.005

VR.1972.006   *'From today painting is dead' : the beginnings of photography* . . . .
[London : Arts Council of Great Britain, 1972].
60, 50 p. : ill., 1 facsim. ; 27 cm.
ISBN: 0900085649
At head of title: Arts Council of Great Britain. — Acknowledgments / Robin Campbell, Norbert Lynton. Includes: Fixing the face / Tristram Powell; Photography as social documentation / Asa Briggs.
EXHIBITION: VX.1972.006

VR.1972.007   *The future of the past : a travelling exhibition organized by the Victorian Society in collaboration with the Central School of Art and Design and circulated by the Victoria and Albert Museum.*
[London : The Society, 1972.]
1 sheet, folded ; 30 x 31 cm. folded to 30 x 11 cm.
"Introduction and the manifesto of the aims of the exhibition . . . contributed by Jane Fawcett, Secretary of the Victorian Society, and Nicholas Boulting, of the Central School of Art and Design"–p. [3]. — First shown at the Central School of Art and Design as part of the Camden Festival, Apr. 1971.

VR.1972.008   *Ivory carvings in early medieval England : with 270 illustrations /* John Beckwith.
London : Harvey, Miller and Redcalf, 1972.
[1], 167, [1] p. : ill. (1 col.) ; 38 cm.
ISBN: 0856020060
Includes bibliographic references and index.
EXHIBITION: VX.1974.013

VR.1972.009   *National Art Library catalogue : author catalogue.*
Boston : G.K. Hall, 1972.
10 v. ; 37 cm.
ISBN: 0816109923

VR.1972.010   *National Art Library catalogue : catalogue of exhibition catalogues.*
Boston : G.K. Hall, 1972.
v, 623 p. ; 37 cm.
ISBN: 0816110220

VR.1972.011   *Papers on the conservation and technology of wood* / N.S. Brommelle,
               J.A. Darrah, A.J. Moncrieff.
               [s.l. : International Council of Museums, 1972.]
               iv, 71 p. ; 30 cm.
               Cover title. — "ICOM Committee on Conservation (Sub-committee Furniture), Madrid,
               October 1972"–cover. — Produced and printed in the V&A Conservation Department,
               by members of staff of the Department." — Stapled sheets.

VR.1972.012   *Supplementary catalogue to an exhibition of modern British
               bookbinding by members of the Designer Bookbinders : the Victoria
               and Albert Museum, London, 14 June–16 July 1972.*
               London : Designer Bookbinders, 1972.
               17 p. ; 24 cm.
               Cover title. — Foreword / Ivor Robinson. — Index of lenders.
               EXHIBITION: VX.1972.013

VR.1972.013   *Winslow Homer, 1836–1910 : a selection from the Cooper-Hewitt
               Collection, Smithsonian Institution.*
               Washington, D.C. : Published for the Cooper-Hewitt Museum of
               Decorative Arts and Design . . . by the Smithsonian Institution Press,
               1972.
               [126] p. : ill. : 22 x 26 cm.
               Foreword / Lisa Taylor. Introduction / Lloyd Goodrich. Winslow Homer's drawings /
               John Wilmerding. Catalog . . . / Elaine Evans Dee. — Index of titles.
               EXHIBITION: VX.1974.030

1973

VR.1973.001   *An American museum of decorative art and design : designs from the
               Cooper-Hewitt Collection, New York : an exhibition mounted by the
               Arts Council of Great Britain at the Victoria and Albert Museum,
               June-August 1973.*
               London : H.M.S.O., 1973.
               [4], vi, 118 p. : chiefly ill. (1 col.). ; 30 cm.
               ISBN: 0901486663
               At head of title: Victoria and Albert Museum. — Foreword / John Pope-Hennessy.
               Introduction / Lisa Taylor.
               EXHIBITION: VX.1973.018

VR.1973.002   *The craftsman's art : published on the occasion of an exhibition of
               new work by British craftsmen at the Victoria & Albert Museum,
               1973.*
               London : Crafts Advisory Committee, 1973.
               104 p. : col. ill. ; 21 x 22 cm.
               ISBN: 090379800X
               Foreword / Gordon Russell. Introduction / James Noel White. Texts: Bookbinding / Ivor
               Robinson. Ceramics / Michael Casson. Furniture / Alan Peters. Glass / Wendy Evans.
               Metal / Leslie Durbin. Woven textiles / Ann Sutton. — List of exhibitors.
               EXHIBITION: VX.1973.009

VR.1973.003   *Indian paintings from the Punjab hills : a survey and history of
               Pahari miniature painting* / by W.G. Archer ; foreword by
               Sherman E. Lee.

London : Delhi : Sotheby Parke Bernet ; Oxford University Press,
1973.
2 v. (xxxiv, 448 p.; vi p., 335 p. of plates) : ill. (2 col.), map ; 31 cm.
ISBN: 0856670022
Vol. 1, Text; vol. 2, Plates. — Bibliography: v. 1, p. 427–431. Glossary. Index and
concordance of Museum numbers. — "the core of this publication is, in effect, a catalog
of the Victoria and Albert Museum's . . . collection . . ."–p. xi.

VR.1973.004   *Saved for the nation : the achievement of the National Art-Collections
Fund, 1903–1973 : Victoria and Albert Museum, 4 October–18
November 1973.*
London : [N.A.C.F.], 1973.
64 p. : ill. ; 25 cm.
ISBN: 0950333409
Catalogue edited by Benedict Nicolson and Francis Sitwell. Foreword / Antony Hornby.
EXHIBITION: VX.1973.026

VR.1973.005   *Victorian children's books, selected from the Library of the Victoria
and Albert Museum, London : arranged for Europalia 73 Great
Britain by the National Book League in co-operation with the British
Council.*
[Brussels : s.n., 1973.]
108 p. : ill. ; 20 x 23 cm.
"The books have been selected and the catalogue compiled by Irene Whalley"– Preface /
Clifford Simmons, Robert De Smet. — Indexes.
EXHIBITION: VX.1973.XXX.001

1974

VR.1974.001   *Danish glass 1814–1914 : the Peter F. Heering collection.*
[Copenhagen : The Collector, 1974.]
71 p. : ill., map ; 20 cm.
Half title: The Peter F. Heering collection of Danish drinking glasses, decanters and
pocket-flasks 1814–1914. — Preface by R.J. Charleston. Includes: Danish glass / Bent
Wolstrup. — Bibliography: p. 71. Glossary.
EXHIBITION: VX.1974.024

VR.1974.002   *The destruction of the country house 1875–1975 /* Roy Strong,
Marcus Binney, John Harris ; the Duke of Bedford . . . [et al.].
London : Thames and Hudson, 1974.
192 p. : ill. ; 26 cm.
ISBN: 0500240949; 0500270052 (pbk.)
Includes: The tale in Scotland / Colin McWilliam. The picture collection / Sir Oliver
Millar. The library / A.N.L. Munby. The park / Marcus Binney. The garden / Miles
Hadfield. The muniment room / Roger Ellis. America: the country house as museum /
Christopher Monkhouse. The economics of the country house / Donald Insall. The
house and the estate / Sir Michael Culme-Seymour. Saving the contents / Peter
Thornton. Woburn Abbey / the Duke of Bedford. Warwick Castle / Lord Brooke.
Knebworth House / David Lytton-Cobbold. Ragley Hall / the Marquess of Hertford.
Castle Howard / George Howard. Goodwood House / the Earl of March. Longford
Castle / the Dowager Countess of Radnor. The preservation societies / Nikolaus
Boulting. The Historic Buildings Councils / I.M. Glennie. The National Trust / Robin
Fedden. Country houses and the law / Nicholas Cooper. — County lists of houses
destroyed / Peter Reid.
EXHIBITION: VX.1974.026

VR.1974.003   *Dominick Labino : a decade of glass craftsmanship, 1964–1974 :*
               Pilkington Glass Museum, Victoria and Albert Museum, the Toledo
               Museum of Art, 1974–1975.
               Toledo : Museum of Art, 1974.
               [59] p. : ill. ; 18 cm.
               Introduction / Daniel E. Hogan. Essay by Otto Wittmann.
               EXHIBITION: VX.1974.027

VR.1974.004   *English influences on Vincent van Gogh : an exhibition organised by*
               the Fine Art Department, University of Nottingham and the Arts
               Council of Great Britain, 1974/5.
               [London : Arts Council of Great Britain, 1974.]
               80 p. : ill., ports. ; 30 cm.
               Preface / Alastair Smart, Norbert Lynton. Acknowledgements / Ronald Pickvance.
               Includes text by V.W. van Gogh. — Includes bibliographic references.
               EXHIBITION: VX.1975.002

VR.1974.005   *George Cruikshank.*
               London : Arts Council of Great Britain, 1974.
               59 p. : ill. (some col.) ; 24 cm.
               ISBN: 0728700131
               Introduction by William Feaver. — Bibliography: p. 45. — In pocket, facsimile reprint
               of: A comic alphabet / designed, etched & published by George Cruikshank. – [London]
               : G. Cruikshank, 1836.
               EXHIBITION: VX.1974.005

VR.1974.006   *Henry Moore : Stonehenge* / introduction, Stephen Spender.
               London : Ganymed Original Editions, 1974.
               [34] p. : chiefly ill. ; 28 cm.
               Suite of lithographs executed between 1971 and 1973.
               EXHIBITION: VX.1975.022

VR.1974.007   *High Victorian design : a travelling exhibition organized by the*
               Victoria & Albert Museum for the National Programme of the
               National Gallery of Canada, Ottawa, 1974–1975 = Le style de la
               grande époque victorienne : une exposition itinérante . . . / by Simon
               Jervis.
               Ottawa : National Gallery of Canada, 1974.
               300 p. : ill. ; 26 cm.
               ISBN: 0888842708
               Preface / Jean Sutherland Boggs. Foreword / Roy Strong. — In English and French. —
               Bibliography: p. 286. Glossary. Index.
               EXHIBITION: VX.1974.XXX.001

VR.1974.008   *High Victorian design = Le style de la grande époque victorienne.*
               Ottawa : National Gallery of Canada for the National Museums of
               Canada, 1974.
               8 p. : ill. ; 43 cm.
               (National Gallery of Canada journal ; no. 2)
               ISBN: 0888842805
               Written by R.H. Hubbard.
               EXHIBITION: VX.1974.XXX.001

VR.1974.009   *Ivory carvings in early medieval England, 700–1200 : 8th May to 7th July 1974 : Victoria and Albert Museum, London.*
London : Arts Council of Great Britain, 1974.
100 p. : ill. ; 21 x 22 cm.
Acknowledgements / Roy Strong, Robin Campbell. Introduction / John Beckwith. — Bibliography: p. 14–15. Index. — "Addendum and corrigendum" slip loosely inserted. — Exhibition and catalogue based on VR.1972.008.
EXHIBITION: VX.1974.013

VR.1974.010   *A report by the Victoria & Albert Museum concerning the furniture in the House of Lords : presented to the Sub-Committee of the Offices Committee on Works of Art in the House of Lords.*
London : Ordered by the House of Lords to be printed [by] H.M.S.O., 1974.
23 p., [7] leaves of plates : ill. (1 col.) ; 25 cm.
(Papers and bills / House of Lords ; HL 133)
ISBN: 0104133759
Cover title: Furniture in the House of Lords. — Preface / Peter Thornton. — Includes bibliographic references.

VR.1974.011   *The Shakers : life and production of a community in the pioneering days of America : an exhibition by the "Neue Sammlung", Munich.*
[München : Die Sammlung, 1974.]
157 p., [59] p. of plates : ill. ; 21 x 22 cm.
The exhibition / Wend Fischer. The Shakers : a brief summary. The Shakers : another America / Karl Mang. Harmony in work and life : the functionalism of the Shakers / Wend Fischer. — Bibliography: p. 133–137
EXHIBITION: VX.1975.011

1975

VR.1975.001   *Art exhibition catalogues of the Victoria and Albert Museum.*
Cambridge : Chadwyck-Healey, 1975.
[ca. 210 microfiches?]
(Art exhibition catalogues on microfiche series)

VR.1975.002   *Back to the drawing board : a Thames Television exhibition at the Victoria & Albert Museum, February-March 1975* / designed by Allan Cameron & Patrick Downing ; assisted by Bill Laslett ; produced by Patrick Downing & John Hambley.
London : Thames Television Ltd., [1975].
64 p. : ill. (some col.), plans, ports. ; 21 cm.
Written and edited by John Hambley, Mick Loftus. Foreword by Lord Aylestone.
EXHIBITION: VX.1975.004

VR.1975.003   *Cambridge plate : an exhibition of silver, silver-gilt and gold plate arranged as a part of the Cambridge Festival 1975, drawn from the holdings of the City of Cambridge, the University of Cambridge, the Colleges, the National Trust (Anglesey Abbey) and the Cambridge Beefsteak Club* / catalogue compiled by R.A. Crighton.

Cambridge : Fitzwilliam Museum, 1975.
96 p. : ill. ; 25 cm.
Foreword / Michael Jaffé. — List of lenders.
EXHIBITION: VX.1975.020

VR.1975.004   *Chinese jade throughout the ages : an exhibition organised by the Arts Council of Great Britain and the Oriental Ceramic Society : 1st May–22nd June 1975, Victoria and Albert Museum.*
[London : The Society], 1975.
[2], 153 p. : ill. (some col.), map ; 28 cm.
ISBN: 0903421135
Foreword / Basil Gray. Introduction / Jessica Rawson, John Ayers. — Bibliography: p. 149–151. Index of lenders.
EXHIBITION: VX.1975.010

VR.1975.005   *Homage to the designers of Diaghilev (1909–1929) : an exhibition for Venice made on behalf of the Theatre Museum, London* / by Richard Buckle.
Venezia : [s.n.], 1975.
xv p., p. 2–16 : ill. ; 22 x 24 cm.
English and Italian parallel texts.
EXHIBITION: VX.1975.XXX.002

VR.1975.006   *Jewellery in Europe : an exhibition of progressive work* / selected by Ralph Turner.
Edinburgh : Scottish Arts Council, 1975.
55, 1 p. : ill., facsims., ports. ; 23 cm.
Introduction / Gerhard Bott. — Includes bibliographies.
EXHIBITION: VX.1976.001

VR.1975.007   *The land : twentieth century landscape photographs* / selected by Bill Brandt ; edited by Mark Haworth-Booth.
London : Gordon Fraser Gallery, 1975.
32 p., 48 p. of plates : ill. ; 23 x 25 cm.
ISBN: 0900406712; 0900406720
Preface / Roy Strong. Introduction / Mark Haworth-Booth. Some speak of a return to nature – I wonder where they could have been? / Jonathan Williams. The gospel of landscape / Professor Aaron Scharf. Return from exile / Keith Critchlow. Poems by Johannes Bobrowski, Pablo Neruda, Ted Hughes, Osip Mandelstam, Jonathan Williams.
EXHIBITION: VX.1975.030

VR.1975.008   *Narrative stone reliefs from Gandhāra in the Victoria and Albert Museum in London : catalogue and attempt at a stylistic history* / Hans Christoph Ackermann.
Rome : IsMEO, 1975.
xii, 206 p., [50] leaves of plates : ill. ; 35 cm.
(Reports and memoirs / Istituto italiano per il Medio ed Estremo Oriente, Centro studi e scavi archeologici in Asia ; 17)
Originally presented as the author's thesis, University of Basle. — Bibliography: p. 177–184. Indexes.

VR.1975.009   *Oriental ceramics : the world's great collections. Vol. 6, Victoria and*
               Albert Museum.
               Tokyo : Kodansha, 1975.
               294 p. : col. ill. ; 37 cm.
               Japanese title: Tōyōtōji taikan : Vikutoria Arubāto Hakubutsukan. — Introduction,
               selection and notes: John G. Ayers. — In Japanese and English.

VR.1975.010   *The prints of Martin Hardie* / edited from the artist's manuscript
               record by Frank Hardie.
               Oxford : Ashmolean Museum, 1975.
               xiii, 83 p. : ill., facsim., port. ; 25 cm.
               ISBN: 0900090243
               Bibliography: p. xi–xiii.
               EXHIBITION: VX.1975.024

VR.1975.011   *Watercolours by Thomas Girtin : Whitworth Art Gallery, University*
               of Manchester, January-February 1975, Victoria and Albert Museum,
               March-April 1975.
               London : [H.M.S.O.? for Whitworth Art Gallery], 1975.
               3–64 p., 48 p. of plates : ill., geneal. table ; 20 x 21 cm.
               ISBN: 0901486868
               Exhibition and catalogue prepared by Francis Hawcroft. Foreword / Reginald Dodwell.
               — Bibliographies: p. 21–24.
               EXHIBITION: VX.1975.006

1976

VR.1976.001   *Caught in the act* / by Nerman ; foreword by Sandy Wilson.
               London : Harrap, 1976.
               72 p. : chiefly ill. ; 22 cm.
               ISBN: 0245529810; 0245529500
               EXHIBITION: VX.1976.XXX.006

VR.1976.002   *Chinese jade throughout the ages : an exhibition organised by the Arts*
               Council of Great Britain and the Oriental Ceramic Society, 1st
               May-22nd June 1975, Victoria and Albert Museum. [New ed.]
               [London] : [The Society], 1976.
               152 p., [108] p. of plates : ill. (some col.), map ; 29 cm.
               Catalogue prepared by Jessica Rawson and John Ayers. Introduction by Basil Gray. —
               Bibliography: p. 149–151. Indexes. — Corrigenda. — Includes an illustration of every
               piece exhibited.
               In: *Transactions of the Oriental Ceramic Society 1973-1974* (1974-1975).
               EXHIBITION: VX.1975.010

VR.1976.003   *English heraldic embroidery and textiles at the Victoria and Albert*
               Museum : a select list with introduction / by Clara Lamb, Robert M.
               Collins, Cedric J. Holyoake.
               London : XIII International Congress of Genealogical and Heraldic
               Sciences, 1976.
               32 p. : ill. ; 21 cm.

VR.1976.004   *Illustrations of the Book of Job : in twenty-one plates* / invented and
               engraved by William Blake . . . .
               [Paris : Trianon Press, 1976.]
               1 portfolio (21 leaves) ; 39 cm.
               Facsimile. — Cover title; label from original cover, dated 1826, mounted on front. —
               The complete edition, with accompanying commentaries, was due to be published in
               1977 but did not appear until 1987. These advance sets of plates were made available
               only at museums and Blake Trust exhibitions.
               EXHIBITION: vx.1976.019

VR.1976.005   *Mārg : a magazine of the arts. Vol. XXIX, no. 4, Sept. 1976.*
               Bombay : J.J. Bhabha for Mārg Publications, [1976].
               70 p., [28] p. of advertisements : ill. (some col.) ; 29 cm.
               Special issue on the Indian collections of the V&A, guest-edited and written by John
               Irwin. Notes by Mārg.

VR.1976.006   *A tonic to the nation : the Festival of Britain, 1951* / edited by Mary
               Banham and Bevis Hillier ; with a prologue by Roy Strong ;
               contributions by Bruce Angrave, Reyner Banham, Gerald Barry, Misha
               Black, Dr J. Bronowski, Hugh Casson, Ian Cox, Jane Drew, Rowland
               Emett, William Feaver, Adrian Forty, Ralph Freeman, James Gardner,
               Frederick Gibberd, Robert Goodden, Charles Hasler, F.H.K. Henrion,
               Antony D. Hippisley Coxe, James Holland, Barbara Jones, Richard
               Levin, Willy de Majo, Victor Pasmore, Brian Peake, John Piper, John
               Ratcliff, Paul Reilly, R.D. Russell ; recollections by Brian Aldiss, Hardy
               Amies, George Backhouse, Roy Fuller, Jack Godfrey-Gilbert, Edward
               Lucie-Smith, George MacBeth, Frank Norman, Charles Plouviez,
               Audrey Russell, Margaret Sheppard Fidler, Arnold Wesker, and others.
               London : Thames & Hudson, 1976.
               200 p. : ill. ; 27 cm.
               ISBN: 0500270791
               Includes: The role of the Design Council before, during and after the Festival / Paul
               Reilly. South Bank exhibition. Pleasure Gardens, Battersea Park. What architecture,
               housing and planning can do for us: Lansbury / Frederick Gibberd. Exhibition of
               Science, South Kensington. Land Travelling Exhibition / Richard Levin. Festival Ship
               'Campania' / James Holland. Exhibition of Industrial Power, Glasgow. Ulster Farm and
               Factory Exhibition, Belfast. The style: 'flimsy . . . effeminate'? / Reyner Banham. Index.
               EXHIBITION: vx.1976.022

1977

VR.1977.001   *1909–1929 : Les ballets russes de Diaghilew : exposition au Centre
               culturel du Marais, Paris, 29 novembre 1977–16 mars 1978 : liste des
               costumes et dessins prêtés par le Victoria and Albert Museum et le
               Theatre Museum à Londres = Diaghilev's Russian ballet : an
               exhibition at the Centre culturel du Marais, Paris, 29 November
               1977–16 March 1978 : costumes and designs from the Victoria and
               Albert Museum and the Theatre Museum, London.*
               [s.l. : s.n.], 1977.
               1 sheet, folded ([8] p.) ; 30 cm.
               Exhibition handlist. — "Crown copyright." — English and French versions on different
               sides of the sheet.
               EXHIBITION: vx.1977.xxx.002

VR.1977.002   *After "Alice" : a hundred years of children's reading in Britain /*
material selected and catalogued by Christine A. Kloet on behalf of the
Youth Libraries Group of the Library Association.
London : Library Association, 1977.
63 p., [3] leaves of plates : ill. ; 25 cm.
ISBN: 0853657408
Bibliography: p. 57. Index.
EXHIBITION: VX.1977.BGM.003

VR.1977.003   *Angliiskoe serebro XVI-XX vekov : iz sobranii Velikobritanii : katalog*
vystavki.
Moskva : Sov. khudozhnik, 1977.
[94] p. : ill. ; 22 cm.
"Sostaviteli kataloga vystavki i avtory vstupitel'nykh statei : sotrudniki Muzeia Viktorii
i Al'berta"–t.p. verso.
EXHIBITION: VX.1977.XXX.003

VR.1977.004   *The art press : two centuries of the art periodical : an exhibition held*
at the Victoria and Albert Museum, London, 8 April–26 September,
1976.
Cambridge : Chadwyck-Healey, 1977.
24 microfiches.
Reproduction of the exhibits.
EXHIBITION: VX.1976.008

VR.1977.005   *Change and decay : the future of our churches /* Marcus Binney and
Peter Burman.
London : Studio Vista, 1977.
192 p. : ill. ; 26 cm.
ISBN: 0289707749; 0289707757 (pbk.)
Introduction / Roy Strong. Includes: England: legacy / Peter Burman. Loss / Marcus
Binney. Scotland / Colin McWilliam. Wales / Elisabeth Beazley. Monuments / John
Physick. Metalwork / Claude Blair and Shirley Bury. Woodwork / Simon Jervis. Stained
glass / Martin Harrison. Ceramics / Michael Archer. Organs / Michael Gillingham.
Churchyards / Pamela Burgess. Liturgy / Thomas Cocke. Archaeology / Richard Morris.
Diocesan Advisory Committees / Tony Bridge. Disposable treasures / R.S. Wingfield-
Digby. The sale of treasures from Catholic churches / James Lees-Milne. The care of
churches / Peter Cleverly. Problems of urban churches / Colin Scott. Repair not
restoration / John Schofield. Church and state / Nicholas Cooper. New uses for churches
/ Patrick Brown. Churches restored / Peter Burman. Churches adapted / Pamela Tudor-
Craig. What the individual can do / Marcus Binney. — Glossary.
EXHIBITION: VX.1977.013

VR.1977.006   *Egyptian objects in the Victoria and Albert Museum /* Barbara Adams.
Warminster : Aris & Phillips, 1977.
[4], 61 p. : ill. ; 30 cm.
(Egyptology today ; no. 3)
ISBN: 0856681032
Includes bibliographic references.

VR.1977.007   *Party pieces : special recipes to celebrate the Queen's Silver Jubilee,*
1952–1977 / by Josceline Dimbleby ; with illustrations by Julia Fryer.
London : Crafts Advisory Committee, 1977.

[i], 20 p. : ill. ; 15 x 21 cm.
ISBN: 0903798174
EXHIBITION: vx.1977.002a

VR.1977.008   *Quarante-deux aquarelles britanniques du Victoria & Albert Museum*
/ John Murdoch.
[Ottawa : Musées nationaux du Canada, 1977.]
87 p. : ill. ; 20 x 21 cm.
ISBN: 0888843429
EXHIBITION: vx.1977.xxx.004

VR.1977.009   *Say when, and what, and how, and why.*
London : Crafts Advisory Committee, 1977.
4 p.
ISBN: 0903798239.
Board game, with instructions. — Unseen.
EXHIBITION: vx.1977.021

VR.1977.010   *The Victoria & Albert Museum collection.*
London : Mindata, 1977.
803 microfiches.
"A photographic record of the principal items in the collection." [1] Dept. of
Architecture and Sculpture.–[2] Ceramics.–[3] Furniture and Woodwork.–[4]
Metalwork.–[5] Textiles.

VR.1977.011   *The Victoria and Albert Museum souvenir guide : with 126
illustrations, 81 in colour.*
London : Designed and produced by Thames and Hudson, 1977.
72 p. : ill. (some col.), plans ; 24 cm.
At foot of title: V&A. — Introduction / Roy Strong.

1978

VR.1978.001   *Adeline Genée : a pictorial record* / by Ivor Guest.
London : Royal Academy of Dancing, 1978.
[60] p. : ill., ports. ; 20 x 25 cm.
Includes: Adeline Genée : centenary exhibition catalogue / Philip Dyer ([12] p.) stapled
in at centre.
EXHIBITION: vx.1978.THM.001

VR.1978.002   *An alphabet* / by William Nicholson.
[Andoversford] : Whittington Press, 1978.
1 portfolio (38 sheets) : all ill. ; 45 cm.
Spine title. — Accompanied by: William Nicholson's An alphabet : an introduction to
the reprint from the original woodblocks / by Edward Craig (11 p. : ill. ; 34 cm.).
EXHIBITION: vx.1978.008

VR.1978.003   *The Burlington magazine. Vol. CXX, no. 902. Special issue devoted to
the Victoria and Albert Museum.*
Includes: The Victoria and Albert Museum, 1978 / Roy Strong. Furniture studies : the
national rôle / Peter Thornton. Department of Prints, Drawings and Photographs, and
Paintings : old problems and new acquisitions; A. Hoskins' and Crosses : work in
progress / John Murdoch, B. Two 'books full of nonsense' and other works by Richard
Doyle / Lionel Lambourne, C. Abstract water-colours of the 1930's / C.M. Kauffmann,

D. Recent acquisitions : photographs / Mark Haworth-Booth. The Indian collections 1798 to 1978 / Robert Skelton. Velázquez's Apsley House portrait : an identification / Enriqueta Harris. Mentmore silver-mounted cabinet / Anna Somers Cocks. Department of Textiles and Dress / Valerie Mendes.

VR.1978.004   *The Cinzano glass collection.*
London : Cinzano, 1978.
[64] p. : chiefly ill. ; 24 cm.
Cover title. — Texts by Peter Lazarus, photographs by Derek Balmer.
EXHIBITION: VX.1978.009

VR.1978.005   *Elizabeth Fritsch : pots about music.*
Leeds : Leeds Art Galleries and the Leeds Art Collections Fund, [1978].
[24] p. : ill. (some col.), port. : 30 cm.
Texts by David Queensberry, Alison Britton, Ian Bennett.
EXHIBITION: VX.1979.012

VR.1978.006   *English engraved silver, 1150 to 1900* / Charles Oman.
London ; Boston : Faber & Faber, 1978.
158 p. : ill. ; 26 cm.
ISBN: 0571104983
Bibliography: p. 154. Index.
EXHIBITION: VX.1978.024

VR.1978.007   *Giambologna, 1529–1608 : sculptor to the Medici : an exhibition organised by the Arts Council of Great Britain and the Kunsthistorisches Museum, Vienna, in association with the Edinburgh Festival Society, the Royal Scottish Museum, and the Victoria & Albert Museum : . . .* / catalogue edited by Charles Avery and Anthony Radcliffe.
[London] : Arts Council of Great Britain, 1978.
239 p. : ill. (some col.), ports. (1 col.) ; 27 cm.
ISBN: 0728701812; 0728701804 (pbk.)
Acknowledgment / Joanna Drew. Essays by Manfred Leithe-Jasper, Katharine Watson. — Bibliography: p. 235-239.
EXHIBITION: VX.1978.021

VR.1978.008   *Henri Cartier-Bresson : his archive of 390 photographs from the Victoria and Albert Museum* / with an essay by Ernst Gombrich.
Edinburgh : Scottish Arts Council, 1978.
40 p. : ill. ; 22 cm.
ISBN: 0902989502
Acknowledgements / Robert Breen. The Cartier-Bresson archive / Mark Haworth-Booth. — Bibliography: p. 39-40. — Catalogued from 2nd imp., rev.
EXHIBITION: VX.1978.XXX.001

VR.1978.009   *The Oxford University Press and the spread of learning, 1478–1978 : an illustrated history* / by Nicolas Barker ; with a preface by Charles Ryskamp.
Oxford : Clarendon Press, 1978.
xiii, 69 p., [103] leaves of plates : chiefly ill. ; 31 cm.
ISBN: 0199510865; 0199510857 (pbk.)

"The Pierpont Morgan Library, the University of Western Ontario, the Victoria and Albert Museum, the Stadt- und Universitätsbibliothek, Frankfurt am Main"–cover of paperback ed. — Includes bibliographic references and index.
EXHIBITION: vx.1978.017

VR.1978.010   *Samuel Palmer, a vision recaptured : the complete etchings and the paintings for Milton and for Virgil.*
London : Trianon Press Facsimiles for the William Blake Trust, 1978.
xiii, 88 p. : ill. (some col.), ports. ; 30 cm. + 1 leaf of plates.
Spine title: Samuel Palmer : commemorative handbook of the exhibition at the Victoria & Albert Museum. — Limited edition of 3826 copies, 1800 numbered 1–1800 with 5 facsimiles of etchings; 2000 unnumbered with one facsimile . . . 26 copies numbered A-Z. — 1 facsimile loosely inserted. — Errata slip inserted. — In protective case.
EXHIBITION: vx.1978.025

VR.1978.011   *Scènes musicales de l'Inde : miniatures de 1590 à 1860 : prêt du Victoria and Albert Museum de Londres : guide de l'exposition, texte bilingue.*
[Nice : Direction des musées de Nice, 1978.]
[28] p. ; 30 cm.
At foot of title : Nice, Action culturelle municipale. — In French and English. — Bibliography: p. [28].
EXHIBITION: vx.1978.xxx.002

VR.1978.012   *Treasures of Indian art at the Victoria and Albert Museum* / John Irwin ; and some notes by Mārg.
Edinburgh ; London : Charles Skilton, 1978.
70 p. : ill. (some col.) ; 29 cm.

VR.1978.013   *Two modern binders : William Matthews & Edgar Mansfield : 12 April until 24 June 1978.*
[London] : Designer Bookbinders, [1978].
[24] p., 8 leaves of plates : ill., ports. ; 25 cm.
Cover title. — Foreword / Philip Smith. Texts signed "B.D.M.", "B.C.M." [i.e. B.D. Maggs?, Bernard Middleton?].
EXHIBITION: vx.1978.011

VR.1978.014   *The young visitor's V & A* / by Ann Gould.
London : Ash and Grant Ltd., 1978.
57, [2] p. : ill. (some col.), plans, ports. (some col.) ; 24 cm.
ISBN: 0904069273
Introduction / Roy Strong.— Index.

1979

VR.1979.001   *Arts of Bengal : the heritage of Bangladesh and eastern India : an exhibition organized by the Whitechapel Art Gallery in collaboration with the Victoria and Albert Museum.*
[London] : Whitechapel Art Gallery, [1979].
80 p. : ill. (some col.) ; 27 cm.
Edited by Robert Skelton and Mark Francis. Forewords by Nicholas Serota and Roy Strong. Includes: Bengal: the historical background / Robert Skelton. Sculpture / John Lowry. Islamic and later Hindu architectural decoration / Robert Skelton. Painting /

Andrew Topsfield. Folk art / Robert Skelton. Textiles / Veronica Murphy. Decorative arts / Susan Stronge. Furniture / Veronica Murphy. — Bibliography: p. 78–80.
EXHIBITION: VX.1979.XXX.004

VR.1979.002   *Bikutoria Ōshitsu hakubutsukan : Yōroppa no dentō kōgei to interia* /
Maeda Masaaki hen.
Tōkyō : Kōdansha, 1979.
178 p. : ill. (some col.) ; 31 cm.
(Sekai no hakubutsukan ; 7)
Series: Wonders of the world's museums. — In slip-case. — General illustrated guide to the V&A.

VR.1979.003   *The Colman collection of silver mustard pots.*
Norwich : Colman Foods, 1979.
143 p. : ill. ; 20 cm.
ISBN: 0950645605
Researched by Honor Godfrey. Introduction / John Culme. — Index to names.
Glossary. — Photographed by John Blomfield.
EXHIBITION: VX.1979.023

VR.1979.004   *The Doulton story : a souvenir booklet produced originally for the exhibition held at the Victoria and Albert Museum, London, 30 May–12 August 1979* / Paul Atterbury & Louise Irvine.
Stoke on Trent : Royal Doulton Tableware, [1979?].
104 p. : ill. ; 18 cm.
Bibliography: p. 104.
EXHIBITION: VX.1979.014

VR.1979.005   *Eileen Gray, designer* / J. Stewart Johnson.
London : Debrett's Peerage for the Museum of Modern Art, New York, 1979.
67 p. : ill. ; 27 cm.
ISBN: 0870703080
Includes bibliographic references.
EXHIBITION: VX.1979.002

VR.1979.006   *The garden : a celebration of one thousand years of British gardening : editor John Harris ; introduction Hugh Johnson.*
London : New Perspectives, 1979.
iv, 192 p. : ill. (some col.), plan ; 23 cm.
ISBN: 0861340167; 0861340175 (pbk.)
Includes: The medieval garden before 1500 / John Harvey. The renaissance garden, 1500–1640 / Roy Strong. John Evelyn's time, 1640 to 1660 / David Jacques. The formal garden, 1660–1710 / John Harris. The landscape garden, 1710–1730 / David Jacques. The flower garden, 1730 to 1830 / John Harris. The gardenesque garden, 1830 to 1890 / Richard Gorer. Victorian garden design / Brent Elliott. The natural garden, 1890 to 1910 / Betty Massingham. English gardens from 1910 to the present day / Russell Page. Illustrating new introductions / Phyllis Edwards. The naming of plants / William T. Stearn. The hunt for new plants / Kenneth Lemmon. The problems of transporting plants / Ray Desmond. Nurseries, nurserymen and seedsmen / John Harvey. Tools of the trade / Kay Sanecki. English gardening books / Rosemary Verey. The herb garden / Kay Sanecki. Physic and botanic gardens / Ray Desmond. Kitchen and vegetable gardens / Joy Larkham.The fruit garden / Ann Bonar. Cottage and suburban gardens / Gillian Darley. Municipal parks and gardens / Clive Wainwright. The garden indoors / Clive Wainwright. Scottish gardens / A.A. Tait. On the conservation of gardens / Marcus Binney. — Added t.p.: A guide to the exhibition by the Victoria and Albert Museum.
EXHIBITION: VX.1979.013

VR.1979.007   *A garden alphabet* / compiled by John Harris in association with the Victoria and Albert Museum for the Garden exhibition.
London : Octopus Books Ltd. in association with the Edgeworth Press, 1979.
[111] p. : ill. (some col.), facsim., plans ; 25 x 31 cm.
ISBN: 0706410823
"contains 24 original engravings from Batty Langley's *Pomona, or, The fruit garden illustrated,* first published in 1729"–t.p. verso.
EXHIBITION: VX.1979.013

VR.1979.008   *Ingres : drawings from the Musée Ingres at Montauban, and other collections.*
[London] : Arts Council of Great Britain, 1979.
48 p. : ill. ; 25 cm.
ISBN: 072748702045
Acknowledgment / Joanna Drew. Text by Pierre Barousse.
EXHIBITION: VX.1979.026

VR.1979.009   *Istra i Dalmacija = Istrie et Dalmatie = Istria and Dalmatia : 1782, Louis François Cassas* / tekst Duško Kečkemet.
Zagreb ; Split : Jugoslavenska akademija znanosti i umjetnosti, 1979.
61 p., [19] leaves of plates : col. ill., maps ; 32 cm.
In English, French and Serbo-Croatian. — Includes bibliographic references. — Watercolours from the V&A's collection.
EXHIBITION: VX.1979.XXX.005

VR.1979.010   *The luxury of good taste : an exhibition of Victorian design 1835–1880 : arranged by students of the Department of Art History and Theory, University of Essex at the Victoria and Albert Museum, March 14th, 1979.*
[London : The Students?, 1979.]
[18] p. ; 30 cm.
Contents: The diffusion of taste. Household taste 1850–1880. Costume 1850–1880. How to lay a cloth. Pugin's Scarisbrooke carver. — Duplicated typescript, stapled. Ill. on cover.
EXHIBITION: VX.1979.005

VR.1979.011   *New glass : a worldwide survey* / . . . organized by the Corning Museum of Glass.
Corning, N.Y. : Museum of Glass, 1979.
288 p. : ill. (some col.), ports. ; 28 cm.
ISBN: 087290069X
Added title: Pilkington presents New glass . . . in conjunction with the Victoria and Albert Museum. — Preface / Thomas S. Buechner. Texts by Antony E. Snow, William Warmus, Russell Lynes. 'Jury statements': Franca Santi Gualteri, Russell Lynes, Werner Schmalenbach, Paul J. Smith. — Bibliography: p. 285–286. Indexes.
EXHIBITION: VX.1981.009

VR.1979.012   *The tale of Mrs Tittlemouse.*
London : Decimus Publishing, 1979.
[50], [9] p. : ill. (some col.) ; 16 cm.
Facsimile of manuscript notebook of Beatrix Potter's, and additional drawings, in the Linder Bequest at the National Art Library. — Includes: The manuscript of Mrs. Tittlemouse : essays / Margaret Lane and Joyce Irene Whalley. — In slip-case. — Limited ed. of 500 numbered copies.

VR.1979.013   *Thames Television's The art of Hollywood : fifty years of art direction*
              / devised and produced by John Hambley and Patrick Downing.
              London : Thames Television, 1979.
              130 p. : ill. (some col.), ports. ; 23 cm.
              Cover title: The art of Hollywood : a Thames Television exhibition at the Victoria and
              Albert Museum. — Bibliography: p. 130. Filmography: p. 110–126.
              EXHIBITION: VX.1979.024

VR.1979.014   *Thirties : British art and design before the war : Hayward Gallery, 25*
              October 1979–13 January 1980 / an exhibition organised by the Arts
              Council in collaboration with the Victoria & Albert Museum.
              [London : Arts Council of Great Britain], 1979.
              [4], 320 p. : ill. (some col.), ports. ; 28 cm.
              ISBN: 0728702169; 0728702150 (pbk.)
              Catalogue edited by Jennifer Hawkins and Marianne Hollis. — The Thirties / A.J.P.
              Taylor. Year by year / Ian Jeffrey. Art at the time / William Feaver. Architecture:
              contrasts of a decade / Charlotte and Tim Benton. Design introduction / Carol Hogben.
              Prints and book illustration / Susan Lambert. Furniture / Simon Jervis. Carpets and
              furnishing textiles / Valerie Mendes. Industrial ceramics and glass / Jennifer Hawkins.
              Studio pottery / David Coachworth. Silverwork and jewellery / Shirley Bury.
              Architectural, decorative and stained glass / Roger Pinkham. Transport and travel /
              Brian Lacey. Photo-journalism: feeling for the past / Ian Jeffrey. — Bibliography: p.
              306–308. Index of lenders, and "index of designers, architects, artists, photographers,
              publishers, manufacturers and selected personalities".
              EXHIBITION: VX.1979.XXX.003

1980

VR.1980.001   *Arthur Rackham, 1867–1939 : illustrations, drawings and*
              watercolours / an exhibition organised by Sheffield City Art
              Galleries . . . .
              [Sheffield] : City Art Galleries, [1980].
              32 p., [21] p. of plates : ill., ports. ; 15 cm.
              ISBN: 0900660503
              Foreword / Frank Constantine. Text by James Hamilton. — Bibliography: p. 23.
              EXHIBITION: VX.1980.001

VR.1980.002   *British textile design in the Victoria and Albert Museum* / directed by
              Donald King . . . ; executive editor, Takahiko Sano.
              Tokyo : Gakken, 1980.
              3 v. : chiefly ill., plates (some col.) ; 38 cm.
              Japanese title: Vikutoria & Arubāto Bijutsukan : Igirisu no shenshoku. — In English
              and Japanese. — v.1. The Middle Ages to the Rococo (1200–1750) / with the
              collaboration of Santina Levey, Natalie Rothstein. v.2. Rococo to Victorian
              (1750–1850) / with the collaboration of Natalie Rothstein, Wendy Hefford. v.3.
              Victorian to modern (1850–1940) / with the collaboration of Linda Parry, Valerie
              Mendes. — Includes bibliographic references.

VR.1980.003   *The early Alinari photographic archive of art & architecture in Italy.*
              London : Mindata, 1980.
              122 microfiches + [14] p.
              Photographs from the V&A collection.

VR.1980.004   *Furniture history. Vol. XVI (1980). The furnishing and decoration of*
              Ham House.

[London] : Furniture History Society, 1980.
194 p., [160] p. of plates : ill., plans ; 25 cm.
ISBN: 090335034 [sic]
By Peter Thornton and Maurice Tomlin. Editorial / Christopher Gilbert. —
Accompanied by v.1980.021. — Includes bibliographic references.

VR.1980.005   *Hendrik Werkman, printer-painter, 1882–1945 : Victoria & Albert*
Museum, South Kensington, 5 March to 27 April, 1980.
[London] : Arts Council of Great Britain, [1980].
1 poster : ill. (1 col.), port. ; 76 x 51 cm. folded to 38 x 26 cm.
ISBN: 0728702312
Text written by Rosemary Miles. — Selected bibliography.
EXHIBITION: vx.1980.002

VR.1980.006   *Old and modern masters of photography : an exhibition of*
photographs selected from the collection in the Victoria and Albert
Museum.
[London] : Arts Council of Great Britain, 1980.
[16] p. : ill. ; 30 cm.
ISBN: 0728702274
Introduction by Mark Haworth-Booth. — Includes bibliography.
EXHIBITIONS: vx.1978.006; vx.1980.xxx.002

VR.1980.007   *Photographs by Bill Brandt* / introduction by Mark Haworth-Booth.
Washington, D.C. : International Exhibitions Foundation, 1980.
[16] p. : ill. ; 30 cm.
Bibliography on inside back cover.
EXHIBITION: vx.1980.xxx.003

VR.1980.008   *Svensk form : Swedish craft and design : an exhibition produced by*
the Swedish Society of Industrial Design in collaboration with the
Swedish Institute.
[s.l. : The Exhibition Organisers?], 1980 (Printed by Upplands
Grafiska AB, Uppsala).
11 p. : ill. ; 42 cm.
Catalogue texts by Helena Dahlback-Lutteman. Foreword by Roy Strong.
EXHIBITION: vx.1980.009

VR.1980.009   *Tapestry : Henry Moore & West Dean : an exhibition at the Victoria*
and Albert Museum, 15th July–25th August 1980.
[s.l.] : Edward James Foundation, 1980.
32 p. : ill. (some col.) ; 19 x 25 cm.
Foreword / Peter Sarginson. Includes text by Edwin Mullins.
EXHIBITION: vx.1980.010

VR.1980.010   *I tre libri dell'arte del vasaio = The three books of the potter's art, by*
Cipriano Piccolpasso : a facsimile of the manuscript in the Victoria
and Albert Museum, London / translated and introduced by Ronald
Lightbown and Alan Caiger-Smith.
London : Scolar Press, 1980.
2 v. (xl, [16], 73 [i.e. 146] p.; xxiv, 122, 1 p., 8 p. of plates : ill. (some
col.), facsims., map ; 32 cm.
ISBN: 0859674525
Bibliography: vol. I, p. xxxix-xl. Glossary. — In slip-case.

VR.1980.011   *Victoria and Albert Museum photographic collection : 1843–1915.*
London : World Microfilms, 1980.
24 microfilm reels + 12 p.
Container title: Early rare photographic collection. — Descriptive list of contents / Mark Haworth-Booth. — A. Photographs. B. Register.

VR.1980.012   *The Victoria and Albert Museum : the making of the collection* / Anna Somers Cocks.
Leicester : Windward, 1980.
186 p. : col. ill. ; 32 cm.
ISBN: 0711200424
Preface / Roy Strong. — Bibliography: p. 182–183. Index.

1981

VR.1981.001   *The art of* Radio times : *an exhibition of original illustrations from 1923 to the present day* / selected by Edward Booth-Clibborn.
London : European Illustration, 1981.
32 p. ; 15 cm.
Foreword / George Howard.
EXHIBITION: VX.1981.012

VR.1981.002   *Artifacts at the end of a decade* / Harry Anderson . . . [et al] ; conceived by Steven Watson ; edited by Carol Huebner and Steven Watson.
[New York : The Editors], 1981.
1 case (44 pieces) : ill. (some col.) ; 38 x 46 cm. + 1 booklet ([55] p. : ill. ; 21 cm.).
Artists' book. Includes pieces by: Harry Anderson, Laurie Anderson, Charles Arnold, John Ashbery, Bern Boyle, Lucinda Childs, Jane Comfort, R. Crumb, Dan Dailey, Jimmy De Sana, Evergon, Sandi Fellman, Benno Friedman, April Greiman, Martha Holt, James Hong, Betsey Johnson, Sonia Katchian, Christopher Knowles, Robert Kushner, Stephanie Brody Lederman, Sol LeWitt, Jacqueline Livingston, Joan Livingston, David Lusby, Joan Lyons, Judy McWillie, Joseph Masheck, Joan Nelsen, Bea Nettles, Jayme Odgers, Richard Olson, Kingsley Parker, Harvey Pekar, Lucio Pozzi, Don Rodan, Martha Rosler, Michael Sorkin, Soul Artists, Stanley Stellar, Michelle Stuart, Benedict Tisa, Curtis Van Buren, David Van Buren, Wendy Von Weise, Philip Warner, Robert Wilson.
EXHIBITION: VX.1990.006

VR.1981.003   *A choice of design, 1850–1980 : fabrics by Warner & Sons Limited.*
[London : The Firm], 1981.
113 p. : ill. (some col.), ports. ; 30 cm.
ISBN: 0950658715
Acknowledgments / Hester Bury. Foreword / Paul Reilly. — Index of designers, and general index.
EXHIBITION: VX.1982.BGM.003

VR.1981.004   *Design in silver 1981 : exhibition of award winners.*
Camberley, Surrey : J. Goddard & Sons Ltd., [1981].
1 sheet, folded ([4] p.) : ill. ; 30 cm.

Addendum [VR.1980.013] *George Wickes 1698–1761 : royal goldsmith* / Elaine Barr. — London: Studio Vista / Christie's, 1980. — xiii, 210 p. : ill., geneal. table, ports.; 26 cm. — ISBN: 028970877x — Includes: The discovery of the Garrard ledgers / Arthur Grimwade. — Bibliography: p. 206. Index.
EXHIBITION: VX.1980.017

At head of title: Goddard's. — Printed on purple; partly in silver and pink.
EXHIBITION: VX.1981.010

VR.1981.005   *D'Oyly Carte : 11 April–26 May 1981, Portsmouth City Museum.*
[Portsmouth : The Museum, 1981.]
15 p. ; 22 cm.
Cover title. — Catalogue by Catherine Haill. — Reproduced typescript, stapled.
EXHIBITION: VX.1981.XXX.001

VR.1981.006   *The English miniature* / John Murdoch, Jim Murrell, Patrick J. Noon,
Roy Strong.
New Haven ; London : Yale University Press, 1981.
vi, 230 p. : ill. (some col.) ; 27 cm.
ISBN: 0300027699; 0300027788 (pbk.)
Check-list inserted (4 p. ; 26 cm.) — Includes bibliographic references.
EXHIBITION: VX.1981.XXX.003

VR.1981.007   *Heraldry now, 1975–1981 : an exhibition of contemporary heraldic
art and design arranged by the Heraldry Society and held at the
Victoria and Albert Museum from 15th April to 31st May 1981.*
[London? : The Society, 1981.]
[24] p. ; 22 x 10 cm.
Cover title. — Foreword / J.P. Brooke-Little. — List of exhibitors.
EXHIBITION: VX.1981.004

VR.1981.008   *Japanische Lackkunst der Gegenwart : Funktion und Design,
Tradition und Modernität am Beispiel Kyotoer Lackmeister = Modern
Japanese lacquer art : a family of Kyoto craftsmen.*
[Köln : Museen der Stadt : Museum für Ostasiatische Kunst,
1981.]
40 p. : chiefly ill. (some col.) ; 26 cm.
"Katalogtext und Gestaltung: Masako Shono." — Foreword by John Ayers. — German
and English parallel text.
EXHIBITION: VX.1981.011

VR.1981.009   *Lucie Rie : a survey of her life and work* / edited by John Houston ;
with photographs by David Cripps.
[London] : Crafts Council, [1981].
92, [4] p. : ill. (some col.) ; 25 cm.
ISBN: 0903798565
Bibliography: p. [94–95]. Index.
EXHIBITION: VX.1982.001

VR.1981.010   *The strange genius of William Burges, 'art-architect', 1827–1881 :
a catalogue to a centenary exhibition organised jointly by the National
Museum of Wales, Cardiff, and the Victoria and Albert Museum in
1981* / edited by J. Mordaunt Crook ; catalogue entries by Mary Axon
and Virginia Glenn.
Cardiff : National Museum of Wales, 1981.
155 p. : ill. ; 24 cm.
ISBN: 0720002591; 0720002346 (pbk.)
Foreword / Douglas A. Bassett, Roy Strong. — Select bibliography: p. 154. — Unseen.
Catalogued from 1982 reprint.
EXHIBITION: VX.1981.015

VR.1981.011   *Summary catalogue of miniatures in the Victoria and Albert Museum :*
               including enamels, plumbagos, silhouettes and other works in related
               media . . . / compiled by Garth Hall ; with Jane Savidge, Jo Macdonald
               and Sarah Postgate.
               Haslemere, Surrey : Emmett, 1981.

               144 p. ; 21 cm.
               ISBN: 0907696015
               Preface by John Murdoch. — Listed by artist, sitter and Museum number. —
               Accompanies VR.1981.013.

VR.1981.012   *Visual catalogue of fashion and costume in the Victoria and Albert*
               Museum.
               Haslemere : Emmett Microform, 1981.
               57 microfiches.
               ISBN: 0907696023
               Photography, Philip Metcalf.

VR.1981.013   *Visual catalogue of miniature paintings in the Victoria and Albert*
               Museum.
               Haslemere : Emmett Microform, 1981.
               42 microfiches.
               (Visual union catalogue of miniatures in Great Britain ; 1)
               ISBN: 0907696007

VR.1981.014   *Vom Penny Dreadful zum Comic : Englische Jugendzeitschriften,*
               Heftchen und Comics von 1855 bis zur Gegenwart.
               Oldenburg : Bibliotheks- und Informationssystem, Universität
               Oldenburg, 1981.
               104 p. : ill. (some col.) ; 24 cm.
               ISBN: 3814200330
               "Eine Ausstellung im Rahmen der 7. Oldenburger Kinder- und Jugenbuchmesse aus den
               Beständen der Universitätsbibliothek und aus Privatbesitz . . . 7 bis 22 November 1981
               Stadtmuseum Oldenburg." — "Ausstellung und Katalog: Kevin Carpenter." —
               Bibliography: p. 100–104.
               EXHIBITION: VX.1983.BGM.002

1982

VR.1982.001   *Art & industry : Boilerhouse Project, Victoria and Albert Museum,*
               January 18th 1982–March 2nd 1982.
               [London] : Conran Foundation, 1982.
               80 p. : ill. ; 22 cm.
               Cover title: Art and industry: a century of design in the products we use. — Foreword /
               Paul Reilly.
               EXHIBITION: VX.1982.BHO.001

VR.1982.002   *The car programme, fifty-two months to job one, or, How they*
               designed the Ford Sierra : an exhibition at the Victoria and Albert
               Museum / text by Stephen Bayley, designed by Conran Associates.
               London : Boilerhouse Project, Victoria and Albert Museum, [1982].
               48 p. ill. (chiefly col.) ; 21 cm.
               EXHIBITION: VX.1982.BHO.005

VR.1982.003   *Family art: essays and a bibliography to accompany an exhibition.*
                Preston : Polytechnic Library & Learning Resources Service, 1982.
                19 p. : ill. ; 30 cm.
                Bibliography: p. 17–19.
                EXHIBITION: VX.1982.BGM.002

VR.1982.004   *The future of the Theatre Museum, together with the minutes of*
                evidence : Fifth report from the Education, Science and Arts
                Committee, Session 1981–82.
                [London : H.M.S.O., 1982.]
                ix, 20 p. ; 25 cm.
                (HC ; 472)
                "Ordered by the House of Commons to be printed, 26th July 1982."

VR.1982.005   *Hamza-nama : vollständige wiedergabe der bekannten Blätter der*
                Handschrift aus den Beständen aller erreichbaren Sammlungen. 2.
                Band, Die Blätter aus dem Victoria & Albert Museum London.
                Graz : Akademische Druck- u. Verlagsanstalt, 1982.
                1 portfolio (9 p., 27 leaves of plates) : col. ill. ; 49 cm.
                (Codices selecti photypice impressi ; v. 52/2)
                Prefaces and captions in English and German.

VR.1982.006   *Humphry Repton, landscape gardener 1752–1818* / George Carter,
                Patrick Goode, Kedrun Laurie.
                Norwich : Sainsbury Centre for Visual Arts, 1982.
                xvi, 176 p. : ill. (some col.), facsims., map, plans, ports. ; 21 x 30 cm.
                ISBN: 0946009031
                Preface / Dorothy Stroud. Includes essay by Stephen Daniels. — Bibliography: p.
                122–127.
                EXHIBITION: VX.1982.010

VR.1982.007   *Images of show business from the Theatre Museum, V&A* / edited by
                James Fowler.
                London : Methuen, 1982.
                [15], 104, [4] p. : ill. (some col.) ; 26 cm.
                ISBN: 041339980X; 0413399907 (pbk.)
                EXHIBITION: VX.1982.THM.002

VR.1982.008   *Inky pinky ponky : children's playground rhymes* / collected by
                Michael Rosen and Susanna Steele ; pictures by Dan Jones.
                London : Granada, 1982.
                [32] p. : col. ill. ; 29 cm.
                ISBN: 0246113197
                EXHIBITION: VX.1982.BGM.005

VR.1982.009   *John Sell Cotman, 1782–1842 : a touring exhibition arranged by the*
                Arts Council of Great Britain . . . .
                London : Arts Council of Great Britain, 1982.
                160 p. : ill. (some col.), ports. ; 24 cm.
                ISBN: 0728703106
                Preface / Joanna Drew. Introduction: Cotman's life and work / Miklos Rajnai. Cotman:
                romantic classicist / David Thompson. Cotman and his patrons / Michael Pidgley.

Cotman and his publication projects / Andrew Hemingway. Cotman and Normandy / Marjorie Allthorpe-Guyton. Watercolours, drawings, oil paintings and etchings / Miklos Rajnai.— Bibliography: p. 35–37.
EXHIBITION: VX.1982.008

VR.1982.010   *John Sell Cotman, 1782–1842 : an Arts Council exhibition organized in collaboration with the Victoria and Albert Museum . . . .*
[London] : Arts Council of Great Britain, [1982].
1 sheet, folded ([3] p.) : ill., port. ; 30 cm.
EXHIBITION: VX.1982.008

VR.1982.011   *Memphis in London.*
[London] : Boilerhouse Project, 1982.
1 sheet, folded (20 p.).
ISBN: 0946410011
Texts by Stephen Bayley, Penny Sparke. Interview with Ettore Sottsass, by Izzika Gaon. — Includes bibliography.
EXHIBITION: VX.1982.BHO.006

VR.1982.012   *The national collection of watercolours in the Victoria and Albert Museum on colour microfiche* / introduced by Michael Kauffmann.
London : Ormonde Publishing, 1982.
82 microfiches + 8 p.
ISBN: 0907716008
Includes index.

VR.1982.013   *Paquin Worth fashion drawings, 1865–1956.*
Haslemere : Emmett Microform, 1982.
60 microfiches + 4 p.
ISBN: 0907696058
The houses of Paquin and Worth / Carla Tscherney. — Index. — Photography, Phil Metcalf. — From the collection of the Prints, Drawings and Paintings Department.

VR.1982.014   *The Pooh sketchbook* / E.H. Shepard ; edited by Brian Sibley ; with a foreword by Sir Roy Strong.
London : Methuen, 1982.
96 p. : ill. ; 24 cm.
ISBN: 0416244203
Later published: New York : Dutton, 1984.
EXHIBITION: VX.1982.012

VR.1982.015   *Sony design.*
London : Conran Foundation, 1982.
84 p., [2] leaves of plates : ill. (some col.), ports. ; 21 cm.
Cover title. — Text by Stephen Bayley.
EXHIBITION: VX.1982.BHO.002

VR.1982.016   *The strange genius of William Burges, 'art-architect', 1827–1881 : a catalogue to a centenary exhibition organised jointly by the National Museum of Wales, Cardiff, and the Victoria and Albert Museum in 1981* / edited by J. Mordaunt Crook ; catalogue entries by Mary Axon and Virginia Glenn.

Cardiff : National Museum of Wales, 1981 (1982 printing).
155 p. : ill. ; 24 cm.
ISBN: 0720002591; 0720002346 (pbk.)
Select bibliography: p. 154.
EXHIBITION: VX.1981.015

VR.1982.017   *The Victoria & Albert Museum collection : Department of Designs.*
London : Mindata, 1982.
172 microfiches.
Includes index.

1983

VR.1983.001   *Aubrey Beardsley = Biazurī–ten.*
Tokyo : Tokyo Shimbun, 1983.
[55] p., [95] p. of plates : ill. (some col.), 1 port. ; 28 cm.
Separate title in English: Aubrey Beardsley exhibition. — Foreword / C.M. Kauffmann.
Message / Michael Barrett. Texts by Brian Reade, Otsuro Sakazaki, Tadanori Yokoo.
Notes by Susan Lambert, Susumu Takagi. — Text in Japanese and English. —
Bibliography: p. [55].
EXHIBITION: VX.1983.XXX.002

VR.1983.002   *British Friends of the Art Museums of Israel : Monday, October 19th,
1983 at the Guildhall, to honour Dame Alicia Markova : private view
of ballet costumes and photographs (by kind permission of the
Theatre Museum, Victoria and Albert Museum).*
London : [The Friends], 1983.
1 v. : port. ; 25 cm.
Includes a catalogue.
EXHIBITION: VX.1983.XXX.004

VR.1983.003   *David Cox, 1783–1859* / selected and catalogued by Stephen
Wildman ; introductory essays by Richard Lockett and John
Murdoch.
[Birmingham] ; London : Birmingham Museums and Art Gallery ;
Distributed by A. Zwemmer, 1983.
136 p., 18 p. of plates : ill. (some col.) ; 22 cm.
ISBN: 0709301146
Includes bibliographic references.
EXHIBITION: VX.1983.023

VR.1983.004   *Design : the problem comes first.* 2nd ed. (French/English)
Copenhagen : Danish Design Council, 1983.
118 p. : ill. (some col.) ; 21 cm.
ISBN: 8787385104
French title: Design : d'abord le problème. — Written by Jens Bernsen. Introduction by
Stephen Bayley. — In English and French.
EXHIBITION: VX.1983.BHO.001

VR.1983.005   *Images for sale : 21 years of graphics, advertising, packaging and
commercials from Design and Art Direction.*
London : Conran Foundation, 1983.

[4] p. : ill. ; 30 cm.
Cover title. — Written and edited by Stephen Bayley. Text by Edward Booth-Clibborn.
EXHIBITION: VX.1983.BHO.003

VR.1983.006   *Japanese ceramics today : masterworks from the Kikuchi collection :*
February 11–April 3, 1983, Smithsonian Institution, Washington,
D.C.; May 1–July 17, 1983, Victoria and Albert Museum,
London.
[s.l. : s.n.], 1983 (Dai Nippon Printing Co.).
131 p. : chiefly col. ill. ; 25 x 26 cm.
Contributors Hayashiya Seizo, Tsuji Kaichi; editing Hakuhodo.
EXHIBITION: VX.1983.009

VR.1983.007   *Kenneth Grange at the Boilerhouse, May 1983.*
[London] : Conran Foundation, [1983].
64 p. : ill. ; 20 x 21 cm.
Edited by Stephen Bayley and Jon Ward.
EXHIBITION: VX.1983.BHO.002

VR.1983.008   *Maestri dell'acquarello inglese : acquarelli del Victoria and Albert*
Museum.
[s.l.] : Gruppo Barclays Bank International ; Roma : F.lli Palombi,
1983.
98 p. : ill. (some col.) ; 24 cm.
Edited by John Murdoch and H. Lee Bimm. Foreword by Ugo Vetere. Presentazione /
G.C. Argan. — Bibliography: p. 98.
EXHIBITION: VX.1983.XXX.003

VR.1983.009   *My father and Edward Ardizzone : a lasting friendship* / by Charles
Booth-Clibborn ; illustrated with Ardizzone Christmas cards.
London : Patrick Hardy, 1983.
48 p. : ill. ; 31 cm.
ISBN: 074440018X
EXHIBITION: VX.1983.027

VR.1983.010   *Philip Garner's Better living catalog.*
London : Sidgwick & Jackson, 1983.
94 p. : ill. (some col.) ; 21 cm.
ISBN: 0283989777
Originally published in the U.S.A., 1982. — Unseen. Record from OCLC.
EXHIBITION: VX.1983.BHO.005

VR.1983.011   *Prompt books and actor's [actors'] copies : Theatre Museum, V&A,*
London.
London : Ormonde, 1983.
583 microfiches + 20 p.

VR.1983.012   *Studio ceramics today : 25th anniversary of the Craftsmen Potters*
Association of Great Britain : Victoria and Albert Museum, London,
S.W.7, October 5–November 27, 1983.
[London : The Association, 1983.]
1 sheet, folded ([6] p.) ; 29 cm.
EXHIBITION: VX.1983.022

VR.1983.013   *Studio ceramics today : a new directory of the work of members of the Craftsmen Potters Association of Great Britain* / edited by Emmanuel Cooper and Eileen Lewenstein.
Potters 6th ed.
London : Craftsmen Potters Association, 1983.
207 p. : ill. ; 25 cm.
ISBN: 0950476730
Foreword by Roy Strong. — Includes: The Victoria and Albert Museum and studio ceramics / Oliver Watson.
EXHIBITION: VX.1983.022

VR.1983.014   *Taste : an exhibition about values in design.*
London : Boilerhouse Project, Victoria and Albert Museum, 1983.
110 p., [24] p. of plates : ill., ports. ; 21 cm.
ISBN: 0946410046
"Written and edited by Stephen Bayley"–t.p. verso. — Includes anthology: Bad taste (1771) / Jean-François [i.e. Jacques-François] Blondel. A house full of horrors (1852) / Henry Morley. Hints on household taste (1872) / Charles Eastlake. How should one dress? (1903) / Adolf Loos. Art and industry (1934) / Herbert Read. The taste of the public (1937) / Niklaus Pevsner. Machine-for-living modern (1954) / T.H. Robsjohn-Gibbings. English commonsense (1967) / Paul Reilly. In praise of tasteless products (1977) / John Pile. Victorian revival (1978) / Jules Lubbock. Don't forget bad taste is popular (1979) / John Blake. A moveable feast (1983) / Glyn[n] Boyd Harte, James Woudhuysen, Sherban Cantacuzino. — Includes bibliographic references.
EXHIBITION: VX.1983.BHO.004

VR.1983.015   *Theatre costume design in the Victoria and Albert Museum.*
Haslemere : Emmett, 1983.
38 microfiches + 1 v. (36 p. ; 23 cm.).
(Fashion, costume & uniforms series ; no. 3)
ISBN: 0907696104
Photography by Philip Metcalf.

VR.1983.016   *The trick that went wrong, or, Fanny & Charles : a Regency episode* / Phillida Gili.
London : Andre Deutsch, 1983.
[26] p. : ill. (some col.) ; 16 x 22 cm.
ISBN: 0233975926
EXHIBITION: VX.1984.BGM.001

VR.1983.017   *The Victoria and Albert Museum Library subject catalogue.*
London : Mindata, 1983.
879 microfiches.

1984

VR.1984.001   *Ausbruch und Abenteuer : deutsche und englische Abenteuerliteratur von Robinson bis Winnetou : Ausstellungskatalog* / Kevin Carpenter und Bernd Steinbrink ; mit Beiträgen von Dennis Butts . . . [et al.].
Oldenburg : Bibliotheks- und Informationssystem der Universität, 1984.
136 p. : ill. (some col.) ; 21 cm.
ISBN: 3814201035

Includes essays: Der unendliche Robinson / Kevin Carpenter. Erlaubte und geheime Blicke auf sittliche und sinnliche Bilder: Robinson Crusoe in den Buchillustrationen / Jens Thiele. Zur Pädagogik in Joachim Heinrich Campes *Robinson der Jüngere* / Klaus Klattenhoff. 'Blood and thunder' / Louis James. Die Entwicklung des englischen Abenteuerromans für die Jugend von Kapitän Marryat bis G.A. Henty / Dennis Butts. Die wilden Früchte des Empire / Jens-Ulrich Davids. Ausgestellte Bücher D, Abenteuerromane für die englische Jugend. Friedrich Gerstäcker und die Südseelegende seiner Zeit / Anselm Maler. Im Reich der Kolportage / Bernd Steinbrink. Der exotische Abenteuerroman des 19. Jahrhunderts in seiner Entwicklung zur Jugendlektüre / Helmut Schmiedt. Karl May und die Karl-May-Forschung / Claus Roxin. — Bibliography: p. 132.
EXHIBITION: VX.1986.BGM.002

VR.1984.002　　　*B————b* / Kit Williams.
London : Cape, 1984.
[32] p. : col. ill. ; 29 cm.
ISBN: 0224019066
The title was eventually revealed to be *Bee on the comb.*
EXHIBITION: VX.1984.BGM.002

VR.1984.003　　　*A catalogue of the puppets and associated material in the British Puppet and Model Theatre Guild collection and in the Guild archives : with a short history of the Guild and an appendix of additional puppet theatre exhibits in the Museum acquired from other sources* / compiled by T.E. Howard.
[London? : The Guild], 1984.
[85] p. ; 30 cm.
The collection became part of the Theatre Museum in 1980.

VR.1984.004　　　*Classical Korean embroideries.*
[London] : Korea-Britain Centennial Committee : International Cultural Society of Korea, [1984].
[40] p., some folded : ill. (some col.) ; 25 cm.
Greetings / Kim Sang Man. Preface / Choi Sunu.
EXHIBITION: VX.1984.004

VR.1984.005　　　*Design at Kingston : an exhibition of work by students from the School of Three-Dimensional Design, Kingston Polytechnic.*
London : Victoria & Albert Museum, 1984.
[22] p. : ill. ; 22 cm.
"Furniture, product, interior, design." — "Boilerhouse Project." — Foreword / Stephen Bayley. [Preface] / Robert Smith. Text by Peter Lloyd Jones.
EXHIBITION: VX.1984.BHO.002

VR.1984.006　　　*Early Korean printing.*
Seoul : Korean Overseas Information Service, [1984?].
82 p. : ill. (some col.), map ; 26 cm.
Text, selections, layout: Sohn Pokee (Powkey). Foreword / Roy Strong.
EXHIBITION: VX.1984.013

VR.1984.007　　　*Edwin Smith : photographs 1935–1971 : with 254 duotone plates and an introduction by Olive Cook.*
[New York] : Thames & Hudson, 1984.
13 p., [253] p. of plates : chiefly ill. ; 28 cm.
ISBN: 0500541000
EXHIBITION: VX.1984.019

VR.1984.008   *From east to west : textiles from G.P. & J. Baker : Victoria & Albert Museum, 9 May–14 Oct. 1984.*
[London] : G.P. & J. Baker, 1984.
160 p. : ill. (some col.) ; 25 cm.
ISBN: 0950929603
By Natalie Rothstein: G.P. & J. Baker – a prologue [and] Introduction to historical textiles. By Linda Parry: The Baker family and G.P. & J. Baker – the first twenty years [and] Pattern-books and precursors / Wendy Hefford. The Baker archives / Audrey Duck. G.P. & J. Baker – 1914 onwards / Frances Hinchcliffe. The Baker studio / Ann Lynch. — Bibliographic references: p. 156–157.
EXHIBITION: VX.1984.010

VR.1984.009   *Handtools : the culture of manual work.*
[London : Conran Foundation, 1984.]
1 sheet, folded ([9] p.) : ill. ; 26 cm.
ISBN: 0946410070
Includes bibliographic references.
EXHIBITION: VX.1984.BHO.001

VR.1984.010   *The House of Worth : fashion designs : a photographic record, 1894–1927.*
London : Mindata, 1984.
150 microfiches.
Originals held at the Archive of Art and Design.

VR.1984.011   *Jewellery Gallery in the Victoria and Albert Museum : a visual catalogue.*
Haslemere : Emmett Microform, 1984.
24 microfiches + [15] p.
ISBN: 0907696139
Includes index.

VR.1984.012   *Robots.*
[London] : Conran Foundation, 1984.
60 p. : ill. ; 21 cm.
ISBN: 0946410089
Written and edited by Stephen Bayley and James Woudhuysen. — Bibliography: p. 60.
EXHIBITION: VX.1984.BHO.003

VR.1984.013   *Visiting museums : a report of a survey of visitors to the Victoria and Albert, Science, National Railway Museums, for the Office of Arts and Libraries* / Patrick Heady.
London : H.M.S.O., 1984.
xiv, 154 p. : ill. ; 30 cm.
(SS (series) ; 1147)
ISBN: 0116910968
Office of Population Censuses and Surveys. Social Surveys Division. — Index.

VR.1984.014   *William Staite Murray* / Malcolm Haslam ; with photographs by David Cripps.
London : Crafts Council : Cleveland County Museum Service, 1984.
96 p. : ill. (some col.) ; 25 cm.
Bibliography: p. 92–93. Index.
EXHIBITION: VX.1985.004

1985

VR.1985.001   *Acuarelas del siglo XX del Victoria & Albert Museum de Londres :*
exposición organizada por el Banco de Bilbao en su la salon de
exposiciones de Madrid, enero-febrero 1985.
[Madrid : El Banco, 1985.]
146 p. : ill. (some col.) ; 26 cm.
Introduction by C.M. Kauffmann. Notes and catalogue: Gilliam [i.e. Gillian] Saunders
and Elizabeth Clunas. — Bibliography: p. 146.
EXHIBITION: VX.1985.XXX.001

VR.1985.002   *Aubrey Beardsley 1872, 1898.*
Milano : Mazzotta, 1985.
215 p. : ill. (some col.), ports. ; 24 cm.
ISBN: 8820206161
"70 opere dal Victoria and Albert Museum"–half-title. — Presentazioni: Alberto Galli e
Guido Aghina, Malcolm Hardy, C.M. Kauffmann. Essays by Renato Barilli, Federica Di
Castro. — Bibliography: p. 205–212. — In slip case.
EXHIBITION: VX.1985.XXX.004

VR.1985.003   *Aubrey Beardsley 1872, 1898 : Roma, 13 marzo, 28 aprile 1985 /*
Soprintendenza speciale alla Galleria nazionale d'arte moderna e
contemporanea ; Victoria and Albert Museum, Londra ; the British
Council.
Rome : Fratelli Palombi, 1985.
234 p. : ill., ports. ; 28 cm.
ISBN: 8876215638
Edited by Brian Reade, Susan Lambert and H. Lee Bimm. Introduction by Brian Reade.
Prefaces by Antonio Gullotti, Lord Bridges, Eraldo Gaudioso, Roy Strong, D.J. Sharp.
— Bibliography: p. 230–234.
EXHIBITION: VX.1985.XXX.002

VR.1985.004   *Gianni Versace at the Victoria and Albert Museum.*
[London : Gianni Versace, 1985.]
53 p. : ill. (some col.) ; 29 cm.
Cover title. — Text in English and Italian. — Published to accompany a study day at the
V&A. — Unseen. Record from OCLC and local information.

VR.1985.005   *The good design guide : 100 best ever products /* text by Stephen
Bayley ; design by Stafford Cliff.
[London] : Conran Foundation, 1985.
102 p. : ill. ; 21 cm.
ISBN: 0946410097
EXHIBITION: VX.1985.BHO.001

VR.1985.006   *Heal's catalogues, 1850–1950, in the Victoria and Albert Museum*
Archive of Art and Design.
Haslemere : Emmett Microform, 1985.
95 microfiches.
(Design history series).
ISBN: 0907696236

VR.1985.007   *Incunabula in the National Art Library.*
[London : Incunabula Short Title Catalogue, 1985.]
31, 8 leaves ; 31 cm.

Spine title. — Consists of annotated imprints from the Incunabula Short Title Catalogue database, bound with: Supplementary list of abbreviations.

VR.1985.008   *Liberty's catalogues 1881–1949 : fashion, design, furnishings.*
London : Mindata, 1985.
142 microfiches.
Catalogues held in the National Art Library.

VR.1985.009   *Masterworks of contemporary American jewelry : sources and concepts.*
[London : American Festival, 1985.]
48 p. : ill. (some col.) ; 22 cm.
Preface by Graham Hughes. Foreword by Oppi Untracht. Introduction by Toni Lesser Wolf. — Selected bibliography: p. 12.
EXHIBITION: VX.1985.010

VR.1985.010   *National characteristics in design.*
London : Boilerhouse Project, 1985.
[34] p. : ill. ; 43 cm.
ISBN: 0946410100
EXHIBITION: VX.1985.BHO.003

VR.1985.011   *Netsuke : Japanese miniature carvings in the Victoria and Albert Museum.*
Haslemere : Emmett Microform, 1985.
7 microfiches + 25 p.
(Oriental art & design series ; v. 1).
ISBN: 0907696090

VR.1985.012   *The Russian Ballet of Serge Diaghilev : the William Beaumont Morris scrapbooks in the Theatre Museum, London.*
Haslemere : Emmett Microform, 1985.
28 microfiches + 1 v.
(Theatre and music series ; no. 3)
ISBN: 0907696228
Index by Caroline Ramsden.

VR.1985.013   *Theatre set designs in the Victoria and Albert Museum.*
Haslemere : Emmett Microform, 1985.
25 microfiches + 1 v. (40 p. ; 23 cm.).
ISBN: 0907696198
From the collection of Prints, Drawings and Paintings.

VR.1985.014   *Yurŏp-ui chŏnt'ong kong ye wa int'eriō : Pikt'oria Wangsil Pangmulgwan = Victoria and Albert Museum.*
Seoul : Han'guk Ilbo, 1985.
178 p. : ill. (some col.) map, port. ; 31 cm.
(Segye-u i Pangmulgwan ; 6)
Cover title: Wonders of the world's museums. — In Korean. — In slip-case. — Originally published in Japanese: VR.1979.002.

1986

VR.1986.001   *14:24 : British youth culture.*
London : Conran Foundation, 1986.
[50] p. : ill. (some col.), facsims., ports. ; 30 cm.
ISBN: 0946410135
Text by Helen Rees. — Bibliography: p. 48.
EXHIBITION: VX.1986.BHO.003

VR.1986.002   *Alexander and John Robert Cozens : the poetry of landscape /*
Kim Sloan.
New Haven : Published in association with the Art Gallery of Ontario
by Yale University Press, 1986.
xii, 180 p. : ill. (some col.) ; 28 cm.
ISBN: 0300038267; 0300038550 (pbk.)
Bibliography: p. 167–177. — Erratum slip inserted.
EXHIBITION: VX.1986.021

VR.1986.003   *American dolls 1840–1985 : the Lawrence Scripps Wilkinson*
collection.
[s.l.] : Mattel UK Ltd., on behalf of the Collection, [1986?].
63 p. : ill. (some col.) ; 25 cm.
ISBN: 1851770674
Cover title. — Foreword / James Ayres. Introduction by Caroline G. Goodfellow.
EXHIBITION: VX.1986.BGM.001

VR.1986.004   *The art periodicals collection at the V&A Museum, 1750–1920.*
Part 1, Ackermann's Repository of art and other periodicals.
London : World Microfilms, [1986].
45 microfilms.
Periodicals held in the National Art Library.

VR.1986.005   *The* Blitz *designer collection : in aid of the Prince's Trust.*
[London : *Blitz* Magazine, 1986.]
[40] p. : ill. ; 30 cm. + 1 sheet, folded.
Programme for fashion gala pasted on to p. [37].
EXHIBITION: VX.1986.012

VR.1986.006   *Coke! : Coca-cola 1886–1986 : designing a megabrand /* Stephen
Bayley.
London : Boilerhouse Project, 1986.
96 p. : ill. (some col.), facsims., ports. ; 21 cm.
ISBN: 0946410127
Bibliography: p. 94–95.
EXHIBITION: VX.1986.BHO.001

VR.1986.007   *Eye for industry : Royal Designers for Industry 1936–1986 /* Fiona
MacCarthy and Patrick Nuttgens.
London : Lund Humphries in association with the Royal Society of
Arts, 1986.
[96] p. : ill. ; 28 cm.

ISBN: 0853315140
Acknowledgments / Kenneth Grange. Introduction / Christopher Lucas. Foreword /
Lord Reilly. The V&A and design / Roy Strong. The influence of science and art upon
productive industry / Simon Tait and Andrew Nahum. The renaissance in British design
/ Patrick Nuttgens. Demi-gods or boffins? the designer's image, 1936 to 1986 / Fiona
MacCarthy. — Includes bibliography and index of RDIs.
EXHIBITION: VX.1986.024

VR.1986.008   *Eye for industry : Royal Designers for Industry 1936–86 : an
               exhibition organised for Industry Year by the Royal Society of Arts in
               association with the Victoria and Albert Museum . . . .*
               [London : The Society, 1986.]
               [6] p. ; 23 x 23 cm.
               Caption title on p. [1].
               EXHIBITION: VX.1986.024

VR.1986.009   *New design for old : an exhibition of new products designed to help
               older people stay independent at home, sponsored by the Helen
               Hamlyn Foundation and the Conran Foundation : Boilerhouse,
               Victoria and Albert Museum, 29th May to 3rd July 1986.*
               [London : The Foundations?], 1986.
               120 p. : ill., ports. ; 21 cm.
               Introduction / Helen Hamlyn. Preface by Eric Midwinter. — Includes report on a
               competition for students linked to the exhibition. — Bibliography: p. 113–115.
               EXHIBITION: VX.1986.BHO.002

VR.1986.010   *Playbills and programmes from London theatres, 1801–1900, in the
               Theatre Museum, London.*
               Cambridge : Chadwyck-Healey, 1983–1986.
               2,997 microfiches.

VR.1986.011   *Summary catalogue of textile designs 1840–1985 in the Victoria and
               Albert Museum.*
               Haslemere, Surrey : Emmett, 1986.
               100 p. ; 21 cm.
               ISBN: 0907696083
               Preface by John Murdoch and Susan Lambert. — Indexes of manufacturers and
               Museum numbers. — Accompanies VR.1986.012.

VR.1986.012   *Textile designs 1840–1985 in the Victoria and Albert Museum.*
               Haslemere : Emmett Microform, 1986.
               25 microfiches.
               (Textiles, wallpapers, surface pattern design series ; no. 3)
               ISBN: 0907696074

VR.1986.013   *Trade catalogues in the Victoria & Albert Museum.*
               London : Mindata, 1986.
               322 microfiches.
               Catalogues in the National Art Library.

VR.1986.014   *Wake up and dream! : costume design for Broadway musicals
               1900–1925, from the Theatre Collection of the Austrian National
               Library = Kostümentwürfe zu Broadway-Musicals 1900–1925 in der
               Theatersammlung des Österreichischen Nationalbibliothek* / by
               Stefanie Munsing Winkelbauer.

Wien : Hermann Bahlhaus, 1986.
60 p. , [36] p. of plates : ill. ; 21 cm.
(Biblos-Schiften ; 137), (Cortina ; 7)
ISBN: 3205063058
Foreword / Oskar Pausch. — In English and German. — Bibliography: p. 60.
EXHIBITION: VX.1988.THM.004

1987

VR.1987.001   *Art & design in Europe and America 1800–1900* / introduction by
Simon Jervis.
London : Herbert Press, 1987.
224 p. : ill. (some col.), ports. ; 25 cm.
ISBN: 0906969735; 0906969751 (pbk.)
Foreword / Simon Jervis. — Designer: Pauline Harrison. — Bibliography: p. 220–221.
Index. — "the gallery's official handbook"–back cover.

VR.1987.002   *The art periodicals collection at the V&A Museum, 1750–1920. Part
2, The artist, 1880–1902,* L'Art *and* Courrier de l'art, *1875–1907, and
other periodicals.*
London : World Microfilms, [1986–1987?].
56 microfilms.
Periodicals held in the National Art Library.

VR.1987.003   *Barbara Johnson's album of fashions and fabrics* / edited by Natalie
Rothstein.
London : Thames and Hudson, 1987.
208 p. : ill. (some col.), facsims., ports. ; 39 cm.
ISBN: 0500014191
Foreword / Sir Roy Strong. Chapters by Natalie Rothstein, Madeleine Ginsburg, Anne
Buck, Jean Hamilton, Avril Hart, James Fowler. — Photographic reproduction of the
album. Includes: The clothing accounts of George Thomson, 1738–48. — Glossary.
Index.

VR.1987.004   Blitz *exposure! : young British photographers, 1980–1987.*
London : Ebury Press, 1987.
[143] p. : chiefly ports. ; 31 cm.
ISBN: 0852236905
"Photographs from *Blitz* magazine"–cover. — Compiled by Simon Tesler & Jeremy
Leslie. — Unseen; record from OCLC.
EXHIBITION: VX.1987.008

VR.1987.005   *English artists [sic] paper : Renaissance to Regency* / John Krill.
London : Trefoil, 1987.
159 p. : ill. (some col.) ; 25 cm.
ISBN: 0862940931
Preface / John Murdoch. — Bibliography: p. 156–159. Index.
EXHIBITION: VX.1987.006

VR.1987.006   *The exhibition of British caricature from Hogarth to Hockney : 24
October–13 December 1987 : the National Museum of Western Art,
Tokyo.*
Tokyo : Kokuritsu Seiyō Bijutsukan, 1987.

145 p. : ill. (some col.), ports ; 27 cm.

Japanese title: Vikutoria & Arubāto Bijutsukan shozō Igirisu no karikachua. — Text mainly in Japanese with introduction and captions in English.

EXHIBITION: VX.1987.XXX.002

VR.1987.007   *The Forster and Dyce collections from the National Art Library at the Victoria and Albert Museum.*
Brighton : Harvester Microform, 1987.
60 microfilm reels.
(Britain's literary heritage)
Manuscripts, 16th–19th centuries.

VR.1987.008   *The Forster and Dyce collections from the National Art Library at the Victoria and Albert Museum, London : an inventory to . . . the Harvester microform collection.*
Brighton : Harvester, 1987.
2 v. (288, 318 p.) ; 21 cm.
(Britain's literary heritage)
ISBN: 0862570549; 0862570646
[1] Part one, 16th & 17th century manuscripts. Part two, 18th century manuscripts. — [2] Parts three and four, Nineteenth century manuscripts. — Publisher's note / William Pidduck. — Accompanies VR.1987.007.

VR.1987.009   *A house full of horrors : with the usual accompaniments* / devised and presented by third-year students of art history . . . .
[Colchester : University of Essex, 1987.]
1 sheet, folded : ill. ; 21 cm.
"Comprising a reconstruction of Examples of false principles of decoration, as originally displayed in a room at Marlborough House, London, being the Ante-chamber to the Museum of Ornamental Manufactures . . . ." — Produced to accompany a display at the University of Essex, 16–27 March 1987.

VR.1987.010   *The image multiplied : five centuries of printed reproductions of paintings and drawings* / Susan Lambert.
London : Trefoil, 1987.
216 p. : ill. (some col.) ; 24 cm.
ISBN: 0862940966
Foreword / John Murdoch. — Bibliography: p. 207–210. Index.
EXHIBITION: VX.1987.017

VR.1987.011   *Local and traditional costumes in the Victoria and Albert Museum.*
[Haslemere] : Emmett Microform, 1987.
51 microfiches + 41 p.
(Fashion, costume and uniforms series ; no. 5)
ISBN: 0907696252
Includes geographical and artist indexes.

VR.1987.012   *Painters and the Derby china works* / John Murdoch, John Twitchett.
London : Trefoil, 1987.
160 p. : ill. (some col.) ; 27 cm.
ISBN: 0862940923
Foreword / Hugh Gibson. Includes: The contribution of Chelsea, 1770–84 / J.V.G. Mallet. — Bibliography: p. 24.
EXHIBITION: VX.1987.004

VR.1987.013   *A practical guide to canvas work from the Victoria and Albert*
               Museum / introduction by Santina Levey ; edited by Linda Parry ;
               technical instructions by Valerie Jackson ; illustrations by
               Jil Shipley.
               London : Unwin Hyman, 1987.
               72 p. : ill. (some col.) ; 20 cm.
               ISBN: 0044400519

VR.1987.014   *A practical guide to patchwork from the Victoria and Albert Museum*
               / edited by Linda Parry ; technical instructions by Valerie Jackson ;
               illustrations by Jil Shipley ; technical adviser: Alyson Morris.
               London : Unwin Hyman, 1987.
               72 p. : ill. (some col.) ; 20 cm.
               ISBN: 0044400500

VR.1987.015   *Salvatore Ferragamo : the art of the shoe, 1927–1960.*
               Florence : Centro Di, 1987.
               263 p. : ill. (chiefly col.) ; 23 cm.
               ISBN 8870381366
               Foreword / Roy Strong. Preface / Kirsten Aschengreen Piacenti. Texts by Valerie
               Mendes, Stefania Ricci, and Deborah Hodges. — Bibliography: p. 259–263. — Lettered
               on cover: Victoria & Albert Museum. — Available in slip-case with Shoemaker of
               dreams: the autobiography of Salvatore Ferragamo.
               EXHIBITION: VX.1987.016

VR.1987.016   *The Theatre Museum, Victoria and Albert Museum* / compiled
               by Alexander Schouvaloff ; preface and introduction by Catherine
               Haill.
               London ; New York : Scala ; Distributed in the U.S.A. by Harper &
               Row, 1987.
               144 p. : ill. (some col.), ports (some col.) ; 29 cm.
               ISBN: 187024804X; 1870248031 (pbk.)
               Index.

VR.1987.017   *"The unknown Beatrix Potter" : a special exhibition of drawings*
               and watercolours from the Linder Bequest, at Beningbrough Hall nr.
               York : June 6th to July 19th, 1987 . . . .
               [London] : National Trust, [1987].
               [6] p. ; 21 cm.
               Cover title. At foot of cover: From the collection of the National Art Library by
               courtesy of the Victoria and Albert Museum, London . . . — Introduction by Janet
               Skidmore and Anne Stevenson Hobbs. — Text on inside covers and on back cover.
               EXHIBITION: VX.1987.XXX.001

1988

VR.1988.001   *The art periodicals collection at the V&A Museum, 1750–1920.* Part
               3, "Art and decoration".
               London : World Microfilms, [1988?].
               28 microfilms.
               Periodicals held in the National Art Library.

VR.1988.002   *Artists in National Parks : an exhibition of art celebrating the national parks of England and Wales.*
London : Dept. of the Environment : Conoco (U.K.) Ltd., [1988?].
24 p. : ill. (chiefly col.), ports. ; 30 cm.
Cover title.
EXHIBITION: vx.1988.008

VR.1988.003   *Avant première : contemporary French furniture* / edited by Garth Hall, Margo Rouard Snowman.
London : Editions Eprouvé, 1988.
95 p. : ill.(some col.), facsims, plans, ports ; 30 cm.
ISBN: 1871649005
Cover title. — Preface / Elizabeth Esteve Coll, Dominique Bozo. Introduction / Garth Hall. The role of VIA / Jean Claude Maugirard. The state as client / Margo Rouard Snowman. French furniture in the eighties / Sophie Anargyros. Designers: Marie Christine Dorner; Elizabeth Garouste, Mattia Bonetti; Pascal Mourgue; Jean Nouvel; Ronald Cecil Sportes; Philippe Starck; Martin Szekely; Jean Michel Wilmotte. — Bibliography: p. 92. — Parallel text in English and French.
EXHIBITION: vx.1988.016

VR.1988.004   *Book Works at the V&A : Book Works presents an exhibition of some recent artists' books at the National Art Library, Victoria and Albert Museum, 16 February–17 April 1988.*
[London] : Book Works, 1988.
[18] p. ; 15 cm.
EXHIBITION: vx.1988.002

VR.1988.005   *British photography : towards a bigger picture* / essays by Mark Haworth-Booth . . .[et al.] ; photographs by Keith Arnatt . . .[et al.].
New York : Aperture Foundation, 1988.
71 p. : ill. (some col.), ports. ; 30 cm.
ISBN: 0893813419
Where we've come from: aspects of postwar British photography / by Mark Haworth-Booth. Landscape and the fall / by Chris Titterington. Thatcher's Britain / the editors. Between frames / by Susan Butler. Other Britains, other Britons / by Gilane Tawadros. Through the looking glass, darkly / by Rosetta Brooks. Romances of decay, elegies for the future / by David Mellor. The B movie phenomenon: British cinema today / by Michael O'Pray.
EXHIBITION: vx.1988.023

VR.1988.006   *Fashion and surrealism* / Richard Martin.
London : Thames and Hudson, 1988.
234 p. : ill. (some col.) ; 32 cm.
ISBN: 0500014442
Includes index. — Originally published: New York : Rizzoli, 1987.
EXHIBITION: vx.1988.010

VR.1988.007   *Forwarding the book in California : an exhibition of West Coast letterpress printers and edition bookbinders sponsored by the Pacific Center for the Book Arts, San Francisco, organized by Linda L. Brownrigg : the National Art Library, the V&A, 5 July–4 September 1988.*
Rhonert Park, [CA] : Vintner's Valley Press, 1988.
1 sheet, folded ; 29 x 61 cm. folded to 29 x 8 cm.
EXHIBITION: vx.1988.011

VR.1988.008   *Gilbert Bayes and the Doulton House frieze.*
                [Stoke on Trent?] : Royal Doulton, [1988?].
                1 sheet ([4] p.) : col. ill. ; 30 cm.
                Published on the occasion of the restoration of the frieze at the V&A.

VR.1988.009   *The graphic language of Neville Brody* / text and captions by Jan
                Wozencroft.
                London : Thames and Hudson, 1988.
                160 p. : chiefly ill. (some col.) ; 31 cm.
                ISBN: 0500274967
                One issue, in white wrappers, printed in Japan, another in pale mauve wrappers, printed
                in Spain. — Bibliography: p. 159.
                EXHIBITION: VX.1988.006

VR.1988.010   *Hizō Ukiyoe taikan, 4. Vikutoria Arubāto Hakubutsukan, I.*
                Tōkyō : Kōdansha, 1988.
                272 p. (some folded) : ill. (some col.) ; 38 cm.
                ISBN: 4061912844
                Added title on box: Ukiyo-e masterpieces in European collections. — Volume editor
                Narazaki Muneshige. Includes text on the Museum's collection of Ukiyo-e by Rupert
                Faulkner. — "Published . . . in co-operation with the Victoria and Albert Museum." —
                In Japanese; captions also in English. — Index of artists. — In silk-covered box.
                Copy note: Accompanied by extra plate, in envelope.

VR.1988.011   *Kaffe Fassett at the V & A : knitting and needlepoint* / photography
                by Steve Lovi.
                London : Century, 1988.
                160 p. : ill. ; 32 cm.
                ISBN: 0712622365
                Examples of work inspired by objects in the V&A. — Index.
                EXHIBITION: VX.1988.018

VR.1988.012   *Koalas, kangaroos and kookaburras : 200 Australian children's book
                illustrations, 1857–1988* / by Robert Holden.
                [Sydney? : s.n., 1988?]
                87 p. : ill. (chiefly col.) ; 21 x 30 cm.
                EXHIBITION: VX.1988.BGM.002

VR.1988.013   *The papers of David Garrick. Part one, Correspondence from the
                Forster collection at the National Art Library, Victoria and Albert
                Museum.*
                London : Research Publications, 1988.
                10 microfilm reels + xi, 169 p.
                (Actors and managers of the English and American stage. Series 2)
                (Britain's literary heritage)
                Includes inventory.

VR.1988.014   *Studies in design & technology* / R.C.A.-V.& A. 1987.
                London : Futures Publications, 1988.
                xxii, 372 p. : ill. ; 21 cm.
                (Working papers / Royal College of Art ; 1)
                ISBN: 1871131006
                Preface / Elizabeth Esteve-Coll. Foreword / Charles Saumarez Smith. Essays: Linoleum:
                a unique floorcovering / Clive Edwards. Warming buildings by hot water : technology

and the home interior, 1880–1910 / Guy Julier. Coin-freed person weighing machines from 1884–1940 / Claudia Kinmonth. The impact of design & manufacture on the appearance of British pillar boxes, 1852–1880 / Caroline Pullee. Drawloom or Jacquard technology in the silk industry c.1730–1830 / Carolyn Sargentson. The production and perception of chromolithographic books in the mid-nineteenth century / Helen Saxbee. Bricks: machine-made decoration / Johanne Vincent. Explorations in the theory and practice of wood engraving in the nineteenth century / Alyson Webb. The role of technology in the function and appearance of waterpoof garments in the nineteenth century / Rhiannon Williams. — Includes bibliographies. Index.

VR.1988.015   *Sun prints* / Linda McCartney ; foreword by Linda McCartney ; introduction by Robert Lassam.
London : Barrie & Jenkins, 1988.
96 p. : chiefly ill., ports. ; 24 cm.
ISBN: 0712621415
Bibliography: p. 96.
EXHIBITION: vx.1988.017

VR.1988.016   *Textiles of the arts and crafts movement* / Linda Parry.
London : Thames and Hudson, 1988.
160 p. : ill. (some col.) ; 26 cm.
ISBN: 0500274975
Bibliography: p. 156.
EXHIBITION: vx.1988.009

VR.1988.017   *A Yarmouth holiday : photographs by Paul Martin* / Mark Haworth-Booth.
London : Nishen, [1988?].
32 p. : chiefly ill ; 25 cm.
(The photo-library ; 4)
ISBN: 1853781045
"The pictures in this booklet are from the Victoria and Albert collection"–p. 32.

1989

VR.1989.001   *Andy Warhol : the Factory years* / Nat Finkelstein.
London : Sidgwick & Jackson, 1989.
[128] p. : ill., ports. ; 28 cm.
ISBN: 0283998717
EXHIBITION: vx.1989.017

VR.1989.002   *Architectural and design history. Part 1, The drawings and manuscripts of A.W.N. Pugin from the Victoria and Albert Museum, London.*
Reading : Research Publications, 1989.
9 microfilm reels.

VR.1989.003   *"Art publishing & art publics today" : transcript of a one-day conference held in the Lecture Theatre of the Victoria and Albert Museum on Saturday 13th May 1989.*
[London : The Conference Organisers?, 1989.]
29 leaves ; 30 cm.

Addendum [VR.1988.018] *The Elton John collection.* — London : Sotheby's, 1988. — 4. v. : ill. (some col.); 27 cm. — Vol. 1, Stage costume and memorabilia. Vol. 2, Art nouveau and art deco. Vol. 4, Diverse collections. — Available as boxed set. Catalogues of sales, 6–9 Sept. 1988. — EXHIBITION: vx.1988.012

Cover title. At head of title: The National Art Library at the Victoria and Albert
Museum and Wimbledon School of Art. — Chairmen: Frank Whitford, Colin Painter.
Speakers: Elizabeth Esteve-Coll, Tim Evans, Ian Breakwell, John A. Walker, Peter
Fuller, Anna Somers Cocks, Marina Vaizey. — Typescript.

VR.1989.004   *Australian fashion : the contemporary art : Twentieth Century
Gallery, Victoria & Albert Museum, London, 7 June–13 August 1989;
and Powerhouse Museum of Applied Arts and Sciences, Sydney, 4
October 1989–24 February 1990.*
Sydney : Powerhouse Museum, 1989.
64 p. : ill. (some col.) ; 29 cm.
ISBN: 1863170022
Prefaces by Marjorie Johnson, Terence Measham, June McCallum, Elizabeth Esteve-
Coll. Text by Jane de Teliga.
EXHIBITION: VX.1989.009

VR.1989.005   *British posters in the Victoria and Albert Museum.*
[Haslemere] : Emmett (with G.K. Hall, in U.S.A.), 1989.
47 microfiches + 1 v. (22 p. ; 23 cm.).
ISBN: 1869934164
Editor, Anne Emmett; photographer, David Gee.

VR.1989.006   *Catalogue [: artist's books / by Ken Campbell].*
[Oxford? : Ken Campbell?, 1989?]
[11] leaves ; 37 cm.
Cover title.
EXHIBITION: VX.1989.001

VR.1989.007   *Contemporary Danish book art : Victoria & Albert Museum,
National Art Library : Helge Ernst, illustrator, Poul Kristensen,
printer, Ole Olsen, bookbinder* / exhibition catalogue by Poul Steen
Larsen. 2nd ed.
Herning : Printed by Poul Kristensen, 1989.
45 p. : ill. (some col.) ; 30 cm.
ISBN: 8774681885; 8774682210
Foreword / Ole Vig Jensen. — Includes bibliographic references. — Text first published
1986.
EXHIBITION: VX.1989.022

VR.1989.008   *The designs of William De Morgan : a catalogue* / by Martin
Greenwood.
Ilminster : Richard Dennis and William E. Wiltshire III, 1989.
256 p. : ill. (some col.), 1 port. ; 31 cm.
ISBN: 0903685248
Bibliography: p. 20. — "The main part of the catalogue represents the Victoria &
Albert Museum's collection"–p. 21.
EXHIBITION: VX.1989.004

VR.1989.009   *Discovering 19th century fashion : a look at the changes in fashion
through the Victoria & Albert Museum's dress collection* / Alexandra
Buxton.
Cambridge : Hobsons, 1989.
48 p. : ill. (some col.) ; 30 cm.
ISBN: 185324161X
Cover title.

VR.1989.010   *The first year at school : an exhibition of photographs by Markéta
                 Luskačová : 1 February to 5 March 1989 at Bethnal Green Museum
                 of Childhood.*
                 London : Thames Television, 1989.
                 1 sheet, folded ([17] p.) : 1 ill. ; 21 cm.
                 "Produced in conjunction with Citizen 2000, the Thames Television series for
                 Channel 4."
                 EXHIBITION: VX.1989.BGM.001

VR.1989.011   *The Forster and Dyce collections from the National Art Library at the
                 Victoria and Albert Museum. Part five, The Charles Dickens
                 manuscripts.*
                 Reading : Research Publications, 1989.
                 16 microfilm reels + 1 v. (40 p. ; 21 cm.).
                 (Britain's literary heritage)
                 ISBN: 0862570956
                 Microfilm bears date: 1988. — In separate vol.: The Forster and Dyce collections from
                 the National Art Library at the Victoria and Albert Museum : an inventory to . . . the
                 Harvester microform collection. — Publisher's note / Caroline Byard-Jones.

VR.1989.012   *French dressing, 1789–1830.*
                 London : Commercial and Cultural Investments, [1989].
                 [20] p. : ill. ; 22 cm.
                 Cover title.
                 EXHIBITION: VX.1989.THM.003

VR.1989.013   *Hizō Ukiyoe taikan, 5. Vikutoria Arubāto Hakubutsukan, II.*
                 Tōkyō : Kōdansha, 1989.
                 289 p. (some folded) : ill. (some col.) ; 38 cm.
                 ISBN: 4061912852
                 Added title on box: Ukiyo-e masterpieces in European collections. — Volume editor
                 Narazaki Muneshige. — Includes text on the Museum's collection of the work of
                 Kuniyoshi by B.W. Robinson. — "Published . . . in co-operation with the Victoria and
                 Albert Museum." — In Japanese; captions also in English. — Index of artists. — In silk-
                 covered box.

VR.1989.014   *Like a one-eyed cat : photographs by Lee Friedlander, 1956–1987 /*
                 text by Rod Slemmons.
                 New York : H.N. Abrams in association with the Seattle Art Museum,
                 1989.
                 119 p. : chiefly ill., ports. ; 30 x 31 cm.
                 ISBN: 0810912740; 0932216323 (Seattle Art Museum, pbk.)
                 Bibliography: p. 119.
                 EXHIBITION: VX.1991.008

VR.1989.015   *The nude : a new perspective* / Gill Saunders.
                 London : Herbert Press, 1989.
                 144 p. : ill. (some col.) ; 24 cm.
                 ISBN: 1871569060; 0906969980 (pbk.)
                 Includes bibliography and index.
                 EXHIBITION: VX.1989.008

VR.1989.016   *Timothy C. Ely : an exhibition of unique and limited edition artist's
                 books : August 16–October 15, 1989, the National Art Library,
                 Victoria & Albert Museum, South Kensington, London.*

[United States : The Artist, 1989.]
1 sheet, folded (p.) : ill., some col. ; 25 cm.
Foreword by Philip Smith.
EXHIBITION: VX.1989.015

VR.1989.017   *Ukiyo-e masterpieces in European collections. 4, Victoria and Albert
               Museum, I /* supervised by Muneshige Narazaki.
               Tōkyō : Kōdansha, 1989.
               272 p., (some folded) : ill. (some col.) ; 38 cm. + 10 p.
               ISBN: 0870118757; 0870118846 (set)
               With separate English supplement: Ukiyo-e in the Victoria and Albert Museum / Rupert
               Faulkner. Notes to the colour plates. — In slip case. — Originally published in Japanese:
               VR.1988.010.

VR.1989.018   *Ukiyo-e masterpieces in European collections. 5, Victoria and Albert
               Museum, II /* supervised by Muneshige Narazaki.
               Tōkyō : Kōdansha, 1989.
               289 p. (some folded) : ill. (some col.) ; 38 cm. + 10 p.
               ISBN: 0870118765; 0870118846 (set)
               With separate English supplement: Kuniyoshi at the Victoria and Albert Museum /
               B.W. Robinson. Notes to the colour plates. — In slip-case. — Originally published in
               Japanese: VR.1989.013.

VR.1989.019   *A vision of Britain : a personal view of architecture /* HRH the Prince
               of Wales.
               London : Doubleday, 1989.
               160 p. : ill. (some col.), port. ; 24 x 30 cm.
               ISBN: 0385 26903X
               Includes index.
               EXHIBITION: VX.1989.018

VR.1989.020   *William Morris and the arts and crafts movement : a source book /* by
               Linda Parry . . . with an essay on textiles of the American arts and
               crafts movement by Gillian Moss . . . .
               London : Studio Editions, 1989.
               22 p., 100 leaves of plates : col. ill. ; 34 cm.
               ISBN: 185170275X
               "Most of the . . . patterns illustrated . . . are taken from the collections of the Victoria
               and Albert Museum"–t.p. verso.

VR.1989.021   *William Morris : from the collections of: Victoria and Albert Museum,
               William Morris Gallery.*
               [Japan] : William Morris Catalogue Committee, [1989].
               188 p. : ill. (chiefly col.), ports. ; 28 cm.
               Includes: William Morris as a designer / Stephen Astley. William Morris : art, work and
               socialism / Norah C. Gillow. William Morris and his Company / Hiroyuki Suzuki. —
               Bibliography: p. 186–188. — In Japanese and English.
               EXHIBITION: VX.1989.XXX.001

1990

VR.1990.001   *Art and television : transcript of a one-day conference held at the*
Victoria and Albert Museum on Saturday 19 May 1990.
[Wimbledon : Wimbledon School of Art?, 1990.]
48 p. ; 30 cm.
Index page: The National Art Library at the V & A and Wimbledon School of Art
present Art and Communication Conference no. 2 . . . . — Contributions by Keith
Alexander, Mike Dibb, Elizabeth Esteve-Coll, Christopher Frayling, Tamara Krikorian,
Graham Murdock.

VR.1990.002   *The art periodicals collection at the V&A Museum, 1750–1920.* Part
4, Christian art I.
London : World Microfilms, [1990].
39 microfilm reels.
Periodicals held in the National Art Library.

VR.1990.003   *Collectif Génération : livres d'artistes.*
[Paris? : Gervais Jassaud?, 1990?]
[8] p. : ill. ; 30 cm.
Chiefly in English. — Texts by John Yau and (in French) Jacques Lepage.
EXHIBITION: VX.1990.008

VR.1990.004   *Domestic idylls : photographs by Lady Hawarden from the Victoria*
and Albert Museum.
[Malibu] : J. Paul Getty Museum, 1990.
1 sheet, folded ([7] p.) : ill. ; 23 cm.
Written by Virginia Dodier.
EXHIBITION: VX.1989.020

VR.1990.005   *Household choices* / edited by Charles Newton & Tim Putnam.
[London] : Futures Publications, 1990.
144 p. : ill., facsims. ; 30 cm.
ISBN: 1871131103
Includes: The breakfast table [photograph] / Edwin Smith. Foreword / John Murdoch.
Ideal home [photographs] / John Taylor. Places in transition : the impact of life events
on the experience of home / Judith and Andrew Sixsmith. Ideal homes : gender and
domestic architecture / Ruth Madigan and Moira Munro. The use of space and home
adaptations by home-based workers / Marjorie Bulos. Making changes / Mary Cooper,
with an introduction by Judith Alfrey. Appropriating the state on the council estate /
Daniel Miller. Variations in marital relations and the implications for women's
experience of the home / Adrian Franklin. Home lives / Kamina Walters, Blackfriars
Photography Project. Families and their technologies : two ethnographic portraits /
Roger Silverstone and David Morley. The empty cocktail cabinet : display in the mid-
century British domestic interior / Judy Attfield. Homemakers and design advice in the
postwar period / Christine Morley. Victimography : framing the homeless? / Syd Jeffers.
Making yourself at home : a study in discourse / Valerie M. Swales. Green ideology :
contruction and consumption in the home / Geoff Warren. First home : an account of
the household choices made by a newly-married couple / Richard Thorn. Documenting
domestic culture by ethnographic interview / Tom Wengraf. The Household choices
project in the museum context / Charles Newton and Tim Putnam. Northfield / Sara
Hinchcliffe. — Includes bibliographic references.
EXHIBITION: VX.1990.005

VR.1990.006   *Lady Hawarden : photographe victorien* / catalogue établi et rédigé
par Virginia Dodier ; traduit de l'anglais par Françoise Heilbrun.
Paris : Réunion des musées nationaux, 1990.

20 p. : ill. ; 26 cm.
(Les dossiers du Musée d'Orsay ; 37)
ISBN: 271182344X
Bibliography: p. 20.
EXHIBITION: vx.1989.020

VR.1990.007   *Masterpieces of painting from the Victoria and Albert Museum.*
[Japan] : Catalogue Committee, 1990.
153 p. : ill. (chiefly col.) ; 28 cm.
Japanese title page: Eikoku Kokuritsu Vikutoria & Arubāto Bijutsukan ten. — Message
/ Sir John Whitehead. [Foreword] / Elizabeth Esteve-Coll. Text by Lionel Lambourne.
EXHIBITION: vx.1990.xxx.003

VR.1990.008   *The Muslim world.*
Haslemere : Emmett, 1989–1990.
169 microfiches + 1 v. (61 p. ; 23 cm.).
ISBN: 1869934156
Prints and drawings by European artists of views of the Near East and North Africa,
from the Searight collection, in the Department of Prints, Drawings and Paintings.
Includes: Traditional costume, from the Department of Designs, Prints and Drawings
and the National Art Library. – Guide in separate vol.

VR.1990.009   *Pierre Cardin : past, present, future* / with an introductory essay by
Valerie Mendes.
London : D. Nishen, 1990.
191 p. : chiefly ill. (some col.), ports. ; 27 cm.
ISBN: 1853780499; 1853780502 (pbk.)
EXHIBITION: vx.1990.024

VR.1990.010   *The poetry of earth : englische Aquarelle der Romantik, 1770–1850 :
Leihgaben des Victoria and Albert Museum London.*
[Berlin] : Staatliche Museen : Nationalgalerie, 1990.
[20] p. : ill., maps ; 30 cm.
Katalogredaktion, Birgit Verwiebe. — Includes bibliographic references. — Unseen.
Record from OCLC.
EXHIBITION: vx.1990.xxx.005

VR.1990.011   *Une saison en enfer* / by Nicholas Rea ; inspired by the poem by
Arthur Rimbaud.
[London] : Nicholas Rea and David Graves, 1990.
[26] leaves : col. ill. ; 57 cm.
Artist's book in an edition of 10 similar but unique copies.
EXHIBITION: vx.1991.004

VR.1990.012   *Silk designs of the eighteenth century in the collection of the Victoria
and Albert Museum, London : with a complete catalogue* / Natalie
Rothstein.
London : Thames and Hudson, 1990.
351 p. : ill. (some col). ; 35 cm.
ISBN: 0500235899
Bibliography: p. 345. Index.

VR.1990.013   *Summary catalogue of British posters to 1988 in the Victoria & Albert
Museum in the Department of Designs, Prints & Drawings.*
Haslemere : Emmett, 1990.

xiii, 129 p. ; 30 cm.
ISBN: 1869934121
Cover title. — Prepared by Margaret Timmers.

VR.1990.014   *Theatre on paper* / Alexander Schouvaloff.
New York : Drawing Center, 1990.
248 p. : ill. (some col.) ; 29 cm.
ISBN: 0856673730
Bibliography: p. 236–239. Indexes.
EXHIBITION: VX.1990.XXX.001

VR.1990.015   *William Morris, designer : designs, prints and drawings by William Morris, his friends and associates from the collections of the Victoria and Albert Museum.*
Newport, Gwent : Newport Museum and Art Gallery, 1990.
1 sheet, folded ([5] p.) : ill. (1 col.), port. ; 14 cm. + 1 sheet, folded ([2] p.)
Note by Sandra Jackaman. Catalogue written by Stephen Astley. — List of works on separate sheet.
EXHIBITION: VX.1989.XXX.006

VR.1990.016   *William Morris : designs, prints and drawings by Morris, his friends and associates : March 31–June 10 1990, Bodelwyddan Castle.*
[Clwyd : Bodelwyddan Castle, 1990.]
1 sheet, folded : ill. (1 col.), port. ; 30 x 42 cm. folded to 30 x 14 cm.
EXHIBITION: VX.1990.XXX.001

1991

VR.1991.001   *50 years of the National Buildings Record, 1941–1991* / with an introduction by Sir John Summerson.
[London] : Trigon in conjunction with the Royal Commission on the Historical Monuments of England, 1991.
iv, 68 p. : ill. ; 26 cm.
ISBN: 0904929272; 0904929280 (pbk.)
Foreword / Tom Hassall. — Index.
EXHIBITION: VX.1991.006

VR.1991.002   *The antique collector. Vol. 63, no. 1, December 1991/January 1992.*
[London] : Guillaume Collis, 1991.
116 p. : ill. (some col.) ; 28 cm.
Issue dedicated mainly to the V&A. — Guest editor: Elizabeth Esteve-Coll.
Includes: Portrait of a populist : Elizabeth Esteve-Coll, Director of the Victoria & Albert Museum / by Brett Gorvy. Museums and cultural reform : the educational rôle of museums / by Elizabeth Esteve-Coll. Gilding the lily : the new Ornament Gallery at the V&A : the language of decoration / by Michael Snodin. Simply inspired : the influence of the V&A collection upon artists and craftspeople / by Susan Morris. Virtue by design : the use of display to enhance museum exhibits / by Robin Cole-Hamilton. Hands on! : teaching today's craftspeople / by Mike Hughes. The obligation to collect : the method of acquisition : the Metalwork Department at the V&A / by Philippa Glanville. — Includes bibliographic references.

VR.1991.003   *Appearances : fashion photography since 1945* / Martin Harrison.
London : Cape, 1991.

312 p. : ill. (some col.) ; 32 cm.
ISBN: 0224030671; 022403068X
Includes bibliographic references.
EXHIBITION: VX.1991.001

VR.1991.004   *The art of selling songs : graphics for the music business, 1690–1990 /*
Kevin Edge.
London : Futures Publications, 1991.
152 p. : ill. (some col.), facsims. ; 30 cm.
ISBN: 1871131030
Bibliography: p. 143–147. Index.
EXHIBITION: VX.1991.002

VR.1991.005   *Betel cutters : from the Samuel Eilenberg collection* / Henry
Brownrigg.
Stuttgart ; London : Hansjörg Mayer, 1991.
135 p. : ill. (some col.), maps ; 23 x 25 cm.
Bibliography: p. 135.
EXHIBITION: VX.1991.019

VR.1991.006   *The box of delights : children's book illustrations by twenty-one
British artists.*
Newport, Gwent : Newport Museum and Art Gallery, 1991.
57 p. : ill., ports. ; 21 cm. + 1 sheet, folded.
Foreword / Sandra Jackaman. Texts by Quentin Blake, Ron van der Meer, Russell
Hoban, C. Walter Hodges. — List of works on separate sheet.
EXHIBITION: VX.1991.BGM.004

VR.1991.007   *Cartoons, comics and caricature : transcript of a one-day conference
held in the Lecture Theatre of the Victoria and Albert Museum on
Saturday 28 September 1991.*
[London : Wimbledon School of Art?, 1991.]
57 p. ; 30 cm.
At head of title: The National Art Library at the V & A and Wimbledon School of Art.
— Index page: Art and Communication Conference number three. — Chairman: Frank
Whitford. Speakers: Peter Blake, Nicholas Garland, Tom Gretton, Richard Reynolds,
Stephen White. Contributions by Mark Haworth-Booth, Oliver Watson, Rowan
Watson.

VR.1991.008   *Fornasetti : designer of dreams* / Patrick Mauriès ; with an essay by
Ettore Sottsass ; foreword by Christopher Wilk.
London : Thames and Hudson, 1991.
285 p. : ill. (some col.), ports. ; 31 cm.
ISBN: 0500092222
EXHIBITION: VX.1991.016

VR.1991.009   *Fyffe Christie, drawings of the school children.*
[London : Save the Children Fund], 1991.
[25] p. : chiefly ports. ; 30 cm.
Introduction by Clare Henry.
EXHIBITION: VX.1991.BGM.003

VR.1991.010   *Japan and China : sources of ceramic design : an exhibition held at the Percival David Foundation of Chinese Art in association with the Victoria and Albert Museum, 17th September 1991–31st January 1992* / R.E. Scott and R.F.J. Faulkner.
London : Percival David Foundation, School of Oriental and African Studies, [1991?].
[20] p. : ill., maps ; 30 cm.
Bibliography: p. [14].
EXHIBITION: VX.1991.XXX.001

VR.1991.011   *The Lichfield Cathedral silver commission.*
Lichfield : Dean and Chapter of Lichfield Cathedral, 1991.
48 p. : ill. (some col.), ports. ; 26 cm.
Foreword / John Harley Lang (Dean). — Marks.
EXHIBITION: VX.1991.020

VR.1991.012   *Visions of Japan.*
Tokyo : Japan Foundation, 1991.
1 case : col. ill. ; 31 cm.
"Given that the exhibition was hardly conventional, it seemed inappropriate to try to produce a catalogue that would document each of the exhibits. Instead a collection of essays, personal observations by Japanese and British writers, has been edited in such a way as to provide a series of layered introductions to Japan, its history and culture, with the volume itself representing another interpretation of Japanese society to be regarded as complementary to the exhibition"–p. v. — Catalogue design: Kijuro Yahagi.
EXHIBITION: VX.1991.015

VR.1991.013   *Visions of Japan.*
[Tokyo : Japan Foundation, 1991.]
1 sheet, folded ([7] p.) : ill. (some col.) ; 36 cm.
EXHIBITION: VX.1991.015

VR.1991.014   *Ziggurat : accordion fold books by Norman B. Colp : 4 December 1991, 15 March 1992, National Art Library, Victoria & Albert Museum.*
[New York] : Norman B. Colp, 1991.
[16] p. : ill., port. ; 11 cm.
Introductory text by Jan van der Wateren.
EXHIBITION: VX.1991.024

1992

VR.1992.001   *Anansi company : a collection of thirteen hand-made wire and card rod-puppets animated in colour and verse* / by Ronald King & Roy Fisher.
London : Circle Press, 1992.
1 portfolio ([16] leaves, folded) : col. ill. ; 40 cm.
ISBN: 0901380687
Artist's book. — Edition of 120 + 3 H.C. + 7 A.P.
EXHIBITION: VX.1993.002

VR.1992.002 *Art of India in the Victoria and Albert Museum.*
Haslemere : Emmett Publishing, 1992.
71 microfiches + 1 v. (221 p. ; 23 cm.)
ISBN: 1869934474 (microfiche); 1869934725 (catalogue)
Cover title: Art of India : paintings and drawings in the Victoria and Albert Museum. —
"The catalogue that accompanies this microfiche was written by curators of the V&A's
Indian and South-east Asian Collection: Rosemary Crill, John Gray [i.e. Guy], Graham
Parlett, Susan Strange [i.e. Stronge] and Deborah Swallow."–p. 3. — Errata slip loosely
inserted.

VR.1992.003 *Bijutsu to dezain no rekishi : Vikutoria & Arubāto Bijutsukan
korekushon = A V & A history of art and design : the Victoria &
Albert Museum collections.*
Osaka : NHK Kinki Media Plan, 1992.
208 p. : col. ill., 1 port. ; 30 cm.
Cover title. — Edited and written by Haruhiko Fujita. — In English and Japanese. —
Includes bibliographic references. — Published in connexion with a series of exhibitions
touring in Japan: VX.1992.XXX.001; VX.1993.XXX.001; VX.1994.XXX.001;
VX.1995.XXX.002; VX.1995.XXX.003.

VR.1992.004 *I codici Forster del Victoria and Albert Museum di Londra : Leonardo
da Vinci* / trascrizione diplomatica e critica di Augusto Marinoni.
Firenze : Giunti Barbèra, 1992.
3 v. : ill., facsims. ; 37 cm.
(Edizione nazionale dei manoscritti e dei disegni di Leonardo da Vinci)
"Sotto gli auspici della Commissione nazionale vinciana." — Each case contains a
facsimile volume, a text volume with critical texts and parallel paleographic
transcription, and a notarized colophon sheet attached to the last vol. — Limited ed. of
998 numbered copies. — Includes bibliographic references and index.

VR.1992.005 *Conservation of leathercraft and related objects : interim symposium
at the Victoria & Albert Museum, London, 24 & 25 June 1992* /
editors, Pieter Hallebeek, Marion Kite, Christopher Calnan.
[London : International Council of Museums Committee for
Conservation, 1992] (London : V&A Printing Section).
64 p. : ill. ; 30 cm.
At head of title: ICOM Committee for Conservation.

VR.1992.006 *Creativity and industry : Queensberry Hunt* / Susannah Walker.
London : Fourth Estate and Wordsearch Ltd. in conjunction with
Blueprint magazine, 1992.
112 p. : ill. (some col.) ; 21 cm.
(A *Blueprint* monograph)
ISBN: 1857020111
EXHIBITION: VX.1992.003

VR.1992.007 *Gates of mystery : the art of holy Russia* / edited by Roderick
Grierson.
Fort Worth, Tex. : InterCultura, [1992?].
336 p. : ill. (some col.) ; 28 cm.
ISBN: 0963537407
Preface / Evgeniia Petrova. Includes: Visions of the invisible: the dual nature of the icon /
Sergei Averintsev. The origins of Russia and its culture / Simon Franklin. The legacy of
beauty: liturgy, art and spirituality in Russia / John Meyendorff. Medieval Russian
painting and Byzantium / Olga Popova. The schools of medieval Russian painting /

Engelina Smirnova. The medieval collection of the State Russian Museum / Liudmila Likhacheva. The technique of old Russian painting / Dariia Maltseva. The history of embroidery technique / Liudmila Likhacheva. The icon, past present and future / Robin Cormack. — Bibliography: p. 328–329. Glossary. Index.
EXHIBITION: VX.1993.030

VR.1992.008   *Jewels of fantasy : costume jewelry of the 20th century* / edited by Deanna Farneti Cera ; with essays by Vivienne Becker, Nicoletta Bocca, Gerda Buxbaum, Deanna Farneti Cera, Melissa Gabardi ; technical section, Rinaldo Albanesi, Vera Maternova, Edward Schwaiger, Alfred M. Weisberg.
New York : Harry N. Abrams, 1992.
408 p. : ill. (chiefly col.) ; 29 cm.
ISBN: 0810931788
Original title: I gioielli della fantasia. Milano : Idea, 1991. — Preface / Daniel Swarovski. Includes: The new century and art nouveau, 1900–1915. The opulence of the poor look: Austria and Germany, 1900–1950. Flights of fancy: the frivolous years, France 1920–1939. The luxury of freedom, the freedom of luxury: the United States, 1935–1968. Bijoux de couture: France 1927–1968. From the artisan's workshop to the International Style: Italy, 1945–1970. The return of the ornament: 1965–present. The history of the manufacture of glass stones and costume jewelry in Bohemia. The history of the production of ornamental jewels in Tyrol. The prominence of Providence, Rhode Island, and the contribution of electroplating. — Bibliography: p. 401–403. Glossary. Index.
EXHIBITION: VX.1992.006

VR.1992.009   *Sporting glory : an exhibition of national trophies at the Victoria and Albert Museum : education booklet.*
London : Issued by the Sporting Glory Exhibition Office, [1992].
12 p. : ill. ; 30 cm.
Cover title. Caption title: Sporting glory : information for teachers. — "devised and compiled by Alex Buck and Jessica Kenny." — Includes bibliographic references.
EXHIBITION: VX.1992.026

VR.1992.010   *Sporting glory : the Courage exhibition of national trophies at the Victoria and Albert Museum.*
London : Sporting Trophies Exhibitions Ltd., [1992].
336 p. : ill. (some col). ; 30 cm.
A message / HRH Prince Edward. Welcome to Sporting Glory / Lord Burghersh. Priceless protection / Group 4 Securitas. Sporting courage / Michael Reynolds. A clear view of sport / Kevin Mahoney. Sporting memories / British Pathe News. Sports Aid Foundation / Noel Nagle. British Sports Association for the Disabled / George Rushforth. History / Dr Helen Clifford. Winners / Robert Blaney. Trophy room / Michael Reynolds. Design / Philippa Glanville. Animal winners / Lionel Lambourne. Team winners / Allan Lamb. Sporting glory : the premier trophies.
EXHIBITION: VX.1992.026

VR.1992.011   *Tennyson : the manuscripts at the Victoria and Albert Museum, the Princeton University Library and the University of Virginia Library* / edited by Christopher Ricks and Aidan Day.
New York ; London : Garland, 1992.
5 xiii, 301 p. : facsims. ; 32 cm.
(The Tennyson archive ; vol. XXX)
ISBN: 0824042298
Manuscripts in the Forster collection, National Art Library.

VR.1992.012   *Vikutoria-chō no eikō : bin'ei no jidai no Eikoku no seikatsu bunka.*
Osaka : NHK Kinki Media Plan, 1992.
[6], 140 p. : ill. (chiefly col.), ports. ; 30 cm.
At head of title: Vikutoria Arubāto Bijutsukan tokubetsuten. — Arts of the Victorians
[title supplied by contributing curators]. — Introduction by Elizabeth Esteve-Coll. Texts
by Paul Greenhalgh, Anna Jackson. Catalogue entries also by: Frances Collard, Ann
Eatwell, Richard Edgcumbe, Wendy Hefford, Greg Irvine, Lionel Lambourne, Susan
McCormack, Anthony North, Jennifer Opie, Linda Parry, Susanna Robson, Gillian
Saunders, Susan Stronge, Chris Titterington, Marjorie Trusted, Eric Turner, Oliver
Watson. — In Japanese. Introduction also in English.
EXHIBITION: VX.1992.XXX.001

1993

VR.1993.001   *Catalogues of the Collection of Prints, Drawings & Paintings in the
Victoria & Albert Museum. Parts 1 & 2.* 2nd ed.
Haslemere : Emmett Publishing, 1993.
627 microfiches + 1 v. (9 p. ; 23 cm.).
ISBN: 1869934563
Introduction / Susan Lambert. Editor, Anne Emmett. Photography, Julius Smit.

VR.1993.002   *Ceramic contemporaries : exhibition catalogue.*
[London : National Association for Ceramics in Higher Education,
1993.]
38, [2] p. : col. ill. ; 21 cm.
Introduction / Martin Smith. Foreword / Paul Greenhalgh.
EXHIBITION: VX.1993.007

VR.1993.003   *Collected works : January–March 1993.*
London : Book Works, [1993].
1 sheet, folded : ill., port. ; 21 cm.
Caption title. — "a series of new commissions . . . by artists and writers for libraries in
the Royal Borough of Kensington and Chelsea." — Includes information about a
performance at the National Art Library, directed by Gary Stevens.
EXHIBITION: VX.1993.001

VR.1993.004   *Fabergé : imperial jeweller* / Géza von Habsburg, Marina Lopato.
St Petersburg ; Washington, D.C. ; London : State Hermitage Museum
and Fabergé Arts Foundation in association with Thames and
Hudson, [1993].
476 p. : ill. (some col.), ports. ; 23 cm.
ISBN: 0500092397
Prefatory statements, etc. by Mikhail Piotrovski, Elizabeth Esteve-Coll, Helmut Ganser
and Patrick J. Choël (of Parfums Fabergé), Fabergé Arts Foundation. Includes essays by:
Carol Aiken, Tatiana Muntian, Anne Odom, Boris Ometov, Karina Orlova and Larisa
Zavadskaia, Paul Schaffer, Galina Smorodinova, Ulla Tillander-Godenhielm, Alexander
von Solodkoff. — Includes: Imperial Easter eggs: a technical study. New light on the
workshop of Henrik Wigström. Fabergé and the Paris 1900 Exposition universelle.
Fabergé drawings in the Hermitage collection. Kshesinskaia's memories. —
Bibliography: p. 462–466. Marks. Index.
EXHIBITION: VX.1994.002

VR.1993.005   *High art and low life* : The Studio *and the fin-de-siècle : incorporating the catalogue to the exhibition . . . Victoria and Albert Museum, 23 June–31 October 1993.*
[London] : Studio International, 1993.
144 p. : ill. (some col.) ; 29 cm.
Cover title. — "*Studio international* special centenary number, Volume 21, number 1022/1023"–contents page ("Number 1021/1023")–spine. — Foreword by Michael Spens. Includes: *The studio* and the arts and crafts movement / Peter Rose. By Lionel Lambourne: The poster and the popular arts of the 1890s. Loïe Fuller. Smoke. *The studio* and Belgium / Bill North. Alphonse Mucha / Tomoko Sato. By Frank Gray: *The studio* and Russia. The time machine [on cinema]. By Stephen Calloway: The colours of a decade. 'The dandyism of the senses'. Charles Conder / Janet McKenzie. 'The love that dare not speak its name' / Emmanuel Cooper. The new woman / Katharine Coombs. *The studio* prize competitions / Barbara Morris. Architecture and The studio / Clive Ashwin. *The studio* recollected in context / Geoffrey Squire. — Includes bibliographic references.
EXHIBITION: VX.1993.017

VR.1993.006   *Indo kyūtei bunka no hana : saimitsuga to dezain no sekai : Vikutoria & Arubāto Bijutsukan ten = The art of the Indian courts : miniature paintings and decorative arts.*
Osaka : NHK Kinki Media Plan, 1993.
181 p. : ill. (chiefly col.), map, ports. ; 30 cm.
Texts by Deborah Swallow and Takashi Koezuka. Catalogue entries supplied by Rosemary Crill, Susan Stronge. — In English and Japanese. — Includes bibliographic references.
EXHIBITION: VX.1993.XXX.001

VR.1993.007   *Kalighat : Indian popular painting, 1800–1930.*
London : South Bank Centre, 1993.
15 p. : ill. ; 16 cm.
ISBN: 1853321206
"Exhibition guide"–cover. — Introduction / Henry Meyric Hughes, Roger Halbert. — Glossary.
EXHIBITION: VX.1994.023

VR.1993.008   *Kalighat : Indian popular painting, 1800–1930* / Balraj Khanna.
London : Redstone Press in association with the South Bank Centre, 1993.
36, [8] p., [51] p. of plates : ill. (some col.) ; 17 cm. + 3 folded posters, 1 postcard.
ISBN: 1870003462
"Today more Kalighat paintings survive in a single western museum – London's Victoria & Albert – than in all of India's museums put together"–p. 8. — Designed by Julian Rothenstein. — Issued in a box.
EXHIBITION: VX.1994.023

VR.1993.009   *Liliane Lijn : poem machines, 1962–1968.*
[London : The Artist, 1993].
[12] p. : ill. ; 15 x 21 cm.
Preface: A hidden harmony / Jan van der Wateren. Liliane Lijn: poem machines / Andrew Wilson.
EXHIBITION: VX.1993.011

VR.1993.010   *The Peter Rabbit trail.*
               [London] : F. Warne & Co., [1993].
               1 sheet, folded : ill. ; 30 cm. + 1 sheet.
               'Adult section' on separate sheet.
               EXHIBITION: vx.1993.027

VR.1993.011   *The street photographs of Roger Mayne.*
               London : Zelda Cheatle, 1993.
               87 p. : chiefly ill., port. ; 28 cm.
               ISBN: 185177002X
               Published on the occasion of an exhibition at the Zelda Cheatle Gallery, Dec.
               1992–Jan.1993. — "Based on the Victoria and Albert Museum catalogue, 1986"
               i.e. v.1986.039.

VR.1993.012   *Two moons : ten years of the Red Hen Press : an exhibition of limited
               edition artist's books : National Art Library, Victoria & Albert
               Museum, London, 6th October 1993–8th January 1994.*
               [s.l. : Shirley Jones, 1993.]
               1 sheet, folded ([5] p.) : ill. ; 18 cm. + 4 postcards.
               EXHIBITION: vx.1993.028

VR.1993.013   *Victoria and Albert Museum catalogue of rings* / by C.C. Oman.
               Ipswich : Anglia, with the permission of the Victoria and Albert
               Museum, 1993.
               xvi, 154 p., [40] p. of plates : ill. ; 26 cm.
               ISBN: 1897874022
               Reprint of v.1930.006

1994

VR.1994.001   *The art periodicals collection at the V&A Museum, 1750–1920. Part
               5, Christian art II.*
               London : World Microfilms, [1994?].
               26 microfilms.
               Periodicals held in the National Art Library.

VR.1994.002   *Ceramic evolution in the middle Ming period : Hongzhi to Wanli
               (1488–1620)* / Rosemary Scott, Rose Kerr = Chi ku ching hui Ming tai
               tzu : Hung-chih chih Wan-li / Su Mei-kuei, Ko Mei-kuei.
               Singapore : Sun Tree Pub., 1994.
               48 p. : col. ill. ; 30 cm.
               ISBN: 9810058934
               In English; title and legends also in Chinese. — Bibliography: p. 48.
               EXHIBITION: vx.1994.XXX.003

VR.1994.003   *Chinese papercuts : a selection* / Ruth Bottomley.
               Singapore ; London : Sun Tree Publishing Ltd., 1994.
               159 p. : col. ill. ; 14 cm.
               (Miniature Sun Tree)
               ISBN: 9810044100
               "The Victoria and Albert Museum papercuts collection portrayed here . . ."–p. 7. —
               Photographs by Ian Thomas. — V&A logo appears on t.p. and back cover. — Paper
               boards, with col. ill.

VR.1994.004 *Eikoku no modan dezain : interia ni miru dentō kakushin.*
Osaka : NHK Kinki Media Plan, 1994.
199 p. : ill. (chiefly col.) ; 30 cm.
At head of title: Vikutoria to Arubāto Bijutsukan ten. — Cover title: British design at
home : the Victoria & Albert Museum. — Edited by Haruhiko Fujita. — Includes:
Introduction / Michael Snodin. British modern design and Japan / Hisao Miyajima.
EXHIBITION: VX.1994.XXX.001

VR.1994.005 *Gates of mystery : the art of holy Russia* / edited by Roderick
Grierson.
Cambridge : Lutterworth, [1994].
336 p. : ill. (some col.) ; 28 cm.
ISBN: 071882900X
Bibliography: p. 328–329. Index. — Reprint of VR.1992.007.
EXHIBITION: VX.1993.030

VR.1994.006 *Hizō Nihon bijutsu taikan. 4, Daiei Toshokan, Ashumorian
Bijutsukan, Vikutoria Arubāto Hakubutsukan.*
Tōkyō : Kōdansha, 1994.
301 p. : ill. (some col.) ; 38 cm.
Cover title: Japanese art : the great European collections. — In Japanese, captions also
in English. — Colophon inserted. — Includes bibliographic references.

VR.1994.007 *Kitaj : a print retrospective.*
[London : Produced by Marlborough Graphics, 1994].
[16] p. : ill., port. ; 21 cm.
Written by Rosemary Miles.
EXHIBITION: VX.1994.015

VR.1994.008 *The peaceful liberators : Jain art from India* / Pratapaditya Pal ; with
contributions by Shridhar Andhare . . . [et al.].
New York : Thames and Hudson ; Los Angeles : Los Angeles County
Museum of Art, 1994.
279 p. : ill. (some col.), map ; 30 cm.
ISBN: 050001650X; 0875871720 (pbk.)
Foreword / William A. Mingst. Includes: Following the Jina, worshiping the Jina: an
essay on Jain rituals / John E. Cort. Are Jains really Hindus? Some parallels and
differences between Jain and Hindu philosophies / Gerald James Larson. Jain
pilgrimage: in memory and celebration of the Jinas / Phyllis Granoff. Jain monumental
painting / Shridhar Andhare. Jain manuscript painting / John Guy. — Bibliography:
p. 262–269. Index.
EXHIBITION: VX.1995.033

VR.1994.009 *Streetstyle : from sidewalk to catwalk* / Ted Polhemus.
London : Thames and Hudson, 1994.
144 p. : ill. (chiefly col.) ; 26 cm.
ISBN: 050027794X
Bibliography: p. 138–142. Index.
EXHIBITION: VX.1994.027

VR.1994.010 *Ten years on : the work of the Camberwell Press, 1984–1994 : the
bibliography . . . .*
London : Camberwell Press, Camberwell College of Arts, 1994.
[46] p. : col. ill. ; 21 cm.
EXHIBITION: VX.1994.030

VR.1994.011   *Umi o watatta Edo no washi : Pākusu korekushon ten, Tabako to Shio no Hakubutsukan, Gifu-shi Rekishi Hakubutsukan.*
Tōkyō : Kami no Hakubutsukan, 1994.
127 p. : ill. (some col.), ports. ; 30 cm.
In Japanese. Introductory messages by John Boyd, Elizabeth Esteve-Coll and Jiro Kawake, also in English. — Includes bibliographic references. — Sir Harry Parkes' collection of Japanese papers, from the V&A and the Royal Botanic Garden, Kew.
EXHIBITION: VX.1994.XXX.002

VR.1994.012   *Warworks : women, photography and the art of war* / Val Williams.
London : Virago, 1994.
96 p. : ill. (some col.), port. ; 28 cm.
ISBN: 1853815918
Includes bibliographic references. Index.
EXHIBITION: VX.1995.001

VR.1994.013   *Women artists in the Victoria and Albert Museum.*
Haslemere : Emmett Publishing, 1994.
20 microfiches + 1 v. (37 p. ; 23 cm.).
ISBN: 1869934571
Summary catalogue by Gill Saunders. Editor, J. Emmett. — Photography, J. Smit.

1995

VR.1995.001   *1970–1995 : the work of the Silversmiths' Studio, San Lorenzo, Milano : an exhibition at the Victoria and Albert Museum.*
Milan : San Lorenzo, 1995.
185, [2] p. : ill., ports. ; 28 cm.
ISBN: 8843554247
Introduction / Marco Bona Castellotti. Craft and industry / Eric Turner. The Silversmith's Studio San Lorenzo / Eric Turner. Silver: forms for today / Angela Vettese. Metallurgy and design for silverware / Pietro Luigi Cavallotti. Notes for the collector / Franco Rizzi. Silversmiths: Franco Albini and Franca Helg, Maria Luisa Belgiojoso, Antonio Piva, Afra and Tobia Scarpa, Lella and Massimo Vignelli.
EXHIBITION: VX.1995.027

VR.1995.002   *American photography 1890–1965, from the Museum of Modern Art, New York* / Peter Galassi ; with an essay by Luc Sante.
New York : Museum of Modern Art : Distributed by H.N. Abrams, 1995.
256 p. : ill. (some col.), ports. ; 30 cm.
ISBN: 081961431 (MoMA, Abrams); 087070401 (MoMA, T&H); 087070141X (pbk.)
Foreword / Richard E. Oldenburg. — Index.
EXHIBITION: VX.1996.034

VR.1995.003   *Goldsmiths, silversmiths and bankers : innovation and the transfer of skill, 1550–1750 : a collection of working papers given at a study day held jointly by the Centre for Metropolitan History and the Victoria and Albert Museum, 24 November 1993* / edited by David Mitchell.
Stroud : Alan Sutton ; London : Centre for Metropolitan History, 1995.

viii, 120 p. : ill. ; 25 cm.
(Working papers series / Centre for Metropolitan History ; no. 2)
Introduction / Philippa Glanville. Innovation and the transfer of skill in the goldsmiths'
trade in Restoration London / David Mitchell. Goldsmiths' apprenticeship during the
first half of the seventeenth century: the situation in Paris / Michèle Bimbenet-Privat.
Training and workshop practice in Zürich in the seventeenth century / Hanspeter Lanz.
Aliens and their impact on the goldsmiths' craft in London in the sixteenth century /
Lien Bich Luu. Balances and goldsmith-bankers: the co-ordination and control of inter-
banker debt clearing in seventeenth-century London / Stephen Quinn. The interaction
between English and Huguenot goldsmiths in the late seventeenth and early eighteenth
centuries / Emma Packer. 'The King's Arms and Feathers' : a case study exploring the
networks of manufacture operating in the London goldsmiths' trade in the eighteenth
century / Helen Clifford. The design of London goldsmiths' shops in the early eighteenth
century / Claire Walsh. The goldsmiths and the London luxury trades, 1550 to 1750 /
John Styles. — Includes bibliographic references.

VR.1995.004   *Igirisu kaiga no 350 nen : Vikutoria & Arubāto Bijutsukan ten = The*
               Victoria & Albert Museum : People and places : British painting
               1550–1900.
               Osaka : NHK Kinki Media Plan, 1995.
               211 p. : ill. (chiefly col.), ports. ; 30 cm.
               Includes: Introduction / Elizabeth Esteve-Coll. Characteristics of British painting / Kozo
               Shioe. — Captions also in English.
               EXHIBITION: VX.1995.XXX.003

VR.1995.005   *The story of glass.*
               Oxford : Reed Interactive, 1995.
               1 computer laser optical disk : col. ; 4¾ in.
               ISBN: 1860450008
               Produced by the V&A, Corning Museum of Glass, New York and Art of Memory. —
               CD-ROM for Windows and Macintosh computers.

VR.1995.006   *Treasures from the courts of Mughal India : exhibition guide.*
               Birmingham : City Council, Dept. of Leisure and Community Services,
               [1995].
               32 p. : ill. (some col.), 1 map ; 30 x 14 cm.
               Written by Raj Pal.
               EXHIBITION: VX.1995.XXX.004

VR.1995.007   *Visions of photography : the best of the Fabergé photography*
               competition : in association with The Guardian.
               [London : The Firm, 1995.]
               [4], 28 p. : ill. (some col.) ; 21 cm.
               Cover title. At foot of title: Fabergé, Paris.
               EXHIBITION: VX.1995.009

VR.1995.008   *Yōroppa senshoku no bi : Vikutoria & Arubāto Bijutsukan = The*
               European art of textiles : the Victoria and Albert Museum.
               Osaka : NHK Kinki Media Plan, 1995.
               215 p. : ill. (chiefly col.) ; 30 cm.
               Includes: A brief history of European textiles / Takahiko Sano. — In Japanese and
               English. — Bibliography: p. 215. Index.
               EXHIBITION: VX.1995.XXX.002

1996

VR.1996.001   *Birds, bats & butterflies in Korean art* / Liz Wilkinson.
U.K. : Sun Tree Publishing, 1996.
119 p. : col. ill. ; 14 cm.
(Miniature Sun Tree)
ISBN: 9810056869
"The motifs illustrated in this book have been taken from artefacts in the Far Eastern
Collection at the Victoria and Albert Museum."–p. 5. — Photographs by Ian Thomas.
— Paper boards, with col. ill. and V&A logo.

VR.1996.002   *Ceramic contemporaries 2 exhibition : 8th February–6th March 1996,
V&A.*
Bath : National Association for Ceramics in Higher Education, 1996.
36 p. : ill. (some col.) ; 21 cm.
ISBN: 0952749009
Cover title. — Introduction / Jane Gibson. Texts by Paul Greenhalgh, Tanya Harrod,
Michael Phillipson, Michael Robinson.
EXHIBITION: vx.1996.004

VR.1996.003   *Embossed images on paper : a display* / conceived and organised by
John Hall . . . .
[Kingston-on-Thames] : Kingston University, 1996.
64 p. : ill. ; 15 x 21 cm.
EXHIBITION: vx.1996.009

VR.1996.004   *Gioielli dall'India : dai Moghul al Novecento : Milano, Galleria
Ottava Piano, La Rinascente piazza Duomo, 8 marzo–13 aprile 1996.*
Milano : La Rinascente, 1996.
235 p. : col. ill. ; 22 cm.
Texts by Kirsten Aschengreen Piacenti, Cristina Del Mare, Binoy Kumar Sahay,
Kamlesh Kumar Sharma, Raj Kumar Tewari, Rita Sharma, Susan Stronge. Includes:
L'arte indiana al Victoria and Albert Museum. Valenza e funzione del gioiello indiano.
Simbologie e disegni negli ornamenti. L'arte degli smalti. La gioielleria Moghul. La
funzione del *navaratna*. L'origine del *nath*. Tecniche di lavorazione. Armi e armature
ornate da pietre preziose. — Bibliography: p. 233–235. Glossary.
EXHIBITION: vx.1996.xxx.001

VR.1996.005   *Landscapes of the spirit : the drawings, prints and books of J.G.
Lubbock.*
[s.l. : The Artist, 1996.]
[8] p., 1 folded leaf of plates : col. ill. ; 21 cm.
Includes bibliography.
EXHIBITION: vx.1996.025

VR.1996.006   *Silk designs of the eighteenth century : from the Victoria and Albert
Museum, London* / edited with an introduction by Clare Browne.
London : Thames and Hudson, 1996.
112 p. : col. ill. ; 30 cm.
ISBN: 0500278806
Illustrations selected from vr.1990.012. — Bibliography: p. 108–109. Index.

VR.1996.007   *The spirit of the staircase : 100 years of print publishing at the Royal
College of Art, 1896–1996 : Victoria and Albert Museum, 7
November 1996–30 March 1997.*

[London] : Royal College of Art, 1996.
1 sheet, folded ([6] p.) : ill. (some col.) ; 30 cm.
Text by Silvie Turner. — Includes prospectus for Twelve artists : the Royal College of
Art centenary year portfolio of prints.
EXHIBITION: VX.1996.035

VR.1996.008   *William Morris at the V&A.*
[London : Evening Standard, 1996.]
[18?] p. : ill., plan ; 28 cm.?
Supplement to the *Evening standard* newspaper, May 1996, available for the duration
of the exhibition.
EXHIBITION: VX.1996.013

PERIODICALS AND PART WORKS

Titles are listed in chronological order of first publication. For explanation of entries see
notes at the head of the V&A Periodicals sequence, p. 387.

VRP.1853.001   [Reports of the Department . . . .]
1853–1899

VRP.1853.001A   *First report of the Department of Practical Art.*
London : Printed by George E. Eyre and William Spottiswoode,
1853.
vii, 390 p. (some folded), [3] folded leaves of plates : plans ; 21 cm.
"Presented to both Houses of Parliament by command of Her Majesty." — Includes:
Catalogue of the articles in the Museum of Manufactures, chiefly purchased from the
Exhibition of 1851; Donations to the Museum; Loans to the Museum, for public
instruction; Museum of Manufactures and Library at Marlborough House; Minute
relating to purchases for the Museum, and encouragement to local museums.

VRP.1853.001B   *Report of the Department of Science and Art.*
London : Printed by George E. Eyre and William Spottiswoode for
H.M.S.O.
Annual, First report (1854)–Forty-sixth report (1899).
46 v : ill., plans ; 22–25 cm.
"Presented to both Houses of Parliament by command of Her Majesty." — From the
Fifth report (1858), entitled Report of the Science and Art Department of the
Committee of Council on Education. — Appendix G: Documents relating to the
administration of the Museum of Art; Appendix H: Report of Mr Wornum on the
Library–First report (1854). Position of reports on the Museum varies until, from the
Twelfth report (1865), Appendix D: South Kensington Museum. — For annual reports
after 1899, see VRP.1900.001.

VRP.1857.001   *Guide to the South Kensington Museum : by authority.*
London : Printed by W. Clowes and Sons.
Quarterly, No. 1, 20th June 1857–no. 9, October 1860?
9? issues : plan ; 33 cm.

Nos. 8 and 9 lack plan. — Advertisements. — Inserted in no. 7 (Sept. 1859): List of objects on loan to the Museum of Ornamental Art [including] Collection of Chinese and Japanese objects of art and manufacture lent by . . . the Earl of Elgin. — Nos. 2–6 unseen.

VRP.1858.001   *The Architectural Museum : report.*
[London : Architectural Museum, South Kensington], 1858–1868.
Annual.
11? issues ; 21 cm.
Included here for the period during which the collection was at South Kensington.

VRP.1867.001   *Fifty etchings of objects of art in the South Kensington Museum.*
London : Arundel Society for Promoting the Knowledge of Art, 1867–1870.
5 v. (each 8 p., [50] leaves of plates) : chiefly ill. ; 40 cm.
At head of title: With the sanction of the Science and Art Department of the Committee of Council on Education. — Half-title: Etchings of objects of art. — First series has 12 p. of text. — Done by the students of the etching class at the Goverment School of Design, South Kensington.
[First series] (1867). Second series (1868). Third series (1869). Fourth series (1869). Fifth series. Jewellery (1870).

VRP.1868.001   *Chromolithographs of the principal objects of art in the South Kensington Museum.*
London : Published by the Arundel Society for Promoting the Knowledge of Art, 1868–1875.
4 v. (each 4 parts) : chiefly ill. ; 58 cm.
Cover title. — At head of title: With the sanction of the Science and Art Department of the Committee of Council on Education, for the use of Schools of Art and amateurs.
Vol. 1. Silver-gilt cup & cover. Della Robbia roundel, Januarius. Pastoral staff. Rock crystal ewer. Vol. 2. Ivory casket from Veroli. Medallion or roundel, Februarius. Silver casket, Limoges enamel. Silver casket, Limoges enamel, the lid. Vol. 3. Ivory triptych. Old English goblet. Enamelled plaque. Ivory casket. Vol. [4]. Soltikoff chasse (Eltenberg reliquary). Gloucester candlestick. Monstrance. Altar cross.

VRP.1881.001   *The South Kensington Museum : examples of the works of art in the Museum, and of the decorations of the building, with brief descriptions.*
London : Sampson Low, Marston, Searle, and Rivington, with the sanction of the Science and Art Department, 1881–1882 (Chiswick Press, printer).
2 v. : ill. ; 33 cm.
Cover title. — Issued in monthly parts, I-XI (1880), XII-XXI (1881), XXII (1882). — Illustrations are mainly etchings; some wood engravings. Parts issued in grey wrappers with architectural border design. Advertisements on back covers.

VRP.1881.002   *Portfolios of industrial art.*
1881–1893   [London] : Produced and published for the Committee of Council on Education, South Kensington Museum by W. Griggs.
Plates issued in parts, in grey wrappers, some with illustration on the cover. Parts consist of two plates, or one double-sized.

VRP.1881.002A   *Portfolio of Indian art.* 1881–[c.1887?].
28 parts : col. ill. ; 37 cm.

Parts 1–10: From drawings in the South Kensington Museum [of Indian craftspeople at work, by J.L. Kipling]. Part 11. Arch of the screen of the Arhai-din-ka Jhonpra mosque at Ajmere, Trellis window at Ahmedabad. Part 12. Shield & belt, Dagger & sheath, H.R.H. The Prince of Wales's collection of presents. Part 13. Fresco decoration; Ornamention in dado, from the mosque of Wazir Khan, Lahore. Part 14. Elevations of the tombs of Shah Jehan and of the Begum Mumtaz-i-Mahal, Taj Mahal, Agra. Part 15. Doorway of screen round the tombs of Shah Jehan and of the Begum Mumtaz-i-Mahal. Parts 16–22. Details from the tombs . . . . Part 23. Glass ware. Part 24. Scarf and Coverlet. Part 25. Gateway and Front of a house . . . . Part 26. Jeypore enamels. Part 27. Ivory casket; Ivory combs. Part 28. Carved and pierced sandstone window, Ahmadebad; Brass censer and tripod stand.

VRP.1881.002B   *Portfolio of Spanish art.* 1881–[1891?].
16 parts : col. ill. ; 37 cm.

Parts 1–8: "From the special loan exhibition of Spanish ornamental art. . . [VX.1881.001]".

Part 1. Point-lace bed-quilt [c.1600]; Embroidered border [17th c.]. Part 2. Altar frontal [17th c.]; Lace table-cover. Part 3. Chest in carved walnut [16th c.]; Bronze fountain-jet. Part 4. Chest in carved walnut [16th c.]; Toledo rapiers. Part 5. Mortuary cope in embroidered black velvet [c. 1560]. Part 6. Embroidered orphrey [c.1580]; Chasuble [16th c.]. Part 7. Cope [or Chasuble?] [17th c.]. Part 8. Altar frontals [c.1500; c.1600]. Part 9. Carpet/cover [17th c.,]. Part 10. Altar frontal, 14th c.; Border or orphrey, early 16th c. Part 11. Bed quilt, 17th c. Part 12. Three borders of napkins. Part 13. Embroideries on velvet, 16th & 17th c. Parts 14, 15. Borders . . . Part 16. Furniture trimming.

VRP.1881.002C   *Portfolio of Russian art.* 1882.
2 parts : col. ill. ; 37 cm.

Part 1. Vestment . . ., 16th c.; Knife & fork . . ., 17th c. Part 2. Bratina; Censer.

VRP.1881.002D   *Portfolio of Flemish art.* 1882–[1890?].
4 parts : col. ill. ; 37 cm.

Part 1. Velvet fabrics. Part 2. Two linen fabrics. Part 3. Orphrey of a chasuble. Part 4. Damask table cover, 18th c.

VRP.1881.002E   *Portfolio of Sicilian art.* 1882–[c.1890].
5 parts : col. ill. ; 37 cm.

Parts 1, 2. Silk & gold damask. Part 3. Damask; Hood of a cope. Parts 4, 5. Silk damasks.

VRP.1881.002F   *Portfolio of French art.* [1882–1892?].
12 parts : ill. (some col.) ; 37 cm.

Part 1. Silk fabrics printed with flowers in colours, 18th century. Parts 2–10: VR.1889.002. Part 11. Portions of stoles.

VRP.1881.002G   *Portfolio of Italian art.* [1882?–1892?].
25 parts : col. ill. ; 37 cm.

Part 1. Bronze medallion: the infant Hercules; Bronze medallion: Hercules bearing the Erymanthian boar. Part 2. Altar or shrine of a female saint from Padua. Part 3. Brocades. Part IV [sic]. Linen embroidered with sprigs; Cushion cover. Part V [sic]. Parts of wall hangings. Part 6. Silk and linen fabrics; silk and gold tissue. Part 7. Silk and linen fabrics. Part 8. Carpet, from a Persian design; Figured damask. Part 9. Linen and woollen brocade; Brocatelle. Part 10. Damask. Part 11. Cloth of gold; Silk brocade. Part 12. Silk and damask; Wool and cotton damask. Part 13. Silk and cotton fabric; Wool and cotton. Part 14. Portion[s] of an altar cloth. Part 15. Wool and cotton fabrics. Part 16. Two brocades. Part 17. Satin brocades. Part 18. Silk embroidery on canvas. Part 19. Brocades. Part 20. Velvet brocade. Velvet on velvet. Part 21. Portion of bed-hangings;

Coverlet. Part 22. Damask, satin; Silk damask. Part 23. Missal cover of enamelled gold; Dish, enamelled copper. Part 24. Tissue; Silk and gold damask. Part 25. Silver-gilt coffret.

VRP.1881.002H   *Portfolio of Swedish art.* [1885?].
5 parts : col. ill. ; 37 cm.
Part 1. Part of a bed-cover dated 1777 and Chair-cushion, early 19th c., made by peasant women of the province of Skåne, Sweden. Part 2. Bag and Chair-cushion, 19th c. Part 3. Part of a border of table-cloth from a Swedish tomb of A.D. 1050, and Chair-cushion, 18th century . . . . Part 4. Carriage-cushion and Part of a bench-cover. Part 5. Rug and Antimacassar.

VRP.1881.002I   *Portfolio of English art.* [1887?].
2 parts : col. ill. ; 37 cm.
Part 1. Silk damask, 18th century; Cover, linen embroidered with silk, 17th century. Part 2. Silk embroidery on quilted linen; Embroidery in coloured silks on linen.

VRP.1881.002J   *Portfolio of Saracenic art.* [1887?–1890?].
4 parts : col. ill. ; 37 cm.
Part 1. Pulpit doors. Part 2. Panel of tiles . . .; Damascus tiles. Part 3. Wall mosaic. Part 4. Tiles.

VRP.1881.002K   *Portfolio of Egyptian art.* [1888–1889].
5 parts : col. ill. ; 37 cm.
Parts 1–4. Egyptian tapestry: One of a pair of angels; piece of a linen cloth. Part 5. Two brocades.

VRP.1881.002L   *Portfolio of German art.* [1888?–1890?].
[8] parts : col. ill. ; 37 cm.
Parts 1, 2. Wall hangings. Part 3. Tapestry. Part 4. Orphrey. Part 5. Damask table covers. Part 6. Damask table covers. Part 7. Linen damasks. Part 8. Embroidery on linen.

VRP.1881.002M   *Portfolio of Chinese art.* [1888–1891].
2 parts : col. ill. ; 37 cm.
Part 1. Part of a screen of lacquered wood. Part 2. Sleeve-pieces and velvet woven pattern.

VRP.1881.002N   *Portfolio of Oriental art.* [1889?–1893?].
9 parts : col. ill. ; 37 cm.
Part 1. Brocades. Part 2. Twilled silk; Silk and linen tissue. Part 3. Satin quilt; Brocade. Part 4. Petticoat, Turco-Greek or Turco-Syrian. Part 5. Hanging or cover, 16th c. Parts 6, 7. Brocades, 16th–17th c. Part 8. Tissues. Part 9. Sacrificial ladle, Cingalese.

VRP.1881.002O   *Portfolio of Persian art.* [1889?–1893?].
22 parts : col. ill. ; 37 cm.
Part 1. Rosewater sprinkler; Water bottle. Part 2. Dish for rice; Dish. Part 3. Silk damask (Brocade?); Wrestler's breeches. Part 4. Carpet, 16th c. Parts 5, 6. Carpet, c.1530. Part 7. Persian velvet carpet, 15th c. Part 8. Printed chintz. Part 9. Carpet, 17th c. Part 10. Dress piece. Part 11. Brocade and velvet. Part 12. Silk damask and silk and linen damask. Part 13. Two dishes. Parts 14–17. Portions of a carpet. Part 18. Flower vase; Water bottle. Part 19. Two water bottles. Part 20–22. Dishes for rice; Bowl.

VRP.1898.001   *Iron work : 53 plates, from objects and drawings in the South Kensington Museum* / reproduced by W. Griggs. 1898.
[London] : Produced and published for the Committee of Council on Education, South Kensington Museum by W. Griggs.
53 leaves of plates (some folded) ; 39 cm.
Photographic illustrations.

VRP.1899.001   *Selected examples of decorative art from South Kensington Museum /*
                edited by F.E. Witthaus.
                London : Longman, Green and Co., 1899.
                6 parts (each 12 plates) : chiefly ill. ; 48 cm.
                "Carved wood-work & furniture, Gesso-work, Sculpture, Bronzes, Silversmith's [sic]
                work, Glass vessels, Textiles fabrics"–portfolio. — Illustrations are photographs. —
                Issued in terra-cotta-coloured wrappers; with cloth covered portfolio for set.

VRP.1900.001   *Report of the Board of Education.*
                London : Printed for H.M.S.O. by Wyman and Sons.
                Annual, 1899/1900 (1900)–1917/18 (1919)
                20 v. ; 25 cm.
                "Presented to Parliament by command of Her Majesty." — In the first Report, for
                1899–1900, the Museum returns appear in Vol. II: Appendix (Secondary education); in
                the second Report, for 1900–1901, in Vol. III: Appendix . . . Reports and returns
                (Museums etc.). Up to Report for 1911/1912, a brief report on the Museum is included
                here, in addition to the documents issued separately (VRP.1902.001 a–d). From Report
                for 1912–1913: "The Annual Report of the Victoria and Albert Museum is issued as a
                separate document." Report for 1916/1917: "Owing to the war the publication of the
                annual report on the Victoria and Albert Museum has been temporarily suspended"
                (p. 84). The Report for 1917/1918 includes a report on the Museum, p. 74–76.

VRP.1902.001   [Reports for the year . . . .]
1902–1922

VRP.1902.001A   *Report for the year . . . on the museums, colleges and institutions*
                under the administration of the Board of Education.
                London : Printed for H.M.S.O. by Wyman and Sons.
                Annual, 1901 (1902)–1902 (1903)
                2 v. : maps ; 25 cm.
                "Presented to Parliament by command of His Majesty." — The Victoria and Albert
                Museum; the Royal College of Science, London; the Royal College of Art, London; the
                Geological Survey of the United Kingdom and Museum of Practical Geology; the Solar
                Physics Committee.

VRP.1902.001B   *Report for the year . . . on the Victoria and Albert Museum, the Royal*
                Colleges of Science and of Art, the Geological Survey and Museum,
                and on the work of the Solar Physics Committee.
                London : Printed for H.M.S.O. by Wyman and Sons.
                Annual, 1903 (1904)–1907 (1908)
                5 v. : maps ; 25 cm.
                At head of title: Board of Education. — "Presented to Parliament by command of His
                Majesty."

VRP.1902.001C   *Reports for the year 1908 on the Royal College of Art, the Victoria*
                and Albert Museum, and the Bethnal Green Museum.
                London : Printed for H.M.S.O. by Eyre and Spottiswoode, 1909.
                55 p. ; 25 cm.
                At head of title: Board of Education. — "Presented to both Houses of Parliament by
                command of His Majesty."

VRP.1902.001D   *Report for the year . . . on the Victoria and Albert Museum and the*
                Bethnal Green Museum.
                London : H.M.S.O. (Printed by Eyre and Spottiswoode).
                Annual, 1909 and 1910 (1911)–1917 (1920).
                8 v. ; 25 cm.
                At head of title: Board of Education. — "Presented to both Houses of Parliament by
                command of His Majesty."

VRP.1902.001E   *Report on the Victoria & Albert Museum for the year 1918.*
London : Published under the authority of H.M.S.O., 1922
("E & S", printer).

5 p. ; 25 cm.

At head of title: Board of Education. — "In view of the urgent need for economy in printing the Board have decided that this and future Reports on the . . . Museum . . . shall be issued in a summarized form . . . included in the annual Review of Principal Acquisitions [VP.1912.001]"– prefatory note / R. Selby-Bigge.

VRP.1904.001   *Portfolio of ivories.*
[London] : Produced and published for the Board of Education by W. Griggs, [1904–1907].

36 parts : ill. ; 38 cm.

Photographic illustrations of objects from the V&A.

EXHIBITIONS AND DISPLAYS OF THE VICTORIA AND ALBERT MUSEUM, 1852–1996

Explanation of entries:

Citation number[a]	vx.1966.XXX[b].002
Title[c]	English domestic silver, 1660–1910
Dates[d]	4 March–24 April
	VENUE[e]: City Hall Art Gallery, Hong Kong
Notes	In association with the British Council, for 'British Week in Hong Kong'.
Cross-reference	PUBLICATION: vr[f].1966.002

[a] Standard prefix, year of exhibition, location if not V&A at South Kensington, running number

[b] AAD   Archive of Art and Design, at Blythe House
BGM   Bethnal Green Museum
BHO   Boilerhouse Project
IND   Indian Section, before moving to main Museum site
THM   Theatre Museum
XXX   External

[c] Exhibition titles may not be authoritative and often appear in variant forms. Where possible, they are taken from official publicity, reports or publications.

[d] Dates are ascertained from official reports, where possible. Significantly conflicting information is given in the notes. Multiple opening dates may be assumed to indicate private or press views. Closing dates often differ from what was first announced. Where dates cannot be approximated, the entry is placed at the end of the main sequence in the known or estimated year.

[e] Venue is given only in the case of 'external' (XXX) exhibitions.

[f] v.   V&A publications list (starts p. 3)
vp.   Periodical publications (p. 387)
vr.   Related publications (p. 409)

1852

VX.1852.001
Examples of false principles in
decoration
September–July 1853
Popularly known as the 'Chamber of Horrors'.
PUBLICATIONS: V.1852.001;
V.1852.005; (Appendix C in each);
V.1853.003

1853

VX.1853.XXX.001
Specimens of cabinet work
27 May–3 September
VENUE: Gore House, Kensington
Held at Gore House due to lack of available space
at Marlborough House.
PUBLICATIONS: V.1853.001;
VR.1871.001

1854

VX.1854.001
Gherardini collection
March–April
This collection of Italian sculpture was afterwards
acquired for the Museum.
PUBLICATION: VR.1854.001

1855

VX.1855.XXX.001
A collection of works of decorative art
1855–1860
The first circulating collection, or 'travelling
museum', "a faithful abstract or
abridgement"–Third report of the Department of
Science and Art (1856), p. 70.
PUBLICATIONS: V.1855.002;
V.1856.002; V.1858.003

1857

[VX.1857]
Manchester Art Treasures Exhibition
"A collection of nearly one thousand objects,
comprising all those obtained from the Bernal sale,
was contributed . . . At the same time, one hundred

and seven objects from the British Museum were
taken charge of by the Department, exhibited along
with the aforementioned specimens"–Fifth report of
the Science and Art Department (1858), p. 69. —
The collection of Jules Soulages was also acquired
for the Exhibition, and later bought in instalments
for the Museum.
PUBLICATION: V.1856.001

1858

VX.1858.001
Photographs and daguerreotypes
Late February–
5th annual exhibition of the Photographic Society
of London, together with an exhibition by the
Societé française de photographie.
PUBLICATION: VR.1858.002

VX.1858.002
Works of art-manufacture designed or
executed by students of the Schools of
Art
June–
Duration: "upwards of four months"–Sixth report
of the Science and Art Department (1859), p. 39.
PUBLICATION: VR.1858.001

1859

VX.1859.001
Drawings by Raphael and Michelangelo,
from Oxford University
Summer
Duration: "during the long vacation"–Seventh
report of the Science and Art Department (1860),
p. 12.

1860

VX.1860.XXX.001
The circulating collection of works of art
1860–1863
"The principal travelling collection has been re-
organized and more than doubled in
extent"–Eighth report of the Science and Art
Department (1862), p. 123. In 1863 the collection
was recalled for examination.
PUBLICATION: V.1860.001;
V.1863.002

1861

VX.1861.001
Chinese silks and embroidery
"obtained by British troops at Pekin during the Chinese war"–*Ninth Report of the Science and Art Department* (1862), p. 121. — This collection was displayed in the Animal Products Museum. — Duration: "more than four months"–ibid.

VX.1861.XXX.001
[Oriental art]
"The loans to the Museum have been numerous, and by the liberality of the owners many of these . . . have been . . . lent to various temporary local exhibitions. Two extensive and valuable collections of . . . Oriental Art . . . [from] the Earl of Elgin and Sir Hope Grant have been thus . . . [lent] for exhibitions at Edinburgh and Bristol."–*Ninth report of the Science and Art Department* (1862), p. 112.

1862

[VX.1862]
London International Exhibition
1 May–15 November
Not a Museum exhibition, but a large scale trade fair, originally planned for the tenth anniversary of the Great Exhibition of 1851. Organised under the aegis of the Society of Arts, held in a building designed by Francis Fowke on the opposite side of Exhibition Road which became part of the South Kensington museum complex.

VX.1862.001
The special exhibition of works of art of the mediaeval, Renaissance, and more recent periods
June–November?
Organised so as to coincide with the International Exhibition (VX.1862, above).
PUBLICATIONS: V.1862.006; V.1862.008; V.1863.003; VR.1862.001

1863

VX.1863.001
The wedding presents accepted by the Prince and Princess of Wales
15 April–4 May
PUBLICATIONS: V.1863.007; VR.1863.001

1864

VX.1864.001
British stained glass, mosaics, etc.
May–
PUBLICATION: V.1864.001

1865

VX.1865.001
The special exhibition of portrait miniatures on loan
5 June–31 October
PUBLICATIONS: V.1865.005; VR.1866.003; VR.1866.004; VR.1867.001

1866

VX.1866.001
The first special exhibition of national portraits
16 April–18 August
PUBLICATIONS: V.1866.002; VR.1866.001; VR.1866.006; VR.1867.001; VR.1867.006

VX.1866.002
The special exhibition of oil paintings, water-colour drawings, architectural and other studies by the late Godfrey Sykes
14 June–March? 1867
Also held at Sheffield School of Art (where Sykes had been both student and master), March 1867, for 2 weeks.
PUBLICATION: V.1866.003

1867

VX.1867.001
The second special exhibition of national portraits
2/3 May–31 August
PUBLICATIONS: V.1867.003; VR.1868.005; VR.1868.006

VX.1867.XXX.001
Food
31 March?–
VENUE: Exposition universelle, Paris

Examples and illustrations from the Food Museum, listed in *Fifteenth report of the Science and Art Department* (1868), pp. 250–251.

VX.1867.XXX.002
Examples of the periodical literature of Great Britain
31 March?–
VENUE: Exposition universelle, Paris
The collection was afterwards transferred to the Education Museum at South Kensington–*Fifteenth report of the Science and Art Department* (1868), p. 248.

1868

VX.1868.001
The third exhibition of national portraits
13 April–22 August
PUBLICATIONS: v.1868.002; v.1868.003; VR.1868.005; VR.1868.006

VX.1868.002
Drawings submitted to an English Art-Union competition
June–July
Held in the Educational Division.

VX.1868.003
Meyrick collection
October–1870
"deposited on loan at a rental . . . One of the most important collection[s] of objects ever received on loan . . . from one individual"–*Sixteenth Report of the Science and Art Department* (1869), pp. 283, 297.
PUBLICATION: v.1869.001

VX.1868.004
Abyssinian objects from the Emperor Theodore
Lent by the Queen, the Admiralty and others.

VX.1868.005
Designs for fans
Entries to a competition for female students at Government drawing schools.

VX.1868.006
Gold and silver-gilt plate from the Royal collections
Previously shown at the Exposition universelle, Paris, 1867.

1869

VX.1869.001
Competition designs for the new Law Courts

VX.1869.002
Illustrated children's books
Many illustrated by Bewick; and 18th century 'little gilt books'. — Held in the Educational Division.

1870

VX.1870.001
The loan exhibition of fans
1 May–
Duration: 6 months.
PUBLICATION: v.1870.003

1871

[VX.1871]
London International Exhibition
1 May–30 September
"The first of a series held under the direction of Her Majesty's Commissioners for the Exhibition of 1851."–*Official catalogue : Fine Arts Department* (1871), t.p. Not organised by the South Kensington Museum but closely associated with it, and held in the building constructed for the Exhibition of 1862, which was also used for Museum collections. — Exhibits in 1871 from the Museum included a collection illustrating food adulteration.

1872

[VX.1872]
London International Exhibition
29 April–19 October
"The second of a series held under the direction of Her Majesty's Commissioners for the Exhibition of 1851."–*Official catalogue : Fine Arts Department* (1872), t.p. See note on 1871 International Exhibition.

VX.1872.001
Selections from the objects of science and art collected by His Royal Highness, together with water-colour sketches and drawings in illustration of the cruise . . . by Messrs. O.W. Brierly and N. Chevalier

[ca. January–April]
The Duke of Edinburgh's cruise round the world in
H.M.S. 'Galatea', 1867–1871.
PUBLICATIONS: v.1872.006;
v.1872.007; v.1872.017; v.1872.023;
v.1872.024; v.1872.025; v.1872.026

VX.1872.002
The special exhibition of ancient musical
instruments
June–
PUBLICATIONS: v.1872.016;
v.1873.006; v.1874.012

VX.1872.003
The loan exhibition of ancient and
modern jewellery and personal
ornament
June–July
PUBLICATIONS: v.1872.015;
v.1873.005

1873

[vx.1873]
London International Exhibition
9 April–31 October
"The third of a series held under the direction of
Her Majesty's Commissioners for the Exhibition of
1851."–*Official catalogue* (1873), t.p. See note on
1871 International Exhibition.

VX.1873.001
The special loan exhibition of decorative
art needlework made before 1800
May–August?
PUBLICATIONS: v.1873.007;
v.1874.007

1874

[vx.1874]
London International Exhibition
4 April–31 October
"The fourth of a series held under the direction of
Her Majesty's Commissioners for the Exhibition of
1851."–*Official catalogue* (1874), t.p. See note on
1871 International Exhibition.

VX.1874.001
The special loan exhibition of enamels on
metal

June–September
PUBLICATIONS: v.1874.008;
v.1875.006

VX.1874.002
A collection of gold and other objects
from Ashanti

VX.1874.XXX.001
Engraved national portraits
"The whole of this collection has been lent for a
limited period for exhibition at
Edinburgh"–*Twenty-second report of the Science
and Art Department* (1875), p. 394.

1876

VX.1876.001
The special loan collection of scientific
apparatus
13 May–31 December
PUBLICATIONS: v.1876.007;
v.1876.008; v.1876.011; v.1876.012;
v.1876.018; v.1876.019; v.1876.020;
v.1876.021; v.1877.002; v.1877.006

VX.1876.BGM.001
Pictures from Dulwich College Picture
Gallery
7 August–February? 1877

1877

VX.1877.001
The Troy collection
Late 1877–1880
Excavations by Heinrich Schliemann at Husserlik.

1878

VX.1878.BGM.001
A special loan collection of furniture
May–May 1879
PUBLICATION: v.1878.003

VX.1878.XXX.001
The Science and Art Department
VENUE: Exposition universelle, Paris
"drawings and specimens illustrating the actions of
the Department in connexion with the Art and
Science Schools . . ."–*Twenty-sixth report of the
Science and Art Department* (1879), p. 559.

1879

VX.1879.BGM.001
The ironwork collection from the South
Kensington Museum

VX.1879.XXX.001
[Cutlery loan?]
1–17 May
VENUE: Cutlers' Company exhibition
"This is the first of the City Companies to which
the Museum has been called upon to contribute for
the promotion of the artistic and technical
handicrafts represented nominally by
them"–*Twenty-seventh Report of the Science and
Art Department* (1880), p. 534.

1881

VX.1881.001
The special loan exhibition of Spanish
and Portuguese ornamental art
June–September
PUBLICATIONS: v.1881.004;
VRP.1881.002b

VX.1881.XXX.001
Indian art and manufactures
Autumn–
VENUE: Kunstgewerbemuseum, Berlin
Objects from South Kensington supplemented by
loans from the Prince of Wales and Earl Lytton. —
Also held at Stockholm, 1882; Copenhagen
1882–3; Amsterdam 1883.

1882

VX.1882.001
Scandinavian art
June–August
PUBLICATIONS: v.1882.004;
v.1883.005

1883

[vx.1883]
Great International Fisheries Exhibition
17 May?–
Not a Museum exhibition. Organised on the site of
the 1862 International Exhibition, under the aegis
of the Commissioners of the Exhibition of 1851. —
Based on the Buckland Museum of Economic Fish
Culture, a private pisciculture collection at South
Kensington.

1884

[vx.1884]
International Health Exhibition
Mid-May–
See first note on the Fisheries Exhibition, 1883. —
Section II, Education, included manufactures,
decorations and designs by students from the
Government Schools of Art.

1885

[vx.1885]
International Inventions Exhibition
4 May–
See first note on the Fisheries Exhibition, 1883. —
Included an exhibition of musical instruments,
manuscripts, books, paintings and engravings
organised by the Society of Arts in the Royal Albert
Hall, Kensington Gore.

1886

[vx.1886]
Colonial and Indian Exhibition
4 May–
See first note on the Fisheries Exhibition, 1883.

1888

VX.1888.BGM.001
Jubilee presents lent by Her Majesty the
Queen
Early months
Subsequently held at the Glasgow International
Exhibition (1888), and circulated.
PUBLICATION: v.1888.007

1890

VX.1890.XXX.001
Indian metalwork
VENUE: Armourers' Company
exhibition

1891

VX.1891.001
Competition designs for the new South
Kensington Museum building
Previously displayed in the tea room at the House
of Commons.

1895

VX.1895.001
Japanese stencil plates
18 January–
Photographic prints. — Duration: a few weeks.

1896

VX.1896.001
Brass rubbings; books of ornament
Summer
Held in the Library "for the benefit of the summer course students"–*Report of the Science and Art Department* (1897), p. xliv.

VX.1896.002
Illuminated manuscripts
Autumn
Lent by William Morris and others.

VX.1896.003
Retrospective exhibition of gold and silver medallists in the National Competitions for students of Government art schools
PUBLICATION: VR.1897.003

VX.1896.BGM.001
A special loan collection of English furniture and figured silks
11/12/13 June–Autumn?
PUBLICATION: V.1896.003

VX.1896.BGM.002
Pictures from the Chantrey Bequest, Royal Academy
To 1897

1898

VX.1898.001
The loan collection of lithographs
21 November–
Held in association with the Society of Arts.
PUBLICATIONS: V.1898.004;
V.1899.006

1901

VX.1901.001
The loan exhibition of modern illustration
12 January–4 May
Held in association with the Society of Arts. Also held at the Museum of Science and Art, Edinburgh, June–September.
PUBLICATIONS: V.1901.002;
VR.1901.001

VX.1901.002
Photographs of historical and architectural subjects and landscape
19 July–4 February 1902
Photographs taken by, and from the collection of, Sir Benjamin Stone, supplemented from the collections of the National Art Library.
PUBLICATION: V.1901.001

1902

VX.1902.001
Coronation art
Summer?
Prints and drawings, some of which are listed in *The museums journal*, Vol. 1 (1901–2), p. 274–5.

1903

VX.1903.001
The loan exhibition of British engraving and etching
13 May–30 September
Held in association with the Society of Arts. Accompanied by a collection of tools and materials used in etching and engraving.
PUBLICATIONS: V.1903.003

1904

VX.1904.001
Paintings by George Morland
May–June
PUBLICATIONS: V.1904.002;
V.1904.003

VX.1904.BGM.001
The first circulating collection of water-colours
May–December
PUBLICATION: V.1904.005

VX.1904.XXX.001
Reproductions of art objects
VENUE: Louisiana Purchase Exposition

1905

VX.1905.001
The loan exhibition of process engraving
14 March–25 June
Later travelled to the Municipal School of Technology, Manchester.
PUBLICATION: V.1905.001

VX.1905.XXX.001
English silversmiths' art
"A collection of electrotype reproductions of plate in the Royal collections and . . . various college and corporate bodies was lent to Toronto"–Report for the year 1905 on the Victoria and Albert Museum . . . (1907), p. 9.

1907

VX.1907.001
Japanese educational exhibition
May
Items lent by Baron Kikuchi to accompany a series of lectures given by him at the University of London. The collection was afterwards circulated until 1911.
PUBLICATION: VR.1907.001

1911

VX.1911.BGM.001
Abyssinian objects
Collection presented to the King by Emperor Menelik as a Coronation gift.

1912

VX.1912.001
Dickens exhibition
March–December
PUBLICATION: V.1912.004

VX.1912.002
Robert Browning centenary display
7 May–early September

VX.1912.003
Cape Town Cathedral memorial record of the Boer War (1899–1902)
23 May–22 June
PUBLICATIONS: V.1912.002;
VR.1912.001

VX.1912.004
Paintings by Peter de Wint and William Hilton
End May–early December

VX.1912.005
French tapestries, carpets and silk fabrics
18 July–11 November
Loan exhibition from the Mobilier national, Paris.
PUBLICATIONS: V.1912.007;
V.1913.009

1913

VX.1913.001
British silhouettes
28 March–December
Lent by Francis Wellesley.

VX.1913.002
Japanese colour prints
6 December–end June 1914
Lent by R. Leicester Harmsworth.
PUBLICATION: V.1913.007

VX.1913.BGM.001
Furniture
"A small collection . . . brought together with a view to placing before the public artistic examples which can be produced at a low cost . . . received on loan from Mr J.H. Whitehouse, M.P."–Report for the year 1913 on the Victoria and Albert Museum and the Bethnal Green Museum (1914), p. 82.

VX.1913.XXX.001
English costume from the collection of Talbot Hughes
November
VENUE: Harrods, London
Collection exhibited in the department store before being presented to the Museum.
PUBLICATION: VR.1913.003

1914

VX.1914.001
Photographs of war damage in France
and Belgium

VX.1914.002
Paintings of the new Calcutta School
April–May
Lent by the Indian Society of Oriental Art,
Calcutta.
PUBLICATION: v.1914.001

VX.1914.003
Miniatures in plumbago etc.
To 1915
Lent by Francis Wellesley.
PUBLICATION: v.1915.001

VX.1914.004
Miniatures
To 1915
Lent by Henry J. Pfungst.
PUBLICATION: v.1915.002

VX.1914.005
Collection of tapestries, carpets,
embroideries and furniture lent by the
Duke of Buccleuch
2 March–6 July
PUBLICATIONS: v.1914.008;
v.1914.009; v.1914.010; v.1915.006;
v.1915.007

VX.1914.006
National Competitions
July–
Annual exhibition of students' work from the
Government schools of art, held on this occasion in
the Museum.
PUBLICATION: vr.1914.001

1915

VX.1915.001
Ivan Meštrović
July–August
PUBLICATION: vr.1915.001

VX.1915.002
Children's exhibition
26 December–23 January 1916
Included "objects having reference to war and
fighting, English dolls' houses . . . dolls illustrating
English costume . . . and a model of a Japanese
palace building . . . graciously lent by Her Royal
Highness Princess Mary"–*Report for the year 1915
on the Victoria and Albert Museum and the Bethnal
Green Museum* (1916), p. 7.

VX.1915.XXX.001
German and Austrian commercial art
March
VENUE: Goldsmiths' Hall, London

VX.1915.XXX.002
British Industries Fair
April
VENUE: Agricultural Hall, London
"The Museum . . . co-operated with the Board of
Trade in connection with the section of
Designs"–*Report for the year 1915 on the Victoria
and Albert Museum and the Bethnal Green
Museum* (1916), p. 8.

1916

VX.1916.001
British Industries Fair
21 February–3 March
In association with the Board of Trade.
PUBLICATION: vr.1916.001

VX.1916.002
Shakespeare tercentenary exhibition
23 April–
PUBLICATIONS: v.1916.006;
v.1916.007

VX.1916.003
Domestic interior paintings and wall-
papers
August
Exhibition intended for children.
PUBLICATION: v.1916.005

VX.1916.004
Children's exhibition
22 December–31 January 1917

VX.1916.005
Miniatures lent by the Duke of Buccleuch
1916–1917
PUBLICATIONS: v.1916.002;
v.1916.004; v.1918.004

VX.1916.006
Modern posters
February?–March?
To coincide with VX.1916.001.

VX.1916.XXX.001
British children's books
"In connection with an exhibition of children's books . . . organised by . . . the Union centrale des arts décoratifs, Paris, the Museum approached various publishers with a view to . . . forming a representative selection of children's books published in the United Kingdom"–*Report for the year 1916* (1917), p. 6.

1917

VX.1917.001
British Industries Fair
26 February–9 March
In association with the Board of Trade.
PUBLICATION: VR.1917.001

VX.1917.002
Modern European pottery and porcelain
Spring

VX.1917.003
Circulation Department exhibition
Spring?

VX.1917.004
Allied war photographs
10 May–14 June
From the Foreign Office.

VX.1917.005
Owen Jones Competition drawings
23 July–25 August
Competition for textile designs organised by the Royal Society of Arts.

VX.1917.006
Drawings, chiefly by Dr. Thomas Monro
[Latter part of the year]
PUBLICATION: V.1917.001

VX.1917.007
Children's exhibition of textiles
Christmas

VX.1917.IND.001
Mogul paintings
February–end December
From the collection of Lady Wantage.

1918

VX.1918.001
Owen Jones Competition drawings
July–August
See note under VX.1917.005.

VX.1918.002
Brass rubbings
PUBLICATION: V.1918.003

1919

VX.1919.001
War memorials
July–1 October
In co-operation with the Royal Academy War Memorials Committee.
PUBLICATIONS: V.1919.003;
VR.1919.001

VX.1919.002
Owen Jones Competition drawings
See note under VX.1917.005.

1920

VX.1920.001
Owen Jones Competition drawings
July–August
See note under VX.1917.005.

VX.1920.002
Old master drawings
Autumn?
PUBLICATION: V.1921.015

VX.1920.003
Spanish art
Late Autumn
Held to coincide with an exhibition at the Royal Academy.

VX.1920.004
English illuminated manuscripts and specimens of medieval book-binding
November–December
Objects lent by Durham and Winchester Cathedrals, and Stonyhurst. "Small but very select"–*Review of the principal acquisitions during the year 1920* (1924), p. 124.

VX.1920.005
Letter-paper and headings designs

1921

VX.1921.001
The Franco-British exhibition of textiles
Spring
Duration: 2 months.
PUBLICATIONS: V.1921.008;
V.1921.009; V.1922.009

VX.1921.002
Models and drawings relating to the art
of the theatre in past and modern times
June

VX.1921.003
Owen Jones Competition drawings
23 July–17 September
See note under VX.1917.005.

VX.1921.004
Wallpapers and posters
July

VX.1921.005
Armenian architecture from the 6th to
the 13th century
Drawings of architectural details and ornament by
A. Fetvadjian.
PUBLICATION: V.1921.001

1922

VX.1922.001
Present day industrial art
16 January–25 February
Organised by the British Institute of Industrial Art.
PUBLICATION: VR.1922.001

VX.1922.002
International theatre exhibition: designs
and models for the modern stage
June–July
"One of the most successful exhibitions ever held
at South Kensington"–*Review of the principal
acquisitions during the year 1922* (1925),
p. 108.
PUBLICATIONS: VR.1922.002;
VR.1922.003; VR.1922.004

VX.1922.003
Owen Jones Competition drawings
29 July–17 September
See note under VX.1917.005.

VX.1922.004
Japanese theatrical art
PUBLICATION: V.1922.012

1923

VX.1923.001
Sacred and secular dances of Bali, and
the marionette theatre of Java
21 April–
Watercolours and drawings by Tyra de Kleen.

VX.1923.002
Owen Jones Competition drawings
Mid-July–17 September
See note under VX.1917.005.

VX.1923.003
Facsimiles of Theban wall-paintings by
Nina de Garis Davies
July–August
Lent by Alan H. Gardiner.
PUBLICATION: V.1923.008

VX.1923.004
Old Colonial architecture in New South
Wales and Tasmania
July–August
Drawings by Hardy Wilson.

VX.1923.005
Drawings by Auguste Ravier
Late Summer?
PUBLICATION: V.1923.010

VX.1923.006
Industrial art today
September?–October
Organised by the British Institute of Industrial
Art.
PUBLICATION: VR.1923.002

VX.1923.007
Association of Old Students of the Royal
College of Art
15 December–19 January 1924
PUBLICATION: VR.1923.001

VX.1923.008
Drawings and tracings of English
medieval wall paintings
From the V&A's collection. Mainly by E.W.
Tristram.

VX.1923.009
Eric Gill: cartoons for the 14 stone panels
of the Stations of the Cross, Westminster
Cathedral

VX.1923.BGM.001
Children's exhibition?
"another gallery containing objects of special
interest to children was arranged"–*Review of the
principal acquisitions during the year 1923* (1926),
p. 107.

1924

VX.1924.001
The Memorial Roll of the Royal Army
Medical Corps, designed by Graily
Hewitt
1–29 February
PUBLICATION: V.1924.015

VX.1924.002
Inigo Jones designs for scenery and
costume for masques, James I–Charles I
May–June
From the library at Chatsworth, lent by the Duke of
Devonshire.

VX.1924.003
Royal Society of Arts competition for
industrial design
June

VX.1924.004
Owen Jones Competition drawings
July–August
See note under VX.1917.005.

VX.1924.005
Royal College of Art Sketch Club
October–November

VX.1924.BGM.001
Bethnal Green Men's Institute
exhibition
12 April–
PUBLICATION: VR.1924.001

VX.1924.BGM.002
Leaves and cuttings from illuminated
manuscripts
Circulation Department exhibition.
PUBLICATION: V.1924.014

VX.1924.BGM.003
Watercolours by Louis François Cassas,
of Roman remains in Istria and Dalmatia

1925

VX.1925.001
Waterloo Bridge: paintings, drawings
and prints, 1817 to the present day
February

VX.1925.002
Civil Service Arts Council exhibition
16 May–1 June
PUBLICATION: VR.1925.001

VX.1925.003
Royal Society of Arts competition for
industrial design
Summer

VX.1925.004
Arms and armour from the collection of
S.J. Whawell

VX.1925.005
Embroideries from the Greek Islands and
Turkey

VX.1925.BGM.001
Bethnal Green Men's Institute exhibition
16 May–16 June

VX.1925.BGM.002
Drawings of Hackney and Bethnal Green
Summer
Recent gift of the Hon. Arthur Villiers.
PUBLICATION: V.1925.004

1926

VX.1926.001
Civil Service Arts Council exhibition
20 March–5 April
PUBLICATION: VR.1926.001

VX.1926.002
Works of art belonging to the Livery
Companies of the City of London
21 July–3 October
PUBLICATIONS: v.1926.003;
v.1927.005

VX.1926.003
Drawings, etchings & woodcuts by
Samuel Palmer and other disciples of
William Blake
20/21 October–January 1927
PUBLICATION: v.1926.002

VX.1926.004
Royal College of Art Sketch Club
October–November

VX.1926.BGM.001
Bethnal Green Men's Institute exhibition
15 April–
PUBLICATION: vr.1926.002

1927

VX.1927.001
Civil Service Arts Council exhibition
19 March–2 April
PUBLICATION: vr.1927.002

VX.1927.002
Modern French and Russian designs for
costume and scenery
March–June
PUBLICATION: v.1927.004

VX.1927.003
Playbills and theatrical prints from the
Gabrielle Enthoven collection
March–June
PUBLICATION: v.1927.004

VX.1927.004
Contemporary French prints
10/11 May–20 June
Held under the auspices of l'Association française
d'expansion et d'échanges artistiques.
PUBLICATION: vr.1927.003

VX.1927.005
William Blake centenary display
Summer

VX.1927.006
Royal College of Art Sketch Club
Early November
Duration: 2 weeks.

VX.1927.BGM.001
Bethnal Green Men's Institute
exhibition
11 April–
Duration: 4 weeks.
PUBLICATION: vr.1927.001

1928

VX.1928.001
Civil Service Arts Council exhibition
17–31 March
PUBLICATION: vr.1928.002

VX.1928.002
Elizabethan embroideries
Spring?
Lent by Lord Leconfield and Mr F. Ward.

VX.1928.003
Gifts made to the nation through the
National Art Collections Fund
Early June

VX.1928.004
Mosaics and frescoes in Kahrié-Djami
Constantinople
Summer
Copied by Dmitri Ismailovitch.
PUBLICATION: v.1928.004

VX.1928.005
Francesco Bartolozzi centenary
exhibition of prints
October–November

VX.1928.006
Royal College of Art Sketch Club

VX.1928.BGM.001
Bethnal Green Men's Institute
exhibition
4 June–
Duration: 4 weeks.
PUBLICATION: vr.1928.001

1929

VX.1929.001
Valentines
13 February–

VX.1929.002
Civil Service Arts Council exhibition
16 March–1 April
PUBLICATION: VR.1929.004

VX.1929.003
Contemporary American prints
14 May–22 June
Under the auspices of the American Federation of
Arts, Washington, D.C.
PUBLICATION: VR.1929.005

VX.1929.004
Miniatures by George Engleheart, J.C.D.
Engleheart and Thomas Richmond
May–June
PUBLICATION: V.1929.006

VX.1929.005
British industrial art for the slender purse
9 November–18 December
Organised by the British Institute of Industrial Art.
PUBLICATION: VR.1929.003

VX.1929.006
Russian icons
16 November–29 December
PUBLICATION: VR.1929.001

VX.1929.BGM.001
Bethnal Green Men's Institute exhibition
10 June–
Duration: 5 weeks.
PUBLICATION: VR.1929.002

1930

VX.1930.001
Royal College of Art Sketch Club
January–February
Exhibition postponed from 1929.

VX.1930.002
Finnish rugs
Mid-February–mid-March
Lent by the National Museum of Finland, Helsinki,
and the Antell Foundation.
PUBLICATION: V.1930.002

VX.1930.003
English mediaeval art
14 May–
PUBLICATIONS: V.1930.009;
V.1930.010; V.1933.002

VX.1930.004
Josiah Wedgwood: bicentenary of his
birth
31 May–13 July
PUBLICATION: V.1930.011

VX.1930.005
Royal College of Art Sketch Club
November–December

VX.1930.006
Drawings, caricatures, relics etc. of Sir
Henry Irving
December–January 1931
Mainly from the Enthoven collection.

VX.1930.BGM.001
Bethnal Green Men's Institute exhibition
19 June–
Duration: 5 weeks.
PUBLICATION: VR.1930.001

VX.1930.BGM.002
Ancient and modern lettering
August–Sept
Circulation Department exhibition.

VX.1930.BGM.003
Margaret Bulley collection of modern
decorative art
Autumn
Loan through the British Institute of Industrial Art.
— "outstanding examples of the advanced school
of present-day decorative art . . . the work of such
modernists as Roger Fry, Duncan Grant, Vanessa
Bell, Mary Hogarth, McKnight Kauffer . . ."–
*Review of the principal acquisitions during the year
1930* (1931), p. 126.

1931

VX.1931.001
Paper casts and photographs of
Byzantine mosaics from the Mosque of
the Omeyyads, Damascus
14 February–14 March
Lent by M. E. de Lorey.
PUBLICATION: V.1931.011

VX.1931.002
English drawings, mainly book illustrations
February

VX.1931.003
Persian and other Near Eastern metalwork
March
Collection of Ralph Harari.

VX.1931.004
Illuminated addresses
Mid-April–mid-June
Organised by the Society of Scribes and Illuminators.

VX.1931.005
Mrs Siddons playbills from the Enthoven collection
6 June–21 August

VX.1931.006
British and foreign posters
22 June–30 September
Supplemented by a loan from the Empire Marketing Board.
PUBLICATION: V.1931.007

VX.1931.007
Lettering in the various crafts
June
Organised by the British Institute of Industrial Art.

VX.1931.008
Royal College of Art Sketch Club
November–December

VX.1931.BGM.001
Bethnal Green Men's Institute exhibition
21 May–
Duration: 4 weeks.
PUBLICATION: VR.1931.001

1932

VX.1932.001
Watercolours by Thomas Rowlandson
January
From the bequest of Captain Desmond Coke. Accompanied by prints and drawings from the Hans Velten bequest.

VX.1932.002
Arms and armour: the G.H. Ramsbottom Bequest
February

VX.1932.003
Civil Service Arts Council exhibition
14–28 March

VX.1932.004
Modern British embroidery
1–30 July
Organised by the British Institute of Industrial Art.
PUBLICATION: VR.1932.002

VX.1932.005
English illustrated children's books
14/15 October–12 November
Organised in collaboration with the National Book Council. "One of the most popular temporary exhibitions held in the Museum . . . the modern books were not shown in cases and could, therefore, be examined by visitors"–*Review of the Principal Acquisitions during the year 1932* (1933), p. 65.
PUBLICATION: VR.1932.003

VX.1932.006
Royal College of Art Sketch Club
November

VX.1932.007
Baxter prints
November–February 1933
From the Francis William Baxter bequest.

VX.1932.008
Covent Garden Theatre bicentenary exhibition
December–March 1933
Playbills and prints from the Gabrielle Enthoven collection.

VX.1932.BGM.001
Bethnal Green Men's Institute exhibition
23 June–
Duration: 6 weeks.
PUBLICATION: VR.1932.001

VX.1932.BGM.002
Fashion plates 1850–1900
November–December

VX.1932.BGM.003
Children's books: early 18th century-
ca.1830
December–
Series of displays selected from VX.1932.005. See
also VX.1933.BGM.001.

Indian Section

VX.1932.IND.001
Sculpture; Mogul and modern paintings;
Tibetan temple pictures
June–September 1933

1933

VX.1933.001
Theatrical designs by Charles Ricketts
January–end March

VX.1933.002
Civil Service Arts Council exhibition
11–25 March

VX.1933.003
Photographs of English medieval
architecture and sculpture
April–May
Lent by the Preussisches Forschungsinstitut für
Kunstgeschichte, Marburg.

VX.1933.004
Edmund Kean centenary display of
playbills and prints
May

VX.1933.005
Woodcuts and wood engravings,
15th–20th centuries
August–November

VX.1933.006
Flower drawings and prints, 16th–20th
centuries
August–December

VX.1933.007
Paintings of a century ago (1830–35)
October–December

VX.1933.008
Royal College of Art Sketch Club
Early December
Duration: first fortnight of December.

VX.1933.009
Drawings and engravings of Victorian
pantomimes
15 December–January 1934

VX.1933.BGM.001
Children's books (i) 19th century; (ii)
20th century
Series of displays selected from VX.1932.005. See
also VX.1932.BGM.003.

VX.1933.IND.001
Siamese and South Indian printed cottons
January–end March
Lent by Prince Damrong of Siam.

1934

VX.1934.001
William Morris centenary exhibition
9 February–8 April
PUBLICATION: V.1934.001

VX.1934.002
British art 1550–1850
February–April
Held to coincide with an exhibition at the Royal
Academy.

VX.1934.003
Paintings, pastels, watercolours and
etchings by Walter James
April–July
The artist, the late Lord Northbourne, had been on
the Museum's Advisory Council.

VX.1934.004
Watercolours, pastels, etchings and
lithographs by J.A. McN. Whistler
April–July

VX.1934.005
English silversmiths' work
June
Held in collaboration with the Council for Art and
Industry.
PUBLICATION: V.1934.002

VX.1934.006
History of line engraving
October–February 1935

VX.1934.007
Royal College of Art Sketch Club
7 November–8 December

VX.1934.BGM.001
Bethnal Green Men's Institute
exhibition
27 October–
PUBLICATION: VR.1934.001

1935

VX.1935.001
Civil Service Arts Council exhibition
20 February–8 March

VX.1935.002
English pottery old and new
April–August
Held in collaboration with the Council for Art and
Industry.
PUBLICATIONS: V.1935.002;
V.1936.006

VX.1935.003
Chinese art: the Eumorfopoulos
collection
April–1936?
The collection was later split between the V&A and
the British Museum.
PUBLICATION: V.1936.003

VX.1935.004
Nigel Playfair memorial exhibition
April–

VX.1935.005
Paintings by foreign artists
June–
19th century European works, excluding French. —
Duration: a few months.

VX.1935.006
Air Force Artists Association
16–26 October

VX.1935.007
History of etching
October–end December

VX.1935.008
Theatre posters
October–end December

VX.1935.009
Royal College of Art Sketch Club
17 November–8 December

VX.1935.BGM.001
London topographical prints and
drawings
16 July–
Including Philip Norman's drawings of old London.

1936

VX.1936.001
Photographs of medieval architecture and
painting in Cyprus
January–February
Photographs taken by C.J.P. Cave.

VX.1936.002
Civil Service Arts Council exhibition
February–March

VX.1936.003
English domestic metalwork
April–June
Held in collaboration with the Council for Art and
Industry.
PUBLICATION: V.1936.007

VX.1936.004
Polish graphic art and textiles
Summer-Autumn
Organised by the Polish Embassy and the Society
for the Propagation of Polish Art Abroad. Textiles
by members of the Ład, a cooperative decorative
artists' society.
PUBLICATION: VR.1936.002

VX.1936.005
Models and designs by Sir Alfred Gilbert
Autumn
PUBLICATION: V.1936.004

VX.1936.006
Children's exhibition
December–January 1937

VX.1936.007
Modern commercial typography
December–January 1937

VX.1936.008
Designs for silhouette films by Lotte
Reiniger

VX.1936.009
Pickwick Papers centenary display

VX.1936.010
Royal College of Art Sketch Club

VX.1936.BGM.001
Bethnal Green Men's Institute exhibition
30 January–
PUBLICATION: VR.1936.001

1937

VX.1937.001
Civil Service Arts Council Coronation
Exhibition
24 March–28 April
PUBLICATION: VR.1937.002

VX.1937.002
Hungarian graphic art
5 May–August
Organised by the Society of Hungarian Painter-
Etchers, Budapest.
PUBLICATION: VR.1937.003

VX.1937.003
Kings and queens of England,
1500–1900
7 May–July?
PUBLICATION: V.1937.003

VX.1937.004
Patchwork quilts
23 September–end October

VX.1937.005
Royal College of Art Sketch Club

VX.1937.BGM.001
Bethnal Green Men's Institute exhibition
21 June–
PUBLICATION: VR.1937.001

1938

VX.1938.001
Northern Graphic Union exhibition
April
"comprising Denmark, Finland, Iceland, Norway,
Sweden"–VR.1938.002.
PUBLICATION: VR.1938.002

VX.1938.002
Technical exhibit of woven and printed
furnishing textiles
31 October–31 December
PUBLICATION: V.1938.010

VX.1938.003
Etchings and drawings by Goya
July?–September?
Held on the occasion of new printings from original
plates lent by the Spanish Government.

VX.1938.004
Flower books and drawings

VX.1938.BGM.001
Bethnal Green Men's Institute exhibition.
28 November–end December?
PUBLICATION: VR.1938.001

1939

VX.1939.001
Early photography
25 January —
PUBLICATIONS: V.1939.001;
V.1939.005

VX.1939.002
Tiles and tilework
18 March–September
Held in collaboration with the Council for Art and
Industry.
PUBLICATION: V.1939.003

1940

VX.1940.001
English posters

1941

VX.1941.001
Arts and crafts
Before July

VX.1941.002
Eric Gill memorial display
January?–

VX.1941.003
Van Dyck tercentenary exhibition
9? December–
Drawings, etchings and photographs. (Paintings
from the National Gallery would have been
exhibited, but they had been placed in safe storage
during the War.)

1942

VX.1942.001
Water colour drawings and sculpture,
1919–1939
March–August
PUBLICATION: V.1942.001

VX.1942.002
Miniatures from the collection of the
Duke of Buccleuch

VX.1942.003
British landscape in oils
18 December–17 January 1943
Touring exhibition organised by the Council for the
Encouragement of Music and the Arts.
PUBLICATION: VR.1942.001

1943

VX.1943.001
Drawings of the old masters from the
Witt collection
January–May
PUBLICATION: V.1943.001

VX.1943.002
Holbein (1497–1543): 4th centenary
[Winter]
A "representative selection" of this exhibition was
later toured by the Council for the Encouragement
of Music and the Arts. See VR.1944.001

1944

VX.1944.001
Recording Britain
Spring–early Summer
Drawings and paintings of Britain made during the
War. Exhibition held to mark their presentation to
the V&A by the Pilgrim Trust.
PUBLICATION: VR.1944.002

1945

VX.1945.001
How to understand modern painting
Before November?
Educational display of photographic reproductions
of contemporary paintings with explanations.
Organised by the Museum of Modern Art, New
York, and presented to the V&A by Mrs Otto
Kahn in preparation for VX.1945.003

VX.1945.002
Edward Johnston memorial exhibition
October–December
PUBLICATION: V.1945.001

VX.1945.003
Picasso, Matisse
1 November–11 January 1946
Organised by l'Association française d'action
artistique and the British Council. Exhibition
touring under the auspices of the British Council
and the Arts Council of Great Britain.
PUBLICATION: VR.1945.001

VX.1945.004
Royal effigies, sculpture & other works
of art from Westminster Abbey
November
PUBLICATION: VR.1945.002

VX.1945.005
Masterpieces of English craftsmanship

1946

VX.1946.001
Works by John Constable
1 February–30 April

VX.1946.002
Photographs of American colonial
architecture
March–
Presented by the Georgian Group.
PUBLICATION: VR.1946.001

VX.1946.003
Style in sculpture
27 March–31 May
PUBLICATION: VR.1947.005

VX.1946.004
Britain can make it
24 September–
Organised by the Council of Industrial Design.
PUBLICATION: VR.1946.002

VX.1946.005
City church plate
December–February 1947
Plate belonging to the churches in the City of
London.

VX.1946.006
Kate Greenaway and Randolph
Caldecott centenary

VX.1946.007
Six hundred years of fashion design.

1947

VX.1947.001
Early examples of glass at the Victoria &
Albert Museum
1 February?–

VX.1947.002
Contemporary British prints and
drawings from the Wakefield collection
of the British Council
12 March–12 April
PUBLICATION: VR.1947.001

VX.1947.003
Masterpieces of French tapestry
29 March–31 May
Organised in association with the Arts Council of
Great Britain.
PUBLICATIONS: VR.1947.002;
VR.1947.003

VX.1947.004
Pictures for schools
22 May–14 June
Organised by the Society for Education in Art.
PUBLICATION: VR.1947.004

VX.1947.005
Nicholas Hilliard and Isaac Oliver: an
exhibition to commemorate the 400th
anniversary of the birth of Nicholas
Hilliard
31 May–31 July
PUBLICATION: V.1947.007

VX.1947.006
Relics of the first Duke of Wellington
18 June–August 1947
PUBLICATION: V.1947.004

VX.1947.007
The human form in Indian sculpture
17/18 September–December?

VX.1947.008
Male costume
8 October–January 1948?

1948

VX.1948.001
British film art
27 February–15 May
Organised by the Society of British Film Art
Directors and Designers.

VX.1948.002
Old master drawings from the Albertina
collection, Vienna
17 April–30 May 1948
Organised by the Arts Council of Great Britain.
PUBLICATIONS: VR.1948.001;
VR.1948.007

VX.1948.003
English pottery and porcelain
5 May–6 or 20 June
Organised by the English Ceramic Circle.
PUBLICATIONS: VR.1948.005;
VR.1949.003

VX.1948.004
English windmills
1 June–29 August

VX.1948.005
Book illustration by Matisse, Picasso and
Rouault
9 June–29 August

VX.1948.006
English church plate
2 July–

VX.1948.007
Sport in art
15 July–14 August

Organised on the occasion of the Olympic Games in London.
PUBLICATIONS: VR.1948.002;
VR.1948.008

VX.1948.008
150 years of lithography, 1798–1948
19 October–31 December

VX.1948.009
Danish art treasures through the ages
28 October–2 January 1949
Organised in association with the Danish Government. — 'Architect of the exhibition': Kaare Klint–VR.1948.003.
PUBLICATIONS: VR.1948.003;
VR.1948.004; VR.1948.006

VX.1948.010
Marion Richardson memorial exhibition
20–29 November
Display of paintings by child pupils of Marion Richardson, organised by the Society for Education in Art. — The Arts Council of Great Britain made a selection from this exhibition, for touring.

1949

VX.1949.001
Book-bindings
15/16 February–18 April
A smaller version was selected for the Circulation Department, V.1949.005.

VX.1949.002
Art for all
6/7 April–30 June
London Transport posters exhibition.
PUBLICATION: VR.1949.001

VX.1949.003
The personal history of David Copperfield
1 May–

VX.1949.004
Colonial views and scenes
June–July
"part of the concerted effort, under the direction of the Colonial Office, to stimulate interest in the colonies"–[exhibition poster]. The British Museum and other institutions participated in 'Colonial Month'.

VX.1949.005
Peter de Wint
30 June–end September

VX.1949.006
The art of the book jacket
5 October–January 1950
An international exhibition of book-jackets from 19 countries. — Part was selected for the Circulation Department. Including showings at the Kunstgewerbemuseum, Zürich, 3 February–4 March 1951; Stedelijk Museum, Amsterdam; Nationalmuseum, Stockholm.
PUBLICATIONS: V.1949.001;
V.1949.002; VR.1951.001;
VR.1951.003

VX.1949.007
Painted panels by John Piper
17/18 November–4 December
Works commissioned for the British Embassy in Rio de Janeiro. Displayed alongside was the only set of furniture designed by Eric Ravilious.

1950

VX.1950.001
French landscape paintings
January–

VX.1950.002
The public house of tomorrow
4–29 April
Exhibition of drawings submitted in a competition to design interiors for pubs. Organised by *Architectural review*.
PUBLICATION: VR.1950.004

VX.1950.003
Handmade furniture
4/5–30 April
Organised by the Rural Industries Bureau.
PUBLICATION: VR.1950.005

VX.1950.004
British stage design
19 April–23 July
Organised by the Association of Theatrical Designers and Craftsmen.
PUBLICATIONS: V.1950.012;
VR.1950.002

VX.1950.005
William & Mary and their time
21 June–20 August
Organised by the Arts Council of Great Britain.
PUBLICATION: VR.1950.006

VX.1950.006
Prints and drawings of birds and
flowers
July–September

VX.1950.007
The Eighth Army memorial window for
Cairo Cathedral
20 September–18 October
Designed by Adrian Gilbert Scott; made by James
Powell & Sons (Whitefriars) Ltd.

VX.1950.008
22nd exhibition of the Arts & Crafts
Exhibition Society
1 November–3 December
PUBLICATION: VR.1950.001

VX.1950.009
Giles Bequest Competition
17 November–December
Prize for coloured woodcuts and lino cuts,
organised jointly with the British Museum.

VX.1950.010
Playing cards and parlour games
6/7 December–4 March 1951

VX.1950.011
Eighteen paintings from the Wellington
Gift
Arts Council of Great Britain touring exhibition.
PUBLICATION: VR.1949.002

VX.1950.012
Polish illustration and book covers
Organised by the Circulation Department and the
Polish Cultural Institute.
PUBLICATION: VR.1950.003

1951

VX.1951.001
Music titles
January
Organised by the Arts Council of Great Britain.

VX.1951.002
Victorian photography from the
Gernsheim collection
1 May–10 October
Organised by the Arts Council of Great Britain on
the occasion of the Festival of Britain.
PUBLICATION: VR.1951.004

VX.1951.003
The Great Exhibition of 1851
3 May–11 October
Centenary exhibition.
PUBLICATIONS: V.1950.617;
V.1964.009

VX.1951.004
British books from Caxton to the present
day
May–30 September
Organised by the National Book League on the
occasion of the Festival of Britain.
PUBLICATION: VR.1951.002

VX.1951.005
Somerset Maugham collection of
theatrical paintings
18/19 July–
Late 18th and early 19th century paintings, notably
by Zoffany, and watercolours; bequeathed to the
National Theatre.

VX.1951.006
BBC drawings: original drawings made
for BBC publications
31 October–31 December

VX.1951.BGM.001
East London churches exhibition
24 May–24 June
Organised by the Bishop of Stepney on the occasion
of the East London Church Congress.

VX.1951.IND.001
Sir William Rothenstein collection of
Indian paintings and drawings
8/9 March–July?

VX.1951.IND.002
A loan exhibition of Persian miniature
paintings, 1300–1900
20/21 December–
Duration: several months.
PUBLICATION: V.1951.003

1952

VX.1952.001
Women's Institutes exhibition of
handicrafts
13–26 March
Organised by the National Federation of Women's
Institutes.
PUBLICATIONS: VR.1952.001;
VR.1952.003

VX.1952.002
The Brunswick art treasures
To 24 August
PUBLICATION: V.1952.005

VX.1952.003
Giles Bequest Competition
September
See note, VX.1950.009. Circulation Department
exhibition.

VX.1952.004
Victorian wall sheets
September

VX.1952.005
Victorian and Edwardian decorative arts
23/24 October–18 January 1953
Held to mark the centenary of the V&A.
PUBLICATIONS: V.1952.006;
V.1952.023

VX.1952.BGM.001
Toy and model soldiers
July–end October

VX.1952.IND.001
Photographs of Indian sculpture, by
Raymond Burnier
12/13 June–
PUBLICATION: VR.1950.007

VX.1952.XXX.001
A hundred early English watercolours
March
VENUE: Municipal Art Gallery,
Middlesbrough, Yorkshire

1953

VX.1953.001
English life: how our ancestors lived from
1700 to 1850
1/2 April–end August

VX.1953.002
Paintings and drawings by John
Constable
16/17 April or 1 May–28 June
PUBLICATION: V.1953.008

VX.1953.003
Fifty years of the National Art
Collections Fund
14 May–mid-August

VX.1953.004
'Art and flowers' display
6–16 June
Over 20,000 flowers sent from Holland, for a
display to mark the Coronation of Queen Elizabeth
II.

VX.1953.005
Royal College of Art students' work
9/10 July–11 August
PUBLICATION: VR.1953.001

VX.1953.006
The collection of John Evelyn
3/4 November–28 February 1954

VX.1953.BGM.001
Thomas Bewick bicentenary exhibition
24/25 September–14 November
PUBLICATION: V.1953.007

VX.1953.IND.001
Indian paintings and drawings (the
Gayer-Anderson gift)
18/19 March–31 August

VX.1953.IND.002
Bazaar paintings from Calcutta
24/25 September–April 1954
For Circulation Department version: see
V.1955.001.
PUBLICATION: V.1953.002

VX.1953.XXX.001
Gothic art
11 July–1 September
VENUE: Peterborough Cathedral
Circulation Department exhibition: "the most
ambitious ever sent on tour by the Victoria and
Albert Museum"–VR.1953.002, p. [1].
PUBLICATION: VR.1953.002

1954

VX.1954.001
Royal plate from Buckingham Palace and
Windsor Castle
18/19 February–19 April
PUBLICATIONS: v.1954.002;
v.1954.012

VX.1954.002
Queen Mary's art treasures from
Marlborough House
26 May–31 December
PUBLICATIONS: v.1954.006;
v.1954.010

VX.1954.003
Early American silverware
1 October–
All pieces made by members of the Ancient and
Honorable Artillery Company of Massachusetts. —
Duration: a few weeks.

VX.1954.004
Rococo art from Bavaria
21/22 October–5 December?
Organised by the Bayerisches Nationalmuseum,
Munich.
PUBLICATIONS: v.1954.004;
v.1954.011

VX.1954.005
International colour woodcuts
17/18 November–16 January 1955
The British Section included the 1954 Giles
Bequest Competition winners (see note,
VX.1950.009).
PUBLICATION: v.1954.007

VX.1954.006
Contemporary American furnishing
fabrics and wallpapers
8–31 December
Circulation Department exhibition?

VX.1954.007
English furniture designs of the 18th and
19th centuries

VX.1954.BGM.001
Puppetry and the toy theatre
22/23 December–20 February 1955

1955

VX.1955.001
Royal College of Art: students' work
from the Departments of Fine Art and
Graphic Design
26/27 January–20 February

VX.1955.002
French theatre art
1 April–31 May
Organised by Valentine Fougère with the aid of
l'Association française d'action artistique.
PUBLICATION: vr.1955.002

VX.1955.003
Contemporary German furnishing fabrics
and wallpapers
22 April–30 June
Circulation Department exhibition.

VX.1955.004
Drawings of the nude
15 June–31 August

VX.1955.005
English theatre art: designs for theatrical
decor and costume in England
1–31 July
PUBLICATION: v.1955.008

VX.1955.006
E. McKnight Kauffer
6/7 October–25 November
Organised by the Society of Industrial Artists, with
the support of the Royal Society of Arts.
PUBLICATION: vr.1955.001

VX.1955.007
Sophie Fedorovitch, 1893–1953: a
memorial exhibition
8/9 December–5 February 1956
Circulation Department exhibition.
PUBLICATION: v.1955.014

VX.1955.XXX.001
Indian paintings from the Victoria and
Albert Museum
7–28 May
VENUE: Arts Council Gallery,
Cambridge
Arts Council touring exhibition.
PUBLICATION: vr.1955.003

VX.1955.XXX.002
English chintz: two centuries of changing taste
December
VENUE: Cotton Board Colour, Design and Style Centre, Manchester
Circulation Department exhibition.
PUBLICATION: V.1955.003;
V.1955.004; V.1967.007

1956

VX.1956.001
Anglo-Jewish art and history
(1656–1956)
6 January–29 February
PUBLICATION: VR.1956.001

VX.1956.002
Oxburgh Hangings: needlework of Mary, Queen of Scots
17 January-
Works owned and conserved by the V&A, shown before return to Oxburgh Hall, Norfolk. — Duration: 2 months.

VX.1956.003
The art of the Chinese goldsmith: the Karl Kempe collection
15 March–early May

VX.1956.004
Contemporary Scandinavian furnishing fabrics and wallpapers
27 March–29 April
Circulation Department exhibition.

VX.1956.005
Handmade furniture
May
Circulation Department exhibition drawn from the collection of the Rural Industries Bureau.

VX.1956.006
Modern American graphic art
7 June–31 July

VX.1956.007
Windows for Coventry: six of the windows for the Cathedral nave
3/4 July–30 September
PUBLICATION: VR.1956.002

VX.1956.008
Exhibition of medieval paintings from Norwich (St. Michael at Plea)
17/18 July–28 October
Organised in conjunction with the Courtauld Institute of Art.
PUBLICATION: V.1956.004

VX.1956.009
Modern tablewares from Germany, Holland and Italy
3 October–4 November
Circulation Department exhibition.

VX.1956.010
Giles Bequest Competition: winning woodcuts
14 November–13 January 1957
See note, VX.1950.009. Circulation Department exhibition.

VX.1956.011
Recent acquisitions
November–

VX.1956.BGM.001
Sketches by John Constable
1 September–30 December

1957

VX.1957.001
Modern Scandinavian tablewares
19 February–31 March
Circulation Department exhibition.

VX.1957.002
William Blake centenary exhibition
3/4 July–7 November

VX.1957.003
English silver 1660–1830
18 September–
Circulation Department exhibition sponsored by the British Council. Travelled to: Rijksmuseum, Amsterdam; Palazzo Venezia, Rome; Musée d'art et d'histoire, Geneva; Danske kunstindustrimuseum, Copenhagen.
PUBLICATIONS: VR.1957.001;
VR.1958.002; VR.1958.003; VR.1958.007

VX.1957.004
25th exhibition of the Arts & Crafts
Exhibition Society
5/6 November–8 December
PUBLICATION: VR.1957.002

VX.1957.005
The English inheritance
20/21 November–31 January 1958
Photographs from ten counties taken by the Royal
Commission on Historical Monuments.

VX.1957.006
C.F.A. Voysey
November–December
Circulation Department exhibition.

VX.1957.BGM.001
Victorian exhibition
9 December–2 March 1958

1958

VX.1958.001
Hildburgh memorial exhibition
29/30 January–30 March

VX.1958.002
[Contemporary?] American prints
19/20 February–7 April
Circulation Department exhibition?

VX.1958.003
Finnish rugs
6/7 March–4 May
Organised by the Finnish Society of Crafts and
Design. "This is the first exhibition in which the
public are encouraged to touch the objects. All the
modern rugs may be stroked . . ."[press release].
PUBLICATION: VR.1958.004

VX.1958.004
Contemporary Norwegian prints
2/3 April–4 May
Circulation Department exhibition in association
with the Royal Norwegian Embassy in London.

VX.1958.005
Selected acquisitions in Engraving,
Illustration and Design
June

VX.1958.006
Japanese art treasures
1/2 July–17 August
Organised by the Arts Council of Great Britain.
PUBLICATION: VR.1958.001

VX.1958.007
The House of Worth: a centenary
exhibition of designs for dresses
(1858–1958)
23/24 July–28 September

VX.1958.008
[Contemporary?] Italian prints
September
Circulation Department exhibition?

VX.1958.009
Masterpieces of Byzantine art
1 October–9 November
Sponsored by the Edinburgh Festival Society in
association with the Royal Scottish Museum where
exhibition was first held, 23 August–13 September
1958. — Exhibition director: David Talbot Rice.
PUBLICATIONS: V.1958.007;
VR.1958.005

VX.1958.010
Turkish, Caucasian and Persian carpets:
the Murray Graham collection
25/26 November–1 January 1959

VX.1958.011
Toys and table games
4/5 December–5 March 1959

VX.1958.012
Fifth Giles Bequest exhibition of
contemporary colour woodcuts and lino
cuts
December
See note, VX.1950.009. Circulation Department
exhibition.

1959

VX.1959.001
Norwegian art treasures
22 January–15 March
Also held at the Royal Scottish Museum,
Edinburgh, October–November 1958.
PUBLICATIONS: V.1959.010;
VR.1958.006

VX.1959.002
Mstislav V. Dobujinsky, 1875–1957:
memorial exhibition
13 March–7 June
PUBLICATION: v.1959.009

VX.1959.003
Rörstrand (1726–1959): three centuries
of Swedish pottery
15/16 April–31 May
Organised with the co-operation of the
Nationalmuseum, Stockholm, in association with
AB Rörstrands Porslinsfabriker.
PUBLICATION: vr.1959.001

VX.1959.004
Graphic art by West Midland students
30 April–24 May
Exhibition of work from the colleges and schools of
art in the West Midlands, organised under the
auspices of the West Midlands Advisory Council
for Technical, Commercial and Art Education.
PUBLICATION: vr.1959.002

VX.1959.005
Two thousand years of silk
9 June–12 July
Circulation Department exhibition.

VX.1959.006
Drawings by Italian artists, 1500–1800
22 June–October

VX.1959.007
Wedgwood bicentenary exhibition,
1759–1959
22/23 June–October?
Closing date extended from 30 August.
PUBLICATION: v.1959.017

VX.1959.008
Twentieth century British water-colours:
from the Tate Gallery and the Victoria &
Albert Museum
12 October–13 December
The Circulation Department made a selection for
touring, before and after.
PUBLICATION: v.1958.016

VX.1959.009
British studio pottery
To 30 November
Circulation Department exhibition.

VX.1959.010
Baxter prints
21 December–21 January 1960

VX.1959.011
Prints by Francesco Bartolozzi
21 December–21 January 1960

VX.1959.012
Wood engraving since Dürer
21 December–28 March 1960

1960

VX.1960.001
Robert Gibbings
28/29 January–28 March
PUBLICATION: v.1960.023

VX.1960.002
The country year: exhibition of
handicrafts
9–29 March
Organised by the National Federation of Women's
Institutes.
PUBLICATION: vr.1960.001;
vr.1960.002

VX.1960.003
Drawings and etchings by Giambattista
Tiepolo
12 April–2 October

VX.1960.004
Modern French tapestries
25/26 April–22 May
Organised by the Minstère des affairs étrangères
and the Association française d'action artistique.
PUBLICATION: vr.1960.003

VX.1960.005
English chintz
17/18 May–17 July
PUBLICATION: v.1960.004

VX.1960.006
A lady of fashion: Heather Firbank
30 September–4 December

VX.1960.007
Rex Whistler: memorial exhibition
12/13 October–18 December

Organised by the Arts Council of Great Britain. —
Included paintings, designs for murals, book-
illustrations and threatre designs.
PUBLICATION: VR.1960.005

VX.1960.008
Mural art today
26/27 October–15 January 1961
Circulation Department exhibition organised by the
Society of Mural Painters.
PUBLICATION: VR.1960.004

VX.1960.009
Swedish graphic art
25? November–
Circulation Department exhibition, lent by the
Swedish Society of Engravers.

VX.1960.010
Giles Bequest Competition
December?–January 1961
See note VX.1950.009. Circulation Department
exhibition.

1961

VX.1961.001
Recent acquisitions: Prints and
Drawings
19/20 January–23 April

VX.1961.002
National art treasures from Korea
22/23 March–7 May
Lent by the Government of the Republic of
Korea (South Korea).
PUBLICATION: VR.1961.001

VX.1961.003
Morris & Co. 1861–1940
10/11–30 April
Touring exhibition organised by the Arts Council of
Great Britain.
PUBLICATION: VR.1961.005

VX.1961.004
Chalon at the theatre
12 April–

VX.1961.005
The rural craftsman
4/5–28 May
Circulation Department exhibition drawn from the
collection of the Rural Industries Bureau.

VX.1961.006
Kuniyoshi centenary exhibition
4/5 May–31 July
The Circulation Department made a selection for
touring.
PUBLICATION: V.1961.006

VX.1961.007
Italian bronze statuettes
26/27 July–1 October
Organised by the Arts Council of Great Britain, in
association with the Italian Ministry of Education
and the Rijksmuseum, Amsterdam. Held
subsequently at the Rijksmuseum, and at Palazzo
Strozzi, Florence.
PUBLICATIONS: VR.1961.003;
VR.1961.004

VX.1961.008
Three centuries of engraved ornament
(1500–1800)
12/13 October–31 March 1962

VX.1961.009
Romanesque art
9 November–end December?
Consisted of the English loans to El arte románico,
the Council of Europe exhibition held at Barcelona
and Santiago, July–October.

VX.1961.010
Finlandia: modern Finnish design
16/17 November–7 January 1962
PUBLICATION: V.1961.005

VX.1961.BGM.001
British journalism: from Weekely newes
(1622) to the death of the News
chronicle (1960)
16/17 May–20 August

VX.1961.XXX.001
International exhibition of modern
jewellery, 1890–1961
26 October–2 December
VENUE: Goldsmiths' Hall, London
Organised in association with the Goldsmiths'
Company.
PUBLICATION: VR.1961.002

VX.1961.XXX.002
Tiepolo drawings
1961–1962
VENUES: National Gallery of Art,

Washington; Worcester Art Museum, Mass.; Museum of Fine Arts, Houston; Los Angeles County Museum; Art Institute of Chicago.

Circulation Department exhibition. Circulated in the United States by the Smithsonian Institution Traveling Exhibition Service.

PUBLICATION: VR.1961.006

1962

VX.1962.001
Modern American wall hangings
15/16 February–
Circulation Department exhibition.
PUBLICATION: V.1962.015

VX.1962.002
International art treasures
1/2 March–29 April
Organised by the International Confederation of Art Dealers, with the British Antique Dealers' Association.
PUBLICATION: VR.1962.003

VX.1962.003
Drawings from the collection of Bruce Ingram
1/2 May–16 August

VX.1962.004
Art of glass
15/16 May–8 July
Exhibition held to commemorate 25 years of the Circle of Glass Collectors.
PUBLICATION: VR.1962.002

VX.1962.005
London 1862: the International Exhibition
19/20 July–30 September
PUBLICATION: V.1962.013

VX.1962.006
Film designs for *Porgy and Bess*
1/2 October–25 April 1963
Closing date extended from 20 January.

VX.1962.007
Recent acquisitions
8 November–December

VX.1962.008
Claude Rotch bequest
6/7 December–February 1963

VX.1962.BGM.001
British transport models
26/27 April–8 July

1963

VX.1963.001
Fans from the Leonard Messel collection, lent by the Countess of Rosse
14/15 March–26 May

VX.1963.002
Drury Lane 1663–1963: three hundred years of theatrical history
4 April–
Duration: 2 months.

VX.1963.003
Art of the armourer
18/19 April–5 May
Organised by the Arms and Armour Society in honour of the third International Congress of Museums of Arms and Military History.
PUBLICATION: VR.1963.001

VX.1963.004
Adam patterns from Carron
9 May–9 June

VX.1963.005
C.R. Ashbee centenary
9 May–

VX.1963.006
Art nouveau designs and posters by Alphonse Mucha
23/24 May–early August?
PUBLICATIONS: V.1963.002;
V.1966.002; V.1967.001

VX.1963.007
Swedish folk art
13/14 June–13 July
From the collections of the Nordiska museet, Stockholm.

VX.1963.008
Swedish silver 1650–1800
13/14 June–1 September
Organised by the Swedish Institute for Cultural Relations.
PUBLICATION: VR.1963.004

VX.1963.009
Enthoven Purchase Fund: the first ten
years
25/26 July–

VX.1963.010
Eisenstein drawings
25/26 September–10 November
Organised by the Friends of the National Film
Archive.
PUBLICATION: VR.1963.002

VX.1963.011
Opus anglicanum
25/26 September–24 November
Organised by the Arts Council of Great Britain.
PUBLICATION: VR.1963.003

VX.1963.012
Omega Workshops 1913–1920
21/22 November–9 February 1964

VX.1963.BGM.001
Polish puppetry, and British puppets past
and present
13/14 May–14 July
Initiated by the Joint International Committee of
the Puppet and Model Theatre Guild and of the
Educational Puppetry Association.
PUBLICATION: v.1963.011

1964

VX.1964.001
The arts of Thailand
6 March–12 April
PUBLICATION: VR.1964.001

VX.1964.002
Shakespeare exhibition
23 April–4 August
Organised by the Arts Council of Great Britain.

VX.1964.003
Townswomen at home
25/26 May–7 June
Organised by the National Union of
Townswomen's Guilds.
PUBLICATION: VR.1964.004

VX.1964.004
Alastair Morton memorial exhibition
1/2–26 July

VX.1964.005
The growth of London, A.D. 43–1964
17 July–30 August
Organised on the occasion of the 20th International
Geographical Congress.
PUBLICATION: VR.1964.003

VX.1964.006
Polish graphic art
August–September
Circulation Department exhibition lent by the
DESA Gallery, Warsaw.

VX.1964.007
Dutch studio pottery
23 September–
Lent by the Royal Netherlands Embassy.

VX.1964.008
Recent acquisitions
8 October–

VX.1964.009
The orange and the rose: Holland and
Britain in the age of observation,
1600–1750
22 October–10 January 1965
Closing date extended from 13 December.
PUBLICATION: v.1964.013

VX.1964.010
Four hundred years of English
handwriting: an exhibition of
manuscripts and copy books
1543–1943
19 November–Summer 1965
National Art Library exhibition.
PUBLICATION: v.1964.008

VX.1964.011
Paintings from Western India
14–22 December

VX.1964.012
Prints illustrating French court
ceremonial from Louis XIV to
Charles X
17 December–March 1965
Loans from the Chalcographie du Louvre,
Paris.

VX.1964.BGM.001
Toys of today
23/24 July–18 October

VX.1964.XXX.001
English silver
7 April–21 June
VENUES: Matsuzakaya department
stores: Ueno, Ōsaka, Shizuoka, Nagoya.
Organisers: Eikoku Bunka Shinkōkai, Nihon Keizai
Shinbunsha.
PUBLICATION: VR.1964.002

1965

VX.1965.001
Tiles
27 February–28 March
Circulation Department exhibition.

VX.1965.002
Weaving for walls
2 April–2 May
Circulation Department exhibition organised with
the Association of Guilds of Weavers, Spinners and
Dyers.
PUBLICATION: V.1965.020

VX.1965.003
Bohemian glass
1/2 April–27 June
Organised through the Czechoslovak Ministry of
Culture and the British Council. Most exhibits from
the Prague Decorative Arts Museum.
PUBLICATIONS: V.1965.002;
V.1965.003

VX.1965.004
Modern prints: accessions
1961–1965
15/16 April–mid July

VX.1965.005
Twentieth century British
watercolours
7 May–6 June
Circulation Department exhibition supplemented
by pictures from the Imperial War Museum.

VX.1965.006
Barry Jackson memorial exhibition
13/14 May–25 July

VX.1965.007
Contemporary Canadian prints
12 June–4 July
Circulation Department exhibition.

VX.1965.008
Chinese painting and calligraphy from
the collection of John M. Crawford Jr.
17/18 June–1 August
Organised by the Arts Council of Great Britain.
PUBLICATION: VR.1965.002

VX.1965.009
Sumerian art
7 August–19 September
Circulation Department exhibition. — Objects from
the British Museum.

VX.1965.010
Pop graphics
23 September–31 October
Circulation Department exhibition.

VX.1965.011
World of the Bible
1 October–28 November
Centenary exhibition of the Palestine Exploration
Fund in co-operation with the British School of
Archaeology in Jerusalem.
PUBLICATION: VR.1965.003

VX.1965.012
Contemporary calligraphy
4/5–28 November
Circulation Department exhibition in association
with the Society of Scribes and Illuminators.

VX.1965.013
Victorian book illustration
18/19 November–April? 1966
From the collections of the National Art Library
and the Department of Prints and Drawings.
PUBLICATION:
VP.1933.001a[Suppl.1967]

VX.1965.014
Modern American woven fabrics
16 December–16 January 1966
Circulation Department exhibition.

1966

VX.1966.001
Russian exhibition
9 February–2 April

VX.1966.002
Clowns and fairies and theatrical designs
11 February–29 May

VX.1966.003
Aubrey Beardsley
20 May–18 September
PUBLICATIONS: v.1966.003;
v.1966.004

VX.1966.004
Islamic jades
16/17 June–31 July
Organised in association with the British
Museum.

VX.1966.005
Opera in London in the mid–19th
century
16/17 June–17 August?
For Circulation Department exhibition see
v.1969.034.

VX.1966.006
American studio pottery
4/5 August–25 September
Circulation Department exhibition.
PUBLICATION: v.1968.002

VX.1966.007
English silversmiths
10 September–23 November

VX.1966.008
Old Sheffield plate (1750–1850)
21 or 29/30 September–13 or 23
November
Organised by the Bowes Museum, Barnard Castle,
and previously held there.
PUBLICATION: VR.1966.003

VX.1966.009
Designs for English church
monuments
3/4 November–29 January 1967
PUBLICATION: v.1969.012

VX.1966.010
Etruscan art
November–December
Circulation Department exhibition. Lent by the
British Museum.

VX.1966.BGM.001
Half a century of modern design,
1900–1950
10/11 November–5 February? 1967

VX.1966.XXX.001
British watercolours, 1750–1850
VENUES: Museum of Fine Arts,
Houston; Pierpont Morgan Library, New
York; Worcester Art Museum,
Massachusetts; William Rockhill Nelson
Gallery of Art, Kansas City; Seattle Art
Museum; California Palace of the Legion
of Honor, San Francisco; St. Louis Art
Museum; Cleveland Museum of Art,
Ohio
Circulated by the International Exhibitions
Foundation.
PUBLICATION: VR.1966.001

VX.1966.XXX.002
English domestic silver, 1660–1910
4 March–24 April
VENUE: Hong Kong City Art Gallery
In association with the British Council, for 'British
Week in Hong Kong'.
PUBLICATION: VR.1966.002

1967

VX.1967.001
Great Britain, USSR
9 February–2 April
Organised by the British Foreign Office and the
Soviet Ministry of Foreign Affairs through the Arts
Council of Great Britain and the V&A.
PUBLICATION: VR.1967.001

VX.1967.002
Graphic work of S.W. Hayter
16/17 February–2 April
PUBLICATIONS: v.1967.008;
v.1967.018

VX.1967.003
New acquisitions, 1965–1966
2/3 March–September

VX.1967.004
Arms and armour
15 March–23 April
Mainly from Glasgow City Museum.

VX.1967.005
Ballet designs and illustrations
(1581–1940)
13 April–1 October
PUBLICATION: v.1967.002

VX.1967.006
Benin bronzes
26 April–4 June
Circulation Department exhibition. Objects lent by
the British Museum.

VX.1967.007
Recent acquisitions of the Circulation
Department
8 June–30 July

VX.1967.008
Six centuries of Persian painting
29/30 June–17 September
From this exhibition the Circulation Department, in
association with the Islamic Art Circle, selected a
touring exhibition of objects from Edmund de
Unger's collection.
PUBLICATION: V.1967.016

VX.1967.009
Photographs by Frederick H. Evans
3 August–10 September
Architectural subjects.

VX.1967.010
Hungarian art treasures: ninth to
seventeenth centuries
10/11 October–14 January 1968
Organised in conjunction with the British Council.
PUBLICATION: V.1967.013

VX.1967.011
Photographs of recent archaeological
excavations in Hungary
11 October–14 January 1968
Organised to accompany VX.1967.010.

VX.1967.012
Edward Gordon Craig, 1872–1966
1/2 November–12 January 1968
PUBLICATION: V.1967.006

VX.1967.013
Turkish art of the Seljuk and Ottoman
periods
7 November–3 December
Organised by the Arts Council of Great Britain.
PUBLICATION: VR.1967.003

VX.1967.014
A Victorian Christmas
December

VX.1967.BGM.001
Polish folk art
4 May–11 June
Organised by the Polish Cultural Institute.

VX.1967.BGM.002
Käthe Kollwitz
8 November–10 December
Organised by the German Arts Council.
PUBLICATION: VR.1967.002

1968

VX.1968.001
The incomparable Max: drawings by
Max Beerbohm (1872–1956)
15/16 January–18 February
Circulation Department exhibition.

VX.1968.002
A selection from the Gabrielle Enthoven
collection
16 January–
Organised to celebrate the anniversary of the
collector's birth.

VX.1968.003
Royal College of Art ceremonial robes
18 January–31 March
Robes designed by Joyce Conwy-Evans, first worn
at the ceremony to adopt the Royal Charter giving
the College university status, 2 November 1967.

VX.1968.004
The art of the postage stamp
19 February–17 March
Circulation Department exhibition.

VX.1968.005
Recent acquisitions
19 February–
Duration: several months.

VX.1968.006
Nineteenth century German drawings
from Düsseldorf
7/8 March–14 April
PUBLICATIONS: V.1968.030;
V.1968.031

VX.1968.007
Dame Marie Rambert collection of ballet
prints

7/8 March–

Duration: several weeks. — The Circulation Department made a selection for a touring exhibition: The romantic ballet.

VX.1968.008
The Wrightsman collection of gold boxes
19 March–

VX.1968.009
Danish design
17/18 April–3 June

Organised by the Danish Society of Arts and Crafts and Industrial Design. — 'Denmark in Britain 68'–VR.1968.004, t.p. verso.
PUBLICATION: VR.1968.004

VX.1968.010
The graphic work of Anthony Gross
26 April–29 September
PUBLICATIONS: V.1968.018;
V.1968.023

VX.1968.011
British Antique Dealers' Association Golden Jubilee
29 April–19 May
PUBLICATION: VR.1968.002

VX.1968.012
Medieval pottery
18 May–30 June

Circulation Department exhibition.
PUBLICATION: V.1966.011

VX.1968.013
Decimal coinage
29 May–

VX.1968.014
Victorian glass
1–31 July

Circulation Department exhibition.
PUBLICATION: V.1967.020

VX.1968.015
English glass
3/4 July–31 August

Organised on the occasion of the Triennial Conference of the International Commission on Glass.
PUBLICATIONS: V.1968.016;
V.1968.019

VX.1968.016
Englishmen in Italy, 1750–1900
16/17 July–22 September

Exhibition of watercolours.
PUBLICATION: V.1968.017

VX.1968.017
Arms from the Bargello
24 September–20 October

Arms and armour from the Museo nazionale, Florence, restored by the V&A conservators after the floods in Florence, 1966.

VX.1968.018
Italian stage designs from the Museo teatrale alla Scala, Milan
17/18 October–25 January 1969
PUBLICATION: V.1968.027

VX.1968.019
Charles Rennie Mackintosh centenary
29/30 October–29 December

Organised by the Scottish Arts Council in association with the Edinburgh Festival Society. Also held during the Edinburgh Festival 1968, at the Royal Scottish Museum, and subsequently in Darmstadt and Zürich under the auspices of the British Council.
PUBLICATION: VR.1968.003

VX.1968.020
English stained glass
October–December

Objects from the 12th Council of Europe Exhibition, L'Europe gothique, held in the Louvre, Paris, April–July

VX.1968.021
American coverlets
14 November–29 December

A John Judkyn Memorial exhibition in association with the American Museum in Britain, Bath.

VX.1968.022
Livres de peintres
19 December–28 June 1969

VX.1968.BGM.001
Bentwood furniture: the work of Michael Thonet (1796–1871)
29 May–30 June

Exhibition designed by Karl and Eva Mang, originally held at the Austrian Building Centre, Vienna. With financial assistance from the Arts Council of Great Britain.
PUBLICATIONS: VR.1965.001;
VR.1968.001

VX.1968.BGM.002
Modern prints: selected from recent
acquisitions of the Prints and Drawings
Department.
19 October–2 March 1969

1969

VX.1969.001
Peter Collingwood, Hans Coper
29 January–2 March
Circulation Department exhibition.
PUBLICATIONS: V.1969.009;
V.1969.010

VX.1969.002
Victorian engravings
31 January–30 April

VX.1969.003
Recent acquisitions: 1969
13 February–
Duration: several months.
PUBLICATION: V.1969.038

VX.1969.004
Photographs by Henri Cartier-Bresson
18/19 March–27 April
Circulation Department exhibition.
PUBLICATION: V.1969.036

VX.1969.005
William Holman Hunt
14/15 May–15 June
Exhibition organised jointly by the Arts Council of
Great Britain and the Walker Art Gallery,
Liverpool, where it was also held.
PUBLICATION: VR.1969.014

VX.1969.006
Festival designs by Inigo Jones
28/29 May–24 August
"Lent . . . by permission of His Grace The Duke of
Devonshire and the Trustees of the Chatsworth
Settlement"–VR.1969.008.
PUBLICATION: VR.1969.008

VX.1969.007
Embroidery today: 62 Group of the
Embroiderers' Guild
5 June–6 July
Circulation Department exhibition.
PUBLICATION: V.1969.017

VX.1969.008
Baroque in Bohemia
9/10 July–14 September
Organised by the National Gallery, Prague, also
held at Birmingham Museum and Art Gallery.
PUBLICATION: VR.1969.002

VX.1969.009
George Stubbs prints
17/18 July–31 August
Organised by the Paul Mellon Foundation; also
held at the Festival Gallery, Aldburgh.
PUBLICATIONS: VR.1969.012;
VR.1969.013

VX.1969.010
Claud Lovat Fraser
11 September–28 December
Circulation Department exhibition. For travelling
version, see V.1970.010
PUBLICATION: V.1969.008

VX.1969.011
German expressionism
20 September–2 November

VX.1969.012
Islamic pottery 800–1400
30 September/1 October–30 November
Organised by the Islamic Art Circle.
PUBLICATION: VR.1969.009

VX.1969.013
Berlioz and the romantic imagination
16/17 October–14 December
Organised with the Arts Council of Great Britain
on behalf of the Berlioz Centenary Committee.
PUBLICATION: VR.1969.003

VX.1969.014
Designs for Berlioz' Les troyens at the
Royal Opera House, by Nicholas
Georgiadis
22 October–9 November

VX.1969.015
Winnie-the-Pooh
17 December–25 January 1970
Designs by E.H. Shepard. — For Circulation
Department exhibition see V.1974.027.

VX.1969.016
Fine printing
1969–1970

VX.1969.BGM.001
Tiepolo drawings
20 March–31 August
Circulation Department exhibition.
PUBLICATION: v.1970.028

VX.1969.BGM.002
Posters then and now
13 November–22 February 1970
Posters of the 1890s and the 1960s.

1970

VX.1970.001
The Harari collection of Japanese
paintings and drawings
14/15 January–22 February
Organised by the Arts Council of Great Britain.
PUBLICATION: vr.1970.003

VX.1970.002
A decade of English naturalism,
1810–1820
15/16 January–1 March
Organised by the School of Fine Arts and Music of
the University of East Anglia; previously held at
Norwich Castle Museum.
PUBLICATION: vr.1969.007

VX.1970.003
The Mount Trust collection of Chinese
art
20/21 January–8 March
Circulation Department exhibition.
PUBLICATIONS: v.1970.024;
v.1971.029

VX.1970.004
Engraved ornament
To June

VX.1970.005
Drawings from the Teyler Museum,
Haarlem
12/13 March– 26 April
PUBLICATION: v.1970.013

VX.1970.006
The Ethiopian tradition
18/19 March–19 April
Circulation Department exhibition organised in
conjunction with the Horniman Museum,
London.

VX.1970.007
Treasures from Althorp
18/19 March–3 May
PUBLICATIONS: v.1970.029;
v.1970.030

VX.1970.008
English creamware
20 April–17 May
Circulation Department exhibition.
PUBLICATION: v.1968.014

VX.1970.009
The art of the book
April–
Selected from the National Art Library's
collections? Cf. note, vx.1979.016.

VX.1970.010
A century of Warner fabrics
1870–1970
27 May–5 July

VX.1970.011
Recent acquisitions 1969–70
28 May–September
PUBLICATION: v.1970.026

VX.1970.012
Charles Dickens: an exhibition to
commemorate the centenary of his
death
9/10 June–20 September
PUBLICATION: v.1970.008

VX.1970.013
The art of Walter Crane
11 July–2 August
Circulation Department exhibition.

VX.1970.014
Modern Swedish ballet
29/30 July–20 September
Organised by the Dansmuseet, Stockholm.
PUBLICATION: v.1970.022

VX.1970.015
Stage costume design
3 August–6 September
Circulation Department exhibition.
PUBLICATION: v.1968.041

VX.1970.016
Art nouveau pewter
12 September–11 October
Circulation Department exhibition.
PUBLICATION: v.1969.003

VX.1970.017
Archibald Knox (1864–1933)
16 September–11 October
With particular reference to his designs for
Liberty's. — Circulation Department exhibition.

VX.1970.018
Adolphe Appia and the new approach to
stage design
7/8 October–10 January 1971
PUBLICATIONS: v.1970.001;
v.1972.001

VX.1970.019
Art and the East India trade,
1500–1857
28/29 October–29 December
Exhibition coincided with a BBC Radio 3 series.
PUBLICATIONS: v.1970.003;
VR.1970.002

VX.1970.020
50 years of postcards, 1870–1920
9/10 December–31 January 1971
Circulation Department exhibition.
PUBLICATION: v.1971.031

VX.1970.021
What the children like
9/10 December–14 February 1971
A selection of children's books, toys and games
from the Renier Collection.
PUBLICATION: v.1970.035

VX.1970.BGM.001
The six wives of Henry VIII: costumes
from the BBC Television series
29 January–15 March
See also VX.1971.002

VX.1970.BGM.002
Silhouettes
August–January 1971

VX.1970.BGM.003
Thomas Rowlandson (1756–1827)
August–January 1971

VX.1970.XXX.001
Modern chairs
22 July–3 August
VENUE: Whitechapel Art Gallery,
London
Circulation Department exhibition.
PUBLICATIONS: v.1971.028;
VR.1970.004; VR.1971.003

1971

VX.1971.001
Themes and variations: the Sketching
Society, 1799–1851
27/28 January–9 May
PUBLICATION: v.1971.039

VX.1971.002
The six wives of Henry VIII: costumes
from the BBC Television series
28/29 January–12 April
See also VX.1970.BGM.001

VX.1971.003
Flöckinger/Herman: jewellery by Gerda
Flöckinger, glass by Sam Herman
9/10 February–28 March
Circulation Department exhibition.
PUBLICATION: v.1971.015

VX.1971.004
Contemporary theatre art in Poland
10 March–5 April
PUBLICATION: v.1971.005

VX.1971.005
Recent acquisitions 1970–71
25 March–19 September
PUBLICATION: v.1971.034

VX.1971.006
Sports photographs by Gerry Cranham
7/8 April–16 May
Circulation Department made a selection for
touring.
PUBLICATION: v.1971.041

VX.1971.007
Watercolours by John Robert Cozens
21/22 April–16 May

Exhibition previously held at the Whitworth Art Gallery, University of Manchester. — "Supported by the Arts Council of Great Britain, the Paul Mellon Centre for Studies in British Art, and the Friends of the Whitworth."–VR.1971.005, t.p.
PUBLICATION: VR.1971.005

VX.1971.008
The decorated page: eight hundred years of illuminated manuscripts and books
12/13 May–10 October
Exhibits from the National Art Library and the Society of Scribes and Illuminators.
PUBLICATION: V.1971.008

VX.1971.009
Design in glass
18 May–9 June
Circulation Department exhibition of work from Edinburgh College of Art; Foley College of Art, Stourbridge; Royal College of Art.
PUBLICATION: V.1970.011

VX.1971.010
The Franco-Prussian War and the Commune in caricature, 1870–71
26/27 May–10 October
PUBLICATION: V.1971.016

VX.1971.011
The ceramic art of China
8/9 June–25 July
Organised by the Arts Council of Great Britain and the Oriental Ceramic Society for the 50th anniversary of the latter's foundation.
PUBLICATION: VR.1971.001

VX.1971.012
Covent Garden: 25 years of opera and ballet, Royal Opera House
18/19 August–10 October
PUBLICATION: V.1971.007

VX.1971.013
Three Americans
August–8 September
Prints by Donald Judd, Robert Graham and Ed Meeley.

VX.1971.014
Fashion: an anthology by Cecil Beaton
13 October–16 January 1972
Costume from the V&A's Dress Collection.
PUBLICATION: V.1971.014

VX.1971.015
Five studio potters
October–7 November
Circulation Department exhibition. — Dan Arbeid, Alan Caiger-Smith, Anthony Hepburn, Gillian Lowndes, Lucie Rie.

VX.1971.016
Homage to Senefelder
3/4 November–30 January 1972
Artists' lithographs from the Felix H. Man collection.
PUBLICATION: V.1971.020

VX.1971.017
dsh, dom sylvester houédard, visual poetries
10 November–5 December
Circulation Department exhibition.
PUBLICATION: V.1971.011

VX.1971.018
Victorian church art
16/17 November–30 January 1972
PUBLICATION: V.1971.050

VX.1971.019
Season's greetings: an exhibition of British biscuit tins, 1868–1939
8/9 December–23 January 1972
Circulation Department exhibition.
PUBLICATION: V.1971.037

VX.1971.BGM.001
Modern prints from the V&A's collection
January–4 April

VX.1971.BGM.002
Kokoschka: prints and drawings
22/23 September–16 January 1972
From the collection of Count Reinhold Bethusy-Huc, on long loan to the Department of Prints and Drawings.
PUBLICATION: V.1971.024

VX.1971.XXX.001
Victorian glass
VENUE: Corning Museum of Glass, New York, and travelling
Circulation Department exhibition, circulated in the U.S.A. by the Smithsonian Institution, Washington, D.C.
PUBLICATION: VR.1971.004

1972

VX.1972.001
John Blake: recent work
26 January–27 February

VX.1972.002
Flemish drawings
9/10 February–26 March
Under the auspices of the Arts Council of Great
Britain, from the Frits Lugt collection, Institut
néerlandais, Paris; also held there and at the
Kunstmuseum, Bern; Bibliothèque royale de
Belgique, Brussels.
PUBLICATION: VR.1972.004

VX.1972.003
Drawings by William Mulready
16/17 February–2 July
PUBLICATION: V.1972.018

VX.1972.004
William Moorcroft (1872–1945)
2 March–3 April
Circulation Department exhibition.
PUBLICATION: V.1972.040

VX.1972.005
Francis Williams Bequest
9 March–23 April
Exhibition of illustrated books organised by the
National Book League. — Artists represented in
this exhibition were invited to submit work for the
exhibition of British children's books held
September–November 1973 at the Bibliothèque
royale, Brussels, as part of the arts festival
Europalia 73 Great Britain.
PUBLICATION: VR.1972.005

VX.1972.006
"From today painting is dead"
16 March–14 May
Exhibition on the beginnings of photography
organised by the Arts Council of Great Britain.
PUBLICATION: VR.1972.006

VX.1972.007
Crafts of Ecuador
6 April–7 May
Circulation Department exhibition.
PUBLICATION: V.1972.015

VX.1972.008
Olivetti 'Save our planet' posters
exhibition
April

VX.1972.009
Recent acquisitions 1971–72
24 April–23 July
PUBLICATION: V.1972.037

VX.1972.010
Recent acquisitions: Circulation
Department
28 April–16 July

VX.1972.011
International ceramics 1972
7/8 June–23 July
Circulation Department in association with the
International Academy of Ceramics.
PUBLICATIONS: V.1972.022;
V.1973.021

VX.1972.012
Martin ware
8 June–23 July
Circulation Department exhibition.
PUBLICATION: V.1971.026

VX.1972.013
Modern British bookbindings
14/15 June–16 July
Works by members of the Designer Bookbinders. —
Also held at: Pierpont Morgan Library, New York;
Newberry Library, Chicago; University Research
Library, U.C.L.A.
PUBLICATIONS: VR.1971.002;
VR.1972.012

VX.1972.014
Australian prints
19/20 July–5 November
PUBLICATION: V.1972.004

VX.1972.015
German posters 1905–1915
26 July–3 September
Circulation Department exhibition.

VX.1972.016
The art of the book
1 August–30 June 1973
Selected from the National Art Library's
collections? Cf. note, VX.1979.016.

VX.1972.017
Neo-classicism in book design
4 September–November

'Aspects of the book': a series of small exhibitions drawn from the collections of the National Art Library, held in the Book Production Gallery, 1972–73. Included displays from the Forster and Dyce Collections, and of 'Historic photographs'. See VX.1972–1973 passim. — Coincides with VX.1972.019.
PUBLICATION: V.1972.002

VX.1972.018
David Hockney: Grimm's fairy tales, a suite of etchings
6 September–15 October
Circulation Department exhibition.
PUBLICATION: V.1972.016

VX.1972.019
The age of neo-classicism
7/8/9 September–19 November
14th exhibition of the Council of Europe. In association with the Arts Council of Great Britain. — Furniture and applied arts sections were held at the V&A; painting, sculpture and architecture sections at the Royal Academy. — See also VX.1972.XXX.001.
PUBLICATIONS: VR.1972.001; VR.1972.002

VX.1972.020
Illuminated manuscripts
September–October
'Aspects of the book, 1972–73': see note, VX.1972.017.

VX.1972.021
Bookbindings: 15th and 16th centuries
September–November
'Aspects of the book, 1972–73': see note, VX.1972.017.

VX.1972.022
The library of John Forster
September–November
'Aspects of the book, 1972–73 (Forster and Dyce)': see note, VX.1972.017.

VX.1972.023
Viscountess Hawarden's photographs of her daughters, ca.1860
September–November
'Aspects of the book, 1972–73 (Historic photographs)': see note, VX.1972.017.

VX.1972.024
The glass of Frederick Carder
18 October–26 November
Organised by the Pilkington Glass Museum.

VX.1972.025
Merlyn Evans: graphic work
16 November–25 February 1973
PUBLICATION: V.1972.020

VX.1972.026
The fable
November–January 1973
'Aspects of the book, 1972–73': see note, VX.1972.017.

VX.1972.027
Louis Wain
6 December–14 January 1973
PUBLICATION: V.1972.027

VX.1972.028
Beatrix Potter: a Christmas exhibition
13/14 December–28 January 1973
PUBLICATIONS: V.1972.005; V.1972.006

VX.1972.029
Augsburg and Venice: Erhard Ratdolt and other 15th century printers
December–January 1973
'Aspects of the book, 1972–73': see note, VX.1972.017.

VX.1972.030
19th century fine bindings
December–February 1973
'Aspects of the book, 1972–73': see note, VX.1972.017.

VX.1972.BGM.001
Venetian glass
5 February–26 March
Objects from the V&A.

VX.1972.BGM.002
Whistler etchings
8–30 April
Circulation Department exhibition.
PUBLICATION: V.1970.036

VX.1972.BGM.003
Sickert etchings
13 May–4 June
Circulation Department exhibition.
PUBLICATION: V.1972.034

VX.1972.BGM.004
Bethnal Green Museum centenary exhibition
23 June–6 August

VX.1972.BGM.005
Olympic posters
19 August–1 October

VX.1972.BGM.006
Matisse lithographs
9 November–31 December
Circulation Department exhibition, from the
collection of the Prints and Drawings Department.
PUBLICATION: V.1972.029

VX.1972.XXX.001
Early neo-classical furniture in Britain,
1755–80
6 September–19 November
VENUE: Osterley Park House
See also VX.1972.019

VX.1972.XXX.002
Indian sculpture
4 December–30 January 1973.
VENUE: Manchester City Art Gallery
"the largest travelling exhibition so far drawn from
the permanent collections of the Museum"–[press
release].
PUBLICATION: V.1971.021

VX.1972.XXX.003
The eighteenth century stage: Britain
VENUE: Second Bi-Annual Conference
of the Canadian Society for Eighteenth-
century Studies
Exhibition lent by the V&A; organised in
association with the Saskatoon Gallery and
Conservatory Corporation, with the assistance of
the British Council.
PUBLICATION: VR.1972.003

1973

VX.1973.001
Treasures from the European
Community
4 January–11 February
"A 'Fanfare for Europe' exhibition"–v.1973.039,
cover.
PUBLICATION: V.1973.039

VX.1973.002
The needle's excellency
17 January–18 February
Circulation Department exhibition.
PUBLICATION: V.1973.029

VX.1973.003
Scenes of English life in the early
decades of the 20th century, by
Agnes B. Warburg
January–March
'Aspects of the book, 1972–73 (Historic
photographs)': see note, VX.1972.017.

VX.1973.004
English writers of the romantic period:
books and manuscripts from the Dyce
and Forster Collections
January–March
'Aspects of the book , 1972–73 (Forster and Dyce)':
see note, VX.1972.017.

VX.1973.005
The compassionate camera: dustbowl
pictures
21/22 February–25 March
Circulation Department exhibition of photographs
taken for the U.S. Farm Security Administration,
1935–1941.
PUBLICATION: V.1973.008

VX.1973.006
Furniture pattern books
February–March
'Aspects of the book, 1972–73': see note,
VX.1972.017.

VX.1973.007
Almanacks, calendars and other
yearbooks
February–April
'Aspects of the book, 1972–73': see note,
VX.1972.017.

VX.1973.008
Recent acquisitions 1972–73
8 March–24 June
PUBLICATION: V.1973.041

VX.1973.009
The craftsman's art
15 March–13 May
Organised in association with the Crafts Advisory
Committee.
PUBLICATION: VR.1973.002

VX.1973.010
Master drawings of the Roman baroque
from the Kunstmuseum Düsseldorf
22 March–15 July

Organised in association with the Scottish Arts Council. Also held at the Talbot Rice Arts Centre, Edinburgh.
PUBLICATION: V.1973.026

VX.1973.011
Books of hours
March–June
'Aspects of the book, 1972–73': see note, VX.1972.017.

VX.1973.012
The Hennells: silversmiths and jewellers, 1735–1973
29 March–29 April
PUBLICATION: V.1973.020

VX.1973.013
The English drama
April–June
'Aspects of the book, 1972–73 (Forster and Dyce)': see note, VX.1972.017.

VX.1973.014
English holiday resorts, from illustrated topographical books, c.1700 to the present
April–June
'Aspects of the book, 1972–73': see note, VX.1972.017.

VX.1973.015
Photographs by Roger Fenton
April–June
'Aspects of the book, 1972–1973 (Historic photographs)': see note, VX.1972.017.

VX.1973.016
Victorian publishers' bindings
May–June
'Aspects of the book, 1972–73': see note, VX.1972.017.

VX.1973.017
The Mortons: three generations of textile creation
7 June–15 July
PUBLICATION: V.1973.027

VX.1973.018
An American museum of decorative art and design
14 June–12 August
Designs from the Cooper-Hewitt Museum, New York. — Organised by the Arts Council of Great Britain.
PUBLICATION: VR.1973.001

VX.1973.019
Jazz seen: the face of black music
20 July–19 August
Circulation Department exhibition of photographs by Valerie Wilmer.
PUBLICATION: V.1973.022

VX.1973.020
Soup tureens from the Campbell collection, USA
25/26 July–9 September
From the Campbell Museum, Camden, New Jersey.

VX.1973.021
'Marble halls': drawings and models for Victorian secular buildings
2 August–28 October
The Circulation Department toured a smaller selection of architectural drawings, entitled 'Victorian buildings'.
PUBLICATIONS: V.1973.025; V.1973.042

VX.1973.022
Phaidon Press Golden Jubilee 1923–1973
22 August–2 September

VX.1973.023
Fine flower prints
6–30 September

VX.1973.024
The floating world: Japanese popular prints, 1700–1900
20 September–25 November
PUBLICATIONS: V.1973.003; V.1973.017

VX.1973.025
150 years of the Royal Asiatic Society
4 October–4 November

VX.1973.026
Saved for the nation: the achievement of the National Art-Collections Fund, 1903–1973
4 October–18 November
Exhibition consisting of objects the Fund enabled the V&A and the British Museum to acquire.
PUBLICATION: VR.1973.004

VX.1973.027
Henry Morris and the Digswell experiment
7/8 November–9 December

VX.1973.028
Plate from the City of London
15 November–16 December
Plate from Goldsmiths' Hall. — Part of an
exhibition held at the Maison du roi, Brussels,
September–November as part of the arts festival
Europalia 73: Great Britain, in Brussels.

VX.1973.029
Old master drawings from Chatsworth
15 November–17 February 1974
Touring exhibition toured in the U.S.A. by the
International Exhibitions Foundation.
PUBLICATION: V.1973.031

VX.1973.030
Secrets of the stage: a Christmas
exhibition
13 December–20 January 1974
PUBLICATION: V.1973.035

VX.1973.031
Edward Ardizzone: a retrospective
exhibition
15 December–13 January 1974
Circulation Department exhibition.
PUBLICATION: V.1973.013

VX.1973.032
A Christmas exhibition
December–January 1974
'Aspects of the book': a series of small exhibitions
drawn from the collections of the National Art
Library, held in its Gallery, 1973–74. 'Aspects of
photography', drawn from the collection of historic
photographs, and displays from the Forster and
Dyce collections, took place alongside. See
VX.1973–74 passim.
PUBLICATION: V.1973.002

VX.1973.033
Elizabethan poetry: a selection of books
and manuscripts from the Dyce collection
December–January 1974
'Aspects of the book, 1973–74 (Dyce Collection)',
though not listed in V.1973.002.

VX.1973.034
Alpine scenery in book illustration
December–February 1974
'Aspects of the book, 1973–74': see note,
VX.1973.032.

VX.1973.035
Aspects of photography: reporting
December–March 1974
See note, VX.1973.032.

VX.1973.036
"Trade & plumb-cake for ever Huzza!":
the publications of John Newbery and
his family
December–March 1974
'Aspects of the book, 1973–74': see note,
VX.1973.032.

VX.1973.037
19th century French publishers' bindings:
cartonnages romantiques from the Renier
Collection
['Aspects of the book, 1973–74
(Renier Collection)', though not listed in
V.1973.002.]

VX.1973.BGM.001
Children's paintings
4 January–4 February
Entries to Shankar's international children's art
competitions, made available from India
House–[press release].

VX.1973.BGM.002
Beatrix Potter
14 February–15 April
Closing date extended from 25 March?
PUBLICATION: V.1972.005

VX.1973.BGM.003
Posters of a lifetime
3 May–29 July 1973
Posters from the Archive of S.H. Benson Ltd
(1893–1971) given to the V&A by Ogilvy Benson
Mather Ltd. — Circulation Department
exhibition.
PUBLICATION: V.1973.032

VX.1973.BGM.004
Victorian engravings: recent acquisitions
from the Department of Prints and
Drawings
9 August–4 November
Circulation Department exhibition?
PUBLICATION: V.1973.043

VX.1973.BGM.005
Modern prints: recent acquisitions from
the Department of Prints and Drawings
22 November–27 January 1974

VX.1973.XXX.001
Victorian children's books from the
Library of the Victoria and Albert
Museum

29 September–13 November
VENUE: Bibliothèque royale, Brussels
"arranged for Europalia 73: Great Britain, by the National Book League in co-operation with the British Council"–VR.1973.005, t.p.
PUBLICATION: VR.1973.005

1974

VX.1974.001
The art of Onisaburō: modern Japanese ceramics, calligraphy & painting
23/24 January–24 March
Organised by the Oomoto Foundation. — Circulation Department exhibition.
PUBLICATION: V.1974.002

VX.1974.002
Drawings by Victor Hugo
14 or 28 February–31 March or 14 April
PUBLICATION: V.1974.014

VX.1974.003
Two contemporary presses (Wild Hawthorn Press, Journeyman Press)
February–April
'Aspects of the book, 1973–74': see note, VX.1973.032.

VX.1974.004
Eighteenth century musical instruments, France and Britain
21 February–24 March
Drawn from the collections of the Conservatoire national supérieur de musique, Paris, the V&A, and the Horniman Museum, London. Toured by the Circulation Department.
PUBLICATIONS: V.1973.014, V.1975.016

VX.1974.005
George Cruikshank
28 February–28 April
Touring exhibition organised by the Arts Council of Great Britain.
PUBLICATION: VR.1974.005

VX.1974.006
Jonathan Swift: a selection of books and manuscripts from the Forster collection
February–May
['Aspects of the book, 1973–74 (Forster Collection)', though not listed in V.1973.002.]

VX.1974.007
Ink in their veins: a sampling of private press publications
March–June
'Aspects of the book, 1973–74': see note, VX.1973.032.

VX.1974.008
The rural chair
10–28 April
Circulation Department exhibition.
PUBLICATION: V.1973.033

VX.1974.009
Aspects of photography: portraits
April–June
See note, V.1973.032.

VX.1974.010
The boast of heraldry
April–June
'Aspects of the book, 1973–74': see note, VX.1973.032.

VX.1974.011
England shown to the children, 1770–1830
April–June
['Aspects of the book, 1973–74 (Renier Collection)'?, though not listed in V.1973.002.]

VX.1974.012
Recent acquisitions: Circulation Department
1 May–8 June

VX.1974.013
Ivory carvings in early medieval England, 700–1200
8 May–7 July
Organised by the Arts Council of Great Britain.
PUBLICATIONS: VR.1972.008; VR.1974.009

VX.1974.014
Early railway prints: from the collection of Mr. and Mrs. M.G. Powell
16 May–22 September
PUBLICATIONS: V.1974.015; V.1979.006

VX.1974.015
Garden and flower books
May–July
'Aspects of the book, 1973–74': see note,
VX.1973.032.

VX.1974.016
Byron
30 May–25 August
PUBLICATIONS: V.1974.007;
V.1974.008

VX.1974.017
Pierre Culot: ceramics
6 June–14 July
Circulation Department exhibition.
PUBLICATION: V.1974.020

VX.1974.018
The fabric of Pop
18 July–18 August
Circulation Department exhibition.
PUBLICATION: V.1974.016

VX.1974.019
Aspects of photography: form and
texture
July–September
See note, VX.1973.032.

VX.1974.020
Illustrations of arts and manufactures
July–September
'Aspects of the book, 1973–74': see note,
VX.1973.032.

VX.1974.021
Natural history and science books,
selected from the Renier Collection of
children's books
July–September
['Aspects of the book, 1973–74 (Renier
Collection)'?, though not listed in V.1973.002.]

VX.1974.022
With pen in hand: a selection of
manuscripts from the Library
July–September
'Aspects of the book, 1973–74': see note,
VX.1973.032.

VX.1974.023
Far Eastern art: recent gifts, purchases
and loans
8 August–29 September

VX.1974.024
Danish glass, 1814–1914: the Peter F.
Heering collection
22 August–29 September or
November
PUBLICATION: VR.1974.001

VX.1974.025
Wood engraving, 1820–60
August–September
'Aspects of the book, 1973–74': see note,
VX.1973.032.

VX.1974.026
The destruction of the country house,
1875–1975
8/9 October–1 December
Organised to launch European Architectural
Heritage Year. — For Circulation Department
exhibition see V.1975.015.
PUBLICATIONS: V.1974.012;
VR.1974.002

VX.1974.027
Dominick Labino
11/12 October–3 November
Organised by and also held at the Toledo Museum
of Art and Pilkington Glass Museum.
PUBLICATION: VR.1974.003

VX.1974.028
Hollywood still photography,
1927–1941, from the collection of John
Kobal
7 November–8 December
Circulation Department exhibition.
PUBLICATION: V.1974.018

VX.1974.029
Recent acquisitions: Department of Prints
and Drawings, and Paintings
19 November–19 January 1975

VX.1974.030
Winslow Homer: watercolours and
drawings
28 November–19 January 1975
Selected from the Cooper-Hewitt Collection,
Smithsonian Institution, Washington, D.C.
PUBLICATION: VR.1972.013

VX.1974.031
Canal boat art
12 December–19 January 1975
Circulation Department exhibition, alternatively
advertised as Barge art.
PUBLICATION: V.1974.009

VX.1974.032
Bodybox
14 December–26 January 1975
Sculpture exhibition for children, organised by the
Education Department
PUBLICATION: V.1974.005

VX.1974.BGM.001
William Moorcroft (1872–1945)
2 February–17 March
Circulation Department exhibition.
PUBLICATION: V.1972.040

VX.1974.BGM.002
The Mount Trust collection of Chinese
art
April–August
Circulation Department exhibition.
PUBLICATIONS: V.1970.024;
V.1971.029

VX.1974.BGM.003
Automobile art: the James Barron
collection
19 September–24 November
PUBLICATION: V.1974.003

VX.1974.BGM.004
Children and their toys in English art
12 December–16 February 1975?
PUBLICATION: V.1974.010

VX.1974.XXX.001
High Victorian design
November–June 1975
VENUES: Winnipeg Art Gallery,
Manitoba; Vancouver Art Gallery;
Glenbow-Alberta Institute, Calgary;
National Gallery of Canada, Ottawa;
Musée du Quebec
Touring exhibition organised by the V&A and the
British Council for the National Programme of the
National Gallery of Canada, Ottawa.
PUBLICATIONS: VR.1974.007;
VR.1974.008

1975

VX.1975.001
Modern British watercolours
23 January–23 February
Circulation Department exhibition.
PUBLICATION: V.1975.031

VX.1975.002
English influences on Vincent van
Gogh
29/30 January–23 February
Touring exhibition organised by the University of
Nottingham Fine Art Department and the Arts
Council of Great Britain.
PUBLICATION: VR.1974.004

VX.1975.003
Joshua Cristall, 1768–1847: an
exhibition of watercolours
13 February–27 April
PUBLICATION: V.1975.026

VX.1975.004
Back to the drawing board
19 February–23 March
Thames Television exhibition of television
design.
PUBLICATION: VR.1975.002

VX.1975.005
Sickert etchings
27 February–23 March
Circulation Department exhibition.
PUBLICATION: V.1972.034

VX.1975.006
Watercolours by Thomas Girtin
13 March–20 April
Organised by the Whitworth Art Gallery,
University of Manchester.
PUBLICATION: VR.1975.011

VX.1975.007
Chinese porcelain figures of musicians
March?–

VX.1975.008
Design review: an international
anthology of design-award-winning
consumer products
27 March–27 April
Circulation Department exhibition.
PUBLICATION: V.1975.012

VX.1975.009
Recent acquisitions: Circulation
Department
1 May–1 June

VX.1975.010
Chinese jade throughout the ages
1 May–23 June
Organised by the Arts Council of Great Britain and
the Oriental Ceramic Society.
PUBLICATIONS: VR.1975.004;
VR.1976.002

VX.1975.011
The Shakers
8 May–15 June
Organised by the Neue Sammlung, Munich.
PUBLICATION: VR.1974.011

VX.1975.012
Alfred Stevens: centenary exhibition
15 May–14 September
PUBLICATIONS: V.1975.001;
V.1975.002

VX.1975.013
The Holy Land, as depicted in nineteenth
and twentieth century books and
paintings
May–June
'Aspects of the book': cf. note, VX.1973.032.

VX.1975.014
Matisse lithographs
12 June–6 July
Circulation Department exhibition.
PUBLICATION: V.1972.029

VX.1975.015
Ben Nicholson: the graphic art
10 July–17 August
Circulation Department exhibition.
PUBLICATION: V.1975.004

VX.1975.016
Mosaics from the Gilbert collection
17 July–14 September
PUBLICATION: V.1975.032

VX.1975.017
Liberty's, 1875–1975: an exhibition to
mark the firm's centenary
31 July–12 October

Circulation Department made a selection for
touring, entitled 'Stile Liberty'.
PUBLICATIONS: V.1975.029;
V.1975.030

VX.1975.018
Art deco: French decorative arts in the
twenties
21 August–28 September
Circulation Department exhibition.
PUBLICATION: V.1974.001

VX.1975.019
The classic fairy tale: drawn from the
Opie collection and the V&A Library
August–September
'Aspects of the book': cf. note, VX.1973.032.

VX.1975.020
Cambridge plate
4 September–5 October
Organised by the Fitzwilliam Museum, Cambridge,
and previously held there.
PUBLICATION: VR.1975.003

VX.1975.021
Constable's Stonehenge
8 October–18 January 1976
For Circulation Department exhibition see
V.1976.014.
PUBLICATION: V.1975.010

VX.1975.022
Henry Moore's Stonehenge
8 October–18 January 1976
PUBLICATION: VR.1974.006

VX.1975.023
John Nixon, 1760–1818
8 October–18 January 1976

VX.1975.024
Martin Hardie, 1875–1952
8 October–18 January 1976
Organised by the Ashmolean Museum, Oxford, and
previously held there.
PUBLICATION: VR.1975.010

VX.1975.025
Wallpaper designs from the Westfries
Museum, Hoorn
8 October–18 January 1976
Also held at the Whitworth Art Gallery, University
of Manchester.
PUBLICATION: V.1975.044

VX.1975.026
Ruskin pottery
9 October–2 November
Exhibits on loan from the Ferneyhough collection of Ruskin pottery, comprising W. Howson Taylor's own collection. — For Circulation Department selected touring version see v.1975.038.

VX.1975.027
Brassaï photographs
October?–

VX.1975.028
Herschorn miniatures
October?–

VX.1975.029
Paul Nash as designer
6 November–7 December
Circulation Department exhibition.
PUBLICATION: v.1975.035

VX.1975.030
The land: 20th century landscape photographs
13 November–15 February 1976
Selected by Bill Brandt. Also held at the National Gallery of Modern Art, Edinburgh; Ulster Museum, Belfast; National Museum of Wales, Cardiff. — For Circulation Department exhibition see v.1976.036.
PUBLICATIONS: v.1975.027; VR.1975.007

VX.1975.031
Arthur Boyd Houghton 1836–1875: painter, illustrator, reporter
19 November–14 February 1976
PUBLICATION: v.1975.003

VX.1975.032
The pack age: a century of wrapping it up
11 December–31 January 1976
Circulation Department exhibition. From the collection of Robert Opie.
PUBLICATION: v.1975.034

VX.1975.033
The makers: artist-craftsmen at work
29 December–3 January 1976
In association with the Crafts Advisory Committee. — 14 craftspeople demonstrating their work in the Museum galleries: Jennifer Boyd-Carpenter (embroiderer), Ann Brunskill (etcher), Brian Fuller (silversmith), Wendy Gould (illuminator), Ann

Hechle (calligrapher), Mo Jupp (potter), Walter Keeler (potter), Nik Lambrinides (gem cutter), John Lawrence (wood engraver), Adrian Pasotti (bookbinder), Kathleen Riley (lacemaker), Diana Springall (embroiderer), Eva Louise Svensson (tapestry weaver), Matthew Tomalin (jeweller).
PUBLICATION: v.1975.045

VX.1975.BGM.001
The designing and making of toys
April–18 May
London College of Furniture students' work.

VX.1975.BGM.002
The thirties: progressive design in ceramics, glass, textiles and wallpapers
24 May–6 June
Circulation Department exhibition.
PUBLICATION: v.1975.041

VX.1975.BGM.003
Corn dollies
24 July–14 September
Circulation Department exhibition.
PUBLICATION: v.1975.011

VX.1975.BGM.004
A gallery of children: the work of Henriette Willebeek le Mair
2 October–30 November
Organised by the Gemeente Museum, Arnhem.
PUBLICATION: v.1975.022

VX.1975.BGM.005
Tin toys from the collection of Anthony Gross
11 December–25 January 1976

VX.1975.THM.001
"A song to sing O"
25 March–31 July
Organised to mark the centenary of the D'Oyly Carte Opera Company.

VX.1975.THM.002
The making of The Wombles
16 December–29 February 1976
Organised in association with the BBC and Film Fair Ltd.

VX.1975.XXX.001
Ellen Terry and Henry Irving
February–July
VENUE: Leighton House, London
Organised by the Theatre Museum.

VX.1975.XXX.002
Homage to the designers of Diaghilev,
1909–1929
15 June–14 September
VENUE: Palazzo Grassi, Venice
'Danza 75 – Incontri internationali della
danza'–VR.1975.005, t.p. — Organised for the
Theatre Museum by Richard Buckle.
PUBLICATION: VR.1975.005

VX.1975.XXX.003
As worn by . . .
Summer
VENUE: Guildhall, Salisbury
Organised by the Theatre Museum for Salisbury
Festival of the Arts.

VX.1975.XXX.004
Sir Lewis Casson centenary
October–June 1976
VENUE: Leighton House, London
Organised by the Theatre Museum.

1976

VX.1976.001
Jewellery in Europe
10 February–28 March
Touring exhibition organised by the Scottish Arts
Council and the Crafts Advisory Committee. Also
held at the Scottish Arts Council Gallery,
Edinburgh; Aberdeen Art Gallery and Museum;
Third Eye Centre, Glasgow; Arnolfini Gallery,
Bristol.
PUBLICATION: VR.1975.006

VX.1976.002
Dr Thomas Monro (1759–1833) and the
Monro Academy
11 February–23 May
PUBLICATION: V.1976.020

VX.1976.003
The rediscovery of an artist: the drawings
of James Jefferys (1751–1784)
11 February–23 May
PUBLICATION: V.1976.048

VX.1976.004
Samuel Beckett by Avigdor Arikha: a
tribute to Samuel Beckett on his 70th
birthday
11 February–23 May
PUBLICATION: V.1976.051

VX.1976.005
Fashion, 1900–1939
25 March–9 May
Organised by the Scottish Arts Council.
PUBLICATIONS: V.1975.018;
V.1976.024

VX.1976.006
Islamic metalwork from Iranian lands
(8th–18th centuries)
31 March/1 April–30 May
Organised for the World of Islam Festival.
PUBLICATION: V.1976.032

VX.1976.007
The thirties: progressive design in
ceramics, glass, textiles and wallpapers
1 April–6 June
Circulation Department exhibition.
PUBLICATION: V.1975.041

VX.1976.008
The art press: two centuries of art
magazines
8 April–26 September
National Art Library exhibition, also offered by
Circulation Department.
PUBLICATIONS: V.1976.008;
VR.1977.004

VX.1976.009
Homage to Kokoschka on his 90th
birthday
6 May–11 July
Prints and drawings lent by Reinhold, Count
Bethusy-Huc.
PUBLICATION: V.1976.030

VX.1976.010
Daumier: eye-witness of an epoch
22/23 June–19 September
Touring exhibition organised by the Arts Council of
Great Britain.
PUBLICATION: V.1976.016

VX.1976.011
Metalwork in the making: a live
exhibition of craftsmen working in metal
28 June–11 July

VX.1976.012
1776: a Londoner's view
4 July–mid-November or December
Domestic decorative arts.

VX.1976.013
American art 1750–1800: towards
independence
14/15 July–26 September
In association with the Arts Council of Great
Britain and Yale University Art Gallery, where the
exhibition was first shown.
PUBLICATIONS: v.1976.002;
v.1976.003

VX.1976.014
Ansel Adams: twentieth-century
American photographs
16 July–29 August
For Circulation Department exhibition see
v.1976.005.
PUBLICATION: v.1976.004

VX.1976.015
Minton, 1798–1910
12 August–10 October
Circulation Department exhibition, in
collaboration with Thomas Goode & Co.
Ltd.
PUBLICATION: v.1976.040

VX.1976.016
The seasons: illustrations to James
Thomson's poem, 1730–1830
9 September–10 October
Circulation Department exhibition from the
collection of Dr Mordechai Omer.
PUBLICATION: v.1976.053

VX.1976.017
Six studio potters
13/14 October–12 December
Circulation Department exhibition. Artists: Gordon
Baldwin, Michael Casson, Hans Coper, Ian
Godfrey, Jacqueline Poncelet, Peter Simpson.
PUBLICATION: v.1977.047

VX.1976.018
Royal College of Art
28 October–14 November
A selection from the Diploma exhibition.

VX.1976.019
Blake's Job: the making of a facsimile
10 November–13 February 1977
Organised by the William Blake Trust and the
Trianon Press, Paris.
PUBLICATION: VR.1976.004

VX.1976.020
Stanbrook Abbey Press and Sir Sydney
Cockerell
10 November–13 February 1977
PUBLICATION: v.1976.056

VX.1976.021
Beatrix Potter: costumes and illustrations
for The tailor of Gloucester
10 November– July? 1977

VX.1976.022
A tonic to the nation: the Festival of
Britain
25 November–3 April 1977
Smaller version selected for Circulation
Department.
PUBLICATIONS: v.1976.063;
VR.1976.006

VX.1976.023
Man-made: demonstrations by thirteen
craftsmen
1 December–30 January 1977
Craftspeople taking part were: Stephen Gottlieb
(lutemaker); Adrian Pasotti (bookbinder); John
Lawrence (wood engraver); Ann Brunskill (etcher);
Ann Hechle (calligrapher); Nik Lambrinides
(glyptic arts); Matthew Tomalin (jeweller); Ray
Silverman (potter); Archie Brennan (tapestry
weaver); Jennifer Boyd-Carpenter (ecclesiastical
embroiderer); Barbara Mullins (handweaver and
spinner); Kathleen Riley and Margaret Susans
(lacemakers); Diana Springall (embroiderer).
PUBLICATIONS: v.1976.037;
v.1976.038; v.1976.065; v.1976.068

VX.1976.024
Worth
2 December–February? 1977
Paris couture house.

VX.1976.025
The artists of Disney
16 December–13 February 1977
Circulation Department exhibition from the Walt
Disney Archive.
PUBLICATION: v.1976.009

VX.1976.BGM.001
Unknown dolls from the Gauder-Anka
Stuttgart collection
2 September–31 October
PUBLICATION: v.1976.064

VX.1976.BGM.002
Jumbo and some other elephants
24/25 November–23 January 1977
PUBLICATION: v.1976.035

VX.1976.THM.001
The Burgtheater, Vienna, 1776–1976
11 March–19 April
Organised by the Austrian Institute.
PUBLICATION: v.1976.001

VX.1976.THM.002
Ballet Rambert
18 May–18 July

VX.1976.THM.003
The Richard Wagner non stop Ring
show
2/3 August–3 October
Offered by Circulation Department as Wagner's
Ring cycle.
PUBLICATION: v.1976.050

VX.1976.THM.004
Jean Hugo designs for the theatre
23 October–5 December
PUBLICATION: v.1976.034

VX.1976.THM.005
Hoffnung and his world of music
20/21 December–27 March 1977
PUBLICATION: v.1976.060

VX.1976.XXX.001
Diaghilev and the Russian ballet
1909–1929
6 January–7 February
VENUE: Leighton House, London
Organised by the Theatre Museum in association
with the Libraries and Amenities Committee of the
Royal Borough of Kensington and Chelsea.

VX.1976.XXX.002
Theatre peepshow
March
VENUE: National Theatre, London
Organised by the Theatre Museum.
PUBLICATION: v.1976.061

VX.1976.XXX.003
[Stand at] Art & Antiques Fair and
Festival
5–12 June
VENUE: Olympia, London

VX.1976.XXX.004
[Stand at] National Committee for
Audio-Visual Aids in Education/
Council for Educational Technology
exhibition
8–11 June
VENUE: Caxton 76 (quincentenary
exhibition, London?)

VX.1976.XXX.005
Dame Sybil Thorndike and Dame Edith
Evans commemoration
June–October
VENUE: Leighton House, London
Organised by the Theatre Museum.

VX.1976.XXX.006
Caught in the act: theatrical caricatures
by Einar Nerman
6 July–16 September
VENUE: Leighton House, London
Organised by the Theatre Museum.
PUBLICATION: vr.1976.001

1977

VX.1977.001
Treasures of the Print Room: acquisitions
1975–6
6 January–17 April
PUBLICATION: v.1977.054

VX.1977.002
Jubilee celebration
27 January–31 December
A series of small exhibitions of contemporary craft
in collaboration with the Crafts Advisory
Committee to celebrate the Queen's Silver Jubilee,
1977.

VX.1977.002A
Good tastes
27 January–6 March
PUBLICATION: vr.1977.007

VX.1977.002B
Presentation pieces [china and glass]
12 March–1 May

VX.1977.002C
Draw the line [graphics]
8 May–26 June

VX.1977.002D
High standards [textiles and banners]
3 July–28 August

VX.1977.002E
Night and day [clocks]
4 September–30 October

VX.1977.002F
Jubilee jewellery
5 November–31 December

VX.1977.003
Chinese blue and white
16/17 February–24 April
Circulation Department exhibition.
PUBLICATION: V.1975.009

VX.1977.004
Recent acquisitions: 20th century textiles
February–July

VX.1977.005
The art of Bernard Leach
2/3 March–8 May
Circulation Department exhibition.
PUBLICATION: V.1977.002

VX.1977.006
Francis Williams Bequest competition
15/16 March–22 May
Illustrated books.

VX.1977.007
A little exhibition of exhibition
catalogues
16 March–31 July

VX.1977.008
Recent acquisitions: Department of
Metalwork
March?–

VX.1977.009
Keith Murray
27/28 April–3 July
Circulation Department exhibition of ceramics.
PUBLICATION: V.1977.027

VX.1977.010
The complete prints of Eduardo Paolozzi:
prints, drawings, collages 1944–77
11 May–29 August
PUBLICATION: V.1977.008

VX.1977.011
Book royalties: a Jubilee display of
Library material concerned with kings &
queens
15 June–31 July

VX.1977.012
Fabergé 1846–1920: goldsmith to the
imperial court of Russia
23 June–23 October
Closing date extended from 25 September.
PUBLICATIONS: V.1977.015;
V.1977.016

VX.1977.013
Change and decay: the future of our
churches
13/14 July–16 October
PUBLICATIONS: V.1977.006;
V.1977.028; V.1977.040; VR.1977.005

VX.1977.014
Textiles for the Church
26 September–January 1978
To coincide with a conference of the Centre
internationale d'étude des textiles anciens.

VX.1977.015
The Bible in British art, 10th to 20th
centuries
28/29 September–8 January 1978
PUBLICATION: V.1977.003

VX.1977.016
The art of the book
28/29 September–24 June 1978
Selected from the National Art Library's
collections. Cf. note, VX.1979.016.

VX.1977.017
Lynton Lamb, 1907–1977
29 September–31 December
To accompany VX.1977.016.

VX.1977.018
Dame Joan Evans memorial exhibition
17 October–20 November
Display of jewellery, commemorating a benefactor
to the V&A Metalwork collection.

VX.1977.019
The wireless show!: 130 classic radio
receivers, 1920s to 1950s
19/20 October–11 December
Circulation Department exhibition, in association
with the British Vintage Wireless Society.
PUBLICATION: V.1977.055

VX.1977.020
Christmas print fair
9 November–21 December
Sale exhibition presented by the Associates of the
V&A with Christie's Contemporary Art.

VX.1977.021
Say when, and what and how and why
15/16 November–12 February 1978
Organised by the Crafts Advisory Committee.
"a game, juxtaposing craft and art and industrial
design and grouping objects to form questions and
invite reactions . . . Pouring vessels will be the
illustrations for this exhibition . . ."– [press release].
PUBLICATION: VR.1977.009

VX.1977.022
"It's not really there, it's painted!":
trompe l'oeil: an artist at work
15 December–8 January 1978
Artist: John Ronayne.

VX.1977.023
Baroque book illustration
National Art Library display.

VX.1977.BGM.001
Scraps
9/10 February–17 April
150 years of stamped, embossed reliefs from the
collection of Alistair Allen.
PUBLICATION: V.1977.046

VX.1977.BGM.002
Jubilation
10 May–4 September
Royal commemorative pottery from the collection
of James Blewitt.
PUBLICATION: V.1977.026

VX.1977.BGM.003
After Alice
28 September–15 January 1978
In association with the Library Association, to
celebrate its centenary.
PUBLICATION: VR.1977.002

VX.1977.THM.001
Royal box: a selection from the Theatre
Museum
2/3 May–2 October
PUBLICATION: V.1977.017

VX.1977.THM.002
Revudeville: non-stop variety at the
Windmill Theatre, 1932–1964
21 November–2 April 1978

VX.1977.XXX.001
Harley Granville Barker
May–
VENUE: National Theatre, London
Touring exhibition organised by the Theatre
Museum.
PUBLICATION: V.1977.048

VX.1977.XXX.002
1909–1929: Diaghilev's Russian ballet
29 November–16 March 1978
VENUE: Centre culturel du Marais, Paris
Costumes and designs from the V&A and the
Theatre Museum. — Organised in co-operation
with the British Council.
PUBLICATION: VR.1977.001

VX.1977.XXX.003
English silver, 16th–20th centuries
VENUES: State Hermitage Museum,
Leningrad; Pushkin Museum, Moscow
PUBLICATION: VR.1977.003

VX.1977.XXX.004
Forty two British watercolours from the
Victoria and Albert Museum
VENUES: Phoenix Art Museum; Utah
Museum of Fine Art; Fine Arts Gallery of
San Diego; Art Gallery of Ontario,
Toronto; National Gallery of Canada,
Ottawa; Art Gallery of Greater Victoria
PUBLICATIONS: V.1977.018;
VR.1977.008

1978

VX.1978.001
Photography in book illustration,
1840–1900
4 January–end February
To accompany VX.1977.016.
PUBLICATION: V.1978.072

VX.1978.002
The Poole potteries
31 January/1 February–9 April
Circulation Department exhibition.
PUBLICATION: V.1978.074

VX.1978.003
Griset's grotesques
31 January/1 February–7 May
'Treasures of the Print Room.'

VX.1978.004
Karl Schmidt-Rottluff (1884–1976):
graphic work from 1907 to 1937
31 January/1 February–7 May
'Treasures of the Print Room.'

VX.1978.005
Mannerist goldsmiths' designs
31 January/1 February–7 May
'Treasures of the Print Room.'

VX.1978.006
Old and modern masters of photography
31 January/1 February–7 May
'Treasures of the Print Room.' See also
VX.1980.XXX.002
PUBLICATION: V.1981.015

VX.1978.007
The printed textiles of William Morris
31 January–16 July
PUBLICATION: V.1978.099

VX.1978.008
The graphic work of William Nicholson
28 February/1 March–9 April
To accompany VX.1977.016. — Marked the
presentation to the National Art Library on long
loan by William Heinemann Ltd. of the original
woodblocks for An alphabet (1898).
PUBLICATIONS: V.1978.038;
VR.1978.002

VX.1978.009
Industry collects: the Cinzano glass
collection
13/15 March–30 May
PUBLICATION: VR.1978.004

VX.1978.010
Habitat and the Observer Easter egg
painting competition
3–16 April

VX.1978.011
Two modern binders: William Matthews
& Edgar Mansfield
12 April–24 June
In association with the Designer Bookbinders.
To accompany VX.1977.016.
PUBLICATION: VR.1978.013

VX.1978.012
Anglo-Jewish silver
9/10 May–9 July
Under the auspices of the Jewish Historical Society
of England.
PUBLICATION: V.1978.003

VX.1978.013
Objects: the V&A collects, 1974–1978
30/31 May–13 August
PUBLICATION: V.1978.065

VX.1978.014
Sir Gilbert Scott (1811–1878), architect
of the Gothic Revival
30/31 May–10 September
PUBLICATION: V.1978.087

VX.1978.015
Photographs by W. Eugene Smith
27/28 June–3 September
Circulation Department exhibition.
PUBLICATION: V.1978.071

VX.1978.016
Yuki
Summer

VX.1978.017
Five centuries of Oxford printing
11/12 July–26 September
Touring exhibition organised by Oxford University
Press.
PUBLICATION: VR.1978.009

VX.1978.018
Cars: colour photographs by Langdon
Clay
25/26 July–24 September
PUBLICATION: V.1978.015

VX.1978.019
John Fowler: a tribute
20 September–March 1979
Tribute to a donor to the V&A Textiles and Dress
collection.

VX.1978.020
Designs for the dream king: the castles
and palaces of Ludwig II of Bavaria
3/4 October–17 December
Organised in association with the Cooper-Hewitt
Museum, New York, where the exhibition was
subsequently held.
PUBLICATION: V.1978.025

VX.1978.021
Giambologna: sculptor to the Medici
4/5 October–16 November
Organised by the Arts Council of Great Britain and
the Kunsthistorisches Museum, Vienna, in
association with the Edinburgh Festival Society, the
Royal Scottish Museum, and the V&A. Held also
at: Royal Scottish Museum, Edinburgh;
Kunsthistorisches Museum, Vienna.
PUBLICATION: VR.1978.007

VX.1978.022
Teaspoons to trains: the designs of Frank
Pick, 1878–1941
17/18 October–10 December
PUBLICATION: V.1978.090

VX.1978.023
The way we live now: designs for
interiors, 1950 to the present day
8 November–25 February 1979
Dates from *Review of the years 1974–1978*,
p. 133. Catalogue gives dates: 7 November–
4 March.
PUBLICATION: V.1978.097

VX.1978.024
English engraved silver
13/14 November–14 January 1979
To celebrate the publication of VR.1978.006.
PUBLICATION: VR.1978.006

VX.1978.025
Samuel Palmer: a vision recaptured
21/22 November–6 May 1979
Organised in association with the William Blake
Trust.
PUBLICATION: VR.1978.010

VX.1978.BGM.001
Toys
14/15 March–17 September
Lent by the Spielzeugmuseum, Sonneberg.
PUBLICATION: V.1978.094

VX.1978.BGM.002
Postcards from the nursery, 1900–1940
31 October/1 November–21 January
1979
From the collection of Dawn and Peter Cope.
PUBLICATION: V.1978.075

VX.1978.THM.001
Adeline Genée, 1878–1970: the
Edwardian ballerina
2/3 May–3 September
PUBLICATION: VR.1978.001

VX.1978.XXX.001
Henri Cartier-Bresson
19 August–10 September
VENUE: Fruitmarket Gallery,
Edinburgh
Organised in association with the Scottish Arts
Council. Also held at Side Photographic Gallery,
Newcastle-on-Tyne and the Hayward Gallery,
London.
PUBLICATION: VR.1978.008

VX.1978.XXX.002
Scènes musicales de l'Inde: miniatures de
1590 à 1860
VENUE: Nice, France
PUBLICATION: VR.1978.011

1979

VX.1979.001
Treasures from Bassetlaw
17 January–December
First in a series of displays of objects from
particular country houses. "The series will begin
with four displays, each lasting one month, devoted
to houses in the Bassetlaw district"–[press release].

VX.1979.002
Eileen Gray
23/24 January–22 April
Also held at the Museum of Modern Art, Oxford.
PUBLICATION: VR.1979.005

VX.1979.003
Vienna in the age of Schubert: the
Biedermeier interior 1815–1848
30/31 January–1 April
Organised by the Österreichisches Museum für
Angewandte Kunst.
PUBLICATIONS: V.1979.021;
V.1979.022; V.1979.023

VX.1979.004
Fans from the East
30/31 January?–15 April?
Organised with the Fan Circle. Also held at
Birmingham Museum and Art Gallery.
PUBLICATION: V.1978.027

VX.1979.005
The luxury of good taste: an exhibition
of Victorian design 1835–1880
14 March
Organised by students of the University of
Essex Department of Art History and Theory
in association with the V&A Education
Department.
PUBLICATION: VR.1979.010

VX.1979.006
Textile arts of France
27 March–December

VX.1979.007
British water-colours
28 March–9 September
'Treasures of the Print Room.'

VX.1979.008
Italian drawings
28 March–9 September
'Treasures of the Print Room.'

VX.1979.009
Wallpapers
28 March–9 September
'Treasures of the Print Room.'

VX.1979.010
Recent ceramics by Richard Batterham
April–1 May

VX.1979.011
The Simpson (Piccadilly) Ltd. gift: an
exhibition of British fashion for winter
1979
30 April–6 May
Previously displayed at Simpson's store.
PUBLICATIONS: VP.1982.001[2]

VX.1979.012
Elizabeth Fritsch: pots about music
2 May–24 June
Touring exhibition organised by Temple Newsam
House, Leeds.
PUBLICATION: VR.1978.005

VX.1979.013
The garden: 1,000 years of British
gardening
23 May–26 August
PUBLICATIONS: VR.1979.006;
VR.1979.007

VX.1979.014
The Doulton story
30 May–12 August
PUBLICATIONS: V.1979.004;
VR.1979.004

VX.1979.015
A history of bookplates in Britain
5/6 June–2 September
Organised in association with the Bookplate
Society.
PUBLICATION: V.1979.003

VX.1979.016
The art of the book: an exhibition of fine
books from the V&A's permanent
collection
5/6 June–28 October
"This . . . is the only treatment of the subject to be
seen in a public gallery in England. It is mounted
from time to time in the V&A's Library
Gallery"–[press release].

VX.1979.017
Some decorative end-papers of the last
eighty years
Summer

VX.1979.018
Masterpieces of cutlery and the art of
eating
11 July–26 August
Organised in conjunction with the Worshipful
Company of Cutlers.
PUBLICATION: V.1979.016

VX.1979.019
Modern glass, 1940–1979
5 September–4 November
To coincide with the first London meeting of the
Association internationale pour l'histoire du verre.

VX.1979.020
Illustrating Ted Hughes
10 September–28 October
PUBLICATION: V.1979.013

VX.1979.021
The open & closed book: contemporary
book arts
11/12 September–18 November
National Art Library exhibition.
PUBLICATION: V.1979.017

VX.1979.022
Photography in printmaking
9/10 October–10 February 1980
PUBLICATION: V.1979.019

VX.1979.023
The Colman collection of silver mustard
pots
23/24 October–2 December
PUBLICATION: VR.1979.003

VX.1979.024
The art of Hollywood
29/30 October–24 January 1980
(opening revised from 16 October)
Organised by Thames Television.
PUBLICATION: VR.1979.013

VX.1979.025
From Hollar to Heideloff: costume and
fashion in books and prints
6 November?–29 January 1980
Organised by the Costume Society.
PUBLICATION: V.1979.012

VX.1979.026
Ingres: drawings from the Musée Ingres
at Montauban and other collections
12 December–24 February 1980
PUBLICATION: VR.1979.008

VX.1979.BGM.001
Puppets of the world
7 March–27 May

VX.1979.XXX.001
[Stand at] Chelsea Flower Show
22–25 May
VENUE: Chelsea Flower Show, London

VX.1979.XXX.002
Parade: dance costumes of three centuries
20 August–14 September
VENUE: Edinburgh College of Art
Organised by the Theatre Museum.
PUBLICATION: V.1979.018

VX.1979.XXX.003
Thirties: British art and design before the
war
25 October–13 January 1980
VENUE: Hayward Gallery, London
Organised in collaboration with the Arts Council of
Great Britain.
PUBLICATION: VR.1979.014

VX.1979.XXX.004
Arts of Bengal: the heritage of
Bangladesh and eastern India
9 November–3 December
VENUE: Whitechapel Art Gallery,
London
Organised in collaboration with the Whitechapel
Art Gallery. Also held at Manchester City Art
Gallery.
PUBLICATION: VR.1979.001

VX.1979.XXX.005
Istria and Dalmatia, 1782: Louis
François Cassas
VENUE: Split, Croatia
Held on the occasion of the VIII Mediterranean
Games.
PUBLICATION: VR.1979.009

1980

VX.1980.001
Arthur Rackham
4/5 March–27 April 1980
Organised by Sheffield City Art Galleries; also held
at Graves Art Gallery, Sheffield; Bristol Museum
and Art Gallery.
PUBLICATION: VR.1980.001

VX.1980.002
Hendrik Werkman, printer-painter,
1882–1945
4/5 March–27 April 1980
Arts Council exhibition, also held at the Mappin
Art Gallery, Sheffield.
PUBLICATION: VR.1980.005

VX.1980.003
Japan style
12/14 March–20 July 1980
Organised in collaboration with the Japan
Foundation.
PUBLICATION: V.1980.029

VX.1980.004
Recent acquisitions: the National Art
Library
18 March–1 June

VX.1980.005
The gold reliquary of Charles the Bold
26 March–1 June
This exhibition had to be cancelled, due to a strike
by contractors, but the reliquary itself was shown
until 25 June.
PUBLICATION: v.1980.020

VX.1980.006
Acquisitions 1977–80: Departments of
Prints, Drawings & Photographs, and
Paintings
3/4 June–9 November
PUBLICATION: v.1980.008

VX.1980.007
Knitting
23 June–14 September

VX.1980.008
The universal penman: a survey of
western calligraphy from the Roman
period to 1980
2 July–28 September or 16 October
National Art Library exhibition.
PUBLICATION: v.1980.038

VX.1980.009
Svensk form
9 July–14 September
Organised by the Swedish Society of Industrial
Design in collaboration with the Swedish Institute.
PUBLICATION: vr.1980.008

VX.1980.010
Tapestry: Henry Moore & West Dean
15/16 July–25 August
PUBLICATION: vr.1980.009

VX.1980.011
Roger Doyle: new work
23 July–3 September
Jewellery and silversmith's work.
PUBLICATION: v.1980.035

VX.1980.012
Tapestries for the nation: acquisitions
1970–1980
6/8 October–end 1981?

VX.1980.013
Princely magnificence: court jewels of the
Renaissance, 1500–1630
13/15 October–1 February 1981
PUBLICATION: v.1980.034

VX.1980.014
Photographs by Donald McCullin
20/22 October–25 January 1981

VX.1980.015
Art in the Boilerhouse
October–

VX.1980.016
Recent acquisitions 1977–1980
3 November–

VX.1980.017
A royal goldsmith: George Wickes
(1698–1761)
10 November–18 January 1981
PUBLICATION: vr.1980.013

VX.1980.018
Ganymed: printing, publishing,
design
18/19 November–31 January 1981
PUBLICATION: v.1980.019

VX.1980.019
Berthold Wolpe: a retrospective survey
18/19 November–1 February or 15
March 1981
PUBLICATION: v.1980.002

VX.1980.BGM.001
British doll artists
6 August–28 September

VX.1980.BGM.002
Book illustration by Gwen White
August–28 September

VX.1980.BGM.003
Spontaneous tapestries by Egyptian
children
7/8 October–30 November

VX.1980.BGM.004
Chad Valley board games, 1887–1935
16 December–1 March 1981
Largely drawn from the collection of Brian Love.

VX.1980.THM.001
Othello
August
'Micro exhibition'–v.1985.042, p. 72.

VX.1980.THM.002
John Lennon
December
'Micro exhibition'–v.1985.042, p. 72. — Organised on the occasion of the subject's death.

VX.1980.XXX.001
English silver ca.1500–1900
24 September–December
VENUES: Museum of Decorative Arts, Belgrade; Museum for Arts and Crafts, Zagreb

VX.1980.XXX.002
Old and modern masters of photography
VENUES: Aberdeen Art Gallery and Museum; Durham Light Infantry Museum and Arts Centre; Herbert Art Gallery and Museum, Coventry; Mappin Art Gallery, Sheffield; Bolton Museum and Art Gallery; Newport Museum and Art Gallery; Towner Art Gallery, Eastbourne
Touring version of vx.1978.006.
PUBLICATION: vr.1980.006

VX.1980.XXX.003
Photographs by Bill Brandt
Touring exhibition drawn from the V&A's collection. Circulated in the U.S.A. by the International Exhibitions Foundation.
PUBLICATION: vr.1980.007

1981

VX.1981.001
Drawing: technique & purpose
27/28 January–26 April or 31 May?
PUBLICATION: v.1981.004

VX.1981.002
Recent acquisitions: Department of Furniture & Woodwork
3 February–3 March

VX.1981.003
Hille: 75 years of British furniture
4 March–31 May
PUBLICATION: v.1981.010

VX.1981.004
Heraldry now, 1975–1981
14/15 April–31 May
Organised by the Heraldry Society.
PUBLICATION: vr.1981.007

VX.1981.005
Old and modern masters of photography
27/28 May–4 October
PUBLICATION: v.1981.015

VX.1981.006
The Chalon brothers: landscape, the theatre and caricature
28 May–4 October 1981
PUBLICATION: v.1981.003

VX.1981.007
The art of the book
23/24 June–30 September?
See note, vx.1979.016.

VX.1981.008
Masterpieces of Serbian goldsmiths' work, 13th–18th centuries
1 July–2 August
Organised in association with the Museum of Decorative Arts, Belgrade.
PUBLICATION: v.1981.012

VX.1981.009
New glass
22 July–11 October
International touring exhibition organised by the Corning Museum of Glass; presented in England by the Pilkington Group in conjunction with the V&A.
PUBLICATION: vr.1979.011

VX.1981.010
Design in silver, 1981
10 August–1 September
Touring exhibition organised by Goddard's.
PUBLICATION: vr.1981.004

VX.1981.011
Modern Japanese lacquer art
8/9 September–8 November
Touring exhibition organised by the Museum für Ostasiatische Kunst, Cologne.
PUBLICATION: vr.1981.008

VX.1981.012
The art of *Radio times*
21 October–21 February 1982
PUBLICATION: vr.1981.001

VX.1981.013
Splendours of the Gonzaga
3/5 November–31 January 1982
"for the first time in a V&A exhibition, a recorded tour will be available"–[press release].
PUBLICATION: V.1981.018

VX.1981.014
Felix Gluck
November–December
Examples of the artist's printmaking, publishing and graphic design, on the occasion of his death.

VX.1981.015
The strange genius of William Burges
16/18 November–17 January 1982
Centenary exhibition, organised in association with the National Museum of Wales, Cardiff and also held there.
PUBLICATIONS: VR.1981.010;
VR.1982.016

VX.1981.016
The art of eating
21 December–
Cookery books.

VX.1981.BGM.001
Cut here: paper cut-out toys and models
17 June–1 November

VX.1981.BGM.002
Ventriloquism: the Valentine Vox collection
20/21 October–21 February 1982

VX.1981.BGM.003
America at play, 1870–1955: toys from the Detroit Antique Toy Museum
1/2 December–28 February 1982
The Lawrence Scripps Wilkinson collection. Toured in Great Britain by the John Judkyn Memorial, Bath, in co-operation with the Detroit Historical Society.
PUBLICATION: V.1981.001

VX.1981.BGM.004
Spirit of Christmas
6 December–2 February 1982

VX.1981.THM.001
Spotlight: four centuries of ballet costume

6/7/8 April–9 August
A tribute to the Royal Ballet. — Closing date extended from 26 July.
PUBLICATION: V.1981.019

VX.1981.THM.002
Royal processions
July
'Micro-exhibition'–v.1985.042, p. 72. — Organised to coincide with the wedding of HRH the Prince of Wales and Lady Diana Spencer.

VX.1981.XXX.001
D'Oyly Carte
11 April–26 May
VENUE: Portsmouth City Museum
Organised by the Theatre Museum.
PUBLICATION: VR.1981.005

VX.1981.XXX.002
Lion of the Punjab
July–September
VENUE: Gunnersbury Park Museum, London
Organised by the Indian Section.

VX.1981.XXX.003
The English miniature
December–September 1982
Exhibition organised by the V&A from its own collections, touring in North America.
PUBLICATION: VR.1981.006

1982

VX.1982.001
Lucie Rie
15/17 February–28 March
PUBLICATIONS: V.1982.025;
VR.1982.010

VX.1982.002
The Indian heritage: court life & arts under Mughal rule
21 April–15 or 22 August
PUBLICATION: V.1982.013

VX.1982.003
India observed: India as viewed by British artists, 1760–1860
26 April–4 July
Organised by the National Art Library as part of the Festival of India.
PUBLICATION: V.1982.012

VX.1982.004
Towards a new iron age
11/12 May–11 July or 1 August
Organised in collaboration with the Crafts Council.
Exhibition toured, 1982–83: Metal Museum,
Memphis; Flint Institute, Michigan; Southern
Illinois University, Carbondale; Mint Museum,
Charlotte, North Carolina; American Craft
Museum, New York.
PUBLICATION: V.1982.031

VX.1982.005
Posy Simmonds cartoons
June?–

VX.1982.006
Francis Williams Bequest competition
9 June–8 July
Illustrated books.

VX.1982.007
Reynolds Stone, 1909–1979
21 July–31 October
National Art Library exhibition.
PUBLICATION: V.1982.027

VX.1982.008
John Sell Cotman, 1782–1842
9/11 August–24 October
Organised by the Arts Council of Great Britain.
Also held at the Whitworth Art Gallery, University
of Manchester; Bristol Museum and Art Gallery.
PUBLICATIONS: VR.1982.009;
VR.1982.010

VX.1982.009
Wendy Ramshaw
5/6 October–16 January 1983
PUBLICATION: V.1982.034

VX.1982.010
Humphry Repton, landscape gardener,
1752–1818
30 November/1 December–20 February
1983
Organised by the Sainsbury Centre for Visual Arts,
University of East Anglia, Norwich, and previously
held there for the 46th Norfolk and Norwich
Triennial Festival.
PUBLICATION: VR.1982.006

VX.1982.011
Modern photography
November–April 1983

VX.1982.012
The Pooh sketchbook
November?–
E.H. Shepard sketches and drawings.
PUBLICATION: VR.1982.014

VX.1982.013
Bernard Moore: master potter,
1850–1935
14/15 December–6 February 1983
PUBLICATION: V.1982.001

VX.1982.014
Japanese country textiles
December–March or June 1983

VX.1982.BGM.001
Indian playing cards
16/17 March–30 May
Organised as part of the Festival of India.
PUBLICATION: V.1982.014

VX.1982.BGM.002
Family art
20 April–20 May
PUBLICATION: VR.1982.003

VX.1982.BGM.003
Warner & Sons fabric designs
16 June–12 September
Touring exhibition organised by the firm.
PUBLICATION: VR.1981.003

VX.1982.BGM.004
Tie-dye and batik by children
29/30 June–12 September
The *Observer* Dyecraft Competition.

VX.1982.BGM.005
Inky pinky ponky
2–31 October
Book illustrations for children by Dan Jones.
PUBLICATION: VR.1982.008

VX.1982.BGM.006
Spirit of Christmas
1 December–16 January 1983

VX.1982.BGM.007
Wire toys from Zimbabwe
1 December–June or August 1983
Loans from Nottingham University Child
Development Research Unit. — Closing date
extended from January.
PUBLICATION: V.1982.035

VX.1982.BHO.001
Art & industry: the products we use
18 January–2 March
PUBLICATION: VR.1982.001

VX.1982.BHO.002
Sony design
24 March–3 June
PUBLICATION: VR.1982.015

VX.1982.BHO.003
Royal flush: a celebration of 100 years of
the water-closet. . .
1 April–

VX.1982.BHO.004
Design: Dieter Rams
1 July–19 August

VX.1982.BHO.005
The car programme
16 October–18 November
On the design of the Ford Sierra.
PUBLICATION: VR.1982.002

VX.1982.BHO.006
Memphis
7 December–10 February 1983
PUBLICATION: VR.1982.011

VX.1982.THM.001
Stravinsky rehearses Stravinsky:
photographs by Laelia Goehr
July
'Micro-exhibition'–V.1985.042, p. 72.
PUBLICATION: V.1982.030

VX.1982.THM.002
Show business
16/17 November–17 April 1983
Also touring, July 1983–May 1984: Mostyn Art
Gallery, Llandudno; Chapter Arts Centre,
Cardiff; Whitworth Art Gallery, University of
Manchester.
PUBLICATION: VR.1982.007

VX.1982.XXX.001
Silk stars of the Theatre Museum
September
VENUE: Liberty's, London

1983

VX.1983.001
Georgina Follett
25/26 January–1 May
PUBLICATION: V.1983.013

VX.1983.002
Illumination, medieval and modern:
manuscripts from the National Art
Library
15/16 March–15 May

VX.1983.003
Personal choice: a celebration of
twentieth century photographs
22/23 March–15 or 22 May
Arts Council of Great Britain touring exhibition;
selected and introduced by photographers, painters,
and writers.
PUBLICATION: V.1983.031

VX.1983.004
Pattern and design: designs for the
decorative arts, 1480–1980
22/23 March–3 July
PUBLICATION: V.1983.029

VX.1983.005
The art of photography: the major
processes, 1840–1914
22/23 March–28 August
PUBLICATION: V.1983.014

VX.1983.006
Tip of the iceberg: changing selection of
prints and drawings
22/23 March–October
Netherlandish drawings, 16th–17th centuries.
Topographical prints and drawings: exotic places.
Avant-garde watercolours, drawings and prints.

VX.1983.007
Henry Cole display
March?–
Duration: ca. 9 months.

VX.1983.008
Drawing in the Italian Renaissance
workshop
29/30 March–15 May
Organised in association with the Arts Council of
Great Britain and Nottingham University Art
Gallery, where the exhibition was first held.
PUBLICATION: V.1983.009

VX.1983.009
Japanese ceramics today: masterworks
from the Kikuchi collection
16/18 May–17 July
Also held at the Smithsonian Institution,
Washington, D.C.
PUBLICATION: VR.1983.006

VX.1983.010
Felix H. Man: 60 years of photography
24 May–24 July
PUBLICATION: V.1983.012

VX.1983.011
The little black dress
8 June–15 April 1984
PUBLICATION: VP.1982.001[4]

VX.1983.012
The common chronicle: an exhibition of
archive treasures from the County
Record Offices of England and Wales
14/15 June–11 September
Organised jointly with the Association of County
Archivists.
PUBLICATION: V.1983.006

VX.1983.013
Diamonds today: award winning pieces
28 June–17 July
Competition sponsored by De Beers.

VX.1983.014
French fashion illustration, 1910–1925
Summer
Organised by the National Art Library to
coincide with the re-opening of the V&A Dress
Collection.

VX.1983.015
Artists of the Tudor court: the portrait
miniature rediscovered, 1520–1620
5/6 July–6 November
PUBLICATION: V.1983.002

VX.1983.016
Joseph Beuys, drawings
27 July–2 October
Also held at Leeds City Art Gallery; Kettle's Yard
Gallery, Cambridge.
PUBLICATION: V.1983.022

VX.1983.017
Costume jewellery
1 August–1 December

VX.1983.018
19th century pressed glass
2/3 August–11 September

VX.1983.019
Fairings: the collection of Florence Dagg
2/3 August–11 September

VX.1983.020
William Eggleston: colour photographs
from the American South
3/4 August–18 September
PUBLICATION: V.1983.046

VX.1983.021
David Bailey: black and white memories
28 September–27 November
Photographs.
PUBLICATION: V.1983.007

VX.1983.022
Studio ceramics today
6 October–27 December
25th anniversary of the Craftsmen Potters
Association of Great Britain.
PUBLICATIONS: VR.1983.013;
VR.1983.014

VX.1983.023
David Cox, 1783–1859: bicentenary
exhibition
8/9 November–8 January 1984
Organised by and also held at Birmingham
Museum and Art Gallery.
PUBLICATION: VR.1983.003

VX.1983.024
Richard Doyle and his family
30 November–26 February 1984
PUBLICATION: V.1983.034

VX.1983.025
Markéta Luskačová: pilgrims
5/6 December–26 February 1984
In 1985 the Arts Council of Great Britain organised
a tour of this exhibition.
PUBLICATION: V.1983.032

VX.1983.026
Islamic bookbindings
13/14 December–4 March 1984
Organised in association with the World of Islam
Festival Trust.
PUBLICATION: V.1983.020

VX.1983.027
A celebration of friendship: Christmas
cards by Edward Ardizzone
15 December–2 February 1984
PUBLICATION: VR.1983.009

VX.1983.028
Russian avant-garde book illustration
and design
National Art Library display. — Dates not
known.

VX.1983.BGM.001
Tie-dye and batik
11 May–11 September
The *Young Observer* Dyecraft Competition.

VX.1983.BGM.002
Penny dreadfuls and comics
1/2 June–2 October
Loan exhibition of English periodicals for children
from the Library of Oldenburg University.
PUBLICATIONS: V.1983.030;
VR.1981.014

VX.1983.BGM.003
Nursery rhymes: books from the Renier
Collection
October–May 1984

VX.1983.BGM.004
Spirit of Christmas
1 December–8 January 1984

VX.1983.BHO.001
Design: the problem comes first
1/2 March–4 April
Touring exhibition organised by the Danish Design
Council.
PUBLICATION: VR.1983.004

VX.1983.BHO.002
Kenneth Grange
3–26 May
PUBLICATION: VR.1983.007

VX.1983.BHO.003
Images for sale
7 June–11 August
Design & art direction exhibition.
PUBLICATION: VR.1983.005

VX.1983.BHO.004
Taste
14 September–24 November
PUBLICATION: VR.1983.014

VX.1983.BHO.005
Philip Garner's *Better living* exhibition
13 December–5 January 1984
PUBLICATION: VR.1983.010

VX.1983.THM.001
A month in the country
1–31 May 1983
PUBLICATION: V.1983.024

VX.1983.THM.002
Oliver Messel
21/22 June–30 October
From the collection of Lord Snowdon.
PUBLICATION: V.1983.027

VX.1983.XXX.001
Scenery from the Diaghilev collection,
and costumes from *The sleeping princess*
June
VENUE: Olympia, London
Organised by the Theatre Museum in connection
with the Fine Art and Antiques Fair.

VX.1983.XXX.002
Aubrey Beardsley
June–September
VENUES: Isetan Museum of Art, Tokyo;
Nabio Gallery; Okazaki City Art
Museum; Funabashi Seibu Museum of
Art
PUBLICATION: VR.1983.001

VX.1983.XXX.003
Maestri dell'acquarello inglese: acquarelli
del Victoria and Albert Museum
September–October
VENUE: Palazzo Braschi, Rome
PUBLICATION: VR.1983.008

VX.1983.XXX.004
Ballet costumes and photographs
19 October
VENUE: Guildhall, London
Organised by the Theatre Museum for the British
Friends of the Art Museums of Israel, to honour
Dame Alicia Markova.
PUBLICATION: VR.1983.002

VX.1983.XXX.005
Photographs by Anthony, reprinted by
Graham Brandon
29 December–14 January 1984
VENUE: Sadler's Wells Theatre, London
Organised by the Theatre Museum.

1984

VX.1984.001
The Platinum Award: award-winning
platinum jewellery
7 January–23 February

VX.1984.002
Wallpapers: four centuries of design
25/26 January–29 April

VX.1984.003
20th century watercolours from the
V&A collection
26 January–20 May

VX.1984.004
Korean embroidery
11 February–15 April
From the collection of Mr and Mrs Huh Dong-
Hwa.
PUBLICATION: VR.1984.004

VX.1984.005
Patricia Meyerowitz: jewellery
3 March–26 April
PUBLICATION: V.1984.022

VX.1984.006
Literary Britain, photographed by Bill
Brandt
6 March–20 May
PUBLICATION: V.1984.018

VX.1984.007
Chinese export watercolours
13/14 March–27 May
PUBLICATION: V.1984.005

VX.1984.008
Rosenthal: a century of porcelain
2/3 May–1 July
First shown at the Kestner Museum, Hanover, and
touring in Germany.
PUBLICATION: V.1984.029

VX.1984.009
Ros Conway: jewellery
5 May–28 June
PUBLICATION: V.1984.028

VX.1984.010
From east to west: a history of the firm of
G.P. & J. Baker
8/9 May–14 October
Organised by the firm and the Department of
Textiles and Dress.
PUBLICATION: VR.1984.008

VX.1984.011
Certain shawls, 1839–1849
12 May–1 March 1985

VX.1984.012
Rococo: art and design in Hogarth's
England
15/16 May–30 September
PUBLICATION: V.1984.026

VX.1984.013
Korean graphic arts
22/23 May–19 August
PUBLICATION: VR.1984.006

VX.1984.014
The golden age of British photography,
1839–1900
5/6 June–19 August
Organised in association with the Alfred Stieglitz
Center, Philadelphia Museum of Art, and held there
27 October–6 January 1985. Also held at: Museum
of Fine Arts, Houston; Minneapolis Institute of
Arts; Pierpont Morgan Library, New York;
Museum of Fine Arts, Boston, May 1985–May
1986.
PUBLICATION: V.1984.011

VX.1984.015
William Kent (1685–1748): designer and
architect
5/6 June–26 August
From the collection of the Prints and Drawings
Department. — Dates from report of the Board of
Trustees (1986). Catalogue gives closing date of 2
September.
PUBLICATION: V.1984.007

VX.1984.016
Office of the future
5 September–14 October
Prototypes by Robin & Stanton, joint third
prizewinner of a French Government design
competition.

VX.1984.017
Modern artists' jewels
11/12 September–1 November
PUBLICATION: V.1984.021

VX.1984.018
The discovery of the Lake District: a
northern Arcadia and its uses
18/19 September–17 January 1985
PUBLICATION: V.1984.006

VX.1984.019
Edwin Smith: photographs
1935–1971
25/26 September–20 January 1985
PUBLICATION: VR.1984.007

VX.1984.020
John Deakin: the salvage of a
photographer
25/26 September–20 January 1985
PUBLICATION: V.1984.015

VX.1984.021
20th century watercolours from the
V&A collection
26 September–18 November
Cf. VX.1984.003

VX.1984.022
Oxtoby's lost rockers
27 October–2 January 1985
Photographs by Miki Slingsby of lost paintings by
David Oxtoby.

VX.1984.023
Marilynn Nicholson: jeweller
3 November–3 January 1985
PUBLICATION: V.1984.019

VX.1984.024
Recent acquisitions: Department of
Textiles, Furnishings and Dress
4 November–7 June 1985

VX.1984.025
John French: fashion photographer
12/14 November–10 March 1985
PUBLICATION: V.1984.016

VX.1984.026
British biscuit tins
1 December–2 February 1985
PUBLICATION: V.1984.004

VX.1984.027
Watercolours by Michael Angelo Rooker
and John Varley
11/12 December–14 April 1985
PUBLICATIONS: V.1984.017;
V.1984.020

VX.1984.028
Selected textiles and their conservation
12 December–March 1985

VX.1984.BGM.001
The trick that went wrong
20 February–31 December
Book illustrations by Phillida Gili.
PUBLICATION: VR.1983.017

VX.1984.BGM.002
The new Kit Williams
23/24 May–23 June
PUBLICATION: VR.1984.002

VX.1984.BGM.003
Jolly hockey sticks: the world of girls'
school fiction
29/30 May–30 September

VX.1984.BGM.004
Spirit of Christmas with the Nutcracker
Prince
1 December–20 January 1985

VX.1984.BHO.001
Handtools: the culture of manual work
20 March–14 June
PUBLICATION: VR.1984.009

VX.1984.BHO.002
Design at Kingston
4/5–11 July
Work by students from the School of Three-
Dimensional Design, Kingston Polytechnic.
PUBLICATION: VR.1984.005

VX.1984.BHO.003
Robots
1 August–25 October 1984
PUBLICATION: VR.1984.012

VX.1984.BHO.004
Post-modern colour
28 November–13 January 1985

VX.1984.THM.001
Ralph Richardson (1902–1983)
January
'Micro exhibition'–v.1985.042, p. 72.

VX.1984.THM.002
Anton Dolin (1964–1983)
June–

VX.1984.THM.003
A midsummer night's dream
July
'Micro exhibition'–v.1985.042, p. 72.

1985

VX.1985.001
Alan Craxford: jeweller
12 January–7 March
PUBLICATION: v.1985.003

VX.1985.002
A vision exchanged: amateurs and
photography in mid-Victorian
England
5/6 February–6 April
Also held at the National Museum of Photography,
Film and Television, Bradford.
PUBLICATION: v.1985.049

VX.1985.003
The people & places of Constantinople:
watercolours by Amadeo Count Preziosi,
1816–1882
5/6 February–9 June
PUBLICATION: v.1985.036

VX.1985.004
William Staite Murray: studio pottery of
the 1920s and 1930s
26/27 February–28 April
Organised by the Cleveland County Museum
Service and also held at the Cleveland
Gallery.
PUBLICATION: vr.1984.014

VX.1985.005
Frances Bendixson: jewellery
16 March–9 May
PUBLICATION: v.1985.016

VX.1985.006
From Manet to Hockney: modern artists'
illustrated books
19/20 March–19 May
National Art Library exhibition.
PUBLICATION: v.1985.017

VX.1985.007
Artists' graphic design before World
War II
21 March–May?
National Art Library display especially from its
collection of jobbing printing organised to coincide
with vx.1985.006.
PUBLICATION: v.1985.004

VX.1985.008
Mouton Rothschild: paintings for the
labels
16/17 April–9 June

VX.1985.009
Sceptical landscapes: photographs of
Park City, Utah, by Lewis Baltz
30 April/1 May–28 July

VX.1985.010
Contemporary American jewellery
11 May–25 July
"This exhibition is part of the American Festival,
the largest celebration of the culture of the United
States ever held in Great Britain"–vr.1985.009,
p. 48.
PUBLICATION: vr.1985.009

VX.1985.011
Louis Vuitton: travelling in style
13/15 May–6 October

VX.1985.012
Bonington, Francia and Wyld, and
Samuel Prout
20/21 May–15 September
PUBLICATION: v.1985.009

VX.1985.013
English caricature
5/6 June–1 September
Exhibition previously circulated to Yale Center for
British Art, New Haven; Library of Congress,
Washington, D.C.; National Library of Canada,
Ottawa.
PUBLICATION: v.1984.008

VX.1985.014
Textiles from the Wellcome collection
8 June–1 December

VX.1985.015
Three English architects: Sir John Soane,
A.W.N. Pugin, J.P. Seddon
25/26 June–27 October

VX.1985.016
20th century costume jewellery from the
Fior collection
27 July–30 August

VX.1985.017
Julia Margaret Cameron: photography
16 August–6 October

VX.1985.018
Jacqueline Mina: jewellery 1973–1985
7 September–7 November
PUBLICATION: v.1985.028

VX.1985.019
Browne muggs: English brown stoneware
11 September–5 January 1986
Closing date extended from 17 November.
PUBLICATION: v.1985.011

VX.1985.020
Shots of style: great fashion photographs,
chosen by David Bailey
25 September–5 January 1986
Dates from *Report of the Board of Trustees . . .*
(1986) p. 59. Dates on catalogue: 9 October–19
January.
PUBLICATIONS: v.1985.039;
vp.1982.001[4]

VX.1985.021
Hats from India
23 October–4 May 1986
Also held at Cartwright Hall, Bradford; Platt Hall,
Manchester; Ashmolean Museum, Oxford.
PUBLICATION: v.1985.021

VX.1985.022
British watercolours: selection from the
national collection
23 October–May 1986

VX.1985.023
Knit one, purl one: historic and
contemporary knitting from the V&A's
collection

22/23 October–5 October 1986
PUBLICATION: v.1985.031

VX.1985.024
Beatrix Potter: the V&A collection
5/6 November–21 February 1986
PUBLICATIONS: v.1985.005;
v.1985.006

VX.1985.025
Acquisitions 1981–1985: Department of
Designs, Prints and Drawings
13 November–2 February 1986
PUBLICATION: v.1985.015

VX.1985.026
Kevin Coates
16 November–9 January 1986
PUBLICATION: v.1985.030

VX.1985.027
Five years of recent Library acquisitions
Dates not known.

VX.1985.028
The Hutton bequest
National Art Library display. — Dates not known.

VX.1985.029
An introduction to the Essex House Press
National Art Library display. — Dates not known.
PUBLICATION: v.1986.026

VX.1985.BGM.001
Tie-dye and batik
11/12 February–21 April
The *Young Observer* Dyecraft Competition
exhibition.

VX.1985.BGM.002
Snoopy and Charlie Brown are 35 years
old
4/5 June–1 September
Drawings by Schulz for the Peanuts comic strip,
from the collection of Jimmy Heineman.

VX.1985.BGM.003
Tall stories . . . to celebrate the
bicentenary of Baron Munchausen
17/18 September–10 November
PUBLICATION: v.1985.043

VX.1985.BGM.004
Spirit of Christmas: the Christmas crib
1 December–12 January 1986

VX.1985.BHO.001
The good design guide
22 January–11 February
PUBLICATION: VR.1985.005

VX.1985.BHO.002
Issey Miyake: 'Bodyworks'
26/27 February–9 April

VX.1985.BHO.003
National characteristics in design
17 April–18 July
PUBLICATION: VR.1985.010

VX.1985.BHO.004
The bag
3 August–3 October
Plastic carrier bags.

VX.1985.BHO.005
The car
17 October–14 November

VX.1985.BHO.006
Natural design: the search for comfort
and efficiency
4 December–27 February

VX.1985.THM.001
Handel in St. Martin's Lane
23 April–16 June
Organised in collaboration with English National
Opera.

VX.1985.THM.002
20th century set and costume design
from the Theatre Museum
9 September–6 April

VX.1985.XXX.001
Acuarelas del siglo XX del Victoria &
Albert Museum de Londres
January–February
VENUE: Banco de Bilbao, Madrid
Organised by the Banca de Bilbao Departamento de
Actividades Culturales.
PUBLICATION: VR.1985.001

VX.1985.XXX.002
Aubrey Beardsley, 1872–1898
13 March–28 April
VENUE: Galleria nazionale d'arte
moderna, Rome
Organised in association with the V&A and the
British Council.
PUBLICATION: VR.1985.003

VX.1985.XXX.003
Pictures from the ballet: Graham
Brandon, photographer
1/2–21 May
VENUE: New Zealand House,
London
Photographs taken for the Theatre Museum
Archive.

VX.1985.XXX.004
Aubrey Beardsley, 1872–1898: 70 opere
dal Victoria and Albert Museum
17 May–16 June
VENUE: Palazzo Bagatti Valsecchio,
Milan
Organised by: Regione Lombardia, Settore
cultura e informazione; British Council Nord Italia;
Comune di Milano, Ripartazione cultura e
spettacolo.
PUBLICATION: VR.1985.002

1986

VX.1986.001
Frank Bauer: jewellery and spectacles
18 January–13 March
PUBLICATION: V.1986.017

VX.1986.002
Characters in cloth: textile portraits
28/29 January–31 December

VX.1986.003
Mainly Mortlake: English tapestry of the
17th century
28/29 January–31 December

VX.1986.004
British textile designs of the 18th and
20th centuries
12 February–22 June

VX.1986.005
French 18th century drawings and Swiss
stained glass design
12 February–22 June
PUBLICATION: V.1986.040

VX.1986.006
The street photographs of Roger Mayne
26 February–1 June
PUBLICATIONS: V.1986.039;
VP.1982.001[5]

VX.1986.007
Chess in art and society
5 March–22 June
PUBLICATION: V.1986.008

VX.1986.008
American potters today
13/14 May–31 August
Organised in conjunction with Garth Clark, Los
Angeles.
PUBLICATION: V.1986.003

VX.1986.009
Ted Tinling
14–17 June
Sportswear designs.
PUBLICATION: V.1986.041

VX.1986.010
Masterpieces of photography:
1839–1980
17/18 June–17 January 1987?
Closing date extended from 30 November?

VX.1986.011
William Mulready, 1786–1863
1/2 July–12 October
PUBLICATION: V.1986.033

VX.1986.012
Blitz designer collection of Levi jackets
10 July–13 October
Held in aid of the Prince's Trust.
PUBLICATION: VR.1986.005

VX.1986.013
Paul and Thomas Sandby
16 July–10 August
PUBLICATION: V.1986.034

VX.1986.014
British International Print Biennale
15/16 July–21 September
A selection of works from the 9th International
Print Biennale held at Cartwright Hall, Bradford,
23 March–22 June 1986.

VX.1986.015
Designs for interiors
26/27 August–12 October
PUBLICATION: V.1986.014

VX.1986.016
E.W. Godwin
26/27 August–12 October

VX.1986.017
Weimar ceramics
23/24 September–23 November
From the collection of Tilmann Buddensieg,
owned by the Germanisches Nationalmuseum,
Nuremberg.

VX.1986.018
New acquisitions: new landscapes
2 October–17 January 1987
Exhibition of photographs.

VX.1986.019
Gerda Flöckinger
14/15 October–30 November
PUBLICATION: V.1986.019

VX.1986.020
The country house described
30 October–24 December
Display organised by the National Art Library to
mark the publication of v.1986.011.
PUBLICATION: V.1986.011

VX.1986.021
Alexander Cozens, 1717–1786
4/5 November–4 January 1987
Organised in association with the Art Gallery of
Ontario, Toronto, where a related exhibition of the
work of Alexander and John Robert Cozens was
held, 30 January–29 March 1987.
PUBLICATIONS: V.1986.002;
VR.1986.002

VX.1986.022
Fashion tracks: clothes from the 1985
Pirelli calendar
4/5 November–30 August 1987

VX.1986.023
Fable books: five hundred years of
illustration
17 November–11 January 1987
PUBLICATION: V.1986.015

VX.1986.024
Eye for industry
25/26 November–8? February 1987
Organised by the Royal Society of Arts in
association with the V&A, for Industry Year. —
Closing date extended from 1 February?
PUBLICATIONS: VR.1986.007;
VR.1986.008

VX.1986.025
The Platinum Award: award-winning
platinum jewellery
10 December–11 January 1987

VX.1986.026
Boydell and the foundation of the British
school of painting
Dates not known.
PUBLICATION: v.1986.006

VX.1986.027
Designs for British dress and furnishing
fabrics: 18th century to the present
Dates not known.
PUBLICATION: v.1986.013

VX.1986.028
An introduction to the Beaumont Press
National Art Library display. — Dates not
known.
PUBLICATION: v.1986.024

VX.1986.029
An introduction to the Doves and
Ashendene Presses
National Art Library display. — Dates not
known.
PUBLICATION: v.1986.025

VX.1986.030
An introduction to the Kelmscott Press
National Art Library display. — Dates not known.
PUBLICATION: v.1986.027

VX.1986.BGM.001
American dolls 1840–1985: the
Lawrence Scripps Wilkinson collection
12 March–8 or 17 June
Collection affiliated to the Detroit Historical
Museum. Circulated in Britain by the John Judkyn
Memorial.
PUBLICATION: VR.1986.003

VX.1986.BGM.002
The world of adventure: English and
German adventure stories from Daniel
Defoe to Karl May
9 July–21 September
Organised by, and previously held at, the University
of Oldenburg.
PUBLICATIONS: v.1986.007;
VR.1984.001

VX.1986.BGM.003
The *Young Observer* children's collage
exhibition
8 October–9 November

VX.1986.BGM.004
Spirit of Christmas: Christmas revels
1 December–18 January 1987

VX.1986.BHO.001
Coke! Coca-cola 1886–1986: designing a
megabrand
9 April–15 May
PUBLICATION: VR.1986.006

VX.1986.BHO.002
New design for old
28 May–3 July
PUBLICATION: VR.1986.009

VX.1986.BHO.003
14:24 – British youth culture
22 July–31 August
PUBLICATION: VR.1986.001

VX.1986.XXX.001
British printmakers, 1960–1985
18 June–13 July
VENUE: Pier Arts Centre, Stromness,
Orkney

1987

VX.1987.001
Irving Penn
13/14 January–8 March
Photographs.

VX.1987.002
An introduction to the Nonesuch Press
19 January–18 May
National Art Library display.
PUBLICATION: v.1986.028

VX.1987.003
Towards a bigger picture [I]
27/28 January–12 July
Photography.

VX.1987.004
Painters and the Derby China Works,
1785–1848
17/18 March–21 June
PUBLICATION: VR.1987.012

VX.1987.005
British hand-coloured prints
17/18 March–5 July
PUBLICATION: V.1987.008

VX.1987.006
English artists' paper
17/18 March–5 July
PUBLICATION: VR.1987.005

VX.1987.007
Zika Ascher: fabric art fashion
14/15 April–14 June
PUBLICATION: V.1987.001

VX.1987.008
Exposure: *Blitz* magazine photographs
14 May–21 June
PUBLICATION: VR.1987.004

VX.1987.009
Susie Cooper productions
2/3 June–6 September
Also held at Stoke on Trent City Museum and Art
Gallery, 4 October–24 December.
PUBLICATION: V.1987.017

VX.1987.010
Wally Gilbert, Thomas Gentille
16/17 June–20 September
Jewellery exhibition.
PUBLICATION: V.1987.021

VX.1987.011
Artists' choice: modern prints to
celebrate 150 years of the Royal College
of Art
7/8 July–20 September

VX.1987.012
W.H. Smith Illustration Awards
15 July–1 November
Annual awards for book and magazine illustration,
after cessation of the quinquennial Francis Williams
Bequest awards. Administered by Leo de Freitas for
the National Art Library.
PUBLICATION: V.1987.002

VX.1987.013
Alvar Aalto
21/22 July–13 September

VX.1987.014
Witness in brass
Held to mark the centenary of the Monumental
Brass Society.
5 August–1 November
PUBLICATION: V.1987.022

VX.1987.015
The royal photographs of Sir Cecil
Beaton
15/16 September–28 February 1988
Closing date extended from 1 February.
PUBLICATION: V.1987.014

VX.1987.016
Salvatore Ferragamo: the art of the shoe,
1927–1960
29/31 October–28 February 1988
Closing date extended from 7 February?
PUBLICATION: VR.1987.015

VX.1987.017
The image multiplied
24/25 November–15 February 1988
PUBLICATION: VR.1987.010

VX.1987.018
Fritz Maierhofer
9 December–6 March 1988
PUBLICATION: V.1987.006

VX.1987.019
From the 1890s to the 1980s: fashion
periodicals in the National Art Library
Dates not known.
PUBLICATION: V.1988.007

VX.1987.020
An introduction to the Golden Cockerel
Press
National Art Library display. — Dates not
known.
PUBLICATION: V.1987.009

VX.1987.021
An introduction to the Gregynog Press
National Art Library display. — Dates not
known.
PUBLICATION: V.1987.010

VX.1987.AAD.001
David Hicks, and J. Bird Iles: records
April–July
Furniture, textile and interior designers' records.

VX.1987.AAD.002
Hugh Easton, stained glass artist: archive
July–August

VX.1987.AAD.003
Charlotte Bondy
11 August–15 September
Aluminium foil packaging designer's autobiography
and designs.

VX.1987.AAD.004
Edith Crapper, illustrator and
miniaturist: archive
16 September–27 October

VX.1987.AAD.005
Fashion ca.1920–1930 in the Archive of
Art and Design
28 October–2 December

VX.1987.AAD.006
Archive of Art and Design Christmas
display
3 December–6 January 1988

VX.1987.BGM.001
The *Young Observer* Dyecraft
Competition sponsored by Dylon
4–28 February

VX.1987.BGM.002
The curators at work on the Palitoy
collection
4 March–23 April

VX.1987.BGM.003
Mr Punch's 325th birthday
29 April–12 May

VX.1987.BGM.004
Judaica from the V&A: a contribution to
the Jewish East End celebration
19/20 May–5 July
This exhibition led to the publication of
v.1991.006.

VX.1987.BGM.005
A calendar of childhood ceremonies
5 August–1 November

VX.1987.BGM.006
Spirit of Christmas: Christmas around
the world
1 December–16 or 18 January 1988
PUBLICATION: v.1987.015

VX.1987.THM.001
Tito Gobbi, Boris Christoff
23 April–25 October

VX.1987.THM.002
The King's pleasures
24 April–2 August
Costumes for the court ballet of Louis XIII.
PUBLICATION: v.1986.012

VX.1987.THM.003
The Theatre Museum unpacks
24 April–27 September
PUBLICATION: v.1987.018

VX.1987.THM.004
John Gielgud: a celebration
13/14 October–28 August 1988

VX.1987.THM.005
Linbury Prize for stage design
18 November–28 January 1988

VX.1987.XXX.001
The unknown Beatrix Potter
6 June–19 July
VENUE: Beningbrough Hall,
Yorkshire
Exhibition of works from the Linder Bequest,
organised by the National Trust in association with
the *Yorkshire post*.
PUBLICATION: VR.1987.017

VX.1987.XXX.002
British caricature from Hogarth to
Hockney
24 October–13 December
VENUE: National Museum of Western
Art, Tokyo
Exhibition mainly of objects from the V&A.
PUBLICATION: VR.1987.006

1988

VX.1988.001
A selection of twentieth century male and
female dress acquired for the Museum
during the 1980s
25 January–
Duration: a year?

VX.1988.002
Book Works at the V&A
16 February–17 April
Exhibition of recent British artists' books.
PUBLICATION: VR.1988.004

VX.1988.003
Richard Redgrave, 1804–1888
15/16 March–26 May
Closing date extended from 22 May? Also held at the Yale Center for British Art, New Haven, 16 June–7 August.
PUBLICATION: V.1988.017

VX.1988.004
Chris Killip
16 March–13 July
Included: In flagrante and The photographer's eye [selection of work by other photographers]. — Closing date extended from 29 May.

VX.1988.005
Faber and Faber poetry: paperbacks designed by Pentagram
Spring?
National Art Library display.

VX.1988.006
The graphic language of Neville Brody
26/27 April–29 May
PUBLICATION: VR.1988.009

VX.1988.007
The art of the *New Yorker*
10/11 May–26 June
Touring exhibition from the U.S.A.

VX.1988.008
Artists in National Parks
22/23 June–4 September
PUBLICATION: VR.1988.002

VX.1988.009
Textiles of the arts and crafts movement
23 June–4 September or 9 October
PUBLICATION: VR.1988.016

VX.1988.010
Fashion and surrealism
29 June–29 August
Closing date extended from 7 August.
PUBLICATIONS: VP.1982.001[Sum 1988]; VR.1988.006

VX.1988.011
Forwarding the book in California
5 July–4 September
National Art Library display organised by Linda L. Brownrigg.
PUBLICATION: VR.1988.007

VX.1988.012
Elton John at the V&A
9–23 August
PUBLICATION: VR.1988.018

VX.1988.013
Highlights from the Photography Collection
24 August–13 November

VX.1988.014
Photographs by women: Clementina Viscountess Hawarden to Cindy Sherman
24 August–13 November

VX.1988.015
From the 1890s to the 1980s: interior design periodicals in the National Art Library
13 September–20 November

VX.1988.016
Avant première: the most contemporary French furniture
11/12 October–8 January 1989
PUBLICATION: VR.1988.003

VX.1988.017
Linda McCartney's Sun prints
8/9–25 November
Photographs.
PUBLICATION: VR.1988.015

VX.1988.018
Kaffe Fassett
15/16 November–29 January 1989
PUBLICATION: VR.1988.011

VX.1988.019
Sock Shop
17 November–June 1989

VX.1988.020
W.H. Smith Illustration Awards
18 November–8 January 1989
See note, VX.1987.012. — Opening date previously announced as 9 November.

VX.1988.021
'Small things' collected by Sir Eduardo
Paolozzi for the Krazy Kat Arkive of
twentieth century popular culture
November–July 1989

VX.1988.022
Hans Joachim Burgert: books, graphic
work and calligraphy
29 November–22 January 1989
National Art Library display.

VX.1988.023
Towards a bigger picture II
30 November–15 January 1989
Photography.
PUBLICATION: VR.1988.005

VX.1988.024
The Burberry story
12 December–20 August 1989
PUBLICATION: V.1988.001

VX.1988.025
Contemporary Danish prints
To February 1990.

VX.1988.026
From the 1890s to the 1980s:
architectural periodicals in the National
Art Library
Dates not known.

VX.1988.027
From the 1890s to the 1980s: modern
art periodicals in the National Art
Library
Dates not known.

VX.1988.AAD.001
Recent acquisitions at the Archive of Art
and Design
7 January–7 March

VX.1988.AAD.002
Dora Lunn, potter: papers and
correspondence
8 March–25 April

VX.1988.AAD.003
Paul Pieter Piech, graphic artist: posters
and papers
26 April–23 June

VX.1988.AAD.004
Knitwear in the 1960s, from the Archive
of Art and Design
24 June–21 December

VX.1988.AAD.005
International Tobacco Company: records
of advertising campaigns
21 December–24 February 1989

VX.1988.BGM.001
Top of the pop-ups: two hundred years
of moveable books
23/24 February–30 April

VX.1988.BGM.002
Koalas, kangaroos and kookaburras:
a century of Australian children's book
illustration
24/25 May–19 June
"almost entirely drawn from the James Hardie
Library's Children's Collection . . . currently being
transformed into the Museum of Australian
Childhood"–VR.1988.012, p. 7.
PUBLICATION: VR.1988.012

VX.1988.BGM.003
Happy and glorious: artwork by today's
children celebrating the accession of
William and Mary
6 July–7 August
Organised by the William and Mary Tercentenary
Trust.

VX.1988.BGM.004
The Hogarth puppets
30/31 August–16 October
Collection of Jan [John Garrett] Bussell and Anne
Hogarth, lent by the Puppet Centre, Battersea Arts
Centre, London.

VX.1988.BGM.005
Tony Hayward's toys from India
22 October–17 November

VX.1988.BGM.006
Happy birthday, Mickey Mouse
1 November–1 December

VX.1988.BGM.007
Spirit of Christmas: the Christmas tree
1 December–15 January 1989

VX.1988.THM.001
A record of pop: images of a decade:
photographs by Harry Hammond
2/3 March–26 June
PUBLICATION: V.1988.016

VX.1988.THM.002
Dance: the world to Australia, Australia
to the world
27/28 July–13 November
Previously held at the Museum of the Performing
Arts, Lincoln Center, New York.

VX.1988.THM.003
Paul Hogarth's Shakespeare
11 August–9 October
Covers of Penguin Books editions of Shakespeare's
works.

VX.1988.THM.004
Wake up and dream!
21 September–15 January 1989
From the Theatre Collection of the Austrian
National Library.
PUBLICATION: VR.1986.014

VX.1988.THM.005
Circus! circus!
14/15 December–2 April 1989
PUBLICATION: V.1988.003

VX.1988.XXX.001
A golden treasury: jewellery from the
Indian subcontinent
24 September–27 November 1988;
12 April–2 June 1989
VENUES: Cartwright Hall, Bradford;
Zamana Gallery, London
PUBLICATION: V.1988.009

1989

VX.1989.001
Ken Campbell: an artist's books
6 February–2 April
National Art Library display.
PUBLICATION: VR.1989.006

VX.1989.002
Photography now
14/15 February–30 April
PUBLICATION: V.1989.012

VX.1989.003
Leon Morris: photographer in residence
1–15 March

VX.1989.004
William De Morgan: designs
15 March–18 June
PUBLICATIONS: VP.1982.001
[Spr 1989]; VR.1989.008

VX.1989.005
Conrad Atkinson: 'Newspaper works'
6 April–
Duration: 6 months? — Prints, Drawings &
Paintings Dept. display.

VX.1989.006
Book art: a selection of 1988 acquisitions
in the National Art Library
12 April–11 June
PUBLICATION: V.1989.001

VX.1989.007
Albert Skira, publisher
12 April–13 August
National Art Library display organised by Valerie
Holman.

VX.1989.008
The nude: a new perspective
24 May–3 September
PUBLICATION: VR.1989.015

VX.1989.009
Australian fashion
7 June–13 August
Organised by the Museum of Applied Arts and
Sciences, Sydney, in association with the Australia
Council and also held at Powerhouse Museum.
PUBLICATION: VR.1989.004

VX.1989.010
Nehru and the making of modern India
8 June–23 July
Presented by the Nehru Centenary Implementation
Committee.

VX.1989.011
From the 1890s to the 1980s: periodicals
in the National Art Library
June
"During 1987–8 the Library held a series of
displays which illustrated the development of the
fashion, architecture, art and interior design
periodicals. This display brings together some of the
themes which have marked the history of magazine

design as it has responded to technical and marketing advances and changes in the habits of reading during the last one hundred years."–v.1989.008.
PUBLICATION: v.1989.008

VX.1989.012
Edward Bawden
26 July–29 October

VX.1989.013
Sources for twentieth century fashion at the Archive of Art and Design
July–December 1990

VX.1989.014
Progress of the worm: 300 years of corkscrews
1 August–8 October

VX.1989.015
Timothy C. Ely
16 August–15 October
National Art Library display of artist's books.
PUBLICATION: vr.1989.016

VX.1989.016
Focus on food
16 August–22 October
This exhibition did not take place.

VX.1989.017
Andy Warhol: the Factory years
6 September–29 Oct or 12 November
Photographs by Nat Finkelstein.
PUBLICATION: vr.1989.001

VX.1989.018
A vision of Britain
8 September–19 November
Organised to demonstrate HRH Prince Charles's views on architecture.
PUBLICATION: vr.1989.019

VX.1989.019
20th century Scandinavian ceramics and glass
20 September–7 January 1990
PUBLICATION: v.1989.013

VX.1989.020
Clementina, Lady Hawarden: photographer
27 September–January 1990

Organised in collaboration with the British Council. Also held at the Musée d'Orsay, Paris, 12 February–29 April 1990; J. Paul Getty Museum, Malibu, 4 December 1990–17 February 1991.
PUBLICATION: vr.1990.006

VX.1989.021
Clouds and flowers
Autumn–April? 1990
Ikats from Turkestan and printed cottons from Persia.

VX.1989.022
Contemporary Danish book art
18 October–25 November
National Art Library display.
PUBLICATION: vr.1989.007

VX.1989.023
Gunnlaugur Briem: lettering artist
29 November–11 January 1990
National Art Library display.

VX.1989.024
China in Persia
End November–end February 1990

VX.1989.025
The Orient observed: images of the Middle East from the Searight collection
6 December–25 February 1990
PUBLICATION: v.1989.009

VX.1989.026
W.H. Smith Illustration Awards
12 December–4 February 1990
See note, vx.1987.012.

VX.1989.027
Pirelli at work
20 December–22 April 1990
Photographs by Chris Killip.

VX.1989.AAD.001
Heber Mathews, potter: photographs and printed material
24 February–28 August

VX.1989.AAD.002
Ronald Grierson, textile designer: annotated designs, photographs and documentary material
29 August–November 1989

VX.1989.AAD.003
Krazy Kat Arkive of Twentieth Century
Popular Culture
November–October 1990

VX.1989.BGM.001
First year at school: photographs by
Markéta Luskačová
1 February–5 March
PUBLICATION: VR.1989.010

VX.1989.BGM.002
Some creative children and what became
of them: Franz Cižek and his art classes
15 March–4 June

VX.1989.BGM.003
Themes from the thirties
21 June–24 September
Pip, Squeak and Wilfred. A tribute to Marjorie
Abbatt. Porcelain children: 'Hummel-figures' from
the Goebel factory. Classroom pictures. Winifred
Gill's puppet theatre.

VX.1989.BGM.004
Penny for the guy: photographs by David
Trainer
18 October–12 November

VX.1989.BGM.005
Play matters
23 October–5 January 1990
Award-winning toys from *What toy?* magazine.
In association with the National Association of Toy
Libraries.

VX.1989.BGM.006
Spirit of Christmas: Christmas characters
29 November–14 January 1990

VX.1989.THM.001
Stage secrets of the Chinese opera
27 February–7 May

VX.1989.THM.002
Shooting stars: the theatre photography
of Houston Rogers
4 May–2 September 1990
PUBLICATION: V.1989.014

VX.1989.THM.003
French dressing, 1789–1830
18 May–1 October 1989
Organised in association with C & W May.
PUBLICATION: VR.1989.012

VX.1989.THM.004
Blues 'n' roots: David Oxtoby, drawings
and mixed media works on paper
19 October–22 April 1990

VX.1989.XXX.001
William Morris
1 March–1 May
VENUES: Isetan Museum of Art, Tokyo;
Daimaru Museum Osaka Umeda
In association with the William Morris Gallery.
Organized in Japan by the Asahi Shimbun.
PUBLICATION: VR.1989.021

VX.1989.XXX.002
Going Dutch: decorative arts from the
age of William & Mary
29 June–4 October
VENUE: Bank of England, London
Objects from the V&A. Curator: Anne Binney.
PUBLICATION: V.1989.005

1990

VX.1990.001
Matthew Tyson: the book as art
16 January–16 February
National Art Library display.

VX.1990.002
Agfa imaging awards
12 February–25 February
Photographs.

VX.1990.003
The plastics age
14 February–29 April
PUBLICATION: V.1990.014

VX.1990.004
Natalie d'Arbeloff: an exhibition of
unique and limited edition artist's books
20 February–3 April
National Art Library display.

VX.1990.005
Household choices: design in domestic
consumption
28 February–June
"part of a major collaborative programme to
document the home in Britain, organised by the
V&A and Middlesex Polytechnic"–VR.1990.005,
cover.
PUBLICATION: VR.1990.005

VX.1990.006
Artifacts at the end of a decade
7 March–29 April
National Art Library display.
PUBLICATIONS: v.1990.002;
VR.1981.002

VX.1990.007
Nicholas Nixon: pictures of people
11 April–24 June
Photographs.

VX.1990.008
Collectif Génération, Paris: livres
d'artistes
12 April–June
National Art Library display.
PUBLICATION: VR.1990.003

VX.1990.009
Posters for freedom: political posters
from Eastern Europe and the USSR
2 May–1 July
An accompanying book was announced but never
published.

VX.1990.010
Direct draw
9 May–24 June
Selection of work by participants in gallery-based
drawing classes at the V&A.

VX.1990.011
The Glasgow style book covers of Talwin
Morris
3 June–13 July
National Art Library display.

VX.1990.012
A fragile walk: artist's books by Les
Bicknell, the Oblivion Boys Press
6 June–13 July or 18 July–24 August
National Art Library display.

VX.1990.013
Collecting for the future: a decade of
contemporary acquisitions
6 June–12 August

VX.1990.014
Alphonse Legros
Early June–Spring 1991

VX.1990.015
Didactics: aspects of photography
11 July–16 September

VX.1990.016
Hogarth Press: graphics from the
holdings of the National Art Library
18 July–24 July and/or 13 November–3
March 1991

VX.1990.017
Recording Britain: a pictorial Domesday
of pre-war Britain
1 August–18 November
Exhibition, also toured "provincial centres around
Britain"–v.1990.015, t.p.
PUBLICATION: v.1990.015

VX.1990.018
Flowered silks
8 August–28 October

VX.1990.019
British studio pottery
10 August–30 September
PUBLICATION: v.1990.005

VX.1990.020
Coracle Press
31 August–7 November
National Art Library display of artists' books.

VX.1990.021
Miss Jones and her fairyland
9 September–13 January 1991
Wedgwood 'fairyland' lustre by Daisy Makeig-
Jones; the Weinstein gift.
PUBLICATION: v.1990.012

VX.1990.022
Edible books by Eva & Co.
19 September–
National Art Library display. Duration: several
weeks, until the objects on display had rotted or
perished.

VX.1990.023
Britain's efforts and ideals in the Great
War
1 October–3 March 1991
Series of lithographs, 1917.

VX.1990.024
Pierre Cardin
10 October–6 January 1991
PUBLICATION: VR.1990.009

VX.1990.025
Paul Strand
11 October–25 November
A touring exhibition organised by the National
Gallery of Art, Washington D.C., was advertised
but cancelled.

VX.1990.026
Christmas then
28 November–27 January or 3 February
1991
Prints, Drawings and Paintings Department display.

VX.1990.027
W.H. Smith Illustration Awards
12 December–24 February 1991
See note, VX.1987.012.

VX.1990.028
The Clarkes: High Wycombe furniture
makers (1893–1986)
December–November 1991

VX.1990.AAD.001
Bertha Sander, interior designer: designs
and papers
October–February 1991

VX.1990.BGM.001
Wishing you well: the Great Ormond
Street Hospital for Sick Children
31 January–25 February

VX.1990.BGM.002
Wooden toys
14 March–29 April
Organised in association with John Gould, London
College of Furniture, City Polytechnic.
PUBLICATION: V.1990.019

VX.1990.BGM.003
Childhood: inward and outward views:
photographs by John Heywood
16 May–15 July

VX.1990.BGM.004
The world of William: Richmal
Crompton's schoolboy hero
1 August–4 November
PUBLICATION: V.1990.020

VX.1990.BGM.005
Big Foot and the baby: children's
sculpture 1990
18 September–15 April 1991

VX.1990.BGM.006
Spirit of Christmas: a white Christmas
1 December–20 January 1991

VX.1990.THM.001
West End meets Broadway: theatre
caricatures by Al Frueh
3 May–21 January 1991
PUBLICATION: V.1990.017

VX.1990.THM.002
Slap: a celebration of stage make-up
13 September–
Duration: indefinite.

VX.1990.XXX.001
William Morris : designs, prints and
drawings by Morris, his friends and
associates
31 March–10 June
VENUE: Bodelwyddan Castle, Clwyd
Exhibits chiefly from the V&A.
PUBLICATION: VR.1990.016

VX.1990.XXX.002
Theatre on paper
7 April–21 July
VENUE: Drawing Center, New York
Drawings from the Theatre Museum.
PUBLICATION: VR.1990.014

VX.1990.XXX.003
Masterpieces of painting from the
Victoria and Albert Museum
September–May 1991
VENUES: Isetan Museum of Art, Tokyo;
Daimaru Museum, Umeda-Osaka;
Hiroshima Museum of Art; Fukuoka Art
Museum; Sogo Museum of Art,
Yokohama; Mie Prefectural Art Museum
PUBLICATION: VR.1990.007

VX.1990.XXX.004
British design, 1790–1990: V&A
7–28 October
VENUE: South Coast Plaza Retail
Center, Orange County, California
PUBLICATION: V.1990.004

VX.1990.XXX.005
Englische Aquarelle der Romantik,
1770–1850: Leihgaben des Victoria and
Albert Museum London

10 October–10 March 1991
VENUES: Nationalgalerie, Berlin;
Schlossmuseum, Gotha; Staatliches
Museum, Schwerin
PUBLICATION: VR.1990.010

VX.1990.XXX.006
William Morris, designer : designs, prints
and drawings . . . from the collections of
the Victoria and Albert Museum
17 November–5 January 1991
VENUE: Newport Museum and Art
Gallery
PUBLICATION: VR.1990.015

1991

VX.1991.001
Appearances: fashion photography since
1945
13 February–28 April
PUBLICATION: VR.1991.003

VX.1991.002
The art of selling songs
20 February–23 June
PUBLICATION: VR.1991.004

VX.1991.003
Agfa imaging awards
27 February?–7 April
Photographs. — Opening date also advertised as
4 March.

VX.1991.004
Nicholas Rea: the art of making the book
12 March–2 June
National Art Library display of work based on
Rimbaud's *Une saison en enfer*.
PUBLICATIONS: V.1991.011;
VR.1990.011

VX.1991.005
Constable in print
3 April–15 September

VX.1991.006
50 years of the National Buildings
Record
12 April–12 May
PUBLICATION: VR.1991.001

VX.1991.007
Puffin's 50th birthday
21 May–7 July
PUBLICATION: V.1991.015

VX.1991.008
Like a one-eyed cat: photographs by
Lee Friedlander, 1956–1987
5 June–26 August
Organised by and first held at Seattle Art Museum,
1989.
PUBLICATION: VR.1989.014

VX.1991.009
Publishing interventions: Stephen Willats,
1965–1991
11 June–28 August
National Art Library display.
PUBLICATION: V.1991.013

VX.1991.010
Wish you were here: the printed seaside
17 July–1 September
Organised by students on the Royal College of
Art/V&A MA Course in the History of Design.

VX.1991.011
A parliament of owls: French graphic
owls from the collection of Walter
Strachan
17 July–22 September

VX.1991.012
Postmodern prints
17 July–27 October

VX.1991.013
Karl Friedrich Schinkel : a universal
man
31 July–27 October
PUBLICATION: V.1991.007

VX.1991.014
American letterpress at the V&A:
Purgatory Pie Press
10 September–24 November

VX.1991.015
Visions of Japan
17 September–5 January 1992
Organised in association with the Japan Festival
Committee and the Japan Foundation. Designers:
Area 1: Kazuhiro Ishii; Area 2: Osamu Ishiyama;
Area 3: Toyo Ito. Art director: Kiguro Yahagi.
PUBLICATIONS: V.1991.021;
VR.1991.012; VR.1991.013

VX.1991.016
Fornasetti
2 October–19 January 1992
PUBLICATION: VR.1991.008

VX.1991.017
Spirits and superheroes: characters from
the Kabuki theatre
4 October–24 November

VX.1991.018
Landscape prints by Francis Vivares
(1709–1780)
16 October–April 1992
PUBLICATION: V.1991.008

VX.1991.019
Betel cutters from the collection of
Samuel Eilenberg
24 October–2 January 1992
PUBLICATION: VR.1991.005

VX.1991.020
Lichfield Cathedral silver
13 November–2 February 1992
PUBLICATION: VR.1991.011

VX.1991.021
The Magi and the gift
20 November–12 January 1992
Prints, Drawings and Paintings Department
display.

VX.1991.022
Fireworks
November–April 1993
Display from the holdings of the Archive of Art and
Design.

VX.1991.023
'Robots playing saxophones'
November–April 1993
Display by Sir Eduardo Paolozzi from the Krazy
Kat Arkive of Twentieth Century Popular Culture
at the Archive of Art and Design.

VX.1991.024
Ziggurat: accordion fold books by
Norman B. Colp
4 December–15 March 1992
National Art Library display.
PUBLICATION: VR.1991.014

VX.1991.025
W.H. Smith Illustration Awards
13 December–23 February 1992
See note, VX.1987.012.

VX.1991.026
Lloyds Bank fashion challenge
December?–12 January 1992
Competition for children.

VX.1991.AAD.001
Women's knitwear design 1930s–1960s,
at the Archive of Art and Design
February–June 1992

VX.1991.BGM.001
A cloth of dreams: photo installations by
Amanda McKittrick
3 February–15 April

VX.1991.BGM.002
Growing pictures: children in art therapy
12 February–12 May

VX.1991.BGM.003
An artist in the classroom: Fyffe
Christie's drawings of school children
29 May–30 June
Held in aid of the Save the Children Fund.
PUBLICATION: VR.1991.009

VX.1991.BGM.004
The box of delights: children's book
illustrations by twenty-one British
artists
17 July–25 August
Previously held at Newport Museum and Art
Gallery, Gwent.
PUBLICATION: VR.1991.006

VX.1991.BGM.005
The Little Angel marionette theatre
18 September–27 October

VX.1991.BGM.006
Spirit of Christmas: Christmas round the
world
1 December–20 January 1992
PUBLICATION: V.1991.014

VX.1991.THM.001
Dance images: photographs by Anthony
Crickmay
29 January–18 October

VX.1991.THM.002
The wind in the willows from page to stage
27 November–
Duration: indefinite.
PUBLICATION: V.1992.024

VX.1991.XXX.001
Japan and China: souces of ceramic design
17 September–31 January 1992
VENUE: Percival David Foundation of Chinese Art, School of Oriental and African Studies, University of London
"Japan Festival 1991"–VR.1991.010.
PUBLICATION: VR.1991.010

1992

VX.1992.001
The art of death: objects from the English death ritual 1500–1800
8 January–22 March
Originally scheduled for 20 March–16 June 1991 but postponed due to the Gulf War.
PUBLICATIONS: V.1991.001;
V.1992.001; V.1992.002

VX.1992.002
Green images: posters and printed ephemera
5 February–25 May
PUBLICATION: V.1992.010

VX.1992.003
Creativity and industry: Queensberry Hunt
6 February–1 May
PUBLICATION: VR.1992.006

VX.1992.004
Textiles from the Festival of Britain, 1951
3 March–26 July

VX.1992.005
More than funny: comics from the National Art Library
11 March–24 May
PUBLICATION: V.1992.016

VX.1992.006
Jewels of fantasy
17/18 March–5 July
PUBLICATION: VR.1992.008

VX.1992.007
Smile: a magazine of multiple origins
20 March–10 August
National Art Library display.
PUBLICATION: V.1992.019

VX.1992.008
Sovereign
3 April–13 September
Organised on the occasion of the anniversary of Queen Elizabeth's coronation, 1952.
PUBLICATIONS: V.1992.021;
V.1992.022

VX.1992.009
The art book: from Vasari to videodisc
13 April
'Open house' organised in the National Art Library for the IFLA Section of Art Libraries 4th European Conference. — Included: Avant-garde periodicals, 1890–1945; Book art; Bookbindings; Oriental collections; Conservation of the art book; NAL displays since 1985; Fable books; Manifestos; Russian illustrated and children's books; Russian theatre; 20th-century bookbinding; Illustrations to *The vicar of Wakefield*, 1798–1971; Vasari; Videodiscs; Women and the art book.

VX.1992.010
W.H. Smith Illustration Awards quinquennial exhibition
15 April–7 June
See note, VX.1987.012. — Retrospective exhibition: 1988–1992.

VX.1992.011
Wild ties: ornamental neckwear
29 April–24 May

VX.1992.012
Election fever – or fatigue
29 April–27 September

VX.1992.013
European watercolours for 1992
13 May–31 January 1993

VX.1992.014
Yuki: 20 years a fashion designer
14 May–20 September
PUBLICATION: V.1992.032

VX.1992.015
Fred Zinnemann: New York City
1932–33
10 June–23 August
Photographs.

VX.1992.016
Vrooom!: automotive designs at the
V&A
17 June–25 September

VX.1992.017
Hair
1 July–1 September
Organised by students on the Royal College
of Art/V&A MA Course in the History of
Design.

VX.1992.018
Textiles by sculptors
10 August–8 November

VX.1992.019
WSAP Editions: artists' books by
students from Wimbledon School of Art
11 August–4 October
National Art Library display.

VX.1992.020
Drawings and watercolours by John
Constable
1 September–30 April 1993

VX.1992.021
Costumes from *The House of Eliott*
25 September–28 March 1993
Costumes for the BBC television drama series,
designed by Joan Wadge.
PUBLICATION: V.1992.008

VX.1992.022
Body impressions
6/7 October–28 March 1993

VX.1992.023
Javier Mariscal: designer
22 October–26 April 1993

VX.1992.024
Tom Phillips: a quest for identity
National Art Library display to coincide with the
artist's retrospective exhibition at the Royal
Academy.
26 October–8 January 1993

VX.1992.025
Christmas revels
18 November–12 January 1993

VX.1992.026
Sporting glory
19 November–12 January 1993
(originally scheduled to run to 14
February)
Closed early due to liquidation of the organising
body.
PUBLICATIONS: VR.1992.009;
VR.1992.010

VX.1992.027
Early Spanish textiles
23 November–29 March 1993

VX.1992.AAD.001
Michael Farr Ltd. & Farr Ergonomics
Ltd., design management companies:
archives
June–May 1993

VX.1992.BGM.001
Trash or treasure: a dip into 400 years of
children's books
28 July–September 1995
PUBLICATIONS: V.1992.025;
V.1993.018

VX.1992.BGM.002
Birth and infancy
11 November–
Interim display pending Museum project for
History of Childhood Gallery.

VX.1992.BGM.003
The winter's trail: a special adventure for
Christmas time
30 November–7 January 1993

VX.1992.THM.001
"Don't clap too hard, it's a very old
building": the Royal Opera House
4 July–
Duration: indefinite.

VX.1992.XXX.001
The arts of the Victorians
October– May 1993
VENUES: Museum of Art, Kobe

Hankyu; Kyoto Municipal Museum of
Art; Daimaru Museum, Tokyo; Fukuoka
City Museum
In association with NHK Kinki Media Plan and
Hankyu department stores.
PUBLICATION: VR.1992.012

1993

VX.1993.001
Cornelia Parker: Reading matter
14 January–15 March
Organised by Book Works at the National Art
Library, as part of 'Collected Works', a series of
exhibitions in libraries in the Kensington area of
London.
PUBLICATION: VR.1993.003

VX.1993.002
Ronald King, Circle Press: *Anansi
company*
20 January–10 March
National Art Library display.
PUBLICATION: VR.1992.001

VX.1993.003
Plans and elevations I
20 January–September
Architectural drawings from the V&A's
collection.

VX.1993.004
African themes
3 February–6 June
Photographs and prints by David Goldblatt, Maud
Sulter and Faisal Ammar Abdu'Allah.

VX.1993.005
Figures: a selection from the V&A
watercolour collection
8 February–29 August

VX.1993.006
Winning hands: V&A/Virgin Atlantic
playing cards
25 February–12 April
Results of a competition to design packs of cards.

VX.1993.007
Ceramic contemporaries
10–31 March
Organised in association with the National
Association for Ceramics in Higher Education.
PUBLICATION: VR.1993.002

VX.1993.008
Ian Breakwell: Free range
17 March–22 August
National Art Library display of the artist's
published works.
PUBLICATION: V.1993.009

VX.1993.009
The quiet light: photographs of Korea by
Mark de Fraeye
24 March–23 May

VX.1993.010
Shared pleasures
5 April–11 July
Lace and embroidery from the collection of
Margaret Simeon.

VX.1993.011
Liliane Lijn: poem machines
20 April–31 July
National Art Library display.
PUBLICATION: VR.1993.009

VX.1993.012
Caricatures from the bequest of
Frank A. Gibson
21 April–12 September

VX.1993.013
Constable and Turner
4 May–31 October

VX.1993.014
Design now: RAAG workshop,
Ahmedabad
5 May–end September

VX.1993.015
Contemporary tradition: the studio of
Asha Sarabhai
6 May–3 October

VX.1993.016
Moghul tent textile project
9 June–4 July

VX.1993.017
High art, low life: *The studio* magazine
and the art of the 1890s
23 June–31 October
PUBLICATION: VR.1993.005

VX.1993.018
Ian and Marcel
8 July–3 January1994
British fashion and interior textile designers.

VX.1993.019
Seven deadly sins: ceramics by Janice
Tchalenko, with Roger Law and Pablo
Bach
14 July–29 November

VX.1993.020
Contemporary Australian tapestry from
the Victorian Tapestry Workshop
25 July–9 January1994

VX.1993.021
The art of the book: recent acquisitions
in the National Art Library
28 July–4 October

VX.1993.022
Interiors: sources for twentieth-century
interior design at the Archive of Art and
Design
4 August–11 May 1994

VX.1993.023
Illumination in manuscripts and books,
ca. 1300–1550
7 September–24 October
Organised by students from Sussex University.

VX.1993.024
Paper, pigment and paste: historic
wallpaper production
22 September–20 March 1994

VX.1993.025
Plans and elevations II
22 September–20 March 1994
Architectural drawings from the V&A's collection.

VX.1993.026
Beatrix Potter and The tailor of
Gloucester
2 October–9 January 1994
PUBLICATION: V.1993.003

VX.1993.027
Peter Rabbit, 1893–1993
2 October–9 January 1994
PUBLICATIONS: V.1993.014;
VR.1993.010

VX.1993.028
Two moons: ten years of the Red Hen
Press
6 October–8 January 1994
National Art Library display.
PUBLICATION: VR.1993.012

VX.1993.029
Design now: Blueprint magazine
7 October–4 April 1994

VX.1993.030
Gates of mystery
20 October–3 January 1994
Touring exhibition organised by Intercultura and
the State Russian Museum in association with the
Walters Art Gallery, Baltimore.
PUBLICATIONS: VR.1992.007;
VR.1994.005

VX.1993.031
Painters of Scotland
3 November–24 April 1994

VX.1993.032
Constable and Salisbury
3 November–1 May 1994

VX.1993.033
150 years of the Christmas card
17 November–9 January 1994

VX.1993.034
W.H. Smith Illustration Awards
15 December–27 February 1994.
See note, VX.1987.012.

VX.1993.AAD.001
Dorothea Braby: designs and papers
May–July

VX.1993.AAD.002
Thomas Cowell, stained glass painter:
archives
21 July–4 October

VX.1993.AAD.003
A selection of carrier bags and plastic
bags
5 October–19 December

VX.1993.AAD.004
Rt. Hon. Baron Reilly, former Director
of the Design Council: archives
20 December–8 April 1994

VX.1993.BGM.001
Play matters: award-winning toys from
the *Good toy guide*. In association with
Play Matters / National Association of
Toy and Leisure Libraries
27/28 July–4 August

VX.1993.BGM.002
Dynamic toys: a touring exhibition from
Banbury Museum
10 August–19 September

VX.1993.BGM.003
The early years
28 October–
Interim display pending Museum project for
History of Childhood Gallery.

VX.1993.BGM.004
Dickens's Christmas world
1 December–6 January 1994

VX.1993.THM.001
16 springs in every seat: the Savoy
Theatre reborn
9 November–
Duration: indefinite.

VX.1993.XXX.001
The arts of the Indian courts
October–June 1994
VENUES: Tokyo Ancient Orient
Museum; Museum of Art, Kobe Hankyu;
Okayama Orient Museum; Museum of
Kyoto; Hong Kong Museum of Art
In association with NHK Kinki Media Plan and
Hankyu department stores.
PUBLICATION: VR.1993.006

1994

VX.1994.001
Hidden pleasures
12 January–13 March
Four hundred years of decorative book end-papers
in the National Art Library.
PUBLICATION: V.1994.007

VX.1994.002
Fabergé: imperial jeweller
26 January–10 April
Previously held at the State Hermitage Museum,
St Petersburg; Musée des arts décoratifs, Paris.
PUBLICATION: VR.1993.004

VX.1994.003
Prospects, thresholds, interiors:
watercolours from a national collection
26 January–15 May
PUBLICATION: V.1994.015

VX.1994.004
Demand for the exotic: English block-
printed furnishing textiles 1790–1810
31 January–9 October

VX.1994.005
The golden age 1730–1760: brass inlaid
furniture by John Channon and his
contemporaries
16 February–24 April
In association with Leeds City Art Gallery, where
the exhibition was first held.
PUBLICATION: V.1993.010

VX.1994.006
Morris Cox and the Gogmagog Press
16 March–30 May
National Art Library display.
PUBLICATION: V.1994.010

VX.1994.007
Walter Strachan, defender of the livre
d'artiste in England: three masters of
copper engraving – Roger Vieillard,
Albert Flocon, Abram Krol
16 March–19 June
National Art Library display.
PUBLICATION: V.1994.024

VX.1994.008
Josef Albers prints
25 March–25 September
PUBLICATION: V.1994.009

VX.1994.009
The architect as designer
30 March–6 November

VX.1994.010
Design now: contemporary textiles
8 April–3 October

VX.1994.011
Constable: sunshine and shadow
4 May–30 October

VX.1994.012
The pencil of nature: watercolour and the
invention of photography
11 May–8 January 1995

VX.1994.013
Americana: a celebration, and, The
anonymous photographer
13 May–10 February 1995
Two selections from the Krazy Kat Arkive of
Twentieth Century Popular Culture.

VX.1994.014
Thoroughly modern minis
17 May–11 June

VX.1994.015
Kitaj: a print retrospective
8 June–9 October
PUBLICATION: VR.1994.007

VX.1994.016
Pugin: a Gothic passion
15 June–11 September
PUBLICATION: V.1994.016

VX.1994.017
20 great photographs of the 20th
century
20 June–29 August

VX.1994.018
Redstone Press: an exhibition of work
22 June–18 September
National Art Library display.

VX.1994.019
Experimenting with the book: the Janus
Press
14 September–27 November
National Art Library display.
PUBLICATION: V.1994.003

VX.1994.020
The first years of the National Art
Library 1837–1853: from the School of
Design to the Department of Practical
Art
21 September–27 November
PUBLICATION: V.1994.005

VX.1994.021
Selling lifestyle: 30 years of Habitat
8 October–2 April 1995
Design Now Room.

VX.1994.022
A fine line: commercial wood
engravings
10 October–26 March 1995
PUBLICATION: V.1994.004

VX.1994.023
Kalighat: Indian popular painting
1800–1930
19 October–15 January 1995
National touring exhibition organised by the South
Bank Centre, London.
PUBLICATIONS: VR.1993.007;
VR.1993.008

VX.1994.024
The finishing touch: passementerie
furnishing trimmings from the sixteenth
to the nineteenth centuries
31 October–9 April 1995

VX.1994.025
Constable and the old masters: drawings
& watercolours
1 November–30 April 1995

VX.1994.026
Studio ceramics 94
5 November–15 January 1995
Organised by the Craft Potters Association for 25
years of *Ceramic Review*.

VX.1994.027
Streetstyle: from sidewalk to catwalk
16 November–19 February 1995
PUBLICATIONS: V.1996.032;
VR.1994.009

VX.1994.028
Young British designers
16 November–19 February 1995
Organised to accompany VX.1994.027.

VX.1994.029
Street photography
17 November–9 January 1995
Organised to accompany VX.1994.027.

VX.1994.030
Ten years on: the work of the
Camberwell Press
30 November–29 January 1995
National Art Library display.
PUBLICATION: VR.1994.010

VX.1994.031
W.H. Smith Illustration Awards
14 December–26 February 1995
See note, VX.1987.012. — Continued by the
National Art Library Illustration Awards, 1995–.

VX.1994.AAD.001
Jacques Groag, architect and Jacqueline
Groag, textile and wallpaper designer:
papers, photographs and illustrations
8 April–6 July

VX.1994.AAD.002
S. London Ltd., furrier: press cuttings,
photographs and seasons' brochures
7 July–20 November

VX.1994.AAD.003
John Shipley's collection of bookjackets
21 November–27 February 1995

VX.1994.BGM.001
Award-winning miniatures
24 January–27 February
British Miniaturist of the Year awards, organised
by *Dolls house and furniture scene*.

VX.1994.BGM.002
Not just a pretty face: dolls by the British
Doll Artists' Association
6 July–1 October

VX.1994.BGM.003
Christmas corner
1 December–8 January 1995

VX.1994.THM.001
The face of theatre
September–
Photographic portraits.

VX.1994.THM.002
Recording performance
11 October–

VX.1994.XXX.001
British design at home
April–November

VENUES: Saitama Prefectural Modern
Art Museum; Museum of Art, Kobe
Hankyu; Kyoto National Museum of
Modern Art; Tokushima Prefectural
Modern Art Museum
In association with NHK Kinki Media Plan and
Hankyu department stores.
PUBLICATION: VR.1994.004

VX.1994.XXX.002
Sir Harry Parkes' collection of Japanese
papers, from the V&A and the Royal
Botanic Gardens, Kew
April–July
VENUES: Tobacco and Salt Museum,
Tokyo; Gifu City Historical Museum
PUBLICATION: VR.1994.011

VX.1994.XXX.003
Ceramic evolution in the middle Ming
period
8 September–7 February 1995
VENUE: Percival David Foundation of
Chinese Art, School of Oriental and
African Studies, University of London
Exhibition drawn from the collections of the
Foundation and the V&A.
PUBLICATION: VR.1994.002

1995

VX.1995.001
Warworks: women, photography and the
art of war
11 January–19 March
PUBLICATION: VR.1994.012

VX.1995.002
The origins of watercolour painting in
England
16 January–18 June
PUBLICATION: V.1995.020

VX.1995.003
New acquisitions for the Photography
Collection
25 January–16 April
PUBLICATION: V.1995.023

VX.1995.004
Early acquisitions for the photography
collection, 1856–1869
25 January–30 April
PUBLICATION: v.1995.023

VX.1995.005
Vandals and enthusiasts: views of
illumination in the 19th century
31 January–30 April
PUBLICATION: v.1995.030

VX.1995.006
The National Art Library and its
buildings from 1837 to the year 2000
1 February–23 April
PUBLICATION: v.1995.019

VX.1995.007
Embroidered jackets
7 March–January 1996

VX.1995.008
Mugs
15 March–29 May

VX.1995.009
Visions of photography: the best of the
Fabergé photography competition
28 March–2 April
PUBLICATION: vr.1995.007

VX.1995.010
From Marcantonio Raimondi to the
postcard: prints of the Raphael cartoons
4 April–17 September
PUBLICATION: v.1995.012

VX.1995.011
The book and beyond: electronic
publishing and the art of the book
7 April–1 October
Design Now Room.
PUBLICATION: v.1995.007

VX.1995.012
A diversity of gifts: four benefactors and
their libraries
26 April–23 July
National Art Library display. — Chauncy Hare
Townshend (1798–1868); Austen Henry Layard
(1817–1894); Emily Francis Strong, Lady Dilke
(1840–1904); Francis William Baxter (1876–1932).
PUBLICATION: v.1995.009

VX.1995.013
The rule of taste: classicism in British
18th-century architecture
26 April–22 October
Display of architectural drawings, prints and
folios.
PUBLICATION: v.1995.024

VX.1995.014
Fabulous fans
1 May–January 1996

VX.1995.015
Lucie Rie memorial display
1 May–28 January 1996

VX.1995.016
Constable and Hampstead
2 May–29 October
PUBLICATION: v.1995.008

VX.1995.017
Picturing plants: a history of botanical
illustration
10 May–24 September
PUBLICATION: v.1995.022

VX.1995.018
The art of stained glass
12 May–3 September
Designs from the Archive of Art and Design.

VX.1995.019
Japanese studio crafts: tradition and the
avant-garde
25 May–3 September
PUBLICATIONS: v.1995.015;
v.1995.016

VX.1995.020
The genius of Wedgwood
8/9 June–17 September
PUBLICATION: v.1995.013

VX.1995.021
20 modern British photographs
14 June–28 August

VX.1995.022
Paul Smith: observations
15 June–12 November
Fashion textiles designer.

VX.1995.023
20 British works on paper, 1980 to
1995
24 June–20 January 1996
PUBLICATION: v.1995.027

VX.1995.024
Japanese woodblock prints I
August–July 1996
Osaka printmakers, late 18th-early 19th centuries.
From the V&A Far Eastern Department
collection.

VX.1995.025
At home in the thirties: the EKCo
collection of trade catalogues
13 September–26 November
National Art Library display.
PUBLICATION: v.1995.004

VX.1995.026
Expressionist prints
5 October–10 March 1996
Mainly German artists, whose work was influenced
by African, Oceanic and other tribal cultures.
Mounted to coincide with the nationwide
Africa 95 festival.
PUBLICATION: v.1995.010

VX.1995.027
Design now: the silver of San Lorenzo
12 October–30 April 1996
PUBLICATIONS: v.1995.025;
VR.1995.001

VX.1995.028
Photographs of African sculpture by
Walker Evans
19 October–7 January 1996
Photographs made at the 1935 exhibition 'African
Negro' art at the Museum of Modern Art, New
York. — Organised for Africa 95: "the nationwide
festival . . . which celebrates the arts of
Africa"–v.1995.002, p. [1].
PUBLICATION: v.1995.021

VX.1995.029
Prints and photographs by artists of
African descent
19 October–7 January 1996
Organised for Africa 95: "the nationwide festival
which celebrates the arts of Africa"–v.1995.002,
p. [1].
PUBLICATION: v.1995.002

VX.1995.030
Constable: 20 great watercolours and
drawings
31 October–30 April 1996
PUBLICATION: v.1995.028

VX.1995.031
Back of the envelope
1 November–24 March 1996
Architectural designs.
PUBLICATION: v.1995.005

VX.1995.032
Emigré designers
13 November–11 August 1996
From the Archive of Art and Design.

VX.1995.033
The peaceful liberators: Jain art from
India
20 November–14 February 1996
Touring exhibition organised by the Los Angeles
County Museum of Art.
PUBLICATION: VR.1994.008

VX.1995.034
Fashion in China 1910–1970: women's
dresses from the Valery Garrett collection
23 November–12 May 1996

VX.1995.035
National Art Library Illustration Awards
1995
11 December–24 February 1996
Annual awards for book and magazine illustration,
previously sponsored by W.H. Smith. Administered
by Leo de Freitas.

VX.1995.AAD.001
Silhouette (Salop) Ltd., underwear and
swimwear manufacturers: catalogues and
promotional material
28 February–31 May

VX.1995.AAD.002
Hyders Ltd., metalwork firm: designs,
photographs and catalogues
1 June–12 December

VX.1995.AAD.003
Betty Newmarch, fashion designer:
sketches, photographs and presscuttings,
1946–1983
13 December–31 March 1996

VX.1995.BGM.001
Award-winning miniatures
21 January–23 February
British Miniaturist of the Year awards, organised
by *Dolls house and miniature scene.*

VX.1995.BGM.002
Breaking away
12 July–
Interim display on adolescence pending Museum
project for History of Childhood Gallery.

VX.1995.BGM.003
Rupert Bear festival
21 October–21 January 1996
Exhibition celebrating 75th anniversary of the
cartoon character.

VX.1995.THM.001
Picturing the players
7 February–
Theatrical paintings from the Somerset Maugham
collection. — Duration: indefinite.

VX.1995.THM.002
Staging Purcell today
21 November–20 May 1996

VX.1995.XXX.001
Camille Silvy: River scene, France –
truth, lies and landscape
28 January–19 March
VENUES: Norwich Castle Museum;
Birmingham City Museum and Art
Gallery; Fox Talbot Museum of
Photography, Lacock
Organised by the V&A; sponsored by the Arts
Council.

VX.1995.XXX.002
The European art of textiles: British and
Continental textiles from 11th century to
the 1990s
February–August
VENUES: Museum of Kyoto; Gunma
Prefectural Museum; Okayama
Prefectural Museum; Museum of Art,
Kobe Hankyu
In association with NHK Kinki Media Plan and
Hankyu department stores.
PUBLICATION: VR.1995.008

VX.1995.XXX.003
People and places: British art 1550–1900
March–November
VENUES: Daimaru Museum, Tokyo;
Wakayama Prefectural Modern Art
Museum; Shizuoka Prefectural Museum;
Museum of Kyoto; Museum of Art, Kobe
Hankyu
In association with NHK Kinki Media Plan and
Hankyu department stores.
PUBLICATION: VR.1995.004

VX.1995.XXX.004
Treasures from the courts of Mughal
India
15 July–24 September
VENUE: Gas Hall, Birmingham City
Museum and Art Gallery
Adapted from VX.1993.XXX.001.
PUBLICATION: VR.1995.006

VX.1995.XXX.005
Voyages and visions
September–March 1996
Smithsonian Institution exhibition touring in the
U.S.A. — Drawn from the Searight collection,
Department of Prints, Drawings and Paintings.
PUBLICATION: V.1995.033

VX.1995.XXX.006
Getting the message across: posters of
protest and propaganda
December–July 1996
VENUES: Gardner Arts Centre,
University of Brighton, Sussex;
Huddersfield Art Gallery; Oriel 31,
Newtown, Powys; Farnham Maltings,
Surrey
Arts Council touring exhibition of posters from the
V&A Prints, Drawings and Paintings Department.

1996

VX.1996.001
The *Woman's hour* quilt
10 January–31 March
Quilt made by listeners to the radio programme, to
celebrate 75 years of women's suffrage in Britain.

VX.1996.002
The exhibition watercolour
29 January–27 May
PUBLICATION: V.1996.015

VX.1996.003
The photography of art and the South
Kensington Museum
1 February–27 May
PUBLICATION: V.1996.024

VX.1996.004
Ceramic contemporaries 2
8 February–6 March
Organised in association with the
National Association for Ceramics in
Higher Education
PUBLICATION: VR.1996.002

VX.1996.005
Leighton as book illustrator
15 February–8 September

VX.1996.006
The Leighton frescoes
15 February–8 September

VX.1996.007
A glimpse of Guatemala: the Maudslay
Bequest
17 February–18 August
19th century Guatemalan textiles.

VX.1996.008
"This is tomorrow"
14 March–28 May
Posters made for an exhibition at the Whitechapel
Art Gallery, London, 1956.

VX.1996.009
Embossed images on paper
28 March–29 October
PUBLICATION: VR.1996.003

VX.1996.010
Arts and crafts architecture
4 April–29 September

VX.1996.011
Marvels of art and cheapness: Liberty
furniture 1880–1910
10 April–1 September
Catalogues and design handbooks.

VX.1996.012
20 unknown Constables
29 April–27 October

VX.1996.013
William Morris
9 May–1 September
"attracted a record number of 216,159 visitors, the
highest achieved by any show at the Museum since
'Britain can make it' [VX.1946.004] drew enormous
post-war crowds"–In-view (January–April 1997)
p. 6. — This exhibition travelled to Japan,
March–August 1997: Kyoto, Tokyo and Nagoya.
PUBLICATIONS: V.1996.040;
V.1996.041; VR.1996.008

VX.1996.014
The vessel and beyond
14 May–15 October
Contemporary Korean ceramics, Design Now Room.

VX.1996.015
Dressing the part: Henry Poole and Co.,
Savile Row tailors
25 May–February 1997

VX.1996.016
The Pre-Raphaelites and early British
photography
3 June–29 September
PUBLICATION: V.1996.025

VX.1996.017
Graphic responses to AIDS
12 June–13 October
PUBLICATION: V.1996.018

VX.1996.018
RCA/V&A Conservation: final year
display
13 June–26 August
Work by M.A. graduates of the Royal College of
Art/V&A Joint Course in Conservation.
PUBLICATION: V.1996.027

VX.1996.019
Ian Stephenson: Mortlake
1 July–31 December
Exhibition of paintings, to celebrate the redisplay
of the Raphael tapestry cartoons at the V&A.

VX.1996.020
Susie Cooper (1902–1995)
15 July–15 September

VX.1996.021
From Utility to prosperity: changing
design at Heal's from the 1930s to the
1950s
12 August–31 May 1997

VX.1996.022
Japanese woodblock prints II
August–1997
Osaka printmakers, late 18th-early 19th centuries.
— From the V&A Far Eastern Department's
collection.

VX.1996.023
Rare and glorious: an introduction to
European textiles
Late August–29 June 1997
Selected from VX.1995.XXX.002.

VX.1996.024
Good taste and true principles: textiles
from the Great Exhibition
30 August–2 March 1997

VX.1996.025
Landscapes of the spirit: drawings, prints
and books by J.G. Lubbock
11 September–24 November
National Art Library display.
PUBLICATION: VR.1996.005

VX.1996.026
Contemporary glass: the Sir Alastair
Pilkington Fund
16 September–January 1997

VX.1996.027
Fine bookbindings: 1960–1990
17 September–5 January 1997
Display of work by the Designer Bookbinders, from
the collections of the National Art Library.

VX.1996.028
Plasticized
30 September–16 December
Plastic tableware, containers and vessels.

VX.1996.029
In pursuit of Old Masters
7 October–30 March 1997
Display about the Arundel Society.
PUBLICATION: V.1996.005

VX.1996.030
Designs for British gold and silver
17 October–3 March 1997
PUBLICATION: V.1996.012

VX.1996.031
Green furniture: ecological design
21 October–13 April 1997
Design Now Room.

VX.1996.032
Collecting Constable: drawings and
watercolours
28 October–27 April 1997
PUBLICATION: V.1996.010

VX.1996.033
First impressions: school work and the
Print Room
30 October–16 February 1997
PUBLICATION: V.1996.016

VX.1996.034
Chairs for a purpose 1700–1900
4 November–July 1997

VX.1996.035
The spirit of the staircase: 100 years of
prints publishing at the Royal College of
Art, 1896–1996
7 November–30 March 1997
Including display of Twelve artists: the Royal
College of Art centenary year portfolio of prints,
1996. — Curated by Tim Mara and Silvie
Turner.
PUBLICATION: VR.1996.007

VX.1996.036
American photography 1890–1965
from the Museum of Modern Art,
New York
14 November–26 January 1997
Touring exhibition.
PUBLICATIONS: V.1996.003;
VR.1995.002

VX.1996.037
Living silver
27 November–2 April 1997
Organised by the Crafts Council in the newly-
reopened Silver Gallery.

VX.1996.038
Treasures of today
27 November–6 April 1997
Display of British silversmiths' work organised
by the Worshipful Company of Goldsmiths in the
newly-reopened Silver Gallery.

VX.1996.039
Alphabet of a century: style, taste and
society in 18th-century London
5 December–5 March 1997

Organised by students from the Royal College of
Art/V&A MA Course in the History of Design,
using material from the Prints, Drawings and
Paintings Department.
PUBLICATION: v.1996.002

VX.1996.040
NALIA Awards [National Art Library
Illustration Awards]
11 December–24 February 1997
See note, VX.1995.035.

VX.1996.AAD.001
V&A Circulation Department
10 February–8 May

VX.1996.AAD.002
Selected sketchbooks from the Archive of
Art and Design's collections
8 May–12 September

VX.1996.AAD.003
Paul Pieter Piech
12 September–28 February 1997

VX.1996.BGM.001
First appearances: additions to the
Museum's collections
2 April–10 March 1997

VX.1996.BGM.002
Christmas gifts
30 November–9 January 1997

VX.1996.THM.001
Visions of Verdi
28 May–30 October

VX.1996.THM.002
Stage design and the Linbury Trust
24 September–May 1998
Designs by Leslie Hurry and Yolande Sonnabend
for productions of *Swan Lake*, and by Linbury
Prizewinner Agnes Treplin.

VX.1996.THM.003
Dressing the part
3 December–November 1997
The art of theatrical costume makers.

VX.1996.XXX.001
Gioielli dall'India, dai Moghul al
Novecento
8 March–13 April
VENUE: Galleria Ottava Piano, Milan
Objects on loan from the V&A and the National
Museum, New Delhi.
PUBLICATION: VR.1996.004

INDEXES

NAME INDEX

Citations may be traced as follows, by their prefixes:

V.	=	Publications of the Victoria and Albert Museum (starts p. 3)
VP.	=	Periodical publications (p. 387). Volume details are given in square brackets.
VR.	=	Publications related to, but not published by, the V&A (p. 409)
VRP.	=	Related periodicals and part works (p. 509)
VX.	=	Exhibitions and displays (p. 517)

All names occurring in the Publications and Exhibitions sequences are indexed. Personal names include authors, editors, artists, collectors, publishers, printers etc. Institutional names include houses, parks and gardens, churches, events (e.g. Great Exhibition) and government departments, as well as museums and galleries, and firms. Names of publications (e.g. newspapers) are in the Title Index.

Personal names
Entries for personal names are gathered under the latest, or most used, version, e.g.

> Blumstein, Madeleine *See* Ginsburg, Madeleine
> Pitcher, William J. C. *See* Wilhelm, C.

Compound surnames are generally listed under the first element. In other cases, cross-references are given:

> Van Gogh, Vincent *See* Gogh, Vincent van

Institutional and corporate names
Cross-references are given from inverted forms:

> Pooley, Alan *See* Alan Pooley Ltd.

Institutional names in languages with non-Roman scripts are entered under their usual English translation, generally with cross-references from a transliteration of the original:

> Gosudarstvennyĭ Ėrmitazh *See* State Hermitage Museum.

Changes in institutional names result in two or more headings:

Photographic Society *Afterwards* Royal Photographic Society

Exceptions
The **South Kensington Museum** entries have been included under the heading **Victoria and Albert Museum,** to avoid two large sequences with a proliferation of cross references between them.

VICTORIA AND ALBERT MUSEUM
Under this heading are indexed publications and exhibitions

> Relating to the Museum as a whole;
> Relating to its constituent collections and administrative departments;
> Relating to particular aspects of it, e.g. *History, Reports.*

The National Art Library, and the branch museums and outstations, are indexed directly under their own names.

Ettlinger, L. D. — VR.1972.002
Eumorfopoulos, George — V.1936.003;
  VX.1935.003
Europalia — VR.1973.005; VX.1972.005;
  VX.1973.028; VX.1973.XXX.001
European Economic Community —
  VX.1973.001
European Illustration — VR.1981.001
Eva & Co — VX.1990.022
Evans, Edith, Dame — VX.1976.XXX.005
Evans, Frederick H. — VX.1967.009
Evans, Joan, Dame — VX.1977.018
Evans, Mark — V.1981.020
Evans, Merlyn — V.1972.020; VX.1972.025
Evans, Tim — VR.1989.003
Evans, Walker — V.1995.021; VX.1995.028
Evans, Wendy — VR.1973.002
Evelyn, John, Sir — VX.1953.006;
  VR.1979.006
Evelyn, Peta — V.1988.013; V.1996.028
Evergon — VR.1981.002
Everington, Judith — V.1993.005
Exeter, Cecil Brownlow, Earl of —
  VP.1994.003[2]
Exner, Wilhelm Franz — VR.1968.001
Exposition internationale des arts décoratifs et
  industriels modernes — VP.1982.001[4]
Exposition universelle de 1867 à Paris —
  V.1868.004; VR.1868.004; VX.1867.XXX.001;
  VX.1867.XXX.002
Exposition universelle internationale de 1878 —
  V.1880.008; VX.1878.XXX.001
Exposition universelle internationale de 1900 —
  VR.1993.004
Eyre and Spottiswoode — V.1852.001;
  V.1852.002; V.1852.003; V.1853.001;
  V.1852.005; V.1852.006; V.1853.002;
  V.1853.003; V.1853.004; V.1853.005;
  V.1854.001; V.1854.002; V.1855.001;
  V.1855.002; V.1855.003; V.1856.001;
  V.1856.002; V.1856.003; V.1856.004;
  V.1856.005; V.1857.002; V.1857.004;
  V.1857.005; V.1857.006; V.1857.007;
  V.1857.008; V.1857.009; V.1857.010;
  V.1858.001; V.1858.005; V.1858.006;
  V.1858.007; V.1858.008; V.1858.009;
  V.1859.001; V.1859.002; V.1859.003;
  V.1859.004; V.1859.005; V.1859.007;
  V.1859.008; V.1860.001; V.1860.002;
  V.1860.003; V.1860.005; V.1860.006;
  V.1860.008; V.1860.009; V.1860.010;
  V.1860.011; V.1861.001; V.1861.003;
  V.1861.005; V.1862.001; V.1862.002;
  V.1862.003; V.1862.005; V.1862.006;
  V.1862.008; V.1863.001; V.1863.003;
  V.1863.004; V.1863.005, 5a; V.1863.006;
  V.1863.007; V.1864.001; V.1864.002;
  V.1864.003; V.1864.004; V.1864.005;
  V.1865.002; V.1865.003; V.1865.004;
  V.1865.006; V.1865.007; V.1866.001;
  V.1866.003; V.1866.004; V.1866.007;
  V.1867.001; V.1867.002; V.1867.005;

V.1867.006; V.1868.001; V.1868.004;
V.1869.001; V.1869.002; V.1869.003;
V.1869.004; V.1869.005; V.1869.006;
V.1869.007; V.1869.008; V.1869.009;
V.1869.010; V.1869.011; V.1870.001;
V.1870.002; V.1870.004; V.1870.005;
V.1870.006; V.1870.007; V.1870.010;
V.1871.001; V.1871.002; V.1871.003;
V.1871.004; V.1871.005; V.1871.006;
V.1872.002; V.1872.003; V.1872.004;
V.1872.005; V.1872.006; V.1872.008;
V.1872.009; V.1872.010; V.1872.011;
V.1872.012; V.1872.013; V.1872.014;
V.1872.017; V.1872.019; V.1872.020;
V.1872.021; V.1872.028; V.1872.029;
V.1872.030; V.1873.001; V.1873.002;
V.1873.003; V.1873.004; V.1873.007;
V.1873.008; V.1873.009; V.1873.010;
V.1873.011; V.1874.001; V.1874.002;
V.1874.003; V.1874.004; V.1874.005;
V.1874.006; V.1874.008; V.1874.009;
V.1874.010; V.1874.011; V.1874.012;
V.1874.013; V.1874.014; V.1874.015;
V.1875.002; V.1875.003; V.1875.004;
V.1875.005; V.1875.007; V.1875.008;
V.1875.009; V.1875.010; V.1875.012;
V.1876.001; V.1876.002; V.1876.003;
V.1876.004; V.1876.005; V.1876.006;
V.1876.008; V.1876.009; V.1876.010;
V.1876.013; V.1876.014; V.1876.026;
V.1876.028; V.1876.029; V.1877.006;
V.1877.007; V.1877.008; V.1877.010;
V.1877.011; V.1877.013; V.1878.001;
V.1878.002; V.1878.003; V.1878.004;
V.1878.005; V.1878.006; V.1878.007;
V.1878.008; V.1878.010; V.1879.001;
V.1879.004; V.1879.007; V.1880.001;
V.1880.003; V.1880.006; V.1880.009;
V.1881.002; V.1881.003; V.1881.005;
V.1881.008; V.1881.009; V.1881.010;
V.1881.012; V.1881.013; V.1881.014;
V.1882.003; V.1882.005; V.1882.006;
V.1882.007; V.1883.001; V.1883.006, 6a;
V.1883.007; V.1883.008; V.1883.009;
V.1883.010; V.1883.011; V.1884.001;
V.1884.002; V.1884.003; V.1884.007;
V.1885.003; V.1885.004; V.1885.005;
V.1886.002; V.1886.004; V.1886.005;
V.1886.006; V.1886.007; V.1887.001;
V.1887.002; V.1887.003; V.1887.004;
V.1887.006; V.1887.007; V.1887.008;
V.1887.009; V.1888.003; V.1888.004;
V.1888.005; V.1888.006; V.1888.008;
V.1888.010; V.1888.011; V.1888.012;
V.1888.015; V.1888.016; V.1889.001;
V.1889.003; V.1889.004; V.1889.005;
V.1889.008; V.1890.001; V.1890.002;
V.1890.003; V.1890.005; V.1890.006;
V.1891.001; V.1891.002; V.1891.003;
V.1891.004; V.1891.005; V.1891.006;
V.1891.007; V.1891.008; V.1891.009;
V.1891.010; V.1891.011; V.1892.001;

*'National' in the name of an institution is British unless indicated otherwise.

Schmiedt, Helmut — VR.1984.001
Schoeser, Mary — V.1993.002
Schofield, John — VR.1977.005
Schofield, Richard — V.1983.009
Schonfield, Zuzanna — VP.1968.001[6]
Schott, Howard — V.1985.013
Schouvaloff, Alexander — V.1983.024;
    V.1983.027; VR.1987.016; VR.1990.014
Schreiber, Charles *and* Charlotte, Lady —
    V.1885.005; V.1915.004; V.1924.004;
    V.1928.002; V.1930.005
Schubert, Franz — V.1979.021; V.1979.022;
    V.1979.023; VX.1979.003
Schulenberg, Fritz von der — V.1985.035
Schulz, Charles M. — VX.1985.BGM.002
Schwaiger, Edward — VR.1992.008
Schwitters, Kurt — V.1986.031
Science Museum — VR.1928.003; VR.1929.006;
    VR.1929.007; VR.1930.002; VR.1984.013
Scolar Press — VR.1980.010
Scott, Adrian Gilbert — VX.1950.007
Scott, Colin — VR.1977.005
Scott, George Gilbert, Sir — V.1978.087;
    VR.1860.001; VX.1978.014
Scott, R. E. (Rosemary) — VR.1991.010;
    VR.1994.002
Scottish Arts Council — V.1973.026;
    V.1975.018; V.1976.024; VR.1968.003;
    VR.1975.005; VR.1975.006; VR.1978.008;
    VX.1968.019; VX.1973.010; VX.1976.001;
    VX.1976.005; VX.1978.XXX.001
Scottish Arts Council Gallery — VX.1976.001
Scottish Education Department — VR.1901.001
Scottish National Gallery of Modern Art —
    VX.1975.030
Scottish National Portrait Gallery — V.1984.011
Scrase, David — VP.1982.001[5]
Scribner, Welford and Armstrong — V.1876.020
Scribner's — VR.1924.002
Scrutton, Hugh — VR.1969.014
Searight, Rodney — V.1989.009; VR.1990.008;
    VX.1989.025; VX.1995.XXX.005
Searight, Sarah — V.1995.033
Seattle Art Museum — VR.1989.014;
    VX.1966.XXX.001; VX.1991.008
Seddon, John Pollard — V.1983.021;
    VX.1985.015
Segerstråle, Lennart — VR.1938.002
Seiberling, Grace — V.1985.049
Seibu Bijutsukan (Funabashi) *See* Funabashi
    Seibu Museum of Art
Seidmann, Gertrud — V.1996.030
Seizo, Hayashiya — VR.1983.006
Sekers, Agi — V.1983.027
Selby-Bigge, R. — VRP.1902.001e
Select Committee on Museums of the Science
    and Art Department — VR.1897.001;
    VR.1897.004; VR.1898.001; VR.1898.003;
    VR.1899.001
Select Committee on the South Kensington
    Museum — VR.1860.001
Seligman, Edgar — V.1966.008; VP.1910.001c

Semper, Gottfried — V.1853.003; V.1854.002
Senefelder, Alois — V.1971.020
September Press — V.1985.041
Sergel, Johan Tobias — VR.1972.002
Serilly, Anne-Marie Louise de — V.1915.014;
    V.1925.011; VP.1982.001[4]
Serota, Nicholas — VR.1979.001
Seton-Watson, R. W. — VR.1915.001
Settore cultura e informazione (Regione
    Lombardia, Italy) — VX.1985.XXX.004
Seymour, Anne — V.1983.022
S.H. Benson Ltd. — VX.1973.BGM.003;
    V.1973.032
Shahjahan, Emperor of India — V.1918.002;
    V.1969.040; V.1978.082; VP.1965.001[II.3]
Shakerley, Geoffrey — V.1984.004; V.1984.025;
    V.1985.020; V.1986.038
Shakespeare, William — V.1916.006;
    V.1916.007; V.1978.083; V.1978.084;
    V.1978.085; V.1978.086; VX.1916.002;
    VX.1964.002; VX.1980.THM.001;
    VX.1984.THM.003; VX.1988.THM.003
Shalloo, Eoin — V.1994.003; V.1995.009
Shankar's International Children's Competition
    — VX.1973.BGM.001
Shapland, H. P. — VR.1910.002
Sharma, Kamlesh Kumar — VR.1996.004
Sharma, Rita — VR.1996.004
Sharman, Lydia — V.1993.017
Sharp, D. J. — VR.1985.003
Sharp, Ivy — VP.1968.001[2; 4]
Sharp, Katherine —VP.1994.003[1; 2]
Sharp, Paul — V.1983.003; V.1983.011;
    V.1983.028; V.1983.042; V.1984.003;
    V.1985.012; V.1985.018; V.1986.009;
    V.1986.032; V.1996.021
Shaw, George Bernard — V.1978.033
Sheasby, Stephen — VP.1991.001[1; 4]
Sheepshanks, John — V.1857.009 See also
    VICTORIA AND ALBERT MUSEUM
    British fine art collections
Sheffield City Art Galleries — VR.1980.001;
    VX.1980.001
Sheffield Government School of Design —
    VX.1866.002
Sheldon, J. M. — VR.1965.003
Shell International Petroleum Co. — V.1989.009
Shelton, R. A. — VR.1964.003
Shenton, Helen — VP.1991.001[6; 9; 13; 15; 20]
Shenval Press — V.1931.005; V.1936.003;
    V.1938.002; V.1938.003; V.1938.005;
    V.1939.004; V.1940.001; V.1946.001;
    V.1947.007; V.1964.013; V.1967.013;
    V.1971.007; VR.1949.001; VR.1965.003
Shepard, Ernest H. — V.1974.027; VR.1982.014;
    VX.1969.015; VX.1982.012
Shepherd, Stanley A. — V.1994.016
Sheppard Fidler, Margaret — VR.1976.006
Sheraton, Thomas — VP.1965.001[IV.1]
Sheridan, Richard Brinsley — V.1978.078
Sherman, Cindy — VX.1988.014
Shestack, Alan — V.1976.002

TITLE INDEX

See general remarks, p. xxvii. Citations may be traced as follows, by their prefixes:

V.	=	Publications of the Victoria and Albert Museum (starts p. 3)
VP.	=	Periodical publications (p. 387). Volume details are given in square brackets.
VR.	=	Publications related to, but not published by, the V&A (p. 409)
VRP.	=	Related periodicals and part works (p. 509)
VX.	=	Exhibitions and displays (p. 517)

Initial articles ('The' etc.) are omitted. The ampersand (&) is treated as interchangeable with 'and'. Subtitles are taken into account in filing.

Titles within titles are italicised (e.g. *Blitz* exposure; Beatrix Potter and *The tailor of Gloucester*).

3 recent gifts of children's books — VP.1933.001a[Suppl. Jan. 1971]

14 : 24 – British youth culture — VR.1986.001; VX.1986.BHO.003

16 springs in every seat — VX.1993.THM.001

17th and 18th century costume — V.1951.007; V.1959.001

17th century Chinese canopied bed — VP.1991.001[11]

19th century costume — V.1951.008

19th century fine bindings — VX.1972.030

19th century French publishers' bindings: cartonnages romantiques from the Renier Collection — VX.1973.037

19th century papier-mâché — V.1973.001

19th century pressed glass — VX.1983.018

20 British works on paper, 1980 to 1995 — VX.1995.023

20 great photographs of the 20th century — VX.1994.017

20 modern British photographs — VX.1995.021

20 unknown Constables — VX.1996.012

20th century: an introduction to women's fashionable dress — V.1983.001

20th century costume jewellery from the Fior collection — VX.1985.016

20th Century Gallery: a teachers' guide — V.1996.001

20th Century Gallery: ideas and information for teachers — V.1993.001

20th century Scandinavian ceramics and glass — VX.1989.019

20th century set and costume design from the Theatre Museum — VX.1985.THM.002

20th century watercolours from the V&A collection — VX.1984.003; VX.1984.021

50 years of postcards, 1870–1920 — VX.1970.020

50 years of the National Buildings Record — VR.1991.001; VX.1991.006

74 children's books from the Guy Little bequest — VP.1933.001a[Suppl. Feb. 1973]

100 great paintings in the Victoria & Albert Museum — V.1985.001

100 masterpieces — V.1930.001; V.1931.001; V.1931.002

100 things to see in the Victoria & Albert Museum — V.1962.001; V.1984.001

150 years of lithography, 1798–1948 — VX.1948.008

150 years of the Christmas card — VX.1993.033

150 years of the Royal Asiatic Society — VX.1973.025

200th anniversary, Burgtheater, Vienna 1776–1976 — V.1976.001

1776: a Londoner's view — VX.1976.012

1909–1929: — VR.1977.001; VX.1977.XXX.002

1970–1995: the work of the Silversmiths' Studio, San Lorenzo — VR.1995.001

1992 — VP.1982.001[Spr. 1989]

5000 years of textiles — V.1993.002

Abridged catalogue of oil paintings by British artists and foreigners working in Great Britain — V.1908.016

SERIES INDEX

This is an index to the main bibliography only (the V-sequence), and includes series devised and published by the Museum. The series are listed in alphabetical order; the individual items in numerical order if numbered, otherwise in alphabetical order. Some reprints or later editions dropped their original series title: items are listed here only if they are known or believed to bear it. Series titles in square brackets are devised by the compiler.

Citations may be traced as follows, by their prefixes:

V.	=	Publications of the Victoria and Albert Museum (starts p. 3)
VP.	=	Periodical publications (p. 387). Volume details are given in square brackets.
VR.	=	Publications related to, but not published by, the V&A (p. 409)
VRP.	=	Related periodicals and part works (p. 509)
VX.	=	Exhibitions and displays (p. 517)

Art handbooks

Entitled South Kensington Museum art handbooks, or from 1899 Victoria and Albert Museum art handbooks. Published for the Museum by Chapman and Hall.

From the Preface to nos. 1–5: "These handbooks are reprints of the dissertations prefixed to the large catalogues of the chief divisions of works of art in the Museum . . . arranged and so far abridged as to bring each into a portable shape. The Lords of the Committee of Council on Education having determined on the publication of them, the editor trusts that they will meet the purpose intended; namely, to be useful, not alone for the collections at South Kensington but . . . by enabling the public at a trifling cost to understand something of the history and character of the subjects treated of." W.M. [i.e. William Maskell].

The binding style was green cloth covered boards with horizontal rules and Museum crest stamped in black, and title in gold; primrose endpapers. Also issued in grey wrappers, usually with advertisements. Some copies are found both cased and with wrappers; some copies are found in case lettered 'Victoria and Albert Museum art handbook' although they appear to predate 1899: either they are stereotyped reprints or sheets were stockpiled and bound later.

From ca. 1908 some reprints were redesignated 'Victoria and Albert Museum handbooks'. These are asterisked.

1. Textile fabrics / Daniel Rock — v.1876.027
2. Ivories ancient and mediaeval / William Maskell — v.1875.011
3. Ancient and modern furniture and woodwork / John Hungerford Pollen — v.1875.001; v.1908.001
4. Maiolica / S. Drury E. Fortnum — v.1875.013; v.1882.008; v.1892.007
5. Musical instruments / Carl Engel — v.1875.014; v.1908.015
6. Manual of design / Richard Redgrave — v.1876.024

The series continued unnumbered:

The art of the Saracens in Egypt / Stanley Lane-Poole — v.1888.001

Bronzes / C. Drury E. Fortnum — v.1877.003

Chinese art / Stephen W. Bushell — v.1904.006; v.1905.003; v.1906.008; v.1909.002; v.1909.003; v.1910.002*; v.1910.003*; v.1914.004*

College and corporation plate / Wilfred Joseph Cripps — v.1881.007

Early Christian art in Ireland / Margaret Stokes — v.1887.005

English earthenware / A.H. Church — v.1884.004; v.1904.007; v.1911.003

English porcelain / A.H. Church — v.1885.001; v.1894.005; v.1898.006; v.1904.008; v.1905.004; v.1911.005*

French pottery / Paul Gasnault and Edouard Garnier — v.1884.005

Glass / Alexander Nesbitt — v.1878.009

Gold and silver smiths' work / John
 Hungerford Pollen — v.1879.002;
 v.1883.003
Handbook of the Dyce and Forster
 collections in the South Kensington
 Museum — v.1880.005
Handbook of the Jones collection in the
 South Kensington Museum — v.1883.004
The industrial arts : historical sketches —
 v.1876.022; v.1888.009
The industrial arts in Spain / Juan F. Riaño
 — v.1879.003; v.1890.004
The industrial arts of Denmark / J.J.A.
 Worsaae — v.1882.004
The industrial arts of India / George C.M.
 Birdwood — v.1880.007; v.1884.006
The industrial arts of Scandinavia in the
 pagan time / Hans Hildebrand —
 v.1883.005; v.1892.006
Ironwork / J. Starkie Gardner
 I, From the earliest times to the end of the
  mediaeval period — v.1893.007;
  v.1907.008; v.1914.012
 II, From the close of the mediaeval period
  to the end of the eighteenth century —
  v.1896.006
Italian wall decorations — v.1901.007
Japanese colour prints / Edward F. Strange —
 v.1904.009; v.1908.013*; v.1910.007;
 v.1913.005*; v.1923.009
Japanese pottery / Augustus W. Franks —
 v.1880.008; v.1885.002; v.1906.010;
 v.1912.006
Persian art / R. Murdoch Smith —
 v.1876.025; v.1880.010
 Precious stones / A.H. Church —
  v.1883.013; v.1905.006; v.1908.018;
  v.1913.011*; v.1924.017*
Russian art and art objects in Russia / Alfred
 Maskell — v.1884.008
Stained glass / Lewis F. Day — v.1903.004;
 v.1913.012*
Tapestry / Alfred de Champeaux —
 v.1878.011; v.1887.010

The arts and living
". . . a unique series . . . approaching the decorative
arts from their users' point of view . . . Devised by
Sir Roy Strong and commissioned and published by
Her Majesty's Stationery Office"— back covers.
 Gaming / Edward T. Joy — v.1982.006
 Getting dressed / Edward T. Joy —
  v.1981.007
 Going to bed / Eileen Harris — v.1981.008
 Keeping warm / Eileen Harris — v.1982.021
 Lighting / Alastair Laing — v.1982.023
 Mourning / Nicholas Penny — v.1981.013
 Writing / Leonee Ormond — v.1981.023

A book of . . .
Series devised by Jennifer Blain and Lesley Burton.
 Birds / introduction by Charles Newton —
  v.1992.003

Dragons & monsters / introduction by Susan
 Stronge — v.1992.004
Sea creatures / introduction by Gill Saunders
 — v.1994.005

Brief guides
All entitled Brief guide to . . . . They are revised
editions of title previously published, not in a series
(see Title Index).
 1. Persian woven fabrics — v.1950.004
 2. Persian embroideries — v.1950.003
 3. Oriental painted, dyed and printed textiles
  — v.1950.002
 3. [sic] Turkish woven fabrics — v.1950.005

[Broadsheets]
"12 broadsheets . . . made possible by a grant
from Mobil." All designed by Omnific, with
drawings by Ron Sandford and plans by
Michael Robinson. Imprint of V&A Associates,
printed by Penshurst Press. Available separately
or together in a slip case.
The art of India : Gallery 41 — v.1980.001
The art of Islam : Galleries 42–47B —
 v.1979.001
Early medieval art : Gallery 43 —
 v.1979.005
English sculpture : Gallery 50 (West) —
 v.1980.012
European art, 1700–1800 : Galleries 4-5-6-7
 — v.1980.013
European baroque : Galleries 1–2 —
 v.1980.014
European baroque : Gallery 3 — v.1980.015
European sculpture : Gallery 50 (East) —
 v.1979.016
Far Eastern Art : Galleries 44–47D —
 v.1979.010
French art, 1700–1800 : Galleries 5-6-7
 (Jones Collection) — v.1980.018
Italian sculpture, 1400–1500 : Galleries
 16–12 — v.1979.028
Music gallery — v.1979.028

Brochures
 1. Three presentation swords in the Victoria
  and Albert Museum, and a group of
  English enamels / Claude Blair —
  v.1972.036
 2. A state bed from Erthig / John Hardy,
  Sheila Landi & Charles D. Wright —
  v.1972.035
 3. Five monuments from Eastwell / John
  Physick — v.1973.016
 4. Sculpture from Troyes in the Victoria and
  Albert Museum / Charles Avery —
  v.1974.022
 5. Photography and the South Kensington
  Museum / John Physick — v.1975.036
 6. Leighton's frescoes in the Victoria and
  Albert Museum / Richard Ormond —
  v.1975.028
 7. Funeral decorations in early eighteenth
  century Rome / Allan Braham —
  v.1975.021

8. Japanese colour-prints / introduction by Arthur W. Ruffy — v.1952.013
9. Costume illustration : the seventeenth and eighteenth centuries / introduction by James Laver — v.1951.007; v.1959.001.
10. English chairs / with an introduction by Ralph Edwards — v.1957.002; v.1970.014; v.1977.011
11. Baroque sculpture / H.D. Molesworth — v.1954.001
12. Roman lettering : a book of alphabets and inscriptions — v.1958.015
13. English printed textiles, 1720–1836 — v.1960.011
14. Samplers / Donald King — v.1960.021; v.1968.038; v.1972.033; v.1977.045
15. Gospel stories in English embroidery — v.1963.009
16. English silversmiths' work, civil and domestic : an introduction / by Charles Oman — v.1965.009
17. The engraved work of Eric Gill — v.1962.009; v.1963.005; v.1970.015; v.1977.012; v.1981.006
18. Art nouveau and Alphonse Mucha / by Brian Reade — v.1963.002; v.1966.002; v.1967.001; v.1976.007
19. The Duke of Wellington in caricature / John Physick — v.1965.006
20. A short history of English furniture — v.1966.017
21. [not identified]
22. [not identified]
23. Paintings at Apsley House / C. M. Kauffmann — v.1965.016
24. Japanese illustrated books / Leonard G. Dawes — v.1972.023
25. English desks and bureaux / J.F. Hayward — v.1968.015
26. [not identified]
27. [not identified]
28. Batiks — v.1969.005
29. Bohemian glass — v.1965.002
30. [not identified]
31. [not identified]
32. Aubrey Beardsley / Brian Reade — v.1966.003; v.1972.003; v.1976.010
33. Persian miniature painting from collections in the British Isles / B.W. Robinson — v.1967.016
34. The engravings of S.W. Hayter / Graham Reynolds — v.1967.008
35. Edward Gordon Craig, 1872–1966 / George Nash — v.1967.006
36. Indian art — v.1969.030; v.1977.023
37. [not identified]
38. Fine illustrations in Western European printed books / T.M. MacRobert — v.1969.023

Large special miscellaneous publications
10. Musical instruments as works of art — v.1968.029
No other titles found in this series.

Leaflets (Department of Textiles and Dress)
1. 20th century : an introduction to women's fashionable dress, 1900 – 1980 / Valerie D. Mendes — v.1983.001
2. English men's fashionable dress / Avril D. Hart — v.1983.010
5. Turkish velvet cushion covers / Jennifer M. Wearden — v.1987.020
No others published in this series?

[Lists of works in the National Art Library]
Entitled: A list of books *or* books and pamphlets *or* books and photographs *or* works on . . . .
Anatomy — v.1886.006
Architecture of the Renaissance and later periods — v.1888.010
Armour and weapons — v.1883.008
Biographies of artists : and of others connected with the history of art — v.1887.007
Catalogues of collections &c, also sale catalogues — v.1888.013
Coins and medals — v.1889.003
Construction, engineering and machinery — v.1889.004
Costume — v.1881.013
Drawing, geometry and perspective — v.1888.011
Furniture — v.1878.010
Gems — v.1886.004
Glass — v.1887.006
Gold and silversmiths' work and jewellery — v.1882.005; v.1887.008
Heraldry — v.1880.009; v.1884.007
Lace and needlework — v.1879.004; v.1888.012
Ornament — v.1882.006; v.1883.010
Painting — v.1881.014; v.1883.011
Pottery and porcelain — v.1875.012; v.1885.004
Sculpture — v.1882.007; v.1886.007
Seals — v.1886.005
Textile fabrics — v.1888.012

Masterpieces
1. Bernini's *Neptune and Triton* — v.1976.011
2. Constable's studies for *The hay-wain* — v.1976.015
3. The Devonshire hunting tapestries — v.1976.018
4. Roubiliac's *Handel* — v.1977.043
5. The Ardabil carpet — v.1976.006
6. The Luck of Edenhall — v.1977.029
7. The Sanchi torso — v.1976.052
8. The great bed of Ware — v.1977.021
9. Donatello's Chellini Madonna — v.1977.010

52. Flowers in English embroidery — v.1932.006; v.1938.008
53. Gothic sculpture — v.1933.010
54. English costume. Part 1, 17th century — v.1937.005
55. English costume. Part 2, 18th century — v.1937.006

Portfolios

Tapestries
I — v.1913.013
II — v.1914.015
III — v.1915.016

Indian drawings : twelve Mogul paintings of the school of Humāyān — Addenda, 1921 (Includes note: "Some years ago a beginning was made in the issue of a series of portfolios containing reproductions, in half-tone or collotype, of important works of art in the Museum, together with explanatory letterpress . . . The outbreak of war necessarily caused the suspension of the scheme, but it is now possible to resume publication . . . Further portfolios will be issued in due course, illustrating other drawings in the Indian Collections . . ."

Indian drawings : thirty Mogul paintings . . . and four panels of calligraphy — v.1922.010

No others published in this series?

[Private presses]

All entitled: "An introduction to the . . . Press : illustrated from material in the National Art Library". Accompanied by displays.

Beaumont Press / Eva White — v.1986.024
Doves and Ashendene Presses / Janet Skidmore — v.1986.025
Essex House Press / Susanna Robson — v.1986.026
Golden Cockerel Press / Julia Bigham — v.1987.009
Gregynog Press / Wendy Fish — v.1987.010
Kelmscott Press / Andrew Isherwood — v.1986.027
Nonesuch Press / Judith Bradfield — v.1986.028

An introduction to the Eragny Press was planned but not published.

Science handbooks

Entitled South Kensington Museum science handbooks, usually with 'Branch Museum, Bethnal Green' added. Published by Chapman and Hall; binding style as the Art handbooks, green cloth covered boards with horizontal rules and Museum crest stamped in black, and title in gold; or grey wrappers.

The analysis and adulteration of foods / James Bell — v.1881.001
Ancient and modern ships / George C.V. Holmes
I, Wooden sailing ships — v.1900.001; v.1906.001
II, The era of steam, iron & steel — v.1906.002

Animal products / P.L. Simmonds — v.1877.001
Catalogue of the Doubleday collection of lepidoptera — v.1877.004; v.1877.005
The chemistry of foods / James Bell — v.1881.006; v.1883.002
Conferences held in connection with the special loan collection of scientific apparatus, 1876 — v.1876.011;
Economic entomology / Andrew Murray — v.1877.009
Food / A.H. Church — v.1876.017; v.1880.004; v.1889.002; v.1893.005
Food-grains of India / A.H. Church — v.1886.001.
Handbook to the special loan collection of scientific apparatus — v.1876.020
Italian wall decorations of the 15th and 16th centuries — v.1901.007
Marine engines and boilers / George C.V. Holmes — v.1889.007
Plain words about water / A.H. Church — v.1877.012; v.1883.012

Small colour books

1. Chinese cloisonné enamels / B.W. Robinson — v.1972.012
2. Tudor & Jacobean miniatures / Graham Reynolds — v.1973.040
3. Jewellery / Shirley Bury — v.1972.024
4. 19th century papier-mâché / Simon Jervis — v.1973.001
5. Limoges painted enamels / Roger Pinkham — v.1974.019
6. Spitalfields silks / Natalie Rothstein — v.1975.040
7. English medieval alabasters / Terence Hodgkinson — v.1976.023
8. Toys / Caroline Goodfellow — v.1975.042
9. Dolls / Caroline Goodfellow — v.1975.014
10. Dolls' houses / Caroline Goodfellow — v.1976.019
11. Chinese tomb figures / Edmund Capon — v.1976.013
12. Playing cards / Frances Hicklin — v.1976.044
13. Pop art / Elizabeth Bailey — v.1976.045
14. Italian Renaissance bronzes / Anthony Radcliffe — v.1976.033
15. Puppets / Caroline Goodfellow — v.1976.046
16. French gold boxes / Charles Truman — v.1977.019
17. Ming porcelains / John Ayers — v.1977.031
18. Tibetan tangkas / John Lowry — v.1977.042
19. The art of fashion, 1600–1939 / Madeleine Ginsburg — v.1978.006
20. Persian oil paintings / B.W. Robinson — v.1977.036

*Similar titles, not apparently identified with the series, are: The Nehru Gallery of Indian Art, 1550–1900 :
a guide for schools — v.1990.013; China : a teacher's pack — v.1993.005; Using the V&A for GCSE and
A-level coursework — v.1993.019; Introducing the V&A : a guide to the collections for teachers —
v.1996.019

SUBJECT INDEX

See general remarks, p. xxvii. Citations may be traced as follows, by their prefixes:

V.	=	Publications of the Victoria and Albert Museum (starts p. 3)
VP.	=	Periodical publications (p. 387). Volume details are given in square brackets.
VR.	=	Publications related to, but not published by, the V&A (p. 409)
VRP.	=	Related periodicals and part works (p. 509)
VX.	=	Exhibitions and displays (p. 517)

Explanation
GLASS[a] — v.1876.023h; VR.1995.005; VX.1962.004
    1970s[b] — VR.1979.011; VX.1981.009
    Bohemia[c] — v.1965.002; v.1965.003; VR.1992.008; VX.1965.003
    British Isles[c] — v.1924.004; v.1926.009; VX.1968.015
        19th century[b] — v.1967.020; VP.1982.001[Spr. 1989]
    France[c]
        See Name Index[g]
        Marinot, Maurice, 1882-1960
    Bibliography[d] — v.1887.006
    Conservation[d] — VP.1991.001[3; 16]
    See also[e] Architectural glass; Pressed glass; Stained glass
GLASS CASES — v.1872.022; v.1876.016; VP.1968.001[4]
GLASS JEWELLERY — VR.1992.008
GLASSES
    See[f] SPECTACLES

Subdivisions
  [a] Main subject heading
  [b] Chronological subdivision, of main heading or of geographical subdivision
  [c] Geographical subdivision
  [d] Topical subdivisions (Bibliography, Conservation, Design, Technique)

Cross-references
  [e] Narrower or related terms (N.B. adjacent related terms are not cross-referred, e.g. GLASS CASES etc.)
  [f] Synonyms

Cross-references to other indexes
  [g] **Names in the subject index**
Proper names are listed here for the purpose of giving extra information about subject coverage. Names are listed under the subject heading/s to which they are relevant in the context of this book; thus the name of J.McN. Whistler is listed under PRINTS and that of Elton John under COLLECTIONS. (Where different items refer to the

work of an individual in different subject areas – e.g. an artist who is also a collector – that person's name is listed only under the most generally applicable index term. Conversely, names appear under multiple countries if necessary, and under multiple subjects if the same item covers their work in those fields.) Dates are added to names of individuals wherever they have been ascertained.

Cross-references also direct the reader to the Title and Series indexes where this is more helpful than duplicating citation numbers:

PANELLING
See Series Index, p. 749
Panelled rooms

In the Series Index the reader can quickly scan all titles relating to the subject.

*Museums and galleries are listed here only if they or their collections are the subject of an exhibition or publication in this book.

PERSIA – ARTS — v.1862.006; v.1873.011;
v.1876.003; v.1876.025; v.1880.010;
vrp.1881.0020
See also Architecture; Calligraphy; Carpets;
Ceramics; Embroidery; Illuminated
manuscripts; Literature; Metalwork;
Ornament; Painting; Textiles
PERU – ARTS
See Textiles
PETER PAN (CHARACTER) — v.1983.008
PEWTER — v.1969.003; vx.1970.016
British Isles — v.1960.002
PHOTOGRAPHIC BOOK ILLUSTRATION —
v.1978.072; vx.1978.001
PHOTOGRAPHIC PRINTS — v.1979.019;
vx.1979.022
PHOTOGRAPHY — v.1968.028; v.1974.018;
v.1981.015; v.1983.031; v.1989.012;
vr.1980.006; vx.1974.019; vx.1978.006;
vx.1980.xxx.002; vx.1981.005;
vx.1982.011; vx.1983.003; vx.1986.010;
vx.1989.002; vx.1990.002; vx.1990.015;
vx.1991.003; vx.1994.017; vx.1994.029;
vx.1995.009; vx.1995.021
19th century — v.1901.001; v.1939.001;
v.1939.005; v.1983.014; v.1985.049;
vr.1951.004; vr.1972.006; vr.1980.011;
vx.1939.001; vx.1951.002; vx.1972.006;
vx.1983.005; vx.1984.014; vx.1985.002;
vx.1994.012; vx.1996.016
20th century — v.1974.025; v.1983.031
1980s — v.1989.012
Belgium
See Name Index
Fraeye, Mark de, 1949–
British Isles — v.1984.011; v.1985.049;
v.1995.002; vr.1858.002; vr.1987.004;
vr.1988.005; vx.1858.001; vx.1984.014;
vx.1985.002; vx.1987.003; vx.1987.008;
vx.1988.023; vx.1993.004; vx.1995.029
See also Name Index
Anthony, Gordon
Association for Historical and Fine Art
Photographers
Bailey, David, 1938–
Beaton, Cecil Walter Hardy, Sir,
1904–1980
Brandon, Graham
Brandt, Bill, 1904–1983
Cameron, Julia Margaret, 1815–1879
Cave, C. J. P., 1871–1950
Cranham, Gerry, 1929–
Crickmay, Anthony
Deakin, John, 1912–1972
Evans, Frederick H., 1853–1943
Fenton, Roger, 1819–1869
French, John, 1907–1966
Frith, Francis, 1822–1898
Hammond, Harry
Hawarden, Clementina, Viscountess,
1822–1865
Hedges, Nick, 1943–

Heywood, John
Jacobs, Sylvester, 1944–
Killip, Christopher, 1946–
Llewellyn, John Dillwyn, 1810–1882
Luskačová, Markéta, 1944–
McCartney, Linda, d. 1998
McCullin, Don, 1935–
McKittrick, Amanda
Martin, Paul, 1864–1944
Mayne, Roger, 1929–
Morris, Leon
Rogers, Houston
Slingby, Miki
Smith, Edwin, 1912–1971
Stone, John Benjamin, Sir, 1838–1914
— v.1901.001; vx.1901.002
Thompson, Charles Thurston,
1818–1868
Trainer, David
Turner, Benjamin Brecknell,
1815–1894
Warburg, Agnes, B., 1872–1953
Wilmer, Val, 1941–
19th century — v.1996.025;
vp.1982.001[Aut. 1988]
1980s — vr.1987.004; vx.1987.008
1990s — vr.1995.007
Czechoslovakia
See Name Index
Luskačová, Markéta, 1944–
France — vr.1858.002; vx.1858.001
See also Name Index
Burnier, Raymond
Cartier-Bresson, Henri, 1908–
Silvy, Camille, 1834–1910
Germany
See Name Index
De Meyer, Adolf, Baron, 1868–1949
Hungary
See Name Index
Brassaï, 1899–1984
Spain
See Name Index
Melián, Christóbal, 1946–
U.S.A. — v.1973.008; v.1974.018;
v.1996.003; vr.1995.002; vx.1996.036;
vx.1996.036
See also Name Index
Adams, Ansel, 1902–1984
Baltz, Lewis, 1945–
Blake, John, 1945–
Clay, Langdon, 1949–
Eggleston, William, 1939–
Evans, Walker, 1903–1975
Finkelstein, Nat
Friedlander, Lee, 1934–
Jacobs, Sylvester, 1944–
McCartney, Linda, d. 1998
Nixon, Nicholas, 1947–
Penn, Irving, 1917–
Sherman, Cindy, 1954–
Smith, W. Eugene, 1918–1978

*Listed here are publishers as *subjects* of exhibitions or publications.